Yearbook of International Humanitarian Law

Volume 13

For further volumes:
http://www.springer.com/series/8912

Michael N. Schmitt
General Editor

Louise Arimatsu
Managing Editor

T. McCormack
Correspondents' Reports Editor

Yearbook of International Humanitarian Law Volume 13, 2010

T·M·C·Asser Press
Cambridge University Press
Springer

General Editor
Michael N. Schmitt
US Naval War College, CNWS-ILD
686 Cushing Road
Newport, RI 02841-1207
USA
email: schmitt@aya.yale.edu

Managing Editor
Louise Arimatsu
The Royal Institute of International Affairs
Chatham House
10 St. James's Square
London SW1Y 4LE
UK
e-mail:
lArimatsu@chathamhouse.org.uk

Correspondents' Reports Editor
T. McCormack
Melbourne Law School
University of Melbourne
Victoria 3010
Australia
e-mail: t.mccormack@unimeb.edu.au

Cover Photograph: US marines on operations in remote southwest Afghanistan
Photographer: John Moore, 2009

ISSN 1389-1359
ISBN 978-90-6704-810-1
DOI 10.1007/978-90-6704-811-8

e-ISSN 1574-096x
e-ISBN 978-90-6704-811-8

This Volume is also available as a journal product through Cambridge University Press. In addition to the electronic version published on www.springerlink, the Yearbook is also available online through the Cambridge Journals Online service.
Published by T.M.C. ASSER PRESS, The Hague, The Netherlands www.asserpress.nl
Produced and distributed for T.M.C. ASSER PRESS, by Springer-Verlag Berlin Heidelberg

Cover design: eStudio Calamar, Berlin/Figueres

Printed on acid-free paper

Springer is part of Springer Science+Business Media (www.springer.com)

Editorial Office

Ms Karin Peters, Editorial Assistant, T.M.C. Asser Instituut
T.M.C. Asser Instituut, P.O. Box 30461, 2500 GL Hague, The Netherlands
YIHL@asser.nl; www.asser.nl; www.wihl.nl

Correspondents

The Yearbook of International Humanitarian Law *extends its sincere thanks and appreciation to its correspondents, without whose assistance the compilation of this volume would not have been possible.*

AFRICA
Major Dan Kuwali, *Burkina Faso, Central African Rep., Côte d'Ivoire, DR Congo, Egypt, Kenya, Liberia, Morocco, Sudan* and *Uganda*
Professor Kamel Filali, *Algeria*
Ms Nadine Fourie, *South Africa*

ASIA-PACIFIC
Ms Nika Dharmadasa, *Australia*
Ms Alison Duxbury, *Australia*
Ms Joanne Lau, *Australia*
Mr James May, *Australia*
Ms Krystina Grinberg, *Australia*
Mr M. Zahurul Haq, *Bangladesh*
Mr Aziz Mohammed, *Fiji*
Ms Treasa Dunworth, *New Zealand*

EUROPE
Dr Thomas Desch, *Austria*
Professor Eric David, *Belgium*
Ms Lelja Vujinović, *Bosnia Herzegovina*
Mr Konstantinos Mastorodimos, *Cyprus* and *Hellas*
Mr Peter Otken, *Denmark*
Professor Paul Tavernier, *France*
Mr Rain Liivoja, Estonia, *Finland* and *Latvia*
Mr Jani Leino, *Finland*
Dr Eszter Kirs, *Hungary*
Mr Ray Murphy, *Ireland*
Ms Rachelle Cera, *Italy*
Dr Valentina Della Fina, *Italy*
Dr Ornella Ferrajola, *Italy*
Ms Silvana Moscatelli, *Italy*
Dr Valeria Eboli, *Italy*
Mr Giovanni Carlo Bruno, *Italy*
Ms Ieva Miluna, *Latvia*
Mr Rytis Satkauskas, *Lithuania*
Professor Antoni Pigrau, *Spain*
Dr Ola Engdahl, *Sweden*
Dr Roberta Arnold, *Switzerland*
Professor Peter Rowe, *United Kingdom*

MIDDLE EAST
Dr Yaël Ronen, *Israel*
Dr Mustafa Mari, *Occupied Palestinian Territories*

NORTH AMERICA
Mr Joseph Rikhof, *Canada*
Mr Burrus M. Carnahan, *USA*
Lieutenant Colonel Chris Jenks, *USA*

CENTRAL AND SOUTH AMERICA
Professor Rafael Prieto Sanjuán, *Colombia*
Mr Juan Pablo Péréz-Léon Avevedo, *Peru*

Contents

Part IV Correspondents' Reports

Part V Documentation

Abbreviations

AALCO	Asian-African Legal Consultative Organization
Abl.	Amtsblatt
AC	Appeal Cases
ACTR	Australian Capital Territory Reports
AD	Annual Digest of Public International Law Cases
Adelaide LR	Adelaide Law Review
ADF	Australian Defence Force
AFDI	Annuaire français de droit international
AFRC	Armed Forces Revolutionary Council (Sierra Leone)
African HRLJ	African Human Rights Law Journal
African JI & CL	African Journal of International and Comparative Law
African YIHL	African Yearbook on International Humanitarian Law
Air Force LR	Air Force Law Review
Air LR	Air Law Review
Airpower J	Airpower Journal
Air Univ. Rev.	Air University Review
AJCL	American Journal of Comparative Law
AJIL	American Journal of International Law
AJLP	Australian Journal of Legal Philosophy
Albany LR	Albany Law Review
All ER	All England Law Reports
ALR	Australian Law Reports
Amer. Crim. LR	American Criminal Law Review
Amer. Univ. JIL & Pol.	American University Journal of International Law and Policy

Amer. Univ. ILJ	American University International Law Journal
Amer. Univ. ILR	American University International Law Review
Amer. Univ. LR	American University Law Review
AMISOM	African Union Mission to Somalia
ANA	Afghanistan National Army
AP	Additional Protocol
AP	Associated Press
APL(s)	Anti-personnel landmine(s)
ARABSAT	Arab Satellite Communications Organization
Arizona JI & CL	Arizona Journal of International and Comparative Law
Army Law.	The Army Lawyer
ASEAN	Association of South East Asian Nations
ASF	African Standby Force
ASIL Proc.	American Society of International Law Proceedings
ATCA	Alien Tort Claims Act (USA)
ATT	Arms Trade Treaty
AU	African Union
AMIB	African Union Mission in Burundi
AMIS	African Union Mission in Sudan
AMISOM	African Union Mission in Somalia
Australian YIL	Australian Yearbook of International Law
Austrian JPIL	Austrian Journal for Public International Law
Austrian Rev. Int. & Eur. L	Austrian Revue of International and European Law
AVM	Anti-vehicle landmine
Berkeley JIL	Berkeley Journal of International Law
B.O.	Boletín Oficial de la República Argentina
BGBl	Bundesgesetzblatt
BGH	Bundesgerichtshof
Boston Univ. ILJ	Boston University International Law Journal
Boston College Int. & Comp. LR	Boston College International and Comparative Law Review
Brooklyn JIL	Brooklyn Journal of International Law
BTF	Balkans Task Force
BverfGE	Bundesverfassungsgericht
BYIL	British Yearbook of International Law

California LR	California Law Review
Calif. Western ILJ	California Western International Law Journal
Can. JL & Jur.	Canadian Journal of Law and Jurisprudence
Canadian YIL	Canadian Yearbook of International Law
Cardozo LR	Cardozo Law Review
Case Western Reserve JIL	Case Western Reserve Journal of International Law
Catholic Univ. LR	Catholic University Law Review
CCW	Convention on Certain Conventional Weapons
CD	Conference on Disarmament
CDF	Civil Defence Forces (Sierra Leone)
CENTCOM	Central Command
Chicago JIL	Chicago Journal of International Law
Chinese JIL	Chinese Journal of International Law
CHR (UN)	Centre for Human Rights
CIA	Central Intelligence Agency
CICC	Coalition for the International Criminal Court
CICR	Comité International de la Croix Rouge
CID	Criminal Investigation Division
CIS	Commonwealth of Independent States
CIVPOL	Civilian Police
CLA	Chief Legal Advisor
CLJ	Criminal Law Journal
CLR	Commonwealth Law Reports
CMAC	Court Martial Appeal Court
Cmnd.	Command Paper
Columbia HRLR	Columbia Human Rights Law Review
Columbia JTL	Columbia Journal of Transnational Law
Columbia LR	Columbia Law Review
Connecticut JIL	Connecticut Journal of International Law
Cornell ILJ	Cornell International Law Journal
Cr. App. R.	Criminal Appeals Reports
CRC	Convention on the Rights of the Child
Criminal LF	Criminal Law Forum
Criminal LR	Criminal Law Review
CSP	Conference of States Parties
CTBT	Comprehensive Test Ban Treaty
CTED	Counter-Terrorism Committee Executive Directorate
CTS	Commonwealth Treaty Series

CWC	Chemical Weapons Convention
Dalhousie LJ	Dalhousie Law Journal
Denver JIL & Pol.	Denver Journal of International Law and Policy
DLR	Dominion Law Reports
DMU	Detainee Management Unit
DoD	Department of Defense (USA)
Drake LR	Drake Law Review
DRC	Democratic Republic of Congo
Duke JCIL	Duke Journal of Comparative and International Law
ECCAS	Economic Community of Central African States
ECCC	Extraordinary Chambers in the Courts of Cambodia
ECHR Rep.	European Convention on Human Rights Reports
ECHR	European Convention on Human Rights
ECOMOG	ECOWAS Cease-Fire Monitoring Group
ECOSOC	United Nations Economic and Social Council
ECOWAS	Economic Community of West African States
ECtHR	European Court on Human Rights
EECC	Eritrea-Ethiopia Claims Commission
EHRR	European Human Rights Reports
Emory ILR	Emory International Law Review
EJIL	European Journal of International Law
ERW	Explosive Remnants of War
EU	European Union
Eur. Ct. HR	European Court of Human Rights
EUFOR	European Union Force
Eur. Comm. HR	European Commission of Human Rights
Eur. J Crime, Crim. L & Crim. Jus.	European Journal of Crime, Criminal Law and Criminal Justice
Ex D	Exchequer Digest
F	Federal
F Supp.	Federal Supplement
FARDC	Armed Forces of the Democratic Republic of the Congo
FCJ	Federal Court of Justice (Canada)
FCR	Federal Court Reports
FDC	Force Detention Centre

FDTL	East Timorese Defence Force
Fed. Reg.	Federal Register (United States)
Fed. Rep.	Federal Reporter
Finnish YIL	Finnish Yearbook of International Law
FNI	Front des Nationalistes et Intégrationistes (Congo)
Fordham ILJ	Fordham International Law Journal
Fordham LR	Fordham Law Review
FPLC	Forces Patriotiques pour la Libération du Congo
FRETILIN	Frente Revolucionaria Timor Lest Independence
FRPI	Force de Résistance Patriotique en Ituri (Congo)
FRY	Federal Republic of Yugoslavia
FYROM	Former Yugoslav Republic of Macedonia
GA	General Assembly (United Nations)
GAOR	General Assembly Official Records
GA Res.	General Assembly Resolution (United Nations)
GC	Geneva Conventions
Georgetown Int. Environ. LR	Georgetown International Environmental Law Review
Georgetown JIL	Georgetown Journal of International Law
Georgia JI & Comp. L	Georgia Journal of International and Comparative Law
German LJ	German Law Journal
GR2P	Global Responsibility to Protect
GW ILR	The George Washington International Law Review
GW JIL and Econ.	The George Washington Journal of International Law and Economics
GU	Gazzetta Ufficiale (Italian Official Gazette)
GYIL	German Yearbook of International Law
Hague YIL	Hague Yearbook of International Law
Harvard ILJ	Harvard International Law Journal
Harvard JHR	Harvard Journal of Human Rights
Harvard JL & Pub. Pol.	Harvard Journal of Law & Public Policy
Harvard JOL	Harvard Journal on Legislation
Harvard LR	Harvard Law Review
Harvard NSJ	Harvard National Security Journal
HCJ	High Court of Justice
HRLJ	Human Rights Law Journal

HRLR	Human Rights Law Review
HRQ	Human Rights Quarterly
I/A Court HR	Inter-American Court of Human Rights
I/A Comm. HR	Inter-American Commission on Human Rights
I/A YBHR	Inter-American Yearbook on Human Rights
ICA	International Council on Archives
ICBL	International Campaign to Ban Landmines
ICBS	International Committee of the Blue Shield
ICC	International Criminal Court
ICCPR	International Covenant on Civil and Political Rights
ICCROM	International Centre for the Study of the Preservation and Restoration of Cultural Property
ICISS	International Commission on Intervention and State Sovereignty
ICJ	International Court of Justice
ICJ Rep.	International Court of Justice Reports
ICLR	International Criminal Law Review
ICLQ	International and Comparative Law Quarterly
ICOM	International Council of Museums
ICOMOS	International Council on Monuments and Sites
ICRC	International Committee of the Red Cross
ICRtoP	International Coalition for the Responsibility to Protect
ICTR	International Criminal Tribunal for Rwanda
ICTY	International Criminal Tribunal for the former Yugoslavia
IDR	International Defense Review
IFLA	International Federation of Library Association and Institutions
IFOR	Implementation Force
IHL	International Humanitarian Law
IJLM	International Journal of Legal Medicine
IJRL	International Journal of Refugee Law
ILAS JI & Comp. L	ILAS Journal of International and Comparative Law
ILC	International Law Commission

ILC Yearbook	Yearbook of the International Law Commission
ILM	International Legal Materials
ILR	International Law Reports
IMO	International Maritime Organization
IMT	International Military Tribunal (in Nuremberg)
IMTFE	International Military Tribunal for the Far East (in Tokyo)
Indian JIL	Indian Journal of International Law
Indiana I & Comp. LR	Indiana International & Comparative Law Review
INTELSAT	International Telecommunications Satellite Organization
Int. LF	International Law Forum
INTERFET	International Force in East Timor
IRA	Irish Republican Army
Iran-US CTR	Iran-United States Claims Tribunal Reports
IRRC	International Review of the Red Cross
ISAF	International Security Assistance Force
Israel LR	Israel Law Review
Israel YB	Israel Yearbook
Israel YB HR	Israel Yearbook on Human Rights
IYIL	Italian Yearbook of International Law
JAMA	Journal of the American Medical Association
J Armed Conflict L	Journal of Armed Conflict Law
JCSL	Journal of Conflict and Security Law
JICL	Journal of International and Comparative Law
JIL & Prac.	Journal of International Law and Practice
J Int. Criminal Justice	Journal of International Criminal Justice
JPI	Judicial Police Inspectors
J Trans. L. & Pol.	Journal of Transnational Law & Policy
J Trauma	The Journal of Trauma
KFOR	Kosovo Force
KLA	Kosovo Liberation Army
LAS	League of Arab States
Leiden JIL	Leiden Journal of International Law
LNTS	League of Nations Treaty Series
LOAC	Law of Armed Conflict

Loy. LA I & CLJ	Loyola of Los Angeles International and Comparative Law Journal
Loyola I & CLJ	Loyola International and Comparative Law Journal
LQR	Law Quarterly Review
Maryland JIL & T	Maryland Journal of International Law and Trade
MCC	Military Criminal Code
Melbourne JIL	Melbourne Journal of International Law
Melbourne Univ. LR	Melbourne University Law Review
Michigan JIL	Michigan Journal of International Law
Michigan LR	Michigan Law Review
Mil. LR	Military Law Review
MINURCAT	United Nations Mission in the Central African Republic and Chad
MINURSO	United Nations Mission for the Referendum in Western Sahara
MINUSTAH	United Nations Stabilization Mission in Haiti
MLR	Modern Law Review
MNF	Multinational Force
Monash LR	Monash Law Review
Moniteur Belge	Belgian Official Parliamentary Journal
MONUC	United Nations Mission in the Democratic Republic of Congo
Moscow JIL	Moscow Journal of International Law
MPYBUNL	Max Planck Yearbook of United Nations Law
MPYIL	Max Planck Yearbook of International Law
MRT	Militair Rechtelijk Tijdschrift
NATO	North Atlantic Treaty Organisation
Naval LR	Naval Law Review
NCOs	Non-Commissioned Officers
Nebraska LR	Nebraska Law Review
New England LR	New England Law Review
NGO	Non-Governmental Organisation
NILR	Netherlands International Law Review
NJ	Nederlandse Jurisprudentie
NLA	Albanian National Liberation Army
NLR	Naval Law Review
Nordic JIL	Nordic Journal of International Law

North Carolina LR	North Carolina Law Review
Northwestern JIHR	Northwestern Journal of International Human Rights
Northwestern Univ. LR	Northwestern University Law Review
Notre Dame JL	Notre Dame Journal of Law
Notre Dame LR	Notre Dame Law Review
NPC	New Penal Code
NQHR	Netherlands Quarterly of Human Rights
NYIL	Netherlands Yearbook of International Law
NY Univ. JIL & Pol.	New York University Journal of International Law and Politics
NY Univ. LR	New York University Law Review
NZLR	New Zealand Law Review
ÖAD	Österreichische Außenpolitische Dokumentation
OAS	Organization of American States
OECS	Organization of Eastern Caribbean States
OEF	Operation Enduring Freedom (Afghanistan)
OIF	Operation Iraqi Freedom
ONU	Organisation des Nations Unies
ONUB	United Nations Operation in Burundi
ONUC	United Nations Operation in the Congo
OPCW	Organisation for the Prohibition of Chemical Weapons
OSA	Operational Support Arrangement
OTP	Office of the Prosecutor (of the ICTR and/or ICTY)
Palestine YIL	Palestine Yearbook of International Law
PCIJ	Permanent Court of Justice
PD	Probate Division, English Law Reports
Penn. State ILR	Pennsylvania State International Law Review
PKF	Peace Keeping Force
PMG	Peace Monitoring Group
POC	Protection of Civilians
POW	Prisoner of War
Proc. ASIL	Proceedings of the American Society of International Law
QB	Queen's Bench

RBDI	Revue Belge de droit international
RDI	Rivista di diritto internazionale
RDPC	Revue de droit pénal et de criminologie
Recueil des Cours	Collected Courses of the Hague Academy of International Law
RGDIP	Revue générale de droit international public
RIAA	Reports of International Arbitral Awards
RICR	Revue International de la Croix Rouge
RPF	Rwandan Patriotic Front
RQDI	Revue Québécoise de Droit International
RSC	Rules of the Supreme Court
RSCDPC	Revue de science criminelle et de droit pénal comparé
RSDIE	Revue Suisse de droit international et de droit européen
RSK	Republic of Serbian Krajina
RUF	Revolutionary United Front (Sierra Leone)
Rutgers LR	Rutgers Law Review
R2P-RtoP	Responsibility to Protect
SADC	South African Development Community
San Diego LR	San Diego Law Review
SASC	South African Security Council
Saskatchewan LR	Saskatchewan Law Review
SC	Security Council
SC CTC	Security Council's Counter-Terrorism Committee
SCOR	Security Council Official Records
SC Res.	Security Council Resolution
SCR	Supreme Court Reports
S. Ct.	Supreme Court Reporter (United States)
SCU	Serious Crimes Unit
SFOR	Stabilization Force
SFRY	Socialist Federal Republic of Yugoslavia
SG	Secretary-General
SIPRI	Stockholm International Peace Research Institute
SOFA	Status of Force Agreement
South African YIL	South African Yearbook of International Law
South Texas LR	South Texas Law Review
Stanford JIL	Stanford Journal of International Law
Stanford JIR	Stanford Journal of International Relations
Stanford LR	Stanford Law Review

Syracuse JIL & Com.	Syracuse Journal of International Law & Commerce
SZIER	Schweizerische Zeitschrift für internationales und europäisches Recht
Tel Aviv Univ. LR	Tel Aviv University Law Review
Temple LR	Temple Law Review
Tennessee LR	Tennessee Law Review
Texas ILJ	Texas International Law Journal
Texas LR	Texas Law Review
TFG	Transitional Federal Government (Somalia)
TIAS	Treaties and other International Acts Series
Tilburg For. LR	Tilburg Foreign Law Review
TLPS	Timorese Police Force
Transn. L & Contemp. Probs.	Transnational Law and Contemporary Problems
TRC Report	Truth and Reconciliation Commission Report (South African)
Tulane JI & Comp. L	Tulane Journal of International & Comparative Law
Tulsa J Comp. & IL	Tulsa Journal of Comparative and International Law
TVF	Trust Fund for Victims
UCLA LR	University of California Los Angeles Law Review
UN	United Nations
UNAKRT	United Nations Assistance to the Khmer Rouge Trial
UNAMA	United Nations Assistance Mission in Afghanistan
UNAMET	United Nations Mission in East Timor
UNAMI	United Nations Assistance Mission for Iraq
UNAMID	United Nations/ African Union Hybrid Operation in Darfur
UNAMIR	United Nations Assistance Mission for Rwanda
UNAMSIL	United Nations Mission in Sierra Leone
UNCHR	United Nations Commission on Human Rights
UNCHS	United Nations Centre for Human Settlements
UNCIVPOL	United Nations Civilian Police

UNCTAD	United Nations Conference on Trade and Development
UN Doc.	United Nations Documents Series
UNDOF	United Nations Disengagement Observer Force
UNDP	United Nations Development Programme
UNEF	United Nations Emergency Force (in the Sinai)
UNEP	United Nations Environment Programme
UNESCO	United Nations Educational, Scientific and Cultural Organisation
UNFICYP	United Nations Force in Cyprus
UNGCI	United Nations Guards Contingent in Iraq
UNHCR	United Nations High Commissioner for Refugees
UNHFOR	United Nations Human Rights Field Office in Rwanda
UNICEF	United Nations (International) Children's (Emergency) Fund
UNIDIR	United Nations Institute for Disarmament Research
UNIFEM	United Nations Development Fund for Women
UNIFIL	United Nations Interim Force in Lebanon
UNIIMOG	United Nations Iran/Iraq Military Observer Group
UNIKOM	United Nations Iraq/Kuwait Observer Mission
UNIPSIL	United Nations Integrated Peacebuilding Office in Sierra Leone
UNITAF	United Nations Unified Task Force
UNITAF	United Nations Task Force (in Somalia)
UNMEE	United Nations Mission in Ethiopia and Eritrea
UNMIL	United Nations Mission in Liberia
UNMIN	United Nations Mission in Nepal
UNMIS	United Nations Mission in Sudan
UNMIT	United Nations Mission in Timor-Leste
UNOCI	United Nations Operations in Côte d'Ivoire
UNOMIG	United Nations Observer Mission in Georgia
UNOMSIL	United Nations Observer Mission in Sierra Leone
UNOSOM	United Nations Operation in Somalia
UNPF	United Nations Peacekeeping Force

UNPOS	United Nations Political Office for Somalia
UNPROFOR	United Nations Protection Force (in Bosnia and Herzegovina)
UNTAC	United Nations Transitional Authority in Cambodia
UNTAET	United Nations Transitional Authority in East Timor
UNTS	United Nations Treaty Series
UNWCC	United Nations War Crimes Commission
Univ. Calif. Davis LR	University of California Davis Law Review
Univ. Chicago LR	University of Chicago Law Review
Univ. Miami I & Comp. LR	University of Miami International & Comparative Law Review
Univ. Pa. J Const. L	University of Pennsylvania Journal of Constitutional Law
Univ. Pitt. LR	University of Pittsburgh Law Review
Univ. Richmond LR	University of Richmond Law Review
USAFA JLS	United States Air Force Academy Journal of Legal Studies
Vanderbilt JTL	Vanderbilt Journal of Transnational Law
VCLT	Vienna Convention on the Law of Treaties
Vermont LR	Vermont Law Review
Virginia JIL	Virginia Journal of International Law
Virginia LR	Virginia Law Review
VWU	Victims and Witness Unit of the Registry (Congo)
Wake Forest LR	Wake Forest Law Review
WBR	Wound Ballistics Review
WCR	War Crimes Reports
WHO	World Health Organisation
Whittier LR	Whittier Law Review
Wisconsin ILJ	Wisconsin International Law Journal
WLR	Weekly Law Reports
Yale HR & Dev. LJ	Yale Human Rights & Development Law Journal
Yale JIL	Yale Journal of International Law
Yale LJ	Yale Law Journal
Yb Eur. Conv. HR	Yearbook of the European Convention of Human Rights
Yb ILC	Yearbook of the International Law Commission

YIHL	Yearbook of International Humanitarian Law
Yug. Rev. IL	Yugoslav Review of International Law
ZaöRV	Zeitschrift für ausländisches öffentliches Recht und Völkerrecht
ZöR	Zeitschrift für öffentliches Recht

Part I
Articles

Chapter 1
Who May Be Killed? Anwar al-Awlaki as a Case Study in the International Legal Regulation of Lethal Force

Robert Chesney

Contents

1.1 Introduction

Anwar al-Awlaki is a dual Yemeni-American citizen who has emerged in recent years as a leading English-language proponent of violent *jihad*, including explicit calls for the indiscriminate murder of Americans. According to the US government, moreover, he also has taken on an operational leadership role with the

---

I wish to thank the editors at the Yearbook of International Humanitarian Law, as well as Professors William Banks, Gary Corn, Ashley Deeks, Kevin Jon Heller, Richard Klingler, Michael Lewis, Marko Milanovic and Matthew Waxman.

R. Chesney (✉)
University of Texas School of Law, Austin, TX, USA
e-mail: rchesney@law.utexas.edu

M.N. Schmitt et al. (eds.), *Yearbook of International Humanitarian Law Volume 13, 2010*, DOI: 10.1007/978-90-6704-811-8_1,

organization al Qaeda in the Arabian Peninsula (AQAP), recruiting and directing individuals to participate in specific acts of violence.

Does international law permit the US government to kill al-Awlaki in these circumstances? The larger issues raised by this question are not new, of course. The use of lethal force in response to terrorism—especially the use of such force by the United States and Israel—has been the subject of extensive scholarship, advocacy, and litigation over the past decade,[1] just as earlier uses of force in response to terrorism spawned their own literatures on this subject.[2] Yet we remain far from consensus. The al-Awlaki scenario accordingly provides an occasion for fresh analysis.

Part 1.2 opens with a discussion of what we know, based on the public record as reflected in media reports and court documents, about AQAP, about al-Awlaki himself, and about the US government's purported decision to place him on a list of individuals who may be targeted with lethal force in certain circumstances.[3] The analysis that follows largely assumes the accuracy of—and depends upon—these asserted facts.

Parts 1.3 and 1.4 review two distinct sets of international law-based objections that might be raised to killing al-Awlaki. Part 1.3 explores objections founded in the UN Charter's restraints on the use of force in international affairs, emphasizing Yemen's potential objections under Article 2(4) of the Charter. I conclude that a substantial case can be made, at least for now, both that Yemen has consented to the use of such force on its territory and that in any event the conditions associated with the right of self-defense enshrined in Article 51 can be satisfied. As to the latter, any attack must conform to the constraints of necessity and proportionality inherent in the self-defense right, and therefore an attack would not be permissible if Yemen is both capable and willing to incapacitate al-Awlaki.

Against that backdrop, Part 1.4 considers whether an attack on al-Awlaki would best be understood as governed by International Humanitarian Law (IHL) or

---

[1] The recent scholarly literature on this topic is substantial. See e.g., Lubell 2010; Melzer 2008; O'Connell 2010; Paust 2010; Blum and Heymann 2010; Anderson 2009; Murphy and Radsan, 2009; Murphy 2009; Cassese 2007b; Kretzmer 2005; Guiora 2004. Reports and statements on the topic from advocacy groups and non-governmental organizations also are numerous. See e.g., Letter from Kenneth Roth, Executive Director of Human Rights Watch, to Barack Obama, President of the United States of America, *Targeted Killings and Unmanned Combat Aircraft Systems (Drones)*, 7 December 2010, available at http://www.hrw.org/sites/default/files/related_material/Letter%20to%20President%20Obama%20-%20Targeted%20Killings%20(1).pdf; Report of the Special Rapporteur on Extrajudicial, Summary or Arbitrary Executions, Philip Alston, Addendum, Study on Targeted Killings, UN Doc. A/HRC/14/24/Add.6, at 3, 54, 85-86 (May 28, 2010). There has been at least one judicial decision directly addressing the topic, from the Israeli High Court's decision in the *Targeted Killings* Case. See HCJ 769/02 *Public Comm. Against Torture in Israel* v *Government of Israel* (*Targeted Killings* Case) [2005], available at http://elyon1.court.gov.il/Files_ENG/02/690/007/a34/02007690.a34.pdf.

[2] See e.g., Sharp 2000; Reisman 1999; Wedgwood 1999; Military Responses to Terrorism 1987, p 287 (transcript of debate sparked by US airstrikes in Libya in 1986); Paust 1986.

[3] Neither this nor any other part of the paper relies in any way upon classified information that may have been released into the public domain by Wikileaks.

International Human Rights Law (IHRL), and whether and when either body of law would actually permit the use of lethal force. Turning first to IHL, I begin with the question whether an attack on al-Awlaki would fall within IHL's field of application. That question is not easily resolved, but I conclude that the better view is that the threshold of armed conflict has been crossed in two relevant respects. First, it has been crossed in Yemen itself as between AQAP on one hand and the US and Yemeni governments on the other. Second, it has been crossed as well with respect to the United States and the larger al Qaeda network—and not only within the geopolitical borders of Afghanistan. Building from these premises, I then proceed to consider whether al-Awlaki could be targeted consistent with IHL's principle of distinction. I conclude that he can be if he is in fact an operational leader within AQAP, as this role would render him a functional combatant in an organized armed group.

Insofar as IHL is indeed applicable to an attack on al-Awlaki, I conclude that IHRL has no separate impact. In recognition of the fact that many critics will not accept the field-of-application analysis noted above, however, I do provide a stand-alone IHRL analysis. The central issues in the IHRL context, I argue, both concern the requirement of necessity inherent in IHRL's protection for the right-to-life, and in particular the notion of temporal necessity. First, does necessity require a strict approach to temporality, such that deadly force can be used only where the target is moments away from killing or seriously injuring others, or instead can the requirement of imminence be relaxed in the limited circumstance in which (i) there is substantial evidence that the individual is planning terrorist attacks, (ii) there is no plausible opportunity to incapacitate the individual with non-lethal means, and (iii) there is no reason to believe a later window of opportunity to act will arise. I conclude the case for the latter approach is compelling. A second question arises, however. Must the state's evidence link the person to a specific plot to carry out a particular attack, or is it enough that the evidence establishes that the person can and will attempt or otherwise be involved in attacks in the future, without specificity as to what the particulars of those attacks might be? The former approach has the virtue of clarity, yet could rarely be satisfied given the clandestine nature of terrorism. The latter approach necessarily runs a greater risk of abuse and thus perhaps justifies an especially high evidentiary threshold, but in any event it is a more realistic and more appropriate approach (particularly from the point of view of the potential victims of future terrorist attacks). Coupled with a strict showing of practical necessity in the sense that there is no realistic opportunity to instead arrest an individual, this analysis leads to the conclusion that al-Awlaki could indeed be targeted consistent with IHRL.

A final note before turning to the substance. This paper does not address the important domestic law questions raised by al-Awlaki's status as an American citizen, such as whether the US Constitution's Fifth Amendment entitles him to certain procedural protections before the government may attempt to kill him or whether AQAP falls within the scope of the September 18, 2001 Authorization for Use of Military Force (though the analysis that follows has implications for the latter question). Nor does it address policy considerations such as whether the use of lethal force by the United States against al-Awlaki or others in Yemen would do more harm than good from a strategic perspective. Finally, this paper is not about drones as such; I do not address the legality of selecting any particular weapons platform—such as an MQ-1 Predator or an MQ-9 Reaper—to carry out an attack.

1.2 Why Might the US Government Target Anwar al-Awlaki?

Before coming to grips with the legal issues, a close review of the underlying fact pattern is in order. I begin below with a sketch of AQAP and its relationship with what we might call 'core al Qaeda' or, simply, 'al Qaeda', a topic that takes on significance in light of the US government's claim that a state of armed conflict exists between it and al Qaeda. Next, I review Anwar al-Awlaki's background and activities. Last, I survey what is known about the use of force by the United States in Yemen in relation to AQAP in general and al-Awlaki in particular.

1.2.1 AQAP in relation to al Qaeda

What is the relationship of the entity now known as AQAP to the entity we label al Qaeda? This is a difficult question for several reasons. As an initial matter, we lack access to the classified intelligence that would be most useful to answering it. Second, it is in any event difficult to map familiar notions of organizational structure on to al Qaeda. It might best be described as a network blending elements of hierarchy and centralization with elements of disaggregation, fluid individual relationships, and franchise-like connections to separate organizations, all against the backdrop of a larger, multi-faceted movement associated with violent Islamist extremism.[4]

For some entities that today bear the al Qaeda 'brand', the relationship is a relatively new phenomenon in which a previously-independent organization has for whatever reason decided to at least portray itself as part of the al Qaeda network. This appears to be the case, for example, with al Qaeda in the Islamic Maghreb (AQIM), which emerged in Algeria in the 1990s under the name the Salafist Group for Preaching and Combat and which aimed to overthrow the Algerian government.[5] The Salafist Group had no particular ties to al Qaeda until a few years ago when under pressure from declining membership and having a new leader, it reached out to al Qaeda.[6] An alliance was announced in September 2006,

---

[4] For a discussion, see Chesney 2007, pp 425, 437-445 (distinguishing al Qaeda from the larger 'global jihad' movement). See also Waxman 2010, pp 447-451 (arguing that disagreements about how to understand al Qaeda's structure complicate efforts to apply IHL).

[5] See Schmitt and Mekhennet 2009.

[6] See Whitlock 2007.

and by January the group had changed its name and reoriented its activities away from just Algeria.[7]

Contrast that with al Qaeda's history of direct involvement in Yemen. According to the 9/11 Commission Report,[8] the key figure in al Qaeda's early relationship to Yemen was Abd al Rahim al Nashiri, a citizen of Saudi Arabia who had fought against the Soviets in Afghanistan and then returned there in the mid-1990s with a group of fighters whom Osama bin Laden attempted to recruit into al Qaeda. Nashiri initially resisted swearing an oath of loyalty to bin Laden, and for a time went to live in Yemen. He later returned to Afghanistan, however, and eventually agreed to join al Qaeda. Sometime in 1998, Nashiri proposed to bin Laden that al Qaeda attack a US Navy vessel in Yemen, and bin Laden agreed. Eventually this resulted in the failed attack on the USS *The Sullivans* in January 2000 and the successful attack on the USS *Cole* in October 2000. Nashiri subsequently became 'chief of al Qaeda operations in and around the Arabian Peninsula', and continued to orchestrate attacks (including the bombing of a French ship) until he was captured in the United Arab Emirates in November 2002.

In the years immediately following Nashiri's capture, al Qaeda's operational activities in Yemen were limited. From roughly 2003 to 2006, al Qaeda focused its efforts on the Arabian Peninsula instead on Saudi Arabia, with Yemenis encouraged to travel to Iraq to fight.[9] Things began to change after some 23 imprisoned al Qaeda members escaped from a jail in Sanaa.[10] Many were recaptured, but two who were not—Nasser Abdul Karim al-Wuhayshi and Qasim al-Raymi—went on to establish 'al Qaeda in Yemen' in order to renew operations there. Wuhayshi had joined al Qaeda in the late 1990s, serving as a 'personal assistant' to bin Laden. Under his leadership, al Qaeda in Yemen began a series of attacks, including the murder of western tourists and an attack on the US embassy in Sanaa in 2008. At the beginning of 2009, moreover, Wuhayshi pronounced that al Qaeda operations in Saudi Arabia and Yemen were merging, and henceforth would operate under the collective heading of AQAP.[11] AQAP has, since then, been remarkably active, including but not limited to its attempt to destroy a US passenger jet bound for Detroit on Christmas Day 2009 and its 'cargo jet' plot in 2010 involving explosives hidden in packages shipped via overnight delivery services. As a Carnegie Endowment report emphasizes, however, the 'raised profile of the current incarnation of the organization should not detract from an awareness of al-Qaeda's enduring presence in Yemen'.[12]

---

[7] See ibid.

[8] The account in this paragraph is drawn from the Final Report of the National Commission on Terrorist Attacks Upon the United States, at pp 152–153.

[9] See e.g., Harris 2010, p 3.

[10] BBCNews, Profile: al-Qaeda in the Arabian Peninsula (31 October 2010), available at http://www.bbc.co.uk/news/world-middle-east-11483095.

[11] See ibid.

[12] See Harris 2010, p 2.

The picture that emerges from this brief sketch is complicated. AQAP appears to be merely the latest iteration of al Qaeda's long-standing operational presence in Yemen, contrasting sharply with the lack of historical ties to al Qaeda when it comes to some other current al Qaeda franchises such as AQIM. On the other hand, AQAP appears to operate without direct lines of control running to bin Laden or other senior al Qaeda leaders. Whether it is best perceived as part-and-parcel of al Qaeda, then, or instead simply an affiliated but independent franchise, would depend on how one defines organizational boundaries in this context in the first place and how one interprets the information available as to this question.

1.2.2 Anwar al-Awlaki in relation to AQAP

At the time of the 9/11 attacks, Anwar al-Awlaki was an imam at a mosque in Northern Virginia. He soon became a public figure of sorts thanks to his public pronouncements condemning the 9/11 attacks from an Islamic perspective.[13] Over time, however, his publicly-stated views appeared to change, taking on an increasingly anti-Western tinge.[14] He left the United States, first for the UK and then later for Yemen. Today al-Awlaki is in hiding in Yemen, and far from denouncing indiscriminate violence he has emerged as a prominent English-language propagandist for violent *jihad*, calling for the indiscriminate murder of Americans and others.[15] According to the US government, moreover, he also has

---

[13] See e.g., Shane and Mekhennet 2010; Washington Post Live Online, 'Understanding Ramadan: The Muslim Month of Fasting With Imam Anwar al-Awlaki, Falls Church Dar Al-hijrah Islamic Center' (19 November 2001), available at http://www.washingtonpost.com/wp-srv/liveonline/01/nation/ramadan_awlaki1119.htm. See also Matthew T. Hall, *Former Local Cleric Seen as 'Bin Laden of the Internet'; Al-Awlaki Headed Mosque on S.D.-La Mesa Border* (Jan. 10, 2010) (noting that al-Awlaki had told *National Geographic* that '[t]here is no way that the people who did this [i.e., the 9/11 attacks] could be Muslim, and if they claim to be Muslim, then they have perverted their religion').

[14] See e.g., Brian Fishman, Anwar al-Awlaki, the Infidel, Jihadica Blog (20 November 2009), available at http://www.jihadica.com/anwar-al-awlaki-the-infidel/ (discussing al-Awlaki's 'personal ideological evolution' with reference to a pre-9/11 episode in which Abdullah al-Faisal, perhaps the most prominent English-language proponent of extremist *jihad,* sharply criticized al-Awlaki's relatively moderate views, as well as a 2004 interview with National Public Radio in which al-Awlaki cited the 2003 invasion of Iraq as having put western Muslims in a position where they are 'torn between solidarity with their religious fellowmen and their fellow citizens'). See also Rob Gifford, National Public Radio All Things Considered, *U.K. Muslims Struggle With Cleric's Radicalization* (24 December 2009) (noting that al-Awlaki was known as a relatively moderate cleric but that his views had grown 'increasingly hostile' to 'the West' over the years), available at http://www.npr.org/templates/story/story.php?storyId=121880241.

[15] See Shane and Mekhennet 2010. See also Alexander Meleagrou-Hitchens, Voice of Terror, www.foreignpolicy.com (18 January 2011) (arguing that al-Awlaki has become the most significant English-language propagandist of *jihad* in terms of Western audiences in particular), available at http://www.foreignpolicy.com/articles/2011/01/18/voice_of_terror. For a collection of al-Awlaki's videos, some with English subtitles or transcripts, see www.memritv.org.

become part of AQAP,[16] and not just as an ideologue or propagandist. The government asserts that he has taken on an operational leadership role in connection with specific attacks.[17]

The government's attention actually had been drawn to al-Awlaki much earlier. The FBI became interested in him in 1999 in light of a position he had held at an Islamic charity suspected of channeling money to extremists and because he had been in at least brief contact with individuals indirectly linked to both bin Laden and Omar Abdel Rahman, the so-called 'Blind Sheik' associated with the 1993 World Trade Center bombing and the 1995 landmarks-and-tunnels plot in New York City.[18] Two of the future 9/11 hijackers had attended a mosque in San Diego where al-Awlaki had been the imam, and apparently spent a substantial amount of time in conference with him.[19] The FBI ultimately concluded that these contacts were innocent, but not everyone involved in the investigation agreed.[20]

In any event, al-Awlaki's extremist views—whether pre-existing or newly developed—would not become widely known to the general public until media reports in late 2009 began to emphasize that the perpetrator of the Fort Hood massacre, Major Nadal Malik Hasan, had been in touch with al-Awlaki by email.[21] Soon thereafter, al-Awlaki gained still further notoriety when media reports asserted that he had been involved with Umar Farouk Abdulmutallab, the would-be 'Christmas Day bomber' who unsuccessfully attempted to ignite an underwear bomb on a flight in 2009.[22]

More recently, the US government has set forth its view that al-Awlaki is not merely a propagandist of *jihad*, but an active member of AQAP. In a declaration filed by the government in connection with the aforementioned ACLU lawsuit, the Director of National Intelligence asserts that:

> 'Anwar al-Aulaqi has pledged an oath of loyalty to AQAP emir Nasir al-Wahishi, and is playing a key role in setting the strategic direction for AQAP. al-Aulaqi has also recruited individuals to join AQAP, facilitated training at camps in Yemen in support of acts of terrorism, and helped focus AQAP's attention on planning attacks on US interests.'[23]

---

[16] See *al-Aulaqi* v *Obama*, No. 10-cv-1469 (D.D.C. 25 September 2010), Opposition to Plaintiff's Motion for Preliminary Injunction and Memorandum in Support of Defendants' Motion to Dismiss, Exhibit 1, Unclassified Declaration in Support of Formal Claim of State Secrets Privilege by James R. Clapper, Director of National Intelligence ('Clapper Declaration'), at § 14, available at http://www.lawfareblog.com/wp-content/uploads/2010/09/Exhibit-1.pdf.

[17] See e.g., Hsu 2010 ('Officials say Aulaqi … was an operational planner in last year's failed Christmas Day bomb plot against a jetliner over Detroit').

[18] See Shane and Mekhennet 2010.

[19] See ibid.

[20] See ibid.

[21] See Shane 2009.

[22] See Johnson et al. 2009.

[23] Clapper Declaration, supra n 16, at § 14.

The declaration adds that al-Awlaki personally instructed Abdulmuttalab 'to detonate an explosive device aboard a US airplane', as part of a larger shift toward an operational leadership role with AQAP.[24]

In May 2010, al-Awlaki for the first time in a public setting expressly endorsed the use of violence not just against American military targets but also against American civilians.[25] When asked whether he supports operations 'target[ing] what the media calls 'innocent civilians,' al-Awlaki responded:

> 'Yes. ... The American people in its entirety takes part in the war, because they elected this administration, and they finance this war. In the recent elections, and in the previous ones, the American people had other options, and could have elected people who did not want war. Nevertheless, these candidates got nothing but a handful of votes. We should examine this issue from the perspective of Islamic law, and this settles the issue—is it permitted or forbidden? If the heroic *mujahid* brother Umar Farouk could have targeted hundreds of soldiers, that would have been wonderful. But we are talking about the realities of war. ...
>
> For 50 years, an entire people—the Muslims in Palestine—has been strangled, with American aid, support, and weapons. Twenty years of siege and then occupation of Iraq, and now, the occupation of Afghanistan. After all this, no one should even ask us about targeting a bunch of Americans who would have been killed in an airplane. Our unsettled account with America includes, at the very least, one million women and children. I'm not even talking about the men. Our unsettled account with America, in women and children alone, has exceeded one million. Those who would have been killed in the plane are a drop in the ocean.'[26]

According to analyst Thomas Hegghammer, al-Awlaki is 'not a top leader in AQAP's domestic operations, but he is arguably the single most important individual behind the group's efforts to carry out operations in the West'.[27] Hegghammer explains that al-Awlaki 'is most likely part of a small AQAP cell—the Foreign Operations Unit—which specializes in international operations and keeps a certain distance to the rest of the organization'.[28] Indeed, he believes al-Awlaki may be the head of that cell, arguing that 'intelligence analysts familiar with his e-mail communications' have long suspected as much:

---

24 See *al-Aulaqi* v *Obama* (D.D.C. 25 September 2010) (Opposition to Plaintiff's Motion for Preliminary Injunction and Memorandum in Support of Defendants' Motion to Dismiss) (hereinafter Government's Brief), at 1 (asserting that 'since late 2009, Anwar al-Aulaqi has taken on an increasingly operational role in AQAP, including preparing Umar Farouk Abdulmutallab in his attempt to detonate an explosive device ... on Christmas Day 2009'), 6 ('Since late 2009, Anwar al-Aulaqi has taken on an increasingly operational role in the group, including preparing Umar Farouk Abdulmutallab, who received instructions from Anwar Al–Aulaqi to detonate an explosive device aboard a US airplane over US airspace and thereafter attempted to do so aboard a Northwest Airlines flight from Amsterdam to Detroit on Christmas Day 2009, for his operation.'), 24 (referring to al-Awlaki as a 'senior operational leader') 29 n. 14 (same), available at http://www.lawfareblog.com/wp-content/uploads/2010/09/usgbrief.pdf.

25 See Lipton 2010. For the video, see http://www.memritv.org/clip/en/2480.htm.

26 Translation available at http://www.memritv.org/clip_transcript/en/2480.htm.

27 Hegghammer 2010.

28 Ibid.

'In public, Awlaki cast himself as an ideologue who supports armed struggle against the West, but is not directly involved in operations. In private, however, he has spent the past year actively recruiting prospective terrorists by e-mail and taking part in face-to-face indoctrination of operatives in Yemen.'[29]

1.2.3 The United States and the use of lethal force in Yemen

It is tempting to begin a discussion of the US government's use of lethal force in Yemen with the November 2002 incident in which, it appears, a US-operated drone fired a Hellfire missile into a vehicle traveling through the desert, killing the occupants.[30] Because of the lengthy fallow period that seems to have followed that attack, however, I will confine the discussion in this subsection to events beginning in late 2009.

The week prior to Abdulmutallab's unsuccessful attempt to take down a passenger jet on Christmas Day 2009, the government of Yemen claimed credit for conducting a pair of attacks on AQAP targets, including an airstrike meant to kill Wuhayshi, al-Shihri, and al-Awlaki.[31] The media reported that the United States also was involved (at least in terms of providing intelligence, but possibly more directly), and this prompted al-Awlaki's father to argue that it is illegal for the United States to attack its own citizens and that his son 'should face trial if he's done something wrong.'[32] Journalists near this time began to focus on whether the United States had orchestrated the attack to kill al-Awlaki and what legal grounds might support such a policy.[33] Then, a few weeks later Dana Priest of the *Washington Post* wrote an article asserting that:

'US military and intelligence agencies are deeply involved in secret joint operations with Yemeni troops who in the past six weeks have killed scores of people, among them six of 15 top leaders of a regional al-Qaeda affiliate, according to senior administration officials.'[34]

Priest described President Obama as having signed off on the December 24th attack on al-Awlaki's house, with the caveat that al-Awlaki was 'not the focus of

[29] Ibid.

[30] See infra n 59 and accompanying text.

[31] See Raghavan and Jaffe 2009.

[32] Ibid.

[33] At a press conference in early January 2010, a reporter asked White House Press Secretary Robert Gibbs whether the government viewed al-Awlaki as merely inspirational or actually an operational figure, and whether the plan was to arrest, capture, or kill him. Gibbs declined to answer, citing intelligence concerns. See Briefing by White House Press Secretary Robert Gibbs, 8 January 2010, 2010 WLNR 525020.

[34] Priest 2010.

the strike'.[35] She went on to reveal, however, that al-Awlaki 'has since been added to a shortlist of US citizens specifically targeted for killing or capture by the [Joint Special Operations Command]'.[36] According to Priest's account:

> 'After the Sept. 11 attacks, Bush gave the CIA, and later the military, authority to kill US citizens abroad if strong evidence existed that an American was involved in organizing or carrying out terrorist actions against the United States or US interests, military and intelligence officials said. The evidence has to meet a certain, defined threshold. The person, for instance, has to pose 'a continuing and imminent threat to US persons and interests,' said one former intelligence official. The Obama administration has adopted the same stance. If a US citizen joins al-Qaeda, 'it doesn't really change anything from the standpoint of whether we can target them,' a senior administration official said. 'They are then part of the enemy.'[37]

Subsequently, Scott Shane of the *New York Times* reported that al-Awlaki had been added to a similar list maintained by the CIA on the ground that he had become personally involved in operational planning, that 'international law permits the use of lethal force against individuals and groups that pose an imminent threat to a country', and that the individuals on the CIA list 'are considered to be military enemies of the United States' within the scope of the Congressional authorization for the use of military force enacted after 9/11.[38]

In late March, State Department Legal Advisor Harold Koh gave a much-noted speech to the American Society of International Law in which he addressed in more detail the legal argument in favor of using lethal force in circumstances such as this.[39] Koh endorsed the propositions that 'the United States is in an armed conflict with al-Qaeda, as well as the Taliban and associated forces' and that the

---

[35] Ibid.

[36] Ibid.

[37] Ibid. The Post subsequently posted a correction with the article: 'The article referred incorrectly to the presence of US citizens on a CIA list of people the agency seeks to kill or capture. After The Post's report was published, a source said that a statement the source made about the CIA list was misunderstood. Additional reporting produced no independent confirmation of the original report, and a CIA spokesman said that The Post's account of the list was incorrect. The military's Joint Special Operations Command maintains a target list that includes several Americans. In recent weeks, US officials have said that the government is prepared to kill US citizens who are believed to be involved in terrorist activities that threaten Americans.' Ibid. (posted at the top of the page).

[38] See Shane 2010. Invoking the principle that an unnamed government official explained that this 'was the standard used in adding names to the list of targets'. Ibid. Testifying before Congress 2 months earlier, Director of National Intelligence Dennis Blair had addressed this topic briefly. He explained that when an element of the Intelligence Community intends to take 'direct action against terrorists' in circumstances involving a US citizen, the relevant official seek 'specific permission' in light of factors including 'whether that American is involved in a group that is trying to attack us, [and] whether that American is a threat to other Americans'. Lake 2010.

[39] See Speech by Harold Hongju Koh, Legal Advisor, US Department of State, to the Annual Meeting of the American Society of International Law, *The Obama Administration and International Law* (25 March 2010), available at http://www.state.gov/s/l/releases/remarks/139119.htm.

United States 'may use force consistent with its inherent right of self-defense under international law'.[40] He then addressed the factors that the United States considers in connection with specific targeting decisions, describing this as a case-by-case process turning on such considerations as 'the imminence of the threat', 'the sovereignty of the other states involved', and 'the willingness and ability of those states to suppress the threat the target poses'.[41] Koh added that the proposed attack must also conform to 'law of war principles' including the principle of '*distinction*, which requires that attacks be limited to military objectives and that civilians or civilian objects shall not be the object of attack', and the principle of '*proportionality*, which prohibits attacks that may be expected to cause incidental loss of civilian life, injury to civilians, damage to civilian objects, or a combination thereof, that would be excessive in relation to the concrete and direct military advantage anticipated'.[42]

As Ken Anderson observed, Koh's comments seemed to affirm not just the existence of an armed conflict between the United States and al Qaeda, but also a long-standing US government position regarding the right to use force in self-defense even absent connections to an existing armed conflict.[43] The *Washington Post* editorial page subsequently praised the speech on similar grounds.[44] Others found his analysis unpersuasive.[45] The American Civil Liberties Union (ACLU), for example, wrote a letter to the President expressing 'profound concern about recent reports indicating that you have authorized a program that contemplates the killing of specific terrorists—including US citizens—located far away from zones of actual armed conflict. If accurately described, this program violates international law ...'[46] Meanwhile, the UN's 'Special Rapporteur on Extrajudicial, Summary or Arbitrary Executions'—Professor Philip Alston of New York University School of Law—produced a report for the UN Human Rights Council that advanced legal arguments relating to the use of force that in many ways appeared to conflict with the views of the US government, above all in connection with the use of force in response to terrorism in locations physically removed from conventional battlefields.[47] As Alston summarized things in a separate statement published on the ACLU's website:

---

[40] Ibid.

[41] Ibid.

[42] Ibid.

[43] Anderson 2010a, b.

[44] Editorial 2010.

[45] See e.g., Heller 2010; Johnson 2010, (citing the ACLU's concern that Koh failed to explain the geographic boundaries of the authority to use force or the criteria for distinguishing legitimate targets from civilians); Milanovic 2010.

[46] Letter from Anthony D. Romero, Executive Director of the American Civil Liberties Union, to Barack Obama, President of the United States, 28 April 2010, at p 1, available at http://www.aclu.org/files/assets/2010-4-28-ACLULettertoPresidentObama.pdf.

[47] See Alston 2010.

> 'The United States has endorsed 'a broad and novel theory that there is a 'law of 9/11' that enables it to legally use force in the territory of other States as part of its inherent right to self-defence on the basis that it is in an armed conflict with al-Qaeda, the Taliban and undefined 'associated forces'. This expansive and open-ended interpretation of the right to self-defence threatens to destroy the prohibition on the use of armed force contained in the UN Charter, which is essential to the rule of law.'[48]

For a time in the fall of 2010, it appeared that the legality of killing al-Awlaki might be put to the test in a judicial forum. In late August, the ACLU joined forces with the Center for Constitutional Rights (CCR) to represent al-Awlaki's father in a suit against President Obama, CIA Director Leon Panetta, and Secretary of Defense Robert Gates, requesting, among other things, (i) a declaratory judgment to the effect that international law forbids the use of lethal force outside of armed conflict except insofar as the targets 'present concrete, specific, and imminent threats to life or physical safety, and there are no means other than lethal force that could reasonably be employed to neutralize the threats',[49] and (ii) an injunction forbidding the use of lethal force against al-Awlaki except on those terms. The suit proved short-lived, however. Ultimately, the court did not reach the merits. Instead, it granted the government's motion to dismiss on the grounds that al-Awlaki's father lacks standing to invoke al-Awlaki's asserted rights and that the arguments in any event present 'political questions' that are not justiciable in the American legal system.[50]

That decision might yet be reversed on appeal, but in the meantime the legal questions generated by the decision to target al-Awlaki remain burning in the realms of policy and academic debate. All of which brings us to the question at hand: how best to think through the many threads of argument woven together under the heading of the international law applicable in the al-Awlaki scenario? A useful first step is to disaggregate those threads, distinguishing among those concerning the UN Charter's restraints on the use of force in international affairs, those involving IHL's *jus in bello* norms, and those involving IHRL.

1.3 Objections Founded in the UN Charter

Would the use of force by the US government against al-Awlaki in Yemen violate the UN Charter rules regarding the use of force in international affairs? The better view is that it would not.

---

[48] Statement of UN Special Rapporteur on US Targeted Killings Without Due Process (3 Augustus 2010, at http://www.aclu.org/national-security/statement-un-special-rapporteur-us-targeted-killings-without-due-process.

[49] *Al-Aulaqi* v *Obama* (D.D.C. 30 August 2010) (Complaint) at 11, available at http://www.aclu.org/files/assets/alaulaqi_v_obama_complaint_0.pdf.

[50] See *Al-Aulaqi* v *Obama*, 727 F.Supp.2d 1 (D.D.C. 2010), available at http://www.lawfareblog.com/wp-content/uploads/2010/12/Al-Aulaqi-Decision-Granting-Motion-to-Dismiss-120710.pdf.

Article 2(4) of the United National Charter provides that member states 'shall refrain in their international relations from the … use of force against the territorial integrity or political independence of any state, or in any other manner inconsistent with the purposes of the United Nations' (which purposes are defined in Article 1 to include, among other things, the goal of 'maintain[ing] international peace and security').[51] Article 2(4) is subject to exceptions, however, including Article 51's preservation of the right of self-defense and the Chapter VII mechanism whereby the Security Council may authorize the use of force.[52] Commentators debate the efficacy of the resulting system,[53] but we can at least say that the general aim was to sharply constrict the circumstances in which force lawfully could be employed across borders.

1.3.1 Has Yemen consented to the use of force?

The legality of a US strike in Yemen at first blush might seem to turn on the plausibility of an Article 51 self-defense argument, there being no applicable Chapter VII Security Council resolution in this setting. But the need to make such an argument drops out if Yemen has effectively consented to the strike.[54] In that circumstance, there is no infringement of Article 2(4) in the first instance—no offense to Yemen's territorial integrity or its political independence, no threat to international peace and security insofar as the rights of member states are concerned—and hence no need to make exculpatory arguments under Article 51.[55]

The public record provides considerable reason to believe that the government of Yemen has given at least some form of consent to at least some uses of lethal force by the United States—or at least to the use of lethal force by US and Yemeni forces acting in cooperation—on Yemen territory. Whether that consent suffices

51 UN Charter, Arts. 1(1), 2(4).

52 See UN Charter Arts. 39, 42, 51.

53 Whether it has served this purpose in actual practice has long been the subject of debate. Compare e.g., Franck 1970, pp 809–810, with Henkin 1971, pp 544–545.

54 See e.g., Alston 2010, p 12 § 37 ('The proposition that a State may consent to the use of force on its territory by another State is not legally controversial.'); Byers 2003, p 9 (asserting, in connection with a 2002 drone strike by the United States in Yemen, that the 'right to intervene by invitation is based on the undisputed fact that a state can freely consent to having foreign armed forces on its territory'); Murphy 2009, p 118; Dinstein 2005, pp 112–114.

55 My position on the doctrinal role played by consent differs from that described by Melzer. Melzer refers to a general consensus to the effect that consent is an 'exculpatory circumstance' justifying action that infringes Article 2(4). See Melzer 2008, pp 41, 75. I argue, in contrast, that where a state consents there is no infringement of Article 2(4) in the first instance and hence no need for exculpation. See also Dinstein 2005, p 112. The result is the same in either case, of course.

for purposes of a UN Charter analysis, and whether in any event it extends to the al-Awlaki scenario are more difficult questions.[56]

Priest reports that '[s]hortly after the Sept. 11, 2001, attacks, [then-CIA Director George] Tenet coaxed [Yemen's President] Saleh into a partnership that would give the CIA and US military units the means to attack terrorist training camps and al-Qaeda targets.'[57] Pursuant to this agreement, the United States provided the Yemen security services with equipment and training, and Saleh in turn gave 'approval to fly Predator drones armed with Hellfire missiles over the country.'[58] This appears to explain how it then came to pass, in November 2002, that a Predator drone was in position to strike and kill a group of al Qaeda suspects—including one who was an American citizen—in a car moving through an isolated stretch of desert in Yemen.[59]

Even if we assume that some degree of consent to lethal strikes existed as of 2002, the extent to which it continues to exist today is subject to some uncertainty in light of the Yemen government's understandable desire to minimize the public's appreciation for the extent of American-Yemeni security cooperation—i.e., its desire for plausible deniability. As Priest recently summarized the situation, the 'broad outlines of the US involvement in Yemen' had become public knowledge at least by the end of 2009 but the full 'extent and nature of the operations' did not become known until she reported in early 2010 that:

> '[i]n a newly built joint operations center, the American advisers are acting as intermediaries between the Yemeni forces and hundreds of US military and intelligence officers working in Washington, Virginia and Tampa and at Fort Meade, Md., to collect, analyze and route intelligence. The combined efforts have resulted in more than two dozen ground raids and airstrikes.'[60]

These revelations put the Saleh administration in a difficult position, as Priest acknowledged:

> 'The far-reaching US role could prove politically challenging for Yemen's president, Ali Abdullah Saleh, who must balance his desire for American support against the possibility

---

[56] I do not mean to suggest that demonstration of effective consent—or of the applicability of self-defense under Article 51—suffices to resolve all the international law questions associated with the al-Awlaki scenario. Part 1.4 below takes up a series of additional concerns sounding in human rights and humanitarian law. Some commentators may object to this sequencing, but I believe it to be the clearest way to proceed. Cf. Statement of Mary Ellen O'Connell, US House of Representatives, Committee on Oversight and Government Reform, Subcommittee on National Security and Foreign Affairs (28 April 2010) (objecting to arguments involving Yemen's consent to a 2002 drone strike on the ground that 'States cannot … give consent to a right they do not have'); O'Connell 2010, pp 16–17 (arguing that consent to use military force in the form of a drone strike would be *ultra vires* absent the existence of armed conflict permitting the consenting state itself to carry out such an attack).

[57] Priest 2010.

[58] Ibid.

[59] See ibid. For an assertion that Yemen's government consented to that attack, see Fisher 2003.

[60] Priest 2010.

> of a backlash by tribal, political and religious groups whose members resent what they see as US interference in Yemen.'[61]

Indeed, just a few weeks earlier Yemen's Deputy Prime Minister for Security and Defense, Rashad al-Alimi, had insisted at a rare press conference 'that there are limits to [Yemen's] military cooperation with the United States, warning that any direct US action in this impoverished Middle East nation could bolster the popularity of Islamic militants.'[62] He conspicuously did not exclude the possibility of further U.S.-directed airstrikes or drone strikes, however.

By late summer 2010, the actual state of affairs became somewhat clearer. The *New York Times* in August published an article describing a 'shadow war' in Yemen in which at least four attacks ostensibly carried out by Yemeni government forces from late 2009 onward in fact had been conducted on a clandestine basis by US military personnel and assets, including cruise missiles and Harrier fighter jets, with the consent in each instance of the Yemeni government.[63] And though these strikes in one instance apparently involved significant civilian casualties, and in another the death of a provincial deputy governor, American officials asserted to the *Times* that President Saleh was 'not so angry as to call for a halt to the clandestine American operations'.[64]

Notably, the same report suggested that an internal US government debate was underway at that time with respect to the possibility of complimenting or even replacing the military's clandestine strikes—which are disclosed to and approved by Yemeni officials—with a CIA covert action program, at least in part in order to 'allow the United States to carry out operations even without the approval of Yemen's government.'[65] Then, after a failed attempt by AQAP to put bombs aboard cargo jets bound for the United States in October 2010, the media reported a new round of debate at the White House concerning the desirability of launching (or in this case, reviving[66]) a CIA-operated drone strike program in Yemen—including the possibility of seeking Yemeni government approval for such

---

[61] See ibid.

[62] Yemen Warns US on Direct Intervention, Washington Post (7 January 2010). 'The statement underscored the rising concern among Yemen's leadership of a domestic backlash that could politically weaken the government and foment more instability. In recent days, top Yemeni officials have publicly downplayed their growing ties to Washington, fearing they will be perceived by their opponents as weak and beholden to the United States'. Ibid.

[63] See Shane, Mazzetti and Worth 2010. The article notes that the White House would have preferred to employ drones for these attacks, in light of their capacity to minimize deaths to innocent bystanders, but that the CIA's compliment of armed drones were tied up with operations in Pakistan. See ibid.

[64] Ibid.

[65] Ibid.

[66] The first new story to break this topic observed that drones had been absent from Yemen for years, apparently because of both the demands of combat elsewhere and the since in the mid-2000s that the presence of al Qaeda in Yemen had diminished. Miller et al. 2010.

strikes.[67] Insofar as this reflected a decision not to use force without notification to the Yemeni government, it might well have stemmed from the fact that President Saleh, according to two anonymous government officials, 'ha[d] shown a willingness to break off cooperation if the US undertakes operations on Yemeni territory without his approval.'[68] A separate, contemporaneous account added that drones actually had been redeployed to Yemen already, albeit under the military rather than the CIA's control, and that Yemen already had consented to their use should appropriate targets be located.[69]

Taken as a whole, these accounts provide substantial support for the following conclusions. First, the government of Yemen is eager for a host of understandable reasons to keep its cooperation with the United States out of the public's eye. Second, the government of Yemen nonetheless not only cooperates closely with US personnel in mounting its own counterterrorism operations but also permits US forces (the CIA in 2002, the military more recently) to use force directly, though subject to some form of notification-and-approval system. In those circumstances, it seems likely that the United States could make out a case for having consent to use force in the al-Awlaki scenario. A final consideration requires attention, however.

Let us assume that the United States government does receive *private* consent from the government of Yemen with respect to using force on its territory to kill al-Awlaki. Is a government's private consent, meant to be withheld from its own public, adequate to discharge the Article 2(4) concern?[70] Or does international law somehow require that consent be public?[71] Some scholars have argued that, as a matter of policy even if not legal obligation, consent ought to be given publicly and explicitly.[72] There are virtues to this position from a normative viewpoint,

---

[67] See e.g., Cloud 2010; Barnes and Entous 2010. The Wall Street Journal account, notably, added the possibility of placing US special forces units under CIA authority in Yemen expressly in order to establish a capacity to conduct ground operations without disclosure to the Yemeni government. See ibid.

[68] See ibid. See also Barnes and Entous 2010, (noting the view of a US official to the effect that the Yemen government 'limit[s] us when we are getting too close,' and reporting that the Yemenis had 'delayed or objected to US operations' in some instances over the past year).

[69] See Miller 2010.

[70] Another issue that can arise with consent is fabrication – as when the request for intervention is made by a puppet government acting under the direction of the intervening state. Dinstein suggests that fabricated consent is invalid. See Dinstein 2005, p 114. There does not appear to be a basis for treating Yemen's consent as an American fabrication, however. Dinstein also notes that a separate issue arises to the extent that consent is coerced, and he specifically notes that there may be a sense of coercion in the scenario in which the intervening state is attempting to suppress terrorism and makes clear that it will intervene in any event on self-defense grounds if consent is not forthcoming; he does not claim, however, that this scenario would actually amount to coercion to the point of invalidating the consent. See ibid.

[71] See Murphy 2009, pp 118–120, for a thorough discussion of this question in the context of Pakistan.

[72] See Alston 2010, p 27 ('If a State commits a targeted killing in the territory of another State, the second State should publicly indicate whether it gave consent, and on what basis.'); National

including that it would remove doubt as to whether consent had been given.[73] This is, after all, an evidentiary issue that proved problematic in the context of the ICJ's consideration of the collective self-defense argument in the *Nicaragua* decision.[74] Requiring public and explicit consent would also tend to make the government of the consenting state more accountable—both domestically and internationally—for such decisions. Such accountability certainly can be viewed in positive terms, yet it also can have a substantial and undesirable cost where, as in both Yemen and Pakistan, it is likely that the domestic response would render cooperation impossible or at least far more difficult. In any event, neither the Charter nor any other instrument addresses this issue, and the case has not been made that state practice supported by *opinio juris* establishes any such requirement; the argument sounds in policy, not legal obligation.[75]

1.3.2 Does the right of self-defense apply?

In the event that a consent argument is unavailing—or becomes so in the future[76]—the question becomes whether the United States nonetheless may act in Yemen pursuant to the right of self-defense preserved in Article 51.

We might begin by asking: self-defense against whom? Certainly not the government of Yemen, which is America's ally (however imperfect or

[73] See Murphy 2009, pp 118–119 (discussing the options for and difficulty of proving private or implicit consent in the context of Pakistan); O'Connell 2010b, p 18 (offering a similar warning).

[74] See Military and Paramilitary Activities in and Against Nicaragua (*Nicaragua* v *US*), Jurisdiction and Admissibility, Judgment, 1984 ICJ 392 (26 November) §§ 165–166 (questioning whether the United States had indeed received a request for assistance from El Salvador, Costa Rica, and Honduras), § 199 (concluding that customary law requires an attacked state to actually request assistance from another state where the latter intervenes on the ground of collective self-defense), §§ 232–236 (concluding that El Salvador had not formally requested assistance until some period after the US intervention in Nicaragua began, and though the court conceded that 'no strict legal conclusions may be drawn from the date' it nonetheless took this as evidence of whether El Salvador previously believed itself to be the subject of an armed attack from Nicaragua).

[75] In the context of Pakistan, Professor O'Connell has raised an important and distinct concern as to the provenance of the host state's consent. Specifically, she has argued that whatever else might be true of consent, it must be the case that consent has been given by the proper domestic authorities rather than, say, some subordinate entity such as a military commander or security service official who may be acting contrary to the preferences of civilian authorities. See O'Connell 2009, ('Pakistani intelligence services or the military have apparently cooperated with the United States on strikes, but under international law, it should be the elected civilian officials who provide a state's consent for foreign military operations'). For present purposes, it suffices to note that the media accounts related above indicate that consent in the Yemeni context flows directly from Yemen's president.

[76] At the time of this writing, a wave of popular protests against authoritarian rule is sweeping through a number of Arab states, prompting President Saleh to declare in early February 2011 that neither he nor his son would seek the presidency in the 2013 election. See Kasinof and Bakri 2011.

constrained) in this endeavor. Rather, the argument is that the United States seeks to engage in self-defense against either al Qaeda or AQAP. But even if we assume that the United States has suffered an armed attack triggering Article 51 self-defense rights against al Qaeda or AQAP, does it follow that the United States can exercise those rights in Yemen's territory without Yemen's consent? I consider these issues in sequence below.

1.3.2.1 Self-defense against al Qaeda

If the United States invokes the right to act in self-defense in the al-Awlaki scenario, is it best to understand this in terms of defense against AQAP in particular or, instead, against al Qaeda more generally? From the US perspective, emphasizing core al Qaeda has advantages and disadvantages. The advantage is the relative ease of establishing that the United States has suffered an armed attack from that group. There seems to be widespread agreement that al Qaeda's 9/11 attacks constituted an 'armed attack' against the United States,[77] notwithstanding much-criticized suggestions by the International Court of Justice in other contexts to the effect that Article 51 should be read atextually to refer only to armed attacks committed by states.[78] Combined with overwhelming reason to believe that al Qaeda intends further attacks (and thus that a responsive use of force would not be

[77] See e.g., UN Sec. Council Res. 1368, S/RES/1368 (12 September 2001) (recognizing, in connection with the 9/11 attacks, 'the inherent right of individual or collective self-defence in accordance with the Charter); Murphy 2009, p 129; Meeting Summary, 'International Law and the Use of Drones,' Summary of the International Law Discussion Group Meeting Held at Chatham House (21 October 2010) (remarks of Michael Schmitt) at pp 5–6, available at http://www.chathamhouse.org.uk/files/17754_il211010drones.pdf; Paust 2009; Jinks 2003b. Mary Ellen O'Connell has argued that '[t]errorist attacks are generally treated as criminal attacks and not as the kind of armed attacks that can give rise to the right of self-defense,' but noting Israel's situation circa 2006 notes exceptions for circumstances in which the pace and nature of the attacks make then 'more than crime' and capable of implicating Article 51. O'Connell 2010, p 5. This raises the question whether the 9/11 attacks (or earlier al Qaeda operations), being part of a considerably more episodic pattern, would count as an armed attack on this model. Cf. ibid., p 3 n.4 (stating that Resolution 1368 'was useful in making a finding that the 9/11 attacks could give rise to a right of self-defense').

[78] The ICJ suggested as much in *Advisory Opinion on the Legal Consequences of the Construction of a Wall in the Occupied Palestinian Territory*, Advisory Opinion, 9 July 2004 [2004] ICJ Rep, § 139 ('Article 51 of the Charter thus recognizes the existence of an inherent right of self-defence in the case of armed attack by one State against another State.'). See also Case Concerning Armed Activities on the Territory of the Congo (*Democratic Republic of Congo* v *Uganda*) 19 December 2005 [2005] ICJ 116 §§ 146–147 (treating the question of the DRC's state responsibility as if dispositive, yet also explicitly reserving decision as to whether and when the right of self-defense extends to 'irregular forces'). For a thorough debunking based on text, state practice, logic, and policy, see Lubell 2010, pp 30–35. See also Wilmshurst 2006, pp 965–971 ('There is no reason to limit a state's right to protect itself to an attack by another state. The right of self-defence is a right to use force to avert an attack. The source of the attack, whether a state or a non-state actor, is irrelevant to the existence of the right.').

a mere matter of revenge), these circumstances suffice to trigger the right of the United States to use force in self-defense vis-a-vis al Qaeda. Focusing on al Qaeda as such also presents a difficulty in the al-Awlaki scenario, however, in that it requires not just linking al-Awlaki to AQAP but also linking AQAP to al Qaeda.

In light of the facts recounted in Part 1.2, there is room for debate regarding AQAP's status as 'part of' al Qaeda. Coming to grips with the organizational structure of a clandestine, non-state actor network of this kind is famously difficult, and international law does not necessarily provide a substantive standard by which to resolve this inquiry.[79] Even if the standard to be applied were clear, moreover, the most pertinent evidence relevant to that task is not likely a matter of public record. In these conditions, it is simply not possible to say that the US government is mistaken when it asserts that AQAP in indeed part-and-parcel of al Qaeda itself.

That said, focusing on AQAP as an extension of al Qaeda does not provide the strongest foundation for concluding that the United States may have Article 51 rights in this context. As I explain below, the argument is stronger when one focuses directly on the course of dealings between the United States and AQAP itself.

1.3.2.2 Self-defense against AQAP

Set aside self-defense arguments based on core al Qaeda and the 9/11 attacks. Can a distinct self-defense argument be mounted based directly on AQAP's own activities? This approach avoids the difficulty of establishing an adequate link between al-Awlaki and core al Qaeda, but it introduces the need to point to AQAP-specific activities as sufficient triggers for Article 51.

Has AQAP engaged in an armed attack against the United States *already*, such that there is no need to broach the question of whether international law permits the *anticipatory* use of force in self-defense in this context? Here we are assuming a categorical distinction between AQAP and core al Qaeda, and hence must focus attention on a much narrower set of attacks. Yet questions of attribution still arise. For example, may we add to AQAP's account the bombing of the *USS Cole* in Yemen in 2000, or the mortar attacks on and car bombing of the US embassy in Yemen conducted by AQAP prior to its adoption of this name? In light of the lineage discussed above in Part 1.2, it seems entirely appropriate to do the latter, and at least defensible to do the former. Combined with AQAP's attempts to destroy both passenger and cargo jets bound for the United States in 2009 and

---

[79] An argument might be made for borrowing the standards provided in international law for attribution to a state of a non-state entity's actions. It is not obvious that it makes sense to transpose such a test to this context, however, and in any event the rules for attribution of state responsibility are not entirely settled themselves. Cf. Cassese 2007a, p 649 (discussing the contrast between the 'effective control' test set forth in *Nicaragua* and the 'overall control' test set forth in *Tadić*).

2010,[80] the United States has a strong case for claiming that it has experienced multiple armed attacks at AQAP's hands. To be sure, none have reached the intensity of the 9/11 attacks in terms of the number of resulting deaths. That is hardly dispositive, however, unless one thinks that the 9/11 attacks somehow constant a floor in terms of the necessary number of casualties involved in the armed attack calculus. The successful attacks emanating out of al Qaeda's Yemen operations have themselves been quite deadly, and those that were foiled would have been at least as destructive. This should suffice.

1.3.2.3 What of Yemen's territorial interests?

What has been said thus far supports no more than the claim that the United States has the right to act in self-defense against both al Qaeda and AQAP in *some* location. It does not automatically follow, however, that the United States can exercise this right in any location whatsoever without respect to the rights of the state in whose territory it proposes to act. Could Yemen properly object under Article 2(4) if it were to withdraw or refuse its consent but the United States nonetheless reached into its territory to kill al-Awlaki?

On current conditions, the answer is no. To be sure, some have argued that a defending state acting under Article 51 may not attack a non-state actor in the territory of another state unless that other state is in a legal sense responsible for the predicate attack.[81] Mary Ellen O'Connell, for example, has written that '[e]stablishing the need for taking defensive action can only justify fighting on the territory of another state if that state is responsible for the on-going attacks,' and that '[i]t may well be that … a group launching significant, on-going attacks has no link to a state and so no state can be the target of defensive counter-attack'.[82] Let us call this the 'strict' position.

Critics of the strict position, in contrast, argue either that (i) there is no need to prove that the host state is legally responsible for the actions of a non-state actor on its territory so long as the defending state confines its response to the personnel or assets of the non-state actor rather than the host state or (ii) the responsibility of the host state is established in any event if it fails to take reasonable steps to suppress

---

[80] That these attempts failed at the last minute should in no way impact their characterization.

[81] See e.g., Meeting Summary, 'International Law and the Use of Drones', Summary of the International Law Discussion Group Meeting Held at Chatham House (21 October 2010) (remarks of Mary Ellen O'Connell) p 3 ('The ICJ has held on several occasions that the armed attack must be attributable to a state where any counterattack in self-defence occurs.'), 4 (The ICJ held in *Congo* v *Uganda* that Congo's failure or inability to take action against militants carrying out sporadic armed attacks in Uganda did not give rise to any right by Uganda to cross the border and attack the groups themselves.'). For additional sources for and against the strict position, see Brunnee and Toope 2010, p 295.

[82] O'Connell 2002, p 899.

the threat posed by the non-state actor.[83] The Chatham House Principles of International law on the use of force in self-defense provide an illustration:

> 'It may be that the state is not responsible for the acts of the terrorists, but it is responsible for any failure to take reasonable steps to prevent the use of its territory as a base for attacks on other states. Its inability to discharge the duty does not relieve it of the duty. ... Thus, where a state is *unable or unwilling* to assert control over a terrorist organisation located in its territory, the state which is a victim of the terrorist attacks would, as a last resort, be permitted to act in self-defence against the terrorist organisation in the state in which it is located.'[84]

This position, notably, is consonant in important respects with the law of neutrality. Under the laws of neutrality, 'the region of war does not include the territories of neutral States, and no hostilities are permissible within neutral boundaries.'[85] Among other things, this means that participants in hostilities must not use the territory of a neutral for troop transit, communications, or recruiting, while the neutral state itself has a corollary obligation to stop the parties from using its territory for operational purposes.[86]

In a similar spirit, Michael Schmitt emphasizes that a state's right of territorial inviolability must be construed in light of its corresponding duty to the international community to ensure that its territory is not used as a base from which to cause harm to others.[87] On this view, the resulting capacity of the victim state to exercise its Article 51 rights on the territory of the host state is narrow, arguably requiring an ultimatum or *demarche* with a reasonable time period for response (though one can readily imagine circumstances where time does not permit this) and certainly requiring that force be limited if possible to the non-state actor rather than the institutions of the host state itself (though the defending state would have to be able to respond with proportional force if the host state used its military to

[83] See e.g., Schmitt, supra n 77, p 6 ('It is true that the ICJ, in the *Wall* and the *Congo* cases, appears to have rejected the notion that the right to self-defence arises against an armed attack by a nonstate actor. Yet, those decisions were highly controversial and widely criticized. Indeed, strong dissenting opinions correctly pointed out that not only was the Court ignoring post 9/11 state practice, but that there was nothing in the text of the Article 51 which would indicate that an armed attack cannot be launched by a nonstate actor.'). See also Lubell 2010, pp 36–42; Paust 2010; Kreß 2010, p 248 (arguing that even prior to 9/11 self-defense extended to attacks from non-state actors) (citing, inter alia, Kreß 1995); Schmitt 2008a, pp 145–149; Dinstein 2005.

[84] Wilmshurst 2006, p 12 (emphasis added). The Chatham House statement expressly rejects a reading of *Democratic Republic of Congo* v *Uganda* that would preclude the use of force against a non-state actor on the territory of the host state absent evidence of the host state's legal responsibility for that non-state actor. It argues that the decision instead supports no more than the conclusion that absent legal responsibility the defending state's self-defense right does not extend to the host state as such. See ibid., at n 81. See also Schmitt, supra n 77, p 5.

[85] Dinstein 2005, p 26.

[86] See ibid. See also Hague Convention (V) Respecting the Rights and Duties of Neutral Powers and Persons in Case of War on Land (1907), Art. 5.

[87] See Schmitt, 'Change Direction', supra n 83, pp 159–162 (citing, inter alia, *Corfu Channel (United Kingdom* v *Albania*), 1949 ICJ 4 (9 April)). See also Schmitt 2008b, pp 20–27.

attempt to stop the Article 51 action).[88] At the risk of oversimplification, in any event, we might collect these views under the heading of the 'broad' position.[89]

Significantly, the strict and broad approaches may not be as far apart as seems at first glance. To be sure, the strict state-responsibility position appears to preclude resort to force under Article 51 in another state's territory except in circumstances of state-sponsored terrorism or its practical equivalent, thus problematically failing to account for the need of states to respond militarily in some circumstances involving genuinely independent terrorist entities.[90] Yet at least some advocates of the strict state-responsibility position endorse a critical exception to that rule. As Mary Ellen O'Connell writes, a defending state may *also* use force against a non-state entity on another state's territory where that state 'cannot control the acts of groups on its territory', even if the state would not otherwise bear legal responsibility for the non-state actors actions.[91] This exception—which she refers to as the 'failed or impotent state'[92]—has direct application to Yemen's Shabwa province, where al-Awlaki is thought to be. The writ of the central government does not truly run there, thus providing ample grounds for the United States to argue that the 'failed or impotent' state exception applies and that it can as a consequence use force in self-defense against AQAP even if one demands satisfaction of the strict state-responsibility standard in other contexts.

[88] See Schmitt 2008a, p 27. Note the difficult question of whether the defending state could avoid the obligation of an ultimatum or *demarche* to the host state in circumstances where the defending state suspects the host state will tip off the non-state actor or even use the warning to enhance its own capacity to repel an attack.

[89] The broad state-responsibility position, as described above, could be viewed simply as a very flexible substantive standard for demonstrating state responsibility or, instead, as an argument against requiring state responsibility in the first instance. The difference matters greatly, in that a finding of state responsibility opens the doors to actions directly targeting the state itself, whereas the point of arguing that state responsibility need not be shown is simply to explain why it is justified to attack the non-state actor within the state's borders, no more and no less. Cf. Schmitt 2008a, p 27 ('It may not strike any targets of the 'host' government, nor anything else unconnected with the terrorist activity.').

[90] See O'Connell 2002, p 900 (arguing that a state is responsible for a non-state actor's armed attack if (i) 'agents of that state were involved', (ii) the state 'sends persons to carry out the attack even if those persons are not the state's officials or agents', and (iii) the state 'has developed sufficiently close links with the group even if it does not control them', (citing the example of 'organizing, coordinating or planning the military actions of the military group, in addition to financing, training and equipping or providing operational support to that group') (quoting *Prosecutor* v *Tadić*, Opinion and Judgment, No. IT-94-1-T, § 137 (7 May 1997)). Cf. Jinks 2003a, pp 144–146 (observing that the US government chose to justify its actions against the Taliban in Afghanistan on grounds of state responsibility resting on a 'harboring'/'supporting' theory rather than the 'overall control' standard of the ICTY in *Tadić* or the 'effective control' standard of the ICJ in *Nicaragua*, and raising objections to this approach).

[91] See supra n 78, p 900–901 (citing the examples of Israeli actions against Hezbollah in Lebanese territory and Turkish and Iranian action against Kurdish entities in the Kurdish regions of Iraq during the interwar period).

[92] See ibid., p 901.

Even with the failed/impotent state exception, of course, important gaps remain between the strict and broad positions. First, the failed/impotent state exception does not necessarily encompass capable-but-unwilling host states (i.e., states that in theory could take effective action but choose not to do so out of sympathy, fear, or otherwise).[93] Even this difference may drop away, however, should one adopt the view that harboring or supporting a terrorist organization in any event suffices to satisfy any state responsibility requirement that might then attach; that is, the difference does not matter if one moves away from the control tests advanced in *Nicaragua* and *Tadić*.[94]

Second, and more problematically, evidentiary disagreements inevitably will arise as to whether the relevant conditions have been satisfied, whatever those conditions may be. As applied to the hypothetical scenario in which Yemen reduces or eliminates its cooperation with the United States, for example, the US government no doubt would argue that Yemen's writ does not effectively run to the Shabwa province and that it is not truly interested in suppressing AQAP in any event, whereas Yemen surely would deny both claims and would point to various actions undertaken against AQAP in that province as evidence. All of which would drive home the point that such disputes ultimately may turn on who if anyone gets to decide them, what standard of proof that decision-maker brings to bear, and what evidence is available. For better or worse, however, '[i]nternational law has no generally-accepted law of evidence' in this circumstance,[95] nor an authoritative forum for addressing such debates (except perhaps in the limited circumstances where the Security Council overcomes obstacles to its involvement or the International Court of Justice can properly assert jurisdiction).

1.3.2.4 Necessity and proportionality as inherent constraints on self-defense in the Article 51 setting

Assume for the sake of argument that the right of the United States to act in self-defense under Article 51 has been triggered (whether by core al Qaeda, AQAP, or both) and that any objection Yemen may have under Article 2(4) has been resolved. The next question is whether the manner in which the United States exercises that right is constrained by any considerations inherent in the self-

---

93 Cf. Schmitt 2008b, p 1. See also Waxman 2009, pp 57–77 (discussing the absence of evidentiary legal standards with respect to use of force, including burdens of proof and their allocation).

94 Cf. Jinks 2003a, pp 145–146 (discussing, and critiquing, the arguable post-9/11 shift away from 'control' to 'harboring' or 'supporting' as a standard for state responsibility). See also Henderson 2010, p 403 (contending that the Obama administration has carried forward the harboring standard).

95 O'Connell 2002, p 895. O'Connell argues for adoption of a clear-and-convincing evidence standard in this context, as a matter of both law and policy. See ibid., pp 895–899.

defense concept itself (separate and apart from the IHL and IHRL considerations discussed below).

Neither Article 51 nor any other aspect of the Charter specifies such restraints. There is substantial consensus, however, that the *customary* right to self-defense enshrined in Article 51 requires compliance with conditions of necessity and proportionality.[96] Just what these elements require, however, and how they relate to identically-named requirements associated with IHL's *jus in bello* provisions and with IHRL, is less clear.

Consider first necessity. In the context of the customary right to self-defense, this element arguably entails two distinct inquiries. According to Murphy, 'the International Court of Justice and scholars typically first consider whether there are peaceful alternatives to self-defense, such as pursuing available diplomatic avenues'.[97] This aspect of the necessity inquiry is primarily a function of both the host state's *willingness* and its *actual capacity* to act effectively to suppress the threat. Both conditions must be satisfied. In most states they would be insofar as al Qaeda is concerned; France, for example, is both perfectly capable and willing to act against any al Qaeda threat that might turn out to be lurking within its borders, and hence the United States could not exercise Article 51 rights there. But not every state is both willing and capable of suppressing threats. Pre-9/11 Afghanistan provides an example of a government (albeit only a de facto regime) arguably able but certainly unwilling to act against al Qaeda. Current-day Somalia provides an example of a government (such as it is) that presumably is willing yet is entirely unable to act against al Qaeda. Pakistan arguably is a mixed case, with difficult questions regarding the extent of its willingness to act in the Federally Administered Tribal Areas and, in any event, substantial doubts surrounding its capacity to do so.[98]

Even if this first aspect of the necessity inquiry is satisfied, at least some observers contend that the analysis must continue with an inquiry into whether

---

96 See e.g., Oil Platforms (*Iran* v *US*) 2003 ICJ (6 November) pp 161, 198; Legality of the Threat or Use of Nuclear Weapons, Advisory Opinion, 1996 ICJ (8 July) pp 226, 245; *Nicaragua*, 1986 ICJ, p 94. See also Alston 2010, p 14; Murphy 2009, p 127; Statement of Kenneth Anderson, US House of Representatives Committee on Oversight and Government Reform, Subcommittee on National Security and Foreign Affairs (18 March 2010) p 5, available at http://www.fas.org/irp/congress/2010_hr/032310anderson.pdf. Note that I do not discuss arguments for an additional requirement of imminence where there has not yet been an actual armed attack and the 'defending' state is acting in an anticipatory mode. That is an important issue, but not one presented here given the attacks that already have been directed at the United States.

97 Murphy 2009, p 127 (citing Dinstein 2005, p 237).

98 See e.g., DeYoung 2010, (discussing conclusion in US government report to the effect that 'Pakistan still has not 'fundamentally changed its strategic calculus' regarding insurgent sanctuaries on its territory' and noting that 'Pakistan has long resisted US urging to launch all-out attacks against Taliban and al-Qaeda redoubts in the [FATA]'), available at http://www.washingtonpost.com/wp-dyn/content/article/2010/12/14/AR2010121407420.html.

attacking a particular target would be useful as a means of preventing further attacks.[99] This inquiry at least partially overlaps with the separate requirement of proportionality, however, and is better dealt with under that heading. Proportionality in self-defense does not require a precise identity between the scale of the predicate attack and the scale of the force the defending state intends to use,[100] but it does require some reasonable degree of relationship between them.[101] Furthermore, some take the view that as time goes by the 'proper *referent* of *ad bellum* proportionality changes with the nature and scope of the conflict.'[102] On this view, the measure of proportionality at some point becomes not the original attack but, rather, 'the object legitimately to be achieved.'[103]

How might one analyze the killing of al-Awlaki under this framework? Consider first whether killing al-Awlaki would be 'necessary' in both the senses described above—i.e., necessary in the sense that Yemen is unable or unwilling to act effectively to suppress the threat he poses, and separately in the sense that targeting him would advance the goal of preventing further attacks. The case for necessity at the *individual* level is relatively strong, assuming that one credits the US government's claims regarding al-Awlaki's 'operational' role in AQAP's violent activities. The more difficult inquiry is the case for necessity in the broader sense in which we examine Yemen's willingness and capacity to suppress AQAP. It is unclear whether the Yemeni government actually is willing to arrest al-Awlaki and otherwise to act to suppress the threat of AQAP.[104] Even if we assume that it is willing, however, that it is not enough without a corresponding capacity to effectuate the arrest. At least for the time being Yemen's weak central government appears to lack the capacity to enforce its will reliably in Shabwa (the province where al-Awlaki and other AQAP members are thought to be) and other relatively

---

[99] See Murphy 2009, p 127 (citing Judith Gardam, Necessity, Proportionality and the Use of Force by States 4–8 (2004)).

[100] See ibid., at p 129 ('"Proportionality" does not require that the force be a mirror image of the initial attack, or that defensive actions be restricted to the particular geographic location in which the initial attack occurred'.).

[101] See Sloane 2009, p 52 ('ad bellum proportionality asks whether the initial resort to force or particular quantum of force used is proportional to the asserted casus belli').

[102] Ibid., at p 68.

[103] Ibid. (citing Higgins 1994). See also Murphy 2009, p 128. But see Anderson 2009, p 5 (referring to the 'customary law standards of necessity and proportionality' in terms of 'necessity in determining whom to target, and proportionality in considering collateral damage,' adding that 'standards in those cases should essentially conform to military standards under the law of war, and in some cases the standard should be still higher').

[104] See Hendawi and al-Haj 2010, (indicating that 'some analysts' believe that Yemen is giving only a 'half-hearted effort' to capture al-Awlaki). Cf. 'Yemen Sentences Awlaki in Absentia,' al Jazeera (Jan. 17, 2011) (noting that Yemen has prosecuted al-Awlaki *in absentia*, sentencing him to ten years' imprisonment), available at http://english.aljazeera.net/news/middleeast/2011/01/201111713355839969.html.

remote provinces where AQAP members enjoy the protection of local tribes.[105] Ironically, if the United States succeeds over time in its efforts to improve the capacities of Yemen's security forces, this answer could change, undermining the self-defense argument under Article 51 in the scenario in which Yemen continues to pursue AQAP but withdraws or refuses to give its consent to some particular uses of force by the US[106]

Next consider the proportionality question. As an initial matter, targeted killing of particular individuals is a relatively small-scale form of self-defense in comparison to, say, regime change and occupation, and certainly in proportion to the violence AQAP has directed and attempted to direct against the United States. But what of the objection that such strikes might be counterproductive in that they might generate sympathy for AQAP and hostility toward both the US and Yemeni governments (because they generate collateral damage, for example)?[107] This is a crucial consideration from a *policy* perspective, but it is difficult if not impossible to see how it could be operationalized with any degree of rigor as a *legal* constraint. Direct US uses of force in Yemen—not to mention resulting civilian deaths—no doubt stoke local grievances and play into extremist propaganda narratives, but it is far from clear how one would translate the existence of this dynamic into a quantifiable output, let alone an output that could be compared with rigor to whatever benefits flow from such attacks.[108] None of this is to say that decisionmakers should ignore the possibility that short-term benefits may be outweighed by long-term costs, of course. That is an entirely appropriate consideration of policy judgment.

Establishing that the United States has the right to use force against al-Awlaki in Yemen by virtue of consent or Article 51 self-defense does not by any means end the analysis. It only resolves objections belonging to Yemen itself under the UN Charter. It remains to be considered whether international law considerations focused on al-Awlaki himself, whether founded in IHL or IHRL, prohibit the United States from killing him.

---

[105] See e.g., *Yemeni Forces Kill Suspected al-Qaeda Militant*, CBC News (Assoc. Press) (13 January 2010) ('The San'a government has little control over Shabwa and large swaths of Yemen…. Powerful, well-armed tribes dominate extensive areas and bitterly resent intrusion by security forces.').

[106] See e.g., Baldor 2010, (discussing military and other aid to Yemen and the 'need to bolster that country's ability to track and battle militants').

[107] Mary Ellen O'Connell makes this argument in the context of drone strikes in Pakistan (though she does so under the rubric of the distinct proportionality inquiry required by IHL's *jus in bello* rules, which I discuss in Part 1.4). See O'Connell 2010, Testimony, supra n 72, p 5.

[108] Cf. Waxman 2008, pp 1365, 1387 and n 76 (citing Final Report to the Prosecutor by the Committee Established to Review the NATO Bombing Campaign Against the Federal Republic of Yugoslavia (1999) § 48).

1.4 Objections Founded in Anwar al-Awlaki's Own Rights

Setting aside objections associated with Yemen's sovereignty, does international law permit the United States to use lethal force against al-Awlaki? In the pages that follow, I first consider whether such an act would fall within IHL's field of application and, if so, to what effect. I then turn to a discussion of the same issues under the heading of IHRL.

Note that I do not also provide in this Part a distinct treatment of self-defense as a separate paradigm potentially governing this question, above and beyond the discussion of self-defense already provided in Part 1.3 above. This is not to suggest that there are no circumstances in which targeted killing is governed in international law primarily by the necessity and proportionality considerations entailed by the self-defense paradigm.[109] On the contrary, those considerations will be the most significant ones (alongside any applicable domestic law) in circumstances where IHL is not applicable and where IHRL has either limited or no applicability (in light of, for example, extraterritoriality considerations). Self-defense, on this view, is not a *substitute* lens through which to consider a particular targeting decision, but rather a *supplemental* one.

1.4.1 Does IHL apply and, if so, to what effect?

Two overarching questions arise under the IHL heading. First, is the al-Awlaki scenario actually within IHL's field of application? Second, would IHL if applicable authorize or forbid killing in this circumstance?

1.4.1.1 Is the al-Awlaki scenario within IHL's field of application?

Writing in the *International Review of the Red Cross*, Sylvain Vite laments that IHL 'does not include a full definition of those situations that fall within its material field of application'.[110] Nonetheless, it is possible to describe conditions that appear to be generally accepted as predicates to recognition of an 'armed conflict' rendering IHL applicable. With respect to IHL governing *international* armed conflict, in Vite's words, 'the level of intensity required for a conflict to be subject to [that law] is very low'; it suffices that there has been a purposeful 'resort

---

109 Cf. Anderson 2010a, b.

110 Vité 2009, p 70. See also Melzer 2008, p 245 (noting absence of definitions for armed conflict and hostilities in IHL treaties).

to armed force between States,' however brief or limited the violence may be.[111] In the *non-international* setting, in contrast, a higher 'threshold of intensity' applies before the label 'armed conflict' attaches, in order to exclude circumstances of mere internal disturbance.[112] Building on the ICTY's *Tadić* decision, among other things, Vite concludes that this threshold breaks down into two key elements: '(a) the intensity of the violence and (b) the organization of the parties'.[113] Both must be 'evaluated on a case-by-case basis by weighing up a host of indicative data.'[114] Intensity, for example, might be assessed by factors including but not limited to the 'duration of the conflict, the frequency of the acts of violence and military operations, the nature of the weapons used, displacement of civilians, territorial control by opposition forces, the number of victims (dead, wounded, displaced persons, etc.)'.[115] Melzer adds that 'the threshold of violence that can be handled with law enforcement must be exceeded, and the use of military means and methods required', but cautions against treating sustained duration as a necessary condition.[116] Organization, in turn, might take into account the existence of a command structure, recruiting capacity, internal rules, and so forth.[117] Other analyses reach comparable conclusions.[118]

It may be that the US government adheres to a broader understanding of IHL's field of application, one encompassing even a single armed attack.[119] But even under a more restrictive approach, the argument that IHL governs the potential use of lethal force against al-Awlaki is strong. There are at least two arguments that should be addressed under this heading. First, one might argue that a stand-alone non-international armed conflict has come into existence in Yemen recently as a result of the increasing intensity of hostilities involving the US and Yemeni governments, on one hand, and AQAP on the other. Second, one might argue in the alternative that an attack on al-Awlaki would in any event be encompassed by a larger, long-running non-international armed conflict between the United States

---

[111] Vité 2009, p 72 and sources cited therein. But see International Law Association Use of Force Committee, 'Final Report on the Meaning of Armed Conflict in International Law', 2010, p 18 ('Use of Force Committee Report), available at http://www.ila-hq.org/download.cfm/docid/2176DC63-D268-4133-8989A664754F9F87. See also Melzer 2008, p 251.

[112] See Vité 2009, p 76; Melzer 2008, p 256.

[113] Vité 2009, p 76 (citing *Prosecutor* v *Tadić*, Case No. IT-94-1-T, Decision on Defence Motion for Interlocutory Appeal on Jurisdiction, 2 October 1995, § 70). See also ICRC Opinion paper 2008.

[114] See Vité 2009, p 76.

[115] See ibid.

[116] Melzer 2008, pp 256–257 (observing that 'even an isolated incident can exceptionally demand the application of IHL relative to non-international armed conflicts, in the instant case due to the particular intensity of the hostilities coupled with the high degree of military organization of the insurgents and the direct involvement of governmental armed forces') (citing the Inter-American Commission on Human Rights decision in *Abella (La Tablada)*.

[117] See Vité 2009, p 77.

[118] See e.g., Use of Force Committee Report, supra n 108.

[119] Cf. Sassoli 2006, pp 7–8.

and al Qaeda, the geographic boundaries of which derive solely from the Article 2(4) and Article 51 considerations discussed previously in Part 1.3.

A. Is there an armed conflict with AQAP in Yemen?

When the US began airstrikes and other, clandestine military interventions in Afghanistan in the fall of 2001, there were few if any who would deny that the circumstances amounted to armed conflict or that IHL governed those particular uses of force (though there was, famously, considerable disagreement as to whether that armed conflict should be categorized as a 'Common Article 2' international armed conflict implicating the full range of IHL, a 'Common Article 3' non-international armed conflict implicating the limited subset of IHL rules applicable in that context, or perhaps something else altogether).[120] In comparison, how do the interactions among the US government, the Yemen government, and AQAP compare?

As described above in Part 1.3, the US military beginning at least in late 2009 and continuing into 2010 on at least four occasions appears to have used airstrikes or ship-launched missiles to attack AQAP targets in Yemen (in addition to the 2003 drone strike attributed in the media to the CIA),[121] and the government of Yemen has to an unclear extent used its own military and security services to carry out attacks against AQAP targets during the same period.[122] AQAP, for its part, has sustained a relatively substantial pace of violence directed at the Yemeni government as well as foreign targets (including but not limited to US targets both within and outside Yemen). AQAP's attacks on US-specific targets are discussed above in Part 1.2.1. In addition, a recent statement from AQAP claimed responsibility in just the second half of 2010 for some 49 violent attacks on Yemeni security and government personnel and installations, including an attack on a regional governor that resulted in the death of eight soldiers in one instance.[123] Of course, one must take such claims with a grain of salt, mindful that they may be

---

[120] See e.g., Corn 2007, p 295; Chesney 2006, pp 708–713; Rona 2003, pp 58–63. For a review of the history of the international/non-international divide in IHL, see Bartels 2009, p 35.

[121] In a recent letter from President Obama to Congress provided 'consistent with' the reporting requirements of the War Powers Resolution, the President wrote that he 'has deployed US combat-equipped forces to assist in enhancing the counterterrorism capabilities of our friends and allies, including special operations and other forces for sensitive operations in various locations around the world'. See 'Letter from the President Regarding the Consolidated War Powers Report' (15 December 2010), available at http://www.whitehouse.gov/the-press-office/2010/12/15/letter-president-regarding-consolidated-war-powers-report. Yemen is not specifically mentioned, though the above-quoted section of the letter concludes by noting that a 'classified annex to this report provides further information'. Ibid. Of course, air and missile strikes in 2009 and 2010 presumably were not launched from within Yemen.

[122] See e.g., Jamjoom 2010.

[123] See 'AQAP Announces Responsibility for 49 Attacks in Yemen During 2010', Yemen Post (1 January 2010), available at http://yemenpost.net/Detail123456789.aspx?ID=3&SubID=2936.

exaggerated, perhaps substantially so. That said, the level of political violence in Yemen is substantial, and AQAP bears responsibility for at least some percentage of it.[124]

Allowing for uncertainties of attribution as to all of the violence described above, the case for satisfaction of the intensity criterion is substantial. Factors cutting in favor of satisfying the intensity criterion include the nature of the weaponry employed by the governments involved (especially the US military's use of air power), the extended period during which this violence has occurred, the frequency with which AQAP has engaged in attacks,[125] and the volume of deaths and injuries as a result of attacks by all parties. Other factors are indeterminate, and at least do not cut *against* a finding of adequate intensity. For example, it is difficult to decide what to make of the frequency-of-attack consideration with respect to uses of force by both governments: we lack good information on the operations of the Yemeni security services, and the frequency of attacks conducted by US forces (four attacks over 1 year that we know of) is a relatively small number in comparison to operations in, say, Afghanistan. Yet these numbers are far from *de minimis*. Similarly, the question of territorial control is a difficult one in this setting. The government's control over Shabwa and other provinces appears to be limited, but it does not follow that AQAP controls that territory; rather, it seems more accurate to say that various tribes control it and that some of these tribes harbor AQAP.[126] Whether that distinction should matter, so long as the state is excluded from control over its territory, is unclear.[127]

The case for satisfaction of the separate criterion of organization likewise is strong despite being subject to debate. This factor is exceedingly difficult to judge from the public record, an inherent problem when it comes to developing an understanding of the organizational structure of a clandestine non-state actor operating in a remote location, not to mention the conceptual uncertainty surrounding the very meaning of organization in such a setting. On one hand, AQAP plainly has a formal leadership structure. As noted in Part 1.2., Wuhayshi functions as the emir, and al-Shihri as his deputy. Other key figures include its military chief (Qassim al-Raymi), its chief bombmaker (Ibrahim Hassan Asiri), its chief ideologue (Ibrahim Suleiman al-Rubaysh), and its chief theologian (Adil al-Abab).[128] AQAP also has a discernible membership structure rooted in the requirement of an oath of allegiance (*bayat*) to Wuhayshi.[129] Gregory Johnsen, who has frequently

---

[124] Cf. Curran et al. 2011, (listing and sourcing dozens of instances of political violence in Yemen in 2010).

[125] Cf. Melzer 2008, p 270 (explaining that the concept of 'attack' encompasses the emplacement of explosive devices).

[126] See e.g., *Al-Awlaki* v *Obama*, No. 10-cv-01469 (D.D.C. Oct. 7, 2010) (Declaration of Prof. Bernard Haykel) § 8.

[127] One might also argue, though, that territorial control is a poor proxy for the 'intensity' inquiry, and should at most be used instead as a loose proxy for the 'organizational' inquiry.

[128] See Johnsen 2010a.

[129] See Johnsen 2010b.

criticized the US government's fixation on AQAP in general and al-Awlaki in particular,[130] nonetheless depicts AQAP as an increasingly cohesive and threatening organization:

> 'The organization, already the most regionally and economically representative of any group in the country, has only grown stronger over the past 3 years. Once disorganized and on the run, today al Qaeda members are putting down roots by marrying into local tribes and *establishing a durable infrastructure that can survive the loss of key commanders*. They have also launched a two-track policy of persuasion and intimidation, first by constructing a narrative of jihad that is broadly popular in Yemen, and second by assassinating or executing security officials who prove too aggressive in their pursuit of al Qaeda fighters.'[131]

To be sure, others take a different view. In a declaration submitted in support of the lawsuit filed by the ACLU on behalf of al-Awlaki's father, Bernard Haykel argues that AQAP 'is a fragmented group ... best understood as ... consisting of separate distinct gangs with different interests and no unified strategy.'[132] AQAP, Haykel continues, 'does not have an organizational chart that lays out its various levels of leadership, command and control or the various committees that manage [its] different affairs'.[133] On this view, AQAP is simply a 'movement', one that 'is not sufficiently coherent to be organized in a stable fashion'.[134]

Which of these views one finds most persuasive would seem to go far in determining whether one thinks that the organization criterion is satisfied in the AQAP scenario. But how to judge between them without additional information, such as classified intelligence available only to the government? In a litigation setting, of course, the allocation and nature of the burden of proof would come into play, as would evidentiary and other procedural rules that might impact the universe of information that a party would be able or willing to put forward to the decisionmaker. Outside that context, however, scholars, government officials, and other participants in the debate are left to grapple with the available information as best they can en route to reaching their own judgments as to whether the substantive legal standard has been satisfied. Ultimately, the most we can reliably say without additional information may simply be that the argument for satisfaction of the organizational criterion is strong yet contested.

130 See ibid.

131 Johnsen Jan./Feb. 2010, (emphasis added).

132 *Al-Awlaki* v *Obama*, No. 10-cv-01469 (D.D.C. 7 October 2010) (Declaration of Prof. Bernard Haykel) § 7.

133 Ibid.

134 Ibid. Haykel elsewhere has observed, on the other hand, that 'Al Qaeda has always had a presence in Yemen. The first attack was in 1992, in Aden, against American troops en route to the relief effort in Somalia. ... Al Qaeda has a longstanding presence in Yemen through marital and ancestral connections. Its members have taken advantage of those links and the protection offered through the tribal system.' See Interview with Bernard Haykel on Yemen, The Browser: Writing Worth Reading (19 January 2011), available at http://thebrowser.com/interviews/bernard-haykel-on-yemen. Haykel's interview does make clear his view that Yemen should not be viewed through an al Qaeda prism. See ibid.

In sum, there is at this time a plausible argument for categorizing the relationship among AQAP and the US and Yemeni governments as a state of armed conflict (of a non-international character).[135] This in not, however, the only argument available for asserting the relevance of IHL to an attack on al-Awlaki.

B. Does IHL apply in Yemen by extension of an armed conflict with al Qaeda in Afghanistan or otherwise?

Imagine that in the midst of the Second World War, the United States learned that an aircraft carrier of the Imperial Japanese Navy was cruising in a remote region of the Pacific Ocean, one that had heretofore seen no hostilities of any kind. Imagine further that by sheer luck the United States had a carrier of its own within striking distance, and dispatched bombers to destroy the Japanese ship. No one would deny that IHL would govern that attack, notwithstanding its geographic remoteness from locations in which America and Japan were then engaged in sustained combat operations. Nor would the analysis change if the United States were to attack a Japanese vessel or military unit that for whatever reason had entered neutral territory in circumstances in which the neutral state proved unable or unwilling to enforce its neutrality.[136] In both cases, the nature and affiliation of the targets compels the conclusion that IHL would govern an attack on them; questions of geopolitical boundaries would enter into the discussion only insofar as the law of neutrality or other host-state sovereignty concerns might arise.

Nonetheless, questions of geography have become increasingly significant to debates over IHL's field of application in recent years thanks to anxieties associated with post-9/11 claims of a 'global war on terror'.[137] When the United States intervened in Afghanistan in the fall of 2001, no one seriously disputed the US government's claim that a state of armed conflict with the Taliban had arisen and that al Qaeda in at least some respects was involved in *that* conflict in *that*

---

[135] The US government largely avoided discussing merits questions in its brief in the *al-Awlaki* litigation. Notably, however, it did not explicitly advance the view that the United States, Yemen, and AQAP are enmeshed in a separate armed conflict (though it did refer to AQAP as a 'co-belligerent' of al Qaeda, as an alternative in the event the court did not accept that AQAP is part-and-parcel of al Qaeda itself; the co-belligerent characterization, arguably, is tantamount to an argument that conditions of armed conflict would be met vis-à-vis AQAP even if analyzed in isolation). See Government's Brief, supra n 24.

[136] These examples are inspired by Professor Michael Lewis, who emphasizes the example of the German pocket battleship the *Graf Spee*, which was penned by the British into the neutral port of Montevideo and then scuttled by her Captain when Uruguay's enforcement of its neutrality obliged him to put to sea. See 'Drone Warfare, Targeted Killings and the Law of Armed Conflict', Panel Discussion at the University of Virginia School of Law (2 November 2010), available at http://www.law.virginia.edu/html/news/2010_fall/drones.htm.

[137] See Waxman 2010, p 443 ('If the non-state terrorist threat is internationally dispersed, how far does self-defense authority extend? Answering these questions depends again on some critical assumptions about the organizational structure of transnational terrorist threats.').

location. But the US government's claim of a distinct armed conflict vis-à-vis al Qaeda alone—one that traced back as far as al Qaeda's 1998 'declaration of war' and that was relevant in contexts well-beyond Afghanistan—proved to be exceptionally controversial; perceptions that the US government claimed the existence of armed conflict not just with al Qaeda but with terrorism in general further aggravated such concerns.[138] The prospect that the United States might on this basis claim authority to kill or detain in circumstances physically removed from Afghanistan itself—as eventually occurred in locations such as Yemen and Somalia[139]—was deeply disturbing to many observers.[140]

The proper way to address such anxieties would be to insist upon rigorous adherence to the Article 2(4) and Article 51 considerations discussed above in Part 1.3. (thereby precluding the US government from resorting to force at its discretion on any state's territory), as well as rigorous adherence to IHL rules governing who may be targeted as an individual matter. Some observers, however, have pursued a different or at least additional line of argument, arguing that IHL's field of application should be geographically confined within the borders of the state(s) in which the predicate conditions for armed conflict (intensity and organization) are at any given moment satisfied[141]—thereby presumably (though not necessarily) leaving the use of force in other locations subject to IHRL.[142] On this model, IHL would govern American uses of force against al Qaeda in Afghanistan but not against al Qaeda in Yemen or anywhere else (so long as we assume that events

[138] Melzer's discussion of the Bush Administration's post-9/11 position illustrates both this perception and this concern. See Melzer 2008, pp 262–267. It is worth emphasizing, however, that the US government in its litigation positions in an array of post-9/11 cases has not claimed such broad authority, but rather has consistently referred to 'al Qaeda, the Taliban, and associated forces.' For a review, see Chesney 2011.

[139] See e.g., Priest 2010, ('Obama has sent US military forces briefly into Somalia as part of an operation to kill Saleh Ali Nabhan ....'); Lake 2010, ('One American ... was killed by a US missile strike in Somalia.').

[140] See e.g., Balendra 2008; Vöneky 2007, p 747; Brooks 2004, p 675. Cf. Arimatsu 2009, p 157, (addressing similar issues in the context of Israel's Gaza Strip operations in 2008–2009).

[141] Consider, for example, Mary Ellen O'Connell's argument that IHL 'has a territorial aspect. It has territorial limits. It exists where (but only where) fighting by organized armed groups is intense and lasts for a significant period'. *Al-Awlaki* v *Obama*, No. 10-cv-01469 (D.D.C. 7 October 2010) (Declaration of Prof. Mary Ellen O'Connell) § 13. Thus the United States may well be able to act under color of IHL against al Qaeda in Afghanistan (given the manifest circumstances of armed conflict there) but it simply does not follow 'that the United States can rely on [IHL] to engage suspected associates of al Qaeda in other countries' such as Yemen without an independent determination of armed conflict in those locations. Ibid., § 14. See also ibid. ('The application of the law of armed conflict [i.e., IHL] depends on the existence of an armed conflict. Armed conflict exists in the territorially limited zone of intense armed fighting by organized armed groups.'). See also Roth Letter, supra n 1 (setting forth the position of Human Rights Watch in opposition to any claim of a geographically-unrestricted definition of an armed conflict with al Qaeda).

[142] As discussed in more detail below in Part 1.4.2, this may be an unsafe assumption insofar as key IHRL conventions are, in the views of some states, inapplicable extraterritorially, leaving IHRL to apply solely on the level of customary law.

there lack the intensity or organization required to make an independent case for the existence of armed conflict), even if we accept for the sake of argument that AQAP is part-and-parcel of al Qaeda or if we assume that undisputed members or leaders of al Qaeda are present elsewhere. On this model, notably, the eventual withdrawal of American forces from Afghanistan sooner or later would remove IHL from the equation even there.

This formalistic approach to IHL's field of application is problematic for several reasons. As an initial matter, the legal foundation for the position is unclear. It cannot easily be derived from treaty language, for example. State practice on this point is indeterminate at best. There are endless examples of a party to an existing armed conflict using force in the territory of another state which until then was not experiencing hostilities within its own borders, in order to prevent establishment of a safe haven.[143] In some such cases, the extraterritorial use of force standing alone was of such intensity as to independently satisfy any requirement that armed conflict exist within the other state's boundaries, making it impossible to say whether application of IHL would rest on that ground or instead on the ground that IHL governs all hostilities among the parties without regard to location.[144] On the other hand, in other instances the level of intensity of the extraterritorial hostilities may be too low to provide an independent foundation for recognition of an armed conflict (consider, e.g., the American special forces raid on an insurgent smuggling operation located in a Syrian village near the border with Iraq in October 2008).[145] Under the strict geographic model, IHL would not govern such raids, yet there is no basis for concluding that states apply or believe they should apply that approach in such circumstances.[146]

Caselaw, meanwhile, does speak to the issue indirectly, but in an indeterminate way. For example, several ICTY Trial Chamber decisions rejected arguments to

[143] See Melzer 2008, pp 259–261 and examples cited therein. Melzer's treatment addresses a distinct issue—i.e., whether a non-international armed conflict necessarily loses its 'non-international' character in such circumstances.

[144] See ibid. p 260 (giving the example of Ugandan attacks on the Lord's Resistance Army in the Sudan (undertaken with Sudan's consent), and noting that 'both the intensity of the confrontation and the extent of the devastation remained those of an armed conflict').

[145] See e.g., Scott Tyson and Knickmeyer 2008.

[146] Ken Anderson summarizes this critique of the pedigree of the strict-geography model: 'I cannot say that these claims—although heroically urged by the advocacy groups and their academic allies—have a basis in the law of war as the US (or really, leading war-fighting states) has traditionally understood it. Certainly the State Department, under Harold Koh, no less, does not even entertain it. And even military lawyers who are very far from defending the Bush administration's war on terror do not endorse the "geographical" limitation. ... Rather, the customary view of the US—and the traditional view of war-fighting states—has always been that the fight can lawfully go wherever the participants go. It goes where they go. "Battlefield" and "theatre of conflict" are not legal terms in the treaty law of war, not as limitations on the armed conflict itself. The law of war accepts as a practical reality that the armed conflict is where hostilities happen to take place, which means, of course, that the armed conflict is a reflection of hostilities and hostilities can be undertaken as a matter of jus in bello where the participants are.' Anderson 2010c.

the effect that IHL should be strictly confined to zones of geographic proximity to the actual conduct of armed activities, concluding instead that it applied throughout territory controlled by a party to the conflict no matter how remote from conflict.[147] On one hand, these decisions rejected the notion that proximity to actual hostilities is the relevant consideration for IHL's application, but on the other hand they did emphasize geographic borders (*de jure* or *de facto*) instead—but only in order to *expand* rather than contract IHL's field of application. These cases simply did not confront the question of whether IHL should also apply when parties to an armed conflict use lethal force against one another in new locations beyond their own respective borders.[148]

Nor is the policy argument for shifting to a strict-geographic model persuasive. On one hand, this approach is simply not necessary in order to prevent states outright from asserting the right to intervene military at their discretion on the territory of others. Article 2(4), in combination with the requirement of necessity entailed in the right of self-defense protected by Article 51, see to that concern adequately; the United States could not use force on a non-consensual basis in France, for example, as there is no basis for questioning France's capacity and will to act against al Qaeda members on its territory. Nor is the strict-geographic approach a sensible way to address concerns about the *individual* scope of targeting authority; such concerns can and should be addressed by a application of the principle of distinction and related concepts from within IHL itself, discussed below. On the other hand, the strict-geographic model does entail certain costs of its own, or at least certain risks. Most problematically, it invites parties to hostilities to position personnel and assets in the territory of other states in order to cloak them with the (potentially) more-protective regime of IHRL,[149] while simultaneously suggesting to states that any attacks they launch on such personnel or assets are more likely to be governed by IHL if the attacks are sustained and of high-intensity. At the same time, we should not assume that the actual effect of limiting IHL's field of application will be to expand the independent field of application of IHRL. The United States, it bears emphasizing, does not accept that its ICCPR obligations apply extraterritorially; removing Common Article 3 and the customary law of war from the analysis of lethal force in places like Yemen or Somalia accordingly may do more to undermine than enhance the goal of subjecting force to legal and humanitarian constraints (though the US military as a matter of policy conducts all operations in view of IHL even when not formally required).

The better view, then, is that when a state of armed conflict exists, attacks carried out by one armed force on the personnel of another should be governed by

147 For an overview, see Cullen 2010, pp 140–141.

148 See ibid.

149 'The reason for this traditional rule is obvious—if the armed conflict is arbitrarily limited in this way, then it invites combatants to use territory outside of the "armed conflict" as a haven.' Anderson 2010c.

IHL without respect to geography. Thus, if one begins from the assumptions that (i) the United States and al Qaeda are engaged in armed conflict at least in Afghanistan and (ii) AQAP is part-and-parcel of al Qaeda, it follows that IHL governs US attacks directed at AQAP in Yemen even if circumstances in Yemen in isolation otherwise would not amount to armed conflict. And conversely, IHL would *not* apply to those same attacks if either (i) the United States and al Qaeda are not engaged in armed conflict in some location or (ii) AQAP is not part-and-parcel of al Qaeda for this purpose.

Notably, this last scenario could well arise in the near future, depending on how events develop in Afghanistan. Just as combat operations in Iraq have drawn down and American forces are likely to be gone by the end of 2011, conventional combat operations in Afghanistan eventually will cease. Though the United States may well continue beyond that point to use drones, special forces, and other means to carry out strikes on al Qaeda targets in various locations including Afghanistan and Pakistan, it is of course possible that the tempo of such operations may be so limited as to raise doubt as to the continued existence of a state of armed conflict with al Qaeda. As discussed in more detail in Part 1.4.1.1, it would depend on how strictly one construes the intensity requirement. Similarly, were the nature of al Qaeda to change such that it cannot be said to satisfy the requirement of minimal organizational coherence, this too could unwind the basis for asserting the existence of armed conflict. None of which is to say that the United States would lose its right to act in self defense under Article 51 (or with the consent of a host state government). It would follow that IHL would no longer govern, however, leaving uses of force subject only to the necessity and proportionality requirements inherent in the right of self-defense (assuming the use of force was an exercise of that right) and, to the extent applicable, IHRL.

I discuss IHRL in considerable detail in Part 1.4.1 below. For the remainder of this subsection, however, I proceed on the assumption that an attack on al-Awlaki would indeed fall within IHL's field of application. But would an attack directed at al-Awlaki then be permitted?

1.4.1.2 Does IHL authorize or forbid killing al-Awlaki?

IHL regulates the use of force within armed conflict in numerous ways, most of which need not be addressed here.[150] One consideration that must be addressed, however, is the principle of distinction.

[150] IHL addresses the permissible means and methods of carrying out an attack, for example, including prohibitions on the use of indiscriminate weaponry or perfidious methods. See Dinstein 2010, pp 126–128, 229–234; Henckaerts and Doswald-Beck 2005, pp 244–250 (Rule 71 on indiscriminate weapons), ibid., pp 221–26 (Rule 65 on perfidy). IHL also requires that any specific attack satisfy the requirements of proportionality, meaning that an attack must not be expected to cause harm to civilians or civilian objects that 'would be excessive in relation to the concrete and direct military advantage anticipated'. Henckaerts and Doswald-Beck ibid., p 46

The principle of distinction is fundamental to IHL.[151] As summarized by the ICRC in its study of customary IHL, the principle requires that 'parties to the conflict must at all times distinguish between civilians and combatants', meaning that '[a]ttacks may only be directed against combatants' and not against civilians—though civilians lose this immunity so long as they are directly participating in hostilities.[152] The question, then, is whether al-Awlaki can be categorized as a combatant, and if not, whether he nonetheless can be said to be a civilian directly participating in hostilities in at least some circumstances.

The task of answering that question is more complicated than one might expect, for four reasons. First, there is disagreement as to whether the combatant category, or some functional equivalent to it, even exists in the context of non-international armed conflict. Second, assuming that the category does exist in the non-international setting at least for purposes of the principle of distinction, there is disagreement as to the conduct or status that places one within it. Third, there is disagreement as to whether combatants may be killed at any time (so long as not *hors de combat*) or if, instead, a 'least harmful means' constraint might apply in at least some circumstances as a result of the requirement of military necessity. And fourth, as to the civilian category, there is disagreement regarding the precise substantive scope and temporal bounds of the direct-participation concept. I consider each of these issues below, mapping them on to the al-Awlaki scenario along the way.

A. Functional combatants in NIAC

IHL draws a sharp distinction between international armed conflict (IAC) and non-international armed-conflict (NIAC). A conflict falls into the IAC category when at least one of the parties on each side of the conflict is a state.[153] The NIAC category, in contrast, encompasses armed conflicts pitting a state against a non-state actor or those pitting non-state actors against one another. Much turns on the distinction, at least in terms of IHL treaty law. Categorization as an IAC brings to bear the full range of provisions contained in the 1949 Geneva Conventions (and, for those

151 The ICJ identified it as one of two 'cardinal principles' of IHL in its 1996 *Nuclear Weapons* opinion, [1996] ICJ Rep., p 257.

152 Henckaerts and Doswald-Beck 2005, p 3 (Rule 1).

153 See Common Article 2. Additional Protocol I seeks to expand the range of the IAC category so as to include those NIACs 'in which peoples are fighting against colonial domination and alien occupation and against racist regimes in the exercise of their right of self-determination, as enshrined in the charter of the United Nations and the declaration on principles of international law concerning friendly relations and co-operation among States in accordance with the Charter of the United Nations.' Protocol Additional to the Geneva Conventions of 12 August 1949, and Relating to the Protection of Victims of International Armed Conflicts (Protocol I), 8 June 1977, Art. 1(4). The United States is not party to AP I, in no small part for this reason. See Newton 2009, pp 323, 349–350.

states party to it, the full range of Additional Protocol I as well). Categorization as a NIAC, in contrast, compels application only of Common Article 3 of the 1949 Conventions (and Additional Protocol II as well, if the state in question is party to that instrument and its higher threshold of application is met).

All of this matters for present purposes because NIAC is the category most likely to apply in relation to the al-Awlaki scenario (assuming one accepts that there is a relevant armed conflict in the first place),[154] and it is often asserted that combatant status does not exist in the NIAC context.[155] As summarized by the ICRC in its study of customary IHL: 'Combatant status ... exists only in international armed conflicts.'[156] It might seem, then, that there is no need to tarry with a discussion of combatancy in the al-Awlaki scenario. But the situation proves more complex on closer inspection.

It certainly is true that states have traditionally resisted recognition of the *combatant's privilege* and eligibility for POW status for non-state actors who take up arms to challenge the state, thereby giving rise to a NIAC. Such armed resistance generally is deemed a criminal act under domestic law, and states have no desire to immunize or legitimize such conduct. As David Kretzmer explains:

> '[s]tates were, and still are, unwilling to grant the *status* of combatants to insurgents and other non-state actors who take part in [NIACs], as doing so would not only afford them an element of legitimacy, but would mean that they enjoy the two 'privileges' of combatants—immunity from criminal liability for fighting, and prisoner-of-war status when apprehended.'[157]

Combatancy has a further consequence, however, one that accrues to the *detriment* rather than the benefit of the combatant. Under the principle of distinction, a combatant lacks immunity from targeting and thus, unlike a civilian, can be targeted without reference to whether he or she is directly participating in hostilities at the time. States have no interest in resisting application of this rule to those who fight on behalf of a non-state actor; on the contrary, they have a tremendous incentive to insist upon it, lest one side of the conflict be deemed targetable at all times while the other enjoys immunity when not actually engaging in the fight.

---

[154] If one takes the view that a stand-alone armed conflict exists involving the US and Yemeni governments on one hand and AQAP on the other, there is no doubt that it would constitute a NIAC. If one instead takes the view that the United States and al Qaeda are engaged in armed conflict (whether just in Afghanistan or more broadly) and that AQAP is part and parcel of al Qaeda for this purpose, the situation is still best described as a NIAC. See e.g., Roberts 2002, pp 204, 211 n. 36 (citing International Committee of the Red Cross, Aide Memoire to United States (19 November 2002) (concluding that the armed conflict in Afghanistan changed from an IAC to a NIAC as of the creation of a new government in June 2002)); *Hamdan* v *Rumsfeld*, 558 US 557, 629–630 (2006) (holding that Common Article 3 applied in relation to an al Qaeda detainee captured in Afghanistan).

[155] See e.g., Olson 2009, pp 197, 208.

[156] Henckaerts and Doswald-Beck 2005, p 11 (Rule 3).

[157] Kretzmer 2005, p 197.

And thus the question arises: can these distinct strands of combatancy—the combatant's privilege, eligibility for POW status, and lack of immunity from targeting—be disaggregated?

The ICRC's recently-published study of customary IHL calls for precisely this approach, and indeed suggests that it is customary law applicable in a NIAC setting. In the very same paragraph that states that there is no 'combatant status' in NIAC, the study expressly asserts that certain individuals nonetheless may be treated as combatants '[f]or purposes of the principle of distinction'.[158] To be sure, the study at this point begins to waffle, stating that this disaggregated approach is indeed the rule for the members of the State's armed forces, yet that state practice somehow 'is not clear as to the situation of members of armed opposition groups'.[159] Other observers, however, have no doubts on this point. Kretzmer argues that it 'seems almost self-evident that in [NIACs] there are indeed combatants, who, as opposed to civilians, may legitimately be targeted by the other side', and that these include the 'members of both the armed forces and the organized armed group' involved in that conflict.[160] Both sets of individuals, he says, may be attacked consistent with the principle of distinction, though it does not follow that they have the combatant's privilege or the right to POW status upon capture.[161] Notably, the ICRC's original commentary on Additional Protocol II expressed much the same view some years ago: 'Those who belong to armed forces *or armed groups* may be attacked at any time.'[162]

Melzer goes further. He not only endorses the disaggregated view—the 'functional combatant' model, in his parlance—as to both the state and non-state forces engaged in NIAC but also characterizes the contrary view (i.e., that all members of organized armed groups in the NIAC setting constitute civilians who may only be targeted while directly participating in hostilities) as 'a misconception of major proportions', one that 'necessarily entails a distortion of the fundamental concepts of 'civilian', 'armed forces' and 'direct participation in hostilities' and, ultimately, leads to irreconcilable contradictions in the interpretation of these terms'.[163] He also makes an important contribution by identifying the foundation of the disaggregated view in state practice. Explicitly rejecting the ICRC study's

---

[158] Henckaerts and Doswald-Beck 2005, p 11 (Rule 3).

[159] Ibid. p 12. The same section of the study notes that the UN General Assembly and other multilateral bodies have used the word 'combatant' in the NIAC setting, and observes that this reflects the view 'that these persons do not enjoy the protection against attack accorded to civilians' (but not that they also are entitled to the combatant's privilege or POW status). Ibid.

[160] Kretzmer 2005, pp 197–198.

[161] See ibid.

[162] ICRC, Commentary on Protocol Additional to the Geneva Conventions of 12 August 1949, and relating to the Protection of Victims of Non-International Armed Conflicts (Protocol II), 8 June 1977, at § 4789 (emphasis added).

[163] Melzer 2008, p 316.

conclusion that state practice on this issue is indeterminate,[164] Melzer argues instead that:

> 'even a cursory glance at almost any non-international armed conflict—be it in South East Asia in the 1960 and 1970s, in Central America in the 1980s, or in Colombia, Sri Lanka, Uganda, Chechnya or the Sudan today—is sufficient to conclude that governmental armed forces do not hesitate to directly attack insurgents even when [the latter] are not engaged in a particular military operation. In practice, these attacks are neither denied by the operating State nor are they internationally condemned as long as they do not cause excessive 'collateral damage.''[165]

The proposition that a 'functional combatant' category exists in NIAC received substantial further support with the publication of the *Interpretive Guidance on the Notion of Direct Participation in Hostilities*, a document written by Melzer under the formal auspices of the ICRC.[166] The *Interpretive Guidance* emerged after a multi-year process involving consultations with a large body of IHL experts from a number of countries in coordination with the ICRC and the TMC Asser Institute. According to the notes from the 2008 experts' meeting, the 'functional membership approach [was] discussed extensively in previous Expert Meetings, and a certain consensus had emerged among many of the participating experts with respect to this issue'.[167] A 'few experts' had objected to recognition of a membership standard in this context, the notes indicate, but by this stage the debate nonetheless had come to focus on the details of how to define membership and certain question of verbiage.[168] Ultimately, an approach tracking Melzer's 'functional combatant' model was adopted in the *Interpretive Guidance*. At least some persons who are members of an 'organized armed group' belonging to the non-state party in a NIAC, on this view, are functional combatants subject to targeting without regarding to direct participation.[169]

---

[164] See ibid., (observing that the customary IHL study appears to rest this conclusion on statements contained in military manuals, and pointing out that states are at pains not to suggest that insurrection and other forms of non-state violence can be legitimate and hence may be expected not to say anything in a manual that might be interpreted otherwise).

[165] Ibid., p 317, Melzer notes that there may be objections to such attacks also on the ground that the targets were not part of the 'military wing' of the enemy entity, but distinguishes this from objecting on the ground that no one should be attacked except while directly participating in hostilities.

[166] See International Committee of the Red Cross, Interpretive Guidance on the Notion of Direct Participation in Hostilities under International Humanitarian Law (2009) (hereinafter Interpretive Guidance).

[167] Summary Report, Fifth Expert Meeting on the Notion of Direct Participation in Hostilities (Geneva, 5/6 February 2008), p 45.

[168] Ibid., pp 45–59.

[169] See Interpretive Guidance, supra n 166, pp 31–35.

Of course the organized armed group-approach does not enjoy universal approval.[170] It is sound, however, in light of its foundation in state practice and the absence of affirmatively contrary treaty language.[171]

What then follows from this approach when applied in the al-Awlaki scenario? If one proceeds from the assumption that AQAP (or al Qaeda) is an organized armed group engaged in an armed conflict with the United States—and that is the working assumption of this section—then at least *some* of its members may constitute functional combatants for the limited purpose of the principle of distinction and, hence, may be targeted without any showing that they are directly participating in hostilities at the time. Indeed, this appears to be precisely the view of the US government, which conspicuously states 'that AQAP is an organized armed group' in its brief in the *al-Awlaki* litigation.[172]

Even if we assume this analysis to be correct, however, it does not automatically follow that *all* AQAP members are functional combatants. Which of them would constitute functional combatants, and would al-Awlaki fall within that group?

B. The indeterminacy of functional combatant status

As noted above in the discussion of the conditions for recognition of an armed conflict, some degree of organizational coherence is necessary in order to be able to say in the first place that a non-state actor constitutes a party to such a conflict. Just because that organizational threshold is crossed, however, does not mean it will be easy to specify which persons associated with that party should be treated as functional combatants for purposes of the principle of distinction. Particularly where the non-state actor employs a decentralized network structure, and does its best to keep its membership and activities secret, difficult sorting questions are bound to arise.[173]

There are several models that could be used to resolve this issue. Melzer, to take one prominent example, argues for adoption of a 'continuous fighting function'

---

[170] Cf. Lubell 2005, pp 737, 748, (noting existence of the arguments for functional combatancy in NIAC and commenting, with or without intended understatement, that 'although they might seem highly controversial, these views nevertheless do still exist and there is not yet enough consensus for them to be ruled out completely').

[171] One might object that it also lacks affirmative *approval* in treaty language, yet it is not clear why that should matter so long as one accepts Melzer's assessment of the relevant customary practice. In this regard, bear in mind Melzer's implied caution against neglect of *customary* IHL: 'the fact that IHL has become one of the most densely codified fields of international law … has given rise to a predominantly positivist approach to the determination of lawful conduct in situations of armed conflict'. Melzer 2006, p 100.

[172] Government's Brief, supra n 24, p 1.

[173] See e.g., Waxman 2010, pp 447–451.

(CFF) test,[174] and in the *Interpretive Guidance* we see this standard adopted under the slightly-more-familiar label 'continuous combat function' (CCF). On this model, not all persons associated with the non-state party would count as combatants for purposes of distinction. Rather, only those members who directly participate in hostilities on a regular base would so qualify; other group members would remain civilian.[175] From a policy perspective, the desirability of this approach of course depends entirely on how one interprets the concept of 'direct participation' and the requirement of continuity. As I will discuss in detail in Part 1.4.1.2 D., below, there is a substantial amount of controversy on this very question. Melzer argues, for example, that the CFF standard would exclude members or an organized armed group who function as 'political and religious leaders, instigators or militants[,] … financial contributors, informants, collaborators, and other service providers',[176] Kenneth Watkin, on the other hand, objects to an approach that would exclude those who perform support functions that routinely are performed by uniformed servicemembers in the regular armed forces.[177] The law on point, unfortunately, is simply not determinate enough to resolve that dispute. It is worth emphasizing, however, that both appear to accept that persons involved in actual operational planning may be covered.[178]

Other models are possible, aside from the CFF/CCF approach. One might, for example, treat all members of a non-state party as functional combatants rather than civilians, regardless of their particular function (either on the theory that function is malleable in such groups or that all functions are sufficiently related to violence for at least some groups). This approach presumably would be most tempting where the entity involved simply lacks fixed organizational divisions or where the entity in any event has little purpose other than to engage in violence. Again, however, IHL at this time does not appear to compel a definitive answer to the question. What is needed is a thorough account of state practice regarding targeting parameters in past NIACs. It may or may not be possible to construct such an account; to the best of my knowledge it has not yet been attempted.

What then is there to say about the al-Awlaki fact pattern, in light of this indeterminacy? One can still offer relative judgments. As an initial matter, the case for targeting him on combatant or combatant-equivalent grounds would be exceptionally weak if he is merely a supporter but not in some sense a member of AQAP or al Qaeda. If the government is correct that he has sworn an oath to

---

[174] More specifically, he argues for resort to this approach in circumstances where it does not make sense from an organizational perspective to analogize the non-state actor's fighting forces to the state's regular armed forces, see Melzer 2008, p 321. The CFF test is, of course, much the same as the 'continuous combat function' (CCF) standard to which the ICRC refers in the Interpretive Guidance, see supra n 166.

[175] Melzer 2008, pp 320–321.

[176] Ibid.

[177] See Watkin 2010.

[178] This implies a relatively flexible conception of direct participation insofar as operational planning activity causes harm, by definition, indirectly.

follow AQAP, however, this will not be the case. If instead the facts show that he has *some* form of membership relationship but is engaged solely in propaganda and generalized recruiting, the case for targeting is stronger yet still relatively weak in the sense that such conduct would fail the CFF/CCF test and probably also most close variations of it. Again, however, the facts described in Part 1.2. suggest that this is not the case. On the contrary, they suggest that al-Awlaki has taken on an operational planning function. Insofar as this is correct, and insofar as it is a recurring function rather than an isolated incident, this would satisfy the CFF/CCF standard.

C. When if ever does a least harmful means test apply?

Let us assume for the sake of argument both that a form of combatancy exists in the NIAC setting and that al-Awlaki's operational role with AQAP suffices to place him in that status. Does it now follow that he may be targeted at any time under IHL? There is one further obstacle to consider. Does IHL in this context require a least-harmful means test, such that the United States could not attempt to kill al-Awlaki so long as it might instead be possible to arrest him?

The suggestion that IHL might contain such an obligation has been sharply criticized,[179] but the matter became less certain in 2006 when the Israeli Supreme Court (sitting as the High Court of Justice) issued an opinion which could be read as asserting that IHL does indeed impose a least-harmful-means test in some contexts.[180]

In the *Targeted Killings* judgment, the court concluded that the relevant conflict was international in nature and that the non-state actors in question were not combatants but rather civilians who, by virtue of both being members of terrorist groups and having a continuing function involving violent acts, had lost their usual immunity from targeting.[181] That is to say, the court in *Targeted Killings* effectively applied a functional combatant test, but without embracing the language of combatancy. It nonetheless concluded that IHL in this setting imposes a least-

[179] See e.g., Hays Parks 2010, (explaining that 'no government has employed a use-of-force continuum with respect to the conduct of its soldiers in engaging enemy combatants or civilians taking a direct part in hostilities. Governments have accepted the treaty prohibitions against perfidy and on denial of quarter, but for very sound reasons have not seen the need for a use-of force continuum in armed conflict.'). Cf. Waxman 2008, pp 1387, 1413–1418 (discussing obligations to consider alternate means during military operations, and arguing that targeting law has evolved towards 'reasonable care' standard and methodologies 'to deal with the practical and moral problems of protecting innocent civilians from injury amid clouds of doubt and misinformation').

[180] See *The Public Committee Against Torture* v *Israel* (HCJ 769/02), Judgment of 14 December 2006 (hereinafter Targeted Killings judgment). Parks argues that the better reading of the opinion is that the court grounded the least-harmful-means test in Israeli domestic law alone. See Hays Parks 2010, p 793.

[181] See ibid., §§ 21, 26, 28, 30, 39.

harmful-means test, however, relying primarily on principles and doctrines derived from Israeli *domestic* law rather than sourcing deriving the principle from an independent IHL source.[182] This approach has generated considerable criticism,[183] but also an attempt at rehabilitation by Nils Melzer in both an article and in his treatise on targeted killing.[184]

Melzer's basic argument is straightforward. The least-harmful-means test, he asserts, follows from the IHL principle of military necessity.[185] Military necessity, in Melzer's view, is an undertheorized and oft-misunderstood principle.[186] It is widely-appreciated that claims of military necessity are *not* a justification for violations of IHL, of course.[187] In contrast, the distinct prohibitory aspect of military necessity—summarized in the US Army Field Manual on the Law of War as 'requir[ing] that [a] belligerent refrain from employing any kind or degree of violence which is not actually necessary for military purposes'[188]—is less well understood.[189] Properly conceived, Melzer argues, it entails a principle of humanity 'which forbids the infliction of suffering, injury or destruction not actually necessary for the accomplishment of legitimate military purposes'.[190] Thus the absence of immunity from targeting—whether for civilians who directly participate in hostilities or for combatants—'does not permit the senseless slaughter of persons not entitled to protection against direct attack where there manifestly is no military necessity to do so'.[191] Rather, it simply means that the attacker has the authority 'to use that kind and degree of force … which is reasonably necessary to achieve a legitimate military purpose with a minimum expenditure of time, life and physical resources'.[192] And by extension, Melzer contends, there is an obligation to attempt an arrest rather than to kill when the circumstances indicate a reasonable probability of success without undue risk.

This claim has been sharply criticized.[193] Even if we assume for the sake of argument that IHL *does* require a least-harmful-means analysis, however, this would not preclude an effort to kill al-Awlaki so long as he remains in remote areas of Yemen beyond the effective writ of the government yet within the

182 See ibid. § 60.

183 See e.g., Ben-Naftali 2007, p 322; Schondorf 2007, p 301.

184 See Melzer 2008, p. 317.

185 See ibid., pp 95–112. Melzer also suggests that the test finds at least a degree of support in the maux superflus principle, see ibid., pp 96–97.

186 See ibid., pp 100–101.

187 See e.g., ibid., p 280, (discussing the discrediting of Kriegsraison geht vor Kriegsmanier).

188 US Army Field Manual 27-10 (1956), § 3 (quoted in Melzer 2008, p 283).

189 See ibid., pp 280–281.

190 Ibid., p 108, (quoting Department of the Air Force, Air Force Pamphlet (AFP 110-31), 'International Law—The Conduct of Armed Conflict and Air Operations' (19 November 1976) § 1–3(2)) (quotation marks omitted).

191 Melzer 2008, p 109.

192 Iibd.

193 See e.g., Hays Parks 2010. For Melzer's response, see Melzer 2010, pp 896–912.

protective—and well-armed—embrace of local tribes. Both the original *Targeted Killings* decision and Melzer's reformulation deny that the least-harmful-means obligation forces armed forces to run inappropriate risks, and both specifically note that the risks to be considered involve not just the prospect of harm to the attacking force but also the possibility that an attempted arrest could put surrounding civilians at greater risk.[194] In al-Awlaki's circumstances, it seems highly likely on the current understanding of the facts that an attempted arrest would be met with armed resistance that almost certainly would result in casualties for the arresting force (and quite possibly for bystanders as well). The US could resort to lethal force in that circumstance even under a least-harmful-means standard.[195] Should al-Awlaki be discovered in an area where the prospects for an arrest were manifestly different, of course, this analysis too would differ.

D. Civilians directly participating in hostilities

Some observers no doubt will reject the threshold proposition that a form of combatancy can exist in NIAC. From their perspective, al-Awlaki necessarily is a civilian whom IHL permits to be targeted only for such time as he directly participates in hostilities (DPH). Could the United States kill al-Awlaki under that paradigm?

The substantive and temporal bounds of DPH are not entirely agreed, unfortunately. As noted above, the ICRC's *Interpretive Guidance* document sought to bring clarity to the DPH issue.[196] But it did not entirely succeed. Many of the experts who participated in the consultations over the years declined to permit their names to be listed in the document, as they did not agree with certain positions it took.[197] Some have since published substantial criticisms.[198]

All that said, at least the basic outlines of DPH are clear enough and adequately identified in the *Interpretive Guidance*. At bottom, DPH refers to 'specific hostile acts carried out by individuals as part of the conduct of hostilities between parties

---

194 See Melzer 2008, pp 110–111. See also Targeted Killings Judgment supra n 180, § 40, Melzer 2010, pp 902–903.

195 Melzer argues that states should be held to a higher standard of certainty regarding the need to resort to lethal force in lieu of a capture attempt where the circumstances resemble a non-combat scenario. See Melzer 2008, p 112. I am doubtful that IHL actually requires this even assuming that it otherwise does entail a least-harmful-means standard as a general proposition. But even so, the al-Awlaki scenario would likely satisfy that standard based on current factual assumptions.

196 The papers of the working group convened by the ICRC and the TMC Asser Institute are collected online at http://www.icrc.org/eng/resources/documents/article/other/direct-participation-article-020709.htm.

197 See Hays Parks 2010, pp 784–785.

198 See for example, the collection of critical essays published in Volume 42 of the New York University Journal of International Law and Politics (2010).

to an armed conflict.'[199] Unpacking that a bit, the *Interpretive Guidance* elaborates that an act of DPH must (i) be likely to cause harm (an adverse effect on military operations or injury to civilians), (ii) involve direct rather than indirect causation of that harm, and (iii) be carried out in support of one party to the conflict and to the detriment of another.[200]

Could al-Awlaki ever be said to have directly participated in hostilities under this standard? Propaganda and ideological activity on behalf of AQAP would not suffice, as the causal link between such activity and harm is, by nature, attenuated. But recall that al-Awlaki is not merely said to be a propagandist. The allegation is that he has taken on an operational leadership position within AQAP, enticing and directing individuals to engage in specific violent acts. The *Interpretive Guidance* states that 'where persons are specifically recruited and trained for the execution of a predetermined hostile act ... such activities [can] be regarded as an integral part of the act and, therefore, as direct participation in hostilities'.[201] It is not precisely clear whether this language means to refer to the act of being so trained alone, or also encompasses providing such training as well. That said, there is not much logic in including the former while excluding the latter, and hence the better reading is the inclusive one. Under it, even if al-Awlaki constitutes a civilian, he might be targeted at least for some period of time (again, assuming the existence of a relevant armed conflict and the accuracy of the allegation of operational leadership).[202] But for precisely how long?

Defining the temporal parameters of such plot-specific leadership activity is almost a metaphysical endeavor. The act of 'participation' could be defined strictly with reference to the moment that al-Awlaki is interacting with the person who actually will carry out an attack, or might at the other end of the spectrum be extended to the entire period during which an operation is conceived, orchestrated, and executed. But however it is measured, al-Awlaki presumably is not engaged in such conduct at *all* times, and perhaps only is engaged in it for brief periods when it does occur. Thus the question arises whether he merely loses civilian immunity from targeting for such times as he is so engaged, or if instead a recurring pattern of engaging in DPH might divest him from targeting immunity on a sustained basis.

The general rule associated with DPH is that one loses immunity from targeting only for such time as the activity constituting DPH lasts.[203] Absent some exception, then, al-Awlaki could be targeted while involved in directing particular plots,

---

199 Interpretive Guidance, supra n166, p 45.

200 See ibid., p 46.

201 Ibid., p 53.

202 Note, however, that there is no good argument for targeting al-Awlaki so long as one understands DPH to refer solely to conduct the temporally-immediate consequence of which is to cause death or injury to others.

203 See ibid., p 70.

but during interim periods would be immune from targeting. There would be, for him, a revolving door of immunity.

Is there, or should there be, an exception to this revolving-door dynamic?[204] The revolving door feature of DPH is relatively unproblematic so long as one accepts the view that a non-state party's armed forces are not civilians but functional combatants for purposes of the principle of distinction; in that case, the revolving-door phenomenon arises only to a limited extent (i.e., in cases involving individuals not associated with the non-state party to the conflict) and might therefore be defended as a worthy price to pay in order to ensure maximum protection for the broader civilian population. And the functional combatant approach is, of course, precisely the approach taken by the ICRC in the *Interpretive Guidance*, as well as by me in Part 1.4.1.2 A., above. If one refuses to recognize a functional combatant category for the armed forces of a non-state party to a NIAC, however, then strict adherence to the revolving-door rule becomes considerably more problematic. If every single person who fights for a non-state party to a NIAC is a civilian who can only be targeted while engaged in DPH, and continuously benefits from revived immunity no matter how routinely they return to the fight, the resulting unlevel playing field would prove untenable in practice, undermining adherence to IHL in general and thereby decreasing protections for genuine civilians. Thus some have argued that at least some if not all members of the armed forces of a non-state party to a NIAC should be deemed to be directly participating at all times (either by expanding the range of conduct qualifying as direct participation so as to encompass some or all kinds of membership, by significantly expanding the temporal duration of the loss of immunity from more discrete acts of DPH, or both).[205] This argument makes sense from a policy perspective, but it remains to be seen whether IHL, *lex ferenda,* will move in that direction. In terms of IHL as it currently exists, the case for targeting al-Awlaki as a civilian direct participant in hostilities would seem to stand or fall on whether one accepts that planning activity can qualify as DPH—an argument that certainly is colorable, though not beyond dispute.

1.4.2 Does IHRL apply and, if so, to what effect?

If as argued above IHL is applicable to an attack on al-Awlaki, then there is no need for a distinct IHRL analysis; pursuant to the *lex specialis* principle, any applicable IHRL right would in that circumstance need to be construed in

[204] See ibid.

[205] The Interpretive Guidance rejects such expansions of DPH, but of course it does so while also embracing the functional combatant concept as an alternative means of addressing this issue. See supra n 166.

conformity with IHL.[206] But if facts were to change, or if one did not accept that IHL applies even on the facts asserted above, a stand-alone IHRL analysis would then be necessary.

As an initial matter, there is no question that IHRL constrains the ability of states to kill. Article 6 of the International Covenant on Civil and Political Rights (ICCPR), for example, provides that '[e]very human being has the inherent right to life,' that '[t]his right shall be protected by law', and that '[n]o one shall be arbitrarily deprived of his life'. The direct relevance of the ICCPR in the al-Awlaki scenario is doubtful, however, since the action at issue would take place in Yemen and the United States has long taken the position that the ICCPR has no extraterritorial application.[207] Others take a different view on the territoriality question, but the persistence of the US interpretation—not to mention its consistency with the plain language of the ICCPR—undermines any claim that the United States somehow has become bound to a broader understanding against its wishes. In light of this, the case for subjecting an attack on al-Awlaki to an IHRL analysis is much stronger if one proceeds instead from the premise that the right to life is a customary norm. Whether this move suffices to escape the extraterritoriality objection is not entirely clear,[208] but for the sake of argument the discussion proceeds as if it does.

Commentators summarizing the conditions that must be satisfied in order to use lethal force under an IHRL right-to-life paradigm typically emphasize three requirements: legality, proportionality, and necessity.[209] I address each in turn.

1.4.2.1 Legality and the domestic law foundation for an attack

Consider first the legality criterion, which requires that there be a domestic law foundation for using lethal force.[210] In al-Awlaki's case, the US government has identified two such foundations, one explicitly and the other only indirectly.

---

[206] For a discussion of *lex specialis* in this context, see Hays Parks, pp 797–798, and sources cites therein at nn 85 and 86.

[207] See e.g., See UN Hum. Rts. Comm., Consideration of Reports Submitted by States Parties Under Article 40 of the Covenant: Initial Reports of States Parties Due in 1993, Addendum: United States of America, 12–25, UN Doc. CCPR/C/81/Add.4 (24 August 1994) (considering US report submitted 29 July 1994) (hereinafter UN Hum. Rts. Comm.).

[208] The 'Law of War Handbook' states that '[i]f a specific human right falls within the category of customary international law, it should be considered a 'fundamental' human right' and as a result 'it is binding on US forces during all overseas operations. See Law of War Handbook 2004, p 279. See also Lubell 2005, pp 737, 741 (noting similar statement in another US military advisory manual). Cf. Hansen 2007, pp 32–33 (arguing that 'if states have agreed that a given human rights treaty applies only within a state's own borders, no party should be forced to provide rights enumerated in the treaty outside its borders' unless the right in question has obtained the status of a 'fundamental' right constituting a 'peremptory norm').

[209] See Melzer 2008, pp 174–175, see also 100–102. Melzer also discusses a requirement of precaution. The precaution requirement arguably could be encompassed by the necessity inquiry, however.

[210] See ibid., p 225.

In a brief submitted in the lawsuit filed by al-Awlaki's father, the government explicitly asserted that an attack on al-Awlaki would be justified under domestic law by the September 18, 2001 Authorization for Use of Military Force statute (AUMF), which authorized the use of 'all necessary and appropriate force' against those entities determined by the president to have been responsible for the 9/11 attacks.[211] As the brief explained, the AUMF would apply in al-Awlaki's case because (i) al-Awlaki has become an operational leader of AQAP and (ii) 'AQAP is an organized armed group that is either part of al Qaeda, or is an associated force, or co-belligerent, of al-Qaeda ...'[212]

Whether this argument persuades depends on two considerations. First, are these factual predicates accurate? I proceed on the assumption that they are, based on the review provided in Part 1.2 above, but note that the argument for legality based on the AUMF would collapse if either al-Awlaki proved not to be part of AQAP or AQAP proved not sufficiently related to al Qaeda so as to come within the AUMF's substantive scope; in that case, it would be necessary to resort to the alternative domestic legal foundation discussed below. In the meantime, however, assuming that the requisite relationship exists, the argument for legality under the AUMF raises a second question: Does the AUMF actually convey (as a matter of domestic law) the authority to use lethal force? If one takes the view that there is an underlying armed conflict with al Qaeda or with AQAP sufficient to implicate IHL, it is easy to answer that question in the affirmative. One can simply argue that the AUMF incorporates IHL by implication (whether as directly controlling law or simply as a source for interpretive insights).[213] But what if one does not believe there is a relevant armed conflict? That is, after all, the working assumption of *this* subsection.

In that case, one could no longer point to IHL as directly relevant. Yet the sweeping delegation of authority to use military force in the plain language of the AUMF would remain, and it is simply not plausible to read that language as conveying *no* authority to use military force or to convey such authority only insofar as the executive branch might choose to use it on a scale sufficient to clearly implicate IHL. Put simply, the AUMF's plain language suffices to convey domestic law authority to use lethal force without an implied precondition that such force be used only if there happens to be a preexisting state of armed conflict or the government is prepared to use force on such a sustained basis so as to generate one; particularly given the recent memory of the Clinton Administration's episodic use of military force against al Qaeda in 1998, the more plausible assumption is that the broad language conferred on the President the authority to engage in both low- and high-intensity uses of force.

What if one rejects this analysis, or if the facts change such that the AUMF no longer remains sufficiently relevant to provide domestic legal authority for an

---

211 See Government's Brief, supra n 24, p 4.

212 Ibid., p 1.

213 Cf. Bradley and Goldsmith 2005, pp 2088–2101 (discussing the interpretive relevance of IHL for the AUMF).

attack on al-Awlaki?[214] In that case, the requirement of legality would have to be satisfied by some *other* domestic law source. Perhaps anticipating such an argument, the government in its brief in *al-Awlaki* writes that:

> '[i]n addition to the AUMF, there are other legal bases under US and international law for the President to authorize the use of force against al Qaeda and AQAP, including the inherent right to national self-defense recognized in international law (see e.g., United Nations Charter Article 51).'[215]

The brief does not elaborate the point, leaving a question as to the alternative 'US' law foundation its authors had in mind. One plausible reading is that they meant for the reference to self-defense under Article 51 to be an example of *both* an international and a US law basis for an attack. This is not an implausible reading, insofar as the UN Charter is deemed to be 'supreme law of the land' under the Supremacy Clause.[216] Even if one rejects it, however, it is not difficult to guess what the authors may otherwise have had in mind. National self-defense is not merely an international law concept under the Charter, but also a domestic constitutional law concept concerning the circumstances in which the President has not just the power but also the duty under Article II of the Constitution to use at least some degree of military force without awaiting legislative authorization.[217] In light of AQAP's repeated attacks on the United States and the certainty that more such attacks will follow, a very strong argument can be made that the President's duty to use force to defend the nation has been implicated, much as was the case when in 1998 when the Clinton Administration, despite lacking any affirmative and explicit legislative authority, used missile strikes in Afghanistan in response to al Qaeda's bombing of two US embassies in Africa. To be sure, AQAP's two most notable attempts to attack the US homeland failed thanks to last-minute interventions. Such good fortune should not, however, enter into the assessment of whether self-defense rights have been triggered at either the domestic or international levels. We should indeed be wary of arguments about self-defense premised on considerably more inchoate threats, but the AQAP threat at least seems more than adequately realized. The legality condition thus is satisfied.[218]

---

[214] Cf. Goldsmith 2010.

[215] Government Brief, supra n 24, pp 4–5.

[216] For a discussion of the complex issues surrounding this point, see Bradley 2008, pp 173–176.

[217] See e.g., The Brig *Amy Warwick* (The Prize Cases), 67 US (2 Black) 635 (1863) (declaring both the right and the duty of the President to use force in defense of the nation when attacked, without awaiting legislative authorization, pursuant to the Constitution). This is not the same, of course, as arguing that the President also may act *contrary* to affirmatively-enacted legislative constraints.

[218] Lubell notes debate as to whether a targeted killing might violate the prohibition on 'assassination' contained in Executive Order 12,333. See Lubell 2010, p 175 and n 35. The better view is that an attack carried out pursuant to an authorization for use of military force or pursuant to Constitutional authority to defend the nation does not constitute an act of 'assassination' even if targeting a specific individual.

1.4.2.2 Proportionality

The next question is whether killing al-Awlaki could be squared with the requirement of proportionality. Proportionality in the IHRL right-to-life context considers whether the 'harm caused is proportionate to the sought objective'.[219] That is, is the benefit to be gained comparable to the taking of a human life? As Lubell wryly—and correctly—notes, 'firing a lethal weapon at someone attempting to avoid a parking ticket can hardly be said to be proportionate'.[220]

In order to satisfy the proportionality requirement, then, the government's 'objection should be the prevention of a real threat to life ...'[221] This appears to be the US government's asserted interest in the al-Awlaki scenario, given the government's claim that al-Awlaki has become personally involved in the recruiting and direction of personnel to carry out particular violent attacks. That is to say, the US government's purpose appears to be to save the lives of those who might otherwise become the victims of an al-Awlaki-directed attack. Absent reason to doubt this purpose, the proportionality requirement appears satisfied.

1.4.2.3 Necessity and the problem of imminence

The final and most vexing question in the IHRL analysis concerns necessity.

In contrast to the IHL discussion above, there is little dispute that a least-harmful-means test does apply here. Melzer, for example, disaggregates necessity into three constituent elements —qualitative, quantitative, and temporal necessity—and weaves the least-harmful-means standard through each.[222]

Qualitative necessity forbids reliance on potentially lethal force unless 'other means remain ineffective or without any promise of achieving the purpose of the operation'.[223] Put another way, qualitative necessity precludes resort to killing where an arrest is plausible. By and large, this IHRL model of necessity tracks the similar aspect of necessity as used in the Article 51 self-defense setting, and by the same token it appears to be satisfied—at least on current factual assumptions—in the al-Awlaki scenario.

Quantitative necessity, in Melzer's formulation, is closely-related. It refers to the requirement that the target should not be killed purposefully where it would be possible instead to 'incapacitate the targeted individual by the use of force which may or may not have lethal consequences'.[224] Again, the al-Awlaki scenario as

[219] Ibid., p 173.

[220] Ibid.

[221] Ibid.

[222] Melzer 2008, p 228.

[223] Ibid.

[224] Ibid.

described in Part 1.1 appears compatible with this standard; it does not appear that a non-lethal option for incapacitating him exists at the current time.

The final strand and most difficult strand in the analysis involves what Melzer calls 'temporal' necessity. Melzer defines this as a requirement that 'at the very moment of [the] application [of lethal force,] it is *not yet* or *no longer* absolutely necessary to achieve the desired purpose in both qualitative and quantitative terms'.[225] Here we come to the real obstacle to justifying an attack on al-Awlaki as compatible with the right to life. It is frequently said that a threat to life must be 'imminent' in order to serve as the predicate for the use of lethal force consistent with IHRL—a consideration best placed under the temporal necessity heading.[226] And since no one alleges that al-Awlaki himself is in the business of pulling triggers, triggering detonations, or otherwise doing anything that would in a strictly immediate since cause death or serious injury, it certainly is not obvious that he poses an 'imminent' threat to life even if one assumes the truth of all the government's allegations against him. But should the temporal aspect of necessity be so strictly construed?

On one hand, deviation from a strict imminence standard threatens to unwind IHRL's protection for the right to life insofar as situations lacking genuine imminence necessarily introduce at least some degree of factual uncertainty as to the individual's future actions.[227] On the other hand, however, enforcement of a strict imminence standard in the context of terrorism very likely would preclude the state from acting—and hence raise questions of both compliance and desirability—in circumstances where (i) there is strong evidence that a person is planning a terrorist attack, (ii) there is little reason to believe the state will know when the point of strict imminence has been reached in connection with a future attack, and (iii) a fleeting opportunity to attack the individual has arisen in the meantime.[228] In that case, the inability to act at that moment most likely would eliminate the possibility of preventing the attack, which is itself a human rights cost in terms of the right to life of the victims of that attack. The scenario is akin to that which Michael Schmitt calls the 'last window of opportunity' in the distinct but related *jus ad bellum* context involving preventive uses of force.[229]

Kretzmer, though expressing deep concern about the risks of alleviating the imminence requirement to any degree, ultimately concludes that there is an irresistible logic to the last window of opportunity concept, at least in contexts where a terrorism suspect operates in another state in circumstances that appear to preclude resort to an attempted arrest. He summarizes:

> '[T]argeting of suspected terrorists must be restricted to cases in which there is credible evidence that the targeted persons are actively involved in planning or preparing further

---

[225] Ibid.

[226] See e.g., Letter from Roth, supra n 1.

[227] See Kretzmer 2005, p 182.

[228] See ibid.

[229] See e.g., Schmitt 2004, p 756.

> terrorist attacks against the victim state and no other operational means of stopping those attacks are available. As there is always a risk that the persons attacked are not in fact terrorists, even in such a case lethal force may be used against the suspected terrorists only when a high probability exists that if immediate action is not taken another opportunity will not be available to frustrate the planned terrorist attacks.'[230]

Tom Malinowski of Human Rights Watch expressed a similar understanding recently, explaining that:

> 'I don't think that the "imminence" rule would require the US to show that an al Qaeda planner was literally on his way to the airport to put a bomb on a plane to Chicago before launching a strike. But it would require an individualized determination that the target is actively involved in planning future attacks (as against simply having been involved in terrorism in the past).'[231]

This strikes an appropriate compromise between the right to life of the potential victims of an anticipated terrorist attack and the right to life of the target of the state's preventive attack. Or at least it may do so, depending on how one construes the requirement that the state have substantial grounds to believe the individuals is planning future terrorist attacks. Does this mean that the state must have proof the person is plotting a specific attack, or is it enough to prove that the person is likely to plot *some* violent attack in the future?

Consider how this issue might be cashed out in relation to an historical example: the US attack on Osama bin Laden and other al Qaeda members in 1998. If we assume for the sake of argument that an IHRL model governed that attack, the question eventually would arise whether the strike satisfied the temporal necessity requirement. On one hand, so far as the public record suggests, there was no claim by the United States that al Qaeda was on the verge of or even contemplating any one particular attack at that moment. On the other hand, it was perfectly obvious that al Qaeda planned to continue to engage in attacks of *some variety* in the future. In short, no one knew then that the attack on the *USS Cole* was forthcoming, still less the attacks of 9/11, yet it was quite clear that *something* would occur sooner or later.

The circumstances today with AQAP and al Awlaki at least arguably are much the same. To insist upon plot-specific knowledge in this context would be to provide only an illusory exception to strict imminence, which is to say no exception at all. The temporal necessity inquiry should be read with a degree of flexibility; the state must have substantial evidence to support the belief that the person in question will in fact be involved in further attacks, but the state should not be expected to stay its hand until plot-specific details emerge.

Al-Awlaki, on this view, can be killed consistent with IHRL so long as the US government does indeed have substantial reason to believe that he will continue to play an operational leadership role in planned attacks against the United States and that he cannot plausibly be incapacitated with sub-lethal means. IHRL in this

---

230 Kretzmer 2005, p 203.

231 Wittes 2010.

specific respect produces much the same result as would IHL, thereby reducing the significance of determining which model controls in the first place.

1.5 Conclusion

The al-Awlaki scenario is a powerful device for coming to grips with international law principles governing lethal force, bringing us face-to-face with that which is determinate and that which is not. As we have seen, a substantial number of important questions fall into the latter camp, though not so many as to preclude the conclusion that the US government most likely could use lethal force against al-Awlaki without violating international law.

At the same time, the case study also brings home the critical role that contested factual predicates play in resolving IHL and IHRL disputes, as well as the collateral point that much of the information most relevant to resolving such disputes consists of classified information available only to the government. This is both inevitable and troubling. The absence of transparency creates an obvious risk of abuse or at least self-serving mistakes, one that will not likely be checked by pre- or post-hoc judicial oversight domestically or internationally. In the final analysis, the power to decide whether the predicates are met as a practical matter lies with the government itself, for good or ill. In that scenario, the extent to which the government has developed internal procedures to vet targeting decisions in accordance with applicable legal rules comes to matter immensely. Of course, those procedures themselves might be wrapped in the cloak of classification, making it impossible to assess them. The US government would do well to maximize their transparency, as so many have urged, if only by providing better information to the public about the abstract nature of and standards associated with its use of lethal force outside of conventional combat contexts.

References

Alston P (2010) Report of the Special Rapporteur on extrajudicial, summary or arbitrary executions, A/HRC?14/24/Add.6. Available at http://www.extrajudicialexecutions.org/application/media/14%20HRC%20Targeted%20Killings%20Report%20%28A.HRC.14.24.Add6%29.pdf

Anderson K (2009) Targeted killing in US counterterrorism strategy and law. In: Wittes B (ed) Legislating the war on terror: an agenda for reform. Brookings Institution Press, Washington DC, p 346

Anderson K (2010a) Bleg for Harold Koh's ASIL speech, Opinio Juris Blog. Available at http://opiniojuris.org/2010/03/25/bleg-for-harold-kohs-asil-speech/

Anderson K (2010b) Assassination, self-defense, and the Koh Speech, The Volokh Conspiracy Blog. Available at http://volokh.com/2010/03/28/assassination-self-defense-and-the-koh-speech/

Anderson K (2010c) The Washington Post on targeted killing and US citizens, The Volokh Conspiracy blog. Available at http://volokh.com/2010/09/06/the-washington-post-on-targeting-killing-and-us-citizens/
Arimatsu L (2009) Territory, boundaries and the law of armed conflict. YIHL 12:157–192
Baldor LC (2010) US officials: military wants to boost aid to Yemen. Washington Post
Balendra N (2008) Defining armed conflict. Cardozo L Rev 29:2461–2516
Barnes JE, Entous A (2010) Yemen covert role pushed: foiled bomb plot heightens talk of putting elite US squads in CIA hands, Wall Street Journal. Available at http://online.wsj.com/article/SB10001424052748704477904575586634028056268.html
Bartels R (2009) Timelines, borderlines and conflicts: the historical evolution of the legal divide between international and non-international armed conflicts. IRRC 873:35–67
Ben-Naftali O (2007) A judgment in the shadow of international criminal law. J Int Criminal Justice 5:322–331
Blum G, Heymann P (2010) Law and policy of targeted killing. Harvard National Security Journal 1:145–170
Bradley CA (2008) Self-execution and treaty duality. Sup Ct Rev pp 131–176
Bradley CA, Goldsmith JL (2005) Congressional authorization and the war on terrorism. Harv L Rev 118:2047–2133
Brooks RE (2004) War everywhere: rights, national security law, and the law of armed conflict in the age of terror. Univ Pa L Rev 153:675 761
Brunnee J, Toope SJ (2010) Legitimacy and legality in international law. Cambridge University Press, Cambridge
Byers M (2003) Letting the exception prove the rule. Ethics and International Affairs 17:9–16
Cassese A (2007a) The Nicaragua and Tadić tests revisited in light of the ICJ Judgment on genocide in Bosnia. EJIL 18:649–668
Cassese A (2007b) On some merits of the Israeli judgment on targeted killings. J Int Criminal Justice 5:339–345
Chesney RM (2006) Leaving Guantánamo: the law of international detainee transfers. Univ Richmond L Rev, pp 657–752
Chesney RM (2007) Beyond conspiracy? anticipatory prosecution and the challenge of unaffiliated terrorism. South Calif L Rev 80:425–502
Chesney RM (2011) Who may be held? Military detention through the habeas lens. Boston College L Rev (forthcoming)
Cloud DS (2010) Obama said to be weighing drone strikes in Yemen. LA Times
Corn GS (2007) Hamdan, Lebanon, and the regulation of hostilities: the need to recognize a hybrid category of armed conflict. Vanderbilt JTL 40:295–355
Cullen A (2010) The concept of non-international armed conflict in international humanitarian law. Cambridge University Press, Cambridge
Curran C, Gallagher J, Knapp P (2011) AQAP and suspected AQAP attack in Yemen Tracker 2010, American Enterprise Institute Critical Threats Project. Available at http://www.criticalthreats.org/yemen/aqap-and-suspected-aqap-attacks-yemen-tracker-2010#_ednref2
DeYoung K (2010) War review cites strides, is less confident of Afghan Governance. Washington Post
Dinstein Y (2005) War, aggression and self-defence, 4th edn. Cambridge University Press, Cambridge
Dinstein Y (2010) The conduct of hostilities under the law of international armed conflict. Cambridge University Press, Cambridge
Editorial (2010) Defending drones: the laws of war and the right to self-defense, Washington Post. Available at http://www.washingtonpost.com/wp-dyn/content/article/2010/04/12/AR2010041204086_pf.html
Fisher I (2003) Threats and responses: the militants: recent attacks in Yemen seen as sign of large terror cell. NY Times
Franck TM (1970) Who killed Article 2(4)? or: changing norms governing the use of force by states. AJIL 64:809

Goldsmith JL (2010) The growing problem of Extra-AUMF threats, Lawfare blog. Available at http://www.lawfareblog.com/2010/09/the-growing-problem-of-extra-aumf-threats/
Guiora A (2004) Targeted killing as active self-defense. Case Western Reserve JIL 36:319–334
Hansen MA (2007) Preventing the emasculation of warfare: halting the expansion of human rights law into armed conflict. Mil L Rev 194:1–65
Harris A (2010) Yemen: on the brink: exploiting grievances: al-Qaeda in the Arabian Peninsula. Carnegie endowment for International Peace Middle East program number 111
Hays Parks W (2010) Part IX of the ICRC 'direct participation in hostilities' study: no mandate, no expertise, and legally incorrect. NY Univ JIL & Pol 42:769–831
Hegghammer T (2010) The case for chasing al-Awlaki, Foreign Policy. Available at http://mideast.foreignpolicy.com/posts/2010/11/24/the_case_for_chasing_al_awlaki
Heller KJ (2010) When bad things happen to good scholars (Koh and the ICC Edition), Opinio Juris Blog. Available at http://opiniojuris.org/2010/03/26/when-bad-things-happen-to-good-scholars-koh-and-the-icc-edition/
Henckaerts J-M, Doswald-Beck L (2005) Customary international humanitarian law, I edn. Cambridge University Press, Cambridge
Hendawi H, al-Haj A (2010) Yemen charges U.S.-Born radical cleric al-Awlaki, Washington Post. Available at http://www.washingtonpost.com/wp-dyn/content/article/2010/11/02/AR2010110200458.html
Henderson C (2010) The 2010 United States National Security Strategy and the Obama Doctrine of 'Necessary Force. JCSL 15:434
Henkin L (1971) The reports of the death of Article 2(4) are greatly exaggerated. AJIL 65:544
Higgins R (1994) Problems and process: international law and how we use it. Clarendon Press, Oxford
Hsu SS (2010) Judge in D.C. tosses suit challenging placement of Yemeni cleric on terror list. Washington Post
ICRC Opinion Paper (2008) How is the term 'armed conflict' defined in international humanitarian law?. Available at http://www.icrc.org/web/eng/siteeng0.nsf/htmlall/armed-conflict-article-170308/$file/Opinion-paper-armedconflict.pdf
Jamjoom M (2010) Yemen launches operation against al Qaeda, CNN.com. Available at http://articles.cnn.com/2010-10-24/world/yemen.counterterror_1_awlaki-yemeni-american-qaeda?_s=PM:WORLD
Jinks D (2003a) Self-defense in an age of terrorism. ASIL Proc 97:141–152
Jinks D (2003b) State responsibility for the acts of private armed groups. Chicago JIL 4:83
Johnsen G (2010a) A false target in Yemen, NY Times. Available at http://www.nytimes.com/2010/11/20/opinion/20johnsen.html?_r=1
Johnsen G (2010b) AQAP: Propaganda and recruiting in Yemen, Big Think.com Waq al-Waq blog. Available at http://bigthink.com/ideas/26254
Johnson K (2010) US defends legality of killing with drones, Wall Street Journal. Available at http://online.wsj.com/article/SB10001424052702303450704575159864237752180.html
Johnson C, DeYoung K and Kornblut AE (2009) Obama cites failures after Detroit incident. Washington Post
Kasinof L, Bakri N (2011) Yemen's leader says he will step down in 2013. NY Times
Kreß C (1995) Gewalverbot and Selbstverteidigungsrecht nach der Satzung der Vereinten Nationen bei staatlicher Verwicklung in Gewaltakte Privater. Duncker & Humblot, Berlin
Kreß C (2010) Some reflections on the international legal framework governing transnational armed conflicts. JCSL 15:245–274
Kretzmer D (2005) Targeted killing of suspected terrorists: extra-judicial executions or legitimate means of defence? EJIL 16:171–212
Lake E (2010) 'Permission' needed to kill US terrorists. Washington Times
Lipton E (2010) U.S.-born cleric justifies the killing of civilians, NY Times. Available at http://www.nytimes.com/2010/05/24/world/middleeast/24awlaki.html
Lubell N (2005) Challenges in applying human rights law to armed conflict. IRRC 860:737–754
Lubell N (2010) Extraterritorial use of force against non-state actors. Oxford University Press, Oxford

Melzer N (2006) Targeted killing or less harmful means?–Israel's high court judgment on targeted killing and the restrictive function of military necessity. YIHL 9:87–116
Melzer N (2008) Targeted killing in international law. Oxford University Press, Oxford
Melzer N (2010) Keeping the balance between military necessity and humanity: a response to four critiques of the ICRC's interpretive guidance on the notion of direct participation in hostilities. NY Univ JIL & Pol. 42:831–916
Milanovic M (2010) Harold Koh on targeted killings, EJIL: Talk! Blog. Available at http://www.ejiltalk.org/harold-koh-on-targeted-killings/
Military responses to terrorism (1987) Panel discussion. ASIL Proc 81:287
Miller G, Jaffe G, DeYoung K (2010) US deploying drones in Yemen to hunt for al-Qaeda, has yet to fire missiles. Washington Post
Murphy SD (2009) The international legality of US military cross-border operations from Afghanistan into Pakistan. Naval War College, International Law Studies 85:109–139
Murphy R, Radsan AJ (2009) Due process and targeted killing of terrorists. Cardozo L Rev 31:405–450
Newton M (2009) Exceptional engagement: protocol I and a world united against terrorism. Texas ILJ 45:323–375
O'Connell ME (2002) Lawful self-defense to terrorism. Univ Pittsburgh L Rev 63:889–908
O'Connell ME (2008) Drones under international law, Washington University Law, Whitney R. Harris World Law Institute International Debate series. Available at http://law.wustl.edu/harris/documents/OConnellFullRemarksNov23.pdf
O'Connell ME (2009) Drones and the law: what we know, IntLawGrrls Blog. Available at http://intlawgrrls.blogspot.com/2009/12/drones-and-law-what-we-know.html
O'Connell ME (2010a) Lawful use of combat drones, US House of Representatives, Committee on Oversight and Government Reform, Subcommittee on National Security and Foreign Affairs. Available at http://www.fas.org/irp/congress/2010_hr/042810oconnell.pdf
O'Connell ME (2010b) Unlawful killing with combat drones: a case study of Pakistan, 2004–2009, in: Bronitt S (ed), Shooting to kill: the law governing lethal force in context (forthcoming Notre Dame Legal Studies Paper No. 09–43). Available at http://ssrn.com/abstract=1501144
Olson LM (2009) Guantánamo habeas review: are the D.C. district court's decisions consistent with ihl internment standards? Case Western Reserve JIL 42:197–243
Paust JJ (1986) Responding lawfully to international terrorism: the use of force abroad. 8 Whittier L Rev, pp 711–733
Paust JJ (2009) Are US attacks in Pakistan an armed attack on Pakistan? A response to Timothy waters, EJILTalk! Blog. Available at http://www.ejiltalk.org/are-us-attacks-in-pakistan-an-armed-attack-on-pakistan-a-response-to-timothy-waters/
Paust JJ (2010) Self-defense targetings of non-state actors and permissibility of US use of drones in Pakistan. Journal of Transnational Law & Policy 19:237–280
Priest D (2010) US military teams, intelligence deeply involved in aiding Yemen on strikes, Washington Post. Available at http://www.washingtonpost.com/wp-dyn/content/article/2010/01/26/AR2010012604239_pf.html
Puls KE (ed) (2004) Law of War Handbook, Charlottesville VA. The Judge Advocate General's Legal Center and School
Raghavan S, Jaffe G (2009) Yemeni airstrike kills 30, targets cleric linked to Ft. Hood attack Washington Post
Reisman WM (1999) International legal responses to terrorism. Houston JIL 22:3–61
Roberts A (2002) The laws of war in the war on terror. Israel YB HR 32:192–245
Rona G (2003) Interesting times for international humanitarian law: challenges from the 'war on terror. The Fletcher Forum of World Affairs 27:55–74
Sassoli M (2006) Transnational armed groups and international humanitarian law, Program on Humanitarian Policy and Conflict Research, Harvard University, occasional paper series. Available at http://www.reliefweb.int/rw/lib.nsf/db900sid/EVOD-6WQFE2/$file/OccasionalPaper6.pdf?openelement

Schmitt MN (2004) US security strategies: a legal assessment. Harvard JL & Public Policy 27:737–763

Schmitt MN (2008a) 'Change Direction' 2006: Israeli operations in Lebanon and international law of self-defense. Michigan JIL 29:127–164

Schmitt MN (2008b) Responding to transnational terrorism under the jus ad bellum: a normative framework. Naval L Rev 56:1–41

Schmitt E, Mekhennet S (2009) Qaeda branch steps up raids in North Africa. NY Times

Schondorf RS (2007) The targeted killings judgment: a preliminary assessment. J Int Criminal Justice 5:301–307

Scott Tyson A and Knickmeyer E (2008) US calls raid a warning to Syria, Washington Post. Available at http://www.washingtonpost.com/wp-dyn/content/article/2008/10/27/AR2008102700511.html

Shane S (2009) Born in U.S., a radical cleric inspires terror. NY Times

Shane S (2010) US approves targeted killing of American cleric. NY Times

Shane S and Mehkennet S (2010) Imam's path from condemning terror to preaching jihad, NY Times. Available at http://www.nytimes.com/2010/05/09/world/09awlaki.html

Shane S, Mazzetti M, Worth RF (2010) Secret assault on terrorism widens on two continents, NY Times. Available at http://www.nytimes.com/2010/08/15/world/15shadowwar.html

Sharp WG (2000) The use of armed force against terrorism: American hegemony or impotence? Chicago JIL 1:37–47

Sloane R (2009) The costs of conflation: preserving the dualism of jus ad bellum and jus in bello in the contemporary law of war. Yale JIL 34:47–112

Vité S (2009) Typology of armed conflicts in international humanitarian law: legal concepts and actual situations. IRRC 873:69–94

Vöneky SNU (2007) Response—The Fight Against Terrorism and the Rules of International Law—Comment on Papers and Speeches of John B. Bellinger, Chief Legal Advisor to the United States State Department. German LJ 8:747–759.

Watkin K (2010) Opportunity lost: organized armed groups and the ICRC 'direct participation in hostilities' interpretive guidance. NY Univ JIL & Pol 42:641–695

Waxman MC (2008) Detention as targeting: standards of certainty and detention of suspected terrorists. Columbia L Rev 108:1365–1430

Waxman MC (2009) The use of force against states that might have weapons of mass destruction. Michigan JIL 31:1–77

Waxman MC (2010) The structure of terrorism threats and the laws of war. Duke JCIL 20: 429–455

Wedgwood R (1999) Responding to terrorism: the strikes against Bin Laden. Yale JIL 24: 559–576

Whitlock C (2007) Group in Algeria turned to al-Qaida for assistance. Washington Post

Wilmshurst E (2006) The Chatham House principles of international law on the use of force in self-defence. ICLQ 55:963–972

Wittes B (2010) Clarification from Tom Malinowski, Lawfare Blog. Available at http://www.lawfareblog.com/2010/11/clarification-from-tom-malinowski/

Chapter 2
Adjudicating Armed Conflict in Domestic Courts: The Experience of Israel's Supreme Court

Galit Raguan

Contents

2.1 Introduction

Until relatively recently, dealing with terror groups and terror activities had been viewed by most nations primarily as an act of law enforcement, regulated by domestic criminal law. Accordingly, in most instances the same codes that applied

I am grateful to Nimrod Karin for his assistance and to Nadav Minkovsky, without whom the writing of this piece would not have been possible.

G. Raguan (✉)
University of California, Boalt Hall, Berkeley, USA
e-mail: galitraguan@gmail.com

to 'ordinary' criminal acts were applied to acts of terrorism. Such crimes were investigated by law enforcement agencies which were also responsible for the apprehension of terrorists. An alleged terrorist would be prosecuted in a regular civilian court of law for crimes such as murder, destruction of property and assault. Specialized terrorism-related offenses were also codified but continued to be drawn from domestic criminal law. When reviewed by the courts, the legitimacy of such counter-terrorism measures was assessed by judges in light of familiar domestic criminal and constitutional legal standards.

In the decade following 9/11,[1] the US has maintained that it is 'at war' with terror organizations, al-Qaeda in particular.[2] More than just a figure of speech,[3] this position carries with it significant legal ramifications. If the 'war on terror' is indeed an armed conflict, then presumably it follows that the legal regime which governs a state's conduct in the course of this conflict is the Law of Armed Conflict. How a country engages in war is rarely regulated by domestic law.[4] Instead, armed conflict is governed almost exclusively by international law. From the actions of soldiers on the battlefield to the selection of military targets and the

---

[1] While some commentators have pointed out that the categorization of the conflict with al-Qaeda as an armed conflict preceded 9/11, Goldsmith 2007, p 104, it is fair to say that the full force and scope of the argument was not made clear by the US administration until after 9/11.

[2] Ibid. at p 103, pp 105–106; Authorization for Use of Military Force, Pub. L. No. 107-40, 115 Stat. 224 (2001) (such acts render it both necessary and appropriate that the United States exercise its rights to self-defense); Military Order of November 13, 2001: Detention, Treatment, and Trial of Certain Non-Citizens in the War against Terrorism, 66 Fed. Reg. 57,883 (16 November 2001) (International terrorists, including members of al Qaida, have carried out attacks on United States… on a scale that has created a state of armed conflict that requires the use of the United States Armed Forces); Letter dated 7 October 2001 from the Permanent Representative of the United States of America to the United Nations addressed to the President of the Security Council, UN Doc. S/2001/946, available at: http://daccess-dds-ny.un.org/doc/UNDOC/GEN/N01/567/85/PDF/N0156785.pdf?OpenElement (reporting to the United Nations Security Council that the US had initiated military action against the al-Qaeda terrorist organization and the *de-facto* Taliban government in Afghanistan pursuant to Article 51 of the United Nations Charter, which guarantees to states the right to use force in self-defense in the event of an armed attack). While the Bush Administration's position was that the US was in a global war against terror, the Obama Administration has narrowed the scope of the conflict to the war against al-Qaeda; Ward and Lake 2009. For a critique of the 'global' and amorphous nature of the Bush administration's armed conflict, see Weiner 2007, p 137.

[3] Weiner 2007, at pp 138–140.

[4] For instance, while the US Constitution does set forth how war is to be declared (US Const. Art. I, § 8 delegates to Congress the power to declare war) and determines that the President is the Commander in Chief (US Const. Art. II, § 2), specific guidance as to the conduct of war is usually found in military manuals or the Uniform Code of Military Justice.

means and methods of warfare—these and many other aspects of an armed conflict are regulated by the Law of Armed Conflict.[5]

However, the application of the Law of Armed Conflict to matters pertaining to counter-terrorism has been far from obvious.[6] Rather, since 2001, it has been the source of extensive legal and political debate in the US and around the world, manifesting in various policy questions, among them: the status and legal rights afforded to detainees apprehended in Afghanistan, the appropriate forum for prosecuting alleged terrorists and the legality of targeted killings. Legal scholars, politicians and human rights groups remain intensely divided as to the legal rules which regulate the 'war on terror'.[7]

If the 'war or terror' is indeed governed by the Law of Armed Conflict,[8] this not only affects the rules governing the situation, but also impacts substantially the

---

[5] Furthermore, armed conflict will often take place outside the sovereign territory of a state, making the application of domestic law largely irrelevant.

[6] See Weiner 2007, pp 140–141. Cf., for instance, Delahunty and Yoo 2010, pp 803–805; Yoo 2006, pp 1–17, (presupposing that the 'war on terrorism' is indeed governed by the laws of war or armed conflict) with Feldman 2002, p 457 (suggesting that the neither the crime or war paradigm necessarily apply exclusively to the conflict with Al-Qaeda).

[7] One only has to look at the first bombing of the World Trade Center in 1993 and compare its legal treatment with that of the 9/11 attacks to realize the difference between these two legal paradigms. While for all intents and purposes the individuals suspected of carrying out the 1993 attack were considered 'terrorists', they were nonetheless apprehended by the FBI, held in custody and tried in the US in accordance with US domestic law. Less than a decade later, following the 9/11 attacks, President Bush announced that the US was at war with al-Qaeda, the same terror organization that had been responsible for the 1993 attack. A UN Security Council resolution supported the position that an armed attack had been perpetrated against the US (SC.Res. 1368, UN Doc. S/RES/1368 (12 September 2001)), and NATO's collective self-defense provision was activated for the first time in history in response to the attack against the US, Press Release, North Atlantic Treaty Organization, Statement by the North Atlantic Council (12 September 2001), available at http://www.nato.int/docu/pr/2001/p01-124e.htm. Apprehension of suspects was carried out primarily by the military and those individuals apprehended and suspected of involvement with al-Qaeda were deemed 'enemy combatants'. The majority of such detainees were held in a detention facility outside the US without the procedural rights afforded to criminal defendants.

[8] In fact, the debate surrounding the appropriate legal regime for the 'war on terror' is not the focus of this Article nor will the justifications for this change in legal treatment be critically analyzed. Rather, the focus is on whether and to what extent this new categorization of the conflict between states and non-state armed groups has affected adjudication by the courts. Nonetheless, it should be noted that the rationales for this change in legal paradigm are not without merit—the scope and intensity of the 9/11 attacks were unprecedented with regard to an act of terror; the organization, structural command and training of al-Qaeda had become quite substantial and similar in nature to that of a militia; and the location of al-Qaeda outside the US made the use of standard law enforcement mechanisms and agencies unrealistic in many respects. The heated legal debate that subsequently ensued regarding the status of detainees for example was not a result of the US position that the Law or Armed Conflict governed the situation, but rather because the Administration adopted the position that essentially *no* law was applicable for handling this 'new' type of conflict.

role of the judiciary in reviewing counter-terrorism policies. Courts have always been reluctant to adjudicate matters pertaining to foreign affairs and the conduct of war.[9] US jurisprudence in particular reflects a certain reluctance to directly apply international law in domestic courts.[10] Hence, there is a high probability that if courts perceive a particular legal challenge as being closely related to an armed conflict and requiring the application of international law in a manner that will affect the conduct of hostilities, they will be deterred from adjudication.

However, this has not been the case in Israel. Since late 2000, Israel has been in a state of escalated hostilities with Palestinian terrorist organizations. As a result, concurrently with the ongoing debate in the US regarding the legal treatment of counter-terrorism policies, similar questions have risen in Israel. The Israeli government has also advanced the position that the violent clash with armed Palestinian groups, particularly with Hamas, has risen to a state of an armed conflict.[11] The Israeli Supreme Court has accepted this position in its judgments. Nonetheless, in doing so, rather than refraining from adjudicating petitions which question the legality of the government's counter-terrorism steps, it has taken a step further and has directly applied the international legal framework which governs armed conflict.

In what is perhaps the Israeli Supreme Court's most prominent decision in this context to date, it ruled substantively on the legality of Israel's targeted killings policy, and in doing so directly applied the principles of the Law of Armed Conflict to Israel's actions. In a subsequent decision, the Court considered the military's fulfillment of its humanitarian obligations during the conduct of hostilities, again in accordance with the Law of Armed Conflict. What is remarkable is that the petition was filed, heard, decided and the opinion published all in the course of ongoing hostilities between Israel and Hamas in the Gaza Strip.

---

[9] See Glennon 1989, p 814; Henkin 1996, pp 208–215; *Gilligan* v *Morgan*, 413 US 1 (1973) (which presented a constitutional challenge to the training and weaponry of the Ohio National Guard); *Goldwater* v *Carter*, 444 US 996 (1979) (in which several members of Congress challenged the President's unilateral notice of termination of a mutual defense treaty with the Republic of China); *Mora* v *McNamara*, 387 F. 2d 862 (DC Cir.), cert. denied, 389 US 934 (1967) (in which the Supreme Court refused to examine the constitutionality of the Vietnam War); *Crockett* v *Reagan*, 720 F. 2d 1355 (DC Cir. 1983) (per curiam), cert. denied, 104 S. Ct. 3533 (1984) (regarding covert activities in Nicaragua). For a general overview of US Supreme Court jurisprudence with regard to foreign affairs, see Lee Boyd 2001, p 277; Slaughter Bruley 2003, p 1980; Franck 1992.

[10] Contra Yoo 1999, p 1979, (arguing that '[a] reading of Article VI [of the Constitution] that does not require self-execution of treaties is consistent with the Supremacy Clause)' with Paust 1988, p 760 (arguing that non-self-execution is a judicial invention at odds with the Constitution and the views of the Framers); Henkin 1984, p 1560 '(International law *is* law of the United States…' [emphasis added]); Henkin 1996, p 201 (arguing that non-self-execution 'runs counter to the language, and spirit, and history' of the Constitution); Vázquez 1992, p 1087 (arguing that the text and history of the Constitution demonstrate that courts may directly enforce treaty provisions in properly brought suits by individuals).

[11] See nn 37–40 infra and accompanying text.

The unique Israeli situation of a prolonged military occupation along Israel's borders has undoubtedly contributed to its Supreme Court's extraordinary jurisprudence. Coupled with procedural aspects of the Israeli Supreme Court's jurisdiction and its permissive rules of standing and justiciability, these characteristics can account for the active approach taken by the Court in relation to other countries. Nonetheless, the Israeli experience provides an intriguing perspective on how domestic courts can, when they choose to do so, adjudicate questions pertaining to the Law of Armed Conflict. If we accept that the 'war on terrorism' is not just a slogan, but also a legal paradigm, similar questions are bound to rise not just in Israel, but also in other countries which encounter threats from non-state actors. The Israeli experience thus provides a relevant case-study.

This Article will focus on how the Israeli Supreme Court has gradually incorporated the Law of Armed Conflict into its judgments when reviewing the Executive's policies, and will trace the historical circumstances and legal developments which have contributed to and enabled the creation of such jurisprudence. It will also address the question of whether the Israeli experience can be utilized by other jurisdictions. Part II of this Article will provide a brief overview of the status of international law in domestic Israeli courts and the legal framework that applies to executive action in Judea and Samaria and the and Gaza Strip. Part III will describe the transition in Israel to an armed conflict paradigm with respect to the Israeli hostilities with Palestinian armed groups, while Part IV will focus on recent Israeli case law in this regard. These cases illustrate the gradual move by the Court toward adjudicating questions which relate more and more closely to the battlefield. Part V will follow with an analysis of the circumstances which have led to this transition in the Israeli context. It will also discuss whether the Israeli experience is comparable to courts in other jurisdictions which encounter similar legal dilemmas.

2.2 The Application of International Law by Domestic Courts in Israel

The Israeli phenomenon of adjudicating questions pertaining to the conduct of hostilities by the military cannot be isolated from the Israeli military occupation in Judea and Samaria (hereinafter also the West Bank) and the Gaza Strip.[12] The prolonged Israeli military presence in these Territories has had a direct contribution to the Israeli Supreme Court's willingness to adjudicate questions pertaining to hostilities. Because Israeli domestic law generally does not apply to these territories, the Court became accustomed long before 2000 to applying international law to executive action and policy in the Territories. This has had a tremendous effect on its

[12] On the legal status of the Gaza Strip in particular following Israel's Disengagement in 2005, see infra nn 65–67 and accompanying text.

treatment of international law in the last decade against the background of the changed nature of the conflict between Israel and Palestinian terrorist groups. Therefore, in order to place the jurisprudence of the Israeli Supreme Court in its proper context, a brief and rudimentary overview of the status of international law in domestic law in Israel and the legal sources applied by Israel's Supreme Court to executive action occurring in the Territories is necessary.[13]

2.2.1 The status of international law in domestic courts in Israel

Different jurisdictions have varying rules regarding the relationship between international and domestic law that will affect the extent to which domestic courts are able to rely on international law. Israel's treatment of international law is similar to that of the United Kingdom,[14] in that both draw a distinction between convention-based and customary international law. Convention or treaty-based law, i.e., those obligations a state takes upon itself by becoming a party to an international agreement, requires active transformation into domestic law through the legislative enactment of a statute. Hence, a treaty obligation does not bind the state of Israel in a domestic court absent a manifestation in its domestic law.[15] Customary international law, i.e., those practices which have formed a consensual custom among nations, is incorporated 'automatically' into domestic law and is applied by the courts, to the extent that no domestic legislation exists to the contrary. In the case of a conflict between a customary international norm and domestic legislation, the latter prevails. Nonetheless, Israeli courts will apply a canon of interpretation whereby the purpose of domestic law is, *inter alia*, to fulfill the provisions of international law and not to contradict it.[16] This is referred to as 'a "presumption of accord" between public international law and local law'.[17]

---

[13] An exhaustive, comprehensive account of the debate regarding the legal and political status of the territories is outside the scope of this Article.

[14] Shaw 2003, pp 129–143.

[15] Crim FH 7048/97 *Anonymous* v *Minister of Defense* [2000] IsrSC 54(1) 721, 742–743.

[16] Ibid.

[17] Ibid. See also CrimA 6182/98 *Sheinbein* v *Attorney General* (unpublished); HCJ 279/51 *Amsterdam* v *Minister of the Treasury* [1952] IsrSC 6 945, 966; CrimA 336/61 *Eichmann* v *Attorney General* [1962] IsrSC 16 2033, 2041; CA 522/70 *Alkotov* v *Shahin* [1971], IsrSC 25 (2) 77, 80, as well as Aharon Barak, *Interpretation in Law*, Vol 2 (Jerusalem, Nevo 1994) (in Hebrew) p 576.

Hence, Israel's courts will make an effort, to the extent possible, to interpret a domestic law provision in a manner that does not contradict international law.[18]

2.2.2 The legal framework applicable to Judea and Samaria and the Gaza Strip

Israel gained military control of the territories known as Judea and Samaria and the Gaza Strip in 1967. These territories (notwithstanding East Jerusalem) were never annexed to the sovereign state of Israel and for many years remained governed by the military authorities of Israel and hence subject to martial law. Although the Territories are not sovereign Israeli territory, the actions of the military and the decisions of the military commander in the Territories are nonetheless subject to judicial scrutiny in Israel, as explained below.

The Israeli Supreme Court is the highest appellate court in Israel. In addition, it also enjoys original jurisdiction over actions by the state or its officials in its capacity as the High Court of Justice (hereinafter HCJ).[19] In such circumstances, it is a court of first and final instance to adjudicate such petitions. Naturally, the fact that a petition against the agencies of the state and state officials can be filed directly with the HCJ has resulted in a heavy case-load for the Court. The Court's tendency over the years to relax its standing requirements,[20] which gradually widened accessibility, has also contributed to the wealth of petitions filed and

[18] A Similar presumption exists in the United Kingdom that legislation is to be construed so as to avoid a conflict with international law; Shaw 2003, p 139. There is also a presumption in the United States that Congress will not legislate contrary to international obligations of the state, so that when an act and a treaty deal with the same subject, the courts will seek to construe them in a manner that will not be contrary to the wording of either; ibid. at p 150; see also Steinhardt 2004, p 6.

[19] Article 15(c) of Israel's Basic Law: the Judiciary provides that the Court: 'shall hear matters in which it deems it necessary to grant relief for the sake of justice...,' Basic Law: Judiciary, 1984, S.H. 78. Furthermore, Article 15(d)(2) sets forth that the Supreme Court, sitting as the High Court of Justice (hereinafter HCJ), shall be competent to order the state and public officials to do or refrain from doing any act, granting the court jurisdiction over persons or bodies 'carrying out public functions under law'. The terms 'Supreme Court' and 'High Court of Justice' will be used interchangeably from hereinafter in the Article. While Israel does not have a constitution, since the state's foundation, the Basic Laws have been enacted piecemeal with the intention of eventually being consolidated into a Constitution. Accordingly, they have been interpreted by the Supreme Court as being superior in status to 'regular' laws enacted by the legislature. The Israeli legislature (Knesset) accordingly enjoys a dual role as both legislator and constitutional drafter. Thus, although the Basic Law: the Judiciary was enacted by the legislature, under certain circumstances it enjoys precedence over 'regular' laws; for a history of the enactment of the Basic Laws and Israel's constitutional regime see Barak-Erez 1995, pp 311–332; Edry 2005, pp 77–113.

[20] See nn. 107–110 infra and accompanying text.

heard by the Court. Thus, for example, in 2008, over 1,600 new petitions were filed with the Court in its HCJ capacity alone.[21]

Over the years, the Court substantiated its broad review powers over executive action, reviewing an ever-increasing number of petitions pertaining to the discretion of the executive branch, determining whether state officials and state policy are reasonable and measured.[22] This trend gradually extended to include petitions pertaining to national security.[23] Based on its general jurisdiction to review executive action, the Court determined in its early years that it had jurisdiction to hear cases pertaining to the actions of the military in the Territories and petitions filed by residents of the West Bank and the Gaza Strip.[24] Since then, the Court has adjudicated numerous petitions on matters pertaining to the military's actions and the decisions of the military commander in the Territories.[25]

The fact that the Territories are not a sovereign part of Israel has meant that domestic Israeli law is inapplicable. Instead, the legal framework that has been applied includes the law in place at the time Israel gained control of the Territories,[26] martial law promulgated by the military commander, and most significantly (for our purposes) international law.[27]

---

[21] The Court System in Israel: Semi-Annual Report 1.7.09-31.12.09, available at http://elyon1.court.gov.il/heb/haba/dochot/doc/7-12_2009.pdf, p 32 (in Hebrew).

[22] For an overview of the Court's scrutiny of the Executive, see Barak-Erez 2002, pp 617–628; Bracha 1991, p 39.

[23] See Barak 2002, pp 148–156 (for a review of the Court's jurisprudence with regard to national security); Bracha 1991; for a translation of terrorism-related judgments of the Supreme Court from recent years, see Israel Ministry of Foreign Affairs, Judgments of the Israel Supreme Court: Fighting Terrorism Within the Law, available at http://www.mfa.gov.il/MFA/government/Law/Legal+Issues+and+Rulings/Fighting+Terrorism+within+the+Law+2-Jan-2005.htm; Vol 2; http://www.mfa.gov.il/MFA/government/Law/Legal + Issues+and+Rulings/Judgments_Israel_Supreme_Court-Fighting_Terrorism_within_Law-Vol_2.htm, Vol 3, http://www.mfa.gov.il/MFA/Terrorism-+Obstacle+to+Peace/Terrorism+and+Islamic+Fundamentalism-/Judgments_Israel_Supreme_Court-Fighting_Terrorism_within_Law-Vol_3.

[24] The Court determined in a number of cases in the 1970 s that since the military commander was a public servant performing a public duty under law, his decisions were subject to the statutory jurisdiction of the Supreme Court in its capacity as the HCJ, HCJ 302/72 *Khelou* v *Government of Israel* [1973] IsrSC 27(2) 169, 176; HCJ 393/82 *Ja'amait Ascan* v *IDF Commander In Judea and Samaria* [1983] IsrSC 37(4) 785, 809; see also Kretzmer 2002, pp 19–20.

[25] See n. 23 supra. See also Negbi 1981, (in Hebrew); Amit-Kohn et al. 1993, pp 59–81; Dotan 1999, pp 322–327. Cf. generally Kretzmer 2002, (for a more critical perspective of the Israeli Supreme Court jurisprudence on legal matters pertaining to the Territories).

[26] E.g., Jordanian law, law from the period of the British mandate, etc.

[27] For an overview of the applicable legal framework to the Territories, see Shamgar 1982, pp 13–60.

While the official (and contested)[28] position of Israel has been that the Territories were legally not under belligerent occupation,[29] it did agree as a matter of policy to abide by the humanitarian treaty obligations applicable to an occupied territory. This includes humanitarian obligations as set forth in the Geneva Convention IV, as well as *any relevant customary international law obligations*. The significance of this is that Israel would be bound by obligations that had become binding under customary law even if these were formalized in treaties it had not ratified. Accordingly, the Supreme Court has routinely examined the actions or decisions of the military commander in light of the humanitarian obligations as set forth in Geneva Convention IV and any obligations in customary international law pertaining to belligerent occupation.[30]

One additional legal source applicable to the Territories deserves mentioning. Although Israel's domestic law generally does not apply to the Territories, the Israeli Supreme Court did determine that some *domestic* legal principles would be applied to military action in the Territories—these are known as the substantive

---

[28] See for example, Roberts 1992, pp 25–85; Mari 2005, pp 358–362.

[29] Hence, the Israeli government formally refers to the Territories as 'Administered' rather than 'Occupied'. The Geneva Convention Relative to the Protection of Civilian Persons in time of War, Art 2, 12 August 1949, 6 UST 3516, 3518, 75 UNTS 287, 288 [hereinafter Geneva Convention IV] provides protection to the civilian population in times of war and also applies to an occupied territory. Article 2 to the Convention, which addresses its application, states, *inter alia*, that '[t]he Convention shall also apply to all cases of partial or total occupation of the territory of a High Contracting Party...', Israel argued that since neither of these regions—the West Bank or the Gaza Strip—had been the territory of a 'High Contracting Party' at the time Israel gained control of them, the Convention did not apply. A similar argument, made by an Israeli scholar shortly after Israel gained control of the Territories, was that since the annexation of the West Bank by Jordan in 1950 (following Israel's War of Independence) had not received international recognition, it was not the sovereign territory of another state when Israel took control of it in 1967. It followed then, according to the author, that Israel was not bound by those parts of the law of occupation whose purpose was to protect the rights of the previous sovereign; however, it was obligated to abide by the humanitarian aspects of belligerent occupation law. See Blum 1968, p 279; Kretzmer 2002, pp 32–34; Amit-Kohn et al. 1993, pp 21–23; Shamgar 1982, pp 31–43; Kelly 1999, pp 156–159.

[30] HCJ 7015/02 *Ajuri* v *IDF Commander in the West Bank* [2002] IsrSC 56(6) 352, 364: '... the parties before us assumed that in the circumstances currently prevailing in the territory under the control of the IDF, the laws of international law concerning belligerent occupation apply... second, the rules of international law that apply in the territory are the customary laws (such as the appendix to the (Fourth) Hague Convention respecting the Laws and Customs of War on Land of 1907, which is commonly regarded as customary law.... With regard to the Fourth Geneva Convention, counsel for the Respondent reargued before us the position of the State of Israel that this convention—which in his opinion does not reflect customary law—does not apply to Judaea and Samaria. Notwithstanding, Mr. Nitzan told us—in accordance with the long established practice of the Government of Israel—that the Government of Israel decided to act in accordance with the humanitarian parts of the Fourth Geneva Convention. In view of this declaration, we do not need to examine the legal arguments concerning this matter, which are not simple, and we may leave these to be decided at a later date. It follows that for the purpose of the petitions before us we are assuming that humanitarian international law—as reflected in the Fourth Geneva Convention (including article 78) and certainly the Fourth Hague Convention—applies in our case.

rules of Israeli administrative law. Over the years, the Court had developed a set of general principles which regulated administrative action domestically—these included an obligation to act under authority granted by law; to ensure procedural fairness; and to exercise administrative discretion reasonably for a proper purpose and on the basis of relevant considerations.[31] In *Al-Taliya* v *Minister of Defense*[32] the Court, in dictum, acknowledged that in addition to customary international law obligations, the military's actions would also be examined 'according to the criteria which this court applies when it reviews the act or omission of any other arm of the executive branch, while taking into account… the duties of the respondents that flow from the nature of their task'.[33] In subsequent jurisprudence, the Court has often opined that 'every soldier carries in his pack both the rules of international law and also the basic principles of Israeli administrative law that are relevant to the issue'.[34]

To summarize, the Israeli Supreme Court's review of military actions and executive policy in the Occupied Territories began shortly after Israel gained control of the West Bank and Gaza in 1967. The Court substantiated its jurisdiction over the Territories based on the statutory authority granted to it to review actions of officials or bodies acting in their official capacity under law. Since domestic Israeli law did not apply to the Territories, the Court in its rulings generally applied customary international law pertaining to belligerent occupation. In addition, the Court reviewed executive and military action in light of a set of controlling principles that have evolved in domestic administrative law.[35] We now turn to the transition into the 'war on terror' paradigm and its effects on adjudication of matters pertaining to military activity in the Territories before the Israeli Supreme Court.

---

[31] For instance, if an Israeli citizen applies for a gun permit from the authorities and is rejected, the responsible agency must act reasonably in rejecting the request. Similarly, if the military commander in the Territories determines that in order to pave a road in the territories, private Palestinian land must expropriated, the Court will first look at any legal obligations pertaining to the situation originating in international law. In addition, this decision will also be examined in light of its reasonableness and proportionality, i.e., was there a real need to expropriate the land; were other options examined; was the owner permitted to present his case; was the land taken no more than was necessary; and does the harm caused by the expropriation outweigh the expected benefits from the road, etc.

[32] HCJ 619/78 [1979] IsrSC 33(3) 505.

[33] Ibid. at p 512; Kretzmer 2002, p 26.

[34] *Ajuri*, IsrSC 56(6) 352 at 365; HCJ 393/82 *Ja'amait Ascan Cooperative Society* v *IDF Commander in Judaea and Samaria* [1983] IsrSC 37(4) 785, 810; HCJ 358/88 *Association for Civil Rights in Israel v Central Commander* [1989] IsrSC 43(2) 529, 536–538; HCJ 4764/04 *Physicians for Human Rights* v *IDF Commander in Gaza* [2004] Dinim 1098 (30) 2004, para 10; HCJ 2056/04 *Beit Sourik Village Council* v *the government of Israel* [2004] IsrSC 58(5) 807, 828.

[35] For an additional resource containing a detailed analysis of the Court's authority to review the decisions of the military commander, as well as the applicable legal sources, see Nathan 1982, pp 109–169.

2.3 The Legal Transition to an 'Armed Conflict' in Israel

Once Israel had gained control of the West Bank and Gaza in 1967, a military administration was established in the Territories. The Israeli military was responsible, in accordance with its humanitarian obligations under the law of belligerent occupation, for public order and security in the Territories. When issues of security arose, various law enforcement means would be employed by the Israel Defense Forces (hereinafter IDF) usually based on military orders promulgated by the military commander and in accordance with humanitarian principles of the laws of belligerent occupation.

The Israeli Supreme Court in its HCJ capacity established its jurisdiction over the decisions of the military commander relatively soon after Israel had gained control over the Territories and has since then engaged in judicial review of the discretion of the military commander in numerous judgments. Decisions and policies implemented by the military in the Territories have been examined by the Court in light of international law (the law of belligerent occupation) and the binding principles of Israeli administrative law.[36]

In 2000, the conflict between the IDF and Palestinians escalated, signified by the outburst of the al-Aqsa Intifada.[37] In the years that followed, the number of terror attacks targeted at Israelis intensified. The IDF in response renewed its military presence in Palestinian cities. Israel crafted various military responses, including aerial attacks, the use of substantial forces for military operations in the Territories, as well as the use of reserve forces. Thousands of Israelis and Palestinians were killed and injured as a result of the hostilities.

The hostilities that broke out in 2000 reached an unprecedented level and intensity in the history of the Israeli-Palestinian conflict. Almost immediately after violence broke out in September 2000, Israel's official position regarding the nature of hostilities with Palestinians began to shift and the government began to formulate its argument that the conflict between the Israeli military and Palestinian

---

[36] See supra n 24 and accompanying text; see also Shamir 1990, pp 784–795; Dotan 1999, pp 326–336 (for figures regarding the number of petitions involving the Palestinian residents of the Territories filed with and adjudicated by the High Court of Justice between 1986 and 1995, a period covering, *inter alia*, the first Intifada; see n 37 infra).

[37] Intifada—literally 'uprising'—is the term used to describe the violent Palestinian campaigns directed at ending the Israeli military occupation. The first Intifada began in 1987 and came to an end with the signing of the Oslo Accords in 1993. It was characterized primarily by violent demonstrations, the throwing of rocks and Molotov cocktails at Israeli soldiers and riot control mechanisms employed by the IDF. The al-Aqsa Intifada, also known as the second Intifada or the 2000 Intifada, began in September 2000 shortly after the failed Camp David Summit between President Clinton, Prime Minister Ehud Barak and Chairman Yasser Arafat. This Intifada was characterized by the deployment of suicide bombers in Israel and the initiation of a rocket campaign from the Gaza Strip directed at Israel (with over 12,000 rockets launched at Israel between 2000 and 2008). This round of violence ultimately resulted in thousands of deaths and casualties for both the Israelis and the Palestinians. This increase in intensity and scope of the violence led to the categorization of the hostilities by Israel as an armed conflict.

armed groups had reached the level of an armed conflict. A comprehensive legal approach to this 'new' armed conflict was developed in a piecemeal fashion by the government of Israel over time.[38] However, an early manifestation of this shift can be traced to the government's position presented in 2001 before the Sharm El Sheikh Fact-Finding Committee (the Mitchell Commission) when it advanced the position that the situation between Israel and Palestinians had risen to an *armed conflict short of war*.[39] In subsequent responses by the government to petitions filed with the Supreme Court pertaining to the IDF's conduct in the Territories, the government began to rely more heavily on the contention that the nature of hostilities—their scope, intensity, level of organization, means—were such that IDF actions were now governed, under these new circumstances, by the Law of Armed Conflict rather than the laws of belligerent occupation[40] or under certain circumstances concurrently with the laws of belligerent occupation.[41]

As early as 2001, the Supreme Court observed that 'for several months now events of actual combat have been taking place in the areas of Judea and Samaria

---

[38] It is interesting to note that in petitions filed with the Supreme Court in support of this position, the government referred, *inter alia*, to the Presidential Order made by President Bush following 9/11, Military Order of 13 November 2001: Detention, Treatment, and Trial of Certain Non-Citizens in the War against Terrorism, 66 Fed. Reg. 57,883, UN Security Council Resolution 1373 which viewed the 9/11 attacks as 'a danger to international peace and security', UN Doc S/RES/1373/2001, available at http://daccess-dds-ny.un.org/doc/UNDOC/GEN/N01/557/43/PDF/N0155743.pdf?OpenElement, and the NATO decision to treat the attacks of 9/11 as such that activates the self-defense of the NATO Treaty; Press Release, North Atlantic Treaty Organization, Statement by the North Atlantic Council (12 September 2001), available at http://www.nato.int/docu/pr/2001/p01-124e.htm; HCJ 769/02 *Public Committee Against Torture in Israel* v *Government of Israel*, Supplementary Brief for the State, 2 February 2003, paras 14–15 (on file with author) (hereinafter *PCATI* v *GoI*).

[39] In Israel's first position paper presented to the Committee, appointed to determine, *inter alia*, the causes of the outbreak of violence, it declared: 'Israel is engaged in an armed conflict short of war. This is not a civilian disturbance or a demonstration or a riot. It is characterized by live-fire attacks on a significant scale both quantitatively and geographically... The attacks are carried out by a well armed and organized militia, under the command of the Palestinian political establishment operating from areas outside Israeli control...' Sharm El Sheikh Fact-Finding Committee First Statement of the Government of Israel [28 December 2000] available at http://www.mfa.gov.il/MFA/MFAArchive/2000_2009/2000/12/Sharm%20el-Sheikh%20Fact-Finding%20Committee%20-%20First%20Sta, para 286.

[40] The distinction between these two legal regimes—the laws of belligerent occupation and the laws of armed conflict—is not purely an academic exercise but carries with it a practical significance. In some aspects it is similar to the distinction between law enforcement and armed conflict. For instance, under the laws of belligerent occupation, if a civilian holding a weapon advances towards a soldier at a checkpoint, the soldier may be required to attempt to disarm and apprehend the individual through calling to him or firing a warning shot and use lethal force only as a last resort for the purpose of self-defense. However, on the battlefield in the course of hostilities, if a soldier encounters a civilian who has picked up arms, the laws of armed conflict consider such a individual a legitimate military target that may be attacked. Hence, the applicable legal regime carries great weight in determining the legality of the act in question.

[41] See nn 50–51 and accompanying text.

and Gaza…'.[42] In a separate case it noted that the damage to property was as 'a result of the combat condition under which the area has been for over two years…,'[43] while in a brief one-page decision dismissing a petition challenging damage to property as a result of the IDF's actions, the Court implicitly accepted that the IDF was acting in accordance with the laws of war.[44] In early 2002, the Supreme Court commented in yet another decision:

> 'Israel finds itself in the middle of difficult battle against a furious wave of terrorism. Israel is exercising its right of self defense. See The Charter of the United Nations, art. 51. This combat is not taking place in a normative void. It is being carried out according to the rules of international law, which provide principles and rules for combat activity.'[45]

Later that year, in *Ajuri* v *IDF Commander in the West Bank*,[46] the Court stated explicitly that '[s]ince the end of September 2000, fierce fighting has been taking place in Judaea, Samaria and the Gaza Strip. *This is not police activity. It is an armed struggle*'.[47] In 2004, in *Beit Sourik Village Council* v *the Government of Israel*, the Court finally used the term 'armed conflict' to describe hostilities between Israel and the Palestinians.[48] The effect of recognizing that the military situation on the ground had changed was the concomitant recognition that the IDF was authorized to act in accordance with the principles dictated by the Law of Armed Conflict.

2.4 The Application of the Law of Armed Conflict by Israel's Supreme Court to Military Activity

By the late 1990s, the Israeli Supreme Court had become relatively comfortable with adjudicating questions pertaining to the military's actions in the Territories and consulting international law in order to discern Israel's legal obligations. Hence, when petitions pertaining to the military continued to flow to the Court's doors after 2000, they seemed familiar and indistinctive. Yet a profound change

---

[42] HCJ 2461/01 *Cna'an* v *IDF Military Commander in Judea and Samaria* [2001] Dinim 364 (7) 2001.

[43] HCJ 8172/02 *Ibrahim* v *IDF Military Commander in the West Bank* [2002] Dinim 737 (38) 2002.

[44] HCJ 9252/00 *Alsake* v *State of Israel* [2001] Dinim 572 (11) 2001 ('In the response… the military picture in the area was laid out before us… According to the state's response, its actions are taken in order to protect villages… *The authority to undertake these various actions is found in the laws of war as determined in the Hague Regulations of 1907*' [emphasis added]).

[45] HCJ 3451/02 *Almandi* v *Minister of Defense* [2002] IsrSC 56(3) 30, 34 [emphasis added].

[46] HCJ 7015/02, [2002] IsrSC 56(6) 352.

[47] Ibid. at 358 [emphasis added].

[48] HCJ 2056/04, [2004] IsrSC 58(5) 807, 815 (These combat operations—which are not regular police operations, but embody all the characteristics of armed conflict…).

had taken place—the nature of the ongoing conflict between Israel and the Palestinians had undergone a transformation, specifically an escalation in scope and intensity that had shifted perception of counter-terrorism efforts from the law enforcement paradigm to that of armed conflict, both in Israel and elsewhere around the world.

The intensity of the hostilities between the IDF and organized, armed Palestinian groups resulted in the Court having to deal with an ever-growing number of petitions involving legal questions pertaining to the conduct of hostilities. This is exemplified by what may be the issue most closely linked to the conduct of hostilities to date—the Court's 2006 adjudication on the merits of Israel's policy of targeted killings. Since then, the Court has continued to examine the military's actions, including those pertaining to the Gaza Strip despite the cessation of Israel's martial rule in the region,[49] as illustrated by the 'real-time' adjudication of petitions pertaining to IDF conduct while hostilities were ongoing in 2009.

2.4.1 Between two paradigms: belligerent occupation and armed conflict

The Israeli government's position regarding the existence of an armed conflict short of war in early petitions did not include a comprehensive approach regarding the legal ramifications of this change in classification. However, with each new petition the government's position was finessed, gaining clarity and depth. It is important to note that although the government advanced the position that the security situation had risen to an armed conflict governed by the Law of Armed Conflict, it did not dismiss the potentially concurrent application of the laws of belligerent occupation. In fact, the government conceded that the laws of belligerent occupation continued to apply to certain matters[50]—those that enjoyed sufficient coverage in the laws of belligerent occupation—as well as in certain areas—those that had remained under Israeli control and governance and had not been transferred to Palestinian responsibility.[51]

Hence, the two legal frameworks would not always be mutually exclusive—while the laws of belligerent occupation could continue to govern certain aspects of governance in the Territories, the government could also resort to the Laws of Armed Conflict in responding to the hostilities. Determining which legal regime

[49] Infra nn 65–66 and accompanying text.

[50] HCJ 769/02 *PCATI* v *GoI*, Supplementary Notice by the State, 2 February 2003 (on file with author), paras 51–54 (on file with author).

[51] Ibid. Prior to 2000, the Israeli military had gradually withdrawn from certain Palestinian cities in accordance with the Oslo Accords and subsequent political agreements of the 1990s. Therefore, it was the State's contention that the laws of belligerent occupation could not apply to areas in which administrative responsibility had been transferred to the Palestinian Authority and the Israeli military no longer had effective control.

applied to a particular matter would therefore require examining that matter *ad hoc* in its specific context. The Supreme Court adopted a similar rationale, although the Court, to a greater extent than the state, has continued to rely on legal principles from various paradigms rather than exclusively on the Law of Armed Conflict.[52]

The petition in *Adalah* v *GOC Central Command*[53] exemplifies the transition—from the government's perspective—from law enforcement/belligerent occupation rationales to armed conflict rationales. The petition, filed in 2002, challenged an army procedure that allowed soldiers conducting arrests to enlist the voluntary assistance of Palestinian civilians to convey messages to wanted individuals in an attempt to convince them to surrender themselves peacefully. While the petitioners in the case relied on the laws of belligerent occupation to challenge the military's policy,[54] the government appeared to justify its actions primarily on the Law of Armed Conflict.[55]

The Supreme Court's decision was handed down in late 2005, by which time the Court had already recognized in several decisions that a state of hostilities existed between the IDF and Palestinian armed groups. Nonetheless, the Court did not adopt the government's position that in this particular case, the military practice was exclusively governed by the Law of Armed Conflict. Rather, it based its decision on the belligerent occupation paradigm in striking down the operational procedure. In the opening sentence of its decision the Court laid out the normative framework by stating that '[a]n army in an area under belligerent occupation is permitted to arrest local residents wanted by it, who endanger its security'.[56] It went on to cite various principles of the laws of belligerent occupation, noting that '[i]ndeed, safeguarding of the lives of the civilian population is *a central value in the humanitarian law applicable to belligerent occupation'*.[57]

---

52 See nn 73–74 supra and accompanying text.

53 HCJ 3799/02 Adalah—The Legal Center for Arab Minority Rights in Israel v GOC Central Command, IDF Dinim 305 (61) 2005.

54 The petitioners' primary claim was that the procedure was at odds 'with the principles of international humanitarian law regarding the military activity of an occupying force in occupied territory,' ibid. at para 13.

55 The State cited the principle of proportionality, which 'require[s] that during the planning of a military activity, every attempt be made to reduce the collateral damage caused as a result of the military activity to those who are not combatants, to the extent possible, under the circumstances,' ibid. at para 17. A related argument made by the government, also derived from the Law of Armed Conflict, was that the 'the IDF prefers to arrest terrorists instead of killing them, *as permitted by the laws of war*,' ibid. at para 16 [emphasis added]. This argument did not directly support the use of civilians by the military to provide early warning to suspected terrorists, but spoke more to the target-ability of those terrorists and the legitimacy of attempting to minimize harm through the early warning procedure, which would allow apprehending rather than targeting them.

56 Ibid. at para 20.

57 Ibid. at para 23 [emphasis added]. The Court further wrote: 'The legality of the 'Early Warning' procedure might draw its validity from the general duty of the occupying army to ensure the dignity and security of the civilian population. It also sits well with the occupying army's power to protect the lives and security of its soldiers. On the other hand stands the occupying army's duty to safeguard the life and dignity of the local civilian sent to relay the warning'.

Hence, while the Court had already conceded that the security situation with the Palestinians had escalated to full-blown hostilities, in this decision it continued nonetheless to apply the laws of belligerent occupation. The Court's ruling reflects the position that the laws of belligerent occupation could continue to apply in certain situations or territories concurrently with the Law of Armed Conflict,[58] a position it would adopt explicitly in later petitions.[59] The decision in this case to apply the former rather than the latter was surely affected by the Court's long tradition of applying the laws of belligerent occupation when engaged in its judicial review of the military's actions in the Territories.

2.4.2 The 'Targeted Killings' case: a landmark decision

Another high-profile petition involving military operations in the Territories was filed with the Supreme Court in 2002 and involved the military's use of preemptive targeted strikes against suspected terrorists.[60] A petition filed a year earlier on the same issue had been dismissed by the Court in a brief, one-paragraph decision which stated that 'the choice of weapons used by the government to thwart murderous terror attacks was not a matter in which the Court intervened, especially in a petition lacking any concrete factual foundation that seeks a sweeping remedy'.[61] Nonetheless, when subsequent petitions were filed later that year raising the issue yet again, the Court requested extensive briefs from the parties addressing various questions of applicable law, both domestic and international, creating the impression that it would deliberate the petition on its merits.[62]

---

[58] See nn 50–51 and accompanying text.

[59] See also HCJ 7957/04 *Mara'abe* v *Prime Minister of Israel* [2005] Dinim 602 (57) 2005, para 17: '[T]he situation in the territory under belligerent occupation is often fluid. Periods of tranquility and calm transform into dynamic periods of combat. When combat takes place, it is carried out according to the rules of international law. "This combat is not being carried out in a normative void. It is being carried out according to the rules of international law, which determine principles and rules for the waging of combat" (see HCJ 3451/02 *Almandi* v *The Minister of Defense*, 56(3) P.D. 30, 34; see also HCJ 3114/02 *Barakeh, M.K.* v *The Minister of Defense*, 56(3) P.D. 11, 16). In such a situation, in which combat activities are taking place in the area under belligerent occupation, the rules applicable to belligerent occupation, as well as the rules applicable to combat activities, will apply to these activities.'

[60] HCJ 769/02 *PCATI* v *GoI* [2006] Dinim 1089 (69) 2006.

[61] HCJ 5872/01, 3114/02 *Barakeh* v *Prime Minister and Minister of Defense* [2002], IsrSC 56(3) 1.

[62] One can speculate as to the reasons for the change in the Court's attitude towards adjudicating the matter. One possible factor may be the different justices appointed to each of the two petitions. Another possibility may be that the justices who first rejected the petition may have hoped that the security situation would improve and that the use of the tactic would be short-lived.

In December 2006, the Court issued its monumental decision regarding the normative legal framework for the targeting of terrorists acting on behalf of non-state groups. The Court's opinion relied heavily on core provisions of the Law of Armed Conflict.[63] It ruled that under certain conditions, targeting of such individuals would be compliant with international law and hence rejected the petition on its merits.[64]

A significant factor to note—and one that will become central in later decisions of the Court discussed below—is that while the case was pending, Israel carried out its unilateral disengagement from the Gaza strip by ending its military presence there and evacuating all Israeli settlements. Martial rule in the Gaza Strip, which had begun in 1967, came to an end.[65] It has been Israel's legal contention since that to the extent there had been a *de-facto* belligerent occupation in Gaza until 2005, the Disengagement had brought the occupation of the Gaza Strip to an end.[66] Today, academics remain divided on the question of the legal status of Gaza.[67] While it is true that Israel's presence in the Gaza Strip ended in 2005, Israel still controls Gaza's air space and waters. Gaza shares a border with Egypt; however, it is heavily dependent on the passage of goods and people into the Strip from Israel, which is tightly regulated by Israel, as well as the passage of people between the Gaza Strip and the West Bank (as there is no territorial contiguity between the two regions). Gaza is also highly dependent on Israel for its supply of basic resources, such as electricity. At the same time, since 2007 the Gaza Strip has been internally controlled exclusively by the terrorist organization Hamas,

---

[63] In short, the Court rejected the State's contention that presently such individuals were viewed as unlawful combatants under the Law of Armed Conflict. Instead, the Court examined the targetability of such individuals within the confines of Article 51(3) of Additional Protocol I to the Fourth Geneva Convention, which recognizes that civilians can be stripped of their protection from targeting if and for such a time as they are directly participating in hostilities.

[64] Due to the Court's permissive rules of standing, which had been substantially relaxed over the years, the petition was heard despite the fact that it was filed by an Israeli non-government organization (hereinafter NGO) and was 'public' in nature. As for the question of justiciability and political question doctrine, the Court analyzed claims of non-justiciability raised by the government over several pages of its decision, consequently concluding that the question at hand was essentially a legal one reviewable by the Court.

[65] Israeli Cabinet Decision No 4235 dated 11 September 2005 (in Hebrew) ('With the withdrawal of IDF forces from these territories, responsibility for them will be transferred to the Palestinian authorities and the military rule in the area will cease.').

[66] HCJ 9132/07 *Al-Bassiouni* v *Prime Minister*, 1 November 2007, Petition for Respondents, paras 4–9 ('Since the Six-Day War the Gaza Strip was held under "belligerent occupation"... as of 12.9.05, at 24:00, the military rule of the IDF in the Gaza Strip ended, and along with it the IDF's belligerent occupation of the Gaza Strip, with all that it entails politically, security-wise and legally.') (on file with author); HCJ 201/09 *Physicians for Human Rights* v *Prime Minister of Israel*, Petition for Respondents, 8 January 2009, para 7 (in Hebrew) ('The Gaza Strip is not under Israeli occupation as of 12.9.05, when the last of IDF forces left the territory of the Gaza Strip following the completion of implementation of the Disengagement plan') (on file with author).

[67] See Shani 2005, p 369; contra Mari 2005, pp 366–368.

which violently seized political control and ousted its opposition.[68] With the cessation of martial law and conclusion of a military government in the Gaza Strip in 2005 on the one hand, and the growing presence of armed terrorist groups in what has become a breeding ground for terrorism under Hamas's rule on the other hand, it is hard to view Israel as having the effective control of an occupier over what happens in Gaza.

The withdrawal of all Israeli troops from the Gaza Strip and end of martial law strengthened substantially the government's position that the applicable legal regime to military action at least in the Gaza Strip (if not in the West Bank as well) could *only* be the Law of Armed Conflict and not the laws of belligerent occupation. Furthermore, this also reinforced the government's claim of non-justiciability—the cessation of belligerent occupation in the Gaza Strip likened the military's actions there with those conducted on foreign soil, and hence well within the core of foreign military actions traditionally considered off-limits to courts (even by the Israeli court).[69] In other words, to the extent that the Court in the past had felt it legitimate to review the military's actions in the Territories due to the prolonged military occupation or the military commander's obligation to administer public life in these Territories—by which it could subject the military commander to the same judicial scrutiny given to other domestic administrative officials—these new circumstances strengthened the argument that there was no longer room for domestic judicial review of the military's activities in the Gaza Strip after September 2005.

The Court nonetheless authored a decision delineating the boundaries for what would be considered legitimate targeted strikes. In doing so, it, *inter alia*, deemed the hostilities between Israel and armed Palestinian groups an international armed conflict governed by the Law of Armed Conflict. However, the Court also applied components outside the armed conflict regime in two respects. First, the Court ruled that a civilian taking a direct part in hostilities could not be attacked if a less harmful means could be employed, namely arrest, interrogation and trial.

---

[68] See International Institute for Strategic Studies, 'Hamas coup in Gaza, 13 *IISS Strategic Comments* (2007) p 1, available at http://www.iiss.org/publications/strategic-comments/past-issues/volume-13-2007/volume-13-issue-5/hamas-coup-in-gaza/; 'Hamas takes full control of Gaza' in BBC News [15 June 2007] available at http://news.bbc.co.uk/2/hi/middle_east/6755299.stm; for an Israeli perspective see the website of the Israel Ministry of Foreign Affairs, 'A year since the Hamas takeover of Gaza' [16 June 2008] http://www.mfa.gov.il/MFA/Terrorism-+Obstacle+to+Peace/Hamas+war+against+Israel/A+year+since+the+Hamas+takeover+of+Gaza+-+June+2008.htm.

[69] See for instance, HCJ 4354/92 *Temple Mount Faithful* v *Prime Minister* [1993] IsrSC 57 (1)37 (challenging the legality of the government's authority to negotiate with Syria in the matter of the Golan Heights); HCJ 6057/99 *MMT Mateh Mutkafei Terror* v *Prime Minister* [1999] Dinim 713 (7) 1999 (unpublished), HCJ 7307/98 *Polack* v *Government of Israel* [1998] Dinim 727 (9) 1998 (unpublished), HCJ 2455/94 *'Betzedek' Organization* v *Government of Israel* (unpublished) (challenging the release of hostages in the framework of a political agreement); HCJ 4877/93 *Irgun Nifgai Terror* v *Government of Israel* Dinim 1492 (1) 1993 (challenging the carrying out of negotiations over the Oslo Accords).

The Court explained that '[i]n our domestic law, that rule is called for by the principle of proportionality'.[70] It went on to note that the availability of such lesser means 'might actually be particularly practical *under the conditions of belligerent occupation*, in which the army controls the area in which the operation takes place...'[71] In addition, the Court decided that following an attack, 'a thorough investigation regarding the precision of the identification of the target and the circumstances of the attack upon him is to be performed (retroactively)'.[72] In substantiating both requirements—the use of a lesser means and the retrospective investigation—the Court cited legal sources derived from human rights law, a separate body of law from that of the Law of Armed Conflict within international law.[73] Thus, in some respects, the Court's references were reminiscent of the previous categorization of terrorism as a criminal activity governed by the law enforcement paradigm.[74]

The relative weight the Court gave the obligation to employ lesser means to apprehend a terrorist, and its reference to a situation of belligerent occupation, were most likely a result of the fact that the petition, when filed in 2002, had challenged the targeted killings policy in general, with regard to both the West Bank and the Gaza Strip. Hence, while a change in the legal status of the Gaza Strip had arguably occurred in 2005, the Court's holding in the case was also applicable to the West Bank, where a military occupation still existed. This may explain to some extent the Court's willingness to adjudicate the issue of targeted killings—a matter at the core of operational military activity—while at the same time relying on legal principles outside the regime of the Law of Armed Conflict proper.

---

70 HCJ 769/02 *PCATI* v *GoI* [2006] Dinim 1089 (69) 2006, para 40.

71 Ibid. [emphasis added].

72 Ibid.

73 The relationship between human rights law and the Law of Armed Conflict (or international humanitarian law as it is also referred to) is an intricate one, beyond the scope of this Article. Opinions vary as to whether the two bodies of law apply concurrently to a situation of armed conflict or whether the Law of Armed Conflict applies exclusively, with additional variants between these two points on the spectrum. On the relationship between human rights law and international humanitarian law in a situation of armed conflict, see generally Watkin 2004, p 1; Hampson 2008, p 549. There are also varying positions as to the applicability of human rights law beyond a state's borders, e.g. to territory under military occupation, Dennis 2005, p 119.

74 In substantiating the investigation requirement, the Court relied in its decision on *McCann* v *United Kingdom*, 21 EHRR 97, at 161, 163 (1995) and *McKerr* v *United Kingdom*, 34 EHRR 553, 559 (2001). In the former case, three members of the IRA were shot to death in the streets of Gibraltar by English agents. In the latter, police officers had shot over 100 rounds at a car and killed three unarmed individuals; claims of a shoot-to-kill policy against suspected terrorists were raised against the government. In both cases the events took place either within the territory of United Kingdom (Northern Ireland) or a territory under its control (Gibraltar). Neither involved the employment of military means nor was considered part of an armed conflict.

2.4.3 A transition completed: armed conflict proper?

This brings us to a series of petitions pertaining exclusively to the Gaza Strip in what can be deemed as the post-Disengagement era. The significance of this distinction is that from a legal perspective, it is the farthest away from the regime of belligerent occupation Israel has been since 1967. In 2007, Hamas (considered to be a terror organization by Israel and many others, among them the US, Canada, and the EU), which had won a parliamentary majority in elections held in Gaza a year earlier, violently overtook the government in the Gaza Strip, and has since that time been estranged politically from the West Bank, where Fatah leaders remain for all intents and purposes exiled. To the extent there has been any interaction between the Israeli and Palestinian leadership in the past three years, it has been between the government of Israel and Palestinian Authority representatives in the West Bank. In the years following the Disengagement, rocket fire from the Gaza Strip into Israel intensified, with over several thousands of rockets fired from the Gaza Strip onto Israeli soil after the Disengagement and until the end of 2008,[75] while weapons and ammunition continue to be smuggled into the Gaza Strip.[76]

These factors assist in illuminating how similar the Gaza Strip has grown in nature after 2005 to an enemy party to an armed conflict. The Supreme Court may have become seasoned at adjudicating matters pertaining to the military's obligations within the context of administering public order and safety in a *de-facto* occupied territory. However, the political and military situation between Israel and the Hamas-controlled Gaza Strip had evolved into something quite different. The government of Israel had already argued in the last of its briefs to the Court in the targeted killings case that the Disengagement from Gaza had turned the hostilities between the IDF and Hamas to the equivalent of a conflict with a foreign adversary.[77] However, despite holding that the hostilities between Israel and Palestinian armed groups were to be treated as an international armed conflict, the Supreme Court nonetheless went on to adjudicate petitions pertaining to this armed conflict.

In late 2007, the government of Israel decided to adopt certain economic restrictions on the Hamas regime in the Gaza Strip which, since Hamas' takeover, has come to be regarded as 'hostile territory'.[78] These restrictions included, *inter alia*, a limitation on the supply of fuel and electricity into the Gaza Strip from

---

[75] IDF Blog, Rocket Attacks towards Israel, available at http://idfspokesperson.com/facts-figures/rocket-attacks-toward-israel/.

[76] Website of Israel Ministry of Foreign Affairs, 'Hamas's illegal attacks on civilians and other unlawful methods of war—legal aspects.' [7 January 2009] available at http://www.mfa.gov.il/MFA/Terrorism-+Obstacle+to+Peace/Hamas+war+against+Israel/Legal_aspects_of_Hamas_methods_7_Jan_2009.htm.

[77] HCJ 769/02 *PCATI* v *GoI*, Supplementary Brief 2 for Respondents, 5 December 2005, para 5–9 (on file with author).

[78] Decision adopted 19 September 2007, as quoted in HCJ 9132/07 *Al Bassiouni* v *Prime Minister* [2008] Dinim 321 (7) 2008, para 2.

Israel[79] to be implemented 'after considering the legal ramifications of the humanitarian situation' in a manner that would 'prevent a humanitarian crisis'.[80] The government's position was that the fuel and electricity supplied by Israel to the Gaza Strip was being used to support terrorist operations, including the launching of rockets into Israel. A controlled reduction in the supply of fuel, it was believed, could damage the terrorist infrastructure and Hamas' ability to operate against Israel without adversely affecting the humanitarian supply of fuel.[81] A petition was filed with the Supreme Court to challenge this decision and its legality in light of Israel's humanitarian obligation towards the Gaza Strip. Much of the hearings before the Court revolved around factual questions—the manner in which the flow of electricity would be reduced, the effect the reduction would have on the civilian population, and the ability to manage and regulate the consumption of electricity inside the Gaza Strip.[82]

As to the applicable legal sources to the matter, the Court stated:

> '[T]he main duties of the State of Israel relating to the residents of the Gaza Strip *derive from the state of armed conflict* that exists between it and the Hamas organization that controls the Gaza Strip; these duties also derive from *the degree of control exercised by the State of Israel* over the border crossings between it and the Gaza Strip, as well as *from the relationship that was created between Israel and the territory of the Gaza Strip after the years of Israeli military rule in the territory*, as a result of which the Gaza Strip is currently almost completely dependent upon the supply of electricity from Israel.'[83]

It further noted that '[t]he state's pleadings in this regard are based upon norms that are part of the customary international law, which set out basic obligations that govern combatant parties during an armed conflict…'[84] The Court then went on to determine, based on the information it had received from the parties as well as alterations that had been made to the reduction plan by the military in the course of the proceedings, that the amounts of electricity and fuel that Israel intended to

---

[79] The Gaza Strip was dependent on Israel for approximately 60% of its electricity supply, 120 megawatt out of 200 megawatt. Seventeen additional megawatts were being supplied at the time by Egypt and the remaining amount was produced within the Strip by Gaza's power plant. Fuel would be purchased by Gaza authorities from private suppliers; however, Israel was responsible for operating the border crossings which allowed fuel to be transferred physically into Gaza.

[80] HCJ 9132/07 *Al Bassiouni* v *Prime Minister*, at para 2.

[81] Ibid. at para 4.

[82] For example, the state contended that if the authorities in Gaza managed the consumption of electricity properly, the flow of electricity to maintain humanitarian needs (such as hospitals and water supply) would continue without interruption. The petitioners argued in response that there was no physical way to reduce the supply of electricity to the Gaza Strip without affecting those services deemed vital, hence causing irreversible harm to the civilian population in Gaza. It is interesting to note that while the Court waited to receive additional information regarding the ability to regulate the flow of electricity in the Gaza Strip, it issued an order mandating that until the aforesaid submissions were received, the plan to reduce the electricity supply to the Gaza Strip would not be implemented.

[83] HCJ 9132/07 *Al Bassiouni* v *Prime Minister*, at para 12 [emphasis added].

[84] Ibid. at para 14.

supply satisfied the humanitarian needs in the Gaza Strip. Accordingly, the petition for injunctive relief was denied.

Hence, while the Court recognized the de-facto cessation of military occupation,[85] it did draw upon two additional sources of legal obligations—the degree of control exercised by Israel over the border crossings to the Gaza Strip and the relationship that was created between Israel and the territory of the Gaza Strip after the years of Israeli military rule in the territory. It seems that the unique situation created as a result of the physical proximity between Israel and the Gaza Strip and the prolonged military occupation of the Strip by Israel had created in the Court's opinion a penumbral source of obligations or rather a heightened level of humanitarian obligation towards the Gaza Strip somewhat beyond the confines of the Law of Armed Conflict.[86]

The peak, to date, of the Court's willingness to adjudicate matters relating to the battlefield appears to be its decision in *Physicians for Human Rights* v *Prime Minister*[87] (hereinafter the *Cast Lead petition*). In late 2008 the IDF initiated a month-long, large-scale military operation in the Gaza Strip, which included both ongoing aerial strikes and the deployment of ground forces. Operation 'Cast Lead' presented the most intense level of hostilities between the IDF and Palestinians in the history of the region. In the course of the Operation, two petitions were filed with the Israeli Supreme Court. The first concerned delays in evacuating Palestinian casualties in the Gaza Strip and claims that medical personnel and ambulances were being attacked by the IDF; the second addressed the shortage of electricity in the Gaza Strip, attributed to the IDF. Two urgent hearings were held within days, in the course of which the state was ordered to submit a more detailed response regarding the efforts it had undertaken to fulfill its humanitarian obligations.[88]

Here too, a large portion of the Court's decision was dedicated to ascertaining the facts, including, for example, the mechanisms that had been set up by the IDF to coordinate humanitarian relief, evacuation and supply to the Gaza Strip; specific repair work to electricity lines; and evacuation efforts of particular individuals (based on real-time information provided by NGOs monitoring the situation and IDF personnel on the ground).[89] The situation changed rapidly even as the petition was pending and

---

[85] In fact, the Court noted (ibid. at para 12) that:

... since September 2005 Israel no longer has effective control over what happens in the Gaza Strip. The military government that was in force in this territory in the past was ended by a decision of the government... In these circumstances... Israel does not have a general duty to ensure the welfare of the residents of the Gaza Strip or to maintain public order in the Gaza Strip under all of the laws of a belligerent occupation under international law.

[86] For a thoughtful analysis and critique of the Al-Bassiouni decision, see Shani 2009, p 101.

[87] HCJ 201/09 Physicians for Human Rights v Prime Minister of Israel [2009] Dinim 901 (7) 2009.

[88] The Court also specifically ordered the state to submit an affidavit by a senior officer responsible for the humanitarian arrangements in the Gaza Strip. The affiant, a colonel who headed the District Coordination Office for the Gaza Strip, also appeared before the Court.

[89] See e.g. para 9 of the decision, HCJ 201/09 *Physicians for Human Rights* v *Prime Minister of Israel* [2009] Dinim 901 (7) 2009.

the Court itself noted on several occasions in the decision the inherent difficulty, in light of ongoing hostilities, in receiving all the necessary information pertaining to the petitioners' claims.[90] Nonetheless, it rejected the state's argument that due to the ongoing hostilities the petition was non-justiciable,[91] and applied to the facts in question the obligations found in customary international law, the application of which was not disputed by either party.[92] The decision was delivered within days and while the operation was still ongoing. The Court determined that the IDF had taken the necessary steps and was prepared to carry out its humanitarian obligations.[93]

Before concluding this section, two additional petitions deserve attention. Unlike the *Cast Lead petition*, which was adjudicated by the Court in the course of intense hostilities, these petitions were less urgent in nature. Nonetheless, they challenged the means and methods of attack used by IDF in its operations. In this regard, they are similar to the targeted killings petition in the sense that all three raise questions that lie at the heart of the Law of Armed Conflict. The first challenged the use of sonic booms by the Israeli Air Force over the Gaza Strip[94] while the second challenged the safety distances (buffer zones) maintained by the military between artillery shelling and civilians or civilian objects.[95] Both petitions pertained exclusively to actions taken by the military in the Gaza Strip, a territory arguably no longer under military occupation.

---

90 HCJ 201/09 *Physicians for Human Rights* v *Prime Minister of Israel* at para 13: Our judicial scrutiny is exercised in such a case while the hostilities are continuing. Naturally this imposes restrictions upon the court's ability to exercise its scrutiny and to ascertain all of the relevant facts at this stage of the hostilities... Indeed, while the hostilities are taking place it is not always possible to obtain all of the information that is required for exercising judicial scrutiny, in view of the dynamic changes that are continually occurring.

91 Ibid. at para 11.

92 In addition, it stated that 'the fundamental rules of Israeli public law also apply', citing previous cases which had been decided in the context of the military occupation, ibid. at para 15. While the application of the principles of Israeli administrative law to the discretion of the military commander in an occupied territory had become a familiar standard in the Court's jurisprudence, continuing to apply these principles to the military's actions where a belligerent occupation no longer exists (assuming this legal position is accepted) is quite a different matter. Admittedly, the Court referenced Israeli administrative law only briefly in the decision and focused primarily on whether actions taken by the IDF had fulfilled obligations set forth in various provisions of customary international law. Nonetheless, the linkage to domestic administrative law shows what a substantial impact the long-term military occupation has had on the Court's jurisprudence, so much so that it continues to attribute to State action domestic legal principles even when it is operating in what has become from a practical perspective a hostile and foreign territory.

93 Ibid., at para 28.

94 HCJ 10265/05 *Physicians for Human Rights* v *Minister of Defense* (unpublished). The sonic booms are presumably used by the military to deter individuals from launching rockets towards Israel for fear of being targeted by the Israeli Air Force.

95 HCJ 3261/06 *Physicians for Human Rights* v *Minister of Defense* (pending). Because of the relative imprecision of artillery fire, firing units are required to keep a minimum safety distance from civilians and civilian objects when discharging artillery fire. According to the petition, the military had narrowed the security buffer zone for artillery shelling from 300 to 100 m away from any civilian presence.

With regard to the sonic booms petition, the Court requested detailed written arguments from the parties, particularly on the questions of the applicable legal regime to the Gaza Strip, the justiciability of the matter and the use of sonic booms under international law. The state argued that following the Disengagement, the legal regime that applied was exclusively the Law of Armed Conflict and that the use of military means in the course of hostilities outside the state was non-justiciable.[96] Since the use of the sonic booms was discontinued as of July 2006, the Court dismissed the petition, which had become theoretical in nature, without prejudice, allowing the petitioners to file it again should the military resume the use of sonic booms.

As for the artillery shelling petition, a response was filed by the state, in which it, *inter alia*, stated that the use of artillery shells in the Gaza Strip had been suspended. To date, the petition remains pending. The renewed use of artillery shells in the Gaza Strip during Operation Cast Lead may perhaps lead to renewed interest in the petition. At any rate, the current status of the petitions is far less significant; like the earlier petitions discussed, of importance is the fact that in both cases the IDF has had to defend its use of military means on its merits.

Although the majority of petitions presented thus far were eventually rejected, their adjudication by the Court nonetheless has significant ramifications for the military. The Court in deciding on the merits of these petitions undertook an in-depth factual examination, which required the government and military to invest resources and valuable time, in the course of hostilities, in gathering data, putting together written responses, obtaining affidavits and appearing before the Court. Furthermore, often times in the course of adjudication of security matters, while a petition is still pending, the parties will make various concessions which will eliminate the need for a court order.[97] Thus, while the petition may be ultimately denied, often times in the course of proceedings the relief sought after is received. The very real threat of immediate litigation before the Israeli Supreme Court regarding actions by the military in the course of hostilities serves in itself as a deterrent when formulating such policy. Moreover, to date, the military has responded to and argued all petitions

96 It also presented its arguments in defense of the petition on its merits.

97 In one such case, HCJ 4764/04 *Physicians for Human Rights* v *IDF Commander in Gaza* [2004] Dinim 1098 (30) 2004, petitioners demanded that the military allow Palestinian civilians to participate in the funerals of relatives. The IDF had originally rejected the request because the individuals were in a neighborhood that had been surrounded by the IDF in the course of operations. In the course of the hearings, the Court demanded that the military find a solution. After the oral arguments before the Court were concluded, several proposals were made by the IDF to allow several family members to participate in the funerals. Each of the proposals was ultimately rejected by petitioners who preferred to hold the funerals after the siege on the neighborhood was lifted, in order to ensure mourning rituals could be carried out in full compliance with Islamic law. The Court noted at para 27 that: '*Prima facie* it would appear that the proposals which he [the IDF representative] made in the end could have been made at an earlier stage. The changing position of the respondent, as it appears from the response of the State Attorney's Office, implies that the matter was not originally taken into account, and the solutions that were proposed were improvisations made up on the spur of the moment. This should not happen. Preparations for dealing with this matter should have been made in advance. A clear procedure should be adopted…'.

challenging its policies. Hence, it seems that the accessibility of the Court alone has an impact on the implementation of the military's policy.

2.5 What Does It All Mean? The Future of Adjudicating Armed Conflict

The decisions of the Israeli Supreme Court discussed in the previous section illustrate the development of the Court's jurisprudence pertaining to questions of armed conflict. However, it would seem that this jurisprudence is a result of a set of legal and factual circumstances unique to Israel. In light of this, one might legitimately ask whether the Israeli experience can be instructive in predicting how other domestic courts, particularly those in the US, will behave if faced with similar legal questions.

2.5.1 Israel

At first glance, the transition in Israel from the law enforcement paradigm to the armed conflict paradigm seems inconsequential. By the year 2000, Israel's Supreme Court was already well-accustomed to reviewing decisions of the military commander because of Israel's long-time military presence in the Territories. Although the government was claiming an armed conflict was now taking place between Israel and the Palestinians, the battlefield essentially had not changed and was one the Court was already familiar with, since it had entertained many petitions in the past pertaining to the Territories. The Court was also experienced at applying international law principles when assessing the military commander's discretion in the Territories, since it had been applying the laws of belligerent occupation since the late 1960s to such petitions. The fact that the government was arguing that in some instances the laws of belligerent occupation continued to apply concurrently with the Law of Armed Conflict helped blur the magnitude of this transition even more. In short, by the beginning of the 21st century, there were probably hundreds of cases on record in Israel in which the Supreme Court had adjudicated petitions against the military; applied international law; and had determined whether or not the military commander's discretion could survive judicial scrutiny.

These factors contributed to making this transition—which was doctrinally significant—seem quite subtle and almost natural. The Israeli Supreme Court, by simply continuing to do what it had had been doing, began adjudicating matters pertaining to the conduct of hostilities by the IDF. The novelty of the situation was made clearer when Israel withdrew entirely its military forces from the Gaza Strip in 2005, ending martial law in the area.[98] Compared with the West Bank which was still subject to Israeli martial law, the Gaza Strip became more removed from Israeli responsibility.

The incursion of IDF forces into the Gaza Strip in late 2008 was the first time a significant Israeli military presence had entered the region in over 3 years. Israel employed extensively its air force and ground forces over a month-long period. It encountered fighting on the ground, as well as cross-border mortar and rocket fire, quite similar to the conflict that had taken place in 2007 between the IDF and Hezbollah in southern Lebanon (a conflict that subsequently became known in Israel as the Second Lebanon War). Yet the judicial review that Operation Cast Lead was subjected to was unlike that of any other armed conflict around the world or previous armed conflicts between Israel and its neighboring countries.

This can no doubt be attributed to the unique circumstances and context of the military conflict between Israel and the Palestinians, which make it distinguishable from other armed conflicts. This is best illustrated by a comparison to the 2006 hostilities between Israel and Hezbollah. Hezbollah, also considered a terrorist entity, carried out rocket attacks in July 2006 from Lebanese territory into Israeli cities and kidnapped several IDF soldiers from Israeli territory near the Lebanese–Israeli border, killing several more in the attack itself. Israel initiated an extensive military operation which was subsequently officially deemed the Second Lebanon War[99] by Israel. In the course of the 5 week operation, despite extensive damage to infrastructure in south Lebanon and loss of life, not a single documented petition pertaining to the conduct of hostilities by the IDF in Lebanon was filed with the Court.[100] There were no challenges to the legal basis for attacking Hezbollah operatives; nor were there any petitions filed contesting the highly-controversial use of cluster munitions by the IDF; or the Israeli naval blockade which burdened the provision of humanitarian aid to Lebanon.

The lack of petitions in the Hezbollah conflict is remarkable in comparison to the frequent petitions challenging military actions in the Gaza Strip. It can most likely be explained by the fact that Lebanon is a sovereign country. In terms of

[98] As noted earlier, Israel withdrew its military presence and considered the belligerent occupation to have ended. However, the Gaza Strip is not recognized as a sovereign state. Claims have been made that Israel still has effective control de-facto of the Gaza Strip due to its control of a majority of the Strip's borders. While the legal status of the Gaza Strip may still be indeterminate in international law, it is uncontested that there is no longer an Israeli military commander who administers the area and that Israeli physical control in the area has diminished substantially; see nn 65–68 and accompanying text.

[99] It is important to in this regard to emphasize that Israel carried out hostilities primarily against Hezbollah—it targeted Hezbollah infrastructure, there were no encounters between the IDF and the Lebanese army in the course of the conflict and the conflict was generally viewed by both countries independently of the state of affairs between Israel and Lebanon.

[100] A petition was filed with the Supreme Court demanding that the government make a formal declaration of war and a state of emergency, HCJ 6204/06 *Beilin* v *Prime Minister of Israel* [2006] Dinim 139 (46) 2006. Both the petition and the decision were limited to questions of constitutional rather than international law.

public perception, the Second Lebanon War fell more squarely within the category of an armed conflict between two nations. Israel's 'duty of care' towards Lebanon was perceived as diminished because of Lebanon's ability to provide assistance to its citizens and the ability of the civilian population to evacuate to areas outside of the immediate combat zone.

The Gaza Strip, on the other hand, is perceived as more dependent on Israel not only because of the prolonged occupation but also because of the physical control Israel still has over most of the Gaza Strip's borders. Moreover, it may be that because of the indeterminate status of the Gaza Strip the Court's involvement in and adjudication of Gaza-related matters was perceived of as less of an intrusion into foreign relations than adjudicating military actions taken by the IDF in the course of a conflict with Hezbollah on Lebanon's territory.[101] Finally, it is highly likely that human rights groups and politically-motivated bodies acting on behalf of the Palestinian residents of the West Bank and the Gaza Strip are simply less invested in the hostilities involving the IDF in other regions of the world.

Whatever the reasons, it seems clear that despite the Court's acceptance that the belligerent occupation in the Gaza Strip has ended and that hostilities between the IDF and Palestinian armed groups are governed by the Law of Armed Conflict, both the Court and the Israeli public still distinguish between this particular armed conflict and others because of its unique circumstances. Hence, the Court's willingness to adjudicate matters pertaining to armed conflict may be limited to those relating to the Palestinian territories.[102] Nonetheless, this is still impressive given the operational issues the Court is willing to adjudicate, such as the targeted killings policy or humanitarian efforts in a combat zone, which are inextricably connected to how the military conducts hostilities.

2.5.2 Is the Israeli experience relevant to other jurisdictions?

There is room to wonder whether the Israeli experience, namely the ongoing development of jurisprudence by Israel's Supreme Court on the adjudication of questions pertaining to armed conflict, will influence the judiciary in other jurisdictions as well. Several factors have contributed to the Court's said jurisprudence.

---

[101] It is important to remember; however, that the Supreme Court in the targeted killings petition categorized the conflict with Palestinian armed groups as an *international* armed conflict.

[102] This proposition could be put to the test should a petition challenge IDF conduct in an armed conflict in a different region or perhaps if a general petition is filed demanding a blanket prohibition on the use of a particular weapon by the IDF, such as cluster munitions. In all probability, absent a particular military operation, the Court will refrain from adjudicating such a theoretical petition, cf., HCJ 8990/02 *Physicians for Human Rights* v *Doron Almog, O.C. Southern Command* [2003] IsrSC 57 (4) 193 (dismissing a petition challenging the legality of flechette munitions on grounds of non-justiciability). Ironically, then, the chances of the Court adjudicating a petition challenging the legality of a particular means or method increases in the course of an armed conflict, when the calls for judicial deference are usual at a high.

First and foremost are the characteristics of the Israeli–Palestinian conflict itself. Other factors that must be considered concern the Court's jurisdiction and accessibility, as well as its jurisprudence on questions of standing and justiciability, all of which determine which cases actually reach the court. Finally, the treatment of international and comparative law by judges may also play a role in the extent to which domestic courts will apply the Law of Armed Conflict. These factors are further developed below.

The Israeli Court's jurisprudence is intrinsically linked to Israel's long-term military occupation in the West Bank and Gaza Strip. Israel has had a military presence in the Territories for over 40 years. Israel shares its borders with the Territories, which are at most 60 km away from Israel's center (and no more than a few kilometers from the Supreme Court). Moreover, military service in Israel is mandatory so that a considerable number of Israelis have served in the military, making it an institution more familiar and accessible to the general public than perhaps in other countries. The military is also much smaller than that of other fighting armies around the world. All of these factors no doubt contribute to the Court's openness to adjudicate questions pertaining to the armed conflict between the IDF and Palestinian armed groups.

The circumstances in other nations with active militaries deployed to combat zones are clearly different. The great distances between the battlefield and the courtroom, such as the one between American, British or Canadian courts and Iraq or Afghanistan, affects the perception of justiciability. It strengthens the sense that a local court has no business reviewing actions taking place so far away in a foreign land. It may even strengthen a judge's fear of interfering in matters in a manner detrimental to security because of an unfamiliarity with the battlefield.[103]

Distance from the battlefield also affects the practical ability to adjudicate because of the difficultly in gathering relevant information and testimony pertaining to the question before the Court. Senior IDF officers have at times attended Supreme Court hearings. There have been instances in which the Court has received information in 'real-time' from IDF personnel in contact with officers 'on

[103] The fact that Guantánamo Bay is so *physically* close to the US and that no hostilities were taking place there no doubt impacted the US Supreme Court justices' position, perhaps subconsciously, that federal courts should exercise jurisdiction over the island and that some constitutional and even statutory protections applied to detainees held there; *Rasul* v *Bush*, 542 US 466 (2004) (determining that the federal habeas corpus statute applied to detainees held at the US military base in Cuba); *Boumediene* v *Bush*, 553 US 723 (2008) (determining that the constitutional provision of habeas corpus has full effect at Guantanamo Bay). *Contra Maqaleh* v *Gates*, 605 F.3d 84 (DC Cir. 2010) (finding that the constitutional writ of habeas corpus did not extend to aliens held in detention in a military detention facility in the Afghan theater of war).

the ground'.[104] This may be harder to execute when the battlefield is a great distance away, although technological advances can provide some practical solutions.

The jurisdiction of the Israeli Supreme Court is such that it is the first (and last) instance to adjudicate a challenge to government or military policy.[105] Combined with the fact that the Court's jurisdiction over such petitions is obligatory, this makes the Court relatively accessible. A petitioner does not have to go through the lower courts before reaching the Supreme Court. Moreover, once a petition has been filed with the Supreme Court, the Court is limited in its ability to tailor its docket. This enables filing and hearing petitions within a matter of days, when necessary.

The structure and jurisdiction of courts in foreign jurisdictions may affect substantially the speed with which cases reach the upper courts, if at all. In the US, for instance, similar suits challenging executive or administrative policy would generally have to go through the district and circuit courts before potentially reaching the US Supreme Court. This makes adjudication of time-sensitive matters by the Supreme Court unlikely (although not impossible).

Furthermore, once a petition for certiorari is filed with the US Supreme Court, the Court may pick and choose the cases it will hear.[106] This enables the Court to steer clear of cases which it considers imprudent to adjudicate without having to resort explicitly to questions of justiciability. Moreover, the abundance of courts in the US exacerbates the complexity of the situation. The fact that there is no single tribunal to adjudicate suits requesting injunctive relief against the military means

[104] In HCJ 4764/04 *Physicians for Human Rights* v *IDF Commander in Gaza* [2004] Dinim 1098 (30) 2004, a petition challenging the military's compliance with its humanitarian obligations in the course of a military operation in the Gaza Strip (prior to the Disengagement), the Head of the District Coordination Office for the Gaza Strip was present in Court to provide oral explanations during the hearing regarding various matters in question, and at times stepped out to receive additional information from his personnel in the area of operations, which he relayed back to the justices. The Court received detailed and changing information in 'real-time', regarding matters such as the number of water wells that were being repaired by the IDF, the flow of water to particular neighborhoods in the Gaza Strip, delays in repairs, the supply of additional water tankers by Israel into the Strip and coordination between the IDF and various NGOs on the matter. Ibid. at para 14: 'While he was explaining this to us, Col. Mordechai was told—and he told us—that six additional water tankers had entered the neighbourhood. We were also told that all the wells are now functioning. Diesel fuel has been brought into the neighbourhood to enable the operation of generators which allow water to be pumped from the wells. As a result of this, there is now running water in all the neighbourhoods of Rafah.

[105] See n 19 supra and accompanying text.

[106] The data gathered distinguishes between petitions filed '*in forma pauperis*', i.e., costs and printing requirements are waived on the basis of a showing of indigence (such 'ifp' are filed primarily by state and federal prisoners), and petitions in which costs are paid by the parties. In the 2001 term, 1886 paid petitions were dockets and 82 (4.3%) were granted; 6037 ifp petitions were docketed and 6 (0.1%) were granted. In the 2006 Term, 1723 paid petitions were docketed and 62 (3.6%) were granted; 7132 ifp petitions were dockets and 15 (0.2%) were granted; Fallon 1991 2009, pp 1462–1463.

that some courts may occasionally or only rarely encounter such petitions, making them all the more reluctant to adjudicate such questions.

Substantive doctrines of standing and justiciability also play a key role. The Israeli Supreme Court has developed over the years relatively lenient standards for substantiating petitioners' standing.[107] In practice, the Court today allows 'public petitioners' to challenge laws or policies which raise concerns regarding the rule of law. This has consequently had a substantial impact on the adjudication of petitions challenging military or executive actions and policies.

The central benefit of the Court's liberal approach to standing is the fact that interest groups can now file petitions challenging military action in the Territories regardless of whether or not they represent a particular individual whose interest has been or could be affected by a particular policy. This is best-illustrated by the petition challenging Israel's targeted killing policy.[108] The petition was filed by two human rights groups and challenged the general policy of Israel to target those individuals considered to be terrorists. Assuming that Israel's target list is likely confidential and undisclosed to the public, it would have been almost impossible to ever substantiate standing had the court insisted on an injury-in-fact showing or one of probable harm. A high-profile terrorist (or alleged terrorist) would have had to convince the Court of the probability of his name being included in such a target list. It is highly doubtful that such a person would be willing to come forward and initiate legal proceedings before an Israeli legal tribunal.[109] It is equally doubtful that the Court, based on traditional rules of standing, would be willing to entertain such a petition.[110]

The importance of the evolution in Israel's standing doctrine cannot be overstated. In the US, for example, attempts to challenge the legality of the NSA wiretap program initiated post-9/11—a legal challenge brought entirely under constitutional law by US citizens—failed precisely on grounds of standing.

---

[107] For an overview of the evolution of the standing doctrine in Israeli law, see HCJ 910/86 *Ressler* v *Minister of Defense* [1988] IsrSC 42(2) 441, 457–472; Barak 2002, pp 106–110; Bracha 1991, p 96.

[108] HCJ 769/02 *PCATI* v *GoI* [2006] Dinim 1089 (69) 2006.

[109] Two human rights groups in the US received permission from the Treasury Department in 2010 to file a lawsuit challenging the reported inclusion on a target-list by the US government of Anwar al-Aulaqi, a militant American-born Islamic cleric. Approval to provide legal services to al-Aulaqi was required as part of the regulation of services provided to individuals and groups subject to anti-terrorism sanctions, see Gerstein 2010. The suit was filed by al-Aulaqi's father Nasser both on his own behalf and as "next friend" of al-Aulaqi. The district court did not recognize the petitioner's standing and the case was therefore dismissed, *Al-Aulaqi* v *Obama*, 2010 US Dist. LEXIS 129601 (D.D.C., 2010).

[110] Assuming that the district court in Al-Aulaqi had recognized the "next friend" status of Nasser al-Aulaqi or if the lawsuit had been filed on behalf of Al-Aulaqi himself directly, it is still uncertain that absent official confirmation by the Government, a court would be willing to accept the presumption that al-Aulaqi is indeed on the US target list for the purpose of establishing standing, see *Al-Aulaqi* v *Obama*, ibid. at n 4.

Plaintiffs were unable to show they had been subjected to wiretaps due to the confidential nature of the program.[111]

Just as the Israeli Supreme Court has been relaxing its standing requirements, the role played by the political question doctrine—another potential barrier to adjudication particularly in matters pertaining to national security—has become less and less substantial.[112] The Court has for the most part adopted an approach that at the heart of most challenges are legal questions, which the Court is capable of examining. In so doing, the Court has stressed on many occasions that it does not replace the discretion of the military commander or the government with its own; rather, it examines whether the executive's exercise of discretion was reasonable. This has led the Israeli Court to adjudicate cases relating to national security previously considered to be off-limits.[113]

Political question doctrine, however, still plays a dominant role in the jurisprudence of other courts, such as the US, in matters pertaining to foreign relations and the military. Hence, it can be assumed that the more closely related a question is to the conduct of hostilities or the laws of war, the slimmer the chances of adjudication by courts in the US. For instance, while the federal courts have been willing to address questions pertaining to the detention of

[111] See *ACLU* v *NSA*, 493 F.3d 644 (6th Cir. 2007) (overturning an earlier district court decision which recognized petitioners' standing and ruled that the government program was constitutional); *cert. denied*, 552 US 1179 (2008); *Amnesty Int'l USA* v *McConnell*, 646 F. Supp. 2d 633 (D.S.D.N.Y. 2009) (dismissing a suit challenging FISA provisions pertaining to wiretaps dismissed for want of standing); See also *Jewel* v *NSA*, 2010 US Dist. LEXIS 5110, 3 (dismissing a challenge to the wiretap program because none of the plaintiffs had alleged 'an injury that is sufficiently particular to those plaintiffs or to a distinct group to which those plaintiffs belong; rather, the harm alleged is a generalized grievance shared in substantially equal measure by all or a large class of citizens').

[112] The political question doctrine assumes that there exist certain issues of constitutional law that are more effectively resolved by the political branches of government and are therefore inappropriate for judicial resolution. See generally Redish 1984, p 1031; Tushnet 2002, p 1204; *Baker* v *Carr*, 369 US 186, 217 (1962); and supra n. 9. For the evolution of justiciability doctrine in Israeli jurisprudence see Barak 2002, pp 98–106; HCJ 910/86 *Ressler* v *Minister of Defense* [1988] IsrSC 42(2) 441, 472–498; Bendor 1997, p 311. See also HCJ 222/68 *National Circles Association* v *Minister of Police* [1970] IsrSC 24(2) 141 (rejecting the claim that the police's decision not to allow prayer at a religious sight is non-justiciable, but dismissing the petition on its merits); HCJ 306/81 *Sharon* v *Knesset Committee* [1981] IsrSC 35(4) 118 (rejecting the claim that the Knesset (Parliament) Committee's decision to suspend a member's privileges is non-justiciable and finding that the Committee exceeded its authority in its decision to suspend a member who had been criminally convicted, but was not sentenced to jail time); HCJ 73/85 *'Kach' Party* v *Hillel—Chairman of the Knesset* [1985] IsrSC 39(3) 141, 162 (finding that 'the issue before us does not raise a non-justiciable political question, but rather a justiciable legal question' and vacating the Knesset Chairman's decision not to allow a one-man party to present a bill dispersing the Knesset).

[113] Barak 2002.

individuals apprehended in the course of the 'war on terror',[114] we are less likely to see judgments regarding the legality of a particular air strike or military target in the near future.[115]

Finally, when attempting to anticipate whether, like Israel, we can expect other domestic jurisdictions to also adjudicate legal questions pertaining to the conduct of hostilities in the foreseeable future, we should not only compare such jurisdictions with the Israeli Supreme Court, but also question whether the Israeli jurisprudence itself will have any bearing on foreign courts. This is dependent to a great extent on foreign courts' attitude towards and receptiveness to comparative law. Those jurisdictions that tend to look at comparative law for legal trends and approaches may perhaps be emboldened by the Israeli Supreme Court jurisprudence pertaining to the application of the Law of Armed Conflict. However, the potential impact of Israeli jurisprudence on those jurisdictions which have adopted a more exceptional, isolationist approach towards the jurisprudence of foreign jurisdictions can be expected to be considerably less significant.

2.6 Conclusion

The Israeli Supreme Court in recent years has engaged in judicial review of questions pertaining to the conduct of hostilities within the context of what it has recognized as an armed conflict between Israel and Palestinian armed groups. This can be attributed to several factors that are unique to Israel, the most prominent being Israel's long-time military presence in the Territories. This military occupation which began in the late 1960s had made the Israeli Court by the 21st century accustomed to adjudicating matters governed by international law and scrutinizing the discretion of military figures. Concurrently, the Court's evolving jurisprudence regarding standing and political question doctrine made the Court overall more accessible to general petitions challenging national security issues. Combined together, these two processes paved the road to adjudication of questions pertaining to the modern battlefield, as at least some counter-terrorism policies, previously considered to be law enforcement actions, have come to be perceived in Israel and elsewhere as part of the armed conflict paradigm.

---

[114] Supra n 103.

[115] *El-Shifa Pharmaceutical Industries Company* v *US*, 402 F. Supp. 2d 267 (D.D.C. 2005) (finding that questions regarding the legality of targeting decisions involving military attacks ordered by the President were likely immune from judicial review under political question doctrine), *aff'd*, 559 F. 3d. 578 (D.C. Cir. 2009), *vacated and hearing reordered en banc*, 2009 US App. LEXIS 17310 (D.C. Cir. Aug. 3, 2009), *dismissal aff'd*, 607 F. 3d 836 (D.C. Cir. 2010).

Although the Israeli legal system may share common-law attributes with other countries such as the US, and perhaps similar threats from non-state actors, they also have divergent jurisprudence on matters of justiciability, as well as different national experiences pertaining to security and distinctly different military arenas. Hence, any analogy to other domestic courts requires extreme caution. Nevertheless, other jurisdictions are also encountering legal challenges to the actions of the military in combat arenas abroad.[116] Even the US federal courts have made a small step toward adjudication of war-related issues primarily in matters pertaining to the detention of individuals,[117] including some analysis of legal requirements derived from international law.[118] To the extent that such jurisdictions are receptive to comparative law, the Israeli experience may prove useful in developing domestic jurisprudence on questions pertaining to the Law of Armed Conflict and its application to executive policy in the 'war on terror'.

References

Amit-Kohn U et al (1993) Israel, the 'Intifada' and the rule of law. Israel Ministry of Defense Publications, Israel

Barak A (2002) Foreword: a judge on judging: the role of a supreme court in a democracy. Harvard Law Rev 116:16–162

Barak-Erez D (1995) From an unwritten to a written constitution: the Israeli challenge in American perspective. Columbia HRLR 26:309–356

Barak-Erez D (2002) Judicial review of politics: the Israeli case. J Law Soc 29:611–631

Bendor AL (1997) Are there any limits to justiciability? The jurisprudential and constitutional controversy in light of the Israeli and American experience. Indiana I & Comp. Law Rev 7:311–377

Blum YZ (1968) The missing reversioner: reflections on the status of Judea and Samaria. Israel Law Rev 3:279–291

Bracha B (1991) Judicial review of security powers in Israel: a new policy of the courts. Stanford JIL 28:39–102

Delahunty RJ, Yoo JC (2010) What is the role of international human rights law in the war of terror. DePaul Law Rev 59:803–849

[116] For example, in 2007 UK's House of Lords addressed the legality of the arrest of a British citizen held in detention in Iraq by British forces as of 2004 in *R—on the application of Al-Jedda (FC) v Secretary of State for Defence* (2007) UKHL 58. The Canadian Supreme Court was asked to rule on the applicability of the Canadian Charter to individuals detained by Canadian forces in Afghanistan, *Amnesty International Canada* v *Chief of the Defense Staff for the Canadian Forces*, 2008 F.C. 336, aff'd 2008 F.C.A. 401. While these suits may not necessarily implicate directly questions of the Law of Armed Conflict, they do relate to the conduct of militaries overseas in situations of hostilities.

[117] This is exemplified, *inter alia*, by the Supreme Court recognizing federal jurisdiction over those incarcerated in Guantanamo Bay, *Rasul* v *Bush*, 542 US 466, 480 (2004); the application of constitutional *habeas corpus* to Guantanamo Bay; *Boumediene* v *Bush*, 553 US 723 (2008).

[118] *Hamdan* v *Rumsfeld*, 548 U.S 557 (2006) (in which the Court examined the legality of the military commissions designated to try unlawful combatants in light of Common Article 3 of the Geneva Conventions).

Dennis M (2005) Application of human rights treaties extraterritorially in times of armed conflict and military occupation. AJIL 99:119–141

Dotan Y (1999) Judicial rhetoric, government lawyers, and human rights: the case of the Israeli high court of justice during the Intifada. Law Soc Rev 33:319–363

Edry YM (2005) The Israeli constitutional revolution/evolution, models of constitutions and a lesson from mistakes and achievements. AJCL 53:77–124

Fallon RH Jr et al (2009) Hart and Wechsler's The federal courts and the federal system, 6th edn. Foundation Press, New York

Feldman N (2002) Choices of law, choices of war. Harvard JL & Pub. Pol. 25:457–485

Franck TM (1992) Political questions/judicial answers: does the rule of law apply to foreign affairs. Princeton University Press, Princeton

Gerstein J (2010) Treasury to allow Anwar al-Awlaki lawsuit. In: Politico (3 August 2010) available at http://www.politico.com/news/stories/0810/40616.html

Glennon MJ (1989) Foreign affairs and the political doctrine question. AJIL 83:814–821

Goldsmith J (2007) The terror presidency: law and judgment inside the Bush Administration. W.W. Norton & Co, New York

Hampson FJ (2008) The relationship between international humanitarian law and human rights law from the perspective of a human rights body. IRRC 90:549–572

Henkin L (1984) International law as law in the United States. Michigan Law Rev 82:1555–1569

Henkin L (1996) Foreign affairs and the US Constitution, 2nd edn. Oxford University Press, New York

Kelly MJ (1999) Restoring and maintaining order in complex peace operations. Kluwer Law International, The Hague

Kretzmer D (2002) The occupation of justice: The supreme court of Israel and the occupied territories. State University of New York Press, Albany

Lee Boyd K (2001) Are human rights political questions. Rutgers Law Rev 53:277–331

Mari M (2005) The Israel disengagement from the Gaza Strip: an end of the occupation? YIHL 8:356–368

Nathan E (1982) The power of supervision of the high court of justice over military government. In: Shamgar M (ed) Military government in the territories administered by Israel 1967–1980: the legal aspects. Alpha Press, Jerusalem, pp 109–169

Negbi M (1981) Justice under occupation: the Israeli supreme court versus the military administration in the occupied territories. Jerusalem, Kanne (in Hebrew)

Paust JJ (1988) Self-executing treaties. AJIL 82:760–783

Redish MH (1984) Judicial review and the 'political question'. Northwestern University LR79:1031–1061

Roberts A (1992) Prolonged military occupation: the Israeli-occupied territories 1967–1988. In: Playfair E (ed) International law and the administration of occupied territories. Clarendon Press, Oxford, pp 25–85

Shamgar M (1982) Legal concepts and problems of the Israeli military government–the initial stage. In: Shamgar M (ed) Military government in the territories administered by Israel 1967–1980: the legal aspects. Alpha Press, Jerusalem, pp 13–60

Shamir R (1990) 'Landmark cases' and the reproduction of legitimacy: the case of Israel's high court of justice. Law Soc Rev 24:781–806

Shani Y (2005) Faraway, so close: the legal status of Gaza after Israel's disengagement. YIHL 8:369–383

Shani Y (2009) The law applicable to non-occupied Gaza: a comment of Bassiouni v the Prime Minister of Israel. Israel Law Rev 42:101–117

Shaw MN (2003) International law, 5th edn. Cambridge University Press, Cambridge

Slaughter Bruley A (2003) Are foreign affairs different? Political questions/judicial answers: does the Rule of Law apply to foreign affairs? Harvard Law Rev 106:1980–2008

Steinhardt RG (2004) International humanitarian law in the courts of the United States: Yamashita, Filartiga, and 9/11. GW ILR 30:1–46

Tushnet M (2002) Law and prudence in the law of justiciability: the transformation and disappearance of the political question doctrine. North Carolina Law Rev 80:1203–1236

Vázquez CM (1992) Treaty-based rights and remedies of individuals. Columbia Law Rev 92:1082–1163

Ward J, Lake E (2009) White house: 'war on terrorism' is over, Washington Times (6 August 2009) available at http://www.washingtontimes.com/news/2009/aug/06/white-house-war-terrorism-over/

Watkin K (2004) Controlling the use of force: a role for human rights norms in contemporary armed conflict. AJIL 98:1–34

Weiner AS (2007) Law, just war, and the international fight against terrorism: is it war? In: Lee S (ed) Intervention, terrorism, and torture: challenges to just war theory in the 21st century. Springer, Dordrecht, pp 137–153

Yoo JC (1999) Globalism and the constitution: treaties, non-self-executing, and the original understanding. Columbia LR 99:1955–2094

Yoo J (2006) War by other means: an insider's account of the war on terror. Atlantic Monthly Press, New York

Chapter 3
Counter-Insurgency Operations in Afghanistan. What about the '*Jus ad Bellum*' and the '*Jus in Bello*': Is the Law Still Accurate?

Chris De Cock

Contents

The views expressed in this paper are those of the author in his personal capacity and do not intend to reflect the views of the DG or of the Ministry of Defense.

C. De Cock (✉)
DG Legal Support & Mediation, Belgian Ministry of Defense, Brussels, Belgium
e-mail: Christian.decock@mil.be

M.N. Schmitt et al. (eds.), *Yearbook of International Humanitarian Law Volume 13, 2010*, DOI: 10.1007/978-90-6704-811-8_3,

3.1 Introduction

The nature of contemporary operations in Afghanistan reflect the complexities of their environment, particularly in the field of terrorism[1] and insurgency[2] and the reaction of states in combating those (new) forms of violence,[3] generally referred to as counterterrorism (hereinafter CT) and counterinsurgency (hereinafter COIN).[4]

Firstly, we need to recognize that the strategic context in which military forces operate has changed dramatically in the last 50 years. Indeed, whereas armies operated mainly within the framework of interstate wars until the Second World War, this changed with the appearance of guerilla warfare where armed groups, when confronted with a technological superior adversary, tried to compensate for their technological disadvantage by drawing their enemies into an environment where they could not use their technological advantages to the fullest. The conflict in Afghanistan demonstrates this changing nature of war. The crucial question concerns the relative importance of violence and persuasion in the choice between war and politics.[5] Although related to the Vietnam War, the wording used by Henry Kissinger remains surprisingly relevant: 'In the process, we lost sight of one of the cardinal maxims of guerilla warfare: the guerilla wins if he does not lose; the conventional army loses if it does not win.'[6] Whereas armies traditionally attempted to destroy the opposing military forces, the main focus of COIN is to isolate the insurgents from the local population by winning the latter's 'hearts and minds'.[7] The insurgents, on the other hand, will try to influence public opinion in our capitals in order to weaken the public support for our deployed troops. In this modern "information age", this Fourth Generation Warfare (hereinafter 4GW) can stand against technologically advanced enemies by using all available networks to convince political decision makers in NATO capitals to withdraw their troops

---

[1] On the definition of terrorism, see: Higgins 1997, pp 130–28; Sorel 2003, pp 365–378; Bennoune 2008, pp 3–61; Acharya 2009, pp 653–679; Di Filippo 2008, pp 533–570; Kalshoven 1985, pp 114–117; Moeckli 2008, pp 157–183.

[2] According to JP 1-02, insurgency is 'an organized movement aimed at the overthrow of a constituted government through the use of subversion and armed conflict'. Compare with the US Government Counterinsurgency Guide, 13 January 2009, available at www.state.gov/t/pm/ppa/pmppt, p 2: 'Insurgency is the organized use of subversion and violence to seize, nullify or challenge political control of a region.'.

[3] Schrijver 2001, p 285.

[4] The US JP 1-02 defines counterinsurgency as those political, economical, military, paramilitary, psychological, and civic actions taken by a government to defeat an insurgency. See also Beckett, cited in Hammes 2006, p 18.

[5] See also the UN High Panel Report, A More Secure World: Our Shared Responsibility, p 164, UN Doc No A/59/565 (2 December 2004), pp 147–148.

[6] Kissinger 1969, p 214.

[7] See also Santopinto 2010, pp 1–6.

instead of defeating them on the battlefield.[8] As in the Iraq and Afghanistan conflicts, hardliners will insist that 'the enemy relies only on bullets and terror applied ruthlessly, while others will argue that deep popular discontent is the key of the insurgency'.[9] Consequently, military commanders need to understand the nature of these 4GW conflicts and plan their military operations accordingly.

Secondly, apart from this new strategic environment, non-state actors act from and in the territory of more than one state, with or without its consent. Examples of such transnational conflicts are the 'new types of terrorism that threatens the world, driven by networks of fanatics determined to inflict maximum civilian and economic damages on distant targets in pursuit of their extremist goals', such as in Iraq or Afghanistan.[10] The presence of transnational actors on the battlefield expanding their scope to more than one state, challenges the '*acquis*' of international (humanitarian) law.[11] Indeed, if members of terrorist organizations or insurgent movements participate directly in hostilities against the armed forces, the question arises to what extent such conflicts qualify as international or non-international armed conflict.[12] If transnational terrorist attacks do not fit in those frameworks, what is then the applicable legal framework?[13]

Whereas the complexity of this new environment is well recognized,[14] there is however disparity in the international community on how to respond to those threats, varying from law enforcement (preventing, detecting and bringing terrorists to justice)[15] to full scale war,[16]or a combination thereof.[17] Nevertheless, recognizing that terrorism constitutes one of the most serious threats against peace and security, the UN Security Council (UNSC) has recalled on different occasions the need to combat terrorism in accordance with applicable international law,

8 Hammes 2004, p 208.

9 Shy and Collier 1986, pp 815–862.

10 Schöndorf uses the term 'extra-state armed conflict', distinguishing that way between the classical interstate and internal armed conflicts, Schondorf 2004, pp 5–7.

11 Waxman 2010, pp 429-455; Rowe 2002.

12 See also Vite 2009, pp 69–94; Schöndorf 2004, pp 1–78; Sharp 2000, pp 37–48.

13 In the *Targeted Killings* case before the Israeli Supreme Court, Israel submitted that 'the question of the classification of the conflict between Israel and the Palestinians is a complicated question, [...]. These law allow striking at persons who are a party to the armed conflict and take an active part in it, whether it is an international or a non-international armed conflict, *and even if it belongs to a new category of armed conflict which has been developing over the last decade in international law: a category of armed conflicts between the State and terrorist organizations.* [Emphasis added] (H.C. 769/02, *Public Committee Against Torture in Israel* v. *Government of Israel*, Judgment of 13 December 2006, para 11).

14 Fahmi 2006, pp 157–167.

15 See Wilkinson 1996, p 5; Benjamin 2009, pp 267–272; Joyner 2003, pp 493–542.

16 Jinks 2003b, p 91.

17 Delbrück 2001, p 12. See also Fitzpatrick 2003, p 9; Kielsgard 2006, pp 249–302; Hoon 2007, pp 107–116.

including IHL and IHRL.[18] According to UN Secretary-General K. Annan, 'Terrorist acts ... constitute grave violations of human rights. Our responses to terrorism, as well as our efforts to thwart it and prevent it should uphold the human rights that terrorists aimed to destroy. Human rights, fundamental freedoms and the rule of law are essential tools in the effort to combat terrorism-not privileges to be sacrificed at a time of tension'.[19]

The aim of this paper is to analyze the rules applicable in COIN operations in Afghanistan. The first part of this article will explore the overall legal framework. Is the Global War on Terror (GWOT) just a rhetorical speech or is there effectively an armed conflict with Al Qaeda and other terrorist organizations? Former President Bush stated that 'international terrorists, including members of Al Qaida, have carried out attacks on United States diplomatic and military personnel and facilities abroad and on citizens and property within the United States on a scale that created a state of armed conflict that requires the use of United States Armed Forces'.[20] The attacks of 9/11 and subsequent events 'confirmed the emergence of a new phenomenon, of transnational networks capable of inflicting deadly violence on targets in geographically distant states. The transnational, rather than international, nature of such networks is evidenced by the fact that their activities, which are also geographically dispersed, are not imputable to a specific state under the international rules of state responsibility.'[21] One of the major problems in the study of terrorism and insurgency relates to the emotive language in approaching the phenomenon and how to describe those involved (terrorists, freedom fighters, criminals, insurgents) or the type of violence (small wars, revolutionary wars, military operations other than war, low intensity conflicts, ...). Subsequent speeches made by former President Bush made the narrative of the war against Al Qaeda clear.[22] In addressing a joint session of the US Congress and the American people, President Bush declared that 'the war on terror begins with Al Qaeda, but it does not end there. It will not end until every terrorist group of global reach has been found, stopped and defeated'.[23]

---

[18] UNSCR S/Res/1267 (1999), UNSCR S/Res/1333 (2000), UNSCR S/Res/1363 (2001), UNSCR S/Res/1373 (2001), UNSCR S/Res/1390 (2002), UNSCR S/Res/1452 (2002), UNSCR S/Res/1455 (2003), UNSCR S/Res/1526 (2004), UNSCR S/Res/1566 (2004), UNSCR S/Res/1617 (2005), UNSCR S/Res/1624 (2005), UNSCR S/Res/1699 (2006), UNSCR S/Res/1730 (2006), UNSCR S/Res/1735 (2006), UNSCR S/Res/1822 (2008) and UNSCR S/Res/1904 (2009). According to ISANGA, the UN resolutions on the applicability of human rights in counter-terrorism confirm the existence of a customary law rule that counter-terrorism measures must conform to human rights, in Isanga 2009, pp 223–255.

[19] K. Annan, UN Doc. SG/SM/8624/-SC7680, 6 March 2003.

[20] Bush 2002, p 252.

[21] International humanitarian law and the challenges of contemporary armed conflicts, Report prepared by the ICRC, 28th International Conference of the Red Cross and Red Crescent, Geneva, 2–6 December 2003.

[22] On the policy of the Bush administration, see Nanda 2009, pp 513–537.

[23] Address of President Bush to a Joint Session of Congress and the American people, 20 September 2001, available at www.whitehouse.gov/news/releases/2001/20010920-!.htlm.

Firstly, we need to recognize that the conflict in Afghanistan raised some controversial questions in relation to the '*jus ad bellum*' and the inherent right of self-defense against non-state actors.[24] In the past, the UNSC condemned the use of force in self-defense against terrorist organizations, such as against South-Africa[25] and Israel (in relation to its raid against the PLO headquarters in Tunis).[26] Secondly, since different military operations take place simultaneously on the territory of Afghanistan, it is necessary to categorize each of them in order to determine the applicable legal framework. Those operations are the US-led operation *Enduring Freedom* (hereinafter OEF), the NATO-led International Security and Assistance Force (ISAF) operation, and finally the internal struggles of the Afghan authorities against both the insurgents and the drug industry.

Whereas the traditional principles of the LOAC – distinction, proportionality, military necessity, and humanity – remain valid in traditional warfare, is it fair to state that in the context of COIN operations, where the main focus shifted from capturing and/or killing enemy combatants to the winning of the 'hearts and minds', the Geneva Conventions and its Additional Protocols are at variance with contemporary military operations when combating enemy fighters who do not distinguish themselves from the civilian population, who seek shelter among that civilian population and whose centre of gravity is not aimed at destroying our regular armies, but winning popular support in our capitals? For instance, when COIN operations are conducted within the context of an armed conflict, what does the principle of distinction means within such asymmetric conflicts? Can we target individual members of terrorist or insurgency movements? When are insurgents directly participating in the conflict? Can we strike those individuals regardless of their active or direct participation in hostilities? In doing so, should we restrain the use of force against persons taking a direct participation in hostilities by limiting the use of force to persons committing hostile acts or display hostile intent? Such limitations, if any, will be translated in a well-defined set of Rules of Engagement (hereinafter ROE). Indeed, the law of (international) armed conflict, aimed at the protection of protected persons and those persons who are considered '*hors de combat*' and the prohibition or limitation of certain means and methods of warfare, consists of a large body of binding international treaty and customary law which must be integrated in the strategic and operational planning of COIN operations. However, in the light of COIN operations, such as in Afghanistan, it remains to be seen to what extent the rules of the LOAC have become obsolete (in the sense that they reflect the applicable legal standards in traditional conflicts between the armed forces of states) or have become less relevant in the context of COIN operations, where 'destruction and capture of enemy forces' as the main Centre of

---

[24] The use of force against terrorist groups is not a novelty, e.g. the Israeli military intervention against Hezbollah in 2006. For an analysis of the applicable *jus ad bellum*, see Schmitt 2008a, b, pp 127, 164.

[25] UNSCR S/Res/387 (1976).

[26] UNSCR S/Res/573 (1985).

Gravity (CoG) has shifted to 'winning the hearts and minds of the local population and their popular support'.[27] This new strategic environment challenges the '*acquis*' of international humanitarian law.

3.2 The Inherent Right of Self-Defense against Al Qaeda: Evolution or Revolution of the *Jus ad Bellum*?

3.2.1 Introduction

The attacks of 9/11 raised some important legal questions in respect of both the '*jus ad bellum*' and the '*jus in bello*'. With regard to the conflict in Afghanistan, the question is to what extent the United States was entitled to use force in exercising its inherent right of self-defense, as enshrined in the UN Charter, to respond to an (armed) attack carried out by a global terrorist organization. By invoking Article 5 of the Washington Treaty and Article 3 of the Inter-American Treaty of Reciprocal Assistance, those Member States accepted that the 9/11 attacks constituted an armed attack triggering the right of self-defense. Noting that the terrorist acts of 9/11 were carried out by Al Qaeda, the following two issues need further clarification:

- If there is a *nexus* between a state and the terrorist organization, did Al Qaeda qualify as *de facto* state organ of the *de facto* Taliban government of the Republic of Afghanistan? Was there substantial assistance or involvement from the Taliban government to Al Qaeda amounting to an armed attack justifying the resort to armed force by the US in exercising its inherent right of self-defense? If so, did the terrorist attacks of 9/11 qualify as an 'armed attack'?
- If no *nexus* with another state exists, does international law authorizes the use of force in self-defense against non-state actors?

3.2.2 Existence of a nexus

Although states have frequently invoked the right of self-defense in relation to their response to the activities of irregular forces fighting wars of insurgency, it is not always easy to characterize those acts as 'armed attacks' justifying the use of armed force in self-defense. This includes indirect attacks, such as the sending by

[27] Victory over terrorists and insurgents will come not from 'capture and kill' operations, but by breaking the cycle of radicalization, recruitment and training, cited in Harting 2008. See also: NATO Nations Approve Civilian Casualty Guidelines, available at http://www.nato.int/cps/en/SID3DC020B28396CC9D/natolive/official_texts_65114.htm?selectedLocale=en,6 August 2010.

or on behalf of a state of armed groups or mercenaries into another state where they carry out 'acts of armed force of such gravity as would constitute an armed attack if conducted by regular forces'.[28] However, in such cases, the *nexus* with another state is clear and unambiguous. Insofar as the 'attack' reaches the level of an 'armed attack', such use of armed force would automatically trigger the right of self-defense against that state since those irregular forces would act as *de facto* state organs of that state (by assimilating them to their regular armed forces).[29]

The International Court of Justice [ICJ] recognized in the *Nicaragua* case that the indirect use of force may trigger the right of self-defense when it reaches a certain level of gravity.[30] Although the ICJ remained silent on what constitutes 'such gravity', it nevertheless clearly stated that it is confined to armed force which reaches the threshold of 'such gravity as to amount to an actual armed attack' that triggers the right of self-defense. According to the ICJ, where a state is involved with the organization of 'armed bands' operating in the territory of another state, this could amount to armed attack 'because of its scale and effects'.[31] The criteria of 'scale and effects' are thus of crucial importance. In its instructions to the military commissions, the US argued that 'A single hostile act or attempted act may provide sufficient basis ... so long as its magnitude or severity rises to the level of an 'armed attack' or an 'act of war', or the number, power, stated intent or organization of the force with which the actor is associated is such that the act or attempted act is tantamount to an attack by armed forces'.[32] Although a single act may not amount to the required 'severity, magnitude or scale and effects', the cumulative effects of apparently independent hostile acts may reach the threshold of an armed attack triggering the right of self-defense.[33] Dinstein argues that not every single incident, scrutinized independently, has to meet the standard of sufficient gravity. A persuasive argument can be made that, should a distinctive pattern of behavior emerge, a series of pin-prick assaults might be weighed in its totality and count for an armed attack.[34] Whereas situations of intense gravity amount to armed attacks, the Court excluded certain activities as not being armed attacks, such as logistical support.[35] According to the ICJ, such forms of assistance 'may be regarded as a threat or use of force, or amount to intervention in the

---

[28] Definition of Aggression, GA Res 3314 (XXIX)(14 December 1974), Article 3, (g).

[29] ICJ, Case concerning Armed Activities on the Territory of the Congo, *Democratic Republic of the Congo* v *Uganda* [2005], para 146, (hereinafter the *Armed Activities* Case).

[30] ICJ, Case Concerning Military and Paramilitary Activities in and against Nicaragua (Merits), [1986] *Gen. List* No 70, para 195 (hereinafter the *Nicaragua* Case)

[31] Ibid. In the same way: Gill 2003, p 30; Dinstein 2005, p 202.

[32] Military Commission Instruction N°2, Crimes and Elements for Trials by Military Commission, 30 April 2003, Section 5(C).

[33] *Armed Activities Case*, supra n 29, para 146: 'The Court is of the view that, on the evidence before it, *even if this series of deplorable acts could be regarded as cumulative in character*, they still remained non-attributable to the DRC.' [Emphasis added].

[34] Dinstein 2005, p 202.

[35] *Nicaragua* Case, supra n 30, para 247.

internal or external affairs of other states'.[36] Finally, when terrorists are sponsored by foreign states, they may be deemed '*de facto* organs' of that state.[37]

3.2.3 Absence of a Nexus

The attacks of 9/11 also raised the question of whether terrorist acts can trigger the inherent right of self-defense, even if no *nexus* with another state exists. Indeed, the findings of the ICJ in its *Advisory Opinion on the Legal Consequences of the Construction of a Wall in the Occupied Palestinian Territory* suggests otherwise. The Court's reasoning that, 'Article 51 of the Charter thus recognizes the existence of an inherent right of self-defense in case of armed attack by one state against another state. However, Israel does not claim that the attacks against it are imputable to a foreign state' supports the view that the right of self-defense is solely confined to armed attacks originating from another state.[38] This conservative position by the Court was, however, subject to much criticism.[39] At the center of the 1986 Schultz doctrine was the issue of the legality of the extra-territorial recourse to force in response to an attack by private actors and directed against terrorists, as opposed to states and their infrastructure. Addressing the issue during a speech at the National Defense University, Schultz stated that 'the Charter's restrictions on the use or threat of force in international relations include a specific exception for the right of self-defense. It is absurd to argue that international law prohibits us from capturing terrorists in international waters and space; from attacking them on the soil of other nations, even for the purpose of rescuing hostages; or from using force against states that support, train and harbor terrorists or guerillas.'[40] This point of view is supported by Dinstein who affirmed that 'self-defense is permitted against the terrorists' bases inside the territory of another state (provided that it is directed against the guilty terrorists rather than against the ineffective local government)'.[41] In the *Case concerning Armed Activities on the Territory of the Congo*, the ICJ unfortunately decided not to address the question

---

[36] Ibid., para 195.

[37] Dinstein 2005, p 203.

[38] ICJ, Advisory Opinion on the Legal Consequences of the Construction of a Wall in the Occupied Palestinian Territory, [2004] *ICJ General List* No. 131, 9 July 2004 (hereinafter: the *Wall* Case).

[39] Judge Higgins, in her *Separate Opinion*, stated that: 'There is, with respect, nothing in the text of Article 51 that thus stipulates that self-defense is available only when an armed attack is made by a State. That qualification is rather a result of the Court so determining in the Nicaragua case.' (paras 33–34). See also the criticism of Judge Kooijmans and Judge Buergenthal in the same case.

[40] Schultz 1986, p 206.

[41] Dinstein 1987, p 146. In the same way Brunnee and Toope 2005; Byers 2002, pp 411–412; Franck 2001, p 840; Dusheine 2008, pp 167–168; van Aggelen 2009, p 26; Jensen 2007, p 272; Schmitt 2008a, b, pp 163–164; Contra Martin 2006, p 294.

'as to whether and under what conditions contemporary international law provides for a right of self-defense against large-scale attacks by irregular forces'.[42] The judgment of the Court, implicitly recognizing that the use of force in self-defense is only admissible insofar the armed attack is carried out by the state (in contrast to organized armed groups), was severely criticized by Judge Kooijmans[43] and Judge Simma.[44]According to Judge Kooijmans 'it would be unreasonable to deny the attacked state the right to self-defense merely because there is no attacker state'. Additionally, he states that 'nothing in the Charter prevents the victim state from exercising its inherent right of self-defense'.[45] On 12 September 2001, the UNSC adopted Resolution 1368 reaffirming 'the inherent right of individual or collective self-defense in accordance with the Charter', which was reaffirmed in UNSCR 1373 providing that all states shall '*take the necessary steps to prevent the commission of terrorist acts*'. It has been argued that these resolutions recognized the inherent right of self-defense against non-state actors [NSA] since no reference was made of an armed attack being carried out by states.[46] This seems to be the position of the United States when on 7 October 2001 it notified the Security Council that it was exercising its right of self-defense in taking action in Afghanistan against the Al Qaeda organization deemed responsible and the Taliban regime in that country which was accused of providing bases for that organization.[47]

The contradictory views referred to above clearly demonstrate the different prevailing opinions on the interpretation of the Charter. On the one hand, the ICJ with its conservative or rather static interpretation of the Charter and, on the other hand, a majority of scholars, states and international organizations calling for a more 'modern' interpretation of the Charter. According to Murphy, three options are possible: 'States and non-state actors can continue to operate under the current system, which tends to view the *jus ad bellum* as a static law unchanged since 1945 [...] States and non-state actors could seek to reaffirm the static *jus ad bellum*, if that remains the consensus position. Finally, if the *status quo* is untenable, and there is no consensus on the static view, then States and non-state

---

42 *Armed Activities* Case, para 147; Tams 2009, pp 359–397.

43 *Armed Activities* Case, Separate Opinion Judge Kooijmans, paras 29–30.

44 Ibid., Separate Opinion Judge Simma, para 11: 'Security Council Resolutions 1368 (2001) and 1373 (2001) cannot but be read as affirmations of the view that large-scale attacks by non-State actors can qualify as "armed attacks" within the meaning of Article 51'.

45 In the same way: Barbour and Salzman 2008, pp 53, 106.

46 *Armed Activities* Case, Separate Opinion Judge Kooijmans, paras 29–30.

47 S/2001/946. See also Dinstein who states that: 'The attacks against the United States on 9/11 were mounted by the Al-Qaeda terrorist organization masterminded from within Taliban-led Afghanistan but not controlled by that State. [...] The fact that terrorist attacks qualify as armed attacks means that they are subject to the full application of Article 51: no more and no less.', in Dinstein 2005, pp 206–208; Contra Saura 2003, p 25.

actors might do well to seek consensus on a re-codification of the *jus ad bellum* to reflect its protean function'.[48]

That being said, it is clear that states have an inherent right of self-defense against armed attacks by non-state actors:

- Against the state and the non-state actors if the acts (armed attack) are attributable to that state;
- Against the non-state actor if the acts cannot be attributed to that state, but if that state is unable or unwilling to "control" the activities of the non-state actor.

3.2.4 Self-defense and the UN Security Council

The issue raised in the context of the ISAF operation is also important in relation to the applicability *ratione temporis* of the right of self-defense. Indeed, Article 51 of the UN Charter is not a 'carte blanche' since it extends the (inherent) right of individual and collective self-defense only 'until the Security Council has taken the measures necessary to maintain international peace and security'. The clause of the Charter reaffirms the primacy of the Security Council to take the necessary measures in the framework of the collective security mechanism.[49] In other words, the right of self-defense is temporary and lasts until such time that the SC takes the necessary measures to restore international peace and security.[50] The question arises as to what extent the establishment of ISAF can be regarded as the 'necessary and effective' measure taken to discontinue the right of self-defense by the United States. Until international peace and security have been effectively and successfully restored, the right of self-defense remains unaffected by collective measures taken by the Security Council.[51] In other words, the establishment of ISAF did not put an end to the military operation OEF, conducted in the exercise of the US inherent right of self-defense. Consequently, both operations ISAF and OEF can legitimately coexist. Only the Security Council can put an end to OEF by an '*affirmative decision, including the concurring votes of the permanent members*'.[52]

---

[48] Murphy 2008, pp 50–51.

[49] Gill 2007, p 119.

[50] Gray 2000, pp 92–94.

[51] Dinstein 2005, p 215.

[52] Alexandrov 1996, p 105.

3.3 Typology of Military Operations in Afghanistan

3.3.1 Introduction

Afghanistan is the theatre of multiple conflicts, each of them regulated by a particular set of legal rules. Firstly, there is the conflict between the Government of the Islamic Republic of Afghanistan [GIRoA] against the insurgents. Secondly, multinational (ISAF) troops, operating under the NATO umbrella, are engaged against the insurgents in support of the Afghan Government and in accordance with the applicable UNSC Resolutions. Thirdly, American forces continue to operate on the territory of Afghanistan against Al Qaeda as part of OEF. Finally, there is the issue of counter narcotic operations (with or without link to the insurgency) conducted by the Afghan authorities with the support of the international community. In such a complex environment, one needs to define the nature of the conflict(s) in order to apply the correct legal standards.

3.3.2 Operation Enduring Freedom

3.3.2.1 October 2001–June 2002

Notwithstanding the controversy on the applicability of the inherent right of self-defense against non-state actors, it is clear that the US intervention in Afghanistan started as an international armed conflict, since the Taliban represented at that time the *de facto* government of Afghanistan. Consequently, the hostilities between them were subject to the law of international armed conflict. Whereas the legal framework is clear between those two belligerents, it still remains controversial as to what body of law applied in the conflict between the Coalition forces and Al Qaeda, as a transnational armed group fighting on the territory of Afghanistan. Can it be said that the applicability of the LOIAC in the relations between the Coalition and the Taliban automatically lead to its applicability in the context of the hostilities against Al Qaeda? If Al Qaeda acted on behalf of the Taliban regime, the situation is clear. In its decision on the merits in the *Tadić* case, the Appeals Chamber of the ICTY noted that 'It is indisputable that an armed conflict is international if it takes place between two or more States. In addition, in case of an internal armed conflict breaking out on the territory of a State, it may become international (or, depending upon the circumstances, be international in character alongside an internal armed conflict) if (i) another State intervenes in that conflict with its troops, or alternatively if (ii) some of the participants in the internal armed conflict act on behalf of that other State.'[53]

[53] *Prosecutor* v *Tadić,* Case No. IT-94-1-A, A. Ch., 15 July 1999, para 84.

As a result, the entire conflict in Afghanistan would have been subject to the LOIAC to the extent that Al Qaeda acted as a governmental organ. In examining Article 4 GC III which defines POW status, the Appeals Chamber in *Tadić* noted that the belligerent parties may use paramilitary units or other irregulars in the conduct of hostilities only on condition that those belligerents are prepared to take responsibility for any infringements committed by such forces. In order for such irregulars to qualify as combatants, control over them by a party to the conflict was required and thus a relationship of dependence and allegiance. Accordingly, the term '*belonging to a party to the conflict*' used in Article 4 GCIII implicitly refers to a control test.[54] However, whether the applicable test is one of effective or overall control remains unclear. The ICJ applied an effective control test in the *Nicaragua* Case to attribute the acts of the *contras* to the United States government. It stated that 'For this conduct to give rise to legal responsibility of the United States, it would in principle have to be proved that that State had effective control of the military or paramilitary operations in the course of which the alleged violations were committed.'[55]

This high threshold was confirmed by the ICJ in the *Case Concerning Armed Activities on the Territory of the Congo,*[56] *and in the Case Concerning the Application of the Convention on the Prevention and Punishment of the Crime of Genocide.*[57] In Tadić, the Appeals Chamber of the ICTY took, however, a totally different approach than the ICJ when it stated that 'in order to attribute the acts of a military or paramilitary group to a State, it must be proved that the State wields overall control over the group, not only by equipping and financing the group, but also by coordinating or helping in the general planning of its military activity. Only then can the State be held internationally accountable for any misconduct of the group. However, it is not necessary that, in addition, the State should also issue, either to the head or to members of the group, instructions for the commission of specific acts contrary to international law.'[58]

On the other hand, if no *nexus* exists between the transnational armed group and the state and their acts cannot be attributed to Afghanistan, the conduct of hostilities against Al Qaeda is governed by the law of non-international armed conflict since the hostilities reached the level of an armed conflict (intensity and organization).[59] According to the ICTY in *Tadić*, an armed conflict exists 'whenever there is a resort to armed force between States or *protracted armed violence*

---

[54] Ibid., paras 94–95.

[55] *Nicaragua* Case, para 115.

[56] *Armed Activities* Case, paras 160–161.

[57] ICJ, Case Concerning the Application of the Convention on the Prevention and Punishment of the Crime of Genocide [2007] *Gen. List* No. 91, para 413. This line of reasoning by the ICJ can also be found in Art. 8 of the International Law Commission's Draft Articles on State Responsibility (Crawford 2002). See also Cassese 2007, pp 649–668, asserting that the ICJ missed a good opportunity to elaborate upon and improve the Nicaragua test.

[58] *Tadić* Case, para 131.

[59] Jinks 2003a, p 9; Downes 2004, p 84.

between governmental authorities and organized armed groups or between such groups within a State' [emphasis added].[60]

The discussion regarding the typology of an extra-territorial armed conflict between a state and a non-state actor is generally focused on the classical dichotomy between international and non-international armed conflicts. Proponents of the international armed conflict will argue that all conflicts which take place outside the territory of that state are international in nature, while proponents of the non-international characterization will argue that all conflicts which are not inter-state conflicts are non-international in nature. In my view, the latter view prevails. Indeed, one could argue that common Article 3 GC apply in all situations which are not governed by common Article 2 GC. The ICRC confirmed that 'the minimum requirements in the case of non-international armed conflict are *a fortiori* applicable in the context of international armed conflicts. It proclaims the guiding principles common to all the Geneva Conventions and from each of them derives the essential provision around which it is built.'[61] The rules contained in Common Article 3 of the Geneva Conventions are considered the '*minimum minimorum*', applicable in all types of armed conflicts.[62] In *Nicaragua*, the ICJ stated that 'Common Article 3 defines certain rules to be applied in the armed conflicts of a non-international character. There is no doubt that, in the event of international armed conflicts, these rules also constitute a minimum yardstick, in addition to the more elaborate rules which are also to apply to international conflicts; and they are rules which, in the Court's opinion, reflect what the Court in 1949 called "elementary considerations of humanity".'[63]A fortiori, common Article 3 will apply in all extra-territorial armed conflicts between a state and NSA.

The concept of armed conflict requires the existence of organized armed groups that are capable of and actually do engage in combat and other military actions against each other. In *Tadić*, the ICTY stated that 'the test applied by the Appeals Chamber to the existence of an armed conflict for the purposes of the rules contained in Common Article 3 focuses on two aspects of a conflict: *the intensity of the conflict and the organization of the parties to the conflict.*[64] In an armed

---

[60] ICTY, *Prosecutor* v *Tadić*, Case No. IT-94-1-T, T.Ch. II, 10 August 1995, para 70.

[61] Pictet (ed) 1958, p 14.

[62] See also ICTY, *Prosecutor* v *Delalić* et al., Case N0. IT-96-21-A, A.Ch., 20 February 2001, paras 147 and 150.

[63] *Nicaragua* Case, supra n 35, para 218. In its Advisory Opinion on the *Legality of the Threat or Use of Nuclear Weapons*, the ICJ reiterated the principle that certain minimum rules are applicable regardless of the nature of the conflict (*Legality of the Threat or Use of Nuclear Weapons*, [1996] ICJ Rep 226, 79).

[64] See also ICTY, *Prosecutor* v *Boškoski*, Case No. IT-04-82-T, T.Ch.II, 10 July 2008, paras 175–292.

conflict of an internal or mixed character, these closely related criteria are used solely for the purpose, as a minimum, of distinguishing an armed conflict from banditry, unorganized and short-lived insurrections, or terrorist activities, which are not subject to international humanitarian law' [emphasis added].[65]

In analyzing the conflict between the US and Al Qaeda, Zemach states that 'the violent conflict between the US and al-Qaeda, notwithstanding its high death toll, cannot be characterized as an armed conflict, as it does not produce the unique pressure of warfare that precludes individualized assessment of dangerousness'.[66] However, the prevailing view is that the conflict between the US and Al Qaeda meets the requirements of a non-international armed conflict. Applying the *Tadić* criteria to the hostilities between the US (and allies) and Al Qaeda can only lead to the conclusion that a state of non-international armed conflict exists.

Consequently, two armed conflicts coexisted: an international armed conflict with the Taliban, and a non-international armed conflict with Al Qaeda.[67]

3.3.2.2 June 2002–…

Noting that an international armed conflict existed in Afghanistan between the US and the Taliban, to what extent did the conflict became non-international after the seizure of power of the Karza government? Although OEF is conducted with the consent of the Afghan authorities, it is clear that OEF is mainly a '*one way street*' operation, conducted by and for the accomplishment of the US national security strategy. Labeled as a CT operation, it remains thus a unilateral operation conducted on the territory of Afghanistan. Most commentators categorize the conflict as a non-international armed conflict, while others consider the conflict as (still) international in nature.[68]

---

[65] ICTY, Opinion and Judgment, *Prosecutor* v *Tadić*, Case No. IT-94-1-T, 7 May 1997, para 562. See also ICTY, Judgment, *Prosecutor* v *Delalić, Mucić, Delić and Landžo*, Case No. IT-96-21-T, T.Ch. II, 16 November 1998, para 184.

[66] Zemach 2010, p 433.

[67] See also: *Nicaragua* Case, supra n 30 para 219.

[68] For an analysis of the Afghan conflict, see in particular Schmitt (ed) 2009a,b. On the nature of the conflict in Afghanistan: non-international armed conflict (ibid., p 308) *versus* international armed conflict (Dinstein 2009, p 51). See also: *Hamdan* v *Rumsfeld*, the US Supreme Court had determined that the armed conflict with Al Qaeda was a conflict 'not of an international character'. Interestingly, the plurality in *Hamdan* held that the 'armed conflict not of an international character' in fact meant 'in contradistinction to a conflict between nations'; Neuman 2003, pp 296–298. See also the interesting position of ZEMACH arguing that 'hostilities that do not meet the threshold of armed conflict-such as the conflict between the United States and al-Qaeda-are governed by human rights law […]', in Zemach 2010, p 428.

3.3.3 Non-international armed conflict

3.3.3.1 Taliban-Northern Alliance (till June 2002)

Even before the US intervention in Afghanistan, a non-international armed conflict opposed the Northern Alliance and the Taliban. Following the US invasion of Afghanistan, the US supported the Northern Alliance in its fight with the Afghan authorities. Although it remains unclear if combined operations were effectively planned and carried out, the support provided by the US to the Northern Alliance can be qualified as a direct intervention in the ongoing non-international armed conflict. However, it cannot be said that the support of the US to the Northern Alliance amounted to the level of 'effective control', in which case the entire conflict would have been internationalized (see *supra*). Consequently, until the eviction of the Taliban, a non-international armed conflict existed between the Northern Alliance and the Taliban, governed by Article 3 Common to the GC and applicable customary international law.

3.3.3.2 ANSF[69]–Taliban (June 2002-...)

After the swearing in of president Karza, the conflict between the Afghan national security forces and the Taliban remained a non-international armed conflict, regulated by Common Article 3 GC and applicable customary international law.[70]

3.3.3.3 Counter-narcotic operations

One of the major challenges for the GIRoA and the international community is the fight against drugs.[71] In the framework of this paper, we will not further develop the legal regime applicable to the fight against narcotics. It suffices to state that counter narcotic operations are subject to domestic and international human rights law as a law enforcement operation. However, it has been asserted that narcotic dealers and facilities can also be subject to military action since the financial profits of this trafficking supports the insurgency. Consequently, they could become a military objective in the sense of Article 52 API. However, one should

---

[69] ANSF: Afghan National Security Forces.

[70] The Islamic Republic of Afghanistan was, at that point in time, not a State Party to Additional Protocol II to the 1949 Geneva Conventions.

[71] This was recognized by the Security Council in several Resolutions, e.g., S/Res/1806 (2008) and S/Res/1890 (2009).

take care not to confuse '*military action*' with '*war sustaining capabilities*'.[72] As correctly stated by Dinstein, the 'war-sustaining' portion is too lax[73] This position accurately reflects the current status of international law, since the connection between military action and drugs exports, required to finance the war effort, is 'too remote'.[74] In the context of the ongoing military operations in Afghanistan, it goes without saying that the disparity between, on the one hand, the US position and, on the other hand, those nations who consider the *nexus* between the narco-industry and the insurgency too remote, inevitably gives rise to some interoperability issues, such as the (positive) identification of military objectives in the targeting process.[75]

3.3.4 ISAF

In the past, the UN Security Council has been actively involved in dealing with terrorism. In the framework of this paper, it should be recalled that even before the events of 9/11, it characterized terrorism as a threat to international peace and security.[76] In the aftermath of 9/11, the UNSC adopted on 12 September 2001 Resolution 1368 noting that it was determined 'to combat by all means threats to international peace and security caused by terrorist attacks' and unequivocally condemned the attack declaring that it regarded such attacks 'like any act of international terrorism, as a threat to international peace and security'. In its Resolution 1373, the UNSC reaffirmed this proposition and the need to combat by all means in accordance with the Charter, threats to international peace and security caused by terrorist acts. More importantly, acting under Chapter VII, the Security Council adopted a series of binding decisions according to which states were called upon to take action against such persons and to cooperate with other states in preventing and suppressing terrorist acts and acting against the perpetrators thereof.

---

[72] Bill and Marsh (eds) 2010, p 20 includes 'war sustaining' activities within the scope of Article 52, (2) of API (Judge Advocate General's School, Operational Law Handbook 10 (2003); US Navy/Marine Corps/Coast Guard, The Commander's Handbook on the Law of Naval Operations, NWP 1-14 M, MCWP 5-2.1, COMDTPUB P5800.7, para 8.1.1, 1995, reprinted in its annotated version as Vol. 73 of the International Law Studies (US Naval War College, 1999).

[73] Dinstein 2004, p 87: 'The American position is that economic targets of the enemy that indirectly but effectively support and sustain the enemy's war-fighting capability may also be attacked. [...] The raw cotton model [...] displays the danger of introducing the slippery-slope concept of "war-sustaining capability".'

[74] Dinstein 2004. In the same way: Doswald-Beck (ed) 1995, p 161.

[75] On the US counter-narcotic strategy in Afghanistan, see Greenspan 2008, pp 493–435.

[76] See UNSCR S/Res/1189 (1998) concerning the bombings of the US embassies in East Africa and UNSCR S/Res/1269 (1999).

In December 2001, the UNSC authorized the establishment of the ISAF in Afghanistan in order to 'assist the Afghan Interim Authority in the maintenance of security in Kabul and its surrounding areas, so that the Afghan Interim Authority as well as the personnel of the United Nations can operate in a secure environment'.[77] The ISAF mandate has since then been broadened and the UNSC subsequently authorized ISAF to 'support the Afghan Transitional Authority and its successors in the maintenance of security in areas of Afghanistan outside of Kabul and its environs, so that the Afghan authorities as well as the personnel of the United Nations and other international civilian personnel engaged, in particular, in reconstruction and humanitarian efforts, can operate in a secure environment, and to provide security assistance for the performance of other tasks in support of the Bonn Agreement.'[78] In February 2006, the UNSC confirmed the geographic expansion of ISAF as well as the support to the Afghan authorities.[79] At the same time, the UNSC also acknowledged the operational synergy between ISAF and OEF, when it expressed 'its support for the Afghan Security Forces, with the assistance of ISAF and the Operation Enduring Freedom coalition in contributing to security in Afghanistan and building the capacity of the Afghan Security Forces, and welcoming the extension of ISAF into Southern Afghanistan, with effect from 31 July 2006, the planned further ISAF expansion into Eastern Afghanistan and the increased coordination between ISAF and the OEF coalition'.[80] In other words, the initial (US) military operation in Afghanistan against the Taliban and Al Qaeda in response to the 9/11 attacks has been "split" into two distinct operations: on the one hand, the continuation of OEF directed against Al Qaeda as a CT operation (mandated under Article 51 of the UN Charter) and, on the other hand, a COIN operation under the ISAF umbrella (mandated by UNSCR 1386 and subsequent UNSC Resolutions).

Based on the applicable UNSC Resolutions, ISAF is authorized to take '*all necessary measures*' to fulfill its mandate.[81] In military terms, this mandate is translated in an operational plan (OPLAN) in which Annex E will detail the precise ROE applicable to the ISAF Forces. The authorization to use force in order to execute the mandate follows from the formulation 'all necessary measures', including the use of force in self-defense, mission accomplishment and force protection (within the limits of the mandate).

Insofar as the ISAF Forces are not taking part in the conflict as a belligerent party, the applicable framework for the use of force is based on the mandate, the

---

[77] UNSCR S/Res/1386 (2001).

[78] UNSCR S/Res/1510 (2003).

[79] UNSCR S/Res/1659 (2006).

[80] UNSCR S/Res/1707 (2006).

[81] UNSCR S/Res/1386 (2001), UNSCR S/Res/1413 (2002), UNSCR S/Res/1444 (2002), UNSCR S/Res/1510 (2003), UNSCR S/Res/1563 (2004), UNSCR S/Res/1623 (2005), UNSCR S/Res/1659 (2006), UNSCR S/Res/1707 (2006), UNSCR S/Res/1746 (2007), UNSCR S/Res/1776 (2007), UNSCR S/Res/1806 (2008), UNSCR S/Res/1817 (2008), UNSCR S/Res/1833 (2008), UNSCR S/Res/1890 (2009), UNSCR S/Res/1894 (2009), and UNSCR S/Res/1917 (2010).

ROE, national and international law, including human rights law. With regard to the actual situation in Afghanistan, especially in South Afghanistan, it is clear that ISAF Forces are engaged in combat operations. As such, ISAF troops are not covered by the 1994 Convention on the Safety of United Nations and Associated Personnel, to the extent that Article 2 provides that the Convention 'will not apply to a UN operation authorized by the Security Council as an enforcement action under Chapter VII in which any of the personnel are engaged as combatants against organized armed forces'.[82] Having regard to the ongoing hostilities in Afghanistan, it is thus obvious that ISAF Forces are engaged therein as combatants. The level of the violence and the organization of the parties involved lead to the conclusion that the hostilities are governed by the law of armed conflict.[83] While recognizing the efforts taken by ISAF and other international forces to minimize the risk of civilian casualties, the UNSC called for compliance with international humanitarian and human rights law and for all appropriate measures to be taken to ensure the protection of civilians. Furthermore, the UNSC urged the continuous review of tactics and procedures. This preoccupation was reaffirmed in other UNSC Resolutions and demonstrates the widespread sense of uneasiness towards the growing number of civilian casualties.[84]

That being said, it is clear that the specific nature of COIN challenges the '*acquis*' of the law of armed conflict, as enshrined in treaty and customary law. In asymmetric conflicts, such as in Afghanistan, where enemy fighters do not distinguish themselves from the civilian population, the question arises to what extent the law of armed conflict is still in line with these new type of conflicts. In other words, is the law of armed conflict still 'well equipped' to answer the legal implications of this changing nature of war?

3.4 The Changing Nature of Military Operations: From Traditional Warfare to Counter-Insurgency

3.4.1 From destroying the enemy to winning the hearts and minds[85]

The nature of COIN demands another approach than the classical attritional approach to which armies have turned historically. Commanders have always recognized 'the need to provide a focus to their planning to avoid dispersal of

---

82 Convention on the Safety of United Nations and Associated Personnel, 1994, 34 ILM 482 (1995), Art. 2(2).

83 *Tadić* Case, supra n 65, para 562. See also ICTY, Judgment, *Prosecutor* v *Delalić, Mucić, Delić and Landžo*, Case No. IT-96-21-T, T.Ch. II, 16 November 1998, para 184.

84 UNSCR S/Res/1674 (2006) and S/Res/1738 (2006).

85 Summers 1989.

resources and provide a coherent benchmark against which conflicting demands can be assessed and prioritized'. This is generally referred to as the Centre of Gravity [CoG], defined as '*the characteristics, capabilities or localities from which a nation, an alliance, a military force or other grouping derives its freedom of action, physical strength or will to fight*'.[86] Historically, commanders have interpreted this as '*something physical that can be destroyed*'. To sum up: of all possible aims in war, the destruction of the enemy's forces always appeared to be as the highest.[87] In 1803, Jomini set down his principles of warfare, stating that '*strategy is the key to warfare; that all strategy is controlled by invariable scientific principles, and that these principles prescribe offensive action to mass forces against weaker enemy forces at some decisive point if strategy is to lead to victory*'.[88] The principle of manoeuvering the mass of an army so as to threaten the 'decisive points' in a theatre of war and then to hurl all available forces against a fraction of the enemy force defending those points was very simple. The Prussian greatest strategist, Von Clausewitz, argued that of all the possible aims at war, the destruction of the enemy's armed forces always appears the first: 'it is the overriding principle of war, and, so far as positive action is concerned, the principal way to achieve our object'.[89] Such direct approaches imply the physical destruction of the enemy's means to make war as a preliminary to the imposition of one's physical will on the enemy. The basic line is clear: in order to defeat the enemy, it is only necessary to defeat his armed forces.[90] The purpose of war was to seek battle and to impose one's own will on the opponent through violence. This has been for a long time the experience in conventional warfare according to the European model. Foch and Ludendorff, two disciples of Von Clausewitz, took him at his word to achieve the 'slaughter' during World War One. The underlying principle that war was aimed at the destruction of the enemy's army is also reflected in the St Petersburg Declaration of 1868 which provides that 'The only legitimate object which states should endeavor to accomplish during war is *to weaken the military forces of the enemy* [emphasis added].'

3.4.2 Guerilla and insurgency

Because revolutions and insurgencies represent a dramatic shift in understanding of the way society is organized, it is not surprising that they result in questions on the best way to counter them.[91] The difficult nature of guerilla warfare led to two

---

86 NATO Glossary of Terms (AAP-6)

87 Peters 2004, pp 24–32.

88 Jomini 1811, p 312.

89 von Clausewitz1984, p 258.

90 von Clausewitz1984, pp 90, 92, 95, 97, 99, 227–229, 236, 248, 259, 489, 527, 577, 596, and 624.

91 See supra nn 15–17. On the outcome of the Afghan conflict, see also Dorronsoro 2010.

different approaches to countering insurgencies: defeating the insurgents versus turning the loyalty of the people. One option is the enemy-centric approach, which generally results in an escalating and indiscriminate use of firepower. Consequently, the result will often be an upward spiral of civilian alienation. Such direct methods imply the physical destruction of the enemy's means to make war as a preliminary to the imposition of one's physical will on the enemy.[92] The other option is the indirect or population-centric approach. Those methods seek to attain the political objective of the conflict by avoiding a frontal clash between opposing forces through political action and security operations. Defeating the insurgency becomes then a matter of "separating the fish from the water" by dividing the insurgents from the local population. Winning that support becomes crucial in a COIN campaign, which should respect the following principles: have a clear political aim, function in accordance with the law (rule of law), adopt an overall plan, give priority to defeating the political subversion and secure its base areas first.[93] Out of the characteristics of COIN (in Afghanistan), a center of gravity develops (support of the population). That is the point against which all our energies should be directed.

3.4.3 COIN Operation: what about the law?

3.4.3.1 Combatant and POW status

The determination of combatant status has become more challenging since most conflicts are no longer waged between the regular armed forces of belligerent states, but between governmental forces and insurgent groups or other organized armed groups. Doubts may arise as to whether persons, having committed hostile acts, have combatant status and consequently may claim and enjoy POW protection once they have fallen into the hands of the enemy. Although terrorists/ insurgents shall generally not be entitled to combatant status, it will nevertheless be necessary to analyze each situation on a case-by-case basis. For example, Al Qaeda members who fought in Afghanistan along with the Taliban forces against the US armed forces could qualify as combatants provided they meet the cumulative criteria of Geneva Convention III. However, the fact that none of them was wearing a distinctive sign (or uniform) is a sufficient element not to confer them POW status if taken prisoner. Since the distinctive sign requirement was not met by the whole group, Al Qaeda failed to qualify the criteria *in se*. If the members of Al Qaeda do not qualify as combatants, what is their status under customary international law? In armed conflicts, all persons who are not combatants remain

---

92 O'Neill 1968, p 185.

93 Thompson 1972, pp 50–60.

civilians.[94] In other words, there is no legal vacuum whereby certain categories of persons, even if categorized as '*enemy combatants*',[95] would not fall under the protection regime of Geneva Convention III or Geneva Convention IV.[96] However, the fact that a person falls under the protection regime of Geneva Convention IV does not provide them with immunity if they have directly engaged in hostilities.

3.4.3.2 Insurgents and their direct participation in hostilities

Combatants and other individuals who directly engage in hostilities are legitimate military targets.[97] The protection from attack afforded to civilians by Article 51 of Additional Protocol I is suspended when and for such time as they directly participate in hostilities.[98] To take a "direct" part in hostilities includes "acts of war which by their nature or purpose are likely to cause actual harm to the personnel and material of the enemy armed forces".[99] As explained by the ICTY in *Kupreškić*: 'The protection of civilians and civilian objects provided by modern international law may cease entirely or be reduced or suspended (...) if a group of civilians takes up arms (...) and engages in fighting against the enemy belligerent, they may be legitimately attacked by the enemy belligerent whether or not they meet the requirements laid down in Article 4(A)(2) of the Third Geneva Convention of 1949'.[100] Article 44(3) of Additional Protocol I states that in order to promote the protection of the civilian population from the effects of hostilities, combatants are obliged to distinguish themselves from the civilian population while they are engaged in an attack or in a military operation preparatory to an attack. It recognizes, however, that there are situations where 'owing to the nature

---

94 HCJ 769/02, supra n 13, at pp 485–488. The Court concluded that members of Palestinian terrorist organizations cannot be considered combatants, and must therefore be considered civilians.

95 According to an Order issued by Wolfowitz, the term 'enemy combatant' shall mean 'an individual who was part of or supporting Taliban or al Qaeda forces, or associated forces that are engaged in hostilities against the United States or its coalition partners. This includes any person who has committed a belligerent act or has directly supported hostilities in aid of enemy armed forces.' (Order of 7 July 2004).

96 On the status and detention of enemy combatants: Cassel 2009; Davidson and Gibson 2009; Deeks 2009; Hakimi 2009; Mc Loughlin et al. 2009; Olson 2009b; Chaffee 2009; Guiora 2009; Olson 2009a; Petty 2009; Waxman 2009; Altenburg Jr 2009; Lohr 2005; Camera 2006a, 2006b; Rona 2008; Sadat 2005; Sadat 2009; Yin 2007; Greenhouse 2008; Nanda 2009; Harris 2003; Roberts 2004; Watkin 2005b; Sassoli 2006.

97 On targeting and immunity of non-combatants, see also Roscini 2005.

98 See also the findings of the Inter-American Commission on Human Rights in the *Abella* Case, IACommHR, 18 November 1997, *Abella* Case, §178.

99 *Strugar* Case, para 178.

100 ICTY, *Prosecutor* v *Kupreškić* et al., Case No. IT-95-16-T, T.Ch.II, 14 January 2000 (hereinafter: *Kupreškić* Case), paras 522–523.

of the hostilities an armed combatant cannot so distinguish himself'. In such cases, the individual shall retain their combatant status provided they carry their arms openly during each military engagement and during such time as they are visible to the adversary while engaged in a military deployment preceding the launching of an attack in which they are to participate. This provision of Protocol I remains very controversial and does in fact provide no added value for military forces in how to deal with insurgents who do not distinguish themselves from the civilian population and seek shelter by intermixing with the civilian population.[101] However, if the protection of the civilian population is to remain a core principle of the law of armed conflict, one cannot accept that insurgents misuse those protective provisions by acting double capped: in other words, where they are a fighter by night and peaceful civilian by day.[102] This protective regime is even more problematic having regard to the interpretation of the ICRC on the notion of DPH under IHL.[103]

According to the DHP Guidance, organized armed groups constitute the armed forces of a non-state party to the conflict (in non-international armed conflict).[104] This is an accurate statement of the law.[105] Indeed, insofar as civilians join organized armed groups (membership) in the context of and in connection with an armed conflict, they lose their protection as civilians and become a legitimate military target for the entire period of the armed conflict, unless they become *hors de combat* or permanently/definitely leave the armed group. Unfortunately, the DPH Guidance goes further by stating that while such armed groups constitute the armed forces of a non-state party, they consist '*only of individuals whose continuous function is to take a direct part in hostilities ("continuous combat function").*[106] By introducing the notion of "*continuous combat function*", the ICRC has created a fundamental discrepancy between, on the one hand, members of the armed forces, who by incorporation become a legitimate target regardless of their function (combatant or non-combatant) and, on the other hand, insurgents who can only be subject to attack when they assume this "*continuous combat function*".' This is not a restatement of the law as it stands today. The DPH Guidance offers no (convincing) arguments at all to support its thesis of why non-combatants, such as cooks and drivers, could be targeted when they are members of the regular armed

101 Jensen 2007.

102 In the same way Dinstein 2004, p 29.

103 Melzer 2009.

104 Melzer 2009, p 36.

105 See also Kretzmer 2005, p 271: 'The logical conclusion of the definition of a non-international armed conflict as one between the armed forces of a state and an organized armed group is that members of *both* the armed forces and the organized armed group are combatants. While these combatants do not enjoy the privileges of combatants in an international armed conflict, *they may be attacked* by the other party to the conflict. [...] According to this view, *if an armed conflict exists between the United States and al-Qaeda, active members of al-Qaeda are combatants who may be targeted*' [Emphasis added].

106 Melzer 2009, p 36.

forces, while those same cooks and drivers would be entitled to civilian protection when performing exactly the same function in an organized armed group. As stated by Mc DONALD, 'the term "direct participation in hostilities" itself is somewhat misleading as it suggests that only direct participation in a literal sense in activities amounting to attacks or which enable the launching of attacks on an enemy are covered. On the contrary, it is generally and increasingly considered that there are many activities which involve a more indirect role for civilians, where the civilian is more than one or more steps (geographically or temporally) away from the actual application of violence (which may be virtual rather than physical) and may not even consider him or herself to be a direct participant in hostilities, and which do not actually involve attacks in the literal or kinetic sense, or where the causality relation is more indirect, yet which are also considered as direct participation in hostilities.'[107]

Instead of closing the gap, the ICRC Guidance might be read as an encouragement for insurgents and terrorists to join such groups since they would only lose their immunity from attack insofar they unambiguously perform a '*continuous combat function*' (in contrast to all other functions which are necessary for the organized armed group in order to fight the regular armed forces). The DPH Guidance is therefore inaccurate, legally incorrect, disconnected from reality and a dangerous regression of the LOAC.[108] Indeed, if the notion of 'direct participation in the hostilities' is to have any meaning at all, a distinction should be made between civilians who take up arms occasionally ('individually') and civilians who are members of organized armed groups ('collectively'). In other words, a different approach should be envisaged to counter the *individual* direct participation in hostilities from the *collective* direct participation in hostilities. In the latter case, the membership approach as envisaged by the ICRC fails on critical issues and is at odds with state practice as well. I firmly support the view that members of organized armed groups cannot shield themselves from military action based on a restrictive interpretation of the concept of 'direct participation in hostilities'. Watkin argues that 'a strong argument can be made that members of a terrorist organization involved in an armed conflict should remain at risk of being targeted as long as they act as "combatants" (albeit without lawful status). Their status as "unprivileged belligerents" would be determined by the participation of their group in an armed conflict and the function that the "individuals" perform within the organization. This could include applying the basic military staff structure (personnel, intelligence, operations, logistics, civil military relations, communications, etc.) to a non-state fighting organization as a form of template to identify where those individual participants might fit.'[109] Such persons are and remain

[107] McDonald 2004, p 16.

[108] For a comprehensive critique of the DPH Study, see in particular Watkin 2010. Other contributions include Schmitt 2010; Boothby 2010; Hays Parks 2010.

[109] Watkin 2005a, pp 312–313.

legitimate targets on a 24/7 basis, regardless their 'continuous combat function', unless they are rendered '*hors de combat*'.

3.4.3.3 The principle of distinction in COIN: how to distinguish?

A. Hostile act/hostile intent

Having regard to the fact that insurgents in Afghanistan remain valid military targets, based on their membership (regardless of their function) of armed groups fighting the multinational forces in Afghanistan, it remains sometimes difficult to distinguish between the insurgents and the civilian population, since the insurgents continuously fail to distinguish themselves from that civilian population.[110] Indeed, status based targeting is only feasible to the extent that the enemy forces comply with their legal obligations to distinguish themselves from the civilian population. Whereas the killing and/or capturing of enemy combatants in armed conflicts remains valid, one needs to recognize that in COIN operations criteria other than status need to be developed,[111] such as the commission of hostile acts (hereinafter HA)[112] or hostile intents (hereinafter HI).[113] It should be recalled that engaging enemy forces under the HA/HI theory is not a substitute for status based targeting. It merely provides additional criteria to engage enemy forces or individuals whose status of 'enemy combatant' cannot be deduced in the absence of the required distinctive sign.[114] Whereas enemy combatants lend a contribution to the war effort and may be killed under the principle of military necessity, the HA/HI based targeting of individuals in COIN operations only supplements this status based killing in the sense that the 'contribution to the enemy's war effort' of some enemy persons can only be observed via the commission of HA/HI.

Secondly, it goes without saying that known members of insurgent groups can be targeted on a 24/7 basis whether or not they personally endanger the lives or

[110] Benvenisti 2010, p 352.

[111] In *Galić*, the Trial Chamber of the ICTY recognized that it may be difficult in certain circumstances to ascertain the status of particular persons in the population. (ICTY, *Prosecutor* v *Stanislav Galić*, Case No. IT-98-29-T, T.Ch.I, 5 December 2003, para 50).

[112] Hostile act is defined as 'an attack or other use of force a nation, the Force or other designated persons or property'. (Mandsager 2009, Appendix 4 to Annex A, p 82). Compare with Bill and Marsh 2010, p 75: 'An attack or other use of force against the United States, U.S. forces, or other designated persons or property. It also includes force used directly to preclude or impede the mission and/or duties of U.S. forces, including the recovery of U.S. personnel or vital U.S. government property.'

[113] Hostile intent is defined as 'the threat of an imminent hostile act' (Mandsager, 2009). Compare with Bill and Marsh 2010, p 75: 'The threat of imminent use of force against the United States, U.S. forces, or other designated persons or property. It also includes the threat of force to preclude or impede the mission and/or duties of U.S. forces, including the recovery of U.S. personnel or vital U.S. government property.'

[114] The term 'enemy combatant' is used here in a generic way.

interests of the other party to the conflict.[115] Engaging persons under HA/HI does not exclude the targeting of insurgents who are members of 'declared hostile forces'.[116] Known leaders and key personnel of insurgent movements do not need to demonstrate any HA/HI in order to be targetable.[117] 'Engagement criteria' under HA/HI theories are merely additional safeguards in order to enhance the protection of the civilian population.[118] Examples of HA/HI include for example the laying of mines or IED,[119] deployment to fighting/shooting positions/rocket launching installations. In practice, it will not always be easy to determine if a particular act constitutes an HA/HI.[120]

B. Minimum force

The aforementioned principles highlight the necessity that COIN forces must use '*minimum force*' in support of the government's effort to establish legitimacy at the expense of the insurgents.[121] Military operations that do not exercise '*minimum force*' instead diminish the support of the local population. The doctrine of minimum force forbids thus 'the use of a sledgehammer to protect the nut inside the shell'.[122] It should be recalled here that the use of the term '*minimum force*' in no way supports the erroneous statement of the ICRC in its DPH Guidance according to which human rights law would prevail over the LOAC in times of armed conflict.[123]

---

115 Kretzmer 2005, p 191.

116 Declared Hostile Force is 'any civilian, paramilitary or military force, or terrorist that has been declared hostile by appropriate U.S. authority', (Bill and Marsh 2010, p 75).

117 In the same way, Bill and Marsh 2010, p 75: 'Once a force has been declared "hostile", U.S. units may engage it without observing a hostile act or demonstrating a hostile intent; i.e. the basis for engagement shifts from conduct to status'.

118 On several occasions, the Security Council reaffirmed the necessity to protect the civilian population in armed conflicts (S/Res/1265 (1999), S/Res/1296 (2000), S/Res/1674 (2006), S/Res/1755 (2007)).

119 IED: Improvised Explosive Devise.

120 See Schmitt 2007, p 58.

121 See also Appendix 5 of Annex A in the ROE Handbook (Mandsager 2009). In the context of this paper, minimum force includes deadly force.

122 Statement made by Addison 2005, p 30.

123 The ICTY observed that in situations falling short of an armed conflict human rights law restricts the usage of lethal force by state agents 'to what is no more than absolutely necessary and which is strictly proportionate to certain objectives'. However, when hostilities amount to an armed conflict 'the question what constitutes an arbitrary deprivation of life is interpreted according to the standards of international humanitarian law, where a different proportionality test applies'. (*Boskoški* Case, supra n 64, para 178).

3.4.3.4 Targeting: close air support in COIN

Since winning the hearts and minds of the civilian population becomes crucial in all COIN campaign, it follows that reducing civilian casualties (hereinafter CIVCAS) will play a major role, especially when powerful air assets are engaged in support of the ground troops, as demonstrated by the tragic Kunduz incident when on 4 September 2009, when a German officer ordered an air strike resulting in the death of up to 142 persons. Aiming at zero CIVCAS will consequently influence both the principles of distinction and proportionality at the tactical and operational level.

A. (Positive) identification

In order to comply with the principle of distinction, a clear distinction should be made between two concepts: identification (ID) and positive identification (PID). The first element of the two prong test to be satisfied is the ID. Identification of the target refers to its geographical location. Both the pilot and the forward air controller (FAC) who will guide the pilot to his objective need to be sure of the target coordinates. The aim is to avoid striking the wrong objective. Identification can be achieved through visual identification, infrared signature, radar signature, electronic signature, etc.[124] PID, on the other hand, refers to the nature of the target as a military objective (Article 52(2) GPI).[125] The difficulty here is to determine who bears the responsibility for the PID: the pilot, the ground force commander (GFC) or the FAC? Both the pilot and the GFC have a role to play. The primary responsibility lies with the GFC. Unless the CAS mission was pre-planned, in which case PID can be performed at an earlier stage, the GFC CAS missions will be flown when ground forces act in self-defense or when confronted with enemy HA/HI. In such cases, he has the primary responsibility to conduct both ID and PID. The pilot, however, based on the information reasonable available to him, will also PID the target before the attack in order to be reasonably sure that the target meets the requirements of a military objective. PID can be achieved visually or by other means, e.g., by querying the FAC.

B. Incidental/collateral damage

Secondly, based on the information from the FAC, the pilot can engage the target provided there is no excessive collateral damage (CD).[126] This CD

[124] Manual on International Law Applicable to Air and Missile Warfare (hereinafter: AMW Manual) 2009, Rule 40.

[125] PID is a reasonable certainty that the proposed target is a legitimate military target Schmitt (ed) 2009a,b, p 316.

[126] In the framework of this article, CD relates both to incidental loss to civilian lives and injury and damage to civilian objects. Technically, the LOAC term of 'incidental loss' refers to persons (death and injury), while the term 'damage' only refers to property. See Article 51(5)(b) API: 'Among others, the following types of attacks are considered as indiscriminate: an attack which may be expected to cause ***incidental loss*** *of civilian life, injury to civilians*, ***damage*** *to civilians objects*, or a combination thereof, which would be excessive [...]' [emphasis added]. In the same way: Article 57(2)(a)(ii) and 57(2)(b) of API.

evaluation constitutes the second prong of the test. Having regard to CIVCAS reduction as a strategic objective in COIN campaigns, planners need to develop formal CDE mechanisms, coupled with appropriate target engagement authority and restrictions on the weaponry used according to the CD assessment. When CD risk is low, engagement approval can be released at lower levels. However, where CD risks are medium to (very) high, the Joint Force Commander will retain target engagement authority at his level or delegate it to his subordinate commanders. In the latter case (where CD risk is high), the use of precision guided weapons is almost inevitable.[127] There are nevertheless situations were formal CDE assessment is not feasible, for example in case of self-defense. In such situations, the CD assessment will primarily be performed by the GFC on the field. From the above, it is clear that the main problem with the principle of proportionality is not whether or not it exists but what it means and how it is to be applied.[128]

3.4.3.5 Means of warfare

Where minimizing incidental damage to civilians and civilian objects is crucial in COIN operations for mission accomplishment and winning the hearts and minds of the population, less lethal capacities can play a major role and therefore constitute a force multiplier. As stated by Colonel Siniscalchi in discussing the need for the greater use of non-lethal weapons and noting the importance of the '*high regard for life in modern democracies*': 'Recent conflicts validate the importance of this factor in modern conflict … President Clinton approved the Bosnia deployment based on the Chairman's projection of a minimum number of civilian casualties. During execution, the target selection and approval process for military operations in Bosnia required extensive, direct involvement from the senior military commanders in an effort to minimize unintended casualties and damage. The desire to minimize [casualties] friendly, civilian, and enemy forces permeates the US decision process.'[129]

A. Riot control agents

An area where the law of armed conflict is affected by the changing nature of warfare concerns the means and methods of warfare. If reducing CIVCAS is a key factor in winning the hearts and minds of the local population, it is clear that this affects the weapons choice in the conduct of hostilities.[130] This has a direct effect

[127] AMW Manual, supra n 124, Rule 8.

[128] Final Report to the Prosecutor by the Committee Established to Review the NATO Bombing Campaign Against the Federal Republic of Yugoslavia, Klip/Sluiter, ALC V, p 22, para 48.

[129] Siniscalshi 1998.

[130] See in particular the US Army/Marine Corps Counterinsurgency Field Manual (The University of Chicago Press, 2007), p. xxv.

on the use of non-lethal weapons (hereinafter NLW)[131] in the sense that if an alternative exists between the use of riot control agents (hereinafter RCA) and lethal weapons, one could claim that the use of NLW is in conformity with the principle of proportionality and, according to the circumstances, better suited to comply with the required use of 'minimum force'. However, the use of NLW is not intended to restrict or prohibit the use of lethal weapons in accordance with the applicable ROEs. Whereas the use of NLW can contribute significantly in minimizing incidental damage to civilians and civilian property, their use is dramatically reduced by existing treaty law. Once again, one can legitimately question the 'obsolete' character of some legal provisions having regard to new technological developments which allow for reduced casualties in war, such as the 1993 Chemical Weapons Convention,[132] the 1972 Biological Weapons Convention, the 1995 Protocol on Blinding Laser Weapons,[133] and the 1997 Convention on the Prohibition of the Use, Stockpiling, Production and Transfer of Anti-Personnel Mines and on their Destruction.[134]

Under Article I of the CWC, states agreed 'never under any circumstances to use chemical weapons'. Moreover, Article I(5) of the CWC expressly provides that 'Each State Party undertakes not to use riot control agents as a method of warfare'. Additionally, Article II(9)(d) of the CWC stipulates that the use of such agents in the context of law enforcement, including domestic riot control purposes, is not prohibited. The exact scope of these provisions is far from clear. Nevertheless, it seems undisputed that in peace operations, the use of RCA is not prohibited under the CWC. Additionally, even in times of armed conflict, the use of RCA remains legal, insofar as they are not used as a 'method of warfare' against enemy combatants.[135] As stated by Ambassador Ledogar during the CWC negotiations: 'There are quite legitimate uses for non-lethal chemicals for law enforcement, in defensive military modes and to safe lives in a variety of circumstances'.[136] Consequently, there are no reasons to assume that the use thereof would be illegal when used for crowd control type interventions (e.g., demonstrations at the main gate of a military compound or manned checkpoints, maintaining public order in occupied territory or in detention facilities, ...), hostage rescue operations and even special search missions (e.g., weapon cashes, ...), provided that such use complies with the basic principles of the law of armed conflict (discrimination, proportionality and unnecessary suffering). In such cases, RCA are not used as a

[131] According to NATO Policy, 'non-lethal weapons' are weapons that 'are explicitly designed and developed to incapacitate or repel personnel, with a low probability of fatality or permanent injury, or to disable equipment with minimal undesired damage or impact on the environment' (hereinafter NLW).

[132] 32 ILM 800.

[133] 19 ILM 1523.

[134] 28 ILM 1507.

[135] Boothby 2009, p 136.

[136] *Contra*: Fidler 2005, p 545.

'method of warfare', but merely as a 'means of warfare'.[137] With regard to other conventional restrictions or prohibitions, the same reasoning applies.[138] Notwithstanding the good intentions of the drafters of arms control regulations, such as the CWC, one cannot disregard the seeming contradiction between, for example, the obligation to restrict/prohibit the use of RCA in times of armed conflict and the obligation to minimize incidental/collateral damage to civilians and civilian property.[139] As we will see, the same applies for the use of expanding bullets.

B. Expanding bullets

Another domain where the use of means of warfare differ according to the classification of the conflict (law enforcement *versus* armed conflict) is the use of expanding bullets. To what extent is the prohibition contained in the Hague Declaration (IV, 3) also applicable in a non-international armed conflict?[140] Having regard to the recurrent tactics of suicide-bombers in Afghanistan against checkpoints, convoys and entry posts, the military advantage of using expanding bullets in order to counter them should not be minimized. In the wording of Haines: 'If there is a clear need effectively to "stop" a suicide bomber, and these weapons are necessary for that purpose, arguably they should be regarded as lawful.'[141] According to the ICRC Customary Law Study, the use of expanding bullets is prohibited, even in non-international armed conflicts.[142] According to the Study, no official contrary state practice was found with respect to non-international armed conflicts, with the possible exception of the United States. However, the absence of state practice does not mean that states consider such use as illegal in non-international armed conflict.[143] In the same way, Boothby states that 'if it is accepted that an expanding bullet is the weapon of choice in certain particular circumstances which may arise both in the context of armed conflict and in law

137 According to Hays Parks, the CWC doesn't prohibit the use of RCA as 'means of warfare'. On the definition of 'means of warfare' versus 'methods of warfare', see Harper who defines 'methods of warfare' as 'methods used to systematically enable or multiply the use of lethal force against hostile enemies' (Harper 2001, pp 154–155. Compare with Schmitt using the term 'instrument of warfare' instead of 'method of warfare' in Schmitt 2000, p 290. Boothby defines 'means of warfare' as 'all weapons, platforms, and associated equipment used directly to deliver force during hostilities' and 'methods of warfare' as 'the way in which weapons are used in hostilities' (Boothby 2009, p 4).

138 Under Article I, (1) of the BWC, States agreed 'never under any circumstances to develop, produce, stockpile or otherwise acquire or retain microbial or other biological agents, or toxins [...]', thereby also denying the use of such agents or toxics (such as fuel degrading agents) against enemy material.

139 Contra Fry 2010, pp 538–539.

140 Declaration (IV, 3) Concerning Expanding Bullets, 1899, (Hague Declaration 3), para 1.

141 Haines 2007, p 272.

142 ICRC Customary Law Study, Vol I, Rule 77.

143 Greenwood 2001, 'There is very little indication in the practice of States that they have necessarily accepted the 1899 treaty as an authoritative statement of custom.'.

enforcement, is it really customary law that that weapon of choice is only to made available when the situation arises in law enforcement environment'?[144]

During the Review Conference of the ICC Statute in Kampala this year, it was agreed that the use of bullets which expand or flatten easily in the human body is also a violation of the laws and customs applicable in armed conflict of a non-international character, whereas the use of expanding ammunition for law enforcement operations is excluded from the ICC's jurisdiction. The understanding was that the crime is only committed 'if the perpetrator employs the bullets *to uselessly aggravate suffering or the wounding effect* upon the target of such bullets, as reflected in customary international law' [Emphasis added].[145] The prohibition on the use expanding bullets in armed conflicts has been interpreted through consistent state practice. This clarifies why current NATO standard projectiles and many other similar projectiles which may in some circumstances deform or fragment are lawful. This also explains why expanding bullets are only forbidden if their use would uselessly aggravate suffering or the wounding effect. Consequently, one cannot regard the use of expanding bullets in armed conflict as uselessly aggravating suffering or the wounding effect if this enhances the protection of the civilian population, e.g. when civilians are used as human shields by enemy fighters. As stated by Greenwood, the protection of combatants from unnecessary suffering is clearly a significant part of international law, but the protection of people who are not combatants at all is surely of far greater significance. One cannot regard suffering as unnecessary if it is inflicted for the purpose of protecting the civilian population. In other words, if the civilian population's protection is enhanced by the use of a particular weapon, then the adverse effects of that weapon on combatants cannot properly be regarded as unnecessary.[146]

3.5 Conclusion

It is submitted that different legal regimes applied in the context of the operations in Afghanistan. Up until the take-over by the new Government of the Islamic Republic of Afghanistan there existed:

- An international armed conflict between the US (and allies) and the Taliban;
- A non-international armed conflict between the US (and allies) and Al Qaeda (Al Qaeda no *de facto* organ of the Taliban);

[144] Boothby 2009, p 149. In the same way: The Manual on the Law of Non-International Armed Conflict With Commentary (IIHL, San Remo, 2006) pp 35–36: 'it is doubtful whether this age-old prohibition can be regarded as applicable in non-international armed conflict'.

[145] Resolution RC/Res.5 Adopted at the 12th Plenary Meeting of the Review Conference of the ICC, held in Kampala, deciding to adopt the amendment to Article 8(2)(e) of the Rome Statute of the International Criminal Court, contained in Annex I of the Resolution, available at http://www.icc-cpi.int/iccdocs/asp_docs/Resolutions/RC-Res.5-ENG.pdf.

[146] Greenwood 2001.

- An internationalized non-international armed conflict between the Northern Alliance and the Taliban.

Today, the situation can be resumed as follows:

- An enforcement action (Chapter VII) between the ISAF and the insurgents, in which ISAF Forces are engaged therein as combatants;
- A non-international armed conflict between the OEF Forces and Al Qaeda;
- A non-international armed conflict between the ANSF and the insurgents;
- A law enforcement operation between the GIRoA and the drug traffickers.

With regard to the conduct of hostilities, particular attention should be paid to the protection of the civilian population in COIN operations. Whereas the focus has shifted from the traditional 'kill and capture' theories to an approach that now looks to winning of the 'hearts and minds' of the population, the use of military force is and remains justifiable and necessary, although the use of 'minimum force' remains the key to success. In situations where insurgents do not comply with their obligations under the law of armed conflict and do not distinguish themselves from the population, self-restraint on the part of the military forces wins hearts and minds. Combatant status based fighting becomes less relevant in COIN operations and leads quite often to disproportionate use of force and excessive collateral damage among the civilian population. Particularly in situations where enemy forces do not distinguish themselves from the civilian population, a HA/HI based approach can reduce the risk of incidental damage. Although such a posture may involve an increased risk for the troops, one should never lose sight of the overall strategic end-state in COIN, namely winning the hearts and minds of the civilian population. Additionally, one should not minimize the advantages of using less-lethal capacities, such as RCA, and expanding bullets in order to enhance the civilian protection.

Finally, all members of organized armed groups in Afghanistan fighting the multinational forces are and remain legitimate military targets 24/7, regardless their function within those groups. As a consequence of their membership, they are precluded from the protections to which all civilians are entitled under international humanitarian law. In case of capture, they will not enjoy POW protection and can be prosecuted for their direct participation in hostilities.

References

Acharya UD (2009) War on terror or terror wars: the problem in defining terrorism. Denver JIL & Pol 37:653–679

Addison M (2005) In: Nagl JA (ed) Learning to eat soup with a knife, counterinsurgency lessons from Malaya and Vietnam. University of Chicago Press, Chicago

Alexandrov SA (1996) Self-defense and the use of force in international law. Kluwer Law International, The Hague

Altenburg JD Jr (2009) Just three mistakes. Case West Reserve JIL 42:11–19

Barbour SA, Salzman ZA (2008) The tangled web: the right of self-defense against non-state actors in the *Armed Activities* Case. NY Univ JIL & Pol (Special Issue) 40:53–106

Benjamin JJ (2009) In pursuit of justice: prosecuting terrorism cases in the Federal Courts, 2009 update and recent developments. Case West Reserve JIL 42:267–272

Bennoune K (2008) Terror/Torture. Berkeley JIL 26:3–61

Benvenisti E (2010) The legal battle to define the law on transnational asymmetric warfare. Duke J Comp & IL 20:339–359

Bill B, Marsh J (eds) (2010) Operational law handbook. Judge Advocate General's Legal Center and School, Charlottesville VA

Boothby WH (2009) Weapons and the law of armed conflict. Oxford University Press, Oxford

Boothby B (2010) And for such time as: the time dimension to direct participation in hostilities. NY Univ JIL & Pol 42:741–767

Brunnee J, Toope S (2005) Terrorism is also disrupting categories of international law, EJIL Forum, available at www.ejil.org/forum_WTC/ny-cassese-03.htlm

Bush GW (2002) Presidential military order on the detention, treatment and trial of certain non-citizens in the war against terrorism, 13 November 2001, Section 1, (a), ILM 41

Byers M (2002) Terrorism, the use of force and international law after 11 September. ICLQ 51:411–412

Camera P (2006a) The Guantanamo gap: can foreign nationals obtain redress for prolonged arbitrary detention and torture suffered outside the United States? Calif West ILJ 36:304–347

Camera S (2006b) The exploitation of legal loopholes in the name of national security: a case study on extraordinary renditions. Calif West ILJ 37:121–142

Cassel D (2009) International human rights law and security detention. Case West Reserve JIL 40:383–401

Cassese A (2007) The *Nicaragua* and *Tadić* tests revisited in light of the ICJ Judgment on genocide in Bosnia. EJIL 18:649–668

Chaffee D (2009) The cost of indefinitely kicking the can: why continued 'prolonged' detention is no solution to Guantánamo. Case West Reserve JIL 42:187–196

Crawford JR (2002) The International Law Commission's articles on state responsibility, Introduction, text and commentaries. Cambridge University Press, Cambridge

Davidson T, Gibson K (2009) Experts meeting on security detention report. Case West Reserve JIL 40:323–381

Deeks AS (2009) Administrative detention in armed conflict. Case West Reserve JIL 40:403–436

Delbrück J (2001) The fight against global terrorism: self-defense or collective security as international police action? Some comments on the international legal implications of the 'war against terrorism. GYIL 44:9–24

Di Filippo M (2008) Terrorist crimes and international co-operation: critical remarks on the definition and inclusion of terrorism in the category of international crimes. EJIL 19:533–570

Dinstein Y (1987) International legal response to terrorism, le droit international à l'heure de sa codification, mélange Roberto Ago, Milan, A. Giuffrè

Dinstein Y (2004) The conduct of hostilities under the law of international armed conflict. Cambridge University Press, Cambridge

Dinstein Y (2005) War, aggression and self-defense. Cambridge University Press, Cambridge

Dinstein Y (2009) Terrorism and Afghanistan. In: Schmitt MN (ed) The war in Afghanistan: a legal analysis, International Law Studies Vol. 85. Naval War College, Newport RI

Dorronsoro G (2010) Afghanistan at the breaking point, Carnegie Endowment for International Peace, available at http://carnegieendowment.org/publications/index.cfm?fa=view&id=42031

Doswald-Beck L (ed) (1995) San Remo manual on international law applicable to armed conflicts at sea. Cambridge Cambridge University Press, pp 114–161

Downes C (2004) Targeted killings' in an age of terror: the legality of the Yemen Strike. JCSL 9:277–294

Dusheine P (2008) Krijgsmacht, geweldgebruik en terreurbestrijding. Een onderzoek naar juridische aspecten van de rol van de strijdkrachten bij de bestrijding van terrorisme. Wolf Legal Publishers, Nijmegen

Fahmi N (2006) Terrorism is the world's problem. Duke J Comp & IL 16:157–167
Fidler DP (2005) The meaning of Moscow: 'Non-lethal' weapons and international law in the early 21st century. IRRC 859:525–552
Fitzpatrick J (2003) Speaking law to power: the war against terrorism and human rights. EJIL 14:241–264
Franck TM (2001) Terrorism and the right of self-defense. AJIL 95:839–843
Fry JD (2010) Gas smells awful: UN forces, riot-control agents, and the Chemical Weapon Convention. Michigan JIL 31:475–559
Gill TD (2003) The eleventh of september and the right in self-defense. In: Heere WP (ed) Terrorisme and the military, International legal implications. TMC Asser Press, The Hague, pp 23–37
Gill TD (2007) The temporal dimension of self-defense: anticipation, pre-emption, prevention and immediacy. In: Schmitt MN, Pejic J (eds) International law and armed conflict: exploring the faultlines. Essays in honour of Yoram Dinstein. Martinus Nijhoff Publishers, Leiden
Gray C (2000) International law and the use of force. Oxford University Press, Oxford
Greenhouse L (2008) The mystery of Guantánamo bay. Berkeley JIL 27:1–21
Greenspan A (2008) Are we fighting the right war. Cardozo J Int Comp Law 16:493–535
Greenwood C (2001) Legal aspects of current regulations. In: Third international workshop on wound ballistics. Thun, Switzerland, 12–20 March 2001
Guiora AM (2009) Not 'by all means necessary': a comparative framework for post 9/11-approaches to counterterrorism. Case West Reserve JIL 42:273–287
Haines S (2007) Weapons, means and methods of warfare. In: Wilmshurst E, Breau S (eds) Perspectives on the ICRC study on Customary international law. British Institute of International and Comparative Law and Cambridge, Cambridge University Press, London
Hakimi M (2009) International standards for detaining terrorism suspects: moving beyond the armed conflict-criminal divide. Case West Reserve JIL 40:593–650
Hammes TX (2004) The sling and the stone. Zenith Press, Stamford, NY
Hammes TX (2006) Countering evolved insurgent networks. Military Rev, July-August:18–26
Harper E (2001) A call for a definition of method of warfare in relation to the Chemical Weapon Convention. Naval Law Rev 48:138–167
Harris GC (2003) Terrorism, war and justice: the concept of the Unlawful enemy combatant. Loy LA I & CLR 26:31–46
Harting S (2008) Meeting America's Security Challenges Beyond Iraq, A conference report, Rand Corporation, 43 pp, available at http://www.rand.org/pubs/conf_proceedings/2008/RAND_CF246.pdf.
Hays Parks W (2010) Part IX of the ICRC 'Direct Participation in Hostilities' study: no mandate, no expertise, and legally incorrect. NY Univ JIL & Pol 42:770–799
Higgins R (1997) The general international law of terrorism. In: Higgins R, Flory M (eds) Terrorism and international law. Routledge, London, pp 13–28
Hoon G (2007) The legal response to global terror. Calif West ILJ 38:107–116
Isanga J (2009) Counter-terrorism and human rights: the emergence of a rule of customary int'l law from UN Resolutions. Denver JIL & Pol 37:223–255
Jensen ET (2007) The ICJ's 'Uganda Wall'. A barrier to the principle of distinction and an entry point for warfare. Denver JIL & Pol 35:241–274
Jinks D (2003a) September 11 and the laws of war. Yale JIL 28:1–49
Jinks D (2003b) State responsibility for the acts of private armed groups. Chic JIL 4:83–96
Jomini A (1811) Traité des grandes opérations militaires, contenant l'histoire des campagnes de Frédéric II, compares à celle de l'empereur Napoléon; avec un recueil des principes généraux de l'art de la guerre, 2nd edn, Vol. 2, Paris
Joyner CC (2003) International extradition and global terrorism: brining international criminals to justice. Loy LA I & Comp LR 25:493–542
Kalshoven F (1985) American Society of International Law: annual meetings proceedings, pp 114–117
Kielsgard MD (2006) A human rights approach to counter-terrorism. Calif West ILJ 36:249–302

Kissinger H (1969) The Vietnam negotiations. Foreign Aff 47/2:214
Kretzmer D (2005) Targeted killing of suspected terrorists: extra-judicial executions or legitimate means of defence? EJIL 16:171–212
Lohr JA (2005) A 'full and fair trial': can the executive ensure it alone? The case for judicial review of trials by Military Commissions at Guantánamo. Duke JCIL 15:387–410
Mandsager D (2009) Rules of engagement handbook. International Institute of Humanitarian Law, IIHL, San Remo
Manual on International Law Applicable to Air and Missile Warfare Bern (2009) Cambridge MA, Humanitarian Policy and Conflict Research
Martin JC (2006) Les règles internationales relatives à la lutte contre le terrorisme. Bruylant, Bruxelles
McLoughlin JP, Noone GP, Noone DC (2009) Security detention, terrorism, and the prevention imperative. Case West Reserve JIL 40:463–505
McDonald A (2004) The challenges to international humanitarian law and the principles of distinction and protection from the increased participation of civilians in hostilities, spotlight on issues of Contemporary Concern in International Humanitarian Law and International Criminal Law, Background working paper at a Round Table in Tehran
Melzer N (2009) Interpretive guidance on the notion of direct participation in hostilities under international humanitarian law. ICRC, Geneva
Moeckli D (2008) The emergence of terrorism as a distinct category in international law. Tex ILJ 44:157–183
Murphy SD (2008) Protean jus ad bellum. Berkeley JIL 27:22–51
Nanda VP (2009) Introductory essay: International Law implications of the United States – War on terror. Denver JIL & Pol 37:513–537
Neuman GL (2003) Humanitarian law and counterterrorist force. EJIL 14:183–298
O'Neill RJ (1968) Vietnam task: the 5th Battalion, Royal Australian Regiment. Southwood Press, Riverwood
Olson LM (2009a) Guantánamo Habeas Review: are the D.C. District Court's decisions consistent with IHL internment standards. Case West Reserve JIL 42:197–243
Olson LM (2009b) Practical challenges of implementing the complementarity between international humanitarian and human rights law, demonstrated by the Procedural Regulation of Internment in Non-International Armed Conflict. Case West Reserve JIL 40:437–461
Peters R (2004) In praise of atrition. Parameters 34:24–32
Petty KA (2009) Are you there, Geneva? It's me, Guantánamo. Case West Reserve JIL 42:171–186
Pictet JS (ed) (1958) The Geneva convention of 12 August 1949 commentary Part IV. ICRC, Geneva
Roberts A (2004) Righting wrongs or wronging rights? The United States and human rights post-September 11. EJIL 15:721–749
Rona G (2008) A bull in a china shop: the war on terror and international law in the United States. Calif West ILJ 39:136–159
Roscini M (2005) Targeting and contemporary aerial bombardment. ICLQ 54:412–444
Rowe P (2002) Responses to terror: the new 'war'. Melb JIL 3:301–321
Sadat LN (2005) Ghost prisoners and black sites: extraordinary renditions and international law. Case West Reserve JIL 37:309–342
Sadat LN (2009) A presumption of guilt: the unlawful enemy combatant and the U.S. war on terror. Denver JIL & Pol 37:539–553
Santopinto F (2010) Afghanistan: échec annoncé d'un changement de stratégie improbable et trop tardif. Les Nouvelles du GRIP 55:1–6
Sassoli M (2006) Transnational armed groups and international humanitarian law, occasional paper series, Harvard University, Cambridge MA, Humanitarian Policy and Conflict Research, 45 pp

Saura J (2003) Some remarks on the use of force against terrorism in contemporary international law and the role of the Security Council. Loy LA I & Comp LR 26:7–30
Schmitt MN (2000) Humanitarian law and the environment. Denver JIL & Pol 28:265–323
Schmitt MN (2008a) 'Change Direction 2006': Israeli operations in Lebanon and the International Law of self-defense. Mich JIL 29:127–164
Schmitt MN (2008b) Current perspectives on regulating means of warfare. Proceedings of the Bruges colloquium, 18–19 October 2007, p 58
Schmitt MN (2009a) Targeting and International Humanitarian Law in Afghanistan. In: Schmitt MN (ed) The war in Afghanistan: a legal analysis, International Law studies, vol 85. Naval War College, Newport RI
Schmitt MN (ed) (2009b) The war in Afghanistan: a legal analysis, International Law Studies Vol 85. Newport RI, Naval War College, 567 pp
Schmitt MN (2010) Deconstructing direct participation in hostilities: the constitutive elements. NY Univ JIL & Pol 42:697–738
Schöndorf RS (2004) Extra-state armed conflict: is there a need for a new legal regime? NY Univ JIL & Pol 37:5–7
Schrijver NJ (2001) Responding to international terrorism: moving the frontiers of international law for 'enduring freedom? NILR 48:271–295
Schultz G (1986) Low-intensity warfare: the challenge of ambiguity, National Defense University. ILM p 206
Sharp WG (2000) The use of armed force against terrorism: American hegemony or impotence. Chic JIL, pp 37–48
Shy J, Collier TW (1986) Revolutionary war. In: Paret P (ed) Makers of modern strategy, from Machiavelli to the nuclear age. Princeton University Press, Princeton, NJ, pp 815–862
Siniscalshi J (1998) Non-lethal technologies: implications for military strategy, occasional paper no. 3, Alabama, Center for Strategy and Technology, Air War College, Air University, Maxwell Air Force Base
Sorel J-M (2003) Some questions about the definition of terrorism and the fight against its financing. EJIL 14:365–378
Summers H (1989) A war is a war is a war is a war. In: Thompson LB (ed) Low intensity conflicts: the pattern of warfare in the modern world. Lexington Books, Lexington
Tams CJ (2009) The use of force against terrorists. EJIL 20:359–397
Thompson RF (1972) Defeating communist insurgency: experiences from Malaya and Vietnam. Chatto & Windus, London
van Aggelen J (2009) The consequences of unlawful preemption and the legal duty to protect the human rights of its victims. Case West Reserve JIL 42:21–89
Vite S (2009) Typology of armed conflicts in international humanitarian law: legal concepts and actual situations. IRRC 873:69–94
von Clausewitz C (1984) On war. In: Howard ME, Paret P (eds and transl), Princeton University Press, Princeton NJ
Watkin K (2005a) Canada/United States military interoperability and humanitarian law issues: land mines, terrorism, military objectives and targeting. Duke J Comp & IL 15:312–313
Watkin K (2005 B) Warriors without rights? Combatants, unprivileged belligerents, and the struggle over legitimacy. occasional paper studies Harvard University, Cambridge MA, Humanitarian Policy and Conflict Research, 75 pp
Watkin K (2010) Opportunity lost: organized armed groups and the ICRC 'Direct participation in hostilities' Interpretive Guidance. NY Univ JIL & Pol 42:642–693
Waxman MC (2009) Guantánamo, habeus corpus, and standards of proof: viewing the law through multiple lenses. Case West Reserve JIL 42:245–266
Waxman MC (2010) The structure of terrorism threats and the laws of war. Duke J Comp & IL 20:429–455
Wilkinson P (1996) The role of the military in combating terrorism in a democratic society. Terror Political Violence 8(3):1–11

Yin T (2007) Distinguishing soldiers and non-state actors: clarifying the Geneva convention's regulation of interrogation of captured combatants through positive inducements. Boston Univ ILJ 26:227–276

Zemach A (2010) The unpleasant responsibilities of international human rights law. Denver JIL & Pol 38:421–461

Chapter 4
Civilian Intelligence Agencies and the Use of Armed Drones

Ian Henderson

> Drones have been credited with eliminating senior leaders of the Taliban and other insurgent groups, and accounts of the recent addition of an American citizen to the target list have received widespread attention. These reports have raised serious questions about whether targeted killing and drone use comport with the relevant international and domestic laws.
> Tierney J, Chairman, Subcommittee on National Security and Foreign Affairs, Opening Statement, Hearing on 'Rise of the Drones II: Examining the Legality of Unmanned Targeting', Committee on Oversight and Government Reform, US House of Representatives (2010), http://oversight.house.gov/index.php?option=com_content&task=view&id=4903&Itemid=30.

Contents

Wing Commander. This paper was written in a personal capacity and does not necessarily represent the views of the Australian Department of Defence or the Australian Defence Force.

I. Henderson (✉)
Royal Australian Air Force, Melbourne, Australia
e-mail: henderis.aus@centcom.mil

M.N. Schmitt et al. (eds.), *Yearbook of International Humanitarian Law Volume 13, 2010*, DOI: 10.1007/978-90-6704-811-8_4,

4.1 Introduction

The use of drones to conduct lethal strikes by the United States against people associated with the Taliban and al Qaeda has been the subject of many recent publications—featuring prominently in the news media and online commentaries[1]; as the subject of two United States House of Representatives sub-committee hearings[2]; and forming a large part of the report by the United Nations Special Rapporteur on extrajudicial, summary or arbitrary executions.[3] Interestingly though, with the first strike widely attributed to the CIA occurred in 2002,[4] the use of this technology is over a decade old. Indeed, the appropriate role for the United States Central Intelligence Agency (CIA) in the use of armed drones, and the legality of the CIA being involved in lethal action, was being discussed even before the capability was ready to be operationally fielded.[5]

Recently, the Legal Adviser for the US Department of State in an address to the American Society of International Law said:

> 'With respect to the subject of targeting, which has been much commented upon in the media and international legal circles, there are obviously limits to what I can say publicly. What I can say *is that it is the considered view of this Administration—and it has certainly been my experience during my time as Legal Adviser—that U.S. targeting practices, including lethal operations conducted with the use of unmanned aerial vehicles, comply with all applicable law, including the laws of war.*'[6]

To analyse this statement, we need to identify what are the legal issues. The Chairman of the US House of Representatives Subcommittee on National Security and Foreign Affairs recently identified, among others, three main questions on the use of armed drones:

a. Who can be a legitimate target?
b. Where can that person be legally targeted?

---

[1] See Solis 2010; Thiesen 2010; Mayer 2009.

[2] See Tierney 2010.

[3] Alston 2010.

[4] 'On 3 November 2002, over the desert near Sanaa, Yemen, a Central Intelligence Agency-controlled Predator drone aircraft tracked an SUV containing six men. One of the six, Qaed Salim Sinan al-Harethi, was known to be a senior al-Qa'ida lieutenant suspected of having played a major role in the 2000 bombing of the destroyer USS Cole. He 'was on a list of "high-value" targets whose elimination, by capture or death, had been called for by President Bush.' The United States and Yemen had tracked al-Harethi's movements for months. Now, away from any inhabited area, the Predator fired a Hellfire missile at the vehicle. The six occupants, including al-Harethi, were killed. Solis 2007, p 130. See also Alston 2010, para 19.

[5] Final Report of the National Commission on Terrorist Attacks Upon the United States, National Commission on Terrorist Attacks Upon the United States, 2004, pp 211–212, www.9-11commission.gov/report/911Report.pdf.

[6] Koh 2010.

c. Does it make a difference if the military carries out an attack, or whether other civilian government entities may legally conduct such attacks?[7]

The focus of this article is on the third question. However, the answer to any one of these questions might vary based on the answers to any other of the questions. A trivial legal answer to each question could be 'anyone', 'anywhere' and 'no', as in the right factual situation with very tightly constrained parameters, there will be a suitable legal authority or legal defence for any person to use an armed drone against another person anywhere in the world.

While the discussion has tended to focus on US activities, and particularly those of the CIA in Pakistan and other regions (e.g., Yemen), the purpose of this article is to discuss the legal issues in a more general context. Much of the detail of many actions by governments is and will remain for some time classified. However, there 'are ways to articulate the legal basis of these policies without having to reveal operational matters ....'[8] And by discussing the legal issues in a general context, hopefully the paper will be useful to a broader audience than one purely concerned with contemporary CIA actions.

4.2 What Are Armed Drones?

The current terminology being used in the US media and other areas debating this issue is 'drone.' Other common terms are unmanned (or uninhabited) aerial vehicle, unmanned (or uninhabited) aircraft system, or the more recent remotely piloted aircraft.[9] When some form of armament is also involved, sometimes the word 'combat' is after unmanned (or uninhabited).[10] Technology-wise:

> 'Unmanned aircraft systems generally consist of (1) multiple aircraft, which can be expendable or recoverable and can carry lethal or non-lethal payloads; (2) a flight control station; (3) information and retrieval or processing stations; and (4) in some cases, wheeled land vehicles that carry launch and recovery platforms.'[11]

Unarmed drones can have a variety of civilian applications.[12] Basic technical data on some of the drones operated by the US military is set out in a recent statement

---

[7] Tierney 2010.

[8] Anderson 2010a, p 11.

[9] Usually abbreviated to 'UAV', 'UAS' and 'RPA' respectively.

[10] Usually abbreviated to 'UCAV.'

[11] Sullivan 2010, p 4.

[12] For a brief discussion on civilian uses and for some statistics on US military use, see Fagan 2010. A very good overview is also available at Program on Humanitarian Policy and Conflict Research, Commentary on the HPCR Manual on International Law Applicable to Air and Missile Warfare, 2009, pp 54–55.

to a US House of Representatives sub-committee.[13] Not all military drones are armed. For example, some carry non-lethal payloads and might engage in only intelligence collection or battlefield surveillance. These surveillance capabilities are also being fielded by groups other than conventional militaries.[14] Relevantly for this paper, the use of armed drones is not limited to military forces. While there is no overt public statement from the US Administration, it is widely assumed that the CIA is using armed drones.[15] Indeed:

> '... the program has grown to such an extent that, according to a Reuters tally, the nearly 60 missiles fired from the CIA's drones in Pakistan in the first 4 months of this year [2010] roughly matched the number fired by all of the drones piloted by the U.S. military in neighboring Afghanistan—the recognized war zone—during the same time period.'[16]

This paper uses the term 'armed drone' to make it clear that the discussion concerns an uninhabited aircraft with a lethal payload. The paper does not deal with systems where there is no human involvement. One or more human beings are involved in piloting the drone and controlling the onboard weapon—it is just that the operators are remote from the aircraft.[17]

4.3 The Applicable Legal Regime

The use of armed drones can be analysed under either domestic or international law. The applicable domestic law for use of force by a civilian intelligence operative would be, as a minimum, the operative's own national domestic law.[18] In addition, other domestic law might also apply—e.g., third-country domestic law might apply if the intelligence operative engages in an act of force:

a. while in a third country;
b. that has an effect in a third country even though initiated from his or her own sovereign territory; or

[13] Fagan 2010, p 17. For a succinct and clear description of some modern military armed drones, see Garlasco 2009, pp 10–12.

[14] 'We already know that during the Israel-Lebanon war in 2006, Hezbollah deployed three surveillance UAVs that it acquired from Iran.' Tierney 2010.

[15] For example, Alston 2010, para 20.

[16] Entous 2010. While there are many reasons why a comparison with operations in Afghanistan may be misleading (not the least of which is that focusing on strikes from drones in Afghanistan is looking at only one available weapon system), this quote does nonetheless provide an example of public perception.

[17] See Anderson 2010a, pp 1–2, who also states that the issues associated with '"Autonomous" firing systems, in which machines might make decisions about the firing of weapons, raise entirely separate issues.'

[18] This is clearly the case where the operator is geographically located on the intelligence operative's own sovereign territory. However, it can also be true where the operator is outside his or her own sovereign territory if the relevant legislation is crafted to deal with the actions of the operator and has extraterritorial effect.

c. where, arguably, a third-country national is adversely affected by the use of force even where both the intelligence operative and third-country national were on the intelligence operative's sovereign territory.

As domestic law by its very nature is particular to each state, this paper will address only international law.[19] However, those aspects of international law that involve the exercise of domestic criminal law jurisdiction are briefly considered.

Are armed drones *legally* different from any other weapon? According to some experts, '[c]ombat drones are battlefield weapons. ... Drones are not lawful for use outside combat zones',[20] while others maintain that the 'use of drones is no different from a pilot dropping a bomb from a fighter jet, or a soldier firing a gun.'[21] In fact, there is no current international law specifically relating to the use of armed drones.[22] For example, if used within an armed conflict, '[f]rom a legal standpoint, the use of a missile fired from a drone aircraft versus one fired from some remote platform with a human pilot makes no difference in battle as ordinarily understood.'[23] The applicable international law is the law that applies to any other weapon or weapon system.[24] For example, if a drone was armed with chemical weapons, the applicable law would be the *Convention on the Prohibition of the Development, Production, Stockpiling and Use of Chemical Weapons and their Destruction*.[25] Alternatively, if armed with 'conventional' munitions, then the general law of targeting would apply (be that treaty law, customary international law or both). If used outside an armed conflict, then any international law that applies to, for example, the firing of a sniper rifle applies to the firing of a weapon from an armed drone. So why such divergent views on the law applicable to the use of are drones? I suggest the explanation put forward by Professor Anderson is correct when he said that 'arguments against drones are really proxy for arguments against the very idea of the CIA using force.'[26] Accordingly, most of the arguments in this article apply equally to a civilian intelligence operative on the ground and using a personal weapon as they do to an agent who may be thousands of miles away operating as part of team controlling and directing the actions of an armed drone.

---

19 For an outline why the use of lethal force by the CIA can be lawful under US domestic law, see Anderson 2009, p 8; Banks 2010.

20 O'Connell 2010a, b, p 13.

21 Shamsi 2010, p 9. See Alston 2010, para 79; Lewis 2010; Paust 2010a, p 4, n 17.

22 Glazier 2010.

23 Anderson 2010a, p 3.

24 Glazier 2010; Garlasco 2009, p 32 ('Unmanned aerial drones ... are covered by the same rules grounded in the laws of war as other weapons systems.'). Putting aside questions not relevant to this paper such as airspace transit rights.

25 Opened for signature on 13 January 1993, 1975 UNTS p 469 (entered into force on 29 April 1997).

26 Anderson 2010b, p 6.

4.4 Resort to the Use of Force

When discussing the use of force (and particularly use of lethal force) by a state, it is helpful to commence by determining what is the legal authority for the *resort* to the use of force. In the context of armed conflicts, this is termed the *jus ad bellum*. A separate question is what law then *governs* (or *regulates*) the application of the use of force. Again, in the context of armed conflicts, this is called the *jus in bello*.[27] The terms themselves are not so important as are the underlying legal concepts.[28] While there are many legal bases on which a state can rely for the resort to the use of force, the one of most interest to this paper is where a state is acting in national self-defence.[29] The starting point for any discussion of the law relating to national self-defence is Article 51 of the *Charter of the United Nations*,[30] being one of the primary sources providing legal authority for the resort to the use of force. Along with Article 51 of the UN Charter, there is also a customary law right of national self-defence,[31] although opinion divides on whether this customary law right is merely coincident or is more expansive than the Article 51 UN Charter right.[32]

The wording of Article 51 itself provides little to no limitations or parameters on what a state may do by way of use of force. What guidance there is comes from state practice, case law and learned commentary. However, that guidance generally covers only the very broad issues of whether the resort to the use of force is *necessary* and whether in the broadest sense the actions taken by the state are

[27] See Nabulsi 2007.

[28] Indeed, while the legal concepts may have existed in some form or another for centuries or even millennia, the 'august solemnity of Latin confers on the terms jus ad bellum and *jus in bello* the misleading appearance of being centuries old. In fact, these expressions were only coined at the time of the League of Nations and were rarely used in doctrine or practice until after the Second World War, in the late 1940s to be precise.' Kolb 1997, n 1.

[29] Another primary source is acting pursuant to a Chapter VII United Nations Security Council resolution that authorises (albeit often in not so many words) the use of lethal force for mission accomplishment.

[30] 'Nothing in the present Charter shall impair the inherent right of individual or collective self-defence if an armed attack occurs against a Member of the United Nations, until the Security Council has taken measures necessary to maintain international peace and security. Measures taken by Members in the exercise of this right of self-defence shall be immediately reported to the Security Council and shall not in any way affect the authority and responsibility of the Security Council under the present Charter to take at any time such action as it deems necessary in order to maintain or restore international peace and security.' (Art. 51 Charter of the United Nations, 24 October 1945, 1 UNTS p XVI (hereinafter UN Charter)).

[31] See Military and Paramilitary Activities in and against Nicaragua (*Nicaragua* v *United States of America*) (Merits) [1986] ICJ Rep 14, paras 193–194; Dinstein 2005, pp 181–182; Schmitt 2008a, p 1.

[32] Dinstein 2005, pp 183–187.

proportional to the threat posed to it.[33] Put another way, there are no clear or explicit limitations in the wording of Article 51 that regulate the *application* of the use of force once the threshold for the *resort* to the use of force has been met. Later in this paper I argue that this statement is correct only where the resort to the use of force by a state crosses the threshold of amounting to an armed conflict. In situations less than armed conflict, I contend that Article 51 does have normative force with respect to not just the resort to the use of force but also governs the application of that force.[34]

Where there is no Chapter VII United Nations Security Council resolution and the threshold for use of force by a state in national self-defence has not been met, there are a number of legal consequences if a state resorts to the use of force. First and most simply put, any use of force by the agents of the state (be they armed forces, civilian intelligence agencies or otherwise) is a breach of the state's international legal obligations. But what about the individuals? Do they attract any personal legal liability? The traditional legal view when analysing such questions in an armed conflict context is that the legal liability of the soldier for the application of force in specific situations is independent of whether there was a general authority to use force at all.[35] In other words, as long as the soldier complies with the *jus in bello*, the fact that there was no *jus ad bellum* legal authority to resort to the use of force is an issue for state liability and not the liability of individual soldiers. With an exception that is not relevant here,[36] that is the current state of the law.

Putting to one side the use of force pursuant to a United Nations Security Council resolution, where the threshold for use of force by a state in national self-defence has been met, then the main question to be addressed in this paper is are there any legal limitations on who can use force on the state's behalf? This question is not subject to a simple answer. I will start by identifying the legal context in which the question needs to be answered. In particular, in what legal paradigm is the state using force?

---

[33] Military and Paramilitary Activities in and against Nicaragua (*Nicaragua* v *United States of America*) (Merits) [1986] ICJ Rep 14, para 194; *Legality of the Threat or Use of Nuclear Weapons* (Advisory Opinion) [1996] ICJ Rep 226, para 41; Case concerning armed activities on the territory of the Congo (*Democratic Republic of the Congo* v *Uganda*) (Judgment) [2005] ICJ Rep 168, para 147. See O'Connell 2007, pp 502–503; Gray 2008, pp 148–150.

[34] Whether or not a United Nations Security Council resolution imposed any limitations on or otherwise regulated the use of force is a matter of interpreting the mandate; while noting, however, that if the use of force pursuant to a mandate amounts to an armed conflict, then the law of armed conflict applies.

[35] See generally Dinstein 2005, pp 156–162. For a thorough analysis of the separation between the *jus ad bellum* and the *jus in bello*, see Moussa 2008, p 963.

[36] I have previously argued that where the *jus ad bellum* is provided by a Chapter VII UN Security Council resolution, then the scope of the Security Council mandate will affect what is a military advantage that may lawfully be sought from any particular attack. Accordingly, the *jus ad bellum* will have some impact on what is lawful under the *jus in bello*—see Henderson 2009, pp 147–154.

Regardless of the context, when a state is engaged in the use of force, human rights law will apply.[37] While the particular rules and source of those rules will vary, a non-derogable fundamental human right is the right to life.[38] So, for the purposes of this paper, the issue is what specific legal paradigm applies (and what is its content) when determining whether or not there has been an arbitrary deprivation of the right to life.[39] There are three primary legal paradigms that require consideration: (1) international armed conflicts; (2) armed conflicts that are non-international in character; and (3) situations short of an armed conflict.[40]

4.5 International Armed Conflict

While the legal paradigm with the clearest laws regulating the use of force is where state B is in an international armed conflict with state C, there is a need to address a matter of nomenclature. There is no perfect generic-term to describe who may lawfully participate in an international armed conflict, although the term 'combatant' is the most widely used. Prior to the 1977 Protocol Additional to the Geneva Conventions of 12 August 1949, and relating to the Protection of Victims of International Armed Conflicts,[41] the term 'combatant' was not defined in treaty law but was in use.[42] However, per Article 2 of the Hague IV Regulations, another class of persons (commonly called a levee en masse) can also be 'belligerents.' Article 4 of the 1949 Geneva Convention Relative to the Treatment of Prisoners of

---

[37] '[T]he fundamental human rights protection of persons apply at all times, in peace, during emergency situations, and in war'—Inter-American Commission on Human Rights, Report on Terrorism and Human Rights, OEA/Ser.L/V/II.116, Doc. 5 Rev. 1 Corr (2002), para 49, available at http://www.cidh.oas.org/Terrorism/Eng/exe.htm.

[38] Lubell 2010, pp 169–170; Melzer 2008, p 189. See also UK Ministry of Defence 2004, para 15.19.1, noting that not all States are parties to the cited treaties.

[39] Melzer 2008, p 92. The term 'arbitrarily deprived' appears in Art. 6.1 of the International Covenant on Civil and Political Rights, opened for signature 19 December 1996, 999 UNTS p. 171 (entered into force 23 March 1976). While not all States are a party to this covenant, it is a useful phrase to adopt in helping to understand the content of the 'right to life.' See ibid. para 61 for a discussion of this concept in the context of an armed conflict. For a recent article reviewing the applicability and relevance of human rights law for US military operations, see Bill 2010, p 54.

[40] For a good analysis of the legal nature of armed conflicts and the legal distinctions between international and non-international armed conflicts, see Sassòli 2006.

[41] Protocol Additional to the Geneva Conventions of 12 August 1949, and relating to the Protection of Victims of International Armed Conflicts, opened for signature 12 December 1977, 1125 UNTS p. 3 (entered into force 7 December 1978) (hereinafter Additional Protocol I).

[42] See for example, Art. 3 Regulations respecting the laws and customs of war on land, annex to Convention (IV) respecting the laws and customs of war on land, signed at The Hague 18 October 1907, 3 Martens Nouveau Recueil (ser. 3) p 461 (entered into force 26 January 1910) (hereinafter Hague IV Regulations).

War[43] defines who is entitled to prisoner of war status. Articles 4.A(1), (2), (3) and (6) of Geneva Convention III are also generally considered to list those groups who may lawfully partake in combat. Unfortunately, Article 4 does not provide a general word or term to describe this group. Article 43(2) of Additional Protocol I provides that members of the armed forces (other than medical personnel and chaplains) are combatants. The Commentary on the Additional Protocols of 8 June 1977 to the Geneva Conventions of 12 August 1949 on this article states: 'All members of the armed forces are combatants, and only members of the armed forces are combatants.'[44] However, while this article might superficially appear to exclusively state who are combatants, on careful reading it is not truly an article that provides a definition for the term *combatants*.[45] Also, the article leaves out a *levee en masse*. The fact that the drafters of Additional Protocol I recognised that members of a *levee en masse* are not civilians is reflected in Article 50(1) Additional Protocol I.

So, either the definition of combatants needs to be expanded to include a *levee en masse* or a more general term for those who may lawfully partake in combat is needed that covers both combatants and a *levee en masse*. At first blush, the term *belligerents* seems suitable.[46] However, *belligerents* is also often used to mean opposing states or groups and not just the individuals engaged in combat.[47] Accordingly, for the purposes of this paper, the term *combatant* will be used to mean any of the persons listed in Articles 4.A(1), (2), (3) and (6) of Geneva Convention III, along with Articles 43 and 44 of Additional Protocol I where that Protocol applies to the conflict.

In international armed conflicts, combatants can legally use lethal force against opposing combatants[48] and civilians who take a direct part in hostilities[49]—even

---

43 Geneva Convention Relative to the Treatment of Prisoners of War, opened for signature 12 August 1949, 75 UNTS p 135 (entered into force 21 October 1950) (hereinafter Geneva Convention III).

44 Sandoz et al. 1987, para 1677.

45 Compare Art. 47(2) that defines a *mercenary* and Art. 50(1) that defines a *civilian*.

46 See for example, the Military Commissions Act of 2009 (10 United States Code Chapter 47A) which uses the terms 'privileged belligerent' and 'unprivileged enemy belligerent' in relation to people and not States or groups.

47 For example, see the definition of 'co-belligerent' in the now repealed Military Commissions Act of 2006 (10 United States Code Chapter 47A) used in relation to States and armed forces rather than individuals.

48 It is clearly lawful to target enemy combatants, although this is not obvious from reading the relevant treaties. Indeed, if one was to read Art. 48 Additional Protocol I and the definition of military objectives in Art. 52 Additional Protocol I, you might conclude that the military personnel of the enemy are not lawful targets. However, as to combatants being lawful targets, see *Prosecutor* v *Galić*, (Trial Chamber) Case No IT-98-29-T (5 December 2003) n 88; *The Public Committee against Torture in Israel* v *The Government of Israel*, HCJ 769/02 (13 December 2006) para 29 (Barak P (emeritus), Rivlin V–P and Beinisch P concurring) available at http://elyon1.court.gov.il/Files_ENG/02/690/007/a34/02007690.a34.pdf; Inter-American Commission on Human Rights, supra n 38, para 100.

49 *Prosecutor* v *Galić*, (Trial Chamber) Case No IT-98-29-T (5 December 2003) para 48.

where those persons are not posing an immediate and direct threat—without attracting either international or domestic criminal liability.[50] It might be presumed therefore that the corollary is true—i.e., that anyone who is not a combatant may not, under international law, use lethal force. Or put in the terms of the law of armed conflict, it might be presumed that international law prohibits the direct participation in hostilities by a civilian. However, the situation is more nuanced than how it appears in most of the commentary on the issue. What is often overlooked, or at least glossed over, is that even inside an armed conflict there are still two distinct legal paradigms: (1) an international; and (2) a non-international armed conflict. Only when the appropriate legal paradigm that is governing the use of force has been established is it possible to answer what is the legal position concerning the direct participation in those hostilities by a civilian (and particularly by a civilian intelligence agent).

In an international armed conflict, direct participation in those hostilities by civilians is not of itself a war crime. There are no treaty provisions prohibiting a civilian from participating in hostilities. Rather, the relevant treaty provisions extend legal rights to combatants when they participate in hostilities.[51] While Article 51(3) Additional Protocol I provides that a civilian who takes a direct part in hostilities loses the protection afforded by section I of Part IV Additional Protocol I, this is not the same as prohibiting, let alone criminalising, civilian participation in hostilities.[52] In an international armed conflict, just because an act is not permitted by the law of armed conflict does not mean that act is a war crime. For example, it is a war crime under the law of armed conflict to misuse the distinctive emblem to facilitate the killing of an enemy soldier. Conversely, failure to 'without delay, take all possible measures to search for and collect the wounded and sick … and to search for the dead'[53] is not a war crime where an individual is liable to punishment.[54] Accordingly, to argue that direct participation in hostilities is a war crime, there is a need to look further than just merely noting that such

---

[50] See *United States* v *List* (hereinafter *Hostages Trial*), reported in United Nations War Crimes Commission, *Law Reports of Trials of War Criminals* (2010) Library of Congress, p 50, available at www.loc.gov/rr/frd/Military_Law/pdf/Law-Reports_Vol-8.pdf.—'It cannot be questioned that acts done in time of war under the military authority of an enemy, cannot involve any criminal liability on the part of officers or soldiers if the acts are not prohibited by the conventional or customary rules of war.' See also Art. 43(2) Additional Protocol I, but noting I am using a more expanded definition of combatant than that used in the article. Of course, that use of force must be in compliance with the *jus in bello* (i.e., the law of armed conflict). The right to use lethal force is a subset of the combatant's privilege, which is a lawful right under international law to participate in hostilities. For a more detailed explanation of the combatant's privilege and it relation to domestic criminal law, see Solf 1983, pp 57–58; Goldman and Tittemore 2002, pp 2–4.

[51] See in particular Arts. 1 and 2 Hague IV Regulations and Art. 43(2) Additional Protocol I.

[52] Contra, Solis 2010.

[53] Art. 15 Geneva Convention for the Amelioration of the Condition of the Wounded and Sick in Armed Forces in the Field, opened for signature 12 August 1949, 75 UNTS p 31 (entered into force 21 October 1950) (hereinafter Geneva Convention I).

[54] Jenks 2010, p 93.

participation is not permitted under the law of armed conflict. Further, nowhere is it defined as a grave breach for a civilian to participate in hostilities.[55] Finally, recent international statutes defining 'war crimes' do not list civilian participation in hostilities as a war crime.[56] The conclusion based on the foregoing was well put by Professor Glazier in his recent testimony to a US House of Representatives sub-committee:

> '... CIA personnel are civilians, not combatants, and do not enjoy any legal right to participate in hostilities on our behalf.[57] It is my opinion, as well as that of most other law of war scholars I know, that those who participate in hostilities without the combatant's privilege do not violate the law of war by doing so, they simply gain no immunity from domestic laws. Under this view CIA drone pilots are liable to prosecution under the law of any jurisdiction where attacks occur for any injuries, deaths, or property damage they cause.'[58]

So, certain actions of CIA personnel may attract domestic criminal liability but not international criminal liability. Of course, the person's action might amount to some other stand-alone war crime (e.g., wilful killing of a protected person). However, in that respect, their liability would be no different from that of an otherwise lawful combatant who had engaged in the wilful killing of a protected person.

Notwithstanding the above points, there is some early case law to support the conclusion that participating in the *fighting* by a civilian is a war crime. 'We think the rule is established that a civilian who aids, abets or participates in the fighting is liable to punishment as a war criminal under the laws of war. Fighting is legitimate only for the combatant personnel of a country.'[59] So, can the judgement in the *Hostages Trial* be reconciled with the above points or is the judgement not good law? The judgement can, with some difficulty, be reconciled with the above points if the concept of aiding, abetting or participating in *fighting* is narrower than that of direct participation in hostilities. Unfortunately, while the *Hostages Trial* is the leading authority on this point, the case was not about the actions of the partisans but of the German officers who were responsible for having the partisans

---

[55] See Art. 50 Geneva Convention I and Art. 85 Additional Protocol I.

[56] See in particular principle VI.(b), Principles of International Law Recognized in the Charter of the Nürnberg Tribunal and in the Judgment of the Tribunal (1950); Art. 3 Updated Statute of the International Criminal Tribunal for the Former Yugoslavia (2009); Art. 8 Rome Statute of the International Criminal Court, opened for signature 17 July 1998, 2187 UNTS p 90 (entered into force 1 July 2002). Watkin notes that 'while killing or wounding treacherously individuals belonging to a hostile nation or army has been identified as a "war crime" under the 1998 Rome Statute of the International Criminal Court, the obligation for a combatant to distinguish himself or herself from the civilian population is not listed as an offense'—Watkin 2005, p 64.

[57] From the context of his overall testimony, it appears that Glazier is referring to a right under international law and at this point was not expressing a view on whether the CIA have legal authority to so act under US domestic law.

[58] Glazier 2010. See Program on Humanitarian Policy and Conflict Research, supra n 13, p 246; Rona 2007.

[59] *Hostages Trial*, supra n 51, p 58.

executed. This might explain why there is no discussion on what amounts to 'aids, abets or participates in the fighting.' However, when reciting the facts of the case the court referred to such actions as damaging transportation and communication lines, surprise attacks, ambushes and that captured German soldiers were often tortured and killed.[60] From this, a conclusion can be drawn that aiding, abetting or participating in fighting is a subset of actions that amount to direct participation in hostilities. The following example might help illustrate the point (even though reasonable people might disagree on how each of the following acts are classified). A person who delivers mortar rounds from a factory to a central ammunition depot is participating in the war effort; and accordingly is only indirectly participating in hostilities. A person who delivers mortar rounds to a magazine at a remote fire base, but not while a fire mission is underway, is directly participating in hostilities but is not aiding, abetting or participating in fighting (at least not as that term is used in the *Hostages Trial*). A person who delivers mortar rounds from a magazine to a mortar team during a fire mission is aiding, abetting or participating in fighting.

An alternative to adopting the above somewhat strained interpretation is to read the judgement in less literal terms. A more plausible explanation is that despite using the term *war crime*, the ruling was really to the effect that unprivileged acts of belligerency remain subject to prosecution under domestic law. As Baxter argues, there can be a tendency to conclude that what is not lawful under international law is, ipso facto, an international crime.[61] Baxter seems to explain the ruling in the *Hostages Trial* in a similar way.[62] In light of subsequent treaty action and learned commentary, this is the preferred understanding of the judgement.[63] Of course, this does not preclude prosecutions for other acts that are war crimes.[64]

The conclusions from the above are that:

a. direct participation in hostilities by a civilian is, of itself, not a crime under international law; and
b. a civilian who directly participates in hostilities does not enjoy any immunity under domestic law to the extent that the actions of the civilian amount to a domestic law crime.[65]

A further example will help illustrate this point. Take the interesting case of civilians acting as coast-watchers in their own territory and thereby providing

---

60 Ibid. p 56.

61 For example, the ruling in *Ex parte Quirin* et al., 317 US 1 (1942) that espionage in war time is a war crime (as opposed to just subject to domestic criminal prosecution) is criticised in Baxter 1951, pp 331 and 340.

62 See Baxter 1951, pp 336 and 338. Unfortunately, Baxter does not clearly say why he distinguishes the ruling in the *Hostages Trial*, but it is probably on the basis of misconstruing the term 'unlawful belligerent' as meaning 'illegal belligerent' – see ibid. pp 331 and 340.

63 See Watkin 2005, p 49. But see, possibly contra, Allison 2007.

64 For example, murdering prisoners – Baxter 1951, p 338.

65 Alston 2010, para 71.

advance warning of the approach of enemy forces.[66] It is clear that such civilians are taking a direct part in hostilities and are liable to attack. Equally though, such activities are almost certainly going to be completely lawful under local domestic law. Nor could the civilians' activities attract lawful sanction under the domestic law of the opposing belligerent.[67] So, the civilians are taking a direct part in hostilities and as such are liable to attack; however, they are not committing any breach of international law and, therefore, do not need to rely on any concept of 'combatant privilege' to avoid prosecution under domestic law. However, if we adapt the example and now assume that the civilians are not just acting as coast-watchers but rather are operating anti-aircraft batteries, the legal analysis changes in one crucial respect. It is now a valid exercise of the opposing belligerent's sovereignty to criminalize the conduct of firing upon its armed forces (even over the high seas or over the territory of the defending State).[68] Now the absence of the combatant's privilege under international law becomes the determining factor. Whereas a combatant complying with the law of armed conflict is immune from prosecution under the domestic law of the opposing belligerent, that is not the case for civilians.

How does the above apply to an employee (or contractor)[69] of a civilian intelligence agency involved in the operation of armed drones during an international armed conflict? First, where that person's activities do not cross the threshold for amounting to taking a direct part in hostilities, that person remains immune from direct attack.[70] Second, where the person's conduct does cross that threshold, that fact alone does not make the person:

a. a 'war criminal' or otherwise liable to prosecution for breaches of international criminal law; nor
b. liable to prosecution for breaches of the domestic law of the opposing belligerent.

Importantly, the conclusion that the person is not liable to prosecution under the domestic law of the opposing belligerent is not contingent upon the person's

---

[66] See for example, the activities of civilians, including clergy, in the Pacific during World War II referred to in Hays Parks 1990, p 132, n 396.

[67] Given the location and nationality of the civilians, there is also no aspect of spying as that activity is understood under the law of armed conflict.

[68] And subject to how one interprets the *Hostages Trial*, it could also be a war crime as the actions would amount to aiding, abetting or participating in fighting.

[69] For a recent discussion of the many and varied activities of contractors in relation to intelligence agencies in the United States, see Priest and Arkin 2010. For the possible involvement of contractors in the CIA use of drones, see Alston 2010, para 20.

[70] Noting, however, that the operation or controlling of armed drones 'during combat operations will almost invariably qualify as direct participation in hostilities' – Program on Humanitarian Policy and Conflict Research, supra n 13, p 122.

whereabouts. The person might be in his or her home country or may be present in the territory of the opposing belligerent.[71]

Third, where the person's actions amount to a domestic law crime under the criminal law of the opposing belligerent, the person is subject to lawful prosecution by that belligerent (as the person does not enjoy the combatant's privilege). Again, the conclusion that the person is liable to prosecution under the domestic law of the opposing belligerent is not contingent upon the person's whereabouts. The person might be in his or her home country, present in the territory of the opposing belligerent or anywhere else for that matter.[72] An important thing about the above third point is that whether the person may be prosecuted under domestic law is wholly independent of whether the person's actions amount to direct participation in hostilities. There is no link between the two. One is a domestic law question and the other is an international law question. The relevance of international law is whether the person enjoys the combatant's privilege. Once that is answered in the negative, the issue becomes one of domestic criminal law or, either alternatively or concurrently, international criminal law—again though, only for stand-alone war crimes that might also have been committed by combatants and not for the (non-existent) crime of 'direct participation in hostilities.'[73]

One interesting exception to the above is the case of civilian members of military aircraft crews as defined in Article 4.A.(4) Geneva Convention III. Such persons are entitled to prisoner of war status. Of course, for our present purposes this would require the drone to be a 'military aircraft' and also for the civilian intelligence operative to be part of the 'crew.'[74] The effect of the article is that where the person's acts are within the limited scope of duties provided for by Article 4.A.(4) Geneva Convention III, then performance of those actions do not expose the person to either international or domestic criminal liability. The person is subject to lawful targeting where his or her actions amount to direct participation in hostilities, but that is not the same as saying the person's actions are criminal. While some have argued that such persons are entitled to prisoner of war status but may concurrently be tried for acts of unprivileged belligerency (even if their acts otherwise complied with the law of armed conflict),[75] I suggest this statement is

[71] An exception to this broad statement is if the person was physically in territory controlled by the opposing belligerent and engaged in espionage.

[72] Of course, this conclusion is subject to the particular terms of the opposing belligerent's criminal law. If there are geographical or other restrictions in that law, then that must be taken into account in determining whether a crime has been committed. However, the general principle remains true.

[73] Although subject to how one interprets the *Hostages Trial*, if the person's actions did amount to aiding, abetting or participating in fighting, that person would be liable for trial for breach of international criminal law.

[74] See the various definitions and rules in Program on Humanitarian Policy and Conflict Research, Manual on International Law Applicable to Air and Missile Warfare (2009), which make it clear that an armed drone (in the Manual referred to as an unmanned combat aerial vehicle) can be a military aircraft and can have a crew.

[75] Goldman and Tittemore 2002, p 4.

true only to the extent that the actions of the person that amount to unprivileged belligerency are actions beyond those envisaged by Article 4.A.(4) Geneva Convention III. Also, it has been argued that where such civilians take a direct part in hostilities, those civilians lose entitlement to prisoner of war status.[76] Again, I suggest this statement is true only to the extent that the actions of the person that amount to taking a direct part in hostilities are actions beyond those envisaged by Article 4.A.(4) Geneva Convention III. One learned commentator states that the functions to be performed by this class of person should be restricted so that they 'cannot be suspected of having taken a direct part in hostilities.'[77] While this make senses for some of the other classes groups mentioned in Article 4.A.(4) Geneva Convention III,[78] it would seem that the whole concept of being a 'civilian members of a military aircraft crews' is almost ipso facto taking a direct part in hostilities. Unfortunately, no examples of the various roles for civilian members of a military aircraft crews are given in the Pictet commentary to Geneva Convention III.[79] To the extent that a civilian member of a military aircraft crew limits his or her actions to that role, then that person should be entitled to prisoner of war status and enjoy immunity from domestic prosecution—while noting that if (as is likely) the role amounts to taking a direct part in hostilities, the person is liable to being targeted.

4.6 Non-International Armed Conflict

In an international armed conflict, both sides are legally equivalent under the law of armed conflict. The principal 'fighters' are referred to as combatants, which is a term with legal significance. However, in a non-international armed conflict both sides do not enjoy legal equivalency.[80] Consequently, the term *combatant* or any comparable term does not appear in the treaty law dealing with non-international armed conflict. Common Article 3 of the Geneva Conventions refers to 'persons taking no active part in hostilities' and 'members of the armed forces who have laid down their arms and those placed hors de combat' in the context of who must be treated humanely (e.g., not attacked). The 1977 Protocol Additional to the Geneva Conventions of 12 August 1949, and relating to the Protection of Victims

---

76 Dinstein 2010, para 115.

77 Ipsen 2008, p 80 at para 319.

78 For example, war correspondents and welfare units.

79 Pictet 1960, pp 64–65.

80 In discussing non-international armed conflicts, I do not include conflicts governed by Additional Protocol I due to Art. 1(4) thereof. Note that non-international armed conflicts are broader than the traditional concept of internal armed conflicts—see Sassòli 2006, pp 8–11; Lubell 2010, p 104.

of Non-International Armed Conflicts[81] refers to 'armed forces', 'dissident armed forces' and 'organized armed groups', but only by way of defining the ambit of application of Additional Protocol II. However, there are no articles in Additional Protocol II that refer to these classes or groups by way of determining the rights and obligations of such groups. A consequence of this is that the use of the term *combatant* in the legal sense of that word is not appropriate and may even be confusing,[82] as using the term *combatant* in a non-international armed conflict would mean using a term with no clear legal or normative meaning *in that context*. If for some reason the term *combatant* is used, that does not mean that opposing forces in a non-international armed conflict gain some sort of legal standing.[83] Nor is it the case that just because a person is subject to being lawfully targeted does that person gain belligerency rights. Being a lawful target is not the same as gaining combatant status.[84]

In this paper, the forces acting on behalf of the government are called the 'government forces' and the other forces (be they dissident armed forces, organised armed groups or others) are called the 'opposing force.' A term like 'insurgent' is not used as that term implies that the opposing force is rising in rebellion or revolt and therefore is part of the state. At least as a matter of nomenclature, it is preferable to leave open the possibility of a non-international armed conflict between a state (the government forces) and a non-state actor that exists outside of the state (the opposing forces).[85] Two different terms are used—rather than a generic term like 'fighter'—as the legal rights of each group are different.

---

[81] Protocol Additional to the Geneva Conventions of 12 August 1949, and relating to the Protection of Victims of Non-International Armed Conflicts, opened for signature 12 December 1977, 1125 UNTS p 609 (entered into force 7 December 1978) (hereinafter Additional Protocol II).

[82] See The Manual 2006, p 4.

[83] Contra O'Connell 2010a,—'To label terrorists "enemy combatants" lifts them out of the status of *criminal* to that of *combatant*, the same category as America's own troops on the battlefield.' O'Connell's comments would have some validity in the context of an international armed conflict, assuming arguendo, that the 'terrorists' also complied with the law of armed conflict.

[84] Lewis 2010.

[85] An example being say an opposing force outside a State that does not want to overthrow the government or gain control over a piece of territory to succeed (typical goals of an insurgency) but may just want to influence the policies (either national or foreign polices) of the government. See Sassòli 2006, pp 8–11; Dinstein 2005, pp 204–208. In the Case concerning armed activities on the territory of the Congo (*Democratic Republic of the Congo* v *Uganda*) (Judgment) [2005] ICJ Rep 168, para 147, the court specifically left open the question of self-defence against non-State actors. In their separate opinions, both Judges Kooijmans and Simma recognised the right under international law to respond against armed attacks from non-State actors (Case concerning armed activities on the territory of the Congo (*Democratic Republic of the Congo* v *Uganda*) (separate opinion of Judge Kooijmans) [2005] ICJ Rep 168, paras 26–31; and Case concerning armed activities on the territory of the Congo (*Democratic Republic of the Congo* v *Uganda*) (separate opinion of Judge Simma) [2005] ICJ Rep 168, paras 12–13. See generally Paust 2010b, p 237.

In a non-international armed conflict, there is no treaty articulation of the concept of the combatant's privilege.[86] There is no equivalent of that part of Article 1 Hague IV Regulations that implies the combatant's privilege in international armed conflict[87]; nor is there in Additional Protocol II an equivalent of Article 43(2) Additional Protocol I. Unless the conflict is an international armed conflict due to the application of Article 1(4) Additional Protocol I, then the current state of the *jus in bello* in a non-international armed conflict is that the non-state actors do not have lawful belligerent status nor enjoy the combatant's privilege.[88]

However, what about the government forces? Do they enjoy a combatant privilege? This question is more than just academic. While government forces who otherwise act lawfully are unlikely to be subject to prosecution by their own government for resorting to the use of armed force, there are at least three scenarios where the issue might arise. First, an opposing force may be successful in overthrowing a government and may then come into power itself. Second, the government forces may use force in the territory of another state and without that state's consent.[89] Third, the government forces may use force in the territory of another state with that state's consent, but the consent may be confidential with a result that there is no status of forces agreement or other like document granting the government forces immunity from prosecution under the domestic law of the territorial state.

I am not aware of a positive assertion in publicly available military manuals or other official sources to the effect that government forces in a non-international armed conflict enjoy the combatant's privilege. Nor does this point seem to be addressed in the learned commentary, with one exception. The highly-respected Kenneth Watkin writes that 'it is logical to conclude that the concept of combatant immunity would apply to the armed forces of the state tasked with using force in a

[86] Solf 1983, p 54.

[87] 'The laws, rights, and duties of war apply not only to armies, but also to militia and volunteer corps ...'—Art. 1 Hague IV Regulations. That this implies the combatant's privilege, see ICRC Commentary, supra n 45, para 1677.

[88] Solf 1983, p 59; Goldman and Tittemore 2002, p 5. See also ICRC Commentary, supra n 45, para 4441; International Institute of Humanitarian Law, supra n 83, pp 40–41. Solf points out that a number of countries have provided for a limited form of combatant's privilege in their domestic legislation on extradition—Solf 1983. In a very good article arguing why the law should be amended (notwithstanding my disagreement with the conclusion, the law is accurately set out and the argument well made), Moussa argues that the denial of 'lawful belligerency' to certain non-State actors in a non-international armed conflict is a threat to 'the validity of the distinction between *jus ad bellum* and *jus in bello*' and that the international law applicable to non-international armed conflict should be amended so that non-State actors would have a combatant status under the *jus in bello* as a way to encourage compliance with other principles and rules of the *jus in bello*—Moussa 2008.

[89] The classic *Caroline* incident so regularly referred to when discussing the law of national self-defence provides an example of an agent of the United Kingdom using force in the territory of the USA against a non-State actor and at a subsequent date being arrested on the territory of the USA—see Schmitt 2008b, p 146.

non-international armed conflict.'[90] No authority is cited. Rather, by his own words, the conclusion is based on logical deduction. Notwithstanding the lack of other commentary to a similar effect, the majority of commentators who discuss the concept of combatant's privilege in the context of non-international armed conflict do so vis-à-vis the opposing forces. Also, while the Customary International Humanitarian Law study does not list such a rule for non-international armed conflicts, it also does not list a rule on combatant's privilege for international armed conflicts even though the existence of such is beyond doubt.[91] Notwithstanding the almost complete absence of writing on this point, I agree with Watkin's conclusion and suggest there is a very persuasive argument in favour of there being the equivalent of a combatant's privilege for government forces in a non-international armed conflict.

The argument starts from the premise that it is lawful for a government to engage in a non-international armed conflict with a non-state actor. And this is not a matter of international law being silent on the issue, but rather there is positive law recognizing this right. Where government forces combat opposing forces on the authorization of their government, they are acting as agents of the state. Surely, therefore, it must be legal for government forces to engage in acts pursuant to government orders (e.g., combat opposing forces) as long as the government forces otherwise comply with the law of armed conflict. Otherwise, a government's right to combat a non-state actor would be somewhat illusory. It makes legal sense for the law to be that government forces enjoy a form of combatant privilege. However, it also makes sense that non-state actors do not enjoy a combatant privilege, as there is no legal right under international law for a non-state actor to engage in a non-international armed conflict. And this line of reasoning is supported by the fact that on the limited occasions where the international community has recognised a right for a non-state actor to take up arms, those conflicts have been given the status of a an international armed conflict[92]; and, therefore, only in such circumstances can the fighters on behalf of the non-state actor can obtain combatant status and the combatant's privilege.

Presuming for current purposes that the equivalent of a combatant's privilege does exist for the government forces, the next relevant question is who may lawfully form the government forces (and thereby lawfully participate in hostilities on behalf of the government)? In particular, is there any legal argument that limits, under international law, the use of force to the military or may the government also authorise other government agents to use lethal force on its behalf? There is nothing explicit in Common Article 3 of the Geneva Conventions that would prevent a government from authorising other government agents to use lethal force on its behalf. Of course, in doing so those government agents would not come

[90] Watkin 2005, p 65.

[91] Henckaerts and Doswald-Beck 2005. Note that while very helpful, the *Customary International Humanitarian Law* study is not authoritative.

[92] See Art. 1(4) Additional Protocol I.

within the limited protections provided by that article as they would be taking an active part in hostilities—which is no different from the fact that members of the armed forces who are still participating in the hostilities also do not come within the ambit of Common Article 3.[93] Also, where the conflict is governed by Additional Protocol II, there is nothing in the Protocol that would prevent a government from authorizing other government agents to use lethal force on its behalf. The application of Additional Protocol II is predicated on the government side involving its 'armed forces',[94] but there is no requirement in Additional Protocol II that *only* the armed forces operate on the government's behalf. Also, the ICRC Commentary on Article 1(1) Additional Protocol II makes it clear that the government armed forces are not limited to military forces.[95]

Importantly, reference to the principle of distinction does not provide a simple answer to the current question. I have already addressed the limited role for common Article 3 of the Geneva conventions in answering this question. The wording of Article 4 Additional Protocol II also provides little assistance. To the extent that Article 4 Additional Protocol II addresses questions of distinction, the divide is between persons who do and persons who do not take a direct part in hostilities—it is not between defined groups or classes of persons.[96] Article 13 Additional Protocol II provides that civilians shall be protected, but it does not define who is a civilian. Nor can one simply assume that a civilian is anyone who is not a member of the armed forces, if for no other reason than Article 1 Additional Protocol II itself identifies that one of the parties to the conflict may be a group other than an 'armed force' when it refers to not only 'armed forces' and 'dissident armed forces' but also to 'organized armed groups.'

The Customary International Humanitarian Law study states that there is a customary international law rule in both an international armed conflict and a non-international armed conflict that:

> 'The parties to the conflict must at all times distinguish between civilians and combatants. Attacks may only be directed against combatants. Attacks must not be directed against civilians.'[97]

However, the Customary International Humanitarian Law study does not identify who is a combatant during a non-international armed conflict.[98] For the reasons discussed above, there is no reason to presume that in a non-international armed

[93] With respect to members of the armed forces, Common Article 3 applies only to those members who have laid down their arms or who are *hors de combat*.

[94] Art. 1(1) Additional Protocol II.

[95] ICRC Commentary, supra n 45, para 4462.

[96] Compare Arts. 43 and 50(1) Additional Protocol I which provide a scheme of distinction, particularly when supplemented by Art. 51(3) Additional Protocol I.

[97] Henckaerts and Doswald-Beck 2005, Rule 1.

[98] Rule 3 of the Customary International Humanitarian Law study (ibid) provides a definition of who is a combatant in an international armed conflict but does not provide such a definition for a non-international armed conflict.

conflict, the class of combatant is limited to members of the military or other armed forces (e.g., police or paramilitary) incorporated into the military. Noting the absence of positive state practice to the contrary, it does not seem likely that states would have chosen to limit themselves via international law as to what forces they can use to combat opposing forces in a non-international armed conflict.[99]

Based on the lack of a treaty provision or other international law imposing any limits or restrictions, the better conclusion is that the government may determine for itself who will operate on its behalf in a non-international armed conflict. Additionally, a government may determine to what extent the government forces distinguish themselves from the civilian population.

Professor Alston states that where CIA personnel conduct targeted drone killings in an armed conflict those 'CIA personnel could be prosecuted for murder under the domestic law of any country in which they conduct targeted drone killings.'[100] Unfortunately, he does not clearly indicate whether this statement was meant to apply to both an international armed conflict and a non-international armed conflict. In the case of an international armed conflict, I agree with him. As discussed above, CIA personnel would not enjoy the combatant's privilege in an international armed conflict. However, the law is not so clear for a non-international armed conflict.

While in an international armed conflict members of the armed forces are required to distinguish themselves from the civilian population,[101] there is no strict legal requirement in a non-international armed conflict for the government forces to wear a uniform or other distinctive sign that shows their status as government forces and not as civilians. And as argued above, nor is it apparent that the government forces could not include civilian intelligence operatives. If, as argued above, an equivalent of the combatant's privilege does exist for government forces in a non-international armed conflict, then it cannot be presumed that this privilege is limited to members of the armed forces wearing a uniform or other distinctive sign. Therefore, it may be that CIA personnel might enjoy the equivalent of a combatant's privilege in a non-international armed conflict when acting on behalf of the government.

---

99 See generally Baxter 1951, p 342, who in the context of an international armed conflict made the comment: 'Consequently the law of nations has not ventured to require of states that they prevent the belligerent activities of their citizenry or that they refrain from the use of secret agents or that these activities upon the part of their military forces or civilian population be punished.' This line of argument applies even more forcefully in the circumstances of a non-international armed conflict where there is not the possibility of States agreeing to limitations in return for other States adopting equal limitations.

100 Alston 2010, para 71.

101 For the obligation for regular armed forces to distinguish themselves in an international armed conflict, see Henderson 2009, pp 81–83; and particularly in relation to the special forces of regular armed forces see Watkin 2005, pp 40–41.

What does the above mean in the context of this paper? If the above conclusions are correct, a civilian intelligence operator may be a member of the government forces and thereby lawfully under international law be involved in the conduct of lethal strikes by armed drones against opposing forces. Also, those strikes might occur in the territory of the state or in the territory of another state.[102] Finally, there is a legal argument that in doing so the civilian intelligence operator has an international law right of immunity from domestic criminal law prosecution.

It has been suggested that CIA operatives and their civilian contractors who arm, operate or pilot drones, or input targeting data over Afghanistan and Pakistan's Tribal Areas directly participate in hostilities and 'are no less unprivileged belligerents than the Taliban and al Qaeda fighters they seek to kill.'[103] Moreover, on the basis of the International Committee of the Red Cross's 2009 guidance on the concept of direct participation in hostilities, it has also been suggested that operatives and contractors 'lose their civilian immunity and may be targeted whenever they may be positively identified … be they located at Pakistan's Shamsi airfield, Creech Air Force Base in Nevada, or Langley, Virginia.'[104] The analysis is not that simple. A civilian who takes a direct part in hostilities during an *international* armed conflict is targetable. It also has no relevant legal significance that they are located far from the battlefield, since what makes them legitimate targets is that their actions directly affect military operations against the enemy.[105] Thus the operator of an armed drone most certainly falls into this category. However, as non-state actors in a *non-international* armed conflict, the Taliban and al Qaeda have no legal right to target anyone, let alone opposing government forces.[106]

Where may a non-international armed conflict occur? While traditionally non-international armed conflicts were thought of as occurring inside the territory of one state, that is no longer the case.[107] Presume that a non-state actor (Group A) is based in state B. Although Group A uses state B's geographic territory as a base to launch attacks against state C, Group A is not otherwise associated with state B or its government. Indeed, state B would be pleased to be rid of Group A, but either politically or due to a lack of capability finds itself unable to take positive action itself. In such circumstances, a non-international armed conflict may occur

[102] The circumstances in which a strike may occur in the territory of another state are discussed below

[103] Horton 2010.

[104] Ibid.

[105] Dinstein 2010, para 373.

[106] While Art. 13(2) Additional Protocol II states that civilians lose the protection afforded by Part IV Additional Protocol II for such time as they take a direct part in hostilities, this must be read in the context of the general law applicable during a non-international armed conflict. In a non-international armed conflict, the opposing force has no lawful right to target *anyone*.

[107] Sassòli 2006, pp 8–11.

between the forces of state C and opposing forces in state B where those opposing forces are not associated with or supported by state B.[108]

In the context of strikes by state C on the territory of state B, factually this might occur with or without the consent of state B. Where a strike occurs without consent, issues of state sovereignty need to be considered. However, that is a state-to-state issue and not a matter that need directly concern our civilian intelligence operative. As this paper is concerned with whether an operator of an armed drone may be committing any criminal offence, consent is somewhat of a red herring in this context. Presume for instance that state B consents to state C using its forces directly against Group A.[109] As Professor O'Connell notes, 'States cannot, however, give consent to a right they do not have.'[110] So while from a pure sovereignty perspective, state B can consent to another state using force inside its borders,[111] that consent cannot transform a non-crime into a crime or vice versa. Consent removes any issues of violations of sovereignty, but consent cannot resolve other international law issues. The true issue is whether a criminal offence has occurred in the first place.

As argued above, there may exist a form of combatant's privilege for government forces in a non-international armed conflict. If so, then the real issue is not about consent but rather whether that privilege extends to taking action against the opposing forces beyond the geographic boundary of the government forces own state. If so, then if it would not have been a criminal offence for an operative for the government forces of state C to have acted against Group A without the consent of state B, then the fact that state B has not consented is irrelevant.

So, does a form of combatant's privilege for government forces in a non-international armed conflict exist where the government forces take action across national boundaries? The first point to note is that the law of armed conflict does not set up legal boundaries where armed conflict may or may not take place beyond those rules relating to neutral states.[112] In this respect, I disagree with the general statement made by O'Connell when she stated that:

> 'The fighting or hostilities of an armed conflict occurs within limited zones, referred to as combat or conflict zones. It is only in such zones that killing enemy combatants or those taking a direct part in hostilities is permissible.'[113]

---

[108] See supra n 86.

[109] Which to use my earlier terminology would be classified as an *opposing force* in a non-international armed conflict.

[110] O'Connell 2010a. See also Shamsi 2010, p 5; Kretzmer 2005, p 205.

[111] Military and Paramilitary Activities in and against Nicaragua (*Nicaragua* v *United States of America*) (Merits) [1986] ICJ Rep 14, para 246; see also Shamsi 2010, p 5.

[112] Blank 2011, pp 8–9. Outside of the law of armed conflict, individual States may have their own treaty obligations limiting conflict zones – e.g., see The Antarctic Treaty, opened for signature 1 December 1959, 402 UNTS p 171 (entered into force 23 June 1961).

[113] O'Connell 2010a. Similar arguments are made in International Law Association, infra n 151, p 32.

There is no rule in the law of armed conflict to that effect.[114] A conflict zone does not define where combat *may* take place, but rather identifies where combat *does* take place. As such, it is a 'non-static environment.'[115] A good example of this point in the context of drone use is the previously discussed civilian operator of a drone located at 'Pakistan's Shamsi airfield, Creech Air Force Base in Nevada, or Langley, Virginia.'[116] In an international armed conflict the civilian operator of a drone, particularly an armed drone, would be taking a direct part in hostilities and, therefore, would be a lawful target notwithstanding that Nevada, Virginia and possibly even Shamsi airfield are outside a combat or conflict zone.

As stated in the ICRC Commentary on direct participation in hostilities in a non-international armed conflict, those who belong to the armed forces and to armed groups may be attacked at any time and the ICRC Commentary makes no reference to any geographic boundary.[117] Indeed, how legally could such a geographic boundary come into existence? If, as suggested by Anderson, it might be based around where there is 'persistent, sustained, intense hostilities', that would mean that a belligerent could not open up a new front and would be precluded from striking the enemy in its rear area. Or it would mean a single strike somewhere was unlawful but a series of strikes would suddenly transform the area into a combat zone and therefore lawful.[118] The main argument in support seems to be based on the requirement of necessity when acting in national self-defence.[119] The correct legal position is that an adversary is liable to attack almost anywhere and at any time (unless, of course, *hors de combat*).[120]

The case law out of the International Criminal Tribunal for the former Yugoslavia (ICTY) and the International Criminal Tribunal for Rwanda (ICTR) on this issue is informative. The ICTR has held that the 'requirements of Common Article 3 and Additional Protocol II apply in the whole territory where the conflict is occurring and are not limited to the "war front" or to the "narrow geographical context of the actual theater of combat operations".'[121] The ICTY has similarly

[114] As examples where no geographic limitations of the type proposed by O'Connell are provided, see Art. 52(2) Additional Protocol I; rule 10 of the San Remo Manual on International Law Applicable to Armed Conflicts at Sea, International Committee of the Red Cross (1994) http://www.icrc.org/Web/Eng/siteeng0.nsf/iwpList375/966627225C719EDCC1256B6600598E0.

[115] Blank 2011, p 3.

[116] Horton 2010.

[117] ICRC Commentary, supra n 45, para 4789. In other words, there is no reference to attacks being limited to combat or conflict zones.

[118] Anderson 2010a, p 5. Anderson was suggesting what he viewed as a middle ground between the one extreme of conflict wherever the enemy is and the other extreme of it being limited to a particular theatre of hostilities.

[119] See Greenwood 2008, p 45 at para 221.

[120] Glazier 2010. See also Alston 2010, para 58.

[121] *Prosecutor* v *Rutaganda*, Case No. ICTR-96-3 (Trial Chamber), 6 December 1999, paras 102–103. This line of authority has been followed in a number of subsequent cases, see most recently *Prosecutor* v *Semanza*, (Trial Chamber) Case No ICTR-97-20-T (15 May 2003), para 367.

held that 'international humanitarian law continues to apply in the whole territory of the warring States or, in the case of internal conflicts, the whole territory under the control of a party, whether or not actual combat takes place there.'[122] And also:

> 'There is no necessary correlation between the area where the actual fighting is taking place and the geographical reach of the laws of war. The laws of war apply in the whole territory of the warring states or, in the case of internal armed conflicts, the whole territory under the control of a party to the conflict, whether or not actual combat takes place there, and continue to apply until a general conclusion of peace or, in the case of internal armed conflicts, until a peaceful settlement is achieved. A violation of the laws or customs of war may therefore occur at a time when and in a place where no fighting is actually taking place.'[123]

Finally, and while not legally conclusive, Professor Lewis also provides some sound military reasons why targeting should not be limited to a defined geographic region as part of his argument as to why such a limitation does not exist in the law of armed conflict.[124] Two examples based on contemporary conflicts will help to illustrate the legal issue.

The conflict between the coalition and Iraq in 2003 was clearly an international armed conflict. As it turned out, the conduct of hostilities predominately occurred in Iraqi territory. However, as a matter of the law of armed conflict, if an Iraqi soldier had conducted an attack on Australian territory against a lawful target (be that an Australian combatant or other military objective like an air base), then as long as that Iraqi soldier otherwise complied with the law of armed conflict, the soldier would not have been committing a criminal offence like murder, or unlawful damage of property but would be protected from criminal prosecution by the combatant's privilege. To take a non-international armed conflict example, the government of Afghanistan, supported by the International Security Assistance Force, is currently in an armed conflict with the Taliban and other forces opposed to the government. For the purposes of this paper, I will presume that this conflict is a non-international armed conflict. If a member of the Afghan army standing on Afghan territory fired a weapon at a member of the Taliban standing on Pakistani territory, that Afghan soldier would not be committing any criminal offence under either international or Afghan domestic law. Equally, if upon receiving fire from within Pakistan the Afghan soldier crossed over into Pakistan to better engage the Taliban shooter and the Afghani soldier was inside Pakistani territory at the time of firing his weapon, it would still be the case that the soldier was not committing

---

[122] *Prosecutor* v *Tadić*, Case No. IT-94-1 (Appeals Chamber), Decision on the Defence Motion for Interlocutory Appeal on Jurisdiction, 2 October 1995, para 70.

[123] *Prosecutor* v *Kunarac, Kovač and Vuković*, (Appeals Chamber) Case No IT-96-23&23/1 (12 June 2002), para 57. See also Case concerning armed activities on the territory of the Congo (*Democratic Republic of the Congo* v *Uganda*) (separate opinion of Judge Simma) [2005] ICJ Rep 168, paras 20–23.

[124] Lewis 2010.

any crime by the act of firing his weapon.[125] This legal analysis is not affected by whether or not Pakistan has given consent for Afghan army operations on Pakistani territory.[126]

Based on the above analysis, Professor Shamsi goes too far when she says:

> 'To the extent Pakistan or Yemen may have consented to U.S. targeted drone killings, they can only do so if they themselves have the legal authority to target and kill particular individuals. Thus, for example, if the United States targets an individual in Pakistan who is not part of an armed conflict against Pakistan, or who does not present a lawful target for Pakistani authorities under law enforcement standards (discussed below), then the U.S. targeting would also be illegal.'[127]

If the individuals being targeted by the US are otherwise lawful targets for the US, then the only issue concerning consent from Pakistan is one of sovereignty. And in appropriate circumstances, the principle of sovereignty may have to give way to another competing interest.[128] This is explained by Anderson when he states:

> 'In this, the President follows the long-standing, traditional view of the US government endorsing, as then-State Department Legal Advisor Abraham Sofaer put it in a speech in 1989, that the United States 'supported the legality of a nation attacking a terrorist base from which attacks on its citizens are being launched, if the host country either is unwilling or unable to stop the terrorists from using its territory for that purpose.'[129]

However, as is made clear above, there is not an unconditional right to violate another's state's sovereignty. First, a right to act in national self-defence must exist. Second, the state where the opposing force is located must have failed to

---

[125] For the argument that international law recognises a right for the State to act in self-defence in such circumstances and that there should be a corresponding form of combatant's privilege for the government armed forces, see supra n 86.

[126] As this example is a *non*-international armed conflict, if Pakistan was taking appropriate steps to prevent the misuse of its territory by the non-State actor, then there would not be a right under international law for the Afghan army forces to cross the border.

[127] Shamsi 2010, p 5.

[128] Alston 2010, paras 34–35; Lubell 2010, 46–48; Schmitt 2008b, pp 158–162. By way of example of the sovereignty issue, it is reported that the Pakistani president complained to the US government that a CIA Predator drone strike on 13 January 2006 inside Pakistan and near the near the Afghanistan border violated Pakistani sovereignty. The attack is reported to have killed 18 people in all, with five to six of those being al Qaeda operatives. The Pakistani president described the attack as 'an unjustified violation of an agreement that Pakistani forces should handle operations against al Qaeda inside their own territory.'—*Musharraf: U.S. attack unjustified* (2006) available at http://edition.cnn.com/2006/WORLD/asiapcf/01/26/musharraf.davos/. The President is also quoted as referring to the violation of Pakistani sovereignty by al Qaeda. How the law applies in the example quoted is complicated by the fact that it would seem that the complaint by the President of Pakistan was not so much that the US had taken action but rather that it had taken action contrary to an agreement reached between the two states.

[129] Sofaer 1989, p 108. The 'United States also supports the right of a state to strike terrorists within the territory of another State where the terrorists are using that territory as a location from which to launch terrorist attacks and where the State involved has failed to respond effectively to a demand that the attacks be stopped.' (ibid).

adequately act in response to a request to do so.[130] Also worth noting in this context is if a state is acting in national self-defence, the geographic location of the target need not as matter of law be in the same state as the state from which the original attack emanated. Suppose state B suffers an attack emanating from state C. As long as an attack on a target in state D meets the requirements of necessity,[131] proportionality and imminence, state B may attack a target in state D regardless of there being no other connection between state C and state D than the presence of the target inside state D.[132] In the above circumstances, it would be lawful for the government forces of state B to engage in the use of force as part of an armed conflict on the territories of state C or D even though a state of armed conflict does not exist between those states.[133]

To summarise the above argument, government forces have a recognised right under international law to use force against opposing force non-state actors. Logically, international law should recognise a form of combatant's privilege for the government forces. In certain circumstances, the government forces can conduct operations against the opposing force in the territory of another state.[134] This is particularly true when consent has been given by that state, but also extends to where that state has been unable or unwilling to prevent the use of its territory by the non-state actors. In such a case, a form of combatant's privilege for the government forces should also exist extraterritorially under international law.[135] International law does not require the government forces to wear a uniform or other distinctive sign when undertaking operations, including operations involving the use of force. International law does not require the government forces to be solely military forces. Logically, therefore, international law should also recognise a form of combatant's privilege for civilian government forces involved in operations against opposing force non-state actors, including where those operations occur, in certain limited circumstances,[136] in the territory of another state. The proceeding argument notwithstanding, it remains the case that the law on a form of combatant's privilege for government forces in a non-international armed conflict

---

[130] See Lubell 2010, pp 46–48; Schmitt 2008a. See also the comments of Michael Lewis during a panel on 'Drone Warfare, Targeted Killings and the Law of Armed Conflict,' sponsored by the Federalist Society and the J.B. Moore Society of International Law, 1 November 2010 (audio available at http://www.law.virginia.edu/html/news/2010_fall/drones.htm) wherein he equates the duties of States that have non-State actors on their territory to the duties of neutrals and rights of belligerents in an international armed conflict. See generally Blank 2011, pp 8–9.

[131] Noting that if state D is cooperating to suppress the threat to state B, it would be unlikely that any use of force by state B on the territory of state D without state D's consent would meet the threshold requirement of 'necessity.'

[132] Lubell 2010, pp 66–68.

[133] Paust 2010b, pp 242.

[134] See supra n 86.

[135] See the argument and reference to state practice from the *Caroline* case in Paust 2010b, pp 278–279.

[136] With consent, or where the territorial state has proved unable or unwilling to prevent the use of its territory by the non-state actor.

is not well enough developed to reach a definitive conclusion on whether such a privilege would extend to cross-border (or other extraterritorial) actions.

4.7 A Third Legal Paradigm for Regulating the Use of Force?

A topical question is whether there is a legal entitlement for a government to use force outside of an armed conflict and in otherwise than a law enforcement activity? In particular, may a government use lethal force in national self-defence where the use of that force is not governed by the law of armed conflict (which is one type of legal paradigm) nor law-enforcement rules (a second type of legal paradigm)[137] but rather is *regulated* by a third legal paradigm?[138] While not a completely new idea, most of the commentary has occurred in only the last few years and predominately in the United States of America.

The Legal Adviser for the US Department of State gave a brief outline for what that third legal paradigm might be when he said: 'But a state that is engaged in an armed conflict or in legitimate self-defense is not required to provide targets with legal process before the state may use lethal force.'[139] His comments have been interpreted as meaning that in certain circumstances, and outside of an armed conflict, a state may use lethal force against a person in national self-defence and not just in the law enforcement paradigm of individual self-defence.[140] For example, Anderson argues that the legal basis for the use of force is not an exclusive binary made up of armed conflict and law enforcement, and that national self-defence is an independent legal basis for the use of force.[141] Importantly, as I understand him, his argument is not just about the *resort* to the use of force, but what legal paradigm *governs* the use of force once force is resorted to by a state. Anderson refers to an example where a state uses force on the territory of another state against a terrorist organisation. He writes that while such use of force might be in the form of an armed conflict, 'it might be something that does not rise to that level of hostilities and thus constitute an act of self-defense use of force

[137] For a detailed explanation of what is meant by 'law enforcement' in the context of distinguishing between the legal paradigms of 'armed conflict' and 'law enforcement', see Melzer 2008, pp 86–90.

[138] It is worth noting that, unfortunately, the Israeli High Court case of *The Public Committee against Torture in Israel* v *The Government of Israel* HCJ 769/02 (13 December 2006) is not helpful on this point. While at first glance it might seem relevant, the court in the case held that an *international armed conflict* existed between Israel and various terrorist organizations (paras 16–18, President Barak).

[139] Koh 2010, [emphasis added].

[140] This is consistent with previous US statements and practice. For a brief review of US and other state practice (mainly Israeli) concerning relying on national self-defence to justify the use of force in response to a terrorist attack, see Gray 2008, pp 195–198.

[141] Anderson 2010a, p 9. See also Anderson 2010c.

simpliciter.'[142] He even makes specific mention of the use of drones by civilian CIA agents not being 'contrary to international law insofar as it is an exercise of lawful self-defense.'[143] From the context, it appears that he was referring to both the resort to use of force and the regulation of that use of force. Anderson also writes that the rules that regulate that use of force would be:

> '... the principles underlying armed conflict rules, distinction and proportionality and, I would add, necessity in the first place in determining to target. Necessity giving rise to self-defense; distinction in defining the target; proportionality in the evaluation of collateral damage.'[144]

While Anderson refers to the 'principles underlying armed conflict rules', it seems that he is not saying those principles apply due to being rules of armed conflict. Rather, he is arguing that the principles that apply do so on a different normative basis but they share a similar normative expression as the rules that apply in an armed conflict. Professor Kretzmer also sets out an argument for what he calls a 'mixed model' between pure law enforcement and clear armed conflict.[145]

Conversely, others argue that there are only two legal paradigms authorising the use of lethal force: armed conflict or law enforcement. For example, Shamsi states that '[t]argeted killings may take place either (a) in the context of armed conflict, in which the more permissive lethal force rules of the laws of war generally apply, or (b) in the context of law enforcement operations, in which more restrictive human rights law applies.'[146] Indeed, later in her statement Shamsi explicitly states that a claim of national self-defence is a legal basis for the use of force addresses only the *jus ad bellum* issue (the resort to the use of force) and that this legal doctrine alone does not provide the *jus in bello* answers (the regulation of that use of force).[147]

One way this question can be answered is by considering whether there is a factual scenario that would legally allow for the use of lethal force but would be neither law enforcement nor armed conflict. One hypothetical example involves a small terrorist organization located in remote territory in state B. The terrorist organization (known by the acronym STO) was recently formed and has little to no affiliation with other terrorist organizations, insurgent non-state actors or state sponsors etc. Perhaps due to civil unrest, an unrelated conflict or for other any

---

[142] Anderson 2010c.

[143] Anderson 2010b, p 6. For a longer exposition of his arguments, see Anderson 2009, pp 11–12.

[144] Anderson 2010c. See also Paust 2010a. On the issue of 'distinction' during the use of lethal force against grave threats, the Inter-American Commission on Human Rights has stated that: ... in peacetime situations, state agents must distinguish between persons who, by their actions, constitute an imminent threat of death or serious injury, or a threat of committing a particularly serious crime involving a grave threat to life, and persons who do not present such a threat, and use force only against the former. (Inter-American Commission on Human Rights, supra n. 38, Executive Summary, para 21) .

[145] Kretzmer 2005.

[146] Shamsi 2010, p 3. See also Melzer 2008, p xiii.

[147] Shamsi 2010, p 6.

other reason, the government forces of state B cannot assert effective control over the area where STO is based. However, STO itself also does not control the territory. There is no intelligence to indicate STO is responsible for previous terrorist attacks, nor has STO claimed responsibility for any such attacks. However, STO maintains a website and through other media opportunities has made it clear that its goals are to force state C to amend its foreign and domestic policies on various issues and that it will pursue those goals through terrorist action.

State C receives highly reliable, classified intelligence that STO is planning to conduct a deadly terrorist attack on a mass public transit system that usually carries a large number of citizens from state C. It is not known whether the attack will occur in the territory of state B, state C, or some other state but the intelligence indicates that the necessary materiel and personnel for the attack are dispersed and are not in the remote region of state B. The attack is planned to occur sometime during a 5 day window following a meeting of key STO hierarchy. There are no details of when that meeting will occur, but state C has through various intelligence means identified the commencement of a gathering of people at a known STO building that has key features that are out of the ordinary from the usual pattern-of-life for that building. Intelligence further indicates that three of the five key hierarchy are present with the whereabouts of the other two undetermined.

State B has no objection to state C taking action against STO but has advised state C in confidential communications that it is unable to do so itself. State B is unwilling for state C to send nationals of state C into state B's territory for direct action against STO, and in any event this has been assessed by state C as being both operationally impractical and could not be done in a timely manner.

The above scenario meets the requirements for allowing state C to act in national self-defence, even though it would be against a non-state actor.[148] Suppose now that state C has the technological capacity to strike the STO building

[148] For a discussion on the *jus ad bellum* legal issues associated with acting in national self-defence against non-State actors, see the separate opinions of Judges Kooijmans and Simma (Case concerning armed activities on the territory of the Congo (*Democratic Republic of the Congo* v *Uganda*) (separate opinion of Judge Kooijmans) [2005] ICJ Rep 168, paras 26–31; and Case concerning armed activities on the territory of the Congo (*Democratic Republic of the Congo* v *Uganda*) (separate opinion of Judge Simma) [2005] ICJ Rep 168, paras 12–13; Lubell 2010, Chapter I; Schmitt 2008a, pp 11–13; Schmitt 2008b; Paust 2010b; and generally Gray 2008, pp 134–143. Probably contra on whether a planned terrorist attack of this nature would be sufficient for a state to invoke the right of national self-defence, see O'Connell 2010b, p 14 As to the lawfulness of acting against an imminent threat, see Report of the High-level Panel on Threats, Challenges and Change, 'A more secure world: Our shared responsibility' (2004) para 188; Lubell 2010, pp 55–63 (a particularly good discussion on 'pre-emptive', 'anticipatory' and 'interceptive'); O'Connell 2007, p 503; Schmitt 2008a, pp 16–19. See also Glazier 2010; Alston 2010, para 45. I acknowledge that Alston might criticize my example as creating a hypothetical that posits 'a rare emergency exception to an absolute prohibition', Alston 2010, para 86. While not suggesting that pre-emptive attacks are lawful, in determining whether a non-state actor is posing an imminent threat, it is worth distinguishing between a state acquiring military capacity (which is something it may lawfully do without thereby demonstrating an intent to attack another state) and a non-state actor acquiring similar capacity (which arguably can be acquired only for a non-lawful purpose).

with a drone-launched missile operated by state C's civilian intelligence agency. This attack would not be classical law enforcement.[149] It is clearly not an international armed conflict as it is not a conflict between states. Even if both states B and C were parties to Additional Protocol II, it is not a non-international armed conflict governed by Additional Protocol II due to not meeting the criteria set out in Article 1(1) thereof.[150] Finally, it would also not amount to any other form of non-international armed conflict.[151] Whether something amounts to an armed conflict is assessed on a case-by-case basis against certain established criteria.[152] The Appeals Chamber for the ICTY has held that 'an armed conflict exists whenever there is a resort to armed force between states or *protracted* armed violence between governmental authorities and organized armed groups or between such groups within a state.'[153]

The Trial Chamber of the ICTY held in relation to the meaning of 'protracted armed violence' that the intensity of the violence may be more determinative than the duration.[154] And particularly in relation to non-international armed conflict, the trial chamber of the ICTR affirmed *Tadić* and then noted that the commentary prepared by the ICRC on Common Article 3 provides useful, albeit not

---

[149] For a discussion on the legal issues for the use of force against terrorist networks outside of the law enforcement paradigm, see Schmitt 2008a.

[150] Further, Additional Protocol II is 'intended to apply only to intense armed fighting and not mere incidents.' (International Law Association, 'Final Report on the Meaning of Armed Conflict in International Law' (2010) p 12, http://www.ila-hq.org/download.cfm/docid/2176DC63-D268-4133-8989A664754F9F87.

[151] See Lubell 2010, p 106.

[152] *Prosecutor* v *Rutaganda*, Case No. ICTR-96-3 (Trial Chamber), 6 December 1999, para 93. For a very good article discussing the types of armed conflicts and the relevant legal tests, see Vite 2009, p 69.

[153] *Prosecutor* v *Tadić*, Case No. IT-94-1 (Appeals Chamber), Decision on the Defence Motion for Interlocutory Appeal on Jurisdiction, 2 October 1995, para 70 [emphasis added]. See also *Prosecutor* v *Kunarac, Kovač and Voković*, Case No. IT-96-23 and IT-96-23/1 (Appeals Chamber), 12 June 2002, para 56. See also *Juan Carlos Abella* v *Argentina*, Case 11.137, Report No. 55/97, Inter-Am. C.H.R., OEA/Ser.L/V/II.98, Doc. 6 rev., 18 November 1997, paras 149–156 (holding that a 30 h confrontation between 42 armed persons inside a military barracks and units of the Argentine military sent to recapture the barracks was an armed conflict). See generally International Law Association, supra n. 151.

[154] *Prosecutor* v *Haradinaj*, Case No. IT-04-84-T, Judgment (Trial Chamber), 3 April 2008, para 49 – 'The criterion of protracted armed violence has therefore been interpreted in practice, including by the Tadić Trial Chamber itself, as referring more to the intensity of the armed violence than to its duration. Trial Chambers have relied on indicative factors relevant for assessing the "intensity" criterion, none of which are, in themselves, essential to establish that the criterion is satisfied. These indicative factors include the number, duration and intensity of individual confrontations; the type of weapons and other military equipment used; the number and calibre of munitions fired; the number of persons and type of forces partaking in the fighting; the number of casualties; the extent of material destruction; and the number of civilians fleeing combat zones. The involvement of the UN Security Council may also be a reflection of the intensity of a conflict.' See also *Prosecutor* v *Boskoski and Tarcolovski*, Case No. IT-04-82-T, Judgment (Trial Chamber), 10 July 2008, para 177.

determinative,[155] criteria for determining when there is a non-international armed conflict.[156] In the scenario as described, there would not be a state of protracted armed violence. In such a circumstance, it is legally possible to have 'an armed attack that is not part of intense armed fighting [and so] is not part of an armed conflict.'[157]

In light of what legal categories a strike by state C on the STO is not, the conclusion must be that in appropriate circumstances it is possible to have a use of lethal force that does not amount to an armed conflict[158] and does not amount to law enforcement. Accordingly, it must be some third category.[159] This conclusion is in agreement with Anderson's views that *armed conflict* and *law enforcement* are not an exclusive binary. Rather, as recognised by the American Civil Liberties Union, there is a third legal regime based on the use of lethal force if it is 'an exercise of "necessary and appropriate force" used only as a last resort to prevent imminent threats.'[160] The imminent threat must also be one that is 'likely to cause death or serious physical injury.'[161]

It is worth noting that while this particular scenario would not amount to an armed conflict, that is due to the limited nature of the strike and is not because it is a counter-terrorist operation. Contrary to some views,[162] there is no legal reason why counter-terrorist operations in response to ongoing terrorist-style attacks cannot amount to an armed conflict.[163] A counter-terrorist operation will usually

---

155 *Prosecutor* v *Boskoski and Tarcolovski*, Case No. IT-04-82-T, Judgment (Trial Chamber), 10 July 2008, para 176.

156 *Prosecutor* v *Akayesu*, Case No. ICTR-96-4-T (Trial Chamber), 2 September 1998, paras 619–620. See also Pictet, 1952, Vol I, pp 49–50.

157 International Law Association, supra n 151, p 8.

158 See Anderson 2010b.

159 See Blum and Heymann 2010, pp 168–170, who discuss the legality of targeted killings that fall outside of both armed conflict and law enforcement; Paust 2010a, p 3 ('the self-defense paradigm is different from both a mere law of war or law enforcement paradigm'). Alston also seems to recognise this as a conceptually possible legal conclusion, albeit he also appears to be critical of the thought process involved and compares it to the ticking time bomb scenario used to justify torture, Alston 2010, para 86.

160 American Civil Liberties Union, Statement, Hearing on 'The Rise of the Drones II: Examining the Legality of Unmanned Targeting', Committee on Oversight and Government Reform, US House of Representatives (2010) p 2, available at http://oversight.house.gov/index.php?option=com_content&task=view&id=4903&Itemid=30.

161 Ibid.

162 For example, see European Commission for Democracy Through Law (Venice Commission), 'Opinion on the International Legal Obligations of Council of Europe Member States in Respect of Secret Detention Facilities and Inter-State Transport of Prisoners', 17 March 2006, Op. No. 363/2005, CDL-AD (2006)009, paras 78–79. See also International Law Association, supra n 151, pp 15 (n 68), 25–26 and 28. However, it maybe that the International Law Association report agrees with my view that the legal issue is about intensity and organisation, not whether an action is characterised as 'terrorism' or 'counter-terrorism.'

163 *Prosecutor* v *Boskoski and Tarcolovski*, Case No. IT-04-82-T, Judgment (Trial Chamber), 10 July 2008, paras 184–190. This point was affirmed on appeal, *Prosecutor* v *Boskoski and Tarcolovski*, Case No. IT-04-82-T, Judgment (Appeal Chamber), 19 May 2010, paras 32–37.

not amount to an armed conflict due to lack of protracted armed violence[164] against an organised group. However, if the objective criteria for an armed conflict are made out,[165] then the violence will amount to an armed conflict. The fact that one side pursues its aims through terrorist-style attacks cannot, of itself, be legally determinative of whether or not the opposing forces are engaged in an armed conflict.[166]

In arguing for this third legal paradigm, I do not conflate the *jus ad bellum* with the *jus in bello*. What I am arguing, and what I believe the State Department Legal Adviser and Anderson were arguing, is that there is a factual situation that falls outside of both armed conflict and law enforcement, and in that third factual circumstance the legal rules that govern the resort to the use of lethal force and that regulate the use of lethal force are reduced to the same basic and fundamental legal principles of necessity and proportionality.[167] Adopting the discourse used in discussing the role of human rights law during an armed conflict, my argument is that in this third legal paradigm the legal concepts of *necessity* and *proportionality* as those concepts are understood in the law relating to national self-defence provide both the *jus ad bellum* and also the *lex specialis* against which to judge whether the use of lethal force was lawful under human rights standards.[168] Indeed, Alston refers to this concept earlier in his report before pursuing a contrary line of argument later in his report.[169]

In this third legal paradigm, the legal concepts of *necessity* and *proportionality* in the context of *regulating* the use of force are the same as how Alston used those terms in his recent report.

> 'A State killing is legal only if it is required to protect life (making lethal force *proportionate*) and there is no other means, such as capture or nonlethal incapacitation, of preventing that threat to life (making lethal force *necessary*). The proportionality requirement limits the permissible level of force based on the threat posed by the suspect to others. The necessity requirement imposes an obligation to minimize the level of force

[164] See *Prosecutor* v *Kordić and Čerkez*, Case No. IT-95-14/2-A, Judgment (Appeals Chamber), 17 December 2004, para 341, which distinguishes 'single acts of terrorism' from being an armed conflict. See also *Prosecutor* v *Boskoski and Tarcolovski*, Case No. IT-04-82-T, Judgment (Trial Chamber), 10 July 2008, para 190 ('while isolated acts of terrorism may not reach the threshold of armed conflict, when there is protracted violence of this type, especially where they require the engagement of the armed forces in hostilities, such acts are relevant to assessing the level of intensity with regard to the existence of an armed conflict').

[165] Which is a factual matter that needs 'to be determined in light of the particular evidence available and on a case-by-case basis', *Prosecutor* v *Boskoski and Tarcolovski*, Case No. IT-04-82-T, Judgment (Trial Chamber), 10 July 2008, para 175.

[166] 'It is immaterial whether the acts of violence perpetrated may or may not be characterised as terrorist in nature.' (*Prosecutor* v *Boskoski and Tarcolovski*, Case No. IT-04-82-T, Judgment (Trial Chamber), 10 July 2008, para 185.).

[167] See Lubell 2010, pp 171 and 257. Contra, see Alston 2010, paras 42–43.

[168] See the succinct and clear discussion on the use of lethal force inside and outside of an armed conflict and the role of human rights law in Schmitt 2010a, pp 41–42.

[169] Alston 2010, para 32 but then see paras 42–43.

used, regardless of the amount that would be proportionate, through, for example, the use of warnings, restraint and capture.'[170]

There is also a need to consider the effects of any use of force on bystanders and their property. It has been suggested that the test would be similar to how the concept of proportionality is used inside an armed conflict, albeit possibly to a higher standard.[171] On this point, I am not certain. In a law enforcement scenario, the assumption is that in most circumstances no collateral injury or damage is legally permissible.[172] At a minimum, compensation is likely to be payable. However, in an armed conflict, a certain level of collateral injury and damage is legally permissible[173] and no legal obligation to pay compensation arises. While not fully embracing the existence of a third legal paradigm, Alston nonetheless states that if a strike resulted in the 'killing of anyone other than the target (family members or others in the vicinity, for example) [that] would be an arbitrary deprivation of life under human rights law and could result in state responsibility *and individual criminal liability*.'[174] Kretzmer has also suggested that the 'presumption should be that suspected terrorists may not be targeted when there is a real danger that civilians will be killed or wounded too.'[175] Noting the lack of any clear authority on this point, at this time the better conclusion is that it is currently uncertain what is the legal principle or rule on this issue. If the concept of a regulating third legal regime is accepted, then more work needs to be done to address this very important aspect on the use of lethal force.

Assuming that there is a third legal paradigm in which a lethal strike could occur outside of both an armed conflict and a law enforcement operation, the next question is who could conduct such a strike. In his statement that dealt with a number of legal issues associated with the use of armed drones, and at a time when the public debate included significant comment on the proper role for the CIA in the operation of armed drones, the State Department Legal Adviser did not touch upon the question of who may operate the armed drones.[176] Likewise, Anderson in his recent statement following on from the State Department Legal Adviser's statement leaves this point unaddressed. Also, testimony to the US House of

170 Ibid., para 32 [emphases in original].

171 Anderson 2010d, p 33. See also Anderson 2010c.

172 In 'domestic law enforcement, the police must hold their fire if they believe that there is a danger to innocent bystanders, except where using lethal force against a suspect is reasonably believed likely to reduce the number of innocent deaths', Blum and Heymann 2010, p 148.

173 For example, see Arts. 51(5)(b) and 57(2)(a)(iii) Additional Protocol I and rule 14 of the Customary International Humanitarian Law (Henckaerts and Doswald-Beck 2005). When assessing the potential loss of civilian life or injury, every civilian is equal and entitled to just as much protection under the principle of proportionality as any other civilian (Henderson 2009, p 192; but see O'Connell 2010b, p 24; while Oeter leaves the question open in Oeter 2008, p 119, at paras 445(3) and 456(3)).

174 Alston 2010, para 86 [emphasis added].

175 Kretzmer 2005, p 204.

176 See Koh 2010.

Representatives sub-committee was given by Professor Radsan on the limitations of strikes by the CIA, but again he suggested no limitation on who could conduct the strikes.[177] The reason why these statements are of interest is that they are some of the clearest statements setting out national self-defence as a governing legal basis for the use of armed force, and the statements were made in the context of a debate about the proper role for the CIA in the use of armed drones. It is notable that the statements did not indicate that there was any restriction as to who could conduct the strike when the statements were made in the context of strikes by the CIA.

Shamsi states that were a CIA operative to conduct a lethal strike this would not be a war-crime but would expose the CIA operative to prosecution under domestic law as the CIA operative does not enjoy the immunity from prosecution provided to the military under the law of armed conflict.[178] While I will return to the issue of criminal liability under domestic law, the statement is support for the view that such actions are not criminal under international law. Also, Watkin's has argued that in certain complex security situations, a military need not wear a uniform to distinguish itself from the civilian population.[179] Importantly, the concept of 'distinction' referred to above in the context of national self-defence[180] concerns directing attacks at appropriate targets—it is not about who may conduct those attacks. This is because the familiar rules from the law of armed conflict on who may conduct attacks during an international armed conflict simply do not apply *de jure*. So, where anti-terrorist operations against Group X do not amount to an armed conflict but rather are merely 'a legitimate act of self-defense in response to a persistent and credible threat',[181] there would be no law of armed conflict issues concerning activities by civilian intelligence operatives.

It appears, therefore, that there is no restriction in international law limiting the use of lethal force to military forces where the strikes are being governed by a third legal paradigm of national self-defence. Accordingly, where a use of force is authorised under international law (e.g., by Article 51 UN Charter) but does not amount to a use of force inside an international armed conflict, it is legal under international law for a CIA operative who is not in uniform, does not carry his or her arms openly etc. to engage in that use of force.[182] Indeed, as the law of armed conflict is not the applicable legal regime, it is also lawful for the CIA operative to employ means and methods that are prohibited under the law of armed conflict but are not otherwise generally prohibited under international law—e.g., to use bullets that expand or easily flatten in the human body.

---

177 Radsan 2010, p 2.

178 Shamsi 2010, p 9 (n 22).

179 Watkin 2005, pp 66-67.

180 See supra n 145.

181 Machon 2006, p 44.

182 Anderson 2010d, p 27.

The absence of a restriction under international law on civilian intelligence agents conducting the lethal strike is not the same legal point as to whether the person who does conduct the strike has the equivalent of the combatant's privilege to be immune from prosecution under domestic law. The existence or otherwise of an immunity from domestic criminal law prosecution is even more problematic in the context of the use of lethal force regulated by the legal paradigm of national self-defence than it is under attacks regulated by the law of non-international armed conflict. There is no treaty article granting such immunity. I am unaware of any recent commentary directly suggesting the existence of a customary international law rule granting such immunity.[183] Also, there is not as clear an overt recognition of the existence of law regulating acts conducted 'purely' under national self-defence as there is for acts conducted in the context of a non-international armed conflict. However, it certainly remains the case that it is lawful for a government to engage in acts of national self-defence, which will have to be executed through its agents. Therefore, to the extent that a government is lawfully acting in national self-defence, and to the extent that an act performed in national self-defence meets the requirements of necessity and proportionality, it seems logical that any act by a government agent should attract immunity from domestic prosecution. Otherwise, like the non-international armed conflict example, a government's right to act in national self-defence would be severely hampered. If the law were otherwise, any agent acting prima facie lawfully on the government's behalf would also have to accept that he or she was exposing his or herself to lawful domestic prosecution.[184] Interestingly, Alston's recent report seems to impliedly suggest such an immunity exists, in that he directly refers to individual criminal liability for 'killing of anyone *other than the target*.'[185]

Of course, the preceding argument is predicated on two assumptions. The first assumption is that there is a third legal paradigm regulating the use of force in addition to law enforcement and armed conflict. If the starting assumption is incorrect, then a person using lethal force on behalf of a state would attract immunity from domestic prosecution only in those circumstances were they either complied with law enforcement rules or were entitled to assert the combatant's privilege under the relevant law of armed conflict. Second, assuming that there is a third legal paradigm regulating the use of force in addition to law enforcement and armed conflict, then the agent's act must have been pursuant to a bona fide act of national self-defence on behalf of the state and must meet the legal requirements of necessity[186] and proportionality. Acts that a government claims are in its national

---

[183] I do note though that Paust argues for the existence of such a rule of immunity on similar grounds as I do in the remainder of this paragraph (Paust 2010b, pp 278–279).

[184] Ibid.

[185] Alston 2010, para 86 [emphasis added].

[186] In particular, that no option other than the use of lethal force existed, Kretzmer 2005, p 203; Schmitt 2010a, p 42; Blum and Heymann 2010, p 169. See also Doswald-Beck 2006, pp 894–898 and 902. While Doswald-Beck's discussion is in the context of international humanitarian law, I suggest her arguments apply *a fortiori* to situations not amounting to an armed conflict.

interests but do not amount to a legitimate act of national self-defence would not attract the immunity. The act must also occur outside of an armed conflict (including a state of occupation), or else the act would have to be assessed against under a different legal paradigm. Finally, force could be used in another state only after having exhausted options to get that other state to effectively respond to the threat posed—otherwise it would not be a legitimate act of national self-defence. Even if all of the previous conditions did apply, at this time the best that can be said is that there is an argument for the existence of an international law rule providing for legal immunity. Whether or not that is the law remains uncertain.

4.8 Non-Military Aircraft Conducting Belligerent Acts

There is one final point concerning the status of the armed drones themselves. As a matter of customary international law, only military aircraft are entitled to engage in belligerent acts during an *international* armed conflict.[187] Where a civilian intelligence agency is operating its own armed drones, then by definition those drones will not be military aircraft.[188] Accordingly, the use of such drones to conduct belligerent acts during an international armed conflict would be a breach of a state's obligations under international law. However, the use of a non-military aircraft to conduct belligerent acts is not of itself a war crime. Also, the above rule concerning military aircraft and belligerent acts applies only during an international armed conflict. There is no corresponding rule for non-international armed conflicts[189] or during acts of national self-defence outside of an armed conflict. Therefore, outside of an international armed conflict, to the extent that use of lethal force by a civilian intelligence operative it otherwise in compliance with international law, it is irrelevant that the armed drone is not a military aircraft.

4.9 Conclusion

It is hard to think of a more important legal issue than the legal authority for the use of lethal force. Concurrently with a state's duty to protect its citizens from foreign threats, people must be protected from illegal acts; and government agents

[187] See Arts. 13 and 16 Hague *Rules of Air Warfare* 1923 and rule 17(a) of the Program on Humanitarian Policy and Conflict Research, supra n 75. As to whether the Hague *Rules of Air Warfare* reflect customary international law see *Prosecutor* v *Galić*, (Trial Chamber) Case No. IT-98-29-T (5 December 2003) n 103; see generally Henderson 2009, pp 26–27. While the *Manual on International Law Applicable to Air and Missile Warfare* is not declarative of what is customary international law, it is highly persuasive.

[188] See the definition of military aircraft at Arts. 3, 14 and 15 Hague *Rules of Air Warfare* 1923 and rule 1.(x) of the *Manual on International Law Applicable to Air and Missile Warfare*, supra n 75.

[189] Program on Humanitarian Policy and Conflict Research, supra n 13, p 101.

acting on behalf of their state should know their own legal position. If there is to be government by rule of law,[190] the law must be known and respected. As inter-state relations are subject to international law, there are legal limits on a state's acts. Where a state chooses to disregard those legal limits, the state cannot expect the actions of its agents, including its intelligence agents, to be exempt for legal consideration.[191] And no one state is entitled to determine the law for all others.[192]

The use of armed drones, and particularly the use by civilian intelligence agencies, has generated significant media and legal interest. The focus of this article has been on the law concerning the operation of armed drones by civilian intelligence agents. Many of the conclusions and arguments also apply to contractors and other persons tasked by a government. However, the fact that lethal force is being employed by armed drones is not a significant legal distinction. There is no unique law applying to armed drones. Rather, the employment of armed drones needs to be analysed under the ordinary principles of international law applying to the resort to the use of force, the rules regulating the use of force and so forth. What is not addressed in this article are any policy considerations concerning whether a particular course of action should be adopted.

Where a state uses lethal force outside of its own borders, that use of force must comply with the UN Charter. Putting to one side Chapter VII UN Security Council resolutions, this will usually mean the law of national self-defence must be considered to determine whether the resort to the use of force was lawful. A separate question from the resort to the use of force is the law that regulates the use of that force. Where the use of force amounts to an armed conflict, that law is predominately the law of armed conflict.

If the armed conflict is of an international character, the law of armed conflict authorises combatants to use lethal force against enemy combatants and civilians taking a direct part in hostilities. Importantly, international law grants combatant

---

190 Which is perhaps never more important a concept than when fighting terrorism, see Sofaer 1989, p 89.

191 See a statement by Anderson in the context of discussing an article by Professor Solis on the issue of the CIA conducting armed drone acts and where Solis had concluded that it was likely a war-crime: 'Professor Solis concludes by stating that the "prosecution of CIA personnel is certainly not suggested". I have trouble understanding why not, if one accepts the legal view of unlawful combatancy by the CIA.' Anderson 2010a, p 9. But see Anderson 2010b, p 4: 'Congress ought to make clear, through pronouncement and resolutions and, even better, through legislation, that any attempts to use international or foreign legal process to go after these officers in pursuit of their duties at the intelligence agencies would be regarded as a serious and unfriendly act toward the United States. It is crucial that the two political branches send a single message that the United States stands behind its self-defense operations as such..'

192 But see Anderson 2010b, p 8: 'Congress needs to clarify its lawfulness, and frankly make clear that countries that seek to gainsay the US's own considered legal view on this topic, including allies and NATO allies, such as unsupervised prosecutors in Spain or elsewhere, will discover that there are consequences.' In fairness, this statement should be read in light of a fuller articulation of the role of the US in developing and interpreting international law in Anderson 2010d, pp 29–30. For an interesting article that devotes many pages to discussing the use and abuse of 'interpretations' of the law of armed conflict, see Schmitt 2008b, p 796.

immunity from domestic criminal law prosecution where the combatant acts within the law of armed conflict. Civilians, including members of civilian intelligence agencies, who engage in acts directly contributing to the use of lethal force, lose protection from attack themselves and have no immunity from domestic criminal law prosecution. The civilians do not, however, by the mere act of directly contributing to the use of lethal force commit a crime under international law (i.e., their acts do not make them war criminals).

If the armed conflict is of a non-international character, the law of armed conflict is silent on who may acts as 'fighters' for the government forces. Accordingly, the government may choose to authorise any of its agents, be they military or civilian, to use lethal force against the opposing force. It is my argument that any agent so authorised by the government enjoys the equivalent of the combatant's immunity from domestic criminal law prosecution where the agent acts within the law of armed conflict. Therefore, unlike in the international armed conflict scenario, members of civilian intelligence agencies who engage in acts directly contributing to the use of lethal force in a non-international armed conflict do have immunity from domestic criminal law prosecution. Also, they retain a form of immunity from attack, in that the opposing force has no lawful right to target anyone, be they military or civilian. And like the international armed conflict scenario, civilian intelligence agents do not by the mere act of directly contributing to the use of lethal force commit a crime under international law.

Where the use of lethal force on behalf of a state does not rise to the threshold of an armed conflict but is also not a law enforcement action, there is a third legal paradigm that regulates the use of force in these circumstances. In this scenario, while not regulated by the law of armed conflict, the legal outcomes for a civilian intelligence agent are functionally the same as those found in a non-international armed conflict. The government may choose to authorise a civilian intelligence agent to use lethal force on its behalf, the agent is not liable to lawful attack, and the agent commits no international law crime where the agent's acts are part of a bona fide act of national self-defence on behalf of a state and those acts meet all applicable legal requirements. While there is an argument that such acts should enjoy immunity from domestic criminal law prosecution, the state of international law on that point is uncertain.

References

Allison E (2007) Comments on 'Military commissions review court misconstruing "unlawful combatant". http://jurist.law.pitt.edu/hotline/2007/09/military-commissions-review-court.php

Alston P (2010) Report of the Special Rapporteur on extrajudicial, summary or arbitrary executions, A/HRC/14/24/Add.6

Anderson K (2009) Targeted killing in U.S. counterterrorism strategy and law, Washington DC, Brookings Institution Press. http://www.brookings.edu/~/media/Files/rc/papers/2009/0511_counterterrorism_anderson/0511_counterterrorism_anderson.pdf

Anderson K (2010a) Statement, hearing on 'Rise of the Drones: Unmanned Systems and the Future of War, Committee on Oversight and Government Reform. US House of Representatives p 11 http://oversight.house.gov/index.php?option=com_content&task=view&id=4840&Itemid=30

Anderson K (2010b) Written testimony, Hearing on 'The Rise of the Drones II: Examining the Legality of Unmanned Targeting.' Committee on Oversight and Government Reform, US House of Representatives p 6. http://oversight.house.gov/index.php?option=com_content&task=view&id=4903&Itemid=30

Anderson K (2010c) Ken's not-yet-response re drone warfare and targeted killing and Professor Alston's Report, Opinio Juris. http://opiniojuris.org/2010/06/03/kens-not-yet-response-re-drone-warfare-and-targeted-killing-and-professor-alstons-report/

Anderson K (2010d) Predators over Pakistan, American University Washington College of Law. http://ssrn.com/abstract=1561229

Banks W (2010) Written testimony, Hearing on 'The Rise of the Drones II: Examining the Legality of Unmanned Targeting', Committee on Oversight and Government Reform. US House of Representatives http://oversight.house.gov/index.php?option=com_content&task=view&id=4903&Itemid=30

Baxter R (1951) So called unprivileged belligerency: spies, guerrillas and saboteurs. BYIL 28:323

Bill B (2010) Human rights: time for greater judge advocate understanding. Army Lawyer, pp 54–68

Blank L (2011) Defining the battlefield in contemporary conflict and counterterrorism: understanding the parameters of the zone of combat. Georgia JI and Comp L 39:1. http://ssrn.com/abstract=1677965

Blum G, Heymann P (2010) Law and policy of targeted killing. Harvard National Security Journal 1:145–170

Dinstein Y (2005) War, aggression and self-defence, 4th edn. Cambridge University Press, Cambridge

Dinstein Y (2010) The conduct of hostilities under the law of international armed Conflict, 2nd edn. Cambridge University Press, Cambridge

Doswald-Beck L (2006) The right to life in armed conflict: does international humanitarian law provide all the answers? IRRC 88/864:881–904

Entous A (2010) Special Report: how the White House learned to love the drone. Reuters http://www.reuters.com/article/idUSTRE64H5SL20100518?feedType=RSS&feedName=topNews

Fagan M (2010) Statement, hearing on 'Rise of the Drones: unmanned systems and the future of war, committee on oversight and government reform, US House of Representatives http://oversight.house.gov/index.php?option=com_content&task=view&id=4840&Itemid=30

Garlasco M (2009) Precisely wrong: Gaza civilians killed by Israeli drone-launched missiles, human rights watch, pp 10–12, http://www.hrw.org/en/reports/2009/06/30/precisely-wrong-0

Glazier D (2010) Written testimony, hearing on 'The Rise of the Drones II: examining the legality of unmanned targeting', committee on oversight and government reform, US House of Representatives. http://oversight.house.gov/index.php?option=com_content&task=view&id=4903&Itemid=30

Goldman RK and Tittemore BD (2002) Unprivileged combatants and the hostilities in Afghanistan: their status and rights under International Humanitarian and Human Rights Law, American Society of International Law: Task Force on Terrorism www.asil.org/taskforce/goldman.pdf

Gray C (2008) International law and the use of force, 3rd edn. Oxford University Press, Oxford

Greenwood C (2008) Scope of application of humanitarian law. In: Fleck D (ed) The handbook of humanitarian law in armed conflicts, 2nd edn. Oxford University Press, Oxford

Hays Parks W (1990) Air war and the law of war. Air Force LR 32:1–225

Henckaerts J, Doswald-Beck L (eds) (2005) Customary international humanitarian law, vol I rules. Cambridge University Press, Cambridge

Henderson I (2009) The contemporary law of targeting. military objectives, proportionality and precautions in attack under Additional Protocol I. Martinus Nijhoff, Leiden

Horton S (2010) The law of armed conflict: six questions for Gary Solis, Harper's Magazine. http://harpers.org/archive/2010/04/hbc-90006912

Ipsen K (2008) Combatants and non-combatants. In: Fleck D (ed) The handbook of humanitarian law in armed conflicts, 2nd edn. Oxford University Press, Oxford
Jenks C (2010) The law and policy implications of 'baited ambushes' utilizing enemy dead and wounded. Army Lawyer, pp 91–94
Koh H (2010) The Obama Administration and International Law, US Department of State. http://www.state.gov/s/l/releases/remarks/139119.htm
Kolb R (1997) Origin of the twin terms jus ad bellum/jus in bello. IRRC 320
Kretzmer D (2005) Targeted killing of suspected terrorists: extra-judicial executions or legitimate means of defence? EJIL 16:171–212
Lewis M (2010) Statement, hearing on 'The Rise of the Drones II: examining the legality of unmanned targeting', Committee on Oversight and Government Reform, US House of Representatives. http://oversight.house.gov/index.php?option=com_content&task=view&id=4903&Itemid=30
Lubell N (2010) Extraterritorial use of force against non-state actors. Oxford University Press, Oxford
Machon M (2006) Targeted killing as an element of U.S. foreign policy in the war on terror, School of Advanced Military Studies
Mayer J (2009) The predator war: what are the risks of the C.I.A.'s covert drone program?. The New Yorker. http://www.newyorker.com/reporting/2009/10/26/091026fa_fact_mayer
Melzer N (2008) Targeted killing in International Law. Oxford University Press, Oxford
Moussa J (2008) Can jus ad bellum override jus in bello? Reaffirming the separation of the two bodies of law. IRRC 90:963–990
Nabulsi K (2007) 'Jus ad Bellum/Jus in Bello', Crimes of War Project. http://www.crimesofwar.org/thebook/jus-ad-bellum.html
O'Connell ME (2007) The ban on the bomb–and bombing: Iran, the U.S., and the international law of self-defense. Syracuse LR 57:497–518
O'Connell ME (2010a) Written testimony, hearing on 'The Rise of the Drones II: examining the legality of unmanned targeting', Committee on Oversight and Government Reform. US House of Representatives http://oversight.house.gov/index.php?option=com_content&task=view&id=4903&Itemid=30
O'Connell ME (2010b) Unlawful killing with combat drones: a case study of Pakistan, 2004–2009, Notre Dame Law School, Legal Studies Research Paper No. 09-43. http://ssrn.com/abstract=1501144
Oeter S (2008) Methods and means of combat. In: Fleck D (ed) The Handbook of Humanitarian Law in Armed Conflicts, 2nd edn. Oxford University Press, Oxford
Paust J (2010a) Permissible self-defense targeting. Denver JIL & Pol. 40. http://ssrn.com/abstract=1707688
Paust J (2010b) Self-defense targetings of non-state actors and permissibility of U.S. drones in Pakistan. Journal of Transnational Law & Policy 19.2, p 237, http://papers.ssrn.com/sol3/papers.cfm?abstract_id=1520717
Pictet J (1952) The Geneva conventions of 12 August 1949: commentary, vol I. ICRC, Geneva
Pictet J (1960) The Geneva conventions of 12 August 1949: commentary, vol III. ICRC, Geneva
Priest D and Arkin W (2010) Top secret America, The Washington Post. http://projects.washingtonpost.com/top-secret-america/
Radsan A (2010) Statement, hearing on 'The Rise of the Drones II: examining the legality of unmanned targeting', Committee on Oversight and Government Reform, US House of Representatives, p 2. http://oversight.house.gov/index.php?option=com_content&task=view&id=4903&Itemid=30
Rona G (2007) Military commissions review court misconstruing 'unlawful combatant.' http://jurist.law.pitt.edu/hotline/2007/09/military-commissions-review-court.php
Sandoz Y, Swinarski C, Zimmerman B (eds) (1987) Commentary on the Additional Protocols of 8 June 1977 to the Geneva conventions of 12 August 1949, Geneva, ICRC, Dordrecht, Nijhoff
Sassòli M (2006) Transnational armed groups and international humanitarian law', Program on Humanitarian Policy and Conflict Research. www.hpcr.org/pdfs/OccasionalPaper6.pdf

Schmitt M (2008a) Responding to transnational terrorism under the jus ad bellum: a normative framework. Naval Law Review 56:1–41

Schmitt M (2008b) 'Change direction' 2006: Israeli operations in Lebanon and the international law of self-defense. Michigan JIL 29:127–164

Schmitt M (2010a) The interpretive guidance on the notion of direct participation in hostilities: a critical analysis. Harvard National Security Journal 1:5–44

Schmitt M (2010b) Military necessity and humanity in international humanitarian law: preserving the delicate balance. Virginia JIL 50(4):796–841

Shamsi H (2010) Statement, hearing on 'The Rise of the Drones II: examining the legality of unmanned targeting.' Committee on Oversight and Government Reform, US House of Representatives p 9. http://oversight.house.gov/index.php?option=com_content&task=view&id=4903&Itemid=30

Sofaer A (1989) Sixth Annual Waldemar A. Solf Lecture in International Law: terrorism, the law, and the national defense. Mil LR 126:89–123

Solf W (1983) The status of combatants in non-international armed conflicts under domestic law and transnational practice. Amer Univ LR 33:53–65

Solis G (2007) Targeted killing and the law of armed conflict. Naval war college review, pp 127–146

Solis G (2010) CIA drone attacks produce America's own unlawful combatants. The Washington Post, 12 March

Sullivan M (2010) DOD Could Achieve Greater Commonality and Efficiencies among Its Unmanned Aircraft Systems, hearing on 'Rise of the Drones: unmanned systems and the future of war, Committee on Oversight and Government Reform, US House of Representatives. p 4 http://oversight.house.gov/index.php?option=com_content&task=view&id=4840&Itemid=30

The Manual of the Law of Armed Conflict (2004) Oxford, UK Ministry of Defence. Oxford University Press

The Manual on the Law of Non-International Armed Conflict, With Commentary (2006) International Institute of Humanitarian Law

Thiesen M (2010) In CIA's drone mission, who will protect the CIA?, American enterprise institute for public policy research. http://www.aei.org/article/102152

Tierney J (2010) Chairman, Subcommittee on National Security and Foreign Affairs, Opening Statement, hearing on 'Rise of the Drones II: examining the legality of unmanned targeting', Committee on Oversight and Government Reform. U.S. House of Representatives http://oversight.house.gov/index.php?option=com_content&task=view&id=4903&Itemid=30

Vite S (2009) Typology of armed conflicts in international humanitarian law: legal concepts and actual situations. IRRC 91:69–94

Watkin K (2005) Warriors without rights? combatants, unprivileged belligerents, and the struggle over legitimacy, Program on Humanitarian Policy and Conflict Research. www.hpcr.org/pdfs/OccasionalPaper2.pdf

Chapter 5
International Humanitarian Law and Bombing Campaigns: Legitimate Military Objectives and Excessive Collateral Damage

Christine Byron

Contents

This article is based on a much updated version of a paper originally given at the Oslo University/Norwegian Red Cross Conference on International Humanitarian Law and International Criminal Law on 5 May 2003. The author would like to thank Mr. David Turns and Dr. Paul Kearns for their helpful comments on earlier drafts. Any remaining errors are, of course, the author's responsibility.

C. Byron (✉)
Cardiff University, Wales, UK
e-mail: ByronC@cardiff.ac.uk

M.N. Schmitt et al. (eds.), *Yearbook of International Humanitarian Law Volume 13, 2010*, DOI: 10.1007/978-90-6704-811-8_5,

5.1 Introduction

Despite the introduction and increasing use of 'smart' bombs,[1] recent bombing campaigns in Iraq, Afghanistan and Serbia, formerly known as the Federal Republic of Yugoslavia (FRY), have resulted in what some commentators consider to be an unacceptably high level of civilian casualties, especially when compared with the low level of combatant casualties in the attacking force.[2] During the most recent Gulf conflict, a conservative estimate suggests that over 1,100 Iraqi civilians died within the first 2 months as a result of aerial bombardment or missile attacks by Coalition forces and that approximately another 600 civilians were killed by unexploded ordinance during the same period.[3] There are no reliable statistics for civilians injured by aerial bombardment and unexploded ordinance in that period but the number is likely to have been many times higher than the number of fatalities.[4]

This paper will focus on the law which applies during international armed conflicts to aerial bombardment or missiles launched from warships in the context of individual criminal responsibility for such bombardment.[5] This necessitates a focus on the rules of aerial bombardment as set out in Additional Protocol I (API) which have been developed by the International Criminal Tribunal for the former Yugoslavia (ICTY) and by the definitions in the Rome Statute of the International Criminal Court (ICC) and in its Elements of Crime, although some comment will also be made as to the duties of non-state parties to API. In this context, first the principle of distinction between civilians and military and civilian objects and military objectives will be considered. This section will include discussion of 'hard cases' such as whether dual use objects or the media (if being used for propaganda) constitute legitimate military objectives. Secondly, the principle of proportionality, that is, the duty not to cause excessive civilian casualties, will be examined and will look at questions such as whether long term collateral damage should be taken into account in the proportionality equation. As part of this section, the duty to take precautions to reduce collateral damage will be considered. Finally, the application of this law to non-international armed conflicts will be briefly assessed.

[1] 'Smart bombs' are capable of being guided after their launch, see Harris 2010.

[2] Dinstein 2002, p 219.

[3] Figures based upon the 'minimum' column of reported deaths by aerial/missile attack in the Iraq Body Count Database between 20 March and 20 May. Available at www.iraqbodycount.org/database/, accessed 28 December 2010.

[4] Some information about civilian casualties in Iraq in March and April 2003 is given on the Project on Defence Alternatives website. www.comw.org/pda/0305iraqcasualtydata.html, accessed 28 December 2010.

[5] State responsibility for bombing campaigns is outside the scope of this article.

5.2 Additional Protocol 1 and the Law on Military Objectives

The prohibition of attacks upon civilians has been recognised at least as far back as the American Civil War.[6] However, during WW2 the practice of 'carpet bombing' of cities, which lead to the deaths of hundreds of thousands of civilians brought this proscription into question.[7] Now the 'basic rule' on distinguishing between civilians and military is contained in Article 48 of the 1977 Additional Protocol 1 (API) to the Geneva Conventions, which states that:

> 'the Parties to the conflict shall at all times distinguish between the civilian population and combatants and between civilian objects and military objectives and accordingly shall direct their operations only against military objectives.'

Article 51(2) of API also states that '[t]he civilian population as such, as well as individual civilians, shall not be the object of attack'.[8] Indeed, Kalshoven comments that this 'basic tenet' of the law of warfare was not doubted by the delegates at the Diplomatic Conference which led to the adoption of Additional Protocol 1 and furthermore this rule on distinction has been accepted as reflecting modern customary international law in the ICRC Study on customary international humanitarian law (hereinafter ICRC Study).[9]

5.2.1 Definition of civilians

API defines 'civilians' negatively, by excluding those defined as combatants in the Geneva Convention and Protocols.[10] One of the commentaries to API emphasises that the definition of civilians also includes individuals linked to the armed forces without being members thereof, such as civilians accompanying, serving and

---

[6] Article 22, Lieber Code, reprinted in Schindler and Toman 1998, p 3.

[7] The Hague Regulations did not expressly prohibit attacks against civilians and Article 22 of the 1923 Hague Rules of Aerial Warfare, reprinted in AJIL 17 (Supp. 1923) p 245, was not legally binding. On 30 September 1938, the League of Nations GA adopted a resolution acknowledging that '[t]he intentional bombing of civilian populations is illegal', but this did not prevent indiscriminate bombing during the Second World War, see Schindler and Toman 1998, pp 221–222.

[8] See also Article 85(3), 1977, Geneva Protocol 1 Additional to the Geneva Conventions of 12 August 1949, and Relating to the Protection of Victims of International Armed Conflicts (API) 1125 UNTS 3.

[9] Kalshoven 1977, p 116; Henckaerts and Doswald-Beck 2005, pp 3–5. See also Greenwood's comments that this principle is 'well established in customary international law', Greenwood 1993, p 70. See also the Report of the United Nations Fact Finding Mission on the Gaza Conflict (hereinafter Goldstone Report), UN Doc A/HRC/12/48, 15 September 2009, para 807.

[10] Article 50(1), API, excludes those persons referred to in Article 4(a)(1), (2), (3) and (6) of Geneva Convention III and those persons referred to in Article 43 of API. On combatant status see generally Clarke et al. 1989, pp 107–135.

transporting the military or employed in munitions work, as well as civilians who have previously taken part in hostilities without combatant status.[11]

API defines the 'civilian population' as comprising all those who are civilians.[12] However, it confirms that:

> '[t]he presence within the civilian population of individuals who do not come within the definition of civilians does not deprive the population of its civilian character.'[13]

Therefore, for example, combatants coming home on leave from the front line during the conflict in the former Yugoslavia would not have deprived their village population of its civilian character. However if the level of combatants within a civilian population had increased to the point where they could be considered a military objective, the legitimacy of the attack would depend on the question of proportionality, which will be addressed later.[14]

Article 51(3) of API provides that civilians are only protected 'unless and for such time as they take a direct part in hostilities'. The expression 'direct part in hostilities' was defined by the International Committee of the Red Cross (ICRC) commentary to API as participation in combatant activities.[15] However, the recent ICRC interpretive guidance on the notion of direct participation in hostilities has expanded this concept.[16] The guidance suggests that in order to lose protection from attack, the acts of the civilians must reach a threshold of harm, in being likely to adversely affect military operations or military capacity of a party to the conflict, that there must be direct causation between the act and the harm likely to occur and that there must be a belligerent nexus, in that the act must be designed to cause the harm in support of one party to the conflict and to the detriment of the other.[17] This definition is not free from controversy with some commentators suggesting that 'these criteria are not a part of existing law and impose inappropriate constraints on the scope of direct participation in hostilities'.[18]

The time during which civilians lose their protection is also a matter of controversy; the ICRC interpretive guidance suggests that '[m]easures preparatory to

---

[11] Bothe et al. 1982, pp 293–294 and see Rogers 1996, pp 8–9.

[12] Article 50(2), API.

[13] Article 50(3), API. See comments by Pocar, that Article 50 generally represents customary international law, Pocar 2002, p 345.

[14] See infra Part 5.3.

[15] Bothe et al. 1982, p 303 and Sandoz et al. (eds) 1987, p 619. See also Program on Humanitarian Policy and Conflict Research at Harvard University (HPCR), Manual on International Law Applicable to Air and Missile Warfare, 15 May 2009 (hereinafter Harvard Manual on Air and Missile Warfare), Rule 29, which contains examples of what may constitute taking a direct part in hostilities.

[16] Melzer 2008, pp 991–1047.

[17] Ibid., p 1016.

[18] HPCR, Commentary on the HPCR Manual on International Law Applicable to Air and Missile Warfare (hereinafter Commentary on the Harvard Manual on Air and Missile Warfare), p 121, para 5 comments that these three criteria 'were not unanimously accepted by the Group of Experts' engaged in the ICRC discussions on direct participation in hostilities.

the execution of a specific act of direct participation in hostilities, as well as the deployment to and the return from the location of its execution, constitute an integral part of that act'.[19] However, the guidance restricts this, in terms of loss of protection, to acts of a 'specific military nature and so closely linked to the subsequent execution of a specific hostile act that they already constitute an integral part of that act' and holds that protection is regained once the individual has physically separated from the operation.[20] The Commentary on the Harvard Manual on Air and Missile Warfare notes the opposing view that 'one could go 'downstream' and 'upstream' as far as the causal connection would stretch'.[21] It is arguable that customary international law lies somewhere between these two extremes. In terms of the definition of direct participation, however, it is rarely disputed that civilians contributing to the war effort in a non-direct manner, such as workers in defence plants, do not lose their protected status.[22]

It is important to note that under Article 51(6) of API, attacks against the civilian population or civilians by way of reprisals are prohibited and so missile attacks against civilians not taking a direct part in hostilities are prohibited in all circumstances. Non-parties to API would be bound by Article 33 of the fourth Geneva Convention which prohibits reprisals against civilians and their property.[23] However, whilst Article 33 would prohibit reprisals against civilians on the territory of the parties to the conflict or in occupied territory, it is unclear whether it would prohibit a reprisal missile attack against civilian populations in the territory of the enemy state. Indeed, Darcy characterises this provision as protecting 'civilians in the hands of the enemy' from reprisals and questions whether 'enemy civilians' are generally protected against reprisals under customary law[24] Whilst the ICTY Trial Chamber in *Kupreškić* proclaimed that Article 51(6) has indeed crystallised into customary international law, the ICRC Study is more tentative, stating that 'there appears, at a minimum, to exist a trend in favour of prohibiting such reprisals'.[25] Nevertheless, it is likely that such an attack would be found morally unacceptable by the international community, irrespective of arguments as to its legality.

Finally, a related issue is the question of what amounts to 'attacks' on civilians. The expression 'attacks' is not confined to offensive actions, but under API in Article 49(1) includes 'acts of violence against the adversary, whether in offence or in defence'. The ICRC commentary explains that this definition essentially equates

[19] Melzer 2008, p 1031.

[20] Ibid., pp 1031–1033.

[21] Commentary on the Harvard Manual on Air and Missile Warfare, p 118.

[22] Bothe et al. 1982, p 303, Sandoz et al. 1987, p 619. However, see Spaight's arguments that such people are 'quasi-combatants', Spaight 1944, p 162. See discussion infra Part 5.3.1.

[23] Geneva Convention Relative to the Protection of Civilian Persons in Time of War of August 12, 1949 (Fourth Geneva Convention), 75 UNTS 287.

[24] Darcy 2003, p 243.

[25] See ICTY Case No. IT-95-16, *Prosecutor* v *Kupreškić* et al., (14 January 2000) (Trial Chamber Judgement), paras 527–534 and criticism of this by Dolzer 2002, pp 357–358. See Henckaerts and Doswald-Beck 2005, p 523.

the word 'attack' with 'combat action',[26] and therefore 'combat action' against civilians, not taking a direct part in hostilities, is prohibited at all times under API.

5.2.2 *Definition of civilian objects/military objectives in API*

Whilst specific civilian objects have been protected by international conventions since the Hague Regulations,[27] the first treaty rule to set out the absolute prohibition that '[c]ivilian objects shall not be the object of attack or of reprisals' was Article 52 of API.[28] It is clear that this principle of distinction between civilian objects and military objects is now considered binding on non-state parties to API.[29] However, as with the question of reprisals against civilians, it is much less certain whether the prohibition on reprisals against civilian objects has crystallised into customary international law.[30]

The definition of civilian objects is a negative one; that is 'objects which are not military objectives'.[31] Therefore, when analysing the nature of civilian objects, the real question becomes: what are military objectives?[32] API defines these as:

> 'those objects which by their nature, location, purpose or use make an effective contribution to military action and whose total or partial destruction, capture or neutralization, in the circumstances ruling at the time, offers a definite military advantage.'[33]

This definition provides a 'two-pronged test'—the objects must both 'make an effective contribution to military action' *and* their neutralisation 'in the circumstances ruling at the time' must offer a 'definite military advantage'.[34] The ICRC Study suggests that this definition is now considered customary international law,[35] and this is supported by the Eritrea Ethiopia Claims Commission Partial Award on the *Western Front, Aerial Bombardment and Related Claims*, in which the Commission found that Article 52(2) 'is a statement of customary international humanitarian law'.[36]

---

[26] Sandoz et al. 1987, p 603 and see Oeter 1999, p 105, para 441(3).

[27] See Article 27, Hague Regulations attached to the 1907 Hague Convention IV Respecting the Laws and Customs of War on Land, reprinted in AJIL 2 (Supp. 1908) p 90.

[28] See Randelzhofer 1982, p 94.

[29] See Henckaerts and Doswald-Beck 2005, p 25 and International Court of Justice Advisory Opinion on the Legality of the Threat or Use of Nuclear Weapons, 8 July 1996, available at www.icj-cij.org/docket/files/95/7495.pdf, accessed 28 December 2010.

[30] See Henckaerts and Doswald-Beck 2005, p 525 and Darcy 2004.

[31] Article 52(1), API.

[32] See von der Heydte 1982, pp 276–279.

[33] Article 52(2), API.

[34] Bothe et al. 1982, p 323.

[35] Henckaerts and Doswald-Beck 2005, p 30.

[36] Eritrea Ethiopia Claims Commission, Partial Award on *Western Front, Aerial Bombardment and Related Claims*, 19 December 2005, para 113, reprinted in (2006) ILM 45:396. See also the identical definition in the Harvard Manual on Air and Missile Warfare in Rule 1(y).

With respect to the first part of this test, the ICRC commentary suggests that objects which by their 'nature' make an effective contribution to military action are 'all objects directly used by the armed forces', such as weapons, equipment, fortifications, staff headquarters and communications centres.[37] 'Location' refers to areas of land that it is strategically important to seize, withhold from enemy possession or force the enemy to retreat from.[38] An example of this would be the hillside above a road which is an important supply route, as those controlling the high ground would be able to prevent enemy vehicles from passing along the roadway.[39] The Commentary on the Harvard Manual on Air and Missile Warfare states in this respect that '[t]he governing criterion is the need to attack a location so as to enhance or safeguard the attacker's operations or to diminish the enemy's options'.[40]

The ICRC commentary states that '[t]he criterion of *purpose* is concerned with the intended future use of an object, while that of *use* is concerned with its present function'.[41] Whilst the criterion of 'use' is fairly clear, with respect to the criterion of 'purpose' the Commentary on the Harvard Manual on Air and Missile Warfare explains that '[t]he key issue in determining purpose is the enemy's intent' and that whilst sometimes that intent is clear, when it is not 'it is necessary to avoid sheer speculation and to rely on hard evidence, based perhaps on intelligence gathering'.[42] The Eritrea Ethiopia Claims Commission considered the concept of 'purpose' in the Partial Award on the *Western Front, Aerial Bombardment and Related Claims*, with regard to the aerial bombardment of the Hirgigo Power Station in Eritrea by Ethiopian aircraft.[43] The Hirgigo plant had been under construction for some time and 'evidence indicated that much of the related transformer and transmission facilities that would be necessary for it to transmit its power around the country were in place' and it was intended to replace an old power plant in supplying power to Massawa which had a port and naval base.[44] The Commission held that the port and naval base at Massawa were military objectives and that 'it follows that the generating facilities providing the electric power needed to operate them were objects that made an effective contribution to military action'.[45] They held that, as the Hirgigo plant was the intended

[37] Sandoz et al. 1987, p 636. See the Harvard Manual on Air and Missile Warfare, Rule 22(a) which gives a similar list of objects which by their nature are military objectives.

[38] Sandoz et al. 1987, p 636.

[39] This is confirmed by UK reservations and understandings to API, available at the ICRC website, www.icrc.org, accessed 28 December 2010. Canada, Germany, Italy, New Zealand and the Netherlands made similarly worded understandings also available at the ICRC website, ibid.

[40] Commentary on the Harvard Manual on Air and Missile Warfare, p 107.

[41] Sandoz et al. 1987, p 636, original emphasis.

[42] Commentary on the Harvard Manual on Air and Missile Warfare, p 107.

[43] Eritrea Ethiopia Claims Commission, Partial Award on *Western Front, Aerial Bombardment and Related Claims*, 19 December 2005, paras 106–121, reprinted in (2006) ILM 45:396.

[44] Ibid., para 118.

[45] Ibid., para 120.

replacement for power generation, it was a military objective on the basis of its future intended use.[46]

With respect to the second part of the test, the terms 'total or partial destruction' and 'capture' are relatively clear. 'Neutralisation' is explained by some commentators in respect of API as denying a location or object to the enemy without necessarily destroying it, perhaps by setting landmines, although clearly, neutralisation by the use of landmines would be restricted for parties to the 1997 Ottawa Convention.[47]

The definite military advantage from this destruction, capture or neutralisation, must be offered 'in the circumstances ruling at the time' and 'not at some hypothetical future time'.[48] The military advantage must be definite, that is, 'a concrete and perceptible military advantage rather than a hypothetical and speculative one',[49] although it need not be related to 'the advantage anticipated by the attacker from the destruction, capture or neutralization of the object' as would be the case in a diversionary attack.[50]

An example of a diversionary attack is the bombing of bridges and railroads by the Allies in the Pas-de-Calais area in the spring of 1944, in order to convince the Germans that the invasion would take place there and so divert the German military effort away from Normandy. However, such an attack would offer a potential advantage (if believed by the adversary) rather than a definite advantage and therefore it has been argued that such attacks are now contrary to API.[51] It is arguable that non Parties to API would have greater scope of action in this respect as they are not bound by the requirement to demonstrate a 'definite' military advantage. Indeed, the US 2002 Joint Doctrine for Targeting omits the word 'definite' and simply requires that the 'total or partial destruction, capture, or neutralization offer a military advantage'.[52] Nevertheless, Roscini opines that the US approach is not consistent with customary international law.[53]

---

[46] Ibid.

[47] Bothe et al. 1982, p 325. See the 1997 Convention on the Prohibition of the Use, Stockpiling, Production and Transfer of Anti-Personnel Mines and on their Destruction (Ottawa Convention) (1997) ILM 36:1507 and also see the 1980 UN Convention on Prohibitions or Restrictions on the Use of Certain Conventional Weapons which may be Deemed to be Excessively Injurious or to Have Indiscriminate Effects, 1342 UNTS 137 and its Protocol II of 1980 or Amended Protocol II of 1996.

[48] Bothe et al. 1982, pp 323–324.

[49] Ibid., pp 325–326.

[50] Ibid., p 325. Although API does not provide a list of military objectives, for examples see Draft Article 24 of the 1923 Hague Rules of Aerial Warfare and Article 8 of the 1954 Hague Convention for the Protection of Cultural Property in the Event of Armed Conflict, 249 UNTS 240.

[51] Meyer 2001, pp 169–170.

[52] Joint Doctrine for Targeting, Joint Publication 3-60, 17 January 2002, Appendix 3, A-3.

[53] Roscini 2005, pp 442–443.

5.2.3 Dual use objects: electricity grids

The air bombardment of Iraq during the 1990–1991 Gulf conflict raised the difficult issue of dual use objects, that is, objects which are contributing to the military campaign as well as supporting ordinary civilian life. In this conflict the Iraqi electrical grid was destroyed in order to deny the military access to electrical power and so weaken their command and control ability. However, the side effect of shutting down the electrical grid was to shut down the water purification and sewage treatment plants and as a result 'epidemics of gastroenteritis, cholera, and typhoid broke out, leading to perhaps as many as 100,000 civilian deaths'.[54]

On this issue the US Department of Defence Report on the legal issues surrounding the Gulf conflict simply stated that:

> '[w]hen objects are used concurrently for civilian and military purposes, they are liable to attack if there is a military advantage to be gained in their attack.'[55]

Greenwood sums up that 'there is no intermediate category of 'dual use' objects: either something is a military object or it is not'.[56] This harsh approach reflects the basic problem of modern conflicts, where many of the necessities of civilian life, such as power and communication lines, are also being used to support the military machine. Nevertheless, with regard to dual use bombardment during the Kosovo crisis, Rowe emphasised the limiting effect of the words *effective* contribution to military action and *definite* military advantage in respect of dual use objects.[57] The fact that an object is of some use to the military is not alone sufficient to justify its being targeted as a military objective, although as commented above the US takes a broader view of military objective by the omission of the word 'definite'.[58]

Roscini comments that in Afghanistan electrical grids were destroyed leaving the cities of Kandahar and Lashkargah without power supplies, but that in the most recent Gulf conflict 'attacks were directed at power distribution facilities instead of generation facilities, and they were carried out with carbon fibre bombs' and that 'the electricity network was largely left undamaged'.[59] The method of disrupting electricity in the later Gulf conflict is to be preferred as attacks on dual use objects such as power grids, as was shown in the 1990–1991 Gulf conflict, are particularly

---

[54] Rizer 2001.

[55] Department of Defence (1992) Conduct of the Persian Gulf War, Final Report to Congress, Washington 1992, Appendix O: The Role of the Law of War (hereinafter, Department of Defence Report) reprinted in (1992) ILM 31:615, p 623.

[56] Greenwood 1993, p 73.

[57] Rowe 2000, pp 151–152.

[58] Ibid. Joint Doctrine for Targeting, Joint Publication 3-60, 17 January 2002, Appendix 3, A-3 and see Department of Defence Report, supra n 55, p 623.

[59] Roscini 2005, p 429, although note that Roscini assumes that the main reason for the avoidance of damage to the power generation facilities in the last Gulf conflict was 'probably in order to facilitate the post-war reconstruction'.

likely to cause civilian casualties and thus raise the issue of whether such casualties will be excessive in light of the military advantage anticipated.[60]

5.2.4 The propaganda machine as a military objective

Another controversial issue which arose as a result of the 1990–1991 Gulf conflict and NATO's bombardment of the Federal Republic of Yugoslavia (FRY), was the targeting of communications. The US Department of Defence report stated that 'microwave towers for everyday, peacetime civilian communications can constitute a vital part of a military command and control system'.[61] Indeed, Oeter observes that '[i]n the case of modern densely interlinked infrastructures of telecommunication, it may be doubted whether any 'unimportant' installation still exists'.[62]

This NATO bombardment of Serbia during the Kosovo crisis led to an assessment by the Office of the Prosecutor (OTP) at the International Criminal Tribunal for the former Yugoslavia (ICTY) of possible breaches of international humanitarian law.[63] The OTP then issued a report on the bombing campaign which included reasoning for the decision not to open a full criminal investigation.[64] The report initially examined the API definition of a military objective and found that this definition is 'generally accepted as part of customary law'.[65] Part of the report considered the NATO bombardment of a state-owned television and radio station in the centre of Belgrade which resulted in the deaths of between ten and seventeen civilians.[66] Whilst the report was equivocal on whether the media, *per se*, could be a legitimate target,[67] importantly it confirmed that 'civilian morale as such' is not a legitimate military objective[68] and that 'merely disseminating propaganda to generate support for the war effort' would not convert the media into a military objective.[69]

---

[60] Proportionality will be discussed in Part 5.3.

[61] Department of Defence Report, supra n 55, p 623.

[62] Oeter 1999, para 443(6).

[63] On the NATO action see generally Lord Robertson 1999; and Kritsiotis 2000.

[64] See Ronzitti 2000.

[65] Final Report to the Prosecutor by the Committee Established to Review the NATO Bombing Campaign against the Federal Republic of Yugoslavia, (13 June 2000), (hereinafter OTP Report) reprinted in (2000) ILM 39:1257, para 42. This interpretation was supported by the ICRC Study, Henckaerts and Doswald-Beck 2005, p 30.

[66] OTP Report supra n 65, paras 71 and 75.

[67] Ibid., para 47.

[68] Ibid., para 55. This is supported by Aldrich 1999, p 150, but see comments by Medenica 2001, p 423.

[69] OTP Report, supra n 65, para 47.

NATO primarily supported its targeting as 'part of a more general attack aimed at disrupting the FRY Command, Control and Communications network'.[70] However, statements from both US and UK officials at the time suggest that this was not necessarily the main motivation for the attack. Ken Bacon, a Pentagon spokesman, reportedly said 'It is a new class of target ... the broad message is that they [the Serbs] should put pressure on their leadership to end this'.[71] Clare Short, a British MP who was at that time International Development Secretary, told reporters 'You know how powerful information is. And the constant stream of completely false information in Serbia is prolonging the war. It's as simple as that'.[72]

Nevertheless, the OTP report accepted that the targeting of the station on a propaganda basis was an incidental, albeit complementary, aim to the legitimate targeting of the station as an attack on Command and Control centres. But it also claimed that:

> '[i]f the media is the nerve system that keeps a war-monger in power and thus perpetuates the war effort, it may fall within the definition of a legitimate military objective.'[73]

This interpretation is problematic as, although the media of dictatorial regimes are often used as part of the control mechanism to sustain the ruling party in power, practically all media display bias in supporting their country during a conflict. Furthermore, use of the emotive term 'war-monger' when deciding upon legitimate targets during a conflict would lead to highly subjective decisions. Therefore, the OTP approach risks opening the way to the bombardment of the media during conflicts as a matter of course. Additionally, as the report acknowledged,

> '[w]hilst stopping such propaganda may serve to demoralize the Yugoslav population and undermine the government's political support, it is unlikely that either of these purposes would offer the 'concrete and direct' military advantage necessary to make them a legitimate military objective.'[74]

It is worth noting that in the aerial bombing phase of the 2003 Gulf Conflict the US and UK also bombed Iraqi television stations. Whilst the US apparently described this as a legitimate targeting of the regime's command and control network, the fact that the bombing occurred only one day after the Iraqi's broadcast footage of US prisoners of war and dead servicemen seems unlikely to have been coincidental.[75] A British national broadsheet newspaper reported this bombing under the heading 'TV Stations bombed to silence Saddam' and commented that the attack was carried out to keep Saddam off the Iraqi televisions screens and thus to 'cut off

---

70 Ibid., para 75.

71 Manyon and Rooney, 1999.

72 Ibid.

73 OTP Report, supra n 65, para 76 and see Fenrick 2001, p 497.

74 OTP Report, supra n 65, para 76 and see Aldrich 1999, p 150.

75 Rooney 2003.

a key prop for his regime'.[76] Whilst the source of the newspaper's interpretation of this attack is unclear, nevertheless, it contributes to the erroneous impression that the media may be attacked in an armed conflict as a matter of course.[77] This impression was reinforced less than a month later when the Baghdad offices of Al-Jazeera were hit by a bomb, killing one journalist and injuring another, leading to speculation that they had been purposely targeted because of Al-Jazeera's anti-American stance.[78]

Unfortunately the targeting of the media has continued in recent conflicts. The Report of the Commission of Inquiry on Lebanon commented that '[t]ransmission stations used by Lebanese television and radio were also the targets of bombing', although it differentiated between the Hezbollah-backed Al-Manar television, which 'is clearly a tool used by Hezbollah in order to broadcast propaganda', and other Lebanese TV stations which the Commission said were not so used.[79] With respect to the bombing of the Al-Manar TV station, the Commission maintained that the dissemination of propaganda alone was not sufficient to convert it into a military target 'unless it is used in a way that makes an "effective contribution to military action" and its destruction in the circumstances at the time offers "a definite military advantage"'.[80] In this respect Stewart comments on the Commission's findings with approval, stating that '[t]he principle of distinction would be diluted to vanishing point if the term "effective contribution to military action" were interpreted as including mere propaganda'.[81]

5.2.5 The economic/financial systems of a state as a military target

An important question is whether a country's economic and financial system could amount to military objectives.[82] Schmitt warns that:

> '[d]isparity also provides an incentive for 'have nots' to define the concept of military objective broadly... [s]ince economic facilities undergird the 'haves' superiority, they will seem particularly lucrative targets.'[83]

---

[76] Ibid.

[77] But see Dworkin's comment that the TV was used to give instructions to Iraqi soldiers, Dworkin 2003.

[78] See Fisk 2003 and Vallely 2003.

[79] Implementation of General Assembly Resolution 60/251 of 15 March 2006 Entitled 'Human Rights Council': Report of the Commission of Inquiry on Lebanon pursuant to Human Rights Council Resolution S-2/1, UN Doc.A/HRC/3/2, 23 November 2006 (hereinafter Commission of Inquiry on Lebanon), paras 140–141.

[80] Ibid., para 142.

[81] Stewart 2007, pp 1048–1049.

[82] Fleck 1997, p 52.

[83] Schmitt 1998, p 65.

At first glance, the ICRC Study appears to support the theory that in certain circumstances, '[e]conomic targets that effectively support military operations' may amount to a military objective, provided that their attack offers a definite military advantage.[84] However, a review of the sources referred to in Part 2 of the Study demonstrates that the illustrations of 'economic' targets cited by states mainly include uncontroversial examples such as industrial installations producing material for armed forces, which are clearly closely connected to the prosecution of the armed conflict.[85]

Nevertheless, the ICRC Study also cites New Zealand's Military Manual which gives the example of the destruction of cotton during the American Civil War as justified 'since the sale of cotton provided funds for almost all Confederate arms and ammunition'.[86] This position that attacking economic 'war-sustaining' targets is lawful under customary international law has been taken by the US since about 1995.[87] The 2007 US Commander's Handbook on the Law of Naval Operations, states in the chapter on the law of targeting that military objectives are those that 'effectively contribute to the enemy's war-fighting or war-sustaining capability' and that '[e]conomic objects of the enemy that indirectly but effectively support and sustain the enemy's war-fighting capability may also be attacked'.[88]

This approach, if accepted, would surely also justify the targeting of a state's banking system, given the reliance that a state may have on that system in order to finance their military campaign. Indeed, the case for an expansive interpretation of military objectives in order to allow the bombardment of financial institutions and businesses is made by a US Air Force Judge Advocate General.[89] She supports her argument by reasoning that the bombardment of such targets would directly affect the morale of the enemy civilians and so encourage them to pressure for regime change or surrender.[90] This approach seems to have been accepted by the Eritrea Ethiopia Claims Commission with respect to the Hirgigo power plant, discussed earlier.[91] The Commission stated that '[t]he infliction of economic losses from

[84] Henckaerts and Doswald-Beck 2005, p 32.

[85] Henckaerts and Doswald-Beck 2005, Volume 2, Part 1, paras 565–572.

[86] New Zealand's Military Manual (1992), para 516(5) cited in Henckaerts and Doswald-Beck 2005, Volume 2, Part 1, para 573.

[87] For the development of the US approach see Holland 2004, pp 44–46.

[88] The Commander's Handbook on the Law of Naval Operations, NWP 1-14 M, July 2007 edition, paras 8.2 and 8.2.5. See similar wording in Joint Doctrine for Targeting, Joint Publication 3-60, 17 January 2002, Appendix 3, A-3. But see the Commentary on the Harvard Manual on Air and Missile Warfare, p 110, which states that the 'majority of the Group of Experts took the position that the connection between revenues from such exports [of oil to neutral States] and military action is too remote'.

[89] Meyer 2001, pp 180–181, in line with and perhaps extending the US approach explained above.

[90] Ibid.

[91] Eritrea Ethiopia Claims Commission, Partial Award on *Western Front, Aerial Bombardment and Related Claims*, 19 December 2005, para 121, reprinted in (2006) ILM 45:396.

attacks against military objectives is a lawful means of achieving a definite military advantage, and there can be few military advantages more evident than effective pressure to end an armed conflict'.[92]

Nevertheless, the definition of military objectives in Article 52 would be stretched to breaking point by the inclusion of financial institutions and banks and other industries whose only link to the conflict is that the Government derives income from them which may assist in the financing of the military campaign. Furthermore, if the expression 'contribution to military action' was interpreted so broadly as to cover any type of contribution to the war effort, then the principle of distinction would become totally illusory.[93] Whilst regime change may be the political objective of an armed conflict, this does not legitimise breaches of humanitarian law, such as the targeting of civilian financial institutions.[94] Indeed, the targeting of civilian institutions in this manner could also breach Article 51(2) of API, which prohibits '[a]cts ... of violence the primary purpose of which is to spread terror among the civilian population'.[95]

5.2.6 The ICTY/International Criminal Court (ICC) and targeting civilians or civilian objectives

Attacks on civilians, in the village of Ahmici, were considered by the ICTY in the case of *Blaškić*.[96] The Trial Chamber stated that in order to constitute an offence the attack must have caused deaths or serious bodily injury, not have been justified by military necessity and have been conducted intentionally in the knowledge that the target was civilian.[97] A similar definition was also given in the *Kordić and Čerkez* case.[98] The proposition that death or serious injury of civilians must result from the incident appears to have been based on Article 85 of API, which confines the grave breach of attacking civilians to situations where death or serious injury has been caused. The defence of military necessity, read into this offence by the tribunal, is questionable. The relevant articles of API do not suggest that there is

[92] Ibid. Although note that the Commission had already found that the power plant was a legitimate military objective on the basis of planned future use of the plant to support naval capability in a major port, ibid., para 120.

[93] This approach is also taken by Watkin 2005, p 17.

[94] But see Meyer 2001, pp 166–167.

[95] This prohibition is also repeated in the Department of the Army, The Law of Land Warfare: Field Manual No. 27-10, para 40(c) and see a similar definition in the USAF Intelligence Targeting Guide: Air Force Pamphlet 14-210, Attachment 4, para A4.2.

[96] ICTY Case No. IT-95-14, *Prosecutor* v *Blaškić*, (3 March 2000) (Trial Chamber Judgement), paras 180 and 414–417.

[97] Ibid., para 180.

[98] ICTY Case No. IT-95-14/2-T, *Prosecutor* v *Kordić and Čerkez*, (26 February 2001) (Trial Chamber Judgement), para 328.

any defence of military necessity in respect of the killing of civilians.[99] Indeed, as has already been stated, under API even reprisal attacks against civilians who are not directly taking part in hostilities are prohibited.[100]

The ICTY also considered attacks upon civilian objects in the cases of *Blaškić* and *Kordić and Čerkez*.[101] The Judgements in both cases defined the offence as the intentional targeting of civilian property which is not justified by military necessity.[102] The Trial Chamber in *Kordić and Čerkez* added that the attack must have resulted in 'extensive damage to civilian objects'.[103] The restriction of this offence to damage to civilian objects not justified by military necessity is in line with the commentary to Article 52 of API.[104] Even civilian objects, such as houses, could become a military objective if the enemy troops were using them as cover to fire from. However, the requirement that the destruction of civilian property must be extensive appears to confuse the offence of attacking civilian objects under Article 52 of API with the grave breach of extensive destruction and appropriation of property under Article 147 of the IV Geneva Convention.[105] Evidence of extensive destruction of civilian objects would, of course, support a finding that the defendant intended to make such objects the target of his attack.[106]

The ICC prohibits attacks against civilians and civilian objects in Article 8(2)(b)(i) and (ii). The Elements of Crimes (EOC), which were adopted by the Assembly of States Parties in order to clarify the offences in the Rome Statute, require that:

1. The perpetrator directed an attack;
2. The object of the attack was a civilian population as such or individual civilians not taking direct part in hostilities/The object of the attack was civilian objects, that is, objects which are not military objectives;
3. The perpetrator intended … [the above] to be the object of the attack;
4. The conduct took place in the context of and was associated with an international armed conflict;
5. The perpetrator was aware of factual circumstances that established the existence of an armed conflict.[107]

---

99 Although civilians may be killed or injured as an incidental result of an attack upon a legitimate military object, see infra Part 5.3.

100 Article 51(6), API and Article 33, Geneva Convention IV and see Aldrich 1981, pp 781–782.

101 *Blaskic*, supra n 96, para 180 and *Kordić and Čerkez*, supra n 98, para 328.

102 Ibid.

103 *Kordić and Čerkez*, supra n 98, para 328.

104 Bothe et al. 1982, p 321.

105 *Kordić and Čerkez*, supra n 98, para 328.

106 Although very minor damage would not be sufficiently 'serious' for prosecution before the ICC, see Article 17(1)(d), Rome Statute of the International Criminal Court, UN Doc A/CONF.183.9 (hereinafter Rome Statute), on admissibility.

107 EOC, Assembly of States Parties to the Rome Statute of the ICC, Official Records, First Session, ICC-ASP/1/3 (3–10 September 2002) (hereinafter EOC), 108, p 130.

Therefore, the EOC confirm that it is not an offence to attack civilians who are taking a 'direct part in hostilities'.[108] This proviso was inserted during the fifth Preparatory Committee meeting prior to the Rome Conference and, as has been discussed, the scope of this phrase is a little uncertain as the ICRC interpretive guidance on the notion of direct participation in hostilities is not universally accepted.[109] Whilst participation in combat activities would clearly deprive civilians of the protection of this section and working in a munitions factory would clearly not,[110] what of civilian engineers working to mend tanks near the front line? In the 'grey' areas between direct participation and indirect participation in hostilities, the ICC will have to take each case on its merits.

The definition of civilian objects is not clear-cut either. Some objects, such as military vehicles and weapons, are clearly military objectives, and others, such as schools and hospitals (when being used for those purposes) are clearly not. API imposes a presumption that:

> 'in cases of doubt whether an object which is normally dedicated to civilian purposes… is being used to make an effective contribution to military action, it shall be presumed not to be so used.'[111]

Whilst this presumption is not mentioned in the Rome Statute or Elements, it would be open to the ICC to hold that this presumption represented customary law.[112] However, whilst the ICRC Study comments that this presumption is contained in numerous military manuals it acknowledges that neither the US nor Israel accept the customary status of this rule.[113]

However, the real legal difficulty for the ICC will probably arise in drawing the line between military objectives and civilian objects in the grey areas of dual use objects. Here it must be remembered that not every object which contributes to the war effort is immediately a legitimate military objective; that the contribution must be *effective* and destruction must produce a *definite* military advantage.[114] Additionally, even if an object constitutes a military objective under this test, if there is anticipated collateral damage, action against it must still be evaluated under the test of proportionality in Article 8(2)(b)(iv).[115]

The *mens rea* of the offence of attacking civilians or civilian objects is set out in the Element requiring that the perpetrator 'intended' the civilians or civilian

---

[108] EOC, p 130.

[109] Preparatory Committee on the Establishment of an ICC, A/AC.249/1997/L.9/Rev.1, (18 December 1997), 3. See discussion supra Part 5.2.1.

[110] Although a munitions factory itself would be a legitimate military target, and thus the civilian workers could be considered as collateral damage in such an attack provided that the rule on proportionality under Article 8(2)(b)(iv), Rome Statute, was not breached.

[111] Article 52(3), API.

[112] See Cottier et al. 1999, p 187.

[113] Henckaerts and Doswald-Beck 2005, pp 35–36.

[114] See Rowe 2000, pp 151–152.

[115] Infra Part 5.3.

objects to be the object of the attack. It appears that recklessness as to civilian injury or damage or destruction to civilian objects would not suffice.[116] Therefore, although the Iraqi use of Scud missiles against Israeli and Saudi cities during the 1990–1991 Gulf conflict was indiscriminate, because the missiles were not capable of being targeted at specific military objects,[117] it would not have breached this Article of the Rome Statute unless it could be proven that an accused Iraqi had intended to make civilians the object of the attack, as opposed to simply being reckless.[118] The argument that the accused must have foreseen that such an attack would amount to an attack against civilians, or that the requisite intention could be inferred from his failure to take precautionary measures (such as more precisely targeted weapons) in the attack, is not a watertight argument.[119] This appears to leave an unfortunate loophole in the Rome Statute, which defendants will no doubt attempt to exploit.

Finally, contrary to the decisions of the ICTY, the EOC do not include a result Element for either offence, so it need not be proven that civilians were actually killed or injured or that civilian objects were in fact destroyed or damaged because of the attack, it would simply have to be proved that the attack had taken place.[120]

5.3 Additional Protocol 1 and the Proportionality Principle

Although the rule of proportionality in the use of force has been acknowledged at least since the destruction of the Caroline in the Canadian Rebellion 1837,[121] the modern rule of proportionality within international humanitarian law is contained in Article 51(5) of API,[122] which prohibits as indiscriminate the launching of:

> 'an attack which may be expected to cause incidental loss of civilian life, injury to civilians or damage to civilian objects, or a combination thereof, which would be excessive in relation to the concrete and direct military advantage anticipated.'

[116] But see arguments of Fenrick in Cottier et al. 1999, p 186.

[117] Such attacks would breach Article 51(4) of API, although Iraq is not a party to API, see Schmitt 1998, p 55.

[118] The Rome Statute does not include jurisdiction over indiscriminate attacks *per se*, but such behaviour would breach Article 51(4), API for States Parties (Iraq is not a State Party to API).

[119] See Dörmann 2001, p 469. The use of such weapons could also be considered under the rule of proportionality of Article 8(2)(b)(iv).

[120] See comments of Dörmann 2001, pp 466–467.

[121] See Harris 1998, pp 894–896.

[122] On state practice on proportionality between these two dates see Fenrick 1982, pp 124–125 and for proportionality in naval warfare, Roucounas 1996, pp 288–289.

Albeit that some commentators have expressed doubts as to whether this precise formulation of the rule of proportionality represents customary international law,[123] the Harvard Manual on Air and Missile Warfare includes in Rule 14 a definition very close to Article 51(5).[124]

The ICRC commentary to API explains that the expression 'concrete and direct military advantage' demonstrates that 'the advantage concerned should be substantial and relatively close'.[125] Indeed, the Commentary on the Harvard Manual states in this respect that 'it is clear for the military advantage to be concrete and direct, it cannot be based merely on hope or speculation'.[126] However in the definition of proportionality in the US Joint Doctrine for Targeting, the words 'concrete and direct' are missing from their definition,[127] but it cannot be maintained that a totally speculative military advantage would satisfy the customary international law in respect of the proportionality equation. Declarations made upon ratification of API have made it clear that the decision on proportionality must be made on the basis of an assessment of 'the information from all sources which is reasonably available to them at the relevant time'.[128] It is clear that the decision of a commander or other person to attack a particular object with a particular weapon may not be judged with hindsight.[129]

A common declaration by several States Parties on the issue of proportionality in API is that:

> 'the military advantage anticipated from an attack is intended to refer to the advantage anticipated from the attack considered as a whole and not only from isolated or particular parts of the attack.'[130]

Doswald-Beck suggests that this approach is acceptable 'if seen within the context of a given tactical operation'.[131] She gives the example of an operation necessitating the destruction of six military objectives, one of which would involve more

---

[123] Infeld 1992, p 119, but see Greenwood 1993, p 77.

[124] Harvard Manual on Air and Missile Warfare, p 10, Rule 14 and see definition in Implementation of General Assembly Resolution 60/251 of 15 March 2006 Entitled 'Human Rights Council', Mission to Lebanon and Israel (7–14 September 2006), UN Doc A/HRC/2/7, 2 October 2006, para 27.

[125] Sandoz et al. 1987, p 684.

[126] Commentary on the Harvard Manual on Air and Missile Warfare, p 92.

[127] Joint Doctrine for Targeting, Joint Publication 3-60, 17 January 2002, Appendix 3, A-4.

[128] UK's declaration para (c), in respect of API, available at www.icrc.org accessed 28 December 2010. Similar declarations were made by Australia, Austria, Belgium, Canada, Germany, Ireland, Italy, New Zealand, Spain and the Netherlands.

[129] Commentary on the Harvard Manual on Air and Missile Warfare, p 91, 'the issue is expectations and not results'.

[130] UK's declaration para (i), in respect of API, available at www.icrc.org accessed 28 December 2010. Similar declarations were made by Australia, Belgium, Canada, Germany, Italy, New Zealand, Spain and the Netherlands. See Oeter 1999, para 444.

[131] Doswald-Beck 1989, pp 156–157.

casualties than the others, but within the context of the operation is an essential objective and so the yardstick would be the number of casualties overall 'in relation to the value of the operation as a whole'.[132] However, Fenrick warns against viewing the attack too broadly as '[i]f military benefit is assessed on too broad a basis ... then it may well be extremely difficult to apply the proportionality equation until the war has ended'.[133]

Nevertheless, an overall view of the attack could be helpful in judging issues such as the height at which planes fly during bombing campaigns. Arguably, there will be more civilian casualties if the planes fly at 15,000 feet, as was the case during part of the NATO bombing of FRY,[134] than if they fly at 7,000.[135] Although precision guided missiles may be accurate irrespective of altitude, as Roberts comments 'in attacks on railway bridges, the time an air-to-ground guided weapon takes to get to the target may also be the time a passenger train takes to get onto the bridge' and in an attack on a road convoy 'it may be impossible at 15,000 feet to be sure that the convoy does not contain, or even consist largely of, the very civilians who are supposedly being protected'.[136]

If a particularly high altitude is adopted for part of a bombing campaign, the inevitable increase in collateral damage must be factored into the proportionality equation.[137] Nevertheless, the Commentary on the Harvard Air and Missile Warfare Manual states correctly that 'indirect effects cannot be taken into account if they are too remote or cannot be reasonably foreseen'.[138] It must also be noted that a lower altitude for the bombing campaign could well result in higher military casualties for the attacking force. In this respect the US Commander's Handbook on the Law of Naval Operations states that the principle of proportionality requires that civilian casualties and damage must be kept to a minimum 'consistent with mission accomplishment and *the security of the force*'.[139]

The proportionality equation is based on the premise that collateral damage must not be excessive compared to the military advantage expected. Factors which must be weighed in this balance include:

---

[132] Ibid.

[133] Fenrick 1982, p 107 and see Gardam 1993, p 407.

[134] OTP Report, para 56 comments on the '15,000 feet minimum altitude adopted for part of the campaign'.

[135] See Roscini 2005, p 415, who states that '[a]t least some bombardments by American aircraft during Operation Enduring Freedom were carried out from above 30,000 feet where anti-aircraft artillery and Stinger missiles could not reach them'.

[136] Roberts 2002, p 415.

[137] Lippman 2002, p 67 and Voon 2001, pp 1104–1105.

[138] Commentary on the Harvard Manual on Air and Missile Warfare, p 91.

[139] The Commander's Handbook on the Law of Naval Operations, NWP I-14 M, July 2007 edition, para 8.3.1, emphasis added.

> 'the military importance of the target or objective, the density of the civilian population in the target area, the likely incidental effects of the attack, including the possible release of hazardous substances, the types of weapon available to attack the target and their accuracy ... and the timing of the attack.'[140]

Additionally, both the Commentary on the Harvard Manual and the Israeli response to the Goldstone Report comment that the security of the attacking forces is a factor which must be weighed in the balance when assessing military advantage.[141]

Schmitt comments upon the difficulty of applying the proportionality equation as, although jurisprudential balancing tests should compare like values, 'proportionality calculations are heterogeneous, for dissimilar value genre—military and humanitarian—are being weighed against each other'.[142] Holland comments on the problems of public reaction to this, in that '[u]ndervaluing expected incidental civilian losses often results in gory pictures. Undervaluing anticipated military advantage usually results in simply a missed targeting opportunity of which the public will likely be unaware'.[143]

5.3.1 The threat to civilians from aerial bombardment

Dinstein comments that, when postulating collateral casualties, planners must take into account several ways in which civilians could be hit.[144] First, they may be inside the target, such as workers in a munitions factory, secondly they may 'live, work or even pass by near a military target' and thirdly a bomb can fall short of its target or a missile may go off course.[145] An example of civilians killed because they lived near a target occurred in the attempts to target Saddam Hussein in the 2003 Gulf war, which according to Human Rights Watch caused dozens of civilian casualties.[146] An example, in the same conflict, of a missile going off course, was the US missile which hit a bus in Western Iraq killing five civilians and injuring

---

[140] Rogers 1996, p 19. With respect to accuracy of weapons available, see Belt 2000, p 150 and Infeld 1992, pp 130–131.

[141] Commentary on the Harvard Manual on Air and Missile Warfare, p 92 and The Operation in Gaza, 27 December 2008 – 18 January 2009, Factual and Legal Aspects, July 2009 (hereinafter Israeli Response to the Goldstone Report), p 39.

[142] Schmitt 1998, p 59.

[143] Holland 2004, p 48. See Shamash 2005–2006, p 134, calling for a much clearer rule of proportionality to resolve this problem.

[144] Dinstein 1997, p 6.

[145] Ibid.

[146] Human Rights Watch 2003, Off Target: The Conduct of the War and Civilian Casualties in Iraq, available at www.hrw.org/reports/2003/usa1203, accessed 28 December 2010.

others.[147] A US spokesman reportedly stated that the real target was a nearby bridge.[148]

A fourth threat to civilians from aerial bombardment is damage caused by defensive measures such as anti-aircraft missiles.[149] A disputed example of this is the bombing of a market in Baghdad's al-Shu'la neighbourhood in the 2003 Gulf Conflict when, according to Amnesty International, 62 civilians were killed.[150] Although the remains of a US missile were found at the scene, the US and UK claimed that the explosion was probably caused by an ageing Iraqi anti-aircraft missile.[151] Finally, another threat to civilians, shown graphically by the injuries to Iraqis in that conflict, is the collapse of houses in the vicinity of military objectives as a result of the shock of explosions.

There have been suggestions that collateral casualties amongst civilians working for the armed forces would carry less weight in the proportionality balance than such casualties amongst 'innocent' civilians, or even that such deaths would not constitute 'collateral civilian casualties'.[152] Whilst there little legal support for this; in reality such civilians would be at more risk than 'innocent' civilians because of their activity in and around military objectives.[153] Nevertheless, in an attack upon a military objective in which civilians are likely to be present, such as a munitions factory, the planning stage should take account of civilian workers and any attack should be timed in order to reduce casualties as much as possible.[154]

An important question with relation to the threat to civilians from aerial bombardment is whether this threat has become practically negligible as a result of the advent of precision guided missiles (PGM's). Unfortunately, although precision guided missiles have capacity to greatly reduce collateral damage, risks to civilians remain. As Hays Parks comments:

---

[147] Amnesty International 2003, Iraq, Civilians under Fire. AI Index:MDE14/071/2003, available at http://web.amnesty.org, accessed 28 December 2010.

[148] Ibid.

[149] See Fenrick 1997, p 547.

[150] Amnesty International, supra n 147.

[151] Ibid. But see Infeld's argument that if the collateral damage is caused by the defending force, then it is not the attacker's responsibility. Infeld 1992, p 132.

[152] Bothe et al. 1982, p 295; Oeter 1999, para 445(3) and Hays Parks 2002, p 291. See also The Commander's Handbook on the Law of Naval Operations, NWP I-14 M, July 2007 edition, para 8.3.2, which states that civilians working in military targets 'may be excluded from the proportionality analysis'.

[153] See Commentary on the Harvard Manual on Air and Missile Warfare, p 93, '[t]he majority of the Group of Experts felt that the principle of proportionality applies to such civilians as in all cases' but some pointed out that when the target is a high-value asset the civilian casualties would not necessarily amount to excessive collateral damage.

[154] For example, the NATO attack on the RTS in Belgrade was timed at just after 2am, *Banković* et al. v *Belgium*, European Court of Human Rights, Grand Chamber Admissibility Decision, Application No 52207/99, 12 December 2001, para 10.

> 'PGM accuracy may be affected by weather and/or defeated by simple countermeasures. Obscurants, such as smoke, may defeat laser-guided bombs, while electro-optical munitions have similar vulnerabilities.'[155]

Even Global Positioning System guided missiles, the accuracy of which is not affected by cloud or smoke, are still susceptible to jamming by low cost jamming devices.[156] In any event, PGM's are only as good as the intelligence which provides the selection of target. They may hit a building with pin-point accuracy, but if the building transpires to be an embassy, then collateral damage, not to say political fallout, may be immense.[157]

5.3.2 Precautions taken to reduce collateral damage

Article 57 of API sets out precautions which should be taken by an attacker in order to ensure that only military objectives are targeted and to reduce collateral damage. The Article requires that those planning an attack 'do everything feasible' to verify that the objects attacked are military objectives and to 'take all feasible precautions' in the choice of means and methods of attack in order to avoid or minimise collateral damage to civilians and civilian objects. Furthermore, attacks which would breach the proportionality principle should be cancelled or suspended and 'effective advance warning' should be given of attacks which may affect the civilian population unless circumstances do not permit. Finally, if there is a choice between several military objectives obtaining a similar military advantage the object which will cause the least collateral damage should be chosen. Greenwood, in his examination of the 1990–1991 Gulf conflict and the customary law applicable at that time, comments that '[m]ost of these provisions were regarded as declaratory of custom before the Gulf conflict'.[158]

In respect of the obligation to do everything feasible to verify that the objects attacked are military objectives, the Commentary on the Harvard Air and Missile Warfare Manual states that commanders must 'utilize all technical assets', such as intelligence, reconnaissance and surveillance systems 'to the extent that these assets are reasonably available, and utilizing them is militarily sound in the context of the overall air campaign'.[159] In this respect Wright states that in Afghanistan 'spy planes were often capable of providing Pentagon officials clear images of small objects with only a 1.5 s time delay'.[160]

---

[155] Hays Parks 2002, p 287.

[156] Belt 2000, p 123.

[157] See infra, discussion on taking all feasible precautions to ensure that the target is not a civilian one, Part 5.3.2.

[158] Greenwood 1993, p 83.

[159] Commentary on the Harvard Manual on Air and Missile Warfare, p 126.

[160] Wright 2003, p 139.

A contentious issue is the extent to which 'all feasible precautions' in minimising collateral damage requires the use of specific weapons and in particular whether it demands the use of Precision Guided Munitions (PGM's) in urban bombing campaigns. Sandoz comments generally that 'if you have the choice between weapons causing more or less collateral damages to obtain the *same* military advantage' then you have an obligation to use those which would cause less collateral damage, even if use of the other weapons in those circumstances would not breach the principle of proportionality *per se*.[161]

Belt has looked specifically at the question of whether customary international law requires the use of PGM's in bombing campaigns over urban areas and concludes that a new customary law principle to that effect has now emerged.[162] However, it must be recognised that a range of commentators, including Hays Parks, Murphy and Infeld, contest this interpretation of customary international law.[163] In its response to the Goldstone Report, Israel stated that eighty per cent of the air missiles fired by Israel in the Gaza Operation were precision guided 'even though it is *not* strictly required under international law'.[164] Rule 8 of the Harvard Air and Missile Warfare Manual states that '[t]here is *no specific obligation* on Belligerent Parties to use precision guided weapons', but recognises that there may be situations in which the requirement to minimise collateral damage 'cannot be fulfilled without using precision guided weapons'.[165]

It is submitted that the key word in this debate is 'feasible'. Are there occasions when it would not be 'feasible' to use PGM's in urban bombing campaigns and should the higher cost of these missiles be a factor which the attacking force may take into account? Given the problems associated with PGM's, such as poor visibility affecting laser guidance or the use of jamming devices to disrupt GPS signals, referred to above, it seems that a hard and fast rule demanding the use of PGM's in urban areas is not 'feasible'.[166] Additionally, Greenwood reluctantly acknowledges that the cost of PGM's and the limit on the number available may also impact upon whether it is 'feasible' to use them in every situation.[167] Nevertheless, the use of a 'dumb' bomb in an urban area, particularly if it resulted in high levels of collateral damage to civilians and civilian objects, should certainly raise questions as to whether API was complied with and whether in the circumstances it really was not 'feasible' to use PGM's.

---

161 Sandoz 2002, p 278.

162 Belt 2000, p 174.

163 Hays Parks 1998, pp 85–86; Murphy 2002, p 240 and Infeld 1992, p 137.

164 Israeli Response to the Goldstone Report, p 97, emphasis added.

165 Harvard Manual on Air and Missile Warfare, p 9, Rule 8, emphasis added. The Commentary on the Harvard Manual on Air and Missile Warfare, p 81, emphasises that 'there exists no obligation in the law of international armed conflict for States to acquire particular types of weapons'.

166 See comments of Murphy 2002, p 242.

167 Greenwood 1993, p 83 and see The Commentary on the Harvard Manual on Air and Missile Warfare, p 81.

In terms of cancelling attacks which may breach the proportionality equation and cause excessive collateral damage, Greenwood states that with respect to the 1990–1991 Gulf conflict:

> 'the coalition acknowledged the legal duty to assess military targets against the criteria of the proportionality principle and to call off attacks if the likely collateral damage was excessive.'[168]

Israel also stated in its response to the Goldstone Report that '[t]he IDF aborted or postponed attacks on Hamas personnel and targets when it appeared that civilians were at risk, at the expense of attaining military advantage'.[169]

The requirement to give 'effective advance warning' to civilians of impending attacks 'unless circumstances do not permit'; has caused controversy with respect to the recent conflicts involving Israel in Gaza and Lebanon. With respect to the Gaza conflict, Israel commented that it used general warnings, 'calling on civilians to stay away from sites where Hamas was conducting combat activities' and regional warnings which 'included a timeframe for the evacuation and designated specific routes for this purpose leading to safe areas'.[170] They achieved this by radio broadcasts, phone calls, the dropping of leaflets and, more controversially, 'firing *warning shots from light weapons that hit the roofs* of the designated targets, before proceeding with the strike'.[171]

The Goldstone Report regarded the requirement to give effective advance warning of attacks to civilians as representing customary international law, recognising that the phrase 'unless circumstances do not permit' allows that there are circumstances where the element of surprise is an essential part of the military operation or that a warning is simply not possible.[172] In terms of the need for the warning to be effective, this was understood as meaning 'that it must reach those who are likely to be in danger from the planned attack … give them sufficient time to react to the warning … clearly explain what they should do to avoid harm and it must be a credible warning'.[173] Furthermore, '[a]s far as possible, warnings should state the location to be affected and where the civilians should seek safety'.[174] The Goldstone Report questioned the effectiveness of Israel's methods, finding that pre-recorded telephone messages 'lacked credibility and clarity, and generated fear and uncertainty' and that leaflets and radio broadcasts mainly told people to leave

---

[168] Greenwood 1993, p 83.

[169] Israeli Response to the Goldstone Report, p 97.

[170] Ibid., p 99.

[171] Ibid., pp 99–100, original emphasis.

[172] Goldstone Report, paras 525–527. The Commission of Inquiry on Lebanon, para 151 concurred with this approach, as did the Commentary on the Harvard Manual on Air and Missile Warfare, pp 132–133.

[173] Goldstone Report, para 528.

[174] Ibid. The Commission of Inquiry on Lebanon, para 157, added to this that 'the message should also give civilians clear time slots for the evacuation linked to guaranteed safe humanitarian exit corridors that they should use'.

their homes and head towards the city centres, so were 'lacking in specificity and clarity' as civilians 'could not tell when they should leave since there was rarely an indication of when attacks would take place'.[175] In addition, the Commission of Inquiry on Lebanon rightly commented that:

> '[a] warning to evacuate does not relieve the military of their ongoing obligation to "take all feasible precautions" to protect civilians who remain behind ... [b]y remaining in place, the people and their property do not suddenly become military objectives which can be attacked.'[176]

With respect to the 'roof knocking' practice of Israel, referred to above, in firing warning shots with light ammunition at roofs before starting the attack proper; the Goldstone Report commented that 'civilians cannot be expected to know whether a small explosion is a warning of an impending attack or part of an actual attack'.[177] The Commentary to the Harvard Air and Missile Warfare Manual states that '[i]n some situations the only feasible method of warning may be to fire warning shots using tracer ammunition, thus inducing people to take cover before the attack',[178] and this may indeed persuade civilians to immediately take cover inside their houses. However, when the civilians are already inside their homes, the Goldstone Report is surely right in its conclusion that 'roof knocking' is not an effective advance warning as, even if the intent is to warn, it is likely 'to cause terror and confuse the affected civilians'.[179]

The requirement to choose the target with the least collateral damage if a choice is possible between several military objectives for a similar military advantage is also the subject of Rule 33 of the Harvard Air and Missile Warfare Manual.[180] The Commentary to the Manual gives the example of an intended attack upon a power generating facility located in the vicinity of civilians or civilian objects but which also gives power to the military.[181] If a temporary disruption of power is the sole objective and if it is possible to attack the transformers or substations serving the power generating facility, then if this will cause less collateral damage, then it should be preferred.[182] The Commentary to the Manual notes, however, that: '[t]here is no requirement to select among several objectives if doing so would be militarily unreasonable'.[183]

---

175 Goldstone Report, paras 529 and 534.

176 Commission of Inquiry on Lebanon, para 158. This is supported by the Commentary on the Harvard Manual on Air and Missile Warfare, p 134.

177 Goldstone Report, para 530.

178 Commentary on the Harvard Manual on Air and Missile Warfare, p 133.

179 Goldstone Report, para 531.

180 Harvard Manual on Air and Missile Warfare, p 17, Rule 33.

181 Commentary on the Harvard Manual on Air and Missile Warfare, pp 128–129.

182 Ibid.

183 Ibid., p 129.

5.3.3 Who should make the proportionality assessment?

Fenrick's solution to this question is that 'the determination of relative values must be that of the "reasonable military commander"'.[184] However, as Schmitt points out, such a value judgement would be affected by the social or cultural background of the commander and whether his side was currently winning or losing the conflict.[185] At the planning stage of a conflict military lawyers often review targets and so can contribute to the decision of whether collateral damage will be excessive.[186] Additionally, new technology may assist in minute-by-minute assessment of risks to non-combatants, such as the use of remotely piloted spy planes.[187]

However, individual soldiers will still have to make proportionality assessments in the heat of battlefield stress with very little time to come to a decision.[188] For example, a pilot may have been ordered to destroy a series of strategically important bridges, but he would surely breach the proportionality principle if he chose to open fire upon one of them at the time when a large convoy of refugees was crossing.[189] Equally he would not be expected to desist from firing upon each target because a single car or person was crossing the bridge at the time.[190] Balancing civilian casualties against military objectives, especially when the lives of troops are directly threatened, is never going to be easy.

5.3.4 Longer term collateral damage and the proportionality principle

After the 1990–1991 Gulf conflict the question arose in as to whether the proportionality equation should take into account longer term collateral damage. Greenwood comments that previously the tendency had been to apply the proportionality principle by 'comparing the immediate military advantage resulting

---

[184] Fenrick 1997, p 546. This is supported by Israel, Israeli Response to the Goldstone Report, p 45.

[185] Schmitt 1999, pp 152 and 157 and see Bothe 2001, p 535.

[186] See Rule 141, ICRC Study, Henckaerts and Doswald-Beck 2005, p 361, which suggests that the use of military lawyers is customary international law, but see Turns 2007, pp 361–362.

[187] Wright 2003, p 139.

[188] See comments on this by Wright 2003, p 146.

[189] Alternatively it could be found that this evidenced an intention to kill the civilians and the soldier could be charged under Article 8(2)(b)(i), Rome Statute.

[190] See the controversy surrounding the NATO pilot who attacked a bridge when a civilian train was crossing it, OTP Report, paras 58–62, although this was primarily discussed in the context of whether the pilot intentionally attacked the civilians.

from an attack with the immediate civilian losses'.[191] However, during the first Gulf conflict there were many more civilian deaths from the longer term results of the destruction of the power grids, 'as hospitals, sewerage plants, water purification facilities and the like ceased to be able to operate', than there were during the actual attacks themselves.[192] Crawford comments that '[n]ever before has there been so much devastation visited upon a civilian population as a result of accurately placed munitions'.[193] Indeed, he estimates that as many as 70,000 non-combatant deaths can be directly attributed to the elimination of Iraq's electrical power.[194] Greenwood argues that these longer term effects must be taken into account when calculating the proportionality equation, but concedes that such side effects may be difficult to predict and may be due to a combination of factors, such as the priority given to military over civilian needs by the opposing power.[195]

Nevertheless, whilst the lessons of the Gulf show that the proportionality equation should not be restricted to the immediate effects of an attack,[196] it is clear that commanders and those planning an attack do not operate with hindsight and can only be expected to take into account the potential side effects which would be apparent at that time.[197] The proportionality equation 'is a forward-looking test based on expectations and information at the time the decision was made',[198] although, as Holland states, '[t]he fact of the controversy over the targeting of enemy civilian electrical systems demonstrates a decreased tolerance of collateral damage'.[199]

5.3.5 *The ICTY/ICC and their approach to excessive collateral damage*

The ICTY discussed the proportionality requirement in the *Blaškić* Judgement, which considered the possible breach of this rule by the defendant during an attack against some villages in central Bosnia.[200] The Trial Chamber held that:

> '[b]y advocating the vigorous use of heavy weapons to seize villages inhabited mainly by civilians, General Blaškić gave orders which had consequences out of all proportion to

[191] Greenwood 1999, p 13.
[192] Ibid., p 12; and Normand and Af Jochnick 1994, pp 400–401 and 404–405.
[193] Crawford III 1997, p 110.
[194] Ibid.
[195] Greenwood 1999, p 13 and Greenwood 1993, p 79. See also comments of Holland 2004, p 61.
[196] Crawford III 1997, p 114.
[197] See Commentary on the Harvard Manual on Air and Missile Warfare, p 91.
[198] Israeli Response to the Goldstone Report, p 45.
[199] Holland 2004, p 62.
[200] *Blaškić*, supra n 96, paras 650–651.

> military necessity and knew that many civilians would inevitably be killed and their homes destroyed.'[201]

This confirms that by using inappropriate and indiscriminate weapons for the target selected, the proportionality rule may be breached.[202] It also demonstrates that the proportionality rule may be breached through excessive damage to civilian objects as well as by wounding or killing civilians.[203] Furthermore, the ICTY in *Galić* confirmed that the proportionality test is a forward-looking test, stating that when determining whether an attack was proportionate, 'it is necessary to examine whether a reasonably well informed person *in the circumstances of the actual perpetrator*, making reasonable use of the information available to him or her, could have expected excessive civilian casualties to result from the attack'.[204]

The ICC formulation of the proportionality principle is contained in Article 8(2)(b)(iv) and prohibits:

> '[i]ntentionally launching an attack in the knowledge that such attack will cause incidental loss of life or injury to civilians or damage to civilian objects … which would be clearly excessive in relation to the concrete and direct overall military advantage anticipated'.

The EOC do not expand much on the definition in the Rome Statute, they simply require that the perpetrator 'launched an attack'.[205] The attack must have been such as to cause:

> 'incidental death or injury to civilians or damage to civilian objects … and that such death, injury or damage would be of such an extent as to be clearly excessive in relation to the concrete and direct overall military advantage anticipated.'[206]

The perpetrator must have known that this incidental death, injury or damage would occur and that it would be clearly excessive in relation to the concrete and direct overall military advantage anticipated.[207]

There are various points of interest in this formulation. First, the EOC require that the collateral damage be 'clearly excessive in relation to the concrete and direct overall military advantage anticipated' and according to the OTP report on NATO action in Yugoslavia the expression 'clearly', 'ensures that criminal responsibility would be entailed only in cases where the excessiveness of the incidental damage was obvious'.[208]

---

201 Ibid., para 651.

202 Bombs delivered at high altitude could be inappropriate weapons, see Lippman 2002 and Voon 2001.

203 See Benvenuti 2001, pp 508–509.

204 ICTY Case No. IT-28-29-T, *Prosecutor* v *Galić*, (5 December 2003) (Trial Chamber Judgement), para 58, emphasis added.

205 EOC, p 131.

206 Ibid.

207 Ibid., pp 131–132.

208 OTP report, para 21 and Lee (ed) 2001, p 148.

This approach is supported by academic commentary, which confirms that, as the Rome Statute was not intended to be used to prosecute 'mere errors of judgement' by commanders in the field, only serious criminal conduct will contravene this article.[209] A footnote to the EOC explains that the expression 'concrete and direct overall military advantage' refers to a 'military advantage that is foreseeable by the perpetrator at the relevant time'.[210] This ensures that the accused will be judged in the light of the information available to him at the time of the decision to attack.[211] According to Watkin, the use of the word 'overall' also 'emphasises the strategic impact of an attack although … "an attack as a whole" must be viewed as a finite event, not to be confused with the entire war'.[212]

Secondly, the mental element of this offence is that the perpetrator knew the attack would cause collateral damage which would be clearly excessive in relation to military advantage anticipated.[213] Therefore, the prosecution must prove that the attack was objectively likely to cause disproportionate collateral damage and show that the perpetrator knew this. A footnote to the EOC explains that this Element requires a value judgement on the part of the perpetrator.[214] Consequently, it must be shown that the perpetrator was aware, as a result of the information available to him at the time, that the collateral damage would be excessive in relation to the military advantage anticipated.[215] The mental element of this offence will doubtless be difficult to prove in all but the clearest of cases and is criticised by Bothe as making the perpetrator 'the judge in his own cause'.[216]

Nevertheless, Dörmann states that the members of the Preparatory Commission accepted that the content of the footnote:

> 'should not benefit a reckless perpetrator who knows perfectly well the anticipated military advantage and the expected incidental injury or damage, but gives no thought to evaluating the latter's possible excessiveness'.[217]

Furthermore, he suggests that in any case:

> 'an unreasonable judgement or an allegation that no judgement was made would, in a case of death, injury or damage clearly excessive to the military advantage anticipated, simply not be credible.'[218]

[209] von Hebel and Robinson 1999, p 111 and Rogers 2000, p 180.

[210] EOC, p 131, fn 36.

[211] See France's interpretative declaration to the Rome Statute, para 7, available at www.icrc.org, accessed 28 December 2010.

[212] Watkin 2005, p 19.

[213] EOC, pp 131–132.

[214] Ibid., p 132, fn 37.

[215] Israel finds that the 'clarifications' of the proportionality test in the Rome Statute reflect customary international law, Israeli Response to the Goldstone Report, p 44.

[216] Bothe 2002, p 400 and see Pejic 2000, p 71 and fn 35.

[217] Dörmann 2001, p 474.

[218] Ibid., p 475.

Finally, although France declared upon ratification of the Rome Statute that Article 8(2)(b) neither regulates nor prohibits the possible use of nuclear weapons,[219] it is clear that nuclear weapons must be used, as must conventional weapons, in accordance with the rule of proportionality.[220] Therefore, use of a nuclear weapon which causes many civilian casualties, a likely scenario because of the very nature of such weapons, could undoubtedly found the basis for a prosecution before the ICC under Article 8(2)(b)(iv).

5.4 Bombing Campaigns in Non-International Armed Conflicts

International humanitarian law is generally less extensive and less specific when it comes to non-international armed conflicts. Historically, states have been jealous of their domestic jurisdiction and unwilling to countenance any interference. Until the 1977 Additional Protocol II (APII) only Common Article 3 of the 1949 Geneva Conventions governed internal conflicts. Common Article 3 is very brief and the only possible bearing it might have on bombing campaigns is the duty to treat non-combatants humanely which, one assumes, would be breached by intentionally bombing civilian populations.

Article 13(2) of APII, in identical wording to Article 51(2) of API, states that: '[t]he civilian population as such, as well as individual civilians, shall not be the object of attack' and the ICRC Study confirms that this is a rule of customary international law irrespective of the nature of the conflict.[221] However, the definition of 'civilians' has caused more difficulties in non-international than international armed conflicts, in particular with respect to non-state actors. The ICRC guidance on the notion of direct participation in hostilities states that 'the decisive criterion for individual membership in an organized armed group [in a non-international armed conflict] is whether a person assumes a continuous function for the group involving his or her direct participation in hostilities', which they termed 'continuous combat function'.[222] Such civilians could be targeted at all times as a result of this, but that unorganised civilians who take up arms should, as with civilians in international armed conflicts, only lose their immunity whilst taking a 'direct part in hostilities'.[223]

---

219 See France's interpretative declaration to the Rome Statute para 2, available at www.icrc.org, accessed 28 December 2010.

220 See Ireland's understanding of Article 55, API, available at www.icrc.org, accessed 28 December 2010, and Burroughs 2000. See also Legality of the Threat or Use of Nuclear Weapons, Advisory Opinion, ICJ Rep (1996) 226, paras 31 and 33.

221 Henckaerts and Doswald-Beck 2005, pp 5–8.

222 Melzer 2008, p 1007.

223 Ibid., p 1009.

It is notable that neither Common Article 3 nor Additional Protocol II specifically prohibits reprisal attacks against those individuals otherwise protected under those instruments. Therefore, these treaties leave open the question of whether a reprisal missile attack may be carried out legitimately against civilians in the area controlled by a non-state party in a non-international armed conflict. As has been commented,[224] this issue is controversial even in international armed conflicts and the fact that the ICRC Study is silent on this question as regards non-international armed conflicts suggests that regretfully reprisals against civilians in such situations may legitimately take place. Nevertheless, as with such action in an international armed conflict, it is likely that such an attack would be morally unacceptable to the international community, irrespective of any arguments as to its legality.

With respect to attacks against civilian objects, neither Common Article 3 nor APII includes a general prohibition against attacking civilian objects in non-international armed conflicts, although objects indispensable to the survival of the civilian population and cultural objects and places of worship are given special protection in APII.[225] Nevertheless, the ICRC Study maintains that a general prohibition against attacking civilian objects in non-international armed conflict exists in customary international law, relying primarily upon the inclusion of this prohibition in more recent treaty law, such as the Amended Protocol II to the Convention on Certain Conventional Weapons, and on the inclusion of such a prohibition in many military manuals.[226]

Furthermore, the ICRC Study also bolsters their assertion that a general prohibition against attacking civilian objects is customary in non-international armed conflicts by reference to judgements of the ICTY, in particular an interlocutory decision in the case of *Kordić and Čerkez* in which the Trial Chamber stated that:

> 'it is indisputable that … the prohibition of indiscriminate attacks or attacks on civilian objects are generally accepted obligations … there is no possible doubt as to the customary status of these specific provisions as they reflect core principles of humanitarian law that can be considered as applying to all armed conflicts, whether intended to apply to international or non-international conflicts.'[227]

Nevertheless, there is neither treaty nor any clear customary prohibition against reprisal bombardment of civilian objects in non international armed conflicts.

The Rome Statute deals with these issues in non-international armed conflicts by including the offence of:

[224] Supra Part 5.2.1.

[225] Articles 14 and 16, APII.

[226] Henckaerts and Doswald-Beck 2005, pp 27–28 (Rule 7).

[227] ICTY Case No. IT-95-14/2, *Prosecutor* v *Kordić and Čerkez* (2 March 1999) (Trial Chamber Decision on the Joint Defence Motion to Dismiss the Amended Indictment for Lack of Jurisdiction based on the Limited Jurisdictional Reach of Articles 2 and 3), para 31.

> 'Intentionally directing attacks against the civilian population as such or against individual civilians not taking direct part in hostilities,'[228]

which is identical in wording to that used with respect to international armed conflicts. However, the Rome Statute fails to include a clear general prohibition against attacks on civilian objects. Attacks are only prohibited against those objects displaying the Red Cross or crescent, or objects associated with humanitarian assistance or peacekeeping mission,[229] or 'buildings dedicated to religion, education, art, science or charitable purposes, historic monuments, hospitals and places where the sick and wounded are collected'.[230]

Nonetheless, the ICRC Study contends that Article 8(2)(e)(xii) which prohibits: *Destroying* or seizing the property of an adversary unless such *destruction* or seizure be imperatively demanded by the necessities of the conflict,[231] suggests that an attack against any civilian object, not imperatively demanded by military necessity would constitute a war crime.[232] Indeed, Kreß also comments upon the confusion regarding the exact ambit of this Article, stating that it appears to introduce a general war crime of attacking civilian objects, 'through the back door … as the term "adversary" used in this provision certainly extends to civilians'.[233]

It must be noted, however, that the Elements of Crime for this Article introduced the requirement that the property in this article must have been 'protected from that destruction or seizure under the international law of armed conflict'.[234] Therefore, unless it can be demonstrated that all civilian objects in non-international armed conflicts are protected under customary international humanitarian law then this article would only add to the protection provided against aerial bombing strikes in that it may protect against the destruction of other objects the destruction of which is prohibited in APII, which in addition to those mentioned above include, dams, dykes and nuclear electrical generating stations,[235] and also foodstuffs, agricultural areas, livestock and drinking water installations.[236]

A notable absence from APII is the prohibition against excessive collateral damage. The Rome Statute also fails to prohibit excessive collateral damage in non-international armed conflicts. However, the Commentary to the San Remo Manual on the Law of Non-International Armed Conflict states that:

---

228 Article 8(2)(e)(i), Rome Statute.

229 Article 8(2)(e)(ii) and (iii), Rome Statute.

230 Article 8(2)(e)(iv), Rome Statute.

231 Emphasis added.

232 Henckaerts and Doswald-Beck 2005, p 27 (Rule 7).

233 Kreß 2001, p 139.

234 EOC, p 155.

235 Article 15, APII.

236 Article 14, APII.

'[t]he relative absence of express mention of proportionality in instruments governing non-international armed conflict should not be construed as meaning that it is inapplicable in such conflict.'[237]

Evidence for the application of the principle of proportionality in a non-international armed conflict can be found in treaty law in the 1996, Amended Protocol II to the Conventional Weapons Convention and the 1999, Second Hague Protocol for the Protection of Cultural Property in the Event of an Armed Conflict.[238] With respect to other sources, the British Military Manual makes it clear that the basic principles of 'military necessity, humanity, distinction and *proportionality*' apply in a non-international armed conflict and the ICRC Study also confirms that the principle of proportionality applies in a non-international armed conflict.[239]

5.5 Conclusion

The law in respect of military targets and excessive collateral damage in international armed conflicts is complex and this paper has only covered some of the issues. However, some important concerns have been raised with regard to the definition of military targets and civilian objects. In particular, only those civilians taking up a direct combatant role can be considered military targets. Therefore, civilians delivering supplies to the armed forces in the field or working in munitions factories should not be considered targets themselves, although they are clearly at greater risk of becoming collateral casualties because of their proximity to legitimate military targets such as munitions.

A critical issue, with regard to military targets, is the question of whether the media can be attacked *per se*. Here it must be stressed that enemy propaganda and civilian morale are *not* by themselves legitimate targets. Although attacks on the media are usually explained as a necessary part of the destruction of the enemy's Command and Control centres, in future such claims should be viewed sceptically particularly where statements to the press suggest that the real reason is to suppress a source of the adversary's propaganda.

This article has also raised important problems with respect to the issue of collateral damage. The proportionality principle is by its nature imprecise and liable to be evaluated differently according to whether those deciding are on the winning or losing side at the time they make the evaluation. Nevertheless, several

237 The Manual on the Law of Non-International Armed Conflict with Commentary, 2006, Rule 2.1.1.4, Proportionality, International Institute of Humanitarian Law, p 22.

238 Protocol on Prohibitions or Restrictions on the Use of Mines, Booby-Traps and Other Devices as amended on 3 May 1996 (Protocol II to the 1980 Convention as amended on 3 May 1996), Article 3(8)(c). Second Protocol to the Hague Convention of 1954 for the Protection of Cultural Property in the Event of Armed Conflict The Hague, 26 March 1999, Article 7(3).

239 The Manual of the Law of Armed Conflict 2004, para 15.5, emphasis added and Henckaerts and Doswald-Beck 2005, pp 48–49.

commentators believe that the current interpretation of this principle is balanced too far towards the interests of the military as in recent conflicts in the Gulf, Afghanistan and Kosovo the civilian casualties far outweighed the casualties taken by the armed forces of those carrying out the attacks.

In order to reduce civilian casualties, it is vital that the lessons from previous conflicts are learnt. Therefore, the longer-term threat to civilians from attacks, particularly on electricity stations, *must* be taken into account when making a proportionality assessment.[240] Additionally, the risk to civilians from collapse of their homes close to military objectives should also be taken into consideration. A possible way to address this latter problem is the use of warnings, where possible, to allow civilians to clear the area, particularly when carrying out attacks upon a state with very little defence against aerial attacks.[241] The warnings must however be effective to be of value in reducing civilian casualties. The increased risks to civilians from mistakes and off-target missiles due to high altitude bombardment must be taken into account as part of the proportionality equation when attacks are planned and lower-level bombing, despite the increased risks to pilots, considered.

Of particular concern is the reduced level of protection for civilian populations during bombing campaigns in non-international armed conflicts. Treaty law protection is minimal and, as has been stated, neither APII nor the Rome Statute of the ICC deals with collateral damage in internal conflicts. The only protection, therefore, from excessive collateral damage in such circumstances would be a finding, as is argued here, that the proportionality principle applies in all circumstances under customary international law.[242]

Finally, it is important to seek the advice of military lawyers during the planning stages of bombing campaigns and to make full use of new technologies which assist in the real-time assessment of risks to civilians. Nevertheless, whilst the aim of international humanitarian law is to reduce civilian casualties as much as possible, it must be accepted that war is destructive; innocent civilians die and their property is destroyed. Closer adherence to the principles of distinction and proportionality can only reduce civilian casualties and will never remove them altogether.

References

Aldrich G (1981) New life for the laws of war. AJIL 75:764–783

Aldrich G (1999) Yugoslavia's television studios as military objectives. Int Law Forum 1:149–150

Belt SW (2000) Missiles over Kosovo: emergence, lex lata, of a customary norm requiring the use of precision guided munitions in urban areas. NLR 47:115–175

240 See comments of Lewis 2003, p 507.

241 See Article 26, Hague Regulations IV 1907, Article 57(2)(c), Department of the Army Field Manual 27-10, The Law of Land Warfare, 25 July 1956, para 43.

242 See Turns 2002, p 145 and Meron 1996, p 244.

Benvenuti P (2001) The ICTY prosecutor and the review of the NATO bombing campaign against the Federal Republic of Yugoslavia. EJIL 12:503–529

Bothe M (2001) The protection of the civilian population and NATO bombing on Yugoslavia: comments on a report to the prosecutor of the ICTY. EJIL 12:531–535

Bothe M (2002) War Crimes. In: Cassese A, Gaeta P, Jones J (eds) The Rome statute of the international criminal court: a commentary, vol I. Oxford University, Oxford

Bothe M, Partsch K, Solf W (1982) New rules for victims of armed conflicts, commentary on the two 1977 protocols additional to the Geneva conventions of 1949. Martinus Nijhoff Publishers, The Hague

Burroughs J (2000) Lawyers' Committee on Nuclear Policy, The French 'interpretative declaration' regarding nuclear weapons. Available at www.lcnp.org/global/french.htm. Accessed 28 Dec 2010

Clarke M, Glynn T, Rogers A (1989) Combatant and prisoner of war status. In: Meyer M (ed) Armed conflict and the new law: aspects of the 1977 Geneva protocols and the 1981 weapons convention. British Institute of International and Comparative Law, London, pp 107–135

Cottier M, Fenrick W, Viseur Sellers P, Zimmerman A (1999) Article 8, war crimes. In: Triffterer O (ed) Commentary on the Rome statute of the international criminal court, observers' notes, article by article. Nomos Verlasgesellschaft, Baden-Baden

Crawford J III (1997) The law of noncombatant immunity and the targeting of national electrical power systems. Fletcher Forum World Aff 21:101–119

Darcy S (2003) The evolution of the law of belligerent reprisals. MLR 175:184–251

Dinstein Y (1997) The laws of air, missile and nuclear warfare. Israel YB HR 27:1–16

Dinstein Y (2002) Discussion. Int Law Stud 78:218–219

Dolzer R (2002) Commentary. Int Law Stud 78:353–359

Dörmann K (2001) Preparatory Commission for the International Criminal Court: the elements of war crimes, part II: other serious violations of the laws and customs applicable in international and non-international armed conflicts. IRRC 842:461–486

Doswald-Beck L (1989) The value of the 1977 Geneva protocols for the protection of civilians. In: Meyer M (ed) Armed conflict and the new law. British Institute for International and Comparative Law, London

Dworkin A (2003) The Iraq war in retrospect. Available at www.crimesofwar.org/onnews/news-iraq3.html. Accessed 28 Dec 2010

Fenrick WJ (1982) The rule of proportionality and Protocol 1 in conventional warfare. Mil LR 98:91–125

Fenrick WJ (1997) Attacking the enemy civilian as a punishable offence. Duke JCIL 7:539–569

Fenrick WJ (2001) Targeting and proportionality during the NATO bombing campaign against Yugoslavia. EJIL 12:489–502

Fisk R (2003) Is there some element in the US military that wants to take out journalists? The Independent, London, 9 April 2003

Fleck D (1997) Strategic bombing and the definition of military objectives. 27 Israel YB HR 27:41–64

Gardam J (1993) Proportionality and force in international law. AJIL 87:391–413

Greenwood C (1993) Customary international law and the first Geneva protocol of 1977 in the Gulf conflict. In: Rowe P (ed) The Gulf war 1990–91 in international and english law. Routledge, London

Greenwood C (1999) A critique of the additional protocols to the Geneva conventions of 1949. In: Durham H, McCormack TLH (eds) The changing face of conflict and the efficacy of international humanitarian law. Kluwer Law International, The Hague

Harris D (1998) Cases and materials on international law, 5th edn edn. Sweet & Maxwell, London

Harris T (2010) How smart bombs work. Available at http://science.howstuffworks.com/smart-bomb.htm. Accessed 28 Dec 2010

Hays Parks W (1998) The protection of civilians from air warfare. Israel YB HR 27:65–112

Hays Parks W (2002) Commentary. Int Law Stud 78:281–285

Henckaerts J, Doswald-Beck L (2005) Customary international humanitarian law. Cambridge University Press, Geneva, ICRC and Cambridge
Holland J (2004) Military objective and collateral damage: their relationship and dynamics. YIHL 7:35–78
Infeld D (1992) Precision-guided munitions demonstrated their pinpoint accuracy in Desert Storm; but is a country obligated to use precision technology to minimize collateral civilian injury and damage. GW JIL and Econ 26:109–141
Kalshoven F (1977) Reaffirmation and development of international humanitarian law applicable in armed conflicts: the Diplomatic Conference, Geneva, 1974–1977: Part 1: combatants and civilians. NYIL 8:107–135
Kreß C (2001) War crimes committed in non-international armed conflict and the emerging system of international criminal justice. In: Fleck D (ed) Humanitarian protection in non-international armed conflicts. International Institute of Humanitarian Law, San Remo, pp 103–177
Kritsiotis D (2000) The Kosovo crisis and NATO's application of armed force against the Federal Republic of Yugoslavia. ICLQ 49:330–359
Lee R (ed) (2001) The International Criminal Court: elements of crimes and rules of procedure and evidence. Transnational Publishers, Ardsley NY
Lewis MW (2003) The law of aerial bombardment in the 1991 Gulf war. AJIL 97:481–509
Lippman M (2002) Aerial attacks on civilians and the humanitarian law of war: technology and terror from World War 1 to Afghanistan. Calif Western ILJ 33:1–67
Manual of the Law of Armed Conflict (2004) UK ministry of defence. Oxford University Press, Oxford
Manyon J, Rooney B (1999) TV attack entirely justified, says Blair, London, The Daily Telegraph, 24 April 1999
Medenica O (2001) Protocol 1 and operation allied force: did NATO abide by principles of proportionality. Loy LA I & CLR 23:329–426
Melzer N (2008) Interpretive guidance on the notion of direct participation in hostilities under international humanitarian law. IRRC 872:991–1047
Meron T (1996) The continuing role of custom in the formation of international humanitarian law. AJIL 90:238–249
Meyer JM (2001) Tearing down the façade: a critical look at the current law on targeting the will of the enemy and air force doctrine. Air Force LR 51:143–170
Murphy J (2002) Legal and ethical dimensions of collateral damage. Int Law Stud 78:229–255
Normand R, Af Jochnick C (1994) The legitimation of violence: a critical analysis of the Gulf war. Harvard ILJ 35:387–416
Oeter S (1999) Methods and means of combat. In: Fleck D (ed) The handbook of humanitarian law in armed conflicts. Oxford University Press, Oxford
Pejic J (2000) The International Criminal Court Statute: an appraisal of the Rome package. Int Lawyer 34:65–84
Pocar F (2002) To what extent is Protocol I customary international law? Int Law Stud 78:337–351
Randelzhofer A (1982) Civilian objects. In: Bernhardt R (ed) Encyclopaedia of public international law, vol 3. North-Holland, Amsterdam
Rizer K (2001) Bombing dual-use targets: legal, ethical, and doctrinal perspectives, air & space power journal—chronicles online journal. Available at www.airpower.maxwell.af.mil/airchronicles/cc/Rizer.html. Accessed 28 Dec 2010
Roberts A (2002) The laws of war after Kosovo. Int Law Stud 78:401–415
Robertson (1999) Kosovo: an account of the crisis. Available at www.unmikonline.org/DPI/html/reports/modlr.html. Accessed 28 Dec 2010
Rogers A (1996) Law on the battlefield. Manchester University Press, Manchester
Rogers A (2000) Zero-casualty warfare. IRRC 837:165–181
Ronzitti N (2000) Is the non liquet of the final report by the committee established to review the NATO bombing campaign against the Federal Republic of Yugoslavia acceptable? IRRC 840:1017–1027

Rooney B (2003) TV stations bombed to silence Saddam, The Daily Telegraph, London, 27 March 2003
Roscini M (2005) Targeting and contemporary aerial bombardment. ICLQ 54:411–444
Roucounas E (1996) Some issues relating to war crimes in air and sea warfare. In: Dinstein Y, Tabory M (eds) War crimes in international law. Kluwer Law International, The Hague
Rowe P (2000) Kosovo 1999: the air campaign – have the provisions of additional Protocol I withstood the test? IRRC 837:147–164
Sandoz Y (2002) Commentary. Int Law Stud 78:273–279
Sandoz C, Swinarski C, Zimmerman B (eds) (1987) Commentary on the additional protocols of 8 June 1977 to the Geneva conventions of 12 August 1949, Geneva, ICRC and Dordrecht, Martinus Nijhoff
Schindler D, Toman J (1998) The laws of armed conflicts, a collection of conventions, resolutions and other documents. Martinus Nijhoff, Dordrecht
Schmitt M (1998) Future war and the principle of discrimination. Israel YB HR 28:51–90
Schmitt M (1999) The principle of discrimination in 21st century warfare. Yale HR & Dev LJ 2:143–182
Shamash H (2005–2006) How much is too much? an examination of the principle of jus in bello proportionality. Israel Def Force Law Rev 2:103–148
Spaight J (1944) Legitimate objectives in air warfare. BYIL 21:158–164
Stewart J (2007) The UN Commission of inquiry on Lebanon. J Int Crim Justice 5:1039–1059
Turns D (2002) At the 'vanishing point' of international humanitarian law: methods and means of warfare in non-international armed conflicts. GYIL 45:115–148
Turns D (2007) Implementation and compliance. In: Wilmshurst E, Breau S (eds) Perspectives on the ICRC study on customary international humanitarian law. British Institute of International and Comparative Law and Cambridge, Cambridge University Press, Chatham House, London
Vallely P (2003) Journalists perish, looters flourish and medics despair in the chaotic jigsaw of war, The Independent, London, 9 April 2003
von der Heydte F (1982) Military objectives. In: Bernhardt R (ed) Encyclopaedia of public international law, vol 3. North-Holland, Amsterdam
von Hebel H, Robinson D (1999) Crimes within the jurisdiction of the court. In: Lee RSK (ed) The International Criminal Court, the making of the Rome statute, issues, negotiations, results. Kluwer Law International, The Hague
Voon T (2001) Pointing the finger: civilian casualties of NATO bombing in the Kosovo conflict. Amer Univ ILR 16:1083–1113
Watkin K (2005) Assessing proportionality: moral complexity and legal rules. YIHL 8:3–53
Wright R (2003) Combating civilian casualties: rules and balancing in the developing law of war. Wake Forest LR 38:129–172

Chapter 6
The Law of Armed Conflict and International Human Rights Law: Some Paradigmatic Differences and Operational Implications

Rob McLaughlin

Contents

6.1 Introduction

Debate over the degree to which International Human Rights Law (IHRL) should legitimately inform and alter the interpretation of the Law of Armed Conflict (LOAC)[1] is increasing in intensity. It is not a new debate—G.I.A.D. Draper was

[1] The terms LOAC and IHL (International Humanitarian Law) will be used interchangeably. LOAC will be preferred, but IHL will be retained in quotes where this is the term that was originally used.

The author wishes to acknowledge the valuable comments provided by Bruce Oswald and Dario Morosini. All errors are of course the author's alone.

R. McLaughlin (✉)
College of Law, Australian National University, Canberra, ACT 0200, Australia
e-mail: rob.mclaughlin1@defence.gov.au

M.N. Schmitt et al. (eds.), *Yearbook of International Humanitarian Law Volume 13, 2010*, DOI: 10.1007/978-90-6704-811-8_6,

considering the issue in 1971,[2] and there have been numerous general statements by the UN recognizing that there is indeed interplay between the two bodies of law.[3] Yet despite a long formative period, the debate—which is now beginning to attract much greater attention jurisprudentially, operationally, and academically—is still being conducted in a procedurally flawed manner. This flawed procedure has two characteristics. First, it is characterized by a process of reverse engineering. By this I mean it is characterized by reasoning from a limited number of particular instances to arrive at a general thesis, followed by the subsequent re-application of this apparent general thesis to other instances. The second procedural characteristic is that the debate is substantially in the form of a one-way argument. I will briefly elaborate on both.

First, in relation to reverse engineering, the debate is currently characterised by a tendency to draw a general concept from specific instances, followed by delving back into the particular with a view to applying it in situations where it was not previously applied. In other words, instances A–L are used to develop a general thesis A–Z, which is then used as justification to reach back into instances M–Z, with a view to altering the applicable law, or at the very least, the way that law is interpreted or applied. As with all debates conducted at the level of generalisation with a view to reverse engineering, this approach to the LOAC-IHRL interplay debate has led to a number of misleading outcomes. The first is a broadening perception that LOAC and IHRL are products of the same legal impulse. However, apart from a 'similar general underlying sense of concern with humanity' (a term both bodies of law use),[4] LOAC and IHRL are fundamentally distinct and different. This perception, I would argue, is merely the most visible manifestation of a project of assimilation which is—to be perfectly blunt—in general aimed at softening, reconceptualising, and renegotiating LOAC by interpretation, infusing it with IHRL norms and attitudes, as opposed to hardening selected components of IHRL so that they can better fit within (and thus have a formidable impact upon) the LOAC paradigm. A recent Casebook on IHRL—Francisco Forrest Martin et al's *International Human Rights and Humanitarian Law: Treaties, Cases, and Analysis*,[5] is indicative of this trend. In their Introduction, the authors declare that:

> 'It is in the nineteenth century that an integration of international human rights law and international humanitarian law that reflects and integrates the ideas, events, and conditions outlined emerges. For example, in the nineteenth century, states began to adopt the practice of outlawing the trafficking of slaves—a human rights concern. In 1868, the St Petersburg Declaration condemned the use of 'dum dum' bullets in war …'[6]

---

[2] Draper 1971a, p 191; Draper 1971b, p 326.

[3] For example, UNSC Resolution 237 (14 June 1967) *On the Situation in the Middle East*, Preambular Paragraph 2—'*Considering* that essential and inalienable human rights should be respected even during the vicissitudes of war …'; a view specifically welcomed with 'great satisfaction' by the General Assembly in UNGA Resolution 2252 (4 July 1967) para 1(b).

[4] I am indebted to Cameron Moore of the University of New England for this very perceptive phrase.

[5] Martin et al. 2006.

[6] Martin et al. 2006, p 3.

LOAC was certainly a visible presence on the legal landscape of the late 1800s, but I tend to more readily accept Steiner and Alston's view that IHRL—as a consciously integrated and coordinated project—is a post-1945 movement.[7] The mere historical co-incidence of the anti-slavery movement (aimed at halting entirely a barbarous practice which inflicted death and suffering) and the prohibition of certain ammunition types (aimed at reducing one particular cause of superfluous and unnecessary suffering, but within a general endorsement of the necessity and legitimacy of inflicting killing and suffering in war) is not necessarily indicative of the early integration of the two streams of law.[8]

The second misleading belief is that there is a general 'spirit' of IHRL which transcends the black-letter application of its core treaties or its defined customary international law elements. To some extent this is so, and a number of IHRL proscriptions and prohibitions are clearly of a *jus cogens* nature—torture being a completely uncontroversial example. Equally clearly, there are specific situations where elements of IHRL treaties are expressed as applicable in situations of armed conflict. In relation to the minimum guarantees necessary for a fair trial, for example, there is little doubt that Article 75(4) of Additional Protocol I to the Geneva Conventions of 1949 (1977) (API) was drafted in light of, and clearly reflects, Article 14 of the International Covenant on Civil and Political Rights (1966) (ICCPR).[9] Hence the comment and jurisprudence around Article 14 ICCPR should be looked to where the scope and meaning of concepts in Article 75(4) API are in dispute. That the ICCPR Article 6 right to life applies in situations of armed conflict by virtue of the non-derogability provisions of ICCPR Article 4(2) is equally crystal clear, although whether this obligation applies extra-territorially is a separate and very contentious question.[10] However, these applications are specific and precise. No-one should doubt that they apply—that they do so is clear from the text, the negotiating history and context, or (depending upon one's view) their status as custom or even *jus cogens*; the only question is how, precisely, they apply. No-one should be in any doubt that most States accept that certain provisions in certain treaties apply during armed conflict because this is what the relevant treaties, or custom,require. The ICJ, it is clear, has adopted an even wider

[7] Steiner and Alston 2000, for example at p v, p 137. See also Droege 2007, p 313—Human Rights Law 'remained, with the exception of minority protection following the First World War, a subject of national law until after the Second World War. With the conclusion of the Second World War human rights became part of international law, starting with the adoption of the Universal Declaration of Human Rights in 1948'. Similarly, Peter Rowe—specifically examining the impact of IHRL on military forces noted that. 'The detailed treatment of human rights is, generally, a post-World War II development'—Rowe 2006, p 5.

[8] See also Bowring 2010, p 485.

[9] Sandoz et al. (eds) 1987, para 3092.

[10] See for example, the comments and materials on this issue—Art 2(1)—at Joseph et al. 2004, paras 4.11–4.15. The US, for example, has recently made a number of comments on this issue—see Second and Third Periodic Report of the United States of America to the UN Committee on Human Rights Concerning the International Covenant on Civil and Political Rights (21 October 2005)—Annex I: Territorial Scope of Application of the Covenant.

view, arguing that IHRL applies 'in toto', and is only trumped where a specific LOAC rule can be considered *lex specialis*.[11]

But the generalising project is about much more than this already generally accepted and legally sustainable assertion that IHRL applies in LOAC where this is what the relevant law expressly states. To say that the ICJ, European Court of Human Rights (ECtHR), Human Rights Committee (HRC) and others are functionally complicit in this generalising project is not to offer a critique—this is, after all, their role.[12] But this should not disguise the fact that the generalising approach is an argument from the specific to the general—by examining a series of specific situations, a general 'rule' is advanced, allowing generalisation which then becomes the new rule upon which analysis is based: '*Once it is established that human rights are applicable to all situations of armed conflict*, how can their relationship with international humanitarian law be described?'.[13] Although it is unlikely that the author so intended, this statement is indicative of the universalizing impulse that underpins the generalising project aimed at 'humanising' LOAC. It does so by going beyond the particular and on towards infusing the entire LOAC paradigm with IHRL—be it IHRL outcomes, processes, concepts or remedies. Droege, concluding her analysis of the interplay between LOAC and IHRL gives us an indication of this aspiration when she observes that '[L]astly, it should be noted that human rights law has more safeguards for the protection of individual rights than humanitarian law, particularly in respect of the right to an individual remedy, to an independent and impartial investigation and to individual reparation'. Whilst I do not agree that this is necessarily so—LOAC does have suitable and sufficient investigative procedures and safeguards, conduct under LOAC certainly is amenable to independent assessment, and with very few (and very specific) exceptions, reparation is not directly addressed in LOAC as it is not a functional component of LOAC—it is where this argument leads that illustrates the aspiration. Thus Droege proposes that '[W]hile not entirely transferable due to the nature of each body of law, this could in the future have an influence on humanitarian law.'[14] Indeed, given that it is accepted that IHRL properly applies in LOAC situations when and where it is expressed as doing so by the relevant specific law, if this aspiration to further 'humanise' LOAC by infusing it with the general paradigmatic influences and attitudes of IHRL were not the aim of the generalising project, what is? That *some* human rights apply to some, and in some cases all, contexts and situations in armed conflict is clearly both desirable and correct. But determining on the basis of those specific instances that there is thus a

---

[11] For example, Legal Consequences of the Construction of a Wall in the Occupied Palestinian Territory, Advisory Opinion, [2004] ICJ Reps 136 at para 106; as reaffirmed in *Case Concerning Armed Activities on the Territory of the Congo (DRC* v *Uganda)* (2005) ICJ (19 December 2006) - for example, at para 119.

[12] See Bowring's critiques of the ICJ and ECtHR in particular: Bowring 2010, pp 486–489, 494–497.

[13] Droege 2007, p 335 (my italics).

[14] Ibid.

general rule that 'human rights' as a collective are applicable to all situations of armed conflict is a step too far.

The second point to make about the procedural flaws in the debate thus far is that most of the jurisprudence relied upon as authority for infusing LOAC with IHRL is procedurally one directional. This is because, as Droege importantly notes, most of these courts, tribunals, and commissions—such as the ECtHR, the Inter-American Court of Human Rights (IACtHR), and the various Committees—'have refused to apply international humanitarian law directly, because their mandate only encompassed the respective applicable human rights treaties'.[15] The *Banković* case is a prime example in that the fact nexus clearly invoked LOAC, but the ECtHR analysed the situation—as it was required and empowered to do—only in terms of the European Convention for the Protection of Human Rights and Fundamental Freedoms (1950) (ECHR).[16] Similarly, the IACtHR judgment in *Bamaca Velasquez* v *Guatemala* (2002) offered an opportunity to assess a matter in the context of applicable LOAC, but maintained its IHRL focus. In that case, the IACtHR tacitly recognised the existence of a non-international armed conflict (NIAC) between Guatemala and the URNG rebel group until the 'Agreement on a definitive ceasefire' in December 1996, and the 'Peace Accord' of March 1997. However, in assessing the 'obligation to repair' owed to the claimants, the Court assessed URNG commander Efrain Bamaca Velasquez's lost income due to detention (he was ultimately disappeared, tortured, and killed). The first period of detention was between his capture in March 1992 and the Peace Accord in March 1997—clearly a period of NIAC. In deciding that it was not 'appropriate to establish compensation regarding the income of the victim during that period', the reason the Court gave was not that LOAC did not require such compensation, but rather that such compensation was not due under applicable IHRL. The reason for this was that had Bamaca Velasquez not been captured, he would have remained a guerrilla commander and thus would not have been earning an income in his normal profession of agriculture.[17] The ECtHR and the IACtHR are not alone—neither is the ICJ immune from this tendency to gloss over the difficult work of

---

[15] Droege 2007, p 321. As Droege notes, the Inter-American Commission on Human Rights is the only such body that has 'expressly assigned itself the competence to apply humanitarian law'—as it did in *Abella* v *Argentina*, Case 11.137, Report No 55/97, Inter-Am. CHR, OEA/Ser.L/V/II.95 Doc 7 rev at 271 (1997). See *Abella* v *Argentina* at, for example, para 148 'The Commission believes that before it can properly evaluate the merits of the petitioner's claims … it must first determine whether the armed confrontation at the base was merely an example of an 'internal disturbance or tensions' or whether it constituted a non-international or internal armed-conflict within the meaning of Article 3 common to the four Geneva conventions …'. And again, at para 164—'The Commission believes that in those situations where the American Convention and humanitarian law instruments apply concurrently, Article 29(b) of the American Convention necessarily require the Commission to take due notice of and, where appropriate, give legal effect to applicable humanitarian law rules'.

[16] *Bankovic* v *Belgium* (2001) XII ECt HR 333 (GC).

[17] *Bamaca Velasquez v Guatemala*, Judgment, Inter-Am Ct HR (Ser C) No 91, 22 February 2002 at paras 29(A)(c), 37–41, 51(a).

applying the detail of LOAC. As Judge Rosalyn Higgins noted in her dissenting opinion in the *Nuclear Weapons* Advisory Opinion (1996):

> 'The Court limits itself to affirming that the principles and rules of humanitarian law apply to nuclear weapons … At no point in its Opinion does the Court engage in the task that is surely at the heart of the question asked: the systematic application of the relevant law to the use or threat of nuclear weapons. It reaches its conclusions without the benefit of detailed analysis. An essential step in the judicial process—that of legal reasoning—has been omitted.'[18]

Further, more recent opportunities to engage with such detailed application of LOAC also appear to have been sidestepped by the ICJ.[19]

This is not to say that IHRL dedicated courts do not appreciate the separate existence and applicability of LOAC. Certainly, in *Kononov* v *Latvia* (2008) for example, the ECtHR did examine the issue of applicable LOAC as at 1944, but this was primarily to establish whether the Latvian courts had applied sufficient forensic detail in their examination of the issues, and with a view to determining if there had been a breach of ECHR Article 7 (no punishment without law).[20] But this is not indicative of an ECtHR trend towards greater application of LOAC in matters that first come before it in an IHRL context—it was merely a necessary incidental ancillary to determining the matter on IHRL grounds. These bodies apply what they have the jurisdiction to apply, not necessarily what should—at first paradigmatic glance—be applied had they the jurisdictional leeway to do so. It is thus no surprise that the generalising project continues to permeate judicial reasoning and academic discourse on the interplay between LOAC and IHRL.[21]

6.2 AIM

The aim of this article is to attempt one contextualisation of the LOAC-IHRL interplay debate by asking: What is the practical effect where the applicability of an IHRL 'approach' (versus a LOAC 'approach') to a discrete issue, or range of conduct, or operational practice, is likely to be asserted? To achieve this, the primary question will be: What are some areas of difference that actually

---

[18] *Legality of the Threat or Use of Nuclear Weapons* (Advisory Opinion) [1996] ICJ Rep 226, dissenting opinion of Judge Rosalyn Higgins at para 9.

[19] See for example, the separate opinion of Judge Rosalyn Higgins in *Legal Consequences of the Construction of a Wall in the Occupied Palestinian Territory* (Advisory Opinion) [2004] at para 24—'Further, the structure of the Opinion, in which humanitarian law and human rights law are not dealt with separately, makes it in my view extremely difficult to see what exactly has been decided by the Court'. See also, as noted previously, Bowring's succinct assessment: Bowring 2010, pp 486–487.

[20] *Kononov* v *Latvia* (Appn No 36376/04) Judgment, 24 July 2008.

[21] See for example, UN Human Rights Committee General Comment No 29, 31 August 2001 at para 3; UN Human Rights Committee General Comment No 31, 26 May 2004 at para 11.

distinguish and separate the LOAC and IHRL paradigms, and do these differences actually have any practical effects upon or implications for operational practice? In pursuing this question, there are many possible avenues of inquiry. A fundamental difference, perhaps the core fundamental difference, between the paradigms is the approach they take to use of lethal force. In LOAC, use of lethal force and highly destructive force is approached in a broadly utilitarian manner which ultimately accepts the legitimacy of incidental death or injury, and collateral damage. In this way, LOAC reflects a positive authorization with restrictions and limitations—a permissive regime—with respect to use of force to achieve military aims. In IHRL, on the other hand, resort to lethal force and highly destructive force is only to be countenanced in very limited situations, for very limited purposes, and in the light of an individually focused approach which is only rarely and reluctantly displaced by a 'broader' necessity argument. IHRL very properly represents a negative approach—a restrictive regime—to use of force, permitting use of such force only exceptionally, and recognizing that use of force by state agents should generally be viewed as fundamentally antithetical to human rights.

Similarly, the fault line of compensation represents another point of departure between LOAC and IHRL. In LOAC, the issue of compensation is viewed in light of the permissive/functional approach to force. This is reflected in the fact that there is no LOAC regime of compensation for loss inflicted upon innocent/blameless parties—death, injury or destruction—where compliance with LOAC is established. Although there is a general requirement to compensate 'if the case demands' (such as where there has been a violation of API or the Geneva Conventions[22]) the requirement is relatively undefined and indefinite. The LOAC paradigm accepts non-compensable losses as part and parcel of the regime. Compensation is a side issue, arising only in the case of breach and, arguably, between states rather than between states and individuals. Certainly, this default position is being amended in practice and in law—in practice, for example, by 'claims' schemes established on some UN operations such as ISAF in Afghanistan[23]; in law, for example, by the obligations under the 2003 Protocol V to the Convention on Certain Conventional Weapons (1980) in relation to clean up of explosive remnants of war, which is effectively a post-conflict compensation regime in situations where there has been no breach of LOAC.[24] In IHRL, however, access to compensation is one of the fundamental remedies available to the harmed or wronged individual.[25] As the UN Human Rights Committee observed in relation to Article 2(3) of the ICCPR:

[22] Additional Protocol II to the Geneva Conventions of 12 August 1949, and Relating to the Protection of Victims of Non-International Armed Conflicts (1977) Art 91.

[23] See for example, Synovitz 2007.

[24] 2003 Protocol on Explosive Remnants of War (Protocol V) to the Convention on Certain Conventional Weapons (1980) at Arts 3, 7, and 8.

[25] For example, International Covenant on Civil and Political Rights (1966) Arts 2(3), 9(5).

> 'Article 2, paragraph 3, requires that States Parties make reparation to individuals whose Covenant rights have been violated. Without reparation to individuals whose Covenant rights have been violated, the obligation to provide an effective remedy, which is central to the efficacy of article 2, paragraph 3, is not discharged.'[26]

Yet another fault line is that LOAC is partially premised upon an assumption of reciprocity—each party's interest in compliance is at least partially underpinned by the hope that the opponent will do likewise.[27] IHRL, on the other hand, is premised primarily upon rights owed vertically by the state to individuals,[28] with attempts to enshrine reciprocal rights owed by the individual to the state or society, and indeed horizontal rights owed by corporations to individuals, being a much more difficult (and indeed in the view of many, dangerous) proposition.[29] In this article, however, I will concentrate on two other faultlines between the LOAC and IHRL paradigms—the *purposes* that underpin each regime, and a measurement yardstick, in terms of the concept of *proportionality*, utilised within each regime. In doing so, I will also attempt to indicate what some of the actual or potential operational effects that follow from adopting an overwhelmingly IHRL approach within the LOAC regime might be.

Before embarking upon this analysis, however, I must make two points clear at the outset. First, in pointing out potential operational effects, I am not necessarily indicating that they are 'bad' or to be avoided—indeed, in some cases, I may agree with or entirely endorse the likely outcome. But my aim is simply to point out issues, rather than to pass a moral or ethical judgment upon the operational burden potentially imposed. Second, my analysis is underpinned by an assumption that a 'human rights' approach will generally trump a LOAC approach ('the beauty contest') in almost any situation where an issue is not characterisable as 'non-negotiably' LOAC. Thus my underlying assumption is as follows: Unless an issue is clearly accepted to be a LOAC governed issue, it should be assumed that it will

---

[26] UN Human Rights Committee General Comment No 31 at para 16.

[27] See for example, the Preamble to Convention (IV) Respecting the Laws and Customs of War on Land (1907) (hereinafter The Hague Convention 1907)—'According to the views of the high contracting Parties, these provisions, the wording of which has been inspired by the desire to diminish the evils of war, as far as military requirements permit, *are intended to serve as a general rule of conduct for the belligerents in their mutual relations* and in their relations with the inhabitants' (my italics).

[28] This has long been recognized as a central paradigmatic element of IHRL—see for example, the majority opinion in *Reservations to the Genocide Convention* (Advisory Opinion, 28 May 1951) [1951] ICJ Rep 15, at 23, available at http://icj-cij.org/docket/files/12/4283.pdf—'Consequently, in a convention of this type, one cannot speak of individual advantages or disadvantages to States, or of the maintenance of a perfect contractual balance between rights and duties'. Similarly, in the dissenting opinion of Judges Guerrero, McNair, Read, and Mo at 46: '[W]hen a common effort is made to promote a great humanitarian object, as in the case of the Genocide Convention, every interested State naturally expects every other interested State not to seek any individual advantage or convenience, but to carry out the measures resolved upon by common accord'.

[29] See below, particularly in relation to the arguments of John H. Knox 2008, on 'horizontal human rights law' in the section on the purpose of IHRL.

(within the next decade) begin to be measured against something closer to the relevant IHRL yardstick, rather the currently applicable LOAC yardstick.[30]

6.3 Paradigmatic Purposes

Cordula Droege, in her excellent study of the interplay between LOAC and IHRL argues that '[H]uman rights and humanitarian law share a common ideal, protection of the dignity and integrity of the person, and many of their guarantees are identical, such as the protection of the right to life, freedom from torture and ill-treatment, the protection of family rights, economic, and/or social rights'.[31] Whilst her argument and examples are persuasive and specifically accurate, I respectfully argue that her conclusion is paradigmatically incorrect. Further, if correct, it is really only functionally so at one end of the LOAC spectrum—a point Droege tacitly concedes when she notes that the 'most frequent examples' that underpin her argument come from 'situations of occupation or non-international armed conflict'.[32] Indeed, as the ICRC's Commentary on the 1977 Additional Protocols notes in relation to APII, the 'irreducible core of human rights also known as 'non-derogable rights' corresponds to the lowest level of protection which can be claimed by anyone at any time. Protocol II contains virtually all the irreducible rights of the Covenant on Civil and Political Rights …'.[33] Similarly, as the Inter-American Commission on Human Rights noted of LOAC and IHRL, in *Abella* v *Argentina* (1997), it is 'during situations of internal armed conflict that these two branches of international law most converge and reinforce each other'.[34]

This is not to say, of course, that NIAC in particular is not as destructive as international armed conflict (IAC), and that a focus on NIAC is inappropriate. Rather, the point is that the traditional approach of LOAC to NIAC has been to distil the much more developed and refined law relating to IAC and to then apply its essences in NIAC—that is to distil and apply from within the paradigm. What Droege's argument tacitly requires is the subversion of this approach in that it argues that the presence of IHRL discourse and applications in NIAC is sufficient justification for it to be drawn further into the core of LOAC—the law relating to IAC. Indeed, the Inter-American Commission on Human Rights—an IHRL

---

[30] *Al-Skeini* and *Al-Jeddah* are indicative of this trend in that the House of Lords, in both cases, maintained that some issues remained non-negotiably LOAC governed (such as civilian deaths caused in the course of exchanges of fire during combat patrols), whilst other issues (such as detention) were to be properly measured against the applicable IHRL yardsticks regardless of the fact that they took place within the context of an armed conflict.

[31] Droege 2007, p 312.

[32] Ibid., p 310.

[33] Sandoz et al. 1987, para 4430.

[34] *Abella* v *Argentina* (1997) at para 160.

body—better characterized the distinct and different provenances of each body of law when it observed in *Abella* v *Argentina* (1997) that:

> 'Although one of their purposes is to prevent warfare, none of these human rights instruments was designed to regulate such situations and, thus, they contain no rules governing the means and methods of warfare... In contrast, international humanitarian law generally does not apply in peacetime, and its fundamental purpose is to place restraints on the conduct of warfare in order to diminish the effects of hostilities.'[35]

6.3.1 The purpose of LOAC

The purpose of LOAC is to authorise and regulate killing, injuring, destruction, and control of people and territory in the course of armed conflict. That the legitimacy of such killing, injuring, destruction, and control is the fundamental fact and assumption underpinning LOAC should be accepted in all of its raw and confronting truth. This is the shadow that stands behind all accurate summaries of the purpose of LOAC. The UK Manual of the Law of Armed Conflict, for example, states that:

> 'The main purpose of the law of armed conflict is to protect combatants and non-combatants from unnecessary suffering and to safeguard the fundamental human rights of persons who are not, or are no longer, taking part in the conflict (such as prisoners of war, the wounded, sick, and shipwrecked) and of civilians... By preventing the degeneration of conflicts into brutality and savagery, the law of armed conflict aids the restoration of peace and the resumption of friendly relations between the belligerents.'[36]

The first point one may note of this paradigmatic purpose is that it is—as many have observed—counter-intuitive.[37] Perhaps one of the reasons people have been so ready to disparage or deny LOAC is to diminish its scope and authority, because LOAC might sometimes appear (depending upon the position one takes) either 'excessively permissive' or alternatively 'inconvenient'. Clausewitz certainly had little time for any law of war, although he had greater respect for the 'customs' of war. In essence, LOAC was less than inconvenient for Clausewitz—it was irrelevant. As he declared in *On War*, '[F]orce to counter opposing force, equips itself with the inventions of art and science. Attached to force are certain self-imposed, imperceptible limitations hardly worth mentioning, known as international law and custom, but they scarcely weaken it'.[38]

---

[35] *Abella* v *Argentina* (1997) at paras 158–159.

[36] The Manual of the Law of Armed Conflict 2004, para 1.8.

[37] Geoffrey Best, in War and Law Since 1945, observed that those 'who are inclined to be sceptical about the possibility of law restraining war will ... find evidence of its having sometimes and to some extent done so; certain periods of history and certain circumstances having been more propitious for it than others'. Best notes that a fair characterisation of LOAC is indeed as one of 'the astonishing paradoxical achievements of civilization': Best 1994, pp 4–9.

[38] Clausewitz 1976, p 75.

Yet the opposing view—that LOAC is far too permissive and allows much greater levels of killing, injury and destruction than it should—is also strongly held. This aspirational view is most recently represented in the ICRC's Interpretive Guidance on the Notion of Direct Participation in Hostilities (2009)—particularly with respect to the 'continuous combat function' criteria for determining the targetable members of organised armed groups.[39] By insisting that trainers in directly and unambiguously military skills—trainers in improvised explosive device (IED) making, trainers in ambush tactics—are in the same category as financiers, recruiters, and propagandists, and thus outside the targetability envelope,[40] the Interpretive Guidance is defying law, practice, and common sense. But it is nevertheless going to be an influential document which will likely bring about an intentionally subtle shift by introducing a new, almost imperceptible limitation into LOAC via a redefinition of its parameters. And the reason this is done, quite clearly, is to rein in what some view as excessive extant authorisations under LOAC. Some advocates of this view will say it has always been so, but simply never overtly expressed in this way. It is those who are up-front and admit that it is an attempt to progressively develop the law who are most intellectually honest. This is not, of course, to say that LOAC does not advance in tandem with society—clearly it does, and (as one example) the area bombing of cities would plainly not be acceptable today. But such LOAC advances and refinements should generally first be detected in State practice. From whichever approach one comes to the debate, however, it should not be forgotten that LOAC's underlying mechanism and purpose is precisely that it is both permissive, and simultaneously inconvenient, when it comes to killing, injuring, destruction, and control. Indeed, the fact that it is subject to both critiques, but that many see it as 'about right' is probably a good indication that it currently strikes a defensible middle line.

Thus the essence of LOAC is that it facilitates killing and destruction, but does so by simultaneously imposing limits upon it. Perhaps the best summation is Article 35 of AP I (1977), which provides:

> 'In armed conflict, the right of the parties to the conflict to choose methods or means of warfare is not unlimited.'[41]

A comparable sentiment is also found in the St Petersburg Declaration of 1868:

> 'Considering that the progress of civilization should have the effect of alleviating as much as possible the calamities of war;
>
> That the only legitimate object which States should endeavour to accomplish during war is to weaken the military forces of the enemy;
>
> That for this purpose it is sufficient to disable the greatest possible number of men ...'[42]

39 Interpretive Guidance 2008, p 33.

40 See for example, Interpretive Guidance 2008, pp 34–35, 53–55, 66–67.

41 Additional Protocol I (1977) Art 31.

42 Declaration Renouncing the Use, in Time of War, of Explosive Projectiles Under 400 Grammes Weight (hereinafter The St. Petersburg Declaration) 29 November/11 December 1868: in (eds) Roberts and Guelff 2000, pp 53–55.

In sum, LOAC facilitates 'disabling the greatest possible number of men', but places limits on *which* men, the *purpose* for doing so, and *how*. In 1900, in *The Paquete Habana*, the US Supreme Court—assessing what LOAC said of the legitimacy of destruction of a belligerent's fishing fleets—observed after a comprehensive recitation and analysis of custom on this point:

> 'The review of precedents and authorities on the subject appears to us abundantly to demonstrate that at the present day, by the general consent of the civilized nations of the world, and independently of any express treaty or other public act, it is an established rule of international law, founded on considerations of humanity to a poor and industrious order of men, and of the mutual convenience of belligerent states, that coast fishing vessels, with their implements and supplies, cargoes and crews, unarmed and honestly pursuing their peaceful calling of catching and bringing in fresh fish, are exempt from capture as a prize of war ...'[43]

The second paradigmatic point one might note of the purposes of LOAC is that it is designed to achieve its aims by focusing upon, and carefully and meticulously distinguishing between, the different rights and responsibilities of collective groups defined by functional characteristics. This is to be distinguished from the self-evident fact that LOAC does indeed reach down—tangibly—into *individual* conduct and individual criminal responsibility. Clearly it does, and despite its limitations in scope and practice, there is currently no more powerful expression of this than the Rome Statute of the International Criminal Court (1998). But it is inescapable that LOAC is defined by opposable collective categories, and that the generation of rights and responsibilities in LOAC is primarily achieved through the juxtaposition of these categories. Thus civilians are distinct from combatants. Military medical and religious personnel are distinct from other military personnel. Civilians taking a direct part in hostilities are distinct from civilians per se. And members of organized armed groups are distinct from other civilians taking a direct part in hostilities. There is no default 'control' group in LOAC. There are two basic functional groups—combatants and civilians—and a number of other sub-groups which are always defined in terms of when they are within, and when without, the targetable envelope. And the prime objective of LOAC is to make sure they remain separate, and are always treated differently.

6.3.2 The purpose of IHRL

The principal purpose of IHRL, as John H. Knox has observed, is 'that it places duties on states to respect the rights of individuals and creates no private duties'.[44] That this remains the case is well borne out in Knox's assessment of two recent attempts at 'horizontal' IHRL—duties borne by an individual to his/her society,

---

[43] *The Paquete Habana* 175 US 677 (1900).

[44] Knox 2008, p 1.

and rights owed by corporations to individuals.[45] Both attempts, he concludes, fail one or both of the tests of 'do no harm' and 'do some good'. Indeed, the draft Declaration on Human Social Responsibilities, he argues, clearly runs the risk of being used by States to limit human rights—the precise opposite of the IHRL project.[46] Thus the paradigmatic view that IHRL exists to facilitate a degree of equalization in power relationships between States and the individuals they govern, through law, remains central to IHRL. This is perhaps nowhere more explicit than in the opening acclamation of the Preamble to the Universal Declaration of Human Rights (1948) (UDHR):

> 'Whereas recognition of the inherent dignity and of the equal and inalienable rights of all members of the human family is the foundation of freedom, justice and peace in the world…
>
> Whereas it is essential, if man is not to be compelled to have recourse, as a last resort, to rebellion against tyranny and oppression, that human rights should be protected by the rule of law …'[47]

Similarly, in General Comment 31 (2004), the UN Human Rights Committee noted explicitly of the ICCPR that '[T]he beneficiaries of the rights recognised by the Covenant are individuals', and that 'the positive obligations on State Parties to ensure Covenant rights will only be fully discharged if individuals are protected by the State, not just against violations of Covenant rights by its agents, but also acts committed by private persons or entities …'.[48] It is therefore clear that the aim of IHRL is to ensure that individuals have a means of ensuring that the State can be held to account by an individual for its conduct in breaching, or allowing other individuals to breach, a human right. Droege declares that '[T]he nature of human rights is universal, and their object and purpose is the protection of the individual from abuse by states'.[49] Jessica Gavron similarly captures the different provenance of each regime: 'While humanitarian law had originated in armed conflict between states and developed international protection for victims of international violence, the subsequent development of human rights law originated principally in the relations between the government and the governed.'[50]

The approach which IHRL adopts in achieving this aim is to start from the fundamental position that all people should be members of the same 'group' in the

---

[45] Respectively, the draft Declaration on Human Social Responsibilities (2003), and the draft Norms on the Responsibilities of Transnational Corporations and Other Business Enterprises with regard to Human Rights (2003).

[46] Knox 2008, pp 2–3, 47.

[47] See also Knox's description of the UDHR's negotiating history on this point, Knox 2008, pp 5–10, outlining the underpinning assumption that '[L]isting individual duties to the state would reinforce the government's authority to use duties to restrict the exercise of rights because it could point to the human rights instrument itself as evidence that duties to obey the law and render service to the state were examples of the "requirements of the State".'.

[48] UN Human Rights Committee General Comment 31, at paras 9 and 8 respectively.

[49] Droege 2007, p 335.

[50] Gavron 2002, p 91.

sense that all should have access to the same, or equivalent manifestations of, specific rights. Differential categorisation is necessary in describing IHRL, and is vital in terms of identifying disadvantage and acting to alleviate this disadvantage. But differential categorization is ultimately anathema to the objective of bringing all to an equivalency of access. This inherent generality of IHRL aims to promote the application of human rights in all, or almost all, circumstances, and equally for all individuals. This is at clear odds with the fundamental premise of LOAC, which is that it applies in extreme situations and creates rules that were never envisaged as having broader, or generalisable, application outside their specific context. Groups in IHRL are founded on attributes rather than function, and there is a 'control group' whose level of access to rights is arguably the benchmark. IHRL endorses differential treatment only in so far as it assists the achievement of equality of access. This is clearly very different to the impetus evident in LOAC, where the maintenance of differential treatment, with the ultimate aim of entrenching differential rights, responsibilities, and protections, is of the very essence.

6.3.3 Operational effects?

There are two immediately apparent potential operational effects that will likely flow from a gradual but persistent infusion of LOAC with IHRL's paradigmatic purposes. These effects are primarily related to paradigmatic default settings. The first is represented by the UK Supreme Court decision in *R (on the application of Smith) (FC) (Respondent)* v *Secretary of State for Defence (Appellant) and another* [2010],[51] where the jurisdictional question, as expressed succinctly in the decision, was '[A]re our armed services abroad, in Iraq, Afghanistan or wherever else they may be called upon to fight, within the United Kingdom's jurisdiction within the meaning of article 1 of the European Convention on Human Rights?... If they are, then the United Kingdom is required to secure to them all the Convention rights and freedoms'.[52] That is, does the UK Human Rights Act (1998) and the ECHR cover a British soldier whilst on patrol in an Iraqi neighbourhood as equally as it applies to him or her whilst inside a UK base or hospital in Iraq? Reversing the Court of Appeal, the majority of the UK Supreme Court held, in essence, that UK service personnel, whilst arguably under the jurisdiction of the ECHR whilst in a UK base in Iraq, are not within its jurisdiction when 'outside the

[51] *R (on the application of Smith) (FC) (Respondent)* v *Secretary of State for Defence (Appellant) and another* [2010] UKSC 29, an appeal from the UK Court of Appeal decision in *R (Smith) and others* v *Secretary of State for Defence* [2009] EWCA Civ 441.

[52] *R (on the application of Smith) (FC) (Respondent)* v *Secretary of State for Defence (Appellant) and another* [2010] per Lord Brown at para 139.

wire' in territory over which the UK does not exercise effective control.[53] As Lord Brown held, '[I]n the end, however, I have concluded that, save in an exceptional case like that of Private Smith himself whose death resulted from his treatment on base, Convention rights do not generally attach to our armed forces serving abroad'.[54]

Thus whilst the Court of Appeal did not arrive at its decision in a contextual vacuum, specifically noting that 'the right to life of a soldier in combat is different from that of a soldier not in combat',[55] the UK Supreme Court held that the ECHR right did not apply, *ab initio*, to a soldier in combat.[56] Certainly it followed from the Court of Appeal's approach that a critical procedural obligation under the Article 2 right to life—that of ensuring an appropriate and adequate 'Article 2 inquest'—applied regardless of whether the potential breach took place inside a British base, or whilst on patrol in Iraq.[57] However, the fact that the UK Supreme Court came to a different conclusion should not lead one to surmise that the need for an analogous level of inquiry might not still be warranted. Certainly, as the House of Lords had previously indicated in *R (Gentle)* v *Prime Minister* [2008], this obligation clearly extended to ensuring 'a procedural obligation to initiate an effective investigation by an independent official body into any death occurring in circumstances in which it appears that [*inter alia*] ... agents of the state are, or may

[53] For example, *R (on the application of Smith) (FC) (Respondent)* v *Secretary of State for Defence (Appellant) and another* [2010] per Lords Phillips at para 55, Hope at para 93, Rodger at para 112, Brown at paras 139–140, and Collins at para 307. Cf Lady Hale at para 136, and Lords Mance at paras 191, 194, 199, and Kerr at para 339. The majority in the UK Supreme Court thus reversed the majority in the UK Court of Appeal, which had previously held that: 'In our judgment, if it is permissible to answer the question posed by Lord Rodger [in *Al-Skeini*], namely whether there was a sufficient link between Private Smith and the UK when he died, on the assumption for this purpose that he died outside the base or a hospital, in a broad and commonsense way, the answer is in our opinion plainly yes ... [T]here is a degree of artificiality in saying that a soldier is protected so long as he remains in the base or military hospital but that he is not protected as soon as he steps outside'—*R (Smith)* v *Secretary of State* [2009] EWCA Civ 441 at para 28.

[54] *R (on the application of Smith) (FC) (Respondent)* v *Secretary of State for Defence (Appellant) and another* [2010] per Lord Brown at para 140.

[55] *R (Smith)* v *Secretary of State* [2009] at para 31.

[56] For example, *R (on the application of Smith) (FC) (Respondent)* v *Secretary of State for Defence (Appellant) and another* [2010] per Lord Rodger at para 120—'I would, however, take an entirely different view of the death of a trained soldier in action—e.g., when a roadside bomb blows up the vehicle in which he is patrolling, or when his observation post is destroyed by a mortar bomb'.

[57] *R (Smith)* v *Secretary of State* [2009] at paras 63–66—The Court cited Lord Bingham's summation of the character of an 'Article 2 inquest': 'The [ECtHR] has repeatedly interpreted article 2 ... as imposing on member states substantive obligations not to take life without justification and also to establish a framework of law, precautions, procedures and means of enforcement which will, to the greatest extent reasonably practicable, protect life'—per Ld Bingham in *R (Gentle)* v *Prime Minister* [2008] UKHL 20 at paras 4–5.

be, in some way implicated'.[58] Such implication can include cases of negligence on the part of state agents—situations which, as Lord Steyn noted in *R (Amin)* v *Secretary of State for the Home Department* [2003], are often actually more complicated to investigate as they may well be founded in systemic problems which need to be identified and rectified in order that others are not deprived of the right to life by a continuing failure.[59]

Although it narrowed the jurisdictional implications of the Court of Appeal's conclusions, the Supreme Court's decision does not fundamentally alter this effect. This is for three reasons. The first is that the Supreme Court majority effectively held that there was little substantive difference, in terms of UK practice, between an inquest and an Article 2 compliant inquest.[60] The second reason is that whilst 'political' decisions (such as procurement decisions) are not properly the subject of such inquests, it is clear that more proximate systemic issues such as actual equipment performance, training and procedures could be.[61] The third reason is that whilst the Supreme Court clearly held that deaths in combat are not prima facie an issue for inquest, this is a rebuttable presumption. For Lord Kerr, it was clear that whilst an inquest into systemic issues may not be appropriate when dealing with the death of a UK service person, this is not the same when dealing with deaths inflicted upon civilians by UK service personnel.[62] For Lord Rodger, whilst a death in combat may not be an incident necessarily requiring such an inquest, where there is any indication of own side complicity or failure—such as that the deaths were the result of friendly fire—this presumption can be rebutted.[63] Similarly, in relation to the issue at play in *Smith* (the adequacy of precautions and treatment with respect to heat stroke) Lords Phillips and Rodger saw this as a proper subject for inquest. Lord Hope similarly found that indications of systemic breach were sufficient to enliven this responsibility.[64]

---

[58] *R (Gentle)* v *Prime Minister* [2008] at para 4. In *R (Smith)* v *Secretary of State* [2009], one of the key questions, as applied to the fact nexus, was 'whether Private Smith's death was caused by a defective system operated by the state to afford adequate protection to human life by ensuring, so far as reasonably practicable, that he was an appropriate person, with proper training and equipment, to expose to the extreme heat of Iraq'—para 70.

[59] *R (Amin)* v *Secretary of State for the Home Department* [2003] UKHL 51 at para 50.

[60] *R (on the application of Smith) (FC) (Respondent)* v *Secretary of State for Defence (Appellant) and another* [2010] per Lord Phillips at paras 78, 87, and Lord Brown at para 152, for example.

[61] *R (on the application of Smith) (FC) (Respondent)* v *Secretary of State for Defence (Appellant) and another* [2010] per Lord Phillips at para 81, Lord Rodger at paras 119, 127, Lord Mance at para 218, Lord Kerr at para 339.

[62] *R (on the application of Smith) (FC) (Respondent)* v *Secretary of State for Defence (Appellant) and another* [2010] per Lord Kerr at para 339.

[63] *R (on the application of Smith) (FC) (Respondent)* v *Secretary of State for Defence (Appellant) and another* [2010] per Lord Rodger at paras 125–127.

[64] *R (on the application of Smith) (FC) (Respondent)* v *Secretary of State for Defence (Appellant) and another* [2010] per Lord Phillips at para 87, and Lord Rodger at para 119; Lord Hope at para 106.

Is this a human rights trump over LOAC that will have the effect of limiting a commander's willingness to take risks? *The Economist* certainly reported that this was the British Army's initial reaction to the Court of Appeal's decision:

> 'Army bosses now fear a flood of litigation from soldier's families and, perhaps worse, that commanding officers will become reluctant to commit troops to anything too risky. The MOD called the ruling an 'attempt to insert lawyers into the chain of command'. Sir Mike Jackson, a former chief of the defence staff, worried that soldiers would feel that "everything they do may 2 or 3 years later be judged coldly in a court of law".'[65]

The fundamentally IHRL based decision by the UK Supreme Court in *Smith*—even though it winds back the Court of Appeal's view—could still have significant potential consequences for LOAC in terms of assessing and conducting merits reviews of training, doctrine, planning and coordination with respect to combat operations. There is a strong ECtHR jurisprudence on the compliance (or otherwise) of training and planning issues in relation to law enforcement operations which involve military forces. *Jordan*,[66] *McCann*,[67] *Stewart*,[68] and *Nachova*[69] are clear examples of the readiness and authority of a human rights-focused Court to delve deeply into training and doctrine, into the planning and execution of operations, and—more significantly—to apply detailed IHRL yardsticks in the course of assessment on the merits.[70] Were this to happen in the context of a combat operation, the risk will be that a court such as the ECtHR—which is focused upon human rights processes, procedures, concepts, measurements, and precedents—will have no option but to review the operation through an IHRL lens. The potential consequence is that the core issues will be dissected using tools from IHRL, and assessed from a perspective other than the LOAC-based perspective (from which they should be addressed). This precedent will then be seized upon as further evidence of a mandated infusion of IHRL into LOAC, in turn generating another cycle of generalised reduction in scope of what was perhaps traditionally understood to be non-negotiably LOAC-governed. Indeed, as Bowring concludes in his analysis of the Chechen cases before the ECtHR, we are probably already there.

The second immediately apparent potential operational effect is one of attitudinal approach. This can be described by reference to the 'Mogadishu line'[71] between a peacebuilding/law enforcement mindset (focused on capacity building

---

[65] 'Soldiers' human rights: The charge of the legal brigade', *The Economist*, 23 May 2009; p 52.

[66] *Jordan* v *United Kingdom* (2001) Appn No. 24746/94 (Judgment 4 May 2001, finalised version 4 Aug 2001).

[67] *McCann* v *United Kingdom* (1996) 21 EHRR 97.

[68] *Stewart* v *UK* (1984) Appn No.10044/82 (Decision 10 Jul 1984).

[69] *Nachova* v *Bulgaria* (2004) 34 EHRR 37.

[70] See Mowbray 2002, p 437.

[71] A most useful and descriptive term coined by General Sir Michael Rose to describe the attitudinal and functional 'line' that is crossed when a force transitions between warfighting and peacekeeping.

and supporting local justice systems towards resolving conflict), and a LOAC mindset (focused upon first establishing supremacy, then security, and then either departing or staying on to re-build). Arguably, the Mogadishu line has ceased to have much relevance as a border between LOAC and non-LOAC governed operations, because most LOAC operations (particularly those taking place within the context of a NIAC) are already substantially infused with IHRL objectives, concepts, and operational drivers. Thus the 'Mogadishu line' is now much more fundamentally about attitudinal shifts *within* what are *prima facie* LOAC governed operations. Where a force element is hunting a Taleban IED layer one day, it could be assisting in building a school the next. Where it conducts a search operation through private residences on one day, it could be facilitating election security the next. Each shift from LOAC based operations to IHRL focused operations requires a shift in attitude and mindset, regardless of the fact that the overall mission of the force is generally an amalgam of both. That is, when seeking to close with and kill or capture the enemy, or to seize and hold ground from the enemy, military forces must still be free to take a LOAC perspective. When reconstructing infrastructure or facilitating education or governance, it is vital that an IHRL sensibility be brought to bear. However, the simple observation that modern NIACs are paradigmatically bi-polar should never obscure the fact it is still nonetheless essential that a purely LOAC governed approach to some issues remains—and is seen to remain—lawful, appropriate, and warranted. The ability to think about groups differentially, to treat them differently, and to ensure those differences are permanently entrenched, is central to LOAC but ultimately antithetical to IHRL.

6.4 Measurement–'Proportionality'

As Thomas Franck recently noted, 'the principle of proportionality has mostly eluded definition in any but the most general terms'. This, as Franck notes, is both a strength and a vulnerability—flexibility versus imprecision. In terms of the interplay between LOAC and IHRL, both attributes are evident. The principle of proportionality is flexible enough to accept that it can be subject to different paradigmatic characterizations. Even more importantly, the principle of proportionality has sufficient paradigm-sensitivity and flexibility that it is considered a good 'fit'. This is key to the concept being internalized by those who apply and are governed by it.[72] But this same universal indeterminacy (which is the inevitable result of conceptual multivalence) leaves significant scope for ill-fitted conceptual osmosis across the dissolving paradigmatic boundary between LOAC and IHRL. And as noted at the outset, the tendency will be for the IHRL concept to infuse LOAC rather than the other way around. But to determine if this is problematic or not, it is first necessary to come to grips with the general shape and features of

[72] Franck 2008, pp 716–717.

'proportionality' within each paradigm, for it is only through understanding these features that the suitability or otherwise of the IHRL concept for application within LOAC can be appreciated.

6.4.1 Proportionality in LOAC

The first feature of proportionality within the LOAC paradigm is that there are actually two manifestations of the concept—the *Jus ad Bellum* manifestation (which is akin to the concept as expressed in just war theory) and the *Jus in Bello* concept (the proportionality calculus balancing military necessity and humanity). For the purposes of this analysis, it is the *Jus in Bello* form of LOAC proportionality that is of central concern, as it is this form of the concept that governs day to day conduct in armed conflict. With this in mind, how is this LOAC concept of proportionality described? The generally accepted 'doctrinal' description of LOAC proportionality is found in the ICRC's 1987 Commentary on Additional Protocol I (1977):

> 'The law of armed conflict is a compromise based on a balance between military necessity, on the one hand, and the requirements of humanity, on the other... Military necessity means the necessity for measures which are essential to attain the goals of war. Consequently a rule of the law of armed conflict cannot be derogated from by invoking military necessity unless this possibility is explicitly provided for by the rule in question. Conversely, when the law of armed conflict does not provide for any prohibition, the Parties to the conflict are in principle free within the constraints of customary law and general principles.'[73]

The first attribute of this form of proportionality is that it is *elastic*—but 'not indefinitely elastic'—such that, as Franck (quoting Theologian Oliver O'Donovan) observes, the concept is almost one of 'not categorically disproportionate' rather than 'proportionate'.[74] This attribute holds up even when LOAC proportionality is described as adopting the least damaging/deleterious option when two or more options for achieving the same objective are available. This process simply allows one to define and discard options as 'disproportionate' by reference to other options with less deleterious effects. In this way options are winnowed. Courses of action are similarly assessed once executed. As the Committee established by the

[73] Sandoz et al. 1987, para 1389. This characterisation has been affirmed in many judicial settings—see for example, Judge Rosalyn Higgins' dissenting opinion in the *Nuclear Weapons* (Advisory Opinion) (1996) at para 14, discussing LOAC 'providing a 'balancing' set of norms' which requires 'a balancing of necessity and humanity'; at para 20, observing that 'the law of armed conflict has been articulated in terms of a broad prohibition—that civilians may not be the object of armed attack—and the question of numbers or suffering (provided always that this primary obligation is met) falls to be considered as part of the 'balancing' or 'equation' between the necessities of war and the requirements of humanity'.

[74] Franck 2008, p 727. This is the descriptor also used on occasion in Sandoz et al. 1987, para 1979, for example. See also Fenrick 2000, p 57.

ICTY Prosecutor to review the NATO air campaign against the Federal Republic of Yugoslavia in 1999 observed in its Report, whilst incidental injury and death resulting from the bombing of the RTS (Serbian TV and Radio Station) in Belgrade on 23 April 1999 was 'unfortunately high', it was not 'clearly disproportionate'.[75] As Schmitt has succinctly noted, '[T]he standard is "excessive" (a comparative concept), not "extensive" (an absolute concept)'.[76]

The second attribute is that LOAC proportionality entails *valuing and comparing* 'apples and oranges'. As Schmitt observes, LOAC proportionality seeks to 'compare tanks destroyed to the number of serious civilian injuries or deaths caused by attacks upon them'.[77] The ICTY Committee similarly concluded that a fundamental attribute of LOAC proportionality is that 'the comparison is often between unlike quantities and values. One cannot easily assess the value of innocent human lives as opposed to capturing a particular military objective.'[78] Furthermore, the valuing and comparing is to be done from a particular, quite discrete perspective. As the ICTY Committee noted:

> 'The answers to these questions are not simple. It may be necessary to resolve them on a case-by-case basis, and the answers may differ depending on the background and values of the decision maker. It is unlikely that a human rights lawyer and an experienced combat commander would assign the same relative values to military advantage and to injury to non-combatants. Further, it is unlikely that military commanders with different doctrinal backgrounds and differing degrees of combat experience or national military histories would always agree in close cases. It is suggested that the determination of relative values must be that of the "reasonable military commander".'[79]

This is a vital component of the valuing and comparing process: The common law 'reasonable person' (who is generally also the IHRL reasonable person) is irrelevant. In LOAC proportionality it is the much more narrowly focussed yardstick of the reasonable military commander which is the central applicable standard.

The third attribute is that in assessing LOAC proportionality, the focus is on *making decisions* in the midst of the fog and friction of armed conflict, with limited time, imperfect information, and subject to the vagaries of conflict where things can and do go wrong, and communications can and do fail.[80] Additional Protocol I

---

[75] Final Report to the Prosecutor by the Committee Established to Review the NATO Bombing Campaign Against the Federal Republic of Yugoslavia, 13 June 2000; para 77, available at http://www.un.org/icty/pressreal/nato061300.htm. For an analysis of the report, see Fenrick 2000. See also, for comment upon some of the LOAC issues associated with targeting during the Kosovo campaign, Rogers 2000, p 165.

[76] Schmitt 2005, p 457.

[77] Schmitt 2006, p 293. See also Schmitt 2005, p 457—'More importantly, how does one compare dissimilar values (civilian harm and military gain) at all, let alone over time in different combat situations and across cultures?'; Fenrick 2000, p 58.

[78] Final Report to the Prosecutor by the Committee Established to Review the NATO Bombing Campaign Against the Federal Republic of Yugoslavia; para 48.

[79] Ibid., para 50. See also the discussion by Fenrick 2000, pp 75–78.

[80] See for example, Rogers 2000.

certainly recognizes and endorses this attribute. Article 57(2) makes it clear that military forces must do 'everything feasible' to verify the status and nature of the objective, 'take all feasible precautions' in planning and executing the attack, 'cancel or suspend' the attack if new counter-balancing information comes to hand or circumstances change, and provide 'effective advance warning ... unless circumstances do not permit'.[81] This is the language of best efforts in time and information constrained (either by scarcity or overload) situations: The time and resources for a test and adjust approach to precaution are often simply not available. This is *not* about best efforts taken within the context of policy assessments, interdepartmental committee meetings and advice, thorough consultation, precautionary measures and phased implementation, and time imperatives measured in weeks or months, not minutes or hours. It is also indicative of the risk of 'second opinions' in retrospective assessments of LOAC proportionality—as Franck argued with respect to the danger avoided by the ICJ in the *Oil Platforms* Case (2003), entering into this aspect of the proportionality debate risks 'being charged with amateurish second-guessing of the tactical and strategic options available to field commanders'.[82] Gleeson CJ's warning on the dangers of hindsight in the High Court of Australia case *Rosenberg* v *Percival* (2001) is most relevant:

> 'A foreseeable risk has eventuated, and a harm has resulted. The particular risk becomes the focus of attention. But at the time of [the conduct] ... there may have been no reason to single it out from a number of adverse contingencies, or to attach to it the significance it later assumed. [There is] ... the danger of a failure, after the event, to take account of the context, before or at the time of the event, in which a contingency was to be evaluated.'[83]

This latitude has long been recognized by courts and tribunals. In the United States Military Tribunal at Nuremberg case of *In re List and Others* (1948)—the 'Hostages Trial'—General Lothar Rendulic had been charged with 'wanton destruction of private and public property in the province of Finnmark, Norway, during the retreat of the XXth Mountain Army commanded by him'. Rendulic argued that his Army's destruction of housing, port installations, power, transport and communications facilities, and forcible relocation of the inhabitants of the Finnmark (with no loss of life directly attributable to the relocations) was proportionate to the military necessity (which was centred upon a perceived imminent attack and takeover of the area by Russian forces). Although found guilty of the other charges on the indictment, he was found not guilty on this specific charge. The Tribunal determined that:

---

[81] Additional Protocol I (1977) Art 57(2).

[82] Franck 2008, p 731. On the context sensitivity of 'feasibility' see also Schmitt 2005, p 460.

[83] *Rosenberg* v *Percival* [2001] HCA 18 at para 16. This was an important component of the standard of assessment applied in a military decision-making context by Commissioner the Honourable Terrence R.H. Cole, AO, RFD, QC in his Report on *The Loss of HMAS SYDNEY II* (Canberra: Commonwealth of Australia, July 2009)—see Chapter 1.

> 'There is evidence in the record that there was no military necessity for this destruction and devastation. An examination of the facts in retrospect can well sustain this conclusion. But we are obliged to judge the situation as it appeared to the defendant at the time. If the facts were such as would justify the action by the exercise of judgment, after giving consideration to all the factors and existing possibilities, even though the conclusion reached may have been faulty, it cannot be said to be criminal. After giving careful consideration to all the evidence on the subject, we are convinced that the defendant cannot be held criminally responsible although, when viewed in retrospect, the danger did not actually exist.'[84]

In elaborating their decision-making process, the Tribunal noted that:

> 'We are not called upon to determine whether urgent military necessity for the devastation and destruction in the province of Finnmark actually existed. We are concerned with the question whether the defendant at the time of its occurrence acted within the limits of honest judgment on the basis of the conditions prevailing at the time. The course of a military operation by the enemy is loaded with uncertainties, such as the numerical strength of the enemy, the quality of his equipment, his fighting spirit, the efficiency and daring of his commanders, and the uncertainty of his intentions. These things when considered with his own military situation provided the facts or want thereof which furnished the basis for the defendant's decision to carry out the 'scorched earth' policy in Finnmark as a precautionary measure against an attack by superior forces. It is our considered opinion that the conditions as they appeared to the defendant at the time were sufficient, upon which he could honestly conclude that urgent military necessity warranted the decision made. This being true, the defendant may have erred in the exercise of his judgment but he was guilty of no criminal act.'

This 'latitude' is equally applicable today. Although it is difficult to find a definitive statement, the ICTY's decision in *Prosecutor* v *Kupreškić and others* (2000) provides some indications. In assessing the three circumstances where the protection provided to civilians and civilian objects 'may cease entirely or be reduced or suspended', the Court referred to the situation where 'although the object of a military attack is comprised of military objectives, belligerents cannot avoid causing so-called collateral damage to civilians …'.[85] This assessment, the Court went on to note, 'has always been applied in conjunction with the principle of proportionality, whereby any incidental (and unintentional) damage to civilians must not be out of proportion to the direct military advantage gained by the military attack'.[86] Importantly, the Court then gave an example:

> 'As an example … regard might be had to considerations such as the cumulative effect of attacks on military objectives causing incidental damage to civilians. *In other words, it may happen that single attacks on military objectives causing incidental damage to civilians, although they may raise doubts as to their lawfulness, nevertheless do not appear on their face to fall foul per se of the loose prescriptions of Articles 57 and 58 (or of the*

[84] *United States of America* v *Wilhelm List* et al. (Case VII) 8 July 1947–19 February 1948—reported as *In re List and Others (Hostages Trial)* (19 February 1948) in Lauterpacht (ed) 1953 pp 647–649.

[85] *Prosecutor* v *Kupreskic and Others*, Judgment (14 January 2000) Case IT-95-16-T at para 522.

[86] Ibid., para 524.

corresponding customary rules). However, in case of repeated attacks, all or most of them falling within the grey area between indisputable legality and unlawfulness, it might be warranted to conclude that the cumulative effect of such acts entails that they may not be in keeping with international law. Indeed, this pattern of military conduct may turn out to jeopardize excessively the lives and assets of civilians, contrary to the demands of humanity.'[87]

The legal issue, as the ICTY pointed out, is to determine whether the conduct was so disproportionate (such as repeated attacks on a village, as opposed to the initial attack) that it falls foul even of the contextually appropriate 'loose prescriptions' applicable to LOAC proportionality.

6.4.2 Proportionality in IHRL

The first comparative attribute of the IHRL concept of proportionality is that it is significantly less *elastic* than its LOAC *Jus in Bello* counterpart. IHRL is characterized by a long list of fairly specific 'trumps',[88] as compared to the single general formula implied by LOAC proportionality (which is more a process than a trump). This predilection for specific limitation as a first step in assessing proportionality in IHRL exists on several levels. First, there are general limitations such as the provisions for derogation in times of national emergency—for example, in the ICCPR and ECHR.[89] However, in a clear limitation of the elasticity permitted by these introductions of proportionality, each specific derogation is only permissible 'to the extent *strictly required* by the exigencies of the situation',[90] and is forensically assessed against this standard. This language of 'strict requirement' is pervasive in IHRL, and stands in marked contrast to the 'loose' proportionality requirements of LOAC. Indeed, Sir Nigel Rodley, a British member of the Human Rights Committee, has persuasively argued that the elasticity of proportionality is further limited in that IHRL requires application of a two limbed test. As Franck records of Rodley's view, he 'emphasizes the duality of the evidentiary threshold: that "such measures [are] subject to the test of proportionality *and the further test* of being required by the exigencies of the situation".'[91] The difference in approach, as compared to LOAC proportionality, could not be more stark.

On the second attribute of proportionality—*comparative units*—IHRL again exhibits a very different approach to LOAC. The first point of distinction is that where LOAC proportionality has been described as valuing and comparing apples

---

87 Ibid., para 526 (my italics). For comment, see Fenrick 2000, pp 59–60.

88 Knox 2008, p 13.

89 ICCPR Art 4(1); ECHR Art 15(1).

90 ICCPR Art 4(1). See also Knox 2008, pp 10–13, where he further analyses this issue.

91 Franck 2008, p 759, quoting Sir Nigel Rodley.

and oranges, IHRL proportionality tends to focus on comparative assessments of like concepts. Within a context that assumes the valid co-existence of both sides of the equation, LOAC attempts to compare and weigh opposites in relation to one another: Tanks destroyed as weighed against civilians killed or injured. IHRL, on the other hand, overtly operates within a broad recognition that the 'opposite' is fundamentally invalid. Based in this assumption, IHRL then attempts to compare and contrast a component within the broad suite of human rights with the totality of protections afforded by that suite of human rights—the right to freedom of (hateful) expression within the totality of the overarching concept of human liberty as expressed through human rights. In many cases, the IHRL assessment thus compares apples with apple cores—one right within a suite of similar rights. As Franck points out of the ECtHR case *Refah Partisi (Welfare Party)* v *Turkey* (2003), for example, 'the Court engaged in a very specific (if controversial) assessment of the proportionality of … an infringement on political rights to the threat posed by the banned party to the state's lawful aim of preserving secularism as a foundational principle of public order'.[92]

The second feature of IHRL units of comparison with regard to proportionality is that it is generally very strict and exclusive as regards what may be taken into account when valuing and comparing. LOAC proportionality mandates that the entirety of the circumstances prevailing at the time, and the commander or decision-maker's assessment in the light of those circumstances, must be taken into account—even if either or both were incomplete or erroneous. IHRL proportionality is much more selective. In the recent ECtHR case *Saadi* v *Italy* (2008),[93] the Court was faced with the question of whether the deportation of a Tunisian national from Italy to Tunisia (where he had been convicted in absentia of terrorism related offences) would offend the ECHR. Italy (with the UK intervening) argued that Saadi presented a real terrorist threat in Italy. Saadi argued that it was 'common knowledge' that individuals detained on terrorism related grounds in Tunisia were subject to torture and persecution. The Court, in determining what could be considered in respect of the proportionality assessment, followed recent precedent and decided that:

> 'The concepts of 'risk' and 'dangerousness' in this context do not lend themselves to a balancing test because they are notions that can only be assessed independently of each other. Either the evidence adduced before the Court reveals that there is a substantial risk if the person is sent back or it does not. The prospect that he may pose a serious threat to the community if not returned does not reduce in any way the degree of risk of ill treatment that the person may be subject to on return.'[94]

Certainly, torture can never be proportionate within LOAC, as is also the case within IHRL—it is an absolute prohibition in both legal paradigms. But the point is more fundamental—it is about the assertion that IHRL does not permit that risk

---

[92] Franck 2008, p 762.

[93] *Saadi* v *Italy* (Appn No 37201/06) ECtHR (GC) 28 February 2008.

[94] Ibid., para 139.

and dangerousness be balanced in relation to each other. As Fiona de Londras summarised of the Court's decision—'[S]ince the Article 3 prohibition is absolute, the danger that an individual might pose to the community cannot be taken into account when assessing the risk to the individual upon transfer'.[95] If we replace 'risk' with 'military necessity' (the risk to the 'opposite'—military mission achievement of not undertaking the act) and 'dangerousness' with 'humanity' (the need to limit to the fullest extent possible the danger to protected people and objects), we arrive at precisely the balancing act that LOAC proportionality explicitly mandates of the commander. LOAC proportionality is eclectic; IHRL proportionality is subject to much tighter controls over what is permissibly within and without the envelope of consideration.

Finally, with respect to *when and how proportionality is assessed*, IHRL is much more geared towards detailed 'second opinions'[96] than LOAC. As Franck argues, this tendency, '[I]n many instances ... requires the tribunal to weigh the actual evidence of situational necessity'.[97] As a consequence, IHRL proportionality is underwritten by a much more intrusive regime of after the fact re-assessment than LOAC proportionality. This is not surprising: In IHRL, the context in which a decision is made generally includes greater time and resources for analysis, discussion, advice and deliberation than is available in LOAC situations. Additionally, the viewpoint adopted is that of the reasonable person in the most general sense—the person on the Clapham Omnibus, subject to the normal vagaries of everyday life, not the military commander subject to the completely abnormal vagaries of armed conflict. Courts, consequently, are much more willing to re-engage with the details and merits of the decision-making process in IHRL than they are in relation to compressed LOAC processes. The 'margin of appreciation' applied by several IHRL courts mitigates this readiness only marginally by comparison to the latitude required by, and properly accorded in, assessing LOAC proportionality. One directly apposite example of this greater predilection to detailed re-assessment and second opinion is provided by the African Charter on Human and People's Rights (1981) which, argues Knox, advocates a number of 'looser' regimes than most other equivalent treaties, and thus tends to be interpreted by its Commission 'in ways that minimize its deviation from the rest of human rights law in these respects'.[98] As the ICTY noted in *Kupreškić*, the 'loose' proportionality assessment inherent in API is the ultimate functional baseline; in IHRL, such looseness is abhorred and tightened through re-interpretation. Thus it is fair to say that the IHRL paradigm tends to assume there has been time and space to make full assessments and to weigh information and options. Assessors are consequently more freely given to finding fault in the analysis of

---

95 Londras 2008, p 616.

96 As described by Franck 2008, p 756, for example.

97 Ibid., p 761.

98 Knox 2008, pp 14–18.

proportionality through detailed re-examination and substitution of their own assessments than is either practicable or warranted in relation to LOAC proportionality.

6.4.3 Operational effects?

The most significant potential operational effect likely to flow from the infusion of LOAC with an IHRL sense of proportionality is the tendency of military legal advisers—in seeking for ever more detailed guidance in order to provide increasingly aware and cautious commanders with greater clarity—to look to where analogies of clarity are provided.[99] This sensitivity to detail will also likely influence courts, tribunals, and opinion formers such as Amnesty International and Human Rights Watch (HRW) as the avenues and appetite for prosecution, and/or judicial or other legal analysis of LOAC based conduct increase. The risk, of course, is that IHRL's detailed jurisprudence on proportionality—particularly where this detail directly addresses operational issues such as planning and training, as with *McCann*, *Jordan*, and many other cases—will be drawn upon analogously and thus introduced into LOAC proportionality. Only slim precedent on the issue of LOAC proportionality has emerged from the ICTY and ICTR. Noting their impending winding-up, unless and until the ICC begins to generate modern jurisprudence on the issue, it is to IHRL courts, tribunals, and committees that people will look when seeking detail with respect to proportionality. The seductive draw that such case law presents—even when it is paradigmatically inappropriate—is not to be underestimated.

An example of this tendency, and the effects which it can have on the interpretation of LOAC proportionality, is offered by the Israel Supreme Court's decision on the building of a section of the security barrier between Israel and the West Bank—*Beit Sourik Village Council* v *Government of Israel* (2004). Although the Court explicitly recognised that the applicable standard of proportionality to be applied was a LOAC standard,[100] in applying this standard, the Court used a fundamentally IHRL approach. This is evident in the actual test of proportionality applied, which the Court defined to be three cumulative sub-tests, all of which were required to be met in order that an act be assessed as 'proportional': Is the objective related to the means; do the means used injure the individual to least extent possible; and is the damage caused to the individual by the means used of

[99] Bowring's analysis of the Chechen cases before the ECtHR points very clearly to how and why this can occur—Bowring 2010, pp 487–489, 494–497.

[100] *Beit Sourik Village Council* v *Government of Israel* HCJ 2056/04, 24 June 2004 at, for example, paras 23 (on the applicable normative framework), 36–37, 48 (proportionality). At para 36, the Court asserted that '[P]roportionality plays a central role in the law regarding armed conflict. During such conflicts, there is a frequently a need to balance military needs with humanitarian considerations'.

proper proportion to the gain brought about by that means.[101] The source of this test (or series of sub-tests) is clearly, and expressly, Israeli administrative law.[102] The form and function of the tests—bearing significant resemblances to Sir Rodley's two-limbed test—is more akin to IHRL proportionality than its LOAC counterpart. The alternative is that the Court was indicating that LOAC proportionality in an occupation context (Geneva Convention IV (1948)/Hague Regulations (1907)) is different to LOAC proportionality per se. This would be a fair and defensible assessment. But the citations referred to by the Court are references to LOAC proportionality per se, and there is no explicit or implicit indication that the Court wished to draw such a distinction.[103]

A second salient example is the recent HRW Letter to Secretary of Defense Robert Gates on US Airstrikes in Azizabad, Afghanistan (dated 15 January 2009).[104] This letter concerned the publicly released Executive Summary (1 October 2008) of an investigation by USAF Brigadier-General Callan into civilian casualties resulting from the US and Afghan engagement in Azizabad in Afghanistan on 21–22 August 2008. The letter also summarises the findings of a HRW investigation into civilian casualty incidents in Afghanistan.[105]

> 'In addition, *had* the US had intelligence from sufficient sources, *they would have* been aware that there was about to be a memorial ceremony in the village where the operation was taking place. The ceremony had drawn many civilians, including persons from outside the village. Reasonable precautions should have uncovered a large civilian presence in the village. It is, therefore, questionable that the close proximity of insurgent forces to civilians was 'unknown' to US and Afghan forces; if it was unknown, then the quality of US intelligence was shockingly poor …
>
> *Given what could be expected to have been known* about the large civilian population in the village at the time, conducting airstrikes over several hours that destroy or damage 12–14 houses in the middle of the night makes high civilian casualties almost inevitable.'[106]

The primary issue arising from this is the apparent application of the IHRL standard of proportionality. The detailed assessment is clearly characterised by a greater willingness to employ hindsight and to assume that an exhaustive analysis attended by time, discussion, and a full grasp of all the relevant facts and circumstances, had been undertaken. The basis of the adopted approach—'had … they would have …'—makes this clear. This is then reapplied to the incident and

---

[101] Ibid., at para 41, and applied at, for example, paras 57–59.

[102] Ibid., at para 39.

[103] See for example, the citations at ibid., at para 37.

[104] Human Rights Watch, Letter to Secretary of Defense Robert Gates on US Airstrikes in Azizabad, Afghanistan (15 January 2009) available at http://www.hrw.org/en/news/2009/01/14/letter-secretary-defense-robert-gates-us-airstrikes-azizabad-afghanistan.

[105] Human Rights Watch, 'Troops in Contact'—Airstrikes and Civilian Deaths in Afghanistan, Human Rights Watch, New York, 2008, available at http://www.hrw.org/sites/default/files/reports/afghanistan0908web_0.pdf.

[106] HRW, Letter to Secretary of Defence Robert Gates (my italics).

used as the standard against which the conduct is measured, as is signalled by the conclusion—'Given what could be expected to have been known …'.

Another example is provided in the HRW report Afghanistan: US Should Act to End Bombing Tragedies (14 May 2009):

> 'Further efforts are needed to minimize civilian casualties. The use of high levels of military firepower in operations to kill or capture mid-level Taliban commanders has frequently resulted in civilian casualties that carry a high cost in terms of public opinion, often for limited military gain. When making proportionality assessments for such attacks, weighing anticipated civilian loss against expected military gain, US forces should consider the relative ease with which insurgent groups have been able to replace mid-level commanders.'[107]

This example offers a further insight into the effect that IHRL tendencies in describing and assessing proportionality could have upon LOAC proportionality. First, the linkage of the statement that civilian casualties 'carry a high cost in terms of public opinion, often for limited military gain' with the assessment of proportionality is not warranted. Public opinion, if it is a factor to be considered in any particular attack, will have been considered at the stage of assessing the discrete element of military necessity—that is, before military necessity is then weighed against humanity in the proportionality assessment. To re-introduce it as a compulsory factor to be used in weighing humanity, or in some form of overriding veto, is to accord it an unwarranted doubling in value. The proper LOAC proportionality assessment is between military necessity and humanity, not military necessity as against public opinion plus humanity. In an IHRL assessment of proportionality, however, such elements as public opinion, morale, and social mores are rightly vital in assessing whether conduct is properly directed. One example is the effect of these factors in assessing 'preservation' of moral health and national security—such as with several ECtHR decisions in relation to prohibitions on homosexuals serving in armed forces. Courts, tribunals, and committees with IHRL jurisdiction properly conduct detailed analysis of the claims made in relation to these matters, and readily substitute their own second opinion on them.[108]

Finally, in the HRW *Troops In Contact Report* (2008), the analysis included the following statement:

---

[107] Human Rights Watch, Afghanistan: US Should Act to End Bombing Tragedies - Civilian Death Toll in May 3 Airstrikes Shows Previous Measures Inadequate (14 May 2009) (my italics) available at http://www.hrw.org/en/news/2009/05/14/afghanistan-us-should-act-end-bombing-tragedies.

[108] See for example, *Smith and Grady* v *UK* (2002) 29 EHRR 493 at paras 75–112, where the ECtHR assessed the issue of a ban on homosexual people serving in the armed forces by reference to the test of 'necessary in a democratic society'. At para 87, for example, the ECtHR, citing previous jurisprudence, affirmed that the 'hallmarks' of a democratic society include pluralism, tolerance, and broadmindedness. See also, *Dudgeon* v *UK* (Appn No 7525/76) Judgment, 22 October 1981 - at paras 58–61, where the ECtHR directly addresses public opinion as a factor to be taken into account in assessing proportionality.

> 'US planes have dropped bombs when they did not know for certain who was in a compound. So long as a valid military target is identified, such attacks are not unlawful on their face, but they raise concerns about whether 'all feasible precautions' have been taken to minimise civilian loss, as required by the laws of war.'[109]

If the attack is 'not unlawful' then it is lawful: Lawfulness in LOAC is not partial or phased—it is an ultimate and absolute assessment. LOAC proportionality arrives at a 'lawful' assessment only subsequent to the 'all feasible precautions' sub-assessment. To suggest that there is a yet further proportionality assessment within the military necessity element effectively requires that 'all feasible' be re-interpreted as 'all', and that if this high—and in LOAC, practically impossible—standard is not met, then an attack should not even be considered. This approach to LOAC proportionality clearly brings into play Sir Nigel Rodley's two limbed test for IHRL proportionality—first, is it proportionate and second, is it strictly required by the exigencies of the situation.[110]

There is a risk that IHRL conceptions of proportionality will continue to infuse our understanding of LOAC proportionality. This risk should be identified and consciously monitored so as to ensure that the paradigmatic functionality of the LOAC concept of proportionality remains clear. The reason this must be done is not to be found in a base need to maintain the flexibility to legitimise attacks, but rather a concern that LOAC proportionality could become so complex and caveated that it is not readily usable by, nor comprehensible to, those who need to make LOAC based decisions in variable and less than ideal circumstances and compressed timeframes. The result could be that such an increasingly complicated standard and test of LOAC proportionality will stop being considered a good paradigmatic 'fit', cease being internalised, and thus become ignored or consciously undermined. As Fenrick very correctly observed:

> 'International humanitarian law, including the law applicable to targeting and proportionality, is a second level barrier against barbarism which comes into force after the first level is breached by the onset of fighting. The success or failure of international humanitarian law must be measured in terms of lives saved and injuries not suffered. It is not measured by the number of prosecutions or the number of convictions.'[111]

6.5 Conclusion

LOAC and IHRL are different. They serve different paradigmatic purposes, and they are subject to different manifestations of proportionality—one of the core concepts shared by, and used for similar purposes within, both paradigms.

---

[109] Human Right Watch, Troops in Contact; pp 30–31.

[110] It should be noted that the HRW Troops In Contact report does indeed clearly note, in the broad, that the 'fog of war' element is important in assessing proportionality after the event (at p 4, for example). However, this recognition is arguably less evident within the discrete analyses of individual incidents which then follows.

[111] Fenrick 2000, pp 79–80.

Furthermore, the dissolving of paradigmatic differences and the infusion of LOAC with IHRL norms could, and most likely will, result in increased operational burdens in terms of resource allocation, decision-making systems, and the balance to be struck between caution and risk. For some, this outcome will be one to be applauded. For others, this outcome will be one to be guarded against. However, regardless of the ethical or moral position one adopts, we should nevertheless be aware that, ultimately, any blurring of paradigmatic distinctions which results in LOAC being considered less 'fit for purpose' by those who must internalise it and use it—governments and militaries—is not necessarily a positive development. But determining whether there are paradigmatic differences between LOAC and IHRL, and indeed whether these differences are of merely theoretical, or more robustly practical consequence, is only step one in the process of moving the debate along. That IHRL has impacts upon LOAC is clear. That IHRL has actual and potential impacts upon operations is also clear. But the debate must now accord some form and shape to the other side of the equation—LOAC—so that we can begin to establish what is to remain within the exclusive preserve of LOAC. It is only once those components of LOAC that are to be considered discernibly and purely LOAC-governed are identified, that we can isolate the proper field of inquiry with respect to setting parameters, and re-negotiating interpretations. Deciding what is non-negotiably LOAC is thus the missing critical step in identifying how to manage those issues which might conceivably sit astride both the LOAC and IHRL paradigms, and be subject to productive, meaningful, and defensible IHRL infusion.

References

Best G (1994) War and law since 1945. Oxford University Press, Oxford

Bowring B (2010) Fragmentation, Lex Specialis and the tensions in the jurisprudence of the European court of human rights. JCSL 14:485–498

Draper GIAD (1971a) The relationship between the human rights regime and the laws of armed conflict. Israel YB HR 1:191

Draper GIAD (1971b) Human rights and the law of war. Va JIL 12:326–342

Droege C (2007) The interplay between international humanitarian law and international human rights law in situations of armed conflict. Israel LR 40:310–355

Fenrick WJ (2000) The law applicable to targeting and proportionality after operation allied force: a view from the outside. YIHL 3:53–80

Franck TM (2008) On proportionality of countermeasures in international law. AJIL 102:715–767

Interpretive Guidance on the Notion of Direct Participation in Hostilities, Reports and Documents (2008) ICRC 872:991–1047

Joseph S, Schultz J, Castan M (2004) The international covenant on civil and political rights: cases, materials, and commentary. Oxford University Press, Oxford

Knox JH (2008) Horizontal human rights law. AJIL 102:1–47

Lauterpacht H (ed) (1953) Annual digest and reports of public international law cases (1948). Butterworth & Co, London, pp 632–653

Londras Fiona de (2008) Saadi v Italy, AJIL 102:610–615

Martin FF et al (2006) International human rights and humanitarian law: treaties, cases, and analysis. Cambridge University Press, Cambridge

Mowbray A (2002) Duties of investigation under the European convention on human rights. ICLQ 51:437–448
Roberts A, Guelff R (eds) (2000) Documents on the law of war, 3rd edn. Oxford University Press, Oxford
Rogers AV (2000) Zero-casualty warfare. IRCR 837:165–181
Rowe P (2006) The impact of human rights law on armed forces. Cambridge University Press, Cambridge
Sandoz Y et al. (eds) (1987) Commentary on the additional protocols of 8 June 1977 to the Geneva conventions of 12 August 1949, Geneva, ICRC, Dordrecht, Martinus Nijhof
Schmitt MN (2005) Precision attack and international humanitarian law. IRRC 859:445–466
Schmitt MN (2006) Fault lines in the law of attack. In: Breau SC, Jachec-Neale A (eds) Testing the boundaries of international humanitarian law. British Institute of International Comparative Law, London, pp 277–307
Steiner HJ, Alston P (2000) International human rights in context: law, politics, morals, 2nd edn. Oxford University Press, Oxford
Synovitz R (2007) Afghanistan: NATO begins fund for civilian war victims, RadioFreeEurope/RadioLiberty, 26 January 2007, at http://www.rferl.org/articleprintview/10740305.html.
The Manual of the Law of Armed Conflict (2004) UK Ministry of Defence, Oxford, Oxford University Press
Von Clausewitz C (1976) On war. In: Howard M, Paret P (eds and trans) Princeton, Princeton University Press

Chapter 7
Unlawful Presence of Protected Persons in Occupied Territory? An Analysis of Israel's Permit Regime and Expulsions from the West Bank under the Law of Occupation

Alon Margalit and Sarah Hibbin

Contents

We wish to thank Professor Iain Scobbie and Louise Arimatsu for their helpful comments and suggestions. Any errors are our own.

A. Margalit (✉) · S. Hibbin
University of London, London, UK
e-mail: am110@soas.ac.uk

S. Hibbin
e-mail: sh84@soas.ac.uk

M.N. Schmitt et al. (eds.), *Yearbook of International Humanitarian Law Volume 13, 2010*, DOI: 10.1007/978-90-6704-811-8_7,

7.1 Introduction

7.1.1 The examined Israeli policy: binding addresses, stay permits and expulsions

On 28 October 2009, Ms Berlanty Azzam, a 22-year-old Palestinian student at Bethlehem University, attended a job interview in Ramallah. On her way back home she was stopped by Israeli soldiers at a check-point near Bethlehem. She was asked to present her ID card, and then questioned about her stay in Bethlehem. The soldiers told Azzam that since her ID card showed her registered address as being in the Gaza Strip, she could not stay in the West Bank without a permit from the Military Commander. Ms Azzam explained that she moved to Bethlehem from Gaza in 2005, when no permit was required in order to move between Gaza and the West Bank, the two parts of the Occupied Palestinian Territory (OPT). Since then she had tried unsuccessfully to change her registered address in the Palestinian Population Registry from Gaza to the West Bank, but was informed by the Palestinian Authority that this could not be done because Israel, the Occupying Power, does not allow such changes to be registered.

The soldiers insisted that Azzam's registered address in Gaza was binding and determinative and thus her presence in the West Bank was unlawful. It was clear to them that her presence in the West Bank did not involve a security concern; however the discussion at the check point as to her status did not last long. Azzam was blindfolded, handcuffed, and loaded into a military jeep. She was expelled to Gaza on the same night, two months before completing her academic degree at Bethlehem University.[1]

A petition to the Israeli High Court of Justice was filed the next day on behalf of Ms Azzam. In the petition Azzam asked the Court to order the Military Commander to enable her return to the West Bank.[2] The petition also emphasized that

[1] For a detailed description of the incident, see Gisha, *As Military Lawyer Gives False Promise, Bethlehem University Student is Blindfolded, Handcuffed, and Taken to Gaza by Force* (Press Release, 29 October 2009), available at http://www.gisha.org/index.php?intLanguage=2&intItemId=1619&intSiteSN=113; Gisha, *High Court to Examine Israel's Refusal to Allow a 21 Year-Old Student to Complete Her BA in Bethlehem* (Press Release, 11 November 2009), available at http://www.gisha.org/index.php?intLanguage=2&intItemId=1632&intSiteSN=113; Lynfield B, Student Expelled to Gaza Strip by Force, *The Independent* (30 October 2009), available at http://www.independent.co.uk/news/world/middle-east/student-expelled-to-gaza-strip-by-force-1811730.html.

[2] HCJ 8731/09 *Azzam* v *the Military Commander of the West Bank* [2009] (Judgment of 9 December 2009, yet not published in English). Available in Hebrew at http://elyon2.court.gov.il/files/09/310/087/V15/09087310.V15.htm.

since 2000 Israel has 'frozen' the Palestinian Population Registry and has not allowed Palestinians to register changes in their place of residence. Moreover, stay permits in the West Bank first began to be issued by the Military Commander in 2007, two years after Azzam had moved to the West Bank.[3] The Military Commander rejected her petition, repeating the argument that since her registered address was in Gaza, she was not entitled to stay in the West Bank without a permit.[4] The Military Commander added that there was a danger that after completion of her studies, Azzam would attempt to remain permanently in the West Bank.

The Israeli High Court, concurring with the Military Commander,[5] added that Azzam had not obtained a permit to leave Gaza for the purpose of academic studies in the West Bank and thus her stay in the West Bank for four years was unlawful.[6] The Court further observed that since the Military Commander does not allow other Gazan students to leave the Gaza Strip in order to study in the

---

[3] On the required procedure to obtain a stay permit in the West Bank, see Gisha, *Restrictions and Removal: Israel's Double Bind Policy for Palestinians Holders of Gaza IDs in the West Bank* (November 2009), available at http://www.gisha.org/index.php?intLanguage=2&intSiteSN=119&intItemId=1635#7. The criteria to obtain such permits are extremely restrictive and most people do not meet them. The procedure specifies that even in patently humanitarian cases, such as an orphan living in Gaza who seeks to reunite with his remaining parent in the West Bank, or an elderly disabled person who requires care by a relative who lives in the West Bank, or married couples who have become separated, Israel will not permit relocation to the West Bank, except under the most exceptional circumstances. The procedure was not introduced in an official Military Order but presented to the Israeli High Court of Justice by the Israeli Government following a petition by an Israeli human rights NGO, see Hamoked and Gisha, *New Procedure: Israel bars Palestinians in Gaza from moving to West Bank* (June 2009), available at http://www.gisha.org/UserFiles/File/publications_/WB_Gaza_Procedure-PositionP-Eng.pdf. For the text of the procedure itself, see Israel Ministry of Defence, *Procedure for Handling Applications by Gaza Strip Residents for Settlement in the Judea and Samaria Area* (8 March 2009), available at http://www.hamoked.org.il/Document.aspx?dID=Documents1234 [in Hebrew]; An English version can be found at Hamoked website http://www.hamoked.org/Document.aspx?dID=Documents1234.

[4] HCJ 8731/09 *Azzam* v *the Military Commander of the West Bank* [2009] para 3.

[5] See Hass A, High Court: Gaza Student Cannot Complete Studies in West Bank, *Haaretz* (9 December 2009), available at http://www.haaretz.com/news/high-court-gaza-student-cannot-complete-studies-in-west-bank-1.2468.

[6] During the court proceedings it was turned out that in 2005 Ms Azzam was granted a five-day-permit to enter Israel in order to cross from Gaza to the West Bank. Land crossing from Gaza to the West Bank is alternatively possible through the territories of Egypt and Jordan. A permit to enter Israeli territory is irrelevant to the relatively new stay permit that Palestinians from Gaza are required to obtain in order to stay and reside in the West Bank, and which is the subject of this paper.

West Bank, Azzam did not deserve more favourable treatment in comparison to other students-petitioners.[7]

Four months later an amendment to Military Order 329 on Prevention of Infiltration was promulgated by the Military Commander in the West Bank.[8] The original Order, which dates from 1969, dealt with the 'Prevention of Infiltration' of people who entered the West Bank from Jordan, Syria, Lebanon and Egypt; namely, those who had come from enemy states with whom Israel was then formally at war. The effect of the amendment is that individuals whose registered address is not in the West Bank (in the 'frozen' Population Registry) will be considered 'infiltrators' should they be found to be present in the West Bank without a stay permit. As infiltrators, they are subject to immediate expulsion from their home in the West Bank and/or to prosecution and criminal sanctions, including a maximum of seven years imprisonment.[9]

The new military legislation formalized the policy of expulsion of Palestinians from the West Bank to Gaza that Israel had carried out sporadically since 2003. The reason given for these expulsions has not been that the individual deportee poses a specific security risk, but rather is based on his or her outdated Gazan registered address and *arguendo* unlawful presence in the West Bank. The requirement to hold a stay permit, and the risk of expulsion in its absence, applies also to individuals who moved to the West Bank *before* 2007, when these permits were first introduced. Despite years of living in the West Bank, their registered address remains as the Gaza Strip, mostly due to the Israeli refusal to register the change, and in some cases, even children subsequently born in the West Bank have

[7] For the restrictions imposed by Israel on the possibility of Palestinian students to access universities outside Gaza, see United Nations Office for the Coordination Of Humanitarian Affairs in the Occupied Palestinian Territory, *Locked In: The Humanitarian Impact Of Two Years Of Blockade On The Gaza Strip* (August 2009) pp 22–23, available at http://www.ochaopt.org/documents/Ocha_opt_Gaza_impact_of_two_years_of_blockade_August_2009_english.pdf; Gisha, *Israel Undermines Higher Education - and its Own Best Interest - in Gaza* (22 October 2007), available at http://www.gisha.org/UserFiles/File/publications_english/Publications%20and%20Reports_English/Appendix%20to%20Press%20Release%2022.10.07_eng.pdf. It should be noted however that in the cases cited by the Israeli High Court in the *Azzam* case, students' request to leave Gaza was refused on security grounds, which are absent in the case at hand. Moreover, in these cited cases the Military Commander imposed restrictions on the students' right to freedom of movement which are permissible due to a security rationale, while Azzam was unlawfully expelled from the West Bank and deported to Gaza as will be discussed below.

[8] See Military Commander Order (329) on Prevention of Infiltration 1969 (as amended in April 2010), Military Legislation, Vol 19, p 665, available at http://www.law.idf.il/487-he/Patzar.aspx?PageNum=17 and also at Vol 233, p 5843 http://www.law.idf.il/487-he/Patzar.aspx?PageNum=11 [both in Hebrew]. The Order is translated into English at http://www.hamoked.org.il/items/112301_eng.pdf.

[9] According to the Military Order on Prevention of Infiltration, expulsions within 72 h are not subject to judicial review.

been registered with the same address as their parents.[10] It is estimated that the recent Military Order exposes tens of thousands of Palestinians to expulsions from the West Bank to the Gaza Strip.[11]

7.1.2 Analysis and structure of this paper

This paper examines the legality of this practice, as illustrated in the *Azzam* case and formalized in the recent military legislation ('the Israeli Policy'), from the perspective of International Humanitarian Law (IHL). Clearly, the Israeli Policy also has important implications for the human rights of the affected Palestinians and it is necessary to examine its lawfulness under International Human Rights Law (IHRL) as well.[12] For instance, the expulsion of Palestinians from their homes in the West Bank to Gaza has significant implications for rights such as the freedom of movement, to property, to education, to work and to an adequate standard of living.[13] In a broader sense the policy also undermines the Palestinian people's right to self-determination, considering the obstacles it imposes on the

---

[10] See HCJ 4019/10 *Hamoked* v *The Military Commander of the West Bank* (still pending, submitted on 25 May 2010 on behalf of Hamoked and 15 other Israeli and Palestinians human rights NGOs), available at http://www.hamoked.org/Document.aspx?dID=Updates1034.

[11] According to Israeli officials 35,000 Palestinians are potential deportees since they are present in the West Bank while their registered address is in Gaza. See Letter from the Coordinator of Israeli Government Activities in the OPT in response to the Israeli NGO Hamoked's Freedom of Information Request (2 June 2010), available at http://www.hamoked.org/Document.aspx?dID=Documents1223; Hass A, 'IDF Order Will Enable Mass Deportation from West Bank' *Haaretz* (11 April 2010), available at http://www.haaretz.co.il/hasen/spages/1162075.html; United Nations Office for the Coordination Of Humanitarian Affairs in the Occupied Palestinian Territory, *The Humanitarian Monitor* (April 2010) pp 13–14, available at http://archive.ochaopt.org/documents/ocha_opt_the_humanitarian_monitor_2010_04_english.pdf.

[12] The Israeli government claims that its human rights obligations do not apply extra-territorially and thus do not apply in the Occupied Palestinian Territories (OPT), see Human Rights Committee, *Report of the Human Rights Committee to the UN General Assembly* (2003, UN Doc. A/58/40) Vol I, para 11, available at http://daccess-dds-ny.un.org/doc/UNDOC/GEN/G03/443/00/PDF/G0344300.pdf?OpenElement. This position has been rejected by both the International Court of Justice and by the Human Rights Committee, each of which affirmed the extra-territorial application of international human rights law to inhabitants of occupied territories, see *Legal Consequences of the Construction of a Wall in the Occupied Palestinian Territory*, Advisory Opinion, ICJ Rep 2004, 136, 180, paras 111–113; Human Rights Committee, *General Comment No. 31: Nature of the General Legal Obligation Imposed on States Parties to the Covenant* (2004, UN Doc. CCPR/C/21/Rev.1/Add.13) para 10. While not formally deciding on the applicability of human rights instruments in the OPT, the Israeli High Court of Justice has based its reasoning on the provisions of these instruments, for example HCJ 7957/04 *Mara'abe* v *Prime Minister of Israel* [2005] para 27.

[13] International Covenant on Civil and Political Rights [1966] arts 6, 12(1); International Covenant on Economic, Social and Cultural Rights [1966] arts 6, 11(1), 13; The Universal Declaration of Human Rights [1948] art 17.

development of Palestinian economic and social life and the potential for demographic alteration in the West Bank.[14] The Israeli High Court previously addressed some of these issues when discussing the damage caused to persons who are forcibly removed from their homes. When considering the legality of assigned residence orders issued by the Military Commander the Court stated:

> 'The fundamental premise is that the displacement of a person from his place of residence and his forcible assignment to another place seriously harms his dignity, his liberty and his property. A person's home is not merely a roof over his head, but it is also a means for the physical and social location of a person, his private life and his social relationships... Several basic human rights are harmed as a result of an involuntary displacement of a person from his home and his residence being assigned to another place, even if this assigned residence does not involve him crossing an international border.'[15]

In addition, there are questions raised about the manner in which the new military legislation in the West Bank has been implemented, particularly in relation to discrimination. While Palestinians living in the West Bank who fail to obtain a stay permit risk expulsion and prosecution if their registered address is not in the West Bank, this does not apply to Israeli-Jewish settlers residing there. They are neither required to hold stay permits, nor are they subject to expulsions or to any other sanctions due to having an 'incompatible' registered address.[16] Further, despite its obligation under the Israeli-Palestinian Interim-Agreement, Israel does not enable Palestinians to register the necessary changes in the Palestinian Population Registry and yet holds them responsible for the consequences, in justifying taking harmful actions against the Palestinian population.[17] Taking into account Israel's ultimate control of the Palestinian Population Registry, this policy raises important legal questions relating to good faith and estoppel. Whilst such legal arguments deserve closer scrutiny, the focus of this paper is restricted to an examination of the legal issues that the Israeli Policy raises with regard to IHL and, in particular, to the law of occupation.

An overview of the application of IHL in the Israeli jurisprudence will be considered in the next section, followed by an analysis of the specific elements of

---

[14] Hamoked and Gisha, *New Procedure: Israel bars Palestinians in Gaza from moving to West Bank* (June 2009), available at http://www.gisha.org/UserFiles/File/publications_/WB_Gaza_Procedure-PositionP-Eng.pdf; Hamoked and B'Teslem, *Separated Entities: Israel Divides Palestinian Population of West Bank and Gaza Strip* (September 2008), available at http://www.btselem.org/Download/200809_Separated_Entities_Eng.pdf.

[15] HCJ 7015/02 *Ajuri* v *IDF Commander in the West Bank* [2002] para 14.

[16] Soon after the Military Order on Prevention of Infiltration (as amended) entered into force in April 2010, the Israeli Military Spokesman announced that it does not apply to Israeli-Jewish Settlers residing in the West Bank, see Hass A, 'IDF Order Will Enable Mass Deportation from West Bank' *Haaretz* (11 April 2010), available at http://www.haaretz.co.il/hasen/spages/1162075.html.

[17] Protocol Concerning Civil Affairs of the Israeli-Palestinian Interim Agreement on the West Bank and the Gaza Strip [1995] Annex III, Art 28, available at http://www.mfa.gov.il/MFA/Peace+Process/Guide+to+the+Peace+Process/The+Israeli-Palestinian+Interim+Agreement+-+Main+P.htm.

the Israeli Policy—expulsions, the requirement to hold a stay permit and the concept of a determinative and binding registered address—in the context of IHL. The third section focuses on the question of expulsions from the West Bank to Gaza and explores the prohibition on forcible transfers and deportations from occupied territory. How this prohibition has been interpreted and applied by the Israeli High Court will then be examined. The fourth section looks at the requirement to hold a stay permit and poses the question of whether a protected person needs permission from the Military Commander in order to be present in the occupied territory. This section further discusses the scope of the definition of a protected person. The fifth section examines the concept of a determinative and binding registered address. It poses the question of whether this concept, in conjunction with the new Military Order on Prevention of Infiltration, falls within the legislative powers of the Israeli Military Commander. Finally, the sixth section provides some concluding observations on the Israeli Policy.

7.2 Application of IHL in the Israeli Jurisprudence

7.2.1 The Hague Regulations and the Fourth Geneva Convention

It is not contested that Israel is the belligerent occupant of the West Bank.[18] Thus the relevant normative framework that applies to the West Bank is the international law regulating belligerent occupation which is contained primarily in the 1907 Hague Convention (IV) respecting the Laws and Customs of War on Land and its annex Regulations concerning the Laws and Customs of War on Land of 1907 ('the Hague Regulations') and in the 1949 Geneva Convention (IV) relative to the Protection of Civilian Persons in Time of War ('the Fourth Geneva Convention'). Israel is not a party to the Hague Regulations, but its High Court has long recognized that its provisions form part of customary international law and that as a result Israel is legally bound by them.[19]

Although Israel became a party to the Fourth Geneva Convention on 6 July 1951, the Convention has not been incorporated into domestic law through parliamentary legislation.[20] Following the June 1967 War and its occupation of the West Bank and the Gaza Strip, the Israeli government took the position that in light of its conventional nature, the Fourth Geneva Convention was not applicable

[18] For a range of views regarding the status of the Gaza Strip after the Israeli redeployment in 2005, see for example, Aronson 2005, p 49; Benvenisti 2009, pp 371–382; Bruderlein 2004; Gisha 2007; Kaliser 2007; Mari 2005, p 356; Scobbie 2004–2005, p 3, reprinted in Kattan (ed) 2008, p 637; Shany 2005, p 369 and Shany 2008 p 68.

[19] HCJ 606/78 *Ayyub* v *Minister of Defence* [1978] PD 33 (2) 113 (*Beth El* case); Kretzmer 2002, p 36.

[20] HCJ 785/87 *Afu* v *IDF Commander in the West Bank* [1988] PD 42(2) 4; HCJ 253/88 *Sejdiah* v *Minister of Defence* [1988] PD 42(3) 801; Dinstein 1988, pp 403, 404.

as a matter of law to the OPT; however it agreed to apply its 'humanitarian provisions' on a *de facto* basis.[21] Based on this *ad hoc* consent, the Israeli High Court has assumed the Convention applies only on a case-by-case basis, without ever ruling on the question of its application and on its legal status *en bloc* as customary international law, although it does recognize that Palestinian civilians, in the West Bank and Gaza, have the status of protected persons within the meaning of the Convention.[22] The international community, including the UN Security Council and the UN General Assembly, have consistently affirmed the applicability of the Fourth Geneva Convention to the OPT, including East Jerusalem,[23] and in 2004 the International Court of Justice unanimously affirmed in the *Legal Consequences of the Construction of a Wall in the Occupied Palestinian Territory* Advisory Opinion that the Convention is applicable in the OPT.[24]

7.2.2 Additional Protocol I

Israel is not a party to the 1977 Protocol Additional to the Geneva Conventions of 12 August 1949 ('Additional Protocol I'). The Israeli High Court has nevertheless consistently held that the Military Commander is bound not only by the Hague Regulations, but also by those provisions of the Fourth Geneva Convention and Additional Protocol I, which reflect customary international law:

> 'International law dealing with the armed conflict between Israel and the terrorist organizations [in the OPT] is entrenched in a number of sources ... The primary sources are as follows: The Fourth Hague Convention (Hague Convention (IV) Respecting the Laws and Customs of War on Land (1907). The provisions of that convention, to which Israel is not a party, are of customary international law status ... Alongside it stands The Fourth Geneva Convention. Israel is party to that convention. It has not been enacted through domestic Israeli legislation. However, its customary provisions constitute part of the law

[21] See Bar-Yaakov 1990, p 485.

[22] HCJ 7015/02 *Ajuri* v *IDF Commander in the West Bank* [2002] para 13; HCJ 2056/04 *Beit Sourik Village Council* v *The Government of Israel* [2004] para 24; HCJ 7957/04 *Mara'abe* v *Prime Minister of Israel* [2005] para 14. The Israeli High Court has indicated that some of the Fourth Geneva Convention's provisions form part of customary international law and, as such, part of Israeli law, see HCJ 769/02 *Public Committee Against Torture in Israel* v *the Government of Israel* [2005] (*Targeted killings* case) para 20.

[23] For Security Council resolutions see SC Resolution 237 of 14 June 1967, SC Resolution 271 of 15 September 1969 and SC Resolution 446 of 22 March 1979. For General Assembly resolutions, see for example GA Resolution 35/122A of 11 December 1980, GA Resolution 56/60 of 10 December 2001 and GA Resolution 58/97 of 9 December 2003. See also Conference of the High Contracting Parties to the Fourth Geneva Convention: Declaration (5 December 2001), available at http://domino.un.org/UNISPAL.NSF/fd807e4666-e3689852570d00069e918/8fc4f064b9be5bad85256c1400722951!OpenDocument.

[24] *Legal Consequences of the Construction of a Wall in the Occupied Palestinian Territory*, Advisory Opinion, ICJ Rep 2004, 136, 177, para 101; see also Declaration of Judge Buergenthal, at 240, para 2.

of the State of Israel ... In addition, the laws of armed conflict are entrenched in 1977 Additional Protocol I to the Geneva Conventions of 12 August 1949 relating to the Protection of Victims of International Armed Conflicts, 8 June 1977. Israel is not party to that protocol, and it was not enacted in domestic Israeli legislation. Of course, the customary provisions of The First Protocol are part of Israeli law.'[25]

7.2.3 Customary IHL

As a general rule, customary international law, unlike conventional law, is automatically incorporated into Israeli domestic law and needs no implementing legislation in order to be justiciable in Israeli courts. It is important however to note a significant caveat to this. According to Israeli jurisprudence, customary international law is part of its legal system provided it does not conflict with primary legislation enacted by the Israeli Parliament (the Knesset).[26] Hence, notwithstanding the customary status of a number of the provisions of the Fourth Geneva Convention and Additional Protocol I, a statute of the Knesset, even if inconsistent with the customary rule, would prevail in an Israeli court. This position was recently summarized in the *Yesh Din* case by President Beinisch of the Israeli High Court:

> '[P]etitioners are now arguing that there is a change in the approach and that it is accepted that the provisions of the [Fourth Geneva] Convention are part of customary law and as such they have a binding status. Whatever is the status of the Geneva Convention, we are ready to accept the argument that the actions of the Military Commander in the area should be examined according to the provisions of the Convention, as the court used to do for years, and that its customary provisions should be respected as part of the existing law ... However, there is no dispute that when an explicit legal provision of the internal Israeli law stands *vis à vis* international law, even when it is customary law, Israeli law prevails.'[27]

A similar proposition has been expressed by the Israeli High Court in other cases where Palestinian-petitioners have invoked the customary status of various provisions of the Fourth Geneva Convention in order to support their causes.[28] The *raison d'être* of this argument is that the supremacy of domestic legislation over

[25] HCJ 769/02 *Public Committee Against Torture in Israel* v *The Government of Israel* [2006] (*Targeted killings* case) para 20 and the sources cited there.

[26] The Israeli approach follows the doctrine of incorporation adopted by English law that determines that 'the rules of international law are incorporated into English law automatically and considered to be part of English law unless they are in conflict with an Act of Parliament', see Fatima 2005, p 405 and the sources cited there.

[27] HCJ 2690/09 *Yesh Din* v *The Military Commander* [2010] para 6 (Judgement of 28 March 2010, yet not published in English, unofficial translation).

[28] For example HCJ 69/81 *Abu Aita* v *The Military Commander* [1983] paras 12–13; HCJ 253/88 *Sejdiah v Minister of Defence* [1988] PD 42(3) 801, 815; HCJ 698/80 *Kawasme* v *Minister of Defence* [1982] PD 35(1) 617, 627.

customary international law guarantees Parliament's supremacy—as the putative sovereign—over the executive branch, preventing the latter from bypassing it and legislating domestically by signing international treaties.[29] Whilst not universal, this is a fairly common practice adopted by states that consider international law and municipal law as separate legal regimes (a dualist model of international law). Nevertheless, it is doubtful whether this proposition is valid in the context of occupied territory and when discussing the recent Israeli Policy in particular.

Firstly, the Israeli Policy is based on orders of the Military Commander, rather than on primary legislation of the Israeli Parliament. The Military Commander is part of the executive branch, being 'the long arm' of the Israeli government in the occupied territory and as noted above, is always bound by international law including treaties to which Israel is party and customary international law.[30] Secondly, as an Occupant is not the sovereign of the occupied territory but only has a temporary right of administration, its own legislature does not possess the power to legislate for the occupied territory.[31] As Kretzmer explains:

> '[T]he rationale for non-application of conventional law in the domestic court does not apply in the case of occupied territory. As such territory is ruled directly by the executive branch of government, which wields executive, legislative and judicial power, enforcing treaties made by that branch of government would in no way undermine the legislative supremacy of parliament.'[32]

This proposition remains valid regardless of whether one is referring to the Fourth Geneva Convention's conventional or customary status. There is no reason to give domestic Israeli legislation, which applies only in Israel, normative priority in the OPT. In the latter, the Occupant's primary legislation does not apply at all and thus cannot override customary international law. To do otherwise would accord the Occupant sovereign rights in occupied territory; this would have important and deleterious consequences not only for the law of occupation but also for other fundamental rules on which the international system is based.[33]

---

[29] Kaiser 2008.

[30] See HCJ 302/72 *Abu Hilo* v *Government of Israel* [1972] PD 27(2) 169, 176; HCJ 698/80 *Kawasme* v *Minister of Defence* [1982] PD 35(1) 617, 636; HCJ 69/81 *Abu Aita* v *The Military Commander* [1983] para 11; HCJ 5973/92 *The Association for Civil Rights in Israel* v *The Minister of Defence* [1993] para 11; Dinstein 1972, pp 331–332 [in Hebrew].

[31] According to Article 43 of the Hague Regulations the Occupying Power must respect, unless absolutely prevented, the laws in force in the occupied territory; See also Sassoli 2005, pp 661, 673; Dinstein 2009, pp 108, 244–245, 247.

[32] Kretzmer 2002, p 40.

[33] Benvenisti for instance, in tracing the origins of the concept of belligerent occupation, notes that it evolved as the mirror image of the concept of sovereignty; a concept which underpins the modern international system. The fact that the occupation of all or part of the territory of another State does not transfer sovereignty to the occupant, as it would have done in an earlier period, could itself therefore be seen an expression of the self-determination of the occupied territory. See Benvenisti 2008, p 621; The Charter of the United Nations [1945] Arts 1(2), 2(1), (4).

The third argument in this regard recalls that the perceived difficulty of the Israeli High Court to reconcile Israeli domestic law with customary international norms, does not absolve Israel and its Military Commander from the obligation to comply with international law.[34] Breaching its rules may have serious implications for Israel's international relations as well as, in some circumstances, from an international criminal law perspective.[35]

7.3 Expulsions of Protected Persons from the West Bank

7.3.1 Article 49(1) of the Fourth Geneva Convention: interpretation

Article 49(1) of the Fourth Geneva Convention provides:

> 'Individual or mass forcible transfers, as well as deportations of protected persons from occupied territory to the territory of the Occupying Power or to that of any other country, occupied or not, are prohibited, regardless of their motive.'

As such, the Military Commander's policy to pursue the expulsion of Palestinians from the West Bank to Gaza would appear to violate the prohibition encapsulated in the provision because of the protected status of the Palestinians.

---

[34] Vienna Convention on the Law of Treaties [1969] art 27 ('a party may not invoke the provisions of its internal law as justification for its failure to perform a treaty').

[35] This paper will not discuss aspects of International Criminal Law however expulsions of protected persons from the West Bank may be considered a 'grave breach' of the Fourth Geneva Convention and a 'war crime' under the Rome Statue of the International Criminal Court (ICC), and thus trigger individual criminal responsibility. See the Fourth Geneva Convention, Art 147; Additional Protocol I, Art 85(4); the Rome Statute of the ICC, Art 8(2)(a)(vii), Art 8(2)(b)(viii). Generally speaking, the commission of serious violations of IHL exposes the perpetrators to investigation and prosecution in foreign courts under the principle of universal jurisdiction and in front of the International Criminal Court, once the responsible State is unable or unwilling to take necessary enforcement measures against them. Israel did not ratify the Rome Statute of the ICC and suspected Israeli violators are generally not subject to its jurisdiction unless the Security Council refers the case to the ICC. On January 2009, the Palestinian Authority lodged a declaration with the Registrar relating to Article 12(3) of the Rome Statute, which allows States not parties to the Statute to accept the Court's jurisdiction. The office of the ICC prosecutor is currently examining whether the Court has jurisdiction in light of uncertainties with respect to the existence or non-existence of a State of Palestine. In case such a recognition will be achieved, the ICC might have jurisdiction to try Israeli soldiers for crimes that are committed on the Palestinian State's territory, see the Rome Statute of the ICC, Art 12, paras (2)(a) and (3); see also *Report of the International Criminal Court* (submitted to the UN General Assembly, 17 September 2009), para 12, available at http://www.icc-cpi.int/NR/rdonlyres/1BC01710-9C2-44AC-8B18-85EE2A 8876EB/281210/A_64_356_ENG2.pdf.

It is clear the prohibition was intended to be absolute—regardless of the motive—and was worded in such a way as to allow no exceptions.[36] The implication of this is that even if security rationales prompted the formulation of the Israeli Policy, the expulsion of Palestinians or any other protected person from the West Bank is not a permissible course of action for Israel to take. As Dinstein puts it, 'even the most compelling security considerations cannot vindicate the deportation of a protected person from an occupied territory'.[37] Article 85(4) of Additional Protocol I further elaborates this absolute prohibition:

> 'In addition to the grave breaches defined in the preceding paragraphs and in the Conventions, the following shall be regarded as grave breaches of this Protocol, when committed willfully and in violation of the Conventions or the Protocol:
> (a) the transfer by the *Occupying* Power of parts of its own civilian population into the territory it occupies, or the deportation or transfer of *all or parts* of the population of the occupied territory *within or outside* this territory, in violation of Article 49 of the Fourth Convention.' [Emphasis added]

Article 49(1) of the Fourth Geneva Convention prohibits individual or group expulsions and covers both transfers to another location within the occupied territory and deportations to any other destination, *occupied or not*, outside this territory.[38] Thus, the broad scope of Article 49(1) makes the debate over the status of the Gaza Strip following Israel's redeployment in September 2005—as occupied or not—immaterial for examining the legality of the expulsions from the West Bank, regardless of their final destination.[39]

Despite the commonly accepted interpretation of Article 49(1) presented above,[40] the Israeli High Court held in 1979 in the *Abu Awad* case, and again in 1988 in the *Afu* case, that Article 49(1) did not apply to the deportation of individuals on security grounds, but rather that it precludes only mass deportations such as those perpetrated by the Nazis during World War II.[41] The Court explicitly rejected an interpretation of Article 49(1) based on the ordinary meaning of the text,[42] declaring that to do so would, in the context of the case before it, lead to a

---

[36] Pictet (ed) 1958, pp 278–280. The exception of 'evacuation' in Article 49 of the Fourth Geneva Convention is inapplicable to the case here as this relates to the temporary evacuation of civilians for their own protection, or when their presence is deemed as an obstacle to military operations.

[37] Dinstein 2009, p 161.

[38] Dinstein 2009, pp 161–162; For a distinction between 'deportations' and 'forcible transfers' see the judgment of the International Criminal Tribunal for the former Yugoslavia in *Prosecutor* v *Simić* [2003] (Trial Chamber Judgment, IT-95-9-T, 17 October 2003) paras 122–123.

[39] For a range of views regarding the status of the Gaza Strip after the Israeli redeployment in 2005, see supra n 18.

[40] For a discussion of the customary interpretation of Article 49(1) see infra Sect. 7.3.2.

[41] HCJ 97/79 *Abu Awad* v *the Military Commander* [1979] para 11; HCJ 785/87 *Afu* v *IDF Commander in the West Bank* [1988] PD 42(2) 4.

[42] Article 31(1) of the Vienna Convention on the Law of Treaties provides that as a general rule: 'A treaty shall be interpreted in good faith in accordance with the ordinary meaning to be given to the terms of the treaty in their context and in the light of its object and purpose.'

manifestly absurd result as it would interfere with the Occupant's duty to enforce law and order.[43] The Court accordingly felt justified under Article 32 of the Vienna Convention on the Law of Treaties[44] in basing its interpretation on the specific historical context in which Article 49(1) of the Fourth Geneva Convention was formulated, and concluded it could only be held to apply in similar circumstances.[45] In coming to this conclusion, Justice Shamgar imported the motivation for a forcible transfer or deportation as a relevant factor into his interpretation of Article 49(1), in contradiction to the actual text of the Article. Dinstein has criticized this for being in denial of the fact that the primacy of the text is the 'cardinal rule for any interpretation ... and it is therefore necessary to submit to 'the *expression* of the parties' intention'.[46] The Court's analysis shall be examined in further detail below but the main point here is to emphasize that its interpretation is inconsistent with a plain reading of the text of Article 49(1) of the Fourth Geneva Convention and of Article 85(4) of Additional Protocol I. Moreover, even according to Shamgar's line of reasoning, the new Israeli Policy is in breach of Article 49(1). As illustrated in the *Azzam* case and the new Military Order on Prevention of Infiltrations, this recent policy is not limited to deportations on security grounds. In fact, it targets *every* Palestinian who is present in the West Bank without a stay permit, whether he or she poses a security risk or not.

At any rate, reference to the *travaux preparatoires* confirms that the ordinary meaning of the text is indeed consistent with the intention of the drafters of the Convention and that it should prevail for interpretative purposes. Although naturally, the horrors meted out to civilian populations in Europe during the Second World War were uppermost in the minds of the drafters and negotiators of this Article, there is no evidence that their intention was to draft a text intended to prohibit only Nazi-style deportations.[47] Other occupations, including *post-war* Allied occupations, also informed discussions at the diplomatic conference in

---

43 HCJ 785/87 *Afu* v *Commander of IDF Forces* [1988] PD 42(2) 4, 31.

44 Article 32 of the Vienna Convention on the Law of Treaties provides that 'Recourse may be had to supplementary means of interpretation, including the preparatory work of the treaty and the circumstances of its conclusion, in order to confirm the meaning resulting from the application of article 31, or to determine the meaning when the interpretation according to article 31: (a) leaves the meaning ambiguous or obscure; or (b) leads to a result which is manifestly absurd or unreasonable.

45 President Shamgar's judgment in HCJ 785/87 *Afu* v *IDF Commander in the West Bank* [1988] PD 42(2) 4. He concluded that 'What concerned the draftsmen of the Convention were the mass deportations for purposes of extermination, mass population transfers for political or ethnic reasons or for forced labour. This concern is the "legislative purpose" and this is the material context', at p 28.

46 Dinstein 2009, p 165 quoting Reuter 1989, pp 74–75.

47 GCIV Meeting references and Dinstein 2009, pp 164–165; Meron 1989, p 49, n 131 ('[T]he object and purpose of Geneva Convention No. IV, a humanitarian instrument par excellence, was not to protect civilian populations against Nazi-type atrocities, but to provide the broadest possible humanitarian protection for civilian victims of future wars and occupations, with their ever-changing circumstances').

Geneva in 1949.[48] The drafters were also clear from the outset that the convention they were drawing up was intended to be flexible enough to be applied in the many different contingencies that war produced, yet robust enough to help guard against both a repeat of the experiences of the World Wars and incidents as yet unimagined.

At the 17th Conference of the International Committee of the Red Cross (ICRC) in Stockholm in 1948, Mr de Truchis de Varennes, the Rapporteur of the Legal Commission observed that:

> '[R]ecent experiences have led to modifications in the [draft] conventions. It has not been easy to make these amendments, for the eventualities which may occur are extremely varied and, unfortunately, possible contingencies in the event of further armed conflicts might well be still more numerous.'[49]

Proposals for and early drafts of a 'Civilians Convention' also *predate* the Second World War. These had their genesis in the experiences of the First World War and the realization that with the advent of modern warfare, battle fields were no longer just that; civilians were as much caught up in war as were combatants, and so were as much in need of humanitarian protection.[50] Already in 1934, at its 15th conference in Tokyo, the ICRC adopted the text of a draft convention designed to meet this need.[51] Importantly, for the purposes of this analysis, this Tokyo draft provided for a strict prohibition on the deportation of civilians from occupied territory.[52] The prohibition against forcible transfers appeared as Article 19b, which provided:

> 'Deportations outside the territory of the occupied State are forbidden, unless they are evacuations intended, on account of the extension of military operations, to ensure the security of the inhabitants.'[53]

The Second World War began before this draft could be considered by states. If there had been any doubt about the effects of modern warfare on civilian populations and the need for their humanitarian protection, the experiences of this

---

[48] See for instance remarks by Mr Clattenburg (US) at the 40th Meeting of Committee III, *Final Record of the Diplomatic Conference of Geneva of 1949*, Vol IIa (1949) p 759.

[49] See 'Report of the Legal Commission', *5th Plenary Meeting in XVII International Conference of the International Committee of the Red Cross* (August 1948) p 70.

[50] For a summary of the process leading up to the Geneva conventions see 'Introduction' in Pictet (ed) 1959, pp 3–9. A good summary of the negotiating history of the Geneva Conventions is given in Best 1994, pp 80–114.

[51] Draft International Convention on the Condition and Protection of Civilians of Enemy Nationality who are on Territory Belonging to or Occupied by a Belligerent, Tokyo (1934) (hereinafter *Tokyo Draft*), available at http://www.icrc.org/ihl.nsf/INTRO/320?OpenDocument.

[52] *Tokyo Draft*, supra n 51, Art 19b. Deportations of civilians from occupied territory had been of concern during the First World War where deportations of French, Belgian and Armenian populations had taken place. See for example the note from the Secretary of State to President Wilson on 15 November 1916 discussing this, pp 40–42 in *FRUS The Lansing Papers 1914–1920*, Vol 1; See also 'Special Supplement' 1917, AJIL 11, p 249 which focuses on the deportation of Belgian civilians to Germany, principally for the purpose of labour.

[53] *Tokyo Draft*, supra n 51, Art 19b.

conflict put them to rest. In the immediate aftermath of the war, the ICRC was determined to revisit the question of the 'Civilians Convention' and to re-examine its Tokyo draft, as well as existing humanitarian conventions in the light of the experiences gained during the conflict.[54] In relation to what was to become Article 49 of the Fourth Geneva Convention, what emerged was an article which deliberately drew a clearer distinction than had the text in the Tokyo draft, between deportations, transfers and evacuations from or within occupied territory.[55] The first paragraph of the draft Article read:

> 'Deportations or transfers *against their will* of protected persons out of occupied territory are prohibited, whether such deportations or transfers are individual or collective, and regardless of their motive.'[56] [Emphasis in original]

At the 1949 Diplomatic Conference in Geneva, Committee III which was charged with negotiations relating to the Civilians Convention, settled on a wording which it felt spelt out with greater clarity the intended prohibition on individual or mass forcible removals or transfers within occupied territory, as well as deportations of protected persons from occupied territory to any other country.[57] It recognizes firstly, that not having any sovereign authority over the local population means that an Occupant does not have the same freedom of action in occupied territory as it has within its own territory,[58] and secondly that there might be circumstances when a protected person might want to be transferred to another part of the occupied territory or to another country.[59]

From the foregoing background, it is clear that the prohibition ultimately embodied in Article 49(1) of the Fourth Geneva Convention is broad and covers

---

[54] See the Report of the Work of the Preliminary Conference of National Red Cross Societies for the Study of the Conventions and of Various Problems Relative to the Red Cross, Geneva 26 July–3 August 1946 (ICRC 1947). This had been preceded by an earlier meeting of experts which met mainly to discuss repatriation issues. The other existing conventions were, of course, the 1929 Geneva Conventions for the Relief of the Wounded and Sick in Armies in the Field and on the Treatment of Prisoners of War, and the Xth Hague Convention of 1907 for the Adaption to Maritime Warfare of the Principles of the Geneva Convention.

[55] See 'Report of the Third Commission: Condition and Protection of Civilians in time of War', *Report on the Work of the Conference of Government Experts for the Study of the Conventions for the Protection of War Victims* (12–26 April 1947) 288–289.

[56] *Revised and New Draft New Conventions for the Protection of War Victims* (ICRC 1948) p 127, Art 45.

[57] 'Report of Committee III to the Plenary Assembly' in *Final Record of the Diplomatic Conference of Geneva of 1949*, Vol IIa (1949) pp 827–828. Article 45 was discussed in the 16th and 40th meetings, pp 664 and 759–760 respectively in the *Final Record*.

[58] This is dealt with separately in Section II (Articles 35–46) of Part III (Status and Treatment of Protected Persons) of the Fourth Geneva Convention concerning the treatment of aliens in the (sovereign) territory of a party to the conflict.

[59] Such was the case for instance with civilians the Allies encountered in concentration camps throughout territories they occupied towards the end and during the aftermath of the war. See remarks for instance by Mr Clattenburg at the 40th Meeting of Committee III, *Final Record of the Diplomatic Conference of Geneva of 1949*, Vol IIa (1949) p 759.

also the deportation of individuals on security grounds. It is therefore not surprising that the Israeli Court's interpretation, that Article 49(1) seeks only to prohibit mass deportations akin to those carried out by Nazis, has drawn heavy, even blistering, criticism not only from leading scholars[60] but even from within the Court itself. For instance, Justice Bach in his separate opinion in the *Afu* case held the language of Article 49(1) to be 'unequivocal and clear'. Whilst he ultimately concurred with the decision to dismiss the petition against deportation in this specific case, it was on the ground that he thought Article 49(1) to be non-justiciable in Israel due to its conventional - as opposed to customary - status and not because he supported the historical analysis adopted by Justice Shamgar.[61] We now turn to discuss the latter argument concerning the binding status of Article 49 of the Fourth Geneva Convention as a customary norm of international law.

7.3.2 Article 49(1) of the Fourth Geneva Convention: customary status

In cases subsequent to the *Abu Awad* and the *Afu* cases, the application of Article 49(1) of the Fourth Geneva Convention in the Israeli High Court was principally rejected on the ground that it does not form part of customary international law, but is merely a conventional norm.[62] As the Fourth Geneva Convention has not been incorporated into Israeli municipal law by Knesset legislation, the argument has been that it does not apply *de jure* in Israeli courts.[63]

As noted above, this approach is questionable as even if the Fourth Geneva Convention is not applicable in the Israeli domestic system (due to lack of incorporation), it certainly applies to the actions of the Israeli Military Commander

---

[60] See Kretzmer 2002, pp 44, 48–51; Meron 1989, p 49, n 131; Arai-Takahashi 2009, pp 338–339; Dinstein 2009, pp 164–165; and Dinstein 1988, p 13; and Dinstein 1980, pp 188, 192–194.

[61] See in particular paragraph 5 of Judge Bach's minority judgment in HCJ 785/87 *Afu* v *IDF Commander in the West Bank* [1988] PD 42(2) 4.

[62] For example, HCJ 253/88 *Sejdiah* v *Minister of Defence* [1988] PD 42(3) 801; Dinstein 1988, p 403; and Dinstein 1980, pp 188, 192–194, contended that Article 49(1) does not posses the status of customary international law and thus it is impossible to invoke the prohibition on deportations and forcible transfers in Israeli courts, in the absence of incorporation of the Fourth Geneva Convention into the domestic legal system by a statute of the Knesset. Dinstein's position was repeatedly cited in Israeli case-law however he does not repeat this argument in his book Dinstein 2009, or in Dinstein 2006, p 1, where he criticizes the methodology and conclusions of the ICRC Study on Customary International Humanitarian Law.

[63] For example HCJ 698/80 *Kawasme* v *Minister of Defence* [1982] PD 35(1) 617, 627 (holding that whatever is the proper interpretation of Article 49 of the Fourth Geneva Convention, the Article is non-customary); Kretzmer 2002, p 167.

outside Israel, in the OPT.[64] Moreover, the Israeli Court's approach suggests that the Court must revisit the question of deportations and transfers of protected persons from occupied territory once Article 49(1) has acquired customary status.

There is an international consensus that the prohibition on forcible transfers and deportations of protected persons from an occupied territory has indeed emerged as a norm of customary international law. Meron argued as early as 1989 that while the customary status of Article 49(1) was 'less clear' in 1949, this prohibition 'has by now come to reflect customary law'.[65] The following developments in international law further support this inference:

(a) The ICRC Study on Customary International Humanitarian Law found the prohibition on forcible transfers and deportations of civilians from occupied territories to be a customary rule. Rule 129A of the Study states as follows:

> 'Parties to an international armed conflict may not deport or forcibly transfer the civilian population of an occupied territory, in whole or in part, unless the security of the civilians involved or imperative military reasons so demand.'[66]

(b) Numerous military manuals, including those of France, Germany, the Netherlands, South Africa, the United Kingdom and the United States, reiterate the prohibition on deportations or forcible transfers of civilians from occupied territories.[67]
(c) Article 6(b) of the 1945 Charter of the International Military Tribunal (Nuremberg) determines that 'deportation to slave labour *or for any other purpose* of civilian population of or in occupied territory' amounts to a war crime.[68] (Emphasis added)
(d) The Fourth Geneva Convention's prohibition on unlawful deportations and transfers is reproduced in the Statute of the International Criminal Tribunal for

---

64 See text accompanying nn 30–35 above.

65 Meron 1989, pp 48–49.

66 Henckaerts and Doswald-Beck 2005, p 457. A database containing the rules and a compendium of practice on which the rules are based is further available at http://www.icrc.org/customary-ihl/eng/docs/home. According to the ICRC Study, a similar prohibition applies in a non-international armed conflict, see Rule 129(B). The prohibition on forcible transfers and deportations continues to apply in times of belligerent occupation as Article 6 of the Fourth Geneva Convention determines that one year after the close of military operations, and to the extent that the occupying State exercises the functions of the government in the occupied territory, it shall be bound for the duration of the occupation by specific articles of the Fourth Geneva Convention, including Article 49. Whilst other parts of the Study attracted some criticism and controversy, none appears to have been directed towards this rule. See for example, Bellinger and Haynes 2007, p 443.

67 See Henckaerts and Doswald-Beck 2005, p 458 and also Vol. II: Practice, pp 2913–2917.

68 UN International Law Commission, 'Principles of International Law Recognized in the Charter of the Nürnberg Tribunal and in the Judgment of the Tribunal, with Commentaries' YB ILC, Vol II, p 376.

the former Yugoslavia and its customary status was acknowledged in the Tribunal's case law.[69]

(e) Under the Rome Statute of the International Criminal Court, 'the deportation or transfer [by the Occupying Power] of all or parts of the population of the occupied territory within or outside this territory' constitutes a war crime in international armed conflict.[70]

(f) More specifically to the OPT, the customary status of the Fourth Geneva Convention, as well as its application in the OPT, have been affirmed by various international tribunals and human rights bodies, including unanimously by the International Court of Justice.[71]

From this list, which is only a sample of practice,[72] it does not appear to be controversial that the prohibition on forcible transfer and deportations, as embodied, *inter alia*, in Article 49(1) of the Fourth Geneva Convention and Article 85(4) of Additional Protocol I, has come to form part of customary international law. Moreover, this norm's content is based on the plain meaning of the text in Article 49(1), and not on the historical interpretation put forward by the Israeli Court in *Abu Awad* and *Afu* cases. The fact that such expulsions are being carried out under the terms set out by a Military Order does not make them lawful. The prohibition on deportations and forcible transfers is absolute and unequivocal, regardless of the motive. As the Military Commander is bound by customary international law without reservation,[73] the Order itself is unlawful.

A final issue in this context is the question whether Israel can exempt itself from a customary rule by invoking the 'persistent objector' principle. This principle provides that a state which persistently objects to a rule of customary international law, *during its formative stages*, will not be bound by that rule when it becomes

[69] Article 2(g) of the Statute of the International Criminal Tribunal for the former Yugoslavia; See also *Prosecutor* v *Krnojelac* [2003] (Appeals Chamber judgment, IT-97-25A, 17 September 2003) paras 220, 222–223; *Prosecutor* v *Stakić* [2003] (Trial Chamber judgment, IT-97-24-T, 31 July 2003) paras 672, 680; *Prosecutor* v *Brđanin* [2004] (Trial Chamber Judgment, IT-99-36-T, 1 September 2004) paras 540–543; *Prosecutor* v *Krstić* [2001] (Trial Chamber Judgment, IT-98-33-T, 2 August 2001) paras 521–522.

[70] The Rome Statute of the International Criminal Court, Art 8(2)(b)(viii). The Israeli High Court of Justice has previously classified the Israeli-Palestinian conflict as an international armed conflict, HCJ 769/02 *Public Committee Against Torture in Israel* v *The Government of Israel* [2006] (*Targeted killings* case) para 18. Israel is not a party to the Rome Statute.

[71] As discussed in detail in the *Legal Consequences of the Construction of a Wall in the Occupied Palestinian Territory*, Advisory Opinion, ICJ Rep 2004, 136, 173–177, paras 90–101.

[72] For a more comprehensive list see the ICRC's continually expanding database of State practice with regards to rule 129, available at http://www.icrc.org/customary-ihl/eng/docs/v2_rul_rule129.

[73] Dinstein 2009, p 113 ('The Occupying Power is barred from introducing (in the name of necessity) new legislation that clashes with the Geneva Convention or the Hague Regulations. Similarly, it cannot leave in place – let alone implement – domestic legislation that collides with them'). See also Greenwood 1992, p 249.

established.[74] Nonetheless, the prohibition on deportations and forcible transfers of civilians from occupied territory had been already established as a customary rule *before* Israel expressed its objection to the rule, both to its interpretation and its customary status. The Israeli objection clearly was not argued earlier than 1967, the year when the Israeli occupation came into being. Further, it seems that Israel's objection has not been sufficiently persistent. On a number of occasions the Israeli High Court did not explicitly reject the argument that Article 49(1) is customary. In order to declare that Article 49(1) does not apply in a particular case, the Court has rather applied its mis-interpretation discussed above or concluded that it is non-justiciable by virtue of a contradictory statute of the Knesset.[75] In short, Israel has not consistently opposed the customary status of Article 49(1).[76]

7.4 The Requirement to Hold a Stay Permit in Occupied Territory

7.4.1 Protected persons are entitled to be present in the Occupied Territory

The *Azzam* case followed by the amended Military Order on Prevention of Infiltration make it clear that the Military Commander demands any Palestinian inhabitant of the West Bank, whose registered address is in the Gaza Strip, to hold a permit in order to stay and reside in the West Bank. This requirement is inconsistent with the position, long accepted by Israel, that the West Bank and Gaza Strip form a single territorial unit, commonly referred to as the Occupied Palestinian Territory. This was formally affirmed in the Israeli-Palestinian Interim Agreement[77] and also by the Israeli High Court:

---

[74] Olufemi 2008, paras 1, 15–16. It must be noted that some authors dispute the legal validity and efficacy of this doctrine, see for example Charney 1985, p 1.

[75] HCJ 97/79 *Abu Awad* v *the Military Commander* [1979] para 11; HCJ 320/80 *Kawasme* v *Minister of Defence* [1981] PD 35(3) 113; HCJ 5973/92 *The Association for Civil Rights in Israel* v *The Minister of Defence* [1993]; HCJ 2690/09 *Yesh Din* v *The Military Commander* [2010] para 6.

[76] Compare with the *Fisheries* case (*UK* v *Norway*), ICJ Rep. 1951, 116, 131.

[77] Israeli-Palestinian Interim Agreement on the West Bank and the Gaza Strip [1995] Art XI, available at http://www.mfa.gov.il/MFA/Peace+Process/Guide+to+the+Peace+Process/The+Israeli-Palestinian+Int-erim+Agreement+-+Main+P.htm. The Agreement was incorporated by the Military Commander into the Military Proclamation (Number 7): The Implementation of The Interim Agreement [1995]. The operation of the Interim Agreement has neither been suspended nor terminated as a legal instrument governing the relationship between Israel and the Palestinians even after the Israeli redeployment from the Gaza Strip and the establishment of Hamas government in Gaza. Israel continues to refer to the Interim-Agreement as an agreement in effect, see for example the Israeli Government's brief in HCJ 726/08 *El-Adluni* v *The Military Commander of the West Bank* [2008] paras 28–29, available at http://www.hamoked.org.il/items/9781.pdf; and Dinstein 2009, p 280.

> 'The two areas are part of mandatory Palestine. They are subject to a belligerent occupation by the State of Israel. From a social and political viewpoint, the two areas are conceived by all concerned as one territorial unit, and the legislation of the military commander in them is identical in content ...'[78]

This position was re-affirmed by the Court in 2007 after both Israel's unilateral disengagement from the Gaza Strip in September 2005, and the establishment of the Hamas government in Gaza in June 2007.[79] Indeed, the inhabitants of the Palestinian occupied territory are entitled to the right to self-determination in both areas that were occupied by Israel in 1967.[80]

Despite the fact that the West Bank and Gaza are a single territorial unit, according to the new Israeli Policy, Palestinians originally from Gaza are not allowed to be present in the West Bank without a permit. The same is true for those who settled in the West Bank before 2007, prior to the introduction of a permit system, and retained their addresses in Gaza as their registered address. Regardless of the current status of Gaza, the introduction of stay permits for Palestinians living in the West Bank and whose registered address remains in Gaza, effectively functions to deny the recognition that they are as much a part of the Palestinian population as are West Bankers. The West Bank and Gaza were traditionally considered a single territorial unit and over the years Palestinians enjoyed free passage between the two parts of the occupied territory.[81] The requirement that Palestinians registered in Gaza hold stay permits in order to reside in the West Bank was first introduced by the Israeli Military Commander in 2007 following the collapse of the Palestinian National Unity Government and the assumption of power by Hamas in Gaza.[82] At around the same time Israel declared Gaza to be a hostile entity.[83] Whilst the freedom of movement of Palestinians has

---

[78] HCJ 7015/02 *Ajuri* v *IDF Commander in the West Bank* [2002] para 22.

[79] HCJ 11120/05 *Hamdan* v *The Southern Military Commander* [2007] para 14 ('We should add that we are assuming that the view of unity of Gaza and the Judea and Samaria area, in the comprehensive Palestinian context ... still stands in principle, but is not manifest in reality, on the ground, in terms of effective, true control by the Palestinian Authority in both areas'), available at http://www.icrc.org/ihl-nat.nsf/46707c419d6bdfa24125673e00508145/125bf9776a200883c125 75bc002b942b!OpenDocument.

[80] The 2004 ICJ advisory opinion upheld the right of the Palestinians to self-determination in the West Bank and Gaza (within the pre 1967 borders), *Legal Consequences of the Construction of a Wall in the Occupied Palestinian Territory* advisory opinion, ICJ Rep 2004, 136, 182–183, para 118. This was a unanimous ruling by the Court.

[81] An entry permit was still required in order to cross from Gaza to the West Bank through Israel's own territory. The new Israeli Policy triggers the problem of retroactivity in case Palestinians are not provided with an opportunity to adjust their status, see the Fourth Geneva Convention, Art 65.

[82] It arguably did not come into force until after this date since the Order was not published properly.

[83] Issacharoff A, 'Israeli Cabinet declares Gaza "hostile territory', *Haaretz* (20 September 2007), available at http://www.haaretz.com/print-edition/news/cabinet-declares-gaza-hostile-territory-1.229665.

been curtailed considerably since the outbreak of the Second Intifada with the closure of the 'safe passage' through Israel to the West Bank,[84] these restrictions can only apply to the ability of Palestinians to *transit* between the two areas and not to their right to be present in either.

The new requirement to hold a permit in the West Bank is not a technical formality that is achieved by mere registration or filling a form. Individuals face major difficulties in obtaining such stay permits, since the procedure to obtain one is vague and very restrictive.[85] Based on available figures, even if they get one, it will only be for a limited period.[86] A stay permit according to the Israeli Policy is however crucial and in its absence, a Palestinian's presence in the West Bank is unlawful. This raises the question of whether members of the local population need permission from the Military Commander to be present in the occupied territory or, in other words, whether such a permit is constitutive for the right of a protected person to enter the territory and to reside there.

As the discussion above demonstrates, the protection granted to protected persons from deportations and forcible transfers is absolute. Therefore, the deportation of a protected person from the West Bank or the transfer against his or her will to another part of the OPT is prohibited, regardless of whether that individual holds a stay permit for the West Bank. A determination by the Military Commander that their presence is lawful is not required in order to be protected.

The classification of forcible transfers and deportations as crimes against humanity and war crimes in the Rome Statute of the International Criminal Court is revealing in this context. Article 7, paragraph 1(d) of the Rome Statute provides that widespread or systematic deportation or forcible transfer of a civilian population is a crime against humanity. The Article further clarifies that the phrase 'Deportation or forcible transfer of population' means 'forced displacement of the persons concerned by expulsion or other coercive acts from the area in which they are lawfully present …'.[87]

---

[84] Btselem and Hamoked, *Gaza Prison: Freedom of Movement to and from the Gaza Strip on the Eve of the Disengagement Plan* (March 2005) 10, available at http://www.btselem.org/Download/200503_Gaza_Prison_English.pdf.

[85] See supra n 3.

[86] Only 388 applications for change of address from Gaza to the West Bank were approved by Israel between 2002 and 2010. See Letter from the Coordinator of Israeli Government Activities in the OPT in response to the Israeli NGO Hamoked's Freedom of Information Request (2 June 2010), available at http://www.hamoked.org/Document.aspx?dID=Documents1223; See also Gisha and Hamoked, *Israel bars Palestinians in Gaza from moving to West Bank* (June 2009), available at http://www.gisha.org/UserFiles/File/publications_/WB_Gaza_Procedure-PositionP-Eng.pdf; For the text of the procedure itself, see Israel Ministry of Defence, *Procedure for handling Applications by Gaza Strip Residents for settlement in the Judea and Samaria Area* (8 March 2009), available at http://www.hamoked.org.il/Document.aspx?dID=Documents1234 [in Hebrew], an English version can be found in Hamoked website http://www.hamoked.org/Document.aspx?dID=Documents1234.

[87] See Rome Statute of the International Criminal Court, Art 7, para 2(d).

As this prohibition also applies in time of peace to the mass deportation of a state's own citizens, the commentary emphasises that lawful presence in a territory is not limited to the position of national law, but also refers to the lawfulness of an individual's presence under international law:

> 'Any other reading would make the definition meaningless as it would permit a government to declare that the people to be transferred were not 'lawfully present' in the area and escape criminal responsibility.'[88]

Since the national law (of the Occupying Power) is not applicable to occupied territory, and the lawfulness of the presence of inhabitants of occupied territories is governed solely by international law which protects them from deportations and forcible transfer, it not surprising that this element of 'lawful presence' in the territory was omitted in Article 8 of the Rome Statute that deals with war crimes:

> 'Contrary to the approach taken for the parallel crime against humanity, States negotiating the Elements of Crimes, took the view that the requirement suggested by some delegations that a protected person must be transferred from his/her 'lawful place of residence' is not an element of the war crime of unlawful deportation or transfer.'[89]

Thus, the protection from deportation or forcible transfer is granted to members of the local population in occupied territory not because the Military Commander has agreed to their presence by issuing stay permits, but rather due to their status as protected persons granted by international law. As the prohibition on deportations and forcible transfers is absolute and stands as long as the occupation lasts, the parallel inference is that protected persons hold an entitlement to be present—to stay and reside—in this occupied territory. Their entitlement is not dependent upon the discretion of the Military Commander, but rather derives from international law. It is attached to a person's status as a protected person under the Fourth Geneva Convention.

This notion is supported by the underlying principle of the law of occupation, that the Occupying Power does not possess sovereignty in the occupied territory but only temporary rights of administration.[90] The principle is further elaborated by Article 47 of the Fourth Geneva Convention which heads the clutch of Articles in Part II, Section III concerning the status and treatment of protected persons in occupied territory and underlines the inviolability of the rights of protected persons as a result of changes an Occupant may try to make in the institutions or government of the occupied territory. As the ICRC Commentary to Article 47 explains:

> 'International law prohibits such actions, which are based solely on the military strength of the Occupying Power and not on a sovereign decision by the occupied State … the traditional concept of occupation (as defined in Article 43 of the Hague Regulations of

[88] Hall 2008, pp 248–250.

[89] Dormann 2008, p 318.

[90] Greenwood 1992, p 251; Sassoli 2005, pp 661, 673; Ben-Naftali et al. 2005, pp 551, 592–594.

1907) according to which the occupying authority was to be considered as merely being a de facto administrator.'[91]

The Military Commander is precluded from promulgating legislation and taking measures in relation to the occupied territory that have a long-term effect designed to outlive the occupation itself. The Occupant is restricted to passing legislation meant to apply only during the occupation and will normally expire at the end of the occupation, unless the legitimate sovereign decides to retain it.[92] In this context, granting citizenship and permanent residency or *a fortiori* revoking such statuses resemble the powers which sovereign governments enjoy in their own territory. Moreover, expelling Palestinians from the West Bank may have a long-term effect and carries the potential of changing the demographic composition in the West Bank taking into account the continuous expansion of Jewish settlements in this territory. This is an effect that will stay after the end of the occupation and may hinder the fulfillment of the Palestinian right to self-determination.[93]

Hence, the constitutive requirement that a protected person must hold a stay permit in order to remain in occupied territory, subject to the Military Commander's discretion, conflicts not only with the prohibition on forcible transfers and deportations of protected persons from occupied territory, but also with the limited powers granted to the Military Commander in order to underline the temporary nature of the occupation. The most compelling conclusion is that a protected person is therefore entitled, in accordance with international law, to be present in the occupied territory and does not need a permit from the Military Commander to fulfill this right.

It is important to remember that in addition to deportation, the Israeli Policy exposes protected persons whose registered address is not in the West Bank and who do not hold a valid West Bank stay permit, to severe criminal sanctions. As the restriction of a protected person's right to be present in occupied territory through the requirement that they hold a stay permit is inconsistent with international law, prosecution and criminal sanctions as a result of not holding such a permit is problematic. Moreover, the threat of criminal prosecution may serve as an effective tool to promote the Israeli Policy of expulsions through the 'voluntary departure' of protected persons from the West Bank. In this context, Article 8 of the Fourth Geneva Convention provides that protected persons cannot, under any circumstances, renounce in part or in entirety the rights secured to them by the Convention. Further, the International Criminal Court's *Elements of Crimes*, for interpreting the crime against humanity of deportation or forcible transfer, clarify that the forcible nature of deportation is not limited to physical force, but may include threat of force such as that caused by fear of violence, duress, detention,

91 Pictet 1958, p 273.

92 Dinstein 2004, p 9.

93 See Greenwood 1992, p 252 ('since belligerent occupation is conceived as a temporary state of affairs, the law seeks to preclude the imposition of measures will pre-empt the final disposition of the territory at the conclusion of the conflict').

psychological oppression or abuse of power, or by taking advantage of a coercive environment.[94] The International Criminal Tribunal for the former Yugoslavia also opined that the term 'forcible transfer' should not be restricted to physical coercion. The determination as to whether a transferred person had a 'real choice' has to be made in the context of all relevant circumstances on a case-by-case basis.[95] In these circumstances, the requirement to hold a stay permit which is almost impossible to obtain, coupled with the threat of criminal prosecution and sanctions, may be considered as expulsions *de facto* and amounts to a violation of Article 49(1) of the Fourth Geneva Convention.

7.4.2 Who is a protected person?

From the discussion above, it is apparent that determining who is a protected person under the Fourth Geneva Convention is crucial since only protected persons possess the entitlement to be present in the occupied territory, regardless of their registered address and/or whether they hold a permit from the Military Commander or not.

The first paragraph of Article 4 of the Fourth Geneva Convention defines *all* those individuals who, 'at a given moment and in any manner whatsoever, find themselves, in the case of a conflict or occupation, in the hands of a Party to the conflict or Occupying Power of which they are not nationals', as protected persons. The text clearly establishes that the relationship between the individual and the relevant Party is key to determining whether someone qualifies, and the words *at a given moment and in any manner whatsoever* were intended to ensure that all situations and cases were covered:

> 'The expression "in the hands of" is used in an extremely general sense ... The mere fact of being in the territory of a Party to the conflict or in occupied territory implies that one is in the power or 'hands' of the Occupying Power.'[96]

The *travaux preparatoires* show that the phrasing of the first paragraph of Article 4 was adopted specifically in order to extend the protection of the Convention to as wide a group of civilians as possible, including to refugees and stateless persons, rather than just those who were enemy nationals, as earlier drafts had proposed.[97] The second paragraph qualifies this admittedly broad casting according to whether or not

---

[94] 'Article 7(1)(e)' in International Criminal Court, *Elements of Crimes* 7, note 12, available at http://www.icc-cpi.int/NR/rdonlyres/9CAEE830-38CF-41D6-AB0B-68E5F9082543/0/Element_of_Crimes_English.pdf.

[95] *Prosecutor* v *Naletilić* [2003] (Trial Chamber judgment, IT-98-34-T, 31 March 2003) para 519.

[96] Pictet 1958, p 47.

[97] See *Final Record of the Diplomatic Conference of Geneva of 1949*, Vol IIa (1949) 814 (Article 4 of the final Convention was listed as Article 3 in the draft text).

the foreign civilian was of enemy, allied or neutral nationality. Only individuals of enemy nationality present in an occupying state's territory and the entire population of occupied territory (whether of enemy or neutral nationality) are automatically granted the status of protected persons. Nationals of neutral states present in the occupying state's national territory are not entitled to claim the status of protected persons under the Convention unless their state has no diplomatic representation there.[98]

Dinstein notes that the blanket protection accorded to civilians in occupied territory in Article 4 indicates that they do not have to be present in the territory from the outset of the occupation in order to qualify; they may arrive at a later date and still be entitled to the protection of the Convention. Nevertheless he asserts that the prohibition on deportation from occupied territory does not apply to infiltrators or even to tourists who remain in the occupied territory after their visa has expired.[99] He contends that 'there is a need to sort out those who arrive lawfully in an occupied territory (after the occupation has begun) from those who do not'. Thus, he continues, 'infiltrators are simply not shielded by the Convention as protected persons', and if after the visa of a tourist has expired, he or she refuses to leave, 'the Occupying Power may compel him [or her] to do so'.[100]

His argument is that the removal of such persons from occupied territory does not amount to deportation but it is an 'exclusion'.[101] This interpretation would appear to strain the meaning of the text of and Article 49(1). Whatever the conceptual difference between the two, it is clear from the *travaux* that what the drafters of the Convention intended was simply that 'deportation' meant the physical relocation of an individual from a territory; they did not intend it as a subtle term of art.[102]

As submitted earlier, a protected person does not need a permit in order to be present in the occupied territory and cannot be deported because he/she does not hold such permit. However, Dinstein suggests that those who enter the occupied territory unlawfully or whose permit has expired are *not* protected persons and thus can be deported. Dinstein's argument may serve a basis for the Israeli Policy. How compelling is Dinstein's proposition, in light of the new Military Order on Prevention of Infiltration, that individuals from Gaza who a) enter the West Bank without a permit (as so-called infiltrators) or b) initially entered the West Bank lawfully but now reside there without a permit (as so-called tourists) are *not* protected persons and thus can be deported? On its face, this interpretation would appear

---

98 See comments by Colonel Du Pasquier, the Rapporteur (Swiss), explaining the changes the Drafting Committee had made to the text. 48th Meeting of Committee III, *Final Record of the Diplomatic Conference of Geneva of 1949*, Vol IIa (1949) p 793.

99 Dinstein 2009, p 167.

100 Ibid. This position was adopted in HCJ 785/87 *Afu* v *IDF Commander in the West Bank* [1988] PD 42(2) 4, 29–31.

101 Dinstein 2009, pp 167–168.

102 The State practice cited by the ICRC in demonstrating the customary status of the prohibition on deportations and forcible transfers (Rule 129a) further supports this. See Section X.3.2 above.

to turn the prohibition of forcible transfers and deportations, and the inferred right of a protected person to be present in the occupied territory, on its head.

A few remarks are worth making here. Firstly, as already noted, the status of a protected person under the Fourth Geneva Convention is determined by that Convention and thus the circumstances in which an individual can lose this status or have it qualified is similarly provided for there. The second and fourth paragraphs of Article 4 define who is not covered by the Convention (those of neutral nationality with normal diplomatic representation present in a state's territory; those of the occupant's nationality in occupied territory; and those already covered by one of the other Geneva Conventions).[103] The absence of a local stay permit from the Military Commander does not fall within these bounds. If the Military Commander was able to deny the status of protected person and its attached protections to inhabitants of the occupied territory, or to make this status subject to different conditions at his own discretion, this would make a mockery of the Convention itself.[104]

Indeed, another issue that deserves clarification concerns unlawful entry into the West Bank and whether it precludes the status of a protected person. The broad definition in Article 4 of the Fourth Geneva Convention makes the exact circumstances of entry to the occupied territory irrelevant to the classification of an individual as a protected person. The Article does not distinguish between lawful and unlawful entry into the territory. As long as individuals are not nationals of the occupying state, their physical presence in the occupied territory is sufficient to entitle them to the status of a protected person. As already discussed, under Article 4, civilians, be they infiltrators or tourists, including those whose visa might have expired, are protected persons as they find themselves *at a given moment and in any manner whatsoever* in the hands of the Occupying Power. The authoritative ICRC Commentary further affirms that travelers, tourists, people who have been shipwrecked and even spies or saboteurs are protected persons.[105] Thus, they are entitled to stay in the occupied territory and cannot be deported, although the Military Commander may take security measures with respect to them.

It is important to emphasize that while individuals definitely suspected in activity hostile to the security of the Occupying Power remain protected persons, they can still be prosecuted and punished.[106] Prosecution also seems possible in

[103] Article 5 provides for the limitation of the full protection of the Convention in the case of individuals detained as spies or saboteurs who pose a risk to the security of the Occupying Power. In addition, under Article 53(3) of Additional Protocol I, a civilian loses their protection from attack if and for such time as they take a direct part in hostilities.

[104] See in particular Article 47 ('protected persons who are in occupied territory shall not be deprived, in any case or in any manner whatsoever, by any change introduced, as a result of the occupation of a territory, into the institutions or government of the said territory ...').

[105] Pictet 1958, p 47.

[106] The Fourth Geneva Convention, Art. 5(2). Article 49(1) also prohibits the transfer of such persons to the territory of the Occupying Power for the reason of criminal prosecution and trial. Following this, Coalition powers in Iraq referred such cases involving protected persons that entered Iraq from abroad to the Central Criminal Court of Iraq in lieu of deporting suspected offenders to their home countries, see Kelly 2003, pp 127, 147–148.

the case of protected persons who, as nationals of other states, entered the occupied territory unlawfully or who stayed there after the expiration of their visa. Unlike protected persons who are nationals of the occupied territory, aliens of neutral states are entitled to leave the occupied territory.[107] In the case of the tourist whose visa has expired, the choice between returning to their home country or facing prosecution seems reasonable—a 'real choice' in the words of the International Criminal Tribunal for the former Yugoslavia[108]—and thus prosecution could not be interpreted as *de facto* deportation. However the ICRC Commentary recalls that as with enemy nationals, the Military Commander cannot expel them against their will:

> '[T]he departure of the protected persons concerned will take place only if they wish to leave. The International Committee's original draft laid down that no protected person could be repatriated against his will ... The point is an important one, for many foreign civilians do not wish to leave a country where they have lived for many years and to which they are attached. This principle applies to all protected persons as defined in Article 4 ...'[109]

To conclude, Palestinians and aliens of neutral states in the occupied territory are protected from deportations as both are protected persons regardless of how they entered the OPT, and whether or not they hold a stay permit from the Military Commander. Generally speaking, while the prohibition on deportation is absolute, it is still permissible to prosecute protected persons from other states for illegal entry or illegal stay, as they have a 'real choice' to go back to their home country. In contrast, nationals of the occupied territory do not have this choice as they are already in their home country. To encourage the voluntary departure of protected persons who are nationals of the occupied territory, through the threat of prosecution and criminal sanctions should they stay, would amount to *de facto* deportation and thus be illegal.

As a final comment on the issue of protected persons, it is worth recalling that the powers of the Occupying Power towards protected persons differ between those in its own territory and those in occupied territory. This can be a source of confusion.[110] This manifests itself with regards to protected persons in two ways. The first is contained in Article 5 of the Fourth Geneva Convention under which an

[107] Fourth Geneva Convention, Art. 48. Protected persons that are national of neutral states *in* the occupied territory are allowed to leave. Their right to leave is subject to Art. 35, meaning that the Occupied Power may refuse to allow the departure in case it is contrary to the national interests of the State.

[108] *Prosecutor* v *Naletilić* [2003] (Trial Chamber Judgment, IT-98-34-T, 31 March 2003) para 519.

[109] Pictet 1958, pp 235, and also at 206–207.

[110] For instance in *Afu,* the Israeli High Court appears to have interpreted Article 49 as if it allowed similar measures to those permitted with regards to aliens present in the Occupant's own national territory. See also HCJ 500/72 *Al-Teen* v *The Minister of Defense* [1973] PD 27(1), pp 481, 484–485.

individual protected person within the national territory of the state (the Occupying Power) who is definitely suspected of or engaged in activities hostile to its security, such as a spy or saboteur, loses the full protections and privileges of the Fourth Geneva Convention, and thus can even be deported, since his conduct would be prejudicial to the security of the state.[111] In occupied territory in contrast, such individuals retain their status as protected persons and may only be regarded as having forfeited rights of communication.

The second principle relates to the distinction between the legitimate interests a state has in its own territory compared to those interests it may have in occupied territory. This is reflected in the structure of the Fourth Geneva Convention, which clearly articulates the status and treatment of protected persons whether in a state's national territory (Articles 35–46), in occupied territory (Articles 47–78) or in either (Articles 27–34). Accordingly there is nothing to prevent a state from exercising its right to deport protected persons from its *own* territory:

> 'This provision shall in no way constitute an obstacle to the repatriation of protected persons or to their return to their country of residence after the cessation of hostilities … The provisions of this Article do not constitute an obstacle to the extradition, in pursuance of extradition treaties concluded before the outbreak of hostilities, of protected persons accused of offences against ordinary criminal law.'[112]

This indeed may be construed as allowing for the deportation of individuals guilty of having committed a criminal offence, and their extradition under treaties concluded before the outbreak of hostilities. The same notion may also underline Dinstein's assertion that the Occupying State is allowed to expel infiltrators and visa-expired tourists even if they *are* protected persons. However, this is possible only when they are present in the Occupant's *own* territory.

In occupied territory, by contrast, the Occupant does not enjoy the same rights. The provisions relating to the treatment of protected persons in *occupied* as opposed to national territory are contained in Section II of Part III of the Fourth Geneva Convention, which includes Article 49. The option of expelling Palestinian inhabitants or other protected persons physically present in the West Bank is simply not open to Israel.

---

[111] Article 5(1) and 5(2), Fourth Geneva Convention. The *ICRC Commentary* explains that the security of the State could not conceivably be put forward as a reason for depriving such persons of the benefit of other provisions, for example, humane treatment and medical attention, Pictet 1958, p 56.

[112] Article 45, Fourth Geneva Convention. See further Pictet 1958, p 266; and discussions in Committee III relating to draft Article 41 (Article 45 of the final text), particularly those made by the US delegate, Mr Clattenburg at p 661; remarks by the Rapporteur, Col. Du Pasquier (Switzerland) at p 776; the general discussion at 809 and the Report of Committee III to the Plenary Assembly at 826–827 in *Final Record of the Diplomatic Conference of Geneva of 1949*, Vol IIa (1949).

7.5 The Concept of 'Determinative and Binding Address'

7.5.1 Determinative and binding address

This section considers the legality of the concept of a determinative registered address introduced by the Israeli Military Commander, and formalized through the 2010 amendment to the Military Order on Prevention of Infiltration. As currently enforced, this concept contains the following elements:

(a) The address registered in the Palestinian Population Registry is determinative and binding in the sense that an individual must live and reside at the location appearing in the Registry.
(b) Moving to another place of residence requires that individuals change their registered address.
(c) Although the Palestinian Authority is responsible for maintaining the Palestinian Population Registry, the procedure for changing registered addresses is, to all intents and purposes, controlled by the Military Commander as it cannot be changed without permission from the Military Commander.
(d) Living in a different location, inconsistent with the registered address, requires the individual to obtain a stay permit from the Military Commander.
(e) Living in a different location, inconsistent with the registered address, without a permit is a criminal offence and exposes the individual to criminal prosecution and possible sanctions.

In practice, Israel does not allow to change addresses in the Palestinian Population Registry, except in exceptional circumstances. Between 2002 and 2010 only 388 applications for change of address from Gaza to the West Bank were approved.[113]

Clearly this concept is Kafkaesque in the way it operates. This paper considers the attempt to clothe deportations or transfers of protected persons, which are prohibited, in a semblance of legality through the formal introduction of new military legislation as illegitimate. Nonetheless, we shall discuss the legality of the Israeli Policy also under Article 43 of the Hague Regulations. This provides:

> 'The authority of the legitimate power having in fact passed into the hands of the occupant, the latter shall take all the measures in his power to restore, and ensure, as far as

---

[113] See Letter from the Coordinator of Israeli Government Activities in the OPT in response to the Israeli NGO Hamoked's Freedom of Information Request (2 June 2010), available at http://www.hamoked.org/files/2010/112281_eng.pdf. Hamoked further report a judgment of the Palestinian Supreme Court on October 2nd 2010, instructing the Palestinian Authority to register notifications in changes of address despite Israel's practice. See Hamoked, 'The Palestinian Supreme Court rules: the Palestinian Civil Affairs Committee must accept Palestinians' notices on change of residence from Gaza to the West Bank in the Palestinian population registry, despite opposition by Israel', 25th October 2010, available at http://www.hamoked.org/Document.aspx?dID=Updates1060.

> possible, public order and life, while respecting, unless absolutely prevented, the laws in force in the country.'[114]

Article 64 of the Fourth Geneva Convention further elaborates that in exercising its powers according to Article 43 of the Hague Regulations, the Occupying Power may promulgate new laws that are necessary in order to protect the security of the occupying forces, as well as to maintain the orderly government of the territory. It is generally accepted that in respect of occupied territory this means that the Military Commander is limited to making orders which relate to security on the one hand, and to the welfare of the local population on the other hand.[115]

In the *Abu Awad* and the *Afu* cases, the Israeli High Court opined that 'Article 49 does not detract from the obligation of an occupying power to preserve public order in the occupied territory, as required by Article 43 of the Hague Regulations.'[116] However, as Kretzmer suggests, to use Article 43 of the Hague Regulation in order to legitimize measures that are inconsistent with the Geneva Conventions 'perverts the very purpose of the Conventions'.[117] The Fourth Geneva Convention aims to limit the measures that the Occupant is able to take in order to protect security, and the prohibition on deportations and forcible transfers is the *lex specialis* with respect to the general rule of Article 43 of the Hague Regulations.[118]

7.5.2 Security considerations

As a security measure, the concept of determinative addresses restricts the freedom of movement of protected persons and enables the Military Commander to control their daily life. Through the Population Registry the Military Commander knows where they physically reside, and any change is subject to the Occupant's permission. Indeed the Military Commander has a fairly wide discretion in the security measures that may be taken in relation to protected persons. As the ICRC Commentary observes:

> 'The various security measures which States might take are not specified; the Article [Article 27 of the Fourth Geneva Convention] merely lays down a general provision.

---

[114] The French text, which is authoritative, refers to the an occupant's duty to restore 'l'ordre et la vie publics' in the territory. The English translation of 'public order and safety' is sometimes criticized for not conveying accurately the meaning of the original. For a discussion on this see Schwenk 1945, p 393, n 1.

[115] HCJ 393/82 *Gamiyat El-Iskan* v *the Military Commander* [1983] para 12; Dinstein 2009, pp 112, 115; Sassoli 2005, pp 661, 673–674; Greenwood 1992, p 263.

[116] HCJ 97/79 *Abu Awad* v *the Military Commander* [1979] para 11; HCJ 785/87 *Afu* v *IDF Commander in the West Bank* [1988] PD 42(2) 4.

[117] Kretzmer 2002, p 60.

[118] Ibid.; Sassoli 2005, pp 661, 664.

> There are a great many measures, ranging from comparatively mild restrictions such as the duty of registering with and reporting periodically to the police authorities, the carrying of identity cards or special papers, or a ban on the carrying of arms, to harsher provisions such as *a prohibition on any change in place of residence without permission*, prohibition of access to certain areas, restrictions of movement, or even assigned residence and internment ...'[119] [Emphasis added]

These various security measures are not to be confused with the principal right of protected persons to be present, stay and reside in the occupied territory. These measures do not include expulsions from the occupied territory which are absolutely prohibited. Other measures, within occupied territory, are permissible only when the Military Commander shows that there is a real security necessity to take them, particularly if the specific measure is recognized as a harsh one.[120] Accordingly, the concept of a determinative address, that so harshly restricts the Palestinians' freedom of movement and their right to choose their residence within the occupied territory, must be necessary for security reasons. Nonetheless, in the case of Ms Azzam, the Military Commander did not suggest that she posed a threat to the security of the occupation regime that necessitated her living in Gaza in accordance with her registered address.

Furthermore, the Israeli Policy and the new Military Order on Prevention of Infiltration apply to *all* Palestinians present in the West Bank. However, particularly harsh security measures can only be taken against individuals on a case-by-case basis. The need to treat each case on its own merits is necessary in order to avoid measures being introduced under the guise of security which are in fact intended to suppress and punish the local population. This was underlined at the 1949 Diplomatic Conference in Geneva. The report of the Committee III which had negotiated the final text for the 'Civilians Convention' to the Plenary Assembly noted that:

> 'In occupied territory, the fact that a national of the Occupied Power harbours resentment against the Occupying Power is likewise insufficient. Moreover, there can be no question of collective measures; the charges must be individual.'[121]

In the light of this, the prohibition on collective punishment as provided by the Hague Regulations[122] requires the Military Commander to show that security measures are taken for the sole purpose of addressing security needs and on an individual basis. It must therefore be demonstrated that the Order on Prevention of Infiltration is intended to ensure the security of both the forces and administration of the Occupying Power. Nonetheless, the security rationale of the new Order remains unclear since it applies indiscriminately and captures even those individuals who pose no security concern.

---

[119] Pictet 1958, p 207.

[120] The Fourth Geneva Convention, Art. 27; Pictet 1958, p 207; Dinstein 2004, pp 6–8.

[121] Comments on draft Article 3A, Report of Committee III to the Plenary Assembly, in *Final Record of the Diplomatic Conference of Geneva of 1949*, Vol IIa (1949) p 815.

[122] 1907 Hague Regulations, Article 50.

The Israeli concept of a determinative and binding registered address is problematic from a further angle. Official data shows that Israel generally refuses to allow changes in the Palestinian Population Registry. Thus, Palestinians are actually forced to stay at the same registered address (in Gaza or elsewhere) in order to avoid potential deportations, prosecution and punishment. The concept of determinative address therefore functions as a *de facto* assigned residence measure.

As already indicated, in exceptional cases, for example where a specific individual poses a security risk, the Military Commander may legitimately issue an order of assigned residence; however, this is subject to a number of requirements and safeguards such as periodic judicial review.[123] The ICRC Commentary further explains:

> 'It will suffice to mention here that as we are dealing with occupied territory, the protected persons concerned will benefit by the provisions of Article 49 and cannot be deported; they can therefore only be interned, or placed in assigned residence, within the frontiers of the occupied country itself. In any case, such measures can only be ordered for real and imperative reasons of security; their exceptional character must be preserved.'[124]

However the Israeli Policy does not meet the criteria required for assign residence orders to be lawful. Even on the basis that as Gaza is a part of the Palestinian territory and therefore removals there from the West Bank do not constitute deportation, then the Military Commander can only assign residence of protected persons within the occupied territory and only for 'real and imperative' security reasons. In the first place, since Israel contends that it is no longer occupies Gaza, it cannot also claim the authority to be able to assign residence there. In the second place, no imperative security concerns were raised as necessitating the removal of *Azzam* nor have they been raised in relation to other individuals residing in the West Bank who are unable to change their registered address from Gaza and have been similarly removed from the West Bank to Gaza, suggesting that it is being used unlawfully as a collective punishment.

7.5.3 Considerations related to civil life in the Occupied Territory

Given the terms of Article 43 of the Hague Regulations and Article 64 of the Fourth Geneva Convention, and in the absence of a convincing security rationale, the only other rationale upon which the Military Commander's practice can be considered *intra vires* is if it serves the benefit of the local population.

The fact that law-enforcement measures limit certain rights of protected persons does not, by itself, invalidate the practice of the Military Commander.

---

[123] 1949 Fourth Geneva Convention, Article 78.

[124] Pictet 1958, p 368. See also HCJ 7015/02 *Ajuri* v *IDF Commander in the West Bank* [2002].

Law-enforcement is a legitimate objective that obviously benefits the local population. It forms part of the Military Commander's duty to restore and ensure public order and life. It is necessary for maintaining the orderly government of the territory.[125] In this respect, maintaining an accurate and updated Population Registry seems a sensible measure. The Israeli Policy, on the other hand, appears to be concerned with freezing the Registry, at least with respect to registered addresses. It imposes harsh restrictions on Palestinians and exposes them to severe sanctions and, as such, it is doubtful that the policy even if justified as a law-enforcement measure can be considered to benefit the local population.

Dinstein indeed warns that 'taking care of the welfare of the local population' may be used as a pretext for a hidden agenda of the Occupying Power. He goes on to suggest that comparing the Military Commander's legislation to the parallel domestic legislation in the Occupying Power's own territory may be used as a 'litmus test' in order to examine whether the Military Commander's policies are intended for the best interest of the local population.[126] The test asks the simple question whether the Occupant had found it necessary and adequate to promulgate similar legislation in its own territory for the welfare of its citizens. The test was adopted by the Israeli High Court in the *Abu Aita* case.[127]

The 1969 Military Commander Order (297) on Identity Card and Population Registry (Judea and Samaria) ('the Palestinian Registry Order') which established the Palestinian Population Registry, is almost identical to the Israeli Population Registry Act of 1965. In both instruments, inhabitants are required to inform the authorities of changes in various personal details, including their address, within 30 days of the change. Failure to do so may constitute an offence and involve a fine or imprisonment.[128] It is important to note that in both laws, a notice on the change of address may be given *after* the actual change of residence occurred, and expulsion from the new address is not mentioned at all as a possible sanction in cases where the necessary notice was not given.

This however is where the similarity ends. There is no parallel policy inside Israel to that which now exists in the West Bank that considers the Population Registry as determinative and binding in regard to personal details, including to the registered place of residence. Israeli citizens are not in practice required to

[125] For instance, imposition of longer prison sentences for acts of looting or sabotage of infrastructure; calling up, if necessary, the inhabitants for police duty to assist the regular police in the maintenance of public order; changes to the traffic code. See Sassoli 2005, pp 661, 678–679.

[126] Dinstein 2009, pp 120–123. He first posited this test in Dinstein 1978, pp 104, 112. For a critique see Roberts 1990, p 94; and Benvenisti 2004, pp 15–16.

[127] HCJ 69/81 *Abu Aita* v *The Military Commander* [1983] para 50; See also Judge Haim Cohen (dissenting) in HCJ 337/71, *The Christian Society for the Holy Places* v *Minister of Defense* [1972] PD 26(1) 574.

[128] The Military Commander Order (297) on Identity Card and Population Registry (Judea and Samaria) 1969, Military Legislation, Vol 17, 609, arts 13, 21, available at http://www.law.idf.il/487-he/Patzar.aspx?PageNum=16; The Israeli Population Registry Act 1965, arts 17, 35.

reside in the same locations as their registered address, nor to ask a priori for a permission in order to move to another address, nor are they required to hold a permit if they choose to live at another location that is different from their registered address. To the best of our knowledge, the criminal provisions of the 1965 Israeli Population Registry Act are not enforced in practice and criminal sanctions are not imposed on individuals who fail to update their address in the Population Registry. In other words, the concept of a determinative and binding registered address does not exist in Israel. In fact, the continuous and consistent position of the Israeli High Court, which has been expressed since 1951, and thus before the Palestinian Registry Order was introduced, is that the data kept in the Israeli Population Registry is merely statistical and accordingly may be inaccurate.[129] Therefore, according to Dinstein's litmus test, there is no basis to argue that the Military Commander's policy is for the benefit of the Palestinian population.

Support for this conclusion can also be found in the negative implications of the Israeli Policy on family life. Article 46 of the Hague Regulations and Article 27 of the Fourth Geneva Convention state that family rights of protected persons must be respected in all circumstances. The ICRC Commentary explains that this obligation 'is intended to safeguard the marriage ties and that community of parents and children' and that 'the family dwelling and home are therefore protected; they cannot be the object of arbitrary interference'.[130] Under the Israeli Policy, an expulsion measure may be enforced against one member of the family whose registered address remains in Gaza, even though the registered addresses of other family members is in the West Bank.[131] In these circumstances, the expulsion tears the family apart.

The prolonged nature of the Israeli occupation adds to the impression that the Israeli Policy cannot be for the benefit of the local population. When considering the Military Commander's powers in a prolonged occupation, the Israeli High Court opined that the Military Commander has greater latitude in the application of his legislative power; however it cautioned that such powers must be used in favor of the changing needs of the civilian population, its welfare and development[132]:

---

[129] HCJ 145/51 *Abu-Ras* v *IDF Galilee Commander* [1951] PD 5 1476, 1478; CA 169/55 *Tzadok* v *Seri* [1956] PD 10 1688, 1689; HCJ 143/62 *Funk-Schlesinger* v *Minister of the Interior* [1963] PD 17 225, 244, 249; HCJ 1779/99 *Berner-Kadish* v *Minister of Interior* [2000] PD 54(2) 368, 383; HCJ 5070/95 *Na'amat* v *Minister of the Interior* [2002] PD 56(2) 721, 735; HCJ 6539/03 *Goldman* v *Ministry of Interior* [2005] PD 59(3) 385.

[130] The obligation to respect family rights is part of customary international law, Pictet 1958, p 200; Henckaerts and Doswald-Beck 2005, pp 379–380 (Rule 105: family life must be respected as far as possible).

[131] For example see recently HCJ 6685/09 *Kahuji* v *the Military Commander* [2010]; HCJ 1266/10 *Kashta* v *the Military Commander* (pending); HCJ 2786/09 *Salem* v *the Military Commander* (pending).

[132] Dinstein 2009, pp 116–118; Greenwood 1992, p 263; While recognizing that prolonged occupations occur frequently, Roberts cautions against treating them as a special category since 'it might suggest that the law of occupation ceases to apply with its full vigour through the passage of time', Roberts 1990, pp 51–52.

> 'In determining the scope of the Military Commander's powers according to the formula of "public order and life" (Article 43), it is appropriate to consider the distinction between short-term military rule and the long-term military rule. It is only natural that in short-term occupation, military-security needs dominate. In contrast, in long-term occupation, local population needs receive more weight[133]
>
> ...
>
> The life of the [local] population, as the life of an individual, do not stop and wait, but are in constant motion, which has a development, growth and change. The military administration can not ignore all that. It may not freeze the life ... Therefore the authority of the military administration extends to take all necessary measures in order to ensure growth, change and development.'[134]

Naturally, over the course of the forty plus years of occupation, many Palestinians have changed their place of residence. As with any person around the world, such changes usually reflect other changes in people's lives, for instance in their marital status, economic situation, employment and education opportunities and other personal and social necessities. A determinative address policy that limits the right to choose the place of residence in occupied territory freezes the development of personal and public life and substantially worsens the life conditions of the Palestinian population. Instead of promoting the well-being of the population living under occupation, it damages the quality of life and the fabric of the community.[135]

7.5.4 Irrelevant consideration

The absence of both a credible security need for the determinative registered address concept and in light of its adverse effect on the well-being of the Palestinian population, the Israeli Policy certainly appears *ultra vires*. In fact, it seems that the Military Commander has based his actions on legally irrelevant considerations. This was evident in the *Ward* case, brought before the Israeli High Court in 2006, before the Policy was formalized by the 2010 amendment to Military Order on Prevention of Infiltration. In this case the petitioner was expelled from the West Bank to Gaza, based on his registered address, after release from internment. The petitioner asked to return to the West Bank but the Military Commander refused. Urging the Court to dismiss the case, the Israeli government expressly argued that:

---

133 HCJ 393/82 *Gamiyat El-Iskan* v *the Military Commander* [1983] para 22 (unofficial translation).

134 Ibid, para 26; see also Benvenisti 2004, pp 11–12.

135 See Gisha, *Restrictions and Removal: Israel's Double Bind Policy for Palestinians Holders of Gaza IDs in the West Bank* (November 2009), available at http://www.gisha.org/index.php?intLanguage=2&intItemId=1635&intSiteSN=119&OldMenu=119#2.

> '[T]he issue of changing the place of residence from the Gaza Strip to the West Bank is a political issue concerning the relationship between Israel and the Palestinian Authority and it was also discussed in the talks held between the parties until recently.'[136]

Israeli Human Rights NGOs add that the Israeli Policy is driven by the aim to further isolate the Gaza Strip, following the establishment of the Hamas government in Gaza, while increasing the geographic and political separation between Gaza and the West Bank.[137] Clearly, political considerations are outside the scope of the Military Commander's legislation powers.

7.6 Conclusion

The very essence of IHL is the protection of the civilian population. It seeks to find a balance between military necessity and the dictates of humanity. Within this body of law, the law relating to occupation aims specifically to protect inhabitants of occupied territory from arbitrary policies of the Occupying Power which are not based on military necessity. To this end, IHL imposes prohibitions in respect of certain behaviour, sometimes in absolute terms, and introduces strict criteria for the operation of the Military Commander which balance the legitimate security needs of the Occupying Power with the interests of the local civilian population. The Israeli Policy discussed in this paper seems to challenge these core principles of the law of occupation. It appears to contradict the basic notion that the civilians living in occupied territory are lawfully present and protected in this territory.

Israel's expulsions of civilians from the West Bank collide with the explicit rule prohibiting forcible transfers or deportations from occupied territory regardless of the motive; a rule which has achieved customary status since its promulgation in the Fourth Geneva Convention of 1949. The current Israeli Policy also appears to authorize the Military Commander to determine who, among the Palestinian inhabitants of the West Bank, is a protected person. Thus it seeks to subordinate entitlements that are granted to protected persons by international law to the discretion of the Military Commander.

Another distortion of IHL concerns the so-called security measures that are taken on a collective basis for no apparent security need, and without adhering to the requisite procedural safeguards. The restrictions on freedom of movement and on the right to freely reside in occupied territory consequently put the development

---

[136] HCJ 3519/05 *Ward* v *Military Commander in the West Bank* [2006] para 3 (unofficial translation). This argument was therefore made before Hamas took over the government of the Gaza Strip in 2007.

[137] Hamoked and Gisha, *New Procedure: Israel bars Palestinians in Gaza from Moving to West Bank* (June 2009), available at http://www.gisha.org/UserFiles/File/publications_/WB_Gaza_Procedure-PositionP-Eng.pdf; Hamoked and B'Teslem, *Separated Entities: Israel Divides Palestinian Population of West Bank and Gaza Strip* (September 2008), available at http://www.btselem.org/Download/200809_Separated_Entities_Eng.pdf.

of Palestinian society in formaldehyde and worsen the life conditions of individuals. In these circumstances, it may well be argued that the Military Commander has exceeded his powers and allegations of a 'hidden agenda' may arise.

Finally, this analysis has focused only on the question of deportations and forcible transfers under the law of occupation. The expulsions from the West Bank however also raise questions relating to human rights, which could be said to have particular relevance during prolonged occupation and may also have serious ramifications in the context of International Criminal Law. The issue therefore merits further investigation to explore the compatibility of the recent Israeli Policies in the West Bank with other areas of international law.

References

Arai-Takahashi Y (2009) The law of occupation. Nijhoff, Leiden

Aronson G (2005) Issues arising from the implementation of Israel's disengagement from the Gaza Strip. J Palest Stud 34:49–63

Bellinger JB, Haynes WJ (2007) A US government response to the International Committee of the red cross study customary international humanitarian law. IRRC 89:443–471

Ben-Naftali O et al (2005) Illegal occupation: framing the occupied Palestinian territory. Berkeley JIL 23:551–614

Benvenisti E (2004) The international law of occupation. Princeton University Press, Princeton

Benvenisti E (2008) The origins of the concept of belligerent occupation. Law Hist Rev 26:621–648

Benvenisti E (2009) The law on the unilateral termination of occupation. In: Giegerich T, Heinz U (eds) A wiser century? Judicial dispute settlement, disarmament and the laws of war 100 years after the second Hague peace conference. Walther Schücking Institute/Duncker & Humblot, Berlin/Leipzig, pp 371–382

Best G (1994) War and law since 1945. Clarendon Press, Oxford

Bruderlein C (2004) Legal aspects of Israel's disengagement plan under International humanitarian law. www.ihlresearch.org/opt/pdfs/briefing3466.pdf

Charney J (1985) The persistent objector rule and the development of customary international law. BYIL 56:1–24

Dinstein Y (1972) Judicial review of the acts of the military commander in the administrated territories. Iyunei Mishpat 3:331 [in Hebrew]

Dinstein Y (1978) The international law of belligerent occupation and human rights. Israeli YB HR 8:104

Dinstein Y (1980) Settlements and deportations in administered territories. Tel Aviv Univ LR 7:188

Dinstein Y (1988) Deportation from administered territories. Tel Aviv Univ LR 13:403 [in Hebrew]

Dinstein Y (2006) The ICRC customary international humanitarian law study. Israel YB HR 36:1–15

Dinstein Y (2009) The international law of belligerent occupation. Cambridge University Press, Cambridge

Fatima S (2005) Using international law in domestic courts. Hart, Oxford

Gisha (2007) Disengaged occupiers: the legal status of Gaza. www.gisha.org/UserFiles/File/Report%20for%20the%20website.pdf

Greenwood C (1992) The administration of occupied territory in international law. In: Playfair E (ed) International law and the administration of occupied territories. Oxford University Press, Oxford

Hall C (2008) Article 7. In: Triffterer O (ed) Commentary to the Rome statute of the international criminal court, 2nd edn. Munchen, Beck

Henckaerts J-M, Doswald-Beck L (2005) Customary international humanitarian law, vol I rules. Cambridge University Press, Cambridge. Available at http://www.icrc.org/web/eng/siteeng0.nsf/htmlall/customary-law-rules-291008/$FILE/custom-ary-law-rules.pdf

Kaiser K (2008) Treaties: direct applicability. In: Wolfrum R (ed) The Max Planck encyclopedia of public international law. Oxford University Press, New York. www.mpepil.com

Kaliser MS (2007) A modern day exodus: international human rights law and international humanitarian law implications of Israel's withdrawal from the Gaza Strip. Indiana I & Comp LR 17:187–228

Kelly MJ (2003) Iraq and the law of occupation: new tests for an old law. YIHL 6:127–165

Kretzmer D (2002) The occupation of justice: the supreme court of Israel and the occupied territories. State University of New York Press, Albany VT

Mari M (2005) The Israeli disengagement from the Gaza Strip: an end of the occupation? YIHL 8:356–368

Meron T (1989) Human rights and humanitarian norms as customary law. Clarendon, Oxford

Olufemi E (2008) Persistent objector. In: Wolfrum R (ed) The Max Planck encyclopedia of public international law. Available at www.mpepil.com

Pictet J (ed) (1958) Commentary on the Geneva conventions of 12 August 1949, vol IV. ICRC, Geneva

Pictet J (ed) (1959) Commentary relative to the protection of civilian persons in time of war. ICRC, Geneva

Reuter P (1989) Introduction to the law of treaties. Pinter, London

Roberts A (1990) Prolonged military occupation: the israeli-occupied territories since 1967. AJIL 84:44

Sassoli M (2005) Legislation and maintenance of public order and civil life by occupying powers. Eur J Int Law 16:661–694

Schwenk EH (1945) Legislative power of the military occupant under Article 43, Hague regulations. Yale LJ 54:393–416

Scobbie I (2004–2005) An intimate disengagement: Israel's withdrawal from Gaza, the law of occupation and of self-determination, yearbook of Islamic and Middle Eastern law 11:3–31, reprinted in Kattan V (ed) (2008) The Palestine question in international law. British Institute of International and Comparative Law, London, pp 637–665

Shany Y (2005) Faraway, so close: the legal status of Gaza after Israel's disengagement. YIHL 8:369–383

Shany Y (2008) Binary law meets complex reality: the occupation of Gaza debate. Israel LR 41:68–86

Part II
Current Developments

Chapter 8
Year in Review

Louise Arimatsu and Mohbuba Choudhury

Contents

Thanks are due to Aleksandra Bojovic for her useful contributions.

L. Arimatsu (✉)
The Royal Institute of International Affairs, London, UK
e-mail: LArimatsu@chathamhouse.org.uk

M. Choudhury
London School of Economics, London, UK
e-mail: Mohbuba.c@gmail.com

M.N. Schmitt et al. (eds.), *Yearbook of International Humanitarian Law Volume 13, 2010*, DOI: 10.1007/978-90-6704-811-8_8,

8.1 Major Developments in IHL in 2010

2010 was characterised by incidents that raised age-old questions pertaining to IHL, albeit in different guises. The increase in the use of unmanned weapon systems, or drones, triggered heated debate on the interplay between *jus ad bellum* and *jus in bello* as well as between IHR and IHL.[1] This raised a host of further questions including: under what conditions does IHL come into operation? Which normative regime—international or non-international—governs the particular armed engagement? And, what is the geographical scope of IHL?

As the armed conflict in Afghanistan continued into its tenth year, questions continued to surface on the characterisation of the conflicts and the different legal regimes that may apply concurrently in complex multi-national operations.[2] In particular, the scope and applicability of IHR in armed conflict has continued to generate debate not least in respect of the conduct of hostilities and detention.[3]

During the first half of the year, international pressure on Israel mounted as the humanitarian situation in Gaza deteriorated, in part as a consequence of Israel's blockade. But it was the Mavi Marmara Incident in May which galvanised the legal community to re-examine the nature of the conflict and to ask, once more, what legal regime and rules apply in the hostilities between Israel and Hamas.[4]

Amidst the armed conflicts that continue to be waged on the DRC's territory and the endemic sexual violence against women for which the DRC has become notorious, the Office of the High Commission for Human Rights released a Mapping Report documenting the most serious violations of IHR and IHL perpetrated during the armed conflicts that raged in the Congo between 1993 and 2003. The Mapping Report serves both as a poignant reminder of the progress that has been made since the maxim *inter arma enim silent leges* was popularised but also of the huge challenges that confront the international community.

8.1.1 Israel's blockade of Gaza and the Mavi Marmara incident

One of the major issues that occupied the international community in 2010 concerned Israel's blockade of Gaza and the subsequent Mavi Marmara incident. Israel's naval blockade of Gaza began in January 2009 after Hamas took office following the legislative elections in the Gaza Strip in 2006. The blockade prevented Gaza from exporting goods and severely restricted imports into the territory. In May 2010 the Free Gaza Movement and the Turkish Humanitarian

---

[1] See Schmitt, this volume pp 311–326; and Chesney, this volume pp 3–60; Henderson, this volume pp 133–174.

[2] De Cock, this volume pp 97–132.

[3] McLaughlin, this volume pp 213–244.

[4] See Focus topic: Kraska, this volume pp 367–396 and Sanger, this volume pp 397–448.

Relief Fund organized a six-ship flotilla, with 700 persons on board, to deliver humanitarian aid to Gaza in order to break Israel's blockade.

On 30 May 2010 Israel offered to unload the cargo in the port of Ashdod in order for the cargo to be inspected; this was offer was refused. On 31 May 2010, the Israeli Navy intercepted the ships in international waters. Five ships were intercepted without incident but a violent confrontation aboard the Mavi Marmara between the IDF forces and passengers led to the death of nine Turkish nationals as well as the wounding of a further fifty-five passengers and nine IDF soldiers.

On 1 June 2010, the President of the Security Council released a statement[5] condemning the acts that had resulted in the loss of civilians and requested the immediate release of the ships and the civilians held by Israel. The Security Council further called for 'a prompt, impartial, credible and transparent investigation conforming to international standards' and reiterated its grave concern at the humanitarian situation in Gaza, stressing the need for sustained and regular flow of goods and people to Gaza as well as unimpeded provision and distribution of humanitarian assistance throughout Gaza.

The Human Rights Council also condemned in the strongest terms the 'outrageous attack' by the Israeli forces against the humanitarian flotilla of ships in resolution 14/1.[6] The resolution expressed grave concern at the deepening humanitarian crisis and called on Israel to immediately lift the siege on Gaza and other occupied territories. The Human Rights Council also decided to dispatch an independent, international fact-finding mission to investigate violations of international humanitarian and human rights law.[7] The fact-finding mission was established in July 2010 with the mandate 'to investigate violations of international law, including international humanitarian law and human rights law, resulting from the interception by the Israeli forces of the humanitarian aid flotilla bound for Gaza on 31 May 2010'.[8] Judge Karl Hudson-Phillips QC, former judge of the International Criminal Court and former Attorney General of Trinidad and Tobago, headed the mission. The other appointed members of the mission included Sir Desmond de Silva QC of the United Kingdom, former Chief Prosecutor of the Special Court for Sierra Leone and Mary Shanthi Dairiam of Malaysia, founding member of the Board of Directors of the International Women's Rights Action Watch Asia Pacific and former member of the Committee on the Elimination of Discrimination Against Women.

The Report of the international fact-finding mission on the Israeli attacks on the flotilla of ships was released in September 2010. Evidence was collated from different sources including eyewitness accounts, forensic reports and interviews with medical and forensic personnel in Turkey, as well as written statements, video

---

5 UN Doc. S/PRST/2010/9, 1 June 2010.

6 HRC Res. 14/1, 23 June 2010, para 1.

7 Ibid., para 8.

8 UN Doc. A/HRC/15/21, 27 September 2010.

film footage and other photographic material relating to the incident. However, the Mission was hampered by Israel's decision not to co-operate.[9]

The Report discussed the permissibility of a blockade under the laws of armed conflict. Referring to the San Remo Manual the report stated that a blockade was illegal if its sole purpose was to starve the civilian population or where the damage to the civilian population is, or may be expected to be, excessive in relation to the concrete and direct military advantage anticipated from the blockade. In evaluating the evidence submitted to the Mission, the Report concluded that it was satisfied that the blockade was inflicting disproportionate damage upon the civilian population in the Gaza Strip. As such, the interception in international waters could not be justified and therefore was illegal.[10] The Report also determined that the passengers on board the Mavi Marmara were 'protected persons' under Article 4 of the Fourth Geneva Convention. The conduct of the Israeli military towards the passengers was not only disproportionate but demonstrated levels of totally 'unnecessary and incredible violence'.[11] In its concluding paragraphs the Report declared that there was clear evidence to support prosecutions for the following crimes within the terms of Article 147 of the Fourth Geneva Convention: wilful killing, torture or inhuman treatment and wilfully causing great suffering or serious injury to body or health. The Report also found that Israel was in violation of a number of its obligations under international human rights law.

On 14 June, Israel established an independent public Commission to examine various aspects of the actions taken by State of Israel to prevent the ships from reaching the Gaza Strip coast. Supreme Court Justice Emeritus Jacob Turkel was appointed to chair the Commission; two foreign experts were also appointed to act as observes. The Turkel Commission Report was published on 23 January 2011.[12]

In August, the UN Secretary General announced the establishment of a separate inquiry into the Mavi Marmara incident, headed by Geoffrey Palmer, the former Prime Minister of New Zealand.

8.1.2 Resolution 13/9 (Tomuschat) Committee

Following the release in October 2009 of the UN Fact-Finding Mission on the Gaza Conflict Report (*Goldstone Report*), the General Assembly adopted resolution 64/10 (1 December 2009) endorsing the report and requested the Secretary-General to transmit it to the Security Council and called upon both the Government of Israel and the Palestinian authorities to take appropriate steps to

[9] Ibid., para 16.

[10] UN Doc. A/HRC/15/21, 27 September 2010, para 53.

[11] Ibid., para 264.

[12] The Turkel Commission Report will be examined in further detail in 2011 YIHL Vol 14.

investigate the serious violations of international humanitarian and international human rights law documented in the report.

On 4 February the Secretary-General submitted a report attaching a paper produced by the government of Israel entitled 'Gaza operation investigations: an update'.[13] The paper, which supplemented and updated an earlier publication, 'The Operation in Gaza: Factual and Legal Aspects', described Israel's procedures for investigating the alleged violations of the law of armed conflict in respect of Operation Cast Lead (27 December 2008–18 January 2009). According to the paper, of the 150 separate incidents investigated by Israel, 36 had been referred for criminal investigation. The paper also noted that of the 34 incidents recorded in the *Goldstone Report*, 22 were already under investigation; the additional 12 were referred to the Military Advocate General's office for further consideration. The vast majority of investigations remained on-going.

As it was not until the 25 January 2010 that Mahmoud Abbas (President of the Palestinian National Authority) authorised the creation of an Independent Investigative Commission (IIC) by Presidential Decree, a report by the Palestinian authorities was not produced until late summer. Meanwhile in March, the General Assembly adopted resolution 64/254 reiterating its call on Israel and Palestine to conduct independent, credible investigations into the serious international law violations perpetrated during the Gaza conflict. In April the UN Human Rights Council adopted resolution 13/9 establishing a committee of independent experts chaired by Professor Christian Tomuschat to monitor and assess any domestic, legal or other proceedings undertaken by both Israel and the Palestinian authorities.

In August the IIC report, together with an update paper from Israel, was submitted with the Secretary-General's second report to the General Assembly.[14]

The Tomuschat Committee released its report in September 2010.[15] The Committee cited Israel's 'lack of cooperation' as having hampered its assessment of the latter's response to conduct investigations that were 'independent, credible and in conformity with international standards'. Consequently it was unable to reach a definitive assessment. While the Committee acknowledged the existence of various mechanisms within the Israeli legal order to investigate allegations of war crimes, concerns were raised as to whether the system was impartial. Further concerns were raised as to the transparency of the process and whether victims were able to access justice. The Committee concluded that Israel had failed to meet its duty to investigate under the ICCPR and CAT; nor had it investigated the actions of those at the highest level of decision-making and whether such actors were complicit in violations of IHL and IHRL. In contrast, the Committee found that the IIC was independent in form and the investigation conducted by it had conformed to international standards. Nonetheless, the IIC's work was hampered

---

13 A/64/651.

14 A/64/890.

15 A/HRC/15/50.

by difficulties in accessing the Gaza Strip and consequently it was unable to investigate the allegations of serious violations of IHL and IHRL in Gaza.

8.1.3 Drones

In March the American Civil Liberties Union filed a lawsuit seeking to enforce a Freedom of Information Act request to the US Defense, State and Justice departments for information regarding the US government's use of armed drones to target individuals in Afghanistan and Pakistan.[16] Under mounting criticism that the use of drones was unlawful, the Legal Advisor to the State Department, Harold Koh, countered each of four main concerns that had been raised in respect of US policy.[17]

Refuting the suggestion that the very *act of targeting particular leaders* of an enemy force in an armed conflict violated the laws of war, Koh referred to US practice during WWII to argue that individuals who are part of such an armed group are belligerents and therefore lawful targets under international law. Koh's argument would have been strengthened had he cited an example of targeting within the context of a non-international armed conflict (NIAC) as both Afghanistan and Iraq are widely accepted as non-international in character. In response to the criticism that the *use of advanced weapons systems* was unlawful, Koh rightly maintained that there is no prohibition under the laws of war on the use of technologically advanced weapons systems in armed conflict so long as they are employed in conformity with the applicable laws of war. The third criticism—that the use of drones amounts to *unlawful extrajudicial killing*—was dismissed on the grounds that a state which is engaged in an armed conflict or in legitimate self-defense is governed by the laws of war and the principles of distinction and proportionality. Finally, that targeting practice violates domestic law insofar as there is a *ban on assassinations* was rejected as inapplicable since the US was engaged in an armed conflict and it was international law that applied. Clearly, each of these counter-arguments relies on the assumption that all such targeted killings have been executed exclusively in the context of an armed conflict. The predominant concern is whether this assumption is sustainable in all situations.

In May, the Special Rapporteur on extrajudicial, summary or arbitrary executions, Philip Alston, presented his 'Study on targeted killings' to the Human Rights Council pursuant to Human Rights Council resolution 8/3.[18] Failure on the part of states to specify the legal justification for their policies, to disclose the safeguards in place to ensure that targeted killings are in fact legal and accurate, or to provide accountability mechanisms for violations were cited as reasons for concern

[16] Available at www.aclu.org.

[17] Available at www.state.gov/s/l/releases/remarks/139119.htm.

[18] A/HRC/14/24/Add.6.

warranting such a report. The Study considers in some detail the applicable legal framework and basic rules that apply to such practice and addresses, *inter alia*: who may lawfully be targeted, when and on what basis; who may conduct a targeted killing; the use of less-than-lethal measures; the use of drones; and the requirement of transparency and accountability.

The Study identifies three potential legal frameworks that may apply. It observes that in the context of armed conflict, IHL applies and targeted killings are lawful when the target is a 'combatant' or 'fighter' or, in the case of a civilian, only for such time as the person 'directly participates in hostilities'. In other words, subject to certain conditions, IHL permits such practice. However, it maintains that regardless of whether the conflict is international or non-international in character, 'the killing must be militarily necessary, the use of force must be proportionate so that any anticipated military advantage is considered in light of the expected harm to civilians in the vicinity, and everything feasible must be done to prevent mistakes and minimize harm to civilians'.

Outside the context of armed conflict, the legality of a killing is governed by human rights standards. According to the Study, a state killing is legal 'only if it is required to protect life (making lethal force proportionate) and there is no other means, such as capture or non-lethal incapacitation, of preventing that threat to life (making lethal force necessary). The proportionality requirement limits the permissible level of force based on the threat posed by the suspect to others. The necessity requirement imposes an obligation to minimize the level of force use, regardless of the amount that would be proportionate, through, for example, the use of warnings, restraint and capture.' It follows that under human rights law, a targeted killing is unlawful since it is never permissible for killing to be the *sole objective* of an operation.

The third legal framework is described as 'the use of inter-state force' and targeted killings in the territory of other states raise issues pertaining to sovereignty. The Study suggests that 'when a State conducts a targeted killing in the territory of another State with which it is not in armed conflict, whether the first State violates the sovereignty of the second is determined by the law applicable to the use of inter-state force while the question of whether the specific killing of the particular individual(s) is legal is governed by IHL and/or human rights law'. The sovereignty of the territorial state is not violated if either (a) it consents, or (b) the targeting state has the right under international law to use force in self-defence under Article 51 of the UN Charter because (i) the territorial state is responsible for an armed attack against the targeting state or (ii) the territorial state is unwilling or unable to stop armed attacks against the targeting state launched from its territory. In such a case, international law permits the use of lethal force in self-defence in response to an 'armed attack' as long as that force is necessary and proportionate. The Study suggests that while the basic rules are not disputed, 'the question of which framework applies, and the interpretation of aspects of the rules have been the subject of significant debate'.

The study concludes with a list of recommendations including the need for states to publicly identify the rules they consider to provide a basis for any targeted killings they undertake; the procedural safeguards that govern such practice and where a targeted killing is exercised in the territory of another state, the territorial state should publicly indicate whether it gave consent and on what basis.

8.1.4 Report of the UN High Commissioner for Human Rights mapping human rights violations in the Democratic Republic of the Congo 1993–2003

On 1 October, a Mapping Report documenting the most serious violations of human rights and international humanitarian law perpetrated in the Democratic Republic of the Congo (DRC) during the decade spanning 1993–2003 was published by the Office of the UN High Commissioner for Human Rights (OHCHR). The report had been prompted by the discovery of three mass graves in the eastern part of the DRC in 2005. In May 2007 the UN Secretary-General approved the terms of reference of the mapping exercise led by the Office of the UN High Commissioner for Human Rights.[19] The exercise had three objectives: (1) to document the most serious violations of human rights and international humanitarian law committed within the territory of the DRC between March 1993 and June 2003; (2) assess the existing capacities within the national justice system to deal appropriately with the violations uncovered; and (3) formulate a series of options aimed at assisting the government of the DRC in identifying appropriate transitional justice mechanisms to deal with the legacy of the violations.

The Report is presented chronologically and is sub-divided into four key periods of violence in the DRC. The first period deals with the internal violence that broke out in the east during the final years of President Mobutu's rule; the second period concerns the armed violence that engulfed the DRC during the First Congo War (1996–1998); the third period covers the Second Congo War and the outbreak of multiple international and non-international armed conflict; and the final 'transition' period focuses on the multiple internal conflicts that continue to persist. Taking each period separately, the Report asks whether the situation amounted to an armed conflict such that IHL applied and from the evidence collated, whether the conflict was international or non-international in scope. The Report concludes that war crimes, crimes against humanity and genocide were perpetrated by the parties to the conflicts during the period under review and, in particular, identifies acts of violence committed against women and sexual violence, violence committed against children, and violence linked to the exploitation of natural resources.

In the third section of the Report, the DRC's justice system is considered in some depth. In concluding that the existing Congolese justice system is unable to deal adequately with the scale of the crimes documented, the Report considers

---

[19] SCR 1794 (2007).

other options, namely, transitional justice mechanisms that could help to combat impunity. These would include: (a) the creation of a hybrid judicial mechanism; (b) the creation of a Truth and Reconciliation Commission; (c) reparation programmes; and (d) reforms of both the legal sector and the security forces.

On its release, the Report was dismissed by Rwanda which had been directly implicated in the mass atrocities.[20] In contrast, it was welcomed by the DRC.

8.2 Protected Persons

8.2.1 Women

In February 2010, the Secretary-General announced the appointment of Margot Wallström of Sweden as the Special Representative on Sexual Violence in Conflict as mandated under SCR 1888 (2009). In her first statement to the Council the Special Representative drew the Council's attention to the situation in the eastern provinces of the Democratic Republic of the Congo and in doing so announced a five-point priority agenda: ending impunity; empowering women; mobilizing political leadership; increasing recognition of rape as a tactic and consequence of conflict; and ensuring a more coherent response from the UN system.[21]

In April 2010, pursuant to a request by the Security Council (SCR 1889 of 2009), the Secretary General issued a report on *Women, Peace and Security* detailing a set of indicators for use at the global level to track the implementation of resolution 1325 (2000).[22] The request was made in response to a concern that 10 years since its adoption, the implementation of SCR 1325 remained slow. Moreover, the lack of 'baseline data and specific, measurable, achievable, relevant and time-bound indicators' was seen as hampering progress. An Inter-Agency Tasks Force was established which, after a comprehensive consultative process, identified 26 indicators. Each of the indicators fall under one of the four thematic areas of the 2008–2009 *UN System-wide Action Plan on implementing SCR1325*: prevention, participation, protection and relief and recovery. In the case of some indicators, the requisite information is already being collated. An example of this is the percentage of reported cases of sexual exploitation and abuse allegedly perpetrated by uniformed and civilian peacekeepers and humanitarian workers that are referred, investigated and acted upon (indicator 4). In contrast, other indicators require the introduction of data collection processes and the development of specialized technical and conceptual tools. An example of this includes documenting the incidence of sexual violence in conflict affected countries (indicator 1).

---

[20] See press statement issued by the Rwanda Ministry of Foreign Affairs and Cooperation on 27 August 2010 on the leaked draft Report.

[21] S/2010/173.

[22] Ibid.

The Secretary-General recommended that the Council urge UN organisations and member states to introduce pilot schemes in order to establish a global system that would facilitate effective tracking of progress and improve decision-making.

In September 2010, the Secretary-General issued the tenth annual report on the implementation of SCR1325.[23] The report includes information on measures taken to improve the capacity of Member States to implement the resolution, a review of the System-wide Action Plan and an update on progress in respect of piloting programmes to take account of the indicators identified in the Secretary-General's April report.

Insofar as implementation by the Council was concerned, it was noted that most reports on peacekeeping missions now include information on actions taken to ensure the participation of women in peace and security and the consequences of armed conflict for women and girls. At the national level, implementation had resulted in a number of states (Canada, Columbia, the Netherlands, Azerbaijan) setting up working groups and task forces while some governments had actively sought to create partnerships with women's organisations (Philippines, Australia, Canada, Sri Lanka). A total of 19 states had developed and adopted national action plans. Civil society organisations at local, regional and international level had been very active over the last 10 years not least in Liberia, Sierra Leone, Sri Lanka, Burundi, and the Gaza Strip.

Given the volume and scattered nature of the activities, the need for a more effective and coordinated implementation programme became evident resulting in the updated *2008–2009 UN System-wide Action Plan* based on five thematic pillars. A central approach under the prevention pillar was to increase the numbers of women police officers and/or to provide gender sensitivity training. As a result, the Department of Peacekeeping Operations (DPKO) had deployed greater numbers of female police officers while the United Nations Population Fund (UNFPA) had supported national police efforts to address and prevent gender-based violence more effectively. UNDP developed a countrywide response in 18 countries to address prevention by ensuring access to legal aid for women, legal information centres, legal aid networks and train female judges, lawyers and prosecutors. UNIFEM prioritised community capacity-building to prevent sexual violence by enabling women's groups in Afghanistan, Haiti, Liberia, Rwanda, Timor-Leste and Uganda to work with the police and judiciary to improve investigation and prosecution outcomes. DPKO developed gender guidelines for police and military peacekeepers on preventing sexual violence.

Following a two day sitting of the Security Council (S/PV.6411) convened to consider the Report of the Secretary-General, the Council requested the Secretary General to propose a strategic framework to guide the UN's implementation over the next decade and, in particular, to recommend policy and institutional reforms to facilitate improved response by the UN to women and peace and security issues.[24]

---

[23] S/2010/498.

[24] S/PRST/2010/22.

8.2.2 Children

In April, the Secretary-General's annual report on Children and Armed Conflict covering the period from January to December 2009 was issued.[25] The Secretary General reported on the measures undertaken by parties to end all violations and abuses committed against children in armed conflict. The measures included action plans signed to end the recruitment and use of child soldiers by a number of groups. The report also provided an update on the implementation of the monitoring and reporting mechanism established by the SCR 1612 as well as information on grave violations committed against children in armed conflicts.

The report listed 59 parties, including 16 persistent violators that recruit or use children, kill or maim children and/or commit rape and other forms of sexual violence against children in situations of armed conflict.[26] In his recommendations the Secretary General called on the Security Council to weigh more vigorous measures against persistent violators for grave violations against children. The report also recommends state parties to the Convention on the Rights of the Child to strengthen national and international measures for the prevention of recruitment of children into armed forces and their use in hostilities.

On 16 June the President of the Security Council issued a statement on children and armed conflict. Taking note of the report of the Secretary General, the President condemned the violations of international law, including humanitarian law, human rights law and refugee law committed against children in situations of armed conflict. The statement expressed the Security Council's readiness to adopt targeted and graduated measures against persistent perpetrators and called on states to take decisive and immediate action through national and international justice mechanisms, with a view to ending impunity for those committing crimes against children.[27]

The Secretary General also issued four country-specific reports on children and armed conflict, concerning Nepal,[28] the Democratic Republic of Congo,[29] Somalia[30] and the Philippines.[31]

---

[25] UN Doc. S/2010/181, 13 April 2010.

[26] Ibid., Annex I and II.

[27] UN Doc. S/PRST/2010/10, 16 June 2010.

[28] UN Doc. S/2010/183, 13 April 2010.

[29] UN Doc. S/2010/369, 9 July 2010.

[30] UN Doc. S/2010/577, 9 November 2010.

[31] UN Doc. S/2010/36, 21 January 2010.

8.3 The United Nations

8.3.1 The Security Council[32]

8.3.1.1 Afghanistan

The Security Council passed two resolutions on Afghanistan in 2010. SCR 1917 extended the mandate of the United Nations Assistance Mission in Afghanistan (UNAMA) for another year until 23 March 2011.[33] The resolution condemned all attacks including the use of improvised explosive devices, suicide attacks, abductions, the targeting of civilians and the use of civilians as human shields by the Taliban and other extremist groups. The resolution also expressed strong concern about the recruitment and use of children by Taliban forces in violation of international law. The Security Council also welcomed the progress made by Afghan and international forces in reducing civilian casualties and reiterated its call for all feasible steps to be taken to ensure the protection of civilians and compliance with international humanitarian and human rights law.

The second meeting on Afghanistan resulted in the adoption of SCR 1943 which extended the mandate of the ISAF force for 1 year until 13 October 2011.[34] In its preamble the resolution expressed serious concern with the high number of civilian casualties and called upon all parties to comply with their obligations under international humanitarian and human rights law. Further, that all appropriate measures be taken to ensure the protection of civilians.

8.3.1.2 Central African Republic and Chad

The Security Council passed three resolutions on the Central African Republic and Chad in 2010, all of which concerned the UN Mission in the Central African Republic and Chad (MINURCAT). On 15 January 2010 the Government of Chad provided a note verbale informing the Secretary General that it wished MINURCAT to withdraw from Chad, this was followed by a letter by the Permanent Representative of Chad stating that it had reconsidered an earlier request for the Mission's withdrawal.[35] SCR 1913 indicated that the discussion of the future of MINURCAT was ongoing and determined that the situation in Chad and surrounding region continued to constitute a threat to international peace and security.

[32] This Year in Review only discusses those situations where the Security Council refers to international humanitarian law.

[33] UN Doc. S/Res. 1917 (2010), 22 March 2010.

[34] UN Doc. S/Res. 1943 (2010), 13 October 2010.

[35] UN Doc. S/2010/115, 3 March 2010.

In its operative paragraph the Security Council agreed to extend the mandate of MINURCAT as set out in SCR 1861 (2009)[36] until 15 May 2010.[37]

Subsequently a report produced by the Secretary General on MINURCAT provided recommendations for a revised mandate for the Mission.[38] The need for a thorough examination of these recommendations was taken into consideration by the Security Council in Resolution 1922 which further extended the mandate of MINURCAT until 26 May 2010.[39]

The Security Council convened again on 25 May 2010 and adopted SCR 1923.[40] The preamble determined that the situation in the region of the border between Sudan, Chad and the Central African Republic constitutes a threat to international peace and security and that, as a result, MINURCAT's mandate would be extended until 31 December 2010. The resolution authorised the military component of MINURCAT to be reduced from 5,200 to 2,200 military personnel (1,900 in Chad and 300 in Central African Republic) and called upon the Secretary General to withdraw all troops, uniformed and civilian components of MINURCAT by 31 December 2010. It also decided that prior to withdrawal of military personnel, MINUCRAT shall be authorised to respond to imminent threats of violence to civilians, provide protection to United Nations personnel and facilities, execute operations to extract United Nations personnel and humanitarian workers in danger. The resolution reaffirmed the obligation of all parties to implement fully the rules and principles of humanitarian law, particularly those regarding humanitarian personnel. It also encouraged MINURCAT and the United Nations country team to continue to assist the Government to prevent the recruitment of refugees and children by armed groups.

8.3.1.3 Côte d'Ivoire

The Security Council met on several occasions to discuss the situation in Côte d'Ivoire. There were a total of five Resolutions adopted during 2010, which expressed concern about continued violations of international humanitarian law. SCR 1911 noted with concern that in spite of the improvements in the overall human rights situation, the persistence of human rights and humanitarian law violations against civilians in different parts of the country, including numerous acts of sexual violence, necessitated that the perpetrators be brought to justice.[41] Acting under Chapter VII the resolution renewed the mandate of the United Nations Operation in Côte d'Ivoire (UNOCI) (and French forces which support

36 UN Doc. S/Res. 1861 (2009), 14 January 2009.

37 UN Doc. S/Res. 1913 (2010), 12 March 2010.

38 UN Doc. S/2010/217, 29 April 2010.

39 UN Doc. S/Res. 1922 (2010), 12 May 2010.

40 UN Doc. S/Res 1923 (2010) 25 May 2010.

41 UN Doc. S/Res. 1911 (2010), 28 January 2010, preamble.

UNOCI) until 31 May 2010, in particular to support the organisation in Côte d'Ivoire of a free, fair, open and transparent election. The Resolution also requests the UNOCI to provide technical and logistical support to the Independent Electoral Commission for the preparation and holding of the elections, to continue to support disarmament and dismantling of militias and to continue to contribute to the promotion and protection of human rights.

In its subsequent resolution,[42] adopted on 27 May 2010, the Security Council refers to the need to examine thoroughly the recommendations for a revised mandate of UNOCI included in the report of the Secretary General.[43] The resolution further determined that the situation in Côte d'Ivoire continues to pose a threat to international peace and security in the region and extended both the mandate of UNOCI and the French forces until 30 June 2010.

On 30 June 2010, the Security Council repeated its concerns over the continued human rights violations against civilians and reiterated its firm condemnation of all violations of human rights and humanitarian law in SCR 1933.[44] In addition, the resolution provided a specific mandate for UNOCI until 31 December 2010 in order to support the parties to implement the Ouagadougou Political Agreement. The mandate requires UNOCI to monitor armed groups, to protect civilians, to monitor the arms embargo, to contribute to the promotion and protection of human rights with special attention to violations committed against children and women with a view to ending impunity, to provide support for humanitarian assistance and to support the organisation of fair and transparent elections. The Security Council also requested the Secretary-General to continue to take the necessary measures to ensure full compliance by UNOCI with the United Nations zero tolerance policy on sexual exploitation and abuses; to keep the Council informed and to urge troop contributing countries to take appropriate preventative action and action to ensure full accountability in cases involving their personnel.

The fourth resolution adopted by the Security Council provided a temporary increase in the level of military and police personnel of UNOCI from 8,650 to 9,150 for a period of up to 6 months.[45] The fifth resolution was passed in October 2010.[46] SCR 1946 once more noted with concern the persistent reports of human rights and humanitarian law violations against civilians. The Security Council decided to renew the measures found in SCR 1572[47] which requires states to prevent the direct or indirect supply, sale or transfer to Côte d'Ivoire of arms or related materials until 30 April 2011.[48] The resolution makes unambiguous, the Security Council's determination that it is fully prepared to impose targeted

---

[42] UN Doc. S/Res. 1924 (2010), 27 May 2010.

[43] UN Doc. S/2010/245, 20 May 2010.

[44] UN Doc. S/Res. 1933 (2010), 30 June 2010.

[45] UN Doc. S/Res. 1942 (2010), 29 September 2010.

[46] UN Doc. S/Res. 1946 (2010), 15 October 2010.

[47] UN Doc. S/Res. 1572 (2004), 15 November 2004, para 7.

[48] UN Doc. S/Res. 1946 (2010), 15 October 2010, para 1.

measures against persons responsible for attacking or obstructing the work of UNOCI and those responsible for serious violations of human rights and international humanitarian law.

8.3.1.4 Democratic Republic of Congo

The Security Council met several times to consider the long-standing armed conflict taking place in the Democratic Republic of Congo. In April, the Special Representative for the DRC and the head of the United Nations Organisation Mission in the Democratic Republic of Congo (MONUC), Alan Dross, briefed the Council on the progress made by the Mission. He stated that progress had been made in protecting the civilian population, disarmament, repatriation and re-integration of armed Congolese and foreign groups, although not consistently across all areas.[49]

In May, the Security Council adopted Resolution 1925[50] expressing great concern for the humanitarian and human rights situation and condemned the targeted attacks against the civilian population, widespread sexual violence and recruitment and use of child soldiers. It stressed the urgent need for the Government of the DRC to end violations of human rights and international humanitarian law, fight impunity and bring the perpetrators to justice. The Security Council also considered the report of the Secretary General[51] and agreed that the DRC was entering a new phase of its transition towards peace consolidation. In its operative paragraph the Council, acting under Chapter VII, decided to extend the mandate of MONUC until 30 June 2010[52] and further decided that in view of the new phase which has been reached, that MONUC would now bear the new title of the United Nations Organisation Stabilization Mission in the Democratic Republic of the Congo (MONUSCO). The resolution provides that MONUSCO would be deployed until 30 June 2011 with a mandate to protect civilians under imminent threat of physical violence emanating from any of the parties engaged in the conflict and is required to take the leading role in stabilisation and peace consolidation.

A further briefing was provided to the Security Council by the Assistant Secretary-General for Peacekeeping (Atul Khare) and the Special Representative on Sexual Violence (Margot Wallstrom) following the mass rapes in North Kivu.[53] Margot Wallstrom reported that the rapes seemed planned and part of a concerted military operation and urged the Council to impose targeted sanctions against the commanders of the armed groups responsible for the gross violations. The

[49] UN Doc. S/PV.6297, 13 April 2010.

[50] UN Doc. S/Res. 1925, 28 May 2010.

[51] UN Doc. S/2010/164, 30 March 2010.

[52] UN Doc. S/Res. 1925, 28 May 2010, para 1.

[53] UN Doc. S/PV.6378, 7 September 2010.

President of the Security Council issued a statement in September reiterating its strong condemnation of the rapes and called upon the Government of the DRC to condemn the atrocities and put an end to impunity.[54]

The second resolution adopted by the Council condemned the continuing illicit flow of weapons within and into the DRC.[55] Acting under Chapter VII the Security Council renewed the arms embargo imposed by SCR 1807[56] until November 2011.

8.3.1.5 Iraq

The Security Council adopted one resolution in respect to Iraq that referred to international humanitarian law. Resolution 1936 extended the mandate of the United Nations Assistance Mission for Iraq (UNAMI) until July 2011.[57] The Council also urged all those concerned, as set forth in international humanitarian law, including the Geneva Conventions and the Hague Regulations, to allow full unimpeded access by humanitarian personnel to all people in need of assistance, and to make available, as far as possible, all necessary facilities for their operations, and to promote the safety, security, and freedom of movement of humanitarian personnel and United Nations and its associated personnel and their assets.

8.3.1.6 Somalia

Given the continuing instability in Somalia, there was significant activity on the part of the Security Council. The first[58] of four resolutions was adopted on 28 January which, in its preamble reiterated its serious concern at the fighting in Somalia and expressed its condemnation in the strongest terms of all acts of violence or abuses committed against civilians in violation of international humanitarian law and human rights law. In its operative paragraphs the Council decided to authorise the Member States of the African Union (AU) to maintain the African Union Mission to Somalia (AMISOM) until January 2011.[59] It also requested the AU to increase its force strength with a view to achieving the originally mandated strength of 8,000 troops.

The second resolution was unanimously adopted in March. In SCR 1916[60] the Council condemned the continuing flow of weapons and ammunition supplies to

---

54 UN Doc. S/PRST/2010/17, 17 September 2010.

55 UN Doc. S/Res. 1952, 29 November 2010.

56 UN Doc. S/Res. 1807, 31 March 2008.

57 UN Doc. S/Res. 1936, 5 August 2010.

58 UN Doc. S/Res. 1910, 28 January 2010.

59 Ibid., para 1.

60 UN Doc. S/Res. 1916, 19 March 2010.

and through Somalia and Eritrea in violation of the arms embargo.[61] The resolution called on all states to comply fully with the arms embargo and extended by 12 months the mandate of the group monitoring those measures. In addition, the mandate of the Monitoring Group was expanded and a further three experts were provided.[62]

The two remaining resolutions adopted by the Security Council concern the piracy situation off the Somali coast. In SCR 1918[63] the Council stated that it continued to be gravely concerned by the threat of piracy and armed robbery at sea against vessels. As a result it called on all states to criminalise piracy under their domestic law and consider the prosecution and imprisonment of convicted pirates apprehended off the coast of Somalia. In August, the President of the Security Council issued a statement[64] in which it welcomed the report[65] of the Secretary-General on possible options to further the aim of prosecuting and imprisoning those responsible for acts of piracy and also welcomed the intention of the Secretary-General to appoint a Special Adviser on Legal Issues Related to Piracy off the Coast of Somalia. In Resolution 1950,[66] the Council once again renewed its call upon states and regional organisations to take part in the fight against piracy.

8.3.1.7 Sudan

The Security Council adopted three resolutions on Sudan in 2010. On 29 April, SCR 1919[67] was adopted extending the mandate of the UN Mission in Sudan (UNMIS) for a further year. The resolution deplored the persistent localised conflict and violence and its effect on civilians, especially within Southern Sudan and called on UNMIS to make full use of its authority to provide improved security to the civilian population.

A further resolution[68] was adopted on 30 July 2010, which expressed deep concern at the deterioration in the security situation in Darfur and demanded that all parties immediately end violence, attacks on civilians, peacekeepers, humanitarian personnel and comply with their obligations under human rights and international humanitarian law. The resolution extended the mandate of the UN Assistance Mission in Darfur (UNAMID) for a further twelve months until 31 July 2011.

---

61 First imposed in UN Doc. S/Res 733, 23 January 1992.

62 UN Doc. S/Res. 1916, 19 March 2010, para 6.

63 UN Doc. S/Res. 1918, 27 April 2010.

64 UN Doc. S/PRST/2010/16, 25 August 2010.

65 UN Doc (S/2010/394).

66 UN Doc. S/Res. 1950, 23 November 2010.

67 UN Doc. S/Res. 1919, 29 April 2010.

68 UN Doc. S/Res. 1935, 30 July 2010.

The final resolution was passed in October 2010.[69] The Security Council once again demanded an immediate and complete cessation of all acts of sexual violence against civilians, recruitment and use of children and indiscriminate attacks on civilians by all parties to the armed conflict. Resolution 1945 also extended the mandate of the Panel of Experts to 19 October 2011 in order to continue monitoring the arms embargo and sanctions on those who impede peace in Sudan.

8.3.1.8 Peacekeeping operations and missions

There are currently 15 UN peacekeeping operations across the world, the majority of which had their mandate extended by Security Council Resolutions in 2010.[70]

Peacekeeping operations have been on the agenda for both the Security Council and the General Assembly. In June 2010 the General Assembly held a thematic debate entitled 'UN Peacekeeping—Looking into the future' to mark the tenth anniversary of the Brahimi Report. The debate addressed the political dimensions of peacekeeping as well as the nexus between security and development to peacebuilding.[71]

In August 2010 the Security Council was briefed by force commanders from missions in Liberia, Sudan, Haiti, the DRC and the Head of the Truce Supervision organisation. The Force Commanders provided a survey of development on their respective missions and stressed to the Security Council the need to address the gap between mandated activity and available resources.[72]

In January, the Department of Peacekeeping Operations (DPKO) and the Department of Field Support (DFS) issued its Interim Standard Operating Procedures on Detention in United Nations Peace Operations. The purpose of the Interim SOPs is to ensure that that persons detained by UN personnel in UN peace operations are handled humanely and in a manner that is consistent with applicable international human right, humanitarian and refugee law, norms and standards. The SOPs is due to be reviewed in January 2011.

DPKO and DFS also issued its first update paper entitled '*The New Horizon Initiative; Progress Report No. 1*' in October. The New Horizon initiative was launched in order to assess the major policy and strategy dilemmas faced by UN Peacekeeping operations and to reinvigorate dialogue with stakeholders. The paper provides an overview of the principal outcomes of the peacekeeping dialogue and implementation efforts in the context of the New Horizon process, as well as ongoing efforts to improve the effectiveness of United Nations peacekeeping.[73]

---

[69] UN Doc. S/Res. 1945, 14 October 2010.

[70] UN Doc. S/Res. 1912 (UNMIT), UN Doc. S/Res. 1941 (UNIPSIL), UN Doc. S/Res. 1927 (MINUSTAH), UN Doc. S/Res. 1937 (UNIFIL), UN Doc. S/Res 1938 (UNMIL).

[71] GA, 64th Meeting, 22 June 2010.

[72] SC, 6370th Meeting, 6 August 2010.

[73] The New Horizon Initiative; Progress Report No. 1, October 2010.

8.3.2 Human Rights Council

In February a joint Study on global practices in relation to secret detention in the context of countering terrorism was released by the Special Rapporteur on the promotion of and protection of human rights and fundamental freedoms while countering terrorism, the Special Rapporteur on torture and other cruel, inhuman or degrading treatment or punishment, the Working Group on arbitrary detention and the Working Group on enforced or involuntary disappearances.[74] The aim of the Study was to examine policy and legal decisions taken by states and 'to illustrate what it means to be secretly detained, how secret detention can facilitate the practice of torture or inhuman and degrading treatment, and how the practice of secret detention has left an indelible mark on the victims and on their families'. The Study concludes that such practice is 'irreconcilably in violation of international human rights law, including during state of emergency and armed conflict'.

In conceding that the right to detain is significantly broader in IHL than IHR, the Study nevertheless observes that the entire system of detention provided for by the Geneva Conventions is founded on the notion that detainees must be registered and held in officially recognized places of detention. Article 70 of the Third Geneva Convention requires that prisoners of war are documented and their whereabouts and health conditions made available to family members and to the country of origin within 1 week. Similarly, Article 106 of the Fourth Geneva Convention establishes near identical procedures for documentation and disclosure of information concerning civilian detainees. However, Article 5 of the Convention permits the detaining power to deny to persons these rights and privileges 'where absolute military security so requires' when an individual found physically in the state's own territory is 'definitely suspected of or engaged in activities hostile to the security of the State' or when an individual in occupied territory is 'detained as a spy or saboteur, or as a person under definite suspicion of activity hostile to the security of the Occupying Power'. Citing the ICRC, the Study emphasizes the exceptional nature of Article 5 which may only be applied on a case by case basis.

8.3.3 The International Criminal Court

On 12 July, the ICC issued a second arrest warrant for President Omar al-Bashir of Sudan on three counts of genocide committed in Darfur.[75] This warrant followed an initial warrant filed against al-Bashir in March 2009, on two counts of war crimes and five counts of crimes against humanity, which made al-Bashir the first sitting head of state to be charged by the ICC. The second warrant is similarly

[74] A/HRC/13/42.

[75] Available at www.icc-cpi.int.

groundbreaking in that it is the first time that the ICC has issued an arrest warrant on a count of genocide. Although Sudan is not party to the Rome Statute, it is nonetheless obligated by SCR 1593 to 'cooperate fully with the Court and Prosecutor, providing them with any necessary assistance'.[76] However, to date, the ICC has been unable to enforce its warrants against al-Bashir.

On 31 March, Pre-Trial Chamber II, by a majority, granted the Prosecutor's request to commence an investigation on crimes against humanity allegedly committed in the Republic of Kenya that took place between 1 June 2005 (the date of entry into force of the statute for Kenya) and 26 November 2009 (the date of the filing of the Request).[77] The evidence presented to the Trial Chamber satisfied the requisite threshold—that it provides a 'reasonable basis' to believe that crimes against humanity have been committed on Kenyan territory.

During the ICC's Review Conference in Kampala (31 May–11 June), the Conference adopted a resolution amending the Rome Statute to include a definition of the crime of aggression and the conditions under which the ICC can exercise jurisdiction over this crime. The actual exercise of jurisdiction is subject to a decision to be taken after 1 January 2017 by the same majority of States Parties as is required for the adoption of an amendment to the Statute.

The definition of aggression agreed by the Conference is based on the UN GAR 3314 of 14 December 1974 and provides:

'1. For the purpose of this Statute, "crime of aggression" means the planning, preparation, initiation or execution, by a person in a position effectively to exercise control over or to direct the political or military action of a state, of an act of aggression which, by its character, gravity and scale, constitutes a manifest violation of the Charter of the United Nations.

2. For the purpose of paragraph 1, "act of aggression" means the use of armed force by a State against the sovereignty, territorial integrity or political independence of another State, or in any other manner inconsistent with the Charter of the United Nations. Any of the following acts, regardless of a declaration of war, shall, in accordance with United Nations General Assembly resolution 3314 (XXIX) of 14 December 1974, qualify as an act of aggression:

(a) The invasion or attack by the armed forces of a State of the territory of another State, or any military occupation, however, temporary, resulting from such invasion or attack, or any annexation by the use of force of the territory of another State or part thereof;
(b) Bombardment by the armed forces of a State against the territory of another State or the use of any weapons by a State against the territory of another State;
(c) The blockade of the ports or coasts of a State by the armed forces of another State;

[76] S/RES/1593 (2005) of 31 March 2005.

[77] Decision of the Pre-Trial Chamber II Pursuant to Article 15 of the Rome Statute, 31 March 2010, ICC-01/09.

(d) An attack by the armed forces of a State on the land, sea or air forces, or marine and air fleets of another State;
(e) The use of armed forces of one State which are within the territory of another State with the agreement of the receiving State, in contravention of the conditions provided for in the agreement or any extension of their presence in such territory beyond the termination of the agreement;
(f) The action of a State in allowing its territory, which it has placed at the disposal of another State, to be used by that other State for perpetrating an act of aggression against a third State;
(g) The sending by or on behalf of a State of armed bands, groups, irregulars or mercenaries, which carry out acts of armed force against another State of such gravity as to amount to the acts listed above, or its substantial involvement therein.'

Insofar as the Court's exercise of jurisdiction is concerned, it was agreed that a situation in which an act of aggression appeared to have occurred could be referred to the Court by the Security Council, acting under Chapter VII; alternatively, in the absence of a determination by the Council that a situation amounting to aggression existed, the Prosecutor would be entitled to initiate an investigation or do so upon request from a State Party. However, this would be subject to a prior authorization from the Pre-Trial Chamber. Moreover, the Court would not have jurisdiction in respect to crimes of aggression committed on the territory of non-States Parties or by their nationals or with regard to States Parties that had declared that they did not accept the Court's jurisdiction over the crime of aggression.

The Conference also adopted a resolution by which it amended Article 8 of the Rome Statute to bring under the Court's jurisdiction the war crime of employing certain poisonous weapons and expanding bullets, asphyxiating or poisonous gases, and all analogous liquids, materials and devices, when committed in armed conflicts not of an international character.[78]

8.4 Regional Organizations

8.4.1 Council of Europe

8.4.1.1 The European Court of Human Rights (ECtHR)

During 2010, the ECtHR rendered a number of judgments in relation to the conflict in Chechnya. In *Suleymanova* v *Russia* the ECtHR found for the applicant in holding that Article 2, which safeguards the right to life and sets out the circumstances where deprivation of life may be justified, had been violated despite

[78] Geiß, this volume pp 337–352.

the existence of an armed conflict.[79] In rejecting the Government's claim that the use of lethal force 'in the course of a counter-terrorist operation' had been no more than 'absolutely necessary', the Court held that 'the use of lethal force had not been accounted for and therefore the Court was not persuaded that the killings constituted a use of force which was no more than absolutely necessary in pursuit of the aims in Article 2'.

In a series of cases relating to disappearances of civilians in the Chechnya conflict, the Court has found Russia in violation of Articles 2, 3, 5 and 13 which concern the right to life, the prohibition against inhuman or degrading treatment, the right to liberty and security and the right to an effective remedy, respectively.[80] Having regard to the previous cases concerning disappearances in Chechnya in the context of the armed conflict, the Court held that 'when a person is detained by unidentified servicemen without any subsequent acknowledgment of the detention this can be regarded as life-threatening'.[81]

8.4.2 Organization of American States

On 8 June, the General Assembly of the Organisation of American States passed a resolution entitled *Promotion of and Respect for International Humanitarian Law*.[82] The Resolution urges member states to honour and fulfil their obligations under international humanitarian law and urges the member states to become parties to the following treaties:

a. The Convention for the Protection of Cultural Property in Time of Armed Conflict (Hague Convention 1954), and its Protocols of 1954 and 1999;
b. The 1968 Convention on the Non-Applicability of Statutory Limitations to War Crimes and Crimes against Humanity;
c. The 1972 Convention on the Prohibition of the Development, Production and Stockpiling of Bacteriological (Biological) and Toxin Weapons and on Their Destruction (Biological Weapons Convention);
d. The 1977 Protocols I and II Additional to the Geneva Conventions of 1949, as well as Additional Protocol III, of 2005, including the declaration contained in Article 90 of Additional Protocol I;

---

[79] *Suleymanova* v *Russia* (9191/06) Judgment 12 May 2010, para 81.

[80] *Guluyeva and Others* v *Russia* (1675/07) Judgment of 11 February; *Dubayev and Bersnukayeva* v *Russia* (30613/05 and 30615/05) Judgments of 11 February; *Suleymanova* v *Russia* (9191/06) Judgment 12 May 2010; *Ilyasova* v *Russia* (26966/06) Judgment 10 June 2010; *Gelayevy* v *Russia* (20216/07) Judgment 15 July 2010; *Akhmatkhanovy* v *Russia* (20147/07) Judgment 22 July 2010; *Dzhabirailova and Dzhabirailova* v *Russia* (15563/06) Judgment 2 December 2010; *Tumayeva and others* v *Russia* (9960/05) Judgment 16 December 2010.
UN Doc. GA/Res. 64/48, 28 October 2009.

[81] *Shakhabova* v *Russia* (39685/06) Judgment 12 May 2010, para 101.

[82] Organisation of American States, AG/RES.2575 (XL-O/10), 8 June 2010.

e. The Convention on Prohibitions or Restrictions on the Use of Certain Conventional Weapons Which May Be Deemed to Be Excessively Injurious or to Have Indiscriminate Effects (CCW) of 1980, including the amendment to Article 1 thereof, adopted in 2001, and the five protocols thereto;
f. The 1989 Convention on the Rights of the Child and the 2000 Optional Protocol thereto on the involvement of children in armed conflict;
g. The 1993 Convention on the Prohibition of the Development, Production, Stockpiling and Use of Chemical Weapons and on Their Destruction (Chemical Weapons Convention);
h. The 1997 Convention on the Prohibition of the Use, Stockpiling, Production and Transfer of Anti-Personnel Mines and on Their Destruction (Ottawa Convention);
i. The 1998 Rome Statute of the International Criminal Court; and
j. The International Convention for the Protection of All Persons from Enforced Disappearance.

It also urges member states to adjust their criminal law in order to meet their obligations under the 1949 Geneva Conventions and, in the case of the states parties to the 1977 Additional Protocol I and the Rome Statute of the International Criminal Court, with respect to the definition of war crimes, universal jurisdiction for these grave breaches, and the responsibility of superiors for the acts of their subordinates, among other pertinent provisions. The resolution further urges member states to adopt all necessary measures to comply with their respective international obligations regarding the recruitment and use of children in armed forces or armed groups and to prevent their participation in hostilities, in accordance with rules and principles of international humanitarian law.

In June, the General Assembly of the Organisation of American States adopted a resolution entitled *Protecting Human Rights and Fundamental Freedoms while Countering Terrorism*[83] which reaffirmed that member states have a duty to ensure that all measures adopted to combat terrorism must be in compliance with international humanitarian law. Further, that states should respect the safeguards concerning the liberty, security, safety and dignity of the person and to treat prisoners in all places of detention in accordance with applicable international law, including human rights law and international humanitarian law.

8.4.3 *African Union*

The Assembly of the African Union in its decision on the Accession of the African countries to the Convention on banning the use of Certain Conventional Weapons with a traumatic effect or which strike indiscriminately[84] invited African states to

[83] Organisation of American States, AG/RES.2580 (XL-O/10) 8 June 2010.

[84] African Union, Assembly Decision 321 (XV) adopted by the fifteenth ordinary session of the Assembly, 27 July 2010, Kampala, Uganda.

accede to this Convention in order to strengthen their contribution to the building and consolidation of international humanitarian law.

8.5 Arms Control and Disarmament

8.5.1 Conventional weapons

8.5.1.1 Small arms and light weapons

Important progress was made in 2010 on the General Assembly resolution[85] concerning the Arms Trade Treaty. The first two Arms Trade Treaty Preparatory Committees were held in July 2010 which considered the elements, guiding principles, goals and objectives, scope, implementation and application of the treaty. The Chair of the Preparatory Committee released a series of papers on treaty elements, principles, goals and objectives which will form the basis of further negotiations at the next Preparatory Committee meeting to take place in February 2011.

Another important development in April 2010 was the consensus on the Kinshasa Convention (otherwise known as the Central Africa Convention for the Control of Small Arms and Light Weapons, their Ammunition, Parts and Components that can be used for their Manufacture, Repair and Assembly) by the United Nations Standing Advisory Committee on Security Questions in Central Africa (UNSAC). This fills a void that provides Central Africa with a legally binding instrument combating the proliferation of small arms and light weapons. In November, at the 31st meeting of UNSAC, the Kinshasa Convention was signed by eight Central African nations (Angola, Cameroon, the Democratic Republic of Congo, Chad, Gabon, the Central African Republic, the Republic of Congo and Sao Tome and Principe). The Kinshasa Convention requires six countries to ratify the Convention before it can come into force. The Convention contains a preamble and nine chapters reflecting the latest developments in the regulation of the trade in small arms and light weapons.[86] The main provisions of the Kinshasa Convention include:

- Authorised transfers between States, subjecting them to strict control exercised by the relevant national authorities.
- The possession of light weapons is prohibited to civilians, and the possession of small arms is subject to an authorisation (licence) delivered by the authorities.
- The manufacture of small arms and light weapons is authorised but subject to control.

[85] UN Doc. GA/Res. 64/48, 28 October 2009.

[86] UN Doc. A/65/176, 28 July 2010.

- National and sub-regional databases must be established and allow for information exchange.
- A tracing mechanism must be established and States are required to limit the number of entry points of weapons on their national territory.[87]

8.5.1.2 Convention on Cluster Munitions

In February the United Nations received the thirtieth instrument of ratification for the Convention on Cluster Munitions. With this step, the Convention entered into force on 1 August 2010, 2 years after its adoption.

8.5.2 Nuclear weapons

8.5.2.1 New Start Treaty and Protocol

In April the United States of America and Russia signed the New Start Treaty which replaces the Strategic Arms Reduction Treaty of 1991. The Treaty commits each party to reduce the number of deployed strategic warheads to 1,550. It also limits the number of deployed delivery vehicles, ballistic missiles and heavy bombers to 700.

8.5.2.2 Review Conference—Treaty on the Non-Proliferation of Nuclear Weapons

In May the States Party to the Treaty on the Non-proliferation of Nuclear Weapons met to review the treaty at the UN Headquarters. A total of 172 states participated in the conference which concluded with a 64 point plan for further action addressing the three pillars of the Treaty, namely; disarmament, non-proliferation and peaceful uses of nuclear energy. The unanimously adopted outcome also contains steps to guide progress on nuclear disarmament, advance non-proliferation and work towards a nuclear-weapon-free zone in the Middle East. The Conference resolved that the nuclear-weapon states commit to further efforts to reduce and eliminate all types of deployed and non-deployed nuclear weapons, including through unilateral, bilateral, regional and multilateral measures. A separate section of the document focused on the Middle East, specifically on implementation of the 1995 Review Conference's resolution on the Middle East.

---

[87] Kinshasa Convention, 23 November 2010.

The final document[88] also endorsed the convening of the next review conference in 2012.

8.5.2.3 Iran's nuclear program

Iran's nuclear program was again the subject of discussion at the Security Council. Resolution 1929[89] noted with serious concern that Iran has constructed an enrichment facility at Qom in breach of its obligations to suspend all enrichment-related activities. The Resolution affirmed that Iran has so far failed to meet the requirements of the International Atomic Energy Agency (IAEA) and that it shall take the steps required by IAEA to build confidence in the exclusively peaceful purpose of its nuclear programme. It further decided under Article 41 of Chapter VII that Iran shall not undertake any activity related to ballistic missiles capable of delivering nuclear weapons and that states shall take all necessary measures to prevent the transfer of technology or technical assistance to Iran related to such activities.

[88] UN Doc. NPT/CONF.2010/50 (Vol 1).

[89] UN Doc. S/Res 1929, 9 June 2010.

Chapter 9
Drone Attacks under the *Jus ad Bellum* And *Jus in Bello*: Clearing the 'Fog of Law'

Michael N. Schmitt

Contents

9.1 Introduction

As the war in Afghanistan and the fight against transnational terrorism wage on with no immediate end in sight, US forces have increasingly turned to drone (technically labeled an unmanned aircraft system or UAS) strikes to target Taliban insurgents and Al Qaeda terrorists, especially in Pakistan's tribal areas of North and South Waziristan. Between 2004 and 2007, a mere nine such attacks were conducted. By contrast, in 2010 there were 118, and by mid-February 2011 US forces had already launched 12.[1] The tactic has proven highly effective in disrupting enemy operations. Since 2004, 32 senior members of al Qaeda and the Taliban have been killed. In 2010, for instance, the US successfully targeted such key figures as Ibne Amin, an al Qaeda linked Swat Taliban commander; Ali

[1] New American Foundation, The Year of the Drone, available at http://counterterrorism.newamerica.net/drones. For comparable data, see Roggio and Mayer 2011.

M. N. Schmitt (✉)
United States Naval War College, Newport, USA
e-mail: schmitt@aya.yale.edu

M.N. Schmitt et al. (eds.), *Yearbook of International Humanitarian Law Volume 13, 2010*, DOI: 10.1007/978-90-6704-811-8_9,

Marjan, a local Lashkar-e-Islam commander; Sheikh al-Fateh, the al Qaeda chief in Afghanistan and Pakistan; Hamza al-Jufi, an al Qaeda commander; Sadam Hussein Al Hussami, an al Qaeda planner and explosives expert; Mohammad Qari Zafar, a Taliban commander wanted in connection with the 2006 Karachi consulate bombing; Sheikh Mansoor, an Egyptian-Canadian al Qaeda leader; Abdul Haq al-Turkistani, an al Qaeda linked leader of the Turkistani Islamic Party; Jamal Saeed Abdul Rahim, wanted for his alleged role in the 1986 hijacking of a Pan American World Airways flight; and Mahmud Mahdi Zeidan, a Jordanian Taliban commander. Overall, US air strikes are estimated to have killed between 1,060 and 1,707 members of al Qaeda, the Taliban and associated groups in the past 6 years.[2]

Although the drone strikes into Pakistan dominate current headlines, they have been employed elsewhere. The first to draw international attention was a 2002 CIA-operated Predator drone strike against a vehicle in Yemen containing al Qaeda operative Ali Qaed Senyan al-Harithi, who was allegedly involved in the bombing of the USS *Cole*. The CIA reportedly mounted the operation with the consent and cooperation of the Yemeni intelligence agency.[3] Since then, drones have been widely employed in both conventional military operations, such as those in Iraq, and in a counter-terrorism or counter-insurgency mode, as in Somalia.

Despite their evident military utility, controversy has erupted over the operations.[4] The State Department's Legal Adviser, Harold Koh, has asserted that 'U.S. targeting practices, including lethal operations with the use of unmanned aerial vehicles, comply with all applicable law, including the laws of war'.[5] Yet Philip Alston, in his role as Special Rapporteur on Extrajudicial, Summary or Arbitrary Executions, has opined that 'outside the context of armed conflict, the use of drones for targeted killing is almost never likely to be legal'.[6]

Most legal criticism focuses on two issues—the use of drones in other states' territory and the incidental civilian deaths caused by the drone attacks. The former derives from the *jus ad bellum*, that aspect of international law restricting the resort to force by states, whereas the latter is based in the *jus in bello* (international humanitarian law), which governs how combat operations may be conducted.

---

[2] Year of the Drone, supra n 1 (data current to 25 February 2011). See also Roggio and Mayer 2010.

[3] Mayer 2009 p 36; Roggio and Mazzetti 2009, A1.

[4] US House of Representatives, Subcommittee on National Security and Foreign Affairs: Written Testimony of Kenneth Anderson, *Rise of the Drones: Unmanned Systems and the Future of War*, 18 March 2010; Testimony of Kenneth Anderson, *Examining the Legality of Unmanned Targeting*, 28 April 2010; Written Testimony of Mary Ellen O'Connell, Lawful Use of Combat Drones, 28 April 2010.

[5] Harold Koh, The Obama Administration and International Law, Remarks at the Annual Meeting of the American Society of International Law, 25 March 2010, available at http://www.state.gov/s/l/releases/remarks/139119.htm.

[6] Report of the Special Rappoteur on Extrajudicial, Summary or Arbitrary Executions, Study on Targeted Killings, 28 May 2010, UN Doc. A/HRC/14/24/Add. 6, at para 85 (hereinafter Alston Report).

Unfortunately, discourse over these and related issues has evidenced serious misunderstanding of the strictures of international law.

This brief article explores both the *jus ad bellum* and *jus in bello* implications of drone attacks. It is intended to clear the 'fog of law' that surrounds the operations, much of it resulting from either misunderstanding of the weapon system or misinterpretation of the applicable law. The article concludes that there is little reason to treat drones as distinct from other weapons systems with regard to the legal consequences of their employment. Nor is there a sound basis for heightened concern as to their use. On the contrary, the use of drones may actually, in certain cases, enhance the protections to which various persons and objects are entitled under international humanitarian law (IHL).

9.2 Drones

The nature and use of drones varies widely. Most are unarmed and used for intelligence, reconnaissance and surveillance (ISR) functions. For instance, the RQ-11B Raven is a 'man-portable' surveillance and reconnaissance drone which is carried in a backpack and has a flight time of nearly an hour and a half. Particularly useful for special operations, the Raven is operated by two individuals and can either be controlled manually or navigate autonomously along a preplanned route. During daylight, it uses a color electro-optical sensor to transmit images to ground forces; at night it can perform the same function using an infrared camera.[7] By contrast, the RQ-4 Global Hawk is a large high-altitude ISR drone operated by a crew of three located far from the battlefield. The Raven is especially useful because of its range of nearly 9,000 nautical miles and its ability to stay over an area for long periods. Its sensors include synthetic aperture radar and electro-optical and medium-wave infrared cameras, and it will eventually have signals (communications) intelligence gathering capability.[8]

Drones used for ISR raise few legal issues beyond that of where they may fly (such as over flight rights in another country's airspace), a limitation that applies equally to manned aircraft. Rather, it is the use of armed drones which has drawn the ire of critics.

The two most prominent armed drones are the Predator and the Reaper. The MQ-1B Predator is medium altitude drone with a range of nearly 700 nautical miles used for close air support (supporting ground forces), air interdiction (striking specific targets) and ISR missions. It is crewed by a pilot and a weapons and sensor operator located beyond the battlefield. The Predator carries the Multi-

[7] United States Air Force, Factsheet—RQ11B Raven, 14 January 2010, available at http://www.af.mil/information/factsheets/factsheet.asp?fsID=10446.

[8] United States Air Force, Factsheet—RQ-4 Global Hawk, 19 November 2009, available at http://www.af.mil/information/factsheets/factsheet.asp?fsID=13225.

spectral Targeting System, or MTS-A, which contains an infrared sensor, a color/monochrome daylight TV camera, an image-intensified TV camera, a laser designator and a laser illuminator. It is armed with two laser-guided AGM-114 Hellfire missiles, which either guide on the internal laser designator or one used by ground forces. The Hellfire missile is a highly accurate system with the ability to engage both personnel and vehicles or other objects.[9]

The MQ-9 Reaper is also commonly relied on to conduct attacks. A medium-to-high altitude system with a range of over 1,000 nautical miles, it, like the Predator and Global Hawk, has the ability to stay aloft for extended periods. The drone carries the MTS-B, a variant of the system used on the Predator. However, in terms of weaponry, it is more versatile than the Predator. For instance, in addition to a suite of four Hellfire missiles, it is capable of employing the GBU-38 Joint Direct Attack Munitions bomb (JDAM) and such laser guided weapons as the GBU-12 Paveway II.[10]

With reference to conducting attacks, drones afford attackers vastly increased capabilities and dramatically expand the options available to them. ISR drones enhance the ability to verify the nature of a target before striking it with other assets (such as manned aircraft or ground assets), thereby diminishing the likelihood of mistaken attacks. Because the drones provide high quality information about the target area in real-time (or near real time), for extended periods and without risk to the operators, they also permit more refined assessments of the likely collateral damage to civilians and civilian objects. The ability of armed drones to observe the target area for long periods before attacking means the operators are better able to verify the nature of a proposed target and strike only when the opportunity to minimize collateral damage is at its height. Further, the fact that armed drones employ very accurate weapons enhances the likelihood of a successful strike, thereby limiting the need for a restrike on the target, which could risk further collateral damage. Obviously, the use of precision-guided weapons also helps attackers to minimize collateral damage.

9.3 The *Jus ad Bellum*

The *jus ad bellum* governs the resort to force by states. Article 2(4) of the UN Charter provides that '[a]ll Members [of the United Nations] shall refrain in their international relations from the threat or use of force against the territorial integrity or political independence of any state, or in any manner inconsistent with the

[9] United States Air Force, Factsheet—MQ-1B Predator, 20 July 2010, available at http://www.af.mil/information/factsheets/factsheet.asp?fsID=122.

[10] United States Air Force, Factsheet—MQ-9 Reaper, 18 August 2010, available at http://www.af.mil/information/factsheets/factsheet.asp?fsID=6405.

Purposes of the United Nations'. This treaty norm is reflective of customary international law and is of a *jus cogens* nature.[11] Reduced to basics, any military action by one state on another's territory which is not otherwise justified in international law is unquestionably a violation of the prohibition.

It is indisputable that one state may employ force in another with the consent of that state.[12] For instance, a state embroiled in an internal conflict with insurgents may request external assistance in restoring order. Contemporary examples include the ongoing US assistance to Iraq and NATO operations in support of the Afghan government. Additionally, a state may consent to defensive operations in its territory by another state, as in the cases of Pakistan, Yemen and Somalia sometimes assenting to US counter-terrorist strikes in their countries.[13] Of course, the territorial state may only grant consent to operations that it could itself legally conduct. Thus, the territorial state cannot lawfully allow attacks that would violate applicable human rights or humanitarian law norms, since it does not itself enjoy such authority.

The legal dilemma arises when the operations are conducted without the territorial state's acquiescence. Pakistan has objected, for instance, to certain of the US drone strikes on the basis that it did not grant prior consent.[14] Similarly, Lebanon protested when Israel mounted large scale operations against Hezbollah forces ensconced in the south of the country in 2006,[15] and the Republic of Congo brought the issue of Ugandan counter-insurgent forays into its territory before the International Court of Justice.[16]

Since the Peace of Westphalia in 1648, sovereignty and the derivative notion of territorial integrity have served as foundational principles of international law. By them, a state enjoys near absolute control over access to its territory. In affirmation, the UN General Assembly has unanimously cited the use of force by a state on the territory of another as an act of aggression.[17] Sovereignty is so essential to the structure of international law that even the lawfulness of intervention to stop an on-going genocide is of questionable legality.

The right of states to use force in self-defense, a customary law right enshrined in Article 51 of the UN Charter, is no less foundational. Article 51 provides that

---

11 See discussion of the issue by the International Court of Justice in Military and Paramilitary Activities in and Against Nicaragua (*Nicaragua* v *US*), 1986 ICJ Rep. 14, paras 187–191 (27 June) (hereinafter *Nicaragua*); On the *jus cogens* nature of the norm, see Draft Articles on the Law of Treaties, Report of the International Law Commission, 18th Session [1996] II ILC Yearbook p 247.

12 Accord, Alston Report, supra n 6, para 35.

13 See e.g., Schmitt and Mazzetti 2009, p 14; Warrick and Finn 2010, p A1.

14 See e.g., Lander 2009, p A9.

15 See discussion in Schmitt 2008a p 127.

16 Armed Activities on the Territory of the Congo (*Dem. Rep. Congo* v *Uganda*), 2005 ICJ Rep. 116 (19 December).

17 Definition of Aggression, GA Res. 3314 (XXIX), UN GAOR 6th Comm., 29th Sess., 2319th plen. mtg., Annex, UN Doc. A/RES/3314 (XXIX) (1975).

'[n]othing in the present Charter shall impair the inherent right of individual or collective self-defence if an armed attack occurs against a Member of the United Nations, until the Security Council has taken measures necessary to maintain international peace and security'. The United States has justified its drone operations occurring outside the context of an armed conflict with another state on the basis of this right.[18] Yet the right of states to act defensively is not unfettered. When terrorists or insurgents seek sanctuary in another state, the right of the victim state to conduct drone or other military operations against them must be tempered by the territorial state's undeniable right to control access to, and activities on, its territory.

International law does not require an either-or resolution of these counterpoised norms. Rather, when principles clash, law seeks that accommodation which best achieves their respective underlying purposes. Although the territorial state need not suffer unconstrained violations of its borders, neither does the victim state have to sit idly by while insurgents and terrorists attack it with impunity from abroad.

A fair balancing of the rights yields a sequential process. The victim state must first ask the sanctuary state to meet its legal duty to ensure its territory is not used to harm other states.[19] If that state complies and is mounting effective operations to remove the threat, then penetration of its territory by the victim state's forces is impermissible. This follows from the principle of necessity, which, together with the principle of proportionality, has been recognized by the International Court of Justice as conditioning the right of self-defence.[20] Necessity requires that no viable alternative to the use of force exist before a state may defend itself forcefully against an armed attack. Therefore, when law enforcement or other measures by the territorial state will serve to safeguard the victim-state from further attacks, its right to resort to military force in self-defence has not matured. Although the concept of necessity is usually conceived of in terms of alternatives available to the state which has fallen victim to an armed attack, there is no reason to limit application to actions taken by that state. The fact that a non-consensual penetration of another state's territory violates that state's sovereign prerogatives reinforces this broader interpretation of the necessity principle.

But if, after being afforded an opportunity to do so, the territorial state fails to take appropriate action, either because it lacks the capability to conduct the operations or simply chooses not to do so (e.g., out of sympathy for the terrorists), the victim state may act militarily in self-defense, including through the use of drones, to put an end to the unlawful activities.[21] Were this not the case,

---

[18] Koh Statement, supra n 5.

[19] On the duty to police one's own territory, see *Corfu Channel* (UK v *Albania*), 1949 ICJ Rep. 4 (9 April).

[20] *Nicaragua*, supra n 11, at 103; Legality of the Threat or Use of Nuclear Weapons, Advisory Opinion, 1996 ICJ Rep. 226, at 245 (8 July); *Oil Platforms* (*Iran* v *US*), 2003 ICJ Rep. 161, at 183, 196–198 (6 November); Congo, supra n 16, p 53.

[21] Accord, Alston Report, supra n 6, para 35. For a more detailed discussion of this approach, see Schmitt 2008b, p 1.

international law would effectively deprive the victim state of any meaningful ability to protect itself.

It is essential to highlight the likely possibility that the territorial state may be willing to conduct actions against the terrorists or insurgents but nevertheless be unable to do so in general or with regard to specific cases. The use of drones is particularly relevant in such circumstances since they often represent a way to react quickly to perishable intelligence or to reach otherwise inaccessible areas. For instance, the territorial state may not have air assets capable of reaching remote areas where terrorists or insurgents are located or, if they do, may not be able to strike them either in a timely fashion (e.g., before they move on) or with sufficient precision to ensure mission success. In these circumstances, the absence of territorial state consent cannot bar action by the victim state, since to do so would be to eviscerate the latter's right of self-defence.

The *jus ad bellum* requirement of proportionality also limits defensive options available to the victim state. Proportionality requires that a state acting defensively employ no more force than reasonably required to overcome a threat. In the context of cross-border operations, this requirement limits the scale and nature of the force employed. For instance, if targeted drone strikes against terrorist camps would suffice to damp down further attacks, it would be unlawful to mount large scale ground operations into the territorial state. The limitation is equally geographical. It would, for example, be unlawful to deploy forces into locations void of terrorists or insurgents. Finally, cross-border operations must be temporally limited in the sense that withdrawal or cessation is required once the threat has been extinguished.

Until the attacks of September 11, 2001, the right of self-defense had been perceived by most experts as applicable only to armed attacks by one state against another. Attacks conducted by non-state entities such as terrorists were deemed matters for law enforcement. This understanding changed overnight. In response to the 9/11 attacks, the UN Security Council, international organizations such as NATO and many individual states took actions that could only be characterized as acknowledging the right of self-defense through military force to counter transnational terrorism.[22] This understanding was subsequently confirmed when Israel attacked Hezbollah in 2006. As with Operation Enduring Freedom, the armed response to 9/11 in Afghanistan, the international community generally acknowledged Israel's right to defend itself against Hezbollah in Operation Change Direction, even though conducted in Lebanon (although some criticized the operation as violating the principle of proportionality).[23]

---

[22] See e.g., UN SC Res. 1368 (12 September 2001); UN SC Res.1372 (28 September 2001); Press Release, North Atlantic Council, 12 September 2001, available at www.nato.int/docu/pr/2001/p01-124e.htm. On the reactions of States and international organizations, see Schmitt 2008, pp 9–11.

[23] See e.g., Kofi Annan, Secretary-General Statement to the Security Council, UN SCOR, 61st Sess., 5492 mtg. at 3, UN Doc. S/PV.5492 (20 July 2006).

Curiously, the International Court of Justice has twice ignored recent state practice by issuing opinions that seemingly require control over such groups by a state before their victim can resort to force in self-defense (as distinct from law enforcement).[24] The opinions have been roundly, and correctly, criticized, and in the key case on the subject three of the Court's judges authored compelling separate opinions condemning that aspect of the holding.[25] While the Court's stance is flawed, its apparent reticence to embrace a robust notion of self-defense is understandable. As with many other international legal norms, the right of self-defense is subject to abuse; indeed, most aggressors tend to couch their unlawful actions in the language of self-defense.

It should be noted that in the event of an international armed conflict (a conflict between states), the law of neutrality provides a separate basis for cross border strikes against armed groups that 'belong' to the opposing party, that is, which 'conduct hostilities on behalf and with the agreement of that party'.[26] Neutral territory may not be used for belligerent purposes and neutral states are obliged to ensure the non-use of their territory for said purposes. This is a longstanding customary law norm which was reflected during the last century in the 1907 Hague Conventions V and XIII, as well as the non-binding Hague Rules of Aerial Warfare.[27]

If a neutral is unable or unwilling to prevent the use of its territory by a belligerent or groups which 'belong' to it, and the consequences of violation of neutral territory are serious, the opposing belligerent party may use force, in the absence of reasonably effective non-forceful measures, to put an end to the misuse of neutral territory to its detriment.[28] The degree of force used cannot exceed that which is necessary to terminate the misuse. Since the use of drones is far less invasive than, for instance, land operations, resort to drones may actually be required by the law of neutrality in certain circumstances. Although the law of neutrality only bears on international armed conflicts, it is reasonable to extend this general approach into non-international armed conflicts that spill-over into neighboring states. The legal basis for doing so is the law of self-defence.

---

[24] Legal Consequences of the Construction of a Wall in the Occupied Palestinian Territory, Advisory Opinion, 2004 ICJ Rep. 136, at 194 (9 July); *Congo*, supra n 16, p 53.

[25] Wall, supra n 24: Sep. Op. Judge Higgins, para 33; Sep. Op. Judge Kooijmans, para 35; Decl. Judge Buergenthal, para 6.

[26] Because the armed groups belong to a belligerent party, their passage into neutral territory is the equivalent of the crossing into that territorial by the armed forces of that party. On the notion of belonging to, see Melzer 2009, p 23.

[27] Convention Respecting the Rights and Duties of Neutral Powers and Persons in Case of War on Land, 18 October 1907, 36 Stat. 2310, 1 Bevans 654; Convention Concerning the Rights and Duties of Neutral Powers in Naval War, 18 October 1907, 205 Consol. T.S. 395, 1 Bevans 723; 1923 Hague Rules of Aerial Warfare, reprinted in AJIL 17, (1923) Supplement 245. For a contemporary adoption of these principles, see Harvard Program on Humanitarian Policy and Conflict Research, Commentary on the HPCR Manual on International Law Applicable to Air and Missile Warfare, Section X (2010) (hereinafter AMW Manual).

[28] AMW Manual, supra n 27, Rule 168(b).

9.4 The *Jus in Bello*

The *jus in bello*, or international humanitarian law, applies only in the event of an armed conflict, whether international or non-international. When operations do not rise to this level, they will be governed by applicable domestic and human rights norms.[29] Two major legal obstacles stand in the way of clarity in this regard. First, the extraterritorial application of human rights norms is a matter of some controversy. Generally, they are viewed as applicable only to areas under the control of a state conducting the operation in question, with some states, such as the United States and Israel, more broadly denying their extraterritorial effect.[30] Second, it is uncertain whether transnational terrorism without any nexus to an ongoing conflict constitutes an "armed conflict" as a matter of law, even when it is of sufficient intensity to otherwise rise to that level. One school of thought argues that it does not and is instead merely highly violent criminality. A second suggests that transnational terrorism should be treated as an international armed conflict, a position adopted to an extent by the Israeli Supreme Court in the *Targeted Killings* case.[31] Finally, the view that such activities are non-international armed conflict appears to increasingly be the preferred characterization. The United States has adopted this stance.[32]

If conducted during an armed conflict, cross border military operations, regardless of the platforms or forces employed, must comport with international humanitarian law. Significant criticism has been leveled against the legality of drone strikes under IHL. Such charges evidence unfortunate misapprehension as to the operational aspects of the strikes and the law that applies to them.

---

[29] See generally, Schmitt 2008c, pp 525–554.

[30] See e.g., UN Human Rights Comm., *Third Periodic Reports of States Parties Due in 2003: United States of America*, at 109, UN Doc. CCPR/C/USA/3 (28 November 2005) (the position taken by the United States regarding the International Covenant on Civil and Political Rights); *Banković and Others* v *Belgium, the Czech Republic, Denmark, France, Germany, Greece, Hungary, Iceland, Italy, Luxembourg, the Netherlands, Norway, Poland, Portugal, Spain, Turkey and the United Kingdom* 123 Eur. Ct. H.R 335, para 71 (2001) (on the control issue).

[31] HCJ [High Court of Justice] 796/02, *Public Committee against Torture in Israel* et al v *Government of Israel* et al., para 21 (13 December 2006).

[32] At the 2010 meeting of the American Society of International Law, State Department Legal; Adviser Harold Koh stated that the 'United States is in an armed conflict with al Qaeda'. Koh statement, supra n 5. Although he did not indicate clearly whether the conflict was international or non-international, references to Common Article 3 of the 1949 Geneva Conventions and the 1977 Additional Protocol II to those conventions suggest the US views the conflict as non international. Further, the United States Supreme Court, in the case of *Hamdan* v *Rumsfeld*, has opined that such conflicts are 'not of an international character'. *Hamdan* v *Rumsfeld*, 548 US 557, 630–631 (2006). Finally, in a Statement to the UN Human Rights Council, the United States confirmed that the conflict with al Qeada was non-international in nature. Report of the United States of America Submitted to the UN High Commissioner for Human Rights In Conjunction with the Universal Periodic Review, UN Doc. A/HRC/WG.6/9/USA/1, 23 August 2010, at para 84.

Some of the controversy surrounds the facts that the drones are piloted from a ground station that may be based thousands of miles away and that the attacks are conducted using video feeds with no human 'eyes on target'. This purportedly results in mistaken attacks or unnecessary civilian casualties. Such counterfactual criticism merits only short shrift. Drone attacks rely on high resolution imagery usually transmitted in real time to a drone crew which, undistracted by any threat, engages the target. When feasible and necessary, drones can be used to carefully monitor the potential target for extended periods before engaging it with precision weapons. Compared to attacks by manned aircraft or ground-based systems, the result is often a significantly reduced risk of misidentifying the target or causing collateral damage to civilians and civilian property. For instance, a drone can track a target, attacking only when he is at some distance from civilians. It can also be used to conduct the 'pattern of life' analysis that is now common in targeting conducted by advanced militaries. In such an analysis, the activities of the civilian population are monitored to assess when and where an attack may be conducted to best avoid causing civilian casualties. Moreover, the weapons employed by drones are generally as good as or better than those carried by manned aircraft. And, because the crew is not at risk, drone operations avoid the stress of combat and its attendant tendency to thicken the fog of war.

Drones are, however, not a panacea. While reliable data is difficult to obtain, civilians have at times been wrongly identified as targetable insurgents or terrorists. It is equally incontestable that many civilians have been killed incidentally during drone strikes.[33] Tragic as such losses are, they do not necessarily render the attacks unlawful. In the confusion of battle, mistakes are inevitable; but they are only unlawful when the attacker has acted unreasonably.[34] For instance, it is sometimes asserted that drone attacks rely on highly questionable human intelligence.[35] If a strike relies on the sort of intelligence that a reasonable attacker would not depend upon in the same or similar circumstances, it is unlawful. But the fact that the attack was conducted using a drone has no bearing on the legality of the operation. It is the unreasonable reliance on suspect intelligence, not the platform used to exploit it, which renders the attack unlawful.

Somewhat curiously, it has been suggested that 'because operators are based thousands of miles away from the battlefield, and undertake operations entirely through computer screens and remote audiofeed, there is a risk of developing a "Playstation" mentality to killing'.[36] Such claims are speculative at best. But even if they are accurate, the assertion misses the point. It is not the mental attitude of the attacker which matters, but rather his or her ability to properly identify lawful

---

[33] One source reports 108 civilian deaths from 2006, while others suggest the figure could be as high as the 500 range. See e.g., Roggio and Mayer 2010, 2011.

[34] AMW Manual, supra n 27, p 86. The Rome Statute excludes criminal liability when a mistake of fact negates the mental element required by the crime. Rome Statute of the International Criminal Court, Art. 32.1, 17 July 1998, 2187 UNTS 90.

[35] See discussion in Alston Report, supra n 6, paras 82–83.

[36] Ibid., para 84.

targets and avoid collateral damage to the extent possible. In other words, it is correct application of the law that will best protect the civilian population. Whether correct application derives from a sense of compassion, commitment to the rule of law, professionalism or a purported desire to win what is perceived as a video game is irrelevant. To the civilian on the ground results matter.

In fact, the IHL which applies to drone strikes is precisely same law which applies to all attacks; generally, the principles and rules governing targeting apply equally in both international and non-international armed conflicts. To begin with, it is unlawful to employ an indiscriminate means of warfare, that is, a weapon or weapon system which cannot be directed at a lawful target or the effects of which cannot be controlled.[37] Since drones employ precision guided munitions such as laser-guided missiles or the JDAM, they are self-evidently not indiscriminate means of warfare. On the contrary, they are far more capable of being aimed at targets than many other weapons systems commonly employed on the battlefield.

However, the indiscriminate use of a discriminate weapon is unlawful. For instance, failing to aim a weapon, such as blindly releasing bombs, constitutes an indiscriminate attack, as does treating clearly 'separated and distinct military objectives located in a city, town, village or other area containing a similar concentration of civilians' as a single military objective.[38] It is difficult to imagine drone operations violating this proscription. In that the weapons they employ are all guided (i.e., they must be directed at something), the very nature of a drone weapon system augurs against the likelihood of such attacks.

Drones could be used to directly attack civilians or civilian objects in violation of the principle of distinction.[39] Yet this is true of every weapon and there is nothing inherent in the drone itself or the method of its use that makes such attacks more likely. Similarly, drones might be used against objects or individuals about which there is disagreement in IHL circles. In light of current drone operations, the situations most likely to raise questions of legality would be either attacks on individuals believed to be members of armed groups, but who do not perform a 'continuous combat function' within the group, or civilians involved in the conflict, but who are not engaged in combat actions at the time of attack (or engaged in activities about which disagreement exists as to whether they comprise 'direct'

[37] Protocol Additional to the Geneva Conventions of 12 August 1949, and Relating to the Protection of Victims of International Armed Conflicts Art. 51.4 (b), 8 June 1977, 1125 UNTS 3 (hereinafter AP I). Certain States, notably the United States and Israel, are not Party to Additional Protocol I. However, many of the rules contained therein reflect customary norms. These norms have been set forth in such publications as the AMW Manual, and in the military manuals of non-party States. Regarding Article 51.4, see, e.g., AMW Manual, supra n 27, Rule 5(a); US Dept. of the Navy, US Marine Corps, US Coast Guard, Commander's Handbook on the Law of Naval Operations, NWP1-14 M, MCWP 5-2.1, COMDTPUB P5800.7, para 9.1.2 (2007) (hereinafter NWP).

[38] AP I, supra n 37, Arts. 51.4 and 51.5; AMW Manual, supra n 27, Rules 13(b), (c); NWP, supra n 37, para 5.3.2.

[39] AP I, supra n 37, Art. 48, 51.1 and 52.1; AMW Manual, supra n 27, Rule 11; NWP, supra n 37, para 8.3.

participation in hostilities).[40] These issues have fueled a firestorm of controversy. Yet, the legal question in such debates is not the weapon system employed, but rather the legal status of its target. That a drone may have been used in the attack is neither here nor there.

When harm to civilians cannot be avoided during an attack on a lawful target, as in the case of civilians who are collocated with the enemy or near military objectives, the *jus in bello* principle of proportionality applies. This principle is wholly distinct from the *jus ad bellum* principle of the same name discussed *supra*. Rather, IHL proportionally prohibits an attack 'which may be expected to cause incidental loss of civilian life, injury to civilians, damage to civilian objects, or a combination thereof, which would be excessive in relation to the concrete and direct military advantage anticipated'.[41]

Two aspects of the rule bear on criticism of the drone strikes. First, it must be understood that the very existence of the principle is an acknowledgement that attacks may in some cases be lawful even when there is absolute certainty that civilians will be killed or injured or that civilian property will be damaged or destroyed. The legal question is whether the civilian harm that an attacker reasonably expects to cause is 'excessive' in light of the military benefits the attacker hopes to attain. Second, proportionality is not assessed with the benefit of hindsight, but instead from the perspective of an attacker in the circumstances. In other words, had the situation been as the attacker reasonably believed it to be, based on intelligence and other information, would the harm have been excessive? Whether it in fact turned out to be excessive, either because the attack caused greater collateral damage than expected or because the mission was less successful than anticipated, is irrelevant as a matter of law.

The paradigmatic case is a drone strike on a building where a major Taliban leader is believed to be hiding. Assume the attacker has reliable intelligence that the home is inhabited by three civilians, reasonably believes that if an attack is delayed the operative will escape, and no alternatives to a drone strike exist. In light of the operative's importance, most commentators would conclude that attacking the individual would be proportionate. Yet, without the knowledge of the attacker, the operative had already fled in the darkness of night and four more civilians entered the house. The ensuing attack kills seven civilians, but no Taliban fighters. In this case, the actual results of the attack would have no bearing on the legality of the strike; it would be proportionate based on the earlier reasonable, albeit mistaken, judgment of the attacker.

When assessing IHL proportionality, the weapon or weapon system used is completely irrelevant. The sole issue is whether the expected civilian casualties or damage were excessive relative to the military gain the attacker reasonably

[40] The ICRC's position on direct participation in hostilities is set forth in Interpretive Guidance, supra n 26. For contrary views on certain of the ICRC's positions, see Boothby 2010, p 741; Hays Parks 2010, p 769; Schmitt 2010a, p 697; Watkin 2010, p 641; Schmitt 2010b, p 5.

[41] AP I, supra n 37, Arts. 52.5(b), 57.2(a)(iii) and 57.2(b); AMW Manual, supra n 27, Rule 14; NWP, supra n 37, para 8.3.1.

anticipated from the strike. A drone strike may violate the rule of proportionality, but only because of the consequences caused, not because a drone conducted the attack. On the other hand, the choice of weapon or weapon system is relevant in the context of the requirement to take 'precautions in attack'. IHL requires an attacker to take 'constant care ... to spare the civilian population, civilians and civilian objects'.[42] This requirement plays out in a variety of ways.

First, an attacker must 'do everything feasible to verify that the objectives to be attacked are neither civilians nor civilian objects'.[43] So long as the attacker has complied with this requirement and still has reasonable grounds to believe the target is a member of the enemy's armed forces, a civilian 'directly participating in hostilities' or a military objective, the attack is lawful.[44] The crux of the requirement is the term 'feasible'. Feasible steps are those which 'are practicable or practically possible, taking into account all circumstances prevailing at the time, including humanitarian and military considerations'.[45] Attackers need not exhaust all possible means to verify the target, but must avail themselves of those that make sense militarily. For instance, if a drone is reasonably available to provide imagery of a target and such imagery would enhance the attacker's ability to ensure it qualifies as a military objective, then the use of a the drone would be required as a matter of law. Of particular note in this regard is the capability of drones to loiter over a target, thereby extending the period during which the status of the target can be verified. Note that the benefits of using the drone must be clear, rather than merely speculative, before the requirement attaches.

During drone attacks, other assets reasonably available to verify a target must be resorted to if doing so would measurably improve verification of the target. In many cases, this may involve coordination with troops on the ground who can observe the target and target area. Since they operate from a different perspective, their observation may offer information unattainable from the air. Again, the requirement is conditioned by feasibility. Troops may not be in the area, the attack may be time-sensitive or troops in the area may be occupied with higher priority tasks (like engaging in combat themselves). Nevertheless, to the extent the use of other means of verifying the target (and assessing likely collateral damage) would make good military sense, they must be so used.

The requirement to take precautions in attack also mandates the use of those feasible means and methods of attack which will minimize harm to civilians and

[42] AP I, supra n 37, Art. 57.1, AMW Manual, supra n 27, Rule 31; NWP, supra n 37, para 8.1.

[43] AP I, supra n 37, Art. 57.2(a)(i); AMW Manual, supra n 27, Rule 32(a); NWP, supra n 37, para 8.1.

[44] Civilians who directly participate in hostilities lose their immunity from attack. AP I, supra n 37, Art. 51.3; AMW Manual, supra n 27, Rule 28; NWP, supra n 37, para 8.2.2.

[45] See e.g., AMW Manual, supra n 27, Rule 1(q); Declarations made by States at the time of ratification, in Roberts and Guelff (eds) 2000, pp 498–512; Amended Protocol on Prohibitions or Restrictions on the Use of Mines, Booby Traps and Other Devices (Amended Protocol II) Art. 3(10), 3 May 1996, S. Treaty Doc. No. 105-1 (1997).

civilian objects, at least to the extent that no military advantage is sacrificed.[46] In this regard, drones loom large. If use of a drone, because it is a relatively precise weapon system and its loiter capability often affords a longer window of opportunity within which to strike, would likely result in less collateral damage than use of other systems (such as a manned aircraft, artillery or ground attack), and if such drone use is militarily feasible, the drone must be employed as a matter of law. Conversely, other systems must be used in lieu of a drone when doing so is feasible and their use will lessen collateral damage without forfeiting military advantage. Since the use of a drone presents no risk to the operator and in light of its unique capabilities, such circumstances will be rare.

Required precautions in attack also include the issuance of 'effective advance warning … of attacks which may affect the civilian population, unless circumstances do not permit'.[47] This requirement does not extend to attacks which only affect civilian property. The rule is subject to an important caveat. It is well accepted that the need for surprise in certain attacks is a circumstance which may preclude the issuance of warnings.[48] When a targeted individual might flee or take cover if a warning is provided to civilians who might be affected, the warning need not be issued. In most drone attacks, surprise is a critical element in mission success.

Finally, significant confusion has surrounded the issue of the status of individuals operating drones, especially intelligence personnel and civilian contractors. Such controversy is misplaced. During an international armed conflict, international law does not prohibit individuals who are not members of the armed forces from engaging in hostilities. Rather, such 'unprivileged belligerents' do not enjoy the rights associated with combatant status, specifically treatment as a prisoner of war and belligerent immunity. The immunity shields a combatant from prosecution for acts which are lawful under IHL but would not be during peacetime, most notably attacking other combatants and destroying property qualifying as a military objective.[49] Those who are not lawful combatants may therefore be prosecuted for acts which are unlawful under the domestic law of a state with jurisdiction over the individual and the offense.[50] Additionally, since they are directly participating in hostilities, they may be attacked.[51] Yet, neither they nor the state using them violate IHL merely on the basis of the fact of their involvement in the conflict. The situation is especially clear in non-international armed conflicts, where the use of law enforcement, civilian intelligence and

---

[46] AP I, supra n 37, Art. 57.2(a)(ii); AMW Manual, supra n 27, Rule 32(b).

[47] AP I, supra n 37, Art. 57.2(c). AMW Manual, supra n 27, Rules 37 and 38; NWP, supra n 37, para 8.9.2.

[48] AMW Manual, supra n 27, p 133; ICRC, Henckaerts and Doswald-Beck (eds) 2005, p 64.

[49] AP I, supra n 37, Art. 43.2: 'Members of the armed forces of a Party to a conflict…are combatants, that is to say, they have the right to participate directly in hostilities'.

[50] See the discussion in Dinstein 2004, pp 27–44.

[51] AP I, supra n 37, Art. 51.3; AMW Manual, supra n 27, Rule 28; NWP, supra n 37, para 8.2.2.

contractor personnel is commonplace. After all, a rebellion is, despite constituting an armed conflict, also a violation of domestic criminal law.

9.5 Concluding Thoughts

Ultimately, any appraisal of the *jus ad bellum* aspects of cross border strikes must proceed on a case-by-case basis. Did the territorial state consent, either explicitly or implicitly, to a specific operation? If not, was a demand made that it comply with its obligation under international law to police its territory? Was there time to seek consent or allow the territorial state's forces to act? Did those forces have the capability to act effectively in the circumstances? How certain were the victim-state's forces that the target was in fact an insurgent or terrorist? What did that state hope to gain through the attack? Did the scope and scale of the victim-state's operations track the extent of the threat it was meant to neutralize?

But these are precisely the same questions asked about any cross-border operation conducted pursuant to the law of self-defense (or the law of neutrality during an international armed conflict). The sole relevance of drones operations is that they may not be mounted if less forceful measures would suffice … and must be conducted if likely to suffice in lieu of more forceful and invasive measures.

The brouhaha over the *jus in bello* issues implicated by drone strikes is equally misguided. Precisely the same law applies to drone operations as those conducted using other weapons and weapon systems. The one area where drones are of particular relevance is with regard to the requirement to take precautions in attack. Here a drone must be used when reasonably available and its use is operationally feasible, but only if such use would minimize likely collateral damage without sacrificing military advantage. Conversely, drones may not be used when other means or methods of warfare that would result in less collateral damage with an equivalent prospect of mission success are available.

Reduced to basics, then, the sole legal issue specific to drone operations under both the *jus ad bellum* and the *jus in bello* is weapon choice. As correctly noted by Special Rapporteur Alston, 'a missile fired from a drone is no different from any other commonly used weapon, including a gun fired by a soldier or a helicopter or gunship that fires missiles. The critical legal question is the same for each weapon: whether its specific use complies with IHL'.[52] Claims to the contrary are the product of poor understanding of drones and their means of employment, a failure to understand application of the law to such operations or simple emotionalism.

Nearly two centuries ago Clausewitz noted that: '[t]he great uncertainty of all data in war is a peculiar difficulty, because all action must, to a certain extent, be planned in a mere twilight, which in addition not infrequently—like the effect of a fog or moonshine—gives to things exaggerated dimensions and unnatural

[52] Alston Report, supra n 6, para 79.

appearance'.[53] Yet, the law applicable to the drone strikes, albeit multifaceted and complex, exists neither in twilight, nor fog. The pundits would do well to consult it more carefully.

References

Boothby B (2010) 'And for such time as': the time dimension to direct participation in hostilities. NY Univ J Int Law Politics 42:741–769

Dinstein Y (2004) The conduct of hostilities under the law of international armed conflict. Cambridge University Press, Cambridge

Hays Parks W (2010) Part IX of the ICRC 'Direct participation in hostilities' Study: no mandate, no expertise, and legally incorrect. NY Univ J Int Law Politics 42:769–831

Henckaerts J-M, Doswald-Beck L (eds) (2005) Customary international humanitarian law, vol. I. Cambridge University Press, Cambridge

Landler M (2009) U.S., Pakistan and Afghanistan to hold regular talks, New York Times, 27 Feb 2009

Mayer J (2009) The predator war, The New Yorker, 26 Oct 2009

Melzer N (2009) Interpretive guidance on the notion of direct participation in hostilities under international humanitarian law. IRRC, Geneva

Risen J, Mazzetti M (2009) C.I.A. said to use outsiders to put bombs on drones, New York Times, 21 August 2009

Roberts A, Guelff R (eds) (2000) Documents on the Laws of War, 3rd edn. Oxford University Press, Oxford

Roggio B, Mayer A (2010) US air campaign in Pakistan heats up, The Long War Journal, available at www.longwarjournal.org/archives/2010/01/analysis_us_air_camp.php

Roggio B, Mayer A (2011) Charting the data for US airstrikes in Pakistan, 2004–2011, The Long War Journal. Available at www.longwarjournal.org/pakistan-strikes.php

Schmitt MN (2008a) 'Change Direction' 2006: Israeli operations in Lebanon and the international law of self-defense. Michigan J Int Law 29:127

Schmitt MN (2008b) Responding to transnational terrorism under the jus ad bellum: a normative framework. Naval Law Rev 56:1

Schmitt MN (2008c) Targeted killings in international law: law enforcement, self-defense and armed conflict. In: Arnold R, Quénivet N (eds) International humanitarian law and human rights law: towards a new merger in international law. Leiden, Brill

Schmitt MN (2010a) Deconstructing direct participation in hostilities: the constitutive elements. NY Univ J Int Law Politics 42:697–739

Schmitt MN (2010b) The interpretive guidance on the notion of direct participation in hostilities: a critical analysis. Harvard NSJ 1:5–44

Schmitt E, Mazzetti M (2009) In a first, US provides Pakistan with drone data, New York Times, 14 May 2009

von Clausewitz C (1832) On war, Berlin, Dümmler

Warrick J, Finn P (2010) CIA director says attacks have hobbled al-Qaeda, Washington Post, 18 March 2010

Watkin KK (2010) Opportunity lost: organized armed groups and the ICRC 'direct participation in hostilities' Interpretive Guidance. NY Univ J Int Law Politics 42:641–695

[53] Clausewitz 1832, vol 2, ch 2 para 24.

Chapter 10
Domestic, Legal or Other Proceedings Undertaken by Both the Government of Israel and the Palestinian Side

Ivana Vuco

Contents

10.1 Introduction

Taking as its starting point United Nations General Assembly Resolution 64/254, the United Nations Human Rights Council's committee of independent experts in international humanitarian and human rights laws was convened to monitor and assess the domestic legal or other proceedings undertaken by both the Government of Israel and the Palestinian side, with an eye to their conformity with international standards.

Consultant on human rights and protection issues; human rights officer with OHCHR and legal advisor with UNHCR in the Secretariat of the Committee until September 2010; senior consultant with UNHCR in Yemen until July 2011. Views expressed in this article are those of the author in her personal capacity.

I. Vuco (✉)
OHCHR, Geneva, Switzerland
e-mail: ivana_vuco@yahoo.com

M.N. Schmitt et al. (eds.), *Yearbook of International Humanitarian Law Volume 13, 2010*, DOI: 10.1007/978-90-6704-811-8_10,

10.2 Overview of the Committee's Creation and Mandate

On 29 September 2009, the United Nations Fact Finding Mission on the Gaza Conflict, otherwise known as the Goldstone Mission, submitted its report (A/HRC/12/48) to the Geneva-based United Nations Human Rights Council. The report set out a number of recommendations, amongst which was that the United Nations Security Council should establish:

> 'an independent committee of experts in International Humanitarian and Human Rights Law to monitor and report on any domestic legal or other proceedings undertaken by the Government of Israel in relation to the aforesaid investigations. Such committee of experts should report at the end of the six-month period to the Security Council on its assessment of relevant domestic proceedings initiated by the Government of Israel, including their progress, effectiveness and genuineness, so that the Security Council may assess whether appropriate action to ensure justice for victims and accountability for perpetrators has been or is being taken at the domestic level. The Security Council should request the committee to report to it at determined intervals, as may be necessary. The committee should be appropriately supported by the Office of the United Nations High Commissioner for Human Rights.'[1]

The Goldstone report was never formally considered by the Security Council. Rather, the UN Human Rights Council (HRC) referred the report to the United Nations General Assembly (UNGA), whereupon the UNGA adopted resolution 64/254[2] calling on the parties to the Gaza conflict to conduct investigations that were independent, credible and in conformity with international standards. At about the same time, on 24 March 2010, the HRC held another session dedicated to the Goldstone report at the conclusion of which its forty-seven members adopted resolution 13/9, which, *inter alia*, called for the establishment of:

> 'a committee of independent experts in international humanitarian and human rights laws to monitor and assess any domestic, legal or other proceedings undertaken by both the Government of Israel and the Palestinian side, in the light of General Assembly resolution 64/254, including the independence, effectiveness, genuineness of these investigations and their conformity with international standards.'[3]

Neither UNGA resolution 64/254 nor HRC resolution 13/9 specify in any amount of detail the origin of the investigative criteria cited in the resolutions, leaving it thus to the Committee experts to determine the appropriateness and applicability of IHL and/or IHRL instruments for the case at hand.

The resolution tasked the Committee to submit its findings to the Council at its 15th session in September 2010. Where the standing up of the Committee was concerned, its establishment was entrusted to the United Nations High

---

[1] Report of the United Nations Fact-Finding Mission on the Gaza Conflict (A/HRC/12/48). Para 1969d.

[2] A/Res/64/254.

[3] A/HRC/13/9 para 9.

Commissioner for Human Rights in Geneva, whose office, in addition to its regular human rights work, also support the work of the HRC.

On 14 June 2010, the High Commissioner for Human Rights announced publically the appointment of the Committee's three members, in particular, Christian Tomuschat, a professor at Humboldt University and former member of the United Nations Human Rights Committee, Mary McGowan Davis, formerly a Justice of the Supreme Court of the State of New York, and Param Cumaraswamy, a Malaysian lawyer and former Special Rapporteur to the Commission on Human Rights on the independence of judges and lawyers. The three experts were selected for their human rights experience. That the Office of the High Commissioner for Human Rights (OHCHR) is inclined towards human rights experts already known to OHCHR should not be surprising—OHCHR, after all, is a principal UN human rights organization—but explains why, in situations where IHL violations are concerned, such committees may be perceived to have a 'human rights bias', owing in part to the fact that human rights experts, in view of some international IHL practitioners, place overt emphasis on human rights norms which change the very essence of the IHL and threaten to make any war-like conduct illegal.

Once established and supported by the secretariat of OHCHR personnel, expert committees and fact-finding missions are expected to make their findings independently from OHCHR. At the same time, owing to the fact that experts serve on non-remunerated basis, and given that much of the analysis undertaken in support of a given committee is performed by OHCHR personnel, the independence of a given committee may, in practice, be less evident.

10.3 Methodology

Whereas the nature and the length of the mandates of expert committees[4] and fact-finding missions vary, they share the common characteristic of being something akin to a research tool employed by the HRC for the purpose of providing the Council with expert advice on issues of immediate concern. As such, the HRC has relatively frequent recourse to such bodies. For instance, in 2009–2010, Council established two fact-finding missions and one expert committee, all of which were concerned specifically with various aspects of the Israeli-Palestinian conflict.[5]

Reports produced by such committees, once adopted by the Council, are published as official HRC documents, and as a general rule, attract significant media

---

[4] Sometimes also referred to as 'commissions of inquiries'.

[5] The HRC's latest fact-finding mission was created following the incident of 31 May 2010, whereby nine passengers of the Turkish ship *Mavi Marmara* were killed by Israeli soldiers while enroute to the Gaza Strip. The International Fact-Finding Mission to Investigate Violations of International Law, Including International Humanitarian and Human Rights Law, Resulting from the Israeli Attacks on the Flotilla of Ships Carrying Humanitarian Assistance was also scheduled to report back to HRC at its 15th session.

attention. The reports are further frequently quoted or referenced by UN agencies and NGOs as authoritative statements of international human rights law (IHRL) and the international humanitarian law (IHL), and a given committee's legal analysis is generally accepted without significant challenge. This sort of implicit confidence in the findings of the committees must be weighed against the difficulties that committees frequently encounter in acquiring the information necessary to fulfill their mandates.

The same point might be made about the Human Rights Council. Created in 2006 from the Commission on Human Rights, the HRC was afforded a strengthened mandate—and limited enforcement powers. For instance, the implementation of the Council's resolutions is a matter left largely to the discretion of individual member states. Moreover, the resolutions of the Council do not necessarily have significant bearing upon the decisions made on like questions by other UN organs, such as the General Assembly and the Security Council. Rather than enforcing adherence to human rights principles, the HRC's principal task is the creation of a forum where universal respect for human rights is promoted principally through dialogue and cooperation between states.[6]

As with similar HRC committees, the Committee of Experts responsible for monitoring and assessing the investigations undertaken by the belligerent parties to the Gaza conflict was established as a formal institution with a narrow mandate of a limited temporal duration. As noted above, the Committee was required to report to the Council where it found 'any domestic, legal or other proceedings undertaken by both the Government of Israel and the Palestinian side'.[7] To this end, the Committee convened for a period of approximately 3 months; during its tenure, the Commissioners undertook a three-day mission to Jordan and a two-day mission to Gaza. Additionally, the Committee conducted consultative interviews with IHL specialists from several countries as well as a thorough-going review of all written submissions and reports concerned with the Israeli and Palestinian investigations. What is more, the Commissioners considered any and all information (including investigations) made by third parties to the conflict with similar legal systems. At the conclusion of this research phase, the Committee produced a report, setting out its mandate and methodology, the applicable law and its conclusions. In accordance with standard practice, at the release of the final report, the Committee held a press conference.

Shortly after it commenced work, the Committee envisioned spending time in both Israel and the territories under Palestinian control, where it hoped to gain access to relevant official documentation and to conduct interviews with individuals concerned with any ongoing investigations. Given the fact that the conflict between the parties remained and continues to remain largely unresolved, the

---

[6] The Human Rights Council's Universal Periodic Review (UPR) is especially instructive in that regard—it is a state-driven, consultative review of member states' human rights reports. The quality of UPR differs significantly from the review process practiced by the UN treaty bodies.

[7] A/HRC/13/9, para 9.

Committee was conscious of the fact that the content of at least some national investigations was likely to be highly confidential, and that, for this reason, the Committee might enjoy only limited access to certain information. Cooperation by the concerned parties and access to relevant officials, however limited, would have enabled the Committee to gain at least a basic understanding of the relevant procedures and practices upon which both the Israeli and Palestinian investigations were being conducted allowing the Committee to draw informed conclusions on the question of whether the investigations were conforming to international standards.

In the event, the Committee faced numerous obstacles in achieving its goals. While some of the obstacles are related to the lack of cooperation by concerned states, others are of a more general nature.

Firstly, HRC committees must typically work against tight deadlines. In practice, this means that over periods seldom exceeding several months[8] committees are expected to carry out all necessary research as well as submit a final report to the HRC. Where additional time is required to identify appropriate or willing experts—as was the case with the Goldstone Mission, for instance—the time available for research and report drafting is correspondingly reduced. As has likewise been noted earlier in this paper, commissioners are expected to work on a voluntary basis, as their time allows. The result of this reliance upon volunteers is that experts often end up juggling several commitments at the same time. Put another way, seldom are commissioners able to commit to a committee on a full-time basis. Where the case at hand was concerned, over a three-month period the commissioners assembled to analyze and report upon the Israeli and Palestinian investigations met for about 16 days, in Geneva, Amman and Gaza. For the rest of the three-month life of the Committee, a substantial number of reports and other documents were collected, reviewed and analyzed by the Committee members in a manner that inevitably depended on an individual member's availability and dedication.

A second and more important factor complicating the work of all HRC committees is the inability of these UN expert bodies to enforce their mandate. Unlike courts, the HRC-convened committees and fact-finding missions cannot summon witnesses and experts. Rather, they are dependent largely upon the goodwill of states that are prepared, for instance, to grant access to territory and official documents that may be of interest to a given panel. It follows from this that the work of HRC-formed bodies is rendered immensely difficult in situations where a member state refuses its cooperation. In this particular case, Israel refused to cooperate with the work of the Committee—as it routinely does where

[8] For instance, the Goldstone Mission carried out its research from early May until the end of September when the report was officially presented to the Human Rights Council on 29 September 2010. The Committee of Experts as a follow up to the Goldstone had even less time of some 3 months to 'monitor and assess' investigations undertaken by the concerned parties. The Flotilla fact-finding mission conducted all its research within the period of 2 months from the moment the Committee members were selected to the moment the report was made public.

investigations into Israeli policies and conduct are called for by the HRC. The Israeli authorities denied access by Committee members to Israel and, by extension to the Israeli-controlled West Bank. The Committee was able to travel to Gaza via Egypt.

Notwithstanding the formal refusal of Israel to cooperate with the work of the Committee, the Commissioners did have several meetings with the Israeli Permanent Representative to United Nations in Geneva, including a number of telephone conversations at the Ambassador's request at a later stage in the Committee's mandate. While several options for cooperation with Israel were discussed during these meetings (some of which would clearly have delayed the submission of the report), none of these options materialized. In the view of the author, Israel was likely weighing the pros and cons of cooperation with the Committee. Typically, Israel would agree to discuss a Committee proposal, only subsequently to reject it. Likewise, Israel had refused to cooperate with the Goldstone Committee as well as the more recent Gaza flotilla fact-finding mission.[9]

Absent formal Israeli cooperation, the Committee made serious efforts to engage Israeli experts. This likewise proved difficult. The Committee of Experts to monitor and assess the Israeli and Palestinian investigations approached a number of Israeli experts—including several with intimate knowledge of the military justice system—with a request for an interview; only two responded positively. It is possible that the Committee's association with the HRC, a body that is viewed by the state of Israel as biased and possessing of an agenda disproportionally dictated by a group of states hostile to Israel, led many of the individuals who had been approached by the Committee to refuse any association with its work.[10]

The cooperation afforded by the authorities in Gaza was marginally better. While willing to provide the Committee with access to the area under its control (i.e., the Gaza strip), the Hamas authorities provided very little useful information. For instance, the authorities in Gaza did not respond to a Committee request for information concerning any and all investigations that might have been undertaken into the conduct of forces loyal to Hamas. In fact, the Gaza authorities clearly thought the entire exercise of the HRC to be prompted by the Israeli attack on the Gaza strip and inferred from this that the Committee ought to deal exclusively with questions of Israeli conduct rather than that of the Palestinian forces. Whatever the explanation, when asked by the Committee about possible investigations of

---

[9] A/HRC/15/21 para 16.

[10] It is often pointed out, for instance, that the Human Rights Council's item 7, which is the 'human rights situation in Palestine and other occupied Arab territories: human rights violations and implications of the Israeli occupation of Palestine and other occupied Arab territories and the Right to self-determination of the Palestinian people' is the only permanent item on HRC's agenda. Furthermore, some twenty UNGA resolutions are annually dedicated to Israel and its conduct in the Palestinian territories; and six of ten emergency sessions of the UNGA have dealt with Israel—while none, as is frequently pointed out, have been held in response to events in Rwanda, Yugoslavia, or Sudan.

violations of the laws of war on the part of Gaza-based armed groups, the Office of the Prosecutor-General in Gaza had no information to share. This led to a paradoxical situation where the Committee's time in Gaza was directed almost exclusively towards the research on undertaken Israeli investigations, and less so on any possible investigative activities carried out by the Gaza authorities.

The highly imperfect measure of cooperation afforded by Hamas and no cooperation afforded by Israel rendered difficult the verification by the Committee of whatever raw data that the Committee had been able to acquire. Here, the Committee relied heavily upon the official submissions of Israel and the Palestinian authorities (from both the West Bank and Gaza) in response to General Assembly resolutions 64/10 and 64/254. The said submissions however left the Committee with many questions on employed procedures and investigative findings that were inadequately addressed within the submissions themselves. In an effort to deal with the myriad outstanding issues, information was collected by the Committee from NGOs and Palestinian witnesses to Israeli military proceedings—this notwithstanding the fact that many of the witnesses and NGOs appeared to possess incomplete information.

On the whole, the Committee was able to acquire substantial amount of information on Israeli investigations from Palestinian and NGO sources—an observation made here without prejudice to the question of the accuracy of the data or the analysis. The lack of official data and direct access to Israeli government sources led some members of the Committee to question whether such a situation of informational imbalance renders the assessment insufficiently reliable. Indeed, there was some discussion within the Committee over the question of whether the *Committee should seek extension or postponement* on the grounds that the Committee could not meet the mandate afforded to it by the HRC.

10.4 Legal Analysis and Findings

The Committee interpreted its mandate to warrant the assessment, to the degree possible, of any criminal, military, administrative or other investigations of allegations of serious violations of IHL and IHRL committed by all parties to the Gaza conflict.

The 452-page Goldstone report cites a plethora of cases where alleged violations of IHL and IHRL were committed by all sides to the conflict. Amongst this number are thirty-six incidents arising from Israeli conduct. These thirty-six incidents constituted the core of the Committee's assessment of the Israeli enquiry into its own conduct during the conflict. Where the Palestinians were concerned, the Committee focused upon the Goldstone report's allegations of indiscriminate attacks against Israeli civilians, the use of human shields, the employment of civilian objects for military purposes, extra-judicial killings and allegations of torture. In contrast to the Goldstone Mission, the Committee was not a fact-finding mission and thus did not see it as being necessary to conduct itself along the lines generally adopted by human-rights and criminal-investigative bodies.

In assessing the incidences and the quality of the investigations (if any) made by the belligerent parties in response to the alleged breaches of IHL and IHRL, the principal question facing the Committee was what standard to apply in assessing any and all investigations that might come to light. In answering this question, the Committee was guided by an earlier conclusion of the HRC. Echoing a formulation expounded by the UN General Assembly, the HRC had ascribed the following criteria as essential in conducting an effective domestic investigation of violations of human rights and IHL: 'independence, effectiveness, genuineness [... and] conformity with international standards'.[11] In the event, neither the HRC nor the General Assembly had specified what they understood the 'international standards' to mean. The legal instruments and jurisprudence, which together constitute the body of IHL, are largely silent on such questions.

IHL appears to consider international investigative standards only insofar as these are relevant to the protection of the rights of suspects and the accused, but remains conspicuously silent on the rights of the victims.[12] While this silence may be a reflection of the age in which IHL standards and rules were codified, contemporary views on the need for providing some form of justice for all victims of conflicts exposes a gap in the law.

There is a growing tendency amongst human rights theoreticians to fill the lacunae in IHL with relevant human rights standards. In this case, the Committee did likewise. In particular, it determined that the silence of IHL on the question of investigative standards ought to be addressed by the application of the relevant human rights instruments. At the same time, the Committee noted that war-like situations do pose certain limitations on the abilities of states to adhere to these principles—a caveat rooted logically enough in key human rights instruments such as the International Covenant on Civil and Political Rights (ICCPR).

Adopting language found in human rights treaties and related instruments, the Committee took the position that the following criteria ought to apply equally to all investigations of violations of IHRL and IHL:

i. Independence and impartiality: identified as independence of investigative bodies and individuals undertaking an investigation from the events or crimes under investigation, and the absence of bias and preconceptions concerning the case at hand.[13]

---

[11] UN General Assembly resolution 64/254 of 26 February 2010, requested all domestic investigations to be 'independent, credible and in conformity with international standards into the serious violations of international humanitarian and international human rights law'. (GA Res 64/254, paras 2 and 3).

[12] In its report, the Committee noted that the ICRC Commentary provides some direction, identifying that the Parties must actively search for and prosecute the accused with speed and that the necessary police action should be taken spontaneously and not merely at the request of another State. The Commentary further specifies that court proceedings should be carried out in a uniform manner and that 'nationals, friends, enemies all should be subject to the same rules of procedure and judged by the same courts' (A/HRC/15/50, para 19).

[13] A/HRC/15/50 paras 22 and 23.

ii. Thoroughness and effectiveness: refers to completeness and comprehensiveness of an investigation which presupposes that all necessary autopsies and medical examinations, site visits and statements are taken as appropriate.[14]
iii. Promptness: identified as a requirement that an investigation should commence and progress with reasonable expedition, even though a determination of whether an investigation has met the standard of reasonableness depends on the specific circumstances of the case. Cases of torture and extrajudicial killings—where medical evidence might disappear—and enforced disappearances—where an individual's life might be in imminent danger—require immediate action.[15]

The Committee's conclusions on the question of the capacity of the belligerent parties to undertake effective and credible investigations differed from those identified by the Goldstone Mission. For instance, the Committee found that the belligerent parties had the capacity as well as the obligation under IHL and IHRL to investigate crimes committed by their nationals. Moreover, it was the view of the Committee that military tribunals might serve as a credible forum through which to investigate alleged crimes, provided that international standards are applied. It was in part for this reason that, unlike the Goldstone Mission, the Committee did not recommend that the investigation of Israeli conduct during the Gaza war be referred to the International Criminal Court (ICC).

The Committee further found that Israel had in fact taken several positive steps to review and/or investigate many cases where war crimes had been alleged by Goldstone and others. Nonetheless, a number of these and other allegations of serious violations of IHL and IHRL by Israel appeared to the Committee to have been inadequately investigated and, in cases where an initial investigation had been launched, summarily dismissed. Moreover, the Committee raised concerns about the application of international standards to the investigative processes that were already underway as well as about the failure of Israel to instigate what in the view of the Committee would be an adequate review of its military doctrine. In the event, the absence of formal Israeli cooperation rendered impossible a thorough-going assessment of these cases. The same could be said of the Palestinian authorities in Gaza: the complete absence of evidence or information on any possible investigations raised serious doubts as to whether any enquiries had been undertaken, and, if they had, whether these enquiries met even minimal international standards.

10.5 Conclusion

Owing to the fact that the HRC committee formed to examine whether the belligerent parties had undertaken meaningful investigations into the conduct of their own forces during the Gaza conflict of December 2008 and January 2009 was able,

[14] Ibid., para 24.
[15] Ibid., para 25.

in the final analysis, to present the HRC with a number of tentative conclusions, in October 2010 the HRC extended the Committee's mandate for another term.[16] The Committee, which is expected to re-commence its work in January 2011, will thus have an opportunity to re-engage with the belligerent parties and build upon its initial findings in a second report to the Council's 16th session in March 2011.

[16] A/HRC/RES/15/6 of 6 October 2010.

Chapter 11
Poison, Gas and Expanding Bullets: The Extension of the List of Prohibited Weapons at the Review Conference of the International Criminal Court in Kampala

Robin Geiβ

Contents

11.1 Introduction

Responses to the recent extension of the list of prohibited weapons at the Review Conference of the International Criminal Court (ICC) in Kampala, Uganda have been rather mixed. Some have hailed the amendments to Article 8 of the Rome Statute as a milestone development. Others speak of a blatant manifestation of the Rome Statute's inability to deal with prohibited weapons in a meaningful and

R. Geiβ (✉)
Professor at the Faculty of Law, University of Potsdam, Potsdam, Germany
e-mail: robin.geiss@uni-potsdam.de

M.N. Schmitt et al. (eds.), *Yearbook of International Humanitarian Law Volume 13, 2010*, DOI: 10.1007/978-90-6704-811-8_11,

up-to-date manner.[1] Certainly, the list of prohibited weapons has been extended in Kampala. But as constructed, does it adequately capture the realities of contemporary armed conflicts? In the pursuance of this question, in a first step, this contribution focuses on what actually happened in Kampala and why it had not already happened in Rome in 1998. In a second step, some light will be shed on what did not happen in Kampala. As is well known, initial proposals for the extension of the list of prohibited weapons had been far more extensive than the list that was ultimately adopted. Thirdly, in a final step this Comment concludes with an assessment of whether the Rome Statute's list of prohibited weapons in its amended form now better corresponds to the realities of contemporary armed conflicts.

11.2 What Happened in Kampala?

As far as the amendments to Article 8 of the ICC Statute are concerned, the story of what happened in Kampala is quickly told. Following a proposal drafted by Belgium,[2] the Kampala Review Conference, by consensus, adopted three crimes regarding the use of prohibited weapons in non-international armed conflict. Specifically, Article 8(2)(e) of the ICC Statute was extended to include the crimes of:

(xiii) Employing poison or poisoned weapons,
(xiv) Employing asphyxiating, poisonous or other gases, and all analogous liquids, materials or devices,
(xv) Employing bullets which expand or flatten easily in the human body.

This can certainly be regarded as an important development in as much as it is the first time that crimes relating to prohibited weapons have been adopted with regard to non-international armed conflicts.[3] In terms of substance, however, the three crimes contain nothing new. They replicate the provisions found in Article 8(2)(b)(xvii), (xviii) and (xix) of the ICC Statute that apply to international armed conflict as adopted in Rome. Moreover, the very same Elements of Crimes apply to

[1] For example, the International Federation for Human Rights (FIDH) has welcomed the harmonisation of rules related to the use of prohibited weapons in international and non-international armed conflicts, see International Federation for Human Rights (FIDH), Press Release of 14 June 2010, Conclusion of landmark ICC Review Conference: Difficult compromise and commitments to be confirmed, available at http://www.iccnow.org/documents/cpi1406a.pdf (last visited November 2010). But for a sharp critique of the results achieved in Kampala see Schabas 2010.

[2] The so-called 'Belgian proposal' is included in Annex III to Resolution ICC-ASP/8/Res.6, 26 November 2009, available at http://www.icc-cpi.int/iccdocs/asp_docs/Resolutions/ICC-ASP-8-Res.6-ENG.pdf (last visited November 2010).

[3] Of course, the ICTY has interpreted Article 3 of its Statute – which refers to the 'employment of poisonous weapons or other weapons calculated to cause unnecessary suffering' – to include war crimes committed either in international and non-international armed conflicts.

both categories of crimes. In accordance with Article 121(5) of the ICC Statute the amendments will enter into force for those State Parties which have accepted them 1 year after the deposit of their instruments of ratification or acceptance.

The proclaimed motivation behind the Belgian proposal was to streamline and standardize the law applicable in international and non-international armed conflicts, to bring Article 8 of the ICC Statute more in line with customary international law and to answer to humanitarian needs in contemporary armed conflicts.[4] The International Committee of the Red Cross (ICRC) has long been of the opinion that the customary law prohibition of the use of poison, gas and expanding bullets also applies to non-international armed conflicts and that infringements of these prohibitions incur individual criminal responsibility.[5] The same position has been endorsed by the International Criminal Tribunal for the former Yugoslavia (ICTY) and by some states.[6] The German 'Völkerstrafgesetzbuch', for example, in force since 2002, criminalizes the use of these weapons in both international and non-international armed conflicts.[7]

11.2.1 Why had it not already happened in Rome?

Of course, all of this begs the question as to why these crimes were not already included in the ICC Statute at the Rome Conference. Notably, an early ICC Draft Statute, adopted by the Preparatory Committee in April 1998, had contained parallel provisions for prohibited weapons in international and non-international armed conflict. In the course of the Rome Conference, however, the weapons provisions pertaining to non-international armed conflicts were dropped. At the time, only Sweden and Australia raised some objections.[8] Evidently, however, the provisions were not dropped because anyone present at the Rome conference

[4] See Assembly of State Parties, 8th Session, Report of the Bureau on the Review Conference, ICC-ASP/8/43/Add.1, Annex I, 10 November 2009, p 2, available at http://www.icc-cpi.int/iccdocs/asp_docs/ASP8/ICC-ASP-8-43-Add.1-ENG.pdf (last visited November 2010).

[5] See only the ICRC Statement at the First Review Conference of the Statute of the International Criminal Court (ICC) Kampala, 31 May—11 June 2010, available at http://www.icc-cpi.int/iccdocs/asp_docs/RC2010/Statements/ICC-RC-gendeba-ICRC-ENG.pdf (last visited November 2010).

[6] In the *Čelebići* case it was stated that: 'The Trial Chamber finds that both the substantive prohibitions in common Article 3 of the Geneva Conventions, and the provisions of the Hague Regulations (which contain both the prohibition of poison and the use of weapons which might cause unnecessary suffering (Article 23 a) and e)) constitute rules of customary international law which may be applied by the International Tribunal to impose individual criminal responsibility for the offences alleged in the Indictment'; *Prosecutor* v *Delalić* et al., IT-96-21-T, Trial Judgment, 16 November 1998, para 316.

[7] See Article 12(1) Nr. 1–3 of the German 'Völkerstrafgesetzbuch', available at http://www.gesetze-im-internet.de/bundesrecht/vstgb/gesamt.pdf (last visited November 2010).

[8] See UN Doc A/CONF.183/C.1/SR.34, paras 4 (Sweden), 108 (Australia).

considered the employment of poison, gas or expanding bullets lawful in non-international armed conflicts. Rather, the weapons listed in the war crimes section applicable to international armed conflicts had become one of the most contentious issues in 1998.[9] Weapons of mass destruction, especially nuclear weapons, were at the heart of the controversy. It seems that a tacit package deal was concluded to appease the opposing sides. As part of this package deal on the one hand nuclear weapons were deleted from the list of prohibited weapons, while on the other hand the regulation of weapons in non-international armed conflict was not pursued any further.

A somewhat similar constellation recurred in the run-up to Kampala. In parallel to the Belgian proposal, Mexico had submitted a proposal pertaining to the prohibition of nuclear weapons. Specifically, Mexico proposed expanding the definition of 'war crimes' under Article 8 of the ICC Statute to include 'employing or threatening to employ nuclear weapons'.[10] Obviously, this contentious issue risked stalling potential progress in respect of other weapons provisions that were to be considered at Kampala. At its 8th meeting in November 2009, the Assembly of State Parties considered Mexico's proposal. Yet, since only a few delegations spoke in favour of the proposal, and in view of the complex political and legal issues involved, it was decided that the issue of nuclear weapons should not be discussed at the Kampala conference and that instead it would be addressed at the 9th session of the Assembly of State Parties in 2010.[11]

With this decision and given that many of the states that had opposed weapons regulations in non-international armed conflicts at the Rome Conference ultimately did not become parties to the ICC Statute, at Kampala, the road was clear for the adoption of the three Belgian proposals. They were adopted by consensus and, with one exception, without any significant debate.

11.2.2 The three categories of prohibited weapons: a closer look

The three categories of prohibited weapons adopted at Kampala correspond to historic categories of prohibited weapons. They constitute specific examples of the general prohibition of weapons that are of a nature likely to cause superfluous injury or unnecessary suffering or are by nature indiscriminate.

---

[9] Cottier 2008, p 412.

[10] See Assembly of State Parties, 8th Session, Report of the Bureau on the Review Conference, ICC-ASP/8/43/Add.1, Annex III, 10 November 2009, pp 9–11, available at http://www.icc-cpi.int/iccdocs/asp_docs/ASP8/ICC-ASP-8-43-Add.1-ENG.pdf (last visited November 2010).

[11] Available at http://www.icc-cpi.int/iccdocs/asp_docs/Resolutions/ICC-ASP-8-Res.6-ENG.pdf. For the permanent members of the Security Council, many members of NATO, and several countries in the Western European and Others Group (WEOG), the inclusion of nuclear weapons has been a deal breaker since the Rome Conference.

11.2.2.1 Poison

The prohibition of poison is one of the oldest prohibitions of a means of warfare in international law. Prohibited since the middle ages, Article 70 of the 1863 Lieber Code provides that 'the use of poison in any manner be it to poison wells, or food, or arms, is wholly excluded from modern warfare'. The ICRC's Customary Law Study found that the prohibition on the use of poison or poisonous weapons applies also in non-international armed conflicts.[12] It is generally accepted that 'employing poison' is to be understood broadly and that the poisoning of water and food supplies is included. The adoption of this war crime was uncontroversial in Rome and it was not contentious in Kampala. The wording of the crime contained in Article 8(2)(b) and (e) of the Rome Statute is drawn from and identical to Article 23(a) of the 1907 Hague Regulations. It is concise and simple and criminalizes '*employing poison or poisoned weapons*'. The only potentially contentious issue is the definition of 'poison' and specifically the question of whether gases and certain biological weapons are covered.[13] In 1998 the Preparatory Commission had wisely avoided the difficult task of defining 'poison'. Instead it adopted a threshold relating to the effects of the substance used. Accordingly, the corresponding Elements of Crimes require that 'the substance was such that it causes death or serious damage to health in the ordinary course of events through its toxic properties'.[14] Since these same Elements of Crimes apply to the amendment, the issue of defining 'poison' was not discussed in Kampala.

11.2.2.2 Asphyxiating, poisonous or other gases

The prohibition on the use of asphyxiating, poisonous or other gases is likewise long-standing. The wording in the Rome Statute is drawn directly from the 1925 Geneva Protocol for the prohibition of the use in war of Asphyxiating, poisonous or other gases, and of Bacteriological Methods of Warfare which in turn reaffirmed earlier prohibitions laid out in the 1899 Hague Declaration concerning Asphyxiating Gases and, for example, Article 171 of the Versailles Peace Treaty.[15] Asphyxiating, poisonous or other gases, as well as analogous liquids, materials or

---

12 Henckaerts and Doswald-Beck 2005.

13 Cottier 2008, para 178.

14 Elements of Crime, ICC-ASP/1/3(part II-B), p. 28, available at http://www.icc-cpi.int/NR/rdonlyres/9CAEE830-38CF-41D6-AB0B-68E5F9082543/0/Element_of_Crimes_English.pdf (last visited November 2010). This of course, changes the nature of the absolute prohibition of poison under the Rome Statute to a prohibition of using a certain substance in a certain way that can be anticipated to create a defined result; see Cottier 2008.

15 Article 171(1) of the Versailles Peace Treaty provides: 'The use of asphyxiating, poisonous or other gases and all analogous liquids, materials or devices being prohibited, their manufacture and importation are strictly forbidden in Germany.' The text is available at http://net.lib.byu.edu/~rdh7/wwi/versa/versa4.html (last visited November 2010).

devices fall within the larger definition of chemical weapons contained in the 1993 chemical weapons convention (CWC).[16] The ICRC Customary Law Study concludes that the prohibition on employing chemical weapons is a customary law rule applicable in international and non-international armed conflicts.[17] During the Rome Conference the most contentious issue pertaining to the prohibition of certain gases was the question of how far the use of riot control agents, such as tear gases, would henceforth be criminalized under the Article 8(2)(b)(xviii) of the ICC Statute.

Already the adoption of the 1925 Gas Protocol had led to a long-standing debate on whether it covered only lethal gases or whether non-toxic and anaesthetic gases were also prohibited. In 1993, the adoption of the CWC brought clarification. The Convention explicitly provides that '[E]ach State Party undertakes not to *use riot control agents* as a method of warfare'.[18] However, one relevant exception to this prohibition was inserted which provides that such agents may be used for 'law enforcement including domestic riot control purposes'.[19] Nevertheless, some ambiguity remains. Although it is now clear that riot control agents are prohibited as a method of warfare but that their use is allowed for law enforcement purposes, the CWC fails to clarify what precisely is meant by 'methods of warfare' or 'law enforcement purposes'.[20]

Thus, at the Rome Conference some states argued that any use of riot control agents in international armed conflict is prohibited, whereas other delegations considered that the use of such agents was permitted in certain circumstances also during armed conflict. In this regard, it was argued that it would be paradoxical if peace-keeping forces striving to control riots in situations where IHL might apply (e.g., UNMIK in Kosovo) could use bullets but not tear gas.[21] But there was also concern that allowing any gas, including non-lethal riot control agents, in armed conflict situations could easily lead to an escalation and culminate in a full out chemical war given that under battlefield conditions it is difficult to determine at first sight what type of gas the enemy is using.[22] As a compromise it was accepted that the gases, substances or devices covered by the crime should be defined only by reference to their effects, namely '*as causing death or serious damage to health in the ordinary course of events*'. This definition was introduced as the second element of the crime. In order to avoid limiting effects on the law governing chemical weapons more generally, a footnote was added to ensure that the

---

[16] Cottier 2008.

[17] Henckaerts and Doswald-Beck 2005.

[18] Article I(5) Convention on the prohibition of the development, production, stockpiling and use of chemical weapons and on their destruction, the text of the Convention is available at http://www.icrc.org/ihl.nsf/FULL/553?OpenDocument (last visited November 2010).

[19] Ibid., Article III(9)(d).

[20] Fry 2010, pp 475, 499.

[21] Cottier 2008, para 180.

[22] Ibid.

Elements were to be considered as being specific only to the war crime in the ICC Statute.[23] Thus, as with the case of poison, the problem was 'resolved' through the definitions contained in the Elements of Crimes. In effect, the explicit reference to a gas, substance or device that causes '*death or serious damage to health in the ordinary course of events*' means that the use of riot-control agents is typically excluded from the ambit of the war crime of using asphyxiating, poisonous or other gases. The use of riot-control gases in the ordinary course of events usually does not cause death or serious damage to health. What is more, by requiring that '*death or serious damage to health*' results from the use of such substances, it would suggest that herbicides—another notoriously contentious issue—are generally not covered by the crime.

That these issues were not tackled head-on but quietly passed over in Kampala is regrettable. It is also rather astounding given that it is in non-international armed conflict where the distinction of law-enforcement- and other military operations is most prevalent and where the question of the use of riot-control agents is far more likely to materialise than in international armed conflicts. On the other hand it must be concluded that the compromise already entailed in the Elements of Crimes, i.e., the reference to a substance's effects in the ordinary course of events, was deemed a suitable compromise also with respect to non-international armed conflicts. As things now stand, the use of riot-control agents in the context of a non-international armed conflict in most circumstances will not amount to a war crime. After all, even in the rare instance that the employment of a riot-control agent leads to death or serious injury, e.g., loss of eyesight in the case of tear gas, in order to amount to a war crime, it would still be necessary to show that this occurred 'in the ordinary course of events'.

11.2.2.3 Expanding bullets

At the Kampala conference, the difficulty in distinguishing so-called law-enforcement operations from the conduct of hostilities came to the fore in a somewhat different context, namely with regard to expanding bullets. Whereas no objections whatsoever had been raised concerning the inclusion of the war crimes of using poison or poisonous gases, some states expressed reservations as to the inclusion of a war crime relating to the use of bullets which expand or flatten easily in the human body. In fact, it seems safe to say that as far as the extension of the list of prohibited weapons is concerned, expanding bullets became 'the' contentious issue in Kampala.

[23] Dörmann 2003, p 285. The footnote reads: 'Nothing in this element [i.e. element 2] shall be interpreted as limiting or prejudicing in any way existing or developing rules of international law with respect to development, production, stockpiling and use of chemical weapons.'.

A. The prohibition of expanding bullets

Historically, the prohibition of expanding bullets was introduced in 1899 by the Hague Declaration concerning the prohibition of using bullets which expand or flatten easily in the human body. The 1899 Declaration was inspired by the sentiments expressed in the 1868 Declaration of St. Petersburg, which aimed to outlaw excessively cruel weapons and constituted a direct reaction to the development of the so-called 'dum-dum bullet'.[24] The wording of Article 8(2)(b) and now 8(2)(e) respectively is drawn from the 1899 Declaration. By way of example these provisions refer to '*bullets with a hard envelope which does not entirely cover the core or is pierced with incisions*'. The German military manual clarifies that the prohibition also applies to projectiles of a nature to burst or deform while penetrating the human body, to projectiles that tumble early in the body, and to the use of shotguns, since shot also causes suffering that is unjustified from the military point of view.[25]

B. Expanding bullets: a useful Means in certain law enforcement operations

Some states were rather reluctant to further extend the ICC's jurisdiction over this crime. They argued that the use of such bullets is necessary and particularly useful in certain law enforcement operations. Indeed, the use of semi-jacketed or hollow-tipped bullets for domestic law-enforcement purposes is said to carry two important advantages.[26] First of all, bullets that expand—unlike the standard military full metal-jacket bullets—tend to remain in the body of the targeted person. This characteristic minimizes the risks for bystanders. Secondly, precisely because all or most of the energy of an expanding bullet is transferred to the body of the targeted person, once hit, the subject is typically instantly immobilized and prevented from firing back. These bullets can be of utility in very specific situations including for example when confronting an armed person in an urban environment, or in a crowd, or alternatively in hostage rescue operations, or during a house-searches. Of course, house and car searches in the vicinity of urban surroundings or hostage-freeing operations are also common operations undertaken by the military in contemporary (asymmetric) armed conflicts. One need not look further than the conflicts in Iraq and Afghanistan for evidence of this trend.

The ICRC Customary Law Study acknowledges that expanding bullets are commonly used by the police in law enforcement situations.[27] In this regard, however, the Study also notes that expanding bullets used by the police are generally fired from a pistol and therefore deposit much less energy than an expanding

---

[24] On Dum-Dum-bullets in general see von Bruns 1898, pp 825–848.

[25] Oeter 2008, para 407.

[26] See also Hampson 2002, para 32.

[27] Henckaerts and Doswald-Beck 2005.

bullet that is fired from a military rifle.[28] The rifles that were being used at the end of the nineteenth century fired a bullet which delivers approximately 3,000 J of energy. The average ammunition for police handguns and machine pistols carries approximately 500 J of energy.[29] Thus the expanding handgun ammunition typically does not cause a wound as large as that caused by an expanding rifle bullet. A bullet carrying 500 J simply does not have the energy to cause a wound as large or as serious as one carrying 3,000 J.[30] In other words, if fired from a handgun expanding bullets do not usually create the type of wound which the drafters of the 1899 Hague Declaration intended to prevent.[31] Against this background it can be argued that most semi-jacketed bullets used in pistols or handguns by law enforcement forces do not constitute a weapon that uselessly aggravates the suffering of persons or renders their death inevitable. Thus, the third element of the crime, which requires that '[t]he perpetrator was aware that the nature of the bullets was such that their employment would uselessly aggravate suffering or the wounding effect',[32] would not be fulfilled if a soldier uses semi-jacketed bullets in a handgun or pistol. However, if used in a military rifle such bullets have shown to create unnecessary suffering or superfluous injury and therefore should be banned not only in situations of armed conflict but also in law enforcement scenarios. Unnecessary suffering is just that: unnecessary; irrespective of whether it is caused in peace or in war-time. Accordingly para 11 (c) of the 1990 Basic Principles on the Use of Force and Firearms by Law Enforcement Officials requires that: '*rules and regulations on the use of firearms by law enforcement officials should include guidelines that … prohibit the use of those firearms and ammunition that cause unwarranted injury or present an unwarranted risk*'.

C. Resolution 5 concerning the amendments to Article 8 of the Rome Statute: constraining the scope of the crime through the backdoor

Notwithstanding this, some states would have liked to insert further exceptions into the Elements of Crimes pertaining to expanding bullets in order to broaden the possibility of their employment in the context of non-international armed conflicts. Indeed, throughout the discussions concerning expanding bullets, the question of whether or not to reopen the Elements of Crimes loomed in the room in Kampala. Ultimately the Elements of Crimes remained untouched. Nevertheless, states' concerns about the criminalization of the use of expanding bullets in

---

[28] Ibid.

[29] See Coupland and Loye 2003, pp136–142.

[30] Ibid.

[31] Ibid.

[32] The elements of crime are available at http://www.icc-cpi.int/NR/rdonlyres/9CAEE830-38CF-41D6-AB0B-68E5F9082543/0/Element_of_Crimes_English.pdf (last visited November 2010).

non-international armed conflicts found expression in Resolution 5 concerning the Amendments to Article 8 of the Rome Statute as it was adopted by the Review Conference on 10 June 2010. It remains to be seen what weight and status states and especially ICC judges will henceforth accord to this Resolution. The Resolution certainly adds—and presumably was intended to do so—some ambiguity. First of all, the seventh unnumbered preambular paragraph of the Resolution considers that the existing Elements of Crimes 'can also help' in the interpretation of the newly adopted crimes pertaining to non-international armed conflicts.[33] The 'can also help' terminology arguably fuels a long-standing debate about the precise role of the Elements of Crimes. As is well known, the Rome Statute already contains a certain ambiguity regarding the role of the Elements of Crimes. Whereas Article 21(1)(a) ICC Statute stipulates that the Court 'shall apply' the Elements of Crimes, Article 9 provides that the Elements of Crimes 'shall assist the Court in the interpretation and application of Articles 6, 7, and 8.' It has been suggested that this linguistic inconsistency can be remedied by combining the two provisions which would then read: the Court 'shall apply' the elements for the purpose of 'assisting the Court …'.[34] The wording contained in Resolution 5, however, seems to accord preference to the terminology entailed in Article 9 of the Statute. What is more, the Resolution appears to further weaken the terms of the Article. After all, Article 9 stipulates that the Elements of Crimes 'shall assist the Court' whereas the Resolution downgrades their role to 'can also help', thereby arguably pushing the door open for the consideration of additional sources of interpretation, such as the Resolution itself.

Resolution 5 in its seventh unnumbered preambular paragraph continues to stipulate that the Elements of Crimes '… specify that the conduct took place in the context of and was associated with an armed conflict, which consequently confirm the *exclusion from the Court's jurisdiction of law enforcement situations.*'[35] Presumably, this is supposed to mean that certain operations carried out by the military in the course of an armed conflict should qualify as law enforcement operations (as opposed to genuine military 'conduct of hostilities' operations) during which soldiers would be permitted to use expanding bullets without fear of criminal prosecution. Of course, it is possible to conduct concurrent law enforcement operations in the context of an ongoing armed conflict. A theft or bank-robbery *prima facie* remain issues of criminal law enforcement irrespective of whether they are carried out in the course of an armed conflict. However, there is a risk that parties to an armed conflict could use the wording in Resolution 5 in order to qualify other operations, i.e., operations that typically have a belligerent nexus, such as for example the house-searches carried out in Afghanistan, per se as law enforcement operations in order to circumvent the jurisdiction of the ICC.

---

[33] Resolution RC/Res. 5, 10 June 2010, preambular § 7.

[34] McAuliffe deGuzman 2008, p 705. See also Rosenne, 2000, pp 167–168.

[35] Resolution RC/Res.5, 10 June 2010, preambular § 7.

Moreover, preambular para 9 of Resolution 5 stipulates that the crime of using expanding bullets is committed '*only* if the perpetrator employs the bullets *to uselessly aggravate* suffering or the wounding effect upon the target of such bullets, as reflected in customary international law'.[36] In this regard, the French delegation, supported by the Canadian, Israeli and American delegations reportedly referred explicitly to the '*specific intent*' to 'uselessly aggravate suffering or the wounding effect' in the target.[37] Of course, any such 'specific intent requirement' is incongruous with the established Elements of Crimes. As mentioned before the third element of crime merely requires that the perpetrator 'was aware that the nature of the bullets was such that their employment would uselessly aggravate suffering or the wounding effect'.[38] A 'specific intent requirement', as opposed to the 'awareness-requirement' that is laid out in the Elements of Crimes, would narrow the scope of the crime considerably.

Amnesty International has already pointed out that a simple Resolution by the Review Conference cannot have any bearing on the Elements of Crimes and that the wording of the Resolution should be understood as being consistent with the knowledge element specified in the Elements of Crimes.[39] This must be right. Article 21 of the ICC Statute establishes a hierarchy of applicable law for the judges of the ICC by providing in para (1)(a) that '[t]he Court shall apply: In the first place, this Statute, Elements of Crimes and its Rules of Procedure and Evidence'. Nevertheless, there can be little doubt that henceforth, in the event of an indictment regarding the use of expanding bullets, defence lawyers will invoke the more restrictive 'specific intent requirement' contained in Resolution 5.

D. Wound ballistics

Before turning to the question of what did not happen in Kampala, a few last words on wound ballistics seem in order. The 1899 Hague Declaration on expanding bullets was generated in view of the state of development of firearms as it stood at the end of the nineteenth century. The prohibition on 'bullets which expand or flatten easily in the human body' arose from the (rudimentary) understanding of wound ballistics at that time.[40] It was an adequate legal instrument for addressing existing humanitarian problems in the early 20th century. Today, however, it can be argued that reference merely to a bullet's construction is no longer sufficient to prevent unnecessarily large wounds. Bullet construction is only one of the factors

[36] Resolution RC/Res.5, 10 June 2010, preambular § 9.

[37] Scheffer 2010.

[38] See supra n 28.

[39] Amnesty International, Public Statement, Comments regarding the language included in the resolution amending Article 8 of the Rome Statute, adopted in plenary on 10 June 2010, available at http://www.iccnow.org/documents/AI_Public_Statement_on_Weapons_Amendment_20100611_SJ.pdf (last visited November 2010).

[40] See Coupland and Loye 2003, p 138.

that determine the size and characteristics of a bullet wound. Bullet velocity is at least as important. The capacity of a bullet to lacerate and crush tissue is determined less by a bullet's construction and more by the kinetic energy it carries.[41]

This understanding was the basis of a Swiss proposal submitted in 2001 to the Second Review Conference of the *Convention on Conventional Weapons* (1980). The proposal argued that the legality of a bullet should be determined by its pattern of energy deposit and not necessarily by its construction.[42] The main cause for concern is so-called high velocity small-calibre ammunition. This type of ammunition typically does not correspond to the narrow technical definitions of expanding bullets but produces similar wounds, owing to a high deposit of energy upon entry in the human body. The 'Swiss proposal' would have ensured that any new bullet, whatever its construction, could be assessed in terms of whether or not its effects are similar to those of a prohibited bullet. However, it was not adopted at the time and has led a rather shadowy existence ever since. In any case, it has rightly been pointed out that if one considers in the absolute the degree of injury and suffering caused by bullets on the modern battlefield,—and not only the size of individual wounds—rate of fire, which is an important design feature of modern military rifles, is probably the most decisive factor.[43] It has been rightly pointed out that as far as can be seen, to date there has been no attempt whatsoever to link the energy deposit from multiple hits to the notion of superfluous injury or unnecessary suffering.[44]

11.3 What Did Not Happen in Kampala?

As far as the extension of the list of prohibited weapons is concerned, ambitions in Kampala were rather moderate. Throughout the conference it was emphasized time and again that the three crimes proposed were not new crimes, that the amendment did not seek to extend the scope of the crimes but merely the jurisdiction of the Court and that in any case the three proposals were part of an ongoing review process that would continue beyond Kampala.

The original Belgian proposal, however, was far more extensive and ambitious.[45] Initially, Belgium had proposed to amend the Statute with regard to both conflict categories, international and non-international armed conflicts, by adding crimes regarding the use of biological and chemical weapons as well as the use of

---

[41] Ibid.

[42] Kneubuehl 1994, pp 26–39; Prokosch 1995, pp 411–425; Second Preparatory Committee for the Second Review Conférence of the 1980 CCW, 'Protocol on the Use of Small Caliber Arms Systems (Draft)', UN Doc. CCW/CONF.II/PC.2/WP.2, 4 April 2001.

[43] See Coupland and Loye 2003, p 139.

[44] Ibid.

[45] United Nations, Reference: C.N.733.2009.TREATIES-8, Belgium: Proposal of Amendments, 29 October 2009 (on file with the author).

anti-personnel mines.[46] Moreover, Belgium had suggested amendments to the weapons defined in Protocols I and IV of the 1980 Conventional Weapons Convention, i.e., the Protocol on Non-Detectable Fragments (I, 1980) and Blinding Laser Weapons (IV, 1995)—and during the very early stages, the Cluster Munitions Convention and Protocols II and III on Mines, Booby-traps and Incendiary Weapons.[47] Belgium's reasoning for these proposals had been that they correspond to treaty prohibitions that had been widely ratified and were considered by an extremely large number of states to have acquired the status of customary international law.[48] The proposed amendments, however, were dropped at the November 2009 session of the Assembly of States Parties for lack of broad consensus. Belgium had always reiterated that it was not the intent of the sponsors to insist for amendments to be transferred to the Review Conference if they do not attract an overwhelming support.[49]

11.4 Does the List of Prohibited Weapons Reflect the Realities of Current Armed Conflicts?

What are the realities of contemporary armed conflicts as far as weapon use is concerned? In non-international armed conflicts one of the most prevalent and available weapons is the AK-47 (so-called 'Kalashnikov') assault rifle arguably followed by the RPG-7, a portable rocket propelled grenade launcher. These weapons are not of direct concern to international humanitarian law; they fall within the ambit of arms control and are potentially subject to regulation by the Arms Trade Treaty that is currently being negotiated under the auspices of the United Nations.[50] Similarly prevalent in Iraq and Afghanistan are the so-called improvised explosive devices (IEDs), also known as 'road-side bombs'. IEDs can either be victim-activated or remote-controlled. IEDs that are victim-activated are widely (and rightly) considered to fall under the prohibition of anti-personnel mines and possibly booby-traps. In any case, although the use of anti-personnel landmines has decreased significantly, they are still being used by some states as well as non-state actors.[51] Anti-personnel landmines in general and IEDs in particular thus remain of concern in contemporary armed conflicts. Although the 1997

46 Ibid., 'Amendment 2', p 5.

47 Ibid., 'Amendment 3', p 6.

48 Ibid., pp 2, 5, 6.

49 Ibid., p 3.

50 United Nations Office for Disarmament Affairs, Towards an Arms Trade Treaty, available at http://www.un.org/disarmament/convarms/ArmsTradeTreaty/html/ATT.shtml (last visited November 2010).

51 International Campaign to Ban Landmines, Land Mine Monitor Report 2010, Executive Summary, p. 1.

Convention on the Prohibition of the Use, Stockpiling, Production and Transfer of Anti-Personnel Mines and on their Destruction, better known as the 'Ottawa Treaty', has not been ratified by a number of key players, it has been ratified by 156 states.[52] Undoubtedly, agreement on a war crime relating to the use of anti-personnel mines in both international and non-international armed conflicts, would have responded to the realities and humanitarian needs of contemporary armed conflicts. The omission of such a crime in the Rome Statute is certainly unfortunate.

On the technologically more advanced end of the weapons spectrum, depleted uranium munitions, cluster munitions and the use of white phosphorous have been at issue in various recent armed conflicts including in Iraq, Afghanistan, Lebanon, Kosovo and during operation Cast Lead in Gaza.[53] These weapons, all of a certain military utility, have remained notoriously controversial in view of their humanitarian impact. Out of these weapons, cluster munitions are the only weapons that are now specifically banned in a treaty. At the time of writing 42 states had ratified the Convention on Cluster Munitions which entered into force on 1 August 2010. Those states that have been most opposed to the Cluster Munitions Convention have also not ratified the Rome Statute. From this perspective there may have even been a chance—however small—to reach agreement on a provision criminalizing the use of cluster munitions in Kampala. But as the Convention was only adopted 2 years ago in May 2008, for many states it would presumably have seemed premature to adopt a criminal law provision on cluster munitions. After all, almost a 100 years have passed between the first codified prohibition on expanding bullets and their criminalization in Rome and Kampala. That the Cluster Munitions Convention was not yet in force at the time of the Kampala Conference—*nota bene* it entered into force 1 month later—no doubt served as a convenient pretext not to consider this issue. Still, a reinforcement of the treaty prohibition on cluster munitions as provided in the Convention with a criminal law provision in the Rome Statute would have been desirable.

Finally, references to weapons of mass destruction were avoided at Kampala. As in 1998 it would not have been possible to deal with chemical and biological weapons—the 'poor man's weapons of mass destruction'—without dealing with nuclear weapons, the classic deal-breaker. Nevertheless, the omission is deplorable and to paraphrase a statement from the Jordanian delegate made at the Rome Conference, it is hard to explain to anyone why bullets which expand or flatten are prohibited while weapons of mass destruction are not.[54]

---

[52] See the ICRC's Treaty Database available at http://www.icrc.org/ihl.nsf/WebSign?ReadForm&id=580&ps=P (last visited November 2010).

[53] See only e.g. Phosphorous Weapons – the ICRC's view, Interview with Peter Herby, Head of the ICRC's Arms Unit, available at http://www.icrc.org/web/eng/siteeng0.nsf/html/weapons-interview-170109 (last visited November 2010); McDonald et al., 2008.

[54] UN Doc. A/CONF.183/C.1/SR.34, para. 80.

11.5 Conclusion

The inability of states to move forward with regard to any of the original Belgian proposals is unfortunate. As it has rightly been pointed out, as things now stand nineteenth century technology is governed by the Rome Statute but twenty-first century technology is largely ignored.[55] Schabas has dubbed this 'a truly dramatic failure of the Rome Statute to incorporate provisions that are meaningful and relevant to modern armed conflict'.[56] Indeed, as far as the list of prohibited weapons is concerned the Kampala Review Conference has merely made good for what should have already been done in Rome. In terms of prohibited weapons the Statute now stands where at the very minimum it should have stood in 1998. But even if the Kampala achievements relating to war crimes only amount to a small step, it is yet another, and therefore important step, towards the streamlining of the law applicable to international and non-international armed conflict in an area where streamlining makes sense. The amendments answer to a humanitarian concern not only of the past but also of the present since there have been proven instances of the use of gas in more recent non-international armed conflicts, albeit rare. In Iraq, for example, non-state armed groups have reportedly used chlorine bombs on at least 10 occasions between January and June 2007, killing and injuring numerous civilians.[57]

Nevertheless, too many major weapons issues were not tackled in Kampala, presumably because too much energy was expended on the quarrels over the crime of aggression. These weapons issues remain dormant in Article 8(2)(b)(xx) ICC Statute which restates the general principle condemning all weapons that are of a nature to cause superfluous injury or unnecessary suffering or which are inherently indiscriminate. For the time being this provision remains an empty shell. It requires an annex that would lay out which specific weapons are encompassed by the general prohibition and thus far no such annex exists. Initial, courageous attempts by Belgium to insert its proposed amendments by way of such an annex were quashed in the very early stages of the discussions. Still, even without an annex this inchoate provision has a function to fulfil. It serves as a permanent reminder of 'unfinished business' and as a 'place-holder' for more elaborate prohibitions in the future. But there is also a problem with this provision. All too easily it could turn into a stumbling block that stymies further progress. The reason is that the general prohibition of weapons that are 'of a nature to cause superfluous injury or unnecessary suffering or which are inherently indiscriminate' as it is laid

---

[55] Schabas 2010.

[56] Ibid.

[57] See only e.g., New York Times, Iraqi Militants Use Chlorine in 3 Bombings, available at http://www.nytimes.com/2007/02/21/world/middleeast/21cnd-baghdad.html?ex=1329714000&en=773c23f16a07847f&ei=5088&partner=rssnyt&emc=rss (last visited November 2010); CBS News, Chlorine Bombs in Iraq makes Hundreds Ill, available at http://www.cbsnews.com/stories/2007/03/18/iraq/main2581781.shtml (last visited November 2010).

out in Article 8(2)(b)(xx) will eventually have to contemplate nuclear weapons. In Kampala, because of the rather glaring gap left after the Rome Conference, it was possible to extend the list of prohibited weapons without touching Article 8(2)(b)(xx) ICC-Statute. At the next review conference, however, this will no longer be possible. There are no more blanks to fill. Next time Article 8(2)(b)(xx) will be the common point of departure for any further amendments concerning prohibited weapons. Then indeed the question about the Rome Statute's ability or inability to deal with contemporary weapons issues in a meaningful way will be brought to the fore.

References

Bruns P von (1898) Über die Wirkung der Bleispitzengeschosse (Dum-Dum-Geschosse). Beiträge zur klinischen Chirurgie 21:825–848

Cottier M (2008) War crimes, Article 8, para 2 a-f. In: Triffterer O (ed) Commentary on the Rome Statute of the International Criminal Court, 2nd edn. Munchen, Beck

Coupland R, Loye D (2003) The 1899 Hague declaration concerning expanding bullets, a treaty effective for more than 100 years faces complex contemporary issues. IRRC 85:136–142

Dörmann K (2003) Elements of War Crimes under the Rome Statute of the International Criminal Court. Cambridge University Press, Cambridge

Fry JD (2010) Gas smells awful: UN forces, riot control agents and the chemical weapons convention. Michigan JIL 31:475–559

Hampson F (2002) Study on human rights protection during situations of armed conflict, internal disturbances and tension, submitted to the Council of Europe, Steering Committee for Human Rights (CDDH), DH-DEV(2002) 1

Henckaerts JM, Doswald-Beck L (2005) Customary International Humanitarian Law, vol I: rules Geneve ICRC. Cambridge, Cambridge University Press

Kneubuehl B (1994) Small caliber weapon systems in: expert meeting on certain weapon systems and on implementation mechanisms in international law, International Committee of the Red Cross. Geneva, pp 26–39

McAuliffe deGuzman M (2008) Article 21. In: Triffterer O (ed) Commentary on the Rome Statute of the International Criminal Court, 2nd edn. Munchen, Beck

McDonald AJM, Kleffner JK, Toebes B (eds) (2008) Depleted uranium weapons and international law. The Hague, Asser Press

Oeter S (2008) In: Fleck D (ed) The Handbook of International Humanitarian Law. 2nd edn, Oxford, Oxford University Press

Prokosch E (1995) The Swiss draft Protocol on small-caliber weapon systems. IRRC 35:411–425

Rosenne S (2000) Poor drafting and imperfect organization: flaws to overcome in the Rome Statute. Virginia JIL 41:164–185

Schabas WA (2010) Prohibited weapons and the Belgian Amendment: symbolic, but of what?, available at: http://iccreviewconference.blogspot.com/2010/05/prohibited-weapons-and-belgian.html

Scheffer D (2010), ASIL Insights: States Parties approve new crimes for International Criminal Court. Available at: http://www.asil.org/insights100622.cfm#_ednref5 (last visited November 2010)

Chapter 12
The US Department of Defense Law of War Manual: An Update

Stephanie Carvin

Contents

12.1 Introduction

One of the major legal instruments the US Department of Defense (DoD) will be relying on in terms of planning and carrying out its activities in the near future is a new law of war military manual which is expected to be published sometime in 2011.[1] While on the surface such a document may not seem of critical interest to those interested in security/strategic studies or to humanitarian activists seeking to ban rather than regulate violence, there are important reasons to place a certain

[1] This was the date suggested to the author by those working on the manual at time of publication. The final date is still to be determined.

This article is based upon research completed while working as an external consultant to the Department of Defense Law of War Working Group from August to December 2009. In addition, the author attended the US Manual International Peer Review Conference at the JAG school in Virginia in May 2009. The author would like to thank Justin Anderson, Anna-Katherine Drake, William H. Boothby, W. Hays Parks for their assistance in the preparation of this article. All errors remain my own.

S. Carvin (✉)
Royal Holloway, University of London, London, UK
e-mail: Stephanie.Carvin@rhul.ac.uk

M.N. Schmitt et al. (eds.), *Yearbook of International Humanitarian Law Volume 13, 2010*, DOI: 10.1007/978-90-6704-811-8_12,

amount of emphasis on this DoD product and to expect that it will have a significant impact, especially on issues that are presently widely debated within the humanitarian legal community.

This article aims briefly to introduce the background of the US military Manual, and illustrate the path taken to bring it to fruition over nearly three decades. It will conclude with a brief description of what the manual will look like when it is eventually published.

12.2 Background

There is no agreed definition as to what, exactly, a law of war military manual is or should look like.[2] Some countries may simply provide a list of all of the treaties to which the state is party with ratification statements.[3] Alternatively, a manual may be a lengthy and statement of the law encompassing political, legal and policy statements.[4] Either way, it is probably fair to suggest that the lowest common denominator of military manuals is a text that provides guidance as to the law of war obligations of the relevant state in times of war and peace. Additionally, they explicitly state the basis of national understanding in explicit terms against which national training in the laws of war and indeed national decision making can be undertaken.

In the case of the United States, the first guidance issued to its armed forces regarding restraints on the use of force was in 1863 as *General Orders 100: Instructions for the Government of Armies of the United States in the Field*, more commonly called *The Lieber Code*. The eponymous *Code* emerged when Francis Lieber, a German who had fought in the Napoleonic Wars and eventually emigrated to the United States, was asked by General H.W. Halleck, General-in-Chief of the Union's armies (who had seen Lieber lecture in New York) to put together a simplified set of rules and guidance for soldiers in the field. In particular, Halleck was interested in guidance to law on the battlefield and in the protection of victims of the conflict. The Code was used throughout the nineteenth century, and was even relied upon to defend the actions of officials and officers during the war and subsequent insurgency in the Philippines from 1899 to 1902.[5]

Yet, the first true Manual that the United States published was not until 1914 (subsequently updated in 1917, 1940 and 1944 to reflect the legal needs and

---

[2] See the discussion of several different national approaches discussed in Hayashi 2008.

[3] For example, none of the Scandinavian Countries currently has a military manual in the true sense of the word.

[4] See for example, the 1958 United Kingdom Manual of Military Law.

[5] Arthur MacArthur, the US Commander in the Philippines partially relied on the *Lieber Code* to justify the harsh treatment of guerrilla soldiers that were captured. Additionally, Major General Smith was charged with 'conduct to the prejudice of good order and discipline' after his order to turn the island of Samar into a 'howling wilderness' and to kill every male over the age of 10. See Karnow 1989; McAllister Linn 1989; and Carvin 2010, pp 76–83.

experiences of the First and Second World Wars.) This Manual was replaced with a new version in 1954 that was produced following the US experiences in the Second World War, the Korean War and to take account of the then-recent US ratification of the 1949 Geneva Conventions. However, the staff assigned to the task, led by R.R. Baxter—a US military lawyer in the army reserves and Harvard Law Professor who would later go on to serve as a judge at the International Court of Justice—were given an extremely short period of time to complete their task. The resulting document, Department of the Army Field Manual FM-27, while adequate, is also sometimes confusing and does not always explain its rationale for the law that it states. For example, sections of the 1949 Geneva Conventions were frequently copied verbatim without any additional commentary on either delicate or sensitive points of law, nor anything on how to actually implement it. Additionally, the new edition broke with the tradition established by previous drafts of US military manuals by removing the explanatory footnotes which had provided context and explanation for the laws stated or interpretations suggested.[6] Ultimately, while minor revisions were made for a re-issue of FM-27 in 1976 to reflect some of the experiences of the Vietnam War, this did not constitute a true update of the Manual.

12.3 The Long Road towards a New Manual

Between 1977 and the present, despite the evolution in the nature of warfighting and the different kinds of conflict the US has engaged in, the Department of Defense has not been able to produce a law of war manual which reflects these changes. As such, it has participated in conflicts in Lebanon, Grenada, Panama, Iraq (twice), Somalia, the Balkans, and Afghanistan (plus occasional peace-enforcement operations abroad) with a manual essentially written in the 1950s. Even then, as mentioned above, this manual was sometimes questionable, or at least failed to provide adequate explanation as to why certain laws were included or excluded. In this sense the United States has not issued a well researched and footnoted war manual for nearly a century.[7]

[6] The explanation for this, provided to the author by Department of Defense employees who knew Baxter and have subsequently worked on producing a new manual, is that, given the severe time-restrictions provided to Baxter and his team, as well as the resource constraints, decisions were made to essentially 'chop' and edit the manual as best they could. Historical experiences and explanatory footnotes were essentially dropped and arguments inserted (subsequently known as 'Baxterisms') without any reasoning or context. This partly explains why the new manual will contain extensive footnotes from selected examples in US military history.

[7] That the United States military has been able to exist for so long without a military manual may beg the question as to whether such a manual is necessary at all. The recent problems over clarity of the law at Abu Ghraib which partially contributed to the scandals there, as well as the increasing use of manuals as evidence of 'custom' by NGOs, the International Committee of the Red Cross (particulary in its 2005 Customary Law Study), and the International Court of Justice suggest otherwise.

Given all of the developments and practice of the twentieth century, it was clear that a complete overhaul would be required. Rather than amending the Army Manual as had been done in 1976, an entirely new product was seen as the best way forward. Between 1949 and the present, nine arms control agreements bearing upon the laws of war and/or IHL treaties had been produced by the international community as well as eight protocols (of which the US has ratified five and six respectively).[8] As W. Hays Parks notes, 'The extent of treaty development made it apparent that a manual new from bottom to top was necessary.'[9]

Unfortunately, starting over meant that any effort to write a new manual had become a massive undertaking. Where the 1954 Manual was put together in a relatively short period of time (albeit with mixed results) a comprehensive review of the applicable laws of war and providing an explanation and examples of US practice would necessarily take years. Beyond this, as will be discussed below, an official DoD Manual applicable to each armed service would naturally require a large amount of negotiation and consultation. Each service and DoD would have to be in complete agreement in terms of the interpretation of law of war treaties.

However, the time and resources required for a manual project in a section of DoD that is constantly short of both meant that it would inevitably be a challenging endeavor. According to Hays Parks, (who is also the editor-in-chief of the new Manual), it was agreed in December 1977 that FM 27-10 should at least be revised after the US signed the Additional Protocols. This revision was to take place concurrently with a review of the Additional Protocols for the Executive branch of the government. However, this work was immediately delayed for

---

[8] The list of treaties, compiled by W. Hays Parks, is as follows. *Asterisk indicates US ratification. The 1954 Hague Convention for the Protection of Cultural Property in the Event of Armed Conflict*, and its First Protocol; the 1972 Convention on the Prohibition of the Development, Production, and Stockpiling of Bacteriological (Biological) and Toxin Weapons*; the 1976 Convention on the Prohibition of Military or any other Hostile Use of Environmental Modification Methods*; the 1977 Protocols I and II additional to the 1949 Geneva Conventions; the 1980 Convention on Certain Conventional Weapons* and its protocols I (non-detectable fragments)*, II (landmines, booby traps, and other devices)*, and III (incendiary weapons)*; the 1993 Convention on the Prohibition of the Development, Production, Stockpiling and Use of Chemical Weapons and on Their Destruction*; the 1995 Protocol IV (Blinding Laser Weapons)* to the 1980 Convention on Certain Conventional Weapons; the 1996 Amended Protocol II to the 1980 Convention on Certain Conventional Weapons*; the 1997 Ottawa Convention on the Prohibition of the Use, Stockpiling, Production and Transfer of Anti-Personnel Mines and on Their Destruction; the 1998 Rome Statute of the International Criminal Court; the 1999 Second Protocol to the 1954 Hague Convention; the 2005 Additional Protocol III to the 1949 Geneva Conventions*; the 2006 Protocol V (Explosive Remnants of War) to the 1980 Convention on Certain Conventional Weapons*. In the main text the 1977 Additional Protocols I and II have been counted as full treaties.

[9] W. Hays Parks, 'National Security Law in Practice: The Department of Defense Law of War Manual'. Speech given to the American Bar Association, Washington DC, 18 November 2010. Comments from text of speech are available at the ABA website http://www.abanet.org/natsecurity/hays_parks_speech11082010.pdf.

3 years as the individuals responsible for it were involved in the negotiation of what became the 1980 Convention on Certain Conventional Weapons (CCW).[10]

On these two points, it is clear that the demands and long-term nature of the project has frequently meant that it has been put aside for short-term needs. This includes day-to-day items which 'pop-up' (everything from opinions on proposed Status of Forces Agreements to clarification on the legality of targeting a particular object in a theatre of operations), to the planning and execution of major wars in the Balkans, Afghanistan and Iraq. As such, Parks estimates that 'At best twenty percent of the time between 1996 and 2010 was dedicated to the manual.'[11] Thus, put most plainly, despite the relative importance of, and reliance on, military manuals within DoD, this project was not truly allocated sufficient resources to enable it to be completed in a short period of time. Despite efforts as early as January 1978 to start the process of drafting a new manual, it is unlikely that this project will come to fruition much before the end of 2011 at the earliest.

Finally, a major reason for the delay may have been the lingering question as to whether the United States would sign and ratify the 1977 Additional Protocols to the Geneva Conventions. The status of the Protocols was not made clear until President Reagan announced in 1987 that ratification for API was not forthcoming.[12] While APII has been sent to the US Senate for ratification, it has not yet acted upon it and is not likely to for some time in the future. In the meantime, the United States has had an ambiguous relationship with API and there can be little doubt that this has affected the drafting and revision of the manual.[13]

Yet to suggest that the US has been negligent in terms of the development and implementation of the laws of war would be, at the very least, an exaggeration. During the time that the US Manual and ratification of the Additional Protocols have been in question, the US spent much of the 1980s working with NATO on producing joint understandings on various national interpretations of the laws of war. In addition, in what has sometimes been described as meetings of 'the Empire Club' (despite the obvious decision of the US to take out 'associate-membership' in 1776) DoD lawyers have constantly met with their counterparts from Australia, Canada, New Zealand and the UK on an informal basis to coordinate legal interpretations and understandings.[14] Finally, internally to the Department of Defense, DoD Directive 5100.77[15] established the Law of War Working Group

---

[10] Ibid.

[11] Ibid.

[12] See Ronald Reagan, 'Message to the Senate Transmitting a Protocol to the 1949 Geneva Conventions', 29 January 1987. The speech is available online at the website of the Ronald Reagan Presidential Library. Available at http://lbj-sage.lbjlib.utexas.edu/archives/speeches/1987/012987B.HTM.

[13] The new manual will have a statement clarifying the US position on API.

[14] Hays Parks, supra n 9. The issue of 'anglo-sphere' participation in the Manual will be discussed further below.

[15] The present Department of Defense Law of War Directive is now DoD 2311.01E as amended 15 November 2010.

which brought legal representatives from all of the service branches together to work on and discuss issues related to humanitarian law such as weapons reviews. This group meets as required within DoD (during 2010 this was approximately twice per month).[16]

12.4 Going Forward

Despite heavy demands on their time, an unclear US position in relation to several international humanitarian law treaties and even, perhaps, 'hostile clients' in the wake of the Vietnam war, military lawyers in DoD continued to press forward with the idea of drafting a new manual that would not only reflect US understanding and practice of IHL but also serve as the definitive DoD authoritative source for all branches of the US military. At the present, some of the service branches have created their own manual-like documents such as US Naval War College's *Commander's Handbook on the Law of Naval Operations* (NWP 1–14 M).[17] Even FM-27-10, although considered authoritative and an important development, is still technically an Army document. Therefore, an important step was taken in 1996 when it was agreed by judge advocate generals in the Army, Navy, Air Force and Marines that there would be a joint manual rather than single-service manuals. As was recognized with this decision, 'the services and DoD needed to speak with a single, authoritative voice'.[18] The result will be a manual more like those of Canada[19] and the UK.[20]

But there were many questions that remained. What should be the scope of the manual? Should it be a simple one-volume project that concentrated on the laws of war, or should it be a comprehensive manual on all aspects of operational law? What form should the manual take? Should it comprise a list of US treaty obligations and relevant articles of the Geneva Conventions? Or should it be more along the lines of the 1914 US and 1958 UK Manuals, complete with lengthy footnotes, examples of practice, history and explanation? And in terms of providing context, is it better to keep the manual as brief and concise as possible, or to give historical illustration?

---

[16] The Directive specifies that the Law of War Working group has the responsibility to produce the Law of War Manual.

[17] Available at http://www.usnwc.edu/getattachment/a9b8e92d-2c8d-4779-9925-0defea93325c/1-14M_(Jul_2007)_(NWP). The Handbook goes beyond a straightforward law of war manual and also discusses policy considerations.

[18] Hays Parks supra n 9. As Hays Parks points out, a joint manual also made sense given the emphasis on joint operations resulting from the 1986 Goldwater-Nichols Act.

[19] See Office of the Judge Advocate General (Canada), Joint Doctrine Manual: Law of Armed Conflict at the Operational and Tactical Levels, 2001, available at http://www.cfd-cdf.forces.gc.ca/sites/page-eng.asp?page=3481.

[20] See Ministry of Defence (United Kingdom), The Manual of the Law of Armed Conflict, 2004.

In addition, more philosophical questions were raised regarding the manual. Who would be using the manual and to what purpose? Out of necessity it would need to be primarily directed to those who would be using it on a daily basis within DoD as well as JAGs in the field who needed to answer a question from their commanders in the middle of the night. But clearly it was also going to be seen by the wider international and humanitarian community as an official statement of DoD regarding their understanding and interpretation of the laws of war. In this sense to what extent did the authors and editors need to mind the fact that the Manual would also represent an example of state practice? And to what extent should technical language be used at the expense of clarity? Should it be aimed solely at lawyers who would be using it the most? Or would it be beneficial to aim to make it universally accessible? And finally, what about the possibility of using the Manual in court cases, particularly those relating to the 'War on Terror'?[21]

12.5 The New Manual: A Brief Description

In terms of a physical description, the new Manual is indicative of the massive undertaking its creation required. It is comprised of approximately 19 chapters and, as of spring 2011, exceeded 1,100 single-spaced pages with more than 3000 footnotes.

As mentioned above, unlike previous US Manuals, the new Manual will be the authoritative DoD source for all service branches. In other words all Army, Navy and Air Force Manuals will have to adhere to the standard set out in the new DoD Manual. This has required significant consultation with the different service branches to ensure that chapters specifically applicable to their area of operations are agreed upon. For the most part this has been done through the Law of War Working Group. However, members of different services have also been heavily involved in writing and editing various chapters of the Manual as well. In addition, service lawyers have played the lead role in drafting chapters most significantly related to their core area of operations. Thus, the Air Force took the lead in writing the Air War chapter, the Navy took the lead in writing the Naval Warfare chapter, etc.

Regarding the scope of the Manual, it is self-consciously limited to the 'laws of war' rather than 'operational law'.[22] The differences between these two concepts is

---

[21] There is no question that the ongoing War on Terror has posed challenges to the drafters of the new Manual. For example, the ongoing situation with detainees in the Global War on Terror has meant that issues relating to the treatment of prisoners of war had to be treated with extra caution in order to present an accurate picture of US legal obligations within the context of an ever changing US policy since 2002.

[22] Also, importantly, it is not concerned with issues related to *jus ad bellum*.

that while the former is geared to the laws of war as reflected in the various law of war treaty obligations of the United States, the latter comprises all legal aspects of military operations and is much broader in scope.[23] The decision to limit the Manual to a more narrow focus (though at over 1100 pages this is an odd description) was made at a 1996 meeting held at the Judge Advocate General's School in Charlottesville, Virginia on the development of the US Manual. Attended by law of war experts from the various branches of the US armed services as well as the key 'the Empire Club' allies of the United States, it was noted that while a law of war manual could be produced as a single volume, 'An operational law manual would require a bookshelf.'[24] Given the already serious crunch on time and resources, an undertaking to produce an operational law manual was unrealistic.

Ultimately, the plan for the new Manual was to go back to the style of earlier Manuals (such as those published by the US between 1914 and 1944, as well as stylistically the UK 1958 Manual). In this sense, the Manual would include not only the law, but also commentary that would provide context and explanation as well as historical examples. Although the drafters of the Manual were well aware that the effort required to do this would be substantial, they decided to proceed on this basis in the hope that this approach would rectify some of the problems that lawyers within DOD and the services found with FM-27. Thus, the new Manual will reflect the fact that its drafters desired to create a product that had a fundamentally different feel to that of its immediate predecessor.

After a lengthy period of writing and revision, the Manual was subjected to a 'Peer Review' in May 2009. Once again this took place at the JAG School in Charlottesville and was attended by representatives from DoD, all of the service branches, high-ranking military lawyers from 'the Empire Club' and distinguished professors from the United States and the United Kingdom.[25] Over 5 days the chapters were read through by the group and subjected to critical scrutiny by all of the attendees. Feedback was given on all aspects of the Manual whether it was on specific details (such as the treatment of prisoners of war, or targeting) or general comments (such as remarks about the organization of a particular chapter). Attendees were urged to be candid and critical, with the expectation that serious and constructive criticism, as well as the occasional heated debate, would, in the end, produce a stronger product.

---

[23] For more information on operational law, see Graham 1987, pp 9–10; Warren 1996, pp 33–73.

[24] Hays Parks, supra n 9. The comments were made by Charles Garraway who was a serving British Army Colonel at the time.

[25] The author served as an official observer and 'historian' at the 2009 Peer Review Conference.

Following the Peer Review, the feedback and comments received were incorporated into the draft Manual's text. This was done with the assistance of a professional non-lawyer editor, Justin Anderson.[26] Once this was completed for each chapter, they were taken back to the Law of War Working Group where they were again discussed and debated before final drafts were produced. As of this writing, the Manual will soon be forwarded to Charles Allen, head of the Office of the General Council, International Affairs, and the DoD General Counsel, Jeh Jonson for their review before forwarding it to the US Secretary of Defense for his approval and release. Although this process has been a lengthy one, it is hoped that having had many eyes critically examine the text will ultimately produce a better produce than otherwise have been the case.[27]

12.6 Conclusion

Ultimately, the approach (if not philosophical underpinnings) of the Manual project may be said to be a belief that merely providing a list of the law of war obligations of the United States would be insufficient. Rather, an approach which combines law, history, and examples as practice would result in a superior Manual—even if this entailed a lengthy period of production. However, it is also important to note that while the emphasis of the new Manual is very much on the historical practice of the United States, there is also a sense among the participants of the Law of War Working Group and those who have spent time either writing, editing or critiquing the Manual (both American and non-American) that it speaks to many of the pressing issues that have emerged since 2001 in terms of the 'War on Terror', and present practice of the laws of war.

On this last point there is no illusion within DoD that the Manual will end up being for 'US-eyes only'. Rather, there is an appreciation and an understanding that the Manual will have an effect beyond US shores. First, particularly within the

---

[26] Anderson, who holds a PhD in War Studies from King's College London, was one of several non-lawyers to participate in the project. Sir Adam Roberts, for example, is a Professor of International Relations, albeit with a long-time expertise in the laws of war. Sir Adam was involved in the Peer Review Process. It was hoped that non-lawyers involved in the project would be able to provide insight beyond legal criticism and help to look at the overall 'big picture' beyond the legal details and provide feedback on the political aspects of the Manual. The author of this article is also not a lawyer.

[27] In this regard one may draw comparisons with the process of drafting the US Army Counterinsurgency Manual (FM 3-24) in 2006. As described by Thomas Ricks, the process involved army officials and counterinsurgency experts as well as academics. General David Patraeus convened a conference in February 2006 at Fort Leavenworth with approximately 135 experts on irregular warfare from not just the military but also representatives from other government agencies such as the CIA and State Department, human rights advocates, academics and high-profile journalists. The Counterinsurgency Manual is available at http://usacac.army.mil/cac2/coin/repository/FM_3-24.pdf.

anglo-sphere (or what has been dubbed 'the Empire Club') there has been a close reliance on each other in developing military manuals. Historically, military lawyers within this group have been inspired by the manuals produced by other countries and frequently copied the style and substance used in one another's manual. For example, one can detect much symmetry between the United States and the UK Manuals over time as just one example.[28]

However, within the wider international community there are also other nations (and possibly non-state actors) which will be using the Manual to see and understand the set of rules and restraints the United States considers itself bound by in armed conflict. Additionally, many NGOs and humanitarian organizations will look and critically examine the new Manual to evaluate how the United States fights its wars and to examine the US position on the laws of war. In this sense it seems clear that the Manual will have an audience that goes well beyond the United States and its armed forces.

These many audiences, and the many purposes to which a military manual may be put to use as outlined above, are indicative of the importance of the document which the Department of Defense will be releasing in 2011 and suggest the relative importance of military manuals as not only vital legal tools for militaries but as important indicators of state understanding and practice of the laws of war. In this sense it is a shame that so few militaries have chosen to produce a military manual, despite the fact that it is a requirement of the 1899 Hague Convention with Respect of the Laws of Customs of War on Land.[29] There is hope that other than making a significant contribution to the understanding of the laws of war that the Manual will inspire other militaries throughout the world to produce their own.

---

[28] For example, the 1958 UK Manual very much resembles in style the 1914 US Manual. While the 1954 US Manual broke this tradition, the new Manual is very much inspired by the style of the 1958 UK Manual (which was replaced in 2004). But there are other examples of cooperation within this group as well. The New Zealand government ended up adopting a law of war manual that was originally intended but ultimately rejected for the Canadian armed forces, written by noted Canadian international legal scholar L.C. Green. Still, a question may be raised as to why only countries the 'anglo-sphere' have played a major consultative role with the US Manual. The short answer is that there is no formal reason as to why this is the case, but at least three good reasons may be suggested as to why such a policy worked for DoD. First, these countries share a martial heritage rooted in British military traditions, as well as the British Articles of War. Second, these countries have frequently fought together in coalitions and they have a good understanding of each other's militaries, traditions and operations. Third, the limited consultation essentially amounted to a continuation of the informal policy of these countries cooperating and outright 'borrowing' military manuals from one another. While each country has its own distinct manual today, there is a similarity in content, interpretation and understanding of the laws of war in these manuals.

[29] Article 1 states 'The High Contracting Parties shall issue instructions to their armed land forces, which shall be in conformity with the 'Regulations respecting the laws and customs of war on land' annexed to the present Convention.' This was reaffirmed at the 1907 Hague Peace Conference. (Article 1 of the 1907 Hague Convention is identical to Article 1 of the 1899 Convention).

References

Carvin S (2010) Prisoners of America's wars: from the early Republic to Guantánamo. Columbia University Press, New York
Graham DE (1987) Operational law—a concept comes of age. The Army Lawyer July, pp 9–10
Hayashi N (2008) National military manuals on the law of armed conflict, FICHL publication series. PRIO, Oslo. http://www.prio.no/Research-and-Publications/Publication/?oid=32950588
Karnow S (1989) In our image: America's empire in the Philippines. Random House, New York
McAllister Linn B (1989) The US army and counterinsurgency in the Philippine War 1899–1902. The University of North Carolina Press, Chapel Hill
Warren ML (1996) Operational law—a concept matures. Mil Law Rev 152:33–37

Part III
Focus Topic: The Gaza Blockade

Chapter 13
Rule Selection in the Case of Israel's Naval Blockade of Gaza: Law of Naval Warfare or Law of the Sea?

James Kraska

Contents

He also is a Senior Associate in the Center for Irregular Warfare and Armed Groups at the Naval War College, a Senior Fellow at the Foreign Policy Research Institute, a Senior Associate of the Institute for Communitarian Policy Studies at George Washington University and a Guest Investigator at the Marine Policy Center, Woods Hole Oceanographic Institution. As the former chief of the International Negotiations Division for the Director of Strategic Plans & Policy, Joint Chiefs of Staff, Commander Kraska led global maritime security strategy and policy for the U.S. armed forces. Commander Kraska recently completed a book on maritime piracy for Praeger Security International, and he is editing a volume on Arctic security for Cambridge University Press. His study, *Maritime Power and the Law of the Sea: Expeditionary Operations in World Politics* recently was published by Oxford University Press in 2011. He earned a doctor of juridical science (J.S.D.) and master of laws (LL.M.) from the University of Virginia Law School and a doctor of jurisprudence (J.D.) from Indiana University Maurer School of Law. The views presented are those of the author and do not reflect the official policy or position of the Department of Defense.

J. Kraska (✉)
International Law Department, Center for Naval Warfare Studies,
U.S. Naval War College, Newport, RI, USA
e-mail: james.kraska@gmail.com

M.N. Schmitt et al. (eds.), *Yearbook of International Humanitarian Law Volume 13, 2010*, DOI: 10.1007/978-90-6704-811-8_13,

13.1 Introduction

On 27 September 2010 the UN Human Rights Council in Geneva released its analysis of the 31 May 2010 boarding of the large passenger liner, *Mavi Marmara*, by forces of the Israeli Navy.[1] The ship was interdicted in the eastern Mediterranean Sea by Israeli commandoes, who rappelled vertically onto the top deck of the ship from a helicopter. The boarding incident and ensuing melee that unfolded on the deck of the ship left several Israeli military members seriously injured and resulted in the death of nine Turkish nationals. The event ignited a firestorm of controversy in international humanitarian law. These sad and unfortunate results raise interdisciplinary questions concerning both fact selection—determining what actually happened, or whose version of the facts are accepted—and rule selection—what was the legal relationship between Israel and the vessel *Mavi Marmara*. Because of the tense stand-off between the Gaza Strip and Israel, however, and the volatile brew of religion, politics and geography that colors choices of fact selection and rule selection, analysis of the incident is especially challenging. The issues of fact selection are more important for resolving questions surrounding the deaths and injuries of persons on board the ship and Israeli naval personnel. Factual claims necessarily are colored by a veneer of subjectivity, and in this case go more toward determining whether the use of force on the part of Israeli commandoes was lawful. The nature of the tactical operation that unfolded on board the ship and the reaction of the vessel's passengers are bitterly disputed, inseparable from who used what force and when.

In contrast to these questions of tactical fact, there is a fairly standard understanding of the strategic landscape upon which the Israeli assault occurred. The facts concerning Israeli's maintenance of a blockade and the resulting interception of the ship are less controversial. Nearly everyone agrees there is some level of armed conflict between the state of Israel and Hamas, the armed group governing the Gaza Strip. What are less clear are the legal implications of the relationship between Israel and Hamas, not over a disagreement with the facts, but rather over a dispute about the law that should apply. Is Israel in an armed struggle with only Hamas, or at war with the Gaza Strip? Is the Gaza Strip part of Israel, or a foreign area (or country) physically or constructively occupied by Israeli forces? Are standards for the use of force derived from international human rights law or international humanitarian law?

In the case of the maritime interception of the *Mavi Marmara*, which is to be sure a single narrow element of the overall relationship between Israel and Hamas or Gaza, the overriding legal issues lay at the intersection of the international law of the sea and the law of naval warfare, which is a subset of international

---

[1] Report of the international fact-finding mission to investigate violations of international law, including international humanitarian and human rights law, resulting from the Israeli attacks on the flotilla of ships carrying humanitarian assistance, UN Doc A/HRC/15/21, 27 September 2010, p 53.

humanitarian law (IHL). Dissecting the legal elements of the raid is important for a better understanding of what happened—and how to prevent a reoccurrence. The report of the Human Rights Council, for example, concluded that the Israeli interception resulted in '... a series of violations of international law, including international humanitarian and human rights law...'[2]

Israel has initiated several investigations into the matter. The Israeli Defense Force (IDF) concluded an inquiry on 12 July 2010, which found that the only way the IDF could have stopped the *Mavi Marmara* was to board the ship, and that the commandoes acted properly.[3] Israel also created a national commission to investigate the incident, which issued its final report exonerating any wrongdoing.[4] In announcing the investigatory commission, Prime Minister Netanyahu stated 'only the Israeli Defence Force (IDF) should question the soldiers, as is generally done in armies around the world'.[5] Turkey has rejected the ability of an Israeli Commission to conduct a thorough investigation. A statement released by the Turkish Ministry of Foreign Affairs in early June 2010 stated: 'Israel does not have the authority to assign a national commission to investigate a crime perpetrated in international waters ...,' and that the inquiry by Tel Aviv 'cannot be impartial, fair, transparent and credible'.[6] Instead, Turkey supported UN Secretary General Ban Ki Moon's call for creation of an independent UN investigation into the matter.

13.2 On Board the Mavi Marmara

Israel's maritime interdiction of the 'freedom flotilla' was designated 'Operation Sea Breeze'. The flotilla set sail from Turkey in May 2010 bound for the Gaza Strip. The stated intentions of the convoy were to deliver humanitarian supplies to the beleaguered people of Gaza, and also to tangibly break the naval blockade of Gaza that was imposed by Israel. A number of nongovernmental groups, led by the

---

[2] Ibid.

[3] Maj. Gen. (Res.) Eiland Submits Conclusions of Military Examination Team Regarding *Mavi Marmara*, 12 July 2010, IDF Blog, 12 July 2010, http://idfspokesperson.com/2010/07/12/maj-gen-res-eiland-submits-conclusions-of-military-examination-team-regarding-mavi-marmara-12-july-2010/.

[4] Justice Emeritus Jacob Türkel, et al., The Public Commission to Examine the Maritime Incident of 31 May 2010, pp 278–279 (The Türkel Commission) January 2010.

[5] The investigation team includes Brig. Gen. (Res.) Aviv Kohavi, the former head of the Operations Division, Brig. Gen. (Res.) Yuval Halamish, former head of the IDF Intelligence and a senior member of the Israeli National Security Council Col. (Res.) Ben Tzion Daabul, the former head of the Israel Navy Operational Branch. Brigadier General Ken Watkins, former Judge Advocate General of the Canadian Armed Forces and Irish Nobel prize holder David Trimble serve as international observers. BG Watkins has been selected to serve as the Stockton Chair of International Law at the US Naval War College for academic year 2010–2011, but the author has not discussed this analysis with him.

[6] Deen 2010.

controversial Turkish charity *İnsan Hak ve Hürriyetleri ve İnsani Yardım Vakfı* (IHH), or Foundation for Human Rights and Freedoms and Humanitarian Relief, announced on 28 April that it intended to sail a flotilla into the coast of the Gaza Strip despite the blockade. Prior to the arrival of the ships in the eastern Mediterranean near Gaza, Israel officially reiterated a standing offer to Turkey to escort the ships into the port of Ashdod, inspect the cargoes and transfer the foreign humanitarian shipments for distribution throughout the Gaza Strip. The offer was declined, however.

The civilian vessels that comprised the relief armada were registered in several nations. The group consisted of the cargo ship *Gazze* (Turkey), the cargo ship *Eleftheri Mesogeios* or *Free Mediterranean* (Greece), the cargo ship *Define Y* (Kiribati), the tourist boat *Sfendonh* (Togo), and the US-flagged yacht, *Alhaya*. The boats were scheduled to arrive in the region on 24 May 2010 together with the Cambodian-flagged *Rachel Corrie*, which departed from Ireland on 17 May with a giant Irish flag painted on the ship along with the words 'Free Gaza'. Due to technical difficulties, the ships began to arrive at the pre-defined gathering point south of Cyprus on Friday, 28 May The largest vessel, the Comoros-flagged passenger ship *Mavi Marmara*, had 561 persons on board, including 67 members of the IHH. The ship also embarked 16 parliamentary members from a variety of nations and 34 media reporters, underscoring the propaganda or public diplomacy aspect of the voyage.

IHH has a checkered reputation. Reports suggest the group has links to Global Jihad in Syria, Iraq, Afghanistan and Chechnya. In 1996, the CIA reported that IHH had connections to violent extreme groups. The organization gained some prominence in the 2001 US prosecution case of an Algerian terrorist convicted of the attempted 31 December 1999 'millennium bombing' plot at Los Angeles International Airport. In the federal prosecution *United States* v *Ahmed Ressam*, French counter-terrorism magistrate Jean-Louis Brougiere testified that 'IHH is a [non-governmental organization], but it was kind of a type of cover-up … [sic] in order to obtain forged documents and also to obtain different forms of infiltration for Mujahedeen in combat … [and recruitment]. And finally, one of the last responsibilities that they had was also to be implicated or involved in weapons trafficking.' Despite this testimony, however, IHH has not been designated a terrorist group by the US Department of State.[7] In 2006, the Danish Institute for International Studies issued a report that stated that during the 1990s the IHH maintained links with al-Qaida and a number of global jihad networks.[8]

The IHH participation in the relief flotilla included purchase of three ships, including the *Mavi Marmara*, as well as providing aid to the Hamas regime in

[7] In a letter to Secretary of State Hillary Clinton, however, the Anti-Defamation League of the United States requested that IHH and another group of 'freedom flotilla' organizers and funders, Union of Good, be designated as Foreign Terrorist Organizations (FTO) under Sect. 219 of the Immigration and Nationality Act. See Robert G. Sugarman and Abraham H. Foxman letter to the Hon. Hillary R. Clinton, 8 June 2010, http://www.adl.org/terrorism/Letter_flotillaorganizers.asp.

[8] Kohlmann 2006. See also Hartman 2010.

preparing to receive the convoy. On 30 May 2010, Bulent Yildrim, president of IHH, told the media that there were children and elderly persons on board the ship, and that the passengers would act as human shields. IHH members on *Mavi Marmara* were armed with an assortment of homemade urban weapons, including pipes, clubs and knives taken from the ship's kitchen and from six cafeterias on board the ship. Steel cables and metal rods sawn from the ship's railings by electric saws, were distributed among IHH members, along with wooden clubs, hammers and other industrial tools, such as large pipe wrenches, that could be used as weapons.[9] Metal screw-nuts were strewn throughout the upper deck to impede the movement of any Israeli naval forces that might come on board.[10] There were a large number of slingshots and ammunition secreted aboard the ship, and flares were also stockpiled in preparation for dazzling night vision devices on helicopters.[11] Later, when commandoes came on board, flares were used to burn soldiers. Israeli authorities uncovered one hundred ceramic protective vests—each imprinted with the Turkish flag—and two hundred gas masks.[12] Eight axes had been removed from the ship's fire-fighting stations and set out as weapons.[13]

After interviewing passengers from the *Mavi Marmara*, Israel's Intelligence and Terrorism Information Center discovered that IHH members riding the ship had prepared for a violent clash with IDF soldiers. The reaction of some of the passengers on the *Mavi Marmara* to the Israeli boarding team apparently was not spontaneous, but rather a pre-planned action orchestrated by a group of hardcore IHH operatives numbering about 40. These principal or dedicated members of IHH

[9] Video—Weaponry Overview and Footage of *Mavi Marmara* Passengers Preparing Weaponry, Israeli Defense Force Spokesperson, 3 June 2010, http://idfspokesperson.com/2010/06/03/video-weaponry-overview-and-footage-of-mavi-marmara-passengers-preparing-weaponry-3-june-2010/; IDF forces met with pre-planned violence when attempting to board flotilla, Israel Ministry of Foreign Affairs, 31 May (Updated 21 June) 2010, http://www.mfa.gov.il/MFA/Government/Communiques/2010/Israel_Navy_warns_flotilla_31-May-2010.htm#weapons. See also Guns may have been thrown overboard, The Jerusalem Post, 4 June 2010, http://www.jpost.com/Israel/Article.aspx?id=177479 (gun sights, coded plans found on *Mavi Marmara*) and Israel Continues In-Depth Investigation into Flotilla Incident, Targeted News Service, 26 September 2010, Israel Condemned for Deadly, CNN 1 June 2010 Tuesday, Cable News Network (CNN), 1 June 2010 (Transcript 060103CN.V11 in NEWS, ALL (English, Full Text), Lexis-Nexis database.

[10] Report on the IHH's preparations for confronting the IDF, Israeli Defense Force, 9 June 2010, http://dover.idf.il/IDF/English/News/today/10/06/0902.htm.

[11] Photos of Bullet Proof Vests, Sawn-Off Rods, Night Vision Goggles and Rifle Scope Found on *Mavi Marmara*, Israeli Defense Force, 2 June 2010, http://idfspokesperson.com/2010/06/02/photos-of-bullet-proof-vests-sawn-off-rods-night-vision-goggles-and-rifle-scope-found-on-mavi-marmara-2-june-2010/ and Katz 2010.

[12] Photos of *Mavi Marmara*'s Equipment and Weapons, Israeli Defense Force, 1 June 2010, http://idfspokesperson.com/2010/06/01/photos-of-the-mavi-marmaras-equipment-and-weapons-1-jun-2010/.

[13] Anshel Pfeffer, Report: 40 IHH activists on *Mavi Marmara* planned violent resistance, Haaretz.com, 10 June 2010, http://www.haaretz.com/print-edition/news/report-40-ihh-activists-on-mavi-marmara-planned-violent-resistance-1.295233.

boarded the ship in the port of Istanbul, and it appears they did so without undergoing a security inspection. Other passengers who boarded in Antalya went on board the ship only after a full inspection. Some of the IHH operatives wore tags on their clothing that stated they were ships security detail. The activists distributed walkie-talkies, and they occupied the upper deck of the vessel as a communications room and command center. Two hours before the Israelis boarded the ship, Yildrim reportedly ordered the formation of a human chain to repel the commandoes. Chairs and clubs were employed to beat back the Israeli boarding team and throw them into the sea.

When small Israeli patrol boats attempted to come alongside the ship for boarding it at the waterline, the IHH operatives removed grappling hooks that were attached by Israelis to facilitate climbing up the side. Israel claims that IHH members seized the sidearm of at least one commando and used it to shoot at the boarding party. One individual Israeli apparently was thrown over a rail, hitting the deck below, and was seriously injured. Eventually, the IDF commandoes opened fire on the attackers. Israel claims the use of deadly force was a reaction to the violence used by IHH to repel the boarding party. In the melee nine IHH protesters were killed and 34 injured. Seven Israeli soldiers were injured, two of them critically. Nonviolent activists also were among the injured. In contrast to the breakdown of order on the decks of the *Mavi Marmara*, the successful boarding of the other vessels in the convoy was without incident. IDF commandoes on the other five ships were met only with passive, nonviolent resistance, and the vessels were either directed or steered into Ashdod for inspection.

In retrospect, the boarding team appears to have been woefully unprepared to establish order on the ship, let alone seize control of the vessel. Israeli commandos were armed with paintballs, shotguns with beanbag ammunition for crowd dispersal, tasers and stun grenades, yet even these non-lethal armaments were not employed effectively. After the incident on the *Mavi Marmara*, all six flotilla vessels were taken to Ashdod and unloaded; their passengers were repatriated. Hamas delayed acceptance of the humanitarian aid from the five smaller ships for several weeks, declining to consent to delivery of the materials at the Kerem Shalom crossing. In mid-June, however, Israel reached agreement with the United Nations to facilitate the transfer of the humanitarian aid from the flotilla. Robert H. Serry, a representative of the UN Secretary General, informed Major General Eitan Dangot, Israel's Coordinator of Government Activities in the Territories (COGAT), that the UN would make arrangements for the transfer of humanitarian goods from the convoy for transfer into the Gaza Strip. Serry also pledged to ensure that the material was used only for humanitarian aid operations. Of the six original vessels that comprised the flotilla, only the *Mavi Marmara* did not have humanitarian supplies on board. Two weeks later, in mid-June 2010, as another flotilla was getting underway from Lebanon with the stated intention of breaking the blockade, Israeli Defense Minister Ehud Barak said in a speech: 'The government of Lebanon … has to prevent war materials, weaponry, ammunitions, explosive charges and so on, which can later lead to violent and dangerous confrontation in case the ship refuses to dock in Ashdod, from finding their way into the ships.'[14] This pronouncement set forth the Israeli government's rationale for intercepting a ship on the high seas.

13.3 Navigating Dichotomy: Law of the Sea and the Law of Naval Warfare

In accordance with Articles 58 and 87 of the 1982 UN Convention on the Law of the Sea (UNCLOS), all ships enjoy the peacetime right of freedom of navigation on the high seas and throughout the exclusive economic zone. Except for provisions of the law of naval warfare that trump the peacetime rules, nations—particularly neutral states—enjoy the same broad freedom of the seas during periods of armed conflict. In challenging the Israeli action, the government of Turkey and the IHH asserted that Israel violated the peacetime right of freedom of navigation of the ships in the convoy. This argument could best be made by the flag states of the vessels boarded—in the case of the *Mavi Marmara* only Comoros, as the state of registry, was in a position to assert this claim. Only the *Gazze* was a Turkish-flagged ship. Although Ankara is not a party to UNCLOS, the right to exercise freedom of navigation is a tenet of a liberal order of the oceans and reflective of customary international law, binding on all nations. In peacetime, freedom of navigation has very few limitations, especially beyond the territorial sea.

In time of armed conflict, although the rules reflected in UNCLOS continue to apply, they share the stage with IHL and more specifically with the law of naval warfare. In effect, during periods of armed conflict, the law of naval warfare is superimposed on the regimes of peacetime oceans law. So while the provisions of UNCLOS are applicable, in time of war the peacetime rules are calibrated by another set of rules governing the rights and duties of parties to conflict at sea. The law of naval warfare helps to regulate relations between neutral states and belligerent states, and the law of blockade is an important element of IHL.[15] Consequently, in some circumstances the law of blockade and its provision for the belligerent right of visit and search provide fidelity to the peacetime framework of navigational freedom.[16]

The right of the parties to an armed conflict to select the methods and means of warfare are not unlimited; the enemy's civilian population may not be targeted for attack. Maritime blockade may be analogized to land-based siege warfare. The law concerning siege on land, and by implication naval blockade, implicate the

[14] Arnon Ben-Dror, The Lebanese Government is Responsible for Every Ship Leaving from its Territory, Israeli Defense Force press release, 17 June 2010, http://dover.idf.il/IDF/English/News/today/10/06/1702.htm.

[15] § 1.3, Helsinki Principles on the Law of Maritime Neutrality, adopted by the International Law Association, Taipei, Taiwan, 30 May 1998, Schindler and Toman 2004, Doc 115, pp 1425–1430 (hereinafter, Helsinki Principles).

[16] Oppenheim 1969, pp 768–769.

principles of distinction and proportionality. Consequently, siege and blockade often give rise to criticism that the measures are inconsistent with the duty of belligerents to protect civilian populations.

13.3.1 Blockade in history

Blockade, or the interdiction of maritime traffic coming from or going to a port or coastline of a belligerent, is a legitimate method of naval warfare and a maritime instrument of economic warfare.[17] Blockade was an enduring feature of the First and Second World Wars. With the Orders-in-Council of 11 March 1915, London instituted a blockade during World War I 'to prevent vessels carrying goods for or coming from Germany'. The British also blockaded the Russian port of Petrograd on 10 October 1919, as part of their intervention in the Russian revolution. In the case of the Petrograd blockade, the British government acted even though it was uncertain whether a 'state of war' existed between the two nations.[18] The concept of blockade also was a feature of the interwar period. On 8 March 1936, for example, the United Kingdom, France, Italy and Germany established a four-power Non-Intervention Patrol to prevent outside involvement in the Spanish Civil War. The Patrol maintained a blockade of the Spanish coastline, with France and Great Britain participating in the Patrol after Italy and Germany dropped out.[19]

Blockade was employed as a method of war by Axis and Allied powers during World War II, and the naval blockades against Germany and Japan devastated the economies of Nazi Germany and Imperial Japan. Since World War II, nations once again resorted to maritime interdiction to enforce maritime blockade during time of armed conflict. The French Navy blockaded Algeria during its struggle with the colony. The United States conducted naval blockades during the Korean War and the Vietnam War (Haiphong Harbor), the latter of which Moscow protested as interference in freedom of navigation.[20] In the 1960s, the Beira Patrol sought to prevent the flow of oil from reaching Rhodesia. But for all of its good intentions, the Patrol found that it was particularly difficult to craft coercive rules of engagement for visit and search on the high seas.[21] Politically, however, there never was a risk that Rhodesia's two supporters—South Africa and Portugal—would forcibly challenge the blockade.[22] The burden for enforcing the Beira Patrol fell on Britain, and by virtue of UN Security Council Resolution 217 of 20

[17] § 5.2.10, Helsinki Principles, supra n 15.

[18] Cable 1981, p 70.

[19] Thomas 2001, p 715.

[20] McDougal and Feliciano 1961, pp 493–495 and Swayze 1977, p 143. Blockade during the Korean War is discussed in Weigley 1973, pp 388–389.

[21] O'Connell 1975, p 174.

[22] Cable 1981, p 126.

November 1965, the United Kingdom was legally entitled to enforce the oil embargo against Rhodesia. Iran and Iraq both blockaded each other's ports during the Iran–Iraq war of the 1980s, with Tehran's order of 1 October 1980 initiating a tit-for-tat tanker war that endangered oil shipping. Iran boarded 1,200 foreign-flagged merchant ships during the early-1980s, including US-flagged vessels, and did so mostly in a professional manner. On the other hand, Iran laid mines in the shipping channels of the Gulf and launched numerous cruise missiles, aviation and small boat attacks against civil neutral shipping, abrogating its responsibilities under the law of armed conflict.

After the Iraqi invasion of Kuwait in August 1990, the UN Security Council adopted resolution 660 (1990), which required withdrawal of Iraqi military forces from Kuwait.[23] Resolution 661 imposed a general embargo on all trade with Iraq and Kuwait, serving as the principal means of inducing Iraqi compliance with resolution 660. Resolution 665 imposed a blockade on Iraq on 25 August 1990, less than a month after the invasion—providing a means to enforce resolution 661.[24] Specifically, resolution 665 authorized states to 'halt all inward and outward maritime shipping in order to inspect and verify their cargoes and destinations', using authority under Chap. VII of the charter.

These contemporary examples illustrate that blockade is part of state practice and that the law concerning blockade has not fallen into desuetude. As part of the conflict with Hamas, the Israeli government has asserted that the 'limitation on the transfer of goods is a central pillar in the means at the disposal of the State of Israel in the armed conflict between it and Hamas', which is known as the Islamic Resistance Movement.[25]

13.4 The Gaza Blockade

The Oslo Accords recognize that the Palestinian Authority (PA) may exercise jurisdiction over the territorial waters off Gaza.[26] Israel, however, was granted the right to maintain external security of the Gaza Strip until such time as there was a final status agreement.[27] Under Article 5(1)(b) of the Gaza-Jericho Agreement, the PA was excluded from exercising functional authority for external security. Article 8 of the Gaza-Jericho Agreement states: 'Israel shall continue to carry the responsibility … for defense against external threats from the sea and from the air

23 UN Security Council Res. 660 (1990) and UN Security resolution 661 (1990).

24 Interestingly, resolution 665 requested states 'cooperating with the Government of Kuwait' while executing the blockade of Iraq also coordinate their actions using the mechanism of the Military Staff Committee in Articles 46 and 47 of the UN charter. The US-led coalition refrained from doing so, however. See Dinstein 2005, p 306.

25 Franks 2010.

26 Article 5, para 1(a), Gaza–Jericho Agreement.

27 Article 5, para 3, ibid.

… and will have all the powers to take the steps necessary to meet this responsibility.' In order to maintain coastal security, three maritime zones were established off Gaza. A central zone extends seaward from the beach to a distance of twenty nautical miles (nm) from the coastline. Along the north and south marine border of the central zone are strips of water adjacent to Egyptian and Israeli territorial seas and measuring one nm in width. The two strips constitute military security areas and are under Israeli authority. The central zone is jointly managed by the government of Israel and the Palestinian Authority, and is open for fishing throughout the zone and for recreational boating out to a distance of three nm from shore. Foreign shipping is not permitted to approach closer than twenty nm from the coastline.

Hamas, which won electoral victory in Gaza in 2006, has consistently opposed the Oslo peace process. The conflict between Israel and Hamas accelerated after the Hamas election success and the subsequent withholding of donor funds and closure of the Gaza strip in 2007. In June 2007, group violently seized control of Gaza from the PA and Israel promptly declared Gaza 'hostile territory'. Hamas was formed in 1987 as the Palestinian branch of the Muslim Brotherhood. The US Department of State has designated Hamas an international terrorist organization, but the group enjoys widespread support and sympathy throughout Gaza, strengthened by a network of social, religious and political patronage. Izz-al-Din al-Qassam Brigades, the military forces of Hamas, are responsible for thousands of missile strikes and hundreds of suicide bombings and terrorist attacks inside Israel and the West Bank. Negotiations between Israel and the PA collapsed in 2002, and Palestinian support for the PA began to erode. Israel imposed intermittent but increasingly restrictive impediments to land and sea entry into Gaza about the same time.[28] On 19 September 2007, Israel issued a communiqué that stated:

> Hamas is a terrorist organization that has taken control of the Gaza Strip and turned it into hostile territory. This organization engages in hostile activity against the State of Israel and its citizens and bears responsibility for this activity. In light of the foregoing, it has been decided to adopt the recommendations that have been presented by the security establishment, including the continuation of military and counter-terrorist operations against the terrorist organization. Additional sanctions will be placed on the Hamas regime in order to restrict the passage of various goods to the Gaza Strip and reduce the supply of fuel and electricity. Restrictions will also be placed on the movement of people to and from the Gaza Strip. The sanctions will be enacted following a legal examination, while taking into account both the humanitarian aspects relevant to the Gaza Strip and the intention to avoid a humanitarian crisis.[29]

---

[28] Prime Minister Ehud Olmert (Communicated by the Prime Minister's Media Adviser) Security Cabinet declares Gaza hostile territory, 19 September 2007, http://www.mfa.gov.il/MFA/Government/Communiques/2007/Security+Cabinet+declares+Gaza+hostile+territory+19-Sep-2007.htm.

[29] At http://www.mfa.gov.il/MFA/Government/Communiques/2007/Security+Cabinet+declares+Gaza+hostile+territory+19-Sep-2007.htm.

The Israeli Security Cabinet's designation of Gaza as 'hostile territory' is a factual (rather than a legal) determination, since Hamas is 'an organization dedicated to the destruction of the State of Israel'.[30] In response to a large increase in the number and frequency of missile attacks into Israel from Gaza throughout 2008, on 27 December the Israeli Air Force launched 'Operation Cast Lead'. Israeli ground troops entered Gaza just days later—on 3 January 2009—the same day the naval blockade was established. The Israeli Navy publicly announced the blockade three days later, and its boundaries were superimposed on the 20 nm Gaza maritime zone.[31] The purpose of the naval blockade was to prevent Hamas from resupplying rockets and other weapons and to stop the infiltration of terrorists into Gaza. The IDF and Hamas were engaged in battle for nearly 3 weeks, and on 21 January 2009, Israeli forces withdrew from the territory. But the naval blockade has persisted.

Since Hamas' takeover of Gaza, Israel limited the import of various goods to Gaza to a 'humanitarian minimum'.[32] All foreign vessels are barred from the Gaza offshore area. Vessels delivering humanitarian supplies to the civilian population are permitted to do so through the land crossings, subject to prior coordination with Israel and inspection of the cargoes. The list of permitted goods includes about 40 items; prior to 2007, about 4,000 items were permitted into Gaza.[33] The humanitarian group Gisha claimed that Israel allowed only 25% of the goods into Gaza than it had before the Hamas takeover.[34] One apparent problem, however, was that there appeared to be no official list of contraband that traders could observe, and Gisha alleges the list was seemingly arbitrary and subject to frequent change without notice. Israel was criticized because decisions on what cargoes were permitted into the Gaza Strip appeared to be made on a case-by-case basis, resulting in eclectic and inconsistent decisions. Gisha claims that items such as newspapers, tea, standard A4 office paper and chocolate were among those reportedly barred (Fig. 13.1 and Table 13.1).

Thus, the contraband list has been criticized as overbroad and illogical. Gisha argued in court that the blockade of Gaza was tantamount to unlawful collective

[30] Behind the Headlines: Israel Designates Gaza a 'Hostile Territory', Israel Ministry of Foreign Affairs, 24 September 2007, http://www.mfa.gov.il/MFA/About+the+Ministry/Behind+the+Headlines/Gaza+designated+a+Hostile+Territory+24-Sep-2007.htm.

[31] State of Israel Ministry of Transport and Road Safety, Notice to Mariners No. 1/2009 Blockade of the Gaza Strip, 6 January 2009, http://en.mot.gov.il/index.php?option=com_content&view=article&id=124:no12009&catid=17:noticetomariners&Itemid=12.

[32] Knickmeyer 2007, p A1. For the current Israeli maritime security notice, see Advisory Notice (Maritime Zone off the Coast of the Gaza Strip), 11 August 2008, No. 6, 13 August 2008.

[33] A complete Israeli list of contraband and acceptable goods in the Gaza blockade emerged from a court case filed in Israel by the Israeli human rights group Gisha. Gisha claimed that prior to the closure, Israel allowed an average of 10,400 trucks to enter Gaza with goods each month, but by the summer of 2010 only 2,500 trucks per month were permitted (Frenkel 2010).

[34] At http://news.bbc.co.uk/2/shared/bsp/hi/pdfs/05_05_10_gazaimports.pdf.

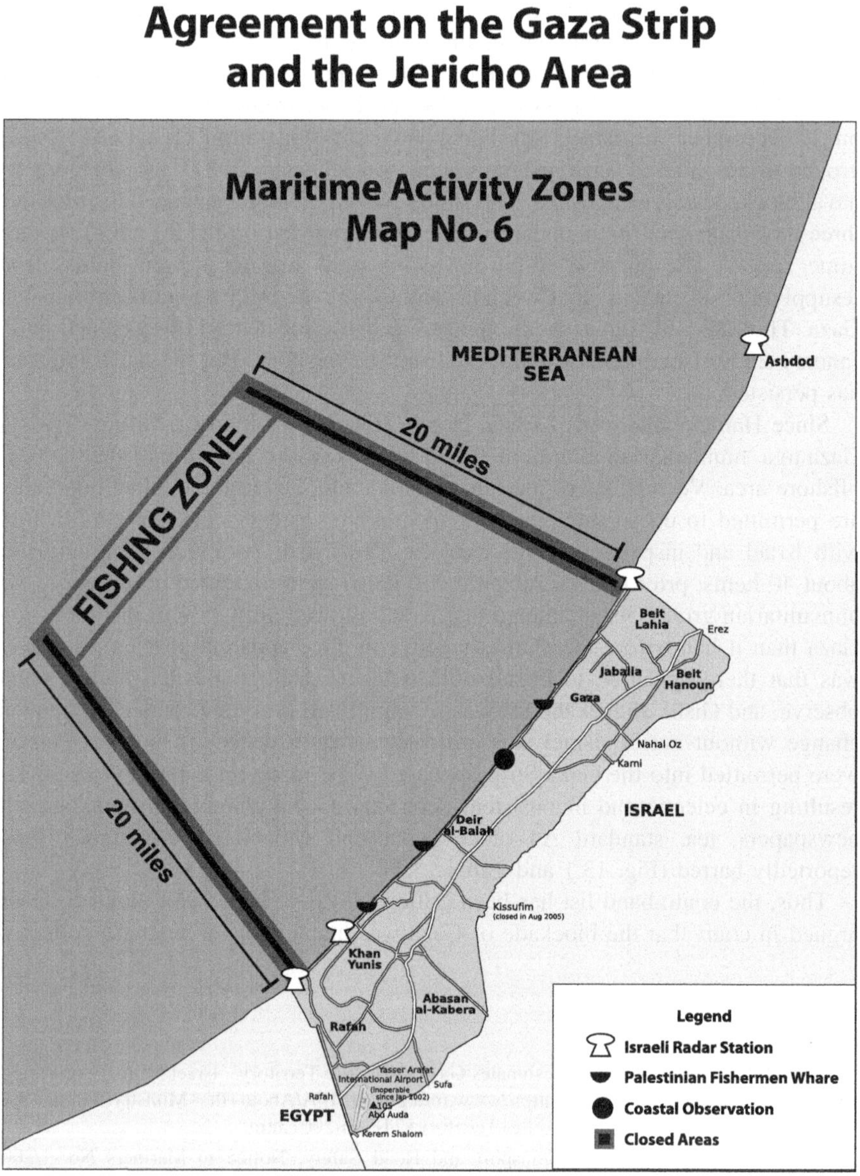

Fig. 13.1 Maritime Activity Zones (*Source* Map No. 6, Agreement on the Gaza Strip and the Jericho Area; see also the Annex appended to the end of this article)

punishment against the civilian population. 'Gisha's position is that the closure is illegal because it punishes civilians in the Gaza Strip for acts they did not commit and for political circumstances beyond their control. The closure inflicts harm to

Table 13.1 Contraband list for the Gaza land crossing as of May 6, 2010

Prohibited	Permitted
Contraband list: Israeli blockade of Gaza	
Steel, cement	Aniseed, cinnamon, black pepper
Coriander, nutmeg, ginger	Fresh fruit, frozen fruit
Canned fruit, dried fruit	Frozen meat and vegetables
Fresh meat	Rice, chickpeas, beans
Seeds and nuts	Frozen fish
Fabric for clothing	Clothes
Fishing rods and ropes for fishing	Animal feed and hay
Chickens and chicken hatcheries	Cartons for transporting chicks
Donkeys, horses, goats and cattle	Chemical fertilizers and pesticides
Musical instruments	Medicine and medical equipment
Newspapers	Wood for doors and window
Construction lumber	

Source Gisha

the civilian population and civilian institutions by blocking the passage of goods necessary for health, well-being, and economic life'.[35]

The Israeli government stated in a document obtained by the media that the blockade is a tool of economic warfare is intended to achieve a political goal. Still, in the aftermath of the *Mavi Marmara* incident, Israel pledged to ease the blockade but would not lift the embargo so long as Hamas remains in control of Gaza.[36] To explain further, Gisha contends that Israel's ban on the entry of raw materials is designed to prevent economic development in the Gaza Strip. For example, Israel allows residents of the Gaza Strip to accept small packages of margarine—a consumer item—but prohibits companies in the region from receiving shipments of large blocks of margarine, because those are used in industrial food manufacture. It is not the product, but rather the purpose, that Gisha claims is banned.

13.5 Law of Blockade

A blockade is a legitimate method of warfare to prevent ingress and egress of all vessels, and it includes the interdiction of all or certain maritime traffic coming from or going to a port or coast of a belligerent party to a conflict.[37] The act of initiating a blockade is tantamount to an act of war, and is one of the enumerated

[35] Gaza Closure Defined: Collective Punishment Position Paper on the International Law Definition of Israeli Restrictions on Movement in and out of the Gaza Strip (Legal Center for the Freedom of Movement, Gisha, December 2008), available at http://gisha.org/UserFiles/File/publications/GazaClosureDefinedEng.pdf.

[36] Frenkel 2010.

[37] Article 5.2.10 [Blockade], Helsinki Principles, supra n 15.

specific acts of aggression that appears in the General Assembly's consensus Definition of Aggression adopted on 14 December 1974.[38] The object of a blockade is the disruption of seaborne transportation links to and from an enemy state. A blockade must meet several criteria, including that it be applied during a state of war or armed conflict.

Senior Israeli officials testified that the legal basis for the blockade was customary international law and the existence of a state of armed conflict between Hamas and Israel. The London Declaration, the *San Remo Manual on International Law Applicable to Armed Conflicts at Sea* and the US Navy's *Commander's Handbook on the Law of Naval Operations* (*Commander's Handbook*) all recognize the application of the law of blockade as an important component of the law of naval warfare.[39] A state imposing a blockade must provide notice to the international community, and a blockade must be effective in order to be lawful.

During the eighteenth century, blockade became a routine practice in European conflict. But the difficulty of blockading long coastlines soon gave rise to the 'paper blockade', in which a nation might declare a blockade, but lack the naval force to effectively maintain it. The early Dutch blockades of England (1662) and France (1672–1673) and the Dutch–English blockade (1689) were regarded as paper blockades. Consequently states agreed in the Declaration of Armed Neutrality (1780) that in order to be lawful, a blockade also must be effective. The French wars opposing Great Britain from 1793 to 1815 included a continental decree issued by Paris on 21 November 1806 with the goal of closing off Europe to British goods. The project proved too ambitious, however, and it was not well-enforced. British and French naval forces blockaded Russia during the Crimean War from 1854 to 1856 in order to coerce Moscow into abandoning its aspirations in Turkey. The 'effectiveness' criterion entered into the law as a requirement in paragraph 4 of the 1856 Paris Declaration Respecting Maritime Law.[40] In the opening salvo of the Spanish–American War, on 21 April 1898, Secretary of the Navy John Long directed US warships of the North Atlantic Squadron to blockade Cuba to wrest control of the island from Madrid. Spain was ill-prepared to defend its possession, and within days the island was locked in a vice grip.[41]

Although much of the law of naval warfare is rather antiquated, the law surrounding naval blockades still has currency. The contemporary international law of blockade emerged from a lack of consensus over the customary international law of prize, which was to be applied by an International Prize Court established

[38] Article 3(c), UNGA Res. 3314, 14 December 1974.

[39] IDF Chief Military Advocate General Staff, Avichai Mandelblit's testimony to the Türkel Committee: Public Commission to Examine the Maritime Incident of May 31, 2010, Session Number 4, 26 August 2010, pp 41–45.

[40] 1856 Paris Declaration Respecting Maritime Law, 16 April 1856, reprinted in AJIL 1 (1907) Supp. 89–90.

[41] Hayes 2006, pp 81–85.

by Hague Convention XII of 1907.[42] In an effort to clarify the customary law relative to prize, ten powers met in a conference in London beginning on 4 December 1908 to determine and codify the rules.[43] The 1909 London Declaration Concerning the Laws of Naval War (the London Declaration) emerged as a product of the meeting. The London Declaration contains 21 provisions concerning 'Blockade in Time of War'.[44] Although the Declaration was never ratified, it is accepted as a general expression of the customary international law of blockade.

Blockade is a lawful measure and is recognized by the UN. After World War II, the UN charter included the concept of naval blockade as a legitimate instrument for the use of force by the UN Security Council. Importantly, the concept of blockade in the charter appears in Article 42 (military sanctions) rather than in Article 41 (economic sanction).[45] Scholars and practitioners in naval warfare similarly have accepted blockade as a legal mechanism during armed conflict. Article 97 of the 1993 *San Remo Manual of International Law Applicable to Armed Conflicts at Sea* also accepts blockade as a lawful tool of naval warfare.[46] Following the 1980–1988 Iran–Iraq War, the International Law Association (ILA) formed a Committee on Maritime Neutrality to consider the rules affecting neutral ships, which suffered heavily during the conflict. Throughout the war, the UN Security Council had called on states to respect the right of neutral shipping to freedom of navigation, but often to little effect.[47] In order to strengthen these rights, the law of blockade was reflected in the Helsinki Principles on the Law of Maritime Neutrality, which were adopted by the ILA at its Taipei Conference on 20 May 1998. In the United States, analysis and practice on the law of blockade is reflected in a manual published by the US Navy, Coast Guard and Marine Corps, the *Commander's Handbook*.[48]

An important element of an effective blockade is to employ 'force sufficient really to prevent access to the enemy coastline'.[49] The date of beginning, period of

[42] International Prize Court, Hague Convention XII (1907) Doc 81, reprinted in Schindler and Toman 2004 Helsinki Principles.

[43] Austria-Hungary, France, Germany, Great Britain, Italy, Japan, Netherlands, Russia, Spain and the United States participated in the conference.

[44] Naval Conference of London, Declaration Concerning the Laws of Naval Warfare, signed at London 26 February 1909, reprinted in Schindler and Toman 2004 Helsinki Principles, Doc 83, pp 1111–1122.

[45] Dinstein 2005, p 295.

[46] § 97, Doswald-Beck 1995, p 178.

[47] UN Security Council Resolutions 540 (1983), 552 (1984), 582 91986) and 598 (1987).

[48] Declaration concerning the Laws of Naval War, 208 Consol. T.S. 338 (1909), available at http://www1.umn.edu/humanrts/instree/1909b.htm. The Commander's Handbook on the Law of Naval Operations (US Navy, Naval Warfare Publication 1–14 M, 2007) (hereinafter, Commander's Handbook), is a product of the International Law Department at the US Naval War College, where I lead a joint effort to revise the document. The revision is planned for release during 2011.

[49] Article 2, London Declaration.

blockade and specific geographic boundaries of a blockade must be published. Neutral vessels must be given some period of time in advance to avoid the blockade, typically between two and 30 days, and failure to provide safe passage from the blockaded coast before initiation of a blockade renders the declaration unlawful.[50] A blockade also may not bar access to neutral coastlines or ports.[51] Furthermore, a blockade must be applied impartially to the ships of all nations, and the blockading belligerent may not discriminate among nations in the enforcement of the blockade.[52]

Weapons, ammunition and other items of military utility constitute 'absolute contraband'.[53] Other goods and material, such as medicine and religious objects, constitute 'free goods' and may not be seized as contraband.[54] Clothing, bedding, and essential foodstuffs and means of shelter for the civilian population generally are considered free goods, provided 'there is not serious reason to believe that such goods will be diverted to other purpose', or accrue a 'definite military advantage' to the enemy.[55] Some scholars retain a third category of 'conditional goods', which are those goods that are considered contraband. Even though not patently military goods, conditional goods are susceptible to being used for a military purpose. In order to consider enumerated conditional goods as contraband, the blockading state must designate them on a published list.[56]

'Starvation of civilians as a method of warfare', may not be the sole purpose of a blockade. Thus, the object of the blockade must be to prohibit war-sustaining goods and cannot be aimed 'solely' at starving the civilian population.[57] A blockade must permit non-belligerent material to flow, but this rule gives rise to inevitable disagreements about dual use items, which may be used by civilians, but also have qualities or uses that may make them 'war sustaining'. Legally, however, the 'war sustaining' element of blockade is actually quite minimal. Article 23 of 1949 Geneva Convention IV, for example, states that blockade must allow 'free passage of all consignments of foodstuffs, clothing and tonics intended for children under fifteen, expectant mothers, and maternity cases', and then only on condition that there be 'no reason for fearing … that a definite advantage may accrue to the military efforts or economy of the enemy'.

A blockade does not target any specific cargo, but rather constitutes a total exclusion of transit into and out of the area or location.[58] But since a naval

---

[50] Article 10, London Declaration.

[51] Article 18, London Declaration.

[52] Article 5, London Declaration.

[53] Article 22, London Declaration.

[54] Article 38, GC II and Article 23(1), 59 and 61, GC IV. See also, § 150, Doswald-Beck 1995, p 217.

[55] GC III and Article 59, GC IV. See also § 150, Doswald-Beck 1995, p 217.

[56] § 149, Doswald-Beck 1995, p 216.

[57] Article 54 (1), Geneva Additional Protocol I (1977) and Article 33, Geneva Convention IV.

[58] Schmitt 1991, p 3.

blockade is imposed for security purposes and not 'solely for the punishment of the civilian population', humanitarian material must be separated from contraband.[59] But the blockading force may prescribe technical arrangements, including visit and search, under which the passage is permitted, in order to ensure that no aid is transferred to the benefit of the enemy, rather than to the civilian population.

In the case of Gaza, the IDF claims that Israel has fulfilled the impartiality and non-discrimination elements of a lawful blockade. Israel has suggested that it has maintained an effective blockade of Gaza, preventing all known vessels from landing in the area, and diverting humanitarian aid shipments through the Israeli port of Ashdod in order to inspect cargo inbound to Gaza. Because the bar for what constitutes 'war sustaining' materiel is so low, it appears in the case of the Gaza blockade that Israel would be within its rights to only permit bare minimum humanitarian supplies for children, pregnant women, and new mothers. Indeed, Israel has adopted this rationale, stating:

> At the heart of (the decision to declare Gaza 'hostile territory') the principle that although Israel remains committed to averting any humanitarian crises, it does not feel required to provide any supplies, which go beyond that. It would be hypocritical to expect Israel to provide anything beyond the basic human needs of a population when a large number of its members, including the authorities, are engaged in systematic hostile activities. While Israel does not wish to see the innocent residents of Gaza harmed, it must protect its own citizens.[60]

There certainly is no legal right for a blockaded people to insist on luxury goods, spices like cinnamon, let alone construction supplies, such as cement, which could be used to construct homes as well as defensive works and bunkers, and steel pipes, which in the past have been used to develop makeshift al-Qassam rocket tubes.[61]

13.6 Enforcement: Belligerent Right of Visit and Search

The right of visit and search is the means by which a belligerent warship or military aircraft may enforce a blockade against an enemy for the purpose of inspecting commercial shipping in order to ascertain the enemy character of the

59 Although blockade is prohibited if 'it has as its sole purpose the starvation of the civilian population,' all of the methods of warfare are subject to proportionality—if the effect on the civilian population is excessive in relation to the lawful military purpose and military benefit. § 102, Doswald-Beck 1995, p 179.

60 Behind the Headlines: Israel Designates Gaza a 'Hostile Territory', Israel Ministry of Foreign Affairs, 24 September 2007, available at http://www.mfa.gov.il/MFA/About+the+Ministry/Behind+the+Headlines/Gaza+designated+a+Hostile+Territory+24-Sep-2007.htm.

61 Qassam rockets are 90–115 mm with a range of 6–12 km. See Rocket threat from the Gaza Strip, 2000–2007, at p 11 (Intelligence and Terrorism Information Center at the Israel Intelligence Heritage & Commemoration Center (IICC), December 2007), available at http://www.terrorism-info.org.il/malam_multimedia/English/eng_n/pdf/rocket_threat_e.pdf.

ship and its cargo. This is a war-time right and a lawful basis for compliant, noncompliant or opposed boarding of foreign-flagged merchant ships at sea. A party to an armed conflict may enforce a blockade against an enemy coastline or port through the belligerent right of visit and search. Visit and search is the process whereby a warship summons to neutral ship to lie to, using the international flag signal (SN or SQ)[62] or firing a blank charge, in order that the warship may determine the enemy character and destination of the ship or its cargo.[63] The summoned neutral merchant ship is required to stop and display her colors, and submit to boarding and inspection of the vessel. As a wartime right, visit and search is entirely separate and distinct from other lawful bases for boarding foreign-flagged ships at sea, including self-defense, authorization by the UN Security Council, boarding as a condition of port entry or boarding under authority of flag-state consent via direct permission, procedures exercised under a bilateral or multilateral maritime security agreement or, in the view of the United States, the consent of the master of the vessel.[64]

Vessels attempting to breach a blockade or resist the exercise of a belligerent's right of visit and search are liable to capture or even risk being sunk.[65] Rule 1710.4 of the *1999 Model Manual of the Law of Armed Conflict for Armed Forces*, published by the International Committee of the Red Cross, for example, indicates that: 'Merchant vessels believed on reasonable ground to be breaching a blockade may be captured and those which, after prior warning, clearly resist capture may be attacked'. Neutral merchant vessels that attempt to breach a blockade or resist attempts to conduct visit and search may be treated as enemy ships.[66] Thus, failure of a neutral ship to submit to visit and search is an assumption of risk for damage or loss of the ship. Naval forces that are conducting visit and search may use force to compel compliance, including deadly force and the destruction of the vessel. Ordinarily, merchant ships should be provided warning so that they may re-route or off-load belligerent cargo. If the warning is ignored by a neutral-flagged merchant ship, however, the Helsinki Principles set forth that:

> Merchant ships flying the flag of a neutral State may be attacked if they are believed on reasonable grounds to be carrying contraband or breaching a blockade, and after prior warning they intentionally and clearly refuse to stop, or intentionally and clearly resist visit, search, capture or diversion.[67]

The blockading state enjoys the belligerent right to capture and condemn neutral or enemy merchant vessels and cargo as prize if they constitute contraband, attempt to breach a blockade, if ships are fraudulently documented, they operate under the

[62] International maritime signal flags for 'SN' are as follows: 'S' is a white flag with a blue square in the center; 'N' is a blue and white checkerboard pattern. 'Q' is a solid yellow flag.

[63] § 5.2.1, Schindler and Toman 2004.

[64] See, e.g., Kraska 2011.

[65] Article 20, London Declaration.

[66] § 7.5.2, Commander's Handbook, supra n 48.

[67] § 5.1.2(3), Helsinki Principles, supra n 15.

control of the enemy, they transport enemy troops or they violate regulations in the immediate area of naval operations.[68] Neutral ships also may be attacked if they engage in belligerent acts on behalf of the enemy or are assimilated into the enemy's intelligence system, such as merchant ships that report the movement of belligerent ships or aid the enemy in targeting of belligerent ships.[69] A merchant vessel also may be attacked if it 'otherwise makes an effective contribution to the enemy's military action'.[70]

A warship may direct the neutral merchant to a port to conduct a shore-side inspection of the ship and cargo. If passengers and crew leave the ship, they are not to be regarded as prisoners of war, but instead should be repatriated as quickly as is feasible. Even the officers and crews of captured neutral merchants vessels who are nationals of a neutral nation do not become prisoners of war and must be repatriated 'as soon as circumstances reasonably permit'.[71] The US Navy has issued additional guidance to its forces conducting visit, board, search and seizure, including a checklist of information that the boarding officer should obtain, such as not only the enemy character of the vessel, but the ports of departure and destination, nature of cargo, manner of employment, and other facts.[72]

13.7 Visit and Search in International Waters

Although a blockade is declared within a defined area, it may be applied virtually worldwide outside of the territorial seas of neutral states. The prohibition against visit and search in neutral territorial waters also includes archipelagic sea lanes of neutral states and straits used for international navigation that are overlapped by the territorial seas of a neutral state. As an exercise of belligerent right and military activities at sea, visit and search may be conducted on the high seas and in any nation's EEZ. These rules makes logical sense, because if a blockading belligerent were forbidden from conducting visit and search in enforcement of a blockade in international waters, then the only place that such activity could occur would be within 12 nm of the shoreline of the belligerent or the enemy—inside the enemy's territorial sea. This interpretation would require an impossibly large force lay down to cover a coastline of any size, as well as compel the blockading belligerent to operate exposed in dangerous littoral waters, enforcing a blockade under the

68 § 14 148, Doswald Beck 1995, pp 212 216.

69 § 5.1.2(4), Helsinki Principles, supra n 15.

70 Ibid.

71 § 7.10.2, Commander's Handbook, supra n 48.

72 Normally, the following papers will be examined: the certificate of national registry, crew list, passenger list, logbook, bill of health clearances, charter party (if chartered), invoices or manifests of cargo, bills of lading, and on occasion, a consular declaration or other certificate of non-contraband carriage certifying the innocence of the cargo. See para 630.23, OPNAVINST 3120.32C CH-6, 26 May 2005.

nose of visual coastal surveillance and vulnerable to all manner of land-based attack. It is no surprise that these naval operational aspects of blockade have meant that blockade occurs in international waters rather than the enemy's territorial sea.

The *Commander's Handbook*, for example, indicates that: 'Attempted breach of blockade occurs from the time a vessel or aircraft leaves a port or airfield with the intention of evading the blockade ... It is immaterial that the vessel or aircraft is at the time of interception bound for neutral territory, if its ultimate destination is the blockaded area.'[73] Similarly, Yoram Dinstein and W. Heintschel von Heinegg are in agreement that neutral merchant ships outside neutral waters are subject to visit and search by belligerent warships in order to determine the enemy character of the cargo and vessel, unless such ships are travelling under convoy of neutral warships.[74]

Visit and search has never been illegal in international waters, although a surprising number of international law scholars have stated as much in the aftermath of the Mari Marmara seizure.[75] To deny Israel the right of blockade would conflate the peacetime international law of the sea with the wartime law of armed conflict and naval warfare. Such a claim constitutes a form of legal minimalism in that it so narrowly prescribes the rule against the interests of the belligerent exercising the blockade as to completely undermine the purpose of the rule. The international law of the sea was never designed to replace or conflict with the law of naval warfare. During the negotiations at the Third UN Convention on the Law of the Sea from 1973 to 1982, for example, delegates roundly rejected the notion that the new Convention set terms either for naval arms control or naval warfare. The law of naval warfare, which developed concurrently with and complementary to the law of the sea in customary international law, was codified long before the first multilateral treaty restated the rules for peacetime law of the sea in 1958. Consequently, the suggestion that the Israeli interception of the 'Freedom Flotilla' in international waters is an unlawful act is incorrect as a matter of law so long as one accepts that the nation enjoyed the right of blockade as a component of the armed conflict with Gaza.

13.8 Blockade in Non-international Armed Conflict

The greatest legal wrinkle in the case of 'Operation Sea Breeze' is whether law of naval warfare applies in the struggle between Israel and Gaza. Blockade is a creature of the law of naval warfare, which applies a priori to international armed

---

[73] § 7.7.4, Commander's Handbook, supra n 48.

[74] Dinstein 2004, p 217. See also Heintschel von Heinegg 1991, pp 283, 299 and Heintschel von Heinegg 1992, pp 89, 115.

[75] See, e.g., at statements by John Quigley, Ohio State University School of Law, Deen 2010, and Michael Byers, They should not have been there: Israel's soldiers may have acted in self-defence, but boarding a flotilla of aid ships on the high seas violated international law, Ottawa Citizen, 3 June 2010.

conflicts (IACs). Common Article 2 of the Geneva Conventions of 1949 states that IAC occurs when one or more states engage in armed conflict with another state, regardless of the intensity of the combat or even in the absence of hostilities. The Geneva Conventions are applicable to IACs involving 'two or more High Contracting Parties, even if a state of war is not recognized by one of them'. No formal declaration of war is required. Common Article 2 also applies in cases of military occupation. Some consider Gaza as occupied by Israel; it is not. There are no Israeli troops in Gaza, which everyone regards as a self-governing enclave cut from the Middle East. The Gaza Strip could be considered part of Egypt, which inherited governance of the area from the British Ottoman protectorate. But Egypt does not want it. An argument could be made that the territory is 'constructively occupied' by virtue of the blockade, but this is rather circular, since the entire analysis is being conducted to determine whether Israel may conduct such a blockade.[76] Article 1(4) of Additional Protocol I of 1977 extends the definition of IAC to include wars of national liberation—armed conflicts in which peoples are fighting against colonial domination, alien occupation or racist regimes in the exercise of their right to self-determination.

But the Gaza Strip is not a traditional *de jure* state, raising the question of whether the conflict between Israel and Gaza is not an IAC, but rather a 'non-international armed conflict' (NIAC). Traditionally, a struggle between two states constitutes IAC, whereas a conflict between a state and non-state entity, such as an insurgency of a terrorist network, constitutes NIAC. The distinction is important because different rule sets apply to IACs and NIACs, and there is some debate as to whether blockade is available as a lawful measure in NIACs. NIACs typically are fought between governmental forces and non-state armed groups, or among such groups only. To further complicate matters, international humanitarian law recognizes a distinction between NIACs within the ambit of common Article 3 of the Geneva Conventions of 1949 and NIACs within the definition set forth in article 1 of Additional Protocol II of 1977.

Common Article 3 applies to 'armed conflicts not of an international character occurring in the territory of one of the High Contracting Parties'. The ICRC suggests that the requirement that the armed conflict occur in the territory of one of the High Contracting Parties has lost its importance in contemporary state practice since the Geneva law is universally accepted, and a conflict 'has to but take place on the territory of one of the Parties to the Convention'.[77] It is not entirely clear, however, that conflict occurring in the Gaza Strip takes place 'on the territory one of the Parties to the Convention'. The definition of NIAC is supplemented by Additional Protocol II of 1977, which contains an even more restrictive definition of the term and therefore is of little help in capturing the Gaza conflict as NIAC.

[76] I am indebted to Eugene Kontorovich, Associate Professor of Law, Northwestern University Law School, for this observation.

[77] How Is the Term 'Armed Conflict' Defined in International Humanitarian Law? International Committee of the Red Cross Opinion Paper at p 3 (International Committee of the Red Cross, March 2008).

Article 1(1) of Additional Protocol II indicates that the treaty applies to armed conflicts, 'which take place in the territory of a High Contracting Party between its armed forces and dissident armed forces or organized armed groups which, under responsible command, exercise such control over a part of its territory as to enable them to carry out sustained and concerted military operations and to implement this Protocol'.

In sum, the Israeli–Gaza conflict does not fit squarely within the definition of IAC because Gaza is not a state, nor within NIAC because the conflict does not take place in the territory of a High Contracting Party—namely, Israel. Gaza is not a High Contracting Party. Some scholars have tried to solve this dilemma by suggesting that the reference in common article 3 to conflicts 'occurring in the territory of one of the High Contracting Parties', and in Article 1 of Protocol II, to conflicts, 'which take place in the territory of a High Contracting Party', are not geographic limitations, but simply recount that treaties apply only to their state parties. The argument is made that if the limitations excluded conflicts that spread over the territory of several states, there would be a gap in NIAC protection. It is incongruous that peoples affected by armed conflict that are spread throughout several states would receive less protection than those in a single state. But even this interpretation does not clearly cover the case of the Gaza Strip, since it is not merely another state, but rather an amorphous, ill-defined entity without any concrete de jure status. The *San Remo Manual on the Law of Non-International Armed Conflict*, for example, excludes from NIAC armed conflicts that extending to the territory of two or more states.[78] The *San Remo Manual* defines NIAC as, 'armed confrontations occurring within the territory of a single State and in which the armed forces of no other State are engaged against the central government'.

In some cases, it appears the rules governing conduct during armed conflict at sea apply in both IAC and NIAC, so the two bodies of law overlap. The law of blockade arose originally as a feature of IAC. If the Gaza conflict constitutes IAC, then the law of blockade applies. If, however, the Gaza conflict constitutes NIAC, the application of the law of blockade is less clear. Reverting attention for the moment to the peacetime international law of the sea, one could question whether there exists a right of blockade beyond the territorial sea during NIAC. It is not clear why parties to a NIAC should be entitled to interfere with foreign-flagged vessels and aircraft beyond the territorial sea. At the same time, it is just as murky why foreign-flagged, purportedly neutral merchant ships, should be immune from visit and search in international waters while fomenting insurrection as part of a NIAC.

In consideration of these issues, there are three particularly prominent applications of the law of blockade to NIAC—the US Civil War, the Spanish Civil War and the French war against Algerian independence. Being sensitive to space limitations, this article addresses in detail only the American Civil War. The conflict has the deepest factual symmetry to the case at hand and richest legal

---

[78] § 1.1.1, Schmitt et al. 2006.

history of the three case studies. During the US Civil War the Union conducted a strangling blockade against the Confederacy. The Northern blockade was initiated only days after the war with the South began. At 0430 on 12 April 1861 43 Confederate guns situated in a ring around Fort Sumter in Charleston Harbor began a bombardment that thrust America into its bloodiest war ever. President Lincoln declared a blockade against Confederate ports 7 days later—on 19 April 1861.[79] The blockade was the most ambitious undertaken by any nation, stretching 3,549 miles along a complex coastal zone comprised of 180 bays, rivers and harbors.[80] The rather novel application of the law of blockade against one's own nation required all of the legal and political skills of the president and Secretary of State William H. Seward. Because of the dismal condition of the US Navy, the blockade served more to put foreign nations on notice not to conduct maritime trade with the South than to actually stop all traffic in and out of the Confederacy. The paucity of Union naval forces and the challenges posed by the extensive coastline call into question the effectiveness of the blockade. Of the 1,300 attempts to break the blockade, 1,000 of were successful.[81]

The Union argued that the Confederate States of America did not form a legitimate sovereign, but rather should be characterized as an insurrection.[82] At the same time, however, the Union boarded and captured Southern merchant ships in international waters. The Confederate commercial ships protested their capture, arguing that that since war can only be conducted between two or more sovereign nations, the Union blockade of the South was unlawful. Initially, European states also questioned the legality of the blockade, echoing the concerns of the Confederacy that Union action was an unlawful impairment of the right of all nations to exercise freedom of the seas during peacetime. British Law Officers stated:

> For the United States to demand the exercise of these belligerent rights, and at the same time to refuse a belligerent status to the enemy was plainly contradictory. In truth the position is as novel and unsound in international law and clearly propounded for the first time for the obvious purpose of giving the United States the advantage of being exclusively recognized by the Neutral State as Belligerent.[83]

But slowly neutral European states began to comply out of practical reasons with the terms of the blockade, submitting their merchant ships to inspection by Union

[79] Rush et al. 1903 Proclamation of President Abraham Lincoln, 19 April 1861, V Official Records of the Union and Confederate Navies in the War of Rebellion, Ser. I, 27 Vols, at p 620.

[80] To make matters worse, nearly one-quarter of U.S. naval officers resigned their commissions and offered their services to the Confederacy (Wagner et al. 2002, p 547).

[81] Wagner et al. 2002, p 548, Referencing statement by historian Stephen R. Wise.

[82] Greater than a riot, which is a 'minor disturbance of the peace … perpetrated by a mob', an insurrection was regarded as an 'organized armed uprising which seriously threatens the stability of government and endangers social order'. There is no recognition of belligerency, and combatants have no immunity for their actions on the field of battle. Insurrection was distinguished from rebellion, which was regarded as a less extensive form of conflict (Randall 1926, p 81).

[83] F.O. 83,2225, reproduced in Smith 1932, pp 309–310.

naval forces. At the same time, however, the Europeans argued that acceptance of the belligerent right of the Union to impose a blockade against the South also triggered for the Confederacy enjoyment of the entire menu of belligerent rights in time of war. The Confederacy was entitled to formal belligerent status, which would have the effect of converting a NIAC into an IAC. In addition to the dilemma posed in the law of armed conflict, there was a related constitutional problem. Blockade is an act of belligerency, yet it was Congress that held the power to declare war. Finessing this point, Lincoln's proclamation included a savings clause, making the blockade operative only 'until Congress shall have assembled and deliberated' on the issue, thereby giving the legislative branch the ultimate authority over whether to maintain the blockade. Eventually, Congress approved the blockade, but that still left the complaint of the English and other neutral nations and the status of the Confederacy as a lawful belligerency.

> According to English reasoning, although Lincoln proclaimed the rebels to be insurrectionists and thus not recognizable under international law as a belligerent power engaged in war, his declared blockade was an act of war, which would have to be conducted against a sovereign state. Thus Lincoln had actually granted belligerency status to the Confederacy and thereby forced foreign powers to do the same. By proclaiming neutrality, England afforded the Confederacy the status of a belligerent power.[84]

The English position—that the blockade converted a NIAC into an IAC—came to be validated by the US Supreme Court. In the 1863 Prize Cases, the Court held that a state of armed conflict existed between the North and the South, even though the Confederacy was not a sovereign state.[85] In the Prize Cases, the owners of seized Confederate merchant vessels sought to have the court recognize that only an insurrection existed between the North and the South, and therefore seizure of their private property was invalid. But the Court rejected this argument, and held that whether a state of war existed, as opposed to a state of insurrection, was determined by the magnitude of the violence attendant t the conflict and not by the language contained in formal declarations.[86] 'The proclamation of blockade itself', the court found, was 'official and conclusive evidence … that a state of war existed …'[87] The Northern blockade and the subsequent British proclamation of neutrality meant that there existed an armed conflict between two belligerents.[88] Therefore the law of blockade applied to the conflict.[89]

But Washington's interest was to deny the Confederacy status as a belligerent, because doing so opened the door to a host of belligerent rights and privileges that

---

[84] Abraham Lincoln: American President; An Online Reference Source, Miller Center of Public Affairs, University of Virginia, available at http://millercenter.org/academic/americanpresident/lincoln/essays/biography/5.

[85] *The Prize Cases*, 67 U.S. 635 (1863).

[86] Ibid.

[87] *The Prize Cases*, (1862), 2 Black 635, 17 L 459, 477.

[88] *The Prize Cases*, 67 U.S. 635 (1863).

[89] Green 1993, p 303.

the South would enjoy. As a belligerent party, the naval forces of the Confederacy stood to benefit from safe harbor, secure credit and contract for warships and other weapons from neutral states. The English Parliament could take up the merits of more active or formal intervention in the war in support of the South.[90] These issues were only the tip of the iceberg, as belligerent status implicated almost every aspect of the conflict, including:

> … [t]he treatment of captured 'insurgents' as criminals instead of prisoners of war; the possible punishment of such 'insurgents' as traitors, and the confiscation of their property; the use of the municipal power over the territory claimed by the insurgents when such territory should be captured; the legality of Confederate captures at sea, and the disposition to be made of the crews of Confederate warships and privateers.[91]

Inevitably, some hybridization of the conflict slowly evolved. Throughout the war, for example, the Union government often afforded Confederate forces belligerent status, particularly when they were captured while in uniform, even though the South was never formally recognized as a belligerent party. On the other hand, captured Southern privateers were hanged as pirates early in the war. The death penalty was imposed on the crews and officers of Confederate naval vessels and privateers operating under letters of marque issued by the Confederate government, in strict accord with Lincoln's blockade proclamation. Later, however, the Union changed this practice as it found it impolitic to punish Confederate sailors as pirates.[92]

13.9 Conclusion

In a more contemporary era, the Spanish Nationalists proclaimed a blockade of Republican ports on 17 November 1936. The Nationalists announced that they would attack international shipping bound for these ports. The blockade was somewhat effective. On 3 December 1936, Britain (really the only major nation genuinely neutral in the conflict) prohibited the export of arms to Spain in British-flagged vessels. Meanwhile, Stalin was supplying war materiel to the Spanish Republic, and the Soviet merchant freighter *Komsomol* was the first Soviet ship to transport armored battle tanks, armored cars and artillery into the country. Eighty-four Soviet ships were stopped and searched by Spanish Nationalists from October 1936 to April 1937. The Canarias, the flagship of the Nationalist Navy, intercepted and sank the *Komsomol* on 14 December 1936.[93] For their part, the Republican forces seized the German vessel *Palos*, which was bound for Nationalist Spain. Even more recently, the 2006 Lebanon War involved an Israeli blockade of the

[90] Abraham Lincoln, supra n 84.

[91] Randall 1926, pp 59–60.

[92] Ibid.

[93] Thomas 2001, pp 432, 555.

coast of Lebanon, but arguably the contest was a transnational NIAC rather than an IAC since the IDF was fighting Hezbollah, a non-state irregular force, and not the national armed forces of Lebanon. The 2006 war was not a war between Israel and Lebanon, *per se*, but rather Israel and Hezbollah—a NIAC in which Israel's prosecution of a blockade was widely accepted by the international community.

The analogy of the American Civil War offers clues for addressing the Israeli blockade of Gaza. The US experience suggests that if Gaza were regarded as a sovereign state, then a state of war—IAC—would exist between Israel and Gaza. In such case, there is no doubt that the imposition of blockade is lawful. But this determination places Israel in the same dilemma experienced by the Union during the Civil War. If Israel avails itself of the right to blockade Hamas, is it also willing to grant Hamas lawful belligerent status? Are Hamas fighters privileged combatants, operating as the armed forces of the 'state' of Gaza? On the other hand, Hamas militants would be entitled to attack Israeli combatants and, if captured, warrant treatment as prisoners of war. Belligerent status however, does not obviate the need for the army of the 'state' of Gaza to comply with the laws of war—something that the group has blatantly failed to do.

If Gaza is not a state, then the conflict may be characterized as a NIAC, even though there are similar definitional shortcomings with this determination. While blockade originated as a legal concept in IAC, usage, state practice and *opinio juris* have caused it to migrate into NIAC. It is not longer the case that the application of the law of blockade and other rules of warfare are restricted only to conflicts in which both parties are states. Gaza is not a nation, but Gaza and Israel certainly are engaged in a war-like struggle. If the law of blockade does not apply in the case of the Israeli armed struggle with Gaza because Gaza is not a 'state', then this produces the absurd result that a nation may defend itself using a lawful instrument recognized by the law of armed conflict in fighting another state, but must voluntarily forgo the option if confronted with an equally powerful entity that does not meet the legal definition. Consequently, the law of blockade applies in the case of Gaza because there is no other rule set that appropriately balances the interests of the belligerents and neutrals. Furthermore, application of blockade law in NIAC in the case at hand dispenses with the rather metaphysical question of the legal status of Gaza.

Annex

Article XI, Annex I, Maritime Activity Zones (Map No. 6), Agreement on the Gaza Strip and the Jericho Area, Declaration of Principles on Interim Self-Government Arrangements [Declaration of Principles (DOP)], 13 September 1993

1. Maritime Activity Zones

    a. Extent of Maritime Activity Zones
    The sea off the coast of the Gaza Strip will be divided into three Maritime

Activity Zones, K, L, and M as shown on map No. 6 attached to this Agreement, and as detailed below:

1. Zones K and M

   a. Zone K extends to 20 nautical miles in the sea from the coast in the northern part of the sea of Gaza and 1.5 nautical miles wide southwards.
   b. Zone M extends to 20 nautical miles in the sea from the coast, and one (1) nautical mile wide from the Egyptian waters.
   c. Subject to the provisions of this paragraph, Zones K and M will be closed areas, in which navigation will be restricted to activity of the Israel Navy.

2. Zone L

   a. Zone L bounded to the south by Zone M and to the north by Zone K extends 20 nautical miles into the sea from the coast.
   b. Zone L will be open for fishing, recreation and economic activities, in accordance with the following provisions:

      (i) Fishing boats will not exit Zone L into the open sea and may have engines of up to a limit of 25 HP for outboard motors and up to a maximum speed of 15 knots for inboard motors. The boats will neither carry weapons nor ammunition nor will they fish with the use of explosives.
      (ii) Recreational boats will be permitted to sail up to a distance of three nautical miles from the coast unless, in special cases, otherwise agreed within the Maritime Coordination and Cooperation Center as referred to in paragraph 3 below. Recreational boats may have engines up to a limit of ten horsepower. Marine motor bikes and water jets will neither be introduced into Zone L nor be operated therein.
      (iii) Foreign vessels entering Zone L will not approach closer than 12 nautical miles from the coast except as regards activities covered in paragraph 4 below.

b. General Rules of the Maritime Activity Zones

   1. The aforementioned fishing boats and recreational boats and their skippers sailing in Zone L shall carry licenses issued by the Palestinian Authority, the format and standards of which will be coordinated through the JSC.
   2. The boats shall have identification markings determined by the Palestinian Authority. The Israeli authorities will be notified through the JSC of these identification markings.
   3. Residents of Israeli settlements in the Gaza Strip fishing in Zone L will carry Israeli licenses and vessel permits.

4. As part of Israel's responsibilities for safety and security within the three Maritime Activity Zones, Israel Navy vessels may sail throughout these zones, as necessary and without limitations, and may take any measures necessary against vessels suspected of being used for terrorist activities or for smuggling arms, ammunition, drugs, goods, or for any other illegal activity. The Palestinian Police will be notified of such actions, and the ensuing procedures will be coordinated through the Maritime Coordination and Cooperation Center.

References

Cable J (1981) Gunboat diplomacy 1919–1979 political applications of limited naval force. Macmillan, London

Deen T (2010) Israeli flotilla attack may violate international, maritime laws, The Island (Sri Lanka), 19 June 2010. http://www.island.lk/index.php?page_cat=article-details&page=article-etails&code_title=335

Dinstein Y (2004) The conduct of hostilities under the Law of International Armed Conflict. Cambridge University Press, Cambridge

Dinstein Y (2005) War, aggression and self-defence, 4th edn. Cambridge University Press, Cambridge

Doswald-Beck L (1995) San Remo manual on international law applicable to armed conflict at sea. IRRC 35:583–594

Franks T (2010) Details of blockade revealed in court case. *BBC News*, 3 May 2010. http://news.bbc.co.uk/2/hi/middle_east/8654337.stm

Frenkel S (2010) Gaza blockade isn't about security. *McClatchey Newspapers*, 9 June 2010. http://www.mcclatchydc.com/2010/06/09/95621/israeli-document-gaza-blockade.html#ixzz0rK8RSa4p

Green LC (1993) The contemporary law of armed conflict. Manchester University Press, Manchester

Hartman B (2010) What is IHH? The Turkish charity that helped plan the Gaza flotilla may be linked to Jihadist groups. *The Jerusalem Post*, 1 June 2010

Hayes ML (2006) The naval blockade of Cuba during the Spanish–American war. In: Elleman BA, Paine SCM (eds) Naval blockades and seapower: strategies and counter-strategies 1805–2005. Routledge, London

Heintschel von Heinegg W (1991) Visit, search, diversion and capture in naval warfare, Part I The traditional law. Can Yearb Int Law 29:283–329

Heintschel von Heinegg W (1992) Visit, search, diversion and capture in naval warfare, Part II Developments since 1945. Can Yearb Int Law 30:89–136

Katz Y (2010) IDF: global jihad links on flotilla. *The Jerusalem Post*, 1 June 2010. http://www.jpost.com/Israel/Article.aspx?id=177169

Knickmeyer E (2007) Gaza straining at Egypt's door: humanitarian, security worries mount. *Washington Post*, 18 June 2007

Kohlmann EF (2006) The role of Islamic Charities in international terrorist recruitment and financing. DIIS working paper no. 2006/7 (Defense Institute of International Studies, 2006). http://www.diis.dk/graphics/Publications/WP2006/DIIS%20WP%202006-7.web.pdf

Kraska J (2010) Broken taillight at sea: the peacetime international law of visit, board, search and seizure. Ocean Coast Law J 16:1–46

McDougal MS, Feliciano FP (1961) Law and minimum world public order: the legal regulation of international coercion. Yale University Press, New Haven

O'Connell DP (1975) The influence of law on sea power. Manchester University Press, Manchester

Oppenheim L (1969) In: Lauterpacht H (ed) International law, vol 2, 7th edn. Longmans, London

Randall J (1926) Constitutional problems under Lincoln. Appleton and Co Publishers, New York

Rush R et al (eds) (1903) Proclamation of President Abraham Lincoln, 19 April 1861, V Official Records of the Union and Confederate Navies in the War of Rebellion at p 620 Ser. I, 27 vols, 1903

Schindler D, Toman J (eds) (2004) Helsinki principles on the law of maritime neutrality, adopted by the International Law Association, Taipei, Taiwan, 30 May 1998, reprinted in The laws of armed conflicts a collection of conventions, resolutions and other documents, Doc 115:1425–1430

Schmitt MN (1991) Blockade law: research design and sources. Hein, Buffalo

Schmitt MN, Garraway CHB, Dinstein Y (eds) (2006) San Remo manual on the law of non-international armed conflict: with commentary, International Institute of Humanitarian Law

Smith HA (1932) Law of nations

Swayze FB (1977) Traditional principles of blockade in modern practice: United States mining of internal and territorial waters of North Vietnam. JAG J 29:143–173

Thomas H (2001) The Spanish civil war, rev edn. Modern Library, New York

Wagner ME, Gallagher GW, Finkelman P (eds) (2002) The library of congress civil war desk reference. Simon and Schuster, New York

Weigley RF (1973) The American way of war a history of United States military strategy and policy. Macmillan, New York

Chapter 14
The Contemporary Law of Blockade and the Gaza Freedom Flotilla

Andrew Sanger

Contents

I am extremely grateful to Dr Louise Arimatsu, Dr Anthony Cullen, Professor James Crawford SC, Ms Blinne Ní Ghrálaigh, Dr Marko Milanovic and Ms Sarah Sadek for their useful comments and discussion on earlier drafts. I am particularly indebted to Dr Louise Arimatsu for her invaluable advice and comments. Usual disclaimers apply.

A. Sanger (✉)
University of Cambridge, London, UK
e-mail: as662@cam.ac.uk

M.N. Schmitt et al. (eds.), *Yearbook of International Humanitarian Law Volume 13, 2010*, DOI: 10.1007/978-90-6704-811-8_14,

14.1 Introduction

In the early hours of 31 May 2010, Israel intercepted six vessels on the high seas carrying humanitarian aid to Gaza (collectively called the 'Gaza Freedom Flotilla'), which resulted in the death of nine civilians and the injury of many more. According to the Free Gaza Movement, the vessels were attempting to cross the Israeli blockade to deliver aid to the blockaded civilians in Gaza.[1] Israel justified its actions by invoking its right to enforce the blockade and prevent contraband from reaching the territory. Nevertheless, the operation prompted moral outrage and a wave of critical statements by governments and international organisations, with many calling on Israel to end the restrictions imposed on Gaza.[2] It also set in motion a highly contested debate on the legality of the blockade and the interception. As with nearly all aspects of the Israeli–Palestinian conflict, the debate involved intense scrutiny of the facts, the rules of international law, and the applicability of these rules to what has undoubtedly become a *sui generis* situation, unparalleled in its duration, complexity and equivocation.

This paper examines the interception from the perspective of international law by considering three pivotal sets of questions: (1) can Israel invoke a *prima facie* right to blockade Gaza? What is the legal basis for this right? What effect, if any, does the characterisation of the Israeli-Hamas conflict have? (2) If Israel does have a *prima facie* right to blockade Gaza, is the blockade legally constituted and maintained? What factors must be taken into consideration? Finally, (3) can Israel lawfully intercept vessels on the high seas without permission of the flag-state? In what circumstances, and under what conditions, can Israel undertake such an operation? Did Israel act lawfully when it intercepted the Flotilla vessels?

In order to address these questions, this paper is divided into five subsections. Section 14.2 presents a cursory account of the factual background to Gaza, the blockade and the interception of the Flotilla vessels. Section 14.3 considers the relevant normative regimes that justify interception of vessels on the high seas, and specifically, the law of blockade. In Sect. 14.4, these legal frameworks are applied to the Israeli-Hamas conflict and the situation in Gaza. The analysis in this section demonstrates the challenges faced when applying established legal norms to a *sui generis* factual situation. The penultimate part outlines the legal framework for

---

[1] 'Blockade' is used in its technical sense to mean an instrument of naval warfare. The UN, Human Rights Watch and many other international bodies and NGOs use the term 'blockade' to refer collectively to (i) Israel's restrictions on the movement of people and goods in or out of Gaza by land, air and sea and (ii) the withholding of financial support, fuel and electricity. See for example, 'the long process of economic and political isolation imposed on the Gaza Strip by Israel… is generally described as a blockade …' and '[t]he blockade comprises measures such as the closure of border crossings, sometimes completely for a number of days, for people, goods and services, and for the provision of fuel and electricity': Human Rights Council, 12th Session, Human Rights in Palestine and Other Occupied Arab Territories, *Report of the United Nations Fact-Finding Missing on the Gaza Conflict*, A/HRC/12/48 (25 September 2009) at p 82.

[2] Black 1 June 2010.

intercepting vessels on the high seas and applies this framework to the interception of the Flotilla vessels.

The paper concludes that although it is likely that Israel's blockade on Gaza is not *prima facie* unlawful, to the extent that the blockade starves the civilian population or prevents that population from receiving supplies necessary for its survival, it is undoubtedly illegal under international law. Any attempt to enforce an illegal blockade or prevent genuine humanitarian aid from reaching a civilian population is prohibited by customary international humanitarian law. Furthermore, states are obliged under customary international law to provide free passage for essential humanitarian supplies.

14.2 Factual Background

It is not the intention of the author to set out a comprehensive and exhaustive account of the Israeli–Palestinian conflict. Nevertheless, key events and background information necessary for the subsequent legal analysis may be briefly summarised.

14.2.1 The Gaza Strip and the Israeli blockade

Following the 6 day War of June 1967, Israel assumed effective control of the Gaza Strip and the West Bank. Prior to 1981 Israeli military commanders directly administered Gaza, but in 1981 and until its disengagement in 2005, the territory was administered by the Israeli Civil Administration, which was established by the Israeli Defence Force.[3] The disengagement was completed on 12 September 2005, when Israel declared that it no longer occupied the territory. Israel subsequently stated that it has been engaged in an ongoing 'armed conflict' with Hamas since October 2000.[4]

In February 2006, Hamas won the legislative election in Gaza Strip and lawfully took power on 15 June 2007. Shortly afterwards, Israel declared the Gaza

[3] See the Revised Disengagement Plan, available on Israel's Ministry of Foreign Affairs website http://www.mfa.gov.il/MFA/Peace+Process/Reference+Documents/Revised+Disengagement+Plan+6-June-2004.htm. See also 'Disengagement Plan—General Outline', 15 April 2004, available at http://www.pmo.gov.il/PMOEng/Archive/Press+Releases/2004/Disengagement+Plan/Disengagement+Plan.htm; and 'Overall concept of the Disengagement Plan', 15 April 2004, available at http://www.pmo.gov.il/PMOEng/Archive/Press+Releases/2004/Disengagement+Plan/DisengagementPlan.htm.

[4] 'The Ongoing Armed Conflict with Hamas', available at http://www.mfa.gov.il/MFA/Terrorism-+Obstacle+to+Peace/Hamas+war+against+Israel/Operation_Gaza_Context_of_Operation_5_Aug_2009.htm#A.

Strip a 'hostile territory'[5] and it was announced that, as well as continuing military and counter-terrorist operations, '[a]dditional sanctions will be placed on the Hamas regime in order to restrict the passage of various goods to the Gaza Strip and reduce the supply of fuel and electricity. Restrictions will also be placed on the movement of people to and from the Gaza Strip.'[6]

Israel borders the south, east and north of Gaza and remains in control of its borders, coastline, airspace, telecommunications, water, electricity, sewage networks and population registry. With Egypt (which borders the southwest of Gaza), Israel also controls the flow of people and property in and out of the Gaza strip. It has complete control over the movement of persons from Gaza to the West Bank, and vice versa. For these reasons, the United Nations, the United States, international human rights organisations and many legal commentators reject Israel's assertion that it is no longer occupying the Gaza Strip.

Over the past 5 years, Israel has implemented strict movement and import/export controls triggering what the United Nations Office for the Coordination of Humanitarian Affairs (UNOCHA) has called 'a protracted human dignity crisis with negative humanitarian consequences'.[7] The UNOCHA has explained that:

> At the heart of this crisis is the degradation in the living conditions of the population, caused by the erosion of livelihoods and the gradual decline in the state of infrastructure, and the quality of vital services in the areas of health, water and sanitation, and education.[8]

In April 2010, the UNOCHA reported that:

> The deterioration of living conditions in the Gaza Strip, mainly as a result of the Israeli blockade continued to be of concern. A new poverty survey conducted by UNRWA showed that the number of Palestine refugees completely unable to secure access to food and lacking the means to purchase even the most basic items, such as soap, school stationary and safe drinking water ('abject poverty') has tripled since the imposition of the blockade…[9]

According to the United Nations Relief and Works Agency (UNRWA), approximately 300,000 Palestine refugees live in conditions of abject poverty, up from 100,000 in early 2007[10]:

---

[5] 'Security cabinet declares Gaza hostile territory', 19 September 2007, available at http://www.mfa.gov.il/MFA/Government/Communiques/2007/Security+Cabinet+declares+Gaza+hostile+territory+19-Sep-2007.htm. This phrase is not recognised by international law.

[6] Ibid.

[7] United Nations Office for the Coordination of Humanitarian Affairs in the occupied Palestinian territory, Special Focus—Locked In: The Humanitarian Impact of Two Years of Blockade on the Gaza Strip (August 2009) p 2.

[8] Ibid.

[9] United Nations Office for the Coordination of Humanitarian Affairs in the occupied Palestinian territory, The Humanitarian Monitor (April 2010) p 2.

[10] Ibid., p 11.

> A decade of socio-economic decline, caused by the policies of closure and blockade, have shattered livelihoods, eroded the productive base and impoverished ordinary people. Jobless and with little hope for employment, the population of Gaza is in large part struggling to survive. The ongoing blockade hampers prospects for long-term improvements and self-reliance.[11]

During May 2010, only 2,558.5 truckloads of imports entered the Gaza Strip, a figure significantly lower than the monthly average prior to the blockade: for example, the average in 2007 was 12,350.[12] Crucially, the number of truckloads of construction, medical, food and fuel supplies entering Gaza falls far below the needs of the population.[13] Examples of items that have been denied to the population at various times include: light bulbs, candles, matches, books, musical instruments, crayons, clothing, shoes, mattresses, sheets, blankets, pasta, tea, certain types of canned food, coffee, chocolate, nuts, certain brands of baby formula, wheat grain, shampoo and conditioner.[14] In addition, livestock (chickens, cows etc.) and building materials such as cement, concrete, gravel, glass, pipes and wood have been regularly refused.[15] The UN has stated that less than one quarter of provisions required for daily needs reaches Gaza and the territory is inadequately supplied with basic provisions necessary for the survival of its population.[16] Exports, required for developing and sustaining a functioning economy, are also largely restricted. UNOCHA has reported that, '[s]ince the imposition of the blockade in June 2007, only 363 truckloads of exports (strawberries and cut flowers) have left Gaza, compared to a monthly average of 1,086 in the first five months of 2007'.[17]

Israel maintains that the civilians of Gaza have access to adequate supplies and provides three justifications for imposing these strict restrictions: (i) to allay security concerns; (ii) as a means by which to exert political pressure; and (iii) as a form of 'economic warfare'.

---

[11] Ibid.

[12] United Nations Office for the Coordination of Humanitarian Affairs in the occupied Palestinian territory, The Humanitarian Monitor (May 2010) p 11.

[13] Ibid., pp 8–14.

[14] See United Nations Office for the Coordination of Humanitarian Affairs in the occupied Palestinian territory, Special Focus—Locked In: The Humanitarian Impact of Two Years of Blockade on the Gaza Strip (August 2009) p 10 and news reports such as: http://news.bbc.co.uk/1/hi/world/middle_east/7545636.stm.

[15] Ibid.

[16] See United Nations Office for the Coordination of Humanitarian Affairs in the occupied Palestinian territory, The Humanitarian Monitor (April 2010) p 2.

[17] United Nations Office for the Coordination of Humanitarian Affairs in the occupied Palestinian territory, Protection of Civilians (29 December 2010–14 January 2011) p 4.

14.2.2 Israel's justifications for imposing a blockade

14.2.2.1 Security concerns

Israel initially justified its strict control of Gaza's borders as a necessary security measure specifically designed to respond to the increasing rocket attacks into southern Israel.[18] As the President of the Israeli Supreme Court made clear:

> The terrorist attacks have intensified and worsened since the Hamas organization secured its control of the Gaza Strip. These attacks include continual firing of rockets and mortar shells toward civilian communities inside the State of Israel, as well as terrorist attacks and attempted terrorist attacks directed against civilians and IDF soldiers both at the border crossings along the fence between the Gaza Strip and the State of Israel, and within the State of Israel...[19]

Rejecting a petition of the High Court requesting a declaration that Israel lacked jurisdiction to intercept the *Mavi Marama* on the high seas, Justice Beinisch explained that security concerns underpinned Israel's restrictive control of Gaza's land and sea borders:

> In light of Hamas' control of the Gaza Strip, Israel has take [*sic*] various steps meant to prevent direct access to the Gaza Strip, including the imposition of a naval blockade on the Strip, which, according to the State's declaration, is meant to block the infiltration of weapons and ammunition into Hamas ranks which have carried out shooting and terrorist attacks in Israeli territory for years with the goal of harming civilians.[20]

14.2.2.2 Political leverage

According to Dov Weisglass, advisor to then Prime Minister of Israel Ehud Olmert, the ultimate objective of Israel's strategy—'to put the Palestinians on a diet, but not to make them die of hunger'—was to encourage the people of Gaza to force Hamas to change its attitude towards Israel or alternatively, to force Hamas out of government.[21] In 2008 Deputy Defense Minister M.K. Matan Vilnai identified another aim of Israel's policy when he announced:

> We are examining the issue [of indirectly negotiating with Hamas for the release of a captured Israeli soldier], and apparently we will need to reduce the scope of goods

---

[18] Such weapons are often transported through a network of tunnels under the border, which, despite the fact that Israeli planes bomb these tunnels on a regular basis, is the only way in which goods essential for the survival of the population can pass into the territory.

[19] HCJ 9132/07 (27 January 2008) per President Beinisch at para 2.

[20] President Beinisch as cited by YNetNews.com, 'High Court rejects flotilla suits: Soldiers defended their lives' (3 June 2010), available at http://www.ynetnews.com/articles/0,7340,L-3898429,00.html.

[21] The Guardian 16 April 2006.

> [permitted entry into the Gaza Strip] and thus create pressure on the Hamas organization, which is deliberately failing to take steps to advance the negotiations.[22]

Recently, in June 2010, Israeli Foreign Minister Avigdor Lieberman was reported as saying that:

> Israel should not lift its blockade on the Gaza Strip unless Hamas agreed to goodwill gestures such as allowing representatives of the Red Cross to visit captive Israeli soldier Gilad Shalit.... Lieberman told Amir Oren and Gabriela Shalev, Israel's ambassadors to the United States and the United Nations, that there was no reason to change the status quo with that regard until Hamas acceded to that minimum request.[23]

14.2.2.3 Economic warfare

Israel also considers the blockade on Gaza to be a form of legitimate 'economic warfare'. A recent government document notes that:

> A country has the right to decide that it chooses not to engage in economic relations or to give economic assistance to the other party to the conflict, or that it wishes to operate using 'economic warfare'.[24]

Another official government document explains that '[t]he limitation on the transfer of goods is a central pillar in the means at the disposal of... Israel in the armed conflict between it and Hamas'.[25]

More recently, US Newspaper *McClatchy* reported that:

> The Israeli government took an additional step... and said the economic warfare is intended to achieve a political goal. A government spokesman, who couldn't be named as a matter of policy, told McClatchy that authorities will continue to ease the blockade but 'could not lift the embargo altogether as long as Hamas remains in control' of Gaza.[26]

In January 2011, *Aftenposten* newspaper reported that three leaked diplomatic cables revealed that Israel briefed the US embassy in Tel Aviv on the Gaza blockade:

> As part of their overall embargo plan against Gaza, Israeli officials have confirmed to (U.S. embassy economic officers) on multiple occasions that they intend to keep the Gazan economy on the brink of collapse without quite pushing it over the edge...[27]

A cable dated 3 November 2008 reported that Israel wanted the Gaza economy 'functioning at the lowest level possible consistent with avoiding a humanitarian crisis'.[28] In order to achieve this goal, Israeli officials employed 'mathematical

---

22 Greenberg 23 September 2008a, b.

23 Haaretz 10 June 2010.

24 Frenkel 9 June 2010.

25 Black 1 June 2010.

26 Frenkel 9 June 2010.

27 Reuters 5 January 2011.

28 Ibid.

formulas to monitor foodstuffs and other basic goods entering the Strip to ensure that the amount of supplies entering was neither less nor more than the amount Israel permitted'.[29] To determine whether a product would be allowed to cross the blockade, several factors were reportedly taken into consideration, including: security, the necessity of the product for meeting humanitarian needs, the product's image (i.e., whether it was a luxury), legal obligations, the impact of the product's use (whether it is used for preservation, reconstruction or development), the sensitivities of the international community and the existence of alternatives.[30]

14.2.3 The Gaza Freedom Flotilla

On 29 May 2010 the Gaza Freedom Flotilla, consisting of six civilian ships[31] with over 700 passengers, including human rights activists, politicians and journalists from over 40 countries,[32] set sail for the Gaza Strip carrying over 10,000 tonnes of humanitarian and construction aid and supplies for Gazan civilians.[33] Passengers went through standard security checks and port authorities supervised the loading of cargo.[34] On 30 May at approximately 22:30, Israeli naval vessels made contact with the Flotilla vessels by radar and radio to request that they discontinue their voyage. Nevertheless, the vessels continued with their journey, followed closely by the Israeli navy.

At 04:00 on Monday 31 May 2010, Israeli naval commandoes rappelled from helicopters onto the *Mavi Marmara,* which was flying a Comoros flag and sailing in international waters, approximately 68 k/m from the coast of Gaza. During the military operation, Israeli commandos opened fire on the passengers, killing nine and seriously injuring approximately fifty individuals.[35] Precisely what occurred on the *Mavi Marmara* is strongly contested. Israel stated that it tried to use non-lethal means and minimal force but was met with resistance. In contrast, those on

---

[29] Hass 26 October 2010.

[30] Ibid.

[31] The intercepted Gaza Freedom Flotilla was made up of the following vessels: *Challenger I*, United States, passenger ship; *Eleftheri Mesogeios*, Greece, cargo ship; *Sfendoni*, Greece, passenger ship; *Mavi Marmara,* Comoros, passenger ship; *Gazze 1*, Turkey, cargo ship; and *Defne Y*, Kiribati, cargo ship.

[32] The majority of the passengers aboard the ships were Turkish citizens. There were also nationals from Britain, Australia, Greece, Canada, Malaysia, Algeria, Serbia, Belgium, Ireland, Norway, Sweden, Kuwait and the United States.

[33] 'Aid supplies' include, amongst other things, medical supplies, food, textiles, toys, paper, pens, books, plastic window frames, diesel generators, concrete, cement for Al Shifa Hospital and other building materials for the reconstruction of, *inter alia*, homes and schools after they were destroyed in Operation Cast Lead, December 2008 to January 2009.

[34] The vessels set sail from Athens, Istanbul and Agios Nikolaos.

[35] Those killed included eight Turkish citizens and one 19-year-old dual Turkish/United States citizen.

board the vessel described an immediate lethal attack with no attempt to minimise civilian causalities. Passengers aboard the other Flotilla vessels also report being shot with rubber bullets, beaten, hooded and cuffed during the course of the operation.[36] All the vessels, including the *Mavi Marmara*, were then towed to the Israeli port of Ashdod.

Following the incident, Israel released a statement to the effect that:

> The organizers of the flotilla scorned Israel's efforts to prevent the vessels from reaching Gaza, via diplomatic dialogue, announcements in advance and declarations over the radio. The organizers of the flotilla similarly rejected Israel's offer to transfer the aid on board directly to Gaza via Israel...[37]

Some in the humanitarian aid community defended the actions of those on board the Flotilla vessels, emphasising that the option of transferring aid through Israel to Gaza was often not available, and that tight restrictions on basic provisions such as paper and pens, and the absolute prohibition of items such as concrete and cement meant that such aid simply did not reach Gaza. Six weeks after the incident, the United Nations Special Coordinator for the Middle East announced that the aid on board the vessels would finally be delivered to UN agencies in Gaza.

14.3 The Normative Frameworks

Was Israel lawfully entitled to intercept the Gaza Freedom Flotilla on the high seas? In order to address the question, this paper proceeds on the basis that the law of armed conflict (LOAC) is the appropriate legal framework within which to assess the conduct of all parties. Nevertheless, the following section briefly considers the alternative legal regime—the law enforcement framework—in order to dismiss its applicability in light of the facts.

In assessing the right to intercept vessels within the LOAC framework, the law of blockade and the effects of the evolution of customary international law on the protection of civilians will merit particular attention. In addition, as the characterisation of the Israeli-Hamas conflict cannot be easily determined and the law of blockade evolved in the context of international armed conflict (IAC), the question of whether blockades may be imposed in non-international armed conflict (NIAC) also requires critical examination.

---

[36] See UN Human Rights Council, Report of the international fact-finding mission to investigate violations of international law, including international humanitarian and human rights law, resulting from the Israeli attacks on the flotilla of ships carrying humanitarian assistance (27 September 2010), UN Doc. A/HRC/15/21 pp 25–36.

[37] Israel's Ministry of Foreign Affairs Website, Justice Ministry statement on High Court of Justice petitions, available at http://www.mfa.gov.il/MFA/Government/Communiques/2010/Justice_Ministry_HCJ_petitions_Gaza_flotilla_1-Jun-2010.htm.

14.3.1 Law enforcement v armed conflict

Established customary international law provides the default position in respect of vessels sailing on the high seas[38]: they are only subject to the jurisdiction of the state whose flag they fly.[39] The Permanent Court of Justice famously held that 'vessels on the high seas are subject to no authority except that of the state whose flag they fly... A corollary of the principle of the freedom of the seas is that a ship on the high seas is assimilated to the territory of the State of the flag of which it flies, for, just as in its own territory, that State exercises its authority up on it, and no other State may do so'.[40] The flag state has exclusive jurisdiction to enforce the rules of its municipal law and those of regional or international law. This rule applies to both warships and vessels owned or operated by the state for the purposes of governmental, non-commercial service.[41] These vessels have 'complete immunity from the jurisdiction of any state other than the flag state'.[42] If a state is not entitled to intercept a vessel flying the flag of another state, any such interception violates the sovereignty of the flag state and constitutes an internationally wrongful act. To intercept vessels on the high seas without permission of the flag state, this default rule must be displaced by an exception provided under international law.

Exceptions can be found under two normative frameworks of international law: (i) the law enforcement framework and (ii) the armed conflict framework. The former provides states with the jurisdiction to enforce the law by intercepting vessels in one of the following situations:

1. The vessel is in the territorial waters of the intercepting state.
2. The vessel is on the high seas and there are reasonable grounds for suspecting that one of the customary international law exceptions codified in Article 22(1) of the Convention on the High Seas 1958 may apply: there are reasonable grounds for suspecting the vessel is engaged in piracy or the slave trade, or the

---

[38] The 'high seas' have been defined in Article 1 of the Convention on the High Seas 1958 (to which Israel is a party) as all parts of the sea that were not included in the territorial sea or the internal waters of a state. This reflected customary international law, although the definition was revised in Article 86 of the 1982 Convention to include all parts of the sea that are not included in the exclusive economic zone, in the territorial sea or in the internal waters of a state, or in the archipelagic waters of an archipelagic state.

[39] Identified as customary international law by the Permanent Court of Justice in the *Case of the SS Lotus* (*France* v *Turkey*), PCIJ Ser A, No. 10, 1927, pp 18–19 and 25. This position is also codified in Article 92 of the UN Convention on the Law of the Sea 1982.

[40] Ibid.

[41] Although warships do possess the right of approach in order to ascertain the nationality of a vessel, this does not incorporate the right to board or visit vessels.

[42] See Articles 8 and 9 of the Convention on the High Seas 1958 (signed by Israel on 29 April 1958 and ratified 6 September 1961) and Articles 95 and 96 of the UN Convention on the Law of the Sea 1982.

vessel is of the same nationality as the warship (even if it is flying a foreign flag/no flag).[43]

3. The vessel is on the high seas and there is a jurisdiction agreement between the intercepting state and the flag state of the intercepted vessel.
4. The intercepting state is acting pursuant to a binding UN Security Council resolution.[44]

The underlying rationale of the law enforcement framework is the desire to enforce a commonly agreed prohibition of specific criminal activity. Vessels used to assist or further that criminal conduct may be intercepted as part of a 'policing operation'. These operations rarely affect the rights and interests of neutral states, but even where they do, it is generally considered that the mutual benefit of enforcing the law outweighs the costs entailed in the temporary interruption to trading and commercial activities.

The armed conflict framework, with which this paper is principally concerned, provides that belligerent States may intercept vessels on the high seas without their permission in order to enforce a legal naval blockade. The purpose of a blockade is to deny an enemy access to the ocean and to obstruct all trade between the enemy and other states. Using a blockade to obstruct enemy trade and travel on the high seas necessarily affects the interests of neutral states: neutral vessels must travel around the blockade and/or must submit to expensive, time-consuming searches of their cargo.[45] As Fraunces observes, '[t]he damaging effects of blockades often lead neutral states to enter conflicts to protect their interests. The law of blockade seeks to minimise this conflict by balancing the competing interests of neutral and blockading states'.[46]

International law permits enforcement of a legally constituted blockade, which may involve intercepting neutral vessels on the high seas. The law of blockade can be found almost entirely in customary international law, having developed out of 'the tension between a blockading state's assertion of a practice and a neutral state's acceptance or rejection of that practice'.[47] Recognising the law developed out of this horizontal negotiation between belligerent and neutral states is important for understanding the evolution of the law.[48] As Mallison and Mallison in their *Survey of the International Law of Naval Blockade* explain:

[43] The content of Article 22(1) has been effectively reproduced in Article 110(1) of the UN Convention on the Law of the Sea 1982 (to which Israel is not a party).

[44] Security Council resolutions passed in connection with the 1990 Iraqi invasion of Kuwait illustrate the law enforcement framework. Shortly after the invasion, UN Security Council resolution 661 imposed a ban on imports to, or exports from, Iraq and occupied Kuwait. Resolution 665 subsequently authorised states cooperating with the government of Kuwait, and with naval forces in the area, to intercept vessels suspected of violating these sanctions. These resolutions provided the law enforcement jurisdiction for warships to police the UN embargo operation, and stop and search vessels suspected of violating the sanctions regime.

[45] Fraunces 1992, 893.

[46] Ibid., pp 893 and 895–900.

[47] Ibid. See also Mallison and Mallison 1976, p 45.

[48] See also Jones 1983, pp 759, 761 and Mallison and Mallison 1976, p 45.

> The naval tactics and strategy of blockade, if accepted over a period of time by other belligerents and by neutrals, become the international law of blockade. The silence and acquiescence of states has typically manifested the acceptance of particular methods of blockade as legally permissible. The function of diplomatic protest is to prevent the law from being made or developed without the assent of the protesting state ... The customary lawmaking process involves a national state acting as claimant through the use of particular methods of blockade and as a decision-maker in appraising the blockade claims of other states.[49]

Thus, the law of blockade exemplifies the decentralised decision- and law-making processes of international law. These processes enabled the law to develop and change in response to new developments in technology and maritime warfare. If the law did not evolve with practice, the legal limitations on blockades may have disappeared altogether.[50] Is it through the common consent of states that permission to intercept neutral vessels on the high seas came to be granted to belligerent states. As Myers explains, 'any inhibition which war places upon a neutral is a matter of custom or provided by treaty and is not considered either legally or theoretically as an inherent right'.[51] Unlike other methods of warfare, states do not have an inherent or inalienable right to blockade; the right is conferred—and managed—through custom.

Consequently, running a blockade is not in itself illegal. If a neutral vessel attempts to run a lawfully established and maintained blockade, it may be stopped, inspected, diverted and/or captured. If the passengers on board the vessel resist capture then, subject to the principles and rules of international humanitarian law, the vessel may be attacked. These actions are permitted on the basis of custom, and as Douglas Owen explained in 1898, they do not make it inherently unlawful for neutrals to run a blockade:

> In one sense, it is not unlawful for neutrals to carry goods to blockaded ports, seeing that, in principle, hostilities between nations A and B do not deprive neutral C of the right to carry on his lawful trade in the accustomed manner. But against this, belligerents enjoy the countervailing right to prohibit interference with the course of hostilities. So that if neutrals choose to attempt such interference by providing the enemy with supplies at blockaded ports, they must do so at their own risk.[52]

The law of blockade reconciles the competing rights and interests of belligerents and neutrals: it enables neutrals to avoid the blockade, ensures the trading interests of one state are not advanced over another, and limits the scope of the blockade so that neutral states are not constrained in their freedom of movement or pursuit of commence any more than is necessary for the success of the legitimate military objective of the blockading state.[53]

---

49 Ibid.

50 Ibid., p 49 also note this observation.

51 Myers 1910, pp 571, 579.

52 Owen 1898, pp 16–17.

53 Myers 1910, p 579.

14.3.2 The law of blockade

A naval blockade is an operation aimed at preventing ingress or egress of all vessels or aircraft, regardless of the nationality of the state, to and from the coast or port of an enemy state.[54] It is one of the oldest methods of naval warfare, designed to 'block supplies to an enemy coast without directly meaning to conquer this coast'.[55] Today, a blockade may be established in two situations: (1) a party to an armed conflict may unilaterally impose a blockade in accordance with the law of maritime warfare; or (2) the Security Council, acting under Chapter VII of the UN Charter, may declare a blockade in response to a threat or breach of international peace or an act of aggression.[56] Heintschel von Heinegg reminds us that regardless of the specific purpose of a blockade (e.g., as economic warfare, part of a military campaign, or pursuant to a Security Council resolution), it is a method of *naval warfare* directed against an enemy's coastline and ports, to which the rules and principles of the law of naval warfare apply.[57]

14.3.2.1 Sources of the law of maritime warfare

The sources of the law of maritime warfare, of which the law of blockade is a part, generally fall within one of three categories: (1) customary international law derived from state practice; (2) treaties and declarations dating from the early twentieth century; and (3) several principles contained in treaties relating to land warfare, which constitute rules of customary international law applicable to naval warfare. Since much of the law of maritime warfare predates the UN Charter, it is necessary when applying it to contemporary conflicts to consider its normative weight in the light of significant developments in public international law, such as the prohibition on the use of force and the evolution of the law of armed conflict through both treaty and customary international law.[58]

The *San Remo Manual on International Law Applicable to Armed Conflicts at Sea* (hereinafter *San Remo Manual*) comprises the most recent attempt by international lawyers and naval experts to restate the rules and principles found in

---

54 US Naval Manual 1997, para 7.7.5; *San Remo Manual*—Explanation, p 176; Heintschel von Heinegg 2008, p 551.

55 Heintschel von Heinegg 2008, p 551.

56 Article 42 of the UN Charter. Blockades should be distinguished from situations where the UNSC has authorised warships to intercept vessels suspected of violating economic sanctions.

57 Heintschel von Heinegg 2008, p 552.

58 GCs and Henckaerts and Doswell-Beck (eds) 2005: 'It was decided not to research customary law applicable to naval warfare as this area of law was recently the subject of a major restatement, namely the San Remo Manual on Naval Warfare. The general rules contained in the manual were nevertheless considered useful for the assessment of the customary nature of rules that apply to all types of warfare'; vol I, p xxxvi.

customary law.[59] Although the participants wanted to provide 'a contemporary restatement of international law applicable to armed conflicts at sea',[60] the *San Remo Manual* also included some progressive legal developments.[61] A restatement and reconsideration of the law was desirable for several reasons: to reflect developments in the law of maritime warfare since 1913, which for the most part had not been incorporated into treaty law; to incorporate and reflect the significant and detailed rules in the 1949 Geneva Conventions, especially the Second Geneva Convention relating to the protection of the wounded, sick and shipwrecked at sea; and because there had not been a more recent codification of the law similar to that of Additional Protocol I to the Geneva Conventions [API] for land warfare (although some of the rules in API apply to naval operations, e.g. the rules relating to medical vessels and aircraft).[62]

The *San Remo Manual* is a private document and not a source of law, but insofar as it restates customary international law it may be considered an expression of the law. It has been beneficial in both representing and influencing state practice. A significant part of the chapter on maritime warfare in the *UK Ministry of Defence Manual of the Law of Armed Conflict* restates or reflects its content.[63] Despite this, the *San Remo Manual* is not exhaustive; earlier treaty instruments, specific provisions of the Geneva Conventions and Additional Protocols, and the practice of States must also be considered.

The *Draft Convention on Rights and Duties of Neutral States in Naval and Aerial War 1939*[64] (hereinafter *Draft Convention*), which predates the Manual, offers some guidance on the substance of the law. The *Draft Convention* is also the work of a private organisation that sought to codify the rules relating to the laws of war (naval war: Articles 83–86; aerial war: Articles 88-112), of neutrality (Articles 4–48, 87) and of prize (Articles 49–82). In some areas, the *Draft Convention* developed rather than restated the law, and the accompanying Comments are careful to indicate where this is the case.

Some treaties, primarily those dating from the early twentieth century, may continue to have relevance for the purposes of this paper,[65] including the

[59] Doswald-Beck (ed) 1995, prepared by international lawyers and naval experts convened by the International Institute of Humanitarian Law, adopted in June 1994.

[60] Doswald-Beck (ed) 1995, p 5.

[61] Ibid.

[62] 'It has to be noted... there was no systematic attempt to include three important areas of the laws of war in this updating process [i.e., Additional Protocol I], to wit the law neutrality, the law of air warfare and the law of naval warfare. But the absence of any attempt to comprehensively codify these areas of the laws of war ... does not mean that the 1977 Protocols have no impact in their field... There are even specific provisions on certain elements of air and or naval warfare': Bothe 1988, p 760.

[63] The Manual of the Law of Armed Conflict 2005 (hereinafter UK Manual) p 348.

[64] Draft Convention on Rights and Duties of Neutral States in Naval and Aerial War (hereafter Draft Convention) 1939, pp 167–817.

[65] UK Manual, p 348.

Declaration of the London Naval Conference 1909 (hereinafter *London Declaration*).[66] Ten Powers participated in the Conference and most of the rules in the *London Declaration* correspond to established practice and decisions of national prize courts. Nevertheless, none of the signatory states ratified the *Declaration*.[67] At the outbreak of the First World War the Allies adopted the articles contained in the *Declaration* relating to the law of blockade (subject to modifications relating to the requirement of presumed knowledge of the existence of a blockade), but the British Maritime Rights Order in Council of 7 July 1916 and the corresponding French decree abandoned the *London Declaration* altogether.[68] Despite not entering into force, many of the provisions of the *London Declaration* are generally recognised as being declaratory of customary international law,[69] and the instrument remains the only collective expression by states of the traditional law of blockade.

14.3.2.2 Conditions for a legal blockade

Traditional international law provides three conditions for the establishment and maintenance of a lawful blockade: the blockade must be declared, it must be impartial, and it must be effectively enforced. With the development of international human rights and humanitarian law, an additional requirement has evolved: the blockade must not have the effect of starving a civilian population.[70]

A blockade must be declared and notified to all belligerents and neutral states.[71] This provides fair warning to neutral states, allowing their vessels to avoid the blockade and the costly and time-consuming stop and search exercise. The declaration must specify the commencement, duration, location, and extent of the blockade, and the period within which vessels of neutral States may leave the blockaded coastline.[72]

In addition, a blockade must be applied impartially to the vessels of all States, including those flying the flag of the blockading state.[73] Thus, 'if a belligerent licenses or knowingly permits its own or any other vessels to pass through the

[66] Final Protocol of the London Naval Conference 1909, p 179. The London Declaration was the initiative of the British government, which convened the main sea powers in order to codify the generally recognised rules of international law relating to prize, including the law of blockade. Articles 1–21 concern the law of blockade.

[67] Bell 1937, p 23.

[68] Lauterpacht (ed) 1952, p 769.

[69] See US Naval Manual 1997, para 7.7.5; and Heintschel von Heinegg 2008, p 552.

[70] The basis for this provision is found in Article 49(3) and Article 54(1) of Additional Protocol I; according to the ICRC these provisions have attained the status of custom: Henckaerts and Doswell-Beck (eds) 2005, p 186. Heintschel von Heinegg 2008, pp 551–558.

[71] San Remo Manual, para 93.

[72] San Remo Manual, para 94.

[73] San Remo Manual, para 100; London Declaration, Article 5.

blockade, the blockade is regarded as raised'.[74] This provision is designed 'to prevent belligerents from using "blockades" as pretexts for furthering their own trade with the enemies' countries at the expense of neutrals…'[75] With the exception of humanitarian relief shipments, permission to enter and leave a blockaded coastline or port may only be granted in exceptional situations.[76] For example, neutral vessels and aircraft in distress are permitted to cross the blockade to reach land, provided they do not discharge or load any cargo.[77]

Paragraph 95 of the *San Remo Manual* requires a blockade to be effectively enforced, the determination of which is a question of fact.[78] Historically this meant a blockade had to be (i) maintained by a force sufficient to prevent access to the enemy coastlines,[79] and (ii) the enforcement cordon—the geographical location of the vessels—had to be located as close to the coastline as possible, thereby minimising interference with neutral trade. These requirements attempted to reconcile the competing interests of belligerent and neutral states. They 'responded to the unwillingness of neutrals to suffer interruptions in trade unless blockading states "possess[ed] the power and resources, and w[ould] incur the hazard and expense" of placing a sufficient number of warships off the enemy coast'.[80] It also helped to distinguish between 'legitimate blockading activity and other activities (including visit and search) that might be carried on illegitimately on the high seas under the guise of blockade'.[81]

The point at which a blockade must be enforced has changed considerably since the First World War, largely as a result of new, more advanced weapons (e.g., underwater mines, self-propelled torpedoes etc.),[82] more sophisticated vehicles (e.g., airplanes, submarines) and new war strategies (e.g., economic warfare, incorporation of merchant vessels into surface naval warfare).[83] Concern over the future use of submarines, mines and aircraft played a significant role in the rejection of the *Draft Convention* by the House of Lords,[84] and throughout the two World Wars the principle of effectiveness was generally ignored.[85] During the First World War, the British administered blockades at a considerable distance

---

[74] London Declaration, Articles 74(2) and 76.

[75] Draft Convention, p 7.

[76] London Declaration, Article 6.

[77] London Declaration, Article 7.

[78] This is supported by Articles 2 ('… a blockade, in order to be binding, must be effective—that is to say, it must be maintained by a force sufficient really to prevent access to the enemy coastline') and 3 ('The question whether a blockade is effective is a question of fact') of the London Declaration.

[79] Draft Convention, Article 2.

[80] Fraunces 1992, pp 893, 897.

[81] UK Manual, p 363.

[82] Heintschel von Heinegg 2006 a, p 277.

[83] Fraunces 1992, pp 893, 895–908 and Mallison and Mallison 1976, pp 45, 48.

[84] Bell 1937, p 23.

[85] Heintschel von Heinegg 2008, p 556; Fraunces 1992, pp 900–901.

from the blockaded coast—'long distance' blockades—and Germany established so-called 'blockading zones', where they would indiscriminately sink all vessels found within a declare zone.[86] These practices represented a radical departure from the traditional rules on effective enforcement of blockades,[87] and were heavily criticised by international lawyers during and after the War.[88] Despite this criticism, they were effective from a military standpoint and subsequently redeployed during the Second World War and in more recent conflicts.

Today, the law on blockade is still derived from state practice, albeit with considerable guidance from the *San Remo Manual*. Consequently, there are 'no criteria that would make possible an abstract determination of the effectiveness of all blockades'.[89] The *San Remo Manual* and the Commentary to Principle 5.2.10 of the Helsinki Principles stipulate that the force maintaining the blockade may be stationed at a distance determined by military requirements.[90] To a large extent, effectiveness will depend upon the circumstances of each case, but it must 'be probable that vessels (and aircraft) will be prevented from entering or leaving the blockaded area'.[91] Heintschel von Heinegg explains that, 'it is no longer necessary for the blockading force to be deployed in close vicinity to the coast; it may also be stationed at some distance seaward as long as ingress or egress continues to be dangerous'.[92] Whether that is the case is a question of fact, but there exists 'an ultimate legal limitation with regard to the area affected. A blockade must be restricted to coastal areas and ports belonging to, occupied by, or under the control of the enemy. It may not be established outside the general area of naval warfare'.[93]

A related question concerns the distance from the blockade that a state may intercept vessels attempting to breach that blockade. To put it another way: when is there an attempted breach of a blockade? The UK and German armed conflict manuals are silent on this question,[94] but the US manual defines an attempted breach as:

> [occurring] from the time a vessel or aircraft leaves a port or airfield with the intention of evading the blockade, and for vessels exiting the blockaded area, continues until the

---

86 Lauterpacht (ed) 1952, pp 791–797.

87 States attempted to justify their practices by claiming they were reprisals; unlawful acts taken in response to a prior unlawful act by the opposing belligerent: Lauterpacht (ed) 1952, pp 791–797; Draft Convention, pp 698–706.

88 Fraunces 1992, pp 893, 901.

89 Heintschel von Heinegg 2006 a, p 277

90 San Remo Manual, Para 96; UK Manual, p 364.

91 Heintschel von Heinegg 2008, p 557. He suggests that this 'result can—to a certain extent—be founded upon Article 3 of the 1909 London Declaration according to which the "question whether a blockade is effective is a question of fact"'.

92 Heintschel von Heinegg 2006b, p 18.

93 Heintschel von Heinegg 2006b, p 18. For the general area of naval warfare see paras 10 and 14 of the San Remo Manual.

94 See also Heintschel von Heinegg 2006b, p 19.

> voyage is completed… It is immaterial that the vessel or aircraft is at the time of interception bound for neutral territory, if its ultimate destination is the blockaded area. There is a presumption of attempted breach of blockade where vessels or aircraft are bound for a neutral port or airfield serving as a point of transit to the blockaded area.[95]

There are persuasive arguments for rejecting this 'continuous voyage' definition.[96] It obviates the requirement of maintaining an effective blockade and risks unnecessarily obstructing access to neutral ports and coastlines. Heintschel von Heinegg suggests that as:

> long as neutral merchant vessels are situated outside the range of operations of the forces maintaining the blockade, and as long as they do not carry contraband or act in a way that makes them liable to attack, the freedoms of navigation and overflight supersede the belligerents' interest in a comprehensive prohibition of imports to their respective enemies.[97]

Finally, as the next section explains, a blockade is not rendered ineffective when humanitarian aid vessels cross the blockade to reach a starving civilian population.

14.3.2.3 Conditions on the operation of a blockade

Blockades necessarily affect both neutral states and the civilian population behind the blockade. While traditional international law was primarily concerned with the interests of states *inter se*, contemporary international law also concerns itself with the interests and protection of individuals. Consequently, international humanitarian law has modified the traditional law of blockade to include the rights and interests of blockaded civilians. Historically, areas under blockade were regarded as a single military objective, but today civilians behind a blockade must be distinguished from legitimate military targets.

To this end, contemporary international law stipulates that a blockade must not have the effect of starving a civilian population. A legal blockade that has this effect will be rendered illegal and cannot be lawfully enforced. The question of whether a blockade is causing a civilian population to starve is one of fact. In addition, if a blockade causes a civilian population to be inadequately provided with food and other objects necessary for its survival, the blockading state is under an obligation to allow humanitarian supplies to pass through the blockade.

Starvation may occur as a consequence of the destruction of food and sources of food *within* a state and/or by imposing blockades or sieges that cut off external food supplies.[98] It has been used throughout history as a method of warfare. As British Foreign Secretary Michael Stewart remarked during the Nigerian-Biafran

---

[95] Department of the Navy (Office of the Chief of Naval Operations), The Commander's Handbook on the Law of Naval Operations, NWP 1–14 M, para 7.7.4.

[96] See also Heintschel von Heinegg 2006b, pp 19–20.

[97] Ibid., p 20.

[98] Rosenblad 1973, pp 252, 266.

War in 1967, '[w]e must accept that, in the whole history of warfare, any nation which has been in a position to starve its enemy out has done so'.[99] Nevertheless, in seeking to balance military necessity with the protection of civilians, modern international law prohibits the use of starvation as a means of warfare against a civilian population. The legal basis for this can be found in two fundamental rules of international humanitarian law: first, civilians must not be directly targeted; and second, any civilian harm resulting from a lawful attack on a military object must be proportionate to the anticipated military advantage.

These rules were codified in Additional Protocol I. Article 54(1), which reflects customary law, unambiguously affirms that 'starvation of civilians as a method of warfare is prohibited', and is applicable in both occupied and non-occupied territories.[100] Additional Protocol II, which applies in non-international armed conflicts, contains a corresponding provision.[101] While there was some doubt in the past about the application of this prohibition to naval blockades,[102] there is no doubt today: Article 49(3) explicitly provides that Article 54 applies to naval blockades if they 'affect the civilian population, individual civilians, or civilian objects on land'. Article 54 also includes a provision that elaborates on the basic rule[103]:

> It is prohibited to attack, destroy, remove or render useless objects indispensable to the survival of the civilian population, such as foodstuffs, agricultural areas for the production of foodstuffs, crops, livestock, drinking water installations and supplies and irrigation works, for the specific purpose of denying them for their sustenance value to the civilian population or to the adverse Party, whatever the motive, whether in order to starve out civilians, to cause them to move away, or for any other motive.[104]

Macalister-Smith explains that this provision is intended not only to 'ensure the survival of the civilian population as such, but also to prevent population displacements which expose civilians to especially high risk'.[105] Furthermore, the

---

[99] Hansard Vol. 786, No. 143 c.953, cited in Rosenblad 1973, pp 252, 253.

[100] Triffterer 2008, p 458; Buckingham 1994, pp 285, 299; and *San Remo Manual*, p 179, para 102(4). Henckaerts and Doswell-Beck (eds) 2005, p 186. The Study notes that international practice includes States there were not, and are still not, party to Additional Protocol I (p 187).

[101] Additional international instruments pertaining to NIACs include the same prohibition; for example, paragraph 6 of the Memorandum of Understanding on the Application of IHL between Croatia and the SFRY, and paragraph 2.5 of a similar Memorandum in relation to the conflict in Bosnia and Herzegovina.

[102] The ICRC Commentary explains that although there is (or was in 1977) 'some uncertainty as regards the present state of the customary law relating to blockade', there is hope that 'the rules relating to blockades will be clarified as part of a future revision of certain aspects of the laws of war at sea, a revision for which there is a great need. Such a reexamination [*sic*] should make it possible to duly take into account the principles put forward in the Protocol which prohibit starvation as a method of warfare': Sandoz, Swinarski and Zimmerman (eds) 1987, p 654, para 2093. The San Remo Manual provides this re-examination by naval law experts.

[103] See also Triffterer 2008, p 458.

[104] Article 54(2), API.

[105] Macalister-Smith 1991, p 10.

legal and factual protection of fixed civilian objects and installations is especially important, '[s]imply because they cannot be moved out of the zone of conflict, [as such] the only available protection is to prohibit attacks against them'.[106]

The rule in Article 54 is reflected in paragraph 102 of the *San Remo Manual*, which sought to restate customary international law on the use of starvation as a means of warfare. Thus, the declaration or establishment of a blockade is prohibited if:

a. It has the sole purpose of starving the civilian population or denying it other objects essential for its survival; *or*
b. The damage to the civil population is, or may be expected to be, excessive in relation to the concrete and direct military advantage anticipated from the blockade.[107]

The word 'sole' in subparagraph (a) means that if a blockade has both the unlawful purpose of starvation together with a lawful military advantage, the provision in (b) applies, rendering the blockade illegal if the effect on the civilian population is excessive in relation to the concrete and direct military advantage.[108] The Commentary explains that whenever a blockade has 'starvation as one of its effects, the starvation effectively triggers the obligation, subject to certain limitations, to allow relief shipments to gain access to the coasts of the blockade belligerent'.[109]

Evidence of state practice in relation to this prohibition can be found in numerous military manuals.[110] The UK *Manual of the Law of Armed Conflict* repeats paragraph 102 of the *San Remo Manual* in its entirety.[111] The Australian Defence Force Manual, Canada's Law of Armed Conflict Manual and the US Commander's Handbook on the Law of Naval Operations state that, '[t]he declaration or establishment of a blockade is prohibited if: (a) it has the sole purpose of starving the civilian population or denying it other objects indispensable for its survival',[112] while New Zealand's Military Manual explains that blockades are not prohibited 'even if it causes some collateral deprivation to the civilian population, so long as starvation is not the specific purpose'.[113] The German Military Manual,

---

[106] Ibid.

[107] San Remo Manual, para 102.

[108] Doswald-Beck (ed) 1995, para 102.4.

[109] Ibid., para 102.3.

[110] See Henckaerts and Doswell-Beck (eds) 2005, § 160 et seq.

[111] UK Military Manual, para 13.74.

[112] Australia, Manual on Law of Armed Conflict, Australian Defence Force Publication, Operations Series, ADFP 37—Interim Edition, 1994, §§ 665 and 666, Canada, The Law of Armed Conflict at the Operational and Tactical Level, Office of the Judge Advocate General, 1999, pp 8–9, §§ 67–68; and United States, The Commander's Handbook on the Law of Naval Operations (July 2007), para 7.7.2.5.

[113] New Zealand, Interim Law of Armed Conflict Manual, DM 112, New Zealand Defence Force, Headquarters, Directorate of Legal Services, Wellington, November 1992, § 504(2), footnote 9.

in a section on blockades, affirms that 'starvation of the civilian population as a method of warfare is prohibited'.[114]

According to the ICRC Commentary to API, 'starvation' is defined by its ordinary meaning (the term "starvation" is generally understood by everyone).[115] The Commentary refers to the Shorter Oxford English Dictionary, which defines starvation as 'the action of starving or subjecting to famine, i.e., to cause to perish of hunger; to deprive of or "keep scantily supplied with food".[116] This definition has been criticised by some experts as being too restrictive[117] and it has been suggested that 'starvation' should be interpreted to include additional objects that are vital to civilian survival.[118] There is little doubt that this must be the correct interpretation as it more accurately reflects paragraph 102(a) of the *San Remo Manual*, which refers to both starvation *and* the denial of objects necessary for civilian survival.

The deliberate starvation of civilians also constitutes a war crime under customary international law.[119] As early as 1919, the Commission on the Responsibility of the Authors of the War included the '[d]eliberate starvation of civilians' as a 'violation of the laws and customs of war' that should be prosecuted.[120] Today, under Article 8(2)(b)(xxv) of the Rome Statute, the following constitutes a war crime in international armed conflicts: 'intentionally using starvation of civilians as a method of warfare by depriving them of objects indispensable to their survival, including wilfully impeding relief supplies as provided for under the Geneva Conventions'.

A corollary of this prohibition on starvation is the obligation, subject to specific limitations, to allow relief shipments to gain access to the coasts of the blockaded territory.[121] This obligation is reflected in paragraph 103 of the *San Remo Manual*, which stipulates that a blockading power must allow free passage of food and other essential supplies necessary for the survival of the civilian population, subject to:

(a) the right to prescribe the technical arrangements, including search, under which such passage is permitted; *and*
(b) the condition that the distribution of such supplies shall be made under the local supervision of a Protecting Power or a humanitarian organization which offers guarantees of impartiality, such as the International Committee of the Red Cross.

---

[114] Germany, Humanitarian Law in Armed Conflicts—Manual, DSK VV207320067, edited by The Federal Ministry of Defence of the Federal Republic of Germany, VR II 3, August 1992, English transaction, § 1051.

[115] Sandoz et al. (eds) 1987, p 653, para 2089.

[116] Ibid.

[117] Triffterer 2008, p 461.

[118] Ibid.; Dörmann 2003, p 363.

[119] Triffterer 2008, p 459.

[120] Commission on the Responsibilities 1920, p 114.

[121] Commentary to paragraph 102 of the San Remo Manual, p 179, para 102.3.

Paragraph 104 also requires that the blockading power allow the passage of medical supplies for the civilian population or for the wounded and sick members of armed forces, subject *only* to the right to prescribe technical arrangements, such as arranging for inspection of the cargo.

The text of these provisions was drawn from Article 23 of the Fourth Geneva Convention and, in particular, Articles 70 and 71 of AP1. Article 23 GCIV imposes a duty on *all* High Contracting Parties to '… allow the free passage of all consignments of medical and hospital stores[122] and objects necessary for religious worship intended only for civilians of another High Contracting Party, even if the latter is its adversary. It shall likewise permit the free passage of all consignments of essential foodstuffs, clothing and tonics intended for children under fifteen, expectant mothers and maternity cases'. Under this provision, '[t]he right to free passage means that the articles and material in question may not be regarded as war contraband and cannot therefore be seized'.[123] This is subject to the conditions laid down in the subparagraphs of Article 23—namely that the supplies reach their intended destination and that the provisions do not confer a direct military advantage to the enemy.[124] The reference to 'even if the latter is its adversary' is intended 'to refer primarily to the relations between the States carrying out a blockade… and the States against whom the blockade is directed'.[125]

Article 70 of AP1 broadens the obligation in Article 23 GCIV to include 'rapid and unimpeded passage of *all* relief consignments, equipment and personnel'.[126] It also provides the basis for paragraph 103 of the *San Remo Manual*, although the text in the *Manual* was adjusted to make it unambiguously clear that the rule is obligatory, and to make it easier to apply in practice.[127] Thus, as the Commentary explains, '[s]implification of the language has allowed the unequivocal statement that the

---

122 According to the ICRC Commentary for Article 23, the expression "consignments of medical and hospital stores" covers consignments of any pharmaceutical products used in either preventive or therapeutic medicine, as well as consignments of medical, dental or surgical instruments or equipment': Pictet (ed) 1958, p 180.

123 Pictet (ed) 1958, p 179.

124 I.e.,… there is no serious reason for fearing 'that a definite advantage may accrue to the military efforts or economy of the enemy through the substitution of the above-mentioned consignments for goods which would otherwise be provided or produced by the enemy or through the release of such material, services or facilities as would otherwise be required for the production of such goods': Article 23(c), Fourth Geneva Convention. Note the ICRC Commentary: 'A distinction is drawn between two classes of consignment: (1) consignments of medical and hospital stores and objects necessary for religious worship; (2) consignments of essential foodstuffs, clothing, and tonics. The former cannot be a means of reinforcing the war economy and can therefore be sent to the civilian population as a whole. On the other hand, consignments which fell into the second category are only entitled to free passage when they are to be used solely by children under fifteen, expectant mothers and maternity cases': Pictet (ed) 1958, p 180.

125 Pictet (ed) 1958, p 181.

126 Article 70(2) AP1 (Emphasis added).

127 Commentary to San Remo Manual, p 180.

blockading power is obliged to allow transit of relief shipments through the blockade'. Furthermore, paragraph 103 only contains two limitations, having dropped the requirement in Article 70 that relief consignments may not be diverted or delayed unnecessarily. It was felt the provision was made redundant by the affirmation in paragraph 103 that blockading powers are obliged to follow this rule.

Article 70 also requires an agreement between the 'parties concerned' to permit free access for humanitarian relief. However, it is not entirely clear whether a blockading State is to be considered a 'party concerned' whose permission is required.[128] Bothe convincingly argues that: (i) a transit State has to provide permission for vessels to pass through its sovereign territory; (ii) a blockading State does not possess this right, but it does have factual power and control over the blockaded area, as demonstrated by the fact that it can obstruct any maritime traffic to and from the blockaded coast; (iii) given the importance attached to factual control in the field of war, for the purposes of Article 70 AP I, there is a persuasive argument that it 'can be equated to the sovereign title to territory possess by a transit State'; and (iv) hence, there is a compelling reason to treat a blockading State as a 'party concerned' under Article 70.[129]

Can a blockading State withhold permission? Article 70 provides that *all* States, including transit states, are under a duty to 'allow and facilitate rapid and unimpeded passageof all relief consignments, equipment and personnel provided in accordance with [Article 70]... even if such assistance is destined for the civilian population of the adverse Party'.[130] The French and US military manuals support this reading.[131] Given this clear duty, the withholding of permission may only be temporary and 'for the reason of overwhelming security concerns'[132]: in other words, states do not possess an 'unfettered discretion'.[133] The state must also 'protect relief consignments and facilitate their rapid distribution'.[134] The ICRC Commentary explains that '[t]he intention of these words is to avoid any harassment, to reduce formalities as far as possible and dispense with any that are superfluous ... Thus the obligation imposed here is relative: the passage of the relief consignments should be as rapid as allowed by the circumstances'.[135]

---

128 Heintschel von Heinegg 2008, p 555.

129 Bothe 1988, pp 763–764.

130 Additional Protocol I, Article 70(2).

131 The French Law of Armed Conflict Manual states that when carrying out a blockade, there is an obligation to 'allow free passage relief indispensible to the survival of the civilian population', Law of Armed Conflict Manual (2001), p 33; the US Naval Handbook states, 'neutral vessels and aircraft engaged in the carriage of qualifying relief supplies for the civilian population... should be authorized to pass through the blockade cordon', Naval Handbook (1995), § 7.7.3.

132 Heintschel von Heinegg 2008, p 555; and Bothe 1988, p 764.

133 For a contrary opinion, see Rauch 1984, pp 91–92: 'The right of transit is dependent upon the consent of the other States concerned and the blockading power, consequently, has an unrestricted discretion to agree or not to the passage of relief consignments'.

134 Artilce 70(4), AP1.

135 Sandoz et al. 1987, p 823, para 2829.

To what extent does this duty of free passage—articulated in Article 23 GCIV, Article 70 AP1 and the *San Remo Manual*—reflect customary international law? The *San Remo Manual* was designed to express the present state of customary international law, but some provisions developed rather than codified the law. It is also not clear that Article 70 reflects customary international law. However, despite this ambiguity, the obligation does appear to be generally accepted by states. States that are not and/or were not at the time party to AP1 have accepted Article 70.[136] Many states have also included the duty in their military manuals and national legislation.[137] Finally, the UN Security Council has, on numerous occasions, called for and/or demanded that states respect this rule without reference to Article 70 or to the specific characterisation of the conflict.[138] This 'widespread, representative and virtually uniform' practice has led Henckaerts to conclude that the duty set out in Article 70 has crystallised into customary international humanitarian law.[139]

To summarise, blockades must satisfy specific conditions in order to be properly constituted: they must be declared, impartial and effectively enforced. However, even if a blockade is legally constituted, it may become illegal if it has the effect of starving a civilian population. Accordingly, blockades may be used to target combatants and prevent full and free trade of an enemy, but they cannot be used to 'starve out' the enemy by targeting its civilian population. A minimum amount of food and items necessary for the survival of a civilian population must be allowed to cross the blockade, subject to inspection and supervision.

---

136 Henckaerts and Doswell-Beck (eds) 2005, p 194.

137 Ibid., pp 186–188.

138 E.g., Res. 688, 5 April 1991, para 3 (the SC 'Insists that Iraq allow immediate access by international humanitarian organizations to all those in need of assistance in all parts of Iraq and to make available all necessary facilities for their operations');

Res. 752, 15 May 1992, para 8 ('Calls on all parties and others concerned to ensure that conditions are established for the effective and unhindered delivery of humanitarian assistance, including safe and secure access to airports …');

Res. 757, 30 May 1992, para 17 ('Demands that all parties and others concerned create immediately the necessary conditions for unimpeded delivery of humanitarian supplies to Sarajevo and other destinations in Bosnia and Herzegovina');

Res. 822, 30 April 1993, para 3 ('Calls for unimpeded access for international humanitarian relief efforts in the region, in particular in all areas affected by the conflict in order to alleviate the suffering of the civilian population …');

Res. 998, 16 June 1995, para 4 ('Demands that all parties allow unimpeded access for humanitarian assistance to all parts of the Republic of Bosnia and Herzegovina');

Res. 1291, 24 February 2000, preamble and para 12 ('Expressing… its deep concern at the limited access of humanitarian workers to refugees and internally displaced persons in some areas of the Democratic Republic of the Congo… Calls on all parties to ensure the safe and unhindered access of relief personnel to all those in need …'); *and*

Res. 1468, 20 March 2003, para 14 ('Demands also that all the parties to the conflict in the Democratic Republic of the Congo, and in particular in Ituri, ensure the security of civilian populations and grant to MONUC and to humanitarian organizations full and unimpeded access to the populations in need').

139 Henckaerts 2005, p 189.

14.3.3 Blockades and non-state actors in a non-international armed conflict

The law of blockade operates in the context of wars between states. It is a right of states to blockade other states, and that right is balanced against the rights and interests of neutral states. International law is silent on whether states can blockade non-state actors, whether non-state actors can blockade state coastlines or ports and what consequences follow for neutral states in respect of interception. However, this silence does not necessarily mean that the law of blockade is irrelevant in non-international armed conflict. The drafters of the *San Remo Manual* explicitly acknowledged and endorsed the possibility of their use in NIACs, with the observation that:

> ... it should be noted that although the provisions of this Manual are primarily meant to apply to international armed conflicts at sea, this has intentionally not been expressly indicated in paragraph 1 in order not to dissuade the implementation of these rules in non-international armed conflicts involving naval operations.[140]

What does state practice tell us about blockades involving non-state actors? First, there are no examples of non-state actors blockading states. This is not surprising given the resources required to effectively maintain a blockade. Second, it is self-evident that a government has the right to intercept any goods travelling within its territorial jurisdiction, especially those destined for a rebel army or insurgent group. South Vietnam mined North Vietnamese ports and territorial waters in May 1972 during the Vietnam conflict, but limited the mining to the 12 miles of claimed North Vietnamese territorial waters (the contiguous zone).[141] Although this conflict had an international character and so the rules of blockade could have been applied, it is nevertheless a clear example of interdiction *within* territorial waters, permitted by international law in both IAC and NIACs.

This internal operation is not the same as extra-territorially blockading an enemy and enforcing that blockade on the high seas. International law offers little guidance on whether, in the context of a NIAC, a government is permitted to deploy its armed forces outside its territorial waters for the purpose of intercepting other vessels. However, there are several nineteenth century examples of states imposing blockades on non-state actors that merit consideration. Although these examples must be understood in light of the legal framework that existed at the time, when it was widely accepted that the regulation of internal rebellions and insurgencies was a matter that fell exclusively within the scope of domestic law, they remain instructive because they provide an exception to this rule. If an internal conflict reached a sufficient severity and scope, it was possible for the non-state actor to be recognised as possessing belligerent status and, as a consequence, the conflict would be governed by international law.

---

[140] Doswald-Beck (ed) 1995, p 73.

[141] See further Mallison and Mallison 1976, pp 50–51.

The recognition of belligerency could be triggered by the government or another state, and could be explicit or implicit. The declaration and enforcement of a blockade by a government against insurgents was considered to imply recognition of their belligerent status. According to Lauterpacht: (i) if war had not already been declared, the blockade functioned as a declaration of war between the government and insurgent forces; (ii) the insurgent forces would thereby be recognised as having the status of belligerents; and (iii) belligerent rights were automatically conferred on the insurgents.[142] In the opinion of some contemporary scholars, 'a blockade is itself evidence that a conflict with a non-state actor is sufficiently serious that the blockading party must treat the non-state actor as a *belligerent*, not as an *insurgent*'.[143]

The principal examples of recognition of belligerency include recognition of the South American Republics in the 1820s and 1830s, Greece in 1825 and the Confederate State during the American Civil War. As Lauterpacht noted, when the South American wars of independence assumed a wider scope, 'Great Britain, notwithstanding the existing Treaty [that prohibited it from exporting arms and war material to the Spanish colonies in America], regarded it as her duty to grant to the insurgents the first essential privilege of recognition of belligerency, i.e., impartial treatment'.[144] In so concluding, Lauterpacht quotes Canning's speech of 16 April 1823, which is instructive in explaining the Government's reasoning:

> In process of time, as those colonies became more powerful, a question arose… to be decided on a due consideration of their *de jure* relation to Spain on the one side, and their *de facto* independence of her, on the other. The law of nations was entirely silent with respect to the course which, under a circumstance so peculiar as the transition of colonies from their allegiance to the parent state, ought to be pursued… It became necessary, therefore, in the Act of 1918, to treat the colonies as actually independent of Spain; and to prohibit mutually, and with respect to both, the aid which had hitherto been prohibited with respect to one alone.[145]

Two observations are warranted. First, law was unable to provide sufficient guidance to neutral states when they were confronted with conflict situations arising out of the right to self-determination. Second, this silence meant that once the violence reached a certain threshold of intensity, states had no choice but to declare their neutrality. The recognition of belligerency doctrine engaged a legal framework that governed the insurgents and enabled states to declare their neutrality in respect of both parties to the conflict. The desire to remain neutral and maintain commercial relations compelled 'a certain *de facto* recognition of the situation even though the conflict was continuing… This gradually emerged as a distinct mode of recognition… [where] the insurgents achieved a separate though temporary status'.[146]

---

142 Lauterpacht 1947, pp 193–199.

143 Heller 2010.

144 Lauterpacht 1947, pp 187.

145 Therry (ed) 1830, Vol. v., p 40.

146 Crawford 2007, p 380.

As Canning's speech reveals, the recognition of belligerency was an exercise in policy, primarily prompted by neutral states that wanted to protect their maritime interests. Threats to their interests were both potential[147] and, if the conflict extended to the open seas, immediate: vital shipping and trading interests may be at risk. Recognition of belligerency also enabled states to provide assistance to belligerents, and provided a resolution to the situation where insurgents clearly had some rights and were not simply pirates or common criminals. As Crawford observes, 'since war was legally permissible, [States] had the option of non-intervention or the commission of an act of war against the metropolitan State'.[148] Recognition therefore had a tripartite effect: 'it formalised the legal status of the insurgents; it gave rise to a duty of non-intervention with respect to both parties and it entailed the acceptance of the exercise of belligerent rights by both.[149]

A model example of belligerent recognition is the Presidential declaration of a blockade during the American Civil War. The Union, while claiming the right to blockade the coasts occupied by the Confederacy, refused to recognise their belligerent status. However, European states subsequently refused to accept this denial and recognised the conflict between the two parties as a state of belligerency, declaring their neutrality in the conflict.[150] Britain took the view that if the necessary factual conditions are fulfilled, the insurgents are entitled to recognition.[151] Lauterpacht explained that, '[t]he British practice, as well as that of other States, leaves no doubt that, apart from other aspects of the question, the insurgents are entitled to recognition inasmuch as acquiescence in the exercise of belligerent rights by the lawful government confers corresponding rights upon the insurgents'.[152] This view was later upheld by the US Supreme Court, which explained that, '[t]he proclamation of blockade is, itself, official and conclusive evidence to the court that a state of war existed which demanded and authorized a recourse to such a measure, under the circumstances peculiar to the case'.[153]

Although this practice was limited, the declaration of a blockade clearly had the effect of transforming the non-international armed conflict into a 'war', or rather, an international armed conflict. Does the same rationale apply in contemporary international law? The doctrine has not been applied for nearly 140 years. The non-recognition of insurgents during the Spanish civil war of 1936–1939, despite

147 The non-state actor may become a state (either by displacing the ruling government or through succession) and neutral states wanted to protect potential future international relations—indeed, in the case of secessionary situations, 'belligerent recognition was sometimes used as a substitute for, rather than an intermediate step towards, recognition of the entity in question as a State': Crawford 2007, p 381.

148 Ibid.

149 Ibid.

150 For an excellent summary of the blockade, the European response and its legal consequences, see: Heller 2010.

151 Lauterpacht 1947, p 188.

152 Ibid.

153 *Prize Cases* (1862) 2 Black 635, 17 L 459 at 477. See also Moir 2008, pp 15–16.

the apparent applicability of the belligerency doctrine, is frequently cited as the point at which the institution fell into disuse.[154] Does this lack of use indicate that the doctrine is no longer valid? Whereas domestic law is valid until repealed by the relevant legislative authority, international law has no comparable system. As Professor Falk remarks, '[a] critical intellectual task is to conceive more fully the problem of overcoming obsolete norms in a legal order that lacks a legislature'.[155] Oglesby undertook this task and convincing applied the civil law concept of 'desuetude' to the recognition of belligerency doctrine.[156]

He posited a quartet of criteria for discerning when non-use of a law has been translated into desuetude: (i) the disuse is of such duration that the disuse itself has become established as custom; (ii) another customary law has been substituted for it; (iii) the contrary practice approaches the universal in its acceptance; and (iv) opportunities must have presented themselves for the law to have been applied.[157] He then examined the belligerency doctrine against this criteria: (a) the time required to formulate a norm of customary law is likely to be enough time for 'custom *contra legem* to harden into law', and the doctrine of belligerency has not been applied by states for a greater period of time than it took for the original custom to form; (b) recognition of insurgency has taken the place of the doctrine; (c) that this contrary custom has met the test of near universal acceptance; and finally (c) in at least two situations where applicable od the doctrine would have been appropriate, it was deliberately not applied.[158] In short: '[w]hen custom disappears on which the law is founded, surely the law itself must disappear'.[159]

Other commentators have reached similar conclusions. It has been argued that by the twentieth century, the recognition of belligerency doctrine 'seemed to become obsolete',[160] and the 'current total disuse of the belligerency doctrine arguably resulted from states resorting to the more flexible concept of insurgency ... [avoiding] the restrictions on behaviour incurred by recognition of belligerency'.[161] Furthermore, the 1949 Geneva Conventions obviated one of the primary

---

[154] See Cullen 2010, p 22. Although one may note that the British Government were recorded as stating on a number of occasions that if the normal rules of civil war applied, 'every precedent would be in favour of granting belligerent rights as was done in the American civil war: Statement by Mr Eden on 25 June 1937, House of Commons Debates, Vol. CCCXXV, col. 1608. In May 1938 Lord Halifax stated before the Council of the League of Nations that '[t]he position was rapidly reached where a state of belligerency existed in fact if not in name, and the normal procedure would have been for other States to assume the rights and obligations of neutrality and for them to recognise the two parties to the civil war were possess of the rights and obligations of belligerents': League of Nations Official Journal, 1938, p. 330.

[155] Falk 1964, p 239.

[156] Oglesby 1971, pp 100–114.

[157] Ibid., p 112.

[158] Ibid., pp 112–113.

[159] Ibid., pp 114.

[160] Bartels 2009, p 17.

[161] Cullen 2010, p 22.

purposes of the doctrine: to allow for international law to regulate the non-international armed conflict. Finally, although there is some academic support for the contemporary relevance of the doctrine, even that support concedes that the doctrine must have been modified as a result of developments in public international law, namely the Geneva Conventions and their Additional Protocols.[162] For example, it is unlikely the doctrine would apply to wars of national liberation that fall within the scope of Article 1(4) of API.[163]

It can be stated with a considerable degree of certainty that the doctrine has fallen into desuetude, but even if one were to accept that it is still valid and can be applied today, it is doubtful the doctrine would apply to the Israeli-Hamas conflict.

14.4 Applying the Normative Frameworks to the Israeli-Hamas Conflict

Is the interception of the Gaza Freedom Flotilla justifiable under either the law enforcement or the armed conflict framework? The interception cannot be justified as a law enforcement operation since none of the applicable exceptions in international law apply. Every passenger underwent security checks similar to those experienced at most commercial airports and docks around the world prior to boarding the vessels, and port authorities supervised the loading of cargo.

Israel expressly invoked the armed conflict framework, declaring that it was in a 'state of armed conflict with the Hamas regime'.[164] Furthermore, the blockade imposed on Gaza since January 2009 can only be justified within the law of armed conflict.[165] Israel claims this blockade provides it with a *prima facie* right to intercept vessels on the high seas. In order to assess whether this claim is sustainable, it is necessary to consider the status of Gaza and the

[162] Lootsteen 2000, pp 109–141.

[163] Although one may argue that if Article 1(4) is, in practice, a 'dead letter', does it still modify the scope of the belligerency doctrine so as to exclude wars where people are fighting to realise their right to self-determination?

[164] Israeli Ministry of Foreign Affairs 31 May 2010, The Gaza flotilla and the maritime blockade of Gaza—Legal background, available at http://www.mfa.gov.il/MFA/Government/Law/Legal+Issues+and+Rulings/Gaza_flotilla_maritime_blockade_Gaza-Legal_background_31-May-2010.htm; Israeli Ministry of Foreign Affairs, MFA legal expert Sarah Weiss Maudi on the legal aspects of Gaza aid, 26 May 2010, available at http://www.mfa.gov.il/MFA/HumanitarianAid/Palestinians/Legal_aspects_Gaza_aid_26-May-2010.htm; Israeli Ministry of Foreign Affairs, 29 July 2009, The Operation in Gaza: Factual and Legal Aspects, available at http://www.mfa.gov.il/MFA/Terrorism-+Obstacle+to+Peace/Hamas+war+against+Israel/Operation_Gaza_Context_of_Operation_5_Aug_2009.htm#A.

[165] Notice to Mariners, No. 1 of 2009, Blockade of Gaza Strip, 3 January 2009. See the official notes on the State of Israel's Ministry of Transport and Road Safety, available at http://199.203.58.11/EN/index.php?option=com_content&view=article&id=124:no12009&catid=17:noticetomariners&Itemid=12.

character of the Israeli-Hamas conflict. This task is beset with difficulties, many of which emerge from the uncertain status of Gaza and Israel's decision not to ratify API.

14.4.1 The character of the Israeli-Hamas conflict: international or non-international?

Israel has maintained an ambiguous position on the character of its conflict with Hamas, describing it as 'sui generis' in nature but without explaining what this means.[166] The UN Human Rights Council Report on the interception of the Flotilla also failed to engage with the problem of identifying the character of the conflict. Yet as Milanovic reminds us, the structure of LOAC is such that international and non-international armed conflicts are separate legal categories: 'an "armed conflict" exists when there is an IAC or a NIAC, not the other way around'.[167]

There is a general consensus that the classification of an armed conflict is determined by the nature of the 'parties' to the conflict. In the case of an international armed conflict, the paradigm party is a state, which is made clear by Common Article 2 to the Geneva Conventions: '[the conventions] apply to all cases of declared war or of any other armed conflict which may arise between two or more of the High Contracting Parties even if the state of war is not recognized by one of them'.[168] Common Article 3 of the Geneva Conventions constituted the formal adoption of a specific legal framework for non-international armed conflicts, although the provision fails to give guidance as to the criteria that must be satisfied.[169] Since common Article 3 refers to 'armed conflict not of an international character occurring in the territory of one of the High Contracting Parties', it has generally been interpreted as including all conflicts that meet the minimum requirements of Article 3, but not the requirements of an international armed conflict. Thus, the definition is structured in the negative: if a conflict is not of an international character, it is a non-international armed conflict.[170] State practice and the jurisprudence of international tribunals have nevertheless filled this 'gap' and, as a result, there is common agreement that an internal armed conflict involves 'protracted armed violence between governmental authorities and

[166] Israel Ministry of Foreign Affairs, 11 July 2009, The Operation in Gaza, 27 December 2008–2018 January 2009: Factual and Legal Aspects, available at http://www.mfa.gov.il/NR/rdonlyres/E89E699D-A435-491B-B2D0-017675DAFEF7/0/GazaOperationwLinks.pdf.

[167] Milanovic 7 May 2010.

[168] Article 2(1) of GCs I to IV: '... which may arise between two or more High Contracting Parties...'.

[169] Moir 2008, pp 6–10.

[170] See Mastorodimos 2010, p 440.

organized armed groups or between such groups within a State'.[171] Although Article 3 only provides a minimum standard of humanitarian protection, over the years many of the rules and principles of international armed conflict have been applied to non-international armed conflicts as a matter of customary international law.[172]

The Israeli-Hamas conflict is between a non-State entity and a State; it therefore does not satisfy the paradigm definition of an international armed conflict. Nevertheless, a *prima facie* NIAC may be transformed into an IAC in three exceptional circumstances.[173] Article 1(4) of API transforms an otherwise non-international armed conflict between a national liberation movement and a State, into an international armed conflict.[174] This provision proved controversial at the Diplomatic Conference of 1974–1977 and has never been applied in practice; it is unlikely that it represents customary international law. The second exception is where another State intervenes directly or indirectly in a civil conflict in support of a non-state actor.[175] The third exception, as discussed above, is the application of the *recognition of belligerency* doctrine.[176]

It is difficult to see that any of these exceptions apply to the Israeli-Hamas conflict. Although the Palestinian people have a right to self-determination,[177] Israel has not ratified Additional Protocol I. Nor is there any evidence to suggest that Hamas is acting on behalf of another state. Finally, the possibility of applying the recognition of belligerency doctrine suffers from two problems. First, there are compelling arguments to suggest the doctrine has in fact fallen into desuetude. Second, even if one accepts the doctrine can be applied today, it is doubtful it could apply to the Israeli-Hamas conflict. The scope of the doctrine will be determined in light of developments in international law, including Article 1(4) of API. Furthermore, the doctrine traditionally applied in the context of civil wars and not alien occupation of a non-state territory. Since none of exceptions appear

---

[171] *Tadić* Case, ICTY IT-94-1, para 70. See ICTY IT-96-21, *Delalić* Case (Judgment of 16 November 1998), § 184 and ICTR IT-96-13-I, *Musema* Case (Judgment of 27 January 2000), § 248. See also Moir 2008, pp 36.

[172] Although the scope of application of AP II is considerably narrower than that of Article 3 of the 1949 Geneva Conventions: see Article 1 of AP II. AP II will only apply to armed conflicts taking place on the territory of a contracting state party, part of which must be under the effective control of the opposing non-state party to the conflict.

[173] See Milanovic 7 May 2010.

[174] The purpose of this provision is to recognise that a people entitled to self-determination, 'whose right is being denied by a state' exhibit a form of sovereignty that requires the application of the law of international armed conflict and the privilege of belligerency. See Milanovic 7 May 2010.

[175] See the overall control test set out in ICTY, Appeals Chamber, *Tadić*, 15 July 1999 (Case no. IT-94-1-A).

[176] Moir 2008, pp 6–10.

[177] Recently affirmed by the UN General Assembly in Res. 65/13 (25 January 2011), UN Doc A/RES/65/13 and by the UN Human Rights Council, HRC Res 13/6, Right of the Palestinian People to Self-determination, UN Doc A/HRC/RES/13/6 (14 April 2010).

to apply to the conflict, is the only option to conclude that the conflict is non-international in nature?

Faced with the challenge of characterising the conflict, the Israeli Supreme Court has conceded that '[a]dmittedly, the classification of the armed conflict between the state of Israel and the Hamas organization as an international conflict raises several difficulties. But in a host of judgments we have regarded this conflict as an international conflict'.[178] The Court has also held that although the Gaza Strip is no longer occupied, Israel remains bound by the customary international law provisions relating to international armed conflict.[179] Although these decisions reflect a desirable approach from a humanitarian point of view, it is unfortunate the Court did not provide a legal basis for its findings.

Neither The UN Human Rights Council Report on the Interception of the Gaza Freedom Flotilla nor the Turkel Commission Report adequately address this problem. Although the Turkel Commission did acknowledge the difficulty of characterising the conflict, it concluded that it would nevertheless examine the blockade 'on the basis of the assumption that the conflict between Israel and Hamas is international in character'.[180] Despite considering the Israeli Supreme Court jurisprudence and recalling that various UN, humanitarian and human rights organisations also refer to the conflict as international in character, the 'assumption' lacked sufficient legal justification.

14.4.2 A sui generis conflict?

The conflict between Israel and Hamas does not posses the necessary attributes to be an international armed conflict but neither does it 'fit' the textual definition found in common article 3. The conflict exhibits several unique attributes: (i) the conflict is between a State and a democratically elected government of a territory that is not yet recognised as a State; (ii) the people of that territory have a recognised international right of self-determination; (iii) the control exerted by Israel on the territory prevents the realisation of that right; and (iv) the territory was never part of Israel: i.e., the conflict has never been a civil war. In addition to these factors, there remains the controversial question of whether Gaza remains occupied by Israel and the extent to which Israel exercises control over the territory. Given these circumstances, can Israel lawfully impose a blockade? Or, to put the question another way, are the hostilities between Israel and Hamas analogous to that of an international armed conflict such that the rules of blockade could apply?

---

[178] *Physicians for Human Rights* v *Prime Minister*, HCJ 201/09 (19 January 2009), para 14.

[179] *Al-Bassiouni* v *Prime Minister*, HCJ 9132/07 (30 January 2008), para 12.

[180] Turkel Report, para 44.

The precise legal status of the Gaza Strip remains highly contested. Israel's voluntary and unilateral disengagement from the Gaza Strip in September 2005 prompted considerable discussion on whether Gaza remains an occupied territory. Article 42 of the Hague Regulations, which reflects customary international law,[181] stipulates that, 'a territory is considered occupied when it is actually placed under the authority of the hostile army. The occupation extends only to the territory where such authority has been established and can be exercised'. The question of whether a territory is occupied is therefore one of fact, based on the factual control exercised over the territory. The debate over whether Gaza remains occupied revolves around the type of control necessary for continued occupation, the extent to which that control must be exercised for territory to remain occupied, and the actual level of effective control exercised by Israel over Gaza.

Israel claims it no longer occupies the Gaza Strip,[182] maintaining that it 'is neither a State nor a territory occupied or controlled by Israel', but rather, it has a 'sui generis' status.[183] Pursuant to the Disengagement Plan, Israel dismantled all military institutions and settlements in Gaza and there is no longer a permanent Israeli military or civilian presence in the territory. However, the Plan also provided that 'Israel will guard and monitor the external land perimeter of the Gaza Strip, will continue to maintain exclusive authority in Gaza air space, and will continue to exercise security activity in the sea off the coast of the Gaza Strip', as well as maintaining an Israeli military presence on the Egyptian/Gaza border, and reserving the right to re-enter Gaza at will.[184]

Israel continues to control six of Gaza's seven land crossings, its maritime borders and airspace, and the movement of goods and persons in and out of the territory. Troops from the Israeli Defence Force regularly enter parts of the territory and/or deploy missile attacks, drones and sonic bombs into Gaza. Israel has declared a 'no-go buffer zone' that stretches deep into Gaza: if Gazans enter this zone, they are shot on sight. Gaza is also dependent on Israel for, *inter alia*, electricity, currency, telephone networks, issuing IDs, and permits to enter and leave the territory. Israel also has sole control of the Palestinian Population Registry, through which the Israeli Army regulates who is classified as a Palestinian and who is a Gazan or West Banker. Since 2000, aside from a limited number of exceptions, Israel has refused to add people to the Palestinian Population Registry.[185]

---

181 *Case concerning Armed Activities on the Territory of the Congo (Democratic Republic of Congo* v *Uganda)*, Judgement of 19 December 2005, ICJ Rep. 2005, para 172.

182 See inter alia: HCJ 9132/07 (27 January 2008) per President Beinisch at para 12.

183 Israel Ministry of Foreign Affairs, 'The Operation in Gaza, 27 December 2008–2018 January 2009. Factual and Legal Aspects' (11 July 2009) available at http://www.mfa.gov.il/NR/rdonlyres/E89E699D-A435-491B-B2D0-017675DAFEF7/0/GazaOperationwLinks.pdf.

184 Available at http://www.mfa.gov.il/MFA/Peace+Process/Reference+Documents/Disengagement+Plan+-+General+Outline.htm (accessed on 7 October 2010).

185 See for example, Dugard, 'Human Rights in Palestine and Other Occupied Arab Territories, Report of the Special Rapporteur John Dugard on the Situation of Human Rights in the Palestinian Territories Occupied since 1967' (21 January 2008) UN Doc A/HRC/7/17, para 11.

It is this direct external control over Gaza and indirect control over life within Gaza that has led the United Nations,[186] the UN General Assembly,[187] the UN Fact Finding Mission to Gaza,[188] international human rights organisations,[189] US Government websites,[190] the UK Foreign and Commonwealth Office[191] and a significant number of legal commentators[192] to reject the argument that Gaza is no longer occupied.

Israel contends that it no longer has effective control of the territory: its troops are not permanently stationed in the territory and it no longer fully administers or

---

186 Seehttp://edition.cnn.com/2009/WORLD/meast/01/06/israel.gaza.occupation.question/index.html: 'The United Nations still calls Gaza "occupied" and '... a reporter pointed out to a U.N. spokesman that the secretary-general had told Arab League representatives that Gaza was still considered occupied. "Yes, the U.N. defines Gaza, the West Bank and East Jerusalem as Occupied Palestinian Territory. No, that definition hasn't changed," the spokesman replied. Farhan Haq, spokesman for the secretary-general, told CNN Monday that the official status of Gaza would change only through a decision of the U.N. Security Council'. See also Human Rights Council Resolution S-9/1 (12 January 2009) A/HRC/S-9/L.1.

187 For example, the UN General Assembly Res 63/96 (18 December 2008), A/RES/63/96.

188 See for example, 'Report of the United Nations High Commissioner for Human Rights on the implementation of the Human Rights Council resolution S-9/1, The Grave Violations of Human Rights in the Occupied Palestinian Territory, Particularly due to the Recent Israeli Military Attacks against the Occupied Gaza Strip' (13 August 2009) A/HRC/12/37. See also the report of the United Nations Fact Finding Mission on the Gaza Conflict: 'Israel has without doubt at all times relevant to the mandate of the Mission exercised effective control over the Gaza Strip. The Mission is of the view that the circumstances of this control establish that the Gaza Strip remains occupied by Israel': 'Report of the United Nations Fact Finding Mission on the Gaza Conflict' (15 September 2009) UN Doc. A/HRC/12/48, 85 para 276.

189 For example, Human Rights Watch, 'Israel: 'Disengagement Will Not End Gaza Occupation', available at http://www.hrw.org/en/news/2004/10/28/israel-disengagement-will-not-end-gaza-occupation.

190 See http://edition.cnn.com/2009/WORLD/meast/01/06/israel.gaza.occupation.question/index.html: 'The CIA World Factbook says: "West Bank and Gaza Strip are Israeli-occupied with current status subject to the Israeli–Palestinian Interim Agreement—permanent status to be determined through further negotiation; Israel removed settlers and military personnel from the Gaza Strip in August 2005". The U.S. State Department Web site also includes Gaza when it discusses the "occupied" territories. State Department spokeswoman Amanda Harper referred CNN Monday to the department's Web site for any questions about the status of Gaza, and she noted that the Web site referred to the 2005 disengagement. When asked the department's position on whether Gaza is still occupied, Harper said she would look into it. She has not yet contacted CNN with any more information'.

191 'Although there is no permanent physical Israeli presence in Gaza, given the significant control Israel has over Gaza's borders, airspace and territorial waters, Israel retains obligations as an occupying power under the Fourth Geneva Convention': UK Foreign and Commonwealth Office, Annual Report on Human Rights 2008—Israel and the Occupied Palestinian Territories (26 March 2009), available at http://www.unhcr.org/refworld/docid/49ce361bc.html accessed 3 February 2011.

192 See Aronson 2005; Benvenisti 2009; Bruderlein 2004; Bashi and Mann 2007; Darcy and Reynolds 2010, pp 211–243; Dinstein 2009, pp 276–280; Kaliser 2007, pp 187–229; Mari 2005, pp 356–368; Scobbie 2004–2005, reprinted in Kattan (ed) 2008, p 637; and Shany 2005, pp 369–383. For a contrary opinion, see Bell and Shefi 2010, pp 268–296.

governs the territory (it does not provide a local administration). Israel also argues that Hamas is now in control of Gaza, and it would require a considerable military operation for Israel to regain control. A comprehensive analysis of the arguments surrounding the occupation debate is outside the scope of this paper.[193] However, it is the opinion of this author that Israel remains the belligerent occupier of Gaza and the relevant provisions of the Fourth Geneva Convention continue to apply.[194]

There are several reasons why the Israeli-Hamas conflict might be better classified as international in character, including historical precedent, the evolution of treaty law in respect of wars of national liberation, Israel's application of the law of IAC as a matter of policy, and Israel's assertion of a right primarily (if not exclusively) associated with IAC.

The factual situation of Gaza may be *sui generis*, but comparable situations are not entirely unknown to international law. Traditionally, wars of national liberation were governed by domestic law and were not subject to international law. Neutral states were prohibited from supporting or aiding rebels or insurgents because this amounted to 'interfering with the domestic affairs of another state'.[195] However, as Abi-Saab observes, wars of national liberation were not always regarded as a purely internal matter: '[o]ne only has to remember the active role played by France in the American war of independence, the acquisition and affirmation of the independence of the Latin American republics behind the double shield of the Monroe Doctrine and ... the proclamation of Greek independence by Great Britain, Russia and France after the destruction of the Egyptian-Ottoman fleet by the British in the battle of Navarino'.[196] Although external interference did not necessarily transform a conflict into an international armed conflict, by the end of the nineteenth century there was some state practice to indicate that some internal conflicts were better governed by the international rules of war (or IAC).

---

[193] For these arguments, see the academic papers in the note above.

[194] Article 6, GCIV. It should be noted that Israel has continually denied it is bound by the Fourth Geneva Convention, but states that it voluntarily takes into account the humanitarian provisions of the Convention (although it does not specify what it means by this). This position runs contrary to Article 4 of the Fourth Geneva Convention, which provides that, '[p]ersons protected by the Convention are those who, at a given moment and in any manner whatsoever, find themselves, in case of a conflict or occupation, in the hands of a Party to the conflict or Occupying Power of which they are not nationals'. The Israeli Supreme Court has held that certain provisions apply (based on the consent of Israel) but did not specify which provisions: HCJ 769/02 *Public Committee Against Torture in Israel* v *the Government of Israel* (2005), para 20. The Court has also determined that Israeli soldiers are subject to the rules of customary international law, HCJ 393/82 *Jami'at Ascan el-Malmun el-Mahdudeh el-Masauliyeh, Communal Society Registered at the Judea and Samaria Area Headquarters* v *The Commander of IDF Forces in the Judea and Samaria Area, Piskey Din* 37(4) 785, p. 810.

[195] As Abi-Saab explains, this positivist position crystallised by the end of the nineteenth century, led by a 'changing international context and the rise of the positivist doctrines of the State both in municipal and in international law', Abi-Saab 1979, p 367.

[196] Ibid.

This practice came to be known as the recognition of belligerency doctrine, which has been discussed above.

More recently, the recognition of self-determination as an international legal principle led to a greater role for international law in wars of national liberation. In the 1960 and 1970s, the General Assembly passed a number of resolutions stipulating that wars of 'national liberation' should be treated as international conflicts.[197] As Cassese explains, these resolutions reinforced a general desire to support the right of self-determination: 'the majority of States pressing for the adoption of the resolutions intended to promote by legal means the fight of liberation movements against colonial and racist regimes as well as military occupants such as Israel'.[198]

By the first session of the Diplomatic Conference on the Reaffirmation and Development of International Humanitarian Law Applicable in Armed Conflicts (hereinafter the Conference), which led to the adoption of API, 'it soon became apparent that there would be a majority for any proposal that struggles by peoples against colonial, alien, or racist domination be treated as international conflicts, for the purposes of Protocol I, and not as internal conflicts, for the purposes of Protocol II'.[199] In 1974, at the first session, a provision that equated wars of national liberation with international conflicts was adopted 70 votes to 21 with 13 abstentions.[200] Opposition to the provision—notably from Western states—gradually receded and by the 1977 plenary session, an agreement, which become Article 1(4) of API, had emerged: 87 states voted in favour, one against (Israel) and 11 abstained.[201] The provision applies, *inter alia*, to armed conflicts where one side is fighting against 'alien occupation', and is therefore directly applicable to the situation between Palestine and Israel:

> The expression "alien occupation" in the sense of this paragraph—as distinct from belligerent occupation in the traditional sense of all or part of the territory of one State being occupied by another State—covers cases of partial or total occupation of a territory which has not yet been fully formed as a State.[202]

This is unsurprising given the provision was 'designed by its sponsors with certain conflicts in mind, specifically those in Palestine and southern Africa, and was drafted in terms fashioned to exclude its application to civil wars within existing states'.[203] Yet Israel never ratified Additional Protocol I and has persistently objected to Article 1(4).[204] Although some scholars have argued that the

---

[197] E.g., Res. 2383, 23 UN GAOR Supp. (No. 18) at 58, UN Doc A/7218 (1968) and GA Res. 3103, 28 UN GOAR Supp. (No. 30) at 142, UN Doc. A/9030 (1973).

[198] Cassese 1984, pp 55, 68–69.

[199] Draper 1979, p 146.

[200] I Diplomatic Conference on the Reaffirmation and Development of International Humanitarian Law Applicable in Armed Conflicts, Geneva 1974–77, Official Records (1977), p 102.

[201] Ibid., p 42.

[202] Sandoz et al. 1987, p 54.

[203] Aldrich 1991, p 6. See also Cassese 1984, pp 55, 71.

[204] Cassese 1984, pp 55, 71.

provision represents the position of customary international law in the mid 1970s,[205] there is insufficient state practice to support this conclusion. Moreover, for present purposes, it must be noted that Israel persistently objected to Article 1(4) during negotiations and voting.[206] However, even though Article 1(4) did not codify customary international law as it stood in 1977, it did receive considerable support from states during negotiations and the subsequent plenary vote.

A third reason for characterising the conflict as international is founded on Israel's own practice. As a matter of policy, Israel applies IAC rules in its armed engagements with Hamas and recognises that the *sui generis* nature of the conflict merits treating the conflict as international in scope.[207] Given its ambiguous position on the character of the conflict, it is somewhat paradoxical that Israel claims a right associated primarily (if not exclusively) with the rules of IAC: i.e. to maintain a blockade and intercept neutral state vessels on the high seas. For this reason, it may be to Israel's advantage that the conflict is treated *in law* as international so as to enable it to conduct itself within the law of armed conflict.

If the conflict cannot be characterised as international, is the Israeli-Hamas conflict analogous to an international armed conflict such that the rules of blockade could be applied? As discussed above, limited historical state practice supports the possibility of imposing blockades in non-international armed conflicts, but doing so impliedly recognised the belligerent status of the non-state actor and transformed the conflict into an international armed conflict. This practice developed out of a desire by neutral states to protect current and future state interests. The need to protect these interests arose from the severity and scope of the conflict. Blockading a non-state actor indicated that the conflict was, to some extent, analogous to an international armed conflict. It was no longer a purely internal matter; it now involved states that wanted to trade and travel within the blockaded area.

Finally, it is arguable that the blockade on Gaza itself acknowledges the conflict as analogous to an international armed conflict (although this argument is circular/ mutually reinforcing[208]). This 'acknowledgement' may be explicit i.e. Israel imposed a blockade on Gaza because it is, in its view, a conflict to which the rules of international armed conflict should apply—or implicit, insofar as blockades are a right logically associated with international armed conflict. Israel cannot impose

---

205 Ibid., p 70. Abi-Saab 1979, p 372.

206 Even Cassese admits that Israel, 'did not become bound by it': Cassese 1984, p 71.

207 Israel 'as a matter of policy applies to its military operations in Gaza the rules of armed conflict governing both international and non-international armed conflicts': Israel Ministry of Foreign Affairs, 'The Operation in Gaza, 27 December 2008–2018 January 2009: Factual and Legal Aspects' (July 2009), available at http://www.mfa.gov.il/NR/rdonlyres/E89E699D-A435-491B-B2D0-017675DAFEF7/0/GazaOperationwLinks.pdf.

208 If Israel has a *prima facie* right to blockade Gaza, this is in *itself* a compelling reason for characterising the conflict as international; for Israel to have a *prima facie* right to blockade Gaza, the conflict must be one that engages the law of international armed conflict.

a blockade without signally that the conflict has gone beyond a non-international armed conflict. Blockades developed within the context of an international armed conflict precisely because they involved other states; they are not an inherent right but a permitted practice. Invoking the law of blockade—which reconciles belligerent and neutral state interests—acknowledges the potential involvement of neutral states: i.e., that the conflict is international in scope. It is noteworthy that neutral states have not disputed Israel's *prima facie* right to blockade Gaza; they have only objected to the manner in which it has been enforced and its effect on the civilian population.

If we accept the *sui generis* factual situation is analogous to that of an international armed conflict (a state and a separate territory for which the people have a recognised right of self-determination), and apply the law of international armed conflict, then Israel has a *prima facie* right to blockade Gaza. Does this mean that only a state in these circumstances can blockade non-state actors or does it mean that each side may blockade the other? Hamas clearly does not have the resources to blockade Israel, but if it did, would this be permitted under the law of blockade? As a matter of logic, permission is hard to deny: if one side has a *prime facie* right to blockade the other, surely this right also extends to the other side? Furthermore, if Hamas possessed sufficient resources to blockade Israel, it would be difficult to deny that the conflict should be treated as international in character, not least because, in addition to the arguments above, Hamas would possess the resources of a *de facto* State.

As the preceding analysis has revealed, there is no straightforward answer to the question of whether Israel has a *prima facie* right to blockade Gaza. If one accepts there is an international armed conflict, then Israel clearly has a right to blockade Gaza. Paradoxically, Israel has not advanced this position, preferring to maintain an ambiguous position on the character of the conflict. This may be explained by its desire to avoid applying the rules relating to combatant status. Although a vast majority of customary international humanitarian law rules are applicable in both international and non-international armed conflict, these rules apply exclusively within the context of an international armed conflict. However, one cannot 'pick and choose' from the two legal regimes: either a conflict is international (engaging international humanitarian law in its entirety) or it is non-international. States cannot take advantage of some rights of international armed conflict (e.g., blockades), while simultaneously denying the applicability of other rights and obligations.

Does the law of blockade extend to *non-international armed conflicts* and if so, does this transform the conflict into an international armed conflict? The law of blockade does not determine the answer to this question. The Turkel Commission concluded it would apply the rules of blockade even if the Israeli-Hamas conflict were a non-international armed conflict. Regrettably, it did not provide a legal argument to support this conclusion, although it was noted that, 'it is likely there will be a willingness on the part of courts and other bodies to recognise that the rules governing the imposition and enforcement of a naval blockade are applicable to non-international armed conflicts'.[209] According to the Commission, the

---

[209] Turkel, para 42.

difficulty in classifying the Israeli-Hezbollah conflict in 2006 'did not stop recognition of the naval blockade that Israel imposed during that conflict'.[210] Furthermore, neutral states have not objected to Israel's *prima facie* right to blockade Gaza; they have only objected to the legality of the blockade itself and the conduct of the Israeli navy in respect of the interception of the Flotilla vessels. Can Israel's practice be regarded as the emergence of a new norm permitting blockades in 'ambiguous' conflicts against non-state actors? It may be recalled that the law of blockade emerged and developed through belligerent state practice and the response of neutrals to this practice. If neutral states did not object to repeated belligerent state practice, then over time that practice became accepted as lawful.

If it is not accepted that (i) the Israeli-Hamas conflict is international in scope or (ii) that the law of blockade can apply to this sui generis conflict, which is analogous to that of an international armed conflict, or (iii) the law of blockade applies to NIACs, then Israel does not have a *prima facie* right to blockade Gaza. On this reading, the interception of the Gaza Freedom Flotilla is an unlawful exercise of jurisdiction over neutral vessels on the high seas and an internationally wrongful act.

14.4.3 The blockade on Gaza

The humanitarian crisis in Gaza, which has left a majority of civilians facing starvation, has resulted from: (i) frequent military operations during which infrastructure, livestock, food supplies and other essential items, including medical supplies were destroyed (internal destruction); and (ii) the blockade and siege on Gaza that prevent humanitarian supplies from reaching the civilian population (external restrictions).[211] The crisis is exacerbated by movement restrictions resulting from the blockade and siege, which prevent civilians from being able to enter Gaza with supplies, or leave the territory in search of supplies. The humanitarian crisis is rooted in a number of mutually reinforcing internal and external elements: military operations, years of economic, political and movement restrictions, the land siege and the blockade.

Although Israel has not declared the sole purpose of the blockade to be starvation of the civilian population of Gaza, it has stated that its policy is to 'put the Palestinians on a diet', to 'keep the Gazan economy on the brink of collapse' and to pressure Gazans into forcing Hamas to change its policy towards Israel.[212]

---

[210] Ibid., para 43.

[211] Shany has argued that the blockade must be considered separately from the land siege: Shany 12 October 2010. However, it is not clear that the blockade and land siege can be separated: (i) they are both mutually reinforcing and (ii) both methods of warfare *have the effect* of starving the civilian population insofar as they prevent food and objects necessary for the survival of the civilian population from reaching the territory.

[212] See Sect. 14.2 above.

These objectives directly target civilians and are prohibited by the law of armed conflict. In addition, if the blockade has the *effect* of starving the civilian population, it is illegal regardless of whether the *sole purpose* of the blockade is starvation of that population.[213]

One of Israel's military objectives has been to 'block the infiltration of weapons and ammunition into Hamas ranks' in order to prevent their use for attacks in Israeli territory.[214] Arguably there are alternative ways to interdict the flow of weapons and ammunition that are not as harmful to the civilian population and less likely to prolong and deepen the humanitarian crisis. For example, Israel would be justified in exercising its right to visit and search vessels sailing to Gaza in order to determine if they are carrying prohibited weapons. Given the availability of this option, which would directly address Israel's military objective and ameliorate the harm caused to civilians, the current maritime blockade may be seen as disproportionate to its anticipated military objective.

In addition, Israel is under an obligation to allow for the free passage of supplies necessary for the survival of the civilian population unless there are overwhelming security concerns at stake. This is a high threshold to meet, especially given that Israel already controls the area that separates Gaza's territorial sea and the high seas, and can therefore easily exercise its right to stop/search vessels for contraband.[215]

To the extent that Israel remains the occupying power of Gaza, the law of belligerent occupation also applies.[216] Many of the rules of belligerent occupation that protect civilians reflect the prohibition of starvation found in general international humanitarian law, but they are more comprehensive in scope and make the occupying power directly responsible for the conditions under which the population lives. Where the rules of warfare provide a duty for states to allow the free passage of essential supplies originating from impartial organisations, the law of belligerent occupation imposes a positive obligation on the occupying power to *provide* these essential supplies. Article 55(1) GCIV stipulates that:

> To the fullest extent of the means available to it, the Occupying Power has the duty of ensuring the food and medical supplies of the population; it should in particular, bring in the necessary foodstuffs, medical stores and other articles if the resources of the occupied territory are inadequate.

The ICRC Commentary emphasises that the spirit behind this provision, 'represents a happy return to the traditional idea of the law of war, according to which

---

213 Heintschel von Heinegg 2008, p 554.

214 Per President Beinisch of the Israeli High Court, available at http://www.ynetnews.com/articles/0,7340,L-3898429,00.html (31 May 2010).

215 The Revised Disengagement Plan of 6 June 2004 states that, 'Israel will guard the perimeter of the Gaza Strip, continue to… patrol the sea off the Gaza Coast'.

216 Israel has never accepted considered itself legally bound by the Fourth Geneva Convention in relation to the occupied Palestinian territories; rather, it has declared that, as a matter of practice, it would honour the 'humanitarian' provisions of the Fourth Geneva Convention.

belligerents sought to destroy the power of the enemy State, and not individuals. The rule that the Occupying Power is responsible for the provision of food and medical supplies for the population places that Power under a definite obligation to maintain at a reasonable level the material conditions under which the population of the occupied territory lives'.[217]

However, the Israeli government claims to owe a substantially lower standard than articulated in Article 55(1), a standard not recognised by international humanitarian law. In *Jaber al Bassiouni Ahmed* et al. v *Prime Minister and Minister of Defence*, President Beinisch noted that the Government,

> ... emphasized that this [duty under IHL to facilitate the transfer of necessary goods to the civilian population in the Gaza Strip] does not oblige them to allow transfer of unnecessary goods or *goods in amounts beyond that necessary for basic humanitarian need* ...[218]

Regrettably, the Court accepted this argument without examining the standards required by international humanitarian law.[219] These objectives do not justify abandoning the humanitarian law requirement of maintaining, at a reasonable level, the conditions under which the population of an occupied territory lives.

In addition to this positive obligation, Article 59 of the GCIV provides that 'if the whole or part of the population of an occupied territory is inadequately supplied, the Occupying Power shall agree to relief schemes on behalf of the said population, and shall facilitate them by all the means at its disposal'. The facilitation of relief consignments under this provision does not relieve the occupying power of its duty under Article 55.[220] The ICRC Commentary explains that:

> [t]he obligation on the Occupying Power to accept such relief is unconditional. In all cases where occupied territory is inadequately supplied the Occupying Power is bound to accept relief supplies destined for the population... The Convention not only lays down that the Occupying Power must 'agree' to relief schemes on behalf of the population, but insists that it must 'facilitate' them by all the means at its disposal. The occupation authorities must therefore co-operate wholeheartedly in the rapid and scrupulous execution of these schemes. For that purpose they have many and varied means at their disposal (transport, stores, facilities for distributing and supervising agencies).[221]

Relief projects may be undertaken by either neutral states or by impartial humanitarian organisations, and *all* contracting parties—not just Israel—have an obligation to ensure the free passage and guaranteed protection of humanitarian relief that travels through their territory. The ICRC Commentary refers to this as the 'keystone of the whole system',[222] and stipulates that humanitarian relief must be allowed to pass through blockades: '[t]he principle of free passage, as set forth in this clause,

---

217 Pictet (ed) 1958, p 310.

218 HCJ 9132/07 (27 January 2008) per President Beinisch at para 15. (emphasis added).

219 HCJ 9132/07 (27 January 2008), paras 1–22; in particular, para 22.

220 Article 60, GCIV.

221 Pictet (ed) 1958, p 320.

222 Ibid., p 321.

means that relief consignments for the population of an occupied territory must be allowed to pass through the blockade; they cannot under any circumstances be declared war contraband or be seized as such by those enforcing the blockade'.[223]

A Power granting free passage to aid consignments destined for territory occupied by an adverse Party to the conflict, does however, have the right to: (i) search the consignments, (ii) regulate their passage according to prescribed times and routes, and (iii) be reasonably satisfied through the Protecting Power that these consignments will be used for the relief of the population and not for the benefit of the Occupying Power.[224] These conditions aim to ensure that aid consignments meet security requirements and do not damage or undermine lawful military operations. However, these rights should not be misused in order to hamper and/or delay the provision of humanitarian aid to the occupied territories.

In summary, Israel has an obligation under the law of blockade and customary international humanitarian law (reflective of Article 23 of GCIV and Article 70 of AP1) to permit the free passage of humanitarian aid to the civilian population behind the Gaza blockade. In addition, the law of belligerent occupation requires Israel to provide essential supplies to the occupied civilian population if their supplies are inadequate and to facilitate, by all means at their disposal, third-party humanitarian aid projects. Indeed, a recent UK Foreign and Commonwealth Office report on Israel and the occupied Palestinian territories reminded Israel that: '[t]he Fourth Geneva Convention is clear that an occupying power must co-operate in facilitating the passage and distribution of relief consignments'.[225]

14.5 Interception of Vessels to Enforce a Blockade

14.5.1 Enforcing a legal blockade

A state may enforce a legal blockade by stopping, inspecting and diverting any vessel that attempts to breach that blockade. A merchant vessel may be captured if it continues to try and run a blockade after an attempt to stop and inspect it has been made. If the passengers resist capture then, subject to the provisions in the *San Remo Manual*, the vessel may be attacked in international waters (although as discussed above, the precise point at which a vessel may be intercepted is not clear).[226]

Three observations can be made. First, this is only an entitlement; it is not a right of attack. A vessel attempting to cross a blockade is not under a correlative duty to

[223] Ibid., p 322.

[224] Article 59, GCIV.

[225] UK Foreign and Commonwealth Office, *Annual Report on Human Rights 2008—Israel and the Occupied Palestinian Territories* (26 March 2009), available at http://www.unhcr.org/refworld/docid/49ce361bc.html, accessed 3 February 2011.

[226] Article 98 of the *San Remo Manual*.

stop or concede to capture; it may resist and try to escape. Neutral vessels that attempt to run a blockade 'are not acting illegally—nor is their national state acting illegally by permitting them to behave in this way—but they run the risk of confiscation if they are caught'.[227] Second, a vessel may only be attacked after (a) an attempt to capture the vessel is made and (b) a prior warning is given. Finally, any attack must be in compliance with the general rules of international armed conflict; for example, civilians are not legitimate military targets while they have civilian status.

The *San Remo Manual* also requires that specific precautions be taken in the event that an attack is attempted:

(a) those who plan, decide upon or execute an attack must take all feasible measures to gather information which will assist in determining whether or not objects which are not military objectives are present in an area of attack;
(b) in the light of the information available to them, those who plan, decide upon or execute an attack shall do everything feasible to ensure that attacks are limited to military objectives;
(c) they shall furthermore take all feasible precautions in the choice of methods and means in order to avoid or minimize collateral casualties or damage; *and*
(d) an attack shall not be launched if it may be expected to cause collateral casualties or damage which world be excessive in relation to the concrete and direct military advantage anticipated from the attack as a whole; an attack shall be cancelled or suspended as soon as it becomes apparent that the collateral casualties or damage would be excessive.

In addition, the *Manual* identifies classes of vessels that are exempt from attack. For example, vessels granted safe conduct by agreement between the belligerent parties, such as vessels engaged in humanitarian missions, include 'vessels carrying supplies indispensable to the survival of the civilian population, and vessels engaged in relief actions and rescue operations'.[228] This is to ensure compliance with the duty of providing safe transport of humanitarian aid necessary for the survival of the civilian population. Furthermore, Article 47 of the *San Remo Manual* prohibits attacks on, *inter alia*, hospital ships, small craft used for coastal rescue operations and other medical transports, passenger vessels when engaged only in carrying civilian passengers, small coastal fishing vessels and small boats engaged in local coastal trade (but they are subject to the regulations of a belligerent naval commander operating in the area and to inspection) and life rafts and life boats.[229]

---

227 Malanczuk 2002, p 350.

228 *San Remo Manual*, Article 47.

229 *San Remo Manual*, Article 47; subject to Article 48—i.e., the vessels must (a) be innocently employed in their normal role; (b) submit to identification and inspection when required; and (c) not intentionally hamper the movement of combatants and obey orders to stop or move out of the way when required. See also other specific provisions outlined in Articles 49 to 58, where such exemption from attack may be removed. Article 58 stipulates that '[i]n case of doubt whether a vessel or aircraft exempt from attack is being used to make an effective contribution to military action, it shall be presumed not to be so used'.

The question of whether the interception of the Gaza Freedom Flotilla was lawful depends on the legal status of the blockade on Gaza and the precise modalities of the attack.

14.5.2 Interception of the Gaza Freedom Flotilla

14.5.2.1 If the blockade on Gaza is lawful

If the blockade on Gaza is lawful, then Israel is entitled to prevent breaches of the blockade. The Gaza Freedom Flotilla vessels, in attempting to run the blockade, could have been attacked and lawfully captured in international waters, subject to the rules of precaution outlined above. After the initial capture was resisted, a general warning could have been dispatched. If the resistance continued, an attack that was not expected to cause collateral causalities or damage excessive in relation to the concrete military objective could have been launched. In this situation, presumably the 'concrete military objective' would have been to ensure the effectiveness of the blockade. Was the death of nine civilians and the injury of fifty more on the *Mavi Marmara* excessive? The answer to this question is a matter of fact that must be considered in light of the anticipated military objective at the time of launching the attack. In retrospect, since the vessels were only carrying humanitarian aid and personnel,[230] Israel arguably had other, non-violent and non-fatal alternatives at its disposal that could have satisfied its military objective. Unless it can be demonstrated that Israel knew this information but nonetheless launched the attack, it is difficult to go further than to suggest that all things considered, the attack appears to have been excessive.

The laws of warfare provide that any armed attack that involves civilians should adhere to certain fundamental rules: force should only be used if necessary, it should be proportionate to the anticipated military advantage, and civilians should not be the direct targets of the attack.[231] In order to balance the use of force against an anticipated military advantage, it is necessary to conduct a proper assessment of the factual situation before the armed operation. This assessment may have involved contacting and working with the Gaza Freedom Flotilla vessels and liaising with neutral port authorities (individuals went through standard security checks and port authorities supervised the loading of cargo). If, on the basis of the information received, Israel wanted to intercept the vessels—either to stop them from crossing the blockade or to obtain further information concerning their cargo and personnel—it could then send its vessels to intercept the Flotilla.

[230] Reports indicate there were no guns or other weapons on board the vessels. Instruments used against the soldiers that attacked the individuals on board on the vessels included wood, maintenance tools and kitchen knives used for preparing food.

[231] *San Remo Manual*, paras 38–46.

As the Israeli vessels approached the Flotilla vessels, all available means should have been used to warn the civilians on board and/or to ascertain the nature of their cargo and personnel. Even if a proper assessment of the factual situation determined lethal force was necessary in order to board or stop the vessels—for example, if intelligence suggested that some passengers were carrying weapons and posed a threat to the lives of the trained soldiers about to board the vessel—the fact that a large number of unarmed civilians were on board should have prompted caution and restraint.

It may be recalled that if blockaded civilians are deprived of essential humanitarian supplies and facing starvation, a blockading state is obliged to permit humanitarian vessels to cross the blockade, subject to its right of search, inspection and direction. If, after intercepting the vessels, Israel determined that only humanitarian aid and personnel were on board, it could then have agreed to allow the vessels to cross the blockade, satisfying both its obligations under IHL and its military objective of maintaining an effective blockade (the passage of humanitarian vessels is a permitted exception to the rules of impartiality and effectiveness).

14.5.2.2 If the blockade on Gaza is unlawful

If the Gaza blockade is unlawful, the interception of the Gaza Freedom Flotilla vessels—and any other neutral state vessels, so long as they do not satisfy a law enforcement exception—is an unlawful exercise of jurisdiction over neutral vessels on the high seas and an internationally wrongful act. It may also amount to an unlawful use of force, prohibited by Article 2(4) of the UN Charter. The interception could only be justified by relying on the right of self-defence, but Israel has not invoked Article 51 of the UN Charter. In any case, it is likely that Israel knew the merchant vessels did not have the means to launch an attack. Faced with an unlawful armed attack, the crew and passengers of the intercepted vessels had the right of personal self-defence, the modalities of which are determined by the domestic law of the flag state, by virtue of its exclusive jurisdiction over the vessel.

14.6 Conclusion

The factual situation of Gaza presents us with significant legal challenges: how do we characterise a conflict between a democratically elected Government within a non-state territory and a State? Does that state continue to occupy Gaza? Is significant external control that translates into significant internal control of that territory enough to satisfy the Article 42 Hague Convention test? How does the occupation affect the legal analysis? Does the characterisation of conflict affect the applicability of the law of blockade? Given the factual situation, can Israel intercept vessels on the high seas without their permission? However, as this paper has sought to demonstrate, some of these challenges are not entirely new to international law. There is historical precedent for bringing wars of national liberation within the scope of international law as international conflicts, for blockading non-state actors during civil wars and for intercepting neutral vessels in these circumstances. Yet, the law today—arguably reflecting an international climate that is not as sympathetic to wars of national liberation as it once was—appears unable to respond as it once did: we no longer have the recognition of belligerency doctrine and its replacement—Article 1(4)—has never been applied.

These challenges are underscored by the blockade on Gaza and the interception of the Gaza Freedom Flotilla. This paper sought to answer the question: can Israel intercept vessels on the high seas without their permission? After dismissing the applicability of the law enforcement framework to the facts, it was necessary to focus on the law of armed conflict. The use of blockades is primarily (if not exclusively) a right associated with the rules of international armed conflict: it enables states to intercept vessels travelling on the high seas, where the flag state has exclusive jurisdiction over the vessel, or within the territorial jurisdiction of an enemy. The law of blockade reconciles the competing rights and interests of belligerent and neutral states.

Can this law of blockade apply in the context of a non-international armed conflict? A government clearly has the right to intercept any vessel travelling within its jurisdiction, but this is not the same as blockading an enemy extra-territoriality and intercepting neutral vessels on the high seas. International law offers little guidance on whether blockades and enforcement interceptions can be undertaken in non-international armed conflicts. There exists some historical precedent of states blockading non-state actors during internal conflicts, but this action impliedly recognised the belligerent status of those actors, transforming the conflict into an international armed conflict.

This leads us to the question of how to characterise the conflict between Hamas and Israel. The *sui generis* situation of Gaza makes it difficult to conclude that the conflict is either international or non-international in character. It has been convincing argued that the recognition of belligerency doctrine has fallen into desuetude, and even if the doctrine does have contemporary relevance, it is unlikely to apply on the facts. Furthermore, Israel has not ratified Additional Protocol I, and Article 1(4) has not been absorbed into customary law.

If one accepts that the conflict between Hamas and Israel is an international armed conflict, then Israel has a *prima facie* right to blockade Gaza. The situation is less clear if the conflict is a non-international armed conflict. There are, however, compelling reasons for treating the situation as analogous to that of an international armed conflict; it was, after all, precisely this situation that Article 1(4) was designed to cover. Furthermore, Israel has stated that it applies both the law of NIAC and IAC; classifying the conflict as international may enable Israel to operate within the law. Finally, neutral states have not objected to the blockade on Gaza *in principle* but they have objected to the manner of the enforcement operation and the effect of the blockade on the civilian population. This apparent acceptance of a *prima facie* right may suggest the law of blockade is evolving to allow states to blockade non-state actors in non-international armed conflicts and/or in conflicts that do not fall neatly within either the international or non-international paradigm.

Assuming Israel has a *prima facie* right to blockade Gaza, one must then consider (i) whether the blockade is legally constituted and (ii) whether the blockade has the effect of starving the civilian population. The law of blockade, traditionally only concerned with balancing the rights of belligerent and neutral states, has shifted in focus as a result of international humanitarian law. A blockade that has the sole purpose of starving the civilian population, or the effect of starving the civilian population such that it is disproportionate to the anticipated military advantage, is unambiguously illegal. It also triggers an obligation to allow vessels carrying humanitarian aid to reach the civilian population.

The humanitarian crisis caused by the blockade has left a majority of Gaza civilians facing starvation. Israel has an obligation to allow vessels carrying humanitarian aid to reach the civilian population, subject to searching their cargo, regulating their route and being satisfied the aid is genuinely humanitarian in character. A blockade that is not properly constituted or has the effect of starving the civilian population cannot be enforced. If Israel had a *prima face* right to blockade Gaza, it may be said with certainty that at the relevant time, its blockade on Gaza was illegal, and as such, Israel was not permitted to intercept the Flotilla vessels. The interception violated the sovereignty of the flag-states concerned and constituted an internationally wrongful act.

On 20 June 2010, in response to international condemnation of the blockade and the interception, Israel's security cabinet announced measures designed to 'ease' the blockade.[232] On 8 December 2010, Israel also announced easing of the restrictions on the export of certain products, 'subject to security and logistical capacity',[233] although as of January 2011, this measure remains unimplemented.[234] Despite these policy changes, the UN reports, 'ongoing restrictions on basic construction materials, impediments to the movement of people as well as exports, continue to impede both economic revival and a significant improvement in the humanitarian situation'.[235] Between 26 December and 1 January 2011, 'a total of 1052 truckloads entered the Gaza Strip, 12 percent above the weekly average of 938 truckloads since the Israeli announcement to ease the blockade on 20 June 2010... [and] only 37 percent of the weekly average of imports recorded

---

[232] Israel Ministry of Foreign Affairs, Briefing: Israel's New Policy Towards Gaza (5 July 2010), available at http://www.mfa.gov.il/MFA/HumanitarianAid/Palestinians/Briefing-Israel_new_policy_towards_Gaza_5-Jul-2010.htm.

[233] United Nations Office for the Coordination of Humanitarian Affairs in the occupied Palestinian territory, The Humanitarian Monitor (November 2010) pp 9–10.

[234] United Nations Office for the Coordination of Humanitarian Affairs in the occupied Palestinian territory, Protection of Civilians (29 December 2010–4 January 2011), pp 3–4.

[235] United Nations Office for the Coordination of Humanitarian Affairs in the occupied Palestinian territory, The Humanitarian Monitor (November 2010) at pp 9–10.

before the imposition of the blockade in June 2007.[236] These 'easing' measures have clearly not succeeded in reversing the humanitarian crisis in Gaza and as such, the blockade remains illegal.

References

Abi-Saab G (1979) Wars of national liberation in the Geneva Conventions and Protocols. Recueil des Cours 165:353–446

Aldrich GH (1991) Prospects for united states ratification of additional protocol I to the 1949 Geneva conventions. AJIL 85:1–20

Aronson G (2005) Issues arising from the implementation of Israel's disengagement from the Gaza Strip. J Palestine Stud 34:49–63

Bartels R (2009) Timelines, borderlines and conflicts: the historical evolution of the legal divide between international and non-international armed conflicts. IRRC 873:35–67

Bashi S, Mann K (2007) Disengaged occupiers: the legal status of Gaza, Tel Aviv, Gisha: Legal Center for Freedom of Movement. Available at http://www.gisha.org/UserFiles/File/Report%20for%20the%20website.pdf

Bell AC (1937) A history of the blockade of Germany and of the countries associated with her in the Great War, Austria-Hungary, Bulgaria, and Turkey, 1914–1918. H.M. Stationery Office, London

Bell A, Shefi D (2010) The mythical post-2005 Israeli occupation of the Gaza Strip. Israel Affairs 16:268–296

Benvenisti E (2009) The law on the unilateral termination of occupation. In: Giegerich T, Heinz U (eds) A wiser century? Judicial dispute settlement, disarmament and the laws of war 100 years after the second Hague peace conference. Walther Schücking Institute, Berlin, Duncker & Humblot

Black I (2010) Flotilla interception looks like a disastrous own goal for Israel, The Guardian. Available at http://www.guardian.co.uk/world/2010/may/31/flotilla-interception-arab-turkish-analysis/ (Accessed 1 June 2010)

Bothe (1988) Commentary on the 1977 Geneva protocol I. In: Ronzitti N (ed), The law of naval warfare: a collection of agreements and documents with commentaries. Nijhoff, Dordrecht

Bruderlein C (2004) Legal aspects of Israel's disengagement plan under international humanitarian law. Available at http://www.ihlresearch.org/opt/pdfs/briefing3466.pdf

Buckingham DE (1994) A recipe for change: towards an integrated approach to food under international law. Pace Int Law Rev 6:285–321

Cassese A (1984) The Geneva protocols of 1977 on the humanitarian law of armed conflict and customary international law. UCLA Pacific Basin Law J 3:55–118

Commission on the responsibilities of the authors of the war on the enforcement of penalties (1920) AJIL 14:95–154

Crawford JR (2007) The creation of states in international law, 2nd edn. Oxford University Press, Oxford

Cullen A (2010) The Concept of non-international armed conflict in international humanitarian law. Cambridge University Press, Cambridge

Darcy S, Reynolds J (2010) 'Otherwise occupied': the status of the Gaza Strip from the perspective of international humanitarian law. JCSL 15:211–243

---

[236] United Nations Office for the Coordination of Humanitarian Affairs in the occupied Palestinian territory, Protection of Civilians (29 December 2010 – 4 January 2011), p 3.

Dinstein Y (2009) The international law of belligerent occupation. Cambridge University Press, Cambridge
Dörmann K (2003) Elements of war crimes under the Rome statute of the international criminal court: sources and commentary. Cambridge University Press, Cambridge
Doswald-Beck L (ed) (1995) San Remo manual on international law applicable to armed conflicts at sea. Cambridge University Press, Cambridge
Draft Convention on Rights and Duties of Neutral States in Naval and Aerial War (1939) AJIL Supplement 33:167–817
Draper GIAD (1979) Wars of national liberation and war criminality. In: Howard M (ed) Restraints in war. Oxford University Press, Oxford
Falk FA (1964) International law of internal law. In: Rosenau JN (ed) International aspects of civil strife. Princeton University Press, Princeton NJ
Final Protocol of the London Naval Conference (1909) 3 AJIL Supplement 3
Fraunces MG (1992) The international law of blockade: new guiding principles in contemporary state practice. Yale LJ 101:893–918
Frenkel S (2010) Israeli document: Gaza blockade isn't about security'. McClatchy Newspapers. Available athttp://www.mcclatchydc.com/2010/06/09/95621/israeli-document-gaza-blockade.html#ixzz0qSOTiCqD Accessed 9 June 2010
Greenberg (2008a) Gaza closure defined: collective punishment. Available at http://gisha.org/UserFiles/File/publications/GazaClosureDefinedEng.pdf Accessed 23 Sept 2008
Greenberg H (2008b) Israel considering reducing the passage of goods to the Strip, Ynet. Available in Hebrew at http://www.ynet.co.il/articles/0,7340,L-3600973,00.html Accessed 23 Sept 2008
Guardian the, Gaza on brink of implosion as aid cut-off starts to bite (2006). Available at http://www.guardian.co.uk/world/2006/apr/16/israel Accessed 16 April 2006
Haaretz (2010) Lieberman: Israel shouldn't lift Gaza siege until Hamas lets Red Cross see Shalit. Available at http://www.haaretz.com/news/diplomacy-defense/lieberman-israel-shouldn-t-lift-gaza-siege-until-hamas-lets-red-cross-see-shalit-1.295342 Accessed 10 June 2010
Halifax EFLW Lord (1938) Leag Nations Off J p 330
Hass A (2010) Israel releases papers detailing formula of Gaza blockade, Haaretz. Available at http://www.haaretz.com/print-edition/news/israel-releases-papers-detailing-formula-of-gaza-blockade-1.321154 Accessed 26 Oct 2010
Heintschel von Heinegg W (2006a) The current state of the law of naval warfare: a fresh look at the San Remo Manual. In: Helm AM (ed) International law studies—The law of war in the 21st century: weaponry and the use of force, Vol 82
Heintschel von Heinegg W (2006b) Naval blockade and international law. In: Elleman BA, Paine SCM (eds) Naval blockades and seapower: strategies and counter-strategies, 1805–2005. Routledge, London
Heintschel von Heinegg W (2008) Blockade: the law of armed conflict at sea. In: Fleck D (ed) The handbook of international humanitarian law, 2nd edn. Oxford University Press, Oxford
Heller KJ (2010) The civil war and the blockade on Gaza (a response to Posner, Opinio Juris. Available at http://opiniojuris.org/2010/06/04/eric-posners-incomplete-editorial-on-the-blockade-of-gaza/ Accessed 4 June 2010
Henckaerts J (2005) Study on customary international law: a contribution to the understanding and respect for the rule of law in armed conflict. IRRC 857:175–212
Henckaerts J, Doswell-Beck L (eds) (2005) Customary international humanitarian law. vols. I, II. Cambridge University Press, Cambridge
Jones TD (1983) The international law of maritime blockade—a measure of naval economic interdiction. Howard Law J 26:759
Kaliser MS (2007) A modern day exodus: international human rights law and international humanitarian law implications of Israel's withdrawal from the Gaza Strip. Indiana I Comp LR 17:187–229
Lauterpacht H (1947) Recognition in international law. Cambridge University Press, Cambridge

Lauterpacht H (ed) (1952) Oppenheim's international law, vol II, 7th edn. Longmans, Green and Co, London

Lootsteen YM (2000) The concept of belligerency in international law. Mil LR 166:109–141

Macalister-Smith P (1991) The protection of the civilian population and the prohibition of starvation as a method of conflict: draft texts relating to international humanitarian assistance. Max Planck Institute for Comparative Public Law and International Law, Heidelberg

Malanczuk P (2002) Akehurst's modern introduction to international law, 7th rev edn. Routledge, New York

Mallison SV, Mallison WT (1976) A survey of the international law of naval blockade. US Naval Institute Proceedings 102:45

Manual of the Law of Armed Conflict (2004) UK Ministry of Defence. Oxford University Press, Oxford

Mari M (2005) The Israeli disengagement from the Gaza Strip: an end of the occupation? YIHL 8:356–368

Mastorodimos K (2010) The character of the conflict in Gaza: another argument towards abolishing the distinction between international and non-international armed conflicts. Int Commun Law Rev pp 437–469

Milanovic M (2010) What exactly internationalizes an internal armed conflict? Eur J Int Law: Talk!. Available at http://www.ejiltalk.org/what-exactly-internationalizes-an-internal-armed-conflict/Accessed 7 May 2010

Moir L (2008) The law of international armed conflict. Cambridge University Press, Cambridge

Myers DP (1910) The legal basis of the rules of blockade in the declaration of London. AJIL 4:571–579

Oglesby RR (1971) Internal war and the search for normative order. Martinus Nijhoff, The Hague, pp 100–114

Owen D (1898) Maritime warfare and merchant-shopping: a summary of the rights of capture at sea. Stevens and Sons Ltd, London

Pictet J (ed) (1958) Commentary: fourth Geneva convention relative to the protection of civilian persons in time of war. International Committee of the Red Cross, Geneva

Rauch E (1984) The protocol additional to the geneva conventions for the protection of victims of international armed conflicts and the United Nations convention on the law of the sea: repercussions on the law of naval warfare. Duncker & Humblot, Berlin

Reuters (2011) WikiLeaks: Israel aimed to keep Gaza economy on brink of collapse, Haaretz. Available at http://www.haaretz.com/news/diplomacy-defense/wikileaks-israel-aimed-to-keep-gaza-economy-on-brink-of-collapse-1.335354. Accessed 5 Jan 2011

Rosenblad E (1973) Starvation as a method of warfare—conditions for regulation by convention. International Lawyer 7:252–270

Sandoz C, Swinarski C, Zimmerman B (eds) (1987) Commentary on the additional protocols of 8 June 1977 to the Geneva conventions of 12 August 1949, Geneva, ICRC and Dordrecht, Martinus Nijhoff

Scobbie I (2004–2005) An intimate disengagement: Israel's withdrawal from Gaza, the law of occupation and of self-determination. Yearbook of Islamic and Middle Eastern Law 11, pp 3–31, reprinted in Kattan V (ed) (2008) The Palestine question in international law, London, British Institute of International and Comparative Law, pp 637–665

Shani Y (2005) Faraway, so close: the legal status of Gaza after Israel's disengagement. YIHL 8:369–383

Shany Y (2010) Know Your Rights! The Flotilla report and international law governing naval blockades. Eur J Int Law: Talk! Available at http://www.ejiltalk.org/know-your-rights-the-flotilla-report-and-international-law-governing-naval-blockades/ Accessed 12 October 2010

Therry R (ed) (1830) The speeches of the Right Hon. George Canning, vol. V. J. Ridgway, London

Triffterer O (2008) Commentary on the Rome statute of the international criminal court: observers' Notes, Article by Article, 2nd edn. Beck, Munchen

Part IV
Correspondents' Reports

Correspondents' Reports

A Guide to State Practice in the Field of International Humanitarian Law

M.N. Schmitt et al. (eds.), *Yearbook of International Humanitarian Law Volume 13, 2010*, DOI: 10.1007/978-90-6704-811-8_15,

Reports Editor at t.mccormack@unimelb.edu.au

2010 alphabetical list of reporters

Giovanni Carlo Bruno, Burrus M. Carnahan, Rachele Cera, Nika Dharmadasa, Valeria Eboli, Ola Engdahl, Ornella Ferrajolo, Valentina Della Fina, Nadine Fourie, M. Zahurul Haq, Chris Jenks, Eszter Kirs, Jani Leino, Rain Liivoja, Konstantinos Mastorodimos, James May, Ieva Miluna, Silvana Moscatelli, Ray Murphy, Antoni Pigrau, Yaël Ronen, Peter Rowe, Rafael A. Prieto Sanjuán, Rytis Satkauskas and Paul Tavernier.

Correspondents' Reports is compiled and edited by Tim McCormack with the excellent assistance of James Ellis, primarily from information provided to the *YIHL* by its correspondents but also drawing on other sources. The section does not purport to be a fully inclusive compilation of all international humanitarian law-related developments in every State, but represents a selection of developments during the calendar year 2010 that have come to the Yearbook's attention. Legal developments from early 2010 that were noted in Volume 12 of the *YIHL* are not repeated here. Readers are thus advised to consult this section in conjunction with Correspondents' Reports in Volume 12. We apologise for this inconvenience. Further, some 2009 humanitarian law-related developments came to our attention after Volume 12 went to press and could not be noted there. For the sake of completeness, we have included them here. Reference is also included to a number of legal developments which are not strictly-speaking related to IHL but which are nonetheless interesting and relevant for our readers, in particular relating to justice issues, jurisdictional questions, *jus ad bellum*, State security, human rights, refugees and internally displaced persons, and terrorism. Where citations or dates or other details have not been provided, they were not available or obtainable. The *YIHL* is actively seeking new correspondents, particularly in Africa, Asia and Latin America. Interested persons or anyone who is willing to contribute information should contact the Reports Editor at t.mccormack@unimelb.edu.au.

AUSTRALIA[1]

Participation in Armed Conflicts—Australian Defence Force and Australian Federal Police Deployments

As reported in the 2008 and 2009 *Yearbook of International Humanitarian Law,*[2] the Australian Defence Force (ADF) and Australian Federal Police (AFP) are deployed in a number of situations around the world. In 2009–2010, ADF deployments peaked at approximately 3500 personnel in 15 operations around the world.[3] The majority of ADF personnel continued to be deployed to Afghanistan as part of Operation Slipper. In 2010, the Australian Federal Police (AFP) deployed 530 officers globally.[4] Twenty-eight AFP officers assisted in training the Afghan National Police.[5] In 2010, six ADF personnel died in operations overseas, including in Afghanistan.[6]

A number of incidents during 2010 involved casualties resulting from ADF operations in Afghanistan. The Department of Defence conducted inquires into incidents, which raised questions about whether targeting decisions properly distinguished between civilians, other non-combatants and combatants.

Government Enquiries—Shooting of Afghan Police during Armed Conflict in Afghanistan

- Australian Government Department of Defence, *Report of an Inquiry Officer into the Shooting of Two Afghan National Policemen* [redacted] (11 August 2009), <www.defence.gov.au/coi/reports/EOF_R.pdf>

On 28 June 2010, the Department of Defence released a report by an inquiry officer. The report considered the shooting of two Afghan National policemen on a motorbike in Afghanistan. On 11 August 2009, the two policemen were shot at a checkpoint patrolled by the ADF. The checkpoint was established to cordon off an area near a roadside. Access had been restricted to the area because another Afghan National policeman claimed he had found a rocket. The inquiry found no wrongdoing by the ADF. The inquiry discussed whether the soldiers were sufficiently familiar with the Afghan police and army uniforms.[7] The report also found

[1] This entry was prepared by Nika Dharmadasa and James May on behalf of the Australian Red Cross International Humanitarian Law Committee (Victorian Division).

[2] See 11 *YIHL* (2008) pp 409–410; 12 *YIHL* (2009) p 455.

[3] Australian Government Department of Defence, *Defence Annual Report 2009–2010* (2010) pp 344–346, <http://www.defence.gov.au/Budget/09-10/dar/index.htm>.

[4] Australian Federal Police, *Statistics of AFP Staff Overseas* (2010), <http://www.afp.gov.au/media-centre/facts-stats/afp-staff-statistics/staff-overseas.aspx>.

[5] Australian Federal Police, *Annual Report 2009–2010* (2010), <http://www.afp.gov.au/media-centre/publications/~/media/afp/pdf/a/afp-annual-report-2009-2010.ashx>.

[6] Australian Government Department of Defence, *Defence Annual Report 2009–2010*, p 3.

[7] Australian Government Department of Defence, *Report of an Inquiry Officer into the Shooting of two Afghan National Policemen* [redacted] (11 August 2009) p 43.

that 'the members involved complied with the law, complied with the ROE [rules of engagement], effectively put into practice their training … and conducted the activity in which they were engaged effectively'.[8] The report did find, however, that the soldiers were unaware that it was mandatory, in tactical circumstances, to fire a warning shot by a pen flare as an alternative to shooting. The inquiry recommended further training in this regard.[9] Finally, it was recommended that no administrative action be taken and no further investigation be conducted against the soldiers or any other person.[10]

Government Enquiries—Civilian Casualties in Armed Conflict—Independent Military Prosecution of Members of the Australian Defence Force

- 'Statement by the Director of Military Prosecutions: 12 February 2009 civilian casualty incident in Afghanistan', <http://www.defence.gov.au/media/DepartmentalTpl.cfm?CurrentId=10896>

On 12 February 2009, six Afghan civilians were killed and four were wounded during a residential compound clearance in an ADF Special Operations Task Group raid targeting a Taliban leader.[11] Five of the civilians killed were children, and children were also amongst the wounded. The soldiers have not been named.

On 27 September 2010, the Director of Military Prosecutions decided, under the *Defence Force Discipline Act 1982* (Cth), to charge three former ADF members with various service offences including manslaughter, dangerous conduct, failing to comply with a lawful general order and prejudicial conduct.[12] The Director of Military Prosecution is designed to provide the ADF with an independent and impartial service, and legal advice on serious allegations under the *Deference Force Discipline Act*.[13]

---

[8] Ibid., para 49.

[9] Ibid., paras 58–59.

[10] Ibid., para 61.

[11] T. Hyland, 'Death and doubt in Afghanistan', *Sydney Morning Herald* (Sydney, Australia) 21 March 2010, <http://www.smh.com.au/world/death-and-doubt-in-afghanistan-20100320-qneg.html>; Australian Defence Force, 'Statement by the Director of Military Prosecutions: 12 February 2009 civilian casualty incident in Afghanistan' (Media Release, 27 September 2010), <http://www.defence.gov.au/media/DepartmentalTpl.cfm?CurrentId=10896>; T. Hyland, 'Deadly Afghan raids expose leadership failings', *The Age* (Melbourne, Australia) 21 March 2010, <http://www.theage.com.au/world/deadly-afghan-raids-expose-leadership-failings-20100320-qn9t.html>.

[12] Australian Defence Force, 'Statement by the Director of Military Prosecutions: 12 February 2009 civilian casualty incident in Afghanistan' (Media Release, 27 September 2010), <http://www.defence.gov.au/media/2010/release1.htmd>; 'Digger charged over Afghan civilian deaths' *ABC News*, 26 November 2010, <http://www.abc.net.au/news/stories/2010/11/26/3077928.htm>. Charges were initially laid against only two soldiers as the third soldier was travelling overseas at the time.

[13] Australian Department of Defence, *Organisations within the military justice system that can provide assistance to ADF members*, <http://www.defence.gov.au/mjs/organisations.htm>.

The manslaughter charge for civilian deaths is the first laid against Australian soldiers in either Afghanistan or Iraq. Further, there appears to be no similar charges brought during the Vietnam War.[14] It is not clear at this stage whether all three accused persons will face the same charges,[15] although reports indicate that only one person may face the manslaughter charge.[16]

It is reported that a central element of the case against the accused surrounds a 'Concept of Operations' document (CONOPS), which is a plan prepared before any major operation to ensure the plan aligns with the tactics, strategy, regulations and legal framework stipulated by the ADF.[17] The 1st Commando regiment searched a house looking for a local Taliban leader, Mullah Noorullah based on a CONOPS. After a first search for Noorullah, the incident occurred in a nearby compound during the second search. Soon after entering the compound, there was gunfire, with Australian soldiers allegedly shooting in an exchange of fire with an Afghan man, Amrullah Khan. The Australian soldiers also used hand grenades, which may have contributed to the ensuing deaths.[18] Khan's family denies that he was a member of the Taliban, and further that any Taliban were present in the village.[19] The former governor of the province in which the incident occurred, Asadullah Hamdan, described Khan as a 'serious Taliban'.[20]

The ground commanders declined to refer the incident to the ADF Investigative Service (ADFIS) within the 24 h following the attack, and it took approximately 6 months for the matter to be transferred to ADFIS.[21]

The issue became more publicised as a result of a SBS Television documentary *Dateline*. Its coverage on 7 March 2010 raised concerns regarding the delay in a formal investigation commencing as well as other administrative matters.[22] On 18 March 2010, the Defence Minister said '[a]ny civilian casualty is a tragedy, but especially so when, as in this case, it involves the deaths of children. The

---

14 R. Epstein et al., 'Army decisions under fire', *The Age* (Melbourne, Australia) 27 March 2010, <http://www.theage.com.au/world/army-decisions-under-fire-20100326-r33j.html>.

15 'Australian soldiers charged over Afghan civilian deaths', *BBC World news online*, 27 March 2010, <http://www.bbc.co.uk/news/world-asia-pacific-11416258>.

16 M. Dodd and J. Kelly, 'Diggers hit back on Afghanistan kill trial', *The Australian* (Sydney, Australia) 28 September 2010, <http://www.theaustralian.com.au/national-affairs/diggers-hit-back-on-afghanistan-kill-trial/story-fn59niix-1225930332529>.

17 R. Epstein et al., 'Army decisions under fire', *The Age* (Melbourne, Australia) 27 March 2010, <http://www.theage.com.au/world/army-decisions-under-fire-20100326-r33j.html>.

18 Ibid.

19 SBS Television, 'Questions from Oruzgan', *Dateline*, 7 March 2010, <http://www.sbs.com.au/dateline/story/transcript/id/600357/n/Questions-from-Oruzgan>.

20 R. Callinan and J. Kelly, 'Fateful Oruzgan grenade was part of training', *The Australian* (Sydney, Australia) 28 August 2010, <http://www.theaustralian.com.au/news/nation/fateful-oruzgan-grenade-was-part-of-training/story-e6frg6nf-1225911089567>. President Hamid Karazi has since removed Hamdan as Governor.

21 SBS Television, 'Questions from Oruzgan', *Dateline*, 7 March 2010, <http://www.sbs.com.au/dateline/story/transcript/id/600357/n/Questions-from-Oruzgan>.

22 Ibid.

Government and the ADF take incidents such as this very, very seriously. It is essential this incident be investigated thoroughly and due process followed'.[23]

The Director of Military Prosecutions has indicated that she intends to seek referral of the charges to the Registrar of Military Justice for a trial by court martial.[24] The use of courts martial as an interim measure until the establishment of the Australian Military Court is reported below in the section '*Legislation—Australian Military Justice*'.[25]

In light of Australia's ratification of the *Rome Statute of the International Criminal Court*, there was concern whether the Chief Prosecutor for the International Criminal Court (ICC) could charge the ADF members involved.[26] In September 2009, the Chief Prosecutor stated he was gathering information about possible war crimes committed by NATO soldiers and insurgents in Afghanistan including 'massive attacks, collateral damage exceeding what is considered proper, and torture'.[27] As at the end of 2010, no formal ICC investigation had been launched into the ADF incident. An ICC spokesperson was unaware of any formal court probe and an Australian Defence Department spokesperson also denied any ICC pressure on the ADF to charge the former soldiers.[28]

The soldiers charged have stated that they intend to defend the charges. The soldiers alleged the casualties were caused by the 'callous and reckless act of an insurgent'[29] who fired at the soldiers from within a room he knew contained women and children, that the building they were targeting contained armed Taliban and that the gunfire came from inside the building and was directed at the Special Operations group.[30]

The process for a trial by court martial is anticipated to start in 2011.

---

[23] Australian Defence Force, 'Ministerial Statement on Afghanistan' (18 March 2010), <http://www.minister.defence.gov.au/FaulknerTranscripttpl.cfm?CurrentId=10055>.

[24] Evidence to Australian Senate Standing Committee on Foreign Affairs, Defence and Trade, Parliament of Australia, Canberra, p 14 (Australian Air Chief Marshal A. Houston), <http://www.aph.gov.au/hansard/senate/commttee/S13305.pdf>.

[25] Australian Department of Defence, *Military Justice Reform*, <http://www.defence.gov.au/mjs/reform.htm>.

[26] ABC News Radio, 'Australian Soldiers charged over Afghan civilian deaths', *PM with Mark Colvin*, 27 September 2010 (Speaker, N. James, Executive Director Australia Defence Association, report by S. Lane), <http://www.abc.net.au/pm/content/2010/s3023133.htm>.

[27] L. Charbonneau, 'ICC prosecutor eyes possible Afghanistan war crimes', *Reuters*, 9 September 2009, <http://www.reuters.com/article/2009/09/09/us-afghanistan-warcrimes-idUSTRE58871K20090909?pageNumber=2&virtualBrandChannel=0&sp=true>.

[28] M. Dodd, 'Special forces soldiers 'should not face charges over Afghan deaths', *The Daily Telegraph* (Sydney, Australia) 1 October 2010, <http://www.dailytelegraph.com.au/news/national/special-forces-soldiers-should-not-face-charges-over-afghan-deaths/story-e6freuzr-1225932624345>.

[29] M. Dodd and J. Kelly, 'Diggers hit back on Afghanistan kill trial', *The Australian* (Sydney, Australia) 28 September 2010, <http://www.theaustralian.com.au/national-affairs/diggers-hit-back-on-afghanistan-kill-trial/story-fn59niix-1225930332529>.

[30] Ibid.

Cases—Alleged Torture of an Australian National

- *Habib* v. *Commonwealth of Australia* [2010] FCAFC 1, <http://www.austlii.edu.au/cgi-bin/sinodisp/au/cases/cth/FCAFC/2010/12.html>

As reported in the 2004 and 2009 *Yearbook of International Humanitarian Law*,[31] Habib is an Australian citizen previously detained in Guantánamo Bay in May 2002, who was then released on 28 January 2005 without charge. Habib alleged he was tortured in Pakistan, Egypt, Afghanistan and at Guantánamo Bay and that the Australian government condoned such conduct through the physical presence of Australian government officials during such incidents.[32] The Australian government argued that Australian courts should refrain from examining the rights and wrongs of the acts of foreign States, which is known as the 'acts of State doctrine'.[33]

The Full Federal Court was asked to decide (among other things) whether the act of state doctrine prevented an Australian court from reviewing the validity of acts of the Commonwealth Executive. In the context of the war on terrorism, it was also a question of whether the doctrine applied to cases involving alleged serious breaches of human rights and international humanitarian law, and whether it was applicable to conduct of the United States government taking place outside that country.[34]

On 25 February 2010, the Full Court unanimously held that the Commonwealth Constitution permitted Australian courts to hear claims of misconduct, including claims of torture, committed by Commonwealth officials in Australia and overseas. The act of state doctrine did not bar a claim for damages based on alleged participation by Commonwealth officials in the alleged torture of Habib at Guantánamo Bay or elsewhere. Torture was found to be an offence both under Australian law and under international criminal law. Jagot J, with whom Black CJ and Perram J agreed, also found that the doctrine could not oust the constitutionally protected independence of Australian courts to determine alleged crimes both for crimes committed by Commonwealth officials and for international crimes such as war crimes and torture as prescribed by Parliament.[35]

On 17 December 2010, the Australian government reached a confidential out of court settlement with Habib and, as a result, the proceedings in the Federal Court were concluded.

Cases—Extradition

- *Zentai* v. *Honourable Brendan O'Connor (No 2)* [2010] FCA 252, <http://www.austlii.edu.au/cgi-bin/sinodisp/au/cases/cth/FCA/2010/252.html>
- *Zentai* v. *Honourable Brendan O'Connor (No 3)* [2010] FCA 691, <http://www.austlii.edu.au/cgi-bin/sinodisp/au/cases/cth/FCA/2010/691.html>

---

31 See 7 *YIHL* (2004) pp 446–448; 12 *YIHL* (2009) p 457.

32 *Habib* v. *Commonwealth of Australia* [2010] FCAFC 12, para 2 (Black CJ).

33 Ibid., paras 72–90.

34 Ibid.

35 Ibid., paras 134–135 (Jagot J). See *Geneva Conventions Act 1957* (Cth); *Crimes (Torture) Act 1988* (Cth).

- *Zentai* v. *Honourable Brendan O'Connor* (*No 4*) [2010] FCA 1385, <http://www.austlii.edu.au/au/cases/cth/FCA/2010/1385.html>

As reported in the 2007, 2008 and 2009 *Yearbook of International Humanitarian Law*,[36] Zentai was alleged by Hungary to have committed a war crime in Budapest on 8 November 1944, namely killing a Jewish man while Zentai was a member of the Hungarian Royal Army. In 2005, a provisional warrant for Zentai's arrest was issued under the *Extradition Act 1988* (Cth), based on an earlier warrant issued by a military judge of the Military Division of the Budapest Metropolitan Court. This request was made pursuant to an extradition treaty between Hungary and Australia (the treaty).[37] After a series of appeals, in 2008, a Magistrate held that Zentai was eligible for surrender to Hungary. In 2009, two further appeals against the legality of the criminal proceedings were dismissed including by the Full Federal Court.[38] On 16 December 2009, Zentai was granted bail subject to conditions.

In 2010, the Australian Minister for Home Affairs[39] decided Zentai should be surrendered to Hungary. Zentai sought judicial review of the Minister's decision in the Federal Court. McKerracher J overturned the Minister's decision.

Zentai argued, on several grounds, that the Minister had made errors of law in his decision. The primary contentions targeted the nature of the allegations themselves. McKerracher J agreed with some of these arguments and allowed the appeal. McKerracher J found that Zentai was not an 'extraditable person' within the meaning of the *Extradition Act* because there were no 'offence or offences against the law of a country that the person is accused of having committed'.[40] Hungary had not charged Zentai with the war crime rather they merely wanted to question him. Zentai argued that being wanted in criminal proceedings that had not passed the purely investigative stage did not render him 'accused'. The fact that Hungary only wanted to question Zentai was only known after the Minister made his decision. Nonetheless, McKerracher J held that the ordinary definition of 'accused' did not include criminal proceedings at the purely investigative stage.[41]

A further and related successful appeal ground related to the status of international criminal law in Hungary in 1944. The Hungarian law retrospectively enacted a war crime but in fact in 1944 no such *war crime*, as distinct from the crime of murder, existed in Hungarian law. The crime of murder was not alleged in the extradition request.[42] Accordingly, there was no qualifying 'extradition offence' within the meaning of the *Extradition Act* because no offence known to

---

36 See 10 *YIHL* (2007) pp 256–257; 11 *YIHL* (2008) pp 417–418; 12 *YIHL* (2009) pp 457–459.

37 *Treaty on Extradition*, Australia–Hungary, signed 25 October 1995, 1985 UNTS 123 (entered into force 25 April 1997); *Extradition (Republic of Hungary) Regulations 1997* (Cth).

38 *Zentai* v. *Republic of Hungary* [2009] FCAFC 139.

39 Acting as a delegate of the Commonwealth Attorney-General.

40 *Extradition Act 1988* (Cth) s. 6(a).

41 *Zentai* v. *Honourable Brendan O'Connor* (*No 3*) [2010] FCA 691, paras 156, 172.

42 Ibid., paras 209–214.

law was actually alleged and the court found that the Minister erred in finding there was such an offence.[43]

The court made a separate finding that Zentai had a valid objection to extradition based on humanitarian grounds. It was argued the extradition of an ill 88-year-old man to be incarcerated for questioning and possible trial in Croatia would be a 'virtual death sentence'.[44] Article 2(f) of the treaty between Australia and Croatia provided that extradition may be refused by the requested state after taking into account (among other things) humanitarian considerations. Several medical reports evidenced Zentai's various medical conditions including risk of stroke and heart failure while one report said international travel would not be life threatening. The court found that departmental advice was deficient because it said that the impact of the trial, including any cognitive impairment which may affect Zentai's ability to defend himself at trial, were matters for Hungary to consider. McKerracher J held the Minister should have considered these matters because the risks of Zentai dying upon extradition were 'very real considerations'.[45] The court found that this failure constituted a jurisdictional error which was 'in effect to totally ignore'[46] the alternative option of prosecuting Zentai in Australia, as permitted under Article 2(a) of the treaty.

McKerracher J subsequently ordered Zentai be released from custody[47] and prohibited the Australian government from extraditing Zentai to Hungary.[48] The Australian government was also ordered to pay Zentai's costs.[49]

At the end of 2010, the Australian government had not lodged an appeal and the period to do so had expired.

Cases—Extradition

- *Republic of Croatia* v. *Snedden* [2010] HCATrans 32, <http://www.austlii.edu.au/cgi-bin/sinodisp/au/cases/cth/HCATrans/2010/32.html>
- *Republic of Croatia* v. *Snedden* [2010] HCA 14, <http://www.austlii.edu.au/cgi-bin/sinodisp/au/cases/cth/HCA/2010/14.html>
- *Vasiljkovic* v. *Honourable Brendan O'Connor* [2010] FCA 1246, <http://www.austlii.edu.au/cgi-bin/sinodisp/au/cases/cth/FCA/2010/1246.html>

As reported in the 2007, 2008 and 2009 *Yearbook of International Humanitarian Law*,[50] Daniel Snedden was sought to be extradited by Croatia for three alleged

---

[43] Ibid., paras 213–214.

[44] Ibid., para 142.

[45] Ibid., para 327.

[46] Ibid., para 344.

[47] As Zentai was already on bail, the order by McKerracher J cancelled bail and Zentai was therefore at full liberty.

[48] As represented in the proceedings by the Minister for Home Affairs and the Commonwealth Attorney-General.

[49] *Zentai* v. *Honourable Brendan O'Connor* (*No 4*) [2010] FCA 1385.

[50] See 10 *YIHL* (2007) pp 285–286; 11 *YIHL* (2008) p 418; 12 *YIHL* (2009) p 459–460.

war crimes in contravention of the *Croatian Basic Penal Code*, namely two crimes against prisoners of war and one crime against civilians.[51] As reported in the 2009 *Yearbook of International Humanitarian Law*, the Full Court of the Federal Court held that Snedden had a valid objection to extradition.[52] Under Croatian law a mitigating factor in sentencing included service in the Croatian army. If tried in Croatia, the court found because Snedden had chosen to fight on the Serbian side there was a real risk his trial or punishment would be prejudiced by reason of his political opinions.[53] The court held there was an extradition objection under section 7(1)(c) of the *Extradition Act*. Snedden was subsequently released from prison on 4 September 2009.[54]

The Australian government appealed to the High Court of Australia. On 30 March 2010, the High Court unanimously allowed the appeal. The Court held that there was no valid extradition objection on the ground that Snedden's trial may be prejudiced by reason of his political opinions. The Croatian sentencing law that provided service in the Croatian army entitled an offender to a reduction in sentence was found not to be based on political opinions.

French CJ traced the history of the law on extradition objections and held that the law required the 'existence of a causal connection between apprehended punishment and the political opinions'.[55] Applying the law to Snedden's case, the mitigating factor of service in the Croatian armed forces did not reflect a risk of unfair trial by Croatian courts. French CJ explained that the question was not whether Snedden served in the Serbian military but whether he did not serve in the Croatian military. Accordingly, 'that does not confer the character of an aggravating factor upon service in the Serbian forces nor thereby upon a political commitment to a Serbian republic advanced by such service. The causal connection was not made out'.[56]

Similar findings were made in the joint judgment of Gummow, Hayne, Crennan, Kiefel and Bell JJ. The joint judgment found that the evidence showed the sentencing law was not based on political opinions.[57] First, war service as a mitigating factor was not uncommon and did not imply homogeneous political opinions in those rendering war service.[58] Second, Serbian forces were not singled out as ineligible for the mitigating factor because it applied to persons who did not serve in any military at all 'irrespective of their personal motives, circumstances or political opinions'.[59] In a separate judgment, Heydon J found there was insufficient

[51] *Vasiljkovic* v. *Commonwealth* [2006] HCA 40. Vasiljkovic is Snedden's Serbian name.

[52] Ibid., paras 55–56.

[53] Ibid., paras 52–55.

[54] Ibid., para 69.

[55] *Republic of Croatia* v. *Snedden* [2010] HCA 14, para 23.

[56] Ibid., para 25.

[57] Ibid., para 72.

[58] Ibid., para 75.

[59] Ibid., paras 76–77.

evidence that the mitigating factor in sentencing actually existed in practice in Croatia and overturned the appeal on that basis alone.[60] The High Court confirmed the Magistrate's original order that Snedden was eligible for surrender for extradition.

In earlier proceedings in February 2010, a summons by Croatia was sought in the High Court for Snedden to surrender his passports and not present at any point of international departure and not leave Australia. French CJ made the orders *ex parte*. During the proceeding, it was disclosed that Snedden's whereabouts were unknown.[61] On 12 May 2010, after absconding, Snedden was arrested in New South Wales by Australian Federal Police and returned to prison.[62]

On 14 September 2010, Snedden sought *habeas corpus* relief in the Federal Court claiming his imprisonment was unlawful and again challenged his eligibility for surrender. On 19 November 2010, Edmonds J dismissed the application finding it had no reasonable prospects of success due to the finality of the High Court's decision (known as *res judicata*).[63]

At the end of 2010, an appeal by Snedden against Edmond J's decision was pending. The Minister for Home Affairs' decision whether to extradite Snedden to Croatia was also awaiting determination.

Legislation—Australian Military Justice

- Military Court of Australia Bill 2010, <http://www.austlii.edu.au/au/legis/cth/bill/mcoab2010314/>

As reported in the 2009 *Yearbook of International Humanitarian Law*,[64] the High Court of Australia found the Australian Military Court as established by the *Defence Legislation Amendment Act 2006* (*Cth*) was unconstitutional.[65] As an interim measure, the Australian Parliament reinstituted the system of courts-martial with review by a Defence Force Magistrate.[66]

In 2010, the Australian government introduced the Military Court of Australia Bill 2010 (Cth) (the Bill). During his Second Reading Speech, the Commonwealth Attorney-General explained the Bill aimed to establish 'the Military Court of Australia in accordance with Chap. III of the Constitution of the Commonwealth of Australia. The Military Court will be created to try all serious service offences

---

60 Ibid., paras 102–103.

61 *Republic of Croatia* v. *Snedden* [2010] HCATrans 32

62 Australian Minister for Home Affairs, 'Daniel Snedden Taken into Custody' (Media Release, 12 May 2010), <http://www.ag.gov.au/www/ministers/oconnor.nsf/Page/MediaReleases_2010_SecondQuarter_12May2010-DanielSneddenTakenIntoCustody>.

63 *Vasiljkovic* v. *Honourable Brendan O'Connor* [2010] FCA 1246, paras 112–114.

64 See 12 *YIHL* (2009) pp 460–461.

65 *Lane* v. *Morrison* [2009] HCA 29. Also see Australian Department of Defence, *Annual Report* 2009–2010 (2010) 'Military Justice Reform', pp 303–305.

66 *Military Justice* (*Interim Measures*) *Act* (*No. 1*) *2009* (Cth); *Military Justice* (*Interim Measures*) *Act* (*No 2*) *2009* (Cth). See for example: *Flynn* v. *Chief of Army* [2010] ADFDAT 1; *Parker* v. *Chief of Air Force* [2010] ADFDAT 2; *Watson* v. *Chief of Army* [2010] AFDAT 3.

… taking into account the important role that discipline has in supporting the operational effectiveness of the ADF'.[67] The 'serious service offences' include murder and mutiny that are heard by federal judges in the Appellate and Superior Division while federal magistrates determine less serious offences.[68] The Attorney-General, after consultation with the Defence Minister, appoints judicial officers until 70 years of age. Such judicial officers must be familiar with the nature of service in the ADF. The court does not have jury trials because civilians sitting in judgment of military officers were considered inappropriate. There were 'almost insurmountable practical barriers to the prosecution of offences'[69] by jury. The Court may also preside overseas where practicable and where the court considers it is in the interests of justice to do so.

On 24 June 2010, the Bill was referred to the Australian Senate Legal and Constitutional Affairs Legislation Committee with a report due by 24 September 2010. The only submission to the Committee argued the Bill may not sufficiently comply with Chap. III of the *Australian Constitution* due to the absence of jury trials, that judicial officers in the General Division were called a 'magistrate' and that judicial tenure was inadequate because there was no proper pension entitlements.[70]

On 19 July 2010, the Governor-General prorogued the Australian Parliament due to a federal election and the Bill lapsed.[71] It is expected another Bill establishing the Court will be introduced in the next Parliament.

Legislation—Cluster Munitions

- Criminal Code Amendment (Cluster Munitions Prohibition) Bill 2010, <http://www.austlii.edu.au/au/legis/cth/bill/ccampb2010545/>

As reported in the 2009 *Yearbook of International Humanitarian Law*,[72] the Australian Parliament ratified the *Convention on Cluster Munitions* (the Convention). The Convention entered into force on 1 August 2010. There remained, however, several outstanding issues for Australia to complete the ratification process, such as amendments to the *Criminal Code Act 1995* (Cth) to provide for offences against the Convention.

---

[67] Explanatory Memoranda, Military Court of Australia Bill 2010, 24 June 2010, <http://parlinfo.aph.gov.au/parlInfo/genpdf/chamber/hansardr/2010-06-24/0022/hansard_frag.pdf;fileType=application%2Fpdf. See also Joint Media Release of Commonwealth Attorney-General and Defence Minister, 24 June 2010, http://www.ag.gov.au/www/ministers/mcclelland.nsf/Page/MediaReleases_2010_SecondQuarter_24June2010-LegislationtoestablishMilitaryCourtofAustralia>.

[68] Military Court of Australia Bill 2010 (Cth) Schedule 3.

[69] Explanatory Memorandum, Military Court of Australia Bill 2010, 'General Outline'.

[70] Submission of Mr Alexander W Street SC, <http://www.aph.gov.au/senate/committee/legcon_ctte/military_court/submissions.htm>.

[71] Senate Australian Legal and Constitutional Affairs Committee, Parliament of Australia, *Report on the Military Court of Australia Bill 2010* (2010), <http://www.aph.gov.au/senate/committee/legcon_ctte/military_court/report/index.htm>.

[72] See 12 *YIHL* (2009) pp 462–463.

On 28 October 2010, the Australian government introduced into Parliament the Criminal Code Amendment (Cluster Munitions Prohibition) Bill 2010 (Cth) (the Bill) and on the same day referred it to the Senate Foreign Affairs, Defence and Trade Legislation Committee. The Bill passed the House of Representatives on 18 November 2010 and was introduced into the Senate on 22 November 2010.[73] The principal aim of the Bill is to create criminal offences relating to cluster munitions and explosive bomblets. The Bill establishes two offences punishable by a maximum of 10 years imprisonment. The first offence is to use, develop, produce, acquire, stockpile, retain, or transfer cluster munitions to any person. The second offence is to assist, encourage or induce another person to do any of those acts. The Bill, however, permits defences to these crimes. Specified members of the ADF or other specified Commonwealth public officials may be authorised by the Defence Minister under the *Explosives Act 1961* (Cth) to acquire or retain specified cluster munitions for training in detection, clearance or destruction techniques, counter—measures and to destroy cluster munitions. Cluster munitions may also be transferred to another country for the same purpose.[74]

Two significant defences to be inserted into the *Criminal Code Act* (Cth) deal with interoperability. As reported in the 2008 and 2009 *Yearbook of International Humanitarian Law*,[75] the Convention intended to permit countries who do not possess and use cluster munitions (such as Australia) to conduct joint military operations with the military forces of countries who do (such as the United States) but significant restrictions applied.[76] The proposed new sections 72.41 and 72.42 in the *Criminal Code* are intended to implement Article 21 of the Convention. Australian military personnel in joint military operations do not commit an offence if 'the act does not consist of expressly requesting the use of a cluster munition in a case where the choice of munitions used is within the Commonwealth's exclusive control'.[77] The military cooperation may entail the use by foreign countries of bases on Australian territory, or the entry of foreign ships or aircraft into Australian territory.[78] The defence only applies to the stockpiling, retention and transfer of cluster munitions, which is intended to implement Article 21(4) of the Convention. It does not apply to the use, development, production or acquisition of cluster munitions by non-Party military forces *while they are in Australian territory*.[79]

---

73 Bill List of 43rd Australian Parliament as at 24 February 2011, Australian Parliament.

74 Criminal Code Amendment (Cluster Munitions Prohibition) Bill 2010 (Cth) Schedule 1 (ss. 72.39, 72.40).

75 See 11 *YIHL* (2008) pp 414–416; 12 *YIHL* (2009) pp 462–463.

76 Ibid. Schedule 1 inserts sections 72.41, 72.42 into Division 72 of the *Criminal Code Act 1995* (Cth).

77 Ibid. Schedule 1, section 72.41(c). Compare Article 21(4) of the Convention.

78 Explanatory Memorandum, Criminal Code Amendment (Cluster Munitions Prohibition) Bill 2010, <http://www.comlaw.gov.au/Details/C2010B00251/Explanatory%20Memorandum/Text>.

79 Section 72.42 of the Bill only refers to 'stockpiling' etc. and not use.

Several submissions to the Senate Committee raised concern about the interoperability provisions.[80] In January 2010, the Australian Red Cross submitted that the provisions were drafted more broadly than needed to cover inadvertent participation by the ADF in the use by other countries of cluster munitions.[81] The submission explained that under the Bill 'Australian personnel could be involved in the refueling of planes carrying cluster munitions or involved in the planning of activities or creation of rules of engagement where the actual use of cluster munitions is not by a State Party to the Convention'.[82] It was argued this could allow the intentional violation of the Convention. Similar concerns were raised in other submissions including Human Rights Watch which explained that the defences should not be allowed because the prohibition on use of cluster munitions still applied during joint military operations.[83] The Australian government responded that Article 21 of the Convention and the Bill were consistent.[84] Further, it was argued that interoperability permitted ADF personnel to participate in a variety of military roles (including senior roles) with nations that used cluster munitions.[85] The Bill remains before the Senate Committee and a report is due in March 2011.[86]

Nika Dharmadasa and James May

BANGLADESH[87]

Cases—War Crimes Trials

- Case against Delwar Hossain Sayedee

---

[80] Submissions made to the Senate Committee of Foreign Affairs, Defence and Trade Committee on the Criminal Code Amendment (Cluster Munitions Prohibition) Bill 2010, (Cth), <http://www.aph.gov.au/senate/committee/fadt_ctte/ccab_cmp_2010/submissions.htm>.

[81] Australian Red Cross, Submission 21 to the Senate Committee of Foreign Affairs, Defence and Trade Committee on the Criminal Code Amendment (Cluster Munitions Prohibition) Bill 2010 (Cth), p 2, <http://www.aph.gov.au/senate/committee/fadt_ctte/ccab_cmp_2010/submissions.htm>. Also see the ICRC submission.

[82] Ibid., p 3.

[83] Human Rights Watch, Submission number 7 to the Senate Committee for Foreign Affairs, Defence and Trade Committee on the Criminal Code Amendment (Cluster Munitions Prohibition) Bill 2010 (Cth), pp 5–8.

[84] Submission on Minister for Foreign Affair, Defence and Attorney-General, Senate Committee for Foreign Affairs, Defence and Trade Committee on the Criminal Code Amendment (Cluster Munitions Prohibition) Bill 2010 (Cth), p 3.

[85] Submission number 24 from the Minister for Defence, Minister for Foreign Affairs and the Commonwealth Attorney-General (undated). Also see 'Additional Information', <http://www.aph.gov.au/senate/committee/fadt_ctte/ccab_cmp_2010/submissions.htm>.

[86] Senate Committee of Foreign Affairs, Defence and Trade Committee, 'Additional Information about the Inquiry', <http://www.aph.gov.au/senate/committee/fadt_ctte/ccab_cmp_2010/info.htm>.

[87] Information and commentaries provided by M. Zahurul Haq, Researcher and PhD Candidate at the Centre for Transnational Crime Prevention, Faculty of Law, University of Wollongong.

On 20 February 2011, the International Crimes Tribunal directed the jail authorities to produce Jamaat-e-Islami (Bangladesh) leader Delwar Hossain Sayedee to appear before it on 15 March 2011 in connection with war crime charges.[88]

Earlier on 29 June 2010, Police arrested Sayedee and three others including party president Motiur Rahman Nizami and his deputy Ali Ahsan Mohammad Mujahid on court order as they failed to appear before the court to face a charge of offending Muslim 'religious sentiment'.[89] Later, charges were brought against them under s 3(2) of the *International Crimes Tribunal Act 1973* for genocide, murder, rape, torture, loot and arson perpetrated during the Liberation War of Bangladesh in 1971.[90]

On 15 February 2011, the prosecution filed a progress report of investigation against Sayedee. Prosecutor Syed Haider Ali told the tribunal that the investigative agency had collected documents on the allegations against the accused.[91] These accusations constituted the inaugural actions of the International Crimes Tribunal for Bangladesh, established in March 2010 with the task of prosecuting those responsible for crimes against humanity during the liberation war of Bangladesh.

The Country's main opposition party and close ally of Jamaat-e-Islami, the BNP, who ruled the country in coalition with Jamaat from 2001 to 2006, demanded the immediate release of the accused leaders claiming that their arrest was 'a heinous example of political repression'.[92] Caitlin Reiger, a senior associate at the International Center for Transitional Justice said that trials of mass atrocities were rarely politically uncontroversial, yet, as she observed, they have produced meaningful results in Sierra Leone, the former Yugoslavia and elsewhere.[93]

Bangladesh's recent initiatives with regard to the mass atrocities have already received international support. The UN agreed to help Bangladesh in the planning stage[94] and in a recent news conference, Stephen Rapp, US Ambassador-at-Large for War Crimes Issues, stated that the 'US Government will help Bangladesh hold an open and transparent war crimes trial with the rights of defence for the accused'.[95]

M. ZAHURUL HAQ

88 'Sayedee to be produced before tribunal Mar 15', *The Daily Star* (Dhaka) Online Edition, 20 February 2011, <http://www.thedailystar.net/newDesign/latest_news.php?nid=28531>.

89 'Police arrest Nizami, Mujahid, Sayeedi on court order', *Bangladesh Sangbad Sangstha* (*BSS*), 29 June 2010, <http://www.bssnews.net/newsDetails.php?cat=0&id=115636$date=2010-06-29&dateCurrent=2010-07-04>.

90 '4 Jamaat leaders produced before tribunal, sent to jail', *The News Today*, 29 July 2010, <http://www.newstoday.com.bd/index.php?option=details&news_id=3420&date=2010-07-30>.

91 *The Daily Star*, supra n 88.

92 S. Sebastian, 'Bangladesh braces for divisive war-crimes trial', *Asia Times Online*, 18 August 2010, <http://www.atimes.com/atimes/South_Asia/LH18Df01.html>.

93 Ibid.

94 'UN to help Bangladesh war crimes trial planning', *AFP*, 7 April 2009, <http://www.google.com/hostednews/afp/article/ALeqM5i8DOGtdoHAJaJQhtR_orq4CmvwOw>.

95 'US offers to help Bangladesh pursue war crimes trial', *BBC News South Asia*, 13 January 2011, <http://www.bbc.co.uk/news/world-south-asia-12183361>.

COLOMBIA[96]

Governmental Policy—New Operational Law Handbook and Rules of Engagement

- Provision No. 056 of 7 December 2009, 'by which an "Operational Law Handbook" is approved' [*Disposición número 056 del 7 de diciembre de 2009, '(p)or la cual se aprueba el 'Manual de derecho operacional'*], Colombian General Commandment of Armed Forces, Manual FF.MM 3-41 Público (not classified, but on file with author).
- Permanent Directives No. 017 of 2009 (without date), 022, of 15 July 2009, and 032, of 16 October 2009 (Classified) [*Directivas permanentes reservadas 017 de 2009* (s.f.)*, 022, del 15 de julio de 2009 y, 032, del 16 de octubre de 2009*], concerning new rules of engagement, National Defence Ministry, quoted by Provision No. 056 (2009) p. 105.

Government policy in relation to IHL can be analysed from two perspectives: on one hand from a strategic or long term planning perspective; and on the other, from an operational perspective. Over the last 8 years (particularly throughout President Uribe's Administration, 2002–2006 and 2006–2010), the Colombian government has adopted various strategies to defeat illegal (guerrilla or paramilitary) armed groups. The prevailing policy was previously known as 'Democratic Security', but as the armed forces secured significant operational results,[97] the government preferred to talk of a strategy of 'Democratic Security Consolidation'. Finally, with the election of a new president (Juan Manuel Santos) who took office in August 2010, the government has labelled its policy 'Defence and Security for Prosperity'.[98]

In relation to an operational perspective, the General Commandment of Armed Forces has formally adopted the first edition of a dedicated manual (Operational Law Handbook) for the Colombian Armed Forces. Although that publication has been developed through a lengthy public discussion with civil society (judicial organs, NGOs and scholars), it is still not widely known across Colombian society generally. Nevertheless, the Manual appears to be well drafted and readily accepted by the Armed Forces.

The first chapter of the Manual outlines the Constitutional authority of the Armed Forces, the second and third chapters deal with the use of force in the framework of IHL and human rights law and the fourth chapter explains the

---

96 Information and commentaries provided by Rafael A. Prieto Sanjuán, Professor of Public International Law and IHL at Pontificia Universidad Javeriana and Universidad Militar Nueva Granada, Bogotá. This report also covers facts and documents concerning 2009, in order to keep the continuity of the author's contribution since 1999.

97 See our precedent Colombia reports in earlier volumes of *YIHL*; Colombian National Defense Ministry, Vice Minister for Strategy and Planning Sectorial Studies Direction, 'Public forces operational results' (12 November 2010), <http://www.mindefensa.gov.co/irj/go/km/docs/Mindefensa/Documentos/descargas/estudios%20sectoriales/info_estadistica/Avance%20de%20la%20Politica%20de%20Defensa%20y%20Seguridad%20ingles.pdf>.

98 Ibid.; 'Logros de la política integral de defensa y seguridad para la prosperidad' (November 2010), <http://www.mindefensa.gov.co/irj/go/km/docs/Mindefensa/Documentos/descargas/estudios%20sectoriales/info_estadistica/Logros%20de%20Politica%20CSD%20Nov%202010.pdf>.

relationship between these two fields of international law in a situation of armed conflict. These opening chapters are directed at a broad audience. However, the remaining chapters of the Handbook address the principal target audience of members of the armed forces.

Hence, Chap. 5 addresses an inventory of different types of military operations beyond—or perhaps more accurately short of armed conflict, incorporating the Rules of Engagement, and paying special attention to the challenges posed in the fight against 'BACRIM' (Criminal Bands)—those emergent illegal armed groups characterised as the successors of demobilised paramilitary groups, but closer in their *modus operandi* to armed gangs and drug trafficking mafias, and sometimes allied to guerrilla groups.[99] The Handbook distinguishes a 'red card' situation for military engagements from a 'blue card' situation for the conduct of security (police) operations. The Manual considers that IHL will be applicable in a red card mission, while human rights law will be the prevailing applicable legal regime for blue card missions. This seems to be an overly simplistic distinction and potentially disregards the complexity of applicable legal regimes in current armed conflicts such as the Colombian one. As an example, troops deployed in a blue mission (police operation), which subsequently evolves into an armed conflict would be required to return to barracks to ask their superiors for a new operation order with a red card, as required by the Manual.[100] This is also a potential problem for deployments that commence as red card missions, with a military objective: what happens if the situation on the field only requires police action or the reestablishment of public order? Unless the red card is downgraded to blue, any use of lethal force against opposing forces will be legal.

Irrespective of the potential operational problems arising under Chap. 5 of the Handbook, Chap. 6 requires coordination between the 'first (military) respondent' and judicial authorities, and also establishes procedures for the demobilisation of combatants, including persons under 18 years of age. Chapter 7 defines the nature, profile, functions and responsibility of the 'operational legal advisor', and finally, Chap. 8 deals with individual and State liability.

Governmental Policy—Conduct of Hostilities

- Operation 'Chameleon', Rescue of four police and military, 13 June 2010, Calamar, Guaviare

---

[99] See Comisión Nacional de Reparación y Reconciliación (Redress and Reconciliation National Commission), *Disidentes, rearmados y emergentes. ¿Bandas criminales o tercera generación paramilitar?* (August 2007), <http://www.cnrr.org.co/new/interior_otros/informe 1 DDR Cnrr.pdf>; Human Rights Watch, *Paramilitaries' Heirs. The New Face of Violence in Colombia* (2010); *El Tiempo*, <http://www.eltiempo.com/Multimedia/especiales_eventos/bacrim>; Colombian National Ministry of Defense, *Operación Diamante: Fuerza Pública Colombiana da de baja a alias 'Chuchillo', cabecilla de la banda criminal ERPAC* (2010), <http://www.mindefensa.gov.co/irj/go/km/docs/Mindefensa/Documentos/descargas/Prensa/especiales/operaciondiamante.html>, exploring Operation 'Diamond', which was undertaken against one of the most redoubtable leaders of these gangs.

[100] General Commandment of Armed Forces, *Manual de derecho operacional* [Operational Law Handbook] Doc. Manual FF.MM 3-41 (7 December 2009) p 11.

- Operation 'Sodom', strike down of 'Mono Jojoy', member of the FARC Secretariat, 23 September 2010, Macarena, Meta

The two following incidents are examples of conduct of hostilities by the Colombian government which demonstrate the application of the strategic and operational planning governmental policies identified above.

Operation 'Chameleon' is the name attributed to the mission of 13 June 2010 by which the Army liberated high ranking police officials, General Luis Herlindo Mendieta and Colonels Enrique Murillo and William Donato, as well as Army Sergeant Arbey Delgado Argoty. Despite unknown details of the operation—in contrast to the well known details of Operation 'Jaque'[101]—media outlets reported that the operation was undertaken by an assault on a guerrilla camp of the 7th Front of the *Fuerzas Armadas Revolucionarias de Colombia—Ejército del Pueblo* (Revolutionary Armed Forces of Colombia—People's Army, or FARC-EP), in the rural municipality of Calamar, department of Guaviare, where these officials were kidnapped and subsequently detained.[102]

Regarding Operation 'Sodom', the most important aspect involved the use of aerial strikes that resulted in the killing of Víctor Julio Suárez, aka Jorge Briceño Suárez, and best known as 'Mono Jojoy', the top FARC military commander and most fearsome member of the Secretariat of the Central High Command (*Secretariado del Estado Mayor Central*). Operation Sodom was initiated at 01:00 a.m. on 23 September 2010 in the Macarena Region (department of Meta), against a camp of the FARC West Bloc. Governmental information indicates that 72 aircraft and seven tonnes of bombs were used against the 'mother of all camps'.[103] In fact, the killing of 'Jojoy' followed an earlier significant attack on the FARC leadership with the killing in the northern Equator Region of the 'Chancellor' and No. 2 FARC Commander, Luis Edgar Devia Silva, aka 'Raúl Reyes', on 1 March 2008 in Operation 'Phoenix'.[104] These two aerial attacks combined to form a 'black

---

[101] See 11 *YIHL* (2008) pp 458, 461–462.

[102] Colombian Army, *Operación Camaleón* (2010), <http://www.ejercito.mil.co/index.php?idcategoria=249417>; General Commandment of Armed Forces, *Operación Camaleón* (13 June 2010), <http://www.cgfm.mil.co/CGFMPortal/operacion_camaleon/1_index_camaleon.html>.

[103] See Colombian Ministry of Defence, *Operación Sodoma: Fuerza Pública colombiana da de baja al número dos y jefe terrorista de las Farc, alias 'El Mono Jojoy'* (2010), <http://www.mindefensa.gov.co/irj/go/km/docs/Mindefensa/Documentos/descargas/Prensa/especiales/OperacionSodoma.html>; General Commandment of Armed Forces, *Operación Sodoma* (2010), <http://www.cgfm.mil.co/CGFMPortal/index.jsp?option=contentDisplay&idCont=1075>.

[104] See R.A. Prieto Sanjuán, 'The Colombia Cross-border Raid: A Solution at the Expense of the Fight Against Terrorism?', *Interest Group on Peace and Security—European Society of International Law* (25 March 2008), <http://igps.wordpress.com/2008/03/25/the-colombia-cross-border-raid-a-solution-at-the-expense-of-the-fight-against-terrorism-article-by-r-prieto-sanjuan>; L.E. Nagle, 'Colombia's Incursion into Ecuadorian Territory: Justified Hot Pursuit or Pugnacious Error?', 17 *Journal of Transnational Law and Policy* (2008) p 359; *Flanklin Guillermo Aisalla Molina* (*Ecuador* v. *Colombia*), Inter-State Petition IP-02, Inter-American Commission on Human Rights, Report No. 112/10, Doc. OEA/Ser.L/V/II.140 (21 October 2010), <http://www.cidh.oas.org/annualrep/2010eng/EC-CO.PI-02ADM.EN.doc>.

month' for the FARC Secretariat, because the supreme chief, Pedro Antonio Marín, best known as Manuel Marulanda Vélez, aka 'Tirofijo'(Surefire or Sure-shot), the 'most ancient guerrilla fighter' died of natural causes 3 weeks later.

Legislation—New Military Criminal Code

- Law 1407 of 17 August 2010, by means of which the Military Criminal Code is enacted [*Ley 1407 del 17 de agosto de 2010, por la cual se expide el Código Penal Militar*]. Published in *Diario Oficial*, no. 47804, 17 August 2010, p. 1, <http://www.secretariasenado.gov.co/senado/basedoc/ley/2010/ley_1407_2010.html>
- Decree 4733 of 23 December 2010 by means of which some errors of Law 1407 of 2010 'by means of which the Military Criminal Code is enacted' are corrected [Dec 4733 del 23 de diciembre de 2010 Por el cual se corrigen yerros de Ley 1407 de 2010 'por la cual se expide el CódigoPenal Militar'], Ministry of National Defence

After more than one decade a new *Colombian Military Criminal Code* has entered in force. Consequently, the main changes regarding the 1999 Code[105] concern the structure of the Judiciary, the trial process itself and the applicable penalties. The new Code establishes 'Guarantee Judges' and an 'Inspector's Office' (*Ministerio Público*). Guarantee judges are in charge of ensuring due process and the legality of evidence admitted by the Court. The Inspector's Office is tasked with ensuring the human rights and fundamental freedoms of all intervenients in the trial process, with monitoring judicial police activities, and with the preservation of defence rights of accused persons, *inter alia*. Additionally, the former position of 'War Auditor' has been replaced by the Military Attorney-General's Office (*Fiscalía General penal militar*) which is authorised to undertake both the investigation and the prosecution through designated military criminal attorneys (*fiscales penales militares delegados ante el Tribunal Superior Militar*) before the High Military Court. Finally, the new Code also creates an Office for Technical Criminal Defence (*Defensoría técnica penal militar*) for accused members of the military as well as for victims in order to guarantee 'equality of arms' with the prosecution.

Thus, the new military criminal justice structure means that the process is entirely of an adversarial nature, integrating principles of oral argument, contradiction, immediacy, concentration and publicity. Hearings previewed are: pre-trial, confirmation of charges, trial preparation, and then, the trial itself by court-martial. Regarding penalties, they are prescribed and can be severe. It is important to note that war crimes and crimes against humanity are excluded from military jurisdiction because such crimes are so egregious that they can never be considered part of the soldiers' or the police officers' official duties.[106] Accordingly, allegations of offences such as extrajudicial executions are dealt with in the civil court system as the following cases illustrate.

---

105 See 2 *YIHL* (1999) p 347.

106 Art. 3 of Law 1407 (2010).

Cases—Extrajudicial Executions

- *Soacha* and other cases concerning extrajudicial executions reported as 'false positives' across the country.[107] Criminal Courts of Cundinamarca Specialised Circuit and Criminal Court of Santander Specialised Circuit (ongoing cases)

Soacha is the name of a southern suburb and a local municipality of Bogotá, the place of residence of some young men whose bodies were presented in Ocaña, a municipality of Norte de Santander (in the northeast of Colombia) as those of alleged guerrilla combatants killed in action. Soacha has also become the name to describe an atrocity because sometime after the killings, investigations revealed that the individuals were actually unemployed youths who were lured by spurious offers of employment, summarily executed and their bodies then displayed to create the false impression of successful counter guerrilla action. Indeed, *Soacha* has became the most scandalous and symbolic case of the protracted armed conflict in Colombia, as well as a glaring exposure of the harmful pressure on the military to produce results in the conduct of hostilities against the guerilla movement. This pressure was so intense that it has caused some members of the military to carry out a number of premeditated civilian murders that have been fraudulently presented as casualties or commonly so-called *falsos positivos* (false positives), better defined as 'unlawful killings of civilians, staged by the security forces to look like lawful killings in combat of guerrillas or criminals'[108]:

> [i]n some cases, civilian victims are lured under false pretences—usually with the promise of a job—by a paid 'recruiter' (a civilian, demobilized armed group member or former soldier) to a remote location. Once there, victims are killed by members of the military, often within a matter of hours or days of when they were last seen by family members. In other cases, the security forces remove victims from their homes or pick them up on patrol or at a roadblock. Victims may also be identified to military members as guerrillas or criminals by 'informers', often in exchange for a monetary reward. Once these victims are killed, the military, with varying degrees of sophistication, then sets up the scene to make it appear like a lawful combat killing. This can involve: placing weapons in the hands of victims; firing weapons from victims' hands; changing their clothes to combat fatigues or other clothing associated with guerrillas; and putting combat boots on victims' feet. The victims are reported by the military and in the press as guerrillas or criminals killed in combat. Victims are often buried without first being identified (*nombre desconocido*) and some are buried in communal graves. Meanwhile, victims' families search desperately—sometimes for many months—for their loved ones. When family members discover what happened and take steps to seek justice, such as reporting a case to officials or discussing the case with the press, they often face intimidation and threats. Some have been killed.[109]

---

[107] See statiscs from NGO, the Attorney-General (*Fiscalía*) and the Office of the Inspector General (*Procuraduría*) quoted in *Report of the Special Rapporteur on extrajudicial, summary or arbitrary executions*, UN Doc. A/HRC/14/24/Add.2, 31 March 2010, fns. 9–15, <http://www.hchr.org.co/documentoseinformes/documentos/relatoresespeciales/2010/A.HRC.14.24.Add.2_EN%20Informe%20Philip%20Alston%20Ejecuciones%20extrajudiciales.pdf>.

[108] Ibid., pp 1, 8.

[109] Ibid., para 11.

Despite the strenuous refusal of authorities that this despicable practice may reflect an official State policy, the pattern, geography and significant number of extrajudicial executions is a source of grave concern to proper authorities, relatives' victims, NGOs and international observers. Notwithstanding that UN Special Rapporteur on Extrajudicial Killings, Philip Alston, did not find 'evidence to suggest that these killings were committed as part of an official policy or that they were ordered by senior Government officials', he did receive:

> detailed and credible reports of such killings from across the country, committed in numerous departments and by a large number of different military units: [t]here have been too many killings [between 1000 and 2300] of a similar nature to characterise them as isolated incidents carried out by individual rogue soldiers or units, or 'bad apples'.[110]

It is important to acknowledge that extrajudicial executions and forced disappearances are a systematic practice of unlawful armed groups. Such practices are reprehensible and rightly condemned. But when those same practices are undertaken by government or military officials against the very civilian population the officials have a constitutional responsibility to protect, the sense of outrage should be exacerbated.[111]

Consequently, important steps have been adopted by authorities and these include: disciplinary sanctions; increased cooperation with and monitoring by the ICRC and the United Nations; the deployment of operational legal advisors in military units (*supra*); enlarged oversight of payments to informers, as well as a temporary special commission to investigate operations (the 'Suárez report'); the appointment of delegated inspectors to army divisions; the introduction of the requirement that deaths in combat be investigated first by judicial police (Directive No. 19); modifying award criteria (Directive No. 142); strengthening of internal command, control, training and evaluation systems (Directive No. 208); and military unit performance criteria (Directive No. 300-28), as well as the creation of a specialised unit in the *Fiscalía* (Attorney General's Office) to deal with alleged extrajudicial executions, and the requirement that military criminal judges transfer cases to the civilian justice system.[112] Nevertheless, despite the impact of those measures on a considerable reduction in the allegations of extrajudicial executions committed by the military, there remain important problems of oversight, transparency and accountability and perhaps

---

110 Ibid., para 14.

111 See supra, Justice Palace case.

112 See Ministry of Defence, *Comprehensive Human Rights and IHL Policy* (2008); Ministry of Defence, *Protecting Rights—Actions and outcomes of the National Security Forces in the protection of human rights 2002–2008* (2009); Ministry of National Defence, *Avances en el cumplimiento de las 15 medidas adoptadas por el ministerio de defense nacional* (*noviembre 2008–mayo 2009*) (2009).

these issues justify an increase in the monitoring activities of the ICC Prosecutor Office on Colombia.[113]

Extradition—From Russia

- *Klein* v. *Russia* (*application no. 24268/08*), Extraditing a convicted Israeli 'mercenary' from Russia to Colombia would breach the convention, European Court of Human Rights, Judgment, 1 April 2010

This case concerns the Israeli national, Gal Yair Klein, who argued that his extradition from Russia, were he was captured in 2007,[114] to Colombia would constitute a 'violation of Article 3 (prohibition of inhuman and degrading treatment) of the European Convention on Human Rights'. Notwithstanding, that the case was decided by the European Court of Human Rights, it is important to note that, in 2001, the accused was convicted *in absentia* by a Colombian criminal court of instruction and training in military and terrorist tactics, and sentenced to 10 years and 8 months' imprisonment.[115] Subsequently, the Prosecutor General of Russia ordered Klein's extradition to Colombia in January 2008, and Mr. Klein appealed the decision, but his appeal was dismissed. Having exhausted Russian internal remedies, Klein's lawyers lodged an application with the European Court of Human Rights on 26 May 2008, in which Mr. Klein repeated his previous allegations, that 'if extradited to Colombia, he would most probably be ill-treated and would face an unfair trial'.[116] Thus, he requested the Court to prevent his extradition to Colombia. The day after the lodgement of the application, the Court indicated to the Russian government under Rule 39 of its Rules, that the extradition should be stayed as an interim measure pending further notice.

Having applied Rule 39 and, following its earlier decisions concerning risks of ill-treatment in a receiving country, the Court decided that 'implementation of the extradition order against the applicant would breach Article 3'. Actually, the Court considered that the applicant:

> feared ill-treatment, on the one hand, because of the poor general human rights situation in Colombia and, on the other hand, because he thought he personally was at a greater risk as

---

[113] See Office of the Prosecutor (Communications, Referrals and Preliminary Examinations) who is examining 'alleged crimes within the jurisdiction of the Court and investigations/proceedings conducted in Colombia against the allegedly most serious perpetrators, paramilitary leaders, politicians, guerrilla leaders and military personnel. The Office is also analysing allegations of international networks supporting armed groups committing crimes in Colombia. See International Criminal Court, *Colombia,* <http://www.icc-cpi.int/menus/icc/structure%20of%20the%20court/office%20of%20the%20prosecutor/comm%20and%20ref/colombia/colombia?lan=en-GB>. See R. A. Prieto Sanjuán, 'A propósito de la plena entrada en vigor del Estatuto de Roma', *Ámbito Jurídico*, 16 al 29 de noviembre de 2009, p 18.

[114] On 27 August 2007, Klein was arrested at Domodedovo Airport, Moscow on the basis of an Interpol notice in order to be transferred to Colombia. See 'Capturan en Rusia a Yair Klein, el mercenario israelí que inició la instrucción de los paramilitares' *Semana*, 28 August 2007, <http://www.semana.com/wf_InfoArticulo.aspx?idArt=101403>.

[115] Tribunal Superior del Distrito Judicial de Manizales, Criminal Chamber, 22 June 2001.

[116] Press release issued by the Registrar.

> a result of the Colombian Vice-President's statement to the media threatening to have the applicant 'rot in jail'.[117]

Despite the inappropriate diplomatic statement of the Vice-President, it should be noted that the judiciary in Colombia is independent and that politicians, no matter how superior, do not exercise authority over Colombian judges. This fact was recognised by the Russian authorities in authorising the extradition and was also recognised by the dissenting judges of the European Court.[118] Additionally, the information relied on by the majority judges about the Colombian human rights situation was indirect and very superficial, especially the information concerning conditions of detention in maximum security prisons.

In sum, once the Court's judgment became final (it was not selected to be referred to the Grand Chamber of the Court),[119] Russia was required to release Mr. Klein, who flew to Tel-Aviv, where he was received as a national hero. Although Klein remains at large, Colombian authorities continue to request his detention and his extradition, or at least, an *exequatur* to enable the serving of Klein's 2001 penalty in Israel.[120]

Cases—Colombian Transitional Justice

- *Prosecutor* v. *Edwar Cobos Téllez, aka 'Diego Vecino', and Uber Enrique Banquéz Martínez, alias 'Juancho dique'*, High Court of Bogotá Judicial District—Justice and Peace Chamber, Bogotá D.C., File: 110016000253200680077, Judgment of 29 June 2010 [*Edwar Cobos Téllez alias de 'Diego Vecino', y Uber Enrique Banquéz Martínez, alias 'Juancho Dique', Tribunal superior del Distrito judicial de Bogotá—Sala de Justicia y Paz Bogotá D.C., Radicación: 110016000253200680077, Sentencia del 29 de junio de 2010, Magistrada Ponente: Uldi Teresa Jimenez Lopez*]
- *Prosecutor* v. *Iván Laverde Zapata, aka 'The Iguana'*, High Court of Bogotá Judicial District—Justice and Peace Chamber, Bogotá D.C., File: 110016000253200680281, Judgment of 2 December 2010 [*Iván Laverde Zapata, alias 'El Iguano', Tribunal Superior del Distrito Judicial de Bogotá—Sala de Justicia y Paz Bogotá D.C., Radicación: 110016000253200680281, Sentencia del 2 de diciembre de 2010, Magistrada Ponente: Uldi Teresa Jimenez Lopez*]

One of the most important events in Colombia's recent history is the peace process initiated by Former President Uribe's Administration between the government and

[117] 'The Mafia's Teacher Awaits Extradition', *Rossiyskaya Gazeta*, August 2007, quoted by the judgment.

[118] See the joint dissenting opinion of Judges Kovler and Hajiyev.

[119] *Convention for the Protection of Human Rights and Fundamental Freedoms,* opened for signature 4 November 1950, 213 UNTS 221, Article 43 (entered into force 3 September 1953) (*European Convention on Human Rights*).

[120] 'Colombia insiste en la extradición de Yair Klein', *Semana*, 27 January 2011, <http://www.semana.com/noticias-nacion/colombia-insiste-extradicion-yair-klein/150829.aspx>.

paramilitary groups. However, 5 years after the implementation of the instrument that established the legal framework facilitating the reinstatement of former combatants into civil society, impunity has become the main threat to the process.[121] Actually, several major leaders of paramilitary groups have been extradited to the United States where they face trial for drug trafficking. In relation to alleged crimes against humanity and war crimes, only three people have been convicted in Colombia.[122]

The first case, best known as the 'Mapuján Case', is that of Mr. Edwar Cobos and Mr. Banquéz Martínez, who were both charged with aggravated homicide and other criminal conduct (deportation, expulsion, transfer or forced displacement of civilians, kidnapping, qualified and aggravated burglary, illegal use of uniforms and ammunition belonging to the Colombian Armed Forces) committed either separately or jointly.[123] The co-accused were both convicted and sentenced to terms of imprisonment of 39 and 38½ years respectively. However, as beneficiaries of the prescribed alternative penalty, both co-accused had their sentences reduced to 8 years of imprisonment—the most severe punishment allowed pursuant to the so-called 'Justice and Peace Act'.[124]

The convicted were both commanders of the United Self Defences of Colombia (USDC). Cobos was commander of the Montes de María Bloc and Martinez was commander of the Canal del Dique (Dock Channel) Front—both militia groups operating under the umbrella of the USDC. In March 2000, Cobos and Martinez led an armed incursion into the village of Maríalabaja, ordering its inhabitants to abandon the town, kidnapping and killing some of them on the road to Yucalito. Martinez was also responsible for similar offenses in 2003 in another village (Múcura Island) facing the north coastal plain. The co-accused were tried as hierarchical superiors but also as material authors of those crimes. But the most interesting procedural aspect of the trial was the integral redress (compensation, satisfaction and non repetition guarantees) for victims, individually and collectively, in the same judgment, occupying half (the second part) of the reasons for sentence.

The second 'peace and justice' judgment was handed down 9 months after the Mapuján case. The accused in this case was Mr. Laverde Zapata, the paramilitary

---

121 For a critical study of the judicial process, see Human Rights Watch, *Breaking the Grip? Obstacles to Justice for Paramilitary Mafias in Colombia* (2008). See R.A. Prieto Sanjuán, 'Internationalising the Colombian Armed Conflict through Humanitarian Law and Transitional Justice' in N. Quenivet and S. Shah-Davis, eds., *International Law and Armed Conflict: Challenges in the 21st Century* (The Hague, T.M.C. Asser Press, 2010) pp 76–94.

122 A first person had been convicted on 19 March 2009 by the High Court of Bogotá, but on 31 July 2009 (file no. 31539) a providence of the Supreme Court (Criminal Chamber Cassation) reversed the decision on the ground of procedural nullities. See *Prosecutor vs. Wilson Salazar Carrascal, aka 'The parrot'*, High Court of Bogotá Judicial District—Justice and Peace Chamber, Bogotá D.C., [*Wilson Salazar Carrascal, alias 'El Loro', Tribunal Superior del Distrito Judicial de Bogotá—Sala de Justicia y Paz Bogotá*].

123 Mr. Cobos Téllez was also found responsible of aggravated conspiracy.

124 See 8 *YIHL* (2005) pp 417–418.

chief of USDC's Catatumbo Bloc (Colombia's northeast). Zapata was sentenced to imprisonment for 40 years (although he also received the statutory alternative sentence of 8 years) after being convicted of multiple offences involving the killing of 140 civilians in 25 massacres, as well as the killing of some judges and four politicians (all war crimes as serious violations of IHL), but also, of crimes of conspiracy, forced displacement, kidnapping, torture, unlawful carriage of weapons, wearing of uniforms belonging to the Colombian Armed Forces, damage to property, deportation, terrorism and extortion. The judgment is currently on appeal to the Supreme Court.

Cases—Links between Politicians and Paramilitaries (*Para Politics*)

Although the justice and peace process has been subject to sustained criticism, one of the more important contributions has been the exposure of some little known aspects of the armed conflict in Colombia,[125] especially, the reconstruction of some contextual (political and social) situations, as well as greater transparency about the links between paramilitaries and certain companies, businessmen or private persons, public officials and politicians. This feature of the Colombian conflict has been labeled 'parapolitics' (*Parapolítica*). Actually, '[b]y November 2009, 249 cases had been initiated against 12 governors, 166 mayors, 13 departmental representatives and 58 councilors' and, of the 268 persons elected for the period of the 2006–2010 legislative term, 120 cases have been filed against parliamentarians or former congresspersons, ten have been sentenced and one acquitted by the Supreme Court in 2010.[126] One of the most resounding cases has been that of Senator Álvaro García Romero who was convicted and sentenced to imprisonment for 40 years for his 'links with paramilitary groups and indirect participation in seven cases of aggravated homicide'.[127]

Cases—Forced Disappearances Following the Palace of Justice Siege

- Final Report of the Truth Commission for the Palace of Justice Events [*Informe final de la Comisión de la Verdad sobre los hechos del Palacio de Justicia*], Bogotá, 17 December 2009, <http://www.verdadpalacio.org.co/Assets/DOCs/INFORME-FINAL-CVPJ.pdf>
- Trial of *Luis Alfonso Plazas Vega* et al., 3rd Criminal Court of the Bogotá Specialised Circuit, 9 June 2010 (on file with author)

---

[125] Besides the discovery of common graves through confessions of certain accused persons, the work of the Comisión Nacional de Reparación y Reconciliación to reconstruct the circumstances around some emblematic massacres has been especially significant. See Comisión Nacional de Reparación y Reconciliación (Redress and Reconciliation National Commission), *La masacre de el Salado: esa guerra no era nuestra* (without date), *Trujillo: una tragedia que no cesa* (2008), *La Rochela: memorias de un crimen contra la justicia* (2010), <http://www.cnrr.org.co/new/libro09.html>.

[126] *Report of the United Nations High Commissioner for Human Rights on the situation of human rights in Colombia*, UN Doc. A/HRC/13/72, 4 March 2010, para 32.

[127] *Report of the United Nations High Commissioner for Human Rights on the situation of human rights in Colombia*, UN Doc. A/HRC/16/22, 3 February 2011, para 45–47.

On 6 November 1985, commandos of the M-19 guerrilla group (19th April Movement) seized the Palace of Justice, site of the *Corte Suprema de Justicia*, the highest court in Colombia. Ostensibly, the seizure was intended to facilitate a trial against the president of the Republic, Belisario Betancourt Cuartas. As a result, hundreds of hostages were detained through the night in the Supreme Court building and an important number of court records including extradition files against supposed mafia leaders as well those located on the last floor of the building, were burned. President Betancourt ordered the Army to end the siege, take control of the building and liberate the hostages. The siege was finally broken but in the process the building was destroyed and, worse, more than 100 people died including 11 Supreme Court Judges, 48 Colombian Soldiers, 35 M-19 commandos and another 11 people unaccounted for.

Consequently, different actions were filed against officials, but victims only obtained administrative compensation. Twenty years after the event, the Supreme Court established an independent extrajudicial commission to determine the truth about these events. The Commission handed down a preliminary report in 2006, a complementary one in 2007, and a final report in 2009. This succession of reports has reconstructed the events of the siege and the retaking of the Justice Building, finding a link between M-19 and drug cartels.[128] The Commission focused on the aftermath of the siege and has attributed individual responsibly for decisions taken during the temporary lack of presidential authority. Unfortunately the Commission has repeatedly asked former President Betancourt to explain his version of events but the former President has consistently refused to appear before the Commission or to provide any information to it about his role in this tragic episode.

Despite the former President's reluctance to co-operate with the Commission, judicial processes against retired military were reopened. Those tried included: the former commander of the 13th Army Brigade in Bogotá, General Jesús Armando Arias Cabrales, who led the operation to retake the building; the commander of the armored cavalry battalion, Colonel Luís Alfonso Plazas Vega, who was personally appointed by General Cabrales to oversee the operation; and B-2 intelligence chief of the 13th Army Brigade, Colonel Edilberto Sánchez.

After a tense and, at times, stormy trial, only Colonel Plazas Vega was convicted of the offences of aggravated forced disappearance and he was sentenced to a term of imprisonment of 30 years. The judgment is currently on appeal.

Some of the most interesting findings in the lengthy (302 pages) written reasons for sentence are related to the criminal responsibility of a hierarchical superior and the theory of 'indirect perpetration', the natural judge principle, the principle of legality (in that the crime of forced disappearance was not incorporated in Colombian criminal law at the time of the facts[129]), and, the issue of statutory

[128] See contra, A. Carrigan, *The Palace of Justice: A Colombian Tragedy* (New York, Four Walls Eight Windows, 1993).

[129] Forced disappearance has just been characterised in Colombia in 2000 (Law 599, Art. 165 Criminal Code) adopting the Inter-American Convention in 2005 and, regarding the Universal Convention, it is pending of ratification by the president (Congress approval in October 2010).

limitations. In dismissing otherwise applicable statutory limitations, the Court relied in part on an argument that forced disappearance has been an international crime at least since the time of the Palace of Justice siege. In an unconvincing argument, the Court reasoned that as the offence constituted an international crime it was not subject to statutory limitations but was instead covered by the *Convention on the Non-Applicability of Statutory Limitations to War Crimes and Crimes Against Humanity*,[130] even though Colombia is not a State party to the treaty.

Cases—Constitutional Challenge to Proposed 'US Military Bases'

- Constitutional challenge to the 'Complementary Agreement for Cooperation and Technical Assistance on Defence and Security Between the Governments of the Republic of Colombia and the United States of America', signed at Bogotá, 30 October 2009 [*Demanda de inconstitucionalidad contra el "Acuerdo complementario para la cooperación y asistencia técnica en defensa y seguridad entre los gobiernos de la República de Colombia y de los Estados Unidos de América", suscrito en Bogotá el 30 de octubre de 2009*] Files D-7964/D-7965 (cumulated). Constitutional Court Providence 288/10, 17 August 2010. M.P.: Jorge Iván Palacio Palacio

After an intense debate at both the national and regional levels, Bogotá and Washington entered into a new bilateral treaty by fast track (simplified treaties) in 2009 to allow for greater military cooperation between the two countries. Litigation was initiated before the Colombian Constitutional Court arguing that the treaty was unconstitutional because Senate approval is required to authorise the 'transit of foreign troops' across Colombian territory specifically as well for the ordinary legal incorporation of treaties generally. The Constitutional Court did not pronounce on the merits of the treaty, but only on procedural form ordering the government to pass the treaty to Congress for its approval.

The most controversial aspect of the treaty envisages US military utilisation of Colombian military bases. Colombian public opinion and the Colombian political opposition were strongly against any such arrangement. The Venezuelan President, Hugo Chávez, even weighed into the Colombian debate arguing that the bilateral treaty represented a plan for extraterritorial 'US Military bases', which his government perceived to be a violation of Colombian sovereignty and a threat (aggression) to neighbouring States including Venezuela. Under the terms of the treaty it can be see that the public debate is political rather than legally substantive. The more significant issue is that US military members, their families and their private contractors are all to enjoy the equivalent of diplomatic or consular privileges and immunities from Colombian national jurisdiction in case of breaches of international or domestic law.

RAFAEL A. PRIETO SANJUÁN

---

[130] UNGA Res. 2391(XXIII), annex, UN GAOR, Supp. No. 18, p 40, UN Doc. A/7218 (1968), 26 November 1968, entered into force 11 November 1970, in accordance with Article VIII.

CYPRUS[131]

Treaty Action—Objection to Reservation to the Incendiary Weapons Protocol

- *Convention on Prohibitions or Restrictions on the Use of Certain Conventional Weapons*, 'Cyprus: Objection to the Reservation Made by the United States of America upon Consenting to be Bound by Protocol III Annexed to the Above Named Convention', C.N.51.2010.TREATIES-5 (Depositary Notification) (5 February 2010), <http://treaties.un.org/doc/Publication/CN/2010/CN.51.2010-Eng.pdf>

Cyprus objected to the reservation of the United States to Protocol III to the *Convention on Certain Conventional Weapons.*[132] The objection is identical in content to the one raised by Hellas.[133]

Treaty Action—Entry into Force for Cyprus of Explosive Remnants of War Protocol

- *Protocol on Explosive Remnants of War to the Convention on Prohibitions or Restrictions on the Use of Certain Conventional Weapons*, 'Cyprus: Consent to be Bound', C.N.160.2010.TREATIES-3 (Depositary Notification) (11 March 2010), <http://treaties.un.org/doc/Publication/CN/2010/CN.160.2010-Eng.pdf>

As reported in the 2009 *Yearbook of International Humanitarian Law,*[134] Cyprus ratified the *Protocol on Explosive Remnants of War to the Convention on Prohibitions or Restrictions on the Use of Certain Conventional Weapons which may be deemed to be Excessively Injurious or to have Indiscriminate Effects.*[135] Cyprus has expressed its consent to be bound to the Secretary General of the United Nations and the Protocol entered into force for Cyprus on 11 September 2010.

Treaty Action—Ratification of the Optional Protocol to the Convention on the Rights of the Child on the Involvement of Children in Armed Conflicts

- Law that Amends the (Ratification) Laws of 1990 and 2000 on the Convention of the Rights of the Child, Law 9(III)/2010, Official Gazette of the Republic of Cyprus, issue 4131, 14 May 2010, <http://www.mof.gov.cy/mof/gpo/gpo.nsf/All/23A67545AD41EBF0C2257723002FB336/$file/4131%2014.5.2010%20PARARTIMA%201o%20MEROS%20III.pdf>

---

[131] Information and commentaries by Konstantinos Mastorodimos, Doctoral candidate, Queen Mary College, University of London and Attorney-at-law, Thessaloniki, Greece. The Report does not cover developments in the self-proclaimed 'Turkish Republic of Northern Cyprus'.

[132] *Protocol on Prohibitions or Restrictions on the Use of Incendiary Weapons*, opened for signature 10 October 1980, 1342 UNTS 171 (entered into force 2 December 1983).

[133] See the current volume of the *YIHL*, Report on Hellas (Greece).

[134] 12 *YIHL* (2009) p 525.

[135] Opened for signature 28 November 2003, 2399 UNTS (entered into force 12 November 2006).

Cyprus ratified the Optional Protocol in 2010. The instrument of ratification was deposited to the UN Secretary General,[136] containing a declaration, reported in the 2008 *Yearbook of International Humanitarian Law*,[137] and an objection. The latter relates to the declaration of Turkey which confines its treaty relations only to states that it recognizes and with which it has diplomatic relations. For Cyprus, Turkey's declaration is a reservation raising 'doubt as to the commitment of Turkey to the object and purpose of the Convention on the Rights of the Child and of the said Protocol'. Nonetheless Cyprus values its objection and Turkey's Declaration as not precluding the entry into force of the Convention of the Rights to the Child or the Optional Protocol between the two states. The Protocol entered into force for Cyprus on 2 August 2010.

Cases—Exhaustion of Local Remedies in Northern Cyprus

- *Demopoulos* v. *Turkey*, European Court of Human Rights, Grand Chamber, Applications No. 46113/99, 3843/02, 13751/02, 13466/03, 14163/04, 10200/04, 19993/04, 21819/04, Admissibility, 1 March 2010

A large number of Cypriot applicants have applied over the years to the European Court of Human Rights with regard to acts and practices of the regime in northern Cyprus. Many of these applications concerned deprivation of property and this violation was acknowledged and remedied by the Court in the past. Thus, indirectly, the Court has provided a leeway for violations of the rule relating to respect of private property in occupied territory.[138] The administration in Northern Cyprus has created, with the encouragement of the Court, an internal body (the Immovable Property Commission) and procedure, which would provide reparation in such cases. Despite the objections by the applicants and the intervening Cypriot government, based, *inter alia*, on the unlawful character of occupation and the ineffectiveness of the procedure, the Court has found that it constitutes an adequate local remedy which the applicants should exhaust before initiating litigation before the European Court of Human Rights.

KONSTANTINOS MASTORODIMOS

---

[136] *Optional Protocol to the Convention on the Rights of the Child on the Involvement of Children in Armed Conflict*, 'Cyprus: Ratification', C.N.562.2010.TREATIES-8 (Depositary Notification) (2 July 2010), <http://treaties.un.org/doc/Publication/CN/2010/CN.562.2010-Eng.pdf>.

[137] 11 *YIHL* (2008) p 464.

[138] *Regulations* annexed to *Hague Convention (IV) Respecting the Laws and Customs of War on Land* of 1907, Art. 46; J.M. Henckaerts and L. Doswald-Beck, *Customary International Humanitarian Law*, (Geneva, ICRC 2005) Vol. I, rule 51, pp 179–182.

ESTONIA[139]

Legislation—Peacetime Rules of Engagement—Renegade Aircraft

- *Organisation of the Defence Force Act* [*Kaitseväe korralduse seadus*], 19 June 2008
- *Deciding on the Use of Force by a Competent Military Commander for National Defence in Time of Peace* [*Pädeva ülema poolt riigi sõjaliseks kaitsmiseks jõu kasutamise otsustamine rahuajal*], Government Regulation, 27 November 2008
- *Use of Force to Deter a Threat Caused by a Civil Aircraft* [*Jõu kasutamine tsiviilõhusõiduki tekitatud ohu tõrjumiseks*], Government Regulation, 11 December 2008

In 2008, the Parliament adopted the *Organisation of the Defence Force Act*, which along with its implementing regulations, entered into force on 1 January 2009. The law deals with the structure and management of the Defence Force, but also with the circumstances of the use of military force. According to the Act, the Defence Force may use armed force: (a) in the interests of national defence; (b) while participating in an international military operation; (c) in demining operations; and (d) to a very limited extent, to maintain security domestically.

Perhaps of wider interest are the circumstances under which military force may be used for national defence. First of all, the Commander-in-Chief of the Defence Force is empowered to authorize the use of force during a 'state of war' declared pursuant to the Constitution.

Second, force may be used in the event of an armed attack against Estonia from abroad. In such circumstances, the Minister of Defense is empowered to authorize the use of force. However, in circumstances where the seeking of instructions from the Minister is either impracticable or impossible, a military commander whose unit has come under attack or who has witnessed the attack first hand may authorize the use of force. He or she may do so strictly to the extent that it is necessary to 'repel or impede' the attack, provided that the attack has progressed into Estonian territory (including territorial waters or airspace) and that all other measures have been exhausted.

Third, force may be used in order to deter a threat emanating from a civilian aircraft—this is the legal basis for taking forcible measures against 'renegade' aircraft. Again, the Minister of Defense, or another designated minister, is the relevant authority. However, he or she may authorize resort to force only if a number of cumulative conditions are met: (i) the aircraft is not flying according to schedule; (ii) the aircraft does not abide by the instruction of air traffic controllers or pilots of State aircraft; (iii) a visual check from a state aircraft or other information give reason to believe that the aircraft would be used to cause the deaths of persons outside the aircraft; (iv) attempts to force the aircraft to leave Estonian airspace or to land have proven ineffective or impracticable; (v) no other measures

---

[139] Information and commentaries by Rain Liivoja (Research Fellow, Asia Pacific Centre for Military Law, Melbourne Law School). These notes cover 2009 and 2010.

are available to prevent the attack by the civilian aircraft; (vi) use of force against the aircraft would result in damage significantly smaller than would presumably be caused by an attack by the civilian aircraft.

Treaty Action and Legislation—Terrorism

- *Council of Europe Convention on the Prevention of Terrorism*, Warsaw, 16 May 2005
- Amendments to the *Penal Code*, 11 March 2009

Estonia ratified the *Council of Europe Convention on the Prevention of Terrorism* on 15 May 2009. In this context, the Parliament amended the *Penal Code* by inserting a new section, which proscribes financing or otherwise knowingly supporting acts of terrorism or terrorist organizations.[140] The amendments took effect on 6 April 2009. Acts of terrorism, belonging to a terrorist organization, as well as preparation of, or incitement to, terrorist acts had been criminalized earlier.[141] The Convention entered into force for Estonia on 1 September 2010.

Treaty Action—Terrorism

- *International Convention for the Suppression of the Financing of Terrorism*, New York, 9 December 1999

Article 2(1)(b) of the *International Convention for the Suppression of the Financing of Terrorism* declares it an offence to provide or collect funds for carrying out:

> [an] act intended to cause death or serious bodily injury to a civilian, or to any other person not taking an active part in the hostilities in a situation of armed conflict, when the purpose of such act, by its nature or context, is to intimidate a population, or to compel a government or an international organization to do or to abstain from doing any act.

On 3 March 2010, when acceding to the Convention, Yemen made a reservation with respect to this provision. On 24 November 2010, Estonia lodged with the depositary the following objection:

> The Government of the Republic of Estonia has carefully examined the reservation made on 3 March 2010 by the Government of Yemen to Article 2(1)(b) of the Convention.
>
> The Government of Estonia wishes to recall that by acceding to the Convention, a State commits itself to suppress the financing of all terrorist acts. The reservation purports to exclude the suppression of the financing of acts of terrorism 'intended to cause death or serious bodily injury to a civilian, or to any other person not taking an active part in the hostilities in a situation of armed conflict' and thus is contrary to the object and purpose of the Convention.
>
> According to customary international law as codified in the Vienna Convention on the Law of Treaties, a reservation incompatible with the object and purpose of the Convention shall not be permitted.
>
> The Government of Estonia therefore objects to the aforesaid reservations made by the Government of the Republic of Yemen to the Convention.

---

[140] *Penal Code*, s. 237-3.

[141] *Penal Code*, ss. 237, 237-1, 237-2.

> This objection shall not preclude the entry into force in its entirety of the Convention as between the Republic of Estonia and the Republic of Yemen.

State Policy—Legal Aspect of Cyber Warfare

- Address by the President of the Republic of Estonia, HE Mr Toomas Hendrik Ilves, to the United Nations General Assembly, 25 September 2009, <http://www.president.ee/en/official-duties/speeches/2688-president-ilves-at-the-64th-session-of-the-general-assembly-of-the-united-nations-in-new-york/index.html>

The President suggested that there had been an increase in global cyber-threats and pointed out that cyber-attacks were becoming both more complex and more frequent. He noted that such cyber-threats endangered not only vital IT-systems but whole communities. He then went on to say that:

> This growing global concern demands both a better coordinated international approach and an enhanced legal domestic framework, including steps to criminalise malevolent cyber acts. Our long-term aim should be the creation of a universal cyber culture—a universally accessible, secure and safe environment for all.

State Policy—Protection of Humanitarian Aid Workers

- Address by the President of the Republic of Estonia, HE Mr Toomas Hendrik Ilves, to the United Nations General Assembly, 29 September 2010, <http://www.president.ee/en/official-duties/speeches/5057-president-of-the-republic-of-estonia-at-the-general-assembly-of-the-united-nations-in-new-york/index.html>

The President spoke of Estonia's concern about the 'increasingly frequent violations of humanitarian principles in conflict zones'. In particular, he mentioned that humanitarian emblems and flags no longer provided adequate protection to the persons working under them. In this light, the President said that '[w]e must step up our efforts and press for increased security for humanitarian aid workers. After all, it is the responsibility of governments to ensure the safety and security of humanitarian personnel working on their territory'.

RAIN LIIVOJA

FINLAND[142]

Cases—Genocide

- *Prosecutor* v. *Bazaramba*, Case No. R 09/404, District Court of Itä-Uusimaa, Judgment, 11 June 2010

In 2007, the Finnish authorities arrested Mr Francoise Bazaramba, a Burundian-born Baptist minister who had settled in Finland, on suspicion of having

[142] Information and commentaries by Jani Leino (Legal Adviser, Finnish Red Cross) and Rain Liivoja (Research Fellow, Asia Pacific Centre for Military Law, Melbourne Law School). These notes cover 2009 and 2010.

participated in the 1994 Rwandan genocide. The Rwandan government sought to have him extradited but Finland refused, citing its obligations under the *Convention for the Protection of Human Rights and Fundamental Freedoms* to ensure that Mr Bazaramba gets a fair trial.

The Finnish Public Prosecutor's Office subsequently charged Mr Bazaramba with genocide, and alternatively with several counts of murder, committed in the Maraba sector of Rwanda. The case proceeded to trial in September 2009. The extensive proceedings involved hearing the testimony of some 70 witnesses, for which purpose the court held public sittings in Rwanda and in Tanzania.[143]

In a judgment handed down on 11 June 2010, the District Court of Itä-Uusimaa found Mr Bazaramba guilty of genocide and sentenced him to life imprisonment. While the court was not convinced that he had personally killed anyone, it found that Mr Bazaramba had on several occasions incited and ordered violence against the Tutsis, coordinated the use of road blocks and night patrols against them, assisted in the burning of their homes, and participated in the distribution of their property—all with the intention of destroying the Tutsis as a group.

The court held that it had jurisdiction to hear the charges of genocide by virtue of the universality principle. Interestingly, the court deemed it necessary to ascertain that Finnish law recognised universal jurisdiction both at the time the judgment was rendered and at the time that the offences were committed. With respect to the alternative charges of murder, the court pointed to a provision of Finnish law that embodies the principle of 'vicarious administration of justice'. This allows Finland to prosecute an offence perpetrated abroad if the offender is found in Finland but cannot be extradited, provided that he was also punishable at the place of commission (which, in this instance, the Rwandan authorities duly confirmed).

The court went on to observe that even though the *Convention on the Prevention and Punishment of the Crime of Genocide* is not directly applicable in the Finnish legal order, its provisions could be used to interpret the provision of Finnish criminal law concerning genocide.[144] In particular, the court held that international sources would be relevant where international law leads to a narrower conception of an offence than national law. In this light and referring in particular to the *Jelisić*[145] case before the ICTY and the *Bagosora*[146] case before the ICTR,

---

[143] See also R. Liivoja, 'Dish of the Day: *Justice sans frontiers à la finlandaise*', 1 *Helsinki Review of Global Governance* (2010) pp 20–22.

[144] In this connection, the court also referred to the principles of interpretation laid down in the *Vienna Convention on the Law of Treaties*, even though, one should add, the Vienna Convention does not directly apply to treaties predating it, such as the *Genocide Convention*.

[145] *Prosecutor* v. *Jelisić*, Case No. IT-95-10-A, ICTY, Appeals Chamber, Judgment, 5 July 2001.

[146] *Prosecutor* v. *Bagosora*, Case No. ICTR-98-41-T, Trial Chamber, Judgment and Sentence, 18 December 2008.

the court rejected the defence's claim that planning constituted an element of the definition of genocide.

A further challenge was posed by the defence's arguments that some of the witnesses—themselves genocide suspects before Rwandan courts—had given their pre-trial statements under torture. While the court conceded that prison conditions in Rwanda had been partly inhumane, it believed this to have resulted from overcrowding, not coercive attempts to extract testimony. However, the court set aside the testimony of two witnesses in light of specific allegations of actual torture.

In sentencing, the judges noted that, had Mr Bazaramba acted without *dolus specialis*, some of his conduct would have amounted to murder. For murder, however, a life imprisonment would be appropriate. Accordingly, the court found it impossible to apply any other punishment in this case.

Both the prosecution and defence have appealed the judgment.

Legislation—Torture

- *Act to Amend the Penal Code*, 4 December 2009, Act of Parliament No. 990/2009

On 1 January 2010, an amendment to the *Criminal Code* entered into force, explicitly criminalising torture. While different acts of torture could previously be punished as, for example aggravated assault, there was no provision criminalising torture as such. The amending legislation inserted a new section into Chap. 11 (War Crimes and Crimes against Humanity) of the *Criminal Code*, which reads as follows:

Section 9a. Torture

1. An official who inflicts severe pain or suffering, whether physical or mental, on a person

   (1) for the purpose of obtaining from him or her or a third person a confession or information;
   (2) for the purpose of punishing him or her for an act he or she or a third person has committed or is suspected of having committed;
   (3) for the purpose of intimidating or coercing him or her or a third person; or
   (4) for any reason based on his or her race, national or ethnic origin, colour, language, sex, age, family ties, sexual preference, genetic origin, disability, state of health, religion, political opinion, political or industrial activity or another comparable circumstance, shall be sentenced for *torture* to imprisonment for at least 2 years and at most 12 years as well as to dismissal (from office).

2. An official with whose consent or acquiescence an act referred to in subsection 1 is committed by a subordinate or by a person who is factually under the command or control of that official, shall also be sentenced for torture.
3. An attempt is punishable.

4. The provisions of this section apply also to a person elected to a public office, to a person exercising public authority and, with the exception of dismissal, to an employee of a public corporation and a foreign public official.[147]

The definition of torture closely follows that of the *Convention against Torture*.[148] However, while the Convention speaks generically about 'discrimination of any kind' as one motivational element for torture, Finnish law supplies an indicative list of discriminatory bases complemented by a reference to 'another comparable circumstance'. The government bill specifically noted that the amendment would not affect the definition of torture as a war crime or as a crime against humanity.

Legislation—Piracy—Detention

- *An Act on the Processing of Criminal Matters of Detainees Suspected of Piracy or Armed Robbery in Connection with the European Union Military Crisis Management Operation EUNAVFOR* [*Laki Euroopan unionin sotilaallisen kriisinhallintaoperaation EUNAVFOR Atalantan yhteydessä merirosvoudesta tai aseellisesta ryöstöstä epäiltyä koskevan rikosasian käsittelystä*], 3 December 2010, Act of Parliament No. 1034/2010

In November 2010, the Finnish Parliament approved Finnish participation in the EU-led EUNAVFOR Operation ATALANTA off the coast of Somalia.[149] In preparation for this participation, legislation was drafted on the treatment of persons suspected of piracy or of armed robbery detained by Finnish troops in the operation.

The government bill submitted in September 2010 noted that, in relation to piracy, Finland could invoke universal jurisdiction.[150] However, the Act established that Finnish authorities would investigate alleged criminal acts for the purposes of prosecution before Finnish courts only when there was a nexus to Finland. In other words, investigation would only occur when the criminal act was directed at a Finnish vessel or person, or the suspect was a Finnish national. In other cases, Finland would hand over the suspects in accordance with agreements made by the EU with third States. However, according to section 4 (decision not to exercise criminal jurisdiction) of the Act, individuals held on a vessel sailing under the Finnish flag may not be handed over to a State where they may face the death penalty, be subjected to torture or some other inhumane or degrading treatment, would not receive a fair trial, or where the receiving State might hand over the suspect to another State where the aforementioned conditions may materialise.

[147] This translation appears in the 'Fifth and Sixth Periodic Reports of Finland under Article 19 of the Convention against Torture and Other Cruel, Inhuman or Degrading Treatment or Punishment, Doc. CAT/C/FIN/5-6 (29 November 2010), para 11.

[148] See *Convention against Torture and Other Cruel, Inhuman or Degrading Treatment or Punishment*, opened for signature 4 February 1985, 1465 UNTS 85, Art. 1(1) (entered into force 26 June 1987).

[149] EK 28/2010 vp (26 November 2010).

[150] HE 117/2010 vp.

According to the government bill, in cases where Finland would not initiate criminal investigations and would not receive adequate assurances as to the treatment of the detainee, the suspect should be let free.

Government Policy—Whether Finland Is 'at War' in Afghanistan

During 2009 and 2010, the media in Finland regularly addressed the nature of the Finnish involvement in Afghanistan as a result of the country's participation in the ISAF operation. In 2009, a researcher at the Finnish Institute of International Affairs published an opinion piece in a leading daily, arguing that Finland was 'at war' because of the actions it is taking in Afghanistan.[151] During 2009 and 2010, Finnish troops serving in Northern Afghanistan were subject to a number of individual armed attacks. One of these attacks resulted in fighting that lasted for several hours. According to news reports Finnish troops also supported the Afghan army in its operations against rebels.

In 2009, when asked whether Finland was indeed engaged in 'war', the Minister for Foreign affairs said, 'Absolutely not, and to my mind it would be irresponsible to claim otherwise. This is a crisis management operation with a UN mandate'.[152] In January 2010 the Minister of Defence was directly asked whether Finland was a party to a war. He responded by stating:

> Legally speaking Finland is involved in a UN mandated crisis management operation and in this respect is not at war. This official determination should not of course obscure the fact that the circumstances are such that one can also come to another conclusion. Legally and politically speaking the answer is no, but the situation is very challenging.[153]

In a policy paper submitted to the Parliament in February 2010, the government outlined that future military participation in the ISAF operation would include the funding and training and mentoring of the Afghan national army.[154] During 2010, Finland increased the number of its military personnel in ISAF from 120 to 195.

Government Policy—Use of Force in International Military Crisis Management

- Rules of Engagement Workgroup Report [ROE-työryhmän raportti], submitted to the Ministry of Defense, 30 September 2010[155]

A working group set up by the Permanent Secretary of Ministry of Defence in March 2010 reviewed national laws and regulations relating to the use of force by

[151] C. Salonius-Pasternak, 'Suomi on paraikaa sotaa käyvä maa', *Helsingin Sanomat*, 24 July 2009, <www.hs.fi/paakirjoitus/artikkeli/1135247907487>.

[152] 'Stubb ja Häkämies: Suomi ei ole sodassa', *Helsingin Sanomat*, 25 July 2009, <www.hs.fi/ulkomaat/artikkeli/1135247928412>.

[153] Mutta onko Suomi sodassa? Kolme kysymystä puolustusministeri Jyri Häkämiehelle. *Helsingin Sanomat*, 19 January 2010, p B1.

[154] Governmental Policy Paper on the Situation in Afghanistan and the Finnish Participation in the ISAF Operation [Valtioneuvoston selonteko Afganistanin tilanteesta ja Suomen osallistumisesta ISAF-operaatioon], VNS 1/2010 vp, 12 February 2010, <http://formin.finland.fi/public/download.aspx?ID=53525&GUID={D85F38F9-9FB4-4938-9513-E59203CB9C16}>.

[155] For the text in Finnish, see <www.defmin.fi/files/1651/101025_ROE_tr_raportti_FINAL.pdf>.

Finnish armed forces participating in international military crisis management. According to the working group's unanimous report submitted in September 2010, there is no need for amendments to current domestic legislation related to the use of force. The working group observed that—along with the rules of engagement of an individual crisis management operation—the principles and restrictions set for the use of force nationally in section 27 (use of force) of the *Act on Military Crisis Management* (Act No. 211/2006) 'must always be in accordance with international law and humanitarian law'. The working group noted that it is important to train all personnel in the rules of engagement prior to deployment.

Government Policy—Comprehensive Crisis Management

- Finland's Comprehensive Crisis Management Strategy, 13 November 2009, Publications of the Ministry for Foreign Affairs 16/2009, <http://formin.finland.fi/public/download.aspx?ID=50401&GUID={BDE426BA-1404-4216-8239-4AAA91BB84A7}>

In November 2009, the Cabinet Committee on Foreign and Security Policy approved Finland's Comprehensive Crisis Management Strategy. Key objectives of the Strategy include enhanced capacity to support security sector reform and rule of law development as well as increased emphasis on human rights and equality issues in crisis management activities. According to its strategic outlines, 'Finland emphasises the importance of respecting international law and the protection of civilians in crises'. According to the Strategy, crisis management personnel's knowledge in human rights and humanitarian law will be strengthened. Crisis management personnel 'must be able to recognise humanitarian law and human rights violations, and react accordingly within the boundaries of their mandate'. In a section titled 'The International Red Cross and other humanitarian actors', the Strategy stipulates that '[i]n international cooperation Finland stresses the need to respect international humanitarian law and the neutral and impartial role of the International Red Cross and other humanitarian actors in armed conflicts'. It is possible that some uses of the expression 'international humanitarian law' in the strategy refer to 'the international law related to humanitarian aid' rather than to 'the law of armed conflict' in its entirety.

Jani Leino and Rain Liivoja

FRANCE[156]

Treaty Implementation—Rome Statute of the International Criminal Court

- Law No. 2010-930 of 9 August 2010 adapting the French Criminal Law to the establishment of the International Criminal Court (*Official Gazette*, 10 August 2010, p. 14678, text No. 1) [Loi no. 2010-930 du 9 aout 2010 portant adaptation

156 Information and commentaries provided by Professor Paul Tavernier, Professor Emeritus Paris-Sud University (Paris XI), Director, Centre de Recherches et d'Etudes sur les droits de l'Homme et le droit humanitaire (CREDHO).

du droit pénal à l'institution de la Cour pénale internationale (*Journal Officiel* du 10 août 2010, p. 14678, texte no. 1)]

- Bill adapting the French Criminal Law to the *Rome Statute*: Senate No. 308 (15 May 2007)
- Senate Patrice Gélard's Report (Laws' Commission), No. 326 (14 May 2008); discussion and adoption on 10 June 2008
- National Assembly. Nicole Ameline's Advisory Report (Commission for Foreign Affairs), No. 1828 (8 July 2009)
- National Assembly Thierry Mariany's Report (Laws' Commission), No. 2517 (19 May 2010); discussion and adoption on 13 July 2010
- Constitutional Council, Decision No. 2010-612 DC of 5 August 2010 (*Official Gazette*, 10 August 2010).

The Bill adapting the French Criminal Law to the *Rome Statute of the International Criminal Court* was first discussed, amended and adopted by the Senate on June 2008.[157] Two years later, on 13 July 2010, it was then discussed by the National Assembly and examined by the Constitutional Council before the law was promulgated and published in the Official Gazette. That protracted procedure indicates that the matter was most sensitive and complicated.

The new Law constitutes the third stage of adapting French Law to the *Rome Statute*: the first stage involved the amendment of the Constitution in 1999[158] and the second stage was the 2002 law on cooperation with the ICC.[159] The 2010 Law comprises ten articles and is divided into three chapters. Chapter I, the most important (Articles 1–7), contains clauses amending the *Criminal Code*. Chapter II (Article 8) modifies the criminal procedure code and Chap. III (Articles 9–10) includes final clauses.

The text adopted by the National Assembly was the same as the one adopted by the Senate in 2008. Several amendments were discussed but they were rejected. Some questions were put before the Constitutional Council by socialist members of Parliament but the law was declared in conformity with the French Constitution. In its decision, the Constitutional Council affirmed that even if the *Rome Statute* is now mentioned explicitly in the Constitution, that does not mean that the Council must review the compatibility of the adapting Law with that Convention. Such a review could be made by the civil and criminal Courts, and the administrative Tribunals.

The *Rome Statute* makes no distinction between war crimes and genocide or crimes against humanity in relation to statutory limitations—in fact statutory limitations are explicitly excluded for all categories of *Rome Statute* crimes. Nevertheless the French Law introduces (Article 7) such a distinction. Moreover Article 462-10 of the *Criminal Code* now provides for an extension of statutory limitations to 30 years for war crimes and 20 years for 'war offences' (délits de

157 See 12 *YIHL* (2009) pp 536–537.

158 See 2 *YIHL*.(1999) p 359.

159 See 5 *YIHL* (2002) p 505.

guerre). The Constitutional Council is of the view that such a double distinction is not contrary to the Constitution.

Another point very much debated involved the exercise of universal jurisdiction, or, as the French government described it, extra-territorial jurisdiction. The most controversial clause required a 'usual place of residence' (résidence habituelle) of the prosecuted person in France. That provision was introduced by the Senate and extends the possibilities for applying universal jurisdiction (beyond a requirement of French nationality—of either the accused or of the victims), but was still considered as too restrictive by some human rights activists. The National Advisory Commission on Human Rights also expressed its concern on that question in an opinion on the implementation of the *Convention against Torture and Other Cruel, Inhuman or Degrading Treatment or Punishment* adopted on 15 April 2010 (plenary session).

The French government emphasized two more points concerning the criminal responsibility of private companies and legal entities (Articles 462-5 and 462-6 of the *Criminal Code*), jurisdiction over which is not provided for in the *Rome Statute*, and the prohibition of recruiting young people below the age of 18 years for military service (Article 7 and new Article 461-7 of the *Criminal Code*) though international law has lowered the bar to 15 years.

It will be interesting to examine in the future how the French Courts and Tribunals will interpret the *Rome Statute* and the French criminal law as the definitions of crimes are sometimes different. The potential for such review by the courts is not excluded because the Constitutional Council only examines the compatibility and the conformity of the Law with the Constitution and not with the *Rome Statute* itself.

Treaty Implementation—Rome Statute of the International Criminal Court

- National Advisory Commission on Human Rights. Opinion on adapting the French Criminal Law to the *Rome Statute of the International Criminal Court* [Commission Nationale consultative des droits de l'Homme (CNCDH): Avis sur l'adaptation de la législation pénale française au Statut de Rome relatif à la Cour pénale internationale]. Adopted on 4 February 2010 (plenary session)

The National Advisory Commission on Human Rights recalled its previous opinions on the subject of implementation of the *Rome Statute* in 2006[160] and 2008[161] and regretted that the French government did not apply the recommendations included in these opinions (see supra on the 2010 Law adapting the French Criminal Law to the establishment of the International Criminal Court).

Treaty Implementation—Cluster Munitions

- Law No. 2010-819 of 20 July 2010 on the elimination of *Cluster Munitions* (*Official Gazette*, 22 July 2010, p 13425, text No. 1) [Loi no. 2010-819 du 20

---

160 See 9 *YIHL* (2006) p 481.

161 See 11 *YIHL* (2008) p 470.

juillet 2010, tendant à l'élimination des armes à sous-munitions, *Journal Officiel*, 21 juillet 2010, p. 13425, texte No. 1]

- Bill No. 113 (2009–2010)
- Senate. Joëlle Garriaud-Maylam's Report (Commission for Foreign Affairs), No. 382 (2009–2010); discussion and adoption on 6 May 2010
- National Assembly. Françoise Hostalier's Report (Defence Commission), No. 2641, discussion and adoption on 6 July 2010

After the adoption in 2009 of a law authorizing ratification of the *Cluster Munitions Convention*[162] the French Parliament adopted on 6 July 2010 a Law aimed at the elimination of *Cluster Munitions* which inserts new provisions into the *Defence Code* (code de la défense) to introduce and translate the Convention's clauses in the French Law, only a few days before the entry into force of the Convention on 1 August 2010.

The National Advisory Commission on Human Rights recommended (see *infra*) full implementation of the Convention and criticized some missing points in the Bill. Several of the Commission's recommendations were included in the final text of the Law, such as the definition of cluster munitions which extends to explosive bomblets. Under section 1, the Definitions in the legislation are the same as the definitions contained in the Oslo Convention.

In section 2 (legal régime), the Bill provides for destruction of French stockpiles of cluster munitions within 8 years consistent with Article 3-2 of the Convention which requires destruction 'as soon as possible'. The temporal precision was added in the final text, as recommended by the National Advisory Commission. The CNCDH recommended the extension of the National Commission on the Elimination of Antipersonnel Mines (CNEMA)'s mandate to include supervision of the law aimed at the elimination of *Cluster Munitions* and Article 2 of the Law includes such a clause.

Treaty Implementation—Cluster Munitions

- National Advisory Commission on Human Rights. Opinion on the preliminary implementation bill of the Oslo Convention on cluster munitions [Commission Nationale consultative des droits de l'Homme (CNCDH): Avis sur le projet de loi tendant à l'élimination des armes à sous-munitions]. Adopted on 15 April 2010 (plenary session).

The National Advisory Commission is generally satisfied with the Bill aiming to eliminate cluster munitions, which introduces the Oslo Convention into French Law. Nevertheless the Commission identifies several clauses which require more precise wording. Most of these clauses were amended in the final text adopted by the French Parliament (see supra).

[162] See 12 *YIHL* (2009) pp 535–536.

Treaty Implementation—Protection of the Red Cross, Red Crescent and Red Crystal Emblems

- National Advisory Commission on Human Rights. Opinion on Protection and Use of the Red Cross, Red Crescent and Red Crystal emblems. [Commission Nationale consultative des droits de l'Homme (CNCDH): Avis sur la protection et l'utilisation des emblèmes de la Croix-Rouge, du Croissant-Rouge et du cristal rouge] Adopted on 15 April 2010 (plenary session).

The Red Cross Emblem was established in the first *Geneva Convention for the Amelioration of the Condition of the Wounded in Armies in the Field* of 1864 and on 17 July 2009 France ratified *Protocol Additional to the Geneva Conventions of 12 August 1949, and Relating to the Adoption of an Additional Distinctive Emblem*, adopted on 8 December 2005.[163]

In a detailed opinion, the National Advisory Commission on Human Rights identifies and explains the laws and regulations applicable in France. Most of the existing laws are old and no longer an adequate implementation of the relevant international instruments. A good example is the Law of 29 July 1913, amended on 6 July 1939. Thus, in the view of the Commission it is necessary to modify the French Laws and to modernize them.

The Commission adopted five recommendations: (1) all three protective emblems must be mentioned in the French Legislation; (2) the criminal law must be amended as suggested by the ICRC in a model law on the emblems; (3) the French Law has to introduce the distinction included in Article 44 of the *Geneva Convention for the Amelioration of the Condition of the Wounded and Sick in Armed Forces in the Field* (*First Geneva Convention*) between the use of the emblems to 'indicate' and the use to 'protect'; (4) the French Law must be amended as regards forgery, encroachment and treachery in using the different emblems; (5) the criminal law must be amended to conform with Article 8(2)(b)(vii) of the *Rome Statute*, which considers as a war crime to make 'improper use of a flag of truce, of the flag or of the military insignia and uniform of the enemy or of the United Nations, as well as of the distinctive emblems of the Geneva Conventions, resulting in death or serious personal injury'.

The fifth recommendation was implemented by the government and Article 461-29 of the *Criminal Code* now punishes as a war crime the improper use of the emblems of the *Geneva Conventions* (see supra).[164]

Cases Cooperation with the International Criminal Court

- *Case of Callixte Mbarushimana*, Criminal Court of Paris, 20 December 2010

---

[163] Law No. 2009-432 of 21 April 2009 authorizing the ratification of Protocol additional to the Geneva Conventions of 12 August 1949, and relating to the Adoption of an additional distinctive emblem (Protocol III) [Loi no. 2009-432 du 21 avril 2009 autorisant la ratification du protocole additionnel aux Conventions de Genève du 12 août 1949 relatif à l'adoption d'un signe distinctif additionnel (protocole III)].

[164] Law No. 2010-930 of 9 August 2010 adapting the French Criminal Law to the establishment of the International Criminal Court, Article 7.

On 20 December 2010, Callixte Mbarushimana, a Rwandan citizen and former UNDP employee, who enjoyed refugee status in France, was indicted by a French Criminal Court for his alleged participation to the genocide in Rwanda in 1994. That procedure was initiated more than 2 years before by the NGO CPCR (Collectif des parties civiles au Rwanda).

In the meantime, Callixte Mbarushimana was also indicted by the International Criminal Court and he was arrested on 10 October 2010 in France under a sealed Warrant issued on 28 September 2010 by the ICC for crimes against humanity and war crimes allegedly committed in 2009 by troops of the FDLR (Democratic Forces for the Liberation of Rwanda) in the Kivus, a province of the Democratic Republic of Congo.

In that case, cooperation between French Authorities and the ICC worked satisfactorily and the proceedings before the French tribunals (concerning the 1994 genocide) were significantly accelerated and boosted by the proceedings before the ICC (concerning the situation in the RDC, brought before the ICC in 2004). That is another side of the complementary jurisdiction of the ICC and a variation on what is provided for in Article 17 of the *Rome Statute*.

Cases—Compensation for Stolen Works of Art during World War II

- *Kaplan* et al. *Case,* Administrative Tribunal, Paris, 25 June 2010 [Tribunal administratif de Paris], text in *Actualité Juridique-Droit Administratif,* 2011, pp 343–347, with observations of Jean-Marie Pontier

The return of or compensation for goods, especially works of art, belonging to citizens of Jewish origin, which were stolen by occupying authorities during World War II raises very difficult questions. The *Kaplan* case provides some insight into the ways of compensation in France. In 1943, in Bordeaux, 151 pieces, including 78 paintings, were stolen and 3 of them were returned after the War. In 1999, a Decree established a Commission to facilitate compensation for stolen goods. That Commission, the so-called Commission for Compensation of Victims of Stealing [Commission d'indemnisation des victimes de spoliations, CIVS] is not a tribunal, but it recommends a solution and proposes an amount for compensation for stealing by occupying authorities or by the Vichy Government.

In that case the applicants claim that the compensation was not adequate and sufficient. Two main points were decided by the administrative tribunal in Paris. The first was the fixing of the date for assessment of the damage and the second concerned the amount of compensation. As regards the critical date for assessment of the loss, the Tribunal says that the loss must be evaluated at the time of spoliation or as soon after as it was possible to evaluate that loss, considering also the monetary depreciation. The Tribunal added that it is not possible to take into account the value of the piece in the current art market.

The second point is related to the amount of compensation. The Administrative Tribunal ruled that complete compensation was not provided for in the 1999 Decree, which provides only for the most precise possible compensation as at the relevant assessment date. Further, the Tribunal said that complete compensation was not possible in this case because of the nature of and circumstances surrounding the stolen pieces—in particular the differences between the objects and also the large time gap which has elapsed since the thefts—so that compensation was awarded for only some of the stolen works. Unfortunately, the Tribunal failed to indicate any criteria for determining which losses were eligible for compensation and which were not.

Prof. Jean-Marie Pontier considered, in the comments of the Administrative Tribunal, that some points still remain to be clarified by the State Council [Conseil d'Etat] if the *Kaplan* case is to proceed before him.

Cases—Article 1(F) of the Refugees Convention and the Alleged Planning of and Complicity in Genocide

- *Agathe Kanziga, Widow Habyarimana* v. *OFPRA [Office Français de Protection des Réfugiés et Apatrides/French Office for Refugees and Stateles Persons Protection]*, State Council [Conseil d'Etat], 16 October 2009. Text in *Revue générale de droit international public,* 2010, pp 662–667, with observations of Cyril Brami.
- *M.K. case*, State Council [Conseil d'Etat], 14 June 2010. text in *Actualité Juridique-Droit Administratif,* 2010, pp 1992–1995, with observations of Rodolphe Mésa and Sébastien Marmin.

Article 1(F) of the 1951 *Convention Relating to the Status of Refugees* reads as follows:

> The provisions of this Convention shall not apply to any person with respect to whom there are serious reasons for considering that: (a) he has committed a crime against peace, a war crime, or a crime against humanity, as defined in the international instruments drawn up to make provision in respect of such crimes.

Moreover Article 3(e) of the 1948 *Convention on the Prevention and Punishment of the Crime of Genocide* provides for punishment of 'complicity in genocide'. There are only a few judicial decisions in France about these provisions.

The State Council, the highest administrative court in France, recently applied and interpreted these two provisions in two cases. In the *M.K.* case. the Council quashed the decision of the Refugees Claims Commission (now National Court for the Right of Asylum) because the motivation was not explicit enough. The Claims Commission is not obliged to decide on guilt, but has to indicate more precisely the factual constituent elements of complicity, as required in the two conventions.

M.K. was refused asylum because he was considered an accomplice in the 1994 Rwanda genocide. In fact he was a beer seller and he continued to sell beer during a 3 month period in a region controlled by genocide authors, as the government encouraged the furnishing of militias and troops with beer for accomplishing their duties. These facts were not sufficient to prove the complicity of M.K. in the perpetration of the genocide.

The *Agathe Kanziga, Widow Habyarimana* case was quite different and more serious, because the role of Mrs Habyarimana in the preparation and planning of the genocide in Rwanda in 1994 is still very controversial. In that case the

Refugees Claims Commission applied Article 1(F)(a) of the 1951 Convention and refused asylum for Mrs Habyarimana. The State Council, as a court of cassation, upheld the decision, because the motivation for the Claims Commission decision was not wrong and was not based on either distorted facts or on mistakes concerning the law. In his comment, Cyril Brami observed that French Law is not very efficient. Mrs Habyarimana first came to France more than 13 years ago and was never taken before a criminal court. Moreover she was refused *de jure* asylum, but she can enjoy *de facto* asylum.

Cases—Prisoner of War Status

- *Manuel Noriega Case*, Paris Criminal Court [Tribunal correctionnel de Paris], 7 July 2010, see Fabien Grech, *Revue générale de droit international public,* 2010-4, p 851.

The former dictator and President of Panama, Manuel Noriega, was convicted on 7 July 2010 of money laundering and sentenced by the Paris Criminal Court to 7 years' imprisonment. He was already sentenced *in absentia* in 1999 to 10 years' imprisonment.

Former General Noriega was extradited from the United States to France on 27 April 2010 after he spent more than 20 years in US jails, with prisoner of war status. He claimed the same status in France, arguing that he could not be deprived of it, but the Ministry of Justice disagreed and denied him such status. Nevertheless the French authorities added that the detention conditions in the French jails are in conformity with the obligations arising pursuant to the *Geneva Conventions*. Moreover, though the French government was not obliged to do so, it authorized ICRC access to Noriega just as the ICRC had done in the US.

The government of Panama has requested the extradition of M. Noriega but first he must serve his current sentence in France.

Cases—Enforced Disappearances in Chile

- *Juan Manuel Contreras Sepulveda* et al. *Case,* Criminal Court of Paris, 17 December 2010

On 17 December 2010, 13 persons were sentenced *in absentia* by the Criminal Court of Paris for the enforced disappearances of four Franco-Chilean citizens: Georges Klein, Etienne Pesle, Alfonso Chanfeau and Jean-Yves Claudet, during the Pinochet dictatorship. The accused were not present during the trial and were not represented by a lawyer. The sentences issued extend from life sentences to 30, 25, 20 and 15 years imprisonment respectively.

The judgment of the Criminal Court of Paris was seen as an 'historic decision' by the FIDH (International Federation for Human Rights) and represents a victory for the victims. It was claimed that the judgment is the first to be delivered by a foreign tribunal identifying and punishing the perpetrators of enforced disappearances in Chile.

PAUL TAVERNIER

HELLAS (GREECE)[165]

Treaty Action—Failure to Destroy Anti-Personnel Land Mines

Hellas, as any party to the *Convention on the Prohibition of the Use, Stockpiling, Production and Transfer of Anti-Personnel Mines and on their Destruction,*[166] has an obligation to destroy anti-personnel mines in stockpile and mined areas. The deadline for its first obligation has expired since 1 March 2008, but Hellas has been unable to respect it.[167]

Treaty Action—Objection to Reservation to the Incendiary Weapons Protocol

- *Convention on Prohibitions or Restrictions on the Use of Certain Conventional Weapons*, 'Greece: Objection to the Reservation Made by the United States of America upon Consenting to be Bound by Protocol III Annexed to the Above Named Convention', C.N.48.2010.TREATIES-2 (Depositary Notification) (2 February 2010), <http://treaties.un.org/doc/Publication/CN/2010/CN.48.2010-Eng.pdf>

Hellas objected to the reservation[168] of the United States to Protocol III to the *Convention on Certain Conventional Weapons.*[169] The US has reserve[d] the right to use incendiary weapons against military objectives located in concentrations of civilians where it is judged that such use would cause fewer casualties and/or less collateral damage than alternative weapons, but in so doing will take all feasible precautions with a view to limiting the incendiary effects to the military objective and to avoiding, and in any event to minimizing, incidental loss of civilian life, injury to civilians and damage to civilian objects.

Hellas judged this reservation as incompatible with the object and purpose of the treaty. Nonetheless its position has not precluded the entry into force of the treaty between the US and Hellas, in its entirety.

165 Information and commentaries by Konstantinos Mastorodimos, Doctoral candidate, Queen Mary College, University of London and Attorney-at-law, Thessaloniki, Greece.

166 Opened for signature 18 September 1997, 2056 UNTS 211 (entered into force 1 March 1999).

167 See Hellenic Republic, *Convention on the Prohibition of the Use, Stockpiling, Production and Transfer of Anti-Personnel Mines and on Their Destruction: Reporting Formats for Article 7* (April 2009), <http://unog.ch/80256EDD006B8954/%28httpAssets%29/B96F01BE74415419C1257752003AA443/$file/Greece+2009.pdf> as well as the Landmine and Cluster Munition Monitor, *Greece* (2010), <http://www.the-monitor.org/index.php/cp/display/region_profiles/profile/71>.

168 *Convention on Prohibitions or Restrictions on the Use of Certain Conventional Weapons*, 'United States of America: Consent to be Bound by Protocol III', C.N.75.2009.TREATIES-1 (Depositary Notification) (21 January 2009), <http://treaties.un.org/doc/Publication/CN/2009/CN.75.2009-Eng.pdf>.

169 *Protocol on Prohibitions or Restrictions on the Use of Incendiary Weapons*, opened for signature 10 October 1980, 1342 UNTS 171 (entered into force 2 December 1983).

Treaty Body Decision—Ability of Greek Nationals to Enforce Domestic Judgments against a Foreign State

- Human Rights Committee, Communication No. 1507/2006, UN Doc. CCPR/C/100/D/1507/2006, 30 November 2010

Relatives of civilian victims of a massacre in occupied Hellas during World War II have brought an action for damages against Germany in Hellenic courts. The legal proceedings ended successfully for the applicants, but their subsequent effort to seize German property did not materialize because the Minister of Justice refused to consent to the enforcement of judgments, as required by the *Code of Civil Procedure*. The applicants have unsuccessfully pursued the issue in Hellenic Courts and in the European Court of Human Rights, claiming the incompatibility of the local law with human rights treaties. The latest episode in this dispute concerned a communication to the Human Rights Committee, where the applicants complained of violation of Articles 2.3 and 14.1 of the *International Covenant on Civil and Political Rights*.[170] The Hellas government argued that the limitation of the said rights is justified due to the customary law nature of immunity from execution in proceedings instituted against a foreign state. The Committee has ruled out the incompatibility of the local law with the Covenant 'without prejudice to future developments of international law'.[171] In their dissenting opinion three Committee members disagreed. They considered that the local law constituted a negation rather than a limitation of any effective remedy. Noting the developments in international human rights law, the dissenters refused to balance state immunity with human rights obligations because there is nothing in international law on the immunity of a foreign State preventing a State Party to the Covenant and the Optional Protocol from itself satisfying the judgment of its judicial authorities and seeking compensatory reparation from the foreign State, in circumstances where the foreign State resists enforcement.[172]

In sum, it appears that the individual right of remedy for violations of international humanitarian and human rights law continues to face significant barriers in its proper realization.

Konstantinos Mastorodimos

HUNGARY[173]

Military Operations—Participation in NATO Operations in Afghanistan

- Resolution 1059/2010 (III. 5.) of the Government on the amendment of Resolution 1014/2010 (I. 28.) of the Government on the amendment of Resolution

170 Opened for signature 16 December 1966, 999 UNTS 171 (entered into force 23 March 1976).

171 Human Rights Committee, Communication No. 1507/2006, UN Doc. CCPR/C/100/D/1507/2006, 30 November 2010, para 10.5.

172 Ibid., para 17.

173 Information and commentaries by Dr. Eszter Kirs, Department of International law, University of Miskolc.

2186/2008 (XII. 29.) of the Government on the continuing Hungarian participation in the military operations of the International Security Assistance Force (ISAF) in Afghanistan [*A Kormány 1059/2010. (III. 5.) Korm. Határozata az afganisztáni Nemzetközi Biztonsági Közreműködő Erők (ISAF) műveleteiben történő további magyar katonai szerepvállalásról szóló 2186/2008. (XII. 29.) Korm. Határozat módosításáról szóló 1014/2010. (I. 28.) Korm. határozat módosításáról*], adopted on 5 March 2010.[174]

- Resolution 1171/2010 (VIII. 18.) of the Government on the amendment of certain resolutions of the Government on the Hungarian participation in the military operations in Afghanistan [*A Kormány 1171/2010. (VIII. 18.) Korm. Határozata egyes afganisztáni katonai szerepvállalásról szóló kormányhatározatok módosításáról*], adopted on 18 August 2010.[175]
- Resolution 1242/2010 (XI. 17.) of the Government on the amendment of certain resolutions of the Government on the Hungarian participation in the military operations of the International Security Assistance Force (ISAF) in Afghanistan [*A Kormány 1242/2010. (XI. 17.) Korm. Határozata az afganisztáni Nemzetközi Biztonsági Közreműködő Erők (ISAF) műveleteiben történő magyar katonai szerepvállalásról szóló egyes kormányhatározatok módosításáról*], adopted on 17 November 2010.[176]

The foregoing resolutions of the government of Hungary provided for the extension of the participation of Hungary in the military operations of the ISAF in Afghanistan until 1 April 2011 and in the enforcement of OMLT (Operational Mentoring and Liaison Team) tasks until 31 August 2011.

Pappné Judit Ábrahám, a 32 year-old soldier belonging to the Hungarian contingent was killed in the province of Baghlan on 23 August 2010.[177]

Training of Security Forces—Participation in EU Operations in Somalia

- Resolution 1100/2010 (IV. 28.) of the Government on the Hungarian military participation in the mission of the European Union for the training of security forces in Somalia (EUTM Somalia) [*A Kormány 1100/2010. (IV. 28.) Korm. Határozata az Európai Uniónak a szomáliai biztonsági erők kiképzésére irányuló missziójához (EUTM Somalia) történő magyar katonai hozzájárulásról*], adopted on 28 April 2010.[178]

---

174 Hungarian Official Gazette (Magyar Közlöny), No. 32 (III. 5.), <http://www.kozlonyok.hu/nkonline/MKPDF/hiteles/mk10032.pdf>.

175 Hungarian Official Gazette (Magyar Közlöny), No. 134 (VIII. 18.), <http://www.kozlonyok.hu/nkonline/MKPDF/hiteles/mk10134.pdf>.

176 Hungarian Official Gazette (Magyar Közlöny), No. 175 (XI. 17.), <http://www.kozlonyok.hu/nkonline/MKPDF/hiteles/mk10175.pdf>.

177 HVG, 'Megöltek egy magyar katonanőt Afganisztánban, három társa megsérült' (23 August 2010), <http://hvg.hu/vilag/20100823_meghalt_magyar_katona>.

178 Hungarian Official Gazette (Magyar Közlöny), No. 63 (IV. 28.), <http://www.kozlonyok.hu/nkonline/MKPDF/hiteles/mk10063.pdf>.

Four servicemen of the Hungarian Armed Forces were deployed by the above mentioned resolution in Uganda to serve the EUTM Somalia from 31 March 2010 to 31 June 2011.

Multilateral Organizations—Senior Hungarian Appointment to NATO

Gábor Iklódy was appointed Assistant Secretary General of the NATO for Emerging Security Challenges. As such, he became the Secretary General's primary advisor on emerging security challenges and their potential implications for the security of the Alliance and a member of the Secretary General's senior management team. He has accomplished his duties in this position from 1 August 2010.[179]

Government Initiative—Prevention of Genocide

The Budapest Centre for the International Prevention of Genocide and other Mass Atrocities was established with contributions from the Hungarian Ministry of Foreign Affairs, the Central European University and the Károli Gáspár University of the Reformed Church.[180] The executive summary of the feasibility study for the establishment of the Center is available on the website of the Ministry of Foreign Affairs.[181]

Eszter Kirs

IRELAND[182]

Government Policy—Withdrawal of Irish Peacekeeping Contingent

- *Ireland withdraws from UN peacekeeping operation in Chad/Central African Republic (MINURCAT)*

In April 2010, the Irish government decided to withdraw its contingent of over 400 peacekeepers from Chad in what was described in UN circles as an 'untimely' and 'unfortunate' decision.[183] The reason given was the lack of certainty about the continuation of the mandate and the approach of the rainy season. The UN was not happy that Ireland pre-empted the decision to withdraw, but the Irish government considered that its options were limited and a decision needed to be made about the future of the mission. The Chad mission was regarded by many Irish personnel

---

[179] NATO, 'Gábor Iklódy' (20 December 2010), <http://www.nato.int/cps/en/SID-31B193E5-0855D573/natolive/who_is_who_66342.htm>.

[180] Ministry of Foreign Affairs, 'Martonyi János és Németh Zsolt beszéde a III. Emberi Jogi Fórumon' (18 October 2010), <http://www.kulugyminiszterium.hu/kum/hu/bal/Aktualis/Szovivoi_nyilatkozatok/20101018_emberjogi_forum_3.htm>.

[181] Ministry of Foreign Affairs, 'Executive Summary—Feasibility Study' (June 2009), <http://www.kulugyminiszterium.hu/kum/en/bal/foreign_policy/protection_human_rights/bp_nepirtas_megelozesi_kozpont/>.

[182] Information provided by Dr Ray Murphy, Irish Centre for Human Rights, National University of Ireland Galway, Ireland.

[183] See C. Lally, 'Troops to be withdrawn from UN Mission in Chad', *The Irish Times* (Dublin) 9 April 2010; R. Murphy, 'Why is UN leaving Chad to banditry and strife?', *The Irish Times* (Dublin) 11 May 2010.

who served there as the most physically challenging mission Ireland had participated into date. The security challenges were compounded by significant logistical issues. Getting enough water, food and fuel were major challenges to the day to day operations of the force. In Ireland, there was some initial opposition to the participation of defence force personnel in what was perceived as a 'French dominated' international force and there were calls to deploy the contingent instead with the AU/UN force in Darfur.[184]

In September 2007, the UN Security Council adopted Resolution 1778 approving the establishment of a multidimensional presence in Chad/Central African Republic.[185] This also provided for the establishment of an EU force (known as EUFOR Chad/CAR) which was authorised 'to take all necessary measures, within its capabilities and its area of operations' to contribute to protecting civilians in danger.[186] In essence, EUFOR was established to provide the military component of the UN mission (MINURCAT). The Security Council reaffirmed the obligation of all parties to implement fully the rules and principles of international humanitarian law.[187]

On 21 February 2008, the Irish Defence Forces troop contribution to the UN mandated, EU led peacekeeping mission commenced. This EU mission was mandated to operate in eastern Chad and work in conjunction with the civilian UN mission in the region (MINURCAT). The military force was authorised to protect refugees, internally displaced persons (IDPs), humanitarian organisations and civilians in danger. The force was intended to create a safe and secure environment whereby humanitarian aid could be delivered and the local population could go about their daily lives. Initially the Irish government authorised a 12-month deployment period commencing on 15 March 2009.

The EU commitment was initiated with the deployment of headquarters staff and an Initial Entry Force. The 97th Infantry Battalion deployed to the mission in May/June 2008 and was the first Irish battalion to become operational in the area of operations along the Chad/Sudan border in south-eastern Chad. Irish forces were involved in some minor confrontations with rebel forces. An incident in June 2008 led to criticism of the alleged failure of Irish troops to protect UNHCR staff and premises from rebel forces.[188] Although the criticism was later withdrawn, it is a good example of the uneasy relationship that sometimes exists between the UN

---

184 See E. Horgan, 'Army tied into questionable peace missions', *The Irish Times* (Dublin) 8 August 2008, p 13. In contrast see T. Kinsella, 'Chad Mission to EU military's peaceful role', *The Irish Times* (Dublin) 9 March 2009.

185 UNSC Res 1778/2007, UN Doc. S/RES/1778, 25 September 2007, para 1.

186 Ibid., para 6.

187 Ibid., para 17.

188 C. Lally, 'Irish troops criticised for failing to protect staff', *The Irish Times* (Dublin) 18 June 2008, p 1. The UNHCR subsequently apologised for the staff members' remarks and 'misinformation' about the incident: see P. Cullen, 'Matter of UN Chad remarks "closed"', *The Irish Times* (Dublin) 21 June 2008; C. Lally, 'O'Dea says troops in Chad face greater risk', *The Irish Times* (Dublin) 27 August 2008.

and other humanitarian workers and the military personnel deployed on the ground to protect them.[189] Unfortunately, such incidents and accusations also make headline news, but subsequent retractions or corrections receive much less attention.[190]

The EU mission was always intended to be a bridging mission while the UN force was being organised for deployment. Security Council Resolution 1861 provided for the withdrawal of EUFOR and the creation of a military component of MINURCAT that would take over from EUFOR.[191] The UN mission assumed command on 15 March 2009 with some nations, including Ireland, remaining in Chad as part of the new UN military component. The 400 Irish troops of the 99th Infantry Battalion came under direct control of the MINURCAT Force Commander and his Irish deputy, Brigadier General Gerald Aherne.

In 2010, the government of Chad called for the withdrawal of MINURCAT. After negotiations, the UN Security Council adopted Resolution 1923 extending the mandate until 31 December 2010.[192] In this way, the Chadian authorities assumed full responsibility for the security and protection of the civilian population in eastern Chad from May 2010 while the UN forces prepared for a phased withdrawal from the rest of the country.

Amnesty International expressed concern about the uncertain security situation that the reduced strength of MINURCAT would create.[193] It cited the heightened risks for organisations delivering humanitarian aid into some areas and the increased risk of children being abducted and recruited as child soldiers. Amnesty International was also critical of the Security Council Resolution which transferred responsibility for the protection of civilians in Eastern Chad to the Chadian authorities.[194] The Resolution outlined the phased withdrawal of MINURCAT from 15 July 2010, with full withdrawal starting in mid October and scheduled to be completed by the end of 2010. It was planned that MINURCAT would have the capacity to protect civilians until October, but only if they were under imminent threat of violence in the immediate vicinity of MINURCAT's bases.[195] Amnesty

---

189 M. Fitzgerald, 'Aid agencies and EU Chad force learn trust in tense security zone', *The Irish Times* (Dublin) 26 November 2008, p 12.

190 Amnesty International, 'UN hands protection of civilians over to Chad' (Press Release, 31 May 2010); Amnesty International, 'UN pullout puts achievement of Irish troops in Chad at risk' (Press Release, 10 May 2010).

191 UNSC Res 1861/2009, UN Doc. S/RES/1861, 14 January 2009, paras 3, 6.

192 UNSC Res 1923/2010, UN Doc. S/RES/1923, 25 May 2010, para 1.

193 Amnesty International, 'UN hands protection of civilians over to Chad' (Press Release, 31 May 2010); Amnesty International, 'UN pullout puts achievement of Irish troops in Chad at risk' (Press Release, 10 May 2010).

194 Amnesty International, 'UN hands protection of civilians over to Chad' (Press Release, 31 May 2010); Amnesty International, 'UN pullout puts achievement of Irish troops in Chad at risk' (Press Release, 10 May 2010); UNSC Res 1923/2010, UN Doc. S/RES./1923, 25 May 2010, paras 10–11.

195 UNSC Res 1923/2010, UN Doc. S/RES/1923, 25 May 2010, para 10.

International was deeply concerned about the Security Council compromise that would see the overall force strength reduced to 1900 troops and a transfer of responsibility for protecting refugees to the Chadian government despite the inability of the Chadian authorities to adequately protect the many thousands of vulnerable people in the region.[196]

From its initial deployment, MINURCAT struggled to achieve full operational capability. Lack of planning was a major flaw and this was apparent in the logistical arrangements for the force. Effective threat assessment and the acquisition of accurate intelligence information proved problematic. Initially it was thought that rebel groups and Janjaweed forces would pose the greatest threat to the mission but in reality banditry presented a far greater risk to security. Neither MINURCAT nor its predecessor, EUFOR, had the mandate to deal with the everyday realities of criminality that were prevalent. EUROR was configured for a more military role to protect vulnerable civilians and was not structured for internal security operations. Although Ireland's unilateral decision to withdraw while the UN was still negotiating with the Chadian authorities did not precipitate the end of MINURCAT, the decision weakened the UN negotiating position and was not well received at the UN Department of Peacekeeping Operations in New York.

Official Report—Ireland and 'Extraordinary Rendition' Flights

- Irish Human Rights Commission publishes final report *'Extraordinary Rendition', A Review of Ireland's Human Rights Obligations*, <http://www.ihrc.ie/download/pdf/ihrc_rendition_report_final.pdf>

The specific functions of the Irish Human Rights Commission (IHRC) are to review the adequacy and effectiveness of law and practice in Ireland relating to human rights and to make recommendations to the government in relation to measures that can be taken to strengthen and protect human rights in the State. The IHRC Final Report on extradition was published in December 2010.[197] The Report concluded that it was known that United States CIA aircraft involved in 'extraordinary rendition' landed and refuelled at Shannon Airport, Ireland. Evidence indicated that such aircraft were not subject to any searches or inspections on Irish soil. The IHRC has been calling for a system of inspection to be put in place since 2005. This is to ensure that Ireland is never, even unwittingly, a party or an accessory to the practice of torture or inhuman or degrading treatment or punishment.[198] The response of the Irish government has been that it has received assurances from the US administration that prisoners have not been and will not be

[196] Ibid. See also, Amnesty International, *No Place for Us Here—Violence Against Refugee Women in Eastern Chad* (September 2009, Index: AFR 20/008/2009); Amnesty International, *Chad: 'We too deserve protection'—Human Rights challenges as UN mission withdraws* (14 July 2010, Index: AFR/20/009/2010).

[197] Irish Human Rights Commission (IHRC), *'Extraordinary Rendition', A Review of Ireland's Human Rights Obligations* (Final Report 2010, Dublin, Ireland).

[198] Ibid., p 2.

transported through Irish territory. In the circumstances, it is the opinion of the government that there is no requirement for a system of aircraft inspections to be put in place. The Irish government considers that the political assurances it has received are sufficient to meet its human rights obligations. It has requested that if any private citizen has evidence that aircraft have been used for 'extraordinary rendition', such information should be given to An Garda Síochána (Irish police) for investigation. In this way, the government appears to have placed the onus of producing evidence regarding suspect aircraft on to Irish citizens, a situation which is unsatisfactory.

The IHRC is of the view that in its approach to 'extraordinary rendition', Ireland is not in compliance with its human rights obligations to prevent torture or inhuman or degrading treatment or punishment. Reliance on the assurances of the US government is inadequate. In order to ensure full compliance with its human rights obligations, the Commission recommended that Ireland put in place a reliable and independently verifiable system of inspection so that no prisoner is ever transported through the country except in accordance with proper legal formalities and the highest observance of human rights standards. Amnesty International has consistently called for an end to the current practice. To date this has not happened. The so-called 'Wikileaks' evelations in late 2010 and early 2011 have added to the controversy owing to reports that members of the government had information relating to such flights.[199]

Legislation—Criminal Procedure

- *Criminal Procedure Act 2010*, No. 27 of 2010, enacted on 20 July 2010, <www.attorneygeneral.ie>

Purposes of Act

This is a lengthy Act that deals with a range of matters relating to criminal procedure. The Act sought primarily to address two major issues, victim impact evidence and the circumstances under which an acquittal may be reversed and a new trial ordered. Both topics have particular relevance for the victims of crime. The opportunity to give victim impact evidence enables a victim to tell about the trauma caused. The reversal of undeserved or erroneous acquittals will assure victims that their quest for justice can be satisfied.[200]

The main purposes of the Act may be summarised as follows. First, to reform the law relating to victim impact evidence and, in particular, to extend the entitlement to make an oral statement (commonly called a victim impact statement) at a sentencing hearing to the family members of homicide victims. Second, to modify the rule against double jeopardy in order to allow a person who has been acquitted of an offence to be re-tried in circumstances where 'new and compelling

---

199 M. Fitzgerald, 'Amnesty claims law on rendition ignored', *The Irish Times* (Dublin) 17 January 2011, p 9.

200 Ireland, *Parliamentary Debates*, Senate (Seanad Eireann), 10 June 2009, Vol. 195, No. 16, Minister for Justice, Equality and Law Reform (Deputy D. Ahern).

evidence' emerges or where the acquittal is tainted due, for example, to corruption or intimidation of witnesses or jurors or perjury. Third, to provide the Director of Public Prosecutions with a right of appeal to the Supreme Court on a 'with prejudice' basis against an acquittal where the acquittal arises from (i) an erroneous ruling by the trial court on a point of law arising during the trial or from (ii) a decision by the Court of Criminal Appeal not to order a re-trial following the quashing of a conviction. Fourth, to provide for a range of procedural amendments dealing with character evidence, notice of intent to adduce expert evidence and disposal of property that is evidence in a trial.

Many of the amendments were the subject of recommendations in the final report of the *Balance in the Criminal Law Review Group* (March 2007).[201]

Important Provisions of Act

Part 2—Impact of Crime on Victim

Sections 4–6 reform the law relating to victim impact evidence. Section 4 amends the *Criminal Justice Act 1993* by the substitution of section 5 of that Act. Formerly, the sentencing court was only required to take into account (and receive evidence where necessary) of the effect of the offence on the direct victim. This evidence was usually in the form of a written report by a medical person. Following the amendment, where the direct victim, as a result of the offence, has died, is ill or otherwise incapacitated, the court is required to take into account the effect of the offence not only on the person directly concerned but also on the family members. In the case of the effect on a child under the age of 14 years, provision is made for the child or the parent/guardian to make the victim impact statement on their behalf. The absence of a victim impact statement shall not give rise to an inference that the offence had little or no impact on the direct victim or the family members, as appropriate.

The range of offences in respect of which the victim impact evidence provisions in this section applies has been expanded to include any offence under the *Non-fatal Offences Against the Person Act 1997*. Many of the offences under the 1997 Act were already within the existing range of offences, but since a number of offences, such as harassment under section 10 and false imprisonment under section 15, do not necessarily involve the use of physical violence or the threat of violence, they did not give rise to an entitlement to make a statement. Such offences can, however, cause substantial emotional distress to the victim. It is for this reason that offences under the 1997 Act have been added. In the interests of justice, provision is made for the court to prohibit the broadcasting or publication of all or part of the victim impact statement.

Part 3—Exceptions to Rule against Double Jeopardy

The rule against double jeopardy provides that no person may be put at risk of being punished twice for the same offence. This Part modifies the rule by allowing

201 <http://www.justice.ie/en/JELR/Pages/Balance_in_criminal_law_report>

the Director of Public Prosecutions to make an application to the Court of Criminal Appeal for a retrial order in respect of a person who is acquitted of an offence on the grounds of 'new and compelling evidence' which emerges post-acquittal or where the acquitted person or another person has been convicted of an offence against the administration of justice in relation to the original proceedings (a 'tainted acquittal').

Where the ground for the re-trial application is 'new and compelling evidence' the scope of the power is restricted to the offences (in this Part referred to as 'relevant offences') specified in the schedule. The relevant offences carry a mandatory or maximum sentence of life imprisonment subject to a limited exception in the case of the offences under the *International Criminal Court Act 2006*. In the case of tainted acquittals the scope is wider and applies in the case of all acquittals following a trial on indictment.

Section 7 defines 'new and compelling evidence' as evidence which was not presented by the prosecution at the proceedings in respect of which the person was acquitted (nor in related appeal proceedings) and could not with the exercise of due diligence, have been presented during those proceedings. It must be reliable, of significant probative value and be such that when taken together with all the other evidence adduced (no matter by whom) in the proceedings concerned, a jury might reasonably be satisfied beyond a reasonable doubt of the person's guilt in respect of the offence concerned.

Section 8 empowers the Director of Public Prosecutions to make an application for a retrial order to the Court of Criminal Appeal in respect of a person who has been acquitted of a relevant offence following a trial on indictment or in related appeal proceedings. The section has prospective application only so that it applies to persons tried and acquitted of a relevant offence on or after the commencement of the section.

The Director of Public Prosecutions may make an application for a retrial order only where it appears to him or her that there is 'new and compelling evidence' and that such an application is in the public interest. The application must be on notice to the acquitted person concerned. However, the hearing may proceed notwithstanding the acquitted person's failure to appear if the court is satisfied that it is, in all the circumstances, in the interests of justice that the application should be heard and determined. Having regard to the person's status as an acquitted person, he or she will remain at liberty (other than where he or she is in prison in connection with another offence) until such time as a retrial order (if any) is made by the court under section 10 and the court makes a decision under section 13 as to whether or not the person should be remanded in custody or on bail pending the hearing of the retrial. The Director of Public Prosecutions may avail of section 8 only on one occasion in relation to an acquitted person's suspected participation in a particular relevant offence.

Section 9 empowers the Director of Public Prosecutions to make an application for a retrial order to the Court of Criminal Appeal in respect of a person who has been acquitted of an offence following a trial on indictment or in related appeal proceedings, and that person or another person has been convicted of an offence against the administration of justice relating to the proceedings which resulted in the acquittal. As under section 8, this section also has prospective application only.

The Director of Public Prosecutions may make an application for a retrial order only where it appears to him or her that there is 'compelling evidence' against the acquitted person and that such an application is in the public interest. An application may not be made where appeal proceedings are pending in relation to the conviction for the offence against the administration of justice. The application must be on notice to the acquitted person concerned. However, the hearing may proceed notwithstanding the acquitted person's failure to appear if the court is satisfied that it is in all the circumstances in the interests of justice that the application should be heard and determined. Having regard to the person's status as an acquitted person, he or she will remain at liberty (other than where he or she is in prison in connection with another offence) until such time as a retrial order (if any) is made by the court under section 10 and the court makes a decision under section 13 as to whether or not the person should be remanded in custody or on bail pending the hearing of the retrial. The Director of Public Prosecutions may avail of section 9 only on one occasion in relation to an acquitted person's suspected participation in a particular offence.

Section 10 deals with the court hearing and determination of an application under section 8 or 9. In the case of an application for a retrial order under section 8 (an application on the basis of 'new and compelling evidence') the court shall grant the order where it is satisfied that there is 'new and compelling evidence' in relation to the acquitted person concerned and that having considered the matters set out in subsection (3) (whether or not it is likely that any retrial could be conducted fairly, the amount of time that has passed since the commission of the offence concerned, the interests of any victim of the offence concerned and any other matters which the court considers relevant) it is in all the circumstances in the interests of justice to grant the order.

In the case of an application for a retrial order under section 9 (an application on the basis of a tainted acquittal) the court shall grant the order where it is satisfied that: there is 'compelling evidence' against the acquitted person, and having considered the matters set out in subsection (3) that it is, in all the circumstances, in the interests of justice to grant the order. In either case, if a retrial order is made, the effect of the order will be to quash the acquittal and direct that the person be re-tried for the offence concerned subject to such conditions and directions (including conditions and directions as to placing a stay on the retrial) as the court considers necessary to safeguard the fairness of the retrial.

Sections 15–18 provide that the Garda Síochána (Irish police) must obtain authorisation from a District Court judge prior to the exercise of certain powers in relation to an acquitted person in connection with an investigation into that person's suspected participation in a relevant offence of which the person has previously been acquitted. An application by the Director of Public Prosecutions for a retrial order on the basis of 'new and compelling evidence' will in practice be preceded by a Garda investigation into that evidence to establish its reliability, substance and so forth. It will be necessary for the Gardaí (police) to be able to exercise standard investigative powers, such as powers of arrest and detention, fingerprinting, taking of forensic samples and search powers in order to conduct its investigation into that new evidence. However, having regard to the status of the suspect as an acquitted person it is necessary to ensure that the exercise of those powers is subject to judicial oversight.

Part 4—Matters Relating to Appeals

Part 4 extends the appeal options available to the prosecution and makes a number of amendments to existing defence appeal provisions.

Section 23 concerns two circumstances: (i) where a person is tried on indictment and acquitted; and (ii) where a person's conviction is quashed on appeal to the Court of Criminal Appeal and the Court does not order a retrial. It provides that the prosecuting authority (most commonly the Director of Public Prosecutions, but on occasion the Attorney General) may appeal the acquittal or as the case may be, the decision not to order a retrial on a 'with prejudice' basis. The appeal is made to the Supreme Court on a question of law. The term 'with prejudice' refers to the possibility that the appeal will result in the acquittal or the decision of the Court of Criminal Appeal not to order a retrial being overturned and a retrial ordered. This appeal option is in addition to the existing 'without prejudice' prosecution appeal right under section 34 of the *Criminal Procedure Act 1967* as amended. The appeal under section 23 is restricted to: (i) rulings which erroneously excluded 'compelling evidence'; or (ii) in the case of judge directed acquittals, rulings which were wrong in law and where the evidence adduced in the proceedings was evidence upon which a jury might reasonably be satisfied beyond a reasonable doubt of the person's guilt in respect of the offence concerned. A jury verdict on the merits of the case based on the reception of all admissible evidence is not subject to appeal under this Part. Notwithstanding that the appeal must be on notice, the hearing may proceed despite the acquitted person's failure to appear if the court is satisfied that it is in all the circumstances in the interests of justice that the appeal should be heard and determined. Having regard to the person's status as an acquitted person, he or she will remain at liberty (other than where he or she is in prison in connection with another offence) until such time as a retrial (if any) is ordered by the court under this section and the court makes a decision under section 26 as to whether or not the person should be remanded in custody or on bail pending the hearing of the retrial. Provision is made for free legal aid for the person who is the subject of the appeal.

Section 35 makes provision for the return or disposal of property which forms part of the evidence in criminal trials. It applies where it is proposed to dispose of property before the trial begins or to return that property to its owner.

Legislation—Money Laundering and Financing of Terrorism

- *Criminal Justice (Money Laundering and Terrorist Financing) Act 2010*, No. 6 of 2010, enacted on 5 May 2010, <www.attorneygeneral.ie>

The main purpose of the Act is to transpose the Third EU Money Laundering Directive[202] and the associated implementing Directive[203] into Irish national law. The Act is also intended to ensure compliance with the recommendations of the third mutual evaluation report on Ireland of the Financial Action Task Force. The Act repeals and re-enacts the anti-money laundering provisions contained in other statutes, principally the provisions relating to money laundering contained in the *Criminal Justice Act 1994*. It also consolidates all of Ireland's anti-money laundering legislation in a single statute. The Act increases the obligations on a wide range of legal persons, including credit and financial institutions, lawyers, accountants, estate agents, trust and company service providers, tax advisers and others in relation to money laundering and terrorist financing. The Act requires designated bodies covered by the legislation to identify customers, to report suspicious transactions to the Irish police and the Revenue Commissioners and to have specific procedures in place to provide to the fullest extent possible for the prevention of money laundering and terrorist financing. It provides that categories of designated bodies in respect of which there is no supervisory or competent authority, will be monitored for the purposes of compliance with the legislation by the Department of Justice, Equality and Law Reform.

Legislation—EU Regulations Governing Chemicals

- *Chemicals (Amendment) Act 2010*, No. 32 of 2010, enacted on 24 November 2010, <www.attorneygeneral.ie>

The main purpose of the Act is to meet EU obligations to implement and enforce certain EU regulations,[204] including the EU regulation on the classification, labelling and packaging of substances and mixtures, known as the CLP (classification, labelling and packaging) regulation,[205] a replacement EU regulation on the export and import of dangerous chemicals implementing the Rotterdam Convention,[206] and periodic technical amendments to these two EU regulations and to the

---

[202] Directive 2005/60/EC of the European Parliament and of the Council of 26 October 2005 on the Prevention of the Use of the Financial System for the Purpose of Money Laundering and Terrorist Financing [2005] OJ L 309/15.

[203] Commission Directive 2006/70/EC of 1 August 2006 laying down implementing measures for Directive 2005/60/EC of the European Parliament and of the Council as regards the definition of 'politically exposed person' and the technical criteria for simplified customer due diligence procedures and for exemption on grounds of a financial activity conducted on an occasional or very limited basis [2006] OJ L 214/29.

[204] Ireland, Parliamentary Debates, Senate (Seanad Eireann), 16 November 2010, Vol. 205, No. 12, Minister of State at the Department of Enterprise, Trade and Innovation (Deputy D. Calleary), <http://debates.oireachtas.ie/seanad/2010/11/16/00006.asp>.

[205] Regulation (EC) No 1272/2008 of the European Parliament and of the Council of 16 December 2008 on classification, labelling and packaging of substances and mixtures, amending and repealing Directives 67/548/EEC and 1999/45/EC, and amending Regulation (EC) No 1907/2006 [2008] OJ L 353/1.

[206] Regulation (EC) No 689/2008 of the European Parliament and of the Council of 17 June 2008 concerning the export and import of dangerous chemicals [2008] OJ L 204/1.

EU Registration, Evaluation, Authorisation and Restriction of Chemicals (REACH) and Detergents Regulations. The Act also includes some minor technical changes to the *Safety, Health and Welfare at Work Act 2005*.

The Act does not amend the *Chemicals Weapons Act 1997* and is not about transposing EU directives. The purpose is to provide an enforcement framework for EU regulations. The provisions of those EU regulations, with which this Act is concerned, are directly applicable in Ireland. They may not be changed or amended by implementing legislation. The provisions of the Act therefore relate only to measures necessary for enforcement.

RAY MURPHY

ISRAEL[207]

Official Inquiries—Gaza Flotilla Investigations

- Internal committee of the Israeli Defence Forces to investigate the maritime incident of 31 May 2010 (the Gaza flotilla incident)

On 7 June 2010, the Chief of General Staff of the Israel Defence Forces (IDF) ordered that an expert command investigation be conducted regarding the events and actions of Operation 'Sea Breeze', i.e., the takeover of the Gaza-bound flotilla that occurred on 31 May 2010, in the course of which nine passengers on board one of the ships (the *Mavi Marmara*) were killed in a violent confrontation with IDF naval commandos.

The Chief of General Staff appointed a special panel, composed of eight IDF officers and headed by Major-General (ret.) Guiora Eiland, which reviewed the preparations for the operation and its execution. The panel examined the conduct of the forces involved in the operation, as well as various related issues: intelligence gathering and assessment, command and control by the General Staff, press relations (handled by the IDF Spokesperson unit), relevant technological alternatives to forcible takeover, and the legal advice prior to and during the operation (provided by the IDF Military Advocate General's Corps).

On 12 July 2010, the panel submitted its classified report to the IDF Chief of General Staff. According to published portions of the report, a lack of cooperation between the IDF's General Staff Intelligence Directorate and the IDF's Navy Intelligence Division led to an under-assessment of the level of resistance that would be encountered on board the *Mavi Marmara*, although it was not clear that greater cooperation would have provided a different assessment. Moreover, the operation was executed on the basis of a rigid plan of action, with no alternative prepared in case of escalation. With regard to technological alternatives, the report concludes that at present there are no effective means for peacefully and safely

[207] Information and commentaries by Dr. Yaël Ronen, Senior Lecturer, Sha'arei Mishpat College. The reporter is grateful to Shlomy Zachary for his assistance in gathering information for the report, and to Yfat Barak, Nimrod Karin and Ido Rosenzweig for their comments and additional information.

interdicting a moving ship on the high seas. The panel's recommendation was to speed up the process of developing and testing suitable operational alternatives. With regard to the performance of the IDF Spokesperson's unit, the report held that it was very well prepared; however, there was a delay in the release of information and footage. This delay resulted from the desire to maintain the credibility of the information released and to protect the privacy of the victims and their relatives, as well as from an unnecessarily cumbersome series of required authorizations. The report concluded that the soldiers on the scene acted properly and that the decisions of the commanders during the operation were reasonable. According to the report, the use of live ammunition by the soldiers was unavoidable under the circumstances, and the conduct of the naval commandos during the entire operation was commendable.

- Public commission to investigate the maritime incident of 31 May 2010 (the Gaza flotilla incident), <http://www.pmo.gov.il/PMO/Secretarial/Decisions/2010/06/des1796.htm>

On 14 June 2010, the Israeli government appointed a public commission to investigate certain aspects of the maritime incident of 31 May 2010 (the Gaza flotilla incident). The commission was chaired by former Supreme Court Justice Yaakov Turkel. Its members were Ambassador Shabtai Rosenne (who passed away during the deliberation of the commission), Major General (ret.) Amos Horev, Ambassador Reuven Merhav, and Professor Miguel Deutch. The commission was accompanied by two international observers, Lord David Trimble, former First Minister of Northern Ireland and Nobel Peace Prize laureate, and Brigadier-General Ken Watkin, former Chief Advocate General of the Canadian Armed Forces.

The commission was mandated to examine whether the actions that had been taken by Israel to prevent the arrival of the flotilla to the Gaza Strip were consistent with international law. In order to answer this question, it was required to issue its findings, *inter alia*, on the security reasons for the imposition of the naval blockade and its compatibility with international law; on the action taken to enforce the blockade, including through use of force, on the day of the incident and its compatibility of international law; and on the actions of the flotilla organizers and its participants, as well as their identity. The commission was also tasked with examining whether Israel's mechanism for investigating alleged violations of IHL was compatible with its obligations under international law.

The commission heard testimonies by government and military officials, by the leader of the opposition party, and by representatives of NGOs. The transcripts of some of these testimonies were published on the commission's internet site. For reasons of state security and maintenance of foreign relations, some of the testimonies were heard *in camera*, either in part or in full. In total the commission heard 26 testimonies during 15 days of hearings, and eleven testimonies *in camera*. The commission also received various submissions by State authorities (including by the special panel headed by Major-General (ret.) Guiora Eiland, see the previous item), most of which were made available on its internet site, as well as by NGOs.

- Testimony of the Military Advocate General (MAG), 26 August 2010, <http://www.turkel-committee.com/index-eng.html>

On the Legal Status of the Gaza Strip

From 1967 to 2000 the Gaza Strip was considered, *grosso modo*, in a state of belligerent occupation. In 2000, in view of the second *intifada*, the situation was redefined by the State as amounting to an 'armed conflict short of war'. Consequently, IDF activity within the Gaza Strip turned from policing and law-enforcement oriented into being governed by the laws on the conduct of hostilities. In September 2005, following the disengagement from the Gaza Strip, the territory in which the armed conflict persisted was no longer under belligerent occupation.

On Economic Restrictive Measures

In September 2007, the Ministerial Committee on National Security declared the Gaza Strip a hostile entity or hostile territory.[208] This led to a policy shift with respect to the flow of goods between the Gaza Strip and Israel: once virtually unrestricted (except for explicit prohibitions stemming from narrow security considerations), now almost entirely prohibited unless required for humanitarian reasons. This 'economic warfare' is intended to weaken the enemy's economy in order to bring it to stop firing rockets at Israel. This measure was considered preferable to fighting that would result in much greater bloodshed. This had no implications on maritime movement, given that since 1967 all goods have entered and exited the Gaza Strip by land, as the Strip has no seaport. However, theoretically, it would have been permissible to impose a naval blockade as an economic warfare measure.

On the Imposition of the Naval Blockade

Since August 2008, various naval vessels have attempted to access the Gaza Strip from the sea. From then until Operation Cast Lead (December 2008 to January 2009), six boats arrived and were permitted to enter the Gaza Strip from the sea. However, this raised concerns that a maritime route would be created and utilized to transport weapons and terrorists.

---

[208] Reported in 10 *YIHL* (2007) p 341.

Under the Interim Agreement, which is still in force, the IDF has exclusive authority in the area up to 20 miles from the coast, including off the Gaza Strip, and no ship is permitted to enter within 20 miles of the coast. What was unclear was whether the Interim Agreement could be relied upon *vis-a-vis* a third party or whether it is only applicable between Israel and the Palestine Liberation Organization.

During active hostilities, a vessel may be instructed to move away from a combat zone even without a formal declaration of combat zone. If the vessel refuses, it may be seized. During periods of relative quiet and tranquility, boarding a vessel is only permissible if there is concrete suspicion of contraband. In view of this requirement and the dispute over what constitutes contraband, the legitimacy of intercepting vessels would have come under much more severe international political criticism. To avoid these, on 3 January 2009, during operation 'Cast Lead', Israel imposed a naval blockade on the Gaza Strip. This raised no negative international reaction.

The principles governing the imposition of a naval blockade, namely, the effectiveness of the proclamation, nondiscrimination and access to the coast of neutral states are governed by customary law, reflected in the *San Remo Manual on International Law Applicable to Armed Conflicts at Sea*,[209] and in the military manuals of various armed forces. The Israeli blockade met all the requirements. As for the requirement of a set duration of the blockade, it is not customary, and in the circumstances, where the conflict is protracted, it is not practicable. As for the requirement of proportionality between the benefit of the blockade and injury to civilians, there is a dispute over whether this is a customary requirement, but given the vitality of the blockade to Israel's security and given that the sea had never been a route for commerce so there was no harm to civilians as a result of its closure, the requirement of proportionality was met.

The objective of the land closure was in fact to induce Hamas to stop firing rockets on Israel, in a manner that was less severe than resort to force. It was not intended to serve as a punishment for the population. Admittedly, a certain degree of suffering was caused to civilians, but this did not exceed the limits of permissibility, as the experience with regard to sanctions against the former Yugoslavia and against Iran demonstrates.

On Preparations for the Flotilla

There was intensive activity to reach the flotilla ships at sea effectively. There is no doubt that the vessels involved in the flotilla were aware of the blockade, particularly as they claimed explicitly that they intended to break the blockade.

The *Mavi Marmara* was unique among the vessels in the flotilla in its large number of passengers. The Turkish organization leading the flotilla, the

---

[209] L. Doswald-Beck, *San Remo Manual on International Law Applicable to Armed Conflicts at Sea* (CUP, 1995).

Foundation for Human Rights and Freedoms and Humanitarian Relief (IHH), supports Hamas and intends to transfer funds to Hamas, and has been declared an unlawful association under Israeli law. This did not mean that all passengers on board the *Mavi Marmara* were saboteurs and terrorists, only that that there are certain administrative and criminal measures available for addressing the activities of the vessel. At no time was there any question of sinking the ship.

At an early stage, the Israeli Navy indicated that military necessity compelled it to act outside the 20-mile blockade-boundary. While undesirable, this was legally permissible given the plausible suspicion that the *Mavi Marmara* and other flotilla vessels were planning to break through the naval blockade. The Military Advocate General (MAG) recommended to act as close as possible to the 20-mile blockade boundary.

A great effort was made to minimize harm to people, including formulation of rules of engagement and examination of issues such as use of less lethal weaponry, use of electronic warfare and disruption by blocking communications broadcasts. The mission instruction was to stop the ship with the least possible public resonance and delegitimization.

The MAG was asked if in a situation where it emerged that the only way to stop the ship was by the use of lethal weaponry despite the absence of a life-threatening situation to the soldiers, the use of lethal weaponry would be permissible. The Chief MAG responded that he would answer this question *in camera*. He noted that while theoretically, sinking a ship to prevent its entry would have been lawful, the principle of proportionality would have prohibited it if it meant killing 650 people who were not terrorists.

On the Conformity of the Inspection and Investigation of Allegations of Violations of the Laws of Combat with International Law

The laws of armed conflict, primarily the *Geneva Conventions*, provide no guidance as to putting into practice the obligation to investigate allegations of violations of the law, and particularly as to the obligation to appoint an external independent body. Therefore one has to turn to a supplementary source. Since the purpose of handling grave breaches is criminal enforcement, the classic supplementary body of law is international criminal law. The *Rome Statute of the International Criminal Court*[210] can serve as an interpretive source despite Israel's non-participation in it. By contrast, international human rights law is inapplicable with respect to armed conflict.

Allegations of violations of the laws of armed conflict are investigated by the Military Police Criminal Investigation Command guided by the Main Military

[210] Opened for signature 17 July 1998, 2187 UNTS 90, Art. 8 (entered into force 1 July 2002).

Prosecution, and by the military courts. These bodies enjoy full professional independence. The Chief MAG is appointed by the Minister of Defense rather than by the Chief of Staff, and is completely independent in law enforcement. The only bodies that can intervene when complaints exist of an error are the State Attorney-General and the High Court of Justice.

Outside the armed conflict context, a case of civilian death raises suspicion that an offence has been committed. Therefore until 2000 any case of civilian death mandated an immediate criminal investigation. In contrast, in the post-2000 situation of *de facto* armed conflict, it 'is the expected result of fighting that civilians get killed', particularly during asymmetric warfare in urban areas. An immediate investigation whenever a civilian is killed would mean thousands of investigations in every incident of fighting. This is inconceivable, incorrect and unnecessary. The means to ascertain the facts is the military debriefing, commonly used by many military forces. In cases where there can be no conceivable justification for the act claimed, such as allegations of pillage, violence towards a prisoner, use of human shields, the case goes directly to a criminal investigation rather than to a preliminary military debriefing.

The *Geneva Conventions*' sole guidance on how to investigate is the obligation to investigate in good faith; the Rome Statute requires that the state investigate 'genuinely'. There is no reason for the investigation not to be carried out through the ordinary channels. Indeed, a change in the accepted procedure for investigation would raise suspicion that perhaps the state does not want to arrive at the truth. The investigation should be independent and impartial.

International human rights law is not applicable to a situation of armed conflict. This is corroborated by the *Convention for the Protection of Human Rights and Fundamental Freedoms*, which does not include armed conflict as a limitation on the right of life, because armed conflict is not within the scope of the Convention. The laws of armed conflict are *lex specialis* with respect to human rights law. Human rights law may fill lacunae, but none exist in the present context. The purpose, nature, and comprehensiveness of human rights law are totally different from those of international criminal law. Human right law offers closure, which is why it provides for victims' participation, and transparency. These are inapplicable to situations of ongoing armed conflict.

- Position paper by the MAG Corps on the legal aspects of the imposition of a naval blockade on the Gaza Strip and its enforcement, submitted to the Public Commission to Examine the Maritime Incident of 31 May 2010, July 2010, <http://www.mag.idf.il/sip storage//FILES/5/915.pdf> (in Hebrew)

On the Legal Status of the Gaza Strip

Belligerent occupation requires the exercise of effective control, although opinions differ whether it must be actual or can also be potential. The termination of belligerent occupation mirrors its beginning: when the occupant is replaced by a different effective government. Israel's disengagement from Gaza was followed by an assumption of power by the Palestinian Authority, and thus the Israeli occupation came to an end as its effective control terminated. The claims that the occupation persists because Israel continues to control movement to and from the Gaza Strip are mistaken, since Israel is merely controlling entry into its own sovereign territory, rather than to the Gaza Strip. Furthermore, Israel does not control the Rafah crossing, i.e., the border passage between the Gaza Strip and Egypt. Finally, control of the air and adjacent sea do not constitute, in and of itself, effective control.

On the Validity of the Israeli-Palestinian Interim Agreement on the West Bank and the Gaza Strip, 28 September 1995

Doubts have been raised as to the validity of the Interim Agreement, for three reasons: the expected replacement of the agreement by a permanent status one; the repeated violations by the Palestinian Authority; and Israel's military operations. Nonetheless, neither party has ever argued that the Agreement is no longer valid. The Israeli cabinet decision on the disengagement stated that the disengagement does not affect the Agreement. At the same time, much of the Agreement became inoperative. Furthermore, the Agreement binds Israel and the PLO and envisages interaction with the Palestinian Authority. Therefore, insofar as the Gaza Strip is concerned, once Hamas came into power, the applicability of the Agreement came under strain. Nonetheless, Israel continues to abide by the Agreement to the extent possible.

Classification of the Armed Conflict with Hamas and Other Palestinian Terrorist Organizations Operating within the Gaza Strip

For many years Israel has avoided taking a formal position as to the classification of the armed conflict with the Palestinians terrorist organizations as international or non-international, deeming this classification largely unnecessary. Israel has applied the laws of belligerent occupation, which apply only under the international armed conflict paradigm. The disengagement from the Gaza Strip has complicated the matter further, but Israel has declared that it abides by the basic principles of the laws of armed conflict that are applicable in both international and non-international conflicts.

Restrictions on Transfer of Goods to the Gaza Strip

Following the disengagement, violent incidents put the lives of personnel operating the land crossings under mortal danger. In addition, the risk posed by entry of military materiel into the Gaza Strip grew. As a result, the import of goods became limited, and it was necessary to prioritize its content. After the Gaza Strip was designated a 'hostile entity', a revision of the policy was instituted. Transfer of goods to and from Israel has become almost entirely prohibited unless required for humanitarian reasons. Legally, these restrictions were merely an expression of the principle of sovereignty. In proceedings before the High Court of Justice, the state nevertheless argued that they constituted economic warfare. Such warfare is customarily conducted through a land siege or naval blockade, and involves the active prevention of entry of goods. Admittedly, Israel prevented importation of goods from third parties, but such importation remained possible through Egypt, via the Rafah crossing between Gaza and Egypt. The naval blockade could have been regarded as economic warfare if it had been directed at the adversary's economic capacity. However, the blockade imposed by Israel was a security measure.

The Laws of Naval Warfare

The laws on naval warfare are stipulated in the London Declaration,[211] widely regarded as customary law, and in the San Remo Manual, also widely regarded as partly reflecting customary law. The laws on naval warfare apply primarily to international armed conflicts, but do not exclude their applicability to other types of conflicts.

A party to a conflict may impose a naval blockade to prevent access by maritime vessels to the territory or exit therefrom, regardless of the existence of concrete knowledge of a military danger emanating from a vessel. Such a blockade is permissible for both military and other reasons, and need not be justified. This measure is available also in non-international armed conflict. When Israel imposed a blockade on the maritime zone off the coast of Lebanon during its 2006 war with Hizbollah, no international objection was voiced. The blockade on the Gaza Strip complied with the four customary requirements, namely a public declaration, effectiveness, non-discrimination and access to the coast of neutral states. Furthermore, the objective of the blockade was military and it was not aimed at starvation of the population, which receives all supplies by land, and for the same reason was proportionate: the military advantage to Israel was significant, while no detriment was caused to the population.

The laws of naval warfare permit the capture of a vessel intending to break the blockade, even outside the blockade perimeter. They also permit the use of force in

---

211 Declaration Concerning the Laws of Naval War, London, 26 February 1909.

case of resistance. If a vessel purports to provide humanitarian supplies, a blockading party may subject it to technical arrangements that ensure that the vessel is not used for the transfer of military material.

Since the imposition of the blockade on 3 January 2009, two ships that attempted to break it were intercepted without violence, brought to Israel and their cargo checked for transfer to Gaza. The ships were not confiscated (nor were the ships captured on 31 May 2010).

In the preparations for the May flotilla, instructions were given to use force only in self defense to avoid an immediate danger to life, and only when no less harmful means are possible. 'Less lethal weapons' were provided. In addition, instruments for communication blocking were made available, so as to minimize the chance of forcible resistance.

- Position paper by the Military Advocate General on Legal and Practical Aspects of Investigating Allegations of Violations of the Laws of Armed Conflict, 19 December 2010, <http://www.mag.idf.il/sip_storage//FILES/9/949.pdf> (in Hebrew)

Under international criminal law, investigations must be independent, impartial, effective and thorough. The requirement of 'independence' is satisfied by functional independence, namely that the law enforcement bodies are independent of the persons investigated and their organizations. This contrasts with organizational independence, where there must be complete dissociation between the law enforcement system and the investigated individuals and their organizations. The promptness of an investigation (in human rights law terms) or its conduct without undue delay (in international criminal law terms) means a pace of investigation that does not substantively harm the effectiveness of the investigation and the capacity to bring the truth to light (and thus does not give rise to doubt as to sincerity and good faith in the investigation). The requirements of effectiveness and thoroughness must be interpreted in light of the difficulties of investigating an incident in a distant arena, outside a state's control and without the ability to summon witnesses and evidence. The requirements that exist only under international human rights law are impracticable in situations of armed conflict.

- Report of the Turkel Commission, Part 1, January–February 2011, <http://www.turkel-committee.com/menu-7.html>

On 23 January 2011, the Turkel Commission submitted the first part of its report to the prime minister. On 8 February, this first part was made public. The following are the main findings of the report.

The Applicable Normative Framework

At the opening of the deliberations on the question of the conditions for imposing and enforcing the naval blockade on the Gaza Strip, the Commission took as the point of departure the following premises that have significance for the applicable legal framework: (1) the conflict between Israel and Hamas is an international one; (a position based on rulings of the Israeli Supreme Court on the one hand, and on the international claim that the Gaza Strip is occupied territory, a status which only exists under the laws of international armed conflict; and (2) Israel's effective control of the Gaza Strip ended when the disengagement was completed in 2005.

Imposition of the Naval Blockade

The Commission concluded that the Government of Israel imposed the naval blockade on the Gaza Strip for military-security reasons. The naval blockade was not imposed in order to restrict the transfer of humanitarian supplies to the Gaza Strip or to disrupt the commercial relations of the Gaza Strip since there is no commercial port on the coast of the Gaza Strip and, consequently, there was in the past no maritime commerce that went via the coast of the Gaza Strip. However, the naval blockade was also regarded as legitimate within the framework of Israel's overall strategy to prevent a legitimization of the Hamas regime in the Gaza Strip. The Commission found that Israel satisfied all formal conditions for imposing a blockade.

In order to assess the humanitarian impact of the naval blockade on the civilian population in Gaza, the Commission also examined the humanitarian impact of Israel's land crossings policy, including the restrictions imposed on entry and exit of goods and movement of people, imposed on the Gaza Strip following the Hamas takeover in 2007. It noted that the land blockade formed part of the overall context in which the naval blockade was imposed, namely Israel's comprehensive strategy against the Hamas regime in the Gaza Strip; that in practice, vessels destined for the Gaza Strip are diverted to Ashdod port in Israel, from where the humanitarian supplies they carry are transported via the land crossings and pursuant to a security check, to the Gaza Strip; and that it is difficult to isolate the effect of the naval blockade on the humanitarian situation in the Gaza Strip from the land crossings policy.

The Commission concluded that the purpose of the land crossings policy was to prevent the entry of weapons, ammunition and military supplies into the Gaza Strip in order to reduce Hamas's attacks on Israel and its citizens; and to achieve a broader strategic goal of 'indirect economic warfare', i.e., to restrict Hamas's economic ability to take military action against Israel. In terms of anticipated military advantage it would appear that the combined measures that were adopted have limited Hamas' capabilities and its speed of rearmament.

The Commission found that Israel took its humanitarian obligations into consideration and planned the restrictions precisely in order to prevent a situation of 'starvation', while operating in close collaboration with the Palestinian Authority, human rights organizations and the international community in order to prevent such a condition. There was no evidence that Israel was trying to deprive the population of the Gaza Strip of food or to annihilate or weaken the population by means of starvation. Similarly, Israel met its obligations regarding the provision of objects essential to the survival of the civilian population and the provision of medical supplies.

The Commission concluded that Israel was in compliance with the requirement of proportionality within the context of placing a naval blockade, especially in view of the extensive steps that it took in order to moderate the humanitarian effects of the naval blockade and the land crossings policy on the population of the Gaza Strip.

However, the Commission warned of the danger that comprehensive restrictions on goods may not be regarded as proportionate in the long term. In this context it took account of changes to the land crossings policy in June 2010, to the effect that items are allowed into the Gaza Strip with the exception of 'weapons, military equipment and problematic dual-purpose items', and on 8 December 2010, to the effect that gradual approval would be given for the export of goods from the Gaza Strip beyond the borders of Israel and to the West Bank. The Commission did not examine new evidence regarding the new land crossings policy and therefore could not assess its effect.

'Collective Punishment'

The Commission stated that the imposition and enforcement of the naval blockade on the Gaza Strip—even when they are considered together with the land crossings policy—do not constitute 'collective punishment' of the population in the Gaza Strip. The purpose of the restrictions on imports into the Gaza Strip was neither solely nor mainly to deprive the civilian population but rather to limit Hamas' abilities—including its economic ability—to carry out attacks against Israel.

Enforcement of the Naval Blockade

Individuals or groups do not have a right to breach a naval blockade that has been established in accordance with the applicable rules governing blockades, even if they consider the blockade illegal because of its impact on the civilian population. The IDF forces were therefore permitted to enforce the naval blockade by capturing the vessels attempting to break it. If a vessel resists capture then, after prior warning, the IDF forces may consider the option of employing force to neutralize them. That said, the IDF forces did not use force against the ships.

Enforcement in International Waters

According to the rules of international humanitarian law, a ship that is purposefully attempting to breach a blockade may be captured wherever it is located, including in international waters. Given the location and announced destination of the flotilla's vessels; the public pronouncements by the flotilla organizers and participants regarding their intention to breach the blockade; and the refusal of the ships' captains to alter their course after they had been warned by the IDF, the Commission concludes that the takeover in international waters was lawful.

Assessment of Takeover Tactics

The experience of other states reveals that the use of intermediate levels of force, such as water cannons and 'shouldering' the vessel, have limited success, and often pose a significant threat to the vessel, its crew and passengers. The means chosen for takeover—descending from helicopters and boarding the deck of the vessels from Morenas—is therefore fully consistent with established naval practice, whether enforcing a blockade or carrying out law enforcement operations.

Use of Force by IDF Soldiers

In response to the severe violence employed against them, the IDF soldiers made use of force, varying in degree from employing stun grenades through the use of less-lethal weapons (i.e., weapons such as paintball guns) to the execution of live fire. During the military preparations for the arrival of the flotilla, the requirement to avoid the use of force, to the extent possible, was emphasized. The authority to use force was limited to two distinct circumstances: 'to prevent the risk of harm to a person', and 'to deal with an attempt to thwart the bringing of a vessel to an Israeli port'. The rules of engagement emphasized that, as a general rule, lethal weapons should not be used unless necessary to avert a real and immediate danger to life, when the danger could be averted by less harmful means. The use of less-lethal weapons was permitted in order to 'neutralize a real danger to human safety or life, emanating from a specific person' and the use of lethal weapons was limited to self-defense.

The use of force in the enforcement of the blockade is to be interpreted in light of the principle of distinction between combatants and civilians under international humanitarian law. Civilians enjoy a general protection against the dangers arising from military operations and shall not be the object of an attack unless and for such time as they take a direct part in hostilities. The use of force against civilians must be guided by the principles of necessity and proportionality linked to the norms of law enforcement based on human rights.

Classification of the Flotilla Participants

The persons who partook in the violence on board the *Mavi Marmara* were direct participants in hostilities. This conclusion was based on, inter alia, the following facts: the IHH activists' resistance to the IDF soldiers' boarding the deck of the *Mavi Marmara* was planned and extremely violent; these actions were not representative of acts associated with civil disobedience or isolated or sporadic acts of violence; the coordinated manner in which the IHH activists met the Israeli soldiers individually fast-roping to the deck (for some of them, even before they reached the deck), indicates a clear intent to oppose violently a capture of the ship, which at that point was a military objective (that is, a vessel breaching a naval blockade and resisting capture). Likewise, the concerted effort on the roof to throw soldiers to other IHH activists that were waiting on the deck below, taken together with the fact that all three captured soldiers were taken to the same location below decks, points to the level of violence, the organization, and the commitment of those activists to the conflict.

Furthermore, this violent activity was directly connected to the ongoing international armed conflict between Israel and Hamas, as breaching the naval blockade would have harmed Israel in its armed conflict with Hamas in the sense that it would have proven that the naval blockade was inefficient, thereby endangering its political and security goals. The IHH activists attempted to execute their plan by employing force against the soldiers of one party of the armed conflict, Israel. Under these circumstances, the Commission has found that the IHH activists participating in the acts of violence on board the *Mavi Marmara* were direct participants in hostilities, at least from the time that the passengers were given the order to return to their cells with the approach of the Navy's vessels, and up to the completion of the ship's takeover.

However, other flotilla participants, who did not actively participate in the violent actions, are not considered to have taken a direct part in hostilities by virtue of their participation in the attempted breach of the blockade alone. Therefore, the principles of necessity and the use of proportionate force associated with law enforcement operations must be applied to the use of force against these civilians.

The Commission has examined every use of force by every single soldier, as reported by more than 40 soldiers and commanders that participated in the takeover of the *Mavi Marmara*, the testimonies of the commanders in charge of the takeover actions of the other vessels participating in the flotilla, as well as the incidents captured on the magnetic media handed over to the Commission. The Commission examined first whether the person against whom force was used was a civilian taking a direct part in hostilities. Where it was determined that the person was a direct participant, assessment of the use of force was first made using the applicable rules of international humanitarian law. If the person against whom the force was used was determined not to have taken a direct part in hostilities, the use of force was assessed solely under law enforcement norms. In light of the fact that the rules of engagement outlined for this operation did not anticipate any of the people on board the ships' decks to be direct participants in hostilities and therefore was based on self-defense principles, as well as the fact that the Israeli government had stated on a number of occasions that the use of force by IDF soldiers was done in self-defense, all uses of force were examined under the norms of law enforcement to determine the degree to which they fell within the scope of those norms, including self-defense or the defense of others.

The Commission noted that its ability to construct a complete picture of the incidents in which force was employed by IDF soldiers was limited for a number of reasons, including the nature of the event, the lack of testimonies by the flotilla participants, and the fact that the scenes in which the events took place did not remain intact. Such an analysis is particularly complex when it is conducted in retrospect. Further, it was clear to the Commission that, especially with respect to the takeover of the *Mavi Marmara*, the IDF soldiers were required to make difficult, split-second decisions regarding the use of force, under conditions of uncertainty, surprise, pressure, and in darkness, with the perception of a real danger to their lives and with only partial information available. In particular, with regards to the nature of the threat and especially in relation to the soldiers fast-roping from the helicopters, it should be noted, *inter alia*, that the IDF soldiers were at a numerical disadvantage in relation to the IHH activists who were equipped with a variety of assault weapons; that the IDF soldiers were equipped with less-lethal weapons (e.g., paintball guns, beanbags) as their primary weapons and their live firearms (pistols or rifles) were used as secondary weapons; and that the attack on the soldiers descending from the first helicopter constituted a real, clear, and immediate threat to the safety and physical well being of their fellow soldiers and themselves. Furthermore, the soldiers were also aware of the fact that some of the IHH activists on board the *Mavi Marmara* were using firearms, which heightened the risk posed to their lives. These factors were taken into account when analyzing the force used during the takeover.

The Commission examined approximately 130 incidents in which force was used. The majority of the uses of force involved warning or deterring fire and less-lethal weapons. Of the total number of uses of force, 16 incidents of hitting the center of bodies with rounds of live fire were reported by the soldiers.

The Commission concluded that the IDF soldiers acted professionally and in a measured manner in the face of extensive and unanticipated violence. This professionalism was evident, among other factors, in their continuing to switch back and forth between less-lethal and lethal weapons in order to address the nature of the violence directed at them.

The Commission found that 127 uses of force investigated appeared to be in conformity with international law. In five of the 127 cases, force appeared to be used against persons taking a direct part in hostilities; however, there was insufficient evidence to conclude that the force used was in accordance with law enforcement norms. In another five cases, the Commission concluded that force appeared to be used in accordance with law enforcement norms, but in two of those cases it did not have sufficient information to determine whether the person against whom force was used was a direct participant in hostilities and in three cases it was determined that the use of force involved a civilian who was not considered a direct participant in hostilities. In an additional six cases, the Commission has concluded that it has insufficient information to be able to make a determination regarding the legality of the use of force. Three out of those six cases also involved the use of live fire; in two cases physical force (kicking) was employed; and in one case there was a strike with the butt of a paintball gun.

The conclusion of the Commission is that despite the fact that several incidents have not been fully clarified, overall the actions undertaken were lawful and in conformity with international law.

Government Policy—Quarrying Activity in Occupied Territory

- Response by the State in *Yesh Din* v. *the Military Commander of Judea and Samaria*, HCJ 2164/09, Supreme Court sitting as the High Court of Justice, 20 May 2010, <http://www.yesh-din.org/userfiles/file/Petitions/Quarries/Quarries%20State%20Response%20May%202010%20ENG.pdf> (unofficial translation)

In response to a petition by an NGO to stop quarrying activity in the Israeli-owned quarries operating in Area C of the West Bank and to freeze licensing and land allocation procedures to open new quarries and expand existing quarries, a submission by the State surveys its practice and position regarding the legality of quarrying activities.

Factual Background

The Palestinian quarries that operated in the West Bank under Jordanian rule exported a substantial part of their produce to Jordan. The commercial ties between the local Palestinian residents and Jordan persisted through the first years of Israeli military administration in the area, with the encouragement of the military administration and in accordance with its policy.

In the mid-1970s a boom of quarry development began in the area, growing until the 1990s, when the question of the quarries arose as part of the negotiations over the Interim Agreement. During that period the amount of minerals transferred from the area into Israel have also risen.

For years quarries have been allocated in the area on a 'first come first serve' basis. An entrepreneur who receives a permit signs a contract with the Custodian of Government and Abandoned Property in the Area (if the quarry is built on land that is government property).

There are presently ten Israeli-owned quarries in Area C, of which eight are active. These quarries were built on land that is government property (state land) allocated by the Civil Administration. There are also in Area C nine active quarries and 20 sawmills and authorized stone mills under Palestinian ownership. Additional Palestinian quarries operate in Areas A and B, but since in those areas the civil powers, including the powers in the area of quarry administration, were transferred to the Palestinian Authority, the Israeli authorities in the area do not presently have a role in administering those quarries. According to Civil Administration figures, 94% of the produce of the Israeli quarries is transferred into the State of Israel, as are 80% of the produce of the Palestinian quarries in Area C (15% is exported abroad and the rest is sold on the local market). The quarries in the area supply 20–30% of Israel's consumption of quarrying materials—gravel as well as various minerals.

The Civil Administration collects fees for the activity of the Israeli quarries in Area C, mainly consisting of royalties. The royalties are calculated by the quantity of produce extracted from the quarry, regardless of its destination. Until 1996, these royalties were recorded in the budget of the Civil Administration. Following the signature of the Interim Agreement in 1995, royalties have been included in the budget of the Israel Land Administration. Simultaneously, the Civil Administration was budgeted directly from the State treasury. However, following an examination undertaken in connection with the petition, a separate registration of the revenues (including royalties collected from quarries) of the Civil Administration has been instituted. As a rule, these revenues were dedicated for the areas of the military government's activity in the area.

The Normative Framework

The powers and authority of the military government, including the Civil Administration, derive from the rules of public international law and specifically the laws of belligerent occupation. The use of government property in a regime of belligerent occupation is governed by Articles 53 and 55 of the Regulations annexed to *Hague Convention (IV) Respecting the Laws and Customs of War on Land* of 1907.[212] The term 'usufruct' in Article 55 essentially reflects the temporary right of use of the property, without substantial detraction from the property's capital and without fundamental change of the property. According to the Petitioner, the meaning of the demand to safeguard the capital is that the occupying power must restrict itself only to '*jus fruendi*', namely to avoid any use that could in any way damage the capital, and therefore the activity of the quarries in the area is inconsistent with the provisions of Article 55 of the Hague Regulations. This approach has certain support in academic writing; but it is inconsistent with state practice and therefore it does not reflect existing law in this matter. Other approaches give a more expansive interpretation to the provisions set forth in Article 55, according to which the occupying power has the right to exploit natural resources within reason.

The Petitioner claims that quarrying in an area under belligerent occupation is subject to a narrow and stiff restriction of the 'principle of continuity', according to

---

212 Opened for signature 18 October 1907, UKTS 9 (1910) (entered into force 26 January 1910) (Hague Regulations).

which it can be done only in such a way that continues the policy and the pace of resource use that existed in the occupied territory prior to the occupation, without the possibility of change by way of expansion and development. This approach freezes the situation that existed at the beginning of the belligerent occupation, and may lead to economic stagnation. A more suitable approach, particularly pertinent to a prolonged occupation, emphasises the reasonableness of use in general, rather than by reference to one historical standard or another. According to this approach, the purpose of the provision set forth in Article 55 of the Hague Regulations is to prevent the occupying power from exhausting the area's resources neglectfully and wastefully, indiscriminately and without economic benefit to the area. Accordingly, Article 55 only prohibits excessive and abusive exploitation that damages the capital of the property. Furthermore, the holder of the right to usufruct may continue to operate economic projects (even ones that involve exhaustive use of natural resources, namely use that damages the capital of the property), if they were active at the time of entering the area. The nature of the quarrying enterprise in Area C is commercial, Israel does not make use of the quarrying materials for its own needs.

A further consideration arises under Article 43 of the Hague Regulations. In a state of prolonged belligerent occupation, the prevailing perception is that the military government acquires additional positive duties in relation to the occupied territory, due to the awareness that treating its control of the area as temporary and transient does not reflect the objective reality on the ground. Moreover, the prolonged belligerent occupation sometimes requires an adjustment of the interpretation of various provisions of international law to the prevailing reality.

In conclusion, there is nothing to preclude the military government, not even in the framework of the provisions of Article 55 of the Hague Regulations, from allowing the extraction of minerals from an area subject to belligerent occupation, if this advances the benefit of the area, and in that framework also the benefit of the population of the area, and as long as it is not a question of wasteful use of the area's resources.

Application to the Facts

At the present pace of quarrying by the Israeli-owned quarries, it will be many hundreds of years before the total quarrying resources in the West Bank are significantly depleted. The activity of the Israeli quarries is therefore a reasonable use of the area's resources.

By registering the royalties as part of the State budget and the budget of the Civil Administration, and thereby financing part of its activity, the Civil Administration fulfills its duty as the military government in an area under belligerent occupation. Since the activity of the quarries that employ Palestinian workers and pay royalties promotes the benefit of the area, there is no preclusion in international law from their continued operation. The fact that most of the produce of the quarries in Area C is sold for use in Israel has no bearing on the matter, because the amount of royalties and leasing fees are recorded in the budget of the Civil Administration.

Policy Changes

Pursuant to the Petitioner's appeal, the State began staff work to explore the question of the quarries in the West Bank. Preliminary changes in policy include:

1. Quarries already operating will continue to do so in the same course in which they are currently operating. Applications to expand existing quarries will be approved only where the quarry is found to have exhausted its quarrying potential in the existing sites, which otherwise would mean closing the quarry. As a rule no new quarries will be established whose main purpose is to extract quarrying materials to sell them in Israel.
2. The possibility is being considered of raising the rate of payment to the West Bank treasury for quarrying products exported to Israel.
3. It was decided to put an emphasis on promoting the rehabilitation of quarries in the area. This will lead in the long run to reducing the impact of the activity of the quarries on the landscape and the environment, and allow the continued use of the land at the end of the quarrying operation for the public good.

Establishment of National Authority—Anti-Personnel Landmines

On 11 and 29 July 2010 the government decided to support a private bill for the establishment of a national authority for landmine clearance.

Investigation of Alleged War Crimes—The Military Incursion in Gaza

- Investigation of allegations of violations of the laws of armed conflict during Operation Cast Lead (December 2008 to January 2009) updates of January 2010 and July 2010, <http://www.mag.idf.il/SIP_STORAGE/files/3/713.pdf>, <http://www.mag.idf.il/SIP_STORAGE/files/4/884.pdf> (in Hebrew)

On 29 January 2010, the Ministry of Foreign Affairs published an update to the July 2009 report,[213] shedding more light on the methods of investigation employed by the IDF, and providing information on the status of the investigations. In July 2010, the Ministry of Foreign Affairs issued a second update report, containing additional information regarding the steps Israel has taken as part of its investigations and the investigations currently underway, as well as an update regarding the operational changes that have been made in the IDF's orders and combat doctrine in order to minimize civilian casualties and damage to civilian property in future operations.

According to the reports, the IDF has initiated over 150 military investigations, which include both criminal and command investigations. The total number of

[213] Reported in 12 *YIHL* (2010) pp 550–553.

criminal investigations by the Military Police Criminal Investigations Department (CID) was 47. The reports elaborate on developments in some specific investigations, related to alleged mistreatment of Palestinian civilians and detainees, alleged targeting of civilian objects and sensitive sites, alleged targeting of civilians, and damage to private property.

The July 2010 Report also provided an update on changes to military operational guidelines that resulted from investigations into aspects of Operation Cast Lead. According to the report, Operation Cast Lead presented complex military challenges in protecting civilians from the hazards of the battlefield. The report holds that Hamas' *modus operandi* of urban warfare and the use of civilian structures as shields contributed to the challenges faced by the Israeli forces. Nonetheless, the IDF conducted an internal self-examination in order to draw the relevant lessons and to improve its ability to protect civilian population from harm in future military operations. This process has resulted in the following two changes:

1. New written procedures regarding the protection of civilians in urban warfare—the IDF's new guidelines emphasize that the protection of civilians is an integral part of a commander's mission. The new procedures and doctrines also specify steps that would better insulate civilian populations and property from combat operations. These steps require thorough research so as to identify and mark existing infrastructure, including installations related to water, food, power, and sewage, as well as other civilian objects and sites. The new written procedures also require the assignment of a Humanitarian Affairs Officer to each combat unit from battalion level and up. This officer will be responsible for advising commanding officer and educating soldiers with regard to protection of civilians, civilian property and infrastructure; planning of humanitarian assistance; coordination of humanitarian movement, and the documentation of humanitarian safeguards employed by the IDF.
2. A new order regulating the destruction of private property for military purposes. The new order, in force from October 2009, provides clear guidelines regarding the circumstances in which civilian structures and agricultural property may be demolished for reasons of military necessity.

Cases—Issues Relating to Imprisonment and Detention of Palestinians

- *Yesh Din—Volunteers for Human Rights and Others* v. *Military Commander in the West Bank and Others* HCJ 2690/09, Israel Supreme Court sitting as High Court of Justice, Judgment of 28 March 2010, <http://elyon1.court.gov.il/files/09/900/026/n05/09026900.n05.htm> (in Hebrew)

In 2009, three NGOs petitioned the High Court of Justice demanding that prisoners and detainees who are residents in the West Bank not be held in facilities within Israel, and that arraignment hearings for such detainees also not be held in courts outside the West Bank.

The petition argues that holding Palestinian detainees in facilities located within Israel, a practice employed by Israeli authorities since 1967 but particularly frequently since the withdrawal of Israeli forces from areas in the West Bank and Gaza Strip in the 1990s, violates the *Geneva Convention Relative to the Protection of Civilian Persons in Time of War* of 1949,[214] particularly Articles 49 and 76, and infringes on detainees' and prisoners' right to due process, right to counsel, as well as visitation rights, as their lawyers and families are unable to meet with them.

In March 2010, the HCJ rejected the petition, relying on its ruling in the *Sajadiya* case,[215] essentially on the same matter, according to which Israeli legislation permitting detention in Israel prevails over public international law, whether conventional or customary.

Moreover, the Court held that the *Geneva Conventions* must be interpreted in light of the circumstances prevailing in the West Bank, the special characteristics of Israel's control over that area and its duration, the region's topography, and the links between Israel and the West Bank. Such a contextual interpretation should focus on the rights of the protected population, including detainees, regardless of the location in which they are being held.

The Court noted that the facilities within Israel in which Palestinian detainees and prisoners are being held are managed by the Israeli Prison Service, and the conditions in these facilities, which are the same as in any other detention facility in Israel, are far better than the conditions in militarily administered facilities in the West Bank, which do not comply as fully with relevant international detention standards. The Court rejected the petition.

- *Hakeem Kanani and Others* v. *The Israel Prison Service*, HCJ 7585/04, Israel Supreme Court sitting as High Court of Justice, Judgment of 25 March 2010, <http://elyon1.court.gov.il/files/04/850/075/r32/04075850.r32.htm> (in Hebrew)

A petition was filed in 2004 on behalf of ten children of Palestinian prisoners convicted of security-related offences against the Israel Prison Service (IPS), demanding the reinstatement of previous visitation procedures, according to which children less than 10 years of age were allowed 15 min of physical contact with their incarcerated parents at the end of family visits. The petition followed severe restrictions on physical contact between security prisoners and their children imposed in May 2002, following incidents in which children were used for smuggling banned objects to their imprisoned parents.

During the proceedings, the petitioners and the IPS agreed to a Court-proposed procedure, with some revision. The Court confirmed the procedure as follows: Generally, direct contact will be allowed for a few minutes between prisoners and their children less than 8 years of age, no less than once every 2 months. The authorities may permit more frequent contact if circumstances merit. This arrangement will be subject to the individual circumstances of the prisoner or

---

214 Opened for signature 12 August 1949, 75 UNTS 287 (entered into force 21 October 1950) (Fourth Geneva Convention).

215 *Sajadyia v. Minister of Defense*, HCJ 253/88, Israel Supreme Court sitting as High Court of Justice, Judgment of 8 November 1988, IsrSC 43(3) 801.

detainee, and so long as there are no substantial changes of circumstances that require its revision.

Cases—Restrictions on Movement of Israelis in the West Bank

- *Akiva Hacohen and Others* v. *Military Commander in the West Bank and Others*, HCJ 4101/10, Israel Supreme Court sitting as High Court of Justice, Judgment of 1 July 2010, <http://elyon1.court.gov.il/files/10/010/041/c07/10041010.c07.htm> (in Hebrew)

The petition addressed the question whether the Military Commander may infringe upon the rights of an Israeli resident of the West Bank through an order of assigned residence issued under the security legislation. The Court responded affirmatively. It also appears to have confirmed the military commission's statement at the lower instance that where the administrative authority to issue the order is grounded in the *Fourth Geneva Convention* (Article 78), the remedy available under the Convention, namely financial support, should be made available also to Israeli nationals.

Cases—Separation Barrier-Fence-Wall

- *Municipal Council of Beit Sahour and Others* v. *Prime Minister and Others*, HCJ 3937/07, Israel Supreme Court sitting as High Court of Justice, Judgment of 4 January 2010, <http://elyon1.court.gov.il/files/07/370/039/n03/07039370.n03.htm> (in Hebrew)
- *Village Council of Mes'ha and Others* v. *Minister of Defense and Others*, HCJ 4387/06, Israel Supreme Court sitting as High Court of Justice, Judgment of 11 April 2010

These two cases both involved petitions against the route of the separation barrier. In HCJ 3937/07, the petitioners argued that the barrier was erected in violation of international law because its aim is to allow the incorporation of the Jerusalem neighbourhood Har Homa (on the non-Israeli side of the Green Line) on the Israeli side of the barrier. They further argued that the barrier causes them disproportionate and grave harm. In HCJ 4387/06, similar claims were made with respect to a segment of the route south of Kalkilya, allegedly planned so as to include on the Israeli side the projected industrial zone of Shomron Gate.

The Court rejected the petitions. It ruled that the applicable legal standards are those established in the *Beit Surik* case.[216] It accepted that the guiding factor in determining the route was security needs, and that the restrictions on the Palestinians' rights were not disproportionate to the legitimate goal of erecting the barrier. The Court noted that the petitions could have been held to be inadmissible, because they were submitted more than four and 3 years (respectively) after the barrier had become operative, a delay that in the circumstances indicated a waiver

[216] Reported in 7 *YIHL* (2004) pp 504–506.

by the petitioners of their right to access the court, and had resulted in significant expenditures by the other party (the State).

- *Ibrahim Saidi and Others* v. *Minister of Defense and Others*, HCJ 6803/08, Israel Supreme Court sitting as High Court of Justice, Judgment of 2 August 2010, <http://elyon1.court.gov.il/files/08/030/068/o09/08068030.o09.htm> (in Hebrew)

The petitioners are Palestinians living outside the municipal boundaries of Jerusalem, in an enclave between the municipal boundary and the Separation Barrier. In January 2010, the enclave was declared part of the Jerusalem Enveloping Area, and made subject to the corresponding restrictive arrangements. The Petitioners object to their detachment from East Jerusalem, where most of them work and study. They requested, among other things, permanent permits to stay in Israel or in Jerusalem, to allow them access by car onto the Israeli side of the Fence, and to allow immediate family members from the West Bank to visit them.

The Court rejected the petition in light of the State's willingness to make certain concessions with respect to the matters raised. The Court noted that the constraints on the petitioners are the result of the security situation, and are a necessary consequence of the State's obligation to protect the lives of its residents.

- *Mhamad Naif Shakir and Others* v. *Military Commander of the West Bank and Others*, HCJ 7337/05, and *State of Israel* v. *Neighbourhood Committee of Sheikh Sa'ed*, HCJ 4343/06, Israel Supreme Court sitting as High Court of Justice, Judgment of 15 March 2010, <http://elyon1.court.gov.il/files/05/370/073/n28/05073370.n28.htm> (in Hebrew)

The petitions in these cases concern the route of the separation barrier in the region of the Sheikh Sa'ed neighbourhood, which lies outside the Jerusalem municipal boundary but is accessible only through Jerusalem. About half of the residents of Sheikh Sa'ed are permanent residents of Israel, while the others are residents of the West Bank. In a previous proceeding, the Appeals Committee under the 1949 Law for Land Registration considered a route of the barrier which would have passed within the Jerusalem municipal boundary, but separated Sheikh Sa'ed from Jerusalem, despite the everyday dependency of the neighbourhood on the city. The Appeals Committee under the 1949 Law for Land Registration rejected a proposal of the State to construct a road linking the neighbourhood with the West Bank village of Swahara as excessively detrimental to the residents of Sheikh Sa'ed and ruled that the State should reconsider a route that would be less detrimental to the residents of Sheikh Sa'ed [217] The present proceedings concern the State's appeal on that ruling and the neighbourhood's objection to the proposed road.

---

[217] Reported in 10 *YIHL* (2007) pp 505–506.

The State argued that maintaining Sheikh Sa'ed on the Israeli side of the barrier would make it subject to the seam line regime, thereby causing significant inconvenience to the non-Israeli residents. The residents responded that the inconvenience to the few non-Israeli residents who do not hold an entry permit into Israel is minor when compared with the inconvenience to the majority Israeli residents if the barrier separates them from the city.

The Court pointed out that maintaining the neighbourhood on the Israeli side, i.e., positioning it within the 'seam line' area between the municipal boundary of Jerusalem and the barrier, would result in significant restrictions on access to Jerusalem. The Court recalled its earlier statements on the need to minimize as much as possible the 'seam line' area. The Court found that the relative detriment in erecting the carrier so that the neighbourhood is on the Palestinian side would not be excessive, and subject to some easing of the restrictions on crossing the barrier between Sheikh Sa'ed and Jerusalem, rejected the petition.

- *Abdelrahman Shaib Rajab and Others* v. *Government of Israel and Others*, HCJ 1882/08, Israel Supreme Court sitting as High Court of Justice, Judgment of 17 August 2010, <http://elyon1.court.gov.il/files/08/820/018/n06/08018820.n06.htm> (in Hebrew)

The petition concerned a segment of the separation barrier in the area near the Tzafa village in the West Bank, the construction of which was completed in 2006. This section of the barrier separates the Palestinian village of Tzafa from the Israeli villages of Kfar Ha'oranim and Kfar Ruth, which are located respectively in the West Bank and in an area of 'no-man's land' (a narrow strip of land situated between the Green Line and the West Bank). The petitioners argued that the route was illegal because it was based not on security needs, but rather on a political interest to expand the Israeli villages in the area. They also claimed that the harm caused to their lives and livelihood by the barrier was disproportionate. In its response, the state conceded that the original plan of the route considered the expansion needs of the two said Israeli villages, and that without those concerns the barrier would have been constructed 100–250 m to the west of its present route. The state claimed, however, that rebuilding the barrier on the alternative route at the present time would cause serious harm to hundreds of acres of fertile agricultural lands, which would have to be seized by the state in order to reconstruct the barrier. The state concluded that comparatively, the advantage of moving the barrier a small distance to the west was outweighed by the harm that would be done to the owners of the lands to be seized in the rerouting process.

The Court held that although the present route did not initially meet the requirements of this proportionality test, the situation should be examined as it is now, and viewed in this light, it is impossible to maintain that rerouting the barrier is less injurious than keeping its present route. The Court therefore rejected the petition.

Cases—Individual Criminal Responsibility for Violations of the Laws of Armed Conflict

- *Military Prosecutor* v. *Staff Sergeants A and B*, Army Military Court (District) 150/10, Judgments of 3 October and 21 November 2010, <www.mag.idf.il/SIP_STORAGE/files/8/948.pdf> (in Hebrew)[218]

On 3 October 2010, two soldiers were convicted by a Military Court of forcing a 9-year-old Palestinian boy to open bags suspected of being booby-trapped (effectively using him as a 'human shield'), in the course of Operation Cast Lead (December 2008 to January 2009). The Court noted that the briefings given to the soldiers prior to their operations were clear and included orders not to harm innocent civilians and to refrain from using civilians as human shields. According to the Court, the soldiers were specifically instructed not to require civilians to inspect anything suspected of being booby trapped. The Court found that the soldiers were ordered to inspect the bags in question, but were not authorized to seek the assistance of civilians, and certainly not children. If a bag was suspected of being booby trapped, the soldiers were supposed to inform their commanders and defuse the device with the assistance of a demolition expert. Although no one was injured in the incident, it was determined that the action, which could potentially have endangered the boy's life, was undertaken without authorization and ran against IDF orders to avoid endangering civilians. On 21 November 2010, the Court published its decision to sentence the soldiers to 3 months of probation and to demote them both from the rank of staff sergeant to sergeant. The Court held that the punishment should reflect the severity of the crime, which violated the important value of human dignity, and tarnished the IDF's image. The Court remarked on the uniqueness of the incident, implying that there were no precedents on which the Court could rely in sentencing the soldiers. Among the circumstances taken into account in the determination of the sentence, the Court noted the intense wartime conditions the soldiers faced prior to the act, their lack of sleep, and the fact that there was no evidence of or claim that the soldiers' intention was to hurt or humiliate the Palestinian boy. Moreover, several high-ranking commanders testified that in their view, the incident should have been handled through disciplinary rather than criminal measures.

- *Military Prosecutor* v. *Lieutenant Colonel A and Staff Sergeant B*, Army Military Court, Special Military Court Case 5/08, Judgment of 15 July 2010, <http://www.mag.idf.il/SIP_STORAGE/files/2/882.pdf> (in Hebrew)

In August 2008, Ashraf Abu Rahma, a resident of the West Bank, was detained, blindfolded and handcuffed following a demonstration in the Ni'ilin area. While he was held by the military unit, Lieutenant-Colonel A said to his subordinate Staff Sergeant B, 'What do you say, shall we shoot him with a rubber bullet?'

---

[218] This entry draws on I. Rosenzweig and Y. Shany, 'Operation "Cast Lead" Update—Two Soldiers Sentenced to Probation [21.11.2010]', Institute for Democracy in Israel, 23 *Terrorism and Democracy Newsletter* (*November 2010*).

Subsequently, Staff Sergeant B shot towards Abu Rahma's feet, from a range of a few meters. Abu Rahma was not injured by the bullet, but his toe was hurt, apparently from ricochets.

The Military Advocate General decided to prosecute the shooting soldier and his commanding officer for 'unbecoming conduct', an offense that does not result in a criminal record. Following a petition to the Supreme Court sitting as High Court of Justice,[219] the indictments were changed to attempted threats and unbecoming conduct for the commanding officer, and illegal use of firearms and unbecoming conduct for the soldier.

In July 2010, the two defendants were convicted of the offenses charged. With respect to the commanding officer, the Court noted that the statement made by the commanding officer, although not intended to result in actual shooting, violated basic values such as human dignity and the morality of the use of military force, and undermined the reputation of the IDF's soldiers and commanders. The Court further emphasized the responsibility of a commander for messages to soldiers which suggest a permission to use force, even if not intended to be such. With respect to the subordinate soldier, the Court ruled that to the extent that he acted upon an order, the order was manifestly illegal and the soldier was prohibited from complying with it.

Cases—Personal Jurisdiction of Military Courts in Occupied Territory

- *Abdelnasser Fathi Sadek Agbaria* v. *the State Attorney and Others* HCJ 3634/10, Israel Supreme Court sitting as High Court of Justice, Judgment of 9 December 2010, <http://elyon1.court.gov.il/files/10/340/036/p11/10036340.p11.pdf> (in Hebrew)

The petitioner, an Israeli Arab national, was indicted before a military court in the West Bank for possession of, and trafficking in, military equipment. He petitioned the Supreme Court against his indictment before the military court on the ground that it was discriminatory, since Jewish Israeli nationals have never been brought to trial in the West Bank but only in Israeli courts. The Court ruled that where a matter falls within the jurisdiction of both Israeli and military courts, the Military Advocate General may opt for the court to which the case has the strongest link. In the circumstances all the links of the matter were to the West Bank, except for the nationality of the defendant.

While this case does not address questions of international humanitarian law directly, it is interesting in that it confirmed the permissibility of indicting nationals of the occupying power before military courts in the occupied territory.

[219] Reported in 12 *YIHL* (2009) pp 564–565.

NGO Reports—Betselem

- 'Void of Responsibility: Israel Military Policy Not to Investigate Killings of Palestinians by Soldiers' (September 2010), <http://www.btselem.org/Download/201009_Void_of_Responsibility_Eng.pdf>
- 'By Hook and by Crook: Israeli Settlement Policy in the West Bank' (July 2010), <http://www.btselem.org/Download/201007_By_Hook_and_by_Crook_Eng.pdf>
- 'B'Tselem Human Rights Review: 1 January 2009 to 30 April 2010' (June 2010), <http://www.btselem.org/Download/2009_Annual_Report_Eng.pdf>

NGO Reports—Gisha

- 'Electricity Shortage in Gaza: Who Turned Out the Lights in Gaza?' (May 2010), <http://www.gisha.org/UserFiles/File/publications/ElectricitypaperEnglish.pdf>

NGO Reports—Physicians for Human Rights-Israel

- '"Humanitarian Minimum"—Israel's Role in Creating Food and Water Insecurity in the Gaza Strip' (December 2010), <http://www.phr.org.il/uploaded/PHR-PHR-Israel_Report_Humanitarian%20Minimum_eng_January_2011.pdf>

NGO Reports—Human Rights Watch Reports

- 'Separate and Unequal: Israel's Discriminatory Treatment of Palestinians in the Occupied Palestinian Territories' (19 December 2010), <http://www.hrw.org/en/reports/2010/12/19/separate-and-unequal-0>
- '"I Lost Everything": Israel's Unlawful Destruction of Property during Operation Cast Lead' (13 May 2010), <http://www.hrw.org/en/reports/2010/05/13/i-lost-everything-0>
- 'Turning a Blind Eye: Impunity for Laws-of-War Violations during the Gaza War' (10 April 2010), <http://www.hrw.org/en/reports/2010/04/11/turning-blind-eye-0>

YAËL RONEN

ITALY[220]

Cases—Italy's Counter-Claim in the Proceedings before the International Court of Justice on the Case Concerning Jurisdictional Immunities of the State (*Germany* v. *Italy*)

- Counter-Memorial of Italy, 22 December 2009, Ch. VII (through which Italy submitted a counter-claim regarding non reparation by Germany for injuries suffered by Italian nationals as a consequence of grave violation of international humanitarian law committed, during World War II, by forces of the German Reich), <http://www.icj-cij.org/docket/files/143/16017.pdf>
- Observations of Italy on the Preliminary Objections of the Federal Republic of Germany Regarding Italy's Counter-Claim, 18 May 2010, <http://www.icj-cij.org/docket/files/143/16021.pdf>

---

220 This Report was prepared by Giovanni Carlo Bruno, Rachele Cera, Valentina Della Fina, Ornella Ferrajolo and Silvana Moscatelli on behalf of the Institute for International Legal Studies of the National Research Council (CNR), Rome.

- Order of the International Court of Justice, 6 July 2010 (through which the Court found Italy's counter-claim inadmissible for lack of jurisdiction) (in *Rivista di diritto internazionale*, 2010, No. 3, p. 831 ff.), <http://www.icj-cij.org/docket/files/143/16027.pdf>

This paper deals with the developments occurring in 2010 in the proceedings instituted by the Federal Republic of Germany before the International Court of Justice against the Italian Republic in 2008.[221] On 22 December 2009, Italy submitted a counter-claim to the Court. This was based on the contention that Germany had not given effective reparation to Italian victims for injuries suffered as a consequence of grave violations of international humanitarian law committed during World War II by forces of the German Reich. Following preliminary objections by Germany, Italy further presented written observations to the Court on 18 May 2010. These documents are discussed below. Finally, we will examine in brief the order delivered by the Court on 6 July 2010, through which Italy's counter-claim was found inadmissible and dismissed.

It should be noted that the dispute pending before the Court relates to the fact that, in recent years, various Italian judicial bodies have declared that Italy holds jurisdiction with regard to claims brought by persons who, during World War II, were deported to Germany to perform forced labour, or otherwise suffered injury as a consequence of serious violations of international humanitarian law committed by forces of Nazi Germany.[222] In the view of the Federal Republic, this judicial practice has disregarded the jurisdictional immunity Germany enjoys as a sovereign State under international law. Accordingly, Germany has asked the Court to declare, *inter alia*, that:

> the Italian Republic's international responsibility is engaged;
>
> … the Italian Republic must, by means of its own choosing, take any and all steps to ensure that all the decisions of its courts and other judicial authorities infringing Germany's sovereign immunity become unenforceable;
>
> … the Italian Republic must take any and all steps to ensure that in the future Italian courts do not entertain legal actions against Germany founded on the occurrences described in request No. 1 above.[223]

---

[221] Cf. G.C. Bruno, 'Cases—Initiation of Proceeding before the International Court of Justice in protest against the Denial of German Immunity in Italian Courts', 11 *YIHL* (2008) p 497 et seq.

[222] This jurisprudence originated from the judgment of the Italian Court of Cassation of 2004 in the *Ferrini* case (*English translation in International Law Reports, Vol. 128, p 658 et seq.*). *See also C. Focarelli, 'Denying Foreign State Immunity for Commission of International Crimes: the Ferrini Decision', International and Comparative Law Quarterly (2005) p 951 et seq.*

[223] *Jurisdictional Immunities of the State* (*Germany* v. *Italy*), Application, ICJ Rep., 23 December 2008, p 18, <http://www.icj-cij.org/docket/files/143/14923.pdf>. Germany's request No. 1 has been that the Court declare that the Italian Republic 'by allowing civil claims based on violations of international humanitarian law by the German Reich during World War II from September 1943 to May 1945, to be brought against the Federal Republic of Germany, committed violations of obligations under international law in that it has failed to respect the jurisdictional immunity which the Federal Republic of Germany enjoys under international law.' See ibid.

In its Counter-Memorial of 22 December 2009, Italy did not limit itself to rebut Germany's claim, but also presented a counter-claim under Article 80 of the Rules of the Court. Through it, Italy complained that Germany has denied effective reparation to Italian victims of international crimes committed by the German Reich. It therefore asked the Court 'to find that Germany has violated its obligation of reparation owed to Italian victims ... and that, accordingly, Germany must cease its wrongful conduct and bear international responsibility for such conduct'.[224] An 'appropriate remedy' for Italy would have been an order of the Court that Germany must offer effective reparation to Italian victims, by means of its own choosing, including a negotiated solution.[225]

As is evident, these requests resulted in extending the subject-matter of the pending dispute. This is, however, a normal consequence of any counter-claim under Article 80 of the Rules of the Court. It was important for the Court assess whether the two eligibility requirements provided in paragraph 1 of Article 80 were met. The Court had, thus, to ascertain whether or not Italy's counter-claim (a) fell within the Court's jurisdiction and (b) was directly connected with the claim of the other party.[226]

On (a), Italy affirmed that Article 1 of the *European Convention for the Peaceful Settlement of Disputes* of 29 April 1957 was the basis of the Court's jurisdiction in respect of the counter-claim.[227] This Article was also invoked by Germany, and recognized by the Court, as being the legal basis of the Court's jurisdiction on the principal claim. It should be noted that the European Convention does not apply to disputes relating to facts or situations prior to its entry into force (Article 27(a)); and that the critical date is, in this instance, 18 April 1961, when the Convention entered into force between Germany and Italy. In the view of the latter, however, this was not an obstacle to the Court's jurisdiction on the counter-claim, because the source of the dispute submitted through it was not crimes committed by Nazi Germany to the prejudice of Italian citizens from September 1943 to May 1945. The source or, the 'real cause' of this dispute was,

---

224 *Jurisdictional Immunities of the State* (*Germany* v. *Italy*),Counter-Memorial of Italy, 22 December 2009, Chap. VII, Sect. I, pp 128 et seq., para 7.2.

225 Ibid., Sect. IV, p 133, para 7.14

226 Cf. International Court of Justice, Rules of Court, adopted on 14 April 1978 and entered into force on 1 July 1978, Article 80, <http://www.icj-cij.org/documents/index.php?p1=4&p2=3&p3=0>.

227 This Article reads: 'The High Contracting Parties shall submit to the judgment of the International Court of Justice all international legal disputes which may arise between them including, in particular, those concerning: (a) the interpretation of a treaty; (b) any question of international law; (c) the existence of any fact which, if established, would constitute a breach of an international obligation; (d) the nature or extent of the reparation to be made for the breach of an international obligation.' Opened for signature 29 April 1957, ETS No. 23 (entered into force 30 April 1958), <http://conventions.coe.int/Treaty/Commun/QueVoulezVous.asp?NT=023&CM=8&DF=23/12/2010&CL=ENG>.

rather, the 'new situation' created by the reparation régime established by Germany, which has allegedly discriminated against Italian victims.[228]

This régime results, more precisely, from the two Agreements regulating certain compensation issues, which were concluded between Germany and Italy in 1961,[229] and from German legislation on reparations, including the most recent Law of 2 August 2000 on the 'Remembrance, Responsibility and Future' Foundation. Under this law, not all the categories of Italian victims of Nazi crimes are entitled to obtain compensation. Accordingly, German courts have rejected some claims brought by Italian nationals. In the opinion of Italy, as all these events are subsequent to the 'critical date', the limitation *ratione temporis* provided in Article 27(a) of the European Convention was not applicable in the case.

Regarding the second requirement prescribed by Article 80, para 1, of the Court's Rules, Italy asserts that the connection between the claim and the counter-claim is the same issue on which Italy relies for rebutting Germany's claim in the proceedings:

> [w]hile Germany has claimed that Italy violated Germany's jurisdictional immunity, Italy submits that no violation has been committed since, under international law, a State responsible for violation of fundamental rules is not entitled to immunity in cases in which, if granted, immunity would be tantamount to exonerating the State from bearing the legal consequences of its unlawful conduct.[230]

Italy further argued that the 1961 Agreements and the compensation measures adopted by Germany 'have proved insufficient', in that they do not cover several categories of Italian victims, 'such as Italian military internees and the victims of massacres perpetrated by German forces during the last months of Second World War'.[231] Accordingly, Germany remains under an obligation to establish an 'appropriate and effective mechanism' for reparation and, thus, to provide Italian victims 'with a legal avenue other than resort to national judges'.[232] In other words, if victims of Nazi crimes have brought claims before national courts, this is because Germany has failed to execute its obligation to provide them with an alternative and effective reparation mechanism. For the same reason, in entertaining these claims, 'Italian judges have lifted State immunity'.[233]

On 10 March 2010, Germany presented some preliminary objections to Italy's counter-claim, contending that it fell outside the scope of the Court's

---

228 Counter-Memorial of Italy, p 129, para 7.4.

229 Treaty on the Settlement of Certain Property-related, Economic and Financial Questions, signed on 2 June 1961 (entered into force on 16 September 1963); Treaty Concerning Compensation for Italian Nationals Subjected to National-Socialist Measures of Persecution, signed on 2 June 1961 (entered into force 31 July 1963) (Annex 3 and Annex 4 to Italy's Counter-memorial).

230 Counter-Memorial of Italy, p 130, para 7.6.

231 Ibid., p 131, para 7.9.

232 Ibid., p 132, para 7.11.

233 Ibid.

jurisdiction.[234] Germany noted that 'the date when the dispute arose is not acknowledged as a relevant criterion under the European Convention', which only takes into consideration 'the facts or situations that entailed the dispute occurred'. These facts or situations were, in this case, 'the unlawful acts and activities committed by German forces and other authorities during the 20 months when Italy was placed under occupation'.[235]

Germany denied that the 1961 Agreements could have created any 'new situation'. In its view, the only issues in dispute between the parties, or the 'real cause' of the dispute brought by Italy through its counter-claim, were differences which arose between the two Governments in the course of the 1970s, about the scope of the waiver clause contained in Article 77, para 4, of the Peace Treaty concluded by the Allied Powers with Italy on 10 February 1947.[236] While the Italian Government maintained that this clause has left room for additional payments, the German Government argues that the clause extinguishes any additional claims. Consequently, the conclusion of the 1961 Agreements was regarded by Germany

> as a gesture of good will designed to put an end to legal fights about compensation due in individual cases'; and 'it is hard to see why a gesture of good will should have brought about a 'new' situation constituting the core of the dispute pending before the Court.[237]

Nor could the Law of 2 August 2000, or its enactment, create any 'new situation'. It is true that this law has not taken into account damages suffered by Italian military internees; however 'no legal claim is derived by Italy from this omission' to assert that Germany has violated its legal obligations vis-à-vis Italy.[238] As a conclusion, Germany can find no other source than the 'horrendous activities' performed during World War II by forces of Nazi Germany as constituting the cause of the dispute. It therefore asked the Court to dismiss Italy's counter-claim, as not falling, *ratione temporis*, within the Court's jurisdiction.[239]

---

[234] *Jurisdictional Immunities of the State* (*Germany* v. *Italy*), Preliminary Objections of the Federal Republic of Germany Regarding Italy's Counter-claim, 10 March 2010. It should be noted that Germany refrained from discussing, at this stage of the proceeding, the second requirement under Article 80, para 1, of the Court's Rules, reserving its position on this issue (ibid., para 3).

[235] Ibid., pp 9 et seq., paras 13–14, pp 11 et seq., para 19.

[236] This clause reads: 'Without prejudice to these and to any other dispositions in favour of Italy and Italian nationals by the Powers occupying Germany, Italy waives on its own behalf and on behalf of Italian nationals all claims against Germany and German nationals outstanding on May 8, 1945, except those arising out of contracts and other obligations entered into, and rights acquired, before 1 September 1939. This waiver shall be deemed to include debts, all intergovernmental claims in respect of arrangements entered into in the course of the war, and all claims for loss and damage arising during the war.' Reproduced *Jurisdictional Immunities of the State* (*Germany* v. *Italy*), Order, ICJ Rep., 6 July 2010, p 4.

[237] *Jurisdictional Immunities of the State* (*Germany* v. *Italy*), Preliminary Objections, ICJ Rep., pp 19–21, paras 30–33.

[238] Ibid., p 23, para 37.

[239] Ibid., p 24, paras 38–39. Other objections raised by Germany have not been taken into account in this paper, as not being strictly necessary to understand the case.

In response to these objections, Italy noted, in its written observations of 18 May 2010:

> Germany simply ignores the distinction, affirmed many times in the Court's jurisprudence, between the source of the rights alleged to have been breached and the source of the dispute, a distinction which is fundamental for the purposes of determining the source or the real cause of the present dispute.[240]
>
> ...
>
> contrary to what Germany appears to suggest, the object of the dispute brought by Italy through its Counter-claim is not whether Germany committed war crimes or crimes against humanity against Italian victims during World War Two. Nor is it whether these crimes gave rise to a duty on Germany to provide reparation. These issues are not in dispute between parties, as Germany has always ... acknowledged its international responsibility deriving from the conduct of the German Reich. Thus, the present dispute did not arise because of the unlawful conduct of German authorities during World War Two. Insofar as this conduct gave rise to Germany's international responsibility, it can be regarded as the source of the right of reparation claimed by Italy.[241]
>
> ...
>
> Italy bases its Counter-claim on a new fact, or, *rectius*, a set of new facts, which all took place after the critical date—18 April 1961—and which are at the origin of a dispute between parties on the issue of the implementation of the obligations of reparation owed to Italian victims of serious violations of international law perpetrated by the German Reich.[242]

Italy's observations principally related to the opposing views of the parties regarding the interpretation of the waiver clause contained in the 1947 Peace Treaty, as well as the interpretation of the 1961 bilateral Agreements. Significantly, these latter, which Germany deems irrelevant to the case, are regarded by Italy as 'a turning point' in the relations between parties, and this for 'at least three different reasons':

> First, through the stipulation of the Agreements Germany waived what it considered to be its right to avail itself of the Italian waiver of all claims (assuming that this waiver could cover serious violations of IHL, which Italy believes it does not). Second, through these Agreements, for the first time after World War Two, Germany agreed to meet Italian claims, thus recognizing that an obligation of reparation towards Italy existed and opening the way for a process of reparation. Third, through the Agreements and in the Agreements themselves, Germany made it clear that these do not exhaust the range of reparations which could be provided to Italian victims, by explicitly recognizing that other avenues remained available (or would become available) under German legislation.[243]

No doubt the Court will return to a discussion of these issues again, and in greater detail, in relation to the principal claim.

---

240 *Jurisdictional Immunities of the State* (*Germany* v. *Italy*), Observations of Italy on the Preliminary Objections of the Federal Republic of Germany Regarding Italy's Counter-claim, ICJ Rep., 18 May 2010, p 7, para 14.

241 Ibid., p 9, para 20.

242 Ibid., p 15, para 35.

243 Ibid., p 17, para 43.

Regarding the counter-claim the Court did not uphold Italy's arguments. In its order of 6 July 2010, the Court recalled, first, its interpretation of Article 27 (a) of the European Convention in a previous case.[244] According to that interpretation, the 'critical date' under the Convention is not the date on which the dispute arose, but the date of the facts or situations to which the dispute relates. Thus, to assess whether or not the 'jurisdictional requirement' under Article 80, para 1, of the Rules of Court was met, the Court had first to identify the subject-matter of the dispute submitted by Italy through its counter-claim. The fact that war crimes and crimes against humanity were committed, between 1943 and 1945, by the Third Reich against Italian nationals was not, *per se*, in dispute between the parties. There were, however, opposing views as to whether and to what extent Germany must give reparation to Italian victims. It followed that crimes committed against Italian nationals during World War II were at the origin of the right claimed by Italy, and as such the 'real cause' of the dispute submitted by way of the counter-claim.[245] The 1961 bilateral Agreements have not changed, in the opinion of the Court, the legal situation of the Italian nationals at issue in the case; this situation is 'inextricably linked', rather, to the scope and the effect of the waiver clause contained in the 1947 Peace Treaty.[246] From this, the Court derived that all the facts and situations to which Italy's counter-claim related occurred prior to the entry into force of the European Convention between the parties. On this basis, the Court dismissed Italy's counter-claim, as not falling within the Court's jurisdiction and being, thus, inadmissible under Article 80, para 1, of the Court's Rules.

This decision was taken almost unanimously (by 13 votes to one). In his dissenting opinion, Judge Cançado Trindade has noted, however, that the case submitted by Italy originated not in the events occurring during World War II, but 'in the initiative of aggrieved individuals, in recent years, to seek justice before domestic tribunals'. Accordingly, the case pending before the Court 'is an inter-State *contentieux* between Germany and Italy, concerning their opposing claim and counter-claim, of State immunity and war reparation, respectively'. In the opinion of this Judge, given that the claim and counter-claim are strictly connected, '[b]y dismissing one of the claims … the Court's majority deprived the Court of the examination and settlement of the dispute in its entirety'.[247]

The Court's decision on the counter-claim does not prejudice, of course, the subsequent procedure. However, as it has been observed by Judge *ad hoc* Gaja in his declaration appended to the order, '[i]n case of a denial of jurisdiction

---

244 *Jurisdictional Immunities of the State* (*Germany* v. *Italy*), Order, ICJ Rep., 6 July 2010, p 7, para 18. The Court refers, here, to the case concerning *Certain Property* (*Liechtenstein* v. *Germany*), Preliminary Objections, ICJ Rep., 10 February 2005, p 25, para 48.

245 *Jurisdictional Immunities of the State* (*Germany* v. *Italy*), Order, ICJ Rep., 6 July 2010, p 8, para 22, p 9, para 26.

246 Ibid., p 10, para 28.

247 *Jurisdictional Immunities of the State* (*Germany* v. *Italy*), Order, ICJ Rep., 6 July 2010, Dissenting opinion of Judge Cançado Trindade, p 29, para 100, <http://www.icj-cij.org/docket/files/143/16031>.

[in relation to the admissibility of a counter-claim], the defendant State would be effectively prevented from bringing to the Court the inadmissible counter-claim as a separate claim'. Taking into account this impact of any decision on jurisdictional matters, the Court could have heard the parties before deciding on the admissibility of the counter-claim, as is provided in the amended text of Article 80 of the Court's Rules, which was applied for the first time in the present case.[248] An oral hearing would have probably helped the Court to identify the subject-matter of the dispute submitted by the counter-claim, as well as the date of the events from which this dispute originated.[249]

ORNELLA FERRAJOLO[250]

Cases—Unauthorized Enlisting or Arming in the Service of a Foreign State

- Judgment of the Assize Court of Bari on the Case 'Prosecutor v. Giovanni Piero Spinelli and Salvatore Stefio' for the Crimes provided by Articles 110 and 288 of the Criminal Code, 16 July 2010 [Corte di assise di Bari, Sentenza relativa al caso 'Procuratore della Repubblica c. Giovanni Piero Spinelli and Salvatore Stefio' per i reati di cui agli artt. 110 e 288 cod. pen., 16 luglio 2010], <http://www.marinacastellaneta.it/blog/wp-content/uploads/2010/10/contractors.pdf>

The Assize Court of Bari decided the case of Giovanni Piero Spinelli and Salvatore Stefio, who were both accused of having committed the crimes covered by Articles 110 and 288 of the *Italian Criminal Code*, i.e., the unauthorized enlisting or arming in the service of a foreign State ('arruolamento o armamento non autorizzato a servizio di uno Stato estero'). In particular, they were accused of the enlistment on Italian territory, without any governmental approval, of four private security guards with the aim of employing them in Iraq in the service of the Anglo-American Armed Forces against foreign armed groups.[251]

---

[248] International Court of Justice, *Rules of Court*, adopted on 14 April 1978 and entered into force on 1 July 1978, Article 80, para 3 (in force since 1 February 2001) reads: 'Where an objection is raised concerning the application of paragraph 1 or whenever the Court deems necessary, the Court shall take its decision thereon after hearing the parties'. This proviso was not present in Article 80 pre-amended version.

[249] *Jurisdictional Immunities of the State* (*Germany* v. *Italy*), Order, ICJ Rep., 6 July 2010, Declaration of Judge *ad hoc* Gaja, <http://www.icj-cij.org/docket/files/143/16033.pdf>.

[250] Ornella Ferrajolo is Senior researcher at the Institute for International Legal Studies of the National Research Council (CNR) of Italy.

[251] They are accused of having used the Presidium Corporation, a firm based in the Seychelles (but controlled by Stefio according to the Prosecutor Giovanni Colangelo) to recruit and send to Iraq the three Italian private security guards Maurizio Agliana, Umberto Cupertino, Fabrizio Quattrocchi, then captured with Stefio, Dridi Forese, a former soldier who then did not participate in the mission during which the others were captured (at that time he was in Baghdad). Notice reported on <http://www.articolo11.org/index2.php?option=com_content&task=view&id=8010&pop=1&page=0&Itemid=7>.

On 19 April 2008 the judge of the preliminary hearing of the Tribunal of Bari accepted as founded the Prosecutor's allegation of the violation of Article 288 and the trial commenced on 3 July 2008.[252]

On 16 July 2010 the Assize Court of Bari dismissed the case against the accused. In the Court's reasoning, the offence in Article 288 of the *Italian Criminal Code* was not committed because there was never any intent to help the foreign State to pursue the military objectives of the international mission. In the view of the judges, the accused were acting only for pecuniary gain and this motivation is not proscribed by the norm. In order to determine whether the conduct of the accused falls within the scope of Article 288, the Court must take into account both the legal status of the enlisted or recruited persons as well as the nature of the activity under scrutiny.

First of all, the judges clarified that Article 288 had to be interpreted in the light of the 1989 *International Convention against the Recruitment, Use, Financing and Training of Mercenaries*,[253] ratified and implemented by Italy pursuant to Law No. 210 of 12 May 1995. The judges also recalled the definition of mercenary contained in the Article 47 of the 1977 *Protocol Additional to the Geneva Conventions of 12 August 1949, and relating to the Protection of Victims of International Armed Conflicts* (*Protocol I*).

Moreover, in so far as the issue of the legal status of the enlisted persons is concerned (and this case was the first time that an Italian judge made such a determination), the Court was of the view that it was incorrect to refer to them as 'Contractors', because technically the contractor is always the firm, while the individuals are just employees.

In so far as the kind of activity is concerned, the Court specified that a distinction has to be made between recruitment and the enlistment. Recruitment is defined in the 1989 *International Convention against the Recruitment, Use, Financing and Training of Mercenaries*, as the search for personnel to employ for military activity. Instead, enlistment as punished by Article 288 of the *Italian Criminal Code*[254] constitutes the final phase of the process—when the recruited person has been appointed and is ready to deploy to the operational theatre. In the view of the Court, Article 288 prohibits only enlistment. The provision presupposes that the employed personnel will deploy for military activity in support of a foreign State.

In the case under review, the accused were employed as security guards for a corporation (especially managers and executives) involved in the business of the post-conflict reconstruction. The Court was of the view that the military nature of

[252] See V. Eboli, Comment on 'Court of Assize of Bari, Order of 24 Avril 2008 committing Salvatore Stefio for trial for the alleged violation of Article 288 of the Penal Code (Unauthorised Recruiting or Arming on Service of a Foreign State)', 11 *YIHL* (2008) pp 511–512.

[253] International Convention against the Recruitment, Use, Financing and Training of Mercenaries, opened for signature 4 December 1989, 2163 UNTS 75 (entered into force 20 October 2001).

[254] Distinction already drawn by the Court of cassation, I penal section, in the decision No. 13597 of 5 March 2009.

the activity is derived from its purpose and not from its inherent nature. Any activity aimed at providing any contribution to military operations can be qualified as 'military'. But it is not the case that simply because a person is armed (even heavily) that he is engaged in military activity. So in this particular case the relevant activity deployed was not a 'military' one.

A description of the envisaged activity, as bodyguards or armed security officers, was contained in some specific Guidelines. The enlisted persons were allowed to use the weapons only for the protection of VIPs, self-defence or the protection of the local population and only if the security agent witnessed acts of violence against the individuals in need of protection. In the view of the Court, the Guidelines excluded the possibility of direct participation in the hostilities.[255] Furthermore the enlisted persons had asked the Coalition Provisional Authority (CPA), at the time being the administrative authority in Iraqi territory, for permission to use the weapons in the territory under the control of the multinational force.[256]

The Assize Court of Bari determined that this kind of activity was excluded from the coverage of Article 288 because the accused did not enlist the employees as combatants but for reasons not connected to the conduct of military operations, even though the envisaged activity was connected to the existence of an armed conflict (as the VIPs the subject of security functions worked in the framework of post-conflict reconstruction).

The Court's decision is important because in Italy there is no law regulating the activities of private military and private security companies. It is clear from this decision that existing law may not adequately cover all exigencies relevant to contemporary armed conflicts.

Valeria Eboli[257]

Cases—Subsidiary Protection Granted to a Former Child Soldier

- Court of Appeal of Naples, Judgment of 17 March 2010, *X* v. *Ministero Interno e Commissione territoriale di Caserta per il riconoscimento dello status di rifugiato*

In the judgment under review, the Court of Appeal of Naples granted subsidiary protection status to a Sierra Leone national, a former child soldier during the civil war in that country (1991–2002).

---

[255] It seems difficult to share the view of the Court on the fact that an eventual intervention of the contractors in defence of the civilians, as provided for in the Guidelines on their employ, does not constitute a direct participation in the hostilities, also bearing in mind the recent study of the ICRC in this regard. See J.M. Henckaerts, L. Doswald-Beck, *Customary International Humanitarian Law* (Cambridge, Cambridge University Press, 2009).

[256] *Prosecutor* v. *Giovanni Piero Spinelli and Salvatore Stefio*, Judgment, p 8.

[257] Valeria Eboli (Ph.D. in International and European Union Law, University 'Sapienza' of Rome) is Adjunct Professor of International Law at the University of Pisa/Italian Naval Academy and Consultant at the Institute of International Legal Studies of the National Research Council (CNR), Rome; Legal Advisor for the Ministry of Defense.

The applicant asked for the recognition of: (a) 'political refugee' status because the individual belonged to a particular social group persecuted and threatened with death; (b) subsidiary protection[258]; (c) humanitarian protection[259]; or, if these different protections were refused, (d) the right of asylum, according to Article 10 of the *Italian Constitution*.

The Territorial Commission for Recognition of International Protection makes assessments of 'grounded applications' for the granting of asylum and political refugee status. If the application is rejected by the Commission, access to courts for judicial review is granted to the applicants.

The Territorial Commission may grant not only asylum and political refugee status, but also subsidiary protection status to a third country national or a stateless person eligible for it, when there is a well-founded fear that the applicant may be persecuted or where there is a real risk of suffering serious harm in the country of origin. Under Legislative Decree No. 251 of 19 November 2007,[260] 'serious harm' can include: death penalty or execution; torture or inhuman or degrading treatment or punishment of an applicant in the country of origin; serious and individual threat to a civilian's life or person by reason of indiscriminate violence in situations of international or internal armed conflict. Subsidiary protection is not available when the person: has committed a crime against peace, a war crime, or a crime against humanity, as defined in the international instruments drawn up to make provision in respect of such crimes; has committed a serious crime (the seriousness being evaluated according to the Italian criminal law); has been guilty of acts contrary to the purposes and principles of the United Nations as set out in the Preamble and Articles 1 and 2 of the *Charter of the United Nations*; or constitutes a danger to the community or to the security of the Member State in which he or she lives.[261]

In the case under examination, the Commission deemed that the applicant was not eligible for subsidiary protection. His/her 'story' (*racconto*, in the original text), the existence of objective evidence (scars, medical certificate on his/her physical and mental health), and the compatibility of the personal history of the applicant with the events occurring in Sierra Leone in the 1990s, were not considered a 'grounded application' for granting international protection, according to the decision of the Territorial Commission in 2008 and the judgment of the Tribunal of Naples (lower court) in 2009.

Conversely, in the opinion of the Court of Appeal, the complexity of evidence and testimony, and in particular the circumstance that the applicant's brother had

---

258 See Legislative Decree No. 25 of 25 January 2008, 'Implementation of the Council Directive 2005/85/EC of 1 December 2005 on minimum standards on procedures in Member States for granting and withdrawing refugee status', Art. 2(f).

259 Ibid., Art. 5(6).

260 Legislative Decree No. 251/2007 implemented the Council Directive 2004/83/EC of 29 April 2004 on minimum standards for the qualification and status of third country nationals or stateless persons as refugees or as persons who otherwise need international protection and the content of the protection granted' (Art. 14).

261 Ibid., Art. 16.

been a commander of the Revolutionary United Front (RUF)—the rebel army which fought against government forces in the war in Sierra Leone—and had committed horrible acts against his nationals, were a reasonable ground for considering the applicant in danger and not adequately protected by local authorities in case of repatriation.

The accused did not qualify for political refugee status because he was not faced with the prospect of persecution based on race, religion, nationality, belonging to a particular social group, or political ideas. However, in the view of the Court the fear of 'serious harm' was concrete and justified the granting of subsidiary protection status.

GIOVANNI CARLO BRUNO[262]

Cases—Duty to Assist Any Person in Danger at Sea

- *Cap Anamur Case*, Tribunal of Agrigento, First Criminal Section, Judgment of 15 February 2010, <http://www.asgi.it/public/parser_download/save/tribunale_agrigento_15022010_1.pdf>, <http://www.asgi.it/public/parser_download/save/tribunale_agrigento_15022010_2.pdf>

The Judgment of the Tribunal of Agrigento[263] marks the end of a long and complex legal case which commenced on 20 June 2004 when the German flagged vessel, the *Cap Anamur*, rescued 37 people on the high sea 46 nautical miles from the Libyan coast, 90 nautical miles from Lampedusa Island (Italy) and 160 nautical miles from Malta. In order to understand the conclusions reached by the Tribunal in this case, it is important briefly to reconstruct the facts.

The *Cap Anamur* belonged to a German humanitarian organization founded in 1979 to carry out missions in the most disadvantaged areas of the world by relying on medical, nursing and technical personnel. The organization purchased the vessel to transport food, medicines, medical equipments and other materials to be used in its humanitarian projects.[264]

In 2004, the President of the organization (Mr. Elias Bierdel), the Captain (Mr. Stefan Schmidt) and the First Officer (Mr. Vladimir Dachkevitch), together with a small crew, began a trip in the Mediterranean Sea directed to Aqaba (Jordan) to unload the *Cap Anamur*'s cargo and transfer it to Baghdad (Iraq) by land. During the voyage the vessel incurred a mechanical breakdown and was obliged to dock in Malta where it was repaired.[265] From 4 to 20 June 2004, the *Cap Anamur* was either at moorings in the port of Valletta or engaged in periods of navigation in the Mediterranean Sea to test the engine. On 20 June 2004, while it was in international waters, the *Cap Anamur*'s crew sighted a group of persons floundering on a raft. Those on the raft were in evident danger because the raft was at the mercy of

---

[262] Giovanni Carlo Bruno is Researcher at the Institute for International Legal Studies, National Research Council (CNR), Naples.

[263] The judgment was pronounced on 7 October 2009, but it was entered on 15 February 2010.

[264] The *Cap Anamur* had a German navigation license for 'cargo ship' and as a 'rescue and support vessel'.

[265] The *Cap Anamur* docked in the port of Valletta from 26 May to 4 June 2004.

the waves and was taking on water. The Captain of the *Cap Anamur* decided to rescue them.[266]

The 37 people on the raft had no identification documents. Most of them claimed to be Sudanese citizens fleeing from the war in their country but one person claimed to be from Sierra Leone and another one from Nigeria. The master of the vessel, Stefan Schmidt, together with the President of the *Cap Anamur* organization, Elias Bierdel, decided to sail to the Italian coast of Sicily to dock at Porto Empedocle, because Lampedusa, for technical reasons, was not considered a suitable port for the vessel. Schmidt and Bierdel choose Italy because they considered it a secure country where the shipwrecked persons could have access to medical and legal assistance, and, above all, enjoy fundamental human rights. According to the reconstruction made by the Tribunal through the *Cap Anamur*'s log book, after the rescue, the vessel held different courses: on 25 June 2004 it approached the port of Marsaxlokk (Malta), the following days it sailed towards Lampedusa, and on 30 June 2004 the vessel arrived 17 nautical miles out from Porto Empedocle where it asked for permission to dock.

On 1 July 2004, the Italian Coast Guard denied authorization to the *Cap Anamur* to enter Italian waters and to have the access to the port.[267] For 11 days, the vessel sailed in international waters near the Italian territorial sea, but during this period the situation on board became difficult. Some of the shipwrecked persons suffered nervous breakdowns and wanted to throw themselves overboard.[268] Furthermore, according to the captain there was a risk of insubordination and revolt against the crew. Only when the Captain issued an emergency call did the Italian authorities grant authorization for the vessel to enter the port and disembark the rescued people on 12 July 2004.

During the 11 days of sailing on the High Seas, a political and diplomatic debate began between Italy, the coastal State, Germany, the flag State, and Malta, the first country approached by the *Cap Anamur* to determine the State responsible for examining the asylum applications,[269] in accordance with Council Regulation (EC)

---

266 See his testimony in the judgment, pp 11 et seq.

267 United Nations Convention on the Law of the Sea, opened for signature 10 December 1982, 1833 *UNTS* 396, Art. 3 (entered into force 16 November 1994) provides 'Every State has the right to establish the breadth of its territorial sea up to a limit not exceeding 12 nautical miles, measured from baselines determined in accordance with this Convention'.

268 The *Cap Anamur* case became also well-known in the media and in international and Italian press. Many journalists visited the vessel and interviewed the captain and the president of the association. The case was also criticized by the United Nations High Commissioner for Refugees (UNHCR). See UNHCR, *Cap Anamur Boat: UNHCR Expresses Strong concern to Italian Authorities* (23 July 2004), <http://www.unhcr.org/4100ec6d9.html>.

269 Rescued people on the *Cap Anamur* applied for political asylum in Germany, their handwritten applications were delivered to a lawyer of the Italian Council for Refugees (Consiglio Italiano per i Rifugiati, <www.cir-onlus.org>) in order to be transmitted to the Federal Office Migration and Refugees in Nuremberg, but Germany did not accept the asylum applications because for the German Ministry of the Interior the applications were to be submitted only on German territory, so those presented on the *Cap Anamur* were null and void.

No. 343/2003 of 18 February 2003 establishing the criteria and mechanisms for determining the Member State responsible for examining an asylum application lodged in one of the Member States by a third-country national. Article 10 of the Regulation establishes that if an asylum seeker has irregularly crossed the border of a Member State by land, sea or air coming from a third country, the Member State thus entered shall be responsible for examining the application for asylum.[270] For Italy and Germany the first port of arrival was Malta because on 25 June 2004, the *Cap Anamur* approached its coasts. However, Malta disagreed with this analysis as its authorities did not receive either any information of the presence on board of irregular immigrants or any request of assistance. It is important to underline that in conformity with UNCLOS, Malta could not exercise criminal and civil jurisdiction over those on the *Cap Anamur*, because foreign ships in territorial waters or ports are self-contained units where coastal States do not exercise effective control, except in the cases established in Articles 27 and 28 UNCLOS.[271] Consequently it is difficult to consider the *Cap Anamur*'s passage towards the port of Marsaxlokk as an entry in Malta in the sense of Article 10 of the Council Regulation (EC) No. 343/2003, even if the vessel was in Maltese territorial waters.[272]

On 12 July 2004, the question was resolved because Italy authorized the vessel's docking at Porto Empedocle. All rescued people made applications for political asylum, declaring themselves to be Sudanese, while Bierdel, Schmidt and Dachkevitch were charged with the crime of aiding illegal immigration provided in Article 12 of the Legislative Decree No. 286/1998[273] and arrested.[274] Italian authorities verified the nationality of the 37 people and found that none of them

---

270 [2003] *OJ* L 50/1, pp 1 et seq. This Regulation and the Commission Regulation (EC) No. 1560/2003 of 2 September 2003 laying down detailed rules for the application of the Council Regulation (EC) No. 343/2003 substituted the 1990 Dublin Convention determining the State Responsible for Examining Applications for Asylum Lodged in one of the Member States of the European Communities, with a new legal regime called 'Dublin II'. On EU law on refugees and asylum, see E. Guild, P. Minderhoud, *Immigration and Criminal Law in the European Union* (Leiden, Martinus Niijhoff Publishers, 2006); V. Della Fina, 'Rifugiati', XV *Enciclopedia giuridica Treccani* (2007); I. Staffans, 'Judicial Protection and the New European Asylum Regime', 12 *European Journal of Migration and Law* (2010) pp 273–297.

271 R. R. Churchill and A. Lowe, *The Law of the Sea* (Manchester, Manchester University Press, 1999).

272 On this aspect of the case see the remarks of S. Trevisanut, 'The Principle of *Non-Refoulement* at Sea and the Effectiveness of Asylum Protection', 12 *Max Plank Yearbook of United Nations Law* (2008) p 227.

273 For the text of the Legislative Decree No. 286/1998, Testo unico delle disposizioni concernenti la disciplina dell'immigrazione e norme sulla condizione dello straniero, <http://www.altalex.com/index.php?idnot=836>.

274 They were released after 5 days. The three members were also accused to have gained money through the rescue mission because the case provoked a worldwide media interest, so they were charged with fraudulent conduct and also false representation to the Italian authorities of the emergency situation on board which determined the issue of the authorization to enter the internal waters of Italy. The Prosecutor asked 4 years imprisonment and the payment of EUR 400,000 in fines.

was Sudanese: 31 were from Ghana and 6 from Nigeria. During a debate in the Parliament on the case, the Italian Minister of the Interior claimed that none of the African people were eligible for political asylum because they were not refugees.[275] Consequently, the Italian authorities rejected all the applications and commenced expulsion proceedings.[276]

After 5 years of litigation, the Tribunal of Agrigento acquitted Bierdel, Schmidt and Dachkevitch rejecting all charges against the three *Cap Anamur* officials.[277] For the Tribunal the master of a ship who rescues immigrants in danger on the high sea and takes them to a safe place cannot be charged with the crime of aiding illegal immigration, because he performs an international obligation and according to Article 51 of the *Italian Penal Code*, conduct made in performance of duty is not punishable.

In its reasoning, the Tribunal recalled all the international treaties ratified by Italy establishing such conduct as a humanitarian duty. In particular, Article 98 of UNCLOS provides that a master of a ship has the duty to assist any person in danger of being lost at sea and to proceed with all possible speed to rescue the persons in distress.[278] The same duty is established in Article V of the 1974 *Convention for the Safety of Life at Sea* (SOLAS)[279] and in Article 10 of the 1989 *International Convention on Salvage*.[280] For the Tribunal the 1979 *International Convention on Maritime Search and Rescue* (SAR) was also relevant because it is based on the principle of international cooperation in maritime search and rescue of persons in distress at sea and it states that each search and rescue region is established by agreement among the Parties concerned.[281]

The judgment emphasized that the aforementioned international obligations are also contained in the *Italian Code of Navigation*. In particular, Article 1158 of the

---

275 'Cap Anamur, espulsi 27 degli immigrati. Pisanu: «Non sono profughi»', L'Unità (Rome, Italy) 22 July 2004, <http://www.meltingpot.org/articolo3286.html>.

276 Only four Ghanaians and one Nigerian were permitted to stay in Italy for humanitarian reasons. The Italian government's decision was criticized by human rights associations. Also the European Court of Human Rights investigated the details of the matter. See MaltaMedia News, *European Court to Examine Cap Anamur Case* (23 July 2004), <http://www.maltamedia.com/cgi-bin/artman/exec/view.cgi?archive=1&num=2704>.

277 Bierdel and Schmidt were acquitted because their conduct was not a crime under the *Italian penal Code*, Dachkevitch was acquitted because he did not commit any of acts charged.

278 Italy ratified and implemented UNCLOS with Law No. 684 of 2 December 1994.

279 Convention for the Safety of Life at Sea, opened for signature 1 November 1974, 1184 UNTS 2 (entered into force 25 May 1980). Italy ratified and implemented the Convention with Law No. 313 of 23 May 1980.

280 International Convention on Salvage, opened for signature 1 July 1989, 1953 UNTS 33479 (entered into force 14 July 1996). Italy ratified and implemented the Convention with Law No. 129 of 12 April 1995.

281 International Convention on Maritime Search and Rescue, opened for signature 1 November 1979, 1405 UNTS 23489 (entered into force 22 June 1985). Italy ratified and implemented the Convention with Law No. 47 of 3 April 1989. The Italian authority responsible to implement SAR is the Ministry of Infrastructure and Transport which acts through the Italian Coast Guard, a corps of the Italian navy, structured in the Italian Maritime Rescue Coordination Center (IMRCC) and 15 sub-centers (IMRSC).

Code provides for the imprisonment of the master of a national or foreign ship who does not assist other ships or persons in distress and Article 490 establishes the duty of rescue.[282]

Furthermore, the Tribunal was of the view that Captain Schmidt acted in conformity with international law when, together with Bierdel, he tried to find a safe place on land for the shipwrecked persons. In the judgment it is explained that according to international law a vessel is only a temporary rescue place. The Tribunal recalled that in conformity with 'IMO Guidelines on the Treatment of Persons Rescued at Sea', adopted on 20 May 2004, a 'place of safety' is a

> location where rescue operations are considered to terminate. It is also a place where the survivors' safety of life is no longer threatened and where their basic human needs (such as food, shelter and medical needs) can be met. Further, it is a place from which transportation arrangements can be made for the survivors' next or final destination.[283]

The IMO Guidelines state very clearly that 'even if the ship is capable of safely accommodating the survivors and may serve as a temporary place of safety, it should be relieved of this responsibility as soon as alternative arrangements can be made'.[284] The Tribunal found that Schmidt and Bierdel legitimately choose Italy as a place of safety, for neither Libya nor Malta gave them sufficient guarantees concerning the rescued people's human rights and their humanitarian assistance. The choice of Italy involved an assessment on the part of Schmidt and Bierdel as to the likely prospects for the irregular passengers to have a fair and objective review of their claims to asylum where the principle of *non-refoulement*, in conformity with 1951 *Convention Relating to the Status of Refugees* (Article 33), would be respected.[285]

The conclusions of the Tribunal of Agrigento on the *Cap Anamur* case represent an important affirmation of the principle that rendering humanitarian assistance by rescuing people in distress at sea does not constitute a crime of aiding illegal immigration.

VALENTINA DELLA FINA[286]

---

282 There are also other relevant provisions in the Italian Code of Navigation, such as Article 69 concerning rescue to ships in danger and shipwrecked persons and Article 70 on the use of ships for rescue.

283 'IMO Guidelines', para 6.12.

284 Ibid., para 6.13.

285 Italy ratified and implemented the 1951 Geneva Convention with Law No. 722 of 24 July 1954. The obligation of *non-refoulement* implies the obligation for the State of refuge not to expel asylum seekers to the countries of persecution until their right to obtain international protection has not been ascertained. For the Italian practice concerning the implementation of the principle of *non-refoulement*, see F. Salerno, 'L'obbligo internazionale dei richiedenti asilo', 3 *Diritti umani e diritto internazionale* (2010); S. Klepp, 'A Contested Asylum System: the European Union between Refugee Protection and Border Control in the Mediterranean Sea', 12 *European Journal of Migration and Law* (2010).

286 Valentina Della Fina is Senior researcher at the Institute for International Legal Studies of the National Research Council (CNR), Rome, and co-ordinates the contributions of the Institute for this Report.

Cases—Prohibition of Extradition to a State Where a Person May Be Subjected to Forced Labour

- Court of Appeal of Trento, detached Section of Bolzano, Judgment No. 48 of 31 March 2010 <http://www.stranieriinitalia.it/briguglio/immigrazione-e-asilo/2010/agosto/corte-app-tn-estradizione.pdf>

The judgment of the Court of Appeal of Trento concerns the case of an Ukrainian who was charged with aggravated robbery in her State of origin (Ukraine) and was subsequently arrested in Italy on 28 January 2010 on a arrest warrant issued by the Tribunal of Kiev on 23 January 2009. Ukraine requested extradition of its national from Italy but the Court of Appeal of Trento denied the application because in the requesting State the offense in question is punishable with punitive labour.[287]

The Court analysed the Ukrainian criminal law, in particular, Article 185(1) of the *Ukrainian Penal Code* which provides that the crime of robbery is punishable by forced labour (up to 2 years) or by imprisonment (up to 3 years), and, Chap. X, Article 51, of the same Code, devoted to 'penalties', which contains a reference to 'correctional labour'.

The Court recalled that Article 4 of the *European Convention for the Protection of Human Rights and Fundamental Freedoms* of 1950 prohibits forced or compulsory labour[288] and that Italy has been a Party to the Convention since 1955.[289] For the Court the granting of the extradition to Ukraine would have been contrary to the *European Convention* and also to Article 698 of the Italian *Code of Criminal Procedure* which prohibits extradition when the defendant can be subjected, *inter alia*, to inhuman or degrading treatment or punishment or acts that violate a fundamental human right.[290] In the reasoning of the Court, forced labour represents a violation of a basic human right, as established by the Court of Cassation in judgment No. 23555 of 19 June 2006 on an analogous case of extradition to Belarus.[291] Furthermore, the Court considered that the defendant may have been subjected to forms of ill-treatment in Ukrainian jails, considering the difficult

[287] On the extradition in international law, see A. Aust, *Handbook of International Law* (Cambridge, Cambridge University Press, 2010) pp 246 et seq.

[288] European Convention for the Protection of Human Rights and Fundamental Freedoms, opened for signature on 4 November 1950, 213 *UNTS* 222 (entered into force on 3 September 1953). Article 4 specifies that for its purposes the expression 'forced or compulsory labour' shall not include: (a) any work required to be done in the ordinary course of detention imposed according to the provisions of Article 5 of this Convention or during conditional release from such detention; (b) any service of a military character or, in case of conscientious objectors in countries where they are recognised, service exacted instead of compulsory military service; (c) any service exacted in case of an emergency or calamity threatening the life or well-being of the community; (d) any work or service which forms part of normal civic obligations.

[289] Italy ratified and implemented the European Convention with Law No. 848 of 4 August 1955.

[290] Article 3 of the European Convention prohibits torture and inhuman or degrading treatment or punishment.

[291] The judgment is available from <http://www.stranieriinitalia.it/briguglio/immigrazione-e-asilo/2010/agosto/sent-cass-23555-2006.html>.

situation of the prisons in Ukraine as documented by an Amnesty International Report of 2009 which is mentioned in the judgment.[292]

In its conclusions the Court of Appeal affirmed respect for human rights, as established in the *European Convention*, as paramount. In the case under examination, the risk that the defendant may have been subjected to forced labour and inhuman or degrading treatment in her State of origin was considered a sufficient basis for rejecting the extradition request.

VALENTINA DELLA FINA

Cases—Prohibition of Expulsion for Humanitarian Protection Reasons

- Supreme Court of Cassation, First Civil Section, Order No. 10636 of 3 May 2010, <www.cortedicassazione.it>

Following the refusal of refugee *status* by the Territorial Commission for Recognition of International Protection in Caserta,[293] a Liberian citizen was found without a lawful permit to stay in Italy and was made subject to expulsion by decree of the Prefect of Caserta of 26 September 2007. Against the decree, the applicant unsuccessfully petitioned a Justice of the Peace (JP) of Caserta, who confirmed the expulsion order by decree of 14 October 2008.

The applicant appealed to the Court of Cassation for judicial review of the decree of the JP. The object of the claim was that the JP did not undertake an effective investigation of the risk of the applicant being persecuted upon return to his country of origin.

The Court of Cassation upheld the claim finding that it is unlawful to validate an expulsion order against an asylum seeker solely on the grounds of the denial of refugee *status* by the Territorial Commission and without examining the

---

292 See Amnesty International, Amnesty International Report 2009: The State of the World's Human Rights (2009) pp 338 et seq. <http://report2009.amnesty.org/sites/report2009.amnesty.org/files/documents/air09-en.pdf>.

293 According to the Legislative Decree No. 25 of 28 January 2008 (partially amended by Legislative Decree No. 159 of 3 October 2008), implementing the Directive 2005/85/EC of the EU Council of 1 December 2005, regarding minimum regulations for procedures applied in the Member States for the purposes of the recognition and the revocation of refugee status, the Territorial Commissions for Recognition of International Protection are set up of four members (two members from the Ministry of the Interior, one representative from the municipality, the province or the region and one representative from UNHCR) and decide on requests for international protection. The applications are preliminarily evaluated on the basis of the information concerning the general situation of the State of origin of the asylum seeker; in case of insufficient information, the Commission can invite the applicant for an interview. [Decreto Legislativo 28 gennaio 2008, n. 25, *Attuazione della direttiva 2005/85/CE recante norme minime per le procedure applicate negli Stati membri ai fini del riconoscimento e della revoca dello status di rifugiato*], published in *Gazzetta Ufficiale* No. 40 of 16 February 2008; [Decreto legislativo 13 ottobre 2008, n. 159, *Modifiche ed integrazioni al decreto legislativo 28 gennaio 2008, n. 25, recante attuazione della direttiva 2005/85/CE relativa alle norme minime per le procedure applicate negli Stati membri ai fini del riconoscimento e della revoca dello status di rifugiato*], published in *Gazzetta Ufficiale* No. 247 of 21 October 2008.

circumstances provided for by law under which expulsion is prohibited. In particular, Legislative Decree No. 286 of 25 July 1998, 'Consolidated Text on Immigration', Article 19 (1), prohibits expulsion or *refoulement* to another State where the individual might be persecuted for various reasons or might be exposed to the risk of expulsion to another country where they would not be protected from persecution.[294]

In this regard, the judges made reference to the long-established rule of the Court of Cassation by which aliens are entitled to the protection of fundamental human rights as foreseen by Article 2 of the *Italian Constitution*. Therefore, the immigration legal system is to be interpreted in conformity with the Constitution and any counterbalance of aliens' fundamental rights with other constitutional interests, whether admitted, does not fall under the competence of the administrative body, but eventually of the legislator acting in accordance to the Constitution.[295]

The turning point of the Court's reasoning is that humanitarian protection, refugee *status* and asylum all have the same legal value, namely fundamental human rights. It is a fact that Legislative Decree No. 286/1998, Article 19, prohibits expulsion with a formula marginally different from that contained in the 1951 *Geneva Convention on the Status of Refugees*, Article 1, to describe the conditions under which refugee *status* is recognised.[296] In the opinion of the Court, this means that the existence of circumstances forbidding expulsion must result in humanitarian protection and a legitimate basis for foreign nationals to stay in Italy.

The legal basis for the human rights of foreign nationals is also envisaged by subsequent Italian laws implementing EU directives. In particular, Article 32 of Legislative Decree No. 251 of 19 November 2007,[297] enumerates the factors which must be examined following a decision of the Territorial Commissions to

---

294 Decreto legislativo 25 luglio 1998, n. 286, Testo unico delle disposizioni concernenti la disciplina dell'immigrazione e norme sulla condizione dello straniero, published in *Gazzetta Ufficiale* No. 191 of 18 August 1998.

295 *Inter alia*, Court of Cassation, United Civil Sections, *Opana* v. *Ministero dell'interno*, Judgment No. 13393 of 9 September 2009, in 92 *Rivista di diritto internazionale* (2009).

296 Convention Relating to the Status of Refugees, opened for signature 28 July 1951, 189 UNTS 137 (*entered into force* 22 April 1954).

297 Legislative Decree No. 251 of 19 November 2007, implementation of the Directive 2004/83/EC of the EU Council of 29 April 2004 regarding minimum regulations on attributing to citizens of third countries or stateless people the status of refugee or person otherwise needing international protection, as well as minimum regulations on the content of the protection recognized. [Decreto legislative 19 novembre 2007, n. 251, Attuazione della direttiva 2004/83/CE recante norme minime sull'attribuzione, a cittadini di Paesi terzi o apolidi, della qualifica del rifugiato o di persona altrimenti bisognosa di protezione internazionale, nonché norme minime sul contenuto della protezione riconosciuta], published in *Gazzetta Ufficiale* No. 3 of 4 January 2008.

deny refugee status or the grant of subsidiary protection.[298] Furthermore, Article 34 affirms the equivalence of subsidiary protection measures and a permit to stay for humanitarian reasons.

The Court cancelled the challenged decree declaring that the JP, by validating the expulsion order because the applicant did not possess a permit to stay, without verifying the existence of conditions excluding expulsion, did not comply with Article 19 of Legislative Decree No. 286/1998.

RACHELE CERA[299]

Cases—Annulment of Expulsion Orders for Rosarno Migrants

- Justice of the Peace of Bari, Order No. 812 of 24 May 2010, <http://www.asgi.it/public/parser_download/save/gdp_bari_2010_812_2.pdf>
- Justice of the Peace of Bari, Order No. 945 of 11 June 2010, <http://www.asgi.it/public/parser_download/save/ordinanza_bari_11_giugno_2010.pdf>

Both orders of the Justice of the Peace (JP) of Bari annulled expulsion decrees adopted against two African migrant farm workers involved in incidents in Rosarno in southern Italy.

In January 2010, there were violent clashes between migrant workers and the local population because of long-standing socio-economic discrimination suffered by migrant workers and a growing xenophobic attitude by the local population towards them. Over a 3 day period, riots caused serious injuries to African and other seasonal migrants, law enforcement officers, and local residents in Rosarno. Over 1000 migrants left the town following the violence, most of them evacuated by law enforcement personnel and deported to the Identification and Expulsion Centre (Centro di identificazione ed espulsione or CIE) in Bari.

The incidents in Rosarno were also a matter of concern during Italy's Universal Periodic Review at the February 2010 UN Human Right Council's (HRC) Session.[300]

The JP deemed that the claimants were made to live and work in inhumane situations and conditions, suffering harassment by their employees, which could lead to the applicability of Legislative Decree No. 286 of 25 July 1998, 'Consolidated Text on Immigration', Article 18, that allows the issuing of a special

---

[298] Legislative Decree No. 25/2008 introduced the institute of subsidiary protection that is granted to either a citizen not belonging to the European Union, or to a stateless person that does not meet the requirements necessary to be recognized as a refugee, but in respect of whom there are reasons to consider that if he or she returns to the country of origin, or to the country in which he or she habitually resided, he or she would effectively risk serious injury, and due to this risk, cannot or does not want to benefit from the protection of that country. Instead, police headquarters may issue a permit of stay for humanitarian reasons whenever the Territorial Commission, while not recognizing the extremes for international protection, indicates 'serious reasons of humanitarian nature' regarding the person requesting asylum.

[299] Rachele Cera is Researcher at the Institute for International Legal Studies of the National Research Council (CNR), Rome.

[300] Human Rights Council, Universal Periodic Review—Italy, UN Doc. A/HRC/WG.6/7/ITA (9 February 2010) <www.ohchr.org/EN/HRBodies/UPR/PAGES/ITSession7.aspx>.

residence permit for social protection to foreigners who have been victims of violence or exploitation from a criminal organisation.[301] The two applicants were able to denounce the inhuman and degrading treatment at work. However, the Ministry of the Interior instructed that Legislative Decree No. 286/1998 does not make the protection *ex* Article 18 conditional on the alien's denunciation or availability to collaborate with police or judicial authorities.[302]

Remarkably, in order No. 945/2010 the JP noted also that the expulsion order 'was issued following a police operation through which the expulsion of numerous foreign citizens who lived and worked in Rosarno was carried out', upholding the complaint that the measure violated the 1963 Protocol No. 4 to the 1950 *Convention for the Protection of Human Rights and Fundamental Freedoms*, Article 4, which forbids the collective expulsion of foreigners.[303] The rationale for this provision is to prevent preordained and systematic measures aimed at compelling aliens, as a group, to leave a country, without demonstrating that the personal circumstances of each of those concerned had been genuinely and individually taken into account.[304] As highlighted in the 2007 Report of the International Law Commission, the key element to define a 'collective expulsion' is not quantitative but qualitative. In particular, it is important to know whether the expulsion was based on discriminatory grounds or whether each of the persons concerned benefited from procedural safeguards applied to them individually.[305]

There were several reasons which led the JP to the view that the expulsions were collective and constituted denial of individually applied procedural safeguards: time, as the expulsion order was issued at the same time as those of several other foreigners picked up and evacuated from Rosarno by the security forces; place, as it was issued alongside others, all of which concerned workers employed

---

301 Decreto legislativo 25 luglio 1998, n. 286, Testo unico delle disposizioni concernenti la disciplina dell'immigrazione e norme sulla condizione dello straniero, published in *Gazzetta Ufficiale* No. 191 of 18 August 1998.

302 Circular of the Ministry of Interior No. Prot. 11050 of 28 May 2007 on Legislative Decree No. 286/1998, Article 18, <www1.interno.it/mininterno/export/sites/default/it/sezioni/servizi/legislazione/_circolari/dip_immigrazione/0997_circolare_n.prot.11050.html_319159486.html>.

303 Protocol No. 4 to the Convention for the Protection of Human Rights and Fundamental Freedoms securing certain rights and freedoms other than those already included in the Convention and in the first Protocol thereto, opened for signature 16 September 1963, 1469 UNTS 263, ETS No. 46 (entered into force 2 May 1968). Italy ratified and implemented the Protocol No. 4 by Decree of the President of the Republic No. 217 of 14 April 1982 [Decreto del Presidente della Repubblica 14 aprile 1982, n. 217, Esecuzione del protocollo n. 4 addizionale della convenzione per la salvaguardia dei diritti dell'uomo e delle libertà fondamentali, che riconosce taluni diritti e libertà oltre quelli che già figurano nella detta convenzione e nel suo primo protocollo addizionale, adottato a Strasburgo il 16 settembre 1963], published in *Gazzetta Ufficiale* No. 124 of 7 May 1982.

304 *Andric* v. *Sweden*, European Court of Human Rights, Application No. 45917/99, 23 February 1999, para 1; ibid., *Conka* v. *Belgium*, European Court of Human Rights, Application No. 51564/99, 5 February 2002, para 63.

305 United Nations, Report of the International Law Commission—59th session, UN Doc. A/62/10 (2007) p 147.

in Rosarno after the police forces' intervention; action, as all the expulsions were part of the same operation by the security forces; reason, as the appellant's expulsion was confirmed for precisely the same reasons as others meted out on the same day, namely illegal entry and residence.[306]

The JP found also that the expulsion orders were provided in languages that the recipients did not understand.

In conclusion, by orders No. 812/2010 and No. 945/2010, the JP of Bari quashed the expulsion orders and, more importantly, affirmed the applicants' right to request a permit to stay for social protection, even if the issue of permits was not within its competence. In fact, as stated in order No. 812/2010, the judge was not permitted to avoid judicial review (*ius dicere*) when the measures of the administrative authority overlook or ignore the individual position the claimant is entitled to.

RACHELE CERA

Cases—Constitutionality of Illegal Presence as an Aggravating Circumstance

- Constitutional Court, Judgment No. 249 of 8 July 2010, <http://www.cortecostituzionale.it/actionPronuncia.do>

The judgment issued by the Constitutional Court on 8 July 2010 concerned the constitutionality of illegal presence as an aggravating circumstance for foreign nationals committing crimes in Italy as provided by Article 61(11-*bis*) of the *Italian Criminal Code*.[307] The requests for constitutional interpretation were submitted to the Constitutional Court by the Tribunal of Livorno by order of 4 February 2010, and by the Tribunal of Ferrara by order of 26 January 2010. Article 61(11-*bis*) covers the common aggravating factors for acts committed by an offender while he is illegally in the Italian territory. This provision was considered by the relevant Tribunals which considered it to be in violation of Articles 3,[308] 25(2)[309] and 27(1), (3)[310] of the *Italian Constitution* in several aspects.[311]

---

[306] D. Belluccio and I. Gjergji, *Rosarno: annullata un'altra espulsione a carico di un cittadino straniero* (18 June 2010), <www.asgi.it/home_asgi.php?n=1063&l=it>.

[307] Para 11-*bis* was introduced by Article 1(f) of the Decree-Law No. 92 of 23 May 2008 and by the Law No. 125 of 24 July 2008.

[308] Article 3 reads: 'All citizens have equal social dignity and are equal before the law, without distinction of sex, race, language, religion, political opinion, personal and social'.

[309] Article 25 states: '1. No one may be withheld from the jurisdiction of the judge previously ascertained by law. 2. No one may be punished except on the basis of a law in force prior to the time when the offence was committed. 3. No one may be subjected to restrictive measures except in those cases provided for by the law'.

[310] Article 27 reads: 'Criminal responsibility is personal. The defendant is not considered guilty until the final judgement is passed. Punishment cannot consist in inhuman treatment and must aim at the rehabilitation of the convicted person'.

[311] On the aspects concerning the constitutional conformity of Article 61 (11-*bis*), see, *inter alia*, L. Masera, 'Profili di costituzionalità della nuova aggravante come applicabile allo straniero irregolare', *Corriere del merito* (2008) pp 1175 et seq.

In its order, the Tribunal of Livorno dealt with a case concerning a foreign national charged with the offence foreseen under Article 13(13) of Legislative Decree no. 286 of 25 July 1998 (Consolidated Text on Immigration)[312] who challenged the aggravating circumstance of his illegal presence on Italian territory according to Article 61(11-*bis*) of the *Criminal Code*. According to the Tribunal, Article 61(11-*bis*) violates Article 3 of the *Italian Constitution*, because the lack of a valid permit of stay cannot be considered a source of danger equivalent to other specified aggravating circumstances. Furthermore, Article 61(11-*bis*) infringes the principle of personal criminal liability, because it results in an increase of punishment based on a personal status rather then on dangerous conduct.

The lack of proportionality of the punitive treatment would have deprived the punishment of its rehabilitative function, so the offender could not have perceived it as helpful for his reintegration into society, but only as a punishment exceeding the degree of his responsibility.

The case dealt with by the Tribunal of Ferrara involved a foreign national accused of drug possession who was sentenced on the basis of the aggravating circumstances pursuant to Article 61(11-*bis*). In this case, the Tribunal of Ferrara alleged a violation of Articles 25(2) and 27(1) of the *Italian Constitution* for the lack of relevant connection between the punishment and the offence and the exclusive reliance upon the personal status of the offender.

According to the Tribunal of Ferrara, the disparity of sentencing for offenders solely on the basis of the legal status of the offender (i.e., whether they are legally or illegally in the territory of the Italian State or whether they are EU or non-EU citizens) could not be justified.

Both Tribunals also considered 'irrational' the presumption that the mere lack of a valid permit of stay in the territory of the State renders an offender more 'dangerous' than an Italian national guilty of the same criminal offence. The Tribunal of Ferrara could find no reason to apply a more severe punishment where there was no connection between the condition of the offender and the committed offence.

The Constitutional Court rejected the constitutional claim submitted by the Tribunal of Livorno. According to the Constitutional Court, no assessment was undertaken to show why an aggravating circumstance based on the illegality of the stay which constitutes a violation of immigration law should not be applied to the offence. It should be noted that according to Article 61 of the *Criminal Code*, common circumstances aggravate the commission of a crime only when they constituting special aggravating circumstances.

By contrast, the Constitutional Court admitted the claim submitted by the Tribunal of Ferrara. In this case, according to the Constitutional Court, the legal status of a foreign national cannot be considered as a valid basis for differential

---

[312] Article 13(13) reads: 'An expelled alien may not return to the State without special authorization of the Minister of the Interior. In case of violation, the alien shall be punished with imprisonment from 1 to 4 years and will be again expelled with immediate accompaniment to the border'.

treatment, especially within the framework of criminal law. The constitutional principle of equality does not admit discrimination between citizens and non-citizens.[313] Thus, any limitations on fundamental rights must be justified on the basis of a primary public interest relevant on a constitutional ground. In addition, the Constitutional Court noted that Article 1(1) of Law No. 94 of 15 July 2009, which excludes the application of aggravating circumstance of clandestine presence to EU citizens, demonstrates, even more clearly, the discriminatory nature of the mentioned provision.[314] Furthermore, the Constitutional Court also affirmed that the quality of unlawful immigrant becomes a 'stigma' and constitutes the basis for punitive differentiated treatment.[315] This is contrary to Article 25 of the *Italian Constitution* which provides that the offender shall be punished for his conduct and not for his personal qualities.

Thus, for the abovementioned reasons, the Constitutional Court declared Article 61(11-*bis*) unconstitutional.

SILVANA MOSCATELLI[316]

Legislation—Italian Participation in International Missions

- Law No. 30 of 5 March 2010, 'Conversion into Law of the Decree-Law No. 1 of 1 January 2010, Urgent Provisions concerning the Extension of the Interventions for Development Cooperation, Support of Peace and Stabilization Processes, and Participation of the Armed and Police Forces in International Missions and Urgent Provisions for the set up of the European External Action Service and for the Defence Agency' [Legge 5 marzo 2010, n. 30 di conversione del Decreto-legge 1 gennaio 2010, n. 1, 'Disposizioni urgenti per la proroga degli interventi di cooperazione allo sviluppo e a sostegno dei processi di pace e di stabilizzazione, nonché delle missioni internazionali delle Forze armate e di polizia e disposizioni urgenti per l'attivazione del Servizio europeo per l'azione esterna e per l'Amministrazione della Difesa']. *E*ntered into force on 6 March 2010.[317] <http://www.parlamento.it/parlam/leggi/10030l.htm>
- Law No. 126 of 3 August 2010, 'Conversion into Law of the Decree-Law No 102 of 6 July 2010, Extension of Time Concerning Interventions for Development Cooperation, Support of Peace and Stabilization Processes, and the

---

313 On this point, see also Judgment n. 62/1994 of the Italian Constitutional Court.

314 For comments on the Law No. 94/2009, so called 'security package', see S. Centonze, *Sicurezza e immigrazione. La nuova disciplina dell'immigrazione dopo il c.d. pacchetto sicurezza* (Milano, Cedam 2009); L. Pepino, 'Le migrazioni, il diritto, il nemico. Considerazioni a margine della Legge 94/2009', in *Diritto, immigrazione e cittadinanza* (2009) pp 9 et seq.

315 On this aspect, see G. Dodaro, 'Discriminazione dello straniero irregolare nell'aggravante comune della clandestinità', 4 *Rivisita italiana di diritto processuale penale* (2008) pp 1634 et seq.

316 Silvana Moscatelli, PhD in Human Rights and International Order, is Consultant at the Institute for International Legal Studies of the National Research Council (CNR), Rome.

317 The Law and the text of the Decree-law as modified by the Law were published in *Gazzetta Ufficiale* No. 55 of 8 March 2010, while the Decree-Law was published in *Gazzetta Ufficiale* No. 4 of 7 January 2010.

Missions of the Armed and Police Forces' [Legge 3 agosto 2010, n. 126 di conversione del Decreto legge 6 luglio 2010, n. 102, 'Proroga degli interventi di cooperazione allo sviluppo e a sostegno dei processi di pace, di stabilizzazione e delle missioni internazionali delle Forze armate e di polizia']. *E*ntered into force on 4 August 2010.[318] <http://www.normattiva.it/dispatcher?service=213&fromurn=yes&datagu=2010-08-11&annoatto=2010&numeroatto=126&task=ricercaatti&elementiperpagina=50&redaz=010G0150&newsearch=1&classeprv=1&paginadamostrare=1&tmstp=1297875588163>

In 2010, the Italian government issued two decrees, later enacted into legislation by Parliament, aimed at authorizing both the participation of the Italian armed forces, police forces, and civilians in international missions and the financing of such missions. The 2010 laws under review concern all the general aspects related to the missions such as the financing, the administrative procedures necessary for deploying military staff abroad, the legal and economic treatment of such staff (including civilians), the criminal law applicable to soldiers and all the humanitarian activities carried out to sustain civilians in the areas of crisis.

Issuing such laws is necessary as Italy still lacks a general legal framework for the regulation of missions abroad. Each year legal acts are needed to authorize and regulate specific missions. Bills providing an overall regulatory system of international missions (including administration, financing, governmental and parliamentary authorizations and humanitarian activities) are still under examination in the Chamber of Deputies.[319] The adoption of those general bills would obviate the need for Parliament to adopt two or more specific laws each year.[320]

Each semester during the year 2010, Italy deployed about 7811 personnel in 22 countries in about 30 missions established by the United Nations (UN), the European Union (EU) and NATO.[321]

By Law No. 30 of 5 March 2010 and Law No. 126 of 3 August 2010, the Parliament regulated the deployment of the aforementioned missions, respectively for the first and the second semester of the year.

---

318 The Law and the text of the Decree-law as modified by the Law were published in *Gazzetta Ufficiale* No. 186 of 11 August 2010, while the Decree-Law was published in *Gazzetta Ufficiale* No. 156 of 7 July 2010.

319 Bills No. A.C. 1820, A.C. 2605 and A.C. 2849, presented in 2008, under examination of the Commissions for Foreign Affairs and Defense of the Italian Chamber of Deputies. For the debate see <http://nuovo.camera.it/126?pdl=1820&tab=1&leg=16>. See V. Della Fina, Comments on the 'Law No. 12 of 24 February 2009, Converting Decree-Law No. 209 of 30 December 2008, Extension of Time concerning the Italian Participation in International Missions' and Law No. 108 of 3 August 2009, Extension of Time Concerning the Italian Participation in International Missions, 12 *YIHL* (2009) pp 579–583.

320 See N. Ronzitti, 'Quale legge organica sulle missioni militari all'estero?', 4 *Rivista di diritto internazionale* (2009) pp 1108–1114.

321 For the Official Report, see <http://www.difesa.it/Operazioni+Militari/Riepilogo_missioni_attività_internazionali_in_corso/>.

The first act (the Law No. 30/2010) authorized the continuation of the Italian participation in international missions until 30 June 2010 for a total expenditure of EUR 814,208,663.

Law No. 30/2010 is divided into four parts: the first Part (Articles 1–4) concerns the interventions for development cooperation in support of peace processes and stabilization and contains the provisions for the activation of the European External Action System; the second Part (Articles 5–8) is dedicated to the international missions of the armed and police forces and contains the regulation of the status of the personnel and provisions regarding the applicable criminal law; the third Part (Article 9) concerns the administration of the defense; and the fourth Part includes financial provisions.

Article 1 authorized the expenditure of EUR 22,300 million for development cooperation activities in Afghanistan and EUR 2 million for Italian participation in the NATO trust fund for the support of the Afghan Army.

Article 2 of Law No. 30/2010 regulated Italian participation in interventions to support peace and stabilization processes in Iraq, Lebanon, Pakistan, Sudan and, Somalia to improve the living conditions of the people and refugees in neighbouring countries and to support civil reconstruction in those countries. Furthermore it authorized the participation of Italy in the NATO Trust Fund for Kosovo and the expenses for the participation in the OSCE cooperation projects (EUR 617,951). It also approved Italian participation in the European Security and Defence Policy (ESDP) initiatives, the EU Special Representatives and the sending of diplomatic staff to the Italian Embassies in Baghdad, Islamabad and Kabul.

Article 4 contains provisions for the European External Action System (EEAS) which should assist the EU High Representative pursuant to Article 27(3) of the *Treaty of Lisbon amending the Treaty on European Union and the Treaty establishing the European Community* which entered into force on 1 December 2010.[322] Article 4 authorized the Ministry for Foreign Affairs to employ a maximum of 50 diplomatic personnel in the framework of the aforementioned System.

As far as the participation of the Italian Armed Forces in international missions is concerned, Article 5 authorized the expenditure of EUR 308,780,721 for the expansion of participation in the *International Security Assistance Force* (ISAF)[323] and EUPOL AFGHANISTAN.

Furthermore, the expenses for the extension of the following missions was also authorized: *United Nations Interim Force in Lebanon* (UNIFIL), including UNIFIL Maritime Task Force, the missions in the Balkans, the Multinational specialized unit (MSU), the European Union Rule of Law Mission in Kosovo (EULEX Kosovo), and Security Force Training Plan in Kosovo; Joint Enterprise in the Balkan area; EU Mission ALTHEA in Bosnia–Herzegovina and the Integrated

322 See M. Fragola, *Il Trattato di Lisbona* (Milan, Giuffrè, 2010). For a description of EEAS, see Council of the European Union, 'Draft Council decision establishing the organisation and functioning of the European External Action Service' (Brussels, 25 March 2010).

323 UNSC Res. 1890/2009, UN Doc. S/RES/1890, 8 October 2009 extended ISAF mandate until 31 October 2010.

Police Unit (IPU) which operates within ALTHEA; Active endeavour in the Mediterranean area, T*emporary International Presence in Hebron* (TIPH 2); Eu*ropean Union Border Assistance Mission in Rafah* (EUBAM Rafah); *UN/ African Union Mission in Darfur* (UNAMID); EUPOL RD Congo and EUSEC RD Congo; *UN Peacekeeping Force in Cyprus* (UNFICYP); the assistance to the Albanian armed forces, EU Monitoring Mission in Georgia (EUMM Georgia); and the EU military operation ATALANTA off the Somali coast.[324] Furthermore, Article 5 also authorized Italian soldiers to give assistance to the Albanian armed forces, assistance and training of Iraqi armed forces, and the deployment of military staff in the United Arab Emirates, Bahrain and Tampa to support missions in Afghanistan and Iraq. It also authorized the expenditure of EUR 2,679,906 for the participation of military personnel of the 'Arma dei Carabinieri' (Carabineers) in the UN Stabilization Mission in Haiti (MINUSTAH). This provision was not contained in the original version of the Decree-Law but was added by the converting Law.

With regard to Italian police participation in international missions, Article 3 authorized the following: *European Union Rule of Law Mission in Kosovo* (EULEX Kosovo) and *UN Mission in Kosovo* (UNMIK); E*uropean Union Police Mission for the Palestinian Territories* (EUPOL COPPS); *European Union Police Mission* (EUPM) in Bosnia–Herzegovina.

Furthermore, the same Article authorized the participation of the Italian customs officers from the 'Guardia di Finanza'[325] in the mission in Libya,[326] the *International Security Assistance Force* (ISAF) and EUPOL Afghanistan; E*uropean Union Rule of Law Mission in Kosovo* (EULEX Kosovo) and UNMIK; EU *Border Assistance Mission in Rafah* (EUBAM Rafah); J*oint Multimodal Operational Units* (JMOUs) in Afghanistan and in the United Arab Emirates.

In relation to criminal law, Article 7 reaffirmed the applicability of the provision contained in Article 5 of the Decree Law No. 209/2008 as converted by Law No. 12/2009. In particular, it stated that the *Military Criminal Code of Peace* applies and also Article 9(3–6) of Decree-Law No. 421 of 2001, as converted into

---

[324] See V. Eboli, Comment on the 'Law No. 100 of 22 July 2009, Conversion into Law of the Decree-Law No. 61 of 15 June 2009, containing Emergency Provisions on the Fight to Piracy', 12 *YIHL* (2009) pp 592–594. The official website of the mission 'Atalanta', where up-to-date information about it can be found, is at <www.consilium.europa.eu/showPage.aspx?id=1518&lang=en>. It started in 2008 with the aim of contributing to the prevention and repression of piracy and armed robbery off the Somali coast.

[325] See V. Eboli, Comment on the 'Law No. 79 of 3 June 2010 'Rules concerning the Appointment of the General Commander of the "Guardia di finanza" Corps and his Participation in Military Operations in Case of War or Military Missions Abroad' in this volume of *YIHL*.

[326] The mission in Libya aimed to maintain ships ceded by Italy to the Libyan government in order to implement the Cooperation Protocol with Libya on Clandestine Immigration and Human Trafficking signed in Tripoli on 29 December 2007 and the Friendship, Partnership and Cooperation Agreement signed in Bengasi on 30 August 2008.

Law No. 6 of 2002.[327] Furthermore Article 7 extended the Italian jurisdiction over crimes committed by foreigners, on the territories or high seas where international missions are carried out, against the Italian State or against its citizens employed on such missions. In this case the crimes committed by foreigners and by the Italian personnel participating in international operations fall within the jurisdiction of the Tribunal of Rome.

In relation to anti-piracy operations, the provision authorized the detention on board of captured persons who have committed, or are suspected of having committed, acts of piracy or armed robbery in the areas where the Italian Navy is present and to seize the vessels of the pirates or armed robbers or the vessels caught perpetrating an act of piracy or an armed robbery and which are in the hands of the pirates, as well as the goods on board.[328] The detention is lawful only for the time necessary for the judicial organs of the State in charge to transfer them and bring them to court, or for any third State wishing to exercise jurisdiction over them when the competent State is unable or unwilling to do so. The related communications and orders can be transmitted by electronic means.

Part III of Law No. 30/2010 on the administration of defence contains miscellaneous provisions, some of which refer to the recruitment of the closest relatives of any deceased military personnel. Part IV indicates the funds upon which the expenses have to be charged.

Law No. 126/2010 was adopted to extend Italian participation in international missions authorized by Law No. 30/2010 from 1 July 2010 to 31 December 2010, with a total expenditure for 2010 of EUR 707,624,498.[329]

Article 1 regulated, in particular, the interventions for development cooperation, in support of peace processes and the enhancement of stabilization in Afghanistan and Pakistan. In so far as the former is concerned, the financial contribution should be especially devolved to the NATO trust fund for the Afghan army and to NATO's Strategic Communications Initiatives. With regard to Pakistan, the resources should finance initiatives in the medical sector, education, infrastructure, and support small and medium enterprises, especially on the border between Afghanistan and Pakistan.

Article 2 authorizes the funding of interventions for the improvement of the living conditions of people and refugees in neighbouring countries and supporting civil reconstruction in Iraq, Lebanon, Pakistan, Sudan and, Somalia and other training activities for the education of the local police personnel in Iraq and for fighting piracy off the Somali coast.

---

327 It concerns the criminal procedure for military personnel arrested in *flagrante delicto* or detained for military crimes.

328 These categories of captured persons are those mentioned by the Article 2 of the Council Joint Action 2008/851/CFSP of 10 November 2008. See V. Eboli, Comment on the 'Law No. 100 of 22 July 2009, 'Conversion into Law of the Decree-Law No. 61 of 15 June 2009, containing Emergency Provisions on the Fight to Piracy', quoted above.

329 The total expenditure for the year 2009 was EUR 509,996,466.

The participation of the armed or police forces in the missions enumerated in Decree-Law No. 1/2010 converted into Law No. 30/2010 is confirmed. This includes the authorization for the 'Guardia di Finanza' personnel in the Joint Multimodal Operational Units (JMOUs) in Afghanistan, Arab United Emirates and Kosovo.

Furthermore, from 1 July 2010 to 31 December 2010, the expenditure of EUR 810,944 for the participation of military personnel in the EU mission EUTM Somalia, set up by decision of the Council 2010/96/EDSP of 15 February 2010 was authorized.

In respect of the treatment of personnel involved in international missions and with regard to the criminal law applicable to military staff, Article 6 recalled again the provisions of Article 5 of the Decree-Law No. 209 of 30 December 2008, converted into Law No. 12 of 24 February 2009. It also recalled the applicability of Article 4, paragraphs 1-sexies and 1-septies of the Decree-Law N. 152 of 4 November 2009, converted into Law No. 197 of 29 December 2009. They contain a clause according to which any soldier who, during the missions, uses, or orders others to use, armed force or other means of coercion for military operational necessities, in conformity with directives, rules of engagement or lawful orders, is not punishable under criminal law.

Valeria Eboli

Legislation—Italian 'Guardia di finanza' Participation in Military Operations in Case of War or Military Missions Abroad

- Law No. 79 of 3 June 2010 'Rules concerning the appointment of the General Commander of the "Guardia di finanza" Corps and his Participation in Military Operations in Case of War or Military Missions Abroad' [Legge 3 giugno 2010 n. 79 'Norme in materia di nomina del Comandante generale del Corpo della guardia di finanza e di attività di concorso del medesimo Corpo alle operazioni militari in caso di guerra e alle missioni militari all'estero']. Entered into force on 4 June 2010.[330] <http://www.normattiva.it/dispatcher?service=213&fromurn=yes&datagu=2010-06-03&annoatto=2010&numeroatto=79&task=ricercaatti&elementiperpagina=50&redaz=010G0102&newsearch=1&classeprv=1&paginadamostrare=1&tmstp=1297876566865>

By Law No. 79/2010, Italy modified the norms concerning the nomination of the General Commander of the 'Guardia di finanza' (Custom police) and stated the rules for his participation in military operations in case of war or military missions abroad.

The 'Guardia di finanza' was founded on 5 October 1774, when the King of Sardinia, Victor Amadeus III, established the 'Light Troops Legion'. It was charged with monitoring cross-border transactions and contributing to military defence.

[330] Published in *Gazzetta Ufficiale* No. 127 of 3 June 2010.

By Law No. 141/1881, the Corps was given a new name 'Royal Guardia di Finanza Corps' and took on the function of 'preventing, suppressing and reporting contraband and any offences and any contravention and transgression to legal and financial regulations' to safeguard the interests of the Financial Authority and to assist in the maintenance of public order and security.[331] In 1923, a special branch of the Royal 'Guardia di finanza' Corps, the so called Investigative Tax Police, was created. Then, in the republican era, Law No. 189/1959 set out the institutional duties of the Corps, and Presidential Decree No. 34/1999, amended and completed it.

The 'Guardia di finanza' is not one of the four Italian institutional armed forces,[332] but has a military status as established by Legislative Decree No. 68/2001, that enhanced its role as a Police Force, granting it powers to enforce economic and financial laws for the safeguarding of the State public budget, the budget of the Italian regions and of local authorities, including fraud against the European Union.

Law No. 79/2010 amended Law No. 189 of 23 April 1959, introducing some novelties regarding both the institutional organization of the Corps and its functions. As far as the former is concerned, Law No. 79/2010 stated that the General Commander will be chosen among the generals of army corps of the 'Guardia di finanza' or of the Army and not only among the generals of army corps of the Army as previously stated. The Commander is appointed by Decree of the President of the Republic and holds the position for a period of 2 years.

The 'Guardia di finanza' operates under the auspices of the Ministry of Economy and Finance (MEF), but in case of participation in war or military missions abroad it operates under the auspices of the Ministry of Defence. Moreover, in case of involvement in these activities, the General Commander of the 'Guardia di finanza' consults with the Defence Chief of Staff to determine the modalities of such participation.

This modification allows a coordinated effort in the military operations abroad and establishes a functional link between the 'Guardia di finanza' and the Ministry of Defence in the case of deployment which should ensure more coherent and effective operational approach. Law No. 79/2010 updates the norms concerning the functioning of the 'Guardia di finanza' by adapting them to the international contemporary context.

Valeria Eboli

Legislation—State Immunity from Italian Jurisdiction

- Law No. 98 of 23 June 2010, 'Converting, with amendments, Decree-Law No. 63 of 28 April 2010 containing Urgent Dispositions on Foreign States Immunity from Italian Jurisdiction and Election of Representative Bodies of Italian Residents Abroad' [Legge 23 giugno 2010, n. 98, *Conversione in legge, con modificazioni, del decreto-legge 28 aprile 2010, n. 63, recante disposizioni*

---

331 See <http://www.gdf.gov.it/GdF_in_English/index.html>.

332 The four Italian armed forces are: Army, Navy, Air Forces and 'Arma dei carabinieri' (Carabineers).

urgenti in tema di immunità di Stati esteri dalla giurisdizione italiana e di elezioni degli organismi rappresentativi degli italiani all'estero]. Entered into force on 27 June 2010[333] <http://www.parlamento.it/elenchileggi/63482/63947/elencoleggi.htm>

Law No. 98 of 23 June 2010 converted Decree-law No. 63 of 28 April 2010, by which the Italian government took action in regard to the suspension of execution measures directed against property of foreign States (Article 1) and the renewal of representative committees of Italian residents abroad (Article 2).[334] It dealt with two heterogeneous issues sharing only one common issue: the competence of the Ministry of Foreign Affairs.[335] This comment is focused on dispositions regarding State immunity from execution.

In particular, by Law No. 98/2010, Italy will suspend the executive force of the judgments rendered against a foreign State if such State initiates action before the International Court of Justice (ICJ) in order to verify its immunity from Italian jurisdiction. Suspension comes to an end once the decision of the ICJ has been rendered and in any case not later than 31 December 2011.

As a consequence, claims for measures of constraint against property of foreign States are not admitted and ongoing proceedings are suspended. Such suspension operates *de jure*, but could also be officially detected by the judge. In this regard, it is established that the judge has a duty to assess whether a suit is underway on matters relating to State immunity from Italian jurisdiction, by requesting information to the Ministry of Foreign Affairs.

The Decree-Law was converted into Law by Parliament, through the introduction of three significant amendments. First, it removed the safeguard clause of Royal Decree-Law No. 1621 of 30 August 1925, converted into Law No. 1263 of 15 July 1926, which prohibited execution against State property without the consent of the Minister of Justice, applying such prohibition solely to those States certified as according reciprocity.[336] This reference was deemed improper since the Law was declared unconstitutional by the Constitutional Court and then abrogated.[337]

---

[333] Published in *Gazzetta Ufficiale* No. 147 of 26 June 2010.

[334] Law No. 98/2010, Article 2, postponed until 31 December 2012 the election of the Committees of Italian Residents Abroad (Comitati degli italiani all'estero—COMITES) and the General Council of Italian Residents Abroad (Consiglio generale degli italiani all'estero—CGIE).

[335] Chamber of Deputies, XVI Legislature, Documentation Dossier 'Immunità degli Stati esteri dalla giurisdizione italiana ed elezioni degli organismi rappresentativi—D.L. 63/2010—A. C. 3443—Elementi di valutazione sulla qualità del testo e su specificità, omogeneità e limiti di contenuto del decreto-legge n. 79 dell'11 maggio 2010', <http://documenti.camera.it/Leg16/Dossier/Testi/CL079.htm>.

[336] Regio Decreto-Legge 30 agosto 1925, n. 1621, Atti esecutivi sopra beni di Stati esteri nel Regno <http://www.prassi.cnr.it/prassi/content.html?id=1653>.

[337] In 1992, the Italian Constitutional Court declared unconstitutional the 1926 Law on the grounds it was not a matter of discretion having regard to reciprocity, but a judicial function to determine whether assets were in public or commercial use. [Corte costituzionale, sentenza 15 luglio 1992, n. 329], published in *Gazzetta Ufficiale* No. 31 of 22 July 1992.

Second, all the references to international organizations have been erased from the text of the Decree since international organizations do not have *locus standi* before the ICJ in contentious cases. Consequently, the Law is now only applicable to States. On the contrary, executive actions against property of international organizations are admitted if it is so set forth by the host agreement with the international organization concerned.

Finally, an important time-limit has been provided for, according to which suspension of judgments and enforcement proceedings will continue until 31 December 2011.

The *occasio legis* is clearly connected to the case currently pending before the ICJ between Italy and the Federal Republic of Germany whereby the latter invoked the responsibility of Italy for violations of international customary law on matters of foreign State immunity.[338] In recent years, Italian courts, including the Supreme Court of Cassation (Corte suprema di cassazione), delivered a number of judgments denying immunity to Germany, since the unlawful acts under consideration consisted of the violation of peremptory norms of international law (namely those protecting human rights). As a consequence, Germany was ordered to compensate the plaintiffs[339] and measures of constraint were decided against its property (such as the judicial mortgage on the German cultural centre in Rome, Villa Vigoni).[340] The Italian government decided that such executive actions could cause significant repercussions on international relations as well as raising unrealistic expectations of compensation among those otherwise entitled to it but for the doctrine of foreign State immunity.[341]

Some argued that Law No. 98/2010 causes an unjustified diminution of the individual right of access to justice, prescribed by Article 24 of the *Italian Constitution*—exacerbated by the fact that Germany did not request the Court to adopt provisional measures *ex* Article 41 of the *Statute of the International Court of*

---

338 O. Ferrajolo, 'Italy's Counter-claim in the Proceeding before the International Court of Justice on the Case Concerning Jurisdictional Immunities of the State (*Germany* v. *Italy*)', in this volume of *YIHL*.

339 In its landmark 2004 decision in the *Ferrini case*, the Supreme Court of Cassation ruled that Italy held jurisdiction with regard to a claim brought by a person who during World War II had been deported to Germany to perform forced labour in the armaments industry. See Corte suprema di cassazione, Sezioni unite civili, *Ferrini* v. *Repubblica federale di Germania*, sentenza 11 marzo 2004, n. 5004, 87 *Rivista di diritto internazionale* (2004).

340 The Court of Cassation confirmed the *exequatur* decree on German property in Italy, issued by the Court of Appeal of Florence, granting reparation to the victims of the Distomo massacre. See G. C. Bruno, 'Court of Cassation, *Sezioni unite civili*, Judgment of 29 May 2008, n. 14199', 11 *YIHL* (2008), pp 496–497.

341 Chamber of Deputies, XVI Legislature, Documentation Dossier 'Immunità degli Stati esteri dalla giurisdizione italiana ed elezioni degli organismi rappresentativi—D.L. 63/2010—A.C. 3443—Elementi di valutazione sulla qualità del testo e su specificità, omogeneità e limiti di contenuto del decreto-legge n. 79 dell'11 maggio 2010', <http://documenti.camera.it/Leg16/Dossier/Testi/CL079.htm>.

Justice.[342] Such a restriction of the right of access to justice has been raised by commentators with different arguments. Some of them make reference to Articles 11 and 80 of the *Italian Constitution*, respectively affirming Italian engagement to cooperate with international organizations and attaching importance to judicial means of international dispute settlement.[343] Others justify a temporary limitation of the right in question by pointing out a pre-eminent public interest to conform the Italian legal system to international general law, as stated in Article 10 of the Constitution, and to not compromise further international relations with a foreign State.[344]

It is also questioned if Law No. 98/2010 would be able to satisfy similar situations others than the specific case of *Germany* v. *Italy*. In fact, the Act refers only to applications pending before the ICJ and is time-limited. Therefore, Law no. 98/2010 probably paves the way to a readjustment of the law of State immunity in Italy in order to clarify the Italian position with regard to controversial and evolutionary aspects of such matters.

A first step in this direction could be the ratification of the 2004 *Convention on Jurisdictional Immunities of States and Their Property*.[345] As suggested by some commentators, Italy could formulate a reservation or declaration upon signature or ratification aimed at conforming to the approach of Italian courts.[346] In particular, such reservation or declaration would affirm that *jus cogens* norms, such as those protecting human rights, are at the peak of the Italian legal order, and they therefore prevail over all other treaty or customary rules, including those pertaining to State immunity.

---

342 N. Ronzitti, 'La prescrizione rischia di mettere in forse l'accesso alla giustizia da parte dei cittadini', *Guida al diritto—Il Sole 24 Ore* (Milan) 15 May 2010, <www.guidaaldiritto.ilsole24ore.com/Doc.aspx? Numero=20&cmd=GuidaDiritto_Archivio&IdDocumento=11636377&Data=2010-05-15&IdFonteDocumentale=53&Sezione=na&Image=tit_guida.gif&MenuOn=menuon>; A. Atteritano, 'Il DL 63/2010 compromette il diritto dell'individuo a una tutela giurisdizionale effettiva', <www.sidi-isil.org/wp-content/uploads/2010/02/Atteritano-DL-Immunit%C3%A0-definitivo1.pdf>.

343 F. Salerno, 'Esecuzione in Italia su beni di Stati stranieri: il decreto-legge 28 aprile 2010, n. 63', <www.sidi-isil.org/wp-content/uploads/2010/02/Salerno-Decreto-legge-28-aprile-2010-_1_.pdf>.

344 E. Sciso, 'L'immunità degli Stati esteri dalla giurisdizione dopo la conversione del decreto-legge 28 aprile n. 63', 93 *Rivista di diritto internazionale* (2010).

345 Convention on Jurisdictional Immunities of States and Their Property, UNGA Res. A/59/38, UN Doc. A/59/508, 2 December 2004 (not yet in force). The Italian Senate adopted an order of the day by which engaged the government to begin the process for ratifying the 2004 Convention before 31 December 2011. Senate of the Republic, XVI Legislature, 'Ordine del Giorno n. G101 al DDL n. 2209', <http://mobile.senato.it/japp/bgt/showdoc/frame.jsp?tipodoc=Emend&leg=16&id=00488093&idoggetto=00586991&parse=no&mobile=si&toc=no>.

346 Sciso,supran.344;N.Ronzitti,'Perlelitisull'immunitàdallagiurisdizioneènecessariolaratificadella Convenzione' Guida al diritto—Il Sole 24 Ore (Milan) 24 luglio 2010, <www.guidaaldiritto.ilsole24ore.com/Doc.aspx?Numero=30&cmd=GuidaDiritto_Archivio&IdDocumento=11797343&Data=2010-07-24&IdFonteDocumentale=53&Sezione=na&Image=tit_guida.gif&MenuOn=menuon>.

An alternative, given the delay in the ratification process of the Convention (at February 2011 only eleven States had ratified), could be the adoption of a new act in line with international law, but enshrining the principles set forth by the Italian courts.[347]

In other words, Law No. 98/2010 does not definitively exhaust the issue of State immunity and the debate on future developments remains open.

RACHELE CERA

Legislation—Ratification by Italy of the European Council Convention on Action against Trafficking in Human Beings

- Law No. 108 of 2 July 2010, 'Ratification and Implementation of the *European Council Convention on Action against Trafficking in Human Beings*, done at Warsaw on 16 May 2005, and Norms on the Adaptation of the Domestic Legal System', <http://www.minori.it/files/legge_2010_n_108.pdf>

On 2 July 2010, the Italian Parliament passed Law No. 108,[348] regarding the ratification and implementation of the Council of Europe *Convention on Action against Trafficking in Human Beings*.[349] This Convention aims at contributing to, and reinforcing at the European level, the implementation of the 2000 *Protocol to Prevent, Suppress and Punish Trafficking in Persons, Especially Women and Children* (Palermo Protocol, supplementing the UN *Convention against Transnational Organized Crime*).[350] The Convention embeds the concept of 'trafficking in persons' agreed upon in the Palermo Protocol,[351] and also takes into account other global and regional treaties, and the EU pertinent legislation.[352] The

[347] Ronzitti, supra n. 346.

[348] Published in *Gazzetta Ufficiale* No. 163 of 15 July 2010.

[349] Opened for signature 16 May 2005, ETS No. 197 (entered into force 1 December 2009), <http://conventions.coe.int/Treaty/EN/Treaties/Html/197.htm>.

[350] Protocol to Prevent, Suppress and Punish Trafficking in Persons, Especially Women and Children, opened for signature 15 November 2000, 2237 UNTS 319 (entered into force 25 December 2003).

[351] Article 4 of the Convention is identical, except for the words 'human beings', to Article 3 of the Palermo Protocol, which reads: Trafficking in persons shall mean the recruitment, transportation, transfer, harbouring or receipt of persons, by means of the threat or use of force or other forms of coercion, of abduction, of fraud, of deception, of the abuse of power or of a position of vulnerability or of the giving or receiving of payments or benefits to achieve the consent of a person having control over another person, for the purpose of exploitation. Exploitation shall include, at a minimum, the exploitation of the prostitution of others or other forms of sexual exploitation, forced labour or services, slavery or practices similar to slavery, servitude or the removal of organs.

[352] Among others: the Convention for the Suppression of the Traffic in Persons and of the Exploitation of the Prostitution of Others of 2 December 1949, the Convention relating to the Status of Refugees of 28 July 1951, the Convention on the Elimination of All Forms of Discrimination against Women of 18 December 1979, the Convention on the Rights of the Child of 20 November 1989 and the Optional Protocol on the Sale of Children, Child Prostitution and Child Pornography of 25 May 2000; the European Convention for the Protection of Human

Convention concentrates on legislative measures and other initiatives (hence the broad term 'action' utilized in the title) to repress and prevent any form of 'new slavery', national or transnational, as constituting a violation of human rights and a crime against humanity. The Convention's purposes include ensuring that any victims of trafficking—women, children, or men—be effectively protected, without discrimination, and receive appropriate assistance in the physical territories of States Parties. Considering that trafficking in human beings is often linked to transnational organized crime, the Convention promotes intergovernmental co-operation in combating this heinous phenomenon, which the Council of Europe considers to be a major contemporary problem both in Europe and around the world.[353]

Italy signed the Convention on 8 June 2005. However, ratification did not follow rapidly.[354] It should be remembered that the Convention falls within the category of those treaties that require amendments to existing national legislation and, thus, Parliamentary approval (Article 80 of Constitution). Several law projects were submitted to this end, in 2008, to the Senate and the Chamber of Deputies, on parliamentary initiative (acts S.476 of 12 May, S.780 of 12 June and S.1135 of 21 October; act C.1917 of 18 November). These were then absorbed into a further draft, introduced into the Senate by the government on 1 March 2010 (acts S.2043; C.3402).[355] This latter draft was then approved, as Law No. 108/2010.

Article 1 of this law authorized the Head of the State to ratify the *Convention on Action against Trafficking in Human Beings*. On this basis, Italy's instrument of ratification was deposited on 29 November 2010. Thus, the Convention will enter into force for Italy on 1 March 2011.[356] On the same date, it will become part of the Italian legal system, by virtue of an implementing order (ordine d'esecuzione), contained in Article 2 of Law No. 108. Article 3 has provided further implementing measures, by amendments to the *Italian Criminal Code*.

Despite the complicated drafting process, Law No. 108/2010 has not introduced, in reality, many important changes. Other relevant innovations had already occurred in national legislation, as a consequence of ratification by Italy of other

---

[353] According to certain estimations, trafficking in persons now represents 'the third largest illicit money making venture in the world after trafficking of weapons and drugs': cf. Council of Europe, Convention on Action Against Trafficking in Human Beings, Explanatory Report (2005), <http://www.coe.int/t/dg2/trafficking/campaign/Source/PDF Conv_197_Trafficking_E.pdf>.

[354] The Convention came into force for a majority of the Council of Europe member states in 2008; and ratification by other states occurred in 2009 and 2010. For the status of signatures and ratifications see <http://conventions.coe.int/Treaty/Commun/ChercheSig.asp?NT=197&CM=1&DF=&CL=ENG>.

[355] This draft-bill was presented jointly, by the Ministers for Foreign Affairs for Justice and for Gender Equality. For the text of all the draft-bills see <http://www.parlamento.it/leg/16/BGT/Schede/Ddliter/35258.htm>.

[356] Under Article 42, para 4, of the Convention, the latter enters into force in respect of any state which has ratified it after entry into force on the international plan, 'on the first day of the month following the expiration of a period of 3 months after the date of the deposit of its instrument of ratification, acceptance or approval'.

treaties on the matter. This fact was clarified by the Parliamentary Committees for Justice and for Foreign and EU Affairs, which jointly examined the draft of the government *ad referendum.*[357] In the opinion of the two Committees, which Parliament has then shared, the domestic legal system was already 'substantially consistent' with the obligations deriving from the Convention for the following reasons.

The concept of 'trafficking in human beings' coincides, as already noted, with that of 'trafficking in persons' under the Palermo Protocol, which Italy has executed through Law No. 146 of 16 March 2006.[358] Moreover, the conduct contained in Article 4 of the Convention is covered by Articles 600, 601 and 602 of the *Criminal Code*, as amended by Law No. 228 of 11 August 2003 (Measures against Trafficking in Persons).[359] These Articles relate to, respectively, 'reduction or maintenance in slavery or servitude' (Article 600), 'trafficking in persons' (Article 601) and 'purchase and sale of slaves' (Article 603). They also provide adequate sanctions for these crimes. Rightly, these provisions have seemed to Parliament sufficient to implement Article 18 of the Convention, under which parties have an obligation to adopt such legislative measures as may be necessary for establishing as criminal offences the acts covered by the Convention, when committed intentionally.

Regarding 'transnational crime', its legal definition—also relevant to the Council of Europe Convention—is found in Law No. 146/2006. Article 3 describes this concept as a crime committed in more than one State, or that, committed in one State, has been prepared, planned, directed or controlled in another State, or has consequences in another State.

Legislative Decree No. 286 of 25 July 1998, containing norms on immigration and on the status of foreigners (so called 'testo unico sull'immigrazione'),[360] also conforms to the Convention's obligations. It establishes, in fact, that persons who carry out activities with the purpose of facilitating illegal immigration are punishable by imprisonment for up to 3 years, except in cases in which their conduct constitutes a more serious crime under national legislation (Article 12, para 1). On the other hand, relief and assistance given in Italy, for humanitarian purposes, to

---

357 'Report of the Joint Meeting of Second and Third Committees' (6 May 2010), <http://www.camera.it/view/doc_viewer_full?url=http%3A//documenti.camera.it/_dati/leg16/lavori/bollet/201005/0506/pdf/0203.pdf&back_to=http%3A//www.camera.it/210%3FslAnnoMese%3D201005%26slGiorno%3D06>.

358 *Gazzetta Ufficiale* No. 85 of 11 April 2006, Ordinary Supplement No. 91, <http://www.parlamento.it/parlam/leggi/06146l.htm>.

359 *Gazzetta Ufficiale* No. 195 of 23 August 2003, <http: //www. normattiva.it/dispatcher?service=213&fromurn=yes&datagu=2003-08-23&annoatto=2003&numeroatto=228&task=ricercaatti&elementiperpagina=50&redaz=003G0248&newsearch=1&classeprv=1&paginadamostrare=1&tmstp=1296818185266>.

360 *Gazzetta Ufficiale* No. 191 of 18 August 1998, Ordinary Supplement No. 139, <http://www.camera.it/parlam/leggi/deleghe/98286dl.htm>.

foreigners in distress who are found, in whatever manner or circumstance, within Italian territory, cannot be qualified as a crime (Article 12, para 2).

Regarding the establishment of appropriate procedures for repressing trafficking in human beings and protecting the victims (Chap. V, Articles 27–31 of the Convention), it was noted by Parliament that the matter falls within the scope of application of Law Decree No. 8 of 1991, converted into Law No. 82 of the same year, and modified by Law No. 45 of 2001.[361] These laws, which pertain to Italian 'anti-mafia' legislation, provide measures to protect witnesses and other persons who collaborate with the judiciary in repressing organized crime (so called 'collaboratori di giustizia'). They do not contain, in reality, specific provisions on the protection of the victims of trafficking in persons, and especially of children, as prescribed in Article 28, paras 3–4, of the Convention.[362] However, further applicable measures are set forth in Law No. 46 of 11 March 2002,[363] and in other laws, through which Italy has implemented the *Optional Protocol on the Sale of Children, Child Prostitution and Child Pornography to the Convention on the Rights of the Child.*

Another issue examined by Parliament has been whether or not the creation of any specialized authority and/or coordinating body was necessary, at the national level, in accordance with Article 29 of the Convention. It has been reputed that this was not the case, because Italian police and the military corps of 'Carabinieri' and 'Guardia di Finanza' also possess specialized competencies for repressing trafficking in persons.

On these bases, Parliament has reached the conclusion that the only provisions of the Convention requiring further legislative measures were contained in Article 20 (Criminalization of Acts Relating to Travel or Identity Documents) and Article 24 (Aggravating Circumstances).[364]

---

361 In *Gazzetta Ufficiale*, respectively: No. 12 of 15 January 1991, No. 64 of 16 March 1991 and No. 58 of 10 March 2001, Ordinary Supplement No. 50.

362 Para 3 reads: 'A child victim shall be afforded special protection measures taking into account the best interests of the child.' Para 4 reads: Each Party shall adopt such legislative or other measures as may be necessary to provide, when necessary, appropriate protection from potential retaliation or intimidation in particular during and after investigation and prosecution of perpetrators, for members of groups, foundations, associations or non-governmental organisations which carry out the activities set out in Article 27, paragraph 3.

363 *Gazzetta Ufficiale* No. 77 of 2 April 2002.

364 Under Article 20: Each Party shall adopt such legislative and other measures as may be necessary to establish as criminal offences the following conducts, when committed intentionally and for the purpose of enabling the trafficking in human beings: (a) forging a travel or identity document; (b) procuring or providing such a document; (c) retaining, removing, concealing, damaging or destroying a travel or identity document of another person. Article 24 establishes: Each Party shall ensure that the following circumstances are regarded as aggravating circumstances in the determination of the penalty for offences established in accordance with Article 18 of this Convention: (a) the offence deliberately or by gross negligence endangered the life of the victim; (b) the offence was committed against a child; (c) the offence was committed by a public official in the performance of her/his duties; (d) the offence was committed within the framework of a criminal organization.

Several acts relating to falsification of documents are dealt with in Articles 476–93 of the *Criminal Code*, which do not however establish them as criminal offences. For this reason, Article 3 of Law No. 108/2010 (Modifications to Criminal Code on the Matter of Trafficking in Persons) has provided an increase in penalty if these acts are committed for the purposes of realizing or facilitating the commission of crimes covered by Articles 600–602.

Moreover, as not all the aggravating circumstances *ex* Article 24 of the Convention were regarded as such in Articles 600–2, Article 3 of Law No. 108 has introduced a further provision into the *Criminal Code* (Article 602 *ter*). The provision allows for an increase in penalty, in either of the following circumstances: (a) the injured person is under the age of 18; (b) the crime is committed for the purposes of the exploitation of the prostitution of others or of the removal of organs; or (c) serious danger to the life, or the physical or mental integrity of the injured person is derived from the crime.

It should be noted, finally, that the commission of a crime by 'criminal organized groups operating in more than one state' was already regarded as an aggravating circumstance in Italian legislation (Article 4 of Law No. 146/2006).[365]

The ratification of the Council of Europe *Convention against Trafficking in Human Beings*, and the implementing measures adopted through Law No. 108/2010 represent a further step in the development of Italian legislation on the matter. They should also be regarded as a response to the recommendations adopted by the Human Right Council in 2010, asking Italy to strengthen efforts to take effective measures to prosecute and punish trafficking in persons, and to provide the victims with adequate assistance.[366] In our opinion, there is, perhaps, too much fragmentation of the applicable norms. This reflects, however, the normative complexity at the international level.

ORNELLA FERRAJOLO

Treaty Action—European Gendarmerie Force

- Ratification and Implementation of the *Declaration of Intent for a European Gendarmerie between France, Italy, Spain, Portugal and the Netherlands concerning the Establishment of a European Gendarmerie Force* (*EGF*), signed in Noordwijk on 17 September 2004
- Ratification and Implementation of the *Treaty between the Kingdom of Spain, the French Republic, the Italian Republic, the Kingdom of the Netherlands and the Portuguese Republic establishing the European Gendarmerie Forces* (*EUROGENFOR*), signed in Velsen on 18 October 2007

---

365 As already noted, Law No. 146/2006 regards the implementation in Italy of the UN Convention against Transnational Organized Crime.

366 Cf. Human Rights Council, Report of the Working Group on the Universal Periodic Review—Italy, UN Doc. A/HRC/14/4 (18 March 2010) p 20, paras 84–85, <http://daccess-dds-ny.un.org/doc/UNDOC/GEN/G10/121/86/PDF/G1012186.pdf?OpenElement>.

- Law No. 84 of 14 May 2010, entered into force on 26 June 2010[367], <http://www.normattiva.it/dispatcher?service=213&fromurn=yes&datagu=2010-06-11&annoatto=2010&numeroatto=84&task=ricercaatti&elementiperpagina=50&redaz=010G0107&newsearch=1&classeprv=1&paginadamostrare=1&tmstp=1298478619632>

The proposal to establish a European Gendarmerie Force was submitted by the French and Italian ministers, at the informal meeting of Ministers of Defence of the European Union (EU) held in Rome on 3–4 October 2003 under the Italian Presidency of the EU, in response to the growing need to deploy international police to maintain order and public safety.

On 17 September 2004, five EU Member States (France, Italy, the Netherlands, Portugal and Spain) signed in Noordwijk the Declaration of Intent for a European Gendarmerie concerning the establishment of a European Gendarmerie Force (EGF), modelled on the French *gendarmes* and the Multinational Specialized Unit (MSU) of the *Carabinieri*.

According to the Declaration of Intent, France, Italy, the Netherlands, Portugal and Spain agreed to provide Europe with a full capability in order to conduct all police missions in crisis management operations within the framework of the Petersberg Declaration,[368] with particular regard to substitution missions.[369] This proposal also aimed to contribute to the development of the European Security and Defence Policy and the creation of an area of freedom, security and justice. It is important to underline that all the aforementioned States possess police forces with a military status capable of carrying out, in accordance with the Nice European Council conclusions,[370] police missions through substitution and/or strengthening of local police. Under the Declaration of Intent, they also proposed to offer a multinational operational structure to those States which intend to join EU operations and to participate in initiatives of international organisations in the area of crisis management.

The establishment of the new EGF became effective through the Treaty between France, Italy, Netherlands, Portugal and Spain, establishing the European Gendarmerie Forces (EUROGENFOR or EGF), signed in Velsen on 18 October 2007. The agreement creates a permanent joint paramilitary force unit to be used for public order and for backing up the military forces. The EGF headquarters is based in Vicenza (Italy) and represents the only permanent structure of the EGF. It

---

367 Published in *Gazzetta Ufficiale* No. 134 of 11 June 2010.

368 For the text of the Declaration, see <http://www.assemblyweu.org/en/documents/sessions_ordinaires/key/declaration_petersberg.php>.

369 Substitution missions carry out executive functions that under normal circumstances would be undertaken by the authorities of the country in which a mission is deployed and usually take place in a more difficult security context. On the specific tasks of substitution missions, see Council of the European Union, Draft Comprehensive EU Concept for Missions in the Field for Rule of Law in Crisis Management (19 November 2002), <http://www.eulex-kosovo.eu/training/material/docs/esdp/consilium/Comprehensive_EU_Concept_for_missions_in_the_field_of_rule_of_law.pdf>.

370 On Nice Council Conclusions, see <http://www.europarl.europa.eu/summits/nice1_en.htm>.

was initially composed of 800 units, drawn from the State Members' paramilitary police: the French *Gendarmerie National*, the Italian *Arma dei Carabinieri,* the Dutch *Koninklijke Marechaussee,* the Portuguese *Guarda Nacional Republicana* and the Spanish *Guardia Civil.* EGF was deployed for the first time in the mission EUFOR 'Althea' in Bosnia–Herzegovina in November 2007.

Article 4 of the EGF agreement indicates the mission and tasks of the EUROGENDFOR. It provides that the EGF can be placed either under civilian authority or under military command and may be used for performing security and public order missions. It also establishes that it can be used to perform security and public order missions, monitoring, advising, mentoring and supervising local police in their day-to-day work, including criminal investigation work.

Members of the EGF are based in their own Member States, but are permanently available for deployment outside the EU's borders within a month, for peace maintenance or crisis management missions, although they may also be deployed by the EU at the request of the UN, NATO, OSCE or other international bodies or an *ad hoc* coalition (Article 5).

The decision body of EGF is the High Level Interdepartmental Committee (CIMIN). According to Article 7, the CIMIN consists of representatives of the appropriate ministries of each Party and the choice of the representatives is a national responsibility. On 1 May 2010, Italy replaced France at the annual Presidency of CIMIN.[371]

In order to fulfil its objectives and accomplish its mission, the EUROGENDFOR has legal capacity within each of the Parties and consequently it may appear in court, where necessary (Article 9).

With reference to criminal and disciplinary jurisdiction, the authorities of each sending State—that is, the State supplying EGF with forces and/or personnel—have the right to exercise all criminal and disciplinary jurisdiction over military and civilian personnel according to the provisions of Article 25 of the Treaty.

With Law No. 84 of 14 May 2010, Italy ratified and implemented the Declaration of Intent and the Treaty on EUROGENDFOR.

EUROGENDFOR represents concrete evidence of cooperation between five European countries determined to contribute to the development of European Security and Defence Policy (ESDP), through the establishment of a multinational structure able to deal with crisis situations in different scenarios.[372]

On 18 December 2008, the CIMIN decided to welcome the Romanian *Jandarmeria* to become a full member of the EGF (Article 42). At present, the EGF consists of six Member States, while Lithuania, Poland were involved as partners (Article 44) and Turkey, as observer (Article 43).

SILVANA MOSCATELLI

[371] On the first meeting under Italian Presidency, see <http://www.carabinieri.it/Internet/Cittadino/Informazioni/Eventi/2010/Maggio/20100520_Cimin_EuroGend>.

[372] On the Italian government position on EGF, see <http://www.governo.it/GovernoInforma/Dossier/gendarmeria_europea/>.

LATVIA[373]

Cases—World War II War Crimes

- *Kononov* v. *Latvia*, European Court of Human Rights, Application No. 36376/04, Judgment, 24 July 2008
- *Kononov* v. *Latvia*, European Court of Human Rights, Grand Chamber, Application No. 36376/04, Judgment, 17 May 2010

In this case, the question before the European Court of Human Rights (ECtHR) was whether the conviction of Mr Vasily Kononov in 2004 for war crimes committed in the Latvian territory during the Second World War violated Article 7 of the *Convention for the Protection of Human Rights and Fundamental Freedoms*, which prohibits the retroactive application of criminal law.[374] In 2008, by a 4—3 majority, a Chamber of the ECtHR found a violation of Article 7. In 2010, by a 14—3 majority, the Grand Chamber reversed the decision.

The underlying criminal case originates from events that transpired in 1944.[375] At that time, the territory of Latvia—which previously had been occupied by, and then annexed to, the Soviet Union—was under German occupation. Soviet guerrillas, known as Red Partisans, operated in the territory behind German lines. A platoon of the Red Partisans, led by Sergeant Kononov, came to believe that the inhabitants of the Mazie Bati village had revealed to the Germans the location of another unit of Red Partisans, who had then been killed by the Germans. Members of Sergeant Kononov's unit, wearing German uniforms to avoid detection, entered Mazie Bati just as its residents were preparing to celebrate Pentecost. Having found weapons supplied by the Germans in a number of farmhouses, the partisans shot six male villagers. They then set fire to several buildings and four more villagers perished in the flames, including a woman in the final stages of pregnancy.

In 1998, the Latvian authorities opened an investigation into the conduct of Mr Kononov. He was prosecuted under a 1993 amendment to the Latvian *Criminal Law* which proscribed war crimes in the following language:

> Any person found guilty of a war crime as defined in the relevant legal conventions, that is to say violations of the laws and customs of war through murder, torture, pillaging from

[373] Information and commentaries by Rain Liivoja (Research Fellow, Asia Pacific Centre for Military Law, Melbourne Law School) and Ieva Miluna (PhD Candidate, University of Amsterdam; Lecturer, Riga Graduate School of Law). These notes cover 2009 and 2010.

[374] Convention for the Protection of Human Rights and Fundamental Freedoms, opened for signature 4 November 1950, 213 UNTS 221, Art. 7 (entered into force 3 September 1953) (ECHR). Article 7 reads: (1) No one shall be held guilty of any criminal offence on account of any act or omission which did not constitute a criminal offence under national or international law at the time when it was committed. Nor shall a heavier penalty be imposed than the one that was applicable at the time the criminal offence was committed. (2) This article shall not prejudice the trial and punishment of any person for any act or omission which, at the time when it was committed, was criminal according the general principles of law recognized by civilized nations.

[375] See 3 *YIHL* (2000) p 546.

> the civil population in an occupied territory or from hostages or prisoners of war, the deportation of such people or their subjection to forced labour, or the unjustified destruction of towns and installations, shall be liable to life imprisonment or to imprisonment for between three and 15 years.[376]

The Latvian courts held that Mr Kononov, by virtue of command responsibility, was responsible for a number of violations of the laws and customs of war: wounding and killing of persons *hors de combat*; treacherous wounding and killing (by making improper use of enemy uniforms); breach of the special protection accorded to women; and an attack against an undefended locality. Mr Kononov was found guilty of war crimes and convicted to 18 months' imprisonment (time already served in pre-trial detention).

Mr Kononov then filed an application with the ECtHR, claiming a violation of Article 7. There were two questions before the court. First, 'whether on 27 May 1944 the applicant's acts constituted offences that were defined with sufficient accessibility and foreseeability by domestic law or international law'.[377] Second, whether the acts, even if proscribed, were statute barred.

As the domestic criminal law in force in Latvian territory in 1944 did not proscribe war crimes, answering the first question led to an analysis of international law. This examination of the law of armed conflict largely focused on the legal status of the persons killed.

The Latvian courts had regarded the villagers as civilians, and the Latvian government maintained this position before the ECtHR.[378] On this view, neither providing information to the Germans, nor having weapons at home and keeping watch at night, deprived the villagers of protection under the law of armed conflict. Such acts did not constitute taking part in military operations and, in any event, at the time of the raid they were not performing any military duty. Hence, the villagers were civilians and killing them amounted to a war crime.

The Chamber—somewhat problematically engaging in a reassessment of the facts—held that the villagers were 'collaborators of the German Army' and could not be regarded as civilians.[379] The raid was 'a targeted military operation consisting in the selective execution of armed collaborators of the Nazi enemy'.[380] Therefore, with respect to the six men, the Chamber did not think it to have been 'adequately demonstrated that the attack ... was per se contrary to the laws and customs of war'.[381] With respect to the women, the Chamber offered two alternative arguments. One option was that they were, like the men, guilty of abusing their civilian status.[382] In the alternative, their execution was an abuse of authority.

---

376 See Criminal Code, s. 68-3 (inserted into the Code on 6 April 1993).

377 *Kononov* v. *Latvia*, Judgment, 24 July 2008, para 116.

378 Ibid., para 78.

379 Ibid., paras 129, 131.

380 Ibid., para 134.

381 Ibid., para 137.

382 Ibid., para 139.

This, according to the idiosyncratic view of the Chamber, meant that the acts were not war crimes but instead constituted ordinary murder,[383] the prosecution of which was barred by a statute of limitations and for which there is no command responsibility. These considerations led to the conclusion that Mr Kononov's acts had either not been criminal or had been time-barred, and that there was therefore a violation of the Convention in his conviction.

The Grand Chamber took a different approach. Rather than taking a definitive stand on the legal status of the villagers, it proceeded from the hypothesis most favourable to Mr Kononov, namely that the villagers were either 'civilians who had participated in hostilities' or combatants.[384] As for the first hypothesis, the Grand Chamber held that '[i]t was also a rule of customary international law in 1944 that civilians could only be attacked *for as long as* they took a direct part in hostilities'.[385] Failing that, 'they remained subject to arrest, fair trial and punishment by military or civilian tribunals for … acts [in violation of *jus in bello*], and their summary execution without that trial would be contrary to the laws and customs of war'.[386] Regarding the hypothesis that the villagers were indeed combatants, the Grand Chamber pointed out that the law in 1944 provided for the humane treatment of prisoners of war and prohibited their ill-treatment and summary execution.[387] Furthermore, if neither of the hypotheses was correct, and the villagers had been civilians, they would have been entitled to even greater protection.[388]

Thus, the Grand Chamber came to the conclusion that the killing of the villagers amounted to a war crime irrespective of their particular legal status.[389] It also agreed with the assessment of Latvian courts that the improper use of enemy uniforms amounted to treachery, that the burning of a pregnant woman to death violated the special protection afforded to women and that the destruction of the farmhouse was an illegal destruction of private property.[390] As concerns the question whether Mr Kononov should have foreseen his prosecution, the Grand Chamber noted that

> even the most cursory reflection by the applicant, would have indicated that, at the very least, the impugned acts risked being counter to the laws and customs of war as understood at that time and, notably, risked constituting war crimes for which, as commander, he could be held individually and criminally accountable.[391]

As regards the statute of limitation, the Grand Chamber essentially argued that since international law did not set a period of limitation for war crimes in 1944 or

383 Ibid., para 140.
384 *Kononov* v. *Latvia*, Judgment, 17 May 2010, para 194.
385 Ibid., para 203 (emphasis in original).
386 Ibid., para 204.
387 Ibid., paras 202, 216.
388 Ibid., para 227.
389 Ibid., paras 216, 227.
390 Ibid., paras 217–219.
391 Ibid., para 238.

at any time thereafter, the crimes could not be considered statute-barred.[392] In a concurring opinion, four judges offered a different line of argument.[393] They noted, first, that a statute of limitation was not really a question of retroactivity under Article 7 of the Convention, but rather a 'purely technical issue more appropriately intertwined with the fairness of proceedings, and Article 6 of the Convention'.[394] They then made the point that it was not the lack of international law in 1944, but rather the development of that law in the subsequent decades that made it permissible for Latvia to prosecute Mr Kononov beyond the statute of limitation attaching to ordinary offences under domestic law.

Military Operations—Latvian National Armed Force Participation in International Military Operations

- Action Plan for the Implementation of the Basic Position for a Comprehensive Latvian Involvement in the Renewal of Afghanistan for the Years 2007–2013[395]
- Parliament Decision, 'On the Prolongation of the Participation of the Latvian National Armed Forces Troops in the North Atlantic Treaty Organisation-led Operation in Afghanistan', 14 October 2010[396]
- Cabinet of Ministers Regulations, 'On the Participation of the Officials of the State Police in the European Union Police Mission in Afghanistan (EUPOL Afghanistan)', 29 January 2009[397]
- Cabinet of Ministers Regulations, 'On the Prolongation of the Participation of the Official of the State Police with Special Rank in the European Union Police Mission in Afghanistan (EUPOL Afghanistan)', 25 November 2009[398]
- Cabinet of Ministers Decision, 'Plan for the Expense Cuts for the Budget Amendments for the Year 2009 and Implementation of Structural Reforms', 13 October 2009[399]

In the years 2009–2010, the National Armed Forces of Latvia continued to participate in the NATO-led International Security Assistance Force (ISAF) in Afghanistan. The Latvian military involvement in this international mission takes place pursuant to the 'Basic Position for Comprehensive Latvian Involvement in the Renewal of Afghanistan for the Years 2007–2013' and the 'Action Plan' of its implementation. The Action Plan also deals with the provision of material–

[392] Ibid., paras 230–233.

[393] *Kononov* v. *Latvia*, Judgment, 17 May 2010 (Joint Concurring Opinion of Judges Rozakis, Tulkens, Spielmann and Jebens).

[394] Ibid., para 7.

[395] For the Latvian text, see <http://www.likumi.lv/doc.php?id=178448>.

[396] For the Latvian text, see <http://titania.saeima.lv/LIVS/SaeimaLIVS_LmP.nsf/0/83E898DEC C7CF81BC22577BC00218E60?OpenDocument>.

[397] For the Latvian text, see <http://www.likumi.lv/doc.php?id=187266>.

[398] For the Latvian text, see <http://www.likumi.lv/doc.php?id=201128>.

[399] For the Latvian text, see <http://www.likumi.lv/doc.php?id=199221>.

technical support to the National Army and National Police of Afghanistan, the participation in Provincial Reconstruction Teams, and the involvement in the European Union police mission (to which Latvia contributed two police officers in 2009 and one police officer in 2010).

In 2009, the National Armed Forces of Latvia also took part in the NATO-lead operation in Kosovo (KFOR), the European Union-led operation in Bosnia and Herzegovina (ALTHEA), the Multinational Battle Group Center in Kosovo (MNTF/MNBG(C)), as well as in the Organisation for Security and Co-operation in Europe (OSCE) Monitoring Mission in Georgia. However, these missions have been discontinued due to budget cuts.

Legislation—Crimes against Humanity and War Crimes

- Amendments to the *Criminal Law*, 21 May 2009[400]

In 2009, the Parliament amended the *Criminal Law* and established individual criminal responsibility for crimes against humanity. A need for the explicit criminalisation of crimes against humanity has become clear in the process of adjudicating conduct that took place in Latvia during the Second World War, which could not be accurately qualified as either genocide or war crimes.

Effective 1 July 2009, Article 71-2 of the *Criminal Law* provides as follows:

> For a person who commits [a] crime against humanity, that is, for an activity which is performed as a part of vast or systematic offensive to civilians and which has been expressed as homicide, extermination, enslavement, deportation or forced movement, unlawful deprivation or limitation of liberty, torture, rape, involvement of a person into sexual slavery, compelling the engaging in prostitution, forced fertilisation or sterilisation, or sexual violence of similar degree of severity, apartheid, persecution of any group of people or union on the basis of political, racial, national, ethnical, cultural, religious or gender affiliation or other reasons which have been recognised as inadmissible in the international law, in relation to any activity indicated in this section or genocide, or war crime or other activity provided for in the international law binding upon the Republic of Latvia, which causes serious physical or mental suffering—the applicable sentence is life imprisonment or deprivation of liberty for a term of not less than three and not exceeding 20 years.[401]

This definition of crimes against humanity largely reflects the definition stipulated in the *Rome Statute of the International Criminal Court*. However, the chapeau of the definition in Latvian law does not reflect the element of knowledge that the act has been committed as a part of a widespread or systematic attack.[402] Also, the list of crimes in the national law does not mention the enforced disappearance of persons. The amendments made in 2009 also redefine war crimes. The new Article 74 of the *Criminal Law* stipulates as follows:

400 For the Latvian text, see <http://www.likumi.lv/doc.php?id=193112>.

401 As translated by the Latvian State Language Centre.

402 See Rome Statute, Art. 7(1).

> For a person who commits [a] war crimes, that is, commits [a] violation of provisions or law [sic], in regard to prohibited conduct in war, comprised in international humanitarian law binding upon the Republic of Latvia, including murder, torture of a person protected by humanitarian law or inhuman treatment of such person, taking of hostages, unlawful deportation, movement, limitation of liberty, unjustifiable destruction of cities and other entities, or other prohibited activity—the applicable sentence is life imprisonment or deprivation of liberty for a term of not less than three and not exceeding 20 years.[403]

Unlike the *Rome Statute*, the definition of war crimes in Latvian law does not include the element of a plan, policy or large-scale commission of offences.[404] The provision fails to criminalise explicitly such grave breaches of the *Geneva Conventions* as wilfully causing great suffering or serious bodily or mental injury, compelling a prisoner of war or other protected person to serve in the armed forces of a hostile power, wilfully depriving a prisoner of war or other protected person of the right to a fair and regular trial. At the same time, the new provision on war crimes leaves the list of violations open by referring to 'other prohibited acts'.

Furthermore, the amendments to the *Criminal Law* in the new Article 74-1 make it punishable to publicly glorify, deny or justify genocide, crimes against humanity, crime against peace or war crimes that have in fact been carried out.

Legislation—Red Cross

- Latvian Red Cross Law, 8 April 2009[405]

This law aims to promote social welfare and respect for international humanitarian law by supporting the Latvian Red Cross Society's cooperation with the State and local government institutions, as well as public participation in the society's work. According to the Law, the basic tasks of the Latvian Red Cross Society include providing assistance to victims of armed conflicts, responding to emergency situations by supporting the victims, searching for disappeared persons, gathering information on burial places during armed conflict, facilitating correspondence with people in conflict zones, and assisting with family reunification. The society also has the general task of popularising humanitarian law and the basic principles of the Red Cross Movement.

The Law provides the national legal basis for the use of the Red Cross emblem. It explicitly states that the Red Cross emblem shall be used in accordance with the *Geneva Conventions* and their *Additional Protocols*, this Law and other regulatory enactment. The Law determines the two functions of the emblem of the Red Cross, those being the protective and indicatory function. The subjects which are entitled

---

403 As translated by the Latvian State Language Centre. Contra the earlier text cited at supra n. 376.

404 See Rome Statute, Art. 8(1).

405 For the Latvian text, see <http://www.likumi.lv/doc.php?id=191208>.

to use the Red Cross emblem as a protective sign are the Latvian Red Cross Society, the National Armed Forces, medical units and other individuals, who in the case of armed conflict are engaged in providing medical assistance for the wounded and sick, as well as transport engaged in their transfer. As an indicative sign, the emblem of the Red Cross may be used by the Latvian Red Cross in fulfilling its tasks of dissemination of international humanitarian law.

Case—Abduction and Rescue Operation of Three Latvian Pilots in Sudan

- Ministry of Foreign Affairs of the Republic of Latvia, 'Government entrusts WFP with freeing Latvian nationals abducted in Sudan', 9 November 2010, <http://www.mfa.gov.lv/en/news/press-releases/2010/november/09-4/>
- Ministry of Foreign Affairs of the Republic of Latvia, 'Foreign Ministry provides further information on hostage crisis in Sudan', 16 December 2010, <http://www.mfa.gov.lv/en/news/press-releases/2010/december/16-3/>
- Ministry of Foreign Affairs of the Republic of Latvia, 'Foreign Minister Ģirts Valdis Kristovskis: Principal task of Foreign Ministry under hostage crisis in Sudan was to bring Latvian citizens back to Latvia alive and unhurt', 21 December 2010, <http://www.mfa.gov.lv/en/news/press-releases/2010/december/21-1/>

On 4 November 2010, three Latvian pilots employed by the United Nations World Food Program (WFP) were abducted in Sudan, in the Darfur region. The Latvian Ministry of Foreign Affairs set up a Crisis-Coordination Centre and asked the WFP to act on behalf of Latvia in any rescue operation. By referring to the UN policy not to pay ransoms, the Latvian government stressed that no ransom would be paid, if demanded.

The pilots were abducted by a group of eight armed persons and taken to an unknown location. For more than a month they were held under armed guard and were subject to a shortage of food and drinking water. However, no physical violence was used against them. According to the official reports, the pilots were subsequently freed in a rescue operation. However, unofficial reports suggest that the pilots incapacitated the kidnappers and escaped.

The Minister of Foreign Affairs, discussing the hostage crisis, stressed that the role of the Ministry of Foreign Affairs had been to bring the Latvian citizens back alive and unhurt. He emphasised that it was the role of the Latvian state to protect its nationals and business interests of Latvian companies in Sudan. The minister concluded that the task to rescue the hostages had been accomplished, but avoided making further comments, as the case was still under investigation by Sudan, the UN and the Counterterrorism Centre of the Security Police of Latvia.

State Practice—Latvia Resettles a Guantánamo Bay Detainee

- Ministry of Foreign Affairs of the Republic of Latvia, 'Latvia responds to US request to receive a Guantanamo detainee' (Press Release, 2 February 2010), <http://www.mfa.gov.lv/en/news/press-releases/2010/february/01-02-03/>

- Question of Members of the Parliament on the Further Fate of the Former Detainee of the Guantanamo Bay Camp in Latvia[406]
- Response of the Minister of Foreign Affairs[407]

In early 2010, at the request of the United States, the government of Latvia decided to resettle a person detained at Guantánamo Bay. The Latvian Ministry of Foreign Affairs explained in a statement that the EU member States, including Latvia, welcomed and politically supported President Barack Obama's decision to close the Guantánamo detention camp and demonstrated their solidarity by admitting detainees into their territories.

The detainee in question was a national of a Central Asian country and had spent more than 5 years in Guantánamo without being charged for terrorist activities. The detainee had agreed to be resettled in Latvia and undertaken to integrate into Latvian society. The Minister of Foreign Affairs assured that he would be guaranteed of all his fundamental rights, including the right to leave the country. However, certain supervisory measures would be imposed.

Ten Members of the Parliament posed a question to the Minister of Foreign Affairs on the status of the former detainee in Latvia. The Minister responded by stating that the detainee would have the status of a stateless person in accordance with Latvian law. The Minister considered that this would not endanger Latvia's bilateral relationship with a State whose national he may be. The Minister stressed the need to observe confidentiality in order not to impede the adaptation and integration process of the detainee.

Treaty Action—Terrorism—Explosive Remnants of War

- *Council of Europe Convention on the Prevention on Terrorism*, Warsaw, 16 May 2005
- *Council of Europe Convention on Laundering, Search, Seizure and Confiscation of the Proceeds from Crime and on the Financing of Terrorism*, Warsaw, 16 May 2005

On 13 November 2008, the Latvian Parliament adopted a Law to ratify the *Council of Europe Convention on the Prevention of Terrorism.*[408] The annotation of the Law reflected the view that the criminalisation of terrorist offences stipulated in the Convention were implemented in Articles 88 and 88-1 of the *Criminal Law* of Latvia (terrorism and financing of terrorism).[409] The Convention entered into force for Latvia on 1 June 2009.

---

406 For the Latvian text, see <http://titania.saeima.lv/LIVS/SaeimaLIVS_LmP.nsf/0/b33d7bafaaf013e3c22576c000406699/$FILE/196.pdf>.

407 For the Latvian text, see <http://titania.saeima.lv/LIVS/SaeimaLIVS_LmP.nsf/0/079503a54329f74dc22576c6003172fd/$FILE/12_5-2-38.pdf>.

408 Law 'On the Council of Europe Convention on the Prevention on Terrorism', 27 November 2008. The Latvian version is available at: <http://www.likumi.lv/doc.php?id=184350&from=off>.

409 Annotation of the Draft Law 'On the Council of Europe Convention on the Prevention of Terrorism'. For the Latvian text, see <http://www.mk.gov.lv/doc/2005/AManot_020608.doc>.

On 17 December 2009, the Latvian Parliament adopted a Law to ratify the *Convention on Laundering, Search, Seizure and Confiscation of the Proceeds from Crime and on the Financing of Terrorism.*[410] The Convention entered into force for Latvia on 1 June 2010.

Treaty Action —Explosive Remnants of War

- *Fifth Protocol on the Explosive Remnant of War to the Conventional Weapons Convention on Prohibitions or Restrictions on the Use of Certain Conventional Weapons Which May Be Deemed to Be Excessively Injurious or to Have Indiscriminate Effects*, Geneva, 28 November 2003

On 16 July 2009, the Latvian Parliament adopted a Law to ratify the *Fifth Protocol to the Conventional Weapons Convention.*[411] The annotation of the Law noted that the accession to the instrument reflected the implementation of the principles of arms control and non-proliferation of weapons of mass destruction.[412] The position of the Ministry of Foreign Affairs is that the Protocol does not have retroactive force, thereby the explosive remnants of war left in the territory of Latvia from the First and the Second World Wars and the problems associated with their neutralisation are not concerned with the implementation of the *Fifth Protocol*. Latvia is a Party to the four protocols of the *Conventional Weapons Convention*. The *Fifth Protocol* entered into force for Latvia on 16 March 2010.

State Policy—Responsibility to Protect

- Address by the President of the Republic of Latvia, H.E. Dr.Valdis Zatlers at the United Nations General Assembly, 24 September 2009, <http://www.president.lv/pk/content/?art_id=14498>

In his 2009 address to the United Nations General Assembly, the President of Latvia expressed support for the concept of The Responsibility to Protect (R2P). Without elaborating on its normative position and basis in international law, the President emphasised the need to contribute to its implementation so that mass atrocities remain a thing of the past.

---

410 Law 'On the Council of Europe Convention on Laundering, Search, Seizure and Confiscation of the Proceeds from Crime and on the Financing of Terrorism', 17 December 2009. For the Latvian text, see <http://www.likumi.lv/doc.php?id=203016&from=off>.

411 Law 'On the Fifth Protocol to the Convention on Prohibitions or Restrictions on the Use of Certain Conventional Weapons which may be deemed to be Excessively Injurious or to have Indiscriminate Effects', 16 July 2009. For the Latvian text, see <http://www.likumi.lv/doc.php?id=195483&from=off>.

412 Annotation of the Draft Law 'On the Fifth Protocol to the Convention on Prohibitions or Restrictions on the Use of Certain Conventional Weapons which may be deemed to be Excessively Injurious or to have Indiscriminate Effects'. For the Latvian text, see <http://www.mk.gov.lv/doc/2005/AManot_030309.737.doc>.

State Policy—Geneva Conventions

- Address by the President of the Republic of Latvia, H.E. Dr. Valdis Zatlers at the United Nations General Assembly, 24 September 2009, <http://www.president.lv/pk/content/?art_id=14498>

In 2009, with reference to the 60th anniversary of the adoption of the *Geneva Conventions*, the President of Latvia observed that the character of armed conflicts is constantly changing. He stressed that new challenges, such as responding to terrorism, arise. The President stated that the *Geneva Conventions* nonetheless remain the bedrock of international humanitarian law, but that the political will to implement them fully is insufficient, as violations of the *Conventions* and human rights still occur.

State Policy—Conflict in Afghanistan

- Address by the President of the Republic of Latvia, H.E. Dr.Valdis Zatlers at the United Nations General Assembly, 24 September 2009, <http://www.president.lv/pk/content/?art_id=14498>
- Statement of the Prime Minister, Mr Valdis Dombrovskis, on National Security, 8 October 2009[413]

The President emphasised that it is crucial to pursue a balanced international involvement in Afghanistan, which would encompass civilian and military efforts. He stated that Latvia contributes both military and civil assistance to the development of Afghanistan. The Prime Minister in his report on national security at the Parliament elaborated that Latvia supports the consolidation of the Afghani National Army and the police.

State Policy—Right to Truth

- Address by the Latvian Ambassador to the United Nations in Geneva, H.E. Jānis Mažeiks at the Human Rights Council panel discussion on the right to truth, 9 March 2010[414]

On 9 March 2010, a panel discussion on the right to truth took place at the Human Rights Council. The topic was not confined to examining the issue of missing and disappeared persons, but encompassed a broader context of gross violations of human rights. The Latvian delegate emphasised the significance of the right to truth in any society that has experienced war, gross violations of human rights or totalitarian repression. He emphasised that Latvia emerged from the oppression of two totalitarian regimes and thus has joined in the efforts in the establishment and clarification of the truth. The Latvian delegate considered that a balance had to be

[413] For the Latvian text, see <http://www.mk.gov.lv/lv/mp/runas-pazinojumi/dombrovska-runas/081009-zinojums-par-nacionalo-drosibu/>.

[414] For a summary, see <http://www.unog.ch/unog/website/news_media.nsf/(httpNewsByYear_en)/38FB083EFA9B70F6C12576E100485D96?OpenDocument>.

achieved between the protection of personal information and the right to truth. However, he expressed the opinion that archives would have to be opened for victims and researchers. He concluded by stating that attempts to glorify a totalitarian past demonstrated the need for further discussion.

RAIN LIIVOJA AND IEVA MILUNA

LITHUANIA[415]

Cases—WWII War Crimes

- *Jevdoksijus Sokolovas*, Kaunas Regional Court decision of 2 July 2010

Jevdoksijus Sokolovas, 82, was convicted on 2 July 2010 of detaining and signing orders that led to the deportation of 15 persons to Siberia in March 1949. Sokolovas conceded that he served as the deputy head of a militia unit in Kruonis and that he was the head of the deportation team, but he also claimed that he could not resist the orders he was given. The Court found Sokolovas guilty of his participation in the deportation of the civilian population. However, he escaped a custodial sentence and was only sentenced to undergo medical treatment due to his poor health. A civil claim for damages, amounting to LTL 20,000 (approximately EUR 6000) attached to the case.[416]

- *Markelis Bulatovas*, Vilnius Regional Court decision of 11 June 2010
- Court of Appeals decision of 23 September 2010

The Vilnius District Court found Markelis Bulatovas, 83, guilty of killing Lithuanian partisans who opposed Soviet rule during the 1950s and 1960s and sentenced him to 7 years in a correctional facility. The Court found that the accused acted in a group with agents of the Ministry of State Security of the Lithuanian SSR. Documents prove that he pretended to be a Lithuanian partisan in 1952–1953 and that he participated in the execution of nine Lithuanian freedom fighters near Ignalina and Švenčionys. Bulatovas confessed he worked for the Ministry of State Security from 1952 to 1960 and that he was present at one of the executions. However, he claimed that he did not fire on the freedom fighters because his gun was stuck.[417]

415 Information and commentaries provided by Rytis Satkauskas, lecturer at Vilnius University.

416 Vyras, ištrėmęs 15 žmonių, yra kaltas, tačiau nenubaustas, <http://kauno.diena.lt/naujienos/kriminalai/vyras-istremes-15-zmoniu-yra-kaltas-taciau-nenubaustas-286971>.

417 Lithuanian court convicts 83-year-old Soviet security agent of genocide: Russia and CIS Business and Financial Newswire (Interfax report, 11 June 2010); Дайнюс Синкявичюс, "Бывшего агента КГБ из Литвы приговорили к семи годам лишения свободы", <http://ru.delfi.lt/news/live/byvshego-agenta-kgb-iz-litvy-prigovorili-k-semi-godam-lisheniya-svobody.d?id=33371333>.

In response to Bulatovas' appeal, the Lithuanian Court of Appeals ordered an examination of the health of the convicted party to ensure that he is able to serve his sentence.[418]

NGO Investigation—Allegations of WWII War Crimes

- Association of Lithuanian Jews, <www.lithuanianjews.org.il>

The Association of Lithuanian Jews accused Lithuanian guerrilla fighters against Soviet oppression of killing Jews.[419] According to the website of the Israel-based association, prominent post-war resistance leaders Juozas Lukša and Adolfas Ramanauskas were among those 3000 Lithuanians who allegedly assisted the Nazis in the Jewish massacre during World War II. The Lithuanian Genocide and Resistance Center[420] denied the allegations, claiming instead that according to the investigation of the facts only 301 of the 1737 examined names could possibly have taken part in the Holocaust. According to the Director of the Center, 'only a court can establish whether they were killers of Jews. Nevertheless, there is evidence that they could have been'. The research of documents revealed new names of persons who could have helped the Nazis in the annihilation of the Jewish population. The materials could be made public in the future. Calculations suggest that about 200,000 Jews of Lithuanian heritage perished during the Nazi genocide in 1941–1944.

Parliamentary Resolution—Reparations for Aggression

- *Resolution on Compensation to the Victims of the USSR Aggression Perpetrated during and after 11–13 January 1991 and to Their Families*, 19 January 2010

On 19 January 2010, the Lithuanian parliament passed the *Resolution on Compensation to the Victims of the USSR Aggression Perpetrated during and after 11–13 January 1991 and to Their Families.*[421] The Resolution recalled the agression of the USSR armed forces on 11–13 January 1991 and called upon the Lithuanian government to apply officially to the government of the Russian Federation for compensation payments to the victims of that aggression and their families.

- Briefing by the Russian Ministry of Foreign Affairs (MFA) on Aggression and Occupation of Baltic States of 29 January 2010

In reply to the Lithuanian Parliamentary Resolution, the Russian Foreign Ministry accused Lithuania of continuing 'to live phobias of the past' and of 'not being

---

418 Дайнюс Синкявичюс"Эксперты выяснят, может ли бывший аг ентМГБ отбывать нак азание", <http://ru.delfi.lt/news/live/eksperty-vyyasnyat-mozhet-li-byvshij-agent-mgb-otbyvat-nakazanie.d?id=36825439>.

419 <http://holocaustinthebaltics.com/wp-content/uploads/2010/09/2010Sept28BNSReportGenocideCenter.pdf>

420 <www.genocid.lt>

421 <http://www3.lrs.lt/pls/inter3/dokpaieska.showdoc_l?p_id=364236>.

interested in remedying bilateral relations'.[422] It also denied the accusation of aggression claiming that '[u]nder international law, aggression can only be a wrongful use of armed force by one state against another, and the UN Security Council gives a legally significant act of aggression qualification, but as of January 1991, an independent Republic of Lithuania did not exist because it was not recognized by any state'. Concerning the relevance of the Treaty between the RSFSR and Lithuania of 29 July 1991 on the Fundamentals of Interstate Relations, in which the attacks of 11–13 January 1991 by the USSR are regarded by both countries as constituting an act of aggression against the sovereign State of Lithuania, the Russian Foreign Ministry explained that '[t]his document at the time of signing was an agreement between two entities of the Soviet federation and, accordingly, could not engender international legal consequences'.

- Russian MFA comments of 19 August 2010 on the Occupation of the Baltic States

In response to a media query on the invitation of the Latvian Foreign Minister that 'Russia's frankness about tragic time and the openness of the Russian archives would be a big step towards recognition (by Russia) of the occupation of the Baltic States', the MFA Spokesman commented that any speculation on the 'so-called occupation of the Baltic States' only causes a serious irritant in bilateral relations. Any attempts by officials in Riga to secure some kind of exclusive right (to access Russian State archives) evokes bewilderment.[423]

Parliamentary Resolution—Forceful Transfer of Persons

- *Resolution on the Persons Transferred to the Occupied Territory of the Republic of Lithuania from the Occupied Territory of the Republic of Poland on the Basis of the Agreement on Resettlement of 10 January 1941 between the USSR and Germany*, 3 June 2010

In its *Resolution on the Persons Transferred to the Occupied Territory of the Republic of Lithuania from the Occupied Territory of the Republic of Poland on the Basis of the Agreement on Resettlement of 10 January 1941 between the USSR and Germany*, the Lithuanian parliament pointed to secret protocols signed by the USSR and Germany on 23 August 1939, 28 September 1939 and 10 January 1941, according to which the territories of Eastern and Central European countries not belonging to the contracting parties were divided between them,

422 Andrei Nesterenko, Russian MFA Spokesman, 'Outcome of the trilateral meeting of Presidents Medvedev, Aliyev and Sargsyan on Nagorno Karabakh' (29 January 2010), <http://www.mid.ru/brp_4.nsf/0/EFE00C59EF3E7ADCC32576BF00288DC3>.

423 Russian Ministry of Foreign Affairs, 'Commentaire d'A.A.Nesterenko, porte-parole du MAE de la Russie, à propos de la question des médias concernant les déclarations d'A.Ronis, Ministre des Affaires Etrangères de la Lettonie, publiées dans le journal «Latvijas Avize»' (19 August 2010), <http://www.ln.mid.ru/brp_4.nsf/7b52686a865d7fd943256999005bcbb4/c3257038003b6dacc32577850033612a?OpenDocument>.

constituting an aggression agreement against the said countries.[424] On the basis of the resettlement agreement and its secret protocol, persons of Lithuanian descent were forcibly transferred from the territory of the Republic of Poland occupied by the German Reich (Suwałki Region) to the territory of the Republic of Lithuania occupied by the USSR. The Lithuanian parliament urged the government of the Republic of Lithuania to initiate consultations with the government of the Federal Republic of Germany on reparations to citizens of the Republic of Lithuania who were forcibly removed from the occupied territory of the Republic of Poland on the basis of the agreement on resettlement of 10 January 1941 between the USSR and Germany. The government was also urged to raise the issue of the responsibility of the Russian Federation as Successor State to the USSR—the other State responsible for this unlawful resettlement—while implementing the Law of the Republic of Lithuania on Compensation for Damage Resulting from the Occupation by the USSR.

RYTIS SATKAUSKAS

SOUTH AFRICA[425]

Legislation—Defence

- *Defence Amendment Act 2010*

The *Defence Amendment Act 2010*,[426] amending the *Defence Act 2002*, was assented to on 7 December 2010. It clarifies who comprises the Military Command of the South African National Defence Force and regulates the appointment of the members of the Force. It also regulates the relationship between members of the Reserve Force and the Defence Force, by requiring members of the Reserve Force to enter into a contract of service. It further requires members of the Reserve Force to comply with a call-up order to report for duty. The Act establishes a Defence Force Service Commission, which is to make recommendations to the Minister of Defence and Military Veterans concerning conditions of service of members of the Defence Force.

Legislation—Transnational Crime

- Prevention and Combating of Trafficking in Persons Bill 2010[427]

This Bill was introduced in the National Assembly on 29 January 2010 in order to give effect to the *United Nations Protocol to Prevent, Suppress and Punish Trafficking in Persons, especially Women and Children, Supplementing the United*

---

[424] <http://www3.lrs.lt/pls/inter3/dokpaieska.showdoc_l?p_id=375044>.

[425] Information and commentaries by Nadine Fourie, Advocate of the High Court of South Africa and member of the Johannesburg Bar.

[426] South Africa, *Government Gazette*, Vol. 546, No. 33866, 9 December 2010, p 2, <http://www.info.gov.za/view/DownloadFileAction?id=137148>.

[427] <http://www.pmg.org.za/files/bills/100316b7-10.pdf>.

Nations Convention against Transnational Organised Crime. It provides for an offence of trafficking in persons and related offences and aims to prevent and combat the trafficking in persons within and across the borders of the Republic. It also provides for measures to protect and assist victims of trafficking. It seeks to establish the Intersectoral Committee on Prevention and Combating of Trafficking in Persons.

Legislation—Immigration and Refugees

- Refugees Amendment Bill 2010[428]

This Bill was introduced in the National Assembly on 20 August 2010. It seeks to amend the *Refugees Act 1998* in order to clarify the way in which unsuccessful applications for asylum are dealt with. The Bill creates a Status Determination Committee that will deal with applications for asylum in terms of the Act, instead of the Refugee Status Determination Officer, as is currently the case. It seeks to ensure that the applications for asylum in terms of the Act are dealt with efficiently and in a less subjective fashion. The Bill also provides for how appeals against unsuccessful applications are dealt with. It clarifies that the Director-General must automatically review applications rejected as being 'manifestly unfounded'. Applications rejected as 'unfounded' may be appealed to the Refugee Appeals Authority.

- Immigration Amendment Bill 2010[429]

The Immigration Amendment Bill was introduced in the National Assembly on 1 October 2010. The Bill seeks to streamline the immigration process by changing certain categories of temporary residence permits to visas. The Bill also seeks to provide that a change in conditions and status of a permit holder may only be made in exceptional circumstances and must be approved by the Minister. The Bill further revises the types of work permits issued under the Act and creates a new category of permit, the critical skills work permit. The Bill provides for the mandatory transmission and use of passenger information, and revises the penal provisions in the Act. The Bill has been criticized for proposing a pre-screening of asylum seekers by immigration officers at border posts, and for imposing harsher criminal penalties for breaching administrative procedures.

Treaty Action—Arms and Arms Control

Thirteen years after it officially opened for signature, the *African Nuclear-Weapon Free Zone Treaty*[430] (Treaty of Pelindaba) came into force with the 28th deposit of its ratification instrument by Burundi on 15 July 2009. The African Treaty bears the name of Pelindaba after the South African nuclear plant at which a number of nuclear warheads were produced that were dismantled after the new

428 <http://www.pmg.org.za/files/bills/100913b30-10.pdf>.

429 <http://www.pmg.org.za/files/bills/b32-2010(immigration).pdf>.

430 Opened for signature 11 April 1996, 35 *ILM* 698 (1996) (entered into force 15 July 2009).

ANC government committed itself to non-proliferation and arms control of all weapons of mass destruction post-1994. The Treaty, which covers the African continent, ensures that nuclear weapons are not developed, produced, tested, or otherwise acquired or stationed in any of the countries on the continent.

On 1 August 2010, the *Convention on Cluster Munitions* came into effect. Cluster munitions were used largely in developing countries, with 11 locations affected by the scourge located on the African continent. At the Africa Regional Seminar on the Implementation of International Humanitarian Law held in South Africa in May 2010, South Africa, which formerly produced and stockpiled clusters munitions, reaffirmed its position that cluster munitions had become obsolete as means of modern warfare.[431]

Participation in Peace Operations—South African National Defence Force Deployments

In 2009–2010, the South African National Defence Force participated in five Peace Support Operations in the Democratic Republic of Congo (DRC), Burundi, Sudan, Nepal and Uganda. The SANDF further participated in two General Military Assistance operations in the DRC and the Central African Republic (CAR). On average, a total of 2894 members, including 148 Reserve members, were deployed in these missions.[432]

Refugees and Asylum Seekers

In 2009, South Africa received the largest number of new asylum requests of any country in the world, with more than 222,000 claims—almost one quarter of applications globally. Most applications were received from Zimbabweans.[433] Of the 158,200 new asylum claims filed internationally by individuals originating from Zimbabwe, 90% were lodged in South Africa.[434] Perhaps not surprisingly then, the largest number of undecided cases at any stage of the application process was also reported by South Africa for the same year, at a staggering 309,800.[435]

---

[431] Ebrahim I Ebrahim, Opening Statement by Deputy Minister of Department of International Relations and Cooperation brahim I Ebrahim at the tenth annual regional seminar on the implementation of International Humanitarian Law, OR Tambo (4 May 2010), <http://www.info.gov.za/speech/DynamicAction?pageid=461&sid=10383&tid=10400>.

[432] Department of Defence, *Annual Report 2010* (2010) pp xvii, 22–23, <http://www.dod.mil.za/documents/annualreports/Annual%20Report%200910f.pdf>.

[433] United Nations High Commissioner for Refugees, 2009 Global Trends: Refugees, Asylum-seekers, Returnees, Internally Displaced Persons and Stateless Persons (2010) p 1, <http://www.reliefweb.int/rw/lib.nsf/db900sid/ASAZ-86EG65/$file/UNHCR_Jun2010.pdf?openelement>.

[434] Ibid., p 18.

[435] Ibid., p 19.

In September 2010, the Department of Home Affairs announced the Zimbabwean Documentation Project. It allowed for undocumented Zimbabweans who had entered the country before 31 May 2010 to regularize their stay by applying for work, study or business permits.

Treaty Action—Internally Displaced Persons

Member States of the African Union met during November 2009 to adopt the *African Union Convention for the Protection and Assistance of Internally Displaced Persons in Africa (Kampala Convention).*[436] The Convention is aimed at the prevention of internal displacement, and the protection and assistance of internally displaced persons.

International Security—Security Council Membership

On 12 October 2010, South Africa was elected as a non-permanent member of the United Nations Security Council.

Cases—Refugees and Asylum Seekers

The years under review saw a number of cases dealing with the unlawful arrest, detention or deportation of 'illegal foreigners'.

- *Koyabe* v. *Minister for Home Affairs*[437]

This judgment of the Constitutional Court deals with the question whether persons declared to be prohibited persons under immigration legislation had to exhaust their internal remedies before reviewing such a decision. It was held that a ministerial review under the *Immigration Act 2002* had to be pursued before the court could be approached on application for judicial review. The *amicus curiae* in the matter contended that the Department had adopted a deliberate and routine strategy of raising the duty to exhaust internal remedies against applicants seeking court orders that they be released from detention or not be deported. The difficulties faced by prohibited persons detained in holding facilities in bringing such internal reviews were often insurmountable. The court held that this issue did not arise in the case under consideration as the applicants had not been detained or deported, but that future challenges on this basis could still be brought.

[436] Opened for signature 22 October 2009 (not yet in force), <http://www.unhcr.org/4ae9bede9.html>.

[437] *Koyabe And Others* v. *Minister for Home Affairs and Others (Lawyers For Human Rights As Amicus Curiae)* 2010 (4) SA 327 (CC) 2010 (4) SA327 (CC), <http://www.saflii.org/za/cases/ZACC/2009/23.pdf>.

- *Jeebhai* v. *Minister of Home Affairs*[438]

In this matter, the Supreme Court of Appeal considered the lawfulness of the arrest and detention of an 'illegal foreigner', Mr Khalid Mahmood Rashid, a Pakistani national. The majority of the court, per Ponnan JA, held that Mr Rashid fell within the definition of 'illegal foreigner'. Moreover, he had perpetrated a fraud in order to facilitate his entry into and sojourn in the Republic. The court accordingly held that his arrest had been authorized by the *Immigration Act*. The court held, however, that the Act did not authorize his detention or deportation, as this had been done without obtaining a warrant. The court emphasized that, as Mr Rashid's detention was therefore *prima facie* unlawful, the onus was on the State to justify the deprivation of Mr Rashid's liberty. This could not be done in the present case. The detention and deportation of Mr Rashid was accordingly declared to have been unlawful.

- *Ulde* v. *Minister of Home Affairs*[439]

This case before the Supreme Court of Appeal dealt with the arrest of an illegal foreigner under s. 34(1) of the *Immigration Act*. The court held that such an arrest was subject to the exercise of a discretion by an immigration officer. The discretion is to be construed in favour of the individual's liberty. This approach is consistent with s. 12(1)(a) of the *South African Constitution* which provides that freedom may not be deprived arbitrarily or without just cause. The court held that, simply put, 'a person may not be deprived of his freedom for unacceptable reasons'. However, once the decision-maker has demonstrated that the discretion has been properly exercised, a court will not interfere, even if it appears that the wrong decision was made.

- *Aruforse* v. *Minister of Home Affairs*[440]

This judgment of the Johannesburg High Court concerned the detention of a Burundian national who had been detained for more than 6 months at the Lindela Holding Facility pending his deportation to Burundi. Mr Aruforse claimed to be an asylum seeker. The court held that there was a dispute of fact about whether or not Mr Aruforse had applied for asylum, and that this dispute could not be resolved in application proceedings. The court nevertheless ordered Mr Aruforse's immediate release from Lindela, holding that his detention was unlawful as the maximum period for which any person may be detained in terms of s. 34(1) of the *Immigration Act* was a period of 120 days. The court emphasized that a detainee had

---

438 *Jeebhai and Others* v. *Minister of Home Affairs and Another* [2009] ZASCA 35; [2009] 3 All SA 103 (SCA); 2009 (5) SA 54 (SCA) (31 March 2009), <http://www.saflii.org/za/cases/ZASCA/2009/35.pdf>.

439 *Ulde* v. *Minister of Home Affairs and Another* [2009] ZASCA 34; 2009 (4) SA 522 (SCA); 2009 (8) BCLR 840 (SCA) (31 March 2009), <http://www.saflii.org/za/cases/ZASCA/2009/34.pdf>.

440 *Aruforse* v. *Minister of Home Affairs* [2010] ZAGPJHC 59; 2010 (6) SA 579 (GSJ); 2011 (1) SACR 69 (GSJ) (25 January 2010), <http://www.saflii.org/za/cases/ZAGPJHC/2010/59.pdf>.

'the absolute right not to be deprived of his freedom for one second longer than necessary by an official who cannot justify his detention'.

- *Arse* v. *Minister of Home Affairs*[441]

In this matter the Supreme Court of Appeal ordered the immediate release of the appellant from the Lindela Holding Facility. The appellant was an asylum seeker from Ethiopia who, according to the founding papers, fled that country due to persecution by reason of his tribal affiliation and political opinion. On arrival in South Africa, he had been provided with an asylum transit permit in terms of s. 23 of the *Immigration Act* so that he could proceed to a Refugee Reception Office to apply for asylum. An asylum transit permit is valid for a period of 14 days. He attempted to gain access to a Refugee Reception Office during that period and in the months thereafter but he did not succeed due to the lengthy queues. He was subsequently arrested and was detained for a week at a police station before being transferred to Lindela where he was detained for 7 months. He applied for asylum in detention. His application was refused and he appealed against this refusal to the Refugee Appeal Board. The Court held that, even if the appellant were an illegal foreigner, he could not be detained under s. 34(1) of the *Immigration Act* for longer than 120 days. Any detention beyond that point would be unlawful. The court further held that once an asylum seeker permit is granted to an applicant for asylum, he can thereafter no longer be regarded as an 'illegal foreigner'. No proceedings may accordingly be instituted or continued against such a person in respect of his unlawful entry into or presence in the country until a decision has been made on his application or he has exhausted his rights of review or appeal.

- *Intercape Ferreira Mainline* v. *Minister of Home Affairs*[442]
- *410 Voortrekker Road Property Holdings CC* v. *Minister of Home Affairs*[443]

These two judgments of the Cape High Court illustrate some of the practical difficulties created by the high volume of asylum applications in South Africa. The matters involve challenges brought by property owners in the area in which the government had established a new refugee reception centre in order to relieve the pressure on existing facilities. These changes were made partly in response to the judgment of the High Court in the matter of *Kiliko* v. *Minister of Home Affairs*,[444] referred to in the 2007 report. The applications were brought on the

---

[441] *Arse* v. *Minister of Home Affairs and Others* [2010] ZASCA 9; 2010 (7) BCLR 640 (SCA); [2010] 3 All SA 261 (SCA) (12 March 2010), <http://www.saflii.org/za/cases/ZASCA/2010/9.pdf>.

[442] *Intercape Ferreira Mainliner (Pty) Ltd and Others* v. *Minister of Home Affairs and Others* [2009] ZAWCHC 100; 2010 (5) SA 367 (WCC) (24 June 2009), <http://www.saflii.org/za/cases/ZAWCHC/2009/100.pdf>.

[443] *410 Voortrekker Road Property Holdings CC* v. *Minister of Home Affairs and Others* [2010] ZAWCHC 87; 2010 (8) BCLR 785 (WCC); [2010] 4 All SA 414 (WCC) (3 May 2010), <http://www.saflii.org/za/cases/ZAWCHC/2010/87.pdf>.

[444] *Kiliko and Others* v. *Minister of Home Affairs and Others* 2006 (4) SA 114 (C).

basis of a breach of city zoning laws as well as the common law of nuisance. In *Mainline,* the court describes how hundreds of asylum seekers stand in queues at reception centres daily, many staying there overnight to be at the front of the next day's queue. This, the judgment says 'is accompanied by the inevitable detritus of people forced to sleep on the streets: the remains of food, makeshift materials to provide rudimentary bedding and warmth, human waste, and general litter'. Apart from noise and health complaints, safety and security concerns were raised by the applicants, with frequent reports of violence and crime, and an incident of police firing rubber bullets at a crowd near the premises. The court held that the operation of the refugee centre was unlawful in that, among other things, it was in breach of zoning regulations and a nuisance in common law. It ordered the government to cease conducting the operations as a refugee reception centre within 3 months.

Some months later, after the reception had been relocated, the matter again came to court in the *Voortrekker Road* matter. The new neighbours of the relocated reception centre again challenged the operation of the refugee reception on essentially the same grounds. Again the court described the conditions under which the centre operated. It held that the centre was operated unlawfully, both on the basis of a breach of statutory zoning provisions and actionable nuisance. It, however, suspended the order to allow the government's position to be regularized by way of amendment to the relevant zoning regulations. It further ordered specific measures in order to address the nuisance created by the centre, including a dramatic increase in staff and provision of sanitation sufficient for the 1500 daily visitors to the centre.

Cases—International Human Rights Standards

- *Von Abo* v. *Government of South Africa*[445]

This matter concerned an application brought by Mr Von Abo, a South African citizen with farming and land interests in Zimbabwe. In 1997, Zimbabwe implemented a new land policy which resulted in his farms being expropriated. Mr Von Abo sought to resist the expropriation and also made numerous requests to the South African government for assistance and diplomatic protection. When such assistance was not forthcoming, Mr Von Abo approached the Pretoria High Court for an order declaring that the government had failed properly to consider his request for diplomatic protection relating to the violation of his rights by the government of Zimbabwe. The court held that the expropriation of his property without payment was in violation of international minimum standards, which are to be afforded to all persons, citizens and foreign nationals alike. It further reconfirmed that it is a principle of international law that a State is entitled to protect its nationals against the wrongs committed by other States contrary to international law. The court found that it would be futile for the applicant to pursue internal remedies within Zimbabwe. The court held that given the 'almost absolute

[445] *Von Abo* v. *Government of the Republic of South Africa and Others* [2008] ZAGPHC 226; 2009 (2) SA 526 (T) (29 July 2008), <http://www.saflii.org/za/cases/ZAGPHC/2008/226.pdf>.

disregard that Government shows even for the orders of its own courts particularly in respect of the expropriation and taking of the farms of white farmers, there are no remedies available to the applicant'. The court held that 'to the extent that it may be suggested that there are any remedies left to exhaust in Zimbabwe, those remedies are not "effective" as that term is understood in international law'.

The court accordingly held that the failure of the government to consider, decide and deal with the applicant's application for diplomatic protection in respect of the violation of his rights by the government of Zimbabwe is inconsistent with the *South African Constitution* and invalid. It was declared further that the applicant had the right to diplomatic protection in respect of the violation of his rights by the government of Zimbabwe. The South African government was ordered to take all necessary steps to have the violation of the applicant's rights remedied, and to report back to the court within 60 days on steps taken in this regard. The possibility of a claim for damages was reserved for consideration at that stage.

The judgment was referred to the Constitutional Court for confirmation,[446] as there was agreement between the parties that an adverse finding about the conduct of the President, who was the second respondent in the proceedings before the High Court, would require a certification process by the Constitutional Court as intended by s. 172(2)(a) of the Constitution. The Constitutional Court, however, disagreed and held that it was unnecessary for the matter to have been referred to it. In essence, diplomatic protection was the responsibility of the government as a whole, and not of the President alone. Moreover, on the facts of this case, it was clear that it was the Department of Foreign Affairs that had dealt with the matter, and not the President, despite the applicant's appeals to the President for diplomatic protection. The court accordingly held that the matter had been erroneously brought to it, and the matter was struck off the roll. The court observed, however, that neither the President, nor any of the government respondents had appealed the decision of the High Court, despite them having an automatic right of appeal. Thus, the order of the High Court remained and Mr Von Abo's relief as contained in the order of that court would not be diminished in any way.

The matter was again before the High Court when the government's report, which it was ordered to provide within 60 days, had to be considered.[447] The court found that the government had not complied with the earlier order and held that the applicant would be entitled to constitutional damages from the South African government for violation of its rights, the quantum of which was referred to oral evidence.

---

446 *Von Abo* v. *President of the Republic of South Africa* [2009] ZACC 15; 2009 (10) BCLR 1052 (CC) 2009 (5) SA 345 (CC) (5 June 2009), <http://www.saflii.org/za/cases/ZACC/2009/15.pdf>.

447 *Von Abo* v. *Government of the Republic of South Africa and Others* (*3106/07*) [2010] ZAGPPHC 4; 2010 (3) SA 269 (GNP); 2010 (7) BCLR 712 (GNP) (5 February 2010), <http://www.saflii.org/cgi-bin/disp.pl?file=za/cases/ZAGPPHC/2010/4.html&query=von%20abo>.

- *Residents of Joe Slovo Community* v. *Thubelisha Homes and others*[448]

This case involved an application for the eviction of approximately 20,000 residents of the Joe Slovo informal settlement in the Western Cape. The application was brought in the Cape High Court by government agencies responsible for housing on the basis that the eviction was required for the purpose of developing affordable housing for poor people. The Court held that the government agencies had complied with the requirements of the *Prevention of Illegal Eviction from and Unlawful Occupation of Land Act 1998* and granted the eviction order.

The Constitutional Court upheld in part an appeal against the order. Its order included that no eviction may take place unless the people evicted are offered alternative accommodation. It also ordered meaningful engagement with individual households before eviction.

The concurring judgment of Ngcobo J, with which two justices concurred, relies on international human rights norms which recognise that development may require evictions. The judgment refers to General Comment No. 7[449] on forced evictions, which states that '[e]victions may be carried out in connection with … development and infrastructure projects … land acquisition measures associated with urban renewal, housing renovation, [and] city beautification programmes'. However, evictions should not result in people being rendered homeless. And where the people affected by the eviction are unable to provide for themselves, 'the [government] must take all appropriate measures, to the maximum of its available resources, to ensure that adequate alternative housing, resettlement or access to productive land, as the case may be, is available'.

NADINE FOURIE

SPAIN[450]

Cases—The Couso Case

- Supreme Court. Criminal Chamber. Appeal No. 2629/2009. Opining Judge: Mr Francisco Monterde Ferrer. Ruling: 13/07/2010. Ruling No. 4222/2010, <http://www.poderjudicial.es/search/doAction?action=contentpdf&databasematch=TS&reference=5697930&links=%222629/2009%22&optimize=20100812>
- National Court. Proceedings 27/2007. Central Investigating Court No. 1. Order of 29 July 2010

---

448 [2009] ZACC 16 (10 June 2009); 2010 (3) SA454 (CC), <http://www.saflii.org/za/cases/ZACC/2009/16.pdf>.

449 Committee on Economic, Social and Cultural Rights, 'General Comment No. 7: The Right to Adequate Housing (Art. 11.1): Forced Eviction', UN Doc. E/1998/22, Annex IV, 14 May 1997, para 7.

450 Information and Commentaries by Antoni Pigrau, Professor of Public International Law at the *Rovira i Virgili University*, Tarragona, Spain.

As reported in the 2007, 2008 and 2009 *Yearbook of International Humanitarian Law*[451] this case concerns the death in Iraq on 8 April 2003, of the Spanish journalist Mr. José Couso Permuy.

This particular decision was delivered in response to the Appeal to the Supreme Court no. 2629/2009 against the Order of 23 October 2009 by the Third Section of the Criminal Chamber of the Spanish National Court, which declared the termination of the proceedings undertaken to ascertain the circumstances of and those allegedly responsible for the death of the journalist Mr. José Couso Permuy.

The Ruling considers various grounds for appeal, including an alleged infringement of Article 24.1 of the *Spanish Constitution*, which covers the right to due process (including a prohibition on a lack of a proper defence, the right to a proper defence and the right to proof of evidence), as well as breach of the law, due to the failure to apply Articles 611.1 and 138 of the *Spanish Penal Code*. Article 611.1 of the *Penal Code* states that it is a crime to 'undertake or order indiscriminate or excessive attacks or to target the civilian population with attacks, reprisals or threats of violence, the main purpose of which is intimidation,' during an armed conflict. Article 138 defines the crime of homicide.

As a result of all the above, the Supreme Court decided to cancel the Order issued by the Third Section of the Criminal Chamber of the Spanish National Court 23 October 2009, which terminated the case and declared the voluntary dismissal of proceedings. Consequently, according to the Supreme Court ruling, 'the proceedings must continue, and the outstanding preparatory enquiries must be undertaken, as well as any others arising from the clarification of the events under investigation'.

As a consequence of the Supreme Court's ruling of 13 July 2010, the Examining Magistrate of the Spanish National Court, Mr. Santiago Pedraz Gómez issued a new indictment on 29 July, against the soldiers allegedly involved in the events.

According to the Order:

> The person who gave the direct order to shoot was Lieutenant Colonel PHILIP DE CAMP, commanding officer of Tank Regiment No. 64 of the Third Armoured Infantry Division of the United States Army, who passed on the order to Captain PHILIP WOLFORD, commanding the Tank Unit of 'A' Company of Tank Regiment No. 64 of the Third Armoured Infantry Division of the United States Army. He authorised Sergeant THOMAS GIBSON, a member of 'A' Company of Tank Regiment No. 64 of the Third Armoured Infantry Division of the United States Army, to physically fire the shot.

The Order also says that 'Previously, on the same day, North American forces had attacked the offices of the two Arab television channels al-Jazeera and Abu Dhabi'.

In his legal reasoning, the Magistrate said that the events:

> could constitute a crime against the international community, as stipulated in Article 611.1 of the Penal Code, as related to Article 608.3 Penal Code, which sets out the protected

---

[451] See antecedents in 10 *YIHL* (2007) pp 437–438; 11 *YIHL* (2008) pp 559–561; 12 *YIHL* (2009) p 623.

> parties, with objective double jeopardy with a crime of homicide, as stated and punishable in Article 138 Penal Code; due to the attack on the civilian population that led to the death of Mr. Couso and the act or threats of violence in order to intimidate the civilian population or journalists

and that there are sufficient grounds to attribute criminal responsibility to the soldiers mentioned above.

The Magistrate ordered the arrest for the purposes of extradition of the United States soldiers Sergeant Thomas Gibson, Captain Philip Wolford and Lieutenant Colonel Philip de Camp, and issued the appropriate international arrest warrants to that end. After this decision was announced, various news items were published in the Spanish newspaper *El País* during the week 29 November to 5 December 2010. In particular the newspaper published telegrams, cables and various communications from the US State Department published by 'Wikileaks,' and related to the behaviour of the Spanish political and judicial authorities aimed apparently at preventing this criminal investigation. The Wikileaks documents suggested that the Spanish authorities were responding to pressure received from various members of the US government. In light of this news, the journalist's family undertook fresh legal action in Spain, and filed suit with the Public Prosecutors' Office on 9 December 2010. This suit contains the relevant information:

> The events brought to the knowledge of this party and which could have criminal relevance may be indicative of the existence of a conspiracy or criminal arrangement between members of the Spanish Civil Service and senior Spanish government officials, on one hand, and employees of a foreign power on the other. The said criminal arrangement would have consisted of the acceptance by Spanish civil servants and politicians holding government posts of various directions and instructions given by United States government employees, especially by diplomatic staff of that power accredited with the embassy of the USA in Spain, as well as by various employees of the State Department of the USA, in order to interfere with the independence and actions of the constitutional authority of the state, the judiciary, seriously hindering the examination of judicial proceedings merely due to the political interests of the USA.

Cases—Repression in China before Beijing Olympic Games

- National Court. Preliminary Proceedings 242/2008. Central Investigating Court no. 1. Order of 26 February 2010

On 26 February 2010, Judge Santiago Pedraz dismissed the criminal proceedings that had commenced with the granting of leave to proceed on 5 August 2008 in a case filed against various Chinese leaders regarding the period of repression against the civilian population in Tibet that began in March of that year. The action was filed by various associations complaining that crimes against humanity were committed against the Tibetan population 3 days before the Beijing Olympic Games began. According to the plaintiffs, the action of the Chinese army led to 'at least 203 deaths, more than 1,000 serious injuries and 5,972 illegal arrests and disappearances'.

The proceedings were dismissed on the basis of the restrictions on the scope of the principle of universal jurisdiction that came into force on 3 November 2009, when Organic Law 1/2009 of 3 November was passed.[452] The judge argued that although the new law does not affect the pre-trial committal phase because it began before the approval of this reform, it would nonetheless 'affect the subsequent trial' and as such 'there would be no sense' in continuing with an investigation that could not conclude with proper trial. The amendment obliges the Spanish National Court only to pursue a case of genocide or crimes against humanity where those presumed responsible 'are in Spain', there are victims 'with Spanish nationality,' or there is some other clear 'relevant connection' with Spain and the case has not been investigated by any other court.

The accused were the Minister of Defence, Lian Guanglie, the Minister of State Security and Deputy Minister of Security, Geng Huichang, and the Minister of Public Security, Meng Jianzhu. The criminal action was also filed against the secretary of the Chinese Communist Party in the Autonomous Region of Tibet, Zhang Qingli, the Politburo member Wang Lequan, the Chairman of the State Ethnic Affairs Commission, Li Dezhu; General Tong Guishan, commander of the People's Liberation Army in the capital of Tíbet, Lhasa, and general Zhan Guihua, political commissar of the military command of Chengdu.

Judge Pedraz's decision was appealed by the plaintiffs, but the appeal was rejected by the Plenary Session of the Criminal Chamber of the Spanish National Court, in its Order of 27 October 2010. Three magistrates dissented from the majority decision—José Ricardo de Prada, Clara Bayarri and Ramón Sáez Valcárcel. All three dissenting members of the Court argued that if the case is not reopened, it should be sent back to Judge Ismael Moreno to examine the alleged genocide perpetrated by the Chinese government in Tibet in the 1980s and the 1990s.

The Court also rejected the plaintiff's application to join these proceedings with other proceedings taking place in the Spanish National Court (also regarding Tibet) due to the lack of a 'legal connection' between the relevant events.

The Judge presiding over the Central Investigating Court number 2, Ismael Moreno, also has had a case open since January 2006 against the Chinese president Jiang Zemin and another six Communist leaders in Tibet and the Chinese government for the genocide allegedly committed in Tibet since 1950.[453]

Regarding this case, on 3 September 2010, the Tibet Support Committee, on its own behalf and on that of its co-plaintiffs (the Casa del Tibet Foundation and Thubten Wangchen) presented a statement requesting that the allegations reported and investigated to date are also classified as serious violations of the *Geneva Conventions*. The provision of evidence from various witnesses has also been proposed. The arguments to justify this request are based on the legal verification of Tibet as an occupied territory, and the mass transfer of population from China (the occupying state) to Tibet (the occupied state) and the existence of crimes

---

452 <http://boe.es/boe/dias/2009/11/04/pdfs/BOE-A-2009-17492.pdf>; see 12 *YIHL* (2009) pp 632–633.

453 See 9 *YIHL* (2006) p 565.

which must be prosecuted in Spain according to international treaties and conventions, such as serious violations of the *Geneva Conventions*.

Cases—Targeted Killing of Salah Shehadeh (Gaza)

- Supreme Court. Criminal Chamber, Second Section. Appeal No. 1979/2009. Opining Judge: Mr. Miguel Colmenero Menéndez de Luarca. Ruling: 04/03/2010. Ruling No.: 3411/2010, <http://www.poderjudicial.es/search/doAction?action=contentpdf&databasematch=TS&reference=5369148&links= %221979/2009%22&optimize=20100415>

On 4 March 2010, the Criminal Chamber of the Supreme Court heard two appeals against the Order of 9 July 2009 by the Second Section of the Criminal Chamber of the Spanish National Court, allowing the remedy of appeal filed by the Public Prosecution Service against the order issued on 4 May 2009 by Central Investigating Court No. 4 in the Preliminary Investigation No. 157/08. The lower court decision confirmed Spanish jurisdiction to ascertain the facts relating to the extrajudicial murder of Salah Shehadeh. The consequence of the decision by the Spanish National Court was the conclusion of the criminal proceedings in Spain.

The Supreme Court rejected the two alleged grounds for appeal: the infringement of the right to a fair trial and the infringement of the right to due process. As regards the former, the Court found no irregularities in the behaviour of the Prosecutor leading to lack of proper representation for the plaintiffs. Regarding the latter, the Court referred to its own jurisprudence to the effect that the right to due process:

> has complex contents that include the right of access to judges and courts, the right to obtain a ruling from them based on the Law and its execution, and the right to the claim concluded being ruled upon within the procedure stipulated by law, without this jurisdiction including the right to obtain a ruling in accordance with the claim (STS 23-12-04)

and that:

> the judicial ruling challenged may only be deemed to infringe the right to due process when the reasoning on which it is based involves a degree of arbitrariness, unreasonableness or error that as a result of its evidence and content, is so apparent and serious that it is clear to any observer that the decision lacks any grounds or reasoning (STS 5-9-03).

The Court determined that 'the appellant has encountered a justified response in terms of the background to the issue under consideration, without prejudice to their legitimate disagreement with the ruling'.

The appeals were rejected as a result of all the above.

Cases—'Gaza Freedom Flotilla'

- National Court. Central Investigating Court no. 5. Order of 30 July 2010

On 23 July 2010, the association *Solidaridad con la Causa Árabe*, representing the Spanish activists Laura Arau, Manuel Espinal and David Segarra, filed suit in the Spanish National Court for war crimes and crimes against humanity against the Israeli Prime Minister Benjamin Netanyahu, a further six members of his government and the commanding officer responsible for boarding the Mavi Marmara, the ship in the *Freedom Flotilla* on which the Spaniards were travelling, which was attempting to break the blockade of Gaza Strip. The Israeli soldiers killed nine aid workers.

As well as Netanyahu, the co-accused include the Minister of Defence, Ehud Barak, the Minister of Foreign Affairs, Abigdor Lieberman, the Minister of Intelligence and Atomic Energy, Dan Meridor, the Minister of Strategic Affairs, Moshe Ya'alon, the Minister of Internal Affairs, Eli Yishai, the Minister without portfolio Benny Bergin and Vice-Admiral Eliezer Marom.

Although nine Turkish activists died during the attack on 31 May as a result of shots fired by the Israeli commandos boarding the 'Mavi Marmara', due to the legislative reform of the scope of universal jurisdiction that limits Spanish competence to cases with Spanish victims, the case focuses on the arrest, deportation and torture allegedly experienced by Segarra, Arau and Espinar. The case places these crimes in a context of a 'generalised and institutionalised attack on Palestinian population, and specifically in the Gaza Strip' to which the fleet 'was transporting aid workers and volunteers, as well as tonnes of humanitarian aid'.

The case also considers that these events might be a crime against persons and assets protected in the event of armed conflict. It states that those travelling on board the ship—aid workers, journalists, parliamentarians, the civilian population in general and those wounded in the boarding operation—are protected according to Article 608 of the *Penal Code* and the international treaties to which Spain is a signatory.

On 30 July 2010, the Spanish National Court Judge Pablo Ruz began a preliminary investigation of the case before deciding whether to allow the case to proceed, and has asked Israel, Turkey and the International Criminal Court (ICC) whether they have begun proceedings as a result of the attack on the *Freedom Flotilla* by Israel in international waters in May 2010. As part of the preliminary investigation, Judge Ruz has also asked the UN for the results of the independent international mission established to investigate what took place.

The request for the results of the independent international mission is due to the strict application of the principle of subsidiarity when exercising universal jurisdiction, as formalised in Spain after the adoption of the first article of Organic Law 1/2009 of 3 November, published in the Official State Bulletin on 4 November 2009.[454]

Cases—Attack on the Ashraf Camp (Iraq)

- National Court. Central Investigating Court no. 4. Order of 27 December 2010

454 <http://boe.es/boe/dias/2009/11/04/pdfs/BOE-A-2009-17492.pdf>; see 12 *YIHL* (2009) pp 632–633.

On 27 December 2010, the Judge of the Central Investigating Court number 4 of the Spanish National Court, Fernando Andreu, gave leave to proceed for a case presented by a group of Spanish human rights lawyers representing the group *People's Mujahedin of Iran* against Lieutenant-Colonel Abdol Hossein Al Shemmari of the Iraqi Army. The applicants allege that Shemmari was responsible for 11 crimes of murder and 36 offences of illegal arrest (in the form of kidnappings), torture and serious injuries inflicted on approximately 500 people who were wounded in the attack on a group of 3500 armed civilians in the camp of Ashraf (Iraq). Around 2000 soldiers participated in the attack on 28–29 July 2009. Numerous Iranian opposition activists belonging to the People's Mujahedin of Iran group live in the camp, located 80 kilometres from the Iranian frontier.

On 8 March 2011, the Judge summoned the accused to give evidence as the defendant for allegedly ordering the attack, and issued a letter of request to the Iraqi authorities to notify Al Shemmari of his ruling.

Judge Andreu has declared himself competent to investigate these events, after asking Iraq to inform him of whether the attack on the refugee camp is being or has been investigated. According to the Order, the response from Baghdad, through the Ministry of Foreign Affairs, is that 'an investigation is underway' and that a commitment has been made 'to finding a solution for the residents of the Ashraf camp in accordance with international law'.

However, the judge considered the Iraqi response to be unsatisfactory, as it 'gives no information on either the authority that is undertaking the investigation, or the date when it began, or of the investigations that have taken place in connection with it, or the results, if in fact there have been any'.

Judge Andreu was acting on the basis of the principle of universal jurisdiction, which allows crimes against humanity committed outside Spain to be investigated providing that certain conditions are met. This case is not related to Spain and there are no Spanish victims, as required by the recently passed parliamentary reform to limit the application of universal jurisdiction in Spain.[455] However, the legislation does allow Spanish courts to try an act that constitutes a crime according to the international treaties and agreements, such as grave breaches of the *Geneva Conventions* of 1949, relating to protection of victims of armed conflict.

Cases—Arrest of former Minister of Guatemala, Carlos Vielmann

- National Court. Central Investigating Court No. 3. Order of 16 December 2010

The former Minister of the Interior Carlos Vielmann, the director of the Penitentiary System Alejandro Giammattei and the ex-deputy director of Criminal Investigation Javier Figueroa are accused of membership of a criminal organisation, and specifically, of participating in the extrajudicial execution of seven

455 Ibid.

prisoners during the Guatemalan Police raid on the Pavón Criminal Rehabilitation Farm on 25 September 2006, and the execution of an additional three prisoners who had escaped from another prison. The International Commission Against Impunity in Guatemala (CICIG), a UN-affiliated body, called on the justice system of Guatemala to arrest Carlos Vielmann. This arrest warrant was issued on 11 August 2010.

Carlos Vielmann was located and arrested in Madrid on 13 October 2010 as a result of the extradition request by the Guatemalan authorities. He was imprisoned in Spain while the extradition was processed. Guatemala had 40 days to provide Spain with the documentation supporting the charges against the ex-minister. However, the Spanish National Court was forced to release him on 23 November, after Guatemala allowed the 40-day period after his arrest to expire without formally applying for his extradition. In fact, the Guatemalan Constitutional Court decided some days beforehand to suspend the extradition process against Vielmann, after accepting an appeal for legal protection presented by the ex-minister's son. At that point, the Head of the CICIG, Francisco Dall'Anese, accused the government of Álvaro Colomo of sabotaging the extradition.

However, the accused was arrested again on 16 December, after a complaint by the CICIG to the Spanish Public Prosecutors' Office, by virtue of which Spanish courts are competent to prosecute crimes against humanity committed abroad by individuals, like Vielmann, who are also Spanish nationals. The prosecutors' office has accused him of 'authorising and supervising' the creation of a 'parallel criminal structure' which carried out the 'extrajudicial execution' of ten prisoners in Guatemala between November 2005 and September 2006.

Vielmann was released by the Spanish National Court Judge Fernando Grande-Marlaska subject to bail of EUR 100,000. After payment, the ex-minister must appear before the Court once a week and may not leave Spain without permission, as his passport has been withdrawn.

Legislation—Reform of the Penal Code

- Organic Law 5/2010 of 22 June, amending Organic Law 10/1995 of 23 November, on the Penal Code. *Official State Bulletin* (BOE) no. 152, 23 June 2010, <http://www.boe.es/boe/dias/2010/06/23/pdfs/BOE-A-2010-9953.pdf>

Organic Law 5/2010 makes numerous changes to Organic Law 10/1995 of 23 November, on the *Penal Code*. The most important of these for current purposes are those concerned with: (a) terrorist crimes; and (b) those concerned with crimes against the international community.

(a) Crimes of Terrorism

There has been a thorough review of the penal treatment of terrorist offences, including the establishment of, membership in or participation in terrorist organisations and groups, as well as the inclusion of new stipulations for compliance with the legislative obligations arising from Council Framework Decision 2008/919/JHA.[456]

The specific treatment of these organisations and groups—now separated from other criminal organisations and groups—is contained in a new Chap. VII of Sect. XXII, which includes Articles 571–580 and is entitled: 'On terrorist organisations and groups and terrorist offences'. The penal consequences of all forms of involvement in terrorism are thus unified in a single chapter.

The first section—Article 571—covers those who promote, establish, organise or lead a terrorist organisation or group, and those who actively participate or form part of the organisation or group. According to the definition:

> terrorist organisations or groups are those groups which have the characteristics of criminal organisations (a group formed by more than two people of a stable nature or for an indefinite period, which systematically and on a coordinated basis allocates various tasks or functions in order to commit crimes) or criminal groups (the union of more than two people which without having any of the characteristics of organisation stipulated above, has the systematic perpetration of offences as its purpose) and have the subversion of the constitutional order or serious disturbances of public order by perpetrating any of the offences listed in the following section as their objective or purpose: crimes of damage or fire, attacks against people, storage of weapons or munitions or the storage of explosive, inflammable, incendiary or asphyxiating substances or devices, or their components, and their manufacture, trafficking, transport or supply in any form, or any other offence with the objective of undermining the constitutional order or seriously disturbing public order, attacks on property, collaboration with the activities or objectives of a terrorist organisation or group, supply or collection of funds with the intention that they are used, or the knowledge that they will be used in full or in part to commit any of the said crimes or for provision to a terrorist organisation or group, praise or justification in any public medium of expression or diffusion of the said crimes, or provocation, conspiracy or intent to commit them.

In accordance with the guidelines of the aforementioned *European Council Framework Decision 2008/919/JHA*, a third stipulation is added to Article 576, expanding the concept of collaboration with a terrorist organisation or group, to include conduct that has to date presented difficulties in terms of legal application: the actions of groups or cells—and even actions by individuals—that have the recruitment, indoctrination, drilling or training of terrorists as their objective.

In accordance with standardised European regulations, the first section of Article 579 includes the public distribution or dissemination by any means of messages or instructions which without necessarily constituting obvious criminal resolve (i.e., provocation, conspiracy or intent to carry out a specific criminal act) are means appropriate to creating the circumstances in which the executive decision to commit a crime could be taken at a given time.

Article 576(b) includes the specific description of the crime of financing terrorism, as well as imprudent conduct of parties with special obligations in terms of

[456] Council Framework Decision 2008/919/JHA of 28 November 2008 amending Framework Decision 2002/475/JHA on combating terrorism [2008] OJ L 330/21, <http://eur-lex.europa.eu/LexUriServ/LexUriServ.do?uri=OJ:L:2008:330:0021:01:EN:HTML>.

collaborating with the government to prevent this financing, in accordance with the regulations on money laundering.

(b) Crimes against the International Community

In recent years, Spain has become a Party to various international conventions, including the *Rome Statute of the International Criminal Court*, the *Convention on the Prohibition of the Use, Stockpiling, Production and Transfer of Anti-Personnel Mines and on their Destruction* of 18 September 1997, the *Convention on the Safety of United Nations and Associated Personnel* of 9 December 1994, the second *Protocol to the Hague Convention for the Protection of Cultural Property in the Event of Armed Conflict* of 26 March 1999, the *Optional Protocol to the Convention on the Rights of the Child on the Involvement of Children in Armed Conflict* of 25 May 2000, and the 2006 *Convention on the Rights of Persons with Disabilities*. It will also become a party to the *Additional Protocol of the Geneva Conventions 12 August 1949 relating to the approval of an additional emblem* (*Protocol III*). This reform aims to adapt Spanish penal legislation to the stipulations of the above international conventions, although some of the offences were already included in the *Penal Code*.

The new offences included in the special penal protection given to women and children in armed conflicts provide for punishment for those committing crimes against a protected individual's sexual freedom, committing acts of rape, sexual slavery, induced or forced prostitution, forced pregnancy, forced sterilization or any other type of sexual aggression and those recruiting or enlisting minors aged under 18 years old or using them to participate directly in the said conflicts.

The legislation adds the crime of 'inflicting intentional hunger on the civilian population as a method of war, depriving it of essential assets for its survival, including arbitrary prevention of aid supplies made in accordance with the Geneva Conventions and its Additional Protocols'.

It also includes as war crimes 'intentional attacks against any member of the United Nations personnel, associated personal or participants in peace or humanitarian assistance missions … or threats of such an attack to oblige a natural or legal person to take or refrain from taking a specific action' and attacks or actions against installations, materials, units, private homes and vehicles of any member of the said personnel or threats of such attacks or hostile actions to oblige a natural or legal person to take or refrain from taking a specific action.

The Red Crystal is added to the distinguishing emblems of the Red Cross and the Red Crescent in cases of improper use of protective or distinctive emblems or signs established and recognised by international treaties to which Spain is a party.

The protection of cultural heritage is reinforced, with the addition of some specific types of crimes, such as the improper use of cultural heritage or places of worship that constitute the cultural or spiritual heritage of peoples in support of a military action and the large-scale appropriation, theft, looting or acts of vandalism against the said cultural heritage or places of worship.

Finally, the legislation ends the tradition of maintaining the criteria for determining the memberships of protected groups contained in the 1948 *Convention on the Prevention and Punishment of the Crime of Genocide* with the somewhat surprising addition allowing a 'group determined by the disability of its members' in Article 607. The disability of members of a group has also been added as grounds for discrimination prohibited as a crime of persecution against humanity in Article 697(b).

A new crime of piracy has also been established within the new Chap. V of the section covering crimes against the international community, a crime that was curiously not included in the *Spanish Penal Code*. This aims to combat the recent numerous episodes of piracy of the coast of East Africa. This is defined according to the stipulations of the *Montego Bay Convention on the Law of the Sea* of 10 December 1982, and the *Convention for the Suppression of Unlawful Acts Against the Safety of Maritime Navigation*, signed in Rome on 10 March 1988.

According to new Article 616 (iii):

> Those using violence, intimidation or deceit to seize, damage or destroy an aircraft, ship or other type of vessel or platform in the sea, or attacking people, cargo or assets on board the same, will be imprisoned for the crime of piracy with a prison sentence of ten to 15 years. The punishment stipulated in this article will in any event be imposed without prejudice to those appropriate to the crimes committed.

Treaty Action—Signing Additional Protocol III (*Red Crystal*)

- Signing *ad Referendum* of the *Protocol for the Creation of the Red Crystal as the New Visible Emblem of Neutrality during Humanitarian Missions,* opened for signature 8 December 2005, 2375 UNTS 237 (entered into force 14 January 2007)

On 2 July 2010, the Council of Ministers authorised the signing *ad referendum* and referred the *Additional Protocol to the Geneva Conventions of 12 August 1949 relating to the Adoption of an Additional Distinctive Emblem* (*Protocol III*) to Parliament. Protocol III was approved at the Diplomatic Conference held in Geneva on 8 December 2005.

The Protocol creates a distinctive emblem in addition to those already in existence, i.e., the Red Cross, the Red Crescent, and the Red Lion and Sun, the visible signs of total neutrality in humanitarian missions in the various armed conflicts, thereby providing protection for these missions.

This new emblem provides an alternative for states that do not identify with any of the emblems mentioned above, or for use in contexts in which the use of another emblem could be considered to have undesired religious, cultural or political connotations.

This new emblem takes the form of a red frame standing on one corner against a white background, and its conditions for use and respect are identical to those stipulated for other signs, as they have the same status.

Treaty Action—Ratification of Protocol for Complete Abolition of the Death Penalty

- Ratification of *Protocol Number 13 to the Convention for the Protection of Human Rights and Fundamental Freedoms, on the Complete Abolition of the Death Penalty,* opened for signature 3 May 2002, ETS No. 187 (entered into force 1 July 2003)

The Spanish representative signed *Protocol Number 13 to the Convention for the protection of Human Rights and Fundamental Freedoms, concerning the abolition of the death penalty in all circumstances*, made in Vilnius on 3 May 2002. After receiving prior authorisation from Parliament stipulated in Article 94.1 of the Constitution, Spain ratified the Protocol on 27 November 2007, and it was published in the Official State Bulletin (BOE) on 30 March 2010.

The following Declaration regarding Gibraltar was included:

> If this Protocol No. 13 to the Convention for the protection of Human rights and Fundamental Freedoms, concerning the abolition of the death penalty in all circumstances were to be extended by the United Kingdom to Gibraltar, Spain would like to make the following declaration:
>
> 1. Gibraltar is a non-autonomous territory whose international relations come under the responsibility of the United Kingdom and which is subject to a decolonisation process in accordance with the relevant decisions and resolutions of the General Assembly of the United Nations.
> 2. The authorities of Gibraltar have a local character and exercise exclusively internal competences which have their origin and their foundation in a distribution and attribution of competences performed by the United Kingdom in compliance with its internal legislation, in its capacity as sovereign State on which the mentioned non-autonomous territory depends.
> 3. As a result, the eventual participation of the Gibraltarian authorities in the application of this Protocol will be understood as carried out exclusively as part of the internal competences of Gibraltar and cannot be considered to modify in any way what was established in Madrid on 27 November 2009.

Treaty Action—Optional Declarations on Enforced Disappearances

- Optional Declarations on the *International Convention for the Protection of All Persons from Enforced Disappearance,* opened for signature 6 February 2007 (entered into force 23 December 2010)

Spain ratified the *International Convention for the Protection of All Persons from Enforced Disappearance* in 2009. On 28 May 2010, the Council of Ministers authorised the declarations stipulated in Articles 31–32 of the *International Convention for the Protection of all Persons from Enforced Disappearance*, adopted by the General Assembly of the United Nations on 20 December 2006, and referred it to Parliament for authorisation.

Articles 31–32 of the Convention include Declarations that the States Parties can make in order to acknowledge the competence of the Committee in its work against enforced disappearances: first, to receive and consider communications from or on behalf of individuals subject to their jurisdiction claiming to be the terms of a violation while the State Party of provisions of the Convention; and second, that each State Party may declare that it recognises the competence of the Committee when it claims that another State is not fulfilling its obligations under the Convention.

Treaty Action—Objection to Reservation on Incendiary Weapons

- Spanish Objection to the Reservation by the United States to the *Protocol on Prohibitions and Restrictions on the Use of Incendiary Weapons*, opened for signature 10 April 1981, 1342 UNTS 137 (entered into force 2 December 1983)

On 26 March 2010, the Council of Ministers was informed of Spain's objection to the reservation and the interpretative declaration formulated by the US regarding *Protocol III on Prohibitions and Restrictions on the Use of Incendiary Weapons to the Convention on Prohibitions or Restrictions on the Use of Certain Conventional Weapons Which May Be Deemed to Be Excessively Injurious or to Have Indiscriminate Effects* and Protocols I, II and III. The Convention was signed by Spain on 10 April 1981 and ratified on 3 December 1993. Spain also ratified the Further Protocols to the Convention: the *Protocol on Non-Detectable Fragments* (*Protocol I*); the *Protocol on Prohibitions and Restrictions on the Use of Mines, Booby Traps and Other Devices, amended in 1996* (*Protocol II, amended*); the *Protocol on Prohibitions or Restrictions on the Use of Incendiary Weapons* (*Protocol III*); the *Protocol on Blinding Laser Weapons* (*Protocol IV*); and the *Protocol on Explosive Remnants of War* (*Protocol V*).

Protocol III defines the terms (incendiary weapon, concentration of civilians, military objectives, civilian objects, and feasible precautions) and the protection of civilians and civilian objects, as well as establishing prohibitions and restrictions on the use of these weapons.

On 21 January 2009, the US, in declaring its consent to be bound by Protocol III, formulated a reservation and an interpretative declaration on the use of incendiary weapons against installations located in concentrations of civilians. Spain considers that the reservation runs counter to the prohibitions contained in Article 2, paragraphs 2–3 of Protocol III due to the incompatibility of the contents of the reservation with the object and purpose of the Protocol.

Treaty Action—Ratification of Cluster Munitions Convention

- Ratification of the *Convention on Cluster Munitions,* opened for signature 3 December 2008 (entered into force 1 August 2010)

The Convention was adopted in Dublin on 30 May 2008. It was signed by the Spanish representative on the same day. The Convention was ratified by Spain on 8 June 2009 and published in the Official State Bulletin (BOE) on 19 March 2010.

Treaty Action—Terrorism Financing Convention

- Ratification of the Council of Europe *Convention on Laundering, Search, Seizure and Confiscation of the Proceeds from Crime and on the Financing of Terrorism,* opened for signature 16 May 2005, ETS No 198 (entered into force 1 May 2008)

On 20 February 2009, the Spanish representative signed the *Convention on Laundering, Search, Seizure and Confiscation of the Proceeds from Crime and on the Financing of Terrorism*, made in Warsaw on 16 May 2005. Parliament subsequently authorised the ratification, according to the stipulations of Article 94.1 of the Constitution. Spain ratified the Convention on 28 December 2009 and it was published in the Official State Bulletin on 26 June 2010.

The ratification was accompanied by following Declaration regarding Gibraltar:

> If this Convention on the laundering, search, seizure and confiscation of the proceeds from crime and the financing of terrorism were to be extended by the United Kingdom to Gibraltar, Spain would like to make the following declaration:
>
> 1. Gibraltar is a non-autonomous territory whose international relations come under the responsibility of the United Kingdom and which is subject to a decolonisation process in accordance with the relevant decisions and resolutions of the General Assembly of the United Nations.
> 2. The authorities of Gibraltar have a local character and exercise exclusively internal competences which have their origin and their foundation in a distribution and attribution of competences performed by the United Kingdom in compliance with its internal legislation, in its capacity as sovereign State on which the mentioned non-autonomous territory depends.
> 3. As a result, the eventual participation of the Gibraltarian authorities in the application of this Protocol will be understood as carried out exclusively as part of the internal competences of Gibraltar and cannot be considered to modify in any way what was established in Madrid on 28 December 2009.

- Spanish Objection to the Reservation by the Republic of Yemen to the *International Convention for the Suppression of the Financing of Terrorism,* opened for signature 10 January 2000, 2178 UNTS 197 (entered into force 10 April 2002)

On 3 December, the Council of Ministers was officially informed of Spain's objection to the reservation by Republic of Yemen to the international convention for the suppression of the financing of terrorism.

Treaty Action—Ratification of NATO Protocol on SOFA

- Ratification of the *Further Additional Protocol to the Agreement between the States Parties to the North Atlantic Treaty and the Other States Participating in the Partnership for Peace Regarding the Status of Their Forces*, opened for signature 19 December 1997 (entered into force 15 April 1999)

On 28 November 2008, the Spanish Government authorised the signing of the Further Additional Protocol to the *Agreement between the States Parties to the North Atlantic Treaty and the Other States Participating in the Partnership for Peace Regarding the Status of Their Forces,* made in Brussels on 19 December 1997. The Protocol extends the provisions contained in the Statute on international military Headquarters established by the North Atlantic Treaty to the countries signing it on a general basis. The Protocol was signed by the Spanish representative in Washington on 9 April 2009. The Council of Ministers sent the Protocol to Parliament on 15 January 2010 for authorisation prior to ratification. After authorisation had been obtained, in accordance with Article 94.1 of the Constitution, Spain ratified the Protocol on 9 July 2010. The protocol was published in the Official State Bulletin (BOE) on 16 September 2010.

Cases—Extradition to Bosnia–Herzegovina

- Case of Veselin Vlahovic

Perhaps the most important case was the arrest and extradition of Veselin Vlahovic. Vlahovic, a Montenegrin, who is also accused of various crimes in Spain, was arrested in Denia (Alicante) on 2 March 2010, by virtue of international arrest warrants issued by the authorities of Serbia, Montenegro and Bosnia–Herzegovina. In Bosnia–Herzegovina, he is sought for allegedly having committed serious crimes against humanity during the war in Bosnia between 1992 and 1995, as a member of the Serbian Armed Forces of the Republika Srpska. In Montenegro, he is sought for trial for alleged murder, torture, inhuman acts, physical and psychological injury, rape, kidnapping and theft against the civilian population during the armed conflict in Bosnia. He is also wanted in order to complete a sentence for robbery. In Serbia, he is wanted for the execution of a sentence of murder. On 9 April 2010, the Council of Ministers gave leave to proceed with the three extradition proceedings under way against Veselin Vlahovic.

On 23 July, the Council of Ministers approved the surrender in extradition to Bosnia–Herzegovina of Veselin Vlahovic, for crimes against persons and assets protected in armed conflicts. Vlahovic, known as 'the monster of Grbavica', is sought for having committed serious crimes against humanity during the war in Bosnia–Herzegovina between 1992 and 1995. He is accused of terrorising the population of Grbavica (Sarajevo) during his time as a member of the Armed Forces of the Republika Srpska, persecuting the civilian population of non-Serb origin, personally killing many people, and committing looting, rape, abuse, torture and other crimes. The defendant, who is being held in provisional custody, is subject to the European Extradition Convention of 13 December 1957. Furthermore, on 1 October 2010 the Council of Ministers approved the continuation of the proceedings for the first extension of the extradition of the Montenegrin national Veselin Vlahovic, as requested by the authorities of Bosnia–Herzegovina. The new allegations date back to 1992, when the defendant, with other members of the 'White Angels,' took 15 members of a family to a Jewish cemetery in the town of Novo Sarajevo, and machine-gunned them. Those who died included a 6-year-old boy and a woman. In July of the same year, he forced a married couple out of their home and killed them both in Grbavica.

The defendant was also sought by the authorities in Serbia, for the crime of murder, and the authorities in Montenegro, for robbery with violence and war crimes. The initial proposal was to hand over Veselin Vlahovic to the authorities of Bosnia–Herzegovina in application of the *European Convention on Extradition* of 1957 to the three petitioning countries, as the relative seriousness of the crimes committed by the defendant in Bosnia–Herzegovina is quantitatively and qualitatively greater. Bosnia–Herzegovina made the application for extradition through diplomatic channels on 8 March 2010, before the other two States did so. The extradition took place on 25 August 2010.

Cases—Extradition to Argentina

- Case of Jorge Alberto Soza

The Spanish Council of Ministers decided on 26 February to extradite Jorge Alberto Soza, an ex-Argentinean soldier, to that country's authorities. Soza, born in Buenos Aires, Argentina on 9 November 1936, holds joint Argentinean and Spanish nationality. He was arrested on 8 July 2009 in Onteniente (Valencia). On 4 September, the Council of Ministers agreed to continue the extradition proceedings by legal means, and on 16 December 2009, the Third Section of the Criminal Chamber of the Spanish National Court agreed to the extradition. He had been free since 15 October 2009 after paying bail for these extradition proceedings. Jorge Alberto Soza is sought by Argentinean justice with regard to alleged crimes of unlawful association, 18 offences of illegal detention committed by government employees, aggravated by a duration of over 15 days, and 17 crimes of torture and other crimes against moral integrity relating to an injury-related crime. The events upon which the extradition and surrender are based occurred between September 1975 and 3 January 1977, when Soza was the deputy chief of the Neuquén Office of the Argentinean federal police.

- Case of Julio Alberto Poch

On 9 April 2010, the Council of Ministers approved the extradition surrender to the Argentinean authorities of Julio Alberto Poch. The Council of Ministers agreed to continue the proceedings by judicial means on 30 October 2009; the Spanish National Court issued an order on 15 January 2010 in which it ruled that the extradition was proper, providing that the appropriate guarantees regarding the imposition of a life sentence were assured and after these guarantees are obtained by the Ministry of Justice and deemed sufficient by the Court, the surrender will take place. Poch, who currently holds Dutch nationality and works as a pilot for the Dutch airline Transavia, was arrested on 22 September 2009 in Manises airport (Valencia), during a stopover between Valencia and Amsterdam. On 7 October, the request for extradition issued by the Argentinean Embassy was received through diplomatic channels, as Julio Alberto Poch is sought by Argentinean Justice in relation to four criminal proceedings investigating events that took place in Argentina between 1976 and 1983, related to 'death flights' and the operations of the Escuela Superior de Mecánica de la Armada, the clandestine centre for detention and torture during the Argentinean dictatorship led by general Videla.

Cases—Extradition to Peru

- Case of Juan Manuel Carranza Laurente

On 4 June, the Council of Ministers approved the extradition to Peru of Juan Manuel Carranza Laurente, who is charged with the crime of terrorism due to his membership of the Shining Path group between 1985 and 1988. Carranza holds double Peruvian and Spanish nationality and had been released on bail. He is alleged to have been a member of the Shining Path terrorist faction of the Communist Party of Peru between 1985 and 1988. He is also accused of having been a member of the organisation's 'Socorro Popular' department until 1997. As reported in the 2009 *Yearbook of International Humanitarian Law,*[457] the criminal process under which he has been accused has been questioned by human rights groups.

Cases—Extradition to Morocco

- Cases of Mohamed Amine Achemlal, Faiçal Herrai, Alí Aarras and Mohamed El Bay

With regard to the applications from Morocco, the government agreed on 22 January 2010 to continue the extradition proceedings for the Moroccan citizen Mohamed Amine Achemlal for crimes of terrorism and false documentation; on 22 October 2010, to continue the extradition proceedings concerning the Moroccan citizen Faiçal Herrai regarding an alleged offence of constitution of a terrorist organisation and aid to terrorism in that country; and on 19 November, the extradition of the Moroccan national Alí Aarras, who also holds Belgian nationality. It refused to extradite the Moroccan national Mohamed El Bay, who also holds Spanish nationality, to the Moroccan authorities.

Cases—Extradition to Turkey

- Case of Irfan Yurtsever

Finally, with regard to the request from the Turkish authorities, the Spanish government decided on 29 October to continue the extradition proceedings for the Armenian national Irfan Yurtsever for alleged crimes involving membership of an armed organisation, murder and kidnapping.

Cases—Extradition from France

Spanish authorities have applied for the extradition of various individuals to face trial in Spain. The following applications all relate to alleged involvement in the terrorist organisation ETA.

- Case of José Lorenzo Ayestaran Legorburu

On 26 March 2010, the Council of Ministers agreed to apply to France for the extradition of the alleged member of ETA José Lorenzo Ayestaran Legorburu, who was arrested on French territory on 28 February 2010, on four counts of murder and involvement in two terrorist attacks. Extradition proceedings rather

---

457 <http://boe.es/boe/dias/2009/11/04/pdfs/BOE-A-2009-17492.pdf>; see 12 *YIHL* (2009) p 636.

than the European Arrest Warrant are being used in the application to France for the surrender of the defendant, as according to Article 32 of the *Council Framework Decision of 13 June 2002, regarding the European arrest warrant and surrender procedures between Member states*, France has made a declaration regarding its continued application of previous extradition systems for events occurring before 1 November 1993, as applies in this case. The Convention, based on Article K.3 of the European Union *Convention on extradition between Member States*, signed in Dublin on 27 September 1996, to which France has been party since 1 July 2005, is therefore applicable to this application. On 23 April, the Council of Ministers agreed to apply to France for the extension of the extradition of José Lorenzo Ayestarán Legorburu, for additional crimes of murder, unlawful possession of weapons and robbery with violence.

- Case of Jesús María Martín Hernando

On 20 May 2010, the Council of Ministers agreed to apply to France for the extradition of Jesús María Martín Hernando, an alleged member of the organisation ETA, for trial in Spain as the alleged perpetrator of an attempted terrorist crime. Martín Hernando, a holder of Spanish nationality, aged 47 years old, born in Santurce (Vizcaya), has been imprisoned in the French penitentiary facility of Tarascon since 2001. This application is also subject to the European Treaty *Convention on extradition between Member states*, signed in Dublin on 27 September 1996, to which France has been a party since 1 July 2005.

- Case of Rafael Caride Simón

On 17 September 2010, the Council of Ministers agreed to apply to France for the extradition of Rafael Caride Simón, an alleged member of the organisation ETA, for crimes of less serious injuries, unlawful possession of explosives, and criminal damage. The Spanish government applied to France for the seventh extension of extradition on 30 April 1993, but the Court of Appeal in Toulouse rejected it in its ruling of 26 June 2002 on grounds of prescription of the events according to French law. A new application for extradition based on the same allegations has been presented at the request of the Central Examining Magistrate's Court No. 1 of the Spanish National Court, as since 1 July 2005, France has been party to the *Convention on extradition between Member States*, signed in Dublin on 27 September 1996, and Article 8.1 of that Convention states that extradition cannot be refused on the grounds that the prosecution or punishment of the person would be statute-barred according to the law of the requested Member State.

- Case of María Soledad Iparraguirre Guenechea

On 24 September 2010, the Council of Ministers agreed to apply to France for an extension of the extradition of María Soledad Iparraguirre Guenechea, an alleged member of the organisation ETA. The extension is requested in order to cover new crimes involving attacks on agents of the security forces, leading to death, injury and harm, committed in 1987. Iparraguirre is currently being held in the French prison of Fresness Allèe Des Thuyas (Paris) while France decides on other previous extradition applications.

- Case of José Francisco Segurola Mayoz

On 3 December 2010, the Council of Ministers agreed to apply to France for the extradition of the member of ETA José Francisco Segurola Mayoz. The application for extradition is based on allegations that on 24 June 1991, the defendant, with three other members of ETA, fired shots against those attending a Flag Swearing ceremony in the Loyola Barracks in San Sebastián. Three people suffered from injuries of varying degrees as a consequence. On 17 December 2010, the Council of Ministers agreed to apply to France once again for the active extradition of the member of ETA José Francisco Segurola Mayoz, for further crimes.

Cases—Extradition from Venezuela

- Case of Arturo Cubillas Fontán

On 29 October 2010, the Council of Ministers agreed to apply to Venezuela for the extradition of Arturo Cubillas Fontán, for crimes of conspiracy to commit terrorist murders and possession of explosives in collaboration with an armed group. The grounds for the application for extradition are that the defendant is suspected of having organised meetings for the exchange of experiences and military training between FARC and ETA. The application was based on the *Treaty of Extradition between the Kingdom of Spain and the Republic of Venezuela* signed in Caracas on 4 January 1989.

Cases—Extradition from Cuba

- Case of José Ángel Urtiaga Martínez

On 3 December 2010, the Council of Ministers agreed to apply to the authorities of Cuba for the active extradition of José Ángel Urtiaga Martínez for the crime of collaboration with an armed terrorist organisation. The defendant is suspected of participation in activities involving training and practice in the use of explosive devices with bombs.

Cases—Extradition from Guatemala

- Case of José Antonio Solares González

On 19 March 2010, the Council of Ministers agreed to apply to Guatemala for the extradition of the Guatemalan citizen José Antonio Solares González, for crimes of genocide committed against the population of that country. Solares González, who is currently in Guatemala, has been sought by Central Examining Magistrate's Court No. 1 of the Spanish National Court due to his alleged responsibility in acts that, in addition to the genocide mentioned above, constitute crimes against moral integrity, terrorism, torture, murder, illegal detention, arson and disregard of public authorities. The defendant was the commander of the military detachment in the town of Rabinal in the department of Baja Verapaz, Guatemala, which committed a number of massacres between 1 January 1981 and 16 April 1983, according to evidence from those convicted and witnesses in other Guatemalan judicial proceedings. In the case of the Rionegro massacres of 13 March 1982, which involved the execution, torture, deprivation of freedom and forced disappearance of 1545 people from the Maya Achi ethnic groups, Solares is subject to criminal proceedings in Guatemala and there has been a warrant for his arrest in the country since April 2003.

Cases—Extradition from South Africa

- Case of Kayumba Nyamwasa

Finally, on 17 September 2010, the Council of Ministers agreed to apply to South Africa for the active extradition of the Rwandan citizen Kayumba Nyamwasa for genocide and other crimes allegedly committed in Rwanda.

Lieutenant General Faustin Kayumba, General of the Rwandan Patriotic Front (FPR) and Rwandan Army former Chief of Staff, participated in systematic and planned attacks against the civilian population, forced disappearances and crimes against international law, organising and carrying out terrorist attacks. He served as Rwandan ambassador in New Delhi, India, but disappeared after a meeting in Kigali in mid-February 2010, thereby losing his diplomatic immunity. He is currently sought by the authorities in Rwanda and in France. The defendant, who is assumed to be in South Africa, is a defendant in criminal proceedings taking place in the Spanish National Court. As well as the accusation of genocide, Nyamwasa is also accused of crimes against humanity, against individuals and assets protected in the event of armed conflict, terrorism and torture. His victims include four Spanish citizens; the missionary Joaquim Vallmajó and the members of the 'Médicos del Mundo' NGO Mª Flors Sirera Fortuny, Manuel Madrazo Osuna and Luis Valtueña Gallego.

According to some sources, Nyamwasa has requested asylum in South Africa on the grounds of political persecution in Rwanda. However, there is currently no extradition treaty between Spain and South Africa. Nyamwasa was shot in the stomach in South Africa in June 2010 and the six people arrested by South African police in relation to the incident were found to be Rwandan.

It should also be remembered that the Rwandan general James Kabarebe—who is also sought by the Spanish National Court—was arrested in South Africa in October 2009, but was released 24 h later without any explanation.

Government Policy—Resettlement Programme for Refugees in Spain for 2010

On 29 January 2010, the Council of Ministers approved the Refugee Resettlement Programme in Spain for 2010, which includes authorisation of the resettlement of 75 refugees in Spain for the year. Resettlement is the process by which a refugee who has fled his/her country of origin due to persecution on the grounds of race, religion or political opinions and has found temporary asylum in another country, is resettled in a third country for permanent protection. The expenses arising from the resettlement of refugees amounted to EUR 2,927,399.86 during the period

2010–2012, of which EUR 694,600 can be financed by the European Fund for Refugees.

Government Policy—Deployment of Additional Military Units in Afghanistan

On 12 February 2010, the Council of Ministers requested the authorisation of the Congress of Deputies for an increase in the Spanish participation in the NATO International Security Assistance Force (ISAF) in Afghanistan, under the mandate of the United Nations. The Congress of Deputies gave its authorisation on 17 February 2010. On 19 February, the Council of Ministers adopted an agreement authorising this increase. This deployment of additional troops consists of three Operational Mentor Liaison Teams (OMLTs), manoeuvre, protection and logistic support teams, and a reinforcement contingent for the ISAF Headquarters. The maximum total for this contingent is 511 troops. The agreement also provides for sending Civil Guard personnel for training and drill of the Afghan police forces. This contingent may not exceed forty individuals.

Government Policy—Contributions to International Organisations

On 10, 17 and 23 December 2010, the Council of Ministers approved various contributions to international organisations, payable by the Development Aid Fund:

- EUR 600,000 for the International Federation of Red Cross and Red Crescent Societies (IFRC)
- EUR 7,000,000 for the International Committee of the Red Cross (ICRC)
- EUR 9,900,000 for the office of the United Nations High Commissioner for Refugees (UNHCR)
- 4,650,000 for the United Nations High Commissioner for Human Rights (UNHCHR)
- Endowment of three Council of Europe programmes: the office of the Human Rights Commissioner (Georgia Programme) with EUR 14,000; Supervision of the execution of sentences by the European Court of Human Rights (EUR 10,000) and promotion of the rights of the gypsy population in Europe (EUR 10,000).
- EUR 60,000 for the International Criminal Court for its programme for victims of the crimes judged in the Court, established in its founding charter.
- EUR 30,000 for the Parliamentary Forum on Small and Light Weapons, which fights against illegal trafficking and the proliferation of firearms.
- EUR 250,000 for the International Institute for Democracy and Electoral Assistance (IDEA), based in Stockholm, an inter-governmental organisation specialising in the execution of governability projects and the promotion of democracy in developing countries. Spain will hold the Presidency in 2011.
- Various United Nations bodies received contributions totalling EUR 515,000. The beneficiaries are:

- The Peacebuilding Fund (EUR 100,000)
- The Mediation Support Unit (EUR 50,000)
- The Democracy Fund (EUR 40,000)
- The Voluntary Trust Fund for Assistance in Mine Action (EUR 50,000)
- The Working Group against Terrorism (EUR 110,000)
- The Office for Disarmament Affairs (EUR 105,000)
- The United Nations Office on Drugs and Crime (EUR 40,000)
- The Trust Fund for the International Criminal Tribunal for Rwanda (EUR 20,000), a contribution for various aspects of a Programme supporting the victims and witnesses infected with the AID/HIV virus.

ANTONI PIGRAU

SWEDEN[458]

Government Inquiry—Review of International Humanitarian Law

- Krigets lagar, SOU 2010:22 (3 May 2010), <http://www.regeringen.se/sb/d/108/a/145115>
- Folkrätt i väpnad konflikt, SOU 2010:72 (29 October 2010), <http://www.regeringen.se/sb/d/108/a/154030>
- Svensk manual i humanitär rätt m.m., Annex to SOU 2010:72 (2010), <http://www.regeringen.se/content/1/c6/15/40/30/113aaee0.pdf>

As reported in 2007, the government decided to establish a committee of inquiry to conduct a systematic review of the rules of international humanitarian law that are legally binding on Sweden, and to review their implementation under Swedish national law. The task also included reviewing education and training in international law against the background of existing convention commitments. A further undertaking involved analysing customary law rules, including conclusions and reasons for them, laid down by the International Committee of the Red Cross in its Customary Law Study. In addition, the committee was asked to investigate the need for a national manual on international humanitarian law, and if judged necessary, to submit a proposal for such a manual. Through supplementary terms of reference, the committee was also instructed to propose any necessary legislative amendments to enable Sweden to ratify the *Protocol Additional to the Geneva Conventions of 12 August 1949 relating to the Adoption of an Additional Distinctive Emblem* (Protocol III), and to review the *Act on the Protection of Certain International Distinctive Emblems of Medical Aid and of International Distinctive Signs of Civil Defence 1953*, as well as suggesting suitable amendments.

In October 2010, the committee submitted its findings to the government, which were contained in three publications. The first is an interim report, consisting of central documents with comments on international law in its application to armed

[458] Information and commentaries by Dr Ola Engdahl, Associate Professor of International Law at the International Law Centre at the Swedish National Defence College, Stockholm.

conflict, neutrality, occupation and peace operations.[459] The second is the main publication and presents the committee's view on the task placed before it.[460] It also comments on recent developments and challenges with regard to IHL, including recommendations for Swedish action and policy in this field, both nationally and internationally. The third publication is a draft manual for the Swedish armed forces on international humanitarian law.[461]

As indicated, the committee of inquiry was established by the government and included members of the Ministry of Defence, Ministry of Foreign Affairs, the Armed Forces and other institutions with vested interests in these matters, such as the National Defence College, the Swedish Civil Contingencies Agency, and the Swedish Red Cross. The findings, however, do not emanate from the government itself. They were presented to it in response to the need to have these issues clarified and have been distributed for referral. In May 2011, it will be up to the government to deal with the findings (in whole or in part) with regard to policy, legislation, and the issuing of instructions or in other ways it deems appropriate. In 1979 a similar committee was instituted to review the situation after the adoption of the two additional Protocols to the four Geneva Conventions. The committee submitted its interim report, The Laws of War[462] in 1979, and its final report, International Law in War,[463] in 1984. The final report has proved highly influential owing to its systematic review of current international humanitarian law and its proposals for the interpretation and application of this branch of law. The committee's analyses and proposals have served as a guide for Sweden's position in this field, and for current national statutes that have a bearing on international humanitarian law.

The main publication, Folkrätt i väpnad konflikt, is in Swedish but its somewhat extensive summary has been translated into English, excerpts of which are reproduced below.

Foundations of international law (Chap. 2)

…

International law and Swedish total defence—a background (Chap. 3)

…

Developments in international law after 1984 (Chap. 4)

…

---

459 Krigets lagar, SOU 2010:22 (3 May 2010), <http://www.regeringen.se/sb/d/108/a/145115>.

460 Folkrätt i väpnad konflikt, SOU 2010:72 (29 October 2010), <http://www.regeringen.se/sb/d/108/a/154030>.

461 Svensk manual i humanitär rätt m.m., Annex to SOU 2010:72 (2010), <http://www.regeringen.se/content/1/c6/15/40/30/113aaee0.pdf>.

462 Krigets lagar, SOU 1979:73.

463 Folkrätten i krig, SOU 1984:56.

The focus of this section lies on the issue of how Sweden has implemented the conventions and protocols that have come into being during this period. We have based our comments on information provided by relevant government agencies and civil society organisations which we have approached in order to identify any shortcomings in Sweden's implementation. In most cases there has not been any particular criticism and nor do we consider there is reason to level any criticism at Sweden's implementation. However, critical views concerning certain treaties have been voiced during our consultations or reached us through other channels. These concern issues such as the fact that Sweden has not yet fulfilled its obligation to sign a Privileges and Immunities Agreement with the Organisation for the Prohibition of Chemical Weapons (OPCW), as stated in the *Convention on the prohibition of the development, production, stockpiling and use of chemical weapons and on their destruction*. We have not become aware of, or otherwise found, any particular reasons not to sign such an agreement. Similar agreements have been signed in other areas. As the full implementation of the Convention requires that an agreement be signed, we recommend that Sweden do so. We have received viewpoints from various sources on the slow process of adapting Swedish criminal legislation to the penal provisions included in *the Rome Statute*. We consider it unfortunate that the processing of the proposals made by the Inquiry on International Criminal Law and Swedish Jurisdiction (Internationella brott och svensk jurisdiktion, SOU 2002:98) has taken so long and that Sweden, as a result of this, does not have the legislation in place that the Statute requires. The issue of adapting Swedish criminal legislation to the Rome Statute is also important in relation to several other treaties, as the regulations in the Statute are associated in several points with issues regulated in these other treaties. This applies to *the Convention on the Safety of United Nations and Associated Personnel, the Convention against Torture and Other Cruel, Inhuman or Degrading Treatment or Punishment, the Convention on the Rights of the Child* (*and its Optional Protocols*) and *the Second Protocol to the Convention for the Protection of Cultural Property in the Event of Armed Conflict*. Criticism has been levelled from various sources at Sweden's implementation of *the Convention against Torture and Other Cruel, Inhuman or Degrading Treatment or Punishment*. This criticism has focused, among other things, on the fact that Sweden has not made torture a criminal offence as defined in the convention, and on the fact that, under Swedish provisions, torture is not exempt from statutory limitations. We note that the issue of the need for amendments to penal provisions has been considered in a legislative context and that, at the time, the assessment was made that no legislative amendments are required. However, we proceed from the assumption that the issue of how *the Convention against Torture and Other Cruel, Inhuman or Degrading Treatment or Punishment* should suitably be incorporated into Swedish law will be considered more closely in connection with the processing of the proposals submitted by the Inquiry on International Criminal Law and Swedish Jurisdiction, and in light of this, we refrain from giving a more detailed account here of our own considerations. We also note that the issue of statutory limitations warrants special consideration in this context. From a range of different sources, including the

United Nations Committee on the Rights of the Child, there has been criticism of and views on how Sweden has implemented *the Convention on the Rights of the Child* and its *Optional Protocol on the Involvement of Children in Armed Conflict.* The views received in this regard are largely beyond the scope of our remit. The issue of the incorporation of the Convention on the Rights of the Child into Swedish law has been discussed in several instances, e.g., 'Putting the best interests of the child first' (Barnets bästa i främsta rummet, SOU 1997:116), which was a broad review of how consistent Swedish legislation and practice were with the Convention on the Rights of the Child. We do not consider there is reason to comment in particular on the implementation of the Convention on the Rights of the Child in Sweden, other than to point out that it is important that Sweden's efforts to deal with the criticism received from the Committee on the Rights of the Child (and that are supported by many Swedish actors as indicated above) continue. In connection with *the Convention for the Protection of Cultural Property in the Event of Armed Conflict*, there has been criticism levelled from various sources at the Swedish Armed Forces' training concerning the protection of cultural property. Our comment on this is that the issue of any shortcomings in training on the requirements laid out in the Convention for the Protection of Cultural Property and its Protocols should be followed up by the Swedish Armed Forces and the civilian agencies responsible for training, in line with the Total Defence International Law Ordinance, particularly in connection with training for peace operations. In the section on Sweden's implementation, we point out how crucial it is that Sweden's efforts to ratify *the Second Protocol to the Convention on the Protection of Cultural Property in the Event of Armed Conflict* and *the Convention on Cluster Munitions* continue. We reiterate our proposals in Chap. 7 with reference to the ratification of *Additional Protocol III to the Geneva Conventions.* In section 4.6 we also make certain comments in connection with issues concerning air warfare, private military companies, 'direct participation', 'the war on terror' and 'unlawful combatants'. With regard to private military companies, we highlight our assessment that Sweden should actively support the Montreux Document on private military and security companies, and where the 'war on terror' and 'unlawful combatants' are concerned, *all* persons participating in hostilities should, in our view, be given protection either under international humanitarian law or human rights. We reject the idea, therefore, that there is a legal vacuum leaving scope to treat certain people without regard for such protection.

International humanitarian law and customary law (Chap. 5)

...

In section 5.3 we give our general assessment of the study and an account of what we have based our analysis of the study's rules on. We stress that we did not interpret our terms of reference in such a way as to mean that we were expected to conduct an independent analysis of all the issues that the customary law study may give rise to. What was relevant within the context of our work was a more general evaluation of the study's approach, a general assessment of the study and of individual rules, as well as of the evidential value of the material gathered and the reliability of the conclusions reported.

…

The aim of this review is to investigate the extent to which the study's results contain new obligations for Sweden under international humanitarian law, and if so, what is required to ensure that Sweden fulfils these obligations. In our view, we can support the principles contained in the study concerning the range of state practice, as well as the criteria for assessing the state practice described in the study. We also consider that the study's assessment of state practice has essentially been conducted in conformity with the general criteria described in the introduction to the study. *Therefore, we proceed from the assumption that there is good reason to accept that the 161 rules contained in the study represent customary law.* In the assessment of what constitutes customary law, we have proceeded from a broad conception of state practice, covering not only concrete acts of state behaviour, but also positions taken at diplomatic conferences, acceptance of treaty rules at such conferences and statements made in the United Nations or in other international fora. We note that in such cases the element of state practice (*usus*) in most cases merges with the manifestation of an *opinio juris*. When evaluating the individual rules, we have mainly focused on assessing the extent to which there is reason to take account of the study and its results when shaping national practice. However, this approach does not allow for a clear dividing line to be maintained between policy and *opinio juris*, and the emphasis has therefore been placed on providing a basis for future *Swedish policy* with regard to the rules proposed. In this case, we have taken our cue from conceptions of justice that appear to be appropriate and desirable from a Swedish point of view.

…

Furthermore, we have found that Sweden has long been pushing for the same rules to apply in non-international and international armed conflicts. We have therefore proceeded from the assumption that the rules contained in the study that are applicable to international armed conflicts according to Swedish *opinio juris* also apply to non-international armed conflicts (where stated in the study), unless there are special reasons otherwise. Concerning the rules whose material content does not correspond to any treaty provision that Sweden is bound by, we have assessed each rule against the background of the Swedish practice that we ourselves have compiled. It should be stressed that this practice is largely of a general nature leaving room for various interpretations, and that for a number of rules there is no Swedish practice that either supports or contradicts the customary law status of the rule in question. If a rule lacks support in Swedish *opinio juris* and is not considered to be a necessary regulation, we have made the assessment that there is no Swedish support for the proposed rule being international customary law. In these situations, we have chosen to proceed from an overall assessment of the rule based on the reasons given in the study. In section 5.4 the study's 161 rules are presented. The presentation and the comments are, like the study itself, divided into six subsections: The Principle of Distinction, Specifically Protected Persons and Objects, Specific Methods of Warfare, Weapons, Treatment of Civilians and Persons Hors de Combat, and Implementation. In each subsection, we begin by placing the rules in their context by providing a short background description and by giving overall views on the area of regulation. We then present and comment on each rule individually. Under the heading *The Principle of Distinction*, 24 rules are presented, divided under six sub-headings: Distinction between Civilians and Combatants, Distinction between Civilian Objects and Military Objectives, Indiscriminate Attacks, Proportionality in Attack, Precautions in Attack, and Precautions against the Effects of Attacks. In our view, all of these rules represent the application of fundamental principles in international humanitarian law and have undoubtedly customary law status. All of these rules—or at least their main features—are also supported by treaties Sweden has ratified. We note in particular that the term 'combatant' is sometimes used in a broader sense than it generally has, which has been indicated in our report through the use of the translation 'stridande' (belligerents) and not 'kombattant' (combatant) in these contexts (see Rule 1). Under the heading *Specifically Protected Persons and Objects*, 21 rules are presented under eight sub-headings: Medical and Religious Personnel and Objects, Humanitarian Relief Personnel and Objects, Journalists, Protected Zones, Cultural Property, Works and Installations Containing Dangerous Forces, and The Natural Environment. Almost all of the rules in this group are covered by agreements that Sweden has ratified, including the Geneva Conventions and their Additional Protocol I, the Regulations concerning the Laws and Customs of War on Land (annex to IV Hague Convention) and the Rome Statute, all of which are largely seen to reflect existing customary law. Some of the rules are considered to have customary law status in the practice of the International Criminal Tribunal for the former Yugoslavia. The study makes extensive references to state practice. Swedish state practice also provides extensive and explicit support for many of the rules. Certain formulations in some of the rules in this subsection may, on first impression, make the rules appear more controversial than they are. We comment in particular on the criticism targeted against Rule 31 (respect for and protection of humanitarian relief personnel), previous Swedish statements concerning protection for journalists (Rule 34), and the lack of treaty support concerning protection for the natural environment (Rules 43–45). Under the heading *Specific Methods of Warfare*, 24 rules are presented under five sub-headings: Denial of Quarter, Destruction and Seizure of Property, Starvation and Access to Humanitarian Relief, Deception, and Communication with the Enemy. Almost all of the rules in this main group have equivalents in agreements that Sweden has ratified, including the St Petersburg Declaration, the Regulations concerning the Laws and Customs of War on Land, the Protocol for the Prohibition of the Use of Asphyxiating, Poisonous or Other Gases, and of Bacteriological Methods of Warfare from 1925, and the Geneva Conventions (and their Additional Protocols), all of which are regarded as reflecting existing customary law. However, we have made the assessment that Rules 64 (prohibition against concluding an agreement to suspend combat with the intention of attacking by a surprise the enemy relying on that agreement) and 66 (right to non-hostile contact with the enemy) lack equivalents in Sweden's treaty-based obligations. In our view, the majority of the rules are relatively uncontroversial for Sweden. However, the rules must be read in the light of what is said in the comments on the rules. Without this, some of the rules may be interpreted as incomplete or more far-reaching than was intended. We comment in particular on criticism levelled against Rules 55 and 56 (on humanitarian relief). Under the heading *Weapons*, 17 rules are presented under eleven sub-headings: General Principles on the Use of Weapons, Poison, Biological Weapons, Chemical Weapons, Expanding Bullets, Exploding Bullets, Weapons Primarily Injuring by Non-Detectable Fragments, Booby-Traps, Landmines, Incendiary Weapons, and Blinding Laser Weapons. All of these rules are based on the fundamental principles on the prohibition of weapons that are indiscriminate and cause unnecessary suffering or superfluous injury. These principles are based, in turn, on the abovementioned principles of distinction, proportionality and precautions in attack. Almost all of the rules are included in treaties that Sweden has ratified, including the St Petersburg Declaration, the Regulations concerning the Laws and Customs of War on Land, the Protocol for the Prohibition of the Use of Asphyxiating, Poisonous or Other Gases, and of Bacteriological Methods of Warfare from 1925 and the Convention on Prohibitions or Restrictions on the Use of Certain Conventional Weapons Which May be Deemed to be Excessively Injurious or to Have Indiscriminate Effects from 1980 and its Protocols, and Additional Protocol I to the Geneva Conventions. The practice described in the study is less extensive concerning several rules than for the majority of the rules in the study. The weapons rules have also been the subject of criticism due to excessively weak support in state practice, especially with regard to non-international conflicts. However, in light of the reasons presented in the study and the material provided, we do not consider it necessary to give any dissenting opinion to that expressed in the study, or to question in more general terms the study's conclusions. We comment in particular on certain issues concerning prohibitions in armed conflict that do not apply in peacetime (Rule 75 on riot-control agents and Rule 77 on expanding bullets) and the admissibility of 12.7 millimetre ammunition (Rule 78 on exploding bullets). Under the heading *Treatment of Civilians and Persons Hors de Combat*, 52 rules are presented under eight sub-headings: Fundamental Guarantees, Combatants and Prisoner-of-War Status, The Wounded, Sick and Shipwrecked, The Dead, Missing Persons, Persons Deprived of Their Liberty, Displacement and Displaced Persons, and Other Persons Afforded Specific Protection. The rules in this main group reflect a fundamental idea in international humanitarian law on the protection of and respect for civilians and persons hors de combat, an idea that has also been expressed in more general terms through the customary law rules in the first part—The Principle of Distinction. All of these rules—or at least their main features—correspond to rules in treaties that Sweden has ratified, including the Regulations concerning the Laws and Customs of War on Land, and the Geneva Conventions and their Additional Protocols.

The rules contained in this main group relate to issues that have long been regarded as customary law. As they correspond with similar rules in the area of human rights, many of these rules have long stood out as having a natural place in Swedish law. The continued applicability of human rights in armed conflicts—irrespective of the type of conflict—supports some of the rules. We comment in particular on the issue of what 'torture' means (Rule 90), the issue of protection for 'voluntary' human shields (Rule 97), the issue of limiting the obligation to release and repatriate prisoners of war after the cessation of active hostilities (Rule 128) and the issue of an age-limit for children (Rules 135, 136 and 137). Under the heading *Implementation*, 23 rules are presented under five sub-headings: Compliance with International Humanitarian Law, Enforcement of International Humanitarian Law, Responsibility and Reparation, Individual Responsibility, and War Crimes. Most of the rules in this main group—or in any case their main features—are included in treaties that Sweden has ratified, including the Hague Conventions and the Geneva Conventions and their Additional Protocols. In our view, the study's rules on the implementation of international humanitarian law are largely uncontroversial and refer to circumstances that have long been considered customary law, at least in relation to states. We comment in particular on the issue of whether reprisals can be allowed (Rules 145 and 148), the issue of what 'serious violations' means (Rule 156) and the associated issue of prohibitions of statutes of limitation (Rule 160).

In the final section (5.5) we stress that the exact scope of customary law will always be subject to differing opinions, but that it is our view that there is no reason to repudiate the assessments made by the ICRC in the study. Most of the rules in the study—at least where international armed conflicts are concerned—are essentially also included in treaties by which Sweden is bound. Moreover, there is every indication that Sweden's position in the issues dealt with by the study is essentially in harmony with the assessments made in the study. The rules that can be claimed to go *beyond Sweden's current obligations in international conflicts* are Rules 43 and 44 (protection of the natural environment), Rule 64 (prohibition against agreement to suspend combat with the intention of attacking by surprise), Rule 66 (right to non-hostile contact with the enemy), Rule 86 (blinding laser weapons), Rule 145 (reprisals), Rule 149 (c) and (d) (state responsibility for violations of international humanitarian law) and Rule 154 (superior's orders). However, none of these rules are of such nature that we consider there to be reason for Sweden to repudiate the study's assessment that they have customary law status. In our view, it should also be possible to base Swedish practice on these rules. Concerning non-international conflicts, we express the view that Sweden—both with regard to the findings of the study and for reasons of expediency—should, as a rule, apply and otherwise maintain the same rules as in international conflicts. States that are not engaged in warfare also have an obligation—alone or together with others—to take action to ensure that the rules of international humanitarian law are respected. *Against this background, we recommend that Sweden supports the rules contained in the study.*

Peace operations (Chap. 6)

...

International emblems in international humanitarian law (Chap. 7)

...

Training and information (Chap. 8)

...

Is a Swedish international humanitarian law manual needed? (Chap. 9)

...

What has been possible within the framework of the resources and time the committee has had at its disposal has simply been to present *a draft of a Swedish manual on international humanitarian law* (*see Annex 7*). This draft may make it easier to assess the extent to which a manual is able to meet the needs mentioned above and function as input when deciding on an appropriate design. We also look at the need for a manual for peace operations in view of the fact that participation in such operations now makes up a major part of the operational activities of the Swedish Armed Forces. The most common situation concerning peace operations in which a Swedish force is participating is that the operation does not take part in armed conflict. The force is then not formally bound by international humanitarian law and therefore a manual in international humanitarian law would not provide any immediate guidance. In our view, however, there is an equally great need for clear and structured guidance concerning peace operations as there is concerning armed conflicts. There are strong arguments to suggest that the legal issues linked to the use of force and coercion in the context of peace operations in which a Swedish force is not participating in armed conflict are so important that a manual should be drawn up for this purpose too. As the aim is for the issue of legal grounds for the use of force and coercion by Swedish military personnel and police officers in peace operations to be dealt with by a special inquiry, we did not consider that it was part of our remit to consider in any detail how such a manual should be designed. In summary, we state, among other things, the following: A manual should not primarily be regarded as an account of positions taken in purely legal terms, rather as *rules and guidelines for the actions of our own armed forces* in armed conflicts. A manual should proceed from the assumption that the same provisions of international humanitarian law are to be observed in the implementation of military operations, *irrespective of whether it is an international or non-international armed conflict*. A manual should not be limited purely to rules of international humanitarian law; it should also include rules based on *human rights*. The law of *neutrality and occupation* should also be included in a manual. However, this was not covered by our inquiry remit in such a way as to give us cause to draw up a proposal on the regulation of these areas in a manual. *The Swedish Armed Forces should have formal responsibility* for both the future drafting and publication of a manual. A manual should be published as a *staff publication* within the Swedish Armed Forces, which would indicate that the rules stated in the manual are not formally binding, but that military commanders are obliged to observe the contents of the manual as guidelines. When drafting the manual, the Swedish Armed Forces should *consult the Swedish Civil Contingencies Agency, the Swedish National Defence College,* and *the Total Defence Council for International Law*, and carry out the work with the *assistance of academically active experts. Experts from other states* should also be consulted. The work to produce a manual should also be carried out under the *supervision of representatives of the ministries concerned.* Sweden has an interest in *clarifying internationally* what is seen in Sweden as applicable international humanitarian law. To what extent this interest should be addressed with the help of regulations in a manual is something that should be assessed when there is a properly functioning manual in place.

Government Inquiry—Peace Operations and the Use of Lethal Force

During the work of the International Law Committee it became clear that the government intended to institute an additional inquiry into the use of force in peace operations. For that reason these matters were only touched upon briefly in the final version of the main publication, Folkrätt i väpnad konflikt. The necessity for such an investigation arose from concerns expressed following Swedish participation in operations of a later date. These involved Swedish forces taking part (primarily) in ISAF and EUNAVFOR. The government had become increasingly aware of the lack of national regulation in respect to the use of force and to the relationship between human rights law and international humanitarian law. This had become particularly clear on questions of detention. Swedish national law does not provide for the explicit support of the use of force by armed personnel in peace operations. Furthermore, this situation has created tension owing to the fact that it is clearly established that Swedish penal law applies to members of its armed forces participating in peace operations. The fact that no legal provision exists authorising coercion by members of the armed forces contributing to peace operations (such as the Swedish police law in relation to the right of the police to use force within the territory of Sweden) raised questions, on the one hand, of criminalisation and on the other, of the rights and duties involved in executing the necessary tasks in a peace operation in order to realise the Security Council's mandate.

In December 2010, the Governmental Inquiry on Peace Operations (Fredsinsatsutredningen)[464] began its work. According to the directives, its members were charged by the government with analysing the legal regulations on the use of force in peace operations and to examine and assemble those aspects of international and national law applicable to peace operations. The question of detentions in such operations was of special interest. The inquiry, moreover, was asked to scrutinise

[464] Dir. Nr. 2010:125 (2010), <http://www.opengov.se/govtrack/dir/2010:125/>.

the applicability of Swedish criminal law to service personnel in international peace operations.

The body was also given the task of assessing whether or not there was a need for specific national legislation on the use of force applicable to those members of the Swedish armed forces participating in peace operations, and if a need existed, to draw up proposals for such legislation. The final report is due to be submitted to the government, at the latest, on 1 December 2011.

OLA ENGDAHL

UNITED KINGDOM[465]

Draft Legislation—Prisoners of War
- The Armed Forces Bill

The constitutional arrangements of the UK require the governing legislation of the armed forces to be renewed every 5 years. The *Armed Forces Act 2006* is therefore due for renewal in 2011.[466] The Armed Forces Bill[467] received its first reading in the House of Commons on 8 December 2010. Of considerable interest is Clause 23 dealing with protected prisoners of war.

It will be recalled that Article 82 of *Geneva Convention Relative to the Treatment of Prisoners of War*[468] requires that prisoners of war 'shall be subject to the laws, regulations and orders in force in the armed forces of the Detaining Power; the Detaining Power shall be justified in taking judicial or disciplinary measures in respect of an offence committed by a prisoner of war against such laws'. Article 102 of GCIII requires that '[a] prisoner of war can be validly sentenced only if the sentence has been pronounced by the same courts according to the same procedure as in the case of members of the armed forces of the Detaining Power'.

The current position in the UK is governed by the *Royal Warrant Governing the Maintenance of Discipline Among Prisoners of War 1958*.[469] It contains two schedules. Schedule 1 deals with the establishment of a 'competent tribunal' in the form of a board of inquiry to determine the status of a prisoner of war should any doubt arise as to his status. It is designed to implement Art 5 of GCIII.[470] The second schedule sets out the *Prisoners of War (Discipline) Regulations 1958*. This

---

465 Peter Rowe, Professor of Law, University of Lancaster, UK.

466 See *Armed Forces Act 2006* (UK) s. 382(4).

467 Bill 122 of 2010–2011.

468 Opened for signature 12 August 1949, 75 UNTS 135 (entered into force 21 October 1950) (GCIII).

469 It is dated 7 August 1958 and was amended in 1965 and 1968.

470 It was invoked in the Gulf war 1990–1991. See G. Risius, 'Prisoners of War in the United Kingdom', in P. Rowe, ed., *The Gulf War 1990–91 in International and English Law* (London, Routledge 1993) pp 289, 295–297. Legal aid was granted to enable a person concerned to be legally represented: at p 297.

schedule is based largely on the *Army Act 1955* (repealed by the *Armed Forces Act 2006*) but it does implement a number of relevant provisions of GCIII.[471]

These Regulations provide for the convening of a prisoner of war court-martial to try a prisoner of war by way of judicial proceedings (as contrasted with disciplinary proceedings).[472] This type of court-martial is *sui generis*. The membership of the court-martial is different from that of courts-martial convened under the *Army Act 1955* when it was in force.[473] The prisoner of war court-martial is clearly different from the Court Martial currently provided by the *Armed Forces Act 2006*. Since the 1958 Regulations there had been a number of challenges brought before the European Court of Human Rights concerning the compatibility of British courts-martial with Article 6 of the *Convention for the Protection of Human Rights and Fundamental Freedoms*.[474] The *Armed Forces Act 2006* consolidated the various statutory step changes to the court-martial system which had been necessary to ensure compatibility.[475]

Clause 23 of the Armed Forces Bill will, if passed in its current form, provide that Her Majesty may issue a Royal Warrant to apply or modify any provision of the *Armed Forces Act 2006* to protected prisoners of war. If achieved this would cause Articles 82 and 102 to be fully implemented into English law. In a Memorandum to the House of Commons Select Committee on Defence, the Ministry of Defence stated that:

> Consideration is being given as to how to provide for a disciplinary system and courts which would meet the requirements of the European Convention and which can deal with disciplinary or criminal offences committed by prisoners of war while in captivity... it is intended to provide a full new regime relating to prisoners of war, derived from the Armed Forces Act 2006.[476]

Since Clause 23 is intended only to give a power to issue a Royal Warrant to achieve the objective discussed above it is possible that no further detail as to the

---

[471] The notes to the schedule show the following Articles in whole or in part: 41–42, 78, 82–98, 100–108. Also included are the grave breaches of each of the *Geneva Conventions*.

[472] This is a distinction drawn in GCIII. See Arts 83, 89, 99. For the relevant parts of the Regulations see Reg. 5 (disciplinary proceedings) and Regs. 7, 25 (judicial proceedings).

[473] Compare Reg. 27 with the *Army Act 1955* (UK) s. 84D.

[474] Opened for signature 4 November 1950, 213 UNTS 221 (entered into force 3 September 1953) (*European Convention on Human Rights*). Article 6 requires that 'in the determination... of any criminal charge against him, everyone is entitled to... an independent and impartial tribunal'.

[475] See generally, P. Rowe, 'Introduction and General Note', Current Law Statutes Annotated, *Armed Forces Act 2006* (London, Sweet & Maxwell 2006); P. Rowe, 'The United Kingdom Armed Forces: The Advance of Human Rights' in S. Hetherington, ed., *Halsbury's Laws of England Centenary Essays 2007* (London, LexisNexis Butterworths 2007) p 41.

[476] The Memorandum is dated 8 September 2010. See <http://www.publications.parliament.uk/pa/cm201011/cmselect/cmdfence/writev/armed/afb01.htm>. House of Commons Library Research Paper 10/85, 17 December 2010, p 15, concluded that the effect of a Royal Warrant made under Clause 23 would be to 'extend the jurisdiction of the Service courts to prisoners of war'.

contents of the proposed Royal Warrant will be provided on the face of the Bill (and, subsequently, the Act).[477]

It may therefore be unknown until the Royal Warrant is issued whether it will give jurisdiction to the Court Martial to try an offence committed prior to capture. The Memorandum from the Ministry of Defence referred to offences committed by prisoners of war 'while in captivity'. A grave breach of the *Geneva Conventions* or of *Protocol Additional to the Geneva Conventions of 12 August 1949, and relating to the Protection of Victims of International Armed Conflicts* (*Protocol I*)[478] will amount to an offence under English law whatever the alleged perpetrator's nationality and whether it is committed in or outside the UK.[479] A person alleged to have committed such an offence and who subsequently becomes a prisoner of war detained by the UK should, like a member of the British armed forces, be subject to trial by the Court Martial.[480] Article 85 of GCIII dictates that a person retains the status of prisoner of war even if convicted of an act[481] committed prior to capture.

It may, however, be that the Royal Warrant will not, in due course, provide any mechanism to try offences alleged to have been committed prior to capture simply because of the practical and procedural difficulties involved. The difficulties involved in the calling of witnesses, who are not themselves prisoners of war, is but one example.[482]

The Royal Warrant will also need to determine what would constitute a 'competent tribunal' for the purposes of Article 5 of GCIII.[483] There is a powerful argument to the effect that such a tribunal should be of the same quality as one envisaged by Article 6 of the *European Convention on Human Rights* simply because if this tribunal decides that a person is not entitled to prisoner of war status he will be subject to national law and liable for any crimes under that law committed prior to capture.[484] The consequences for an individual of a decision made by this tribunal are likely to be more severe than that of a periodical review panel established to determine whether a protected civilian should be released from

---

[477] As to the procedure for issuing secondary legislation under the Armed Forces Act 2006, see s. 373.

[478] Opened for signature 8 June 1977, 1125 UNTS 3 (entered into force 7 December 1978).

[479] See Geneva Conventions Act 1957 (UK) s. 1.

[480] The explanatory note 1(a) to Reg. 7 of the 1958 Regulations assumed that it caught grave breaches committed before or after capture.

[481] This need not necessarily amount to a grave breach but it is suggested that the act should amount to a crime over which (in this case) the UK has jurisdiction at the time it was committed.

[482] See GCIII, Art. 105.

[483] Along with Additional Protocol I, Art. 45. The board of inquiry referred to by Colonel Risius (see supra n. 470) has now been replaced by a service inquiry. See Armed Forces Act 2006 (UK) s. 343; Armed Forces (Service Inquiries) Regulations 2008 (UK) SI 2008/1651.

[484] For examples see *Osman Bin Mohamed Ali* v. *Public Prosecutor* [1969] 1 AC 430; *Public Prosecutor* v. *Oi Hee Koi* [1968] AC 829.

detention. In the latter case it may be sufficient if a judicial type decision is made without the involvement of a judicial officer.[485]

It has become more common in recent times for the armed forces to detain civilians rather than prisoners of war. The governments in both Iraq and in Afghanistan requested States to remain on their respective territories after an international armed conflict or occupation to assist them with defeating insurgencies. Civilians detained by UK armed forces in Iraq have sought to challenge the lawfulness of their detention or to claim that they had been ill-treated in detention.[486] Whilst the civilians under consideration cannot be entitled to the status of prisoner of war it is not unknown for a State to declare that they should be treated *as if* they were.[487] It may be that the proposed Royal Warrant should go beyond implementation of GCIII and include, *mutatis mutandis*, civilians detained by UK armed forces whether during an international or a non-international armed conflict (or other state of emergency taking place outside the UK). The importance of doing so lies in the fact that the Royal Warrant can implement one or more Articles of the *Geneva Conventions* of 1949 or their *Additional Protocols* of 1977 directly into English law and by so doing make them part of that law which soldiers must obey.[488] Standing orders, or any other form of military directives, will not therefore be able to take any precedence over that law. This action may go some way to prevent possible ill-treatment of civilian detainees.[489] It would, however, clearly be important to stress that such civilians would not actually become prisoners of war.

Legislation—Ratification of Treaties
- *Constitutional Reform and Governance Act 2010*

The ratification of treaties has always been based under the Royal prerogative, the effect of which is that a Minister of the Crown makes the decision whether to ratify a treaty or not to do so. Since 1921 treaties have had to be laid before Parliament for 21 days before any ratification can take place.[490] The Act puts these procedures

---

[485] See *Al-Jedda* v. *Secretary of State for Defence* [2010] EWCA Civ 758.

[486] See *R* (*Mousa*) v. *Secretary of State for Defence* [2010] EWHC 3304 (Admin).

[487] See *Amnesty International Canada* v. *Chief of the Defence Staff of Canadian Forces* 2008 FC 336, paras 166, 171 (Mactavish J.).

[488] It may not be necessary to create any additional criminal offences but a statutory-based regime for the treatment of civilian detainees would cure any uncertainty as to how they should be treated.

[489] See below discussion of *R* (*Mousa*) v. *Secretary of State for Defence* [2010] EWHC 3304 (Admin).

[490] See Explanatory Notes to ss. 20–5 of the Act. For the background to the Act see: 11 *YIHL* (2008) p 572; Government Response to the Report of the Joint Committee on the Draft Constitutional Renewal Bill, Cm 7690 (2009) p 30; Government Response to the Report of the Public Administration Select Committee on the Draft Constitutional Renewal Bill, Cm 7688 (2009) pp 14–15.

in statutory form[491] and it enables either House of Parliament to resolve that a particular treaty should not be ratified although the Minister can, nevertheless, decide to ratify it.

Legislation—To Enable Ratification of the Cluster Munitions Convention
- *The Cluster Munitions (Prohibitions) Act 2010*

This Act enabled the UK to ratify the *Convention on Cluster Munitions.*[492] It also establishes a number of offences under English law which can be committed in the UK or elsewhere.[493]

Cases—Civilian Detainees in Iraq Transferred to Iraqi Authorities
- *Al-Saadoon and Mufdhi* v. *United Kingdom*, European Court of Human Rights, Application No 61498/08, Judgment, 2 March 2010

The decisions of the courts in England and an earlier decision of the European Court of Human Rights relating to these two applicants were discussed in earlier volumes of the Yearbook.[494] It will be recalled that they were two Iraqi nationals arrested and detained by British armed forces in Iraq in 2003 as persons suspected of killing two British soldiers whom they had captured. The two British soldiers would have been entitled to prisoner of war status since their capture occurred during the international armed conflict between the coalition States and the government forces of Iraq.[495]

The Basra Criminal Court had decided that the applicants should be transferred to the Iraqi High Tribunal (IHT) for trial. The decisions of the English courts related to an application for judicial review by Al-Saadoon and Mufdhi to prevent their transfer. Ultimately, the English Court of Appeal ruled that they should be transferred. In 2009, the European Court of Human Rights ordered, by way of an application for interim measures, that they should not.[496] The British government failed to comply with the interim measure ordered by the Court and transferred the applicants to the IHT.[497]

---

[491] The procedure was previously known as the Ponsonby Rule. The Minister is now required to explain the provisions of the treaty and the reason why ratification is sought.

[492] Opened for signature 3 December 2008, 48 ILM 357 (entered into force 1 August 2010). The UK ratified the Convention on 4 May 2010.

[493] The offences are set out in s. 2 and the jurisdiction of the UK courts in s. 4.

[494] See 11 *YIHL* (2008) p 577; 12 *YIHL* (2009) pp 678–680.

[495] The English courts would have had jurisdiction to try these two individuals had they been transferred to the UK. See Geneva Conventions Act 1957 (UK) s. 1. The British military authorities would have had no jurisdiction to try them in Iraq since, as civilians, they would not have been subject to British military law.

[496] See European Court of Human Rights, Rules of Court (July 2009) Rule 39. See also discussion of these proceedings in 12 *YIHL* (2009) p 679.

[497] The facts of the transfer are set out in *Al-Saadoon and Mufdhi* v. *United Kingdom*, Judgment, 2 March 2010, paras 78–81. See also the partly dissenting view of Judge Bratza discussed infra. The government repeated its reasons for transferring the applicants in Responding to Human Rights Judgments: Government Response to the Joint Committee on Human Rights Fifteenth Report of Session 2009-10, Cm 7892 (2010) para 26.

The key issues before the European Court of Human Rights in 2010 were whether the applicants remained within the jurisdiction of the UK for the purposes of Article 1 of the *European Convention on Human Rights* despite the mandate for the British presence in Iraq ending at the end of December 2008 and whether the risk of the death penalty being imposed should the applicants be convicted by the IHT must result in a refusal to make the transfer.

The Court held that the two applicants were within the jurisdiction of the UK immediately before their transfer to the Iraqi authorities. The argument of the UK government that, 'in accordance with well established principles of international law, they had no option but to respect Iraqi sovereignty and transfer the applicants, who were Iraqi nationals held on Iraqi territory, to the custody of the Iraqi courts when so requested'[498] was rejected. The Court took the view that 'a Contracting Party is responsible under Article 1 of the Convention for all acts and omissions of its organs regardless of whether the act or omission in question was a consequence of domestic law or of the necessity to comply with international legal obligations'.[499]

In a partly dissenting opinion Judge Bratza referred to the 'special circumstances' of this case. These were that the 'two applicants were held by a contingent of a multinational force on foreign sovereign territory, whose mandate to remain on the territory had expired and who had no continuing power or authority to detain or remove from the territory nationals of the foreign State concerned'. A request by the UK for the referral of this case to the Grand Chamber of the European Court of Human Rights was made, upon which a decision is awaited.

The facts suggested that there was a substantial risk of the applicants being sentenced to death before the IHT. In these circumstances the Court would not

---

[498] *Al-Saadoon and Mufdhi* v. *United Kingdom*, Judgment, 2 March 2010, para 138. According to the European Court of Human Rights at para 67 of the judgment, the Court of Appeal had concluded that the UK was: 'not exercising jurisdiction over the appellants within the meaning of ECHR, Article 1... In essence the United Kingdom detains the appellants only at the request and to the order of the IHT, and is obliged to return them to the custody of the IHT by force of arrangements made between the United Kingdom and Iraq, and the United Kingdom has no discretionary power of its own to hold, release or return the appellants. They are acting purely as agents of the IHT'.

[499] *Al-Saadoon and Mufdhi* v. *United Kingdom*, Judgment, 2 March 2010, para 128. The effect of this is that a State by entering into a treaty, prior or subsequent to becoming a party to the European Convention on Human Rights, cannot limit its obligations to those within its jurisdiction under the Convention. By way of example the Court referred in the same paragraph to *Soering* v. *United Kingdom* (1989) 11 EHRR 439 where it had held that the United Kingdom must not repatriate a fugitive from the US because of the risk of the death penalty being imposed on him in a subsequent trial. This ruling was made in spite of the UK's obligations to the US under the Extradition Treaty, United Kingdom–United States, signed 8 June 1972, 1049 UNTS 167 (entered into force 21 January 1977). Compare, however, where there is a conflict of obligations between the Charter of the United Nations and the European Convention on Human Rights. See (*Al-Jedda*) v. *Secretary of State for Defence* [2007] UKHL 58.

permit a State to transfer an applicant who was within its jurisdiction.[500] It concluded that the UK had failed to comply with the interim measure, that it was in breach of Article 3 of the Convention[501] and that it had failed to provide the applicants with an effective remedy.[502]

Cases—Whether Civilian Detainees Should Be Transferred to the Afghan Authorities

- *R* (*Evans*) v. *Secretary of State for Defence* [2010] EWHC 1445 (Admin) (Divisional Court)

In this case an individual sought to prevent, by way of judicial review, the Secretary of State from transferring Afghan nationals, detained by British armed forces in Afghanistan, to the appropriate authorities in Afghanistan. Her argument was, essentially, that any transferees would be subject to a real risk of 'torture or serious mistreatment'[503] in Afghan custody and that no further transfers should take place. If successful, the effect would be that detainees would have to be released.

The Court noted the power to detain Afghan nationals issued by the International Stabilisation Assistance Force (ISAF) and drew attention to the fact that 'the UK's policy reflects that of ISAF'.[504] The Secretary of State had argued that:

> the counter-insurgency campaign in southern Afghanistan is challenging and highly dangerous, with a particular high threat from improvised explosive devices, ambushes and snipers... Detention operations are central to the efforts of the UK forces to protect themselves and local civilians from such attacks. They are also crucial to the UK's wider contribution to assisting the Afghan Government to bring security and stability to the country, for example by enabling insurgents to be prosecuted before the Afghan courts and by providing the opportunity for the gathering of intelligence.[505]

---

[500] See *Soering* v. *United Kingdom* (1989) 11 EHRR 439; Protocol No. 13 to the Convention for the Protection of Human Rights and Fundamental Freedoms, concerning the abolition of the death penalty in all circumstances, opened for signature 3 May 2002, 2246 UNTS 110 (entered into force 1 July 2003).

[501] This prohibits torture, inhuman or degrading treatment, which in this case involved mental suffering caused by the fear of execution. See *Al-Saadoon and Mufdhi* v. *United Kingdom*, Judgment, 2 March 2010, para 171.

[502] See the European Convention on Human Rights, Art 13. This occurred because the transfer of the applicants to the Iraqi authorities prevented them from exercising a right of appeal from the decision of the Court of Appeal.

[503] *R* (*Evans*) v. *Secretary of State for Defence* [2010] EWHC 1445 (Admin), para 1. The detainees were transferred into the custody of Afghanistan's National Directorate of Security (NDS): at para 27.

[504] Ibid., para 20. The policy of the UK (along with those other States forming part of the coalition and party to the European Convention on Human Rights) was to ensure that those within its jurisdiction were not transferred if a substantial risk of a breach of Article 3 of the Convention might occur while in Afghan custody.

[505] Ibid., para 23.

In addition, the Secretary of State had argued that although this case was concerned only with Afghan nationals detained by UK armed forces, it could have 'serious implications for joint operations conducted by the UK and for the position of other ISAF partners'.[506]

The Court considered the nature of the individual institutions of NDS in Afghanistan to which the British military authorities had transferred those whom it had detained. It concluded that transfers could be made to certain NDS facilities but not, at present, to NDS Kabul.[507] The Memorandum of Understanding between the UK and the government of Afghanistan[508] had provided for monitoring by British military officials of the transferred detainees in Afghan custody on a regular basis with each individual having the right to a private interview. This was some assurance that once transferred the detainees would not be subjected to torture, inhuman or degrading treatment consistent with the guarantees in Article 3 of the *European Convention on Human Rights*.[509]

These two cases illustrate the problems which States face when they detain a civilian whilst conducting military operations outside their own territory. Once detained within a military base, a civilian comes within the jurisdiction of a State party to the *European Convention on Human Rights*.[510] The detaining State may then be faced with the problem that it cannot transfer him or her to the proper authorities of that individual's own State, either because there is a substantial risk that that individual would face torture, inhuman, degrading treatment or an unfair trial or both.[511]

It may be that this is an issue which receives less consideration than it deserves when a State undertakes military operations outside its own territory. The short term detention of civilians, often on suspicion of having committed a criminal offence, is a clearly foreseeable event during military operations, particularly where a non-international armed conflict is taking place on the territory concerned. Participating States will hardly wish to find themselves in a position where they

---

[506] Ibid., para 268. Compare the view of the UK with that of Canada on the safety of transferring detainees to NDS Kandahar: at para 318.

[507] The Court considered, but rejected, seeking an assurance from the Afghan authorities that detainees would not be further transferred by them. The Court concluded that 'we doubt whether such a 'condition would be unrealistic'. See ibid., para 320.

[508] See House of Commons Foreign Affairs Committee, Visit to Guantanamo Bay, Second Report, Session 2006–2007, HC 44, Appendix 3, para 4. The Memorandum is dated 23 April 2006. See UK, Parliamentary Debates, House of Commons, 26 February 2009, Vol. 488, col. 396.

[509] As to the 'Catch 22' situation of merely asking for assurance of the State to whom the detainees are transferred see *R* (*Evans*) v. *Secretary of State for Defence* [2010] EWHC 1445 (Admin), para 248.

[510] See *R* (*Al-Skeini and others*) v. *Secretary of State for Defence* [2007] UKHL 26. Decision of the Grand Chamber awaited in *Al-Skeini* v. *United Kingdom*. The same result may occur in relation to the national law of other States. See *Amnesty International Canada* v. *Chief of the Defence Staff of the Canadian Forces* 2008 FC 336.

[511] *Brown* v. *Government of Rwanda* [2009] EWHC 770 (Admin), discussed in 12 *YIHL* (2009) pp 681–682.

can neither transfer detainees to the proper authorities of their own State nor try them in their own courts. The only alternative would then be to release them, thereby rendering the process of detaining them of little value.

Moreover, in both cases the purpose of the transfer was to enable the Afghan authorities to place the individuals on trial (or release them if there was insufficient evidence to prosecute). There does not appear from any of the cases any discussion of whether the Afghan criminal judicial system would provide a trial consistent with Article 6 of the *European Convention on Human Rights*. There is certainly some evidence that might put a transferring State on its guard.[512] This was the ground upon which the Divisional Court in England refused to extradite a number of Rwanda nationals to face trial for their alleged participation in the genocide there.[513]

Cases—Was Detention of Civilian Contrary to Iraqi Law?
- *Al-Jedda* v. *Secretary of State for Defence* [2010] EWCA Civ 758

The essential facts in this case were discussed earlier.[514] Mr Al-Jedda had been detained in Iraq by British armed forces as a security detainee[515] and claimed that he should be able to test the lawfulness of his detention under the *Human Rights Act 1998*.[516] The House of Lords held that the obligations of the UK 'had been displaced by its obligations under the UN Charter'.[517]

In these proceedings Mr Al-Jedda argued that his detention by the British military authorities was contrary to Iraqi law from 20 May 2006[518] to 30 December 2007, the date of his release. The Court of Appeal held that it was not. By way of analogy Elias LJ referred to Article 78 of *Geneva Convention Relative*

---

512 See UNSC Res 1917/2010, UN Doc. S/RES/1917, 22 March 2010, para 30, which referred to 'accelerating the establishment of a fair and transparent judicial system'.

513 See *Brown* v. *Government of Rwanda* [2009] EWHC 770 (Admin).

514 10 *YIHL* (2007) p 448; 12 *YIHL* (2009) p 680. It should be remembered that Mr Al-Jedda also held British nationality. The Court of Appeal concluded that the Secretary of State could not plead 'act of State'. Elias LJ took the view that it was 'difficult to see how even the interests of state can justify the arbitrary and uncontrolled internment of a British subject'. See *Al-Jedda* v. *Secretary of State for Defence* [2010] EWCA Civ 758, para 213.

515 Compare a person detained on the basis of an allegation of a criminal offence. See the two cases discussed above.

516 This Act implemented into English law the rights and fundamental freedoms to be found in the European Convention on Human Rights.

517 *Al-Jedda* v. *Secretary of State for Defence* [2010] EWCA Civ 758, para 2 (Arden LJ). The House of Lords held that this was the effect of UNSC Res 1546/2004, UN Doc. S/RES/1546, 8 June 2004. This case has been referred to the Grand Chamber of the European Court of Human Rights. An oral hearing was held on 9 June 2010 and judgment is expected in 2011.

518 This was the date when the Iraqi Constitution came into force. See *Al-Jedda* v. *Secretary of State for Defence* [2010] EWCA Civ 758, para 134 (Elias LJ). It had been alleged that some of the rules concerned with his detention conflicted with that Constitution.

to the Protection of Civilian Persons in Time of War.[519] This provides that a protected person subjected to assigned residence or internment in occupied territory has a right to a periodical review by a 'competent body'.

The specific issue was whether a 'competent body' should be composed of a judge or whether it was sufficient if it proceeded in a way which 'concentrates on what the judicial oversight is designed to achieve'.[520] Elias LJ concluded that 'the essence of the right (conferred in the Iraqi Constitution) requires not the involvement of a judge; rather it requires that the decision displays the essential features of these typically judicial characteristics'.[521] In dealing specifically with Article 78 of GCIV he concluded that a 'competent body' could include the commanding officer acting jointly with a panel set up for the purpose. It was not therefore necessary to involve a judge. Indeed, he went on to say that 'non-judicial procedures may be capable of better serving a detainee than would judicial procedures, where the reason for the detention is the threat to security. Judges are not in the best position to assess whether national security is threatened or not'.[522]

Cases—Whether British Soldier within the Jurisdiction of the UK When Conducting Military Operations and Away from Base

- *R* (*Smith*) (*FC*) v. *Secretary of State for Defence* [2010] UKSC 29

The earlier judgments in this case were discussed in the 2008 and 2009 volumes of the *Yearbook of International Humanitarian Law.*[523] Private Smith died of hyperthermia on a British base in Iraq. An inquest had been conducted in the UK when his body was repatriated. The issue before the Supreme Court was whether a British soldier could remain 'within the jurisdiction'[524] of the UK while serving on active service abroad when *outside his base*. The Secretary of State had conceded that Private Smith was within the jurisdiction of the UK since he had died on a British base. His mother was therefore entitled to a fresh inquest based upon Article 2 of the *European Convention on Human Rights* (the right to life). The Supreme Court held that the mere death of a soldier on active service did not raise a presumption of a breach of Article 2. It would be necessary to show

---

[519] Opened for signature 12 August 1949, 75 UNTS 287 (entered into force 21 October 1950) (GCIV).

[520] *Al-Jedda* v. *Secretary of State for Defence* [2010] EWCA Civ 758, para 148 (Elias LJ).

[521] Ibid.

[522] Ibid., para 152. The reasons given by Elias LJ were supported by Sir John Dyson, SCJ, at para 126, and formed the majority view in the case.

[523] See 12 *YIHL* (2009) p 677; 11 *YIHL* (2008) p 576.

[524] See European Convention on Human Rights, Article 1. If this Article is satisfied a person is entitled, within English law, to the rights accorded by the Human Rights Act 1998. The most significant in this context is Article 2 (the right to life), which includes an obligation on the State to provide an adequate system to protect life. See 11 *YIHL* (2008) p 576.

'circumstances that give ground for suspicion that the State may have breached a substantive obligation imposed by article 2'.[525]

On an interpretation of the jurisprudence of the European Court of Human Rights and on the wider issue raised, a majority (6:3)[526] concluded that a British soldier was not within the jurisdiction of the UK should he die or be killed[527] during military operations away from his or her base.[528] This case was concerned with the type of inquest to be held in relation to a soldier who died abroad during the course of military operations. A related question, and not forming part of the instant judgment, is that of whether a soldier could sue for alleged negligence during the conduct of military operations or whether 'combat immunity applies'.[529]

Cases—Call for an Investigation into the Treatment of Detainees in UK Custody Abroad

- *R (Mousa)* v. *Secretary of State for Defence* [2010] EWHC 3304 (Admin)

Mr Mousa was a representative of a group of about one hundred other Iraqi civilians, who alleged ill-treatment by British armed forces when detained in Iraq. He sought judicial review to compel the Secretary of State to hold an investigation of the type required by Article 3 of the *European Convention on Human Rights* into these allegations.[530]

The Court was informed that the Secretary of State had set up two related investigatory bodies, the Iraq Historic Allegations Team (IHAT) and the Iraq

---

525 See *R (Smith) (FC)* v. *Secretary of State for Defence* [2010] UKSC 29, para 84 (Lord Phillips). The requirements of an 'Article 2' investigation are set out by Lord Phillips at para 64.

526 The decision of the Grand Chamber of the European Court of Human Rights in the joined cases of *R (Al Skeini)* v. *Secretary of State for Defence* [2007] UKHL 26; *R (Al-Jedda)* v. *Secretary of State for Defence* [2007] UKHL 58 is expected in 2011. These cases dealt with the issue of 'within jurisdiction' for the purposes of the Human Rights Act 1998 and have been based, in turn, upon the interpretation of the relevant jurisprudence of the European Court of Human Rights relating to Art 1 of the Convention.

527 See generally, P. Rowe, 'The Obligation of a State under International Law to Protect Members of its Own Armed Forces During Armed Conflict or Occupation', 9 *YIHL* (2006) p 3.

528 A powerful argument presented by Lords Mance and Kerr (both of whom dissented on this issue) was that if a British soldier died away from his base on military operations (in this case in Iraq) he would not be within the jurisdiction of any State. See *R (Smith) (FC)* v. *Secretary of State for Defence* [2010] UKSC 29, para 191 (Lord Mance); para 317 (Lord Kerr).

529 See *Mulcahy* v. *Ministry of Defence* [1996] QB 732; *Bici* v. *Ministry of Defence* [2004] EWHC 786 (QB); *Multiple Claimants* v. *Ministry of Defence* [2003] EWHC 1134 (QB), para 16.1(b).

530 Article 3 prohibits torture, inhuman or degrading treatment. The European Court of Human Rights has held on many occasions that States have an obligation to investigate where credible allegations of such treatment are made. For the ingredients of an investigation under Article 2 or 3 of the Convention recently stated see *Israilova* v. *Russia*, European Court of Human Rights, Application No. 35079/04, Judgment, 28 October 2010, para 111. For their application in English law to a case similar to that under discussion see also *R (Al-Sweady)* v. *Secretary of State for Defence* [2009] EWHC 2387 (Admin), para 54.

Historic Allegations Panel (IHAP).[531] The function of the IHAT, led by a civilian, is to conduct criminal investigations into allegations made in the course of the judicial review proceedings. It is envisaged that IHAP will deal with 'the proper and effective handling of information and consider the results of investigations by IHAT … [and] identify wider issues to be brought to the attention of … Ministers'.[532]

An issue before the Court was whether the IHAT investigations could be sufficiently independent of the chain of command for the purposes of an Article 3 investigation. It concluded that they could be since under the *Armed Forces Act 2006* the result of investigations relating to serious crimes had to be passed to the Director of Service Prosecutions, a civilian, for a decision.[533]

The Court was also aware that two public inquiries had also been established by the Secretary of State for Defence. These were the Baha Mousa Inquiry under the chairmanship of a retired Court of Appeal Judge (Rt Hon Sir William Gage)[534] and the Al Sweady Inquiry, due to commence its work in 2011.[535]

The Secretary of State had argued that a public inquiry should not be ordered into the allegations made by Mr Mousa and the other potential claimants at the present time given the investigatory work of the IHAT, which may lead to prosecution of some of the soldiers involved. Moreover, the IHAT may establish facts and lead to the settlement of civilian claims. An investigation of allegations of systemic ill-treatment was also to be considered by the Baha Mousa public inquiry.

The Court concluded that:

> the investigative obligation under article 3 does not require the Secretary of State to establish an immediate public inquiry. It is possible that a public inquiry will be required in due course, but the need for an inquiry and the precise scope of the issues that any such inquiry should cover can lawfully be left for decision at a future date.[536]

Cases—Disqualification from Refugee Status If Alleged War Criminal

- *R (JS) (Sri Lanka)* v. *Secretary of State for the Home Department* [2010] UKSC 15

The decision of the Court of Appeal in this case was discussed in 2009 *Yearbook of International Humanitarian Law*.[537] On appeal to the Supreme Court the case was remitted to the Secretary of State to make a fresh decision based on the reasoning of the Supreme Court and not of the Court of Appeal.

---

531 *R (Mousa)* v. *Secretary of State for Defence* [2010] EWHC 3304 (Admin), para 3.

532 Ibid., para 17.

533 Ibid., para 67. Compare the view of the court which gave permission for judicial review in this case: *Mousa* v. *Secretary of State for Defence* [2010] EWHC 1823, para 23.

534 Oral hearings were concluded on 14 October 2010. The website of the Inquiry can be found at <http://www.bahamousainquiry.org/index.htm>.

535 This inquiry was conceded by the Secretary of State for Defence following *R (Al Sweady)* v. *Secretary of State for Defence* [2009] EWHC 2387 (Admin). It has yet to begin oral hearings.

536 *R (Mousa)* v. *Secretary of State for Defence* [2010] EWHC 3304 (Admin), para 134.

537 12 *YIHL* (2009) p 683.

The issue was whether the applicant was disqualified under Article 1F(a) of the *Refugee Convention* on the basis that he had been a member of the LTTE in Sri Lanka. Any liability on his part for the commission of war crimes or crimes against humanity would depend on whether he could be considered to be a participant in any such crimes. The Supreme Court relied on Articles 25(3) and 30 of the *Rome Statute of the International Criminal Court.*

Lord Hope (with whom the other Supreme Court judges agreed) concluded that a person would be disqualified (under Article 1F(a) of the Convention) from refugee status if 'there were serious reasons for considering him voluntarily to have contributed in a significant way to the organisation's ability to pursue its purpose of committing war crimes, aware that his assistance will in fact further that purpose'.[538]

In considering the issue of the *mens rea* required Lord Hope concluded that '[a]s article 30 of the ICC Statute makes plain, if a person is aware that in the ordinary course of events a particular consequence will follow from his actions, he is taken to have acted with both knowledge and intention'.[539]

In arriving at his conclusion, Lord Hope made it plain that by merely joining the LTTE and, thereby being part of an organisation (the LTTE) which had taken up arms against the Sri Lankan Government, the applicant had not committed war crimes.[540]

Treaty Action—Denunciation of a European Treaty

- *Western European Alliance (WEA) Brussels Treaty 1948*

The UK denounced,[541] as from 1 June 2010, the *Western European Alliance (WEA) Brussels Treaty 1948*[542] and all other instruments based on that treaty.

Treaty Action—Bilateral Defence Co-operation with France

- *Treaty Between the United Kingdom and the French Republic for Defence and Security Co-operation*

The UK and the Republic of France signed a new treaty for defence co-operation between themselves.[543] The treaty provides that:

1. The deployment and employment of the armed forces of each Party shall remain a national responsibility at all times.

538 *R (JS) (Sri Lanka)* v. *Secretary of State for the Home Department* [2010] UKSC 15, para 38.

539 Ibid., para 36.

540 Lord Hope stated that 'nor of course ... is military action against government forces to be regarded as a war crime'. Ibid., para 27.

541 See Cm 7952 (2010).

542 Treaty for Collaboration in Economic, Social and Cultural Matters and for Collective Self-Defence, signed 17 March 1948, 19 UNTS 52 (entered into force 25 August 1948).

543 Treaty for Defence and Security Co-operation, United Kingdom–France, signed 2 November 2010, Cm 7976 (2010).

2. … The Parties shall form, in advance of deployment or employment, a common understanding of the purpose and legal basis under international law for such deployment or employment and appropriate and complementary rules of engagement.
3. Appropriate command and control arrangements shall be agreed by both Parties for all bilateral deployments or operations.[544]

Government Policy—Future Character of Conflict

- *Securing Britain in an Age of Uncertainty: the Strategic Defence and Security Review*, Cm 7948 (2010)

The Strategic Defence and Security Review held by the British Government in 2010 considered the future character of conflict. It concluded that:

> Globalisation increases the likelihood of conflict involving non- and failed-state actors… asymmetric factors such as economic, cyber and proxy actions instead of direct military confrontation will play an increasing part, as both state and non-state adversaries seek an edge over those who overmatch them in conventional capacity. As a result, the difference between state-on-state warfare or irregular conflict are dramatically reducing.[545]

Government Policy—Small Arms and Light Weapons

- UK Foreign and Commonwealth Office, *Annual Report on Human Rights 2009*, Cm 7805 (2010)

The policy of the UK Government was stated as follows: 'The UK is committed to tackling the uncontrolled spread and accumulation of SALW [small arms and light weapons]'.[546]

Government Policy—Detention of Civilians in Afghanistan

- UK Foreign and Commonwealth Office, *Annual Report on Human Rights 2009*, Cm 7805 (2010)
- UK, *Parliamentary Debates*, House of Lords, 1 March 2010

The UK government made the following statement:

> In accordance with ISAF [International Stabilisation Assistance Force] guidelines, UK forces release captured persons or transfer them to the Afghan authorities within 96 h of detention. In exceptional circumstances and with ministerial approval, UK armed forces may detain beyond 96 h where necessary.[547]

---

[544] Ibid., Art 5.

[545] UK, Securing Britain in an Age of Uncertainty: The Strategic Defence and Security Review, Cm 7948 (2010) p 16.

[546] UK Foreign and Commonwealth Office, Annual Report on Human Rights 2009, Cm 7805 (2010) p 49.

[547] Ibid., p 85.

A Government Minister gave the following written answer:

> ISAF … in Afghanistan is not responsible for charging or prosecuting detainees. ISAF forces are mandated to either transfer detainees to the Afghan Government for prosecution through their judicial system or release them. As a sovereign nation, responsibility for prosecution lies with the Government of Afghanistan. The question of how many prisoners detained without charge or prospects of trial by the Governments of Afghanistan and the US is a matter for these Governments to answer… the UK will continue to work with the Afghan authorities to build capacity within their detention and judicial systems. The Government of Afghanistan will decide what review procedures should be put in place.[548]

Ministerial Statements—Gaza: Applicability of the Fourth Geneva Convention 1949

- UK, *Parliamentary Debates*, House of Commons, 5 February 2010

In response to a question in the House of Commons concerning the 'compatibility of Israel's blockade of Gaza with the provisions of the Fourth Geneva Convention' a Government minister gave a written response:

> We have serious concerns about the Israeli restrictions on Gaza and the impact they have on the lives of Gazans. Although there is no permanent physical Israeli presence in Gaza, given the significant control that Israel has over Gaza's borders, airspace and territorial waters, Israel retains obligations under the fourth Geneva Convention as an occupying power. The fourth Convention is clear that an occupying power must co-operate in allowing the passage and distribution of relief supplies. The restrictions currently imposed on the passage of relief supplies are, as we see it, a disproportionate response to the security threat.[549]

Ministerial Statements—Israeli Occupied Territories: House Demolitions

- UK, *Parliamentary Debates*, House of Commons, 7 June 2010

A Government minister made the following written statement:

> I would like to make clear, with few exceptions, house demolitions in occupied territory, including in East Jerusalem, are in direct contravention of article 53 of the fourth Geneva Convention.[550]

Ministerial Statements—Gaza: War Crimes

- UK, *Parliamentary Debates*, House of Commons, 29 March 2010

---

548 UK, Parliamentary Debates, House of Lords, 1 March 2010, Vol. 717, col. WA317.

549 UK, Parliamentary Debates, House of Commons, 5 February 2010, Vol. 505, col. 556W. See also UK, Parliamentary Debates, House of Commons, 7 June 2010, Vol. 511, col. 25W; UK, Parliamentary Debates, House of Lords, 18 November 2010, Vol. 715, col. WA233 concerning 'the need for further measures to secure change on the ground, including speeding up of imports for UN-led reconstruction, particularly schools'.

550 UK, Parliamentary Debates, House of Commons, 7 June 2010, Vol. 511, col. 27 W. See also UK, Parliamentary Debates, House of Lords, 18 November 2010, Vol. 715, col. WA237 in which a government minister, quoting from 'the UN humanitarian report to date (9 November)' stated that '315 Palestinian-owned structures have been demolished in East Jerusalem and Area C'.

The Secretary of State for Foreign and Commonwealth Affairs made the following comment to a petition:

> Although under the Geneva Conventions Act the UK has jurisdiction to prosecute war crimes in an international conflict, we consider that it is the primary responsibility of the parties involved to investigate such allegations. The Report of the UN Human Rights Council-mandated Fact-Finding Mission on Gaza (the Goldstone Report) and the UN General Assembly also made it clear that the parties should do so. From the outset we have called for the very serious allegations about conduct of the Gaza conflict by both sides to be impartially investigated by the parties to the conflict.[551]

Ministerial Statements—War Crimes Allegation: Sri Lanka
- UK, *Parliamentary Debates*, House of Lords, 18 November 2010

A government Minister made the following written statement:

> we have called for an independent and credible process to examine allegations of war crimes by both sides in Sri Lanka … under international law, it is the primary responsibility of the state against whose forces allegations are made to investigate possible war crimes committed by its own forces.[552]

Ministerial Statements—Law of Armed Conflict Training
- UK, *Parliamentary Debates*, House of Commons, 8 September 2010

A government Minister issued the following written statement:

> In addition to annual Law of Armed Conflict training, all Service personnel are required to complete mandatory pre-deployment training. An element of these training activities is specific to the rules of engagement for a given location and the requirements and responsibilities for compliance with the Geneva Conventions and their additional protocols. Service personnel will not be deployed to an area of conflict without knowing how they may engage an enemy and what international laws their actions are subject to.[553]

PETER ROWE

UNITED STATES OF AMERICA[554]

Official Legal Positions—International Criminal Court; Detention and Targeting of Hostile Belligerents

---

[551] UK, Parliamentary Debates, House of Commons, 29 March 2010, Vol. 507, col. 17P.

[552] UK, Parliamentary Debates, House of Lords, 18 November 2010, Vol. 715, col. WA244. See also UK, Parliamentary Debates, House of Commons, 16 March 2010, Vol. 507, col. 791W in which the relevant government minister stated that: officials from the Foreign and Commonwealth Office hold regular discussions with US officials on the need for a credible process to address reports of violations of international humanitarian law by both sides during the military conflict in northern Sri Lanka. We believe this could play an important role towards national reconciliation.

[553] UK, Parliamentary Debates, House of Commons, 8 September 2010, Vol. 515, col. 539W.

[554] Information and commentaries by Burrus M. Carnahan, Professorial Lecturer in Law, The George Washington University, Washington, DC, USA and Lieutenant Colonel Chris Jenks, United States Army, Judge Advocate Generals' Corps. The entry does not necessarily reflect the views of the Judge Advocate General's Corps, the United States Army, or the Department of Defense.

- Speech of Harold Koh, Legal Adviser, US Department of State, 'The Obama Administration and International Law', 25 March 2010, <http://www.state.gov/s/l/releases/remarks/139119.htm>

In March 2010, the Legal Adviser to the Department of State, Harold Koh, delivered an address to the annual meeting of the American Society of International Law in Washington, DC. The Society is the leading professional organization of international law practitioners and academics in the United States, and the Legal Adviser is the principal authority on international law within the US government. Historically, statements by the Legal Adviser to the Society's annual meeting have been used to expound authoritative positions of the US on international legal issues.

On this occasion, Mr Koh addressed the position of the current administration on three major issues—the International Criminal Court (ICC), the holding of detainees at the Guantánamo Naval Base in Cuba, and drone attacks on individuals believed to be terrorist leaders. Without committing the US to become a party to the ICC Statute, Mr. Koh expressed a more positive policy toward the Court than had been adopted by previous administrations:

> Even as a non-State party, the United States believes that it can be a valuable partner and ally in the cause of advancing international justice. The Obama Administration has been actively looking at ways that the U.S. can, consistent with U.S. law, assist the ICC in fulfilling its historic charge of providing justice to those who have endured crimes of epic savagery and scope. And as Ambassador Rapp announced in New York, we would like to meet with the Prosecutor at the ICC to examine whether there are specific ways that the United States might be able to support the particular prosecutions that are already underway in the Democratic Republic of Congo, Sudan, Central African Republic, and Uganda.

Mr Koh's statement on this occasion was later supplemented by a more nuanced expression of support for the ICC in the UN Security Council, where the US representative noted that '[t]he primary responsibility for ensuring accountability' for violations of international humanitarian law still "lies with states", but that the international community must also "be prepared to take action against those who violate international humanitarian law"'. In this regard, she noted that the 'International Criminal Court plays a key role in bringing perpetrators of the worst atrocities to justice'.[555]

In continuity with previous US administrations, Mr Koh expressed continuing opposition to adopting a definition of the crime of aggression for the ICC:

> In particular, we are concerned that adopting a definition of aggression at this point in the court's history could divert the ICC from its core mission, and potentially politicize and

[555] R. DiCarlo, 'Remarks by Ambassador Rosemary DiCarlo, U.S. Deputy Permanent Representative to the United Nations, during a Security Council Debate on the Protection of Civilians' (Speech delivered at New York, 22 November 2010), <http://usun.state.gov/briefing/statements/2010/151752.htm>.

> weaken this young institution. Among the States Parties we found strongly held, yet divergent, views on many fundamental and unresolved questions.

Mr Koh then turned to what he referred to as 'the law of 9/11', the controversial legal policies arising from the US response to the attacks on that date against the World Trade Center and the Pentagon. While noting that the government was still committed to closing the detention facility at Guantánamo, he defended continued confinement of those being held there, based on the international laws of war:

> As a nation at war, we must comply with the laws of war, but detention of enemy belligerents to prevent them from returning to hostilities is a well-recognized feature of the conduct of armed conflict, as the drafters of Common Article 3 and Additional Protocol II recognized …

Invoking Common Article 3 and *Protocol Additional to the Geneva Conventions of 12 August 1949, and relating to the Protection of Victims of non-International Armed Conflicts* (*Protocol II*)[556] firmly establishes that the Obama administration regards its operations against Al Qaida, the Taliban and similar organizations as part of a non-international armed conflict. The reference to Additional Protocol II is rather unusual for an American official, since the US is not a party to that treaty. However, the Protocol had been submitted to the US Senate for advice and consent to ratification by President Ronald Reagan in 1987, and no US administration has ever expressed opposition to its eventual ratification.

Mr Koh made it clear that the decision to continue detention of specific individuals was reached on a case-by-case basis, based on their relationship to non-state organizations hostile to the US:

> In sum, we have based our authority to detain … on whether the factual record in the particular case meets the legal standard. This includes, but is not limited to, whether an individual joined with or became part of al Qaeda or Taliban forces or associated forces, which can be demonstrated by relevant evidence of formal or functional membership, which may include an oath of loyalty, training with al Qaeda, or taking positions with enemy forces. Often these factors operate in combination. While we disagree with the International Committee of the Red Cross on some of the particulars, our general approach of looking at 'functional' membership in an armed group has been endorsed not only by the federal courts, but also is consistent with the approach taken in the targeting context by the ICRC in its recent study on Direct Participation in Hostilities.

The International Committee of the Red Cross study Mr Koh referred to concluded that '[i]n non-international armed conflict, organized armed groups constitute the armed forces of a non-State party to the conflict and consist only of individuals whose continuous function it is to take a direct part in hostilities ("continuous combat function")'.[557]

---

[556] Opened for signature 8 June 1977, 1125 UNTS 609 (entered into force 7 December 1978) (Additional Protocol II).

[557] International Committee of the Red Cross, Interpretive Guidance on the Notion of Direct Participation in Hostilities under International Humanitarian Law (2009) p 16.

The increased use of drones to attack and kill specific targeted persons has been one of the most controversial policies of the Obama Administration. Mr Koh based his defense of this practice both on the existence of an armed conflict *and* on the inherent right to self-defense:

> As ... a matter of international law, the United States is in an armed conflict with al Qaeda, as well as the Taliban and associated forces, in response to the horrific 9/11 attacks, and may use force consistent with its inherent right to self-defense under international law.

This approach has been criticized as blurring, rather than clarifying, the legal basis for attacking individual members of armed groups. The following critique is typical:

> Although Koh clearly refers to an ongoing armed conflict, he also offers the broader notion of self-defence as an alternative justification ... What is striking in Koh's speech is that the existence of an armed conflict and the broader right of self-defence are both offered as possible justifications without any attempt to delineate the boundary between the two: it is not clear how far Koh is claiming that the purported armed conflict against al-Qaeda and the Taliban extends. Does it cover military actions in Pakistan? Somalia and Yemen? The ambiguity here is consistent with the continued lack of a definitive statement from the administration about the precise legal contours of its fight against al-Qaeda ...[558]

Whether based on self-defense or on the existence of an armed conflict, Mr Koh argued that US drone strikes against individuals were lawful under international humanitarian law:

> This Administration has carefully reviewed the rules governing targeting operations to ensure that these operations are conducted consistently with law of war principles, including:
>
> First, the principle of *distinction*, which requires that attacks be limited to military objectives and that civilians or civilian objects shall not be the object of the attack; and
>
> Second, the principle of *proportionality*, which prohibits attacks that may be expected to cause incidental loss of civilian life, injury to civilians, damage to civilian objects, or a combination thereof, that would be excessive in relation to the concrete and direct military advantage anticipated.

Finally, he briefly addressed specific objections to targeting individuals under international and US domestic law. Of the three critiques based on international law, the first two were quickly disposed of:

> First, some have suggested that the very act of targeting a particular leader of an enemy force in an armed conflict must violate the laws of war. But individuals who are part of such an armed group are belligerents and, therefore, lawful targets under international law.
>
> ...
>
> Second, some have challenged *the very use of advanced weapons systems*, such as unmanned aerial vehicles, for lethal operations. But the rules that govern targeting do not turn on the type of weapon system used, and there is no prohibition under the laws of war on the use of technologically advanced weapons systems in armed conflict.

---

558 A. Dworkin, 'Obama Administration Announces Legal Basis for Drone Attacks' (30 March 2010), <www.crimesofwar.org>.

Here Mr Koh appears to be on firm legal ground. Weapons are not presumptively unlawful merely because they are new, and the US Department of Defense requires the armed forces to conduct a legal review of all new weapon systems to ensure that they comply with international humanitarian law.[559] Targeting of individual enemies is an accepted method of warfare, and is not unlawful unless perfidy or treachery is involved.[560]

The response to the final objection is somewhat more problematic:

> Third, some have argued that the use of lethal force against specific individuals fails to provide adequate process and thus constitutes *unlawful extrajudicial killing*. But a state that is engaged in an armed conflict or in legitimate self-defense is not required to provide targets with legal process before the state may use lethal force ... In my experience, the principles of distinction and proportionality that the United States applies are ... implemented rigorously throughout the planning and execution of lethal operations to ensure that such operations are conducted in accordance with all applicable law.

This objection arises from tension between international humanitarian law, which governs armed conflicts, and international human rights law, which may apply both in war and peace. It has been argued that targeting individuals is a form of extrajudicial killing, prohibited by human rights law.

> There is a strong argument that, when the state has sufficient control to target individuals outside battlefield conditions, human rights principles must also form part of the equation in determining when the deliberate taking of life is legitimate. Although the United States has historically resisted the idea that human rights apply outside a state's own territory or during armed conflict, these positions are now rejected by mainstream legal opinion around the world, though there is little consensus about the precise way that human rights obligations apply in such circumstances. Human rights principles would impose a much higher threshold for the use of lethal force than is generally thought to apply under the laws of armed conflict: for instance, the taking of life would have to be absolutely necessary in every case, rather than merely being allowed under the military law concepts of distinction and proportionality.[561]

In fact, the current US position is that both humanitarian law and human rights law may apply during armed conflict, but that 'the applicable rules for the protection of individuals and conduct of hostilities in armed conflict outside a nation's territory are typically found in international humanitarian law'.[562] This approach is similar to that adopted by the International Court of Justice in its advisory opinion on the

---

559 The review process was initiated by a 1974 Department of Defense Instruction to the armed forces. The contents of the Instruction can be found in the Digest of United States Practice in International Law 1974 (Department of State Publication 8809) pp 710–711.

560 See the extensive Memorandum of Law on assassination issued on 2 November 1989, by the International Law Branch of the Office of the Judge Advocate General, US Army. See Cumulative Digest of United States Practice in International Law 1981–1988 (Department of State Publication 10120) Vol. III, pp 3411–3421.

561 Dworkin, supra n. 558.

562 'Explanation of Vote by a US Advisor on the Extrajudicial Summary or Arbitrary Executions Resolution (A/C.3/65/L.29), UN General Assembly Third Committee' (16 November 2010), <http://usun.state.gov/briefing/statements/2010/151133.htm>.

use of nuclear weapons. Conceding that in principle 'the right not arbitrarily to be deprived of one's life applies also in hostilities,' the Court then stated that in armed conflict '[t]he test of what is an arbitrary deprivation of life' is 'to be determined by the applicable *lex specialis*, namely, the law applicable in armed conflict which is designed to regulate the conduct of hostilities'.[563]

The most noted critic of drone strikes as extrajudicial killing is Philip Alston, the United Nations Special Rapporteur on extrajudicial, summary or arbitrary executions. Alston has attacked targeted killing by the US, Israel and Russia as violations of human rights law, and in particular has called for more 'transparency and accountability' in the operation of these programs:

> Meeting the legal requirements of transparency and accountability for targeted killing need not impose an onerous burden upon the States concerned. The minimum requirements are: disclosure of the legal criteria for who can be targeted and killed; the legal justification for where in the world, and when, such killings are permitted to occur; the precautions in place to ensure that the killings are legal; and what follow-up there is when civilians are illegally killed.[564]

Mr Alston makes it easy to understand why Legal Adviser Koh, along with other government officials, prefers to look primarily to international humanitarian law, or the law of war, rather than human rights law, to regulate military operations. Even if the US government published all the information and standards Alston calls for, it is difficult to believe that this information would not then become the subject of even more criticism for not meeting other human rights standards, e.g., by failing to provide for a hearing before a neutral magistrate, or by failing to demonstrate in every case that capture, rather than killing, was impossible. More stringent standards would be called for, and eventually the published criteria would be used by potential targets to evade attack.

Complete 'transparency' in the planning and conduct of military operations is something no government at war has ever tolerated. International humanitarian law does not require transparency in conducting attacks, with the possible exception of Art. 57(c) of *Protocol Additional to the Geneva Conventions of 12 August 1949, and relating to the Protection of Victims of International Armed Conflicts* (Protocol I),[565] which states that 'effective advance warning shall be given of attacks which may affect the civilian population'. Even that limited call for transparency is inapplicable if the attacker finds that 'circumstances do not permit'. For an example of a military situation where circumstances may permit, or even require, 'transparency', see General McChrystal's Tactical Directive on night raids in Afghanistan, discussed elsewhere in this report.

---

[563] Legality of the Use by a State of Nuclear Weapons in Armed Conflict, Advisory Opinion, ICJ Rep., 1996, p 26, para 25.

[564] Interim report of the Special Rapporteur on extrajudicial, summary or arbitrary executions, UN Doc A/65/321, 23 August 2010, para 16.

[565] Opened for signature 8 June 1977, 1125 UNTS 3 (entered into force 7 December 1978) (Additional Protocol I).

Cases—US Supreme Court—Sovereign and Official Immunity for Violations of International Humanitarian Law

- *Samantar* v. *Yousuf*, 560 US (2010), 130 S. Ct. 2278, <http://www.supremecourt.gov/opinions/09pdf/08-1555.pdf>

Mohamed Ali Samantar was the First Vice President and Minister of Defense of Somalia from 1980 to 1986, and from 1987 to 1990 he served as its Prime Minister. He later moved to the US, where he was sued by several Somalis who alleged that while holding these offices he had authorized torture and extrajudicial killing of either themselves or members of their families. In defense, Samatar argued that the US courts lacked jurisdiction under the *Foreign Sovereign Immunities Act* of 1976 (FSIA).[566]

Prior to passage of the FSIA, whenever the immunity from suit of a foreign government had come into issue, US courts had requested advice from the State Department on a case by case basis. This practice tended to politicize recognition of sovereign immunity, and the FSIA was enacted to remove the executive branch of the US government from the process by codifying the customary international law of sovereign immunity as recognized by the US. In essence, the FSIA permits lawsuits against foreign sovereigns for commercial activity, but bars suits based on the governmental functions of a foreign state or 'an agency or instrumentality of a foreign state'. Samantar argued that, as First Vice President, Minister of Defense and Prime Minister, he had acted as an agency or instrumentality of the Somali state.

Intermediate appellate courts had reached conflicting conclusions on whether the FSIA granted immunity to individual foreign officials. The Supreme Court settled the issue by holding that the FSIA did not apply to suits against foreign officials in their personal capacities, and remanded the case to the trial court for further proceedings. The Court noted that Samantar might still be immune from suit under the common law doctrine of 'foreign official immunity', but expressly refrained from ruling on the applicability of that defense to the acts of torture and extrajudicial killing alleged here.

Cases—US Supreme Court—Punishing Aid to 'Terrorist Organizations'

- *Holder* v. *Humanitarian Law Project*, 561 US (2010), 130 S. Ct. 2705, <http://www.supremecourt.gov/opinions/09pdf/08-1498.pdf>

Under US law it is a crime to provide 'material support or resources' to any group designated by the Secretary of State as a 'foreign terrorist organization'.[567] The term 'material support or resources' is broadly defined as:

> any property, tangible or intangible, or service, including currency or monetary instruments or financial securities, financial services, lodging, training, expert advice or assistance, safe houses, false documentation or identification, communications equipment,

[566] 28 USC §§1330, 1602 et seq.

[567] 18 USC §2339B.

> facilities, weapons, lethal substances, explosives, personnel … and transportation, except medicine or religious materials.

In 1997, the Secretary so designated 30 groups, including the Kurdistan Workers' Party (also known as the Partiya Karkeran Kurdistan, or PKK) and the Liberation Tigers of Tamil Eelam (LTTE). Thereafter, several individuals and groups, claiming that they wanted to provide the PKK and LTTE with money, other tangible aid, legal training and political advocacy in support of the humanitarian and political activity of those organizations, sued the US to prevent the application of this statue to the proposed activities. The plaintiffs claimed that the statute was constitutionally vague, and that its application to the non-terrorist activities of the PKK and LTTE would infringe the plaintiffs' rights to freedom of speech and association under the US Constitution. In particular, the plaintiffs proposed to 'train members of [the] PKK on how to use humanitarian and international law to peacefully resolve disputes', and to 'teach PKK members how to petition various representative bodies such as the United Nations for relief'.

The Supreme Court rejected the plaintiffs' claims, and held that Congress had the constitutional power to prohibit the proposed support to the PKK and LTTE. As to the prohibition on monetary support, the Court noted that 'money is fungible', and that funds 'raised ostensibly for charitable purposes have in the past been redirected by some terrorist groups to fund the purchase of arms and explosives'. Training in international law and dispute settlement could also be abused by these groups.

> It is wholly foreseeable that the PKK could use the 'specific skill[s]' that plaintiffs propose to impart … as part of a broader strategy to promote terrorism. The PKK could, for example, pursue peaceful negotiation as a means of buying time to recover from short-term setbacks, lulling opponents into complacency, and ultimately preparing for renewed attacks. … A foreign terrorist organization introduced to the structures of the international legal system might use the information to threaten, manipulate, and disrupt. This possibility is real, not remote.

The Court saw a similar danger in teaching the PKK techniques to obtain 'relief', a term 'which plaintiffs never define with any specificity, and which could readily include monetary aid'.

Three of the nine justices dissented. The majority responded as follows:

> The dissent seems unwilling to entertain the prospect that training and advising a designated foreign terrorist organization on how to take advantage of international entities might benefit that organization in a way that facilitates its terrorist activities. In the dissent's world, such training is all to the good. Congress and the Executive, however, have concluded that we live in a different world: one in which the designated foreign terrorist organizations 'are so tainted by their criminal conduct that any contribution to such an organization facilitates that conduct'.

However, the majority also warned the government that the Court might find that the statute had been abused in other situations:

> All this is not to say that any future applications of the material-support statute to speech or advocacy will survive [constitutional] scrutiny. It is also not to say that any other statute

> relating to speech and terrorism would satisfy the First Amendment [to the US Constitution]. In particular, we in no way suggest that a regulation of independent speech would pass constitutional muster, even if the Government were to show that such speech benefits foreign terrorist organizations. We also do not suggest that Congress could extend the same prohibition on material support at issue here to domestic organizations. We simply hold that, in prohibiting the particular forms of support that plaintiffs seek to provide to foreign terrorist groups, [this statute] does not violate the freedom of speech.

Government Policy—Detention and Punishment of Hostile Belligerents

- Final Report of the Guantánamo Review Task Force, 22 January 2010, <http://www.justice.gov/ag/guantanamo-review-final-report.pdf>

As part of his effort to close the detention facility at Guantánamo, on 22 January 2009, President Obama ordered the creation of a high-level executive task force to review the cases of all the detainees held there and recommend appropriate action in each case. Chaired by the Attorney General, the task force included representatives of the Department of Defense, the Director of National Intelligence, the Department of State, the Joint Chiefs of Staff of the armed forces, and the Department of Homeland Security. The task force reached its decisions by unanimous consent. Its final report was submitted on 22 January 2010, exactly 1 year after its establishment.

Of the 240 individuals held at the Guantánamo Naval Base, the task force approved the transfer of 126 to other countries, either their home countries or third states willing to accept them. Prosecution was initially found to be appropriate in 44 cases. By the time of the final report, eight of these cases had been disposed of without prosecution, leaving 36 still subject to trial, either before a civilian court for violations of US criminal statutes, or before a military commission for 'offenses under the laws of war'.

Forty-eight detainees were 'determined to be too dangerous to transfer but not feasible for prosecution'. These would continue to be held in US custody without trial. The task force found that these 48 met 'three core criteria' for continued detention:

> First, the totality of available information—including credible information that might not be admissible in a criminal prosecution—indicated that the detainee poses a high level of threat that cannot be mitigated sufficiently except through continued detention; second, prosecution of the detainee in a federal criminal court or a military commission did not appear feasible; and third, notwithstanding the infeasibility of criminal prosecution, there is a lawful basis for the detainee's detention ...[568]

The task force based its decisions on the lawfulness of continued detention on the 'Authorization for Use of Military Force' (AUMF) passed by the US Congress in response to the 11 September 2001 attacks, and on a holding by the US Supreme Court that the AUMF gave the government the power 'to capture and detain

[568] Final Report of the Guantánamo Review Task Force (22 January 2010) p 23.

combatants' to prevent them from returning to the field of battle and taking up arms once again.[569]

Finally, 30 detainees from Yemen were approved for 'conditional' continued detention. The President had suspended detainee transfers to Yemen based on concerns over the security conditions in that country. These Yemenis might be returned to their home country after those concerns are resolved at some time in the future.

Government Policy—Use of Nuclear Weapons

- Department of Defense, *Nuclear Posture Review Report*, April 2010, <http://www.defense.gov/npr>

During the negotiation of the Nuclear Non-Proliferation Treaty[570] (NPT) in the UN Eighteen-Nation Disarmament Committee, countries without nuclear weapons (non-nuclear weapon states) sought assurances from the nuclear powers (nuclear weapon states) that, if they gave up the right to acquire nuclear weapons for themselves, nuclear weapons would not be used against them. Such a commitment was not included in the text of the NPT, but the five nuclear weapon states recognized in the NPT (China, France, the Soviet Union, the United Kingdom and the US) later issued policy statements, referred to as 'negative security assurances', in an effort to meet this demand from the non-nuclear weapon states party to the Treaty.

The first negative security assurance statement was issued by the US at the 1978 UN General Assembly Special Session on Disarmament. Heavily influenced by the Cold War environment, it stated that the US would not use nuclear weapons against a non-nuclear weapon state party to the NPT 'except in the case of an … attack on the United States, its territories, its armed forces or other troops, its allies, or on a State towards which it has a security commitment, carried out or sustained by such a non-nuclear-weapon State in association or alliance with a nuclear-weapon State'. This exception referred to the non-nuclear weapon state allies of the Soviet Union in the Warsaw Pact. If the non-nuclear weapon state members of the Warsaw Pact attacked the NATO allies in Western Europe, the US had expressly retained the option of using tactical nuclear weapons against them. The other nuclear weapon state members of NATO, France and the UK, later issued similar negative security assurance statements.

The US most recently reaffirmed its negative security assurance policy in 1995. Although never included in its negative security assurance statements to NPT parties, in the past the US has also taken the position that nuclear weapons might be used in response to an attack with chemical or biological weapons.

The Soviet Union's negative security assurance statement was similarly influenced by the Cold War. It promised not to attack NPT non-nuclear weapon states

---

569 Ibid., pp 7–8.

570 Treaty on the Non-Proliferation of Nuclear Weapons, opened for signature 1 July 1968, 729 UNTS 161 (entered into force 5 March 1970).

with nuclear weapons, unless they had nuclear weapons on their territory, an obvious attempt to discourage non-nuclear weapon state NATO members from allowing the US to station nuclear weapons in their countries. After the dissolution of the Warsaw Pact and the fall of the Soviet Union, the Russian Federation announced a negative security assurance policy similar to that of the NATO powers.

In April 2010, the first major revision of the US negative security assurance policy in over 30 years was announced in the *Nuclear Posture Review Report*. The Report, issued by the Secretary of Defense in consultation with the Secretaries of State and Energy, is intended to be a comprehensive assessment and statement of US nuclear weapons policy and strategy for the foreseeable future. The last *Nuclear Posture Review Report* had been issued in 2001.

After reviewing the old negative security assurance policy, the *Report* notes that 'after the United States gave up its own chemical and biological weapons (CBW) pursuant to international treaties (while some states continued to possess or pursue them) the United States reserved the right to employ nuclear weapons to deter CBW attack on the United States and its allies and partners'. Recently, however, 'improvements in missile defenses and counter-weapons of mass destruction capabilities have strengthened deterrence and defense against CBW attack'.

> Given these developments, the role of U.S. nuclear weapons to deter and respond to non-nuclear attacks—conventional, biological, or chemical—has declined significantly. To that end, the United States is now prepared to strengthen its long-standing 'negative security assurance' by declaring that the United States will not use or threaten to use nuclear weapons against non-nuclear weapons states that are party to the Nuclear Non-Proliferation Treaty (NPT) and in compliance with their nuclear non-proliferation obligations.[571]

According to news reports, US officials have identified Iran and North Korea as countries not in compliance with nuclear non-proliferation obligations. As stated in the *Report*, the US would not regard these countries as covered by the new policy.[572]

> In the case of countries not covered by this assurance—states that possess nuclear weapons and states not in compliance with their nuclear non-proliferation obligations—there remains a narrow range of contingencies in which U.S. nuclear weapons may still play a role in deterring a conventional or CBW attack against the United States or its allies and partners.[573]

---

[571] Department of Defense, Nuclear Posture Review Report (April 2010) p 15.

[572] D. Sanger and P. Baker, 'Obama Limits When U.S. Would Use Nuclear Arms', *The New York Times* (New York, US) 6 April 2010, <http://www.nytimes.com/2010/04/06/world/06arms.html>; 'All bets are off if US under biological attack, warns Hillary Clinton', *NEWS.COM.AU* (Australia) 12 April 2010, <http://www.news.com.au/world/all-bets-are-off-if-us-under-biological-attack-warns-hillary-clinton/story-e6frfkyi-1225852529473>.

[573] Department of Defense, supra n. 571, p 16.

The US also reserves the option of reconsidering its policy if attacked or threatened with biological weapon:

> Given the catastrophic potential of biological weapons and the rapid pace of bio-technology development, the United States reserves the right to make any adjustment in the assurance that may be warranted by the evolution and proliferation of the biological weapons threat and U.S. capacities to counter that threat.[574]

'If we can prove that a biological attack originated in a country that attacked us, then all bets are off', Secretary of State Hillary Clinton has been quoted as saying in an interview on American television.[575]

Government Policy—Protection of Civilians in Afghanistan

- International Security Assistance Force (ISAF) Public Information Office News Release 5 March 2010, *ISAF Issues Guidance on Night Raids in Afghanistan*, <http://www.centcom.mil/en/press-releases/isaf-issues-guidance-on-night-raids-in-afghanistan.html>
- COMISAF's Counterinsurgency Guidance, 1 August 2010, <https://afghancoin.harmonieweb.org/Lists/Announcements/Attachments/7/100801_COMISAF_COIN_Guidance.pdf>
- ISAF Public Information Office News Release, 4 August 2010, *Updated Tactical Directive: Emphasizes 'Disciplined Use of Force'*. <http://www.isaf.nato.int/article/isaf-releases/updated-tactical-directive-emphasizes-disciplined-use-of-force.html>

As the US armed forces draw down from their combat role in Iraq, increased resources and attention have been devoted to the conflict in Afghanistan. During 2010, the Commanding Generals of US Forces—Afghanistan, Stanley McChrystal and his successor in command David Petraeus—issued several directives stressing the importance of respecting and protecting the civilian population. Some of these directives are classified, but the unclassified portions have been published in news releases from the International Security Assistance Force Public Information Office. The Commanding General, US Forces–Afghanistan also serves as Commander of the NATO International Security Assistance Force, or ISAF.

In March, General McChrystal issued a new Tactical Directive governing the conduct of night raids by all ISAF units operating in Afghanistan. A 'night raid' was defined as 'any offensive operation involving entry into a compound, residence, building or structure that occurs in the period between nautical twilight and nautical dawn'. Unclassified portions of the Tactical Directive include the following:

> We know from experience that operations conducted at night are an essential component of our campaign delivering often decisive effects in disrupting and defeating some of the

[574] Ibid.

[575] 'All bets are off if US under biological attack, warns Hillary Clinton', supra n. 572.

> most dangerous insurgent groups. More importantly, the data supports that night raids reduce the potential for civilian casualties.
>
> That said, in the Afghan culture, a man's home is more than just his residence. It represents his family and protecting it is closely intertwined with his honor. He has been conditioned to respond aggressively in defense of his home and his guests whenever he perceives his home or honor is threatened. In a similar situation, most of us would do the same. This reaction is compounded when our forces invade his home at night, particularly when women are present. Instinctive responses to defend his home and family are sometimes interpreted as insurgent acts, with tragic results. Even when there is no damage or injuries, Afghans can feel deeply violated and dishonored, making winning their support that much more difficult.
>
> Despite their effectiveness and operational value, night raids come at a steep cost in terms of the perceptions of the Afghan people. The myths, distortions and propaganda arising out of night raids often have little to do with the reality—few Afghans have been directly affected by night raids, but nearly every Afghan I talk to mentions them as the single greatest irritant. Night raids must be conducted with even greater care, additional constraints, and standardization throughout Afghanistan.
>
> The first and most preferable course of action is to explore all other feasible options before effecting a night raid that targets compounds and residences.
>
> ...
>
> To minimize the ability of the insurgency to foster resentment and ill-will, the use of night raids must be tactically sound, judiciously used, and as transparent as possible. If possible, local elders should be incorporated into the process to ensure that the actual facts are related to the local populace.

On 1 August 2010, shortly after he had taken command in Afghanistan, General Petraeus issued an unclassified four-page letter directed to all 'Soldiers, Sailors, Airmen, Marines, and Civilians of NATO ISAF and US Forces–Afghanistan', setting out the General's guidance on conducting counter-insurgency operations. The guidance provided in the letter includes the following:

> *Secure and serve the population.* The decisive terrain is the human terrain. The people are the center of gravity. Only by providing them security and earning their trust and confidence can the Afghan government and ISAF prevail.
>
> ...
>
> *Fight hard and fight with discipline.* Hunt the enemy aggressively, but use only the firepower needed to win a fight. We can't win without fighting, but we also cannot kill or capture our way to victory. Moreover, if we kill civilians or damage their property in the course of our operations, we will create more enemies than our operations eliminate. That's exactly what the Taliban want. Don't fall into their trap. We must continue our efforts to reduce civilian casualties to an absolute minimum.
>
> ...
>
> *Be a good guest.* Treat the Afghan people and their property with respect. Think about how we drive, how we patrol, how we relate to people, and how we help the community. View our actions through the eyes of the Afghans and, together with our partners, consult with elders before pursuing new initiatives and operations.

General Petraeus also issued a revised Tactical Directive on 1 August 2010, providing additional guidance on the use of force during operations under his command. Subordinate commanders were instructed not to restrict this guidance without General Petraeus' approval. Unclassified portions of the Directive include the following guidance:

> We must continue—indeed, redouble—our efforts to reduce the loss of innocent civilian life to an absolute minimum. *Every Afghan civilian death diminishes our cause.* If we use excessive force or operate contrary to our counterinsurgency principles, tactical victories may prove to be strategic setbacks.[576]
>
> ...
>
> Prior to the use of fires [e.g., artillery or air strikes], the commander approving the strike must determine that no civilians are present. If unable to assess the risk of civilian presence, fires are prohibited, except under ... two conditions ...

The specific conditions were deleted from the press release and remain classified for reasons of operational security; however, they reportedly relate to the risk to ISAF and Afghan forces in particular situations.

> Protecting the Afghan people does require killing, capturing, or turning the insurgents ... But we must fight with great discipline and tactical patience. We must balance our pursuit of the enemy with our efforts to minimize loss of innocent civilian life, and with our obligation to protect our troops ... In so doing, however, we must remember that it is a moral imperative both to protect Afghan civilians and to bring all assets to bear to protect our men and women in uniform and the Afghan security forces with whom we are fighting shoulder-to-shoulder when they are in a tough spot.

Successfully balancing the duty to protect civilians against the need to protect friendly forces will obviously require good judgment and great discretion on the part of junior officers in the field.

BURRUS M. CARNAHAN[577]

Government Reports—Afghanistan Casualties

- Congressional Research Service, *Afghanistan Casualties: Military Forces and Civilians*, R41084 (3 February 2011)[578]

The Congressional Research Service issues a report which collects statistics from a variety of sources on casualties from Operation Enduring Freedom in Afghanistan. The report, which is periodically updated, reflects different categories of casualties, including American, coalition partners, and parses out Afghan casualties between Afghan civilians, the Afghan national army, and the Afghan national police.

Cases—United States Military Justice System

In 2010, the United States military remained deployed in two combat theatres: Iraq as part of Operation New Dawn; and Afghanistan as part of Operation Enduring Freedom. Over the course of 2010 the number of US service members in each

576 Emphasis in original.

577 Information and commentaries by Burrus M. Carnahan, Professorial Lecturer in Law, The George Washington University, Washington, DC, USA.

578 S. Chesser, 'Afghanistan Casualties: Military Forces and Civilians' (Congressional Research Services, 3 February 2011), <http://www.fas.org/sgp/crs/natsec/R41084.pdf>.

theatre inverted from years past such that there is now a greater number deployed to and in support of operations in Afghanistan than in Iraq.

Pinpointing examples of US enforcement of its obligations under various international humanitarian law agreements and treaties is challenging, both legally and practically. Legally there are questions of how the conflicts are characterized and which agreements apply.[579] Practically, the US military will ordinarily charge a person subject to the *Uniform Code of Military Justice* with a specific violation of that code[580] rather than a violation of the law of war.[581]

The military cases which follow are illustrative of how the US utilizes its military justice system where the victim is either Afghani or Iraqi and the offense occurred during an operational combat deployment. By way of brief introduction, US policy is that 'efforts should be made to maximize the exercise of court-martial jurisdiction over persons subject to the [UCMJ] to the extent possible'.[582] As a result, the cases which follow are examples of just that—the exercise of court-martial jurisdiction by the US military over its service members (as opposed to jurisdiction exercised by US Federal or State Courts).

Service members who receive a punitive discharge (meaning the characterization of the military service is either a bad conduct or a dishonorable discharge) and/or are sentenced to 180 days or more confinement are entitled to appellate review of their court-martial by a service specific appellate court. Subject to those qualifiers, that appeal is one of right. Following action by a service appellate court, service members may petition for review by first the Court of Appeals for the Armed Forces (CAAF) and then by the United States Supreme Court although, both those levels of appeal are discretionary.

---

[579] The US answer is largely policy based. Pursuant to Department of Defense Directive 2311.01E, 'DoD Law of War Program', it is DoD policy that 'members of DoD components comply with the law of war during all armed conflicts however such conflicts are characterized, and in all other military operations', §4.1. Under this policy, the law of war is defined as 'encompass[ing] all international law for the conduct of hostilities binding on the United States or its individual citizens, including treaties and international agreements to which the United States is a party, and applicable customary international law', §3.1. See <http://www.fas.org/irp/doddir/dod/d2311_01e.pdf>. This policy generally results in the application of international armed conflict standards of conduct in all conflicts, 'no matter how characterized.' This approach also provides criminal sanctions for those actions that could be characterized as 'grave breaches' of the Geneva Conventions or Common Article 3 [accord the U.S. War Crimes Act 18 USC 2441]; other violations of the law of armed conflict may result in criminal or administrative sanctions: see, e.g., Geneva Convention Relative to the Protection of Civilian Persons in Time of War, opened for signature 12 August 1949, 75 UNTS 287, Art. 146 (entered into force 21 October 1950), which describes the requirement for 'suppression of all acts contrary to the … convention'.

[580] Uniform Code of Military Justice, 10 USC §801 et seq (UCMJ), <http://www.law.cornell.edu/uscode/usc_sup_01_10_10_A_20_II_30_47.html>.

[581] Rule for Court Martial 307(c)(2) Charge (discussion).

[582] Rule for Court Martial 201(d) Exclusive and nonexclusive jurisdiction (discussion).

United States Air Force

- *United States* v. *Flores* [2010] 69 M.J. 651 United States Air Force Court of Criminal Appeals

Flores, a non-commissioned officer in the US Air Force, was court-martialed in 2007 for misconduct committed while serving as a detention facility guard at Camp Bucca, Iraq. Then Staff Sergeant Flores' misconduct included 'blatant violations'[583] of lawful orders which prohibited photographing and videotaping detainees and fraternizing with or acting with undue familiarity towards any detainee. Flores was a 'quad shift leader and was entrusted with up to 250 detainees … [a]s such, she was responsible for ensuring that the detainees in her quad were treated with dignity and respect and that the detainees received food, medical care, and other support'.[584] Flores was charged with four specifications of failure to obey a lawful order and two specifications of false official statement in violation of the UCMJ. She pled guilty and was found guilty by a military judge of two specifications of failure to obey a lawful order stemming from her inappropriate conduct towards and relationship with an Iraqi detainee. She was also found guilty of the other two specifications of failure to obey a lawful order and the specifications of false official statement. A military judge sentenced her to a bad-conduct discharge, confinement for 6 months, and reduction to the lowest enlisted grade.

In 2010, the United States Air Force Court of Criminal Appeals (A.F. Ct. Crim. App.) heard Flores' appeal, which alleged legal and factual insufficiencies at her court-martial and that improper comments by the military prosecutor deprived her of a fair trial. The Court of Appeals however found that a 'plethora of evidence' supported the charges against the appellant and that the Court was convinced beyond a reasonable doubt of her guilt. The Court did however determine that one of the prosecutor's comments on Flores' constitutional right to remain silent constituted error. But the Court held that there was no material prejudice to the appellant and that the error was harmless beyond a reasonable doubt. The Court ruled that the court-martial findings and sentence were correct in law and fact and thus affirmed.

- *United States* v. *Flores* [2011] 69 M.J. 366 United States Court of Appeals for the Armed Forces

While technically just outside the 2010 reporting period, the CAAF granted Flores petition for review and issued its ruling on 9 February 2011. The appeal focused exclusively on the A.F. Ct. Crim. App's ruling that only one of the prosecutor's comments at the court-martial constituted error, and harmless error at that. In a majority opinion, the CAAF held that more than just one of the prosecutor's comments constituted error but that even the cumulative errors were harmless

583 *United States* v. *Flores* [2010] 69 M.J. 651, p 653.

584 Ibid.

beyond a reasonable doubt given the 'overwhelming' evidence of Flores' guilt.[585] The CAAF affirmed the A.F. Ct. Crim. App'.s decision.

United States Army

- *United States* v. *Graner* [2010] 69 M.J. 104 United States Court of Appeals for the Armed Forces

Graner, an enlisted soldier in the US Army, was court-martialed in 2005 for his role in the mistreatment of prisoners at Abu Ghraib prison in Iraq. Then Specialist Graner was a military policeman at Abu Ghraib who 'exploited his position … in order to abuse and demean Iraqi detainees'.[586] Graner was involved in a host of impermissible actions towards detainees, including, among others: punching a detainee unconscious, forcing naked detainees into a human pyramid, placing a leash around a detainee's neck, and taking pictures of detainees forced to masturbate or simulate fellatio with other detainees.

He was charged with conspiracy to maltreat prisoners, maltreatment, dereliction of duty by failing to protect detainees under his charge from abuse, assault with a means likely to produce death or grievous bodily harm, assault consummated by battery, and committing an indecent act, in violation of the UCMJ. Contrary to his pleas, a general court-martial comprised of members found him guilty and sentenced him to a dishonorable discharge, confinement for 10 years, reduction to the lowest enlisted grade, and forfeiture of all pay and allowances.

On review in 2009, the ACCA affirmed the findings and sentence. The Court of Appeals for the Armed Forces (CAAF) granted Graner's petition for review. Graner argued that the military judge erred at the court-martial by failing to compel the military prosecutor to produce various memoranda between high level United States Government officials which Graner claimed authorized the manner in which he treated detainees. He also claimed error in the military judge's denial of his request that a US Army intelligence officer be allowed to testify that superiors had authorized rough treatment of detainees and curtailment of the testimony of a defense expert on the use of force.

The CAAF held that Graner failed to establish the relevance of the various documents at issue and also failed to properly request their production as specified by the Rules for Court-Martial. The CAAF also upheld the denial of the intelligence officer's expected testimony 'given the total lack of evidence connecting' the testimony and Graner's conduct. Finally, the CAAF agreed with the restriction of defense expert's testimony as the expert had an insufficient basis for his conclusions that the naked human pyramid and neck leashes were reasonable uses of force. The CAAF affirmed the decision of the ACCA.

---

[585] *United States* v. *Flores* [2011] 69 M.J. 366 p 19. One Judge dissented, agreeing with the majority in affirming the A.F. Ct. Crim. App. decision but disagreeing with how the majority applied the plain error doctrine.

[586] *United States* v. *Graner* [2010] 69 M.J. 104, p 106.

- *United States* v. *Harman* [2010] 68 M.J. 325 United States Court of Appeals for the Armed Forces

Harman, an enlisted soldier in the US Army, was court-martialed in 2005 for her role in the mistreatment of prisoners at Abu Ghraib prison in Iraq. Then Specialist Harman was a guard at Abu Ghraib and was involved in a host of impermissible actions towards detainees, including, among others: after a hooded detainee was placed on a box, affixing his fingers with wires and telling him he would be electrocuted if he fell off; taking pictures of and posing in front of a naked human pyramid of detainees other guards had forced the detainees into, and writing 'I'm a rapist [sic]' on a detainee's naked thigh. She was charged with conspiracy to maltreat prisoners, maltreatment, and dereliction of duty by failing to protect detainees from abuse, cruelty, and maltreatment in violation of the UCMJ. Contrary to her pleas, a general court-martial comprised of members found her guilty and sentenced her to a bad-conduct discharge, confinement for 6 months, reduction to the lowest enlisted grade, and forfeiture of all pay and allowances.

On review in 2008, the ACCA affirmed the findings and sentence. The CAAF granted Harman's petition for review. Harman argued that her conduct was legally insufficient for a conspiracy conviction and that her lack of proper training should preclude her conviction for maltreatment. As to conspiracy, the CAAF held that Harman actively participated in the abuse and stressed the ACCA's conclusions that Harman's 'smiling face, when seen with the "thumbs up" hand signals [in front of the detainee "pyramid"], shows approval and encouragement to her co-conspirators as they maltreated the prisoners'.[587] In rejecting Harman's argument concerning her lack of training, the CAAF noted that Harman had received 'training in the care, custody and control of detainees as well as in the basic requirements of the Geneva Conventions regarding their treatment'.[588] The CAAF affirmed the decision of the ACCA.

- *United States* v. *Maynulet* [2010] 68 M.J. 374 United States Court of Appeals for the Armed Forces

Maynulet, a commissioned officer in the US Army, was court-martialed in 2005 for killing a purportedly mortally injured and unarmed insurgent in Iraq in 2004. Maynulet was serving as a company commander of an armor company and was instructed to set up a traffic control point as part of an operation to kill or capture a high value target (HVT). Following a high speed chase, the vehicle believed to contain the HVT crashed into a wall. Members of Maynulet's company found only the driver still in the car and with a readily apparent grievous head injury from the crash. A US Army medic told Captain Maynulet that the driver would not survive. Captain Maynulet then shot the driver in the head, killing him. He was charged with assault with intent to commit voluntary manslaughter in violation of the

---

587 *United States* v. *Harman* [2010] 68 M.J. 325, p 327.

588 Ibid., p 328.

UCMJ. Contrary to his pleas, a general court-martial comprised of members found him guilty and sentenced him to dismissal from the US Army.

In 2008, the US Army Court of Criminal Appeals (ACCA) reviewed and affirmed the case. The CAAF granted Maynulet's petition for review. Throughout the proceedings Maynulet acknowledged that he had shot and killed the driver, indeed the incident was captured on video by an unmanned aerial vehicle. Maynulet claimed that he thought he was authorized to shoot the driver under the international humanitarian law concept of preventing unnecessary suffering and that even if that was not the case, because he believed his actions were consistent with predeployment legal training, that the court-martial panel should have received a mistake of law instruction. The panel was not so instructed, a decision first the ACCA and then the CAAF upheld. As the CAAF stated:

> the problem with [Maynulet's] argument is that the record is devoid of any erroneous pronouncements or interpretations of military law or the law of armed conflict upon which he could have reasonably relied to justify his killing of the injured driver. The best [Maynulet] can argue is that he had a subjective belief as to what the law allowed. However, this if the very kind of mistake rejected by the general rule regarding mistake of law.[589]

The CAAF affirmed the decision of the ACCA.

- *United States* v. *Smith* [2010] 68 M.J. 316 United States Court of Appeals for the Armed Forces

Smith, a non-commissioned officer in the US Army, was court-martialed in 2006 for his role in the mistreatment of prisoners at Abu Ghraib prison in Iraq. Then Sergeant Smith was a military working dog (MWD) handler who, contrary to the training he received at the dog handler course, employed his working dog, unmuzzled and barking, directly in front of a detainee's face, and removing the detainee's hood with its teeth. He was charged with conspiracy to maltreat prisoners, maltreatment, dereliction of duty, and indecent acts in violation of the UCMJ. Contrary to his pleas, a general court-martial comprised of members found him guilty and sentenced him to a bad-conduct discharge, confinement for 179 days, reduction to the lowest enlisted grade, and forfeiture of $750 pay per month for 3 months.

On review in 2008, the ACCA dismissed the charges alleging indecent acts and dereliction of duty, while affirming the remaining findings and the sentence. The CAAF granted Smith's petition for review. Throughout the proceedings, Smith claimed that his brigade commander had ordered the use of MWDs in conjunction with interrogations and that the military judge's failure to instruct the court-martial panel on obedience to lawful orders constituted reversible error. While there was evidence that MWDs were used in conjunction with at least one interrogation, that use did not involve Smith nor use of a MWD in the manner in which Smith did. Smith also claimed that he could not be guilty of maltreatment because, for, among

589 *United States* v. *Maynulet* [2010] 68 M.J. 374, pp 376–377.

other reasons, the detainees were not subject to his orders. The CAAF, in dismissing this argument, *sua sponte* referred to the Geneva Conventions for the general proposition that 'detainees are obliged to follow the lawful orders of their captors'.[590] The CAAF affirmed the decision of the ACCA.

- *United States* v. *Girouard* [2010] 2010 WL 3529415 United States Army Court of Criminal Appeals (unpublished)

Girouard, a noncommissioned officer in the US Army, was court-martialed in 2007 for ordering two subordinate soldiers to kill three recently captured Iraqi detainees. Then Staff Sergeant Girouard was a squad leader in an infantry unit conducting an air assault operation in the Sunni Triangle area of Iraq in May 2006. The unit conducted the operation under rules of engagement (ROE) and guidance from their commander that all military aged males in the objective area were hostile and to be killed. During the operation, members of Girouard's squad captured and secured three such military aged males. Shortly thereafter, Girouard held a squad meeting where he informed his soldiers that the unit first sergeant (1SG) had inquired why the detainees had not been killed during what the 1SG mistakenly thought had been a firefight. Girouard also relayed one squad member's desire to kill the detainees to the rest of the squad. The squad interpreted Girouard's comments as a 'suggested plan to kill the detainees' with which some of the squad expressed approval and others disapproval. Girouard assigned two of the soldiers who expressed approval the responsibility to guard the detainees. Those soldiers, Hunsaker and Clagett, then cut the ties off the detainees, forced them to run, and then shot all three detainees. A third member of the squad, Graber, responding to the gunfire found one of the detainees mortally wounded but still alive and shot him in the head, killing him.[591]

Girouard was charged with conspiracy to obstruct justice, violating a lawful order, obstruction of justice and negligent homicide in violation of the UCMJ. Contrary to his pleas, a general court-martial comprised of members found him guilty and sentenced him to a dishonorable discharge, confinement for 10 years, reduction to the lowest enlisted grade, and forfeiture of all pay and allowances.

On appeal to the ACCA, Girouard claimed that the military prosecutor had failed to prove beyond a reasonable doubt that his conduct proximately caused the detainees' deaths. While acknowledging the existence of the 'kill all military aged males' ROE, the ACCA ruled Girourard, and the members of his squad, knew that

[590] *United States* v. *Smith* (2010) 68 M.J. 316, fn. 8. The military prosecutor 'did not introduce the Geneva Conventions into evidence at trial, nor … brief or argue … as to whether, how, and if the Third or Fourth Geneva Convention applied in the context of Abu Ghraib'. See ibid.

[591] All three were court-martialed in 2007. Hunsaker and Clagget pled and were found guilty of conspiracy to commit murder, attempted premeditated murder, and premeditated murder. Although they were sentenced to confinement for life, a pretrial agreement with the military authority which convened the courts-martial reduced their sentences to 18 years. Graber was found guilty of aggravated assault with a dangerous weapon and sentenced to 9 months confinement.

the ROE 'did not authorize the killing of [military aged males] once they had been detained, and that the killing of detainees under their control was an unlawful act'.[592] Noting that Girouard was an experienced squad leader, the ACCA held that the detainees' deaths following the squad meeting was reasonably foreseeable and that a reasonably prudent person in Girouard's position would have kept the detainees under his control and not placed them with a subordinate who openly expressed a desire to kill them. The ACCA affirmed the findings and sentence.

While likely to be the subject of the 2011 report, the following ongoing US Army military justice cases bear noting:

- *United States* v. *Stevens* [2010] Ft. Lewis, Washington

As at the time of submission of this report, twelve US Army Soldiers from the same unit face up to 76 charges under the UCMJ stemming from a wide range of alleged misconduct while deployed in Kandahar Province, Afghanistan, including killing Afghan civilians and taking body parts as trophies.[593] The first of the trials, involving US Army Staff Sergeant Stevens, occurred in December, 2010.[594] Stevens pled and was found guilty of lying to investigators, shooting in the direction of two Afghan men, and throwing a grenade despite the absence of a threat. He was sentenced to 9 months confinement, a bad conduct discharge, reduction to the lowest enlisted grad and forfeiture of all pay and allowance.

- *United States* v. *Miller* [2011] Ft. Campbell, Kentucky

In June 2011, Sergeant Derrick Miller is scheduled to stand trial by court-martial for allegedly murdering an Afghan male in 2010.[595]

United States Marine Corps

- *United States* v. *Hutchins* [2010] 68 M.J. 623 United States Navy-Marine Corps Court of Criminal Appeals

Hutchins, a non-commissioned officer in the US Marine Corps, was court-martialed in 2007 stemming from the kidnap and murder of an Iraqi man near Hamdaniyah, Iraq in 2006.[596] Then Sergeant Hutchins was serving as a squad

---

[592] *United States* v. *Girouard* [2010] 2010 WL 3529415, p 1.

[593] M. Archbold, 'Grisly Details in Charges Against Soldiers', *The Olympian* (Olympia, US) 9 September 2010, <http://www.theolympian.com/2010/09/09/1363486/grisly-details-in-charges-against.html#>.

[594] 'Soldier Pleads Guilty to Some Charges in Afghan Killing; Gets 9 Months', *CNN*, 1 December 2010, <http://articles.cnn.com/2010-12-01/justice/afghanistan.sport.killings_1_first-soldier-stevens-afghan-men?_s=PM:CRIME>.

[595] E. Graham-Harrison, 'U.S. Soldier Faces Trial For Afghan Civilian Murder', *Reuters*, 23 February 2011, <http://www.reuters.com/article/2011/02/23/us-afghanistan-civilian-idUSTRE71M1C420110223>.

[596] Six other Marines, members of Sergeant Hutchins' squad, and a Navy corpsman were court-martialed for various offenses related to the kidnap and murder.

leader and led six of his Marines and a Navy Corpsman to drag a retired Iraqi policeman from his home, kill him, and plant a shovel and an AK-47 near the body in an effort to support the false claim that he was an insurgent.

Hutchins was charged with conspiracy, making a false official statement, unpremeditated murder and larceny in violation of the UCMJ. Contrary to his pleas, a general court-martial comprised of members found him guilty and sentenced him to a dishonorable discharge, confinement for 11 years, and reduction to the lowest enlisted grade.

In 2010, the US Navy-Marine Corps Court of Criminal Appeals heard Hutchins' appeal. The Court exclusively focused on whether the departure of Hutchins' military defense from active duty prior to trial constituted good cause for severing the attorney–client relationship, whether Hutchins had voluntarily consented to severing the relationship, and the presumptions of prejudice which follow. The Court ruled that Hutchins had not consented, that departing active duty was not good cause, and that there was a presumption of prejudice. The Court set aside the findings and sentence. As a result, in the spring of 2010, Hutchins was released from confinement and assigned duties at Camp Pendleton, California.

- *United States* v. *Hutchins* [2011] 69 M.J. 282 United States Court of Appeals for the Armed Forces

While technically just outside the 2010 reporting period, The Judge Advocate General of the Navy certified the case to the CAAF, which issued its ruling on 11 January 2011. The CAAF reversed the Navy-Marine Corps Court of Criminal Appeals, focusing on the same issue, the departure of Hutchins' military defense counsel from active duty before his court-martial. The CAAF held that while the military judge erred in failing 'to ensure that the record accurately reflected the reasons for the absence', that the error did not materially prejudice Hutchins.[597] The CAAF stressed that notwithstanding the issue of the military defense counsel, Hutchins was represented by two other attorneys, a civilian with nearly 30 years experience whom Hutchins had selected and a Lieutenant Colonel Judge Advocate who had previously served as a regional defense counsel. Moreover, after the departure of the third defense counsel, Hutchins was provided a substitute, another Lieutenant Colonel Judge Advocate, this one with 6 years of military justice experience and civilian experience as a public defender. Because the Navy-Marine Corps Court had only considered the defense counsel issue and Hutchins had raised other challenges to the findings and sentence, the CAAF remanded the case for further review. As a result of the CAAFs action, on 18 February 2011, Hutchins returned to confinement to serve the remainder of his sentence while renewing the challenge to his conviction at the Navy-Marine Corps Court of Appeals.[598]

---

597 *United States* v. *Hutchins* [2011] 69 M.J. 282, pp 291, 293.

598 'Camp Pendleton Marine Returns to Brig for 2006 Killing of Iraqi', *LA Times* (Los Angeles, US) 18 February 2011, <http://latimesblogs.latimes.com/lanow/2011/02/marines-brig-lawrence-hutchins-iraq.html>.

United States Navy

- *United States* v. *Keefe, Huertas, and McCabe* [2010]

Keefe, Huertas, and McCabe are Special Warfare Operators (SEALs) in the US Navy who were separately court-martialed in 2010 for the alleged assault of a detainee they captured in Iraq. The three Sailors were part of a team that captured Ahmed Hashim Abed, who was purportedly involved in the murder and mutilation of four US security contractors (two of whom were former Navy SEALs) in Fallujah, Iraq, in 2004. Following Abed's capture, McCabe allegedly assaulted Abed, and Huertas and Keefe allegedly both failed to stop the assault and later lied about the incident. McCabe was charged with assault, dereliction of duty, and making a false official statement in violation of the UCMJ. Huertas and Keefe were charged with dereliction of duty and false official statement in violation of the UCMJ. In three separate special courts-martial comprised of members, each was acquitted. Media reports claimed that the court-martial panels heard 'too many differences between the testimony of a sailor who claimed he witnessed the … assault at a U.S. base outside Fallujah, Iraq, and statements from a half dozen others who denied his account'.[599]

Legislation—Terrorist Detention

- *Terrorist Review Detention Reform Act*

A bill to provide for habeas corpus review for certain enemy belligerents against the United States was introduced in the US Congress in 2010.[600] The bill is still in committee. The bill would, among other things, result in the US Congress defining who is subject to detention, the quantum of evidence required for that detention, and the process of and limitations on detainees challenging their detention through petition for a writ of habeas corpus.

CHRIS JENKS[601]

---

[599] L. Jakes, 'Military Jury Clears SEAL in Iraq Abuse Case', *Associated Press*, 22 April 2010, <http://www.navytimes.com/news/2010/04/ap_navy_seal_court_martial_042210/> (referring to Huertas' court-martial); 'Second Navy SEAL Found Not Guilty of Prisoner Abuse', *NY Post* (New York, US) 23 April 2010, <http://www.nypost.com/p/news/international/second_navy_seal_found_not_guilty_SrdAXqEHg9ItuIidpBLVGJ?CMP=OTC-rss&FEEDNAME=> (referring to Keefe's court-martial); 'Navy SEAL Acquitted of Assaulting Iraqi Detainee', *CNN*, 6 May 2010, <http://articles.cnn.com/2010-05-06/justice/virginia.navy.seal.trial_1_iraqi-detainee-two-other-navy-seals-assaulting?_s=PM:CRIME> (referring to McCabe's court-martial).

[600] L. Graham, 'Terrorist Detention Review Reform Act', 111th US Congress, 4 August 2010, <http://www.govtrack.us/congress/bill.xpd?bill=s111-3707>. The 111th Congress is no longer in session, having been replaced by the 112th. In the United States, proposed bills which have not been passed by the end of one Congress are cleared but may be reintroduced in the next Congress.

[601] This entry was prepared by Lieutenant Colonel Chris Jenks, United States Army, Judge Advocate Generals' Corps. The entry does not necessarily reflect the views of the Judge Advocate General's Corps, the United States Army, or the Department of Defense.

Part V
Documentation

Classification Scheme

Part Zero	International humanitarian law in general
Part One	Sources and general principles
Part Two	Conflicts, armed forces and combatants
Part Three	Protected persons
Part Four	Methods, means and types of warfare
Part Five	Termination of armed conflicts
Part Six	International criminal law
Part Seven	Implementation of IHL
Part Eight	The law of neutrality
Part Nine	International organisations and international actions
Part Ten	Regional organisations and actions
Part Eleven	Arms control and disarmament
Part Twelve	Conflict prevention and resolution
Part Thirteen	Related fields

M.N. Schmitt et al. (eds.), *Yearbook of International Humanitarian Law Volume 13, 2010*, DOI: 10.1007/978-90-6704-811-8_16,

0.	**Zero:**	**International Humanitarian Law in General**
1.	**One:**	**Sources and General Principles**
1.1	I	Sources
1.11		A. Pre-Hague
1.12		B. Hague Law
1.13		C. Geneva Law
1.14		D. Post-1977 Developments
1.15		E. Customary Law
1.2	II	General Principles
1.21		A. Martens Clause
1.22		B. Superfluous Injury and Unnecessary Suffering
1.23		C. Principle of Distinction
1.24		D. Prohibition of Indiscriminate Attacks
1.25		E. Principle of Proportionality
1.26		F. Principle of Precaution
1.27		G. Military Necessity
2.	**Two:**	**Conflicts, Armed Forces and Combatants**
2.1	I	Types of Conflicts
2.11		A. International
2.12		B. Non-international
2.13		C. Other
2.2	II	Types of Actor(s)
2.21		A. Armed Forces and Combatant Status
2.22		B. Non-State Actors
2.23		C. Specific Groups
2.231		1. Mercenaries
2.232		2. Spies
2.233		3. Contractors/Private Military Companies
2.234		4. Other
3.	**Three:**	**Protected Persons**
3.1	I	Types of Protected Persons
3.11		A. Wounded, Sick and Shipwrecked
3.12		B. Prisoners of War
3.13		C. Civilian Population
3.131		1. Civilians Generally
3.132		2. Women and Children
3.133		3. Medical and Religious Personnel

3.134		4. Journalists
3.135		5. Other
3.2	II	Specific Situations and Prohibitions
3.21		A. Internment
3.22		B. Occupation
3.23		C. Prohibition of Collective Punishment
3.24		D. Prohibition of Deportation and Transfer
3.25		E. Reprisals
4.	**Four:**	**Methods, Means and Types of Warfare**
4.1	I	Methods and Means of Warfare
4.11		A. Basic Rules
4.111		1. Existing Weapons
4.1111		a. Conventional Weapons
4.11111		i. Mines
4.11112		ii. Small weapons and others
4.1112		b. Weapons of Mass Destruction
4.11121		i. Nuclear weapons
4.11122		ii. Chemical and biological weapons
4.112		2. New Weapons
4.113		3. Prohibition of Perfidy
4.114		4. Emblems and Safeguards of Persons hors de combat
4.12		B. Direct and Indiscriminate Attacks
4.13		C. Precautionary Measures
4.14		D. Protection of Civilian and Other Specified Objects
4.141		1. Specifically Protected Objects
4.142		2. Cultural Property and Places of Worship
4.143		3. Works and Installations Containing Dangerous Forces
4.144		4. The Natural Environment
4.145		5. Localities and Zones
4.146		6. Civil Defence
4.15		E. Medical Assistance
4.16		F. Humanitarian Assistance Operations
4.2	II	Specific Types of Warfare
4.21		A. Land Warfare
4.22		B. Air and Missile Warfare
4.23		C. Naval Warfare

5.	**Five:**	**Termination of Armed Conflicts**
5.1	I	Ceasefire, Armistices and Peace Agreements
5.2	II	War Crimes Commissions
5.3	III	Amnesties, Truth and Reconciliation Commissions
5.4	IV	Reparations/Compensation
5.5	V	Military Commissions and Tribunals
6.	**Six:**	**International Criminal Law**
6.1	I	The Crimes
6.11		A. War Crimes
6.12		B. Genocide
6.13		C. Crimes against Humanity
6.14		D. Aggression
6.15		E. Terrorism
6.16		F. Other
6.2	II	General Principles, Including Defences
6.21		A. Nullum Crimen Sine Lege and Nulla Poena Sine Lege
6.22		B. Individual Criminal Responsibility
6.23		C. Superior/Command Responsibility
6.24		D. Irrelevance of Official Capacity
6.25		E. Non-Retroactivity of Criminal Law
6.26		F. Non-Applicability of Statutory Limitations
6.27		G. Grounds for Excluding Criminal Responsibility
6.3	III	Repression of Breaches
6.31		A. International and Internationalised Courts
6.311		1. Nuremberg and Tokyo
6.312		2. International Criminal Tribunal for the former Yugoslavia
6.313		3. International Criminal Tribunal for Rwanda
6.314		4. International Criminal Court
6.315		5. East Timor's Special Panels for Serious Crimes
6.316		6. Kosovo's Internationalised Courts
6.317		7. Special Court for Sierra Leone
6.318		8. Extraordinary Chambers for Cambodia
6.319		9. Iraqi Special Tribunal
6.320		10. Special Tribunal for Lebanon
6.32		B. National Courts
6.4	IV	Victims of Crimes

7.	**Seven:**	**Implementation of IHL**
7.1	I	National Policy Statements
7.2	II	National Law
7.21		A. Legislation to Implement IHL Treaties
7.22		B. Legislation to Implement Obligations vis-à-vis the International Criminal Court and International Criminal Tribunals
7.23		C. Military Manuals/National Instructions/Codes of Conduct
7.24		D. Role of Defence Force Legal Advisers
7.3	III	Protecting Powers
7.4	IV	ICRC
7.5	V	Fact-Finding, Including the International Fact-Finding Commission
7.6	VI	Dissemination
7.7	VII	Training and Education
8.	**Eight:**	**The Law of Neutrality**
8.1	I	The Rights and Duties of Nationals
8.2	II	War on Land
8.3	III	Naval Warfare
8.4	IV	Aerial Warfare
9.	**Nine:**	**International Organisations and International Actions**
9.1	I	International Organisations
9.11		A. United Nations Organisation
9.12		B. Other
9.2	II	International Actions
9.21		A. Peacekeeping
9.22		B. Peace Enforcement and Peace Building
9.23		C. Fact-Finding and Monitoring
9.24		D. Humanitarian and Other Interventions
9.25		E. Sanctions
10.	**Ten:**	**Regional Organisations and Actions**
10.1	I	European
10.2	II	American
10.3	III	Asian
10.4	IV	African

11.	**Eleven:**	**Arms Control and Disarmament**
11.1	I	Conventional Weapons
11.11		A. Mines
11.12		B. Small Weapons and Others
11.13		C. Production and Transfer
11.2	II	Weapons of Mass Destruction
11.21		A. Nuclear Weapons
11.22		B. Chemical and Biological Weapons
11.23		C. New Types
12.	**Twelve:**	**Conflict Prevention and Resolution**
12.1	I	Conflict Prevention
12.2	II	Conflict Resolution
12.3	III	The Peace Movement
13.	**Thirteen:**	**Related Fields**
13.1	I	Jus Ad Bellum
13.2	II	The Law Relating to Terrorism and Counter-Terrorism
13.3	III	Military Law
13.4	IV	Human Rights Law
13.5	V	Refugee Law

Bibliography 2010

1. International Humanitarian Law in General

Books

- Andersen, Elizabeth and David M. Crane, *Proceedings of the Third International Humanitarian Law Dialogs*, No. 42 (Washington, American Society of International Law 2010) 291 pp.
- Besson, Samantha and John Tassioulas, *The Philosophy of International Law* (Oxford, Oxford University Press 2010) 632 pp.
- Carlton-Ford, Steven and Morten G. Ender, eds., *The Routledge Handbook of War and Society: Iraq and Afghanistan* (Abingdon, Routledge 2010) 320 pp.
- Chukwu, Iheke, *Appraisal of the United Nation's Goldstone Report on the Gaza Conflict: War crimes, International Humanitarian Law and Fact Finding Mission* (Saarbrucken, Lambert Academic Publishing 2010) 144 pp.
- Evans, M.D. *International Law*, 3rd edn. (Oxford, Oxford University Press) 936 pp.
- Gill, Terry and Dieter Fleck, *The Handbook of the International Law of Military Operations* (Oxford, Oxford University Press 2010) 728 pp.
- Hayashi, Nobuo, *National Military Manuals on the Law of Armed Conflict*, 2nd edn. (Brussels, Torkel Opsahl 2010) 278 pp.
- Heintschel von Heinegg, Wolff and Volker Epping, *International Humanitarian Law Facing New Challenges: Symposium in Honour of Knut Ipsen* (New York, Springer 2010) 280 pp.
- Kellenberger, Jakob, *Humanitären Völkerrechts (International Humanitarian Law)* (Frauenfeld, Huber 2010) 359 pp.

The bibliography was compiled by Aleksandra Bojovic, Mohbuba Choudhury, Manuela Melandri and Andrew Sanger. Aleksandra Bojovic holds an LLM in Public International Law from the London School of Economics and Political Science and is a Doctoral Candidate in International Economic Law at the London School of Economics and Political Science. Mohbuba Choudhury holds a BA (Hons) from the University of Oxford and an LLM in Public International Law from the London School of Economics and Political Science. Manuela Melandri is a Doctoral Candidate at the University College of London. Andrew Sanger holds an LLM in Public International Law from the London School of Economics and Political Science and is a Doctoral Candidate in International Law at the University of Cambridge.

- Linero, Gabriel Jose Angulo, *The Effects of Armed Conflict on the Right to Education: Colombia in Focus* (Saarbrucken, Lambert Academic Publishing 2010) 64 pp.
- Matheson, Micahel, J., *Rules and Institutions of International Humanitarian Law* (Leiden, Brill 2010) 1072 pp.
- Naert, Frederik, *International Law Aspects of the EE's Security and Defence Policy, with a Particular Focus on the Law of Armed Conflict and Human Rights* (Antwerp, Intersentia 2010) 682 pp.
- Pedrozo R.A., ed., *The War in Iraq: A Legal Analysis, International Law Studies* Vol. 86 (Newport RI, Naval War College 2010) 518 pp.
- Schmitt, Michael N., *Essays on Law and War at the Fault Lines* (London, Cameron May 2010) 650 pp.
- Solis, Gary. D., *The Law of Armed Conflict: International Humanitarian Law in War* (Cambridge, Cambridge University Press 2010) 692 pp.
- Thurer, D., *International Humanitarian Law, Theory, Practice, Context* (Leiden, Brill 2011)
- Yildiz, Kerim and Susan Breau, *The Kurdish Conflict: International Humanitarian Law and Post-Conflict Mechanisms* (Abingdon, Routledge 2010) 354 pp.

Articles

- Abrahams, David, 'A synopsis of urban violence in South Africa', 92 *International Review of the Red Cross* (2010) pp. 495–520
- Arimatsu, L., 'Territory, Boundaries and the Law of Armed Conflict', 12 *Yearbook of International Humanitarian Law* (2009) pp. 157–192
- Bangerter, Oliver, 'Territorial gangs and their consequences for humanitarian players', 92 *International Review of the Red Cross* (2010) pp. 387–406
- Barnidge, Robert P., Jr., 'Islam and International Humanitarian Law: A Question of Compatibility?', 40 *Israel Yearbook on Human Rights* (2010) pp. 257–274
- Benvenisti, Eyal, 'The Legal Battle to Define the Law on Transnational Asymmetric Warfare', 20(3) *Duke Journal of Comparative and International Law* (2010) pp. 339–360
- Bill, Brian, 'Detention Operations in Iraq: A View from the Ground', 40 *Israel Yearbook on Human Rights* (2010) pp. 67–116
- Bisharat, George, E., 'Israel's Invasion of Gaza in International Law', 38(1) *Denver Journal of International Law and Policy* (2010) pp. 41–114
- Bismuth, Régis, 'Mapping a Responsibility of Corporations for Violations of International Humanitarian Law Sailing Between International and Domestic Legal Orders', 38(2) *Denver Journal of International Law and Policy* (2010) pp. 203–226
- Blank, L.R., 'The Application of IHL in the Goldstone Report: a Critical Commentary', 12 *Yearbook of International Humanitarian Law* (2009) pp. 347–402

- Bourbonniere, Michel, 'The Clausewitz Nebulae: The Legitimacy of Military Activities in Outer Space During Armed Conflicts', 40 *Israel Yearbook on Human Rights* (2010) pp. 243–256
- Breau, S.C., 'The Year in Review', 12 *Yearbook of International Humanitarian Law* (2009) pp. 195–232
- Chevalier-Watts, Juliet, 'Has human rights law become lex specialis for the European Court of Human Rights in right to life cases arising from internal armed conflicts?', 14(4) *International Journal of Human Rights* (2010) pp. 584–602
- Clarke, Ben, 'Securing Compliance with International Humanitarian Law: The Promise and Limits of Contemporary Enforcement Mechanisms', 1(1) *Journal of International Humanitarian Legal Studies* (2010) pp. 213–220
- Corn, G.S. and E.T. Jensen, 'The Obama Administration's first year and IHL: A pragmatist reclaims the high ground', 12 *Yearbook of International Humanitarian Law* (2009) pp. 263–286
- Del Mar, Katherine, 'The requirement of "belonging" under international humanitarian law', 21(1) *European Journal of International Law* (2010) pp. 105–124
- Dinstein, Yoram, 'Concluding Remarks: The Influence of the Conflict in Iraq on International Law', 40 *Israel Yearbook on Human Rights* (2010) pp. 203–218
- Duijsens, Raimond, 'Humanitarian challenges of urbanisation', 92 *International Review of the Red Cross* (2010) pp. 351–368
- European Centre for Law and Justice, 'Legal Memorandum Answering the UN Human Rights Council's Report on the Goldstone Fact-Finding Mission on the Gaza Conflict', 40 *Israel Yearbook on Human Rights* (2010)
- Gharagozli, Behnam, 'War of Words or a Regional Disaster: The Legality of Israeli and Iranian Military Options', 33 *Hastings International and Comparative Law Review* (2010) pp 203–244
- Giosa, Laura María, 'First Colloquium on International Humanitarian Law and International Criminal Law: "The Geneva Conventions: Commemorating their Sixtieth Anniversary"', 1(1) *Journal of International Humanitarian Legal Studies* (2010) pp. 221–223
- Goodman, R., 'Controlling the Recourse to War by Modifying *Jus in Bello*', 12 *Yearbook of International Humanitarian Law* (2009) pp. 53–84
- Greenwood, Christopher, 'The Law of War (International Humanitarian Law)', in Evans M.D., ed., *International Law*, 3rd edn. (Oxford, Oxford University Press 2010) pp. 783–812
- Harroff-Tavel, 'Violence and humanitarian action in urban areas: new challenges, new approaches', 92 *International Review of the Red Cross* (2010) pp. 329–350
- Hauck, Pierre and Sven Peterke, 'Organized crime and gang violence in national and international law', 92 *International Review of the Red Cross* (2010) pp. 407–436
- Hazen, Jennifer M., 'Understanding gangs as armed groups', 92 *International Review of the Red Cross* (2010) pp. 369–386

- John-Hopkins, Michael, 'Regulating the conduct of urban warfare: lessons from contemporary asymmetric armed conflicts', 92 *International Review of the Red Cross* (2010) pp. 469–493
- Kanwar, Vivek, 'Post-Human Humanitarian Law: The Law of War in the Age of Robotic Warfare', 2 *Harvard Journal of National Security* (2010)
- Kreß, Claus, 'Some Reflections on the International Legal Framework Governing Transnational Armed Conflicts', 15(2) *Journal of Conflict and Security Law* (2010) pp. 245–274
- Lefkowitz, David, 'Jus in Bello through the Lens of Individual Moral Responsibility: McMahan on Killing in War', 1(1) *Transnational Legal Theory* (2010) pp. 121–126
- Mastorodimos, Konstantinos, 'The Character of the Conflict in Gaza: Another Argument towards Abolishing the Distinction between International and Non-international Armed Conflicts', 12(4) *International Community Law Review* (2010) pp. 437–469
- McMaham, Jeff, 'Laws of War', in Besson, Samantha and John Tassioulas, eds., *The Philosophy of International Law* (Oxford, Oxford University Press 2010) pp. 493–510
- Peterke, Sven, 'Urban Insurgency, "Drug War" and International Humanitarian Law: The Case of Rio de Janeiro', 1(1) *Journal of International Humanitarian Legal Studies* (2010) pp. 165–187
- Rostow, Nicholas, 'The Human Rights Council (Goldstone) Report and International Law', 40 *Israel Yearbook on Human Rights* (2010) pp. 275–306
- Samson, Elizabeth, 'Is Gaza Occupied?: Redefining the Status of Gaza Under International Law', 25 *American University International Law Review* (2010) pp. 915–967
- Schmitt, Michael N., 'Investigating Violations of International Law in Armed Conflict', 2(1) *Harvard National Security Journal* (2010) pp. 31–34
- Shue, Henry, 'Laws of War', in Besson, Samantha and John Tassioulas, eds., *The Philosophy of International Law* (Oxford, Oxford University Press 2010) pp. 511–530
- Solomon, Solon, 'The Great Oxymoron: Jus In Bello Violations as Legitimate Non-Forcible Measures of Self-Defense: The Post-Disengagement Israeli Measures towards Gaza as a Case Study', 9(3) *Chinese Journal of International Law* (2010) pp. 501–536
- Stephens, Dale, 'Blurring the Lines: the Interpretation, Discourse and Application of the Law of Armed Conflict', 12 *Yearbook of International Humanitarian Law* (2009) pp. 85–118
- Stephens, Dale, 'Military involvement in law enforcement', 92 *International Review of the Red Cross* (2010) pp. 453–468
- Tougas, M., 'Some Comments and Observations on the Montreux Document', 12 *Yearbook of International Humanitarian Law* (2009) pp. 321–345
- Turns, David, 'The International Humanitarian Law Classification of Armed Conflicts in Iraq since 2003', in Pedrozo R.A., ed., *The War in Iraq: A Legal*

Analysis International Law Studies, Vol. 86 (Newport RI, Naval War College 2010) pp. 97–126
- Turns, David, 'The International Humanitarian Law Classification of Armed Conflicts in Iraq Since 2003', 40 *Israel Yearbook on Human Rights* (2010) pp. 39–66
- Van Laer, Tania, 'Damage to energy resources during armed conflict: towards a new regime', 3 *International Energy Law Review* (2010) pp. 64–72
- Vautravers, Alexandre, 'Military operations in urban areas', 92 *International Review of the Red Cross* (2010) pp. 437–452
- Warren, Marc, 'The "Fog of War": The Law of Armed Conflict in Operation Iraqi Freedom', in Pedrozo R.A., ed., *The War in Iraq: A Legal Analysis, International Law Studies* Vol. 86 (Newport RI, Naval War College 2010) pp. 167–208
- Weissbrodt, David, 'The Approach of the Committee on the Elimination of Racial Discrimination to Interpreting and Applying International Humanitarian Law', 19(2) *Minnesota Journal of International Law* (2010) pp. 327–362
- Zyberi, Gentian, 'Provisional measures of the International Court of Justice in armed conflict situations', 23(3) *Leiden Journal of International Law* (2010) pp. 571–584

1.13 Geneva Law

Books

- Perrigo, Sarah and Jim Whitman, eds., *The Geneva Conventions Under Assault* (London, Pluto Press 2010) 272 pp.
- Solis, Gary D., *Geneva Conventions* (US, Kaplan Trade 2010) 320 pp.

Articles

- Focarelli, Carlo, 'Common article 1 of the 1949 Geneva Conventions: a soap bubble', 21(1) *European Journal of International Law* (2010) pp. 125–171
- Meyer, Michael and Charles Garraway, 'The Geneva Conventions and United Nations Personnel (Protocols) Act 2009: A Move Away from the Minimalist Approach', 59(1) *International and Comparative Law Quarterly* (2010) pp. 171–180

1.27 Military Necessity

Articles

- Bill, B.J., 'The Rendulic "Rule": Military Necessity, Commander's Knowledge, and Methods of Warfare', 12 *Yearbook of International Humanitarian Law* (2009) pp. 119–155

- Hayashi, Nobuo, 'Requirements of Military Necessity in International Humanitarian Law and International Criminal Law', 28 *Boston University International Law Journal* (2010) pp. 39–140
- Melzer, Nils, 'Keeping the Balance between Military Necessity and Humanity: A Response to Four Critiques of the ICRC's Interpretive Guidance on the Notion of Direct Participation in Hostilities', 42 *New York University Journal of International Law and Policy* (2010) pp. 831–916
- Schmitt, Michael N., 'Military Necessity and Humanity in International Humanitarian Law: Preserving the Delicate Balance', 50 *Virginia Journal of International Law* (2010) pp. 795–840

2. Conflicts, Armed Forces and Combatants

Books

- Chandran, Suba D. and Chari, P.R, *Armed Conflicts in South Asia* (Abingdon, Routledge 2010) 192 pp.
- Crawford, Emily, *The treatment of Combatants and insurgents under the law of armed conflict* (Oxford, Oxford University Press 2010) 240 pp.
- Dinstein, Yoram, *The conduct of hostilities under the law of International Armed Conflict* (Cambridge, Cambridge University Press 2010) 328 pp.
- Gill, Terry and Dieter Fleck, *The Handbook of the International Law of Military Operations* (Oxford, Oxford University Press 2010) 688 pp.
- Quenivet, Noelle and Shilan Shah-Davis, *International Law and Armed Conflict; Challenges in the 21st Century* (The Hague, T.M.C Asser Press 2010) 462 pp.
- Solis, Gary, *The Law of Armed Conflict; International Humanitarian Law in War* (Cambridge, Cambridge University Press 2010) 692 pp.

Articles

- Bassiouni, Cherif M, 'Legal status of US forces in Iraq from 2003–2008', 11 *Chicago Journal of International Law* (2010) pp. 1–39
- Bilkova, Veronika, 'Treat them as they deserve?! Three approaches to armed opposition groups under current international law', 4 *Human Rights and International Legal Discourse* (2010) pp. 111–126
- Blank, Laurie and Amos Guiora, 'Teaching an old dog new tricks; Operationalizing the law of armed conflict in new warfare', 1 *Harvard National Security Journal* (2010) pp. 45–86
- Del Mar, Katherine, 'The requirement of 'belonging' under international humanitarian law', 21 *European Journal of International Law* (2010) pp. 105–124
- Glabe, Ensign Scott L., 'Conflict classification and detainee treatment in the war against Al-Qaeda', *The Army Lawyer* (2010) pp. 112–117

2.11 International Armed Conflicts

Books

- Dinstein, Yoram, *The Conduct of Hostilities under the Law of International Armed Conflict*, 2nd edn. (Cambridge, Cambridge University Press 2010) 328 pp.

Articles

- Dinstein, Yoram, 'The influence of the conflict in Iraq on International Law', 40 *Israel Yearbook on Human Rights* (2010) pp. 203–218
- Kress, Claus, 'Some reflections on the international legal framework governing transnational armed conflicts', 15 *Journal of Conflict and Security Law* (2010) pp. 245–274
- Turns, David, 'The International Humanitarian Law Classification of Armed Conflicts in Iraq since 2003', 40 *Israel Yearbook on Human Rights* (2010) pp. 39–66

2.12 Non-international Armed Conflicts

Books

- Cullen, Anthony, *The Concept of Non-International Armed Conflict in International Humanitarian Law* (Cambridge, Cambridge University Press 2010) 234 pp.
- La Haye, Eve, *War Crimes in internal armed conflicts* (Cambridge, Cambridge University Press 2010) 448 pp.

Articles

- Colassis, Laurent, 'The Role of the International Committee of the Red Cross in Stability Operations in Iraq', 40 *Israel Yearbook on Human Rights* (2010) pp. 183–202
- Guan, Jing, 'ICC's jurisdiction over war crimes in Internal Armed Conflicts; an insurmountable obstacle to China's accession', 28 *Penn State International Law Review* (2010) pp. 703–754
- John-Hopkins, Michael, 'Regulating the conduct of urban warfare; lessons from contemporary asymmetric armed conflicts', 92 *International Review of the Red Cross* (2010) pp. 469–495

2.13 Other: Occupation

Articles

- Darcy, Shane and John Reynolds, 'An Enduring Occupation: The Status of the Gaza Strip from the Perspective of International Humanitarian Law', 15 *Journal of Conflict and Security Law* (2010) pp. 211–243

2.21 Armed Forces and Combatant Status

Books

- Crawford, Emily, *The Treatment of Combatants and Insurgents under the Law of Armed Conflict* (Oxford, Oxford University Press 2010) 250 pp.

Articles

- Akande, Dapo, 'Clearing the fog of war? The ICRC's interpretive guidance on direct participation in hostilities', 59 *International and Comparative Law Quarterly* (2010) pp. 180–192
- Al-Duaij, Nada, 'Volunteer Human Shields in International Humanitarian Law', 12 *Oregon Review of International Law* (2010) pp. 117–140
- Boothby, Bill, 'And for such time as; the time dimension to direct participation in hostilities', 42 *New York University Journal of International Law and Politics* (2010) pp. 741–768
- Goodman, Ryan and Derek Jinks, 'ICRC Interpretive Guidance on the notion of direct participation of hostilities under International Humanitarian Law; an introduction to the forum', 42 *New York University Journal of International Law and Politics* (2010) pp. 637–640
- Gregory, E. John, 'Trying Unlawful Combatants at General Courts-Martial: Amending the UCMJ in Light of the Military Commissions Experience', 1 *Military Law Review* (2010) pp. 150–188
- Melzer, Nils, 'Keeping the Balance between Military Necessity and Humanity: A Response to Four Critiques of the ICRC's Interpretive Guidance on the Notion of Direct Participation in Hostilities', 42 *New York University Journal of International Law and Politics* (2010) pp. 831–916
- Mortlock, David, 'Definite Detention: The Scope of the President's Authority to Detain Enemy Combatants', 4 *Harvard Law and Policy Review* (2010) pp. 375–404
- Parks, W. Hays, 'Part IX of the ICRC Direct Participation in hostilities study: No mandate, no expertise, and legally incorrect', 42 *New York University Journal of International Law and Politics* (2010) pp. 769–830
- Schmitt, Michael N., 'Deconstructing Direct Participation in Hostilities: The Constitutive Elements', 42 *New York University Journal of International Law and Politics* (2010) pp. 697–740
- Watkin, Kenneth, 'Opportunity Lost: Organized Armed Groups and the ICRC Direct Participation in Hostilities Interpretive Guidance', 42 *New York University Journal of International Law and Politics* (2010) pp. 641–696
- Watts, Sean, 'Combatant Status and Computer Network Attacks', 50 *Virginia Journal of International Law* (2010) pp. 391–448
- Williamson, Jamie A, 'Challenges of Twenty-First Century Conflicts: A look at direct participation in hostilities', 20 *Duke Journal of Comparative and International Law* (2010) pp. 457–472

2.22 Private Military Companies/Mercenaries/Non-state Actors

Books

- Chenoweth, Erica, Adria Lawrence and Stathis Kalyvas, *Rethinking Violence: States and Non-State Actors in Conflict* (Cambridge MA, MIT Press 2010) 400 pp.
- International Institute of Humanitarian Law, *Non-State Actors and International Humanitarian Law. Organized armed groups: a challenge for the 21st century* (Milan, Franco Angeli 2010) 256 pp.
- Ortiz, Carlos, *Private Armed Forces and Global Security: A Guide to the Issues* (Santa Barbara, Greenwood Press 2010) 250 pp.

Articles

- Chapman, Katherin J., 'Untouchables: Private Military Contractors' Criminal Accountability under the UCMJ', 63 *Vanderbilt Law Review* (2010) pp. 1047–1080
- Dickinson, Laura A., 'Military Lawyers, Private Contractors, and the Problem of International Law Compliance', 42 *New York University Journal of International Law and Politics* (2010) pp. 355–388
- Ebrahim, Adam, 'Going to War with the Army You Can Afford: The United States, International Law and the Private Military Industry', 28 *Boston University International Law Journal* (2010) pp. 181–218
- Guilfoyle, Douglas, 'The Laws of War and the Fight against Somali Piracy: Combatants or Criminals?', 11(1) *Melbourne Journal of International Law* (2010) pp. 141–153
- Heintschel von Heinegg, Wolff, 'Repressing Piracy and Armed Robbery at Sea—Towards a New International Legal Regime', 40 *Israel Yearbook on Human Rights* (2010) pp. 219–242
- Kidane, Won, 'The Status of Private Military Contractors Under International Humanitarian Law', 38(3) *Denver Journal of International Law and Policy* (2010) pp. 361–419
- Kemp, John S., 'Private Military Firms and Responses to Their Accountability Gap', 32 *Washington University Journal of Law and Policy* (2010) pp. 489–514
- Mehra, Amol, 'Bridging Accountability Gaps—The Proliferation of Private Military and Security Companies and Ensuring Accountability for Human Rights Violations', 22 *Pacific McGeorge Global Business & Development Law Journal* (2010) pp. 323–332
- Pattison, James, 'Outsourcing the responsibility to protect: humanitarian intervention and private military and security companies', 2 *International Theory* (2010) pp. 1–31
- Paust, Jordan J., 'Self-Defense Targetings of Non-State Actors and Permissibility of U.S. Use of Drones in Pakistan', 19 *Journal of Transnational Law & Policy* (2010) pp. 237–280

- Rose, Cecily, 'Emerging Norma: The Duty of States to Provide Reparation for Human Rights Violations by Non-State Actors', 33 *Hastings International and Comparative Law Review* (2010) pp. 307–344
- Van Steenberghe, Raphael, 'Self-Defence in Response to Attacks by Non-state Actors in the Light of Recent State Practice: A Step Forward?', 23 *Leiden Journal of International Law* (2010) pp. 183–208
- Wittels, Stephen, 'From Dogs of War to Soldiers of Peace: Evaluating Private Military and Security Companies as a Civilian Protection Force', 12 *Journal of Military and Strategic Studies* (2010) pp. 130–182

3.12 Prisoners of War

Articles

- Morris-Frazier, Jerica M., 'Missing in Actions: Prisoners of War at Guantánamo Bay', 13 *University of the District of Columbia Law Review* (2010) pp. 155–178
- Pinzauti, Giulia, 'Protective Prisoners of War: The Mrkšić et al. Appeals Judgment', 8 *Journal of International Criminal Justice* (201) pp. 199–219

3.13 Civilian Population

Books

- Primoratz, Igor, *Civilian Immunity in War* (Oxford, Oxford University Press 2010) 288 pp.

Articles

- Balcells, Laia, 'Rivalry and Revenge: Violence against Civilians in Conventional Civil Wars', 54(2) *International Studies Quarterly* (2010) pp. 291–313
- Blocq, Daniel, 'Western Soldiers and the Protection of Local Civilians in UN Peacekeeping Operations: Is a Nationalist Orientation in the Armed Forces Hindering Our Preparedness to Fight?', 36 *Armed Forces & Society* (2010) pp. 290–309
- Jones, Samuel Vincent, 'Ethics of Letting Civilians Die in Afghanistan: The False Dichotomy between Hobbesian and Kantian Rescue Paradigms', 59 *DePaul Law Review* (2010) pp. 899–942
- Lie, Jon Harald Sande and Benjamin de Carvalho, 'Between Culture and Concept: The Protection of Civilians in Sudan', 14 *Journal of International Peacekeeping* (2010) pp. 60–85
- Modirzadeh, Naz K., 'Dark Sides of Convergence: A Pro-Civilian Critique of the Extraterritorial Application of Human Rights Law in Armed Conflict', 86 *International Law Studies Series US Naval War College* (2010) pp. 349–410

- Roberts, A., 'The Civilian in Modern War', 12 *Yearbook of International Humanitarian Law* (2009) pp. 13–51
- Ronen, Yael, 'Superior Responsibility of Civilians for International Crimes Committed in Civilian Settings', 43 *Vanderbilt Journal of Transnational Law* (2010) pp. 313–356
- Schmitt, Michael N., 'Deconstructing Direct Participation in Hostilities: The Constitutive Elements', 42 *New York University Journal of International Law and Politics* (2010) pp. 697–740
- Schmitt, Michael N., 'Interpretive Guidance on the Notion of Direct Participation in Hostilities: A Critical Analysis', 1 *Harvard National Security Journal* (2010) pp. 5–44
- Stigali, Dan E., 'Thickest Grey: Assessing the Status of the Civilian Response Corps under the Law of International Armed Conflict and the U.S. Approach to Targeting Civilians', 25 *American University International Law Review* (2010) pp. 885–914
- Taylor, Richard S., 'Capture versus Kill Debate: Is the Principle of Humanity Now Part of the Targeting Analysis When Attacking Civilians Who are Directly Participating in Hostilities', *Army Lawyer* (2010) pp. 103–111
- Wills, Siobhan, 'The obligations due to former 'protected persons' in conflicts that have ceased to be international; the People's Mujahedin Organisation of Iran', 15 *Journal of Conflict and Security Law* (2010) pp. 117–139
- Wood, Reed M., 'Rebel capability and strategic violence against civilians', 47 *Journal of Peace Research* (2010) pp. 601–614

3.132 Women and Children

Books

- Njita, Wilson, *Sexual Violence Against Women in Situations of Armed Conflict: Sexual Violence against Women and Girls* (Saarbrucken, Lambert Academic Publishing 2010) 64 pp.

Articles

- Banderage, Asoka, 'Women, Armed Conflict, and Peacemaking in Sri Lanka: Toward a Political Economy Perspective', 2 *Asian Politics & Policy* (2010) pp. 653–667
- Cahn, Naomi, Dina Haynes and Fionnuala Ni Aolain, 'Returning Home: Women in Post-Conflict Societies', 39 *University of Baltimore Law Review* (2010) pp. 339–370
- Gardam, Judith, 'War, Law, Terror, Nothing New for Women', 32 *Australian Feminist Law Journal* (2010) pp. 61–76
- Goldstoff, Melissa Goldenberg, 'Security Council Resolution 1820: An Imperfect but Necessary Resolution to Protect Civilians from Rape in War Zones', 16 *Cardozo Journal of Law & Gender* (2010) pp. 491–518

- Konge, Paolo, 'International Crimes & Child Soldiers', 16 *Southwestern Journal of International Law* (2010) pp. 41–74
- Lewis, Dustin A., 'Unrecognized Victims: Sexual Violence against Men in Conflict Settings under International Law', 27 *Wisconsin International Law Journal* (2009–2010) pp. 1–50
- Rosen, David M., 'Dilemma of Child Soldiers', 10 *Insights on Law and Society* (2010) pp. 6–9
- Ryan, Daniel, 'International Law and Laws of War and International Criminal Law—Prosecution of Child Soldiers—Untied States v. Omar Ahmed Khadr', 33 *Suffolk Transnational Law Review* (2010) pp. 175–186
- Shepherd, Laura J., 'Women, armed conflict and language—Gender, violence and discourse', 92 *International Review of the Red Cross* (2010) pp. 143–159
- Waschefort, Gus, 'Justice for Child Soldiers? The RUF Trial of the Special Court for Sierra Leone', 1 *Journal of International Humanitarian Legal Studies* (2010) pp. 189–204

3.25 Reprisals

Articles

- Newton, Michael A, 'Reconsidering Reprisals', 20 *Duke Journal of Comparative and International Law* (2010) pp. 361–388

4. Methods, Means and Types of Warfare

Articles

- Boothby, William, 'Weapons and the Law of Armed Conflict', 21 *European Journal of International Law* (2010) pp. 483–486

4.1111 Conventional Weapons

Articles

- Reeves, Major Shane R., 'How White Phosphorus Use is 'incendiary' for counter-insurgency operations', *Army Lawyer* (2010) pp. 84–91

4.11122 Chemical and Biological Weapons

Articles

- Fry, James D., 'Sovereign Equality under the Chemical Weapons Convention: doughnuts over holes', 15 *Journal of Conflict and Security Law* (2010) pp. 45–63
- Fry, James D., 'Gas smells awful; UN forces, riot control agents, and the Chemical Weapons Convention', 31 *Michigan Journal of International Law* (2010) pp. 475–558
- Millet, Piers, 'The Biological Weapons; securing biology in the twenty-first century', 15 *Journal of Conflict and Security Law* (2010) pp. 25–43
- Wallach, Evan J., 'Tiny Problem with huge implications—Nanotech agents as Enablers or Substitutes for banned Chemical Weapons; is a new Treaty needed', 33 *Fordham International Law Journal* (2010) pp. 858–956

4.11121 Nuclear Weapons

Articles

- Anastassov, Anguel, 'Are nuclear weapons illegal? The role of public international law and the International Court of Justice', 15 *Journal of Conflict and Security Law* (2010) pp. 65–87
- Brown, Andrew and Loma Arnold, 'The quirks of nuclear deterrence', 24 *International Relations* (2010) pp. 293–312
- Tkacik, Michael, 'Pakistan's nuclear weapons program and implications for US national security', 24 *International Relations* (2010) pp. 175–217
- Duarte, Sergio, 'Nuclear weapons and the rule of law', 33 *Fordham International Law Journal* (2010) pp. 573–584

4.112 New Weapons

Articles

- Blank, Laurie and Amos Guiora, 'Teaching an Old Dog New Tricks: Operationalizing the Law of Armed Conflict in New Warfare', 1(1) *Harvard National Security Journal* (2010) pp. 45–85
- Lin, Herbert S., 'Offensive cyber operations and the use of force', 4 *Journal of National Security Law and Policy* (2010) pp. 63–86
- Kanuck, Sean, 'Sovereign discourse on cyber conflict under International Law', 88 *Texas Law Review* (2010) pp. 1571–1598
- Watts, Sean, 'Combatant Status and Computer Network Attack', 50 *Virginia Journal of International Law* (2010) pp. 391–448

4.142 Cultural Property and Places of Worship

Books

- O'Keefe, Roger, *The Protection of Cultural Property in Armed Conflict* (Cambridge, Cambridge University Press 2010) 430 pp.

Articles

- Van Der Auwera, Sigrid, 'Peace operations and the protection of cultural property during and after armed conflict', 17 *International Peacekeeping* (2010) pp. 3–16

4.144 Natural Environment

Books

- United Nations Environment Programme, *Protecting the Environment During Armed Conflict: An Inventory and Analysis of International Law* (UNEP 2010) 83 pp.

Articles

- Lujala, Paivi, 'The spoils of nature: armed civil conflict and rebel access to natural resources', 47 *Journal of Peace Research* (2010) pp. 15–28
- Van Laer, Tania, 'Damage to energy resources during armed conflict; towards a new regime', 3 *International Energy Law Review* (2010) pp. 64–72

4.16 Humanitarian Assistance Operations

Books

- Oswald, Bruce, Helen Durham and Adrian Bates, *Documents on the Law of UN Peace Operations* (Oxford, Oxford University Press 2010) 624 pp.

4.22 Air and Missile Warfare

Books

- Gill Terry and Dieter Fleck, *The Handbook of the International Law of Military Operations* (Oxford, Oxford University Press 2010) 657 pp.

Articles

- Jr. Dunlap, Charles J., 'Come the revolution; A legal perspective on air operations in Iraq', 40 *Israel Yearbook on Human Rights* (2010) pp. 141–158
- Schmitt, Michael N., 'Air Law and Military Operations', in Gill T. and Fleck D., eds., *The Handbook of the International Law of Military Operations* (Oxford, Oxford University Press 2010) ch. 18.

4.23 Naval Warfare

Articles

- Armstrong, Benjamin, 'The most daring act of the age; Principles for Naval Irregular Warfare', 63 *Naval War College Review* (2010) pp. 106–119

5.1 Ceasefire, Armistices and Peace Agreements

Articles

- Bell, Christine and Catherine O'Rourke, 'Peace Agreements or Pieces of Paper? The Impact of UNSC Resolution 1325 on Peace Processes and Their Agreements', 59 *International and Comparative Law Quarterly* (2010) pp. 941–980

5.3 Amnesties

Articles

- Guzman Dalbora, Jose Luis, 'The Treatment of International Crimes in Chilean Jurisprudence', 10 *International Criminal Law Review* (2010) pp. 535–547
- Holtermann, Jacob V. H., 'The End of "The End of Impunity"? The International Criminal Court and the Challenge from Truth Commissions', 16 *Res Publica* (2010) pp. 209–225
- Parenti, Pablo F., 'The Prosecution of International Crimes in Argentina', 10 *International Criminal Law Review* (2010) pp. 491–507
- Zapito Barbeito, Monica, 'Investigating the Crimes of the Franco Regime: Legal Possibilities, Obligations of the Spanish State and Duties Towards Victims', 10 *International Criminal Law Review* (2010) pp. 243–274

5.7 Reparation and Compensation

Books

- Samy, Shahira, *Reparations to Palestinian Refugees: A Comparative Perspective* (London, Routledge 2010) 181 pp.

Articles

- Pogany, Istvan, 'International Human Rights Law, Reparatory Justice and the Re-Ordering of Memory in Central and Eastern Europe', 10 *Human Rights Law Review* (2010) pp. 397–428
- Samy, Shahira, 'Would "Sorry" Repair My Loss? Why Palestinian Refugees Should Seek an Apology for Their Displacement', 14 *International Journal of Human Rights* (2010) pp. 364–377
- Xavier Fellmeth, Aaron, 'Below-Market Interest in International Claims against States', 13 *Journal of International Economic Law* (2010) pp. 423–457
- Zegveld, Liesbeth, 'Victim's Reparations Claims and International Criminal Courts', 8 *Journal of International Criminal Justice* (2010) pp. 79–111

5.5 Military Commissions and Tribunals

Books

- Graham, David E. 'Military Commissions as the Forum to Prosecute Acts of Terrorism and Other Violations of the Laws of War', in Moore, John N. and Robert F. Turner, *Legal Issues in the Struggle Against Terror* (Durham NC, Carolina Academic Press 2010) pp. 3–34
- Morris, Lawrence J, *Military Justice: A Guide to the Issues* (Westport CT, Praeger 2010) 211 pp.

Articles

- Boister, Neil, 'The Application of Collective and Comprehensive Criminal Responsibility for Aggression at the Tokyo International Military Tribunal: The Measure of the Crime of Aggression?', 8 *Journal of International Criminal Justice* (2010) pp. 425–447
- Jenkins, David, 'The Closure of Guantanamo Bay: What Next for the Detainees?', *Public Law* (2010) pp. 46–60
- Mettraux, Guenael, 'A Little-Known Case from the American Civil War: The War Crimes Trial of Major General John H. Gee', 8 *Journal of International Criminal Justice* (2010) pp. 1035–1058

6.25 Non-retroactivity of Statutory Limitations

Books

- Fijalkowski, Agata, *From Old Times to New Europe* (Farnham, Ashgate 2010) 243 pp.

9.11 Fact-Finding Commission

Books

- Chukwu, Iheke, *Appraisal of the United Nations Goldstone Report on the Gaza Conflict; War crimes, International Humanitarian Law and Fact-finding mission* (Saarbrücken, Lambert Academic Publishing 2010) 144 pp.

Articles

- 'Report on UN Fact-finding mission on the Gaza conflict', 2 *European Human Rights Law Review* (2010) pp. 125–148

9.11 United Nations Organisation

Books

- Conforti, Benedetto and Carlo Focarelli, *The Law and Practice of the United Nations*, (4th edn. (Leiden, Martinus Nijhoff 2010) 449 pp.

Articles

- Costantinides, Aristotle, 'Human Rights Obligations and Accountability of Armed Opposition Groups: The Practice of the UN Security Council', 4 *Human Rights and International Legal Discourse* (2010) pp. 89–110
- Garraway, Charles, 'The Geneva Conventions and United Nations Personnel (Protocols) Act 2009. A Move Away from the Minimalist Approach', 59 *International and Comparative Law Quarterly* (2010) pp. 171–180
- Ng, Trina, 'Safeguarding Peace and Security in Our Warming World: A Role for the Security Council', 15 *Journal of Conflict and Security Law* (2010) pp. 275–300

9.12 International Committee of the Red Cross

Books

- Borda, Aldo Zammit, *International Humanitarian Law and the International Red Cross and Red Crescent Movement* (Abingdon, Routledge 2010) 224 pp.

– Connolly, Sean, *The International Red Cross* (London: Franklin Watts 2010) 48 pp.

Articles

– Colassis, Laurent, 'The role of the International Committee of the Red Cross in Stability Operations in Iraq', 40 *Israel Yearbook on Human Rights* (2010) pp. 183–202
– Fenrick, W.J., 'ICRC Guidance on Direct Participation in Hostilities', 12 *Yearbook of International Humanitarian Law* (2009) pp. 287–300
– Gazzini, Tarcisio, 'A unique non-state actor; the International Committee of the Red Cross', 4 *Human Rights and International Legal Discourse* (2010) pp. 32–46

9.2 International Actions: The Law of Neutrality

Books

– Botha, Neville, Michèle Olivier and Delarey van Tonder, eds., *Multilateralism and International Law with Western Sahara as A Case Study* (Pretoria, Verloren van Themaat Centre, University of South Africa 2010) 283 pp.

Articles

– Donoghue, Aoife, 'Neutrality and Multilateralism after the First World War', 15 *Journal of Conflict and Security Law* (2010) pp. 141–168
– Kreß, Claus, 'Some Reflections on the International Legal Framework Governing Transnational Armed Conflict', 15 *Journal of Conflict and Security Law* (2010) pp. 245–274

9.21 Peacekeeping

Books

– Charlesworth, Hilary and Jean-Marc Coicaud, eds., *Fault Lines of International Legitimacy* (Cambridge, Cambridge University Press 2010) 406 pp.

Articles

– Bangura, Mohamed A., 'Prosecuting the Crime of Attack on Peacekeepers: A Prosecutor's Challenge', 23 *Leiden Journal of International Law* (2010) pp. 165–181
– Johnstone, Ian, 'The UN Security Council, Regional Arrangements, and Peacekeeping Operations', in Charlesworth, Hilary and Jean-Marc Coicaud,

eds., *Fault Lines of International Legitimacy* (Cambridge, Cambridge University Press 2010) pp. 175–203
- Odello, Marco, 'Tackling Criminal Acts in Peacekeeping Operations: The Accountability of Peacekeepers', 15 *Journal of Conflict and Security Law* (2010) pp. 347–391
- Suntharalingam, Nishkala, 'The UN Security Council, Regional Arrangements, and Peacekeeping Operations', in Charlesworth, Hilary and Jean-Marc Coicaud, eds., *Fault Lines of International Legitimacy* (Cambridge, Cambridge University Press 2010) pp. 204–238

9.22 Peace Enforcement and Peace Building

Books

- Tondini, Matteo, *Statebuilding and Justice Reform: Post-Conflict Reconstruction in Afghanistan* (London, Routledge 2010) 167 pp.

Articles

- Cameron, Lindsey and Rebecca Everly, 'Conceptualizing the Administration of Territory by International Actors', 21 *European Journal of International Law* (2010) pp. 221–244
- Chesterman, Simon, 'International Territorial Administration and the Limits of Law', 23 *Leiden Journal of International Law* (2010) pp. 437–447
- Orford, Anne, 'International Territorial Administration and the Management of Decolonization', 59 *International and Comparative Law Quarterly* (2010) pp. 227–249

9.25 Sanctions

Books

- Charlesworth, Hilary and Jean-Marc Coicaud, *Fault Lines of International Legitimacy* (Cambridge, Cambridge University Press 2010) 406 pp.
- Gordon, Joy, *Invisibile War: The United States and the Iraq Sanctions* (Cambridge MA, Harvard University Press 2010) 359 pp.
- Katselli Proukaki, Elena, *The Problem of Enforcement in International Law: Countermeasures, The Non-Injured State and The Idea of International Community* (London, Routledge 2010) 331 pp.
- Portela, Clara, *European Union Sanctions and Foreign Policy: When and Why Do They Work?* (London, Routledge 2010) 206 pp.
- Spadoni, Paolo, *Failed Sanctions: Why The US Embargo against Cuba Could Never Work* (Gainesville FL, University Press of Florida 2010) 230 pp.

- Taylor, Brendan, *American Sanctions in the Asia–Pacific* (London, Routledge 2010) 170 pp.

Articles

- Godinho, Jorge, 'When Worlds Collide: Enforcing United Nations Security Council Asset Freezes in the EU Legal Order', 16 *European Law Journal* (2010) pp. 67–93
- Matsukuma, Jun, 'The Legitimacy of Economic Sanctions: An Analysis of Humanitarian Exemptions of Sanctions Regimes and The Right to Minimum Sustenance', in Charlesworth, Hilary and Jean-Marc Coicaud, eds., *Fault Lines of International Legitimacy* (Cambridge, Cambridge University Press 2010) pp. 360–388
- Stenhammar, Fredrik, 'United Nations Targeted Sanctions, The International Rule of Law and the European Court of Justice's Judgement in Kadi and al-Barakaat', 79 *Nordic Journal of International Law* (2010) pp. 113–140
- Tzanakopoulos, Antonios, 'United Nations Sanctions in Domestic Courts: From Interpretation to Defiance in Abdelrazik v. Canada (Minister of Foreign Affairs)', 8 *Journal of International Criminal Justice* (2010) pp. 249–267
- Wilde, Ralph, 'The legitimacy of economic sanctions: an analysis of humanitarian exemptions of sanctions regimes and the right to minimum sustenance', in Charlesworth, Hilary and Jean-Marc Coicaud, eds., *Fault Lines of International Legitimacy* (Cambridge, Cambridge University Press 2010) pp. 327–359.

9.24 Humanitarian and Other Interventions

Books

- Bellamy, Alex and Sara E. Davies, *The Responsibility to Protect and International Law* (London, Routledge 2010) 224 pp.
- Buchanan, Allen E., *Human Rights, Legitimacy and the Use of Force* (Oxford, Oxford University Press 2010) 332 pp.
- Cimbala, Stephen G. and Peter K. Foster, *Multinational Military Intervention: NATO Policy, Strategy and Burden Sharing* (Farnham, Ashgate 2010) 233 pp.
- Charlesworth, Hilary and Jean-Marc Coicaud, eds., *Fault Lines of International Legitimacy* (Cambridge, Cambridge University Press 2010) 406 pp.
- Giorgetti, Chiara, *A Principled Approach to State Failure: International Community Actions in Emergency Situations* (Leiden, Martinus Nijhoff 2010) 198 pp.
- Helmke, Belinda, *Under Attack: Challenges to The Rules Governing The International Use of Force* (Farnham, Ashgate 2010) 296 pp.
- James, Erica C., *Democratic Insecurities: Violence, Trauma and Intervention in Haiti* (Berkeley California, University of California Press 2010) 357 pp.
- Podikiska, Bradley F., *Acting Alone: A Scientific Study of American Hegemony and Unilateral Use of Force Decision Making* (Lanham MD, Lexington Books 2010) 255 pp.

Articles

- Baker, Gideon, 'The "Double Law" of Hospitality: Rethinking Cosmopolitan Ethics in Humanitarian Intervention', 24 *International Relations* (2010) pp. 87–103
- Benjamin, Dave, 'Sudan and the Resort to Regional Arrangements: Putting an Effect to The Responsibility to Protect?', 14 *International Journal of Human Rights* (2010) pp. 233–245
- Chimni, Bhupinder Singh, 'Determining How The Legitimacy of Intervention Is Discussed: A Case Study of International Territorial Administration', in Charlesworth, Hilary and Jean-Marc Coicaud, *Fault Lines of International Legitimacy* (Cambridge, Cambridge University Press 2010) pp. 303–226
- Coicaud, Jean-Marc, 'Intervention In a "Divided World": Axes of Legitimacy', in Charlesworth, Hilary and Jean-Marc Coicaud, *Fault Lines of International Legitimacy* (Cambridge, Cambridge University Press 2010) pp. 115–145
- Elliott, Lorraine, 'Sovereignty, Rights, and Armed Intervention: a Dialectical Perspective', in Charlesworth, Hilary and Jean-Marc Coicaud, *Fault Lines of International Legitimacy* (Cambridge, Cambridge University Press 2010) pp. 279–302
- Greer, Steven and Nikolaos Tsagourias, 'Next Steps', 160 *New Law Journal* (2010) p. 475
- Stein, Lord, 'The Legality of The Invasion of Iraq' 1 *European Human Rights Law Review* (2010) pp. 1–7
- White, Nigel D., 'International Law, The United Kingdom and Decisions to Deploy Troops Overseas', 59 *International and Comparative Law Quarterly* (2010) pp. 814–823

10.1 European

Books

- Popescu, Nicu, *EU Foreign Policy and Post-Soviet Conflicts* (London, Routledge 2010) 176 pp.
- Wade, Marianne and Almir Maljević, *A War on Terror? The European Stance on a New Threat, Changing Laws and Human Rights Implications* (New York, Springer 2010) 554 pp.

Articles

- Drieskens, Edith, 'Beyond Chapter VIII: Limits and Opportunities for Regional Representations at the UN Security Council', 7 *International Organizations Law Review* (2010) pp. 149–169
- Koutrakos, Panos, 'EU Law: External Relations', 59 *International and Comparative Law Quarterly* (2010) pp. 481–489

- Lambert, Helene and Theo Farrell, 'The Changing Character of Armed Conflict and The Implications for Refugee Protection Jurisprudence', 22 *International Journal of Refugee Law* (2010) pp. 237–273
- Lenaerts, Koen, 'The Contribution of the European Court of Justice to The Area of Freedom, Security and Justice', 59 *International and Comparative Law Quarterly* (2010) pp. 255–301
- Osterdahl, Inger, 'The Use of Force: Sweden, the *Jus ad Bellum* and The European Security and Defense Policy', 79 *Nordic Journal of International Law* (2010) pp. 141–188
- Toje, Asle, 'The EU Security Strategy Revised: Europe Hedging Its Bets', 15 *European Foreign Affairs Review* (2010) pp. 171–190

10.4 African

Articles

- Chernor Jalloh, Charles, 'Universal Jurisdiction, Universal Prescription? A Preliminary Assessment of The African Union Perspective on Universal Jurisdiction', 21 *Criminal Law Forum* (2010) pp. 1–65

11.1 Conventional Weapons

Books

- Nystuen, Gro and Stuart Casey-Maslen, *The Convention on Cluster Munitions: A Commentary* (Oxford, Oxford University Press 2010) 864 pp.

Articles

- Anzalone, Joseph, 'Virtue of a proportional response; The United States stance against the Convention in Cluster Munitions', 22 *Pace International Law Review* (2010) pp. 183–212
- Barak, Eitan, 'None to be trusted; Israel's use of Cluster Munitions in the second Lebanon war and the case for the Convention on Cluster Munition', 25 *American University International Law Review* (2010) pp. 423–484

11.2 Weapons of Mass Destruction

Articles

- Garvey, Jack, 'Nuclear containment for the twenty-first century: a mandatory international nuclear forensics data bank', 15 *Journal of Conflict and Security Law* (2010) pp. 301–346

- Grotto, Andrew 'Why do states that oppose nuclear proliferation resist new non-proliferation obligations; three logics of non-proliferation decision-making', 18 *Cardozo Journal of International and Comparative Law* (2010) pp. 1–44
- Hosur, Prashant, 'Indo-US Civilian Nuclear Agreement', 65 *International Journal* (2010) pp. 435–450
- Singh, Anita, 'India-Canada Civilian Nuclear deal; Implications for Canadian Foreign Policy', 65 *International Journal* (2010) pp. 233–254

12.1 Conflict Prevention

Books

- Gross, Eva and Anna E. Juncos, *EU Conflict Prevention and Crisis Management; Roles, Institutions and Policies* (Abingdon, Routledge 2010) 192 pp.
- Ledberg, Sofia, Alec Forss and Niklas Swanstrom, *Conflict Prevention and Management in North East Asia; the Korean Penninsula and Taiwan Strait in comparison* (Newcastle u T, Cambridge Scholars Publishing 2010) 290 pp.

Article

- Kydd, Andrew H, 'Rational Approaches to Conflict Prevention and Resolution', 13 *Annual Review of Political Science* (2010) pp. 101–121

12.2 Conflict Resolution

Books

- Breau, Susan and Kerim Yildiz, *The Kurdish Conflict; International Humanitarian Law and Post Conflict mechanisms* (Abingdon, Routledge 2010) 376 pp.

Articles

- De Brabandere, Eric, 'Responsibility for post-conflict reforms; a critical assessment of Jus Post Bellum as a legal concept' 43 *Vanderbilt Journal of Transnational Law* (2010) pp. 119–150

13.1 Jus Ad Bellum

Books

- Henderson, Christian, *The Persistent Advocate and the Use of Force: The Impact of the United States upon the Jus ad Bellum in the Post Cold War Era* (Farnham, Ashgate 2010) 230 pp.

- Moir, Lindsay, *Reappraising the Resort to Force: International Law, Jus ad Bellum and the War on Terror* (Oxford, Hart 2010) 176 pp.

Articles

- Bakken, Tim, 'Nations' Use of Force outside Self-Defense', 8 *Georgetown Journal of Law & Public Policy* (2010) pp. 451–470
- Corn, Geoffrey and Dennis Gyllensporre, 'International Legality, the Use of Military Force, and Burdens of Persuasion: Self-Defense, the Initiation of Hostilities, and the Impact of Choice between Two Evils on the Perception of International Legitimacy', 30 *Pace Law Review* (2010) pp. 484–543
- Henderson, Christian and James A. Green, 'The *Jus Ad Bellum* and Entities Short of Statehood in the Report on the Conflict in Georgia', 59 *International and Comparative Law Quarterly* (2010) pp. 129–139
- Murphy, John F., 'Iraq and the 'Fog of Law'', 86 *International Law Studies, US Naval War College* (2010) pp. 19–41
- Osterdahl, Inger, 'The Use of Force: Sweden, the *Jus ad Bellum* and The European Security and Defense Policy', 79 *Nordic Journal of International Law* (2010) pp. 141–188
- Pedrozo, Raul, 'Legal Bases for Military Operations in Iraq', 40 *Israel Yearbook on Human Rights* (2010) pp. 45–68
- Perina, Alexandra, 'Legal Bases for Coalition Combat Operations in Iraq, May 2003-Present', 86 *International Law Studies, US Naval War College* (2010) pp. 81–96
- Rocheleau, Jordy, 'From Aggression to Just Occupation? The Temporal Application of *Jus Ad Bellum* Principles and the Case of Iraq', 9 *Journal of Military Ethics* (2010) pp. 123–138
- Shah, Sikander Ahmed, 'War on Terrorism: Self Defense, Operation Enduring Freedom, and the Legality of U.S. Drone Attacks in Pakistan', 9 *Washington University Global Studies Law Review* (2010) pp. 77–130
- Solomon, Solon, 'The Great Oxymoron: Jus in Bello Violations as Legitimate Non-Forcible Measures of Self-Defense: The Post-Disengagement Israeli Measures towards Gaza as a Case Study', 9 *Chinese Journal of International Law* (2010) pp. 501–536
- Wall, Andru E., 'Was the 2003 Invasion of Iraq Legal?', 40 *Israel Yearbook on Human Rights* (2010) pp. 69–80

13.2 The Law Relating to Terrorism and Counter-Terrorism

Books

- Blum, Gabriella, *Laws, Outlaws, and Terrorists: Lessons from the War on Terrorism* (Cambridge, MIT Press 2010) 232 pp.

– Brahimi, Alia, *Jihad and Just War in the War on Terror* (Oxford, Oxford University Press 2010) 336 pp.
– Jemaneh, Kokebe W., *Armed Conflict in the Wilderness of Humanitarian Law: Fighting Transnational Terrorism in the No-man's-Land of International Humanitarian Law* (Saarbrucken, VDM Publishing 2010) 128 pp.
– Harmon, Christopher C., Andrew N. Pratt and S. Gorka, eds., *Toward a Grand Strategy against Terrorism* (New York NY, Dushkin/McGraw-Hill 2010) 448 pp.
– Tegamaisho, Prosper, *Protection of Terrorism Suspects under International Humanitarian Law: A Case Study of Guantanamo Bay* (Saarbrucken, Lambert Academic Publishing 2010) 80 pp.
– Wabuyabo, Justus, *Humanitarian Law and the War Against International Terrorism: Challenges and opportunities since September 11, 2001* (Saarbrucken, Lambert Academic Publishing 2010) 136 pp.

Articles

– Bellinger III, John B., 'Terrorism and Changes to the Laws of War', 20(3) *Duke Journal of Comparative and International Law* (2010) pp. 331–338
– Schmitt, Michael N. and Dean Dwigans, 'International Law and Counterterrorism', in Harmon, Christopher C., Andrew N. Pratt and S. Gorka, eds., *Toward a Grand Strategy against Terrorism* (New York NY, Dushkin/McGraw-Hill 2010) pp. 86–102
– Waxman, Matthew C., 'The Structure of Terrorism Threats and the Laws of War', 20(3) *Duke Journal of Comparative and International Law* (2010) pp. 429–456

13.4 International Human Rights Law

Books

– Dickson, Brice, *The European Convention on Human Rights and the Conflict in Northern Ireland* (Oxford, Oxford University Press 2010) 472 pp.
– Holgernes, Honne Tord, *Challenges in applying human rights law to armed conflict; the relationship between international human rights law and international humanitarian law* (Saarbrucken, Lambert Academic Publishing 2010) 64 pp.
– Sriram, Lekha Chandra, Olga Martin-Ortega and Johanna Hermann, *War, Conflict and Human Rights; Theory and Practice* (Abingdon, Routledge 2010) 272 pp.

Articles

– Chevalier-Watts, Juliet, 'Has human rights law become lex specialis for the European Court of Human Rights in right to life cases arising from internal

armed conflicts?', 14 *International Journal of Human Rights* (2010) pp. 584–602
- Mastorodimos, Konstantinos, 'The utility and limits of International Human Rights Law and International Humanitarian Law's parallel applicability', 3 *USAK Yearbook of International Politics and Law* (2010) pp. 123–144
- Murdie, Amanda and David Davis, 'Problematic potential; The human rights consequences of peacekeeping interventions in civil wars', 32(1) *Human Rights Quarterly* (2010) pp. 49–72
- Rose, Cecily, 'Emerging norma: the duty of states to provide reparations for human rights violations by non-state actors', 33 *Hastings International and Comparative Law Review* (2010) pp. 307–344
- Tomuschat, Christian, 'Human Rights and International Humanitarian law', 21 *European Journal of International Law* (2010) pp. 15–23
- Weissbrodt, David, 'Role of the Human Rights Committee in interpreting and developing humanitarian law', 31 *University of Pennsylvania Journal of International Law* (2010) pp. 1185–1238

13.5 Refugee Law

Articles

- Lambert, Helene and Theo Farrell, 'The changing character of armed conflict and the implications for refugee protection jurisprudence', 22 *International Journal of Refugee Law* (2010) pp. 237–273

Table of Cases*

INTERNATIONAL

*The table of cases was compiled by Mrs C.C. Diepeveen, Middelburg, The Netherlands.

M.N. Schmitt et al. (eds.), *Yearbook of International Humanitarian Law Volume 13, 2010*, DOI: 10.1007/978-90-6704-811-8,

NATIONAL

Index

The Index was compiled by Mrs. C.C. Diepeveen, Middelburg, The Netherlands.

The Index contains references to all matters of substance dealt with in the text of the articles. Detailed references to cases dealt with will be found in the accompanying Table of Cases. The section on correspondents' Reports is also indexed, but for information on the practice of individual states regarding detailed aspects of international humanitarian law the reader should consult the index under the states concerned. Footnotes containing substantive material are also indexed, as are references to the work of scholars the first time such work is listed.

M.N. Schmitt et al. (eds.), *Yearbook of International Humanitarian Law Volume 13, 2010*, DOI: 10.1007/978-90-6704-811-8,

C

F

H

M

V

The manufacturer's authorised representative in the EU is Springer Nature Customer Service Centre GmbH, Europaplatz 3, 69115 Heidelberg, Germany. If you have any concerns regarding our products, please contact ProductSafety@springernature.com

Printed and bound by CPI Group (UK) Ltd, Croydon, CR0 4YY
30/09/2026
02225447-0020